Marcus Tullius aut Cicero

M. Tullii Ciceronis orationes

Marcus Tullius aut Cicero

M. Tullii Ciceronis orationes

ISBN/EAN: 9783742844156

Manufactured in Europe, USA, Canada, Australia, Japa

Cover: Foto ©Thomas Meinert / pixelio.de

Manufactured and distributed by brebook publishing software
(www.brebook.com)

Marcus Tullius aut Cicero

M. Tullii Ciceronis orationes

BIBLIOTHECA CLASSICA.

EDITED BY

GEORGE LONG, M.A.

FORMERLY FELLOW OF TRINITY COLLEGE, CAMBRIDGE,

AND THE

REV. A. J. MACLEANE, M.A.

TRINITY COLLEGE, CAMBRIDGE.

VOL. I.

M. TULLII CICERONIS ORATIONES.

WITH A

COMMENTARY BY GEORGE LONG.

VOL. I.

VERRINARUM LIBRI SEPTEM.

Second Edition.

LONDON:

WHITTAKER AND CO. AVE MARIA LANE;

GEORGE BELL, FLEET STREET.

1862.

LONDON:

GILBERT AND RIVINGTON, PRINTERS,

ST. JOHN'S SQUARE.

M. TULLII CICERONIS

ORATIONES.

WITH

A COMMENTARY

BY

GEORGE LONG.

VOL. I.

VERRINARUM LIBRI SEPTEM.

Second Edition.

LONDON:
WHITTAKER AND CO. AVE MARIA LANE;
GEORGE BELL, FLEET STREET.
1862.

PREFACE.

The text of this edition of Cicero's orations against Verres approaches nearest to that of Zumpt's edition of 1831, which is entitled, "M. Tullii Ciceronis Verrinarum Libri Septem. Ad fidem codicum manu scriptorum recensuit et explicavit Car. Timoth. Zumptius." The variations from the text of Zumpt are indicated in the notes. I have not intentionally omitted to notice any important variation; but I have omitted to notice some which are of no importance at all, or matters perfectly indifferent.

I used for printing from, after I had corrected it to suit my purpose, the English reprint of Zumpt, third edition, 1847. I supposed that the third edition of a work, printed in 1847, would not be a reprint of Zumpt's first and minor edition, but that it would contain all the improvements of the larger edition of 1831. I soon discovered, however, that this was not so; and I merely mention the circumstance because there are a few readings in Zumpt's larger edition, in the Divinatio, which I prefer to those which I have retained. They are, however, of very little importance. The most important differences between the English reprint of Zumpt and his larger edition, occur in the orations which come after the Divinatio. The whole amount of difference

between the English reprint and Zumpt's larger edition is considerable; and nearly all the variations of the larger edition are improvements. The English reprint is very correct in the typography, and very bad in the punctuation, which fault, however, may be perhaps mainly chargeable on the German original, which I never saw.

The history of the text of the Verrine orations is given in Zumpt's Preface. Readers of Cicero are greatly indebted to him for what he has done. Indeed, we who can now read these orations with comparative ease, are apt to forget how much we owe to a long series of scholars. Zumpt's edition is what is commonly called a critical edition, the main object of which is the establishment of the text. For this purpose Zumpt collated two of the Wolfenbüttel MSS., which he calls Guelff. 1, 2. But he derived most advantage from the "Lagomarsinianae novem codicum Florentinorum collationes." The fragments of the Verrine orations, which were published by A. Mai, 1828, from a Vatican Palimpsest, did not reach Germany early enough for Zumpt to use them, except for the fifth and last of the Verrine orations. Zumpt has given in an Appendix (Appendix variantium lectionum et supplementa annotationis) the readings of the Vatican MS. "This Appendix," he says, "contains 'farrago variantium lectionum e codicibus MSS. et editionibus petitarum, quibus in annotatione usi non sumus, aut uti noluimus.'" The Vatican fragments contain parts of the following books:—Act. ii. Lib. 1, 2, 3, 4, 5. The MS. to which these fragments belong is of high antiquity and undoubted value. Zumpt considers the Cod. Vat. as the parent of Par. B. and Lag. 29, which he further considers to be the parents of the inferior MSS. There are many gross blunders in the Cod. Vat., which prove that it must be, in parts, at least, a carelessly made copy from a good original. All the other MSS. Zumpt considers as the progeny of a "Cod. antiquus deperditus," a respectable ancestor who lives only in his descendants. As to Guelf. 1, Madvig is of opinion that Zumpt rates it too high.

As I have often referred to the MSS., the following extract from Zumpt may be useful. His conclusion is this:

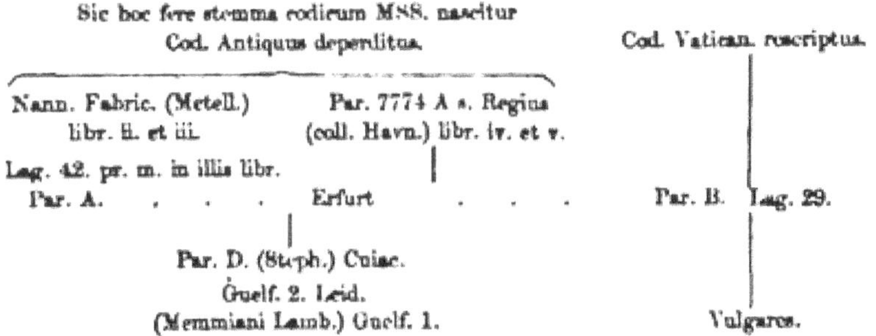

Fabric. and Metell. are the same MS. Par. 7774 A is the same as Regius. I am not sure that Zumpt always agrees with himself about the value of Lag. 29. In a note on Lib. 3. c. 76, he calls Lag. 29. 42. Paris A. B. "quatuor meliores nostri." In another place (Lib. 5. c. 46), he calls Lag. 29, "minime fidelis;" and again (Lib. 4. c. 37), he calls it "infidelis quamvis ex fidelissimo ductus."

The edition of Cicero's orations by Klotz, to which I have often referred, is in three vols. 8vo, with notes in German. At the foot of the page he has given the variations of Orelli's edition. In his Preface to the second volume (Leipzig, 1837), which contains the Verrine orations, the editor explains what he has done for the text. He states that he owes much to a careful examination of the Vatican fragments published by Mai. I have noted some of the chief variations in the text of Klotz, except in the fifth book of the Verrines, where I have noticed very few.

For the second book of the Verrines, I made use of the notes to the edition by F. Creuzer and G. H. Moser, Göttingen, 1847. The occasional references in the notes to this edition will show how far I am indebted to Creuzer and Moser. Their commentary is copious, and sometimes useful.

For the fifth book I used the separate edition of this oration

by J. C. Orelli, Leipzig, 1831. The text of this oration has been carefully and judiciously revised by the editor. Orelli used for this edition two collations of the Codex Regius of the ninth century, N. 7774. A. 1; one collation is the "Havniensis," or Copenhagen collatio, which is contained in the Epistola Critica of Madvig; the other was made for Orelli, at Paris, by a learned youth (eruditus juvenis) of Basle, named Hanhart. Orelli also used a new and accurate collation of the Cod. Leidensis, presented to him by Bake; the fragments of the Vatican Palimpsest of Mai; and a MS. of St. Gallen. These MSS. are referred to by Orelli under the following abbreviations:—R., Codex Regius; L., Leidensis; V., Palimpsestus Vaticanus; G., Codex Sangallensis. The labours of Zumpt, Orelli, and Madvig, have probably settled the text of this oration as well as it can be settled.

The Opuscula Academica of J. N. Madvig, Copenhagen, 1834, contain an essay, entitled "De locis aliquot Ciceronis orationum Verrinarum dissertatio critica." It is referred to several times in these notes.

With respect to the commentary of Asconius on part of these orations, which I have often cited, I have used the text of Orelli's edition of Cicero. This commentary contains both good and bad matter; and in its present shape it is not the genuine commentary of Asconius. This subject has been well examined by Madvig in his essay, "De Q. Asconii Pediani et aliorum veterum interpretum in Ciceronis orationes Commentariis Disputatio Critica, Copenhagen, 1828."

It was my intention, conformably to the plan of this series of editions, to take a text such as Zumpt's, and merely to make notes on it. But a careful study of these orations convinced me that I could not adopt any one text. Though this has no pretensions to be a critical edition, the text has cost me a great deal of labour; and that kind of labour which is not seen. In many passages, I have no doubt that the text which I have

given may be improved, for I do not consider that the text of these orations is yet finally settled.

In the matter of orthography I have done nothing. The orthography of Latin texts still remains to be settled; and there is a prospect that, in a few years, when the Latin language has been more studied, and is better understood, our printed texts will differ considerably in orthography from what they now are. Though I have not followed Zumpt in the mode of writing some words which he undoubtedly writes correctly, I have still refrained from writing "concio" for "contio," as the English reprint of Zumpt does.

The notes are intended to explain the text. I have passed over no passage where I found a difficulty myself, and very few where others have found a difficulty. If I have often made notes where some readers may not think them necessary, I have done so because I know by experience that many students will require such assistance. I have not intentionally concealed any obligations that I owe to other editors or commentators. Indeed, in the matter of acknowledgment, I have gone further than is necessary; for the modern commentators, whom I often cite, have derived much of their materials from the earlier commentators.

The Excursus may be unsuitable for younger students; and, indeed, they were not designed for them. If some of them are in parts obscure, I believe the fault is chiefly in the matter; and I can't help that. Any person may see that the subjects discussed in them are necessary to the understanding of Cicero's text; and those who are competent to form an opinion will look with indulgence on any errors that I have committed in treating such subjects for the first time in an edition of Cicero for the use of Englishmen.

GEORGE LONG.

BRIGHTON COLLEGE,
Sept. 1, 1851.

PREFACE TO THE SECOND EDITION.

I HAVE used for the revision of this volume the edition of Cicero's orations by I. G. Baiter and C. Halm. The Verrine orations are edited by C. A. Iordan, who has carefully described the MSS., and given a valuable collation of them. There is also a "Supplementum Apparatus Critici ad Quattuor libros priores orationum Verrinarum" by C. Halm (pp. 443—461).

Iordan's edition of the Verrine orations appears to contain all that can be done for the text. The variations are given so fully and carefully that a diligent reader may find instruction in studying them, and may exercise his own judgment on the text. The passages which are doubtful are now reduced to a small number.

I have looked at all the readings, and in some cases I have altered the text of my first edition, but the number of passages which I have altered is small. I have not always followed Iordan's text, for I believe that he is sometimes wrong.

I have selected a considerable number of the most important variations, both to justify the readings which I have chosen, and for the instruction of the reader. The MSS. variations are sometimes valuable, even when they are manifestly wrong, for they show how blunders are made in transcription, and that even the best manuscripts contain some singular errors.

I have examined all the notes, added much new matter, and

corrected some mistakes. I wish I could say that I have cleared the book of all errors; but as that is not possible, I must be content with having done my best to explain one of the most valuable monuments either of ancient or modern literature.

Having received many remarks from diligent students of Cicero, I have made use of them whenever I could; and in some cases where I could not, I have given additional reasons for keeping the explanation which I had already given.

I shall have no opportunity of revising this volume a third time. With all its defects, and I have no doubt that they are many, I hope it may assist the readers of Cicero. Some years hence somebody will take these orations in hand again, and if he shall find that what I have done is useful, he may improve it by striking out all that is useless or incorrect.

GEORGE LONG.

BRIGHTON COLLEGE,
Dec. 28, 1861.

CONTENTS.

INTRODUCTION

TO THE

ORATIONS AGAINST C. VERRES.

In the year B.C. 70, in the consulship of Cn. Pompeius Magnus and M. Licinius Crassus, M. Tullius Cicero was a candidate for the curule aedileship, and in the same year the Sicilians selected him for their patronus in the prosecution of C. Verres for mal-administration during his three years' government of Sicily. C. Verres was the son of C. Verres, a Roman senator, who was still living at the time when his son was governor of Sicily. The gentile name of C. Verres is never mentioned, and he probably had no other name than Verres. It is merely a conjecture, supported by no evidence, that his gentile name was Cornelius. His assumed relationship to the Caecilii Metelli is rather disproved by the passages usually cited to prove it. (Act. ii. Lib. 2. c. 26, 56.) Verres had a wife, Vettia, who bore him a daughter and a son. The son, though he had not attained the age to assume the 'toga virilis,' accompanied his father to Sicily, and was a witness of his scandalous conduct. (Lib. 3. c. 9, 68, 71.)

In the Verrine Orations Cicero represents Verres as an ignorant, brutal, and licentious man. He even gives him no credit for taste, though be had a passion for works of art; but here the orator has perhaps gone too far, for that Verres had some taste is proved by Cicero himself. Of the earlier part of his life Cicero says little: he professes to pass over the sins of his youth as things notorious.

Cicero says that Verres was the quaestor of the consul Cn. Papirius Carbo, in Cisalpine Gaul, fourteen years before the trial (B.C. 70), and he declares that all the acts of Verres from his quaestorship should furnish matter for the accusation. (Act. ii. Lib. 1. c. 12.) Accordingly the orator distributes his charges under four heads: the quaestorship of Verres; his legatio in Asia; his praetura urbana; and his government of Sicily. If Verres was quaestor to Carbo in B.C. 84, this was in the second consulship of Carbo; but Cicero appears to have made a mistake as to the fourteen years. For, as Drumann observes, it was in B.C. 82

that Carbo, then consul for the third time, was in Cisalpine Gaul, and this must be the year in which Verres was his quaestor. In his capacity of quaestor Verres was treacherous to the consul, and also embezzled the public money. (Act. ii. Lib. 1. c. 13—16.) After the defeat and death of Carbo, whom Cn. Pompeius caught in Sicily (B.C. 82) and put to death, Verres joined Sulla's party. Sulla sent him to Beneventum, probably to be out of the way, and he gave him certain estates which had belonged to the proscribed of Beneventum. He paid Verres, says Cicero, for his treachery, but he would not trust him. Verres soon found fresh employment. Cn. Cornelius Dolabella, praetor of Cilicia (B.C. 80, 79), an unprincipled, greedy fellow, made Verres one of his legati; and, after the death of the quaestor C. Malleolus, he appointed him proquaestor. The governor and his quaestor were a worthy pair, who kept one another in countenance. Cicero (Act. ii. Lib. 1. c. 17, &c.) has given a lively sketch of this period of the administration of Verres. He betrayed Dolabella as he had betrayed Carbo. When Dolabella was prosecuted (B.C. 78) by M. Aemilius Scaurus for repetundae, Verres, his companion in knavery, bargained with the accuser for his own safety on the terms of giving evidence against his old master. (Act. i. c. 4: Lib. 1. c. 38.) Hortensius defended Dolabella, but he was convicted and went into exile.

Verres had enriched himself in Asia, and he is said to have used his wealth in buying votes when he was a candidate for the praetorship. He was praetor in B.C. 74, and had the urbana jurisdictio. Under his praetorship (Lib. 1. c. 40, &c.) justice was sold, and the praetor's interest was purchased by applying to his mistress Chelidon. Cicero gives many instances of the praetor's greediness and unscrupulous ways of getting money. In B.C. 73 Verres obtained the propraetorship of Sicily, one of the most fertile of the Roman provinces, and the most abundant in works of art. The governor did not neglect this opportunity of filling his pockets with Sicilian gold, and his house with the choicest works of the Greek artists. Verres held the government of Sicily for three years, owing to the praetor Q. Arrius, who ought to have taken his place at the close of the year B.C. 73, being engaged in the war against Spartacus. (Lib. 4. c. 20.) He went to Sicily, says Cicero, with the settled purpose of plundering it, and neither the contest between the Romans and the Carthaginians for the possession of Sicily, nor the two servile wars, had caused so much misery in the island as the misgovernment of a Roman praetor. Verres ruined the corn-growers, beggared the farmers-general (publicani), and robbed both temples and private houses of the works of art, which the Greeks of Sicily prized even more than their money. Cicero has treated of the Sicilian government of Verres under four heads: his administration of justice (Lib. 2); his

administration with respect to the corn (frumentum) of Sicily (Lib. 3); his plunder of works of art (Lib. 4); and his cruelty (Lib. 5).

Verres was succeeded in his government of Sicily by L. Caecilius Metellus (B.C. 70). He carried most of his plunder to Rome in a vessel which the people of Messana built for him; for this city had received some favours from Verres, and had been a depôt for part of his ill-gotten property. The Sicilians, having determined to prosecute their late praetor for his mal-administration, chose Cicero to conduct the prosecution. Cicero had been quaestor B.C. 75, under the praetor Sex. Peducaeus, in the Lilybaean or western district of the island, and he had gained the good-will of the people by his upright conduct. On taking leave of the Sicilians in B.C. 74, he promised them his assistance, if ever they should want it, and all the cities of the island now called upon him to redeem his promise, Syracuse and Messana excepted. This was a great opportunity for Cicero, and he eagerly seized it, as the whole tenor of these speeches shows, notwithstanding certain rhetorical flourishes about his unwillingness to change his practice of defending the accused, in order to become a public prosecutor. Verres had the support of Q. and M. Metelli, the brethren of L. Metellus, now the propraetor of Sicily. The great orator Q. Hortensius was to defend Verres, who had many friends among the optimates or senatorian party, and contrived also to gain the support of L. Metellus, who, as governor of Sicily, did what he could for him. The senators generally disliked such a prosecution as that with which Verres was threatened: many of them had enriched themselves at the expense of the provinces; and others, who had not, hoped to have the opportunity. The reforms of the Dictator Sulla had deprived the equites of the power of sitting as judices, and made the senators only eligible; but the senators had often abused their power, and acquitted great criminals of their own body. At the time when the prosecution of Verres was preparing, there was a loud outcry against the judicial body, and a demand for its reformation. Cicero saw, and he told the judices who sat on the trial of Verres, that the result would be the condemnation or absolution of their own body. If they convicted Verres, it was a triumph for Cicero to have brought to punishment the plunderer of Sicily, to have vindicated the purity of the Judicia, and to have humbled the arrogance of Hortensius, the tyrant of the courts. If Verres was acquitted, it would not be for want of industry or ability in the patron of the Sicilians, but through the corruption of the senatorial body, out of whom the judices were chosen. In either way Cicero could not fail to gain the favour of the equites, the class to which he belonged, and the class from which, from the time of the Gracchi to the legislation of Sulla, the judices had been chosen. The mass of the people too would be on his side, if for no other reasons, from hatred to those who possessed

the political power. It was a safer policy for an ambitious Roman, who was not yet ennobled, to gain the good-will of those whose votes might raise him to the highest honours of the state, than to serve the senatorial party. When Cicero had taken his place among the nobiles, by having filled a curule magistracy, it would be easy for him to gain the good-will of the optimates; for such a class, however proud and exclusive, has a secret pleasure in seeing its ranks recruited by men who can infuse fresh vigour into an effete body.

In the year B.C. 70 the praetor M'. Acilius Glabrio presided in the trials for repetundae, and early in the year Cicero applied to him for permission to prosecute Verres. But at the same time Q. Caecilius Niger claimed to be the prosecutor of Verres, or at least to be one of the prosecutors (Div. 15), probably prompted by Hortensius. The prosecution in the hands of Caecilius would either have failed for want of being properly conducted, or through the bad faith of the prosecutor. Caecilius was a Roman citizen, but probably a Sicilian by birth, and he had been quaestor under Verres for the district of Lilybaeum. He urged that Verres had done him wrong, that he was therefore his enemy, that he was well acquainted with the facts of the governor's misconduct, and, for all these reasons, he was the fittest person to conduct the prosecution. The first question to be decided was, whether Cicero or Caecilius should conduct the prosecution. The first of Cicero's Verrine Orations, entitled 'De Divinatione,' was therefore in defence of himself and against Caecilius. He had to support his own claims as the chosen advocate of the Sicilians, and to destroy those of Caecilius, whom the Sicilians rejected; to show his opponent's unfitness, without urging his own qualifications beyond the limits of a modest confidence: and he did all this well. The decision was in favour of Cicero, and he conducted the prosecution alone. Halm infers from a passage in the orations (Act. ii. Lib. 4. c. 65) that Cicero's cousin Lucius was his subscriptor, or assistant in the prosecution, but that is more than can be inferred from Cicero's words.

Cicero asked and obtained from the praetor Glabrio one hundred and ten days for a voyage to Sicily to collect evidence against Verres; but a new device was resorted to by his opponents. At the instigation of Verres (Act. i. c. 2, 3), a person proposed to institute a prosecution which concerned Achaea, and a senator was selected as the man to be prosecuted; but Cicero does not mention his name. This person asked for only one hundred and eight days for going to Achaea and returning to Rome. If he returned within the hundred and eight days, and commenced his prosecution, Cicero's attack on Verres must be deferred, and perhaps it might be put off until the next year. But this trick failed. The false prosecutor never got as far as Brundusium, while Cicero

hurried to Sicily, and made the best use of his time, with the assistance of L. Cicero, the son of his father's brother. He traversed Sicily from west to east, and was every where joyfully received, except at Syracuse, where, however, he collected some important evidence, and at Messana, where the city did not receive him with the hospitality to which a Roman senator was entitled. (Act. ii. Lib. 4. c. 11.) Cicero travelled through Sicily and collected his evidence in fifty days. (Act. i. c. 2.) He was back again at Rome long before Verres and his friends expected him, ready to commence the prosecution, with a crowd of witnesses, and a mass of documentary evidence.

The trial was conducted under the presidency of M'. Acilius Glabrio, the praetor urbanus, a man of integrity. In settling the list of judices (judicum consilium) for the trial, Verres, being a senator, had the power, according to the Cornelia Lex de Repetundis, of challenging more than three judices; those who were not senators could only challenge three. The advocates of Verres availed themselves of this privilege, and Cicero mentions the names of six persons whom Verres rejected. Cicero also rejected some of the judices. (Lib. 1. c. 7.) But the result was, that the list as finally settled left Verres no hope of acquittal, for his guilt was notorious, and the judices were too honest to be bribed. In Act. i. c. 10 Cicero names eight of the judices, whom he calls 'almost the whole body;' and from various passages in the orations the names of twelve judices are collected. It may therefore be inferred that the number was not much more than twelve.

Q. Metellus and Q. Hortensius were elected consuls for the following year, B.C. 69, with the aid of the Sicilian gold of Verres, as Cicero insinuates. The election was made before the trial began. (Act. i. c. 6.) M. Metellus was elected a praetor for the following year, and the lot gave him the duty of presiding at trials for the offence of repetundae. The object of the friends of Verres was now to get the trial deferred to the next year, and to exclude Cicero from the curule aedileship by bribing the voters. Cicero had thus a personal motive for pushing the prosecution vigorously against a man whose stolen money was to deprive him of the object of his ambition. The friends of Verres had still hopes that the trial might be thrown over to the next year, when Q. Metellus and Q. Hortensius would be in office. M. Metellus would be sitting in the place of M'. Acilius Glabrio, and a dishonest set of judices could be packed. Cicero was however elected curule aedile, after the delivery of the Divinatio, as appears from the speech itself (Div. c. 22), and before the trial began (Act. i. c. 9). The Pseudo-Asconius, in the argument of the Divinatio, incorrectly calls him 'designatus aedilis.' Cicero then was aedilis designatus when he conducted the prosecution, and Hor-

tensius consul designatus was Verres' advocate. (Brutus, c. 92; Act. i. c. 13.)

The trial began on the 5th of Sextilis (August), according to the unreformed Calendar. The games of Cn. Pompeius in celebration of the successful termination of the war against Sertorius were to begin on the 15th of August and to last fifteen days; and these games would be followed by the Romani Ludi, which began on the 4th of September, and lasted fourteen days, with an interval of two days between the two sets of Romani Ludi. The opponents of Cicero expected that they should not have to begin the defence until these games were over. They would easily occupy with talking and legal quibbles all the time between the Romani Ludi and the Ludi of Victoria, which began on the 27th of October and lasted five days. The Plebeii Ludi in November would next follow, very little time would be left for business during the current year, and finally the trial, as they expected, would be postponed to the next, when M. Metellus would be praetor. (Act. i. c. 10.) But instead of delivering an elaborate speech, which he had prepared, Cicero opened his case briefly in the first Verrine oration (Actio Prima), and then stated the chief charges against Verres, confirming each statement as he went on by an examination of witnesses, and the production of documentary evidence. Hortensius occasionally interrupted the witnesses to make some objections, but the evidence was too strong for him, and he saw that a defence was impossible. He did not cross-examine any of Cicero's witnesses. (Act. ii. Lib. 5. c. 59.) Cicero only took nine days for the prosecution; and before the nine days were over, Verres left Rome for Marseille, and the judices condemned him to exile, and to make full compensation in damages. The assessment of the damages (litis aestimatio) came afterwards, as was usual in such cases. It seems that the Sicilians did not obtain full satisfaction; and we may assume that Verres thought it better to leave Rome with what he could take with him, than to wait for the result of the assessment and perhaps lose all that he had, and also run the risk of other prosecutions.

The oration entitled 'Divinatio,' and the 'Actio Prima,' were the only Verrine Orations which were spoken. Cicero wrote the other five after the trial. He has handled his matter so skilfully that, if we were unacquainted with this fact, we should never suspect that we were reading a rhetorical exercise; for such the five last Verrine Orations are, though the orator doubtless wished to leave to posterity not only a sample of his art, but a merciless exposure of the plunderer of Sicily, of his eloquent advocate, and of the senatorian body who had attempted to save him. Cicero however has transgressed the limits of his subject in the first of the five orations, which is chiefly on Verres' praetorship at Rome,

a matter entirely distinct from the prosecution for his misgovernment of Sicily; but the exposure of Verres in all the acts of his administration was consistent with his general design in publishing orations which were never delivered. At the time when Cicero wrote these Orations the *Lex* Aurelia, which made the judices eligible from the senate, the equites, and the tribuni aerarii, was promulgated. It is also possible, as Drumann observes, that the *Lex* was even enacted, though Cicero in direct terms speaks only of its promulgation (Act. ii. Lib. 2. c. 71; Lib 3. c. 96; Lib. 5. c. 69), and threatens that Aurelius Cotta would carry his *Lex* if Verres was acquitted. Now Verres, we know, was actually convicted at the time when Cicero wrote these words; and as Cicero represents Verres as still on his trial, in order to give to his Orations the air of being really delivered, so he would consistently represent the Aurelia *Lex* as not enacted, but only promulgated.

Verres lived in banishment until the proscription of the Triumviri, B.C. 43. He carried with him some of the works of art which he had collected during his official career, if the story is true that M. Antonius put his name in the proscription-lists because he would not give up to him his Corinthian vessels. (Plin. *Hist. Nat.* 34, c. 2; Seneca, *Suasor.* 6.) It seems unlikely that this was the only cause of his being proscribed; and yet it is not easy to suggest a good reason why such a man shared the fate of many who were better than himself, or why Antonius was his enemy. The same story adds that he died with courage, and not before he heard of the death of Cicero, the most illustrious victim of the vengeance of Antonius.

Drumann (Geschichte Roms, v. p. 263—328) has included in his Life of M. Tullius Cicero an Abstract of the Verrine Orations, and a History of the Prosecution of Verres. Halm also in his edition of Cicero's 'Reden gegen Q. Caecilius,' &c., Leipzig, 1852, has written a useful introduction to the Verrine Orations.

M. TULLII CICERONIS

IN

Q. CAECILIUM ORATIO

DE

ACCUSATORE IN C. VERREM CONSTITUENDO,

QUAE

DIVINATIO

DICITUR.

The Sicilians, with the exception of the Syracusans and the Mamertini, had asked Cicero to conduct their case against Verres; and, after he had consented, he applied to the praetor M'. Acilius Glabrio, who during this year presided in the Quaestiones perpetuae de pecuniis repetundis, for permission to be the accuser. Q. Caecilius Niger also put in his claim, though the Sicilians had not asked him, and did not want him. There were sufficient reasons why injured parties should not have the power of naming the person who should conduct their case, when the prosecution was a matter which concerned the public interest. There had sometimes been collusion between the guilty persons and those who came to demand satisfaction of them, or to bring them to punishment. The accused would secretly compound with their prosecutors for a sum of money, and the trial would be so managed as to result in an acquittal, and so the criminal would be secured against further risk. To prevent such an impudent fraud, the Lex, which defined each particular offence for which a man might be brought to a Judicium Publicum, provided that the Judices should choose the accuser, at least in cases where more than one person claimed the office. The practice was maintained under the Empire, as we see from a passage of Ulpian (Dig. 48. 2. 16): "Si plures exsistant qui eundem publicis judiciis accusare volunt, judex eligere debet eum qui accuset; causa scilicet cognita, aestimatis accusatorum personis vel de dignitate vel ex eo quod interest, vel aetate, vel moribus, vel alia justa de causa."

There is no evidence that Glabrio presided in this preliminary inquiry, nor that the Judices were those who sat on the trial of Verres. It seems, however, most likely that Glabrio would preside; and Cicero says (Act. ii. Lib. 1. c. 6), that several of those who were Judices on the trial of Verres had also acted as Judices in this preliminary inquiry. This is all that can be affirmed in the absence of direct evidence. The decision of the Judices in such a matter as this was not founded on any evidence, but on the speeches of the rival claimants, each of whom supported his own case by argument, and endeavoured to weaken the claim of his opponent. The Judices had to form their judgment, as well as they could, on what they thus heard. This 'actio de accusatore constituendo' was called 'Divinatio,' or divining; apparently because the Judices could do no more than make a kind of guess or probable conclusion as to the fitness of the opposing claimants. Asconius (commonly called Pseudo-Asconius) in his argument

gives some other reasons, one of which is founded on the statement that the Judices were 'injurati,' not sworn; which, if there is no other evidence than that of this Asconius, we may doubt. Quintilian (*Inst. Or.* vii. 4. § 33) says that such 'judicia' were called 'Divinationes.' The term 'Divinatio' is also explained in the same way by the grammarian Gabius Bassus (Gellius, ii. 4): "Divinatio judicium appellatur, quoniam divinet quodammodo judex oportet quam sententiam sese ferre par sit:" the Judices must guess, as Gellius explains the meaning of Bassus, because they had little to found their judgment upon. The name 'Divinatio' expressed the whole proceeding, the result of which was the selection of an accuser; and it was also used to signify the speech made on the occasion by the opposing claimants. C. Julius Caesar, the dictator, composed a 'Divinatio' (Sueton. *Julius Caesar*, c. 55).

The Actio Prima against Verres was delivered on the 5th of August, A.U.C. 684, or B.C. 70 (c. 10). A prosecutor, as already observed, had asked and obtained a period of 108 days in order to go to Achaea to collect materials for a prosecution (Act. ii. Lib. 1. c. 11); and though Cicero says that he never went to Achaea, we may perhaps conclude that Cicero could not commence his attack until the 108 days had expired. He himself had 110 days allowed for his journey to Sicily to collect evidence, and, though he was back again at Rome before the expiration of the time, the accuser who had only asked for 108 days had the priority over him, and Cicero must wait to see whether he really meant to avail himself of this advantage. If these conclusions are right, the period of 108 days reckoned back from the 5th of August will fix the time of the delivery of the 'Divinatio' somewhere in the latter part of April of the unreformed Calendar.

The edition of the Verrine orations in Baiter and Halm's edition of Orelli's Cicero is by C. A. Iordan.

The following is Iordan's description of the MSS. and editions which he has used.

I. Codices Meliores:

G 1 = Guelferbytanus antiquior, membranaceus.

G 2 = Guelferbytanus secundus, chartaceus. Ambo codices post Zumptium accurate contulimus, non paucos ejus errores correximus.

Ld = Leidensis a Petr. Burmanno negligenter collatus—Cum ex eodem fonte quo G. 1. 2. deductus sit, denuo eum conferre non erat operae pretium. Horum trium codicum consensum significavimus G 3.

s = Vetus codex C. Stephani, sine dubio ex numero Parisiensium, praestantissimus. Editionem C. Stephani significavimus St.

λ = Vetus codex Lambini, item praestantissimus, plerumque cum s conspirans.

D = Parisiensis nr. 7823, de quo v. Zumptium p. xii. Videtur non differre a Stephaniano.

Lg. 29 = Lagomarsinianus nr. 29, membranaceus Saec. xv., qui medium quendam locum tenet inter meliores et deteriores codices, sed propius tamen ad meliores accedit.

C = Cuiacianus, ex quo varias lectiones aliquot enotavit Lambinus, sicut ex codicibus Memmianis, quos significavimus codd. Lbi.

A = Pseudo-Asconius.

S = Scholiasta Gronovianus.

II. Codices Deteriores (dtt):

Huc sunt referendi Lagomarsiniani octo reliqui 1. 5. 6. 14. 27. 42. 45. 48, duo Palatini Gruteri, codex Ursini, codex Hotomani, duo Franciani Graevii, Innocentianus Garatonii, Meiningensis Facii, Huydecoperanus (H), Oxoniensis (ψ), tres Parisienses Lallemandi, quorum quidem incerta ac dubia est fides et auctoritas.

ctt = ceteri codices noti et diligenter collati, in quorum numero sunt maxime habendi

G. 1. 2. Lagomarsiniani omnes, H. Mein. ψ. Editionem Lambini 1566 significavimus L, Garatonii curas secundas, Ravennae asservatas et a Tych. Mommsenio mecum communicatas Garat. II, editionem Orellianam priorem O, editionem Klotzii Teubnerianam a. 1852. Kl.

I. Si quis vestrum, judices, aut eorum qui adsunt, forte miratur me, qui tot annos in causis judiciisque publicis ita sim versatus ut defenderim multos, laeserim neminem, subito nunc mutata voluntate ad accusandum descenderim, is si mei consilii causam rationemque cognoverit, una et id quod facio probabit, et in hac causa profecto neminem praeponendum mihi esse actorem putabit. Quum quaestor in Sicilia fuissem, judices, itaque ex ea provincia decessissem ut Siculis omnibus jucundam diuturnamque memoriam quaesturae nominisque mei relinquerem, factum est uti quum summum in veteribus patronis multis tum nonnullum etiam in me praesidium suis fortunis constitutum esse arbitrarentur. Qui nunc populati atque vexati cuncti ad me publice saepe venerunt, ut suarum fortunarum omnium causam defensionemque susciperem; me saepe

1. *miratur me,—descenderim*] Asconius, now commonly called Pseudo-Asconius, mentions a reading 'descendere,' which is the reading of some MSS., and has been adopted by Zumpt and Iordan. Asconius observes that 'descenderim' is a kind of soloecism, unless we prefix 'et' or 'idem' to 'subito.' But the text is right, and it would be spoilt by this interpolation, as well as by the change of 'descenderim' into 'descendere.' For Cicero does not mean to say, 'if any of you are surprised—that I have all at once descended to be an accuser;' but he says, 'if any of you are surprised at *me*, that I who for so many years, &c., now all at once have descended, &c.' Cicero had appeared as an advocate in the courts as early as B.C. 81; and there are still extant two orations which he delivered in B.C. 81 and 80. (See Pro P. Quintio; Pro S. Roscio Am., vol. ii.; and Brutus, c. 91).

judiciisque publicis] See the Excursus on the 'Iudicia Publica.'

actorem] 'Actor' is a general term for one who is a plaintiff. In a 'causa publica' the 'actor' was usually called 'accusator.' Here it means no more than the manager of the prosecution: as in c. 4, "Siculos omnes actorem suae causae." According to some, 'actor' is properly the plaintiff in actions 'in personam,' and 'petitor' the plaintiff in actions 'in rem.' But the general sense of the verb 'agere' is in favour of the supposition that 'actor' is the most general term that can be used.

decessissem] 'Decedere' is the word applied to a governor of a province, who leaves it when his term of office is expired; and it appears that it was also applicable to a quaestor leaving his province (c. 9). There is a reading 'discessissem,' G 3 ψ.

veteribus patronis] These old patroni, or protectors of the Sicilians, were the Marcelli (Act. ii. Lib. 4. c. 40), the Scipiones, and the Metelli. M. Marcellus, the conqueror of Syracuse, preserved the captured city. The younger Scipio Africanus restored to the Sicilians the works of art which the Carthaginians had carried away; and Metellus Celer and Nepos had on a former occasion given the Sicilians their protection in the prosecution of the praetor M. Lepidus (Asconius). It was usual for a province or for particular provincial cities to choose protectors (patroni) among the great families of Rome.

cuncti] "Simul omnes, quasi conjuncti" (Asconius). The commentator has indicated the etymology of the word; for 'cunctus' is 'coniunctus' or 'coiunctus.' See Pro Archia, c. 1. It is accordingly equivalent to 'universi' (c. 4). Compare 'universa provincia' (c. 5).

publice] 'Publice' means sent on a 'public mission,' deputed by the inhabitants of the island, or the cities of the island. This is a common usage of the word; and like the Greek κοινῇ. (See Caesar, B. G. i. 16; vi. 12; vii. 55.)

esse pollicitum, saepe ostendisse dicebant, si quod tempus accidisset quo tempore aliquid a me requirerent, commodis eorum me non defuturum. Venisse tempus aiebant non jam ut commoda sua sed ut vitam salutemque totius provinciae defenderem; sese jam ne deos quidem in suis urbibus ad quos confugerent habere, quod eorum simulacra sanctissima C. Verres ex delubris religiosissimis sustulisset; quas res luxuries in flagitiis, crudelitas in suppliciis, avaritia in rapinis, superbia in contumeliis efficere potuisset, eas omnes sese hoc uno praetore per triennium pertulisse; rogare et orare ne illos supplices aspernarer, quos me incolumi nemini supplices esse oporteret.

II. Tuli graviter et acerbe, judices, in eum me locum adduci ut aut eos homines spes falleret qui opem a me atque auxilium petissent, aut ego qui me ad defendendos homines ab ineunte adolescentia dedissem, tempore atque officio coactus ad accusandum traducerer. Dicebam habere eos actorem Q. Caecilium, qui praesertim quaestor in sua provincia [post me quaestorem] fuisset. Quo ego adjumento sperabam hanc a me posse molestiam dimoveri, id mihi erat adversarium maxime. Nam illi multo mihi hoc facilius remisissent, si istum non nossent, aut si iste apud eos quaestor non fuisset. Adductus sum, judices, officio, fide, misericordia, multorum bonorum exemplo, vetere consuetudine institutoque majorum, ut onus hujus laboris atque officii non ex meo sed ex meorum necessariorum tempore mihi suscipiendum putarem. Quo in negotio tamen illa me res, judices, consolatur, quod haec quae videtur esse accusatio mea non potius accusatio quam defensio est existimanda.

pollicitum] Cicero says 'saepe;' that he had often declared his readiness to serve the Sicilians; but Asconius refers this observation particularly to the address which he made to the Sicilians at Lilybaeum on retiring from the quaestorship of that division of the island. Klotz observes that Arusianus Messus has preserved some fragments of this speech (ed. Lindem. p. 226). The word 'polliceri' is a word of 'proffering,' 'voluntary proposing' (c. 6), and differs from 'promittere,' which implies an answer to an offer which had been made.

2. *qui praesertim*] 'Praesertim' is a word of emphasis, and often put in clauses with 'quum' and 'si;' and its place is generally after the word to which it gives emphasis. (See De Am. c. 4, and Seyffert's note.) But in c. 11 we have 'praesertim tanta.' Cicero says in substance, 'I told them that they might take Q. Caecilius to manage their case, especially as he had been,' &c.—'dimoveri:' 'demoveri,' 6 Lgg. Iordan.

istum—iste] Cicero in this oration generally refers to Caecilius, when he uses this pronoun; and in like manner in the following orations he uses 'iste' when he refers to Verres. It is not exactly a word of contempt in these cases, though, if he had been speaking of persons whom he respected, he might have used 'ille.' The 'iste' is the man whom I have mentioned to you, he whom you know.

ex meo tempore] 'Not out of regard to my interests, but to those of my friends.' Comp. Act. i. c. 11, 'ex istius tempore.' 'Ex tempore' has a different meaning (Act. ii. Lib. 3. c. 71). So we may compare 'jure,' and 'pro meo jure.'

Defendo enim multos mortales, multas civitates, provinciam Siciliam totam. Quamobrem quia mihi unus est accusandus, propemodum manere in instituto meo videor, et non omnino a defendendis hominibus sublevandisque discedere. Quod si hanc causam tam idoneam, tam illustrem, tam gravem non haberem; si aut hoc a me Siculi non petissent, aut mihi cum Siculis causa tantae necessitudinis non intercederet, et hoc quod facio me rei publicae causa facere profiterer, ut homo singulari cupiditate, audacia, scelere praeditus, cujus furta atque flagitia non in Sicilia solum sed in Achaia, Asia, Cilicia, Pamphylia, Romae denique ante oculos omnium maxima turpissimaque nossemus, me agente in judicium vocaretur; quis tandem esset qui meum factum aut consilium posset reprehendere?

III. Quid est, pro deum hominumque fidem, in quo ego rei publicae plus hoc tempore prodesse possim? Quid est quod aut populo Romano gratius esse debeat, aut sociis exterisque nationibus optatius esse possit, aut saluti fortunisque omnium magis accommodatum sit? Populatae, vexatae, funditus eversae provinciae: socii stipendiariique populi Romani afflicti, miseri, jam non salutis spem

sublevandis] A like use of 'sublevare,' 'to raise up,' occurs in c. 3 and 4. In conformity with the generalizing sense of Roman expressions, the word means either to 'raise up for the purpose of supporting,' or 'to raise up for the purpose of taking away, or removing,' as in Cicero De Am. c. 24. See note in Seyffert's edition, who compares the double use of 'sublevare' with that of the German verb 'heben.'

3. *pro deum hominumque fidem*] What did the Romans understand by this expression, which we find so difficult to translate? We must accept the Roman notion of 'fides,' which Cicero (De Off. i. 7) defines to be the 'foundation of justice,' that is, of just conduct or of the discharge of duty (Or. Part. 22), for so he explains 'justitia,' considered with reference to the conduct of individuals. Further, in the same passage of the De Officiis, he defines 'fides' to be 'dictorum conventorumque constantia et veritas,' or stedfastness and truth in all that we say and all that we promise. It is opposed to 'fraus,' one of the forms of 'injustitia.' The sense of the passage then is this: 'What is there, in the name of all that is truthful in the sight of gods and men,' &c. 'Fides et religio' often go together. Act. ii. Lib. 1. c. 8, 'fidem vestram ac religionem.' That the phrase should be used on less solemn occasions, with little or no regard to its meaning, is not surprising. See Ter. Andr. i. 5, 11; Hauton. i. 1, 9. Juvenal xiii. 31.

socii stipendiariique] The term 'socii' is often used in conjunction with 'Latini' or 'Nomen Latinum' (De Am. c. 3), to denote the free inhabitants of Italy who were in some sense under the dominion of Rome. The full enumeration of the inhabitants of Italy who were within the Roman dominion before the Social War, B.C. 90, was 'Cives Romani, Latini, et Socii.' The 'Cives Romani' were the citizens of Rome, the citizens of Roman colonies, and the inhabitants of Municipia, without any respect to their particular nationality. The Latini were the citizens of the old towns of the Latin nation, with the exception of those which had become Municipia; the numerous Coloniae Latinae were also comprehended under the term Latini. The Socii were the rest of the inhabitants of Italy, all of whom before the Social War became subject to Rome, and belonged to various nations. The term Socii would seem to imply something of a 'foedus,' by which they were connected with the Roman state. The Provinciales were the free subjects of Rome beyond the limits of Italy, and of course the term comprehended the Sicilians among others. Before the Social War there were only two classes of people

sed solatium exitii quaerunt. Qui judicia manere apud ordinem senatorium volunt, queruntur accusatores se idoneos non habere; qui accusare possunt, judiciorum severitatem desiderant. Populus Romanus interea, tametsi multis incommodis difficultatibusque affectus est, tamen nihil aeque in re publica atque illam veterem judiciorum vim gravitatemque requirit. Judiciorum desiderio tri-

within the Roman dominions, marked by a distinct *political* name, and these were Cives and Peregrini, for the term Peregrini comprised Latini, Socii, and Provinciales. After the Social War the Civitas was extended to all Italy, and even comprehended Gallia Cispadana, which, as is known, was not at that time included in the term Italia. Finally, even Gallia Transpadana obtained the Civitas in Cicero's lifetime. The class of Latini and Socii, as above defined, had now disappeared: they were Cives Romani. But a new class of Latini was formed—a class which, except in name, had no relationship to the former Latini: they had the Commercium, but not the Connubium. Henceforward we find three political classes in the Roman state—Cives, who had the Commercium and Connubium; Latini, who had only the Commercium; and Peregrini, who had neither. The Sicilians were Peregrini after the Social War, and at the time when Cicero was delivering this oration. When Cicero calls the Sicilians Socii, he uses the word just in the same sense as he does when he speaks of the Socii of the province of Asia (Ad Q. Fr. i. 1. c. 1); but not in the same sense in which he uses the word in another place (De Am. c. 3), when he is speaking of the Populus Romanus, Socii et Latini, of the time of Scipio Africanus the younger. He says that the inhabitants of Asia, of that province, consist of Socii, that is natives, and Cives, who were either Publicani or Negotiatores residing in the province. He calls the Romans resident in Asia, in one passage, Provinciales (Ad Q. Fr. i. 1. c. 5), but he only means men who are residing in a province, and not in Italy. The term Socii may have been applied to Peregrini out of Italy before the Social War; but, if that was the case, the Socii of Italy must have been distinguished from other Socii by the term Italici, which term, indeed, designates Italian Socii, without the addition of the word Socii. Cicero here speaks of Socii in the provinces as opposed to Stipendiarii, and he probably means those who had a 'foedus' or treaty with Rome. The Stipendiarii were those who were designated simply by a term which expressed their liability to make certain fixed payments, arbitrarily imposed, without any 'foedus' or terms of compact. The Socii might either be subject to fixed payments, or might be free from them; but the circumstance of their having a 'foedus' with Rome distinguished them from those who had not, and gave them a higher rank. This subject is discussed by Savigny, Vermischte Schriften, vol. i. Jus Italicum.

judicia manere] See the Excursus on the Judicia Publica.

aeque—atque] This form is common; it signifies 'so much as' (c. 12). The position of 'nihil' shows how it is to be understood: 'Nothing that you can name and that former energy and dignity of the judicia are called for in an equal degree.' Cicero (Brutus, 71) says, "qui tibi sunt aeque noti ac mihi." Compare Act. ii. Lib. 3. c. 19, "aequam partem tibi ac Populo Romano."

tribunicia potestas] L. Cornelius Sulla, during his dictatorship (B.C. 82—79), among other constitutional changes, got a law passed which deprived the Tribuni plebis of the power of proposing a Lex in the Comitia Tributa, and left them only their 'jus intercessionis.' They were deprived of that power which the Romans expressed by the words 'agere cum populo,' that is, the power of holding meetings and addressing the people either on the matter of a proposed Lex or on any public business. The voice of the tribunes was freedom of speech, which a tyrant feared then as he now fears the freedom of printing. The suppression of the tribunitian power was the destruction of Roman liberty. Sulla's law was repealed (B.C. 70) in the consulship of Cn. Pompeius Magnus and M. Licinius Crassus, a measure which Cicero, in another place, says that he could not commend (De Leg. iii. 9). The 'incommoda,' just before mentioned, are the various measures of Sulla, and the enactment as to the Tribuni plebis among the rest. Asconius explains the 'difficultates' to be the consequences of Sulla's proscriptions, the loss of property, and the other sufferings that he inflicted on his opponents.

'Incommodis' seems to us a vague word in this passage. Perhaps as it stands first,

bunicia potestas efflagitata est; judiciorum levitate ordo quoque alius ad res judicandas postulatur; judicum culpa atque dedecore etiam censorium nomen, quod asperius antea populo videri solebat, id nunc poscitur, id jam populare et plausibile factum est. In hac libidine hominum nocentissimorum, in populi Romani quotidiana querimonia, judiciorum infamia, totius ordinis offensione, quum hoc unum his tot incommodis remedium esse arbitrarer, ut homines idonei atque integri causam rei publicae legumque susciperent, fateor me salutis omnium causa ad eam partem accessisse rei publicae sublevandae quae maxime laboraret.

Nunc quoniam quibus rebus adductus ad causam accesserim demonstravi, dicendum necessario est de contentione nostra, ut in constituendo accusatore quid sequi possitis habeatis. Ego sic intelligo, judices: quum de pecuniis repetundis nomen cujuspiam deferatur, si certamen inter aliquos sit cui potissimum delatio detur, haec duo in primis spectari oportere; quem maxime velint actorem esse ii quibus factae esse dicantur injuriae, et quem minime velit is qui eas injurias fecisse arguatur. IV. In hac causa, judices, tametsi utrumque esse arbitror perspicuum, tamen de utroque dicam, et de eo prius quod apud vos plurimum debet valere, hoc est, de voluntate eorum quibus injuriae factae sunt, quorum causa

it should mean less than 'difficultatibus.' The Romans often use 'incommodum,' and in many cases it means a great deal more than we should suppose that it meant, if we looked to its etymological sense only. In Act. ii. Lib. 3. c. 50 it means 'loss.' Caesar often uses the word in the sense of a 'defeat' (i. 13; vii. 29).

ordo quoque alius] The 'ordo equestris' and the 'tribuni aerarii,' to whom with the 'senatores' the Lex Aurelia of B.C. 70 gave the judicial authority, which at the trial of Verres was in the hands of the 'senators' only. (See Introduction.)

censorium nomen] According to the Schol. Gronov., p. 384, ed. Orelli, Sulla abolished the censorship. However this may be, there were no censors from the dictatorship of Sulla to B.C. 70, the first consulship of Cn. Pompeius Magnus. The last lustrum preceding that of B.C. 70 was in B.C. 86.

plausibile] That which merits 'plaudite,' the word with which the Roman comedian generally concluded his plays, and by which he solicited the applause of the spectators. We have no equivalent word; for 'plausible' is a different thing.

offensio] In Act. i. c. 12, there occurs, 'in odium offensionemque populi Romani irruere,' where 'offensio' is the feeling, the aversion, and disgust of the subject which is expressed by the genitive case. The expression 'pedis offensio,' the striking of the foot against an obstacle, shows the primary sense of the word. Here the 'totius ordinis offensio' is the stumbling of the Senatorian ordo, their impinging on something, their false, unsteady step. See 'offensione,' c. 7 and 13.

nomen cujuspiam deferatur,] 'Nomen deferre,' or simply 'deferre,' in one of its senses, means to accuse, but only by virtue of its implication with the context; for 'deferre' also means to hand in or give in a man's name with the view of doing him a service, as in Cicero (Pro Balbo, c. 28), "Caesar in praetura, in consulatu praefectum fabrum detulit." See the use of 'rem defert,' Act. ii. Lib. 2. c. 71. In the sense of bringing a charge we have the words 'delatio,' 'delator.'

cujuspiam] In the next chapter we have 'cujusquam.' There seems little doubt that the terminations 'piam' and 'quam' are the same. The MSS. have often both in the same passage.

judicium de pecuniis repetundis est constitutum. Siciliam provinciam C. Verres per triennium depopulatus esse, Siculorum civitates vastasse, domos exinanisse, fana spoliasse dicitur. Adsunt, queruntur Siculi universi; ad meam fidem quam habent spectatam jam et cognitam confugiunt; auxilium sibi per me a vobis atque a populi Romani legibus petunt; me defensorem calamitatum suarum, me ultorem injuriarum, me cognitorem juris sui, me actorem causae totius esse voluerunt. Utrum, Q. Caecili, hoc dicis, me non Siculorum rogatu ad causam accedere, an optimorum fidelissimorumque sociorum voluntatem apud hos gravem esse non oportere? Si id audebis dicere, quod C. Verres cui te inimicum esse simulas maxime existimari vult, Siculos hoc a me non petisse, primum causam inimici tui sublevabis, de quo non praejudicium sed plane

4. *constitutum.*] He means *this* trial for repetundae is allowed, in consequence of the 'postulatio,' demand, of a prosecutor being admitted (recepta) by the praetor. If he had been speaking of the establishment of the 'quaestio perpetua' he would have said 'institutum.' See c. 21.

cognitorem juris sui,] One man could represent another, as plaintiff or defendant, in a suit, and act for him. If such an agent or attorney was appointed by a party to a suit for a particular case in the presence of the opposing party, he was called 'cognitor' (Pro Q. Roscio Com. c. 11). It was not necessary that the 'cognitor' must be present when he was appointed (Gaius, iv. 83, &c.). The 'cognitor' in all respects represented the person who had appointed him. A 'procurator' was an agent who was appointed by an absent party (Act. ii. Lib. 2. c. 24), and he was bound to give security that his principal would ratify all that he did (Gaius, iv. 98; Dig. 46. tit. 8; Puchta, *Instit.* ii. § 156). The term 'cognitor' is only applied to private or civil suits. Cicero here intends to show that he represented the Sicilians in every respect, for every demand; he was their 'representative for the recovery of their just claims.' Asconius has a note on 'patronus,' 'advocatus,' 'cognitor,' 'procurator,' which is short, but quite correct. The writer of this particular note was not Pseudo-Asconius.

Si id audebis, &c.] "If you shall dare to say what C. Verres, whose enemy you pretend to be, would have people above all things believe, that the Sicilians have not requested me to undertake their prosecution, in the first place you will be helping the cause of your own enemy, as to whom it is not a 'praejudicium,' but really a 'judicium' that is now considered to have been made, inasmuch as it is the universal belief that all the Sicilians have looked out for a manager of their case to prosecute Verres for his unlawful acts." Orelli has 'actorem me suae causae,' which was Menard's conjecture, but 'me' is not in the MSS., nor is it necessary. Caecilius might deny that Cicero was selected as the advocate of the Sicilians; but that would not disprove the truth of the general opinion that the Sicilians had sought an advocate, for every body believed that they had, and the advocate was not Caecilius, at least. The bare fact of all Sicily agreeing to choose some one to prosecute their case, Cicero says further, must be considered a condemnation of Verres. The word 'praejudicium' cannot be translated by an English noun. The name of the Roman form of action called 'praejudicium,' or 'actio praejudicialis,' is derived from the circumstance that it had no 'condemnatio' as a consequence, but its end was to establish the existence of a fact, or facts, which might serve as the foundation of further proceedings (Gaius, iv. 44, 94; Dig. 25. tit. 3. s. 1, 3). Cicero's use of the word may be hardly exact, but he means this: 'the fact of the Sicilians having all agreed to choose some manager or other of their case, a fact which may be considered as certain, is no mere preliminary to the trial; it is the condemnation of Verres.'—The form 'percrebuit' is probably correct, though 'percrebruit' may be the true etymological form. The MSS. here have both forms. The reason for the omission of the last 'r' is plain (Lib. 2. c. 3, note).

judicium jam factum putatur, quod ita percrebuit Siculos omnes actorem suae causae contra illius injurias quaesisse. Hoc si tu inimicus ejus factum negabis, quod ipse cui maxime haec res obstat negare non audet, videto ne nimium familiariter inimicitias exercere videare. Deinde sunt testes viri clarissimi nostrae civitatis quos omnes a me nominari non est necesse: eos qui adsunt appellabo; quos, si mentirer, testes esse impudentiae meae minime vellem. Scit is qui est in consilio C. Marcellus; scit is quem adesse video Cn. Lentulus Marcellinus; quorum fide atque praesidio Siculi maxime nituntur, quod omnino Marcellorum nomini tota illa provincia adjuncta est. Hi sciunt hoc non modo a me petitum esse, sed ita saepe et ita vehementer esse petitum ut aut causa mihi suscipienda fuerit aut officium necessitudinis repudiandum. Sed quid ego his testibus utor, quasi res dubia aut obscura sit? Adsunt homines ex tota provincia nobilissimi qui praesentes vos orant atque obsecrant, judices, ut in actore causae suae deligendo vestrum judicium ab suo judicio ne discrepet. Omnium civitatum totius Siciliae legationes adsunt praeter duas civitates, quarum duarum, si adessent, duo crimina vel maxima minuerentur quae cum his civitatibus C. Verri communicata sunt. At enim cur a me potissimum hoc praesidium petiverunt? Si esset dubium petissent [a me praesidium] necne, dicerem cur petissent. Nunc vero quum id ita perspicuum sit ut oculis judicare possitis, nescio cur hoc mihi detrimento esse debeat, si id mihi objiciatur me potis-

videto ne] 'You must take care, that you be not considered to be a friend while you are merely pretending to be an enemy.' The 'videto' is more emphatic and imperative than 'vide,' and it may be appropriately called the imperative mood, as opposed to the weaker form 'vide,' which may be called the jussive mood.—*Key's Latin Grammar*, 1st Ed. See also 2d Ed.

qui est in consilio] C. Marcellus was one of the 'judices,' whom Cicero was addressing. The body of the 'judices' was called a 'consilium;' "Cum consilio causam Mamertinorum cognoscit, et de consilii sententia . . . pronuntiat" (Act. ii. Lib. 5. c. 21). Cn. Cornelius Lentulus Marcellinus was originally a Marcellus, and he had passed by adoption into the family of the Lentuli; but the form Marcell*inus* added to his name indicated his original family. He was afterwards consul, B.C. 56. Of Marcellinus he says 'quem adesse video:' he was one of the 'corona populi circum subsellia stans,' as Asconius explains the expression 'eorum qui adsunt,' c. 1.

maxime nituntur] Zumpt and Klotz have 'maxime utuntur,' the reading of the MSS.

praeter duas civitates,] The two states were the Syracusani (Act. ii. Lib. 2. c. 14, &c.) and the Mamertini (Lib. 5. c. 17). These passages will explain why these two cities did not take a part in the prosecution of Verres.

cum his . . communicata sunt] 'shared between these towns and Verres.' Their crime and his was one, but the guilt of these towns would have been diminished, if they had joined in the prosecution of Verres.

necne,] This is one of the rarer forms of expressing a disjunctive proposition by 'necne' only; the most common form is 'utrum—an.' Comp. the form c. 14, 'utrum velis, factum esse necne,' &c.

oculis judicare possitis,] "ut oculis in utram partem fluat judicari non possit." Caesar, B. G. i. 12.

simum esse delectum. Verum id mihi non sumo, judices, et hoc non modo in oratione mea non pono, sed ne in opinione quidem cujusquam relinquo, me omnibus patronis esse praepositum. Non ita est: sed uniuscujusque temporis, valetudinis, facultatis ad agendum ducta ratio est. Mea fuit semper haec in hac re voluntas et sententia, quemvis ut hoc mallem de iis qui essent idonei suscipere quam me, me ut mallem quam neminem.

V. Reliquum est jam ut illud quaeramus, quum hoc constet Siculos a me petisse, ecquid hanc rem apud vos animosque vestros valere oporteat, ecquid auctoritatis apud vos in suo jure repetundo socii populi Romani supplices vestri habere debeant. De quo quid ego plura commemorem? quasi vero dubium sit quin tota lex de pecuniis repetundis sociorum causa constituta sit. Nam civibus quum sunt ereptae pecuniae, civili fere actione et privato jure repetuntur: haec lex socialis est; hoc jus nationum exterarum est; hanc habent arcem minus aliquanto nunc quidem munitam quam antea, verumtamen, si qua reliqua spes est quae sociorum animos consolari possit, ea tota in hac lege posita est, cujus legis non modo a populo Romano sed etiam ab ultimis nationibus jampridem severi custodes requiruntur. Quis ergo est qui neget oportere eorum arbitratu lege agi quorum causa lex sit constituta? Sicilia tota, si

patronis] Here Cicero by implication calls himself a 'patronus,' which is equivalent to 'orator,' the person who managed a cause before the 'judices' and delivered the speech. The 'advocatus' of Cicero's time was a person who gave his legal advice and was present at a trial, without taking any further part.

neminem.] As Asconius remarks, Caecilius is comprehended under 'nemo.' Caecilius was a nobody. The position of 'nemo' at the end of a sentence is a common form of emphatic expression.

5. *ecquid*] This 'ec' prefixed to 'quis,' 'quid,' seems to vary the sense somewhat. It is used both in direct and in indirect forms. Compare 'ecquis unquam,' c. 17. The translation is, 'whether this matter ought to have any influence with you,' &c.

in suo jure repetundo] 'In recovering their rights,' that is, in getting their rights acknowledged by a competent jurisdiction, and in obtaining satisfaction or compensation for their wrongs. Conformably to this meaning is the title of the 'Lex de pecuniis repetundis,' which Cicero affirms to have been enacted entirely for the benefit of the 'Socii;' though the fact is that a Roman citizen also might avail himself of it. See the Excursus on the 'Leges de pecuniis repetundis.'

civili fere actione . . repetuntur] Generally a Roman citizen would sue to recover damages or compensation under the 'Jus civile,' that is, the peculiar law of the Romans; for, though every 'Lex' was a part of the 'Jus Civile Romanorum' in its wider sense, Cicero means to call this 'Lex de repetundis' rather a 'Lex' enacted for the benefit of the 'Socii' (lex socialis), than as properly a part of the 'Jus Civile Romanorum.' He adds, 'privato jure;' that is, the injured Roman would sue simply as an individual for damages and satisfaction. The words 'repetere,' 'repetitio' are the technical terms for the recovery of damages in all cases (Dig. 12. 6. 7; 12. 5. 4. § 2) civil and private as well as public. The nature of the Roman division of law into 'Publicum' and 'Privatum' is explained in the Excursus on the 'Judicia Publica.'

lege agi] 'that the prosecution should be conducted according to law,' here according to the special Lex. 'Lege agere' means generally, to proceed by legal means. Act. ii. Lib. 2. c. 16.

una voce loqueretur, hoc diceret: Quod auri, quod argenti, quod ornamentorum in meis urbibus, sedibus, delubris [fuit]; quod in unaquaque re beneficio senatus populique Romani juris habui, id mihi tu, C. Verres, eripuisti atque abstulisti; quo nomine abs te sestertium millies ex lege repeto. Si universa, ut dixi, provincia loqui posset, hac voce uteretur: quoniam id non poterat, harum rerum actorem quem idoneum esse arbitrata est ipsa delegit. In ejusmodi re quisquam tam impudens reperietur qui ad alienam causam invitis iis quorum negotium est accedere aut adspirare audeat?

VI. Si tibi, Q. Caecili, hoc Siculi dicerent: Te non novimus; nescimus qui sis; numquam te antea vidimus; sine nos per eum nostras fortunas defendere cujus fides est nobis cognita; nonne id dicerent quod cuivis probare deberent? Nunc hoc dicunt: utrumque se nosse; alterum se cupere defensorem esse fortunarum suarum, alterum plane nolle. Cur nolint, etiamsi taceant, satis dicunt. Verum non tacent. Tamen his invitissimis te offeres? tamen in aliena causa loquere? tamen eos defendes qui se ab omnibus desertos potius quam abs te defensos esse malunt? tamen iis operam tuam pollicebere qui te neque velle sua causa, nec, si cupias, posse arbitrantur? Cur eorum spem exiguam reliquarum fortunarum, quam habent in legis et in judicii severitate positam, vi extorquere conaris? cur te interponis invitissimis iis quibus maxime

beneficio senatus, &c.] The Romans allowed the Sicilians to retain the 'Leges Hieronicae,' and gave them also rules for the general administration of the island, which were made by Rupilius and ten commissioners, B.C. 132. Verres violated all these rules which the Roman state gave the Sicilians for their benefit and protection (Lib. 2).

sestertium millies] Milies, or milliens, a thousand times a hundred thousand 'sestertes.' Asconius remarks that Cicero has been blamed (by critics) for claiming a thousand here, and only four hundred in other places (Act. i. c. 18; Act. ii. Lib. 1. c. 10). Without adopting all or any of the old commentators' explanations, it is enough to observe that Cicero says here, that the amount of damages which he claimed was one thousand. In the two other passages, he says that Verres had wrongfully taken four hundred. All that can be inferred then is, that he here claims higher damages than the actual damages; as to which, see the Excursus 'De pecuniis repetundis.'

Si universa . . loqui posset . . uteretur: quoniam . . non poterat,] If any person is in danger of misunderstanding 'posset' and 'uteretur,' the word 'poterat' may help to save him from it. 'If, as I said, the province could have spoken with one voice (for this is the meaning), it would have spoken as I have just done: since it could not, it has chosen,' &c. Compare 'dicerent' in the next chapter. This form of the imperfect is often used to express an impossible hypothesis.

6. *Cur nolint, etiamsi taceant, satis dicunt.*] 'Why they would not choose to have you, they tell you plain enough, even if they should be silent.'—'taceant' G3 r, 'tacerent' dtt.

Tamen his] So 'tamen' is sometimes placed at the beginning of a sentence, 'Tamen eum adducam,' Ter. And. i. 4. 4.

velle sua causa,] 'Velle' is thus used elliptically with an ablative, as "credo tua causa velle Lentulum" (ad Q. Fr. i. 4, 5); and also 'cupere,' as "cujus causa omnia cum cupio, tum mehercule etiam debeo" (ad Fam. xiii. 75). (Halm.)

lex consultum esse vult? cur de quibus in provincia non optime es meritus, eos nunc plane fortunis omnibus conaris evertere? cur his non modo persequendi juris sui sed etiam deplorandae calamitatis adimis potestatem? Nam te actore quem eorum adfuturum putas, quos intelligis non ut per te alium sed ut per aliquem te ipsum ulciscantur laborare?

VII. At enim solidum id est ut me Siculi maxime velint: alterum illud, credo, obscurum est, a quo Verres minime se accusari velit. Ecquis umquam tam palam de honore, tam vehementer de salute sua contendit quam ille atque illius amici [ut] ne haec mihi delatio detur? Sunt multa quae Verres in me esse arbitratur, quae scit in te, Q. Caecili, non esse; quae cujusmodi in utroque nostrum sint paullo post commemorabo. Nunc tantum id dicam quod tacitus tu mihi assentiare; nullam rem in me esse quam ille contemnat; nullam in te quam pertimescat. Itaque magnus ille defensor et amicus ejus tibi suffragatur, me oppugnat; aperte a judicibus petit ut tu mihi anteponare, et ait hoc se honeste sine ulla invidia ac sine ulla offensione contendere. Non enim, inquit, illud peto, quod soleo

lex consultum esse vult?] 'Vult' expresses the design or purpose of the law, conformably to the general sense of 'velle,' which is not the 'wish,' but the 'will.' 'Cupere' is the 'desire,' 'velle' is the 'resolve,' 'optare' is the 'choice' or 'selection' out of various things presented of one that seems the best. See c. 14, 'potestatem optionemque.' The distinction of 'cupiditas' and 'voluntas' is clear.

cur his] 'cur iis,' Iordan; a matter of indifference here: the words 'ii' and 'hi' are constantly confounded or interchanged in the MSS. A little further on Orelli had 'Num te actore,' &c., which is the reading of some inferior MSS., and 'nunc' of one MS. But 'nam,' the reading of Klotz, Zumpt, and Iordan, appears to be the true reading; and 'nam' is easily confounded with 'num,' and 'num' with 'nunc.' If we read 'num,' the word 'quem' has the force of an enclitic without having its place, which should be next to 'num;' for the interrogation lies in the 'num.' But the interrogation ought to be in the 'quem,' and that can only be by reading 'nam.' This use of 'nam,' not to express an inference, but a transition to a thing on which the speaker does not intend to dwell, is very common. Comp. De Am. c. 27, 'Nam quid de studiis,' &c., and c. 13, 'nam quibusdam,' &c., and Seyffert's note. —'per aliquem:' Zumpt, Klotz, and Iordan have 'per alium aliquem,' the reading of Gl 2 D C s.

7. *At enim solidum &c.*] Comp. c. 4, 'At enim cur,' which means, 'well, but it may be said why,' &c. Here it means, 'well, suppose this be established that,' &c. 'The other thing, I suppose, is not clear,' &c., which is said ironically, 'credo' being often thus employed. All the known MSS. have 'solum,' which may have arisen from an abbreviation of 'solidum.' But Lambinus affirms that some MSS. have 'solidum.' It is curious to see how the commentators have handled this matter in the Variorum edition.

'Solidum' means 'whole,' 'entire,' or, if we choose, 'clear,' as opposed to 'obscurum.' The sense is this: 'well, you grant me all this that,' &c., 'you acknowledge that this admission is completely due to me;' in which sense it is very near akin to the legal sense of 'solidum' in an 'obligatio,' where there may be several debtors, and each bound in the whole sum to the creditor (Dig. 45. 2. 3). Klotz, Zumpt, and Iordan have 'solum,' which I don't understand.

amicus ejus tibi] Hortensius is meant, and the word 'Hortensius' is inserted after 'tibi' by some editors, though it is omitted in the best MSS.

invidia . . offensione] 'without bringing any ill-will or disfavour on the Judices.'

quum vehementius contendi impetrare, reus ut absolvatur non peto; sed ut potius ab hoc quam ab illo accusetur, id peto. Da mihi hoc; concede quod facile est, quod honestum, quod non invidiosum; quod quum dederis, sine ullo tuo periculo, sine infamia illud dederis, ut is absolvatur cujus ego causa laboro. Et ait idem, ut aliquis metus adjunctus sit ad gratiam, certos esse in consilio quibus ostendi tabellas velit; id esse perfacile; non enim singulos ferre sententias, sed universos constituere; ceratam unicuique tabellam dari cera legitima, non illa infami ac nefaria. Atque is non tam propter Verrem laborat quam quod eum minime res tota delectat. Videt enim, si a pueris nobilibus quos adhuc elusit, si a quadruplatoribus quos non sine causa contempsit semper ac pro nihilo putavit, accusandi voluntas ad viros fortes spectatosque homines translata sit, sese in judiciis diutius dominari non posse. VIII. Huic ego

quum vehementius contendi] Asconius explains these words to mean 'quum pecuniam judicibus dedi,' and adds, that Cicero does not say this in direct terms, because he introduces Hortensius as speaking. Klotz thinks that the false Asconius is right —I do not.

aliquis metus, &c.] This sentence is not very clear, though the general meaning is plain. The 'gratia' is the bribery; but it was not enough to bribe, it was necessary to secure the rogue's voting as he had promised. The 'judices' voted by ballot; and Hortensius is supposed to say that he has persons among the 'judices' who will look at the 'tabellae,' or voting-tablets, of the doubtful men, and see that they vote as they have promised. The words 'id esse perfacile' are not clear, and 'non enim,' &c. cannot refer to them. He says that the 'judices' do not severally place their tablets in the box (cista), but put them in altogether; which is no reason why it would be easier to see how they voted. The words 'non enim' must refer to 'ostendi tabellas velit.' He would have the 'tabellae' shown to certain trustworthy rogues among the 'judices,' and this could easily be managed; and the reason for its being necessary is that the 'judices' put their tablets in all in a lump; they must, therefore, show them first, that the certain rogues might know how the rest voted. Another reason is added why they must show them, in order that their votes may be known. They had all got tablets of 'cera legitima,' all of one colour, all alike, so that a man's vote could not be known from the colour of the tablets, which had been given him, and on which he must write his vote. The fact that this infamous coloured tablet (Act. i. c. 13) was not used, or going to be used, on this occasion, has nothing to do with the 'perfacile,' but with the 'ostendi tabellas velit,' which was 'perfacile.' "You have got your 'cera legitima,'" says Hortensius with a sneer, "you have the uniform tablets, which the 'lex' (for that is the meaning of 'legitima') requires; you have not got that infamous and wicked tablet of divers colours," he adds sarcastically, "but yet I will find out how you vote. I have men among you, who will look after you."

pueris nobilibus] Youngsters who belonged to the nobility, sons of men who had filled curule offices. The old commentator mentions the case of Appius Claudius Pulcher, a noble youth, who accused Terentius Varro (B.C. 75) of 'repetundae,' and failed, owing to the management of Hortensius, who employed these tablets of different colours for the purpose of discovering whether the 'judices' whom he bribed, voted as they promised. See Rein, Das Criminalrecht der Römer, p. 653.

quadruplatoribus] 'Quadruplatores' were probably those who undertook prosecutions in those cases in which some 'lex' gave them a portion of the penalty or damages; as in 'qui tam' actions in England, where a man sues for a penalty, part for the crown, and part for himself. "Majores enim nostri hoc sic habuerunt et ita in legibus posuerunt, furem dupli condemnari, foeneratorem quadrupli," Cato de Re Rustica, 1. Whatever may be the original sense of the word, Cicero means men who prosecute only for their own profit. See Tacit. Ann. iv. 20; and Rein, Das Criminalrecht der Römer, p. 809.

homini jam ante denuntio, si a me causam hanc vos agi volueritis, rationem illi defendendi totam esse mutandam; et ita tamen mutandam ut meliore et honestiore conditione sit quam qua ipse esse vult; ut imitetur homines eos quos ipse vidit amplissimos, L. Crassum et M. Antonium, qui nihil se arbitrabantur ad judicia causasque amicorum praeter fidem et ingenium afferre oportere. Nihil erit quod me agente arbitretur judicium sine magno multorum periculo posse corrumpi. Ego in hoc judicio mihi Siculorum causam receptam, populi Romani susceptam esse arbitror, ut mihi non unus homo improbus opprimendus sit, id quod Siculi petiverunt, sed omnino omnis improbitas, id quod populus Romanus jamdiu flagitat, exstinguenda atque delenda sit. In quo [ego] quid eniti aut quid efficere possim malo in aliorum spe relinquere quam in oratione mea ponere.

Tu vero, Caecili, quid potes? quo tempore aut qua in re non modo ceteris specimen aliquod dedisti, sed tute tui periculum fecisti? In mentem tibi non venit quid negotii sit causam publicam sustinere, vitam alterius totam explicare atque eam non modo in animis judicum sed etiam in oculis conspectuque omnium exponere, sociorum salutem, commoda provinciarum, vim legum, gravitatem judiciorum defendere? IX. Cognosce ex me, quoniam hoc primum tempus discendi nactus es, quam multa esse oporteat in eo qui alterum accuset; ex quibus si unum aliquod in te cognoveris, ego jam tibi ipse istuc quod expetis mea voluntate concedam. Primum integritatem atque innocentiam singularem. Nihil est enim quod minus ferendum sit quam rationem ab altero vitae reposcere eum qui non possit suae reddere. Hic ego de te plura non dicam: unum illud credo omnes animadvertere, te adhuc ab nullis nisi ab Siculis potuisse cognosci; Siculos hoc dicere, quum eidem sint irati cui tu te inimicum esse dicis, sese tamen te actore ad judicium non

8. *denuntio*] A word which Cicero often uses. It means 'to give a person notice.' It has not a technical meaning here, but is used in a general sense. It has, however, often the signification of giving legal notice. Pro Caecina, c. 7 and 32. Compare the use of 'denuntiare' in De Sen. c. 6.

ut meliore, &c.] 'ut meliore et honestiore conditione, quam qua ipse vult, imitetur homines.' Iordan.

L. Crassum, &c.] L. Licinius Crassus, and M. Antonius, the two great orators whom Cicero introduces in his treatise De Oratore.

receptam—susceptam] Quite misexplained by Asconius. 'Recipere' is to undertake what a man is asked to undertake, or it signifies the undertaking of that which he is by some antecedent bound to undertake; so that the *re*, according to this explanation, has its proper force. 'Suscipere' has no reference at all to the cause or motive: it states a fact simply, or as a consequence, for 'qui recipit suscipit.' Zumpt refers to the like use of 'recipere' and 'suscipere' in Act. ii. Lib. 2. c. 1; and Klotz to the De Oratore, ii. 24, "in quo est illa quidem magna offensio vel negligentiae susceptis rebus vel perfidiae receptis." See also Act. i. c. 12.

adfuturos. Quare negent ex me non audies: hos patere id suspicari quod necesse est. Illi quidem, ut est hominum genus nimis acutum et suspiciosum, non te ex Sicilia litteras in Verrem deportare velle arbitrantur, sed quod iisdem litteris illius praetura et tua quaestura consignata sit, asportare te velle ex Sicilia litteras suspicantur. Deinde accusatorem firmum verumque esse oportet. Eum ego si te putem cupere esse, facile intelligo esse non posse. Nec ea dico quae, si dicam, tamen infirmare non possis, te antequam de Sicilia decesseris in gratiam redisse cum Verre; Potamonem scribam et familiarem tuum retentum esse a Verre in provincia, quum tu decederes; M. Caecilium, fratrem tuum, lectissimum atque ornatissimum adolescentem, non modo non adesse neque tecum tuas injurias persequi, sed esse cum Verre, et cum illo familiarissime atque amicissime vivere. Sunt et haec et alia in te falsi accusatoris signa permulta, quibus ego nunc non utor: hoc dico, te, si maxime cupias, tamen verum accusatorem esse non posse. Video enim permulta esse crimina quorum tibi societas cum Verre ejusmodi est ut ea in accusando attingere non audeas.

X. Queritur Sicilia tota C. Verrem ab aratoribus, quum frumentum sibi in cellam imperavisset, et quum esset tritici modius HS II, pro frumento in modios singulos duodenos sestertios exegisse.

9. *ut est hominum genus*] Klotz remarks that Cicero casts a slight censure on the sharpness and jealousy of the Sicilians, to let Caecilius know what he may expect, if he obtrudes himself on them as their 'patronus.' As to the use of 'ut,' compare De Sen. c. 4, 'ut in homine Romano;' De Or. iii. 18; and Caesar, B. G. iii. 8. vii. 22.

deportare—asportare] The false Asconius explains 'deportare' correctly enough, as far as he goes, 'ut mutet locum;' as to 'asportare' he says, 'ut intereat.' 'Deportare,' or 'deferre,' means to bring the documents to Rome, or such other place as the person was ordered to bring them to, who received a commission for that purpose. (Act. ii. Lib. 2. c. 26. Lib. 4. c. 42.) 'Asportare,' says Klotz, is 'to carry off,' not for any particular purpose, but simply 'to carry away.' So far the explanation is true; but the word seems to mean by implication here, to carry away with the intention of suppressing. It is used again, Act. ii. Lib. 2. c. 36; Lib. 3. c. 12; Lib. 4. c. 41.

scribam] A 'scriba' is a public clerk or writer, such as were employed in keeping the public accounts and copying. See what Cicero says of them, Act. ii. Lib. 3. c. 78, 79. The body of 'Scribae' was numerous, and had considerable influence at Rome, as they were employed in all branches of administration. They were divided into Decuriae, a kind of associations or corporations. The various magistrates, such as quaestors, aediles, and so forth, had Scribae attached to them.

10. *Queritur, &c.*] The cultivators (aratores) besides paying their tenths were required to furnish a certain quantity of grain for the praetor's use, for his 'cella' or storehouse (see De Sen. c. 16, for the general use of 'cella'); but he took money instead, and when wheat was two sestertii the modius, he made them pay him twelve. (See Act. ii. Lib. 2. c. 60; Lib. 3. c. 81.) Cicero has already urged several reasons against the fitness of Caecilius to be the accuser, which have not much weight, and this is weaker than the rest. It is true that he charges Caecilius with doing the same thing that Verres did, but he does not come to particulars.

'Frumentum imperare' means to impose on them a requisition. See Caesar, B. G. vi. 4. As to 'Aratores,' see Lib. iii.

Magnum crimen, ingens pecunia, furtum impudens, injuria non ferenda. Ego hoc uno crimine illum condemnem necesse est: tu, Caecili, quid facies? Utrum hoc tantum crimen praetermittes an objicies? Si objicies, idne alteri crimini dabis quod eodem tempore in eadem provincia tu ipse fecisti? Audebis ita accusare alterum ut quo minus tute condemnere recusare non possis? Sin praetermittes, qualis erit ista tua accusatio, quae domestici periculi metu certissimi et maximi criminis non modo suspicionem verum etiam mentionem ipsam pertimescat? Emptum est ex S. C. frumentum ab Siculis praetore Verre, pro quo frumento pecunia omnis soluta non est. Grave est hoc crimen in Verrem, grave me agente; te accusante nullum. Eras enim tu quaestor; pecuniam publicam tu tractabas; ex qua, etiamsi cuperet praetor, tamen ne qua deductio fieret magna ex parte tua potestas erat. Hujus quoque igitur criminis te accusante mentio nulla fiet. Silebitur toto judicio de maximis et notissimis illius furtis et injuriis. Mihi crede, Caecili, non potest in accusando socios vere defendere is qui cum reo criminum societate conjunctus est. Mancipes a civitatibus pro frumento pecuniam exegerunt. Quid, hoc Verre praetore factum est solum?

domestici] 'your own.' So Cicero writes 'domesticum incommodum,' 'a man's own loss.'

Emptum est, &c.] A quantity of corn had been purchased in Sicily by an order of the Senate, probably for the victualling of Rome, after the fashion of the time; and it was not all paid for; and Caecilius, as the quaestor, had the handling of the money. Klotz remarks that this charge also is a feeble one; for the quaestor was bound to obey the praetor's orders. He had indeed the care of the money, and must account for it to the Aerarium; but he must obey the orders of the praetor as to payment or non-payment. He quotes, in support of this, a passage of Polybius (vi. 12), to prove that the quaestor at Rome must make the payments which the consul ordered him to make. But this is not quite decisive. It might be, that in the case of corn purchased for Rome he was absolutely bound to pay, and that he was provided with money for the purpose. However this may be, it is true, as Klotz remarks, that Cicero's expression, 'magna ex parte tua potestas erat,' is but a feeble way of affirming the quaestor's responsibility in the matter. But Klotz, in his zeal to defend Caecilius, goes a little too far. He argues, from what Cicero says at the end of the next chapter, that the authority of the praetor over the quaestor was supreme. But it does not follow, that if Verres could prevent Caecilius from doing wrong, he could prevent him from doing right: if he could prevent him from paying money when he ought not, or from mis-applying money, it does not follow that he could prevent him from paying it when he ought, or from applying it properly. Again, in the matter of the Mancipes at the end of this chapter, Cicero says that Caecilius could have prevented the fraud. Whether this is true or not, it makes Cicero consistent.

Mancipes] Here they are the farmers (fermiers généraux), who paid a sum of money to the state for the right of levying certain imposts. 'Manceps' means generally a person who purchases any thing from the state, or agrees to pay a certain sum by way of farm or the like (Festus v. Manceps; and Act. ii. Lib. 1. c. 64; Pro S. Roscio Am. c. 8). These Mancipes paid a certain sum for the right of collecting certain imposts in kind, but not to take money instead (Act. ii. Lib. 3. c. 71), "Praesertim quum ex iisdem agris ejusdem anni frumentum ex decumis Romam mancipes advexissent." See Cicero, Pro Cn. Plancio, c. 26, ed. Wunder.

Non; sed etiam quaestore Caecilio. Quid igitur daturus es huic crimini quod et potuisti prohibere ne fieret, et debuisti? an totum id relinques? Ergo id omnino Verres in judicio suo non audiet, quod quum faciebat quemadmodum defensurus esset non reperiebat.

XI. Atque ego haec quae in medio posita sunt commemoro. Sunt alia magis occulta furta, quae ille ut istius, credo, animos atque impetus retardaret benignissime cum quaestore suo communicavit. Haec tu scis ad me esse delata, quae si velim proferre, facile omnes intelligent vobis inter vos non modo voluntatem fuisse conjunctam, sed ne praedam quidem adhuc esse divisam. Quapropter si tibi indicium postulas dari quod tecum una feceris, concedo, si id lege permittitur; sin autem de accusatione dicimus, concedas oportet iis qui nullo suo peccato impediuntur quo minus alterius peccata demonstrare possint. Ac vide quantum interfuturum sit inter meam et tuam accusationem. Ego etiam quae tu sine Verre commisisti Verri crimini daturus sum quod te non prohibuerit, quum summam ipse haberet potestatem: tu contra ne quae ille quidem fecit objicies, ne qua ex parte conjunctus cum eo reperiare.

Quid illa, Caecili, contemnendane tibi videntur esse sine quibus

Quid igitur daturus es] The omission of the ? after 'Quid' in 'Quid hoc,' and its omission here after 'igitur,' will probably cause a difficulty to some readers; but when they are accustomed to it they will find it clear enough. See Act. ii. Lib. 1. c. 55, note.

11. *in medio posita*] here means 'that which is plain,' as appears from the words which follow. The various senses of 'in medio' are collected in Forcellini.

magis occulta] The note of Asconius is not a bad one: "inepte a quibusdam quaeritur quae sint: nulla sunt enim," &c. It is said oratorically, that is, falsely. 'Ille,' &c., is Verres, at present the more remote person. 'Istius' is the man whom you have before you.

si velim—intelligent] No various reading is given, but the general usage of the language requires 'intelligant' in such cases; but I am not, for that reason, convinced that 'intelligent' is wrong. There are many similar examples, if the MSS. may be trusted; for in such a matter their authority is not great: 'nec si cupias, licebit,' Act. ii. Lib. 2. c. 69. See Heindorf's note on Horace, 1 Sat. i. 15, "Si quis deus, En ego, dicat," &c.

non modo—sed ne—quidem] This is not a case in which 'non modo' is equivalent to 'non modo non,' if it ever is. This means; 'all will see that between you two there was not, in a manner (that is, I will not say there was, merely), a union of will, but that even the booty is not yet divided: you have still accounts between you to settle.' But this use of 'non modo' requires a particular investigation. See Excursus on Non modo.

indicium] 'Index' is an informer, a witness, and one who was privy to the act of which he is a witness, as Asconius explains it; but Caecilius could not be an 'index,' as Cicero says; at least he adds, he will accept him, if the law (lex) permits it. "Vettius reus quum esset damnatus erat indicium postulaturus," Ad Att. ii. 24. See In Vatin. c. 11, and note, vol. iv.

concedas oportet] 'Oportet' is thus used with the subjunctive, as well as with the infinitive; generally without 'ut' when with the subjunctive. Comp. Act. ii. Lib. 3. c. 83.

Quid illa, &c.] The usual absurd pointing is 'Quid? illa,' &c. The reader may

causa sustineri praesertim tanta nullo modo potest? aliqua facultas agendi, aliqua dicendi consuetudo, aliqua in foro, judiciis, legibus, aut ratio aut exercitatio. Intelligo quam scopuloso difficilique in loco verser. Nam quum omnis arrogantia odiosa est, tum illa ingenii atque eloquentiae multo molestissima. Quamobrem nihil dico de meo ingenio; neque est quod possim dicere; neque, si esset, dicerem. Aut enim id mihi satis est quod est de me opinionis, quidquid est; aut si id parum est, ego majus id commemorando facere non possum. XII. De te, Caecili, jam mehercule hoc extra hanc contentionem certamenque nostrum familiariter tecum loquar, tu ipse quemadmodum existimes vide etiam atque etiam; et tu te collige, et qui sis et quid facere possis considera. Putasne te posse de maximis acerbissimisque rebus, quum causam sociorum fortunasque provinciae, jus populi Romani gravitatemque judicii legumque susceperis, tot res, tam graves, tam varias, voce, memoria, consilio, ingenio sustinere? Putasne te posse quae C. Verres in quaestura, quae in legatione, quae in praetura, quae Romae, quae in Italia, quae in Achaia, Asia, Pamphyliaque peccarit, ea quemadmodum locis temporibusque divisa sint, sic criminibus et oratione distinguere? Putasne posse id quod in ejusmodi reo maxime necessarium est facere, ut quae ille libidinose, quae nefarie, quae crudeliter fecerit, ea aeque acerba et indigna videantur esse iis qui audient atque illis visa sunt qui senserunt? Magna sunt ea quae dico, mihi crede; noli haec contemnere. Dicenda, demonstranda, explicanda sunt omnia: causa non solum exponenda, sed etiam graviter copioseque agenda est: perficiendum est, si quid agere aut perficere vis,

pause after 'Quid,' if he likes; but the interrogation is 'Quid illa,' and it is resumed by 'contemnendane.'

scopuloso — loco] A reading 'scrupuloso' is cited by Zumpt from one MS. I think that it is the true reading. 'Scopulosus' and 'scrupulosus' seem to have been occasionally confounded in the MSS. Ausonius has the expression 'scrupulosus locus;' and Festus (v. Scrupi) says: "scrupulosam rem dicimus quae aliquid habet in se asperi," 'rough, as a place with gravel.' Cicero (De Or. iii. 19) speaks of 'mare scopulosum;' but a 'locus scopulosus' is not so easy to understand. Iordan has 'scopuloso,' and no notice of the reading or supposed reading 'scrupuloso.' The use of 'scrupulus' is well known (Pro S. Roscio Am. c. 2).

12. *Pamphyliaque peccarit,*] 'Patrarit,' Orelli. But 'peccarit' has the authority of the better MSS.; and 'patrarit' is not used thus by Cicero, as Zumpt says.

quemadmodum — sic] These are two of the terms of a comparison which Cicero often uses, and he places 'quemadmodum' first; and this is its place, for it occupies the position that the relative clause often does with respect to the corresponding clause which follows.

Dicenda, demonstranda,] 'Every thing must be mentioned, precisely stated, fully unfolded.' 'Demonstrare' does not correspond to the English word to 'demonstrate.' See c. 14; and Act. i. c. 8, "demonstrat qua iste oratione usus esset."

perficere vis,] This is Orelli's reading. Zumpt, Klotz, and Iordan have 'proficere.' This and like words have been frequently confounded, owing to the MS. abbreviations for 'pro,' 'per,' 'prae,' being nearly the same. See the Index Siglarum in

ut homines te non solum audiant, verum etiam libenter studioseque audiant. In quo si te multum natura adjuvaret, si optimis a pueritia disciplinis atque artibus studuisses et in his elaborasses, si litteras Graecas Athenis non Lilybaei, Latinas Romae non in Sicilia didicisses, tamen esset magnum tantam causam, tam exspectatam et diligentia consequi, et memoria complecti, et oratione expromere, et voce ac viribus sustinere. Fortasse dices, Quid ergo haec in te sunt omnia? Utinam quidem essent: verumtamen ut esse possent magno studio mihi a pueritia est elaboratum. Quod si ego haec propter magnitudinem rerum ac difficultatem assequi non potui, qui in omni vita nihil aliud egi; quam longe tu te ab his rebus abesse arbitrare, quas non modo antea nunquam cogitasti, sed ne nunc quidem quum in eas ingrederis quae et quantae sint suspicari potes? XIII. Ego qui, sicut omnes sciunt, in foro judiciisque ita verser ut ejusdem aetatis aut nemo aut pauci plures causas defenderint, et qui omne tempus quod mihi ab amicorum negotiis datur in his studiis laboribusque consumam, quo paratior ad usum forensem promptiorque esse possim; tamen, ita mihi deos velim propitios ut quum illius temporis mihi venit in mentem quo die citato

Goeschen's Gaius. The reader may choose which he will have in this passage, for the MSS. are divided.

litteras Graecas, &c.] Cicero exults over his poor opponent, whose Greek and Latin were equally bad. His Greek was the dialect of Lilybaeum, not the pure language of Athens; and his Latin was picked up in Sicily, not learned in Rome. Plautus (Pers. iii. 1. 66) has a sneer on the Greek dialect of Sicily. 'expromere:' 'exponere' dtt. But Hahn suggests 'exprimere,' which may be the true reading.

13. *Ego qui . . . verser . . . consumam,*] There is a reading 'versor' G2 Ld, but no various reading 'consumo.' It does not seem easy to explain the use of the subjunctive here, and to reconcile it with the indicative 'qui nihil aliud egi,' which occurs at the end of the preceding chapter. But the two cases are different; and I observe, by way of suggestion, that the use of the indicative or subjunctive seems to depend, in such cases, in some degree on the position which the 'qui' has in the sentence. The indicative 'qui . . . egi,' is a positive affirmation: 'if I have not been able to accomplish this, I who have laboured at nothing else all my life.' The words 'qui . . . egi' are an emphatic description of the 'ego' as the subject of 'assequi non potui.' The other sentence is of this form, 'for my part, though I have been engaged' (ego qui . . . verser) . . . , still I am not only much excited in my mind (tamen . . . non solum commoveor animo). The words 'qui . . . verser' &c. are not a description of the 'ego,' but matter contingent and subordinate, a circumstance affecting the 'ego,' and one which makes the affirmation in the sentence (commoveor, perhorresco) more striking. This use of 'qui' and the subjunctive, in place of which modern writers of Latin often use 'quum,' is a great nicety in the Latin language.

ita mihi deos velim, &c.] This is a usual form of solemn asseveration: 'so may the gods help me, as what I say is true.' But in this formula the 'ut' may be omitted, "ita me dii bene ament, non nihil timeo," Ter. Eun. i. 1. 1.

quum illius temporis mihi venit, &c.] There are other examples of 'mihi venit in mentem' with a genitive, which is probably an elliptical expression, the nominative, on which the genitive should depend, being omitted. Act. ii. Lib. 1. c. 18, "non dubito quin . . tuorum tibi scelerum veniat in mentem." (Pro P. Quintio, c. 2; Pro P. Sulla, c. 6.) It is also a form of expression which Terence uses; and Cicero was a great reader of Terence.

reo mihi dicendum sit, non solum commoveor animo, sed etiam toto corpore perhorresco. Jam nunc mente et cogitatione prospicio quae tum studia hominum, qui concursus futuri sint; quantam exspectationem magnitudo judicii sit allatura; quantam auditorum multitudinem infamia C. Verris concitatura; quantam denique audientiam orationi meae improbitas illius factura sit. Quae quum cogito, jam nunc timeo quidnam pro offensione hominum, qui illi inimici infensique sunt, et exspectatione omnium et magnitudine rerum dignum eloqui possim. Tu horum nihil metuis, nihil cogitas, nihil laboras? si quid ex vetere aliqua oratione, IOVEM EGO OPTIMVM MAXIMVM, aut, VELLEM, SI FIERI POTVISSET, IVDICES, aut aliquid ejusmodi ediscere potueris, praeclare te paratum in judicium venturum arbitraris? Ac si tibi nemo responsurus esset, tamen

citato reo] 'Citare' is the word used to signify a person being called upon to appear in court by a 'praeco,' after he has been summoned in due form, as by the praetor's 'edictum,' for instance. Klotz refers to Act. ii. Lib. 2. c. 38, 40.

non solum commoveor animo, sed etiam] 'Sed etiam' stands in this position with respect to 'solus' not only when it is used as an adverb, but also when it is used as an adjective; "nec mihi soli versatur ante oculos sed etiam posteris," &c. (De Am. c. 27.) 'Verum' is also used after 'non solum,' as 'sed' is. As 'solus' means 'single,' 'whole,' 'entire,' it is used with 'non' in those forms in which the writer intends not only to affirm something, but to add that this is not all; that there is something more. 'Non solum' is properly enough rendered 'not solely,' 'singly,' or 'not only:' but it leads to great confusion when 'non modo' is also translated 'not only,' though it is sometimes used like 'non solum;' "non modo praesentia verum etiam futura bella delevit" (De Am. c. 3).

Cicero's admission of the feeling that he had when a case was called on, is evidence of his sincere devotion to his profession of an orator, and his consciousness of the duty that he undertook. Such feelings are, with very few exceptions, shared by all men of real merit, especially at the commencement of their career as an advocate or public speaker. Those who begin any arduous duties with perfect self-confidence and no misgivings of themselves are not the men who ultimately obtain the highest and best deserved distinction. Klotz refers to the following passages in which Cicero speaks of himself to the same effect as in this passage: De Orat. i. 26; Pro Cluentio, c. 18; Pro Rege Deiotaro, c. 1; Pro Sex. Roscio Amerino, c. 4.

factura sit.] Orelli, Zumpt, &c., have simply 'factura.' Klotz observes, "*factura*, errore opinor typographi inde a D. Lambino propagato." Iordan says '*sit* om. dtt.'

Quae quum cogito, jam nunc timeo] This is a good example of 'quum' being used with the indicative, when the object is to denote an event contemporaneous with another circumstance, which is also expressed by the present tense.

'Quidnam' is one of the forms of 'qui' to which 'nam' is added, and it appears to give emphasis to the expression, whether it is used interrogatively or not, as in this instance. The words 'ubinam,' 'utinam,' are other examples of the addition of 'nam' to the forms of 'qui;' for such 'ubi' and 'uti' are. The meaning of this passage is: 'as soon as I think of all this, I begin to fear that I shall hardly be able to utter any thing commensurate with (pro),' &c.

ex vetere aliqua, &c.] Cicero supposes his adversary so barren in invention as to be compelled to resort to some trite form of commencing his address, which might be well enough as it was originally used, but is ridiculous when it is a mere imitation. Servius (ad Aen. xi. 301) says that the people of old always began their orations with an invocation of the gods, and he adds, "sicut sunt omnes orationes Catonis et Gracchi; nam generale caput in omnibus legimus. Unde Cicero per irrisionem ait: Si quis ex vetere" (ed. Masv.) &c.

VELLEM, SI FIERI] Comp. Pro P. Sulla, c. 1, 'Maxime vellem' &c.

ipsam causam, ut ego arbitror, demonstrare non posses. Nunc ne illud quidem cogitas, tibi cum homine disertissimo et ad dicendum paratissimo futurum esse certamen, quicum modo disserendum, modo omni ratione pugnandum certandumque sit? Cujus ego ingenium ita laudo ut non pertimescam, ita probo ut me ab eo delectari facilius quam decipi putem posse. XIV. Nunquam ille me opprimet consilio; nunquam ullo artificio pervertet; nunquam ingenio me suo labefactare atque infirmare conabitur. Novi omnes hominis petitiones rationesque dicendi: saepe in iisdem, saepe in contrariis causis versati sumus. Ita contra me ille dicet, quamvis sit ingeniosus, ut nonnullum etiam de suo ingenio judicium fieri arbitretur. Te vero, Caecili, quemadmodum sit elusurus, quam omni ratione jactaturus, videre jam videor: quoties ille tibi potestatem optionemque facturus sit ut eligas utrum velis, factum esse necne, verum esse an falsum; utrum dixeris, id contra te futurum. Qui tibi aestus, qui error, quae tenebrae, dii immortales! erunt homini minime malo? Quid quum accusationis tuae membra dividere coeperit, et in digitis suis singulas partes causae constituere? Quid quum unumquidque transigere, expedire, absolvere? Ipse profecto metuere incipies ne innocenti periculum facesseris. Quid quum commiserari, conqueri, et ex illius invidia deonerare aliquid et in te trajicere coeperit, commemorare quaestoris cum praetore

Nunc ne illud quidem cogitas,] When a proposition is going to be laid down, it is Cicero's fashion to introduce it in this manner by the word 'illud.' Examples are abundant.

14. *opprimet*] 'he will never surprise me,' 'take me at a disadvantage.' See Act. ii. Lib. 3. c. 91, 'mors oppressit.'—'nunquam . . . pervertet,' 'he will never trip me up.'

potestatem optionemque] 'optio et potestas,' In Vat. c. 17; where the order of the words is different.

accusationis tuae membra dividere] Klotz refers to the following passages in which the skill of Hortensius in anatomizing a cause is mentioned: Quintil. Inst. Or. iv. 5; Cicero's Hortensius, quoted by Nonius, p. 364; and Brutus, c. 88, "duas quidem res (attulerat Q. Hortensius) quas nemo alius: partitiones, quibus de rebus dicturus esset, et collectiones, memor et quae essent dicta contra quaeque ipse dixisset" (ed. Meyer). See also Pro P. Quintio, c. 10, vol. ii.: "Faciam quod te saepe animadverti facere, Hortensi; totam causae meae dictionem certas in partes dividam" &c.

transigere, expedire, absolvere?] The best service that a commentator can render is to explain, when he can, such words as these, in which lies the great difficulty of the Latin language. Asconius has attempted it, and perhaps he has come near to the sense of the passage. 'What, when he shall begin with each several head (of your charge), summarily settling one, explaining away another, clearing away a third.' 'Transigere' in this passage seems to mean to 'settle or dispose of' promptly, at once, by directly denying or admitting, or in some way; as in Act. ii. Lib. 4. c. 16, 'quod verbo transigere possum.' The Latin language has a mode of dealing with generalities which the English has not. The Latin reaches the understanding, but it often refuses all expression in another tongue, at least in ours.

facesseris.] "*facessieris* Lg 29 atque ita in quibusdam codd. inventum esse testatur Prisc. i. p. 505, qui tamen cum Diomede, Capro, Charisio alteram formam quam h. l. optimi codd. tuentur, praeferendam censet." Jordan. But the regular form would be 'facessiveris.'

quaestoris cum praetore] Cicero uses a climax, as it is called: "the intimate rela-

necessitudinem constitutam, morem majorum, sortis religionem, poterisne ejus orationis subire invidiam? Vide modo; etiam atque etiam considera. Mihi enim videtur periculum fore ne ille non modo verbis te obruat, sed gestu ipso ac motu corporis praestringat aciem ingenii tui, teque ab institutis tuis cogitationibusque abducat. Atque hujusce rei judicium jam continuo video futurum. Si enim mihi hodie respondere ad haec quae dico potueris, si ab isto libro quem tibi magister ludi nescio qui ex alienis orationibus compositum dedit verbo uno discesseris, posse te et illi quoque judicio non deesse et causae atque officio tuo satisfacere arbitrabor: sin mecum in hac prolusione nihil fueris, quem te in ipsa pugna cum acerrimo adversario fore putemus?

XV. Esto: ipse nihil est, nihil potest. At venit paratus cum subscriptoribus exercitatis et disertis. Est tamen hoc aliquid; tametsi non est satis. Omnibus enim rebus is qui princeps in agendo est ornatissimus et paratissimus esse debet. Verumtamen

tionship that has been established between a 'quaestor' and his 'praetor,' the usage of our ancestors, the sanctity of the lot." The intimate relationship is first mentioned as a well-known thing; then ancient usage, which gave it strength; and, finally, the sanctity of the lot, for that which in form was submitted to the decision of chance was, in effect, the will of the gods. (Phil. iii. c. 10, vol. iv.) Comp. c. 20, "quicum me sors . . . quicum me deorum judicium . . . conjunxerat." As to the 'provinciae' of the 'quaestores' being determined by lot, see c. 19, 'conjunctionem sortis.'—'constitutam more maj.' J. Gronov.

poterisne ejus orationis, &c.] Klotz has altered the passage thus; 'poterisne ejus orationi subire? Invidiam vide,' &c.: and he says that he has been the first to correct this passage in conformity with infallible critical evidence. The grounds of his correction are stated in his preface. The text of Orelli, Zumpt, and Iordan is the same as this. Asconius read 'orationi,' and perhaps omitted 'invidiam.'

praestringat] Probably the true reading may be 'perstringat' (see c. 12; and Forcellini, praestringere, perstringere). The primary notion of 'stringere' (stric) seems to be 'to hold fast or tight, to press close upon' (Ovid, Met. iv. 135. 560); and the compound, 'perstringere,' is accordingly used to signify the deadening of the active energies of the body or the mind, as through fear, or by the rapid motion of weapons used in assault, which is the metaphor employed by Cicero. Asconius quotes a passage of Plautus, Miles Gloriosus, i. 1. 3:

"Ut, ubi usus veniat, contra conserta manu
Praestringat oculorum aciem in acie hostibus."

The metaphor is resumed a little further on, where Cicero speaks of the matter in dispute between him and Caecilius as a 'prolusio,' a mere playing or skirmishing compared with the real battle (pugna) which he would have to fight with Hortensius. Comp. De Or. ii. 80; De Sen. c. 12.

ab institutis tuis] 'from what thou hast planned, conceived.' He will make Caecilius forget all that he intends to say. See 'instituere,' c. 21, note.

15. *At venit*] 'Suppose it to be admitted that Caecilius is nobody. But, it will be urged, he comes prepared with practised and eloquent supporters.' 'At' in this, as in most cases, adds something, the effect of which is to diminish or destroy the force of what has been admitted. 'At' occurs again at the beginning of c. 17. The distinction between 'at' and 'sed' will easily be made out by a careful reader.

A 'subscriptor' (qui subscribit) is he who assists the first or principal prosecutor, and writes his name at the end of the charge under that of the principal prosecutor. "Gabinium de ambitu reum fecit P. Sulla subscribente privigno Memmio" (Ad Q. Fr. iii. 3). See Pro M. Fonteio, c. 16, and 'subscribere,' Forcellini.

L. Apulcium esse video proximum subscriptorem, hominem non aetate sed usu forensi atque exercitatione tironem. Deinde, ut opinor, habet Alienum, hunc tamen ab subselliis, qui quid in dicendo posset nunquam satis attendi; in clamando quidem video eum esse bene robustum atque exercitatum. In hoc spes tuae sunt omnes: hic, si tu eris actor constitutus, totum judicium sustinebit. At ne is quidem tantum contendet in dicendo quantum potest, sed consulet laudi et existimationi tuae, et ex eo quod ipse potest in dicendo aliquantum remittet ut tu tamen aliquid esse videare. Ut in actoribus Graecis fieri videmus, saepe illum qui est secundarum aut tertiarum partium, quum possit aliquanto clarius dicere quam ipse primarum, multum summittere, ut ille princeps quam maxime excellat; sic faciet Alienus; tibi serviet, tibi lenocinabitur; minus aliquanto contendet quam potest. Jam hoc considerate cujusmodi accusatores in tanto judicio simus habituri, quum et ipse Alienus ex ea facultate si quam habet aliquantum detracturus sit, et Caecilius tum denique se aliquid futurum putet, si Alienus minus vehemens fuerit et sibi primas in dicendo partes concesserit. Quartum

ab subselliis,] This expression is explained to signify 'a man practised in the courts.' 'Subsellium,' from 'sella,' means apparently a continuity of seats, a bench, called 'subsellium,' with reference to something higher. 'Subsellia,' the seats of the 'judices,' are sometimes opposed to the tribunal of the presiding judge (In Vatin. c. 14). Cicero says that Alienus had no other knowledge of conducting a cause than what he got by sitting on the 'subsellia;' but in this passage it cannot mean the 'subsellia' of the 'judices.' It is used, in its more general sense, for any seats occupied by witnesses and others, as in Pro Q. Rosc. Amer. c. 6, "Quorum alterum sedere in accusatorum subselliis vides." See also De Or. i. 62.

quid . . . posset . . . attendi;] "habuit attendere quae res maxime tanta negotia sustinuisset," Sall. Cat. 53. See Act. ii. Lib. 3. c. 5, note.

At ne] 'Ac ne' Iordan, with most of the MSS. It is often very difficult to determine whether 'at' or 'ac' is the true reading.

Ut in actoribus Graecis] The allusion is to Greek plays and Greek actors; and to the πρωταγωνιστής, δευτεραγωνιστής, and τριταγωνιστής, who took the first, second, and third parts. See Heindorf's note on Horace, 'posset qui ferre secundas' (1 Sat. ix. 46); and Ars Poet. 192. Cicero explains his own meaning. 'Actor' has a double sense.

summittere,] 'Lower the voice,' or, generally, 'put a restraint on their powers.' Comp. De Am. c. 20, "ut ii qui superiores sunt summittere se debent in amicitia, sic quodam modo inferiores extollere;" a passage which has sometimes been misunderstood. See Seyffert's note on it.—'lenocinabitur:' Cicero uses an odious word, somewhat difficult to render. A 'leno' is one who gets his living by the prostitution of slaves, or by assisting in illicit cohabitation. Terence in his Phormio has a 'leno.' 'Alienus,' says Cicero, 'will act like one who plays a second part; he will be your slave, your pimp.' See Act. ii. Lib. 1. c. 12.

et sibi primas] Most of the MSS. have 'tibi,' which is evidently a mistake.

Quartum] Zumpt, quoted by Klotz, remarks that it was usual to have four 'accusatores;' and we might almost safely make the inference from this passage. "Defenderunt Scaurum sex patroni, cum ad id tempus raro quisquam pluribus quam quatuor uteretur: ac post bella civilia ante legem Juliam ad duodenos patronos est perventum" (Ascon. in Scaur. p. 20, ed. Orell.).—'moratorum' is an emendation of Cujacius; the MSS. have 'oratorum' or 'meatorum.' The correctness of the emendation is supposed to be confirmed by the context and the words of Asconius,

quem sit habiturus non video, nisi quem forte ex illo grege moratorum qui subscriptionem sibi postularunt, cuicunque vos delationem dedissetis. Ex quibus alienissimis hominibus ita paratus venis ut tibi hospes aliquis sit recipiendus. Quibus ego non sum tantum honorem habiturus ut ad ea quae dixerint certo loco aut singulatim unicuique respondeam. Sic breviter, quoniam non consulto sed casu in eorum mentionem incidi, quasi praeteriens satisfaciam universis. XVI. Tantane vobis inopia videor esse amicorum ut mihi non ex his quos mecum adduxerim sed de populo subscriptor addatur? vobis autem tanta inopia reorum est ut mihi causam praeripere conemini potius quam aliquos a columna Maenia vestri ordinis reos reperiatis? Custodem, inquit, Tullio me apponite. Quid mihi quam multis custodibus opus erit, si te semel ad meas capsas admisero, qui non solum ne quid enunties sed etiam ne quid auferas custodiendus sis? Sed de isto custode toto sic vobis brevissime respondebo; non esse hos tales viros commissuros ut ad causam tantam a me susceptam, mihi creditam, quisquam sub-

"obturbatores quosdam sordidosque candidos significat, qui adhibebantur ad moram faciendam dum meliores advocati reperirentur." Manutius thinks there is no reason to alter 'oratorum.'

alienissimis] Cicero after his fashion is playing on the name of Alienus, and he is speaking sarcastically when he says 'paratus.' The sense of the passage is this: 'You come prepared to accept any of these men, who are perfect strangers to you, just as if you had to receive some strange guest into your house.' 'Ex quibus' does not depend on 'paratus.' These words mean no more here than if we were to say 'ex eo numero.' A man would choose his 'subscriptores' among his friends, but Caecilius must get whom he can, just as if he opened his door to receive the first stranger who presented himself.

singulatim] The MSS. have this form, and also 'singillatim,' and 'sigillatim.' It is possible that all three forms were in use, but 'singulatim' has the recommendation of being conformable to the word 'singuli,' the root of which is '*sim*.'

16. *de populo*] That is, one of the crowd, any body.

a columna Maenia] "'ad columnam Maeniam,' A. Parr. Lall. codd. (?) Urs. 'a columna Maenia' Franc. pr. 'a columna aenea.' s. 'aenea' cett. codd. noti, etiam r" (Jordan); who has 'ad columnam Maeniam.' 'Rather than seek for some criminal of your class (slaves and the like) at the column of Maenius.' As to Maenius, see Heindorf, Horace, 1 Sat. i. 101. The tradition was that he was a spendthrift, who sold his house on the Forum to the censors Cato the Elder and Flaccus, for the purpose of a basilica being built there, but reserved one column, on the summit of which he might build or place a balcony to secure a view of the gladiatorial games. Compare Asconius and the Scholium of Porphyrio on Horace, 1 Sat. iii. 21. At this column, the 'triumviri capitales,' it is said, used to punish thieves and slaves. (Pro Cluentio, c. 13.) But it appears that the Scholiasts have confounded the Maenius of Horace with C. Maenius, the conqueror of the Latins, in whose honour this 'columna Maenia' was placed (Livy, viii. 13) near the Puteal Libonis at the entrance of the Forum.

capsas] These were vessels of cylindrical form, of wood or other material, with a rounded top or covering, used for the keeping of rolls and documents, of which Cicero had collected a large store to serve for evidence against Verres. See Horace, 1 Sat. iv. 22, and the drawings from Pompeii.

ad causam . . . adspirare] Comp. c. 6, 'accedere aut aspirare,' where 'accedere' and 'adspirare' are different things, as the 'aut' shows. 'Accedere' is 'to come near;' 'adspirare,' 'to breathe towards,'

scriptor me invito adspirare possit. Etenim fides mea custodem repudiat, diligentia speculatorem reformidat.

Verum ut ad te, Caecili, redeam, quam multa te deficiant vides: quam multa sint in te quae reus nocens in accusatore suo cupiat esse profecto jam intelligis. Quid ad haec dici potest? non enim quaero quid tu dicturus sis; video mihi non te sed hunc librum esse responsurum quem monitor tuus hic tenet, qui si te recte monere volet, suadebit tibi ut hinc discedas neque mihi verbum ullum respondeas. Quid enim dices? an id quod dictitas, injuriam tibi fecisse Verrem? Arbitror: neque enim esset verisimile, quum omnibus Siculis faceret injurias, te illi unum eximium cui consuleret fuisse. Sed ceteri Siculi ultorem suarum injuriarum invenerunt; tu dum tuas injurias per te, id quod non potes, persequi conaris, id agis ut ceterorum quoque injuriae sint impunitae atque inultae: et hoc te praeterit non id solum spectari solere qui debeat, sed etiam illud, qui possit ulcisci; in quo utrumque sit, eum superiorem esse; in quo alterum, in eo non quid is velit sed quid facere possit quaeri solere. Quod si ei potissimum censes permitti oportere accusandi potestatem cui maximam C. Verres injuriam fecerit, utrum tandem censes hos judices gravius ferre oportere te ab illo esse laesum, an provinciam Siciliam esse vexatam ac perditam? Opinor, concedes multo hoc et esse gravius et ab omnibus ferri gravius oportere. Concede igitur ut tibi anteponatur in accusando provincia. Nam provincia accusat, quum is agit causam quem sibi

means 'to attempt to approach.' We have adopted the word in the same sense.

reus nocens] A 'reus' might be 'nocens' or 'innocens,' for 'reus' is merely the accused. He is opposed to 'accusator.' But 'reus' may mean the defendant in a civil action; and, indeed, both parties, plaintiff and defendant, may be called 'rei.' (Cic. De Or. ii. 43.) If several persons respectively were entitled to enforce an 'obligatio,' or liable to perform it, they were 'rei:' "et stipulandi et promittendi duo pluresve rei fieri possunt," Inst. iii. 16. See Unterholzner, Lehre des Römischen Rechts von Schuldverhältnissen, i. 174. 'Creditor' and 'debitor' are the names which in the Roman Law as fully developed signify the parties who stand opposed to one another in an Obligatio, and these are the legal terms used to express these two parties, whatever may be the origin of the Obligatio. 'Reus' is the common expression for both (Dig. 45. 2. 1, 16; Festus, v. 'reus,' and v. 'contestari'). (Savigny, Obligationenrecht, i. p. 15.) There seems to be no explanation of the word 'reus,' except by referring it to 'res.'

eximium] 'Eximius' means 'selected,' 'excepted,' as the context shows, and its relationship to 'exim-ere,' which must be compared with 'adim-ere,' 'subim-ere,' that is, 'sum-ere.' Terence (Hec. i. 1. 9) writes: "Ph. Utin' eximium neminem habeam? Sy. Neminem."

non id . . . sed etiam illud,] See the note on c. 13, as to 'illud.' The proper demonstrative opposed to 'ille' is 'hic.' But 'is' and 'ille' are often used in contrast by Cicero when his object is simply to denote two things in some way opposed or contrasted. See the end of c. 21, and De Oratore, ii. 72; Pro Cn. Plancio, c. 3; Ter. Hauton. i. 2. 21: "Qui uti scit, ei bona: illi, qui non utitur recte, mala."

hos judices] Orelli has 'hoc judices.' Klotz says that 'hoc judices' is a typographical error, originating with Ernesti and Beck. Gl has 'hos iudices,' the true reading.

illa defensorem sui juris, ultorem injuriarum, actorem causae totius adoptavit.

XVII. At eam tibi C. Verres fecit injuriam quae ceterorum quoque animos posset alieno incommodo commovere. Minime: nam id quoque ad rem pertinere arbitror, qualis injuria dicatur, quae causa inimicitiarum proferatur. Cognoscite ex me; nam iste eam profecto, nisi plane nihil sapit, nunquam proferet. Agonis est quaedam Lilybaetana, liberta Veneris Erycinae; quae mulier ante hunc quaestorem copiosa plane et locuples fuit. Ab hac praefectus Antonii quidam symphoniacos servos abducebat per injuriam,

adoptavit.] 'has selected by its own choice.' See 'optionem' c. 14. We have adopted the word in nearly the same sense. The Romans also used 'adoptare' to express the adoption of a child (Gaius, i. 97).

17. *liberta Veneris*] Agonis had been a slave attached to the temple of Venus at Mount Eryx, in Sicily (Act. ii. Lib. 2. c. 8); she had been one of the class whom the Greeks called *ἱερόδουλοι*, of which Strabo speaks (p. 272, ed. Casaub.). See Polybius (i. 55). Slaves were possessed both by individuals, and by the state, and other bodies, as municipal towns and temples. Klotz refers to Cicero, Pro Cluentio, c. 15, for similar instances. This woman had been manumitted, and had herself become a slave-holder; and, to save her property, she pretended that she and all that she had belonged to the goddess, that is, were dedicated to the service of religion, and so were of the class of sacred things. Strabo's account of the great temple at Comana (ed. Casaub. 535, 536, 558) is instructive. The priest occupied a good piece of land, which was attached to the temple, and he enjoyed the revenue of it. He was next in rank to the king, and generally a member of the royal family. At the time of Strabo's visit, this opulent priest had six thousand slaves, men and women, all working for him. The people all about the temple were the subjects of the king, but also owed obedience in sacred matters, we may suppose, to the priest. When Cn. Pompeius made Archelaus priest of Comana, he deprived him of the power of selling the slaves, who thus became 'adscripti glebae.' There was another place in this happy country, held by another priest, who ranked next to him of Comana, but he had only three thousand slaves. His land was good, and the labour of his people brought him in fifteen talents clear by the year. Both these good places were for life. (See also Strabo, p. 532, and p. 577.) The Temple of Venus at Corinth possessed above a thousand female slaves, courtezans, whom both men and women dedicated to the goddess; "and it was by reason of them," adds the grave philosopher, with the utmost simplicity (p. 378), "that the city was much frequented and enriched, for the seafaring folks readily eased themselves of their money." We may now understand what the temple at Eryx was, and the 'Venerei,' or slaves of Venus. There was probably a college of Venerei at Pompeii, as we infer from the following words found in an inscription on a building there: COL. VEN. COR.

In the year 1776, there still existed on the flanks of the Jura an abbey of Bernardins, who held in servitude a large number of peasants. The men were not slaves, but they were serfs of the abbot and his convent, and in a worse condition than real slaves. The number of these serfs attached to religious houses in France was very considerable; some say more than fifty thousand; but this may be an exaggeration. The revolution broke their chains.

Orelli reads, 'Agonis est quaedam;' Zumpt and Iordan have 'Agonis quaedam est,' the reading of G 1 2 Lg 29 St. The matter seems a trifle; but Orelli is perhaps right. As to the form, compare Cic. Ad Div. xiii. 30, 'L. Manlius est Sosis;' 'C. Sulpicius Olympus fuit' (Act. ii. Lib. 1. c. 48; but also Act. ii. Lib. 4. c. 22).

symphoniacos servos] Asconius states that they were slaves who gave the signal, the 'celeusma,' to the rowers; and also sounded the trumpets in a naval fight. See Pro Milone, c. 21. This Antonius was M. Antonius Creticus, who, in B.C. 74, during his proprietorship, had almost unlimited authority over the sea and the coast region. See Act. ii. Lib. 2. c. 3, and Lib. 3. c. 91.

quibus se in classe uti velle dicebat. Tum illa, ut mos in Sicilia est omnium Venereorum, et eorum qui a Venere se liberaverunt, ut praefecto illi religionem Veneris nomenque objiceret, dixit et se et [omnia] sua Veneris esse. Ubi hoc quaestori Caecilio viro optimo et homini aequissimo nuntiatum est, vocari ad se Agonidem jubet; judicium dat statim, SI PARET EAM SE ET SVA VENERIS ESSE DIXISSE. Judicant recuperatores id quod necesse erat; neque enim

Venereorum,] 'Veneriorum,' Iordan. We may infer from 'liberaverunt' that these slaves sometimes got their liberty by paying the price of their value, or in some other way.—'nomenque:' 'nomine,' Iordan. The word 'religionem' means an answer to the claim of the praefectus, which was founded on the relation of the slaves to their former mistress, who after their manumission would be their 'patrona.' See note on 'Veneris esse.'

VENERIS ESSE] A deity was considered as a person, like a human person, and accordingly he could possess property. It was an easy transition to consider the deity who was worshipped in any particular temple as having the character of an artificial person, or what we call very absurdly a corporation, and still more absurdly, when the artificial person is a church, we call it a corporation sole. It is the characteristic of all artificial persons to have the capacity to hold property and to be represented by real persons; and indeed this capacity is the essence of the notion of an artificial person. (Dig. 3. 4. 1. § 1.) Under the later Roman system it was not permitted for a man to make gods his heredes, that is, he could not bequeath his property to a temple, except such gods as some senatusconsultum or imperial constitution allowed a man to leave his property to. (Ulpian, Fr. xxii. § 6.) This rule of law, mentioned by Ulpian, was perhaps not a rule of law which allowed in some cases what had previously been forbidden in all cases; but it seems more likely that it was a rule of law which limited the capacity of testators to give and of religious bodies to take by testament. It is curious to trace the adaptation of Roman notions to Christian institutions, of the corporate character of a Roman temple to a Christian church. All this is well explained by Savigny (System, &c. vol. ii. Iuristische Personen).

As soon as Caecilius was informed of the statement of Agonis, he appointed a judicial inquiry, that is, he named judices (judicium dat) to inquire about the fact, 'si paret,' if it should appear that Agonis had said so. 'Si paret' refers to that part of the formula called the 'intentio,' that is, that part of the formal instructions which the magistrate gave to the 'judices,' in which part the claim of a plaintiff was expressed. But in some cases, as in this of Agonis, the 'judex' was not required to examine whether a certain thing belonged to the plaintiff, or a certain demand was due from the defendant; but he had simply to ascertain a fact, and thereupon to condemn or absolve. In such a case the formula was said to be 'in factum concepta;' and it was in this shape—"Judex esto: si paret A. A. apud N. N. mensam argenteam deposuisse eamque dolo malo Numerii Negidii Aulo Agerio redditam non esse, quanti ea res erit tantam pecuniam N. N. Ao Ao condemnato." The passages which explain this matter are Gaius, iv. 45–47. Klotz and Zumpt read 'si paret,' which is the true legal formula. 'Paret,' being misunderstood by the copyists, was corrupted. The old editions have 'pateret.' 'Pareret' is a correction of Lambinus. Orelli has 'pareret.'

recuperatores] The 'recuperatores' belonged to the 'judices privati.' It is said that 'recuperatores' were originally appointed in cases of dispute between Romans and Peregrini, and were appointed for each occasion as it arose. But this distinction disappeared in course of time, for we read of 'recuperatores' in cases where Roman citizens only were concerned, and of 'judices' in cases where Peregrini only were concerned. After the Lex Aebutia, of uncertain date, the 'judices' generally were called either 'judices' or 'recuperatores;' and as to the 'recuperatores,' properly so called, we collect from various passages that they were appointed in certain particular cases. In the later period, at least in the time of Gaius, there was generally only one 'judex' appointed, but the 'recuperatores' were always several, sometimes three (Act. ii. Lib. 3. c. 12); and thus Gaius (iv. 105) opposes the 'recuperatoria judicia' to those 'sub uno judice.' Much has been written on the 'recuperatores,'

erat cuiquam dubium quin illa dixisset. Iste in possessionem bonorum mulieris mittit; ipsam Veneri in servitutem adjudicat; deinde bona vendit; pecuniam redigit. Ita dum pauca mancipia Veneris nomine Agonis ac religione retinere vult, fortunas omnes libertatemque suam istius injuria perdidit. Lilybaeum Verres venit postea; rem cognoscit; factum improbat; cogit quaestorem suum pecuniam quam ex Agonidis bonis redegisset, eam mulieri omnem adnumerare et reddere. Est adhuc, id quod vos omnes admirari video, non Verres sed Q. Mucius. Quid enim facere potuit elegantius ad hominum existimationem, aequius ad levandum mulieris calamitatem, vehementius ad quaestoris libidinem coercendam? Summe haec omnia mihi videntur esse laudanda. Sed [repente] e vestigio ex homine tamquam aliquo Circaeo poculo factus est Verres. Redit ad se atque ad mores suos. Nam ex illa pecunia magnam partem ad se vertit; mulieri reddidit quantulum visum est.

XVIII. Hic tu si laesum te a Verre esse dicis, patiar et con-

and more than is worth repeating. The reader may consult Puchta, *Instit.*; and, for various references as to 'recuperatores,' Rein, *Das Römische Privatrecht*, p. 420; and Klotz, in his notes on Cicero, Pro Caecina, vol. i. p. 464, who appears to have collected nearly all that can be said. Consistently with the etymology of the word, 'recuperatores,' or 'reciperatores' (recoverers), were employed in cases where a fact easy to be established was the only matter in question, or where a very speedy decision was required, as in the 'Interdictum de vi hominibus armatis,' and in the 'Actio Injuriarum' (Gellius, xx. 1). The mode of proceeding before them was the same as before a 'judex.'

mittit;] This is the usual word in such a case. Jordan following G 1 Lal D has 'intrat.' G 2 has 'intrat vel mittit,' one of which words is a gloss. The dtt have 'mittit,' and in this instance the worse are the better.

pecuniam redigit.] This term is applied to getting in money, as when a man got in all his debts, and to converting property into money by sale (Livy, v. c. 16; Hor. Epod. 2. 69). Caecilius proceeded harshly against Agonis in taking her at her word, and adjudicating her to Venus. As to her property, it does not appear that Caecilius had appropriated it to himself, for Cicero says 'redigit;' and if he had said all that he ought to have said, perhaps he ought to have added 'in publicum.' However, 'redigere,' in itself, does not imply misappropriation. Cicero afterwards says 'reddere,' but that will not prove that Caecilius had taken the money for his own use. Comp. Act. ii. Lib. 2. c. 36.

Q. Mucius.] This is Q. Mucius Scaevola, consul B.C. 95, and Pontifex Maximus, one of the most illustrious among the great names of Rome. As proconsul of Asia he left behind him an eternal remembrance of his wise and equitable administration. 'Verres,' says Cicero, 'all at once became a Q. Mucius.' There is another allusion to Q. Mucius, Act. ii. Lib. 2. c. 13; and also c. 10, 21.

'Elegantius' means more fit, or better adapted, to satisfy men's opinion. Act. ii. Lib. 3. c. 61.

e vestigio] 'on the track, immediately.' Servius Sulpicius uses the same expression in a letter to Cicero (Ad Fam. iv. 12), 'e vestigio eo sum profectus.' The word 'repente' looks like the gloss of 'e vestigio,' as Manutius and others have suggested.

Circaeo poculo] The name of 'Verres,' which signifies a 'boar-pig,' furnished Cicero with the opportunity of making this allusion to the story of Circe, whose magic drink changed men into hogs (Od. x. 137).

ad se vertit;] Zumpt reads 'partem avertit,' which may be right. Orelli, Klotz, and Jordan have 'ad se vertit;' but in Act. ii. Lib. 1. c. 4, in a like case, 'avertisse.' Lambinus suspects that the true reading is 'averrit.' He would make Cicero guilty of another insipid joke.

18. *laesum*] "Injuria semper injusta est: laedi etiam aliquis juste potest, nam

cedam: si injuriam tibi factam quereris, defendam et negabo. Denique de injuria quae tibi facta sit neminem nostrum graviorem judicem esse oportet quam te ipsum cui facta dicitur. Si tu cum illo postea in gratiam redisti, si domi illius aliquoties fuisti, si ille apud te postea coenavit, utrum te perfidiosum an praevaricatorem existimari mavis? Video esse necesse alterutrum: sed ego tecum in eo non pugnabo quo minus utrum velis eligas. Quod si ne injuriae quidem quae tibi ab illo facta sit causa remanet, quid habes quod possis dicere quamobrem non modo mihi sed cuiquam anteponare? nisi forte illud quod dicturum te esse audio, quaestorem illius fuisse; quae causa gravis esset, si certares mecum uter nostrum illi amicior esse deberet: in contentione suscipiendarum inimicitiarum ridiculum est putare causam necessitudinis ad inferendum periculum justam videri oportere. Etenim si plurimas a praetore tuo injurias accepisses, tamen eas ferendo majorem laudem quam ulciscendo mererere: quum vero nullum illius in vita rectius factum sit quam id quod tu injuriam appellas, hi statuent hanc causam, quam ne in alio quidem probarent, in te justam ad necessitudinem violandam videri? qui si summam injuriam ab illo accepisti, tamen, quoniam quaestor ejus fuisti, non potes eum sine ulla vituperatione accusare; si vero non ulla tibi facta est injuria, sine scelere eum accusare non potes. Quare quum incertum sit de injuria, quemquam horum esse putas qui non malit te sine vituperatione quam cum scelere discedere?

et qui jure damnantur, laeduntur," says Asconius; that is, 'laedere' implies no legal wrong.—'graviorem vindicem,' Orelli, instead of 'graviorem judicem.' It is easy to see that 'vindicem' (uindicem) and 'judicem' (iudicem) may be confounded in the MSS. But here the evidence is in favour of 'judicem.' At the beginning of c. 18 Orelli has 'Hic . . dices.'

perfidiosum, &c.] 'Treacherous' (perfidiosus), or a 'praevaricator,' one who wished to undertake the prosecution of Verres only for the purpose of securing his acquittal. Cicero (Or. Part. c. 36) gives a definition of 'praevaricator;' and Marcianus (Dig. 48. 16. 1) says "praevaricatorem eum esse ostendimus qui colludit cum reo," &c. 'Praevaricari' is properly said of one who goes shuffling along, and not in a straight line; who is 'varus;' 'which,' says Heindorf (Hor. 1 Sat. iii. 47), 'expresses a divergence like the letter V;' for he is 'varus,' as Celsus says, whose foot 'intus inclinatur.'

remanet,] 'remains' after all that has happened. Not 'manet.' The 're' in 'remanere' refers to the consequence of some antecedent, which is one of the usual meanings of 'red' in composition. See In Cat. i. c. 13, vol. iii., and 'reticere,' Act. ii. Lib. 1. c. 35.

causam necessitudinis] 'It is ridiculous to suppose that the ground or reason of your close intimacy, as praetor and quaestor, is a sufficient (justam) ground for your bringing him into peril.' 'Justus,' though formed from 'jus,' has a wide meaning, and signifies any thing which is complete or sufficient in its kind. Thus: 'In amicitia parum justus' (De Am. c. 20), 'one who does not fulfil all the conditions of a perfect friend.' Compare what follows in this chapter: 'justam ad necessitudinem violandam videri;' and 'justiorem' in c. 19.

discedere?] This word is often used to express the getting out of an affair, coming off, as we say, in a certain way, and gene-

XIX. Ac vide quid differat inter meam opinionem et tuam. Tu quum omnibus rebus inferior sis, hac una in re te mihi anteferri putas oportere, quod quaestor illius fueris: ego, si superior ceteris rebus esses, hanc unam ob causam te accusatorem repudiari putarem oportere. Sic enim a majoribus nostris accepimus, praetorem quaestori suo parentis loco esse oportere; nullam neque justiorem neque graviorem causam necessitudinis posse reperiri quam conjunctionem sortis, quam provinciae, quam officii, quam publici muneris societatem. Quamobrem si jure posses eum accusare, tamen, quum is tibi parentis numero fuisset, id pie facere non posses: quum vero neque injuriam acceperis et praetori tuo periculum crees, fatearis necesse est te illi injustum impiumque bellum inferre conari. Etenim ista quaestura ad eam rem valet ut elaborandum tibi in ratione reddenda sit quamobrem eum cui quaestor fueris accuses; non ut ob eam ipsam causam postulandum sit ut tibi potissimum accusatio detur. Neque fere unquam venit in contentionem de accusando qui quaestor fuisset quin repudiaretur. Itaque neque L. Philoni in C. Servilium nominis deferendi potestas

rally badly. Cicero has just said that a quaestor could not avoid some blame in prosecuting his praetor, even if he had sustained the greatest wrongs from him: if he had received none, to prosecute him was a crime. He concludes thus: 'Do you think that there is any of these judices who would not rather that you should come off in this contest with me without any blame at all by being rejected as the prosecutor, than with the criminality which you would bear if you were appointed the prosecutor?' Cicero says of M. Antonius, after he had been addressing the people, 'turpissime . . discessit' (Ad Div. xii. 3). Comp. c. 22, 'ut turpissime . . discedat.'

19. *una in re*] Zumpt omits 'in.'—'h. l. is paulo insolentius dictum est' (Iordan).

conjunctionem sortis,] Cicero, Ad Q. Fr. i. 1, c. 3, "quaestorem habes non tuo judicio delectum sed eum quem sors dedit." Compare Act. ii. Lib. 1. c. 13.

parentis numero] He has just said 'parentis loco.' The Romans wrote both ways; and also 'in cohortis praetoriae loco.' Caesar, B. G. i. 42. In Act. ii. Lib. 2. c. 53, Cicero writes 'numero et loco;' and in Act. i. c. 5, 'in hostium numero.'

pie] 'As he had been to you in the place of a father, you could not do it consistently with filial duty (pie).' Cicero says (Orat. Part. 22), "justitia erga deos religio, erga parentes pietas nominatur." Justitia is the performance of a man's duty.

injustum impiumque bellum] Klotz refers to Hotmann's note, who remarks that the allusion is to the Roman law of war, according to which no war was 'justum et pium' unless declared according to the Jus Feciale, with certain solemnities. Caecilius is represented as a quaestor declaring an 'injustum et impium bellum' against his praetor.

eum cui quaestor] 'For that quaestorship of yours is a sufficient reason so far as this, that you will have to use all diligence in showing on what ground you bring a charge against a man whose quaestor you have been; it is not a sufficient reason why you should demand the prosecution to be entrusted to you of all others.'—My object in making these attempts at translation, is to show the difficulty of it, rather than to offer a model. The difficulty lies in such forms as 'ad eam rem valet,' which have a meaning most comprehensive, and yet exact. (Comp. in Cat. iii. 12; Pro P. Sulla, c. 28.) Our language is often totally inadequate to render Roman expressions; and it is losing daily, instead of gaining, in comprehensiveness and precision. Klotz and Zumpt have 'quamobrem, qui quaestor ejus fueris,' the reading of most of the MSS., and it may be right.

est data, neque M. Aurelio Scauro in L. Flaccum, neque Cn. Pompeio in T. Albucium; quorum nemo propter indignitatem repudiatus est, sed ne libido violandae necessitudinis auctoritate judicum comprobaretur. Atque ille Cn. Pompeius ita cum C. Julio contendit ut tu mecum. Quaestor enim Albucii fuerat, ut tu Verris. Julius hoc secum auctoritatis ad accusandum afferebat, quod ut hoc tempore nos ab Siculis, sic tum ille ab Sardis rogatus ad causam accesserat. Semper haec causa plurimum valuit, semper haec ratio accusandi fuit honestissima, pro sociis, pro salute provinciae, pro exterarum nationum commodis inimicitias suscipere, ad periculum accedere, operam, studium, laborem interponere.

XX. Etenim si probabilis est eorum causa qui injurias suas persequi volunt, qua in re dolori suo non rei publicae commodis serviunt, quanto illa honestior causa est, quae non solum probabilis videri sed etiam grata esse debet, nulla privatim accepta injuria sociorum atque amicorum populi Romani dolore atque injuriis commoveri? Nuper quum in P. Gabinium vir fortissimus et innocentissimus L. Piso delationem nominis postularet, et contra Q. Caecilius peteret isque se veteres inimicitias jam diu susceptas persequi diceret, quum auctoritas et dignitas Pisonis valebat plurimum, tum illa erat causa justissima, quod eum sibi Achaei patronum adoptarunt. Etenim quum lex ipsa de pecuniis repetundis sociorum atque amicorum populi Romani patrona sit, iniquum est non eum legis judiciique actorem idoneum maxime putari quem actorem causae suae socii defensoremque fortunarum suarum potissimum esse voluerunt. An quod ad commemorandum est honestius,

Cn. Pompeio] This Cn. Pompeius is the father of Magnus. Pompeius had been the quaestor of T. Albucius in Sardinia, and he was not allowed to be his prosecutor. The prosecutor who was preferred to Pompeius was C. Julius Caesar Strabo (B.C. 103), a clever advocate, and a witty man. He is one of the speakers in Cicero's dialogue on oratory.

20. *probabilis*] Cicero (De Invent. c. 29) says: "probabile est id quod fere solet fieri, aut quod in opinione positum est, aut quod habet in se ad haec quandam similitudinem, sive id falsum est sive verum." When Livy (40. c. 29) speaks of a 'probabile mendacium,' he means a lie that has the semblance of truth. When 'probabile' refers to opinion, it is that which opinion gives its approval to.

P. Gabinium] P. Gabinius Capito had been praetor in Achaea; or perhaps he was governor of Macedonia and had with it also the administration of Achaea; for it appears that Achaea was first made a separate province only a short time before the end of the republic, or perhaps not before the time of Augustus. Gabinius (see Pro Flacco, c. 26, vol. iii.) was prosecuted for Repetundae, B.C. 88, and condemned. This Piso is mentioned in Lib. i. c. 46.

patrona] The feminine form of 'patronus.' A woman might be the 'patrona' of a 'libertus' in the same sense in which a man might be 'patronus.' Cicero calls the Lex de Repetundis by a kind of personification the 'patrona of the socii,' and he argues that it would be unfair not to allow the 'socii' to choose their agent to maintain the cause of their 'patrona,' the Lex de Repetundis.

id ad probandum non multo videri debet aequius? Utra igitur est splendidior, utra illustrior commemoratio? Accusavi eum cui quaestor fueram, quicum me sors consuetudoque majorum, quicum me deorum hominumque judicium conjunxerat? an, Accusavi rogatu sociorum atque amicorum; delectus sum ab universa provincia qui ejus jura fortunasque defenderem? Dubitare quisquam potest quin honestius sit eorum causa apud quos quaestor fueris quam cum cujus quaestor fueris accusare? Clarissimi viri nostrae civitatis temporibus optimis hoc sibi amplissimum pulcherrimumque ducebant, ab hospitibus clientibusque suis, ab exteris nationibus, quae in amicitiam populi Romani ditionemque essent, injurias propulsare eorumque fortunas defendere. M. Catonem illum Sapientem, clarissimum virum et prudentissimum, cum multis graves inimicitias gessisse accepimus propter Hispanorum apud quos consul fuerat injurias. Nuper Cn. Domitium scimus M. Silano diem dixisse propter unius hominis Aegritomari paterni amici atque hospitis injurias. XXI. Neque enim magis animos hominum nocentium res unquam ulla commovit quam haec majorum consuetudo longo intervallo repetita ac relata, sociorum querimoniae delatae ad hominem non inertissimum, susceptae ab eo qui videbatur eorum fortunas fide diligentiaque sua posse defendere. Hoc timent homines; hoc laborant; hoc institui atque adeo institutum referri ac renovari

jura fortunasque] 'Rights and interests,' as we might say. 'Jus,' besides its sense of 'law' generally, has the sense of 'a right,' or 'legal faculty.' The plural number, 'jura,' is used also to signify rules of law generally, even legal provisions contained within a 'lex.' And it also means 'rights' generally, as 'jus' means a particular right. 'Fortunae' is often used by the Latin writers in the plural number, but in a sense different from the singular, 'fortuna,' which very seldom means 'goods' or 'property,' though 'fortunae' does. Comp. Act. ii. Lib. 1. 44, 'bona fortunasque.' Horace (1 Ep. 5) says, "Quo mihi fortunam, si non conceditur uti?" See Bentley's note.

in amicitiam . . essent,] The readings 'issent' and 'venissent' have been proposed.—'venissent' cod. Urs. (Iordan.) See Act. ii. Lib. 2. c. 27.

M. Catonem illum Sapientem,] M. Porcius Cato, the censor, of whom he says in the De Amicitia, c. 2, "propterea quasi cognomen jam habebat in senectute sapientis." Asconius says that Cato prosecuted Ser. Galba and P. Furius for maladministration among the Lusitani. The prosecution of Ser. Sulpicius Galba took place shortly before Cato's death, B.C. 149; but that of P. Furius Philus at a much earlier date, B.C. 172.

M. Silano] This is the true reading, not D. which the MSS. have. Compare Act. ii. Lib. 2. c. 47. M. Junius Silanus was consul B.C. 109, and therefore the trial must have taken place a long time before the trial of Verres. The date of Silanus' prosecution is fixed at B.C. 104. But 'nuper' appears to be said by comparison with the remoter instance of Cato. —'diem dicere' is the ordinary expression to signify the commencement of a criminal prosecution against a man, to appoint a day for his appearance in court (Pro Sex. Roscio Amer. c. 12). It seems to be equivalent to 'in judicium vocare,' c. 21.

21. *atque adeo institutum*] 'They are troubled at the establishment of a fashion, and more than this (adeo), that an established fashion should be revived.' 'Instituere' is a word of grounding and fixing, applied to education, for instance (bene institui), the establishment of a plan,

moleste ferunt: putant fore ut, si paulatim haec consuetudo serpere ac prodire coeperit, per homines honestissimos virosque fortissimos, non imperitos adolescentulos aut illiusmodi quadruplatores, leges judiciaque administrentur. Cujus consuetudinis atque instituti patres majoresque nostros non poenitebat tum quum P. Lentulus, is qui princeps senatus fuit, accusabat M' Aquillium subscriptore C. Rutilio Rufo; aut cum P. Africanus, homo virtute, fortuna, gloria, rebus gestis amplissimus, posteaquam bis consul et censor fuerat, L. Cottam in judicium vocabat. Jure tum florebat populi Romani nomen; jure auctoritas hujus imperii civitatisque majestas

the laying of the foundation of a thing (see Caesar, B. G. iv. 17, v. 40, vi. 9; Cicero, Pro Murena, c. 9, 'tu actionem instituis'): altogether a different word in its use from 'constituere.' 'Adeo,' that is, 'ad eo,' is often a word of emphasis, of which numerous examples occur in these orations.

serpere] Said of an unperceived progress rather than of a slow progress. See Seyffert's note on De Am. c. 12, 'serpit deinde res.' Compare Act. ii. Lib. 3. c. 76, "ita serpit illud insitum natura malum:" and Lib. 2. c. 22.

non imperitos adolescentulos] Plutarch (Life of Lucullus, c. 1): "Lucullus, while he was still a youth, before he was a candidate for a magistracy and engaged in public life, made it his first business to bring to trial his father's accuser, Servilius the Augur, as a public offender; and the matter appeared to the Romans to be creditable to Lucullus, and they used to speak of that trial as a memorable thing. It was indeed the popular notion, that to prefer an accusation was a reputable measure, even when there was no foundation for it, and they were glad to see the young men fastening on old offenders, like well-bred whelps laying hold of wild beasts."

tum quum] These words are used emphatically to denote a coincidence of events, and 'quum' in such case has the indicative. "Expertus igitur es istius perfidiam tum quum se ad inimicos tuos contulit," Act. ii. Lib. 1. c. 30.

P. Lentulus,] M' Aquillius, consul of the year B.C. 129, was prosecuted for Repetundae, on his return from Asia after the defeat of Aristonicus. He was acquitted, by bribing the 'judices,' it is said (Appian, *Bell. Civ.* i. 22). This P. Lentulus was the grandfather of P. Lentulus Sura, who was strangled in prison in Cicero's consulship, B.C. 63. Asconius says that he was the father, but he is mistaken. Lentulus is here named Princeps Senatus. The Princeps Senatus was the Senator whose name was written first on the Censorian list, and this distinction was usually given to the oldest 'vir censorius.' It was also the general practice for the Princeps Senatus to be first called on to deliver his opinion in the Senate on any matter in debate, when there were no 'consules designati.' (Becker, Handbuch, ii. 2. 399. 425.)

P. Africanus,] Africanus, the younger, prosecuted L. Cotta in B.C. 131, at least not earlier (for Scipio triumphed over the Numantini B.C. 132). This L. Aurelius Cotta also escaped, and by the same means as M' Aquillius (Appian, *Bell. Civ.* i. 22). Cicero (Pro Murena, c. 28) attributes his acquittal to the unwillingness of the 'judices' to allow a man to be destroyed by so terrible an opponent as Scipio; a kind of feeling of pity at the disproportion between the power of the accuser and the weakness of the accused. L. Cotta, the son, who was consul B.C. 119, is supposed to be the Cotta who is meant, and not the father of the same name, who was consul B.C. 144. (Meyer, *Orat. Roman. Fragm.* p. 186, sec. ed.)

Jure, &c.] 'Jure' means 'justly,' 'rightly,' in the sense of 'there was good or sufficient cause.' 'Jure,' in its largest sense, is right (τὸ δίκαιον); and in its limited sense of 'law,' that is, positive institution, it is implied that positive law is conformable to a higher standard.

'Auctoritas' and 'majestas' are two untranslateable words, which are generally disposed of in a summary, and a slovenly way. They must both be explained by reference to the political notions of the Romans. The 'auctoritas' of a thing or a person, is the weight that is attached to the idea or constitution of the thing, or to the character or office of the person. 'Majestas,' literally, the magnitude of a thing, is its

gravis habebatur. Nemo mirabatur in Africano illo, quod in me nunc homine parvis opibus ac facultatibus praedito simulant sese mirari, quum moleste ferunt. Quid sibi iste vult? accusatoremne se existimari qui antea defendere consueverat? nunc praesertim ea jam aetate quum aedilitatem petat? Ego vero et aetatis non modo meae sed multo etiam superioris et honoris amplissimi puto esse, et accusare improbos et miseros calamitososque defendere. Et profecto aut hoc remedium est aegrotae ac prope desperatae rei publicae, judiciisque corruptis et contaminatis paucorum vitio ac turpitudine, homines ad legum defensionem judiciorumque auctoritatem quam honestissimos et integerrimos diligentissimosque accedere; aut, si ne hoc quidem prodesse poterit, profecto nulla unquam medicina his tot incommodis reperietur. Nulla salus rei publicae major est quam eos qui alterum accusant non minus de laude, de honore, de fama sua, quam illos qui accusantur de capite ac fortunis suis pertimescere. Itaque semper ii diligentissime laboriosissimeque accusarunt, qui seipsos in discrimen existimationis venire arbitrati sunt.

XXII. Quamobrem hoc statuere, judices, debetis, Q. Caecilium, de quo nulla unquam opinio fuerit nullaque in hoc ipso judicio exspectatio futura sit, qui neque ut ante collectam famam conservet neque uti reliqui temporis spem confirmet laborat, non nimis hanc causam severe, non nimis accurate, non nimis diligenter acturum. Habet enim nihil quod in offensione deperdat; ut turpissime

fulness and completeness; and the 'majestas Romani Imperii' or 'Populi Romani,' is all that composes that Imperium or Populus. A public functionary was said to impair the 'majestas' of the 'imperium' by misconducting any business of the state, or to betray it. ('Majestas vestra . . . hostibus tradita,' Sall. *Jug.* 31.) The term 'imperium' is derived from the oldest institutions of Rome, and has no connexion with 'empire' in the modern sense. Rome had an 'imperium' under the Republic. A praetor in his province exercised 'imperium.' Act. i. c. 5, 'imperio istius.'

defendere consueverat?] It ought perhaps to be 'consueverit;' but I find no notice of any various reading, except 'consuerat.'

honoris amplissimi] 'even of the highest office,' a higher office than the 'aedileship.' The high offices (magistratus) of the Roman state were called 'honores.' In c. 22, 'habet honorem quem petimus.' In Act. i. c. 4, 'quaestura, primus gradus honoris.'

aut—aut,] Either this is the remedy, or there is none. This is the force of the disjunctive 'aut,' which proposes two things, of which both are not true, or both not possible, or the like.

22. *nulla . . opinio*] 'about whom no public opinion has yet been formed' (Halm); which is the meaning. He had done nothing by which people could form any opinion about him.

severe,] The notion of 'severus' is strict or severe in the sense of 'serious;' but 'severus' is not 'tristis.' 'Accurate' means 'with care, painstakingly, laboriously.' 'Accurata oratio' is elaborate, laboured, like the Greek ἀκριβής (De Am. c. 7).

in offensione] 'if he fails,' a metaphor derived from stumbling. He says, shortly after, 'si tantulum offensum titubatumque sit.' 'Nihil requiret,' 'he will miss nothing,' or, as Asconius says, 'he won't feel the want

flagitiosissimeque discedat, nihil de suis veteribus ornamentis requiret. A nobis multos obsides habet populus Romanus, quos ut incolumes conservare, tueri, confirmare ac recuperare possimus omni ratione erit dimicandum. Habet honorem quem petimus; habet spem quam propositam nobis habemus; habet existimationem multo sudore, labore, vigiliisque collectam; ut, si in hac causa nostrum officium ac diligentiam probaverimus, haec quae dixi retinere per populum Romanum incolumia ac salva possimus; si tantulum offensum titubatumque sit, ut ea quae singulatim ac diu collecta sunt, uno tempore universa perdamus. Quapropter, judices, vestrum est deligere quem existimetis facillime posse magnitudinem causae ac judicii sustinere fide, diligentia, consilio, auctoritate. Vos si mihi Q. Caecilium anteposueritis, ego me dignitate superatum non arbitrabor: populus Romanus ne tam honestam, tam severam, diligentemque accusationem neque vobis placuisse neque ordini vestro placere arbitretur, providete.

of that which he never had.' "Ita bonis esse viribus extremo tempore aetatis ut adolescentiam non requireret" (De Sen. c. 9; and 'requiras,' c. 10).

honorem quem petimus;] Compare c. 21, 'quum aedilitatem petat.' Cicero was therefore a 'petitor' or candidate, when he delivered this speech; and yet the argument of Asconius incorrectly calls him 'designatus aedilis.'

singulatim] This word is contrasted with 'universa,' things taken singly, contrasted with things viewed as one.

Quapropter,] This is 'quam (rem) propter,' not 'quae propter;' as 'propterea,' its correlative, is 'propter eam.' We have the forms 'postquam,' 'praeterquam,' 'tamquam,' 'quamquam,' all of one family. It is not surprising that the Romans made so much use of this form 'quam,' which we may assume to have originally implied 'rem,' for 'res' itself is a word which they use on all occasions when they wish to express themselves with the utmost generality. When words come into common use, their origin is forgotten, and they serve many purposes for which their original meaning would seem to render them ill suited.

I. REPETUNDAE.

The Crimen Repetundarum Pecuniarum in Cicero's time comprehended, among other things, the offence committed by a Roman provincial governor in getting money or other valuable things by illegal means from the subjects and Socii of Rome. The direct object of the prosecution to which such a governor was liable, was the recovery of the money which he had taken; and hence the term Repetundae (res repetere). But the word 'Repetundae' is also used to express the illegal act for which compensation was sought. In the earlier periods of the Roman State the legal offence of Repetundae did not exist, for the Roman magistrates were seldom long absent from Rome; and when they did leave Rome for a time, it was only to carry on war against their near neighbours. It was during the second Punic war that the first instances occur of complaints made against the behaviour of Roman commanders in distant parts. An instance of this is mentioned by Livy (xxix. 8—16, &c.) when the Locri of Italy complained to the Roman Senate of the misconduct of the legatus Q. Pleminius. The senate sent commissioners to inquire into the affair on the spot, and they brought Pleminius, and others who were as guilty as himself, in chains to Rome. Pleminius died in prison before the Populus had pronounced judgment (prius—quam judicium de eo populi perficeretur). The Lex Porcia, probably proposed by M. Porcius Cato about B.C. 198, was the first legislative act on the abuse of their power by provincial governors. The terms of this Lex are supposed to be referred to by Livy (xxxii. 27); but this is hardly a correct interpretation of the passage. There was, however, a Lex Porcia, which is cited in the Plebiscitum de Thermensibus[1], which limited the amount of what governors could demand of the provincials: and it is possible that the prohibition mentioned by Cicero (Verr. Act. ii. Lib. 4. c. 5) may have been contained in the Lex Porcia; or, as some

[1] This part of the Plebiscitum is worth quoting as a specimen of legislative form and of the Roman language: NEIVE QVEIS MAGISTRATVS PROVE MAGISTRATV LEGATVS NEV QVIS ALIVS FACITO NEIVE IMPERATO QVO QVID MAGIS IEI DENT PRAEBEANT AB IEISVE AVFERATVR NISEI QVOD EOS EX LEGE PORTIA DARE PRAEBERE OPORTET OPORTEBIT. So it stands in Sigonius (De Jure Antiquo, &c., p. 318).

critics say, in the Lex Calpurnia. The Lex Porcia however appears to have done little towards checking or preventing exorbitant demands on the subjects and allies of Rome.

There were however means of punishing magistrates who were guilty of mal-administration. The Senate, as the chief administrative body in the State, could itself examine into any case of mal-administration and punish a criminal; or the Senate could empower persons to examine into complaints and do justice (Liv. xxxix. 3; xliii. 2). The Senate also could give authority to the Tribuni Plebis to prosecute a guilty person before the Comitia Tributa (judicium Publicum); as in the case of C. Lucretius whom two of the Tribuni Plebis prosecuted (ad populum accusarunt: Liv. xliii. 10). Livy adds: "comitiis habitis omnes quinque et triginta tribus eum condemnarunt." In the case mentioned by Livy (xliii. 2) the Senate empowered L. Canuleius, a Praetor, to appoint Recuperatores from the Senate, who should determine, on hearing the evidence, what amount was to be recovered from the accused. This was an instance in which Recuperatores were employed in conformity, as it appears, with their original functions of deciding in cases where Peregrini had a pecuniary demand against Romans, or Romans against Peregrini. (Div. c. 17.)

All these modes of procedure being found insufficient, a permanent court was formed for the trial of those Provincial magistrates who had been guilty of illegal acts which came under the denomination of Repetundae; and thus originated the Quaestio Perpetua de Pecuniis Repetundis. The Lex Calpurnia, which established this court, was proposed and carried by the Tribunus Plebis, L. Calpurnius Piso Frugi, B.C. 149. This Lex empowered Peregrini only to maintain an Actio of Repetundae. Roman citizens in the like case could recover by the usual form of proceedings (civili fere actione, Cic. Div. c. 5). As to the form of procedure, the court consisted of the Praetor Peregrinus as president, and of a certain, but not an ascertained, number of Senators who sat as Judices during a year, whence the name Quaestio Perpetua. These Judices must not be confounded with Recuperatores, who were appointed only for each particular case. Yet we read of Recuperatores being sometimes employed in the case of Repetundae, as for instance under the Lex Acilia. There was a Lex Junia de Repetundis, passed after the Calpurnia; but neither the time when it was enacted, nor the matter of it is known. Some fix the date at B.C. 126.

The Lex Servilia[1] (B.C. 106, or somewhere between 106—100, as some

[1] The fragments of the Lex Servilia of Glaucia were edited and explained by Klenze, Berlin, 1825, and this is the best edition. Two fragments of this Lex are said to be at Vienna, four at Naples, and the seventh, which was once at Paris, has disappeared. The learned C. Sigonius published a part of this Lex in his work De Antiquo Jure Populi

suppose) proposed by C. Servilius Glaucia, a Tribunus Plebis, made material additions to the Quaestio de Repetundis. It made not only provincial Magistratus, but all Magistratus and even Judices liable to prosecution for misconduct in the administration of justice. The chapters of the Lex contained many particular provisions; the chief of which was the following (c. 1): "quantum—ablatum captum coactum conciliatum aversumve sit, de ea re eius petitio nominisque delatio esto." The time fixed for the trial of matters which concerned the provincials was the summer months before the Kalends of September, in order that the proceedings might not be interrupted by the numerous holidays, if they were commenced later (Cic. Act. i. c. 10). After the 'nominis delatio,' or formal commencement of the proceedings, the Praetor named the persons (patroni, actores) who were to conduct the prosecution on the part of the complainants; but Peregrini might conduct their own case if they liked. Klenze is of opinion, that kings and free peoples, who were complainants, had the choice of conducting their case either by their Legati or by Patroni; but individual Peregrini and subject peoples were required to have Patroni. The Judices, the whole number of whom was 450 (the numerals CDL occur several times in the fragment of the Servilia Lex), were annually appointed by the Praetor, whose duty it was to preside in this court; and their names with the addition of the designation of their tribe were put on a tablet (album) in a public place. The accuser and the accused selected each 100 Judices from the list; and each had to challenge 50, so that 100 remained[1]. This took place twenty days after the 'nominis delatio,' and the names of the 100 Judices were placed on a tablet. The accused had to give 'vadimonium' or security for his appearance, and if he went into exile before the verdict was given, he was condemned to pay the amount of damages mentioned in the declaration. The Judices were required to give their votes in writing. One of the chapters related to the reward for the accusers, which in the case of a Peregrinus was the conferring of the 'civitas' on one at whose instance a Roman was convicted of Repetundae (Cic. Pro Balbo, c. 24). The Lex also provided for a second hearing by means of a 'comperendinatio' (Verr. Act. ii. Lib. 1. c. 9). It also provided, like the Lex Calpurnia, that a Roman citizen might have his civil action (legis actio sacramento) to recover damages, or might proceed criminally. Peregrini were not allowed to have this 'legis actio,' which was a mode of proceeding strictly Roman, that is, peculiar to Roman citizens. The Servilia Lex expresses the difference between these two

Romani, Bologna, 1574. He says "cujus fragmentum ego, cum Patavii profiterer, reperi in nobilissimo Petri Bembi Cardinalis musaeo in aeneis tabulis vetustissimis incisum."

[1] So it is stated by Rein, Das Criminalrecht der Römer, p. 618.

modes of proceeding by the words: "de ea re petitio nominisve delatio esto."

The penalty of the Lex was double the amount of what the accused was convicted of having wrongfully taken. There is nothing in the Lex which shows that exile was added as a penalty, though it appears that after the passing of this Lex some persons were condemned to exile. This was the case with T. Albucius B.C. 103, and P. Rutilius Rufus. But there is a difference of opinion among scholars on this matter of exile. That any criminal might leave Rome before sentence was pronounced, and that this was followed by the 'aquae et ignis interdictio,' is well ascertained; but this is a different thing from a formal sentence of exile. After the judgment followed the 'litis aestimatio' or the assessing of the amount of damages, whether the accused had gone into exile or not. If the man who was convicted was unable to pay the damages, or if he was dead, those were liable to pay to whose hands the money of the criminal had come (ad quos pervenit), heredes and the like.

The Lex Acilia, proposed by the Tribunus Plebis M' Acilius Glabrio, was enacted B.C. 101. Some writers make the Lex Acilia precede the Servilia in the order of time, to which there is this objection, that the Acilia is not mentioned in the fragments of the Servilia, while the Calpurnia and Junia are mentioned. Besides this, it would not have been necessary for the Cornelia to restore the second 'actio,' if the Acilia had preceded the Servilia.

The Acilia did not allow either 'comperendinatio' or 'ampliatio.' Cicero says (Verr. Act. ii. Lib. 1. c. 9): "ego tibi illam Aciliam legem restituo, qua lege multi semel accusati, semel dicta causa, semel auditis testibus condemnati sunt."

During the Dictatorship of Sulla (B.C. 81) was enacted the Lex Cornelia, the basis of which was the Servilia. This Lex contained the provision, that if a provincial governor got or received money for the purpose of having statues erected to him, he should be liable to a prosecution, if the statues were not set up within five years. The aediles were also forbidden to borrow statues from the provinces for the decoration of their spectacles at Rome, or to take money for this purpose. These and other regulations are stated to have been contained in the Cornelia Lex. The penalty of exile was still retained, as it is inferred from Cicero's expression (Verr. Act. ii. Lib. 2. c. 31), "retinete hominem in civitate," &c., and as it is stated by Asconius (Act. i. c. 13). The pecuniary damages, which were assessed in the 'litis aestimatio,' after the condemnation of the accused, were increased to four times the actual amount of what the accused had wrongfully taken, and payment could be demanded even from those to whose hands it could be proved that any part of the ill-gotten money or valuables had come, or as the Romans

expressed it, "ad quos ea pecunia pervenit" (Cic. Ad Div. viii. 8). Zumpt reconciles the statement of Cicero (Divin. c. 5), that Sicily claimed 'sestertium millies' from Verres, with the statement in another passage that Verres had illegally robbed the Sicilians of 'quadringenties sestertium,' by assuming that the Lex Cornelia made the damages two and a half the amount of what had been illegally taken. I am not aware that there is any other foundation for this assumption than the fact that Cicero will thus be made consistent. But that is not a satisfactory way of settling differences. (See the note on Divin. c. 5.) The amount stated in the Divinatio may have been exaggerated, or there may have been reasons for claiming less than the amount mentioned in a speech which was no part of the judicial proceedings. The Lex empowered the Praetor to allow a second Actio, if the Judices could not come to a decision on the first hearing; and the Judices were not to be chosen by the prosecutor and the accused, but were determined by lot. The Judices were taken from the Senators. An alteration was also made as to the challenge of the Judices, as we may collect from Cicero (Verr. Act. i. c. 7).

The Lex Julia de Repetundis was enacted in the first consulship of C. Julius Cæsar B.C. 59; and consequently after the trial of Verres.

The provisions of some of these Leges, the Cornelia for instance, appear to be very doubtful, and the conclusions of writers, from scattered passages, are uncertain. (Rein, Das Criminalrecht der Römer, p. 604, &c.; Dict. of Greek and Roman Antiquities, art. Repetundae; Orelli's Cicero, Index Legum).

II. JUDICIA.

The terms Jus Publicum and Jus Privatum were used by the Romans to express the whole body of law which exists in a state. The opposition between Jus Publicum and Jus Privatum is shown by the words of Ulpian (Dig. 1. 1. 1. § 2): "Publicum jus est quod ad statum Rei Romanae spectat, privatum quod ad singulorum utilitatem." (Comp. Justin. Inst. 1. 1. 1.) The Jus Publicum has the State for its object, the political organization of a people. The Jus Privatum comprehends the whole of the legal relations in which individuals stand to one another. The two divisions are distinct enough and intelligible, whatever objections may be made to the terms by which they are designated. The notion of a State is not indeed limited to the department of Law; but one of the purposes of the existence of a State is to give reality to the idea of Law. And this is effected in two ways. If an individual's rights are invaded, the State protects him and gives him redress; and the mode by which this is accomplished comprehends the rules of Civil Procedure. The State also exercises its activity without respect to the interests of individuals by inflicting punishment for the violation of positive Law: and the rules according to which this is done comprehend Criminal Law and Criminal Procedure. The Romans comprehended under Jus Publicum, both Civil Procedure, Criminal Law and Criminal Procedure. The activity of the State, by means of those to whom power is delegated, is as manifest in Civil Procedure as it is in Criminal Procedure. But the direct object in Civil Procedure is to establish the right of an individual or to give him compensation for a wrong: in Criminal Procedure the direct object is the punishment of an individual for the general interest.

Publicum Jus comprehended the Law which concerned religion (Jus Sacrum); and if ever Jus Publicum and Sacrum are opposed to one another, it is only for the purpose of marking the distinction between the rules of Law that relate to things which concern religion, and to things which do not concern religion.

One of the Leges Valeriae declared that no Roman Magistratus should have the power of putting to death or whipping a Roman citizen without

an appeal (provocatio) to the popular assembly (comitia centuriata). Thus the supreme jurisdiction in criminal matters was secured to the people. Afterwards the Tributa Comitia in some way got the power of judging high offences against the State. The distinction between Public crimes (publica crimina) and Private injuries (privata delicta) corresponds to the distinction in the mode of procedure. The State as such, that is the people in their 'comitia,' judged all such offences as were directly opposed to the interests of the State. The Publica Crimina ultimately comprehended numerous offences, the complete list of which belongs to a later period than that which we are considering (Dig. 48. tit. 1). Among them were Perduellio or treason (in a sense), murder and Parricidium, Repetundae, Ambitus, and many others. 'Delicta' were the subjects of actions, and belonged to the competence of the Ordo Judiciorum Privatorum. 'Delicta' comprehended 'furtum,' 'rapina,' 'injuria,' and 'damnum injuria' (Gaius, iii. 182; Justin. Inst. iv. 1).

The administration of criminal justice was thus in the hands of the people and exercised in the Comitia. The offences which were cognizable, were chiefly determined and defined by custom. As to the Leges which preceded the Twelve Tables we know little, and the Twelve Tables themselves, if they were sufficient for the time, soon required to have their deficiencies supplied. They did not comprise every offence which the moral and religious notions of the people considered as worthy of punishment; and this defect was not made up by direct legislation. The power of the people, who were the judges in their Comitia, was not limited as that of the Judices in the time of Cicero by particular Leges. The Magistratus, who prosecuted before the Comitia, prepared a bill of indictment, in which the offence and the penalty were comprised; and the judges, that is, the people, might accept or reject his Rogatio. The offence might be one which opinion considered deserving of punishment, according to a just interpretation or extension of the provisions of the Twelve Tables, or it might be something new, which opinion declared to be deserving of punishment. Such instances of punishment served as precedents, both as to the crime and the punishment. This development of the criminal law is precisely what might be expected in a State, where the assembled people gave judgment, and when legislation was still very imperfect. A code which minutely defines crimes and fixes punishments never can exist in the early period of a nation's history. The trials before the Comitia would gradually lead to the establishment of forms of procedure and the more exact definition of crimes; and though the early criminal law of Rome had no systematic character, it does not follow that it was not practically good for the time.

The legislation of Rome in the department of Criminal Law is very scanty for the period which precedes the Lex Calpurnia. Leges were enacted to prevent Ambitus, or the improper means of obtaining the votes of the people at elections, and on some few other matters. The difficulty of a trial before a public body would increase when the guilt or innocence of a man did not depend on a single fact, but on many facts and many witnesses; and the impartiality of the popular vote would often be disturbed by the spirit of faction. The Senate, as the administrative body, had or assumed the power of appointing special commissioners to inquire into offences, which belonged to the cognizance of the Comitia; and these special commissions may have suggested the establishment of a permanent court for the trial of offences. A Quaestio Perpetua was first established by the Lex Calpurnia (B.C. 149). The term Perpetua in the Quaestio Perpetua is to be understood in the same way as Perpetuum in the Edictum Perpetuum. The Quaestio Perpetua was a court which had permanence during the term of office of the Magistratus who was the president of it. Perpetua accordingly is the same as Annua, and the court thus established was so called in opposition to those which were established for a special occasion and with a special president, Quaesitor or Quaestor. These Quaestiones perpetuae, or permanent courts, were afterwards extended to other offences besides that of Repetundae; and this was fully effected by the legislation of Sulla. His legislation established or confirmed nine Quaestiones. The Quaestio Perpetua was an improvement on the courts of the Comitia; but though the people lost most of their judicial power, the Comitia were still considered the supreme judges, and they still exercised the judicial functions in some cases, as in that of Perduellio.

The criminal trials at Rome were now conducted pursuant to the several Leges, which were applicable to them. Each Lex defined the crime, determined the punishment, and contained provisions as to the constitution of the court before which an accused person was to be tried. There was no code which comprehended all the matters which came under the denomination of Publica Crimina; but certain Leges, commonly called Leges Judiciariae, contained certain general regulations as to the mode of procedure.

The establishment of a Quaestio Perpetua by the Lex Calpurnia gave the Senatorius Ordo a power which they had before only exercised occasionally. Before the enactment of the Lex Calpurnia, the Senate possessed a concurrent jurisdiction with the Comitia, as we have already seen; for crimes were tried either by the assembled people, or by a Consilium of Senators under the presidency of one or more magistrates

who were empowered to act as a special commission. The appointment of such special commissions by the Senate was apparently an encroachment on the popular power, and the establishment of a Quaestio Perpetua was nothing more than the giving of a regular form to what was done occasionally. As the higher personages of the State were chiefly the objects of criminal prosecutions, the Senate would be inclined to secure as far as possible the jurisdiction over those who were either members of their own body or connected with those who were. In a Quaestio Perpetua the Judices were still the Senators, a certain number of whom were annually selected by the Praetor, as it appears, and their names were entered on a list, the Album Judicum Selectorum. Out of this body were taken by lot the requisite number of Judices for each trial. The Senators were often partial judges in the case of members of their own body; and the Populares or popular leaders attempted to wrest from them their judicial power. The Lex Sempronia, B.C. 122, of C. Gracchus, took away the judicial power from the Senators and gave it to the Equites, from which body the Praetor was required to take the Judices. According to Cicero the people were satisfied with the Equites. But in trials for Repetundae nothing was gained by the change, for the governors in the provinces winked at the exactions of the Publicani, who belonged to the equestrian order, the object of the governors being to secure the favour of that body from whom their Judices must be chosen, if they were ever prosecuted for mal-administration (Cic. Verr. Act. ii. Lib. 3. c. 41). The Lex Servilia Caepionis, B.C. 106, repealed the Lex Sempronia; but the Lex Servilia Glaucia Repetundarum again excluded the Senators from the Judicia[1]. This Lex did not give the Judicia to the Equites in express terms, but it accomplished this object by excluding others. The Praetor had the power of naming 450 Judices, but he could not name any person who was or had been Tribunus Plebis, Quaestor, Triumvir Capitalis, Tribunus Militum in one of the first four legions, or Triumvir agris dandis assignandis, or any one who had been or was in the Senate, any person who was Infamis, any person who was under thirty or above sixty years of age, any person who did not reside in Rome or in the immediate neighbourhood, any father, brother, or son of any person who was or had been a member of the Senate, or any person who was absent beyond seas. M. Livius Drusus, Tribunus Plebis, proposed and carried a Lex Judiciaria, B.C. 91, which distributed the judicial power between the Senate and the Equites; but the Senate declared this and all the other Leges Liviae invalid on the ground of not

[1] The date of the Servilia Glaucia is not certain. It was certainly enacted after the Servilia Caepionis. See p. 44.

having been enacted in due form. The Lex Plautia, B.C. 89, enacted that fifteen Judices should be elected from each tribe, without any respect to the class of persons. When the party of the Optimates under Sulla had got all the power in their hands, a Lex Cornelia (B.C. 80) again gave the Judicia to the Senate. This Lex Cornelia was repealed by the Aurelia, B.C. 70, the agitation for which was going on at the time of the prosecution of Verres. The Aurelia made the Judices eligible from the Senators, Equites, and Tribuni Aerarii. A Lex Julia subsequently deprived the Tribuni Aerarii of the judicial functions, and gave them to the Senators and Equites.

It is plain from this sketch that the disputes as to the constitution of the Judicia and the class of persons from whom the Judices were to be chosen, did not relate to the Judicia Privata, a term which we find used by Cicero (Top. 17). The Romans had a permanent court for the decision of many civil actions, called the court of the Centumviri, the origin and constitution of which are very uncertain. At the time when we are best acquainted with it, this court had a very extensive jurisdiction, especially in matters relating to an Hereditas. Cicero in a passage of the De Oratore (i. 38) enumerates some of the many questions which belonged to the jurisdiction of this court; and from this passage we may conclude that at one time at least, this court decided on all matters in dispute with respect to property in land. At an earlier period, however, private persons, who held no official situation, were appointed by a magistrate for the hearing and determining of civil actions; and such Judices were called Privati, as being opposed to those who acted as Judices by virtue of any office. There might be various reasons for the appointment of such Judices Privati. The permanent courts might not be adapted for the investigation of all questions; or they might not have time; or cases might arise in which some particular kind of knowledge was necessary in order to enable a Judex to come to a just decision; and finally the intercourse between Romans and Peregrini might render this form of procedure necessary in many cases. A Lex Pinaria of early date (Gaius, v. 15), in the case of a Legis Actio Sacramento, allowed the parties to apply for a Judex, whom the Praetor named within thirty days after the application; and this appears to be the earliest notice that we have of the appointment of a Judex, though it does not follow that this Lex established the practice. It is certain that the practice of appointing a Judex for the hearing and determining of matters between individuals, was well adapted to the wants of the Romans, and that the practice gradually was extended, and the permanent courts for the decision of civil matters were much less employed. This change may have originated in the circumstance of the permanent

courts retaining their old practice and their original constitution, without being capable of adapting themselves to the alterations in the social state and to the changes in the habits of the Romans. People, if left alone, can find out what they want better than any legislator; and there are few countries at the present day in which the old courts would not be soon superseded by something better suited to the wants of the people, if the free development of a nation's activity was not fettered by those who hold power, and particularly by those who are interested in maintaining existing forms of procedure. The notion of justice, which is in all people, and is developed by their social progress, finally led the Romans to the transferring of the Officium Judicis to private persons, named for the occasion, and generally in each case to a single person. In certain cases, several Judices were appointed, under the name of Recuperatores, whose functions appear to have been limited to particular kinds of actions. It does not belong to the present inquiry to explain, how the Magistratus controlled and directed a Judex in the hearing and determining of a case. The references at the end will give the necessary information on this matter to those who will take the pains to look for it.

Many persons would naturally (natura) be excluded from the Officium Judicis, as idiots, deaf people, and Impuberes; or by custom, that is, opinion in a persistent form (moribus), as women, slaves; or by special rule, as Infames (Dig. 5. 1. 12). It does not follow that all who were not specially excluded had the capacity of acting as Judex; and the Praetor might by virtue of the power of his office extend the exceptions. Yet the nature of the institution of a Judex seems to require that there should be the freest possible selection of persons; and this was particularly so in the case of that class of Judices who were called Arbitri (see Cicero, Pro Rosc. Com. c. 4, and Top. 17); and apparently in the case of Recuperatores also. There were two classes of Arbitri; and one class were those who by the Formula were empowered to decide what one party should do or make good to another 'ex fide bona,' or 'quantum aequius melius id dari,' or 'ut inter bonos agier oportet.' This class of actions was finally comprehended under the name of 'bonae fidei judicia.' The Romans had a tact for legal precision; but they had likewise a nice sense of what is just. They knew that many of the transactions of life cannot be bound down to the rigid formulae of a legal rule. Our legal formalists can see nothing beyond the narrow circle within which they intrench themselves. If the case in hand does not fit their formula, no legal redress for a wrong which the common understanding (communis sensus) of mankind pronounces to be a wrong, no legal establishment of a right, which the like sense pronounces to be one. By means of their 'bonae fidei judicia,' the Romans kept a mean between the refusal of

justice and the laxity of no legal rule. Their law existed less in the written text than in the understanding of the people, the true depository of a large part of law, and that mainly which relates to the multifarious concerns of life which come under the legal denomination of Contracts, or the popular and wider term of Agreements.

It has been observed that the Leges Judiciariae did not relate to civil actions, but to Criminal procedure. We cannot suppose that the Senators who originally were the Judices in the Publica Judicia were excluded from being Judices in civil actions. Polybius (vi. 17) says that from the body of the Senate were appointed judges (κριταί) of most both public and private matters (συναλλαγμάτων), which involved any magnitude of charge (ἐγκλημάτων); a statement too vague to build any thing upon. It is at least certain that the Leges Judiciariae had nothing to do with civil cases or actions. Besides these it would be absurd to suppose that the Senatorian body would have maintained such a vigorous contest about the Judicia in order to maintain their right to act as Judices in matters that concerned the ordinary transactions of a Roman plebeian, such as buying and selling, pledging, and the like. Augustus certainly, or perhaps Caesar, extended the institution of the Judices Selecti to the Judicia Privata; and the Judices for these matters also were from that time taken from the Album Judicum Selectorum. This arrangement made the Officium Judicis a duty incumbent upon all who were included in the Album. It was not simply a distinction: it was also a burden; yet of course the office would be viewed by the citizens generally as honourable (1 Hor. Sat. iv. 123).

Though so many offences against the State were brought under the cognizance of the Quaestiones Perpetuae, the Judicia Populi, or trials before the Comitia, still existed in Cicero's time for the offence of Perduellio (Populus Romanus judicabit, &c. In Verr. Act. ii. Lib. 5. c. 69). If Verres should escape the prosecution for Repetundae, and prosecutions for other offences also before the permanent courts, Cicero threatens to bring him before the Populus Romanus, before the thirty-five Tribes (Act. ii. Lib. 1. c. 5). In Cicero's consulship, B.C. 63, C. Rabirius was prosecuted for Perduellio; and when C. Julius Caesar and L. Julius Caesar were appointed Duumviri Perduellionis by the Praetor instead of by the Populus, Rabirius, on being condemned, appealed to the Populus in the Comitia Centuriata, and Cicero made a speech in his defence, part of which is extant. An instance of an appeal of this kind is in the story of M. Horatius in Livy (i. 26).

The object of these remarks was to explain the nature of the court before which Verres was tried; but it seemed also necessary to show that the Judices Privati were distinct from the Judices in the Quaestiones Perpetuae. There are several matters relating to the Publica Judicia

which have been either briefly treated here, or omitted, the object not being to say all that could be said, but as much as will serve to explain these orations. There is a dissertation by Ph. Invernizius, intitled 'De Publicis et Criminalibus Judiciis" (reprinted at Leipzig, 1846), but it is not a critical performance.—(Savigny, System des Heut. Röm. Rechts, Vol. i.; Puchta, Instit.; Rein, Das Criminalrecht der Römer; the article JUDEX in Smith's Dict. of Antiquities, by G. L. As to the Publica Judicia, see also the last Title of the Institutions of Justinian, De Publicis Judiciis).

ACCUSATIONIS

IN

C. VERREM

ACTIO PRIMA.

"Haec oratio iisdem codicibus quibus Divinatio in Caecilium continetur. Parisiensis D tamen ad hanc orationem et ad Actionis secundae libros non est collatus nisi paucis locis. Aliquoties apud Zumptium enotatae sunt variae scripturae ex codd. Par. nr. 7776 (B) et nr (7786) (C)" (Iordan). See the Introduction.

I. Quod erat optandum maxime, judices, et quod unum ad invidiam vestri ordinis infamiamque judiciorum sedandam maxime pertinebat, id non humano consilio sed prope divinitus datum atque oblatum vobis summo rei publicae tempore videtur. Inveteravit enim jam opinio perniciosa rei publicae vobisque periculosa, quae non modo Romae sed et apud exteras nationes omnium sermone percrebuit, his judiciis quae nunc sunt pecuniosum hominem, quamvis sit nocens, neminem posse damnari. Nunc in ipso discrimine ordinis judiciorumque vestrorum, quum sint parati qui contionibus et legibus hanc invidiam senatus inflammare conentur, reus in

1. *vestri ordinis*] Klotz has 'nostri.' Cicero had been Quaestor, and he was now 'aedilis designatus;' he could therefore say 'nostri.'—'vobis:' 'nobis,' G1 6 Lgg. al.

summo . . . tempore] Comp. Divin. c. 2, 'ex meo tempore;' Pro Archia, c. 6; and the numerous passages in which Cicero uses this word.—'Inveteravit:' comp. Caesar's use of this word, B. G. ii. 1. v. 41.

sed et] 'sed etiam,' Iordan, who also has 'percrebruit.' The MSS. are divided as usual. See Divin. c. 4.

his . . . quae nunc sunt] Orelli and Zumpt have 'sint.' The Romans could use either form of expression in such a clause, though the two forms have not the same meaning. If the emphasis is placed on the verb, it should be 'sunt,' and the word 'nunc' shows that 'sunt' is emphatical. When Cicero does not intend to dwell particularly on the fact, expressed by a clause 'qui' and a verb, he seems generally to use the subjunctive. There is no other explanation of his reason for using the indicative or subjunctive in many of the sentences in these orations.

contionibus et legibus] Klotz adopts in his text, like Orelli, the false form 'concionibus,' but the true one, 'contionibus,' in his note on this passage. Zumpt has 'contionibus.' There is also a reading 'contentionibus.' Besides the evidence of the Bacchanalian inscription, where we have the form 'coventio,' of which 'contio' is a shortened form, there is the evidence of the

judicium adductus est C. Verres, homo vita atque factis omnium jam opinione damnatus, pecuniae magnitudine, sua spe et praedicatione absolutus. Huic ego causae, judices, cum summa voluntate et exspectatione populi Romani actor accessi, non ut augerem invidiam ordinis, sed ut infamiae communi succurrerem. Adduxi enim hominem in quo reconciliare existimationem judiciorum amissam, redire in gratiam cum populo Romano, satisfacere exteris nationibus possetis; depeculatorem aerarii, vexatorem Asiae atque Pamphyliae, praedonem juris urbani, labem atque perniciem provinciae Siciliae. De quo si vos severe ac religiose judicaveritis, auctoritas ea quae in vobis remanere debet haerebit; sin istius ingentes divitiae judiciorum religionem veritatemque perfregerint, ego hoc tamen assequar ut judicium potius rei publicae quam aut reus judicibus aut accusator reo defuisse videatur.

II. Equidem, ut de me confitear, judices, quum multae mihi a C. Verre insidiae terra marique factae sint, quas partim mea diligentia devitarim, partim amicorum studio officioque reppulerim, nunquam tamen neque tantum periculum mihi adire visus sum neque tanto opere pertimui ut nunc in ipso judicio. Neque tantum me exspectatio accusationis meae concursusque tantae multitudinis, quibus ego rebus vehementissime perturbor, commovet, quantum

MSS. in many cases, though Orelli and others take no notice of it. See Seyffert's note on the De Am. c. 25, where he has the true form 'contio,' and Pro Milone, c. 2. The 'invidia senatus' is the bad repute of the senate, which was increased by the speeches made on the occasion of proposing the Lex Aurelia; for this was the year in which this measure was proposed and carried by L. Aurelius Cotta, supported by Cn. Pompeius. Compare Act. ii. Lib. 3. c. 96, where he alludes to Cotta's agitation about his 'lex.' The 'lex' was not promulgated, in the Roman sense, till after the Actio Prima against Verres (Act. ii. Lib. 5. c. 69).

reconciliare] 'Conciliare' is to bring together, and 'reconciliare' has the same relation to it that 'reducere' has to 'ducere.' Here it means to 'recover' or 'restore.' 'In quo' belongs to the examples of 'in pueris,' 'in perfecto viro' (De Am. c. 2). The English language here requires some change in the form of expression: 'for I have brought before you a man who will give you the opportunity of recovering the character of the Judicia, which is lost.' As to the primary sense of 'reconciliare,' see Plautus, Capt. Prol. 32.

praedonem juris urbani,] A poorish kind of play on the word 'praetor, for he is alluding to the misconduct of Verres as Praetor Urbanus. G3 s have only 'juris,' and Iordan omits 'urbani.'—'remanere:' see Divin. c. 18.

labem] The primary meaning of this word, as its etymology indicates (lab-i), is a sinking or falling; as, for instance, the sinking of the earth, 'labes agri Privernatis' (De Divin. 1. 43). Comp. De Am. c. 12. The use of the word by the Roman law writers confirms this explanation (Dig. 19. 2. 62).

2. *insidiae terra marique*] Asconius, the false one, takes all this literally, and explains it by some amplification, after the manner of many of the scholiasts, who treat us with the text over again in another shape. Cicero has the same rhetorical flourish in Act. ii. Lib. 2. c. 40. He means to say that Verres formed designs against his life when he went to Sicily to get evidence.—'reppulerim:' Iordan, who cites no MSS., but I assume that the MSS. have this way of writing.

quibus ego rebus] When there might be any ambiguity or want of precision in using the relative only, or when the re-

istius insidiae nefariae quas uno tempore mihi, vobis, M' Glabrioni praetori, sociis, exteris nationibus, ordini, nomini denique senatorio facere conatur; qui ita dictitat, iis esse metuendum qui quod ipsis solis satis esset surripuissent, se tantum eripuisse ut id multis satis esse possit; nihil esse tam sanctum quod non violari, nihil tam munitum quod non expugnari pecunia possit. Quod si quam audax est ad conandum, tam esset obscurus in agendo, fortasse aliqua in re nos aliquando fefellisset. Verum hoc adhuc percommode cadit, quod cum incredibili ejus audacia singularis stultitia conjuncta est. Nam ut apertus in corripiendis pecuniis fuit, sic in spe corrumpendi judicii perspicua sua consilia conatusque omnibus fecit. Semel ait se in vita pertimuisse tum quum primum reus a me factus sit; quod quum e provincia recens esset invidiaque et infamia non recenti sed vetere ac diuturna flagraret, tum ad judicium corrumpendum tempus alienum offenderet. Itaque quum ego diem in Sicilia inquirendi perexiguam postulavissem, invenit iste qui sibi in Achaiam biduo breviorem diem postularet, non ut is idem conficeret diligentia et industria sua, quod ego meo labore et vigiliis consecutus sum; etenim ille Achaicus inquisitor ne Brundisium quidem pervenit; ego Siciliam totam quinquaginta diebus sic obii ut omnium populorum privatorumque literas injuriasque cognoscerem; ut perspi-

ference is to all that is comprised in the antecedent part and not to a single word or words, the Romans write 'quae res,' 'quibus rebus.' Caesar always writes in this way.

obscurus] Zumpt has 'astutus,' on the authority of only one MS., G1. There is something to say in favour of 'astutus,' but 'obscurus' gives at least as good a meaning.

audacia . . . stultitia] See Cicero's remark "quod aut ii, qui ad fraudem callidi sunt," Pro Cluentio, c. 65, vol. ii.

reus a me] 'a me reus' Iordan, and the better MSS. This variation in the order of two or three consecutive words continually occurs in the MSS., and it is often impossible to determine in what order the author placed them. I think that 'reus' should stand first, but others may read the passage differently.

diem . . . inquirendi] Halm, who is followed by Iordan, has altered this to 'inquirendi in Siciliam,' and he refers to Act. i. Lib. 1. c. 11, 'in Siciliam,' which is not exactly the same thing. But I have no doubt that Halm's Latin is right, and that the MSS. reading is Latin too.

diem . . . perexiguam] 'Dies feminino genere tempus,' says Asconius; that is, it is used in the feminine gender to signify many days, or a long time. He adds, "et ideo diminutive *diecula* dicitur breve tempus et mora. Dies horarum xii generis masculini est: unde *hodie* dicimus quasi *hoc die*." This is true: but 'dies' is also feminine, when it is a day fixed by authority or legal form. 'Dies,' the natural day, the time from sunrise to sunset, is masculine. See Caesar, B. G. i. 6.

invenit iste qui] Asconius, our only guide here, gives the various opinions as to the names of the prosecutor and accused to whom Cicero alludes; but the names are immaterial. See Introd.

populorum . . . cognoscerem ;] Cicero, in this short time, made himself acquainted with the written statements, and with the wrongs, of every community and every private person. 'Cognoscere' is a word of examination and investigation, for the purpose of knowing. So the French use it: 'les tribunaux connaissent de tous les crimes.' 'Agnoscere' is a word of recognition, of knowledge declared upon sight or inspection. 'Verres cognoscebat, Verres

cuum cuivis esse posset hominem ab isto quaesitum esse non qui reum suum adduceret, sed qui meum tempus obsideret.

III. Nunc homo audacissimus atque amentissimus hoc cogitat. Intelligit me ita paratum atque instructum in judicium venire ut non modo in auribus vestris sed in oculis omnium sua furta atque flagitia defixurus sim. Videt senatores multos esse testes audaciae suae; videt multos equites Romanos, frequentes praeterea cives atque socios, quibus ipse insignes injurias fecerit: videt etiam tot, tam graves ab amicissimis civitatibus legationes cum publicis auctoritatibus ac testimoniis convenisse. Quae quum ita sint, usque eo de omnibus bonis male existimat, usque eo senatoria judicia perdita profligataque esse arbitratur ut hoc palam dictitet, non sine causa se cupidum pecuniae fuisse, quoniam in pecunia tantum praesidium experiatur esse; sese, id quod difficillimum fuerit, tempus ipsum emisse judicii sui quo cetera facilius emere postea posset, ut, quoniam criminum vim subterfugere nullo modo poterat, procellam temporis devitaret. Quod si non modo in causa, verum in aliquo honesto praesidio, aut in alicujus eloquentia aut gratia spem aliquam collocasset, profecto non haec omnia colligeret atque aucuparetur; non usque eo despiceret contemneretque ordinem senatorium ut arbitratu ejus deligeretur ex senatu qui reus fieret, qui, dum hic quae opus essent compararet, causam interea ante eum diceret. Quibus ego rebus quid iste speret et quo animum intendat facile perspicio: quamobrem vero se confidat aliquid proficere posse hoc praetore et hoc consilio intelligere non possum. Unum illud intelligo, quod populus Romanus in rejectione judicum judicavit, ea spe istum fuisse praeditum ut omnem rationem salutis in pecunia

judicabat' (Act. ii. Lib. 2. c. 10). The distinction, though not always made, is substantially true. See Forcellini 'Agnoscere,' and Seyffert, De Am. c. 2; and 'cognoscere' and 'recognoscere,' Act. i. c. 5.

3. *ac testimoniis*] omitted by Jordan, being found only in dtt. Asconius explains 'auctoritatibus' by 'publicis literis,' public documents.

tempus . . . judicii] "id est, dilationem temporis impetrasse. *Judicium suum* autem debemus intelligere sibi aptum, et e contrario ait: *alienum tempus offenderet*" (c. 2) Ascon.

arbitratu ejus] 'at his pleasure,' according to his own choice and will. Comp. De Am. c. 1. The words 'ex senatu qui reus fieret' are explained by the last part of c. 2. See Introd.

dum hic quae opus essent] 'Hic', is Verres, who is represented as contriving that another accused should be engaged in defending himself, that he might have time to prepare his own defence, by bribery and so forth.

in rejectione judicum] In making his challenge of the 'judices,' Verres showed that he relied on bribery, for he left those unchallenged whom he, and apparently others also, considered most likely to be purchased. 'Rejicere,' 'to throw back or out,' is the word which the Romans used to express the removal of a 'judex' by the right of challenge. See (Ad Att. i. 16) Cicero's account of the trial of Clodius. —'in pecunia constitueret:' the dtt have 'poneret,' which is just as good in itself, but not so good here, because there is less evidence for it.

constitueret; hoc erepto praesidio ut nullam sibi rem adjumento fore arbitraretur.

IV. Etenim quod est ingenium tantum, quae tanta facultas dicendi aut copia quae istius vitam, tot vitiis flagitiisque convictam, jam pridem omnium voluntate judicioque damnatum, aliqua ex parte possit defendere? Cujus ut adolescentiae maculas ignominiasque praeteream, quaestura, primus gradus honoris, quid aliud habet in se nisi Cn. Carbonem spoliatum a quaestore suo pecunia publica, nudatum et proditum consulem, desertum exercitum, relictam provinciam, sortis necessitudinem religionemque violatam? cujus legatio exitium fuit Asiae totius et Pamphyliae, quibus in provinciis multas domos, plurimas urbes, omnia fana depopulatus est, quum in Cn. Dolabellam suum scelus illud pristinum renovavit et instauravit quaestorium; quum eum cui legatus et pro quaestore fuisset, et in invidiam suis maleficiis adduxit, et in ipsis periculis non solum deseruit, sed etiam oppugnavit ac prodidit: cujus praetura urbana aedium sacrarum fuit publicorumque operum depopulatio, simul in jure dicundo bonorum possessionumque contra omnium instituta addictio et condonatio. Jam vero omnium vitiorum suorum plurima et maxima constituit monumenta et indicia in provincia Sicilia, quam iste per triennium ita [vastavit,] vexavit,

4. *convictam,*] Zumpt has 'conjunctam.' The MSS. are of little authority here, for 'conuictam' and 'coniunctam' are easily confounded. The sense is 'a life against which there is the evidence of so many crimes and abominations.' The use of 'convincere' and 'condemnare' in Act. ii. Lib. 1. c. 1, shows that 'convictam' may be the true reading here. Comp. Act. ii. Lib. 1. c. 9, 'tam multis testibus convictus.' 'In convictos maleficii servos' (Act. ii. Lib. 5. c. 53) is a different thing. Zumpt shows that 'convictum testimonio, judicio,' &c., is Cicero's language; but he maintains that 'vita' cannot be 'convicta vitiis,' but must be 'convicta vitiorum,' by something else, which is expressed in the ablative. But he is mistaken. Caesar (B. G. i. 40) writes "aut aliquo facinore comperto avaritiam esse convictam;" where however many good MSS. have 'coniunctam.' Cicero, Pro P. Quintio, c. 25, writes, "volo inauditum facinus ipsius qui id commisit voce convinci."

Cn. Carbonem] See Introd.

sortis necessitudinem &c.] See Divin. c. 19.

depopulatus] 'depeculatus' Orelli.

legatus et pro quaestore] Here two functions are mentioned, that of 'legatus,' and that of 'pro quaestore,' or the office of 'quaestor' filled by one who was not 'quaestor.' Comp. Act. ii. Lib. 1. c. 15. It seems that a man who had been 'quaestor' might be appointed, without the election of the people, when from any cause the office of 'quaestor' became vacant in a province.

oppugnavit] See Introd.

in jure dicundo] These words express the 'praetor's' office, which was 'jus dicere.' Excursus iv. 'Addictio' (see Addicere, Forcellini, for examples) is the term which expresses the praetor's adjudication, that is, his sentence, by which he gave effect to the right that he declared. 'Condonatio' means the remitting of the adjudication, or not making it, when he ought to make it; for, when a right is established, it is the duty of him who declares the law to make such order as shall give it effect. 'Bona' is the most comprehensive Roman term to express property, to express every thing to which a man has any right (Dig. 50. 16. 49); a term which in this sense has passed into languages derived from the Roman, and in a limited legal sense into our own. See Blens, Comyns, Digest. The Germans have a better term, 'Vermögen.'

vastavit,] Only G1 is quoted as autho-

ac perdidit, ut ea restitui in antiquum statum nullo modo possit, vix autem per multos annos innocentesque praetores aliqua ex parte recreari aliquando posse videatur. Hoc praetore Siculi neque suas leges, neque nostra senatusconsulta, neque communia jura tenuerunt. Tantum quisque habet in Sicilia quantum hominis avarissimi et libidinosissimi aut imprudentiam subterfugit aut satietati superfuit.

V. Nulla res per triennium nisi ad nutum istius judicata est; nulla res tam patria cujusquam atque avita fuit quae non ab eo imperio istius abjudicaretur. Innumerabiles pecuniae ex aratorum bonis novo nefarioque instituto coactae; socii fidelissimi in hostium numero existimati; cives Romani servilem in modum cruciati et necati; homines nocentissimi propter pecunias judicio liberati; honestissimi atque integerrimi absentes rei facti, indicta causa damnati et ejecti; portus munitissimi, maximae tutissimaeque urbes piratis praedonibusque patefactae; nautae militesque Siculorum, socii nostri atque amici, fame necati; classes optimae atque opportunissimae cum magna ignominia populi Romani amissae et perditae. Idem iste praetor monumenta antiquissima partim regum locupletissimorum, quae illi ornamento urbibus esse voluerunt, partim etiam nostrorum imperatorum, quae victores civitatibus Siculis aut dederunt aut reddiderunt, spoliavit nudavitque omnia. Neque hoc solum in statuis ornamentisque publicis fecit, sed etiam delubra omnia sanctissimis religionibus consecrata depopulatus est;

rity for 'vastavit.' Comp. Divin. c. 3, "populatae, vexatae, funditus eversae provinciae," which passage Asconius quotes in his note on 'vexavit.'

communia jura] Literally, 'common rights.' He says that under Verres the Sicilians did not maintain their own laws, nor the privileges given to them by the Roman senate, nor such rights as are respected every where, every where at least where the Romans ruled. I suppose that this is his meaning; or he may mean such rights as all peoples have.

5. *abjudicaretur.*] 'Abjudicare' is opposed to 'adjudicare,' which occurs in the Divin. c. 17. As to the use of 'tam' with 'patria' and 'avita,' comp. Act. ii. Lib. 1. c. 37. The sense of the passage is this: 'there was nothing to which a man had all the title that he could have from father or remoter ancestor, of which he was not deprived, under the form of legal proceeding during this man's administration.' 'Ab eo' refers to 'cujusquam.' Comp. Cic. 2. Agr. c. 16, 'a Populo Romano abjudicabit.' Instead of 'patria' Klotz reads 'patrita;' on which Iordan says, "*patrita* Man. et Klotz (ad Tuscul. Addit. p. 25, ex libris nescio quibus Fabritii)." Ld. has 'paterna.' But 'patria' is right, and there are other examples of its being used in this sense.

aratorum] See Act. ii. Lib. 3.

absentes rei facti,] "Ut Sthenius et Heraclius," Ascon. All these general charges are explained by particular instances in the five books of the Actio Secunda.

regum] Such as Agathocles and Hiero. —'imperatorum:' Scipio and Marcellus. (Ascon.)

depopulatus] 'depeculatus' Orelli, and it may be the right reading. The Romans use 'religionibus' in the plural when they mean religious ceremonials and usages. See Act. ii. Lib. 1. c. 3, 'religiones caerimoniaeque,' and Caesar, B. G. vi. 16.

deum denique nullum Siculis qui ei paulo magis affabre atque antiquo artificio factus videretur reliquit. In stupris vero et flagitiis nefarias ejus libidines commemorare pudore deterreor; simul illorum calamitatem commemorando augere nolo, quibus liberos conjugesque suas integras ab istius petulantia conservare non licitum est. At enim haec ita commissa sunt ab isto ut non cognita sint ab hominibus. Hominem esse arbitror neminem qui nomen istius audierit quin facta quoque ejus nefaria commemorare possit, ut mihi magis timendum sit ne multa crimina praetermittere quam ne qua in istum fingere existimer. Neque enim mihi videtur haec multitudo quae ad audiendum convenit cognoscere ex me causam voluisse, sed ea quae scit mecum recognoscere.

VI. Quae quum ita sint, iste homo amens ac perditus alia mecum ratione pugnat. Non id agit ut alicujus eloquentiam mihi opponat; non gratia, non auctoritate cujusquam, non potentia nititur. Simulat his se rebus confidere; sed video quid agat, neque enim agit occultissime; proponit inania mihi nobilitatis, hoc est hominum arrogantium nomina, qui non tam me impediunt quod nobiles sunt quam adjuvant quod noti sunt. Simulat se eorum praesidio confidere, quum interea aliud quiddam jam diu machinetur. Quam

liberos] This comprehensive term must be here limited to 'daughters,' as Klotz remarks, for Verres is no where charged with unnatural passions.

At enim] 'But, it may be said, all this he has done in such wise as not to be known to people.' Cicero has given, in general terms, a catalogue of the enormities of Verres, enough, if true, to cover him with infamy. To anticipate an objection, that he ought to be more particular in his statements, for all these crimes could not be known to every body, he adds what follows, 'Hominem esse,' &c. The reading 'hominibus' is only in Lg. 29, but Halm says that he thinks it is the true reading, and I think he is right. The other MSS. have 'omnibus;' but there is little force in saying that they were not known to every body. 'Hominibus' and 'omnibus' are often confounded. Lg. 29 has also 'arbitror esse neminem.' But the repetition of the word gives more force to the passage, and the position of 'hominem' is a reason for preferring 'hominibus.'

recognoscere.] 'Cognoscere ex me causam' means 'to be informed of the facts of the case by me.' 'Recognoscere,' as he explains it by 'ea quae scit,' means a fresh consideration of a thing which is known.

6. *Quae quum ita sint,*] One of Cicero's usual formulae, and hardly worth notice, except to show that 'ita' is generally a word of reference, like 'is,' to what has preceded.

proponit inania . . . nobilitatis,] The generality of Roman terms is one of the great difficulties of the language, which sometimes makes it almost impossible to translate. 'While he is really doing one thing,' says Cicero, 'he attempts to deceive me by the show of another thing.' 'To divert my attention, he puts before me the unsubstantials of nobility, that is, the names of arrogant men.' He appears not to mean by 'inania,' that 'nobilitas,' or the condition of being 'nobilis,' was a 'res inanis;' but these names of his noble defenders were unsubstantial things, the real substance of his defence being his command of money to bribe with. A 'nobilis,' in the time of Cicero, was a man whose father or ancestors had enjoyed a Curule office. A plebeian, who was the first member of his family who attained a Curule office, also became 'nobilis,' and was the founder of the 'nobilitas' of his family. See Act. ii. 3. c. 4, note on 'novus homo.'

spem nunc habeat in manibus et quid moliatur breviter jam, judices, vobis exponam. Sed prius ut ab initio res ab eo constituta sit, quaeso, cognoscite. Ut primum e provincia rediit, redemptio est hujus judicii facta grandi pecunia. Ea mansit in conditione atque pacto usque ad eum finem dum judices rejecti sunt. Posteaquam rejectio judicum facta est, quod et in sortitione istius spem fortuna populi Romani et in rejiciendis judicibus mea diligentia istorum impudentiam vicerat, renuntiata est tota conductio. Praeclare se res habebat. Libelli nominum vestrorum consiliique hujus in manibus erant omnium. Nulla nota, nullus color, nullae sordes videbantur his sententiis allini posse; quum iste repente ex alacri atque laeto sic erat humilis atque demissus ut non modo populo

Ut primum . . . rediit,] 'Ut,' with 'primum' and without, and 'ubi' also, are used with the indicative perfect, to indicate 'as soon as.' Act. ii. Lib. 1. c. 6, 'Romam ut ex Sicilia redii.'

redemptio] 'Redimere,' like 'conducere,' is applied to one who undertakes to do something for a sum of money. 'Conductio' and 'locatio' are the correlatives, which express the contract by which a sum of money (merces) is agreed to be paid for the use of a thing, or to be received for the doing of something (Gaius, iii. 142, &c.; Dig. 19. tit. 2). 'Some one,' says Cicero, 'made an agreement with Verres, by which he undertook to see him through his difficulties for a sum of money.' This is called the 'redemptio hujus judicii,' the 'bargain to save him harmless in the trial.' But the bargain was not made complete; 'it remained subject to a condition, and in the form of a pact, or bare agreement, until the Judices were challenged.' A 'conditio' is an uncertain future event, upon which something else is made to depend. Here the 'conditio' was the constitution of the Consilium; for, if such a body of Judices was finally selected for the trial as the 'redemptor' could have no hope of corrupting, the bargain would be useless. 'Pactum' is the most general Roman term for any agreement, but it applied particularly to those agreements for which the Romans had no special name, and which were not classed under any head of contracts. The agreement, being for an illegal purpose, could not be a contract: it could not be a case of 'locatio et conductio,' though Cicero treats it as if it could, without troubling himself about the strict propriety of his language. Klotz, who writes 'condicio,' takes it to contain the root of 'condicere,' the 'i' being shortened, as in 'maledĭcus.' There is a great dispute about the writing of this word, but analogy is in favour of 'conditio,' and it contains the word 'da,' as 'traditio' does. All the MSS. have 'ea mansit in ditione,' or 'dictione,' which is a manifest blunder; and 'conditione' is the true reading, which Asconius and S have preserved. After the Consilium was determined by the Sortitio or choosing by lot of a certain number, followed by the challenges, 'it was apparent' says Cicero, 'that nothing could be done with the Judices; and the Conductio, or undertaking, was given up (renuntiata) by the man or men who had undertaken it.' Iordan has 'renuntiata est tota condicio,' and he says, "condicio Asconii edd. vett. et MS. Leid. Agroetius p. 2274. P: dicio G1; conclusio G2 Ld; *conductio*, vulgo O." The MSS. authority then can hardly decide the question, though we learn from Halm that all the Lgg. have 'conductio.' The 'conditio' had failed, and there is no sense in saying 'renuntiata est tota conditio.' It was the bargain about which the notice was given.

fortuna populi Romani] After 'Romani' Klotz adds 'perfregerat.'

Libelli nominum &c.] Lists of the names of all the Judices, of whom the Consilium, as finally constituted, consisted, were circulated in some way; at least, as Cicero says, every body had them. Asconius has a note here, which is one of the better kind. The words 'nulla nota,' &c., are explained by reference to Divin. c. 7, 'cera legitima:' and 'his sententiis' means the 'tabellae' on which these Judices were to give their vote.

sic erat humilis &c.] 'Sic' often appears in the place which 'ita' may occupy, followed by 'ut.' The difference appears

Romano sed etiam sibi ipse condemnatus videretur. Ecce autem repente his diebus paucis comitiis consularibus factis eadem illa vetera consilia pecunia majore repetuntur, eademque vestrae famae fortunisque omnium insidiae per eosdem homines comparantur. Quae res primo, judices, pertenui nobis argumento indicioque patefacta est; post aperto suspicionis introitu ad omnia intima istorum consilia sine ullo errore pervenimus.

VII. Nam ut Hortensius consul designatus domum reducebatur e campo cum maxima frequentia ac multitudine, fit obviam casu ei multitudini C. Curio, quem ego hominem honoris potius quam contumeliae causa nominatum volo. Etenim ea dicam quae ille si commemorari noluisset, non tanto in conventu tam aperte palamque dixisset; quae tamen a me pedetemptim cauteque dicentur ut et amicitiae nostrae et dignitatis illius habita ratio esse intelligatur. Videt ad ipsum fornicem Fabianum in turba Verrem. Appellat hominem et ei voce maxima [victoriam] gratulatur. Ipsi Hortensio qui consul erat factus, propinquis necessariisque ejus qui tum aderant, verbum nullum facit; cum hoc consistit, hunc amplexatur, hunc jubet sine cura esse. Renuntio, inquit, tibi te hodiernis comitiis esse absolutum. Quod quum tam multi homines honestissimi audissent, statim ad me defertur; immo vero, ut quisque me viderat, narrabat. Aliis illud indignum, aliis ridiculum videbatur; ridiculum iis qui istius causam in testium fide, in criminum ratione, in judicum potestate, non in comitiis consularibus positam arbitrabantur; indignum iis qui altius perspiciebant et hanc gratulationem ad judicium corrumpendum spectare videbant. Etenim sic

to be that 'sic' is an emphatic, or, so to speak, a demonstrative adverb, whereas 'ita,' conformably to its meaning, is either less emphatic, or indicates the mode or manner of which 'ut,' and what follows, is the exposition; as we observe where 'id' is used, followed by 'ut,' as in c. 6, 'non id agit ut . . . opponat.' However, though the distinction between 'sic' and 'ita' is clear enough, perhaps it is not always strictly observed. A passage in Cicero (Ad Q. Fr. i. 1. 1), "qui . . . ita negotiantur ut locupletes sint," will explain what is here said as to 'ita.' 'Sic' in this passage would hardly do. In c. 8 of this speech we have 'ita loquebatur;' and yet we have 'sic' in a like sense in the next chapter, 'sic ratiocinabantur,' c. 7.

his paucis diebus] 'within the last few days.' See c. 8, and Introd. p. 5.

7. *C. Curio,*] C. Scribonius Curio, consul B.C. 76, and an orator. Cicero mentions him in the Brutus, c. 59. (Meyer, Fragment. Orat. Rom. p. 347, 2nd ed.) He was the father of the Curio who perished in Africa B.C. 49.

honoris . . . causa] 'out of respect,' 'respectfully,' a common formula. See Act. ii. Lib. 5. c. 7; Phil. ii. c. 44; Caesar, B. G. ii. 15. HONORIS VIRTVTISQVE CAVSSA occurs in inscriptions.

ad . . . fornicem Fabianum] Near the arch of Fabius, which stood in the Via Sacra (comp. Pro Plancio, c. 7; De Or. ii. 66), and was erected by Q. Fabius Maximus, the censor, who conquered the Allobroges. Fabius was consul B.C. 121, and censor, B.C. 108.

victoriam] Zumpt and Iordan omit 'victoriam.'

immo vero,] See Act. ii. Lib. 1. c. 1, note.

videbant.] G3 r; 'arbitrabantur' dit. Madvig argues that Cicero would not apply

ratiocinabantur, sic honestissimi homines inter se et mecum loquebantur: Aperte jam ac perspicue nulla esse judicia: qui reus pridie jam ipse se condemnatum putabat, is, posteaquam defensor ejus consul est factus, absolvitur. Quid igitur quod tota Sicilia, quod omnes Siculi, omnes negotiatores, omnes publicae privataeque literae Romae sunt, nihilne id valebit? Nihil invito consule designato. Quid judices non crimina, non testes, non existimationem populi Romani sequentur? Non: omnia in unius potestate ac moderatione vertentur.

VIII. Vere loquar, judices: vehementer me haec res commovebat. Optimus enim quisque ita loquebatur: Iste quidem tibi eripietur; sed nos non tenebimus judicia diutius. Etenim quis poterit Verre absoluto de transferendis judiciis recusare? Erat omnibus molestum: neque eos tam istius hominis perditi subita laetitia quam hominis amplissimi nova gratulatio commovebat. Cupiebam dissimulare me id moleste ferre; cupiebam animi dolorem vultu tegere et taciturnitate celare. Ecce autem illis ipsis diebus, quum praetores designati sortirentur, et M. Metello obtigisset ut is de pecuniis repetundis quaereret, nuntiatur mihi tantam isti gratulationem esse factam ut is domum quoque pueros mitteret qui uxori suae nuntiarent. Sane ne haec quidem mihi res placebat; neque

the same word 'arbitrabantur' to those who did not see clearly the real state of the case, and to those 'qui altius perspiciebant,' to whom the word 'videbant' was most aptly applied. There is great weight in this; but if Cicero wrote 'videbant,' we must suppose that some copyist substituted 'arbitrabantur' for 'videbant,' which would be a curious mistake. If Cicero did use 'arbitrabantur' twice, it is very easy to suppose that somebody put 'videbant' in place of the second 'arbitrabantur.'

negotiatores,] These men were Romans, who carried on a money-lending and a banking business in the provinces, and had also mercantile transactions there. They are different from 'mercatores,' who travelled or sailed with their wares. Cicero (Ad Q. Frat. i. 1, 1) enumerates, among the classes of men who composed the population of the province of Asia, 'socii' or native inhabitants, 'publicani' or farmers of the revenue, and those who 'ita negotiantur ut locupletes sint.' See the Asiatic inscription quoted in the note Pro Fonteio, c. 5, vol. ii. 'Negotia habere' (Cic. Ad Fam. xiii. 30) applies to a 'negotiator' (and Horace, 1 Sat. 7, 4.)

8. *transferendis judiciis*] "transferring the 'judicia,' the office of 'judices,' from the senators." See Introd.

illis ipsis diebus,] Asconius reads 'his diebus paucis.' He observes that the consular 'comitia' took place on the 27th of July, and the trial began on the nones or 5th of August. He adds that the 'sortitio' of the 'praetors' took place shortly after the 'comitia consularia,' the 'comitia praetoria' having, of course, preceded the 'sortitio.' The use of the ablative 'his diebus' expresses a measure of time by which two events are separated, 'within these few days;' and, if the reading 'illis ipsis diebus' is right, it means "within those very few days, between the 'comitia' and the 'sortitio.'" The 'praetors,' who were at this period eight in number, determined by lot (sortirentur) what functions they should severally exercise; and the lot had given to M. Metellus, one of the praetors elect (designati) for the next year, the office of holding the 'quaestiones de rebus repetundis;' and, if the trial of Verres could have been put off to the next year, M. Metellus would have presided instead of M' Acilius Glabrio. (Introd.)

[tamen] tanto opere quid in hac sorte metuendum mihi esset intelligebam. Unum illud ex hominibus certis, ex quibus omnia comperi, reperiebam: fiscos complures cum pecunia Siciliensi a quodam senatore ad equitem Romanum esse translatos; ex his quasi x fiscos ad senatorem illum relictos esse comitiorum meorum nomine; divisores omnium tribuum noctu ad istum vocatos. Ex quibus quidam, qui se omnia mea causa debere arbitrabatur, eadem illa nocte ad me venit; demonstrat qua iste oratione usus esset; commemorasse istum quam liberaliter eos tractasset etiam antea quum ipse praeturam petisset et proximis consularibus praetoriisque comitiis; deinde continuo esse pollicitum quantam vellent pecuniam, si me aedilitate dejecissent. Hic alios negasse audere, alios respondisse non putare id perfici posse; inventum tamen esse fortem amicum ex eadem familia, Q. Verrem Romilia, ex optima

fiscos complures cum pecunia] 'several baskets with Sicilian money;' filled with some of the Sicilian plunder of Verres. 'Fiscus' signified a basket or receptacle of wicker-work, which the Romans used for the holding and conveying of large sums of money, particularly for the purposes of the 'aerarium' or treasury. Mai, quoted by Klotz, says that in the Vatican Museum such a Fiscus full of money is represented cut on a stone, with a vessel near it to take out the pieces of money with, and the inscription VIATOR AD AERARIVM. (See the passages Act. ii. Lib. 3. c. 85; and c. 79, 'qui fiscum sustulit.') In the Republican period the State, considered as possessing property, was indicated by the term 'aerarium,' for all the functions of the State with respect to property were resolvable into receiving money into the 'aerarium' and paying it out. Under the Empire, that which the emperor was entitled to, as emperor, from the provinces under his administration, got the name of Fiscus; and that to which the Senate was entitled in respect of those provinces which they administered retained the name of 'aerarium.' The name 'fiscus' appears to have been applied to the emperor's treasury, because his 'fisci' were more spoken of than those of the Senate; and finally, when all power was concentrated in the emperor, the term 'fiscus' was used to denote the whole property of the State; and it then signified what 'aerarium' did in the republican period. (Savigny, System des Heut. Röm. Rechts, ii. p. 272; and Dict. of Antiqus. Fiscus.)

a quodam senatore &c.] Asconius observes that some foolishly ask about the names of the persons to whom Cicero alludes, as if all this were true.

ex his . . relictos] Zumpt has a note to explain this. Several 'fisci' were sent by a senator to an 'eques.' Out of these 'several' about ten were left with the senator; not a very exact way of speaking. All of them seem to have been deposited with the senator, who kept about ten of them and sent the rest away, I suppose, for some purpose.

ad . . illum . . relictos] So 'ad' is used. See In Cat. i. c. 8, vol. iii.

comitiorum &c.] 'For the purpose of preventing my being elected curule aedile' by bribery. The comitia aedilicia, says Asconius, followed the consularia and praetoria, which is plain from this story.

divisores] Asconius asks if all the tribes had their own 'legitimi divisores,' such as the 'magistri curiarum' referred to by Plautus (Aul. i. 1, 30), or criminal 'divisores,' and he adds that, if Cicero meant criminal 'divisores,' he would not have said that one of them was dear to him. This is a sample of the trifling which is mixed up with better matter. The 'divisores' were the men who managed the distribution of bribery money, of whom we read in the oration Pro Cn. Plancio, c. 18, 19.

omnia . . debere] We must supply 'facere,' says Asconius. See Divin. c. 6; and most of the MSS. have 'facere debere.'

Q. Verrem Romilia,] or 'Romulea,' as Zumpt has it and Gl. The note of Asconius on this passage is good: "Q. Verrem is a proper name, Romilia is the name of a tribe, in the ablative case,—ut sit ex Ro-

divisorum disciplina, patris istius discipulum atque amicum, qui HS quingentis millibus depositis id se perfecturum polliceretur; et fuisse tamen nonnullos qui se una facturos esse dicerent. Quae quum ita essent, sane benevolo animo me ut magno opere caverem praemonebat.

IX. Sollicitabar rebus maximis uno atque eo perexiguo tempore. Urgebant comitia, et in his ipsis oppugnabar grandi pecunia. Instabat judicium; ei quoque negotio fisci Siciliensce minabantur. Agere quae ad judicium pertinebant libere comitiorum motu deterrebar: petitioni toto animo servire propter judicium non licebat. Minari denique divisoribus ratio non erat, propterea quod eos intelligere videbam me hoc judicio districtum atque obligatum futurum. Atque hoc ipso tempore Siculis denuntiatum esse audio primum ab Hortensio, domum ad illum ut venirent: Siculos in eo sane liberos fuisse, qui quamobrem arcesserentur quum intelligerent, non venisse. Interea comitia nostra, quorum iste se ut ceterorum hoc anno comitiorum dominum esse arbitrabatur, haberi coepta sunt. Cursare iste homo potens cum filio blando et gratioso circum tribus; paternos amicos, hoc est divisores, appellare omnes et convenire. Quod quum esset intellectum et animadversum,

milia," &c. This mode of referring a man to his tribe was usual, when the object was to designate him very particularly. When Cicero (Phil. ix. 7) moved that a monument should be erected to the memory of Servius Sulpicius, he commenced in the following terms: "Quum Ser. Sulpicius Q. F. Lemonia Rufus." Sulpicius was of the Tribus Lemonia.

fuisse tamen] 'tamen' is the MSS. reading, but G1 has 'tm̄,' and G2 has 'tn̄.' Iordan has 'tum,' a conjecture of Benecke.

9. *propter judicium*] Omitted by G3 s λ and by Iordan.

districtum &c.] 'Destrictum,' G1 2 Lg 29 A. "At vulgatam tuetur consuetudo Tulliana." (Iordan.) "Districtus potest et sine vinculis in diversum manu ducentium ferri." (Ascon.) He is said to be 'districtus' (distracted), who is so held by several things as to be unable to turn one way or the other. 'Obligatum' must be taken in its literal sense of 'bound,' or the nearly related sense of 'altogether engaged and occupied.' Shortly after he says, 'animo . . vacuo et soluto.' Now as 'solvere' is the correlative of 'obligare,' 'vacuus' appears to be the correlative of 'districtus.' An 'obligatio,' in the legal sense, is terminated by 'solutio,' 'performance or payment.'

Siculos . . sane . . non venisse] This passage caused a difficulty to Asconius, who proposes to read 'venissent;' and, if we observe that the next word begins with 'int,' it is possible that the 'nt' of 'venissent' might accidentally have been omitted. But the text is right, and we can hardly omit the 'qui,' as some critics propose. Cicero says; 'I hear, or I admit, that the Sicilians were left to do as they liked in that matter, and that when they knew why they were sent for, they did not go.' 'Qui' is the nominative to 'intelligerent.'

'Arcessere' is compounded of the preposition 'ar' (ad), which occurs in the Bacchanalian inscription, in the verb 'arfuisse' (adfuisse), and 'cessere,' which is formed from 'ci-ere,' as 'facessere' from 'fac-ere,' and 'lacessere' from 'lac-ere.'

convenire.] 'Quasi de promissorum debito,' says Asconius; and correctly. For 'convenire,' in one of its senses, is 'in jus vocare,' 'agere cum aliquo,' or to sue, as the passages cited from the Digest by Forcellini show. But, when Asconius says that 'appellare' means 'quasi familiares,' this is hardly consistent. If 'convenire' is to have this technical meaning, 'appellare' may also mean to call on a debtor to pay what he owes. Cic. Ad Att. i. 8, "Tulliola tuum munusculum flagitat et me ut

fecit animo libentissimo populus Romanus ut, cujus divitiae me de fide deducere non potuissent, ne ejusdem pecunia de honore dejicerer. Posteaquam illa petitionis magna cura liberatus sum, animo coepi multo magis vacuo ac soluto nihil aliud nisi de judicio agere et cogitare. Reperio, judices, haec ab istis consilia inita et constituta, ut quacunque opus esset ratione res ita duceretur ut apud M. Metellum praetorem causa diceretur. In eo esse haec commoda; primum M. Metellum amicissimum; deinde Hortensium consulem non solum, sed etiam Q. Metellum, qui quam isti sit amicus attendite; dedit enim praerogativam suae voluntatis ejusmodi ut isti pro praerogativis jam reddidisse videatur. An me taciturum tantis de rebus existimavistis, et me in tanto rei publicae existimationisque meae periculo cuiquam consulturum potius quam officio et dignitati meae? Arcessit alter consul designatus Siculos: veniunt nonnulli propterea quod L. Metellus esset praetor in Sicilia. Cum iis ita loquitur: se consulem esse; fratrem suum alterum Siciliam provinciam obtinere, alterum esse quaesiturum de pecuniis repetundis: Verri ne noceri possit multis rationibus esse provisum.

X. Quid est, quaeso, Metelle, judicium corrumpere, si hoc non est? testes, praesertim Siculos, timidos homines et afflictos, non solum auctoritate deterrere sed etiam consulari metu et duorum

sponsorem appellat."—'dejiceret,' G1, Iordan.

non solum,] "amicissimum, sed etiam Q. Metellum consulem amicissimum." This is Iordan's explanation, and the true explanation, I think, which makes all attempts at correction unnecessary. Halm says that Iordan's explanation proves that the passage is corrupt.

praerogativam &c.] The figure is 'dilogia,' according to the pedantic expression of Asconius, 'quum ambiguum dictum duas res significat.' 'For Metellus gave such an intimation of his disposition (towards Verres) that he may be considered to have made it a return for the first votes which Verres secured for him.' Orelli reads 'eam' for 'jam' (iam), and it may be the true reading. The tribe, which by lot obtained the right of voting first at the Comitia, was called 'praerogativa,' because 'prima rogaretur,' it was first called on to vote; (comp. Pro Cn. Plancio, c. 20, and Livy, x. 22;) and the Centuriae, which were contained in the 'tribus praerogativa,' and voted first, were also called 'praerogativae' (Pro Cn. Plancio, c. 33). As the vote of the first 'centuriae' in a manner determined the election, or gave some indication of the turn which the voting would take, it was a matter of importance to secure these votes, in order that the 'centuriae,' which voted after them (to which the term 'jure vocatae' was applied), might be thus influenced. Hence 'praerogativa' came to be used in the sense of a sign or probable indication of the future, as in a letter of Cato to Cicero (Ad Fam. xv. 5), and in Pro Cn. Plancio, c. 20.

provinciam obtinere,] 'to hold the government of a province:' 'to obtain' is not the meaning. 'Quaesiturum de pecuniis repetundis,' that is, 'would preside in the Quaestio de pecuniis repetundis.' See Excursus i. 'Quaesitor' occurs in the next chapter, and is correctly explained by Asconius, "praetor de pecuniis repetundis quaestionem exercens;" and he quotes Virgil, Aen. vi. 432, 'Quaesitor Minos urnam movet.'

praetorum potestate? Quid faceres pro innocente homine et propinquo, quum propter hominem perditissimum atque alienissimum de officio ac dignitate decedis, et committis ut quod ille dictitat alicui qui te ignorat verum esse videatur? Nam hoc Verrem dicere aiebant, te non fato ut ceteros ex vestra familia sed opera sua consulem factum. Duo igitur consules et quaesitor erunt ex illius voluntate. Non solum effugiemus, inquit, hominem in quaerendo nimium diligentem, nimium servientem populi existimationi, M' Glabrionem: accedit nobis etiam illud; judex est M. Caesonius, collega nostri accusatoris, homo in rebus judicandis spectatus et cognitus; quem minime expediat esse in eo consilio quod conemur aliqua ratione corrumpere, propterea quod jam antea, quum judex in Juniano consilio fuisset, turpissimum illud facinus non solum graviter tulit, sed etiam in medium protulit. Hunc judicem ex Kal. Januar. non habebimus. Q. Manlium et Q. Cornificium, duos severissimos atque integerrimos judices, quod tribuni plebis tum erunt, judices non habebimus. P. Sulpicius, judex tristis et integer magistratum ineat necesse est Nonis Decembr. M. Cro-

10. *qui te ignorat*] This is the reading of Orelli. Zumpt, Klotz, and Jordan have 'ignoret.' It is one of those cases in which, as far as we can judge, usage was somewhat unsettled. I think that 'alicui qui te ignorat' is intended to be a positive affirmation.

te non fato] According to Asconius, the old poet Naevius said of the Metelli,

"Fato Metelli Romae fiunt consules;"

to which Metellus, the then consul, replied,

"Dabunt malum Metelli Naevio poetae."

It is said that Q. Metellus, consul B.C. 206, a contemporary of Cn. Naevius, was one of those who were the cause of Naevius being banished from Italy. It is, however, argued, that this verse, 'Fato,' &c., could hardly be by Naevius, the author of the poem on the Punic War, as it was in his lifetime that two of the Metelli were the first of their family who attained the highest honours of the state. It is concluded, then, that the verse, 'Fato Metelli,' &c., was a saying current among the people, and that Cicero alludes to it.

M. Caesonius,] Caesonius was now one of the 'judices;' but, as he was elected 'aedilis' with Cicero for the following year, he could not, during his office, act as 'judex,' if the trial should be deferred to the next year, which was the great object of Verres, as Cicero says. It appears from what follows, that the 'aediles,' as well as the 'consuls' and 'praetors,' at this time entered on their office on the 1st of January. C. Junius was the 'quaesitor' under a 'Lex Cornelia,' on the occasion of A. Cluentius prosecuting his step-father Oppianicus, who was convicted of an attempt to poison, as it was believed, through some of the 'judices' being bribed by Cluentius. Caesonius, however, one of the 'judices' in that trial, was innocent, and, according to Cicero, helped to expose the villainy (Rein, Das Criminalrecht der Römer, p. 429, 654).

Q. Manlium et Q. Cornificium,] It is not said here when the 'tribuni plebis' entered on their office, nor can we assume that it was the Nones of December, for Asconius, who observes that P. Sulpicius would enter on his office of 'tribunus plebis' on that day, has drawn a false conclusion, or barely asserted what is not true. If P. Sulpicius had been a tribune, he would have been mentioned with L. Manlius and Q. Cornificius. Klotz is inclined to the opinion of the scholiast of Gronovius, that P. Sulpicius may have been a 'quaestor.' It appears that the tribunes entered on their office before the consuls (De Leg. Agr. ii. 5). Cicero was on terms of intimacy with the son of this Cornificius, to whom he addressed several letters (Ad Fam. xii. 17, 18, 19).

pereius ex acerrima illa equestri familia et disciplina, L. Cassius ex familia quum ad ceteras res tum ad judicandum severissima, Cn. Tremellius homo summa religione et diligentia, tres hi homines veteres tribuni militares sunt designati; ex Kal. Januar. non judicabunt. Subsortiemur etiam in M. Metelli locum, quoniam is huic ipsi quaestioni praefuturus est. Ita secundum Kalendas Januar. et praetore et prope toto consilio commutato, magnas accusatoris minas magnamque judicii exspectationem ad nostrum arbitrium libidinemque eludemus. Nonae sunt hodie Sextiles. Hora octava convenire coepistis. Hunc diem jam ne numerant quidem. Decem dies sunt ante ludos votivos quos Cn. Pompeius facturus est. Hi ludi dies quindecim auferent; deinde continuo Romani consequentur. Ita prope XL diebus interpositis, tum denique se ad ea quae a nobis dicta erunt responsuros esse arbitrantur: deinde se ducturos et dicendo et excusando facile ad ludos Victoriae. Cum his plebeios esse conjunctos; secundum quos aut nulli aut perpauci dies ad agendum futuri sunt. Ita defessa ac refrigerata accusatione

L. Cassius &c.] "Inde sunt leges Cassiae tabellariae de suffragiis libere ferendis non voce, sed tabula. Inde ille Cassius qui in cognoscendis criminalibus causis in primis quaerendum esse dicebat, Cui bono." (Ascon.) See Pro S. Rosc. Amerino, c. 30, and the note.

tribuni militares] Those chief officers of a legion, 'tribuni militum,' or 'militares,' who were elected by the people, were called, says Asconius, 'Comitiati;' and those who were appointed in the army by the commander were called 'Rufuli.' The exact meaning of the word 'veteres' is not clear. Zumpt supposes that it means "exercitati, rerum judiciorumque gnari." Asconius says 'graves et severi,' and perhaps he is right. 'Veteres' may have the sense of 'antiqui,' men of the old time, of the old stamp (see Pro Sestio, c. 3, note).

Subsortiemur] 'Subsortiri' is the word used to express the choosing of 'judices' to take the place of those who were challenged (rejecti), or became incapable of acting as 'judices,' in consequence of holding a 'magistratus.' See Act. ii. Lib. 1. c. 19, 61; Pro Cluentio, c. 34.

secundum] Here the meaning of the word 'secundus' (sequundus) is clearly shown, and in a passage which shortly after follows, 'secundum quos,' 'after which;' from which notion of 'following' are derived the various senses of 'secundum.'

prope toto &c.] See Introd.

Cn. Pompeius] The games which Cn. Pompeius had vowed, as Asconius says, if he should conquer Sertorius. Sertorius was now dead. The war in Spain ended in B.C. 72. (Introd.)

deinde continuo] Then, 'without any interruption,' for this is the meaning of 'continuus.' The 'Ludi Romani,' or 'Circenses Magni,' were celebrated in the Circus Maximus, between the 1st and the 19th of September, it is said. From the 16th of August to the 19th of September makes thirty-five days, which Cicero in round numbers calls nearly forty.

excusando - - Victoriae.] These 'Ludi Victoriae' were instituted by L. Cornelius Sulla after his victory over the Samnites (Vell. Paterc. ii. 27); and they began on the 27th of October. By talking, and availing themselves of legal technical grounds for delay, they would push on the matter to the end of October. 'Excusare' and 'excusatio' are the terms for legal grounds of excuse, which, in this instance, mean legal causes of delay in answering. In the Fragmenta Vaticana there is a long chapter, 'De Excusatione,' the matter of which, though not applicable to this case, shows what the meaning of the term is.

plebeios] These games began on the 4th and lasted to the 17th of November; and thus the year would be near an end.

rem integram ad M. Metellum praetorem esse venturam. Quem ego hominem, si ejus fidei diffisus essem, judicem non retinuissem; nunc tamen hoc animo sum ut eo judice quam praetore hanc rem transigi malim, et jurato suam quam injurato aliorum tabellas committere.

XI. Nunc ego, judices, jam vos consulo quid mihi faciendum putetis; id enim consilii mihi profecto taciti dabitis quod egomet mihi necessario capiendum intelligo. Si utar ad dicendum meo legitimo tempore, mei laboris industriae diligentiaeque capiam fructum, et ex accusatione perficiam ut nemo unquam post hominum memoriam paratior, vigilantior, compositior ad judicium venisse videatur. Sed in hac laude industriae meae reus ne elabatur summum periculum est. Quid est igitur quod fieri possit? non obscurum, opinor, neque absconditum. Fructum istum laudis, qui ex perpetua oratione percipi potuit, in alia tempora reservemus: nunc hominem tabulis, testibus, privatis publicisque literis auctoritatibusque accusemus. Res omnis mihi tecum erit, Hortensi. Dicam

jurato] Metellus, as a 'judex,' was sworn, but he would not be required to take an oath when presiding as 'praetor' in the following year. As a 'judex,' he would only have his own 'tabella' or 'voting tablet' to look after, which Cicero says he would rather trust him with on his oath, than have him as 'praetor' unsworn, and with the influence over the votes which his office would give him. Though the 'praetor' did not take an oath, a 'quaesitor,' or 'judex quaestionis,' who acted for the 'praetor,' took an oath (Pro Cluent. c. 33), as Klotz observes.

11. *legitimo tempore,*] 'all the time which the law (lex) allowed;' that is, the 'lex de repetundis.' 'Legitimus' must not be translated 'legal,' for 'legal' is a more comprehensive term than 'legitimus,' which means, according to some 'lex,' that is, some special enactment. So the Romans said 'quaestio legitima,' Pro Archia, c. 2. The following passage from Gaius will explain this term (i. § 155): "quibus testamento quidem tutor datus non sit, iis ex lege xii agnati sunt tutores, qui vocantur legitimi." They were called 'legitimi,' because they derived their office from the Lex Duodecim Tabularum. See also Gaius, iv. § 103. The term 'pactum' has already been explained. When an agreement was concluded in some form which did not belong to the head either of 'res,' 'verba,' 'literae,' or 'consensus' (Gaius iii. 89), it was simply a 'pactum,' and could not be the foundation of an action, though it might be an answer or plea (exceptio) to an action. But some 'pacta' were, by particular 'leges' or enactments, made the ground of actions, which is expressed thus (Dig. 2. 14. 6): "Legitima conventio est quae lege aliqua confirmatur," &c. Comp. Act. ii. Lib. 1. c. 9, "de meis legitimis horis remittam. Nisi omni tempore quod mihi lege concessum est," &c.

perpetua oratione] A 'perpetua oratio' is a continuous oration, uninterrupted by the reading of evidence or the examination of witnesses. The notion of 'perpetuus' is uninterrupted, and has no reference to 'perpetual' in the English sense. 'Perpetuus' is equivalent to 'continuus,' and so it appears in the funeral inscriptions, when it is used to denote the number of 'ollae' in a continuous row which were appropriated to a person in a monumentum (Fabretti, Inscript. Antiq. p. 11):

L . AVCCITA . HERA . OLLAS
SINGVLARES . PERPETVAS
V . SIBI . ET . SVIS

where Fabretti shows that Reinesius misunderstood the sense of 'perpetuas,' which Fabretti proves by other examples to be synonymous with 'continuas,' 'continentes,' and 'ex ordine.' See Excursus iv., Edicta Magistratuum.

auctoritatibusque] Cicero intends to establish his case by 'tabulae,' documentary evidence; 'testibus,' by witnesses; and by the letters and other confirmatory writ-

aperte. Si te mecum dicendo ac diluendis criminibus in hac causa contendere putarem, ego quoque in accusando atque in explicandis criminibus operam consumerem; nunc quoniam pugnare contra me instituisti, non tam ex tua natura quam ex istius tempore et causa, malitiose, necesse est istiusmodi rationi aliquo consilio obsistere. Tua ratio est ut secundum binos ludos mihi respondere incipias; mea ut ante primos ludos comperendinem. Ita fiet ut tua ista ratio existimetur astuta, meum hoc consilium necessarium.

XII. Verum illud quod institueram dicere, mihi rem tecum esse, hujusmodi est. Ego quum hanc causam Siculorum rogatu recepissem, idque mihi amplum et praeclarum existimassem, eos velle meae fidei diligentiaeque periculum facere qui innocentiae abstinentiaeque fecissent; tum suscepto negotio majus mihi quiddam proposui, in quo meam in rem publicam voluntatem populus Romanus perspicere posset. Nam illud mihi nequaquam dignum industria conatuque meo videbatur, istum a me in judicium jam omnium judicio condemnatum vocari, nisi ista tua intolerabilis potentia et ea cupiditas, qua per hosce annos in quibusdam judiciis usus es,

ten evidence of private persons and public bodies. The word 'auctoritas' must be explained by reference to its general sense of that which gives credibility to a thing, or confirms a thing or gives it the completeness which is required for any purposes. Thus, the 'auctoritas' of a tutor, that is, his sanction, his approbation, gives to the act of the 'pupillus,' which without it would be insufficient, its full legal effect. Cicero accordingly seems to mean by 'auctoritatibusque' every kind of confirmatory testimony which does not exactly come within the meaning of the terms which he has already used. See c. 3.

instituisti,] See Divin. c. 21, note.—'ex istius tempore:' see Divin. c. 2, note.

malitiose,] Klotz has a useful note on the technical sense of 'malitia' (Pro Caecina, c. 1). Its literal signification of 'badness' does not express its meaning here. It is that badness in the purpose which consists in a man availing himself of a legal right, or of legal forms, in a manner which morality condemns; for nothing is clearer than that a man may make an immoral use of a legal right. Klotz refers to the following passages, which will assist the reader in ascertaining the notion of 'malitia:' Tuscul. Disput. iv. 15, "nam malitia certe cujusdam," &c.; and De Off. iii. 17, "eaque malitia quae vult illa quidem videri se esse prudentiam, sed abest ab ea distatque plurimum." The character of the word is shown by the company which it keeps; its companions are 'calliditas, fraus, et calumnia.' Cicero (De Nat. Deorum, iii. 30) calls the 'judicium de dolo malo,' which C. Aquilius introduced, the broom or besom (everriculum) for sweeping away all 'malitiae.' Ulpian, Ad Edictum (Dig. 4. 3. 1), uses 'malitia' in this technical sense: "hoc edicto Praetor adversus varios et dolosos qui aliis obfuerunt calliditate quadam subvenit, ne vel illis malitia sua sit lucrosa vel istis simplicitas damnosa."

binos ludos] See Introd.

comperendinem.] 'Comperendinare' is to put off a thing to the third day (perendie); and, according to Festus, "res comperendinata significat judicium in tertium diem constitutum." Cicero says that his adversary's design was to defer his answer until after the two first 'ludi' were over; while his own plan was to have his own speech, and his adversary's too, over before the commencement of the first 'ludi,' and so to come to the 'comperendinatio.' What this means is explained in a note to Act. ii. Lib. 1. c. 9.

12. *hujusmodi*] 'of this kind' or 'fashion.' The Romans use this word as if it were an adjective undeclined. So they used 'hujuscemodi,' 'ejusmodi,' 'istiusmodi.'

cupiditas,] 'corruptionem judicum significat.' (Ascon.)

etiam in istius hominis desperati causa interponeretur. Nunc vero quoniam haec te omnis dominatio regnumque judiciorum tanto opere delectat, et sunt homines quos libidinis infamiaeque suae neque pudeat neque taedeat, qui quasi de industria in odium offensionemque populi Romani irruere videantur, hoc me profiteor suscepisse magnum fortasse onus et mihi periculosum, verumtamen dignum in quo omnes nervos aetatis industriaeque meae contenderem. Quoniam totus ordo paucorum improbitate et audacia premitur et urgetur infamia judiciorum, profiteor huic generi hominum me inimicum, accusatorem odiosum, assiduum, acerbum adversarium. Hoc mihi sumo, hoc mihi deposco quod agam in magistratu, quod agam ex eo loco ex quo me populus Romanus ex Kal. Januar. secum agere de re publica ac de hominibus improbis voluit; hoc munus aedilitatis meae populo Romano amplissimum pulcherrimumque polliceor. Moneo, praedico, ante denuntio, qui

ex eo loco . . secum agere] 'De Rostris scilicet,' says Asconius. Cicero threatens to bring any persons who should be guilty of bribery on this occasion before the 'Populus,' that is, before a 'Judicium Populi,' after entering on his office of Curule Aedile. It is a matter of doubt with some of the commentators whether he could do it. 'Agere cum populo' means to propose a measure to the 'Populus' (Gellius, xiii. 15). Niebuhr (Roman Hist. vol. iii. Engl. transl.) has some remarks on the powers of the curule aediles as public prosecutors. Zumpt refers to Liv. xxv. c. 2; xxxiii. c. 42; xxxv. c. 10.

munus aedilitatis] Asconius sees here some allusion to the name of Verres, which signifies a boar pig, but it is difficult for other people to see it. Schuetz has a note on this passage of Asconius. Part of the 'munus' of the curule aedileship consisted in the exhibition of shows to the people; but Cicero says that the best thing that he can show the people will be the prosecution of the 'improbi.' 'Munus' is a word which implies a duty or obligation to discharge certain functions, in consequence of holding a certain office, or sustaining a certain character (persona). The sense in which 'munus' is used in the Digest (50. tit. 4, 'de Muneribus et Honoribus') helps to explain the general meaning of the term. It is often used in the plural number to express the plays, fights of gladiators, and other spectacles with which the Roman people were amused. Cicero (Phil. ii. 45) says, "muneribus, monumentis, congiariis, epulis multitudinem imperitam delenierat."

Moneo &c.] Klotz considers these words to be formal words of threatening a judicial prosecution, and also of declaring war; and he refers to Terence, Andria, Prolog. 22, "Dehinc ut quiescant porro moneo et desinant Maledicere." But 'monere' and 'praedicere' are words of common use; and so is 'denuntiare,' as in Cicero (Ad Fam. xi. 25). The words 'deponere,' and the rest, have a technical sense, which appears to be rightly indicated by Asconius, and expounded by Klotz. Cicero comprehends in these words all the means and all the persons employed in corruption. 'Deponere' is to deposit a sum of money in the hands of a person, which money is to be paid to the bribed, if they do their work. 'Recipere,' a word which implies engagement or undertaking, may refer to him who undertakes to pay the 'judices' a certain sum for their votes; and he would be not the accused himself, but the agent of the accused. Zumpt says, "mihi quidem recipere videtur sequester ab eo qui deponit pecuniam;" which I do not assent to. 'Accipere' clearly applies to him who is bribed, to the 'judex.' But Lg 29 has 'aut accipere aut recipere,' on which Halm says, "hanc optimam lectionem, quam Iord. immerito sprevit, etiam Pseudo-Asconium in suo exemplo habuisse ex ejus interpretatione facile apparet." It is true that Asconius explains 'accipere' before 'recipere,' but whatever may be the order of the words, I do not think that it will alter the meaning of the passage.

aut deponere aut recipere aut accipere aut polliceri aut sequestres aut interpretes corrumpendi judicii solent esse, quique ad hanc rem aut potentiam aut impudentiam suam professi sunt, abstineant in hoc judicio manus animosque ab hoc scelere nefario.

XIII. Erit tum consul Hortensius cum summo imperio et potestate, ego autem aedilis, hoc est, paulo amplius quam privatus; tamen hujusmodi haec res est, quam me acturum esse polliceor, ita populo Romano grata atque jucunda ut ipse consul in hac causa prae me minus etiam, si fieri possit, quam privatus esse videatur. Omnia non modo commemorabuntur, sed etiam expositis certis rebus agentur, quae inter decem annos, posteaquam judicia ad senatum translata sunt, in rebus judicandis nefarie flagitioseque facta sunt. Cognoscet ex me populus Romanus quid sit quamobrem, quum equester ordo judicaret annos prope quinquaginta continuos, nullo judice equite Romano judicante ne tenuissima quidem suspicio acceptae pecuniae ob rem judicandam constituta sit; quid sit quod judiciis ad senatorium ordinem translatis sublataque populi Romani in unumquemque vestrum potestate Q.

'Polliceri' is not so clear. It is misexplained by Klotz, who makes it signify the promise of the 'judex' to him who proposes the bribe to him; but this is not the meaning of 'polliceri' (note on Divin. c. 1). Cicero's words are general, and yet particular enough, without descending to a minute examination of them. 'Polliceri' here means, as usual, to make a proffer, and it may mean either a proffer of the 'judices' to sell their votes, or a proffer of the corrupter to buy the votes. 'Sequestres' are the persons in whose hands money is deposited, to be afterwards distributed among the bribed; and 'interpretes' were the managers and brokers of the bargain.

13. *cum summo imperio &c.*] The consuls had both 'imperium' and 'potestas;' and they had the 'summum imperium.' Some 'magistratus,' the tribunes, for instance, had only 'potestas.' We can say 'consularis potestas,' or 'tribunicia potestas' (c. 15), and 'imperium consulare,' but not 'imperium tribunicium.' 'Summo cum imperio' could be applied to a 'propraetor' in his provincial administration, for he had full power, both civil and military (Cic. Ad Q. Fr. i. 1, 2). The 'summum imperium' included the highest judicial authority, in the Roman sense (Dig. 2. tit. 1, de Jurisdictione). See Excursus iv.

sed etiam . . . agentur,] This is one of those Roman expressions which are very difficult to translate, owing to their having a generality, for which we have nothing corresponding. The orator says, 'every thing shall be, I do not say simply told, but, after certain matters are set forth, every thing shall, in every possible way, be brought before you, which,' &c. Comp. Div. c. 12, "causa non solum exponenda sed etiam graviter copioseque agenda est," &c.

decem annos,] Ten years, in round numbers, since Sulla transferred the 'judicia' to the senate. The real time was somewhat above eleven years. The 'prope quinquaginta annos' is also an exaggeration, for the real time was about forty-one years, during which the Equites exercised the Judicia under the Lex Sempronia of C. Gracchus.

nullo judice &c.] This is the reading of all the MSS. Zumpt and Jordan have 'in nullo judice.' 'Locus corruptus,' says Orelli. Klotz points it thus: 'nullo judice, equite Romano judicante.' The simplest change would be to write 'nulla.' Madvig proposes 'in nullo judice ne tenuissima,' &c.

sublataque . . potestate] As Asconius explains it, the appeal to the 'populus,' that is, to the 'tribuni plebis.'

Calidius damnatus dixerit, minoris HS tricies praetorium hominem honeste non posse damnari; quid sit quod, P. Septimio senatore damnato Q. Hortensio praetore de pecuniis repetundis lis aestimata sit eo nomine quod ille ob rem judicandam pecuniam accepisset; quod in C. Herennio, quod in C. Popillio, senatoribus, qui ambo peculatus damnati sunt; quod in M. Atilio, qui de majestate damnatus est, hoc planum factum est, eos pecuniam ob rem judicandam accepisse; quod inventi sunt senatores qui C. Verre praetore urbano sortiente exirent in eum reum quem incognita causa condemnarent; quod inventus est senator, qui quum judex esset, in eodem judicio et ab reo pecuniam acciperet quam judicibus divideret, et ab accusatore ut reum condemnaret? Jam vero quomodo ego illam labem, ignominiam, calamitatemque totius ordinis conquerar, hoc factum esse in hac civitate, quum senatorius ordo judicaret,

Q. Calidius] He had been praetor in Spain, B.C. 78, and was tried on a charge of Repetundae, and condemned. His 'judices,' it appeared, were bribed with a moderate sum to convict him; and the accused said that a man of his rank could not be convicted honourably to the 'judices' for less than 'tricies;' which was as much as to say that, if they sold themselves, they ought to get a good price. Zumpt reads "HS $\overline{xxx}$;" and adds, "mihi nunc $\overline{xxx}$, i. e. quae singuli judices acceperint satis videtur, siquidem in causa Cluentiana, c. 26, quadragena dabantur." 'HSXXX codd. plerique.'

lis aestimata sit] The 'litis aestimatio' in criminal matters was this: if a person was condemned in a criminal trial, it might be necessary in some cases, as in trials for Repetundae, and for receiving a bribe as a 'judex' (ob judicandum), to ascertain and assess the damages or amount which the condemned person had to pay; and this was the 'litis aestimatio.' This man, P. Septimius Scaevola, was tried B.C. 72, but it does not appear on what charge. In the 'litis aestimatio' account was taken, it is said, of his having received a bribe in his capacity of 'judex' (ob rem judicandam). Cicero alludes to him in the Pro Cluentio, c. 41.

ob rem judicandam] Comp. Pro Rabirio Post. c. 7.

peculatus] 'Peculatus' is the offence of a man appropriating public money (pecunia publica) to his own use. Atilius was convicted on a charge of Majestas, as Cicero observes; and it further appears that he and the others, Herennius and Popillius, had also been guilty of receiving bribes as 'judices.' This, as Asconius remarks, will answer the question, What connexion is there between a man being convicted of 'peculatus' by the senatorian 'judices' and the charge of judicial corruption against the same 'judices?' "Respondebimus litis aestimationem [fieri] non solum ex titulo propositi criminis, sed etiam ex aliis probationibus, quae ex ante actis rebus apud judices constiterint. Hi peculatus crimine proposito etiam quas judicando pecunias ceperant reddiderant."

sortiente] This word expresses the praetor's activity in his office as presiding at a trial. The case alluded to in the words 'exirent in eum reum,' is that of Oppianicus, whom one of the 'judices' was charged with voting against, though he had not heard the evidence. Though Cicero uses the plural 'exirent,' there was only one person to whom the charge did apply, and even he (C. Fidiculanius Falcula) was acquitted of the charge, as Cicero tells us (Pro Cluentio, c. 37). Though he was generally suspected to have been guilty, it suited Cicero's purpose, when speaking for Cluentius, to consider him innocent.

'Exirent in eum reum' means 'were hostile to,' or something of the kind. Forcellini explains 'exire in aliquem' by 'infesto animo ire,' but he gives examples only from Statius.

qui quum judex esset, in eodem judicio] This man, who was charged with taking money in the Judicium Junianum from both sides, was C. Aelius Staienus or Stalenus, who is mentioned in the oration Pro Cluentio, c. 24, &c.

ut discoloribus signis juratorum hominum sententiae notarentur? Haec omnia me diligenter severeque acturum esse polliceor.

XIV. Quo me tandem animo fore putetis, si quid in hoc ipso judicio intellexero simili aliqua ratione esse violatum atque commissum? quum [praesertim] planum facere multis testibus possim, C. Verrem in Sicilia multis audientibus saepe dixisse, se habere hominem potentem cujus fiducia provinciam spoliaret; neque sibi soli pecuniam quaerere, sed ita triennium illud praeturae Siciliensis distributum habere, ut secum praeclare agi diceret, si unius anni quaestum in rem suam converteret, alterum patronis et defensoribus [suis] traderet, tertium illum uberrimum quaestuosissimumque annum totum judicibus reservaret. Ex quo mihi venit in mentem illud dicere quod apud M' Glabrionem nuper quum in rejiciendis judicibus commemorassem, intellexi vehementer populum Romanum commoveri, me arbitrari fore uti nationes exterae legatos ad populum Romanum mitterent, ut lex de pecuniis repetundis judiciumque tolleretur: si enim judicia nulla sint, tantum unumquemque ablaturum putant quantum sibi ac liberis suis satis esse arbitretur: nunc quod ejusmodi judicia sint, tantum unumquemque auferre quantum sibi, patronis, advocatis, praetori, judicibus satis futurum sit; hoc profecto infinitum esse: se avarissimi hominis cupiditati satisfacere posse, nocentissimae victoriae non posse. O commemoranda judicia praeclarumque existimationem nostri ordinis! quum socii populi Romani judicia de pecuniis repetundis fieri nolunt, quae a majoribus nostris sociorum causa comparata sunt.

discoloribus signis] See Divin. c. 7. These 'signa' are the 'cerae' of different colours.

14. *putetis,*] 'putatis' L. in marg. 1584, Lordan. The codd. have 'putetis.'

ut secum praeclare agi &c.] This is one of the uses of this almost universal term 'agere.' Verres said 'that he should think that he came off very well.' The same expression occurs in another place (De Am. c. 3), where the gravity of the subject requires a somewhat different rendering. See also Act. ii. Lib. 1. c. 4, 'praeclare nobiscum actum iri.'

quod apud M' Glabrionem] The word 'quod' depends directly on 'commemorassem,' though the word 'commoveri' also must be connected with it; but its grammatical case is determined by 'commemorassem.' The ordinary placing of a comma after 'nuper,' and another after 'commemorassem,' is absurd.

si . . . sint, . . . putant] This is not an exception to the rule that 'si' is used with a subjunctive to suppose a non-existing case, and that the corresponding clause must have the subjunctive also, as in 'Tu si hic sis, aliter sentias.' In this case, 'putant' is a positive opinion. 'They think that, if there were no judicia, every man would take only what he thought to be sufficient,' &c. See Key's Latin Gram. § 1213, &c. Orelli has 'arbitrentur.'

nocentissimae] Lordan has 'nocentissimi:' the reading of S. The codd. have 'nocentissimae.' The reading at first sight appears specious, as 'nocentissimi' would correspond to 'avarissimi.' But 'avarissimus' is sufficient, and the word 'cupiditas,' 'greediness,' has for its counterpart not 'victoriae,' but 'nocentissimae victoriae.'

sociorum causa] See Divin. c. 5.

An iste unquam de se bonam spem habuisset, nisi de vobis malam opinionem animo imbibisset? Quo majore etiam, si fieri potest, apud vos odio esse debet quam est apud populum Romanum, quum in avaritia, scelere, perjurio vos sui similes esse arbitretur.

XV. Cui loco, per deos immortales, judices, consulite ac providete. Moneo praedicoque id quod intelligo, tempus opportunissimum vobis hoc divinitus datum esse, ut odio, invidia, infamia, turpitudine totum ordinem liberetis. Nulla in judiciis severitas, nulla religio, nulla denique jam existimantur esse judicia. Itaque a populo Romano contemnimur, despicimur: gravi diuturnaque jam flagramus infamia. Neque enim ullam aliam ob causam populus Romanus tribuniciam potestatem tanto studio requisivit, quam quum poscebat, verbo illam poscere videbatur, re vera judicia poscebat. Neque hoc Q. Catulum hominem sapientissimum atque amplissimum fugit, qui Cn. Pompeio, viro fortissimo et clarissimo, de tribunicia potestate referente, quum esset sententiam rogatus, hoc initio est summa cum auctoritate usus: Patres conscriptos judicia male et flagitiose tueri; quod si in rebus judicandis populi Romani existimationi satisfacere voluissent, non tanto opere homines fuisse tribuniciam potestatem desideraturos. Ipse denique Cn. Pompeius, quum primum contionem ad urbem consul designatus

15. *Cui loco,*] This is another of these general words, which here signifies a 'matter' or 'part of the subject of discourse.' The reference is to the words at the end of the preceding chapter: he thinks that you are as bad as he is. 'Now I entreat you to find an answer to this assumption.'—'tempus hoc vobis divinitus datum esse:' Klotz, Zumpt, Iordan.

contemnimur &c.] Klotz observes that Cicero could say 'contemnimur' since his quaestorship, by which he obtained admission to the Senate; and he refers to Act. ii. Lib. 4. c. 11, "qui honos non homini solum habetur, sed primum populo Romano cujus beneficio nos in hunc ordinem venimus."

referente,] This is the word used to signify the proposing of a matter to the Senate. Ad Fam. xvi. 11, "Sed Lentulus consul . . dixit se relaturum." 'Sententiam rogare' is said of the consul or other magistrate who called on a senator for his opinion. Klotz refers to Vell. Pater. ii. 30, and Suetonius, Caesar. 5, as to the restoration of the 'Tribunicia Potestas' in the first consulship of Cn. Pompeius, in B.C. 70, the same year in which Cicero delivered this oration. 'Patres conscripti,' as equivalent to 'Senatores,' occurs in Pro Cn. Plancio, c. 25, In L. Pison. c. 8 (Zumpt). See Divin. c. 3, note.

ad urbem] On which Asconius falsely remarks 'in urbe.' Cn. Pompeius after returning from the war against Sertorius in Spain, where he had proconsular power, waited outside of the city, because he was expecting the honour of a triumph, and he could not enter the city while he held this 'imperium' until the Senate had granted him a triumph. As 'consul designatus' he therefore addressed the people (contio) outside of the walls. Cicero, who was expecting a triumph after his Cilician victories, says in a letter to Tiro (Ad Fam. xvi. 11), "ego ad urbem accessi pridie Nonas Januarias." The phrases are: 'ad urbem accedere, venire, esse.' Klotz refers to Cort, Sallust. Catilin. 30. Comp. Act. ii. Lib. 2. c. 6. See also De Imp. Cn. Pomp. c. 21, and the note. Klotz observes that 'Romae' is a more general expression, and is not the same as 'in urbe.' Paulus, Dig. 50. 16. 2, "Urbis appellatio muris, Romae autem continentibus aedificiis finitur, quod latius patet."

habuit, ubi id quod maxime exspectari videbatur ostendit, se tribuniciam potestatem restituturum, factus est in eo strepitus et grata contionis admurmuratio. Idem in eadem contione quum dixisset populatas vexatasque esse provincias, judicia autem turpia ac flagitiosa fieri; ei rei se providere ac consulere velle; tum vero non strepitu sed maximo clamore suam populus Romanus significavit voluntatem.

XVI. Nunc autem homines in speculis sunt: observant quemadmodum sese unusquisque vestrum gerat in retinenda religione conservandisque legibus. Vident adhuc post legem tribuniciam unum senatorem vel tenuissimum esse damnatum; quod tametsi non reprehendunt, tamen magno opere quod laudent non habent. Nulla est enim laus ibi esse integrum ubi nemo est qui aut possit aut conetur corrumpere. Hoc est judicium in quo vos de reo, populus Romanus de vobis judicabit. In hoc homine statuetur possitne senatoribus judicantibus homo nocentissimus pecuniosissimusque damnari. Deinde est ejusmodi reus, in quo homine nihil sit praeter summa peccata maximamque pecuniam, ut, si liberatus sit, nulla alia suspicio nisi ea quae turpissima est residere possit: non gratia, non cognatione, non aliis recte factis, non denique aliquo mediocri vitio tot tantaque ejus vitia sublevata esse videbuntur. Postremo ego causam sic agam, judices; ejusmodi res ita notas, ita testatas, ita magnas, ita manifestas proferam ut nemo a vobis ut istum absolvatis per gratiam conetur contendere. Habeo autem certam viam atque rationem qua omnes illorum conatus investigare et consequi possim: ita res a me agetur ut in eorum consiliis omnibus non modo aures hominum sed etiam oculi [Populi Romani] interesse videantur. Vos aliquot jam per annos concep-

in eo] 'at that,' on the occasion of his saying this.

16. *in speculis sunt*:] 'they are on the look-out.' A 'specula' (σκοπιά) is a tower or any lofty place, from which we command a view. Cicero calls Narbo Martius (Narbonne), a Roman colony in Gallia, a 'specula' (Pro Fonteio, c. 1). Strabo describes a 'specula' on the summit of Tmolus: ὁ Τμῶλος εὔδαιμον ὄρος ἐν τῇ ἀκρωρείᾳ σκοπὴν ἔχον ἐξέδραν λευκοῦ λίθου Περσῶν ἔργον ἀφ' οὗ κατοπτεύεται τὰ κύκλῳ πεδία (ed. Cas. 625). See Hom. Od. x. 97; Pro Deiotaro, c. 8, 'in speculis fuisse;' and Ovid, Her. xviii. 11,

"Adscensurus eram, nisi quod quum vincula prorae
Solveret in speculis omnis Abydos erat."

unum senatorem] Asconius says it was Dolabella. Manutius observes that the old commentator was mistaken. Asconius read 'unum hominem vel.' Iordan writes 'unum senatorem, *hominem* vel.'

residere] 'remain fixed.' It is the second conjugation, as in the passage of Caesar, B. G. vii. 77, 'residere;' and In Cat. i. c. 13, vol. iii., 'residebit,' and the note.

vitia sublevata] 'so many and such monstrous vices of Verres will not be considered as cleared away,' &c. See Divin. c. 2: and as to the different senses of the word 'tollere' also, see Heindorf, Hor. 1 Sat. iv. 11.

oculi [Populi Romani]] 'populus Romanus' G1 2 r, Iordan: 'oculi populi,' vulg.

tam huic ordini turpitudinem atque infamiam delere ac tollere potestis. Constat inter omnes post haec [constituta] judicia quibus nunc utimur nullum hoc splendore atque hac dignitate consilium fuisse. Hic si quid erit offensum, omnes homines non jam ex eodem ordine alios magis idoneos, quod fieri non potest, sed alium omnino ordinem ad res judicandas quaerendum arbitrabuntur.

XVII. Quapropter primum ab diis immortalibus, quod sperare mihi videor, hoc idem, judices, peto ut in hoc judicio nemo improbus praeter eum qui jampridem inventus est reperiatur: deinde, si plures improbi fuerint, hoc vobis, hoc populo Romano, judices, confirmo, vitam mehercule mihi prius quam vim perseverantiamque ad illorum improbitatem persequendam defuturum. Verum quod ego laboribus, periculis, inimicitiisque meis tum quum admissum erit dedecus, severe me persecuturum esse polliceor, id ne accidat tu tua auctoritate, sapientia, diligentia, M' Glabrio, potes providere. Suscipe causam judiciorum; suscipe causam severitatis, integritatis, fidei, religionis; suscipe causam senatus, ut is hoc judicio probatus cum populo Romano et in laude et in gratia esse possit. Cogita [qui sis], quo loco sis, quid dare populo Romano, quid reddere majoribus tuis debeas; fac tibi paternae legis Aciliae veniat in mentem, qua lege populus Romanus de pecuniis repetundis optimis judiciis severissimisque judicibus usus est. Circumstant te summae auctoritates quae te oblivisci laudis domesticae non sinant, quae te noctes diesque commoneant fortissimum tibi patrem, sapientissimum avum, gravissimum socerum fuisse. Quare si Glabrionis patris vim et acrimoniam ceperis ad resistendum hominibus audacissimis; si avi Scaevolae prudentiam ad prospiciendas insidias quae tunc atque

Fritzsche proposes to omit 'populi Romani;' and this is a good suggestion.

[*constituta*] *judicia*] The dtt omit 'constituta.' I suspect that the dtt are right here, or that we should read 'instituta.'

17. *peto*] 'opto' G3 ι codd. Lambini, and Jordan, who refers to In Cat. ii. c. 7, 'a diis immortalibus optabo.'

[*qui sis*] Ascon. The words are not in our MSS.

legis Aciliae] The 'Lex Acilia de repetundis' which was proposed and carried by M' Acilius Glabrio, 'tribunus plebis,' the father of the Glabrio who presided as praetor at this trial of Verres. See Excursus I.—'legis . . . in mentem:' see Divin. c. 13. There is a reading 'leges . . . veniant,' G3 ι, a signal instance in which the better MSS. are the worse.

avi Scaevolae] Glabrio the father married a daughter of P. Scaevola, who was therefore the grandfather of this Glabrio. Asconius says that this was Scaevola, the learned jurist, who was consul with Cn. Piso (B.C. 133), the year in which Tiberius Gracchus was killed. But Piso's name was Lucius. Klotz says that the false Asconius takes this Scaevola to be Quintus; but the falsity is not on the side of Asconius, for he means the Scaevola who was consul B.C. 133, the same that Klotz means. Manutius and Garatoni changed 'Cn. Pisone' in the text of Asconius into 'L. Pisone,' which is the true name; but Asconius may have made a mistake in the praenomen.

M. Aemilius Scaurus was Princeps Senatus, and this M' Glabrio married his daughter Aemilia; but Sulla, who married the widow of Scaurus, took away Aemilia the daughter from Glabrio and gave her to

horum famae comparantur; si soceri Scauri constantiam ut ne quis te de vera et certa possit sententia demovere; intelliget populus Romanus integerrimo atque honestissimo praetore delectoque consilio nocenti reo magnitudinem pecuniae plus habuisse momenti ad suspicionem criminis quam ad rationem salutis.

XVIII. Mihi certum est non committere ut in hac causa praetor nobis consiliumque mutetur. Non patiar rem in id tempus adduci, ut Siculi, quos adhuc servi designatorum consulum non moverunt, quum eos novo exemplo universos arcessérent, eos tum lictores consulum vocent; ut homines miseri, antea socii atque amici populi Romani, nunc servi ac supplices, non modo jus suum fortunasque omnes eorum imperio amittant, verum etiam deplorandi juris sui potestatem non habeant. Non sinam profecto causa a me perorata, quadraginta diebus interpositis, tum nobis denique responderi quum accusatio nostra in oblivionem diuturnitatis adducta sit: non committam ut tum haec res judicetur quum haec frequentia totius Italiae Roma discesserit, quae convenit uno tempore undique, comitio-

wife to Cn. Pompeius Magnus, as Plutarch tells us in the life of Sulla, c. 33. Klotz observes that Scaurus is still called the father-in-law of Glabrio, because Glabrio's son by Aemilia was still living, and consequently the affinity according to Roman notions still subsisted. He observes, in a note on the Pro P. Quintio, c. 6, that the Romans considered affinity only to exist so long as either the woman whom a man had married was alive, or at least the children of the marriage; and he refers to the Pro Sestio, c. 3. See the note on Pro P. Quintio, c. 6, vol. ii.

demovere;] 'dimovere' Gl Ld Lg 42.—'momenti:' 'more force or effect,' an example of the original sense of the word.

18. *ut Siculi,*] Madvig proposes to omit 'Siculi,' though all the MSS. have it; and Iordan has omitted it. The correction is specious, but like some other corrections of the same excellent critic, it is not true. We might suppose that some copyist inserted the word, or wrote it in the margin by way of explanation. But if we look carefully at the passage, we may see that Cicero would hardly omit to name the Sicilians, and that the mention of their name adds force to the passage. He says 'ut Siculi —,' and then he interposes 'quos adhuc . . . vocent.' He resumes with 'ut homines miseri,' which corresponds to 'ut Siculi.'

eorum] That is, the 'consules.' Orelli remarks 'sine causa suspectum Ern.' Cicero might have repeated 'consulum.' If he did not, he must use 'eorum.' Klotz remarks that Ernesti would refer 'eorum' to 'lictores,' which seems hardly credible. The ambiguity of 'eorum,' if there is any, is shared by all languages.

quadraginta diebus] "Iis qui sunt per binos ludos, votivos atque Romanos, quos alii bini consecuturi erant, Victoriae atque plebeii" (Ascon.). See Introd.

responderi] Klotz has 'respondere,' which he says is the reading of the best MSS. But according to Iordan 'respondere' is not the reading of any MS. Orelli has 'respondeant.' Klotz rightly understood the words in a general sense, and he applies them generally to the answer or defence, and not to any particular person: but for that 'responderi' is the true word. It corresponds in its generalizing form to 'causa perorata.' Zumpt and Iordan say that 'responderi' is a correction of Lambinus.

comitiorum &c.] Asconius, as usual, has a kind of paraphrase, which contains little more than the original; but he adds that the censors were Gellius and Lentulus. A census was held in this year, B.C. 70, by the censors L. Gellius Poplicola and Cn. Cornelius Lentulus Clodianus. As to the censorship see Divin. c. 3. The preceding censorship was in B.C. 86. After the enactment of the 'Lex Julia' (B.C. 90), by which the 'Civitas' was given to the 'Socii' and 'Latini,' all the inhabitants of Italy were not required to come to Rome to the cen-

rum, ludorum, censendique causa. Hujus judicii et laudis fructum et offensionis periculum vestrum; laborem sollicitudinemque nostram; scientiam quid agatur memoriamque quid a quoque dictum sit, omnium puto esse oportere. Faciam hoc non novum sed ab iis qui nunc principes nostrae civitatis sunt ante factum, ut testibus utar statim: illud a me novum, judices, cognoscetis, quod ita testes constituam ut crimen totum explicem; ubi id interrogando, argu-

sus, but the census was taken in the remoter places at least, and the results were forwarded to Rome. This is the opinion of Mazocchi, no great authority indeed, but it seems probable enough (Mazocchi, Tab. Herac. p. 455). They must have come however to vote at the Comitia, and yet it is impossible that any except the rich could bear the expense and would take the trouble of coming annually to the elections from remote parts of Italy and staying some time in Rome. But I know no evidence that the votes were taken at the place of a man's residence and forwarded to Rome.—'ludorum' is an emendation of Manutius derived from the text of Asconius. The MSS. have 'iudiciorum.' I do not know why the people should come 'judiciorum causa;' nor how we must explain the fact of all the MSS. having 'iudiciorum,' if Cicero wrote 'ludorum.'

censendique causa.] The verb 'censere' is applied to the office of the censors in making registers of the citizens and of their property. It is also applied to the citizens giving in their names, the names of their 'familia,' and the particulars of their property, as in the oration Pro Flacco, c. 32, "in qua tribu denique ista praedia censuisti?" 'Censendi causa' here means for the purpose of giving in the particulars which were required. See Forcellini.

scientiam quid agatur &c.] This resembles a Greek form of expression, so far as this, that in Greek the noun sometimes has the same effect on the construction as if it were a verb.

principes] Asconius says that Cicero alludes to the prosecution of L. Cotta by the brothers M. and L. Lucullus who "non usi sunt perpetua oratione, sed interrogatione testium causam peregerunt" (comp. Cicero, De Off. ii. 14; Acad. Pr. ii. at the beginning). Zumpt thinks that Asconius is mistaken as to Cotta being prosecuted, and that we must follow the authority of Plutarch (*Lucullus*, c. 1), who speaks of the prosecution of Servilius. But Plutarch mentions only one prosecutor, L. Lucullus, in the case of Servilius. Asconius speaks of two prosecutors.

ut testibus utar statim:] 'I will examine my witnesses at once, from the very commencement.' It is easy to perceive that the position of words in Latin sentences is determined by their relative value in the sentence, and that such a word as 'statim' may stand as it does here, when the orator terminates with it as the emphatic word. Thus in the De Am. c. 26 'eaque ipsa concludamus aliquando.'

ubi id interrogando,] Klotz reads, 'ut ubi id,' &c. Hotmann saw the difficulty of this passage, but he has not removed it by suggesting the transposition of 'interrogando' so that it shall stand between 'ut' and 'crimen' in the preceding line; for the words 'eadem interrogandi facultas, argumentandi dicendique' at the end of the sentence appear to correspond to 'interrogando, argumentis atque oratione.' The difficulty lies in the words 'tum testes ad crimen accommodem.' Cicero says, that there will be something new in his mode of proceeding, which novelty will not consist in examining the witnesses from the first, for this had been done before. The novelty is this. 'I will so arrange my witnesses as to unfold the nature of the charge in general.' He then adds, 'and when by my examination, my arguments, and my discourse, I have established it, I will then apply my witnesses to the (particular) charge,' that of 'Repetundae.' He says shortly afterwards, 'Haec primae actionis,' &c.: 'The charge in the first Actio will be as follows;' and then, after stating the general charge against Verres, he adds, 'and besides I charge him with illegally carrying off from Sicily "quadringenties sestertiûm."' He seems, therefore, to say that he will first establish the general character of his misconduct (totum crimen), which he afterwards expresses by 'multa libidinose, multa crudeliter,' &c.; and then he will apply his witnesses to the proof, *the* 'crimen,' which was Repetundae; or, as he otherwise expresses it, 'quadringenties sestertiûm ex Sicilia contra leges abstulisse.' This may be the meaning of the

mentis atque oratione firmavero, tum testes ad crimen accommodem; ut nihil inter illam usitatam accusationem atque hanc novam intersit, nisi quod in illa tunc quum omnia dicta sunt testes dantur, hic in singulas res dabuntur; ut illis quoque eadem interrogandi facultas, argumentandi dicendique sit. Si quis erit qui perpetuam orationem accusationemque desideret, altera actione audiet: nunc id quod facimus, ea ratione facimus ut malitiae illorum consilio nostro occurramus, necessario fieri intelligat. Haec primae actionis erit accusatio. Dicimus C. Verrem, quum multa libidinose, multa crudeliter in cives Romanos atque socios, multa in deos hominesque nefarie fecerit, tum praeterea quadringenties sestertiûm ex Sicilia contra leges abstulisse. Hoc testibus, hoc tabulis privatis publicisque auctoritatibus ita vobis planum faciemus, ut hoc statuatis, etiamsi spatium ad dicendum nostro commodo vacuosque dies habuissemus, tamen oratione longa nihil opus fuisse. Dixi.

passage; and the interpretation is consistent with the facts, for in this trial Verres was prosecuted for Repetundae, and not for other offences; though Cicero, in order to aggravate the odium against him, exposed all his public life, and even that part of it which had no relation at all to the conduct of Verres in Sicily or to the particular charge, which was a demand of so much money against him as illegally gotten in Sicily. In another passage (Act. ii. Lib. 1. c. 11), he reminds his (supposed) hearers of the way in which he had proceeded in the 'prior actio:' "Etenim sic me ipsum egisse memoria tenetis, ut in testibus interrogandis omnia crimina proponerem et explicarem, ut quum rem totam in medio posuissem tum denique testem interrogarem." He also (Act. ii. Lib. 3. c. 44) says, "De Aetnensibus perpauca dicam; dixerunt enim ipsi priore actione publice," which means that the men sent by the Aetnenses had been examined, and had given their evidence on behalf of their town (publice). Zumpt maintains the correctness of this passage against Hotmann and those who have followed him. But his explanation is not quite the same as mine. Madvig omits 'interrogando.'

illam usitatam . . testes dantur,] Compare the passage in the Pro Flacco, c. 10, 'Nam antea,' &c., vol. iii. and the note.

nunc id quod facimus,] Asconius found this passage as obscure as 'illa in fine orationis pro Ligario;' and he adds 'nisi forte *facimus* semel ponitur.' Camerarius reads 'ea enim ratione.' Klotz thinks that he does the best service to this passage by pointing it thus: "nunc id, quod facimus, ea ratione facimus, ut malitiae illorum consilio nostro occurramus: necessario fieri intelligat." He explains the 'asyndeton,' 'necessario . . intelligat,' by supposing that the 'ut' extends its force to it, so that 'intelligat' depends upon 'ut' as well as 'occurramus' does. I have no hesitation in rejecting this explanation. It is plain that 'necessario fieri intelligat' is connected with 'nunc id quod facimus;' and if the intermediate words are omitted, the sense is 'now let him understand that what we are doing is done of necessity.' Now there is no great difficulty in understanding the words 'ea ratione . . occurramus,' as being interposed as a rapidly delivered parenthesis between the two extremes, the connexion of which seems to me very clear. Zumpt points it thus: "nunc id, quod facimus (ea ratione facimus, ut malitiae illorum consilio nostro occurramus) necessario fieri intelligat," and Iordan does the same, but he has adopted 'intelliget,' an unnecessary alteration by Fritzsche.

Dixi.] It was the practice, says Asconius, of the ancient orators to say 'Dixi' when they had done speaking; and for the praetor to pronounce the word 'dixerunt' when both parties had finished. Perhaps Asconius meant to say 'praeco' for 'praetor,' as he ought to have done (Act. ii. Lib. 2. c. 30); and it is printed 'praeco' in the corrected text of Asconius (ed. Orelli).

The old commentator thinks that 'Dixi' is appropriately said here by the orator, who wished to impress his opponents with the brevity of his speech, which was to be immediately followed by the examination of the witnesses, and the production of the documentary evidence.

Asconius adds, "Non autem ibi finitur prima actio. Inducentur enim dehinc a Tullio testes, quorum verba in oratione conscribere nullius elegantiae fuit. Multis autem diebus prima actio celebrata est, dum testes Verris producuntur criminum diversorum, dum recitantur publicae privataeque literae: quibus rebus adeo stupefactus Hortensius dicitur, ut rationem defensionis omitteret, adeo perculsus Verres ut abiret in exilium sua sponte. Nec quid amplius in judicio gestum est, nisi quod Tullius metuens ne tantum negotium paene tacitum praeteriret, finxit Verrem comperendinationi praesto fuisse, ut his defensus accusaretur iterum. Et quemadmodum victoriae consuluerat brevitate dicendi, ita laudem eloquentiae tamquam repetita accusatione est consecutus reliquorum conscriptione librorum qui caeterus consequuntur."

ACTIONIS SECUNDAE

IN C. VERREM

LIBER PRIMUS.

DE PRAETURA URBANA.

INTRODUCTION.

The five books of the Actio Secunda were written after Verres' trial was ended, as already stated (p. 6); and Cicero wrote them in such a form that they might be read as if they had been delivered at the trial of Verres. If he observed in writing them the same rules which he would have observed in delivering them, or, to express the same thing for clearness' sake in other words, if he intended these five orations to be such orations as he might have delivered or would have delivered, if Verres' trial had continued, we must form a very unfavourable opinion of Roman procedure in such trials as this.

Verres was prosecuted solely for maladministration in his Sicilian province, and Cicero went to Sicily to collect evidence against him. But in this oration, De Praetura Urbana, Cicero speaks not only of Verres' misconduct as Praetor Urbanus at Rome, but he even goes back to the time of his quaestorship under Carbo (c. 12, and note), and to the crimes which he committed while he was legatus of Dolabella (c. 15). Nor does Cicero confine himself to general statements and to general abuse of Verres for his acts as quaestor and legatus: he even produces evidence against Verres, that is, he affects to produce evidence; and, as I have said, if he wrote as he would have spoken if the trial had continued, he would have produced evidence against Verres about his misconduct as quaestor and legatus. In c. 14 he refers to written evidence about the accounts of Verres in his office of quaestor. In c. 21 he refers to the accounts of P. Servilius in order to contrast them with the accounts of Verres. In c. 31 he produces documentary evidence about the scandalous conduct of Verres in the affair of Lampsacus; and in c. 34 in the matter of Verres' behaviour to the

Milesians, while he was Dolabella's legatus, he says that he will omit the mention of certain things, and will leave them to the testimony of witnesses who were still to be heard ('eaque omnia testibus integra reservabo;' see also the end of c. 35). In c. 40 he apologizes for saying so little about Verres as Praetor Urbanus, and he adds that he has reserved some things, which relate to the Praetura Urbana, for the witnesses to tell. All this talk and all this evidence have nothing to do with the matters for which Verres was prosecuted.

But Cicero writes (c. 28) as if evidence had been given even in the Prior Actio about the affair of Lampsacus, and in c. 31 he affirms that he had produced and examined witnesses on this matter. Again in c. 48 he refers to the evidence that had been given in the Prior Actio about the case of Ligur, which was a charge of misconduct against Verres in his Urban Praetorship.

In the second book (c. 1) Cicero comes, as he says, to the real business, to the case of Sicily and Verres' three years' maladministration; and this is the subject of the third, fourth, and fifth books also. In the last four books Cicero confines himself to the proper matter of the prosecution. But he still speaks of fresh evidence to be heard from Sicilian witnesses (2. c. 33); though a great deal of evidence had been given in the Prior Actio both by individuals and by those who were commissioned to give evidence on behalf of Sicilian towns (2. c. 49). There are many other passages to the same effect (2. c. 65), (2. c. 76, 'tum quum eos ipsos produxero qui dederunt;' and 3. c. 9.) Cicero also in these last four orations often refers to documentary evidence then produced for the first time about the conduct of Verres in Sicily, and makes his remarks on it (3. c. 10, and c. 17).

The matter then stands thus, as Cicero states it. After the speech here called the Actio Prima, evidence was given both about the maladministration of Verres in Sicily, for which he was on his trial, and for other previous misconduct, not in Sicily, and for which he was not on his trial. I do not understand why Cicero produced evidence in the Prior Actio about matters which did not pertain to the prosecution that he had undertaken; but still this speech was delivered. The first book of the Second Actio is wholly unconnected with the real matter of the prosecution. The speech and the evidence referred to in it have no relation to the charges on which Cicero undertook to be the prosecutor of Verres. Though the Roman procedure gave very great licence to a prosecutor and allowed him to say much, which he did not prove and sometimes could not prove, of which Cicero's orations furnish plenty of instances, I do not believe that such a speech as this De Praetura Urbana could have been delivered, or that the presiding magistrate could have tolerated the production of so much evidence which could lead to no conviction, when there was

evidence enough on the real charges to ensure the condemnation of Verres. I conclude that Cicero when he wrote the Actio Secunda wished to expose the whole life of Verres, and also to give to these five rhetorical exercises, as far as he could, the appearance of being real speeches. And on the whole he has succeeded well in producing this general impression, and it is fortunate for us that we possess such an instructive and amusing piece of writing as his Second Actio. But he has not written this Second Actio with a strict observation of what he would have said, if he had spoken these orations; and the first book, which is on the Praetura Urbana and other extraneous matters, though valuable to us, spoils the effect, which we suppose that Cicero intended to produce. But we cannot doubt that so accomplished an advocate and writer knew what he was doing. As the five books were written only to be read, we may suppose that he was careless about confining himself strictly to his case. His purpose was to show what a villain Verres was all through his public life, and to let his readers see how he could deal with him.

[Those who have the inclination may read the Preface of the Pseudo-Asconius to this oration (ed. Orelli, p. 154). It begins "Deinceps haec omnia non dicta sed scripta sunt contra eum, quod [ita] factum est: Fingit Cicero adesse in judicio Verrem comperendinatum, respondere citatum et defendi."]

ACTIONIS SECUNDAE

IN C. VERREM

LIBER PRIMUS.

DE PRAETURA URBANA.

Haec oratio iisdem quibus superior continetur codicibus. G1 desinit § 105 (c. 41), G2 Ld s § 111 (c. 43). Ad cap. xvii. commemoratur fragmentum Palimpsesti Taurinensis (P. T.), quod incipit a verbis . . *que iter fecit*, desinit in verbis: *non participem C. Ver.* cf. Peyron. fragmm. p. 216—A § 105 (c. 41) incipiunt fragmenta Palimpsesti Vaticani (V) a Maio edita. (Auctores class. e Vatt. codd. Tom. ii. p. 390 sqq. Romae, 1828.) Sunt autem haec:

1. § 105 (c. 41) *docet hominem*—§ 114 (c. 44) *usitata satis.*
2. § 119 (c. 46) *videbantur, quod*—§ 130 (c. 50) *locarisset.*
3. § 137 (c. 52) *Venit ad Ch.*—§ 139 (c. 53) *esse deferre.*
4. § 142 (c. 54) *bonis praedibus*—§ 148 (c. 56) *existimationem con* . . 5. § 150 (c. 57) *tabulae praedam*—§ 153 (c. 58) *ut illorum.* 6. *Q. Curtium*—*subsortiebatur.* Ubi Maius editionis scripturae auctoritatem codicis non diserte adscripsit, signo eV (i. e. editio Vaticana) usi sumus. Nam quamquam Maius sese rem diligenter egisse cunctumque codicem in adversaria rettulisse typisque edendum curasse dicit, tamen interdum jure dubitari videtur satisne accurate codicis scripturam in editione expresserit —Scholiasta Gronovianus desinit § 62 (c. 24). (Iordan.)

I. Neminem vestrum ignorare arbitror, judices, hunc per hosce dies sermonem vulgi atque hanc opinionem populi Romani fuisse, C. Verrem altera actione responsurum non esse neque ad judicium adfuturum. Quae fama non idcirco solum emanarat quod iste certe statuerat ac deliberaverat non adesse, verum etiam quod nemo quemquam tam audacem, tam amentem, tam impudentem fore arbitrabatur qui tam nefariis criminibus, tam multis testibus convictus, ora judicum adspicere aut os suum populo Romano ostendere auderet. Est idem Verres qui fuit semper, ut ad audendum projectus, sic paratus ad audiendum. Praesto est, respondet, defenditur. Ne hoc quidem sibi reliqui facit ut in rebus turpissimis

1. *audendum—audiendum.*] A rhetorical play on words, a trick not worth imitating. So he writes 'impudentiae suae pudentem exitum.'

respondet.] That is, 'answers to his name,' when he is called by the 'praeco' (Asconius).

quum manifesto teneatur, si reticeat et abeit, tamen impudentiae suae pudentem exitum quaesisse videatur. Patior, judices, et non moleste fero me laboris mei, vos virtutis vestrae fructum esse laturos. Nam si iste id fecisset quod primo statuerat, ut non adesset, minus aliquanto quam mihi opus esset cognosceretur quid ego in hac accusatione comparanda constituendaque elaborassem; vestra vero laus tenuis plane atque obscura, judices, esset. Neque [enim] hoc a vobis populus Romanus exspectat neque eo potest esse contentus, si condemnatus sit is qui adesse noluerit, et si fortes fueritis in eo quem nemo sit ausus defendere. Immo vero adsit,

primo] G12 ; and Iordan have 'prius.' Lal 'primus.'

Immo vero] This word may be taken either affirmatively or negatively, according to the words to which we suppose it to refer. This apparent inconsistency is explained by considering 'immo' to be a shorter form of 'in modo,' for 'modus' is a word that is very often attached to another word. There is 'admodum,' 'dummodo,' 'tantummodo,' 'ejusmodi,' &c. 'Illico' is an example of 'in' attached to another word of ordinary use (in loco). 'Immo' may be taken in this passage as an affirmation, strengthened by 'vero,' as in the phrase 'ego vero ;' and it refers to the word 'adesse.' 'Yes, indeed, let him appear, let him answer.' In c. 32, there is again 'Immo vero ab hominibus,' &c., here a reference to the preceding sentence shows that it may be translated; 'No, indeed, not so, but by men of the gentlest disposition.' In Act. ii. Lib. 4. c. 42, "Quid hoc nos dicimus? Immo vero ipse praesens :"—'Well, is it I who say this? No, indeed, he is here himself to say it.' Comp. Act. ii. Lib. 4. c. 46. In Act. ii. Lib. 3. c. 10, "Quid omne? plus immo etiam, inquit, si volet :"—'What all? yes, and more too, he says, if he shall choose.' The literal rendering would be, 'What all? more indeed, in a manner, he says, if he shall choose.' Some of the best instances of the use of 'immo' occur in Terence; as in Andr. 3, 5, 12, "Pa. Nempe ut modo. D. Immo melius spero :"—'Pa. Ay, as you did just now. D. No, better I hope;' or, 'Yes, and better I hope.' It is often indifferent whether a man says Yes or No to a question, if he adds something by way of explanation; for neither Yes nor No alone fully expresses what he has to say. Andr. 1, 2, 30, "quid hoc intellextin' an nondum etiam ne hoc quidem? D. Immo callide." Here are two questions : which must Davus be considered as answering? 'Well, do you understand this, or don't you yet understand even this?' 'Yes,' says Davus, replying to the first part, 'I understand it very well.' 'No,' says Davus, replying to the second part, 'I do understand it very well.' The following passage is clear: Hauton. 1, 1, 4, "M. filium unicum adolescentulum Habeo. Ah! quid dixi habere me? immo habui, Chreme." 'I have an only son, a youth : ah! why did I say that I have? No, I had, Chremes;' or, 'Yes, I had, Chremes :' where 'No' is a denial of 'have ;' 'Yes' is an affirmation of 'had.' 'Modo' is often a monosyllable in the verse of Terence, which shows that the Romans in speaking abbreviated it, like many other words. They would pronounce 'in modo,' 'immo,' and so they wrote it; and they might on the same principle have written 'dummodo,' 'dummo.' The MSS. abbreviation of 'modo' is ṁ in the MS. of Gaius, where 'hoc modo' is written ho cṁ in the specimen in Lachmann's edition.

It has been objected (Parry's Terence, p. 52) to this explanation of 'immo' that the expression 'in modo' does not occur. That objection is weighty, if 'immo' is not 'in modo.' But if 'immo' is 'in modo,' then the objection is not true. It is also asked if the 'ablative modo' ever occurs as a monosyllable in Plautus or Terence. The answer is that 'modo' does, and people may call it ablative or not, as they like. The true form of the word is 'immo' as far as I can ascertain, and not 'imo.' But the critics are not agreed on this matter. There is however no doubt about the way in which 'immo' is used; and the suggestion that it is a correlative word to 'summus,' and means 'in the lowest degree,' 'by no means,' is a false explanation, for it will spoil the

respondeat; summis opibus, summo studio potentissimorum hominum defendatur; certet mea diligentia cum illorum omnium cupiditate, vestra integritas cum istius pecunia, testium constantia cum illius patronorum minis atque potentia: tum demum illa omnia victa videbuntur quum in contentionem certamenque venerint. Absens si iste esset damnatus, non tam ipse sibi consuluisse quam invidisse vestrae laudi videretur.

II. Neque enim salus ulla rei publicae major hoc tempore reperiri potest quam populum Romanum intelligere, diligenter rejectis ab accusatore judicibus socios, leges, rem publicam, senatorio consilio maxime posse defendi: neque tanta fortunis omnium pernicies potest accidere quam opinione populi Romani rationem veritatis, integritatis, fidei, religionis ab hoc ordine abjudicari. Itaque mihi videor, judices, magnam et maxime aegram et prope depositam rei publicae partem suscepisse, neque in eo magis meae quam vestrae laudi existimationique servisse. Accessi enim ad invidiam judiciorum levandam vituperationemque tollendam, ut quum haec res pro voluntate populi Romani esset judicata, aliqua ex parte mea diligentia constituta auctoritas judiciorum videretur; postremo, ut esset hoc judicatum, ut finis aliquando judiciariae controversiae constitueretur. Etenim sine dubio, judices, in hac causa ea res in discrimen adducitur. Reus est enim nocentissimus, qui si condemnatur, desinent homines dicere his judiciis pecuniam plurimum posse; sin absolvitur, desinemus nos de judiciis transferendis recusare. Tametsi de absolutione istius neque ipse jam sperat, nec populus Romanus metuit: de impudentia singulari quod adest, quod respondet, sunt qui mirentur; mihi pro cetera ejus audacia

meaning of some passages, as Plautus, Aulul. iv. 10, 34, 'Negas? Ly. Pernego immo.'

istius] 'illius' G12 r, Iordan. The MSS. have, I suppose, 'illius patronorum.' I think that the true reading is 'istius' in both cases.

2. *senatorio consilio*] A 'consilium' of 'judices' taken from the senators.

abjudicari.] See Act. i. c. 5: 'nor is there any calamity which can befall the interests of all the citizens so great, as for the opinion of the Roman people to declare that the Senatorian Ordo has no regard to truth, integrity, good faith, and religion.' 'Accidere' is the certain correction of Manutius. The MSS. have 'accedere.' The two words are often confounded.

prope depositam] 'Depositam' has a sense almost like 'desperatus.' A person is 'depositus' who is placed on the ground with little hope that he will rise again. Ovid says (Ep. Pont. ii. 2, 47), 'Jam prope depositus, certe jam frigidus.' Cicero uses 'suscipere,' 'to take up,' to raise, as the opposite of 'deponere.'

ut esset] codd. 'utut esset,' Muret., Guilielm., Iordan, who thinks that Muretus has not set the text quite right, for 'postremo,' he says, is wrongly placed in "in altero membro, quod haud scio an usquam alibi reperiatur. Itaque ante *postremo* lacunam esse suspicor."

pro cetera &c.] 'Considering,' 'in respect of.' See Caesar, B. G. vi. 19, "Funera sunt pro cultu Gallorum magnifica." Cicero Ad Div. iv. 2, 'pro ea copia' &c.

atque amentia ne hoc quidem mirandum videtur. Multa enim et in deos et in homines impie nefarieque commisit, quorum scelerum poenis agitatur et a mente consilioque deducitur.

III. Agunt eum praecipitem poenae civium Romanorum, quos partim securi percussit, partim in vinculis necavit, partim implorantes jura libertatis et civitatis in crucem sustulit. Rapiunt eum ad supplicium dii patrii, quod iste unus inventus est qui e complexu parentum abreptos filios ad necem duceret, et parentes pretium pro sepultura liberum posceret. Religiones vero caerimoniaeque omnium sacrorum fanorumque violatae, simulacraque deorum quae non modo ex suis templis ablata sunt, sed etiam jacent in tenebris ab isto retrusa atque abdita, consistere ejus animum sine furore atque amentia non sinunt. Neque iste mihi videtur se ad damnationem solum offerre, neque hoc avaritiae supplicio communi qui se tot sceleribus obstrinxerit contentus esse: singularem quandam poenam istius immanis atque importuna natura desiderat. Non id solum quaeritur ut isto damnato bona restituantur iis quibus erepta sunt, sed et religiones deorum immortalium expiandae, et civium Romanorum cruciatus multorumque innocentium sanguis istius supplicio luendus est. Non enim furem sed ereptorem, non adulterum sed expugnatorem pudicitiae, non sacrilegum sed hostem sacrorum religionumque, non sicarium sed crudelissimum carnificem civium sociorumque in vestrum judicium adduximus, ut ego hunc unum ejusmodi reum post hominum memoriam fuisse arbitrer cui damnari expediret.

IV. Nam quis hoc non intelliget istum absolutum diis hominibusque invitis, tamen ex manibus populi Romani eripi nullo modo

3. *quos partim*] 'part of whom.' 'Partim' is used as a noun undeclined. See Pro Fonteio, c. 12, vol. ii., and De Prov. Cons. c. 10, vol. iv.

sacrilegum] One who lays his hands on sacred things, things set apart for religious purposes. Among other divisions of things, the Romans had a division of 'res divini juris,' or things set apart for the purposes of religion, and 'res humani juris,' things which were not (Gaius, ii. 1, &c.). A 'sacrilegus' is one 'qui sacra legit,' i. e. 'furatur,' one who robs temples or steals sacred things. In the Imperial period the word obtained the wider signification of any offence against religion. The Lex Julia Peculatus brought 'Sacrilegium' under the denomination or penalties of 'Peculatus.' And Cicero, c. 4, seems to include the offence of temple-robbing under 'Peculatus.'

cui damnari expediret.] "Because," says Asconius, "there was a less penalty in being condemned in this trial, than in an assembly of the Roman people and in the punishment which they might inflict;" an interpretation which, as Klotz remarks, is confirmed by the words 'Nam quis,' &c. Cicero means to say that Verres, if acquitted in this trial, would be punished by the 'Populus Romanus' by a special vote. Whether he threatens Verres with a regular proceeding by a kind of bill of pains and penalties, or with some irregular vengeance of the Roman people, does not seem quite clear. But one of the two seems to be meant. Zumpt gives it another meaning: "ut animus furiis agitatus quiesceret soluta poena. V. Gronov. ad Tacit. Ann. xv. 68."

posse? Quis hoc non perspicit praeclare nobiscum actum iri, si populus Romanus istius unius supplicio contentus fuerit ac non sic statuerit, non istum majus in sese scelus concepisse, quum fana spoliarit, quum tot homines innocentes necarit, quum cives Romanos morte, cruciatu, cruce affecerit, quum praedonum duces accepta pecunia dimiserit, quam eos si qui istum tot, tantis, tam nefariis sceleribus coopertum jurati sententia sua liberarint? Non est, non est in hoc homine cuiquam peccandi locus, judices: non is est reus, non id tempus, non id consilium, metuo ne quid arrogantius apud tales viros videar dicere, ne actor quidem est is cui reus tam nocens, tam perditus, tam victus, aut occulte surripi aut impune eripi possit. His ego judicibus non probabo C. Verrem contra leges pecuniam cepisse? sustinebunt tales viri se tot senatoribus, tot equitibus Romanis, tot civitatibus, tot hominibus honestissimis ex tam illustri provincia, tot populorum privatorumque literis non credidisse? tantae populi Romani voluntati restitisse? Sustineant. Reperiemus, si istum vivum ad aliud judicium perducere poterimus, quibus probemus istum in quaestura pecuniam publicam Cn. Carboni consuli datam avertisse, quibus persuadeamus istum alieno nomine a quaestoribus urbanis, quod priore actione didicistis, pecuniam abstulisse. Erunt qui et in eo quoque audaciam ejus reprehendant, quod aliquot nominibus de capite quantum commodum fuerit frumenti decumani detraxerit. Erunt etiam fortasse, judices, qui

4. *in hoc homine*] 'in this man's case;' like 'si fortes fueritis in eo,' c. 1.

tam victus,] "Emendandum est 'tam convictus,' ut locum affert rhetor incertus in Anecdotis Parisinis rhetor. p. 3, quae nuper Ekstenius publicavit" (Halm).

contra leges pecuniam cepisse?] The general expression of taking money contrary to (particular) 'leges,' must here mean such a taking of money as was the ground of a prosecution for 'Repetundae.' Compare the passage in the oration Pro M. Scauro, c. 21, "adversus leges pecuniarum captarum reum fecit repetundarum lege quam tulit Servilius Glaucia." In this passage 'pecuniam' is the reading of G12 Lg 27 29; and 'pecunias' of the ditt. The Romans used both forms. Sallust, Jug. 32, writes 'pecuniae captae arcessebant.'

ad aliud judicium] 'Populi scilicet et equitum Romanorum,' says Asconius, but he is mistaken. Cicero threatens him with a prosecution for 'peculatus,' for misemploying public money, as the words at the beginning of the next chapter show, and the words 'illum ejus peculatum,' near the end of this chapter.

alieno nomine] Asconius makes a guess that 'alieno nomine' means in the name of Carbo or his army; and another, that he got the money to buy corn in Sicily, and did not pay for it; which cannot be the meaning in this passage.

'Aliquot nominibus' means under certain heads or entries; as in c. 38, 'his nominibus solis,' &c. Cicero (De Am. c. 25), says, "multis nominibus est hoc vitium notandum," &c.

de capite—frumenti decumani] That is, he remitted as much as he pleased of the 'frumentum decumanum,' which was due to the Roman people.

quantum commodum fuerit] This means 'quantum libuerit,' 'just as much as he pleased;' as in Act. ii. Lib. 2. c. 13, "quod civis cum cive ageret, aut eum judicem quem commodum erat, haruspicem, medicum suum dabat; aut," &c.; where Asconius quotes Terence, Adelph. 1, 2, 38, "Amat?

illum ejus peculatum vel acerrime vindicandum putent, quod iste M. Marcelli et P. Africani monumenta, quae nomine illorum, re vera populi Romani et erant et habebantur, ex fanis religiosissimis et ex urbibus sociorum atque amicorum non dubitaverit auferre.

V. Emerserit ex peculatus etiam judicio, meditetur de ducibus hostium quos accepta pecunia liberavit; videat quid de illis respondeat quos in eorum locum subditos domi suae reservavit; quaerat non solum quemadmodum nostro crimini, verum etiam quo pacto suae confessioni possit mederi; meminerit se priore actione, clamore populi Romani infesto atque inimico excitatum, confessum esse duces praedonum a se securi non esse percussos, se jam tum esse veritum ne sibi crimini daretur eos ab se pecunia liberatos; fateatur id quod negari non potest, se privatum hominem praedonum duces vivos atque incolumes domi suae, posteaquam Romam redierit, usquedum per me licuerit, tenuisse. Hoc in illo majestatis judicio si licuisse sibi ostenderit, ego oportuisse concedam. Ex hoc quoque evaserit, proficiscar eo quo me jampridem vocat populus Romanus. De jure

dabitur a me argentum dum erit commodum." Act. ii. Lib. 1. c. 26, 'quos ei commodum sit invitet;' and c. 44.

M. Marcelli &c.] The works of art which M. Marcellus gave up to the Siculi, and those which Scipio Africanus brought back from Carthage, and restored to them.

5. *Emerserit*] This tense is often so placed. 'Suppose him to escape from the prosecution for Peculatus;' which might be considered to be an elliptical expression, some word being understood. Compare 'ex hoc evaserit' in this chapter: and c. 14, 'fuerit aliis.' See Heindorf, Horat. 1 Sat. i. 45, note. But the present indicative, and even the perfect, are used to express a condition without 'si;' and 'emerserit' may be the second future of the indicative.

per me licuerit,] 'So long as I allowed it;' that is, 'I was the hindrance to its being done any longer.' 'Per me licet;' 'You may do it for me, I won't hinder you.' 'Habeat per me,' c. 12.

majestatis judicio] The acts just mentioned would be sufficient to found a prosecution for 'Majestas' against Verres, who had saved the enemies of the state. The 'Majestas' of the Roman state is its 'integrity;' and the 'Majestas Populi Romani' is the whole of that which constituted the Roman state. To impair (minuere) this 'Majestas' was an offence; and it might be impaired by any act which directly tended to damage the state, as such. The old name for any act which was directly injurious to the state was 'Perduellio,' and the offender was called 'Perduellis.' Trials for 'Perduellio' took place even in the later times of the Republic, as in the case of C. Popilius Laenas, B.C. 107, and of M. Junius Silanus, consul B.C. 109. By the words 'apud Populum Romanum,' which follow in this chapter, Cicero threatens Verres with a prosecution before the Roman people, for putting to death a Roman citizen; and here the guilt of Verres would be decided by the 'suffragia Populi Romani.' Cicero promises to bring him before the 'Populus Romanus,' in his capacity of aedile, when he should have entered on his office; and the charge would be that of 'Perduellio.'—Cicero here speaks of a 'Majestatis judicium' as a distinct thing from 'Perduellio;' at least, distinct in the form of procedure. Though the notion of 'Majestas minuta' was involved in that of 'Perduellio,' special 'leges' had defined 'Majestas' more particularly, and made it a Quaestio. The first was a Lex Apuleia (B.C. 102 or 100), which was followed by a Lex Cornelia, and this by a Lex Julia, which Lex Julia continued to be the fundamental Lex on this subject under the empire (Dig. 48, tit. 4).—The subject of 'Perduellio' and 'Majestas' is discussed with great minuteness by Rein, Das Criminalrecht der Römer.

De jure . . judicium,] 'For the Roman people think that the jurisdiction in matters

enim libertatis et civitatis suum putat esse judicium, et recte putat. Confringat iste sane vi sua consilia senatoria, quaestiones omnium perrumpat, evolet ex vestra severitate; mihi credite, arctioribus apud populum Romanum laqueis tenebitur. Credet iis equitibus Romanis populus Romanus, qui ad vos antea producti testes ipsis inspectantibus ab isto civem Romanum qui cognitores homines honestos daret sublatum esse in crucem dixerunt. Credent omnes v et xxx tribus homini gravissimo atque ornatissimo M. Annio, qui se praesente civem Romanum securi percussum esse dixit. Audietur a populo Romano vir primarius, eques Romanus, L. Flavius, qui suum familiarem Herennium, negotiatorem ex Africa, quum [cum] Syracusis amplius centum cives Romani cognoscerent lacrimantesque defenderent, pro testimonio dixit securi esse percussum. Probabit fidem et auctoritatem et religionem suam L. Suetius, homo omnibus ornamentis praeditus, qui juratus apud vos dixit multos cives Romanos in lautumiis istius imperio crudelissime per vim morte esse multatos. Hanc ego causam quum agam beneficio populi Romani de loco superiore, non vereor ne aut istum vis ulla ex populi Romani suffragiis eripere, aut a me ullum munus aedilitatis amplius aut gratius populo Romano esse possit.

VI. Quapropter omnes in hoc judicio conentur omnia: nihil est jam quod in hac causa peccare quisquam, judices, nisi vestro periculo possit. Mea quidem ratio quum in praeteritis rebus est cognita, tum

affecting liberty and citizenship belongs to them' (suum). 'Suum' is the predicate, as its position shows. 'Jus libertatis et civitatis' is 'the law which relates to liberty and citizenship.'

recte putat.] Zumpt has 'ratione putat' from G1. Both are good Latin, and it is merely a question of probability, which is decided in favour of 'recte' by the MSS.

quum [cum]] 'Eum,' says Halm, is not in the 'boni libri,' and Bake conjectures that we should read 'quem' in place of 'quum cum.'

amplius centum] This is one of the adverbs which is often used without 'quam' after it, and the case is not affected by 'amplius.' 'Non amplius' is used the same way. See Caesar, B. G. i. 38. 41; ii. 16. 'Plus' and 'minus' are used the same way. 'Cognoscerent' means 'were witnesses to his character,' &c. Lib. 5. c. 65, 'cognoscerent.'

lautumiis] These were the extensive stone-quarries of Syracuse, which Thucydides (vii. 86) calls λιθοτομίαι. The Athenians, who were taken prisoners in the Sicilian expedition, were placed in these quarries, where they endured dreadful sufferings. The stone for the construction of Syracuse was taken from these quarries.

beneficio populi Romani] 'By the favour or grant of the Roman people,' who conferred the 'honores' by their votes, and were said to confer a 'beneficium.' Cicero says, Act. ii. Lib. 4. c. 11, speaking of the senatorial rank, "populo Romano cujus beneficio nos in hunc ordinem venimus." See De Imp. Cn. Pompeii, c. 19; Pro Murena, c. 1; In Vatin. c. 5; Sallust, Jug. 31. The word had other significations among the Romans, as that of some special grant or favour. The history of it may be traced from the republican, through the imperial period, and into the middle ages, when it signified a fief, and also, as now, an ecclesiastical preferment (*Beneficium*, Dict. of Antiqs.). Cicero declares what he will do when he enters on his office of aedile, when he will address the people from the Rostra (de loco superiore).

in reliquis explorata atque provisa est. Ego meum studium in rem publicam jam illo tempore ostendi, quum longo intervallo veterem consuetudinem rettuli, et rogatu sociorum atque amicorum populi Romani, meorum autem necessariorum, nomen hominis audacissimi detuli. Quod meum factum lectissimi viri atque ornatissimi, quo in numero e vobis complures fuere, ita probaverunt ut ei, qui istius quaestor fuisset et ab isto laesus inimicitias justas persequeretur, non modo deferendi nominis sed ne subscribendi quidem, quum id postularet, facerent potestatem. In Siciliam sum inquirendi causa profectus, quo in negotio industriam meam celeritas reditionis, diligentiam multitudo literarum et testium declaravit; pudorem vero ac religionem, quod, quum venissem senator ad socios populi Romani, qui in ea provincia quaestor fuissem, ad hospites meos ac necessarios causae communis defensor deverti potius quam ad eos qui a me auxilium petivissent. Nemini meus adventus labori aut sumptui neque publice neque privatim fuit. Vim in inquirendo tantam habui quantam mihi lex dabat, non quantam habere poteram istorum studio quos iste vexarat. Romam ut ex Sicilia redii, quum

6. *meorum autem*] This passage shows the sense of 'autem,' which is not that of direct opposition, but of addition: it expresses something further or more, and it never stands first in a sentence. See Cic. De Am. c. 8, 'Quis est qui,' &c., followed by 'Quis autem est qui.'

quo in numero] He alludes to the question that was settled by the Divinatio, when the 'consilium,' or 'judices,' determined that Cicero should be the accuser. Some of the present 'consilium' were the same persons, and some were not. The 'consilium' which was formed for the decision on the Divinatio may have been the same which was formed for the trial, but if so, it was changed to some extent by the 'rejectio' or challenges. Zumpt has 'quo e numero,' the reading of G12 r λ.

inimicitias justas] Asconius asks if 'justas' means 'magnas,' and he refers to the use of 'injusto' in Virgil, Georg. iii. 347. The answer is that it does not mean 'magnas;' it means 'well founded, sufficient.' 'Justas' might be taken ironically here; or, if not, Cicero does not scruple now to say that Verres had wronged his 'quaestor,' though he denied it in the Divinatio; and thus he adds one more to the long list of the offences of Verres.

reditionis,] Caesar, B. G. i. 5, has 'domum reditionis spe sublata.'

pudorem . . ac religionem,] 'Pudorem' may be translated 'his modesty,' or 'his absence of all assumption,' in not claiming the public hospitality, to which he was entitled as a senator; and this, though he came on so important business. Here we learn that Cicero was now a senator, which is evidence, if any were wanted, that he acquired a seat in the senate after being 'quaestor.' But how is 'religio' to be understood? for the word must have a distinct meaning, and we must interpret it by reference to the general sense of the word, which implies a reference to divine powers, or to the gods. The duty which Cicero had undertaken was one that he was bound to discharge faithfully, both in the judgment of men, and in the judgment of the gods, to whom he was responsible. His sense of duty towards the gods prevented him from burdening an oppressed and pillaged people with any expense. He alleges it as a proof of his modesty and his religious (in the meaning already explained) sense of his duty, that he put neither communities, nor individual Sicilians, to any cost on his account. A senator, when he travelled not on public business, might still have a kind of nominal commission, called a 'legatio libera,' by virtue of which he was received at the public cost of the province, or of the towns, which he visited. Comp. Act. ii. Lib. 4. c. 11.

istorum studio] The MSS. have 'istorum,' which Zumpt alters to 'illorum,' and

iste atque istius amici, homines lauti et urbani, sermones hujuscemodi dissipassent quo animos testium retardarent, me magna pecunia a vera accusatione esse deductum, tametsi probabatur nemini, quod et ex Sicilia testes erant ii qui quaestorem me in provincia cognoverant, et hinc homines maxime illustres qui, ut ipsi noti sunt, sic nostrum unumquemque optime norunt; tamen usque eo timui ne quis de mea fide atque integritate dubitaret, donec ad rejiciendos judices venimus.

VII. Sciebam in rejiciendis judicibus nonnullos memoria nostra pactionis suspicionem non vitasse, quum in ipsa accusatione eorum industria ac diligentia probaretur. Ita rejeci judices ut hoc constet, post hunc statum rei publicae quo nunc utimur simili splendore et dignitate consilium nullum fuisse. Quam iste laudem communem ait sibi esse mecum, qui quum P. Galbam judicem rejecisset, M. Lucretium retinuit; et, quum ejus patronus ex eo quaereret, cur suos familiarissimos, Sex. Peducaeum, Q. Considium, Q. Junium rejici passus esset, respondit quod eos in judicando nimium sui juris sententiaeque cognosceret. Itaque judicibus rejectis sperabam jam onus meum vobiscum esse commune; putabam non solum notis sed etiam ignotis probatam meam fidem esse et diligentiam. Quod

Iordan follows him. Zumpt says, "nam si Verres *iste*, non possunt illi, qui ei opponuntur, et ipsi *isti* vocari." But why not?

lauti et urbani,] It might be supposed that these words were spoken ironically; but that supposition is not necessary. 'Lautus,' a form of 'lavatus,' 'well washed' or 'clean,' had numerous derived significations, the history of which it is not easy to trace, and even in modern languages, in like cases, it is often a matter of difficulty. The sense here is perhaps 'sharp' or 'clever,' as in the passage of Caecilius quoted by Cicero, De Am. c. 26, 'emunxeris lautissime.' In Act. ii. Lib. 1. c. 25, there is 'parum laute,' which the context explains. 'Urbanus' is explained by Klotz in this passage to signify one who possesses the cunning and sharpness which are supposed to characterize towns' people as opposed to country folks; and he refers to Quintilian, Inst. Or. vi. 3, § 105, for a definition of 'urbanus,' as then understood. Zumpt refers to a passage in Cicero's letters (Ad Fam. iii. 8): "te hominem non solum sapientem, verum etiam, ut nunc loquimur, urbanum." See Heindorf, Horat. 1 Sat. iv. 90; and Pro Sestio, c. 54, note on 'favor.'

7. *post hunc statum &c.*] Since Sulla's changes, ten years before. The 'rejectio' of the 'judices' was the test of Cicero's integrity in the prosecution, for he made it apparent that he wished to have an honest 'consilium.' When Cicero says that Verres claimed credit too, he means, of course, to deny his claim; for P. Galba, whom he rejected, was an honest man, and Lucretius, whom he kept, was not. Asconius tells us, whether it is a guess, or whether he had authority for it, that Lucretius was afterwards rejected by Cicero, for the accused had the first challenge. The reason which Asconius gives for affirming that Lucretius was rejected by Cicero is sufficient, for Cicero could not speak disparagingly of any 'judex' who was retained; and, indeed, he eulogizes the whole 'consilium.' The reason which Verres is alleged to have given for allowing the rejection of the other three, which means, as Asconius says, rejecting them himself,—that they were men too independent (sui juris), is another sarcastic refutation of the claim of Verres.

cognosceret.] 'cognosset' Lg 29, Iordan. 'cognoscet' s. 'cognosceret' ctt. "Saepissime hae formae hoc modo a librariis commutantur" (Iordan).

notis sed etiam ignotis] See Pro Plancio, c. 17. "ignotis te judicibus uti malle quam notis judicavisti."

me non fefellit. Nam comitiis meis, quum iste infinita largitione contra me uteretur, populus Romanus judicavit istius pecuniam, quae apud me contra fidem meam nihil potuisset, apud se contra honorem meum nihil posse debere. Quo quidem die primum, judices, citati in hunc reum consedistis, quis tam inimicus huic ordini fuit, quis tam novarum rerum, judiciorum, judicumque cupidus qui non conspectu consessuque vestro commoveretur? Quum in eo vestra dignitas mihi fructum diligentiae referret, id sum assecutus ut una hora qua coepi dicere reo audaci, pecunioso, profuso, perdito, spem judicii corrumpendi praeciderem; ut primo die testium tanto numero citato populus Romanus judicaret isto absoluto rem publicam stare non posse; ut alter dies amicis istius ac defensoribus non modo spem victoriae sed etiam voluntatem defensionis auferret; ut tertius dies sic hominem prosterneret ut morbo simulato non quid responderet sed quemadmodum non responderet deliberaret; deinde reliquis diebus, his criminibus, his testibus et urbanis et provincialibus sic obrutus atque oppressus est ut his ludorum diebus interpositis nemo istum comperendinatum sed condemnatum judicaret.

VIII. Quapropter ego quod ad me attinet, judices, vici: non enim spolia C. Verris sed existimationem populi Romani concupivi. Meum fuit cum causa accedere ad accusandum: quae causa fuit honestior quam a tam illustri provincia defensorem constitui et deligi? rei publicae consulere: quid [tandem] rei publicae honestius quam in tanta invidia judiciorum adducere hominem cujus damnatione totus ordo cum populo Romano et in laude et in gratia posset esse? ostendere ac persuadere hominem nocentem adductum esse: quis est in populo Romano qui hoc non ex priore actione abstulerit,

in hunc reum consedistis,] This may be compared with 'exirent in eum reum' Act. i. c. 13, and 'in eum judices essent' Lib. 2. c. 73.

conspectu] 'aspectu' G12; Lg 29: 'conspectu' dtt. See Pro Plancio, c. 1, 'conspectus et consessus.' Iordan truly says "solet autem Cicero verba ab iisdem syllabis incipientia componere," and yet he writes 'aspectu.'

una hora . . . dicere] 'within one hour after I began to speak.' Comp. Act. ii. Lib. 2. c. 15, 'diebus xxx . . . quibus,' and Caesar, B. G. iii. 23, iv. 18.

isto absoluto] The correction of Zumpt. The MSS. have 'ipso.' The two words are often confounded in the MSS. 'Ipso,' Orell.

8. *cum causa*] 'Cui rei contrarium est *sine causa*,' Asconius. 'Sine causa' occurs at the end of this chapter. Cicero says (De Or. ii. 60), "quod nos cum causa dicimus, illi sine causa." See Act. ii. 4. c. 51, note.

In place of 'justior,' Orelli's reading, Zumpt and Iordan have 'honestior.'

'Quid tandem rei publicae,' Zumpt. 'Quid jam' &c., Orelli.—'quid tam e republica quam,' Madvig's correction, Iordan. All the MSS. retain 'honestius.' The error lies in the word between 'quid' and 'rei.'

ex priore actione abstulerit,] 'has learned or understood,' an expression of ordinary life, as Zumpt remarks. See examples in Forcellini.

omnium ante damnatorum scelera, furta, flagitia, si unum in locum conferantur, vix cum hujus parva parte aequari conferrique posse? Vos quod ad vestram famam, existimationem, salutemque communem pertinet, judices, prospicite atque consulite. Splendor vester facit ut peccare sine summo rei publicae detrimento ac periculo non possitis. Non enim potest sperare populus Romanus esse alios in senatu qui recte possint judicare, vos si non potueritis. Necesse est, quum de toto ordine desperarit, aliud genus hominum atque aliam rationem judiciorum requirat. Hoc si vobis ideo levius videtur quod putatis onus esse grave et incommodum judicare, intelligere debetis primum interesse, utrum id onus vosmet ipsi rejeceritis, an, quod probare populo Romano fidem vestram et religionem non potueritis, eo vobis judicandi potestas erepta sit; deinde etiam illud cogitare, quanto periculo venturi simus ad eos judices quos propter odium nostri populus Romanus de nobis voluerit judicare. Verum vobis dicam id quod intellexi, judices: homines scitote esse quosdam, quos tantum odium nostri ordinis teneat ut hoc palam jam dictitent, se istum quem sciant esse hominem improbissimum hoc uno nomine absolvi velle, ut ab senatu judicia per ignominiam turpitudinemque auferantur. Haec me pluribus verbis, judices, vobiscum agere coëgit non timor meus de vestra fide, sed spes illorum nova, quae quum Verrem a porta subito ad judicium retraxisset, nonnulli suspicati sunt non sine causa illius consilium tam repente esse mutatum.

IX. Nunc ne novo querimoniae genere uti possit Hortensius et ea dicere, opprimi reum de quo nihil dicat accusator; nihil esse tam periculosum fortunis innocentium quam tacere adversarios; et

nostri . . nobis] 'vestri—vobis,' Orelli.

Haec me] 'Haec me res,' the reading of all the known MSS. 'Delevit *res* Naugerius in Aldina.' According to the text 'haec' is the accusative. According to that of Klotz 'haec res' refers to what was said in the preceding sentence; but, 'haec res' not being sufficiently forcible, Cicero explains himself by declaring that it is not any fear that they will not discharge their duty, but the 'spes illorum nova,' that is, 'the thing,' 'haec res.' This reading and exposition of Klotz, I reject without any hesitation.

a porta subito] Cicero gives an air of reality to the speech by speaking of Verres as if he had set out to leave Rome, and was induced to return to wait the result of his trial.

9. *Nunc ne &c.*] Cicero still gives the colour of reality to his speech, by declaring that he will now make a formal continuous speech, which he did not do in the Actio Prima. And he says, in a sarcastic manner, (hic tu fortasse eris diligens) to Hortensius, 'you will perhaps look sharply to see that I take up all the time that the "lex" allows me;' whereas a man can refuse to avail himself of an advantage; he may forego it, if he pleases.—In place of 'non quoniam hoc sit necesse,' the reading of the MSS., Klotz and Iordan have 'non quo jam,' &c., which is a conjecture of Madvig. 'Abusus ero' means 'consumed,' for 'abuti' means 'to use a thing which is consumed in the use.' Comp. Cic. Top. 3, where the word 'abusus' is opposed to 'usus,' and Ulpian, Dig. 7. 5. 5.

ne aliter quam ego velim meum laudet ingenium, quum dicat me, si multa dixissem, sublevaturum fuisse eum quem contra dicerem; quia non dixerim, perdidisse—morem illi geram, utar oratione perpetua; non quoniam hoc sit necesse, verum ut experiar utrum ille ferat molestius me tunc tacuisse an nunc dicere. Hic tu fortasse eris diligens ne quam ego horam de meis legitimis horis remittam; nisi omni tempore quod mihi lege concessum est abusus ero, querere, deum atque hominum fidem implorabis, circumveniri C. Verrem quod accusator nolit tamdiu quamdiu liceat dicere. Quod mihi lex mea causa det, eo mihi non uti non licebit? Nam accusandi mihi tempus mea causa datum est, ut possem oratione mea crimina causamque explicare: hoc si non utor, non tibi injuriam facio, sed de meo jure aliquid et commodo detraho.—Causam enim, inquit, cognosci oportet.—Ea re quidem quod aliter condemnari reus, quamvis sit nocens, non potest. Id igitur tu moleste tulisti, a me aliquid factum esse quo minus iste condemnari posset? Nam causa cognita multi possunt absolvi: incognita quidem condemnari nemo potest.—Adimo enim comperendinatum.—Quod habet lex in se

deum atque hominum fidem] See Divin. c. 3.

det,] 'dedit' Asconius, Iordan. Either 'dedit' or 'det' is Latin. I prefer the reading of all the MSS., and I can see no probability that if Cicero wrote 'dedit,' all the MSS. should have 'det.'

Causam enim, &c. . . . Adimo enim &c.] 'Enim' has a reference to what has been said, 'hoc si non utor,' &c. It is a supposed answer: 'Yes, but it is necessary for the case to be investigated.' To which supposed answer, Cicero rejoins: 'Admitted, so far as this, that a guilty man cannot be condemned without the case being investigated; but you surely will not make it a ground of complaint, that I have done any thing, the tendency of which is to prevent your client's condemnation.' The word 'enim' certainly does not mean 'for.' It is a word of reference, that is, it respects something that has gone before; but it is not strictly a word of inference. (Comp. Pro Q. Rosc. Am. c. 9; Pro Caecina, c. 7; Pro Rabirio Post. c. 14; Caesar, B. G. v. 7, 'Ille enim' &c.) Cicero often begins his sentences with 'Etenim,' the meaning of which is much nearer 'and indeed,' 'in truth,' than 'for.' The words 'Adimo enim comperendinatum' is another supposed objection: 'You say that I prevent the Comperendinatio;' to which Cicero replies: 'the very thing in the Lex that is most burdensome, that the cause should be heard twice, the very rule which was established,' &c. There is no difficulty in the second 'quod aut,' which Orelli placed in brackets, and Ernesti, who mistook the whole passage, changed into 'id aut.' Iordan also says 'Locus vix sanus.' I think it is quite sound.

comperendinatum.] The adjourning of a trial to the third day; the deferring of the verdict; hence also the arguing of the cause after it was thus adjourned. The word is compounded of 'con' and 'perendinus,' for there are the adjective 'perendinus' and the form 'perendie,' like 'pridie,' 'postridie.' The word 'perendie' means the day after the morrow, as appears from Cicero to Atticus, xii. 44; and from a passage in the oration Pro Murena, c. 12, "tot homines, tam ingeniosos per tot annos statuere non potuisse utrum diem tertium an perendinum dici oporteret." See Gellius, x. 24. When 'dies tertius' is equivalent to 'dies perendinus,' the first day and the last are included in the reckoning, and there is one day in the middle. The etymology of 'perendie' is unknown. Asconius has a note on what follows, the matter of which is apparently only derived from his notion of the meaning of the text. He says that when the trial was adjourned, the accused spoke first, after having already replied in the previous proceedings, and the prosecutor then spoke

molestissimum, bis ut causa dicatur, quod aut mea causa potius est constitutum quam tua, aut nihilo tua potius quam mea. Nam si bis dicere est commodum, certe utriusque commune est; si eum qui posterius dixit opus est redargui, accusatoris causa ut bis ageretur constitutum est. Verum, ut opinor, Glaucia primus tulit ut comperendinaretur reus; antea vel judicari primo poterat vel amplius pronuntiari. Utram igitur putas legem meliorem? opinor illam veterem, qua vel cito absolvi vel tarde condemnari licebat. Ego tibi illam Aciliam legem restituo, qua lege multi semel accusati, semel dicta causa, semel auditis testibus, condemnati sunt, nequaquam tam manifestis neque tantis criminibus quantis tu convinceris. Puta te non hac tam atroci sed illa lege mitissima causam dicere. Accusabo; respondebis: testibus editis, ita mittam in consilium

again, so that the two speeches for the defence came between the two speeches for the prosecution. But this is absurd. Cicero argues that the 'comperendinatio' was rather intended for the advantage of the prosecutor, for he would have the opportunity of replying to his adversary's defence. 'Si eum qui posterius dixit' is evidently the speaker for the defence, for the speech for the prosecution was delivered first, and, if there was no 'comperendinatio,' the matter was ready for the decision of the 'consilium,' when the prosecutor had spoken first and the speaker for the defence had replied. If, argues Cicero, the object or purpose (opus) is for the second speaker to be replied to, then it is clear that the 'secunda actio' (ut bis ageretur) was intended for the benefit of the prosecutor. It could not be intended for the benefit of the accused; for, if the prosecutor brought forward no new matter in his second speech, the defendant would gain less by a second reply, than the prosecutor would by enforcing his original arguments and answering the answer of his adversary. And, if he did bring forward new matter, it must be something that he had neglected to bring forward before, or something that he had in the mean time discovered; in neither of which cases would the second 'actio' be for the benefit of the accused.

Glaucia] C. Servilius Glaucia who proposed (tulit) the 'lex' that bears his name. (Ex. i. ii.) Zumpt agrees with Ernesti in making the Acilia prior to the Servilia Lex. When Cicero says 'ut opinor,' he does not mean to express a doubt. He speaks as a man who does not concern himself very particularly about the history of changes in law: he takes it for granted that it is so. Before the Lex Servilia the 'judices' either gave their votes at once, or declared an 'ampliatio,' an adjournment to another day, which might be a more distant day than the 'dies perendinus.' The 'ampliatio' depended on the choice of the 'judices.' The 'comperendinatio' was fixed by this 'lex.' The old law, says Cicero, permitted the 'judices' either to acquit at once, or to defer their decision for some time. He professes to restore in effect the Lex Acilia, which was enacted on the proposal of Acilius Glabrio, the father of the 'praetor' who presided at this trial; and this 'lex' allowed no 'comperendinatio' or 'ampliatio.' But he says to Hortensius: imagine the proceedings to be not according to this severe law, but according to that old and very lenient law. Suppose this to be the case; Cicero will then make his charge, Hortensius will answer; and, after the witnesses are produced, Cicero will bring the 'judices' to their vote; for that is 'mittere in consilium:' and he says that even if the 'lex' were to allow an 'ampliatio,' they would be ashamed to avail themselves of it. Verres was prosecuted under the Lex Cornelia, which we must suppose to have contained the provisions of the Servilia, except as to the class from which the 'judices' were to be chosen. Orelli, Klotz, and Iordan have 'legem molliorem.' 'Moliorem' Lg. 29; 'meliorem' G 1 2, Zumpt. Iordan does not say what the other MSS. have.

ut, etiamsi lex ampliandi faciat potestatem, tamen isti turpe sibi existiment non primo judicare.

X. Verum si causam cognosci opus est, parumne cognita est? Dissimulamus, Hortensi, quod saepe experti in dicendo sumus. Quis nos magno opere attendit unquam in hoc quidem genere causarum ubi aliquid ereptum aut ablatum a quopiam dicitur? nonne aut in tabulis aut in testibus omnis exspectatio judicum est? Dixi prima actione me planum esse facturum C. Verrem HS quadringenties contra leges abstulisse. Quid hoc planius egissem, si ita narrassem? Dio quidam fuit Halesinus, qui, quum ejus filio praetore Sacerdote hereditas a propinquo permagna venisset, nihil habuit tum neque negotii neque controversiae. Verres simulac tetigit provinciam, statim Messana literas dedit, Dionem evocavit, calumniatores ex sinu suo apposuit qui illam hereditatem Veneri Erycinae commissam esse dicerent: hac de re ostendit seipsum cogniturum. Possum deinceps totam rem explicare, deinde ad extremum id quod accidit dicere, Dionem HS decies centena millia numerasse ut causam certissimam obtineret; praeterea greges equarum ejus

isti] Halm proposes 'ipsi.'

10. *nos . . . attendit*] 'pays much attention to what we say.' See Act. ii. 3. c. 5.

a quopiam] 'from any person,' as Zumpt suggests, for he says that Cicero uses the ablative with a preposition in this sense; and he refers to c. 4, 'a quaestoribus urbanis,' &c.; c. 8, 'ab senatu,' &c.; and to other passages.

contra leges] 'contra legem' Orelli; but there is better authority for 'leges.' Zumpt refers to Act. i. c. 18; and to c. 4 of this oration, 'contra leges,' &c. As to the sum 'HS quadringenties,' see Excursus I. Repetundae.

Messana literas dedit,] 'addressed letters from Messana.' 'Dare literas' is the common expression for sending a letter, that is, giving it 'tabellario,' to the letter-carrier. The place from which the letter is sent is usually put in the ablative; but sometimes in the genitive, if the texts are right. Cic. Ad Q. Fr. ii. 15. The MSS. reading 'Messanam' is obviously a mistake.

calumniatores] A 'calumniator,' or 'calumniosus,' is one who knowingly and purposely, and with fraudulent design, schemes to trouble another (Paulus, Rec. Sent. i. 5. 1. Comp. Marcianus, Dig. 48. 16. 1, and Gaius, iv. 178). The word 'calumnia' contains the root 'calv' or 'calu,' which appears in the Fragments of the Twelve Tables, and shows the original meaning of the word: 'si calvitur pedemve struit' (Dirksen, *Uebersicht, &c., der Zwölf-Tafel-Fragmente*, p. 144; and Gaius, Dig. 50. 16. 233). As to 'calumnia,' compare Cic. Ad Q. Fr. i. 1. c. 9, "illam acerbissimam ministram praetorum avaritiae calumniam;" Pro S. Rosc. Am. c. 19, 20; Pro Caecina, c. 21; De Domo, c. 14.

hereditatem . . . commissam] This 'hereditas,' or property of a deceased person, was, it was alleged, to be forfeited, and came to the temple of Venus at Eryx. The alleged cause of forfeiture might be the non-performance of a condition. This use of 'commissus' is not uncommon in Cicero (Act. ii. Lib. 2. c. 14; and Lib. 3. c. 12; Ad Fam. xiii. 56), and also in the law writers (Dig. 39, tit. 4).

greges equarum] "*greges equorum* Lg 42. Debebat saltem Zumptius et qui eum secuti sunt, cum hanc lectionem negligerent, vulgatam *equarum* argumentis tueri" (Hahn), who refers to ii. 2. c. 6. If Zumpt had taken the reading 'equorum,' there would have been some occasion to defend it by arguments. What would be the use of 'greges equorum?' They were mares for breeding.

istum abigendos curasse, argenti vestisque stragulae quod fuerit curasse auferendum. Haec neque quum ego dicerem, neque quum tu negares, magni momenti nostra esset oratio. Quo tempore igitur aures judex erigeret animumque attenderet? Quum Dio ipse prodiret, quum ceteri, qui tum in Sicilia negotiis Dionis interfuissent; quum per eos ipsos dies per quos causam Dio diceret reperiretur pecunias sumpsisse mutuas, nomina sua exegisse, praedia vendidisse; quum tabulae virorum bonorum proferrentur; quum, qui pecuniam Dioni dederunt, dicerent se jam tum audisse eos nummos sumi ut Verri darentur; quum amici, hospites, patroni Dionis, homines honestissimi, haec eadem se audisse dicerent. Opinor, quum haec fierent, tum vos audiretis, sicut audistis; tum causa agi vere videretur. Sic a me sunt acta omnia priore actione ut in criminibus omnibus nullum esset, in quo quisquam vestrum perpetuam accusationem requireret. Nego esse quidquam a testibus dictum quod aut vestrum cuipiam esset obscurum, aut cujusquam oratoris eloquentiam quaereret.

XI. Etenim sic me ipsum egisse memoria tenetis ut in testibus interrogandis omnia crimina proponerem et explicarem, ut, quum

pecunias sumpsisse mutuas,] 'to have borrowed money.' 'Pecuniae mutuae' is money borrowed; and 'mutuum' is the general name for that Roman form of contract, by which things which were consumed in the use were borrowed, as money, wine, oil, and the like. In the case of a 'mutuum,' the thing borrowed became the property of the borrower, and he had only to return things of the same kind and value. (Gaius, iii. 90.)—'nomina sua exegisse:' 'had got in his debts' (see also c. 36). 'Nomen' is the entry in a book, which is one of the kinds of evidence of a debt. Its technical meaning is explained hereafter. Cicero uses 'exigere' in De Am. c. 9, in a sense derived from this notion of getting in a debt.—'praedia vendidisse:' 'sold his estates in land.' 'Praedium' is either 'urbanum' or 'rusticum.' A building on a 'praedium urbanum' is 'aedes:' on a 'praedium rusticum,' it is 'villa' (Dig. 50. 16. 27. 115. 211).

dicerent se jam tum audisse] "Apud antiquos et de auditione testimonium dicebatur," Ascon.: a piece of information extracted from the text. We may certainly infer that this hearsay evidence was received. Yet we may assume that the Romans had sense enough to give to such evidence its proper value. The words 'apud antiquos,' perhaps, indicate that the author of the above note lived a long time after Cicero, and later than the real Asconius, who appears to have died in the latter part of the first century, A.D.

quum haec fierent, &c.] Klotz changes 'tum vos audiretis' into 'cum vos audiretis,' which is the reading of G2, and he makes 'tum causa agi vere videretur' the second member of the sentence. He says there is no sense in the common reading.

cuipiam] "'cuiquam' conj. Heindorf ad N. D. p. 290. Bake ad Legg. p. 668 [Sic utique flagitat jam ratio rhetorica]" (Jordan). I suppose he means that the 'ratio rhetorica' requires 'quidquam . . . cuiquam,' with an emphasis on both words.

11. *omnia crimina*] 'all the charges.' Comp. Divin. c. 12, 'criminibus et oratione.' But 'crimen' was also used to signify both the charge, or accusation, and the matter, which was the foundation of the 'crimen.' There is a general distinction between 'crimen' and 'delictum;' for 'crimen' is properly applied to such matters as were the subject of 'judicia publica.' This passage seems to throw some light on the passage in Act. i. c. 18. He here uses the expression 'in testibus interrogandis' to express the whole of that part of the proceeding which related to the examination of witnesses;

rem totam in medio posuissem, tum denique testem interrogarem. Itaque non modo vos quibus est judicandum nostra crimina tenetis, sed etiam populus Romanus totam accusationem causamque cognovit. Tametsi ita de meo facto loquor, quasi ego illud mea voluntate potius quam vestra injuria adductus fecerim. Interposuistis accusatorem, qui, quum ego mihi c et x dies solos in Siciliam postulassem, c et VIII sibi in Achaiam postularet. Menses mihi tres quum eripuissetis ad agendum maxime appositos, reliquum omne tempus hujus anni me vobis remissurum putastis, ut, quum horis nostris nos essemus usi, tu binis ludis interpositis quadragesimo post die responderes, deinde ita tempus duceretur ut a M' Glabrione praetore et a magna parte horum judicum ad praetorem alium judicesque alios veniremus. Hoc si ego non vidissem, si me non omnes noti ignotique monuissent id agi, id cogitari, in eo laborari ut res in illud tempus rejiceretur, credo, si meis horis in accusando uti voluissem, vererer ne mihi crimina non suppeterent, ne oratio deesset, ne vox viresque deficerent, ne, quem nemo prima actione defendere ausus esset, eum ego bis accusare non possem. Ego meum consilium quum judicibus, tum populo Romano probavi; nemo est qui alia ratione istorum injuriae atque impudentiae potuisse obsisti arbitretur. Etenim qua stultitia fuissem, si, quam diem, qui istum eripiendum redemerunt, in cautione viderunt, quum ita caverent, "si post Kalendas Jan. in consilium iretur," in

and that part included the statement of the charges, and the setting forth of them, which was followed by the examination of the witnesses. So that he appears to call this part of the proceedings, the 'examination of the witnesses;' which included both the statement of the facts to be proved, and the real examination of the witnesses.

in medio posuissem,] Orelli has 'proposuissem,' the reading of the dtt. Zumpt remarks, that 'in medio proponere' is not used in any other passage of Cicero.

binis ludis &c.] See Introduction to the Verrine orations.

in eo laborari] Zumpt has 'elaborari.' He says "vulgo *laborari*, id esset in angustiis versari, quod nullum verum est." 'Id elaborari,' Klotz, which is the reading of Lg. 42; 'in eo elaborari' G3 ; and Iordan; 'in eo laborari' dtt, which are here the better, as they sometimes are. Either 'id' or 'in eo laborari' is the true reading.

si, quam diem, &c.] 'for what a fool I should have been, if, when the men who undertook to save Verres by corrupting the Judices contemplated a particular time in fixing the terms of their undertaking, the terms being to this effect, "provided the Judices should not give their verdict until after the first of January"—what a fool I should have been, to stumble on that very time, when it was in my power to avoid it.' What he says is plain enough; but it is not so easy to express it. As to 'quam diem,' see Act. i. c. 2.

'Cavere,' as Forcellini observes, is a forensic word. 'Cavere alicui' is said of a 'jurisconsultus,' whose advice is given for the protection of his client (Pro Caecina, c. 27). 'Cavere sibi' is to get security, that is, legal security of some kind for oneself. 'Cavere ab aliquo' is to get security from a person (Act. ii. Lib. 2. c. 23), 'ab sese cavent.' 'Cavere' is also used by the law writers with a dative and accusative, to express the giving to a person security to some amount, as in Dig. 29. 2. 88, "Singuli heredes Sempronio caverunt summam, qua quisque condemnatus erat." To whom then does 'caverent' apply in this

eam diem ego, quum potuissem vitare, incidissem? Nunc mihi temporis ejus quod mihi ad dicendum datur, quoniam in animo est causam omnem exponere, habenda ratio est diligenter.

XII. Itaque primum illum actum istius vitae turpissimum et flagitiosissimum praetermittam. Nihil a me de pueritiae suae flagitiis [peccatisque] audiet, nihil ex illa impura adolescentia sua, quae qualis fuerit aut meministis aut ex eo quem sui simillimum produxit recognoscere potestis. Omnia praeteribo quae mihi turpia dictu videbuntur, neque solum quid istum audire, verum etiam quid me deceat dicere considerabo. Vos, quaeso, date hoc et concedite pudori meo, ut aliquam partem de istius impudentia reticere possim. Omne illud tempus, quod fuit antequam iste ad magistratus remque publicam accessit, habeat per me solutum ac liberum. Sileatur de nocturnis ejus bacchationibus ac vigiliis; lenonum, aleatorum, perductorum nulla mentio fiat; damna, dedecora, quae res patris ejus, aetas ipsius pertulit, praetereantur; lucretur indicia veteris infamiae; patiatur ejus vita reliqua me hanc tantam jacturam criminum facere. Quaestor Cn. Papirio consule

passage, and what is its sense? The subject of it is the same as that of 'redemerant,' those who undertook to get Verres off; and 'caverent' implies a 'cautio' for their own benefit, not a 'cautio' as to the sum of money, for the money-terms are not the question here; but a 'cautio' as to time, for the 'redemptio' was 'sub conditione,' provided the affair was postponed till after the first of January. See Act. i. c. 6, note on 'redemptio.'

12. [*peccatisque*]] Zumpt omits. Also G 3 1 and Iordan.

quem . . . produxit] As Zumpt remarks, Verres produced his son at the trial, or is here supposed to have brought him into court; and as to this Roman fashion, he refers to Quintilian, Inst. Or. xi. c. 3, § 174. The purpose of Cicero's foul abuse of the son is explained by Asconius after his fashion. It has been suggested to me that 'produxit' may mean 'genuit' in this passage. I think it is possible that Cicero purposely used a word which may have two meanings. There is no doubt that it can mean 'in judicium produxit,' and also 'genuit.' "Audientem dicto, mater, produxisti filiam," Plaut. Asin. iii. 1. 40.

reticere] See Divin. c. 18, note on 'remanet.'

lenonum, &c.] See Divin. c. 15. The Lex Julia de Adulteriis made 'lenocinium' a punishable offence; but the 'lex' did not apply to those who got their living by the prostitution of slaves (Rein, Das Criminalrecht der Römer, p. 880). The meaning of 'perductores' may be collected from the context. Comp. Hor. 2 Sat. v. 77.

lucretur indicia &c.] 'let him have the benefit of all the evidence of his old infamy;' that is, let nothing be said of it.

Cn. Papirio consule] Asconius says 'legitur tamen et *consuli*;' which reading Orelli has and Iordan. In favour of 'consule,' Klotz remarks, that after the murder of Cinna, B.C. 84, Cn. Papirius Carbo was sole consul, and that the time of the quaestorship of Verres is thus more distinctly marked. As Carbo was consul for the second time B.C. 84, and this oration was delivered (that is, supposed to be delivered) B.C. 70, Zumpt observes that Cicero, according to the common Roman way of reckoning, should have said fifteen. But the Romans were not consistent as to including both extremes in reckoning. See Savigny, System des Heut. Röm. Rechts, iv. Beylage xi., whose remarks have reference to the use of the ordinal numbers, first, second, and so on; but the remarks are applicable also to the use of the cardinal numbers in some cases. However, it appears that Verres was 'quaestor' to Carbo in B.C. 82 (Introd.).

fuisti abhinc annos quatuordecim: ex ea die ad hanc diem quae fecisti in judicium voco. Hora nulla vacua a furto, scelere, crudelitate, flagitio reperietur. Hi sunt anni consumpti in quaestura, et legatione Asiatica, et praetura urbana, et praetura Siciliensi. Quare haec eadem erit quadripartita distributio totius accusationis meae.

XIII. Quaestor ex senatusconsulto provinciam sortitus es: obtigit tibi consularis, ut cum consule Cn. Carbone esses eamque provinciam obtineres. Erat tum dissensio civium, de qua nihil sum dicturus quid sentire debueris: unum hoc dico, in ejusmodi tempore ac sorte statuere te debuisse utrum malles sentire atque defendere. Carbo graviter ferebat sibi quaestorem obtigisse, hominem singulari luxuria atque inertia; verumtamen ornabat eum beneficiis officiisque omnibus. Ne diutius teneam, pecunia attributa, numerata est: profectus est quaestor in provinciam: venit exspectatus in Galliam ad exercitum consularem cum pecunia. Simulac primum ei occasio visa est, cognoscite hominis principium magistratuum gerendorum et rei publicae administrandae, aversa pecunia publica quaestor consulem, exercitum, sortem, provinciamque deseruit. Video quid egerim: erigit se, sperat sibi auram posse aliquam afflari in hoc crimine voluntatis [assensionisque] eorum quibus Cn. Carbonis mortui nomen odio sit, quibus illam relictionem proditionemque consulis sui gratam sperat fore. Quasi vero id cupiditate defendendae nobilitatis aut studio partium fecerit, ac non apertissime consulem, exercitum, provinciamque compilarit, et propter impudentissimum furtum aufugerit. Est enim obscurum et ejusmodi factum ejus ut possit aliquis suspicari C. Verrem, quod

ex ea die ad hanc diem . . . quadripartita distributio] Three of these four divisions had nothing to do with the case of Verres, who was prosecuted only for his maladministration in his praetorship of Sicily.

13. *dissensio civium,*] The civil war between Sulla and the partizans of Marius. The orator purposely touches lightly on this matter. A little further on he speaks of 'Cn. Carbonis mortui,' but, as Zumpt observes, he was put to death at Lilybaeum by the order of Cn. Pompeius, B.C. 82. (See Ad Fam. ix. 21; and Plutarch, Pomp. c. 10.)

beneficiis] 'beneficiis officiisque' Zumpt, Iordan. 'Officiisque' om. dtt.

attributa,] A word used to express the payment of money out of the 'aerarium' to a 'quaestor' or other person. As to 'aversa,' see Divin. 17, note; and Act. ii. Lib. 3. c. 69, 'frumenti numerum- -aversum.' This use of the word appears in the 'oneris aversi actio,' Dig. 19. 2. 31. The word 'sortem' refers to the mode in which the quaestor became attached to his consul, which involved 'religio.'

[*assensionisque*]] Zumpt has 'dissensionisque.' 'Assensionisque,' which reading has generally been adopted since the time of P. Manutius, rests only on the 'lemma' of Asconius. Zumpt also reads 'afflare,' and contends that 'auram afflari' cannot be said. I do not see how 'dissensionis' can be explained.

Est enim obscurum] To prevent any obscurity, it may be remarked that Cicero is speaking ironically.

ferre novos homines non potuerit, ad nobilitatem, hoc est ad suos, transisse, nihil fecisse propter pecuniam. Videamus rationes quemadmodum rettulerit. Jam ipse ostendet quamobrem Cn. Carbonem reliquerit: jam se ipse indicabit.

XIV. Primum brevitatem cognoscite.—Accepi, inquit, HS vicies ducenta triginta quinque millia quadringentos XVII nummos: dedi stipendio, frumento, legatis, pro quaestore, cohorti praetoriae, HS mille sexcenta triginta quinque millia quadringentos XVII nummos: reliqui Arimini HS sexcenta millia.—Hoc est rationes referre? hoc modo aut ego, aut tu, Hortensi, aut quisquam omnium rettulit? Quid hoc est? quae impudentia? quae audacia? quod exemplum ex tot hominum rationibus relatis hujuscemodi est? Illa tamen HS sexcenta millia, quae ne falso quidem potuit quibus data essent describere, quae se Arimini scribit reliquisse, quae ipsa HS sexcenta millia reliqua facta sunt, neque Carbo attigit neque Sulla vidit neque in aerarium relata sunt. Oppidum sibi elegit Ariminum, quod tum quum iste rationes referebat oppressum direptumque erat: non suspicabatur, id quod nunc sentiet, satis multos ex illa calamitate Ariminensium testes nobis in hanc rem reliquos esse. Recita denuo. P. LENTVLO L. TRIARIO QVAESTORIBVS VRBANIS RES

14. *vicies*] As the reading stands, the sum which Verres returned as expended by him, added to the amount which he said that he left at Ariminum, makes up the whole amount which he had received. From this it appears that 'vicies' is correctly explained to signify 'vicies centena millia.' In c. 10 there is 'HS decies centena millia,' for which 'decies' alone might be, and generally is, used. Horace says, 'decies centena dedisses' (1 Sat. iii. 15, and Heindorf's note).

cohorti praetoriae,] The term 'praetoria' was applied, whether the commander was 'consul' or 'praetor,' for every commander of an army was originally called 'praetor.' 'Cohors praetoria' is rightly explained by Asconius, 'comitibus consularibus,' those who were the commander's or governor's staff, the persons of higher rank immediately about him. The 'comites et adjutores' were the 'praetoria cohors' (Cic. Ad Q. Fr. i. 1. c. 3); and the inferior officers or functionaries were said to be 'quasi ex cohorte praetoris.'—'Pro quaestore,' Asconius' reading, is the right reading: he paid or retained this sum, 'pro officio quaestoris,' in respect of his office. The reading 'pro quaestori' is absurd, for a 'quaestor' would not say that he paid himself. The MSS. are said to have 'pro quaestoribus.' Some editors have been misled apparently by the other dative cases: 'I disbursed for the soldiers' pay, for corn, for or to Legati; on my own account, as Quaestor, I disbursed or retained,' &c.

Ariminum,] Rimini, south of Ravenna. This town, as Asconius says, was given up by P. Tullius Albinovanus, one of the Marian faction, to Sulla's party, B.C. 81, who plundered it; which circumstance, according to Cicero, accounts for Verres selecting Ariminum as the alleged place of deposit.

Recita] This is the word used for a public reading of letters addressed to the senate, and the like. (See Forcellini.)

QVAESTORIBVS VRBANIS] The two Urbani quaestores, who stayed in Rome, and had the management of the 'aerarium.' A lively picture of Cato's activity during his office is drawn by Plutarch (Cato Min. c. 16, &c.) This Lentulus was guilty of embezzlement of money in some capacity (Plutarch, Cicero, c. 17), and he was afterwards executed for his share in the conspiracy of Catilina. L. Triarius afterwards served under L. Lucullus in the Mithridatic war, and was defeated by Mithridates (Plutarch, Pomp. c. 35).

RES RATIONVM &c.] Manutius omits

RATIONVM RELATARVM. Recita. EX SENATVS CONSVLTO. Ut hoc pacto rationem referre liceret, eo Sullanus repente factus est, non ut honos et dignitas nobilitati restitueretur. Quod si illinc inanis profugisses, tamen ista tua fuga nefaria, proditio consulis tui conscelerata judicaretur.—Malus civis, improbus consul, seditiosus homo Cn. Carbo fuit.—Fuerit aliis. Tibi quando esse coepit? Posteaquam tibi pecuniam, rem frumentariam, rationes omnes suas exercitumque commisit. Nam si tibi antea displicuisset, idem fecisses quod anno post M. Piso. Quaestor quum L. Scipioni consuli obtigisset, non attigit pecuniam, non ad exercitum profectus est; quod de re publica sensit, ita sensit ut nec fidem suam nec morem majorum nec necessitudinem sortis laederet. XV. Etenim si haec perturbare omnia ac permiscere volumus, totam vitam periculosam, invidiosam, infestamque reddemus; si nullam religionem sors habebit, nullam societatem conjunctio secundae dubiaeque fortunae, nullam auctoritatem mores atque instituta majorum. Omnium est communis inimicus qui fuit hostis suorum. Nemo unquam sapiens proditori credendum putavit. Ipse Sulla, cui adventus istius gratissimus esse debuit, ab se hominem atque ab exercitu suo removit: Beneventi esse jussit apud eos quos suis partibus amicissimos esse intelligebat, ubi iste summae rei causaeque nocere nihil posset. Ei postea praemia tamen liberaliter tribuit: bona quaedam proscriptorum in agro Beneventano diripienda concessit: habuit honorem ut proditori, non ut amico fidem. Nunc quamvis sint homines qui mortuum Cn. Carbonem oderint, tamen hi debent, non quid illi accidere voluerint,

'res,' and Hotmann proposed to alter 'res' to 'Verris.' 'Res rationum' is the 'matter of the accounts;' a form of expression sometimes used, though such expressions as 'res divina, frumentaria,' &c., are the usual forms. (See Forcellini, Res.)

M. Piso.] He was quaestor (B.C. 83) to the consul L. Cornelius Scipio, whom he left for the party of Sulla. Scipio's troops deserted him through the intrigues of Sulla. Piso was at this time (B.C. 70) proconsul in Spain, and in B.C. 69 he had a triumph.

Quaestor quum] Bake suspects that 'qui' ought to stand before 'Quaestor,' and this is a good suggestion.

15. *invidiosam,*] Codd. 'insidiosam,' the conjecture of Lambinus adopted by Iordan. I do not see why 'invidiosam' should not stand.

nullam religionem sors] See Divin. c. 14.

proscriptorum] The 'proscripti' were those whose names 'proscribebantur,' were put up in public. Plutarch, in his Life of Sulla (c. 31), has drawn a picture of these dreadful times, when the signal for a man's murder, and the seizure of his property, was the appearance of his name in the proscription lists. 'Proscribere' is a word used generally for any public notice which is put up, as an auction, for instance, and Ulpian (Dig. 14. 3. 11) has defined the word.

habuit honorem] 'he rewarded him like a traitor, but he did not trust him as a friend.' Zumpt correctly explains the sense of 'honos,' which here means a fee or pay for service, as in Cic. Ad Fam. xvi. 9. 'Curio misi ut medico honos haberetur.' From this sense of the word came 'honorarium.' (See Ulpian, Dig. 11. 6. 1.)

sed quid ipsis in tali re metuendum sit, cogitare. Commune est hoc malum, communis metus, commune periculum. Nullae sunt occultiores insidiae quam eae quae latent in simulatione officii aut in aliquo necessitudinis nomine. Nam eum qui palam est adversarius facile cavendo vitare possis: hoc vero occultum, intestinum ac domesticum malum, non modo non exsistit, verum etiam opprimit antequam prospicere atque explorare potueris. Itane vero? tu, quum quaestor ad exercitum missus sis, custos non solum pecuniae, sed etiam consulis, particeps omnium rerum consiliorumque fueris, habitus sis in liberum loco, sicut mos majorum ferebat, repente relinquas, deseras, ad adversarios transeas? O scelus! O portentum in ultimas terras exportandum! Non enim potest ea natura quae tantum facinus commiserit hoc uno scelere esse contenta: necesse est semper aliquid ejusmodi moliatur: necesse est in simili audacia perfidiaque versetur. Itaque idem iste quem Cn. Dolabella

in aliquo necessitudinis nomine.] 'in some name or title of intimacy.' The name or title of relation, friend, associate in any office brings men together, and if a knave takes advantage of this opportunity, he is a most mischievous man. Hence every body understands the danger that he is in from his friends, under which name we foolishly include all who have easy access to a man's privacy. Experience proves that we suffer more from those who are called friends than from those who are our open enemies. So it is well said:

"Di che mi fido, mi guarda Iddio:
Di che mi non fido, mi guarderò io."

non modo non exsistit,] All the MSS. have this reading, and yet Zumpt and Iordan omit the 'non' before 'exsistit.' Zumpt's remark that nothing is more common than for 'non' to be incorrectly added or omitted in the MSS., is true; and there are no where more instances of it than in the Digest. But he gives the passage a meaning which is contrary to what Cicero intends to say: "non modo existit, antequam prospicias, verum etiam opprimit, antequam cavere possis." But Cicero does not intend to say this: he says that this evil does not show itself, but crushes you, before you can have the opportunity of looking at it, and seeing what it is. It does not even give warning: it comes upon you unawares. Madvig (Opuscula Academica, p. 326) approves of the omission of this 'non,' on the authority of Augustinus, De Civ. Dei, lib. 19. 5, who has, however, 'non solum.' According to the supposed reading of Augustinus, then, the sense is this: 'it shows itself, and that is not all; it even crushes you before,' &c., which is plain nonsense. Zumpt and Madvig make the passage like other passages in these speeches, where 'non modo' is followed by 'verum etiam,' without any negative interposed. It would be just as consistent to strike out the 'non' before 'adesse' in Div. c. 9, 'non modo non adesse,' &c. Asconius has 'non modo existit' in his lemma, and he explains it 'emergit, oritur, exsurgit.' On 'non modo non exsistit' Madvig says, "Verum certe existit et oritur antequam opprimit: perversa est igitur sententia; ne quis enim *existit* putet esse *adparet*, primum ita dici hoc quidem loco *existit* vix potest; deinde inanis est sententia, occulta non adparere; postremo propter *verum etiam* haec dici absolute non possunt, sed ad *antequam* pertinent." There is nothing in the 'primum,' which assumes that 'exsistit' can scarcely mean what it must mean if we read 'non exsistit.' (See 'exsistat' c. 37.) The 'deinde' is still feebler, for it is of the nature of 'occulta' not to appear, and the very point of Cicero's remark is that the danger being concealed does not show itself, as many other dangers do. 'Postremo' again assumes the matter in dispute, for if we read 'non exsistit' the negative is absolute and has no reference to 'antequam.' The sense is that the danger never does show itself: it brings on a man's ruin before he can guard against it.

postea C. Malleolo occiso pro quaestore habuit,—haud scio an major etiam haec necessitudo fuerit quam illa Carbonis, ac plus judicium voluntatis valere quam sortis debeat,—idem in Cn. Dolabellam qui in Cn. Carbonem fuit. Nam quae in ipsum valebant crimina, contulit in illum, causamque illius omnem ad inimicos accusatoresque detulit: ipse in eum cui legatus, cui pro quaestore fuerat, inimicissimum atque improbissimum testimonium dixit. Ille miser quum esset Cn. Dolabella quum proditione istius nefaria, quum improbo ac falso ejusdem testimonio, tum multo [etiam] ex maxima parte istius furtorum ac flagitiorum invidia conflagravit.

XVI. Quid hoc homine faciatis, aut ad quam spem tam perfidiosum, tam importunum animal reservetis? qui in Cn. Carbone sortem, in Cn. Dolabella voluntatem neglexerit ac violarit, eosque ambos non solum deseruerit, sed etiam prodiderit atque oppugnarit. Nolite, quaeso, judices, brevitate orationis meae potius quam rerum ipsarum magnitudine crimina ponderare. Mihi enim properandum necessario est ut omnia vobis quae mihi constituta sunt possim exponere. Quamobrem quaestura istius demonstrata primique magistratus et furto et scelere perspecto reliqua attendite. In quibus illud tempus Sullanarum proscriptionum ac rapinarum praetermittam; neque ego istum sibi ex communi calamitate defensionem ullam sinam sumere: suis eum certis propriisque criminibus accusabo. Quamobrem hoc omni tempore Sullano ex accusatione circumscripto legationem ejus praeclaram cognoscite.

XVII. Posteaquam Cn. Dolabellae provincia Cilicia constituta est, O dii immortales! quanta iste cupiditate, quibus allegationibus illam sibi legationem expugnavit; id quod Cn. Dolabellae princi-

C. Malleolo occiso] "Oratorie pro mortuo occisum dixit," Asconius.

quae in ipsum] See Introd. to the Verrine orations.

Ille . . Cn. Dolabella] All the MSS. Naugerius and many others erase 'Cn. Dolabella.' Some propose to erase 'ille' and keep 'Cn. Dolabella.' I see no objection to the MSS. reading.

16. *Quid hoc homine faciatis,*] 'What can you do with such a fellow?' The ablative is used the same way with the passive 'factum,' and with the verb 'fio,' as 'quid me' or 'de me fiet?' 'Quid illo myoparone factum sit,' c. 35. (See Forcellini.)

in Cn. Carbone . . in Cn. Dolabella] 'in Cn. Carbonem . . Cn. Dolabellam,' in all the MSS. and all the old editions; but it is a mistake. Zumpt explains 'voluntatem neglexerit' to refer to the 'voluntas' of Verres, and the 'judicium voluntatis,' in c. 15, also to mean the 'voluntas' of Verres. It seems to me to mean the 'voluntas' of Dolabella.

ambos] 'ambo,' G 1 s Lg. 29 C, Iordan.

quae mihi constituta sunt] 'which it is my business,' 'which I have undertaken to lay before you.'

circumscripto] "Sublato, circumducto ac praetermisso" (Asconius). See Act. ii. Lib. 2. c. 31. Zumpt also refers to Cic. De Fin. iii. 9, § 31.

17. *allegationibus . . legationem*] One of Cicero's plays on words, in which he indulged more than good taste can approve. The Cilician praetorship of Dolabella belonged to B.C. 80, and probably to 79 also.

pium maximae calamitatis fuit. Nam ut [iste] profectus est, quacunque iter fecit, ejusmodi fuit non ut legatus populi Romani sed ut quaedam calamitas pervadere videretur. In Achaia—praetermittam minora omnia quorum simile forsitan alius quoque aliquid aliquando fecerit: nihil dicam nisi singulare, nisi id quod si in alium reum diceretur incredibile videretur—magistratum Sicyonium nummos poposcit. Ne sit hoc crimen in Verrem: fecerunt alii. Quum ille non daret, animadvertit. Improbum, sed non inauditum. Genus animadversionis videte: quaeretis ex quo genere hominem istum judicetis. Ignem ex lignis viridibus atque humidis in loco angusto fieri jussit: ibi hominem ingenuum, domi nobilem, populi Romani socium atque amicum, fumo excrutiatum, semivivum reliquit. Jam quae iste signa, quas tabulas pictas ex Achaia sustulerit, non dicam hoc loco: est alius mihi locus ad hanc ejus cupiditatem demonstrandam separatus. Athenis audistis ex aede Minervae grande auri pondus ablatum. Dictum hoc est in Cn. Dolabellae judicio. Dictum? etiam aestimatum. Hujus consilii non modo participem C. Verrem sed principem fuisse reperietis. Delum venit. Ibi ex fano Apollinis religiosissimo noctu clam sustulit signa pulcherrima atque antiquissima, eaque in onerariam navem suam conjicienda curavit. Postridie quum fanum spoliatum viderent ii qui Delum incolebant, graviter ferebant: est enim tanta apud eos ejus fani religio atque antiquitas ut in eo loco ipsum Apollinem natum esse arbitrentur. Verbum tamen facere non audebant, ne forte ea res ad Dolabellam ipsum pertineret.

XVIII. Tum subito tempestates coortae sunt maximae, judices, ut non modo proficisci quum cuperet Dolabella non posset, sed vix in oppido consisteret; ita magni fluctus ejiciebantur. Hic navis illa praedonis istius, onusta signis religiosis, expulsa atque ejecta

calamitas] 'like a tempest.' See Act. ii. Lib. 3. c. 98.

animadvertit.] This sense of the word is explained by Cicero: 'he punished;' and he tells us the kind of punishment (animadversio). The complete expression would be 'in eum animadvertit' (Caesar, B. G. i. 19).—'ex quo genere hominem:' 'hominum,' conj. Hot. and Orelli.

ingenuum,] 'free by birth,' not a mere manumitted slave, which would have been bad enough. As to the definition of 'ingenuus,' see Gaius (i. 11).

est alius mihi locus] In Act. ii. Lib. 4, De Signis; but he does not speak of the Achaean spoils, and it would have been out of place, if he had spoken of the Achaean statues there. The orator forgot himself, when he wrote these words, 'est alius' &c. Orelli reads 'ad hanc . . . servatus.'

etiam aestimatum.] 'it was not only said, but proved:' the amount stolen was assessed and ascertained.

non modo] P T omit 'modo,' and Iordan omits it.

Apollinem natum] So the story is told in the so-called Homeric Hymn to Apollo, and in the Hymn of Callimachus.

18. *ita magni fluctus*] 'such great waves were thrown up,' or 'so great waves,' as some say. 'Ita' is thus sometimes used with an adjective, as in Cic. De Sen. c. 20, 'non ita longa;' Ad Q. Fr. i. 1. c. 11, 'non ita acer-

fluctu frangitur: in littore signa illa Apollinis reperiuntur: jussu Dolabellae reponuntur: tempestas sedatur: Dolabella Delo proficiscitur. Non dubito quin, tametsi nullus in te sensus humanitatis, nulla ratio unquam fuit religionis, nunc tamen in metu periculoque tuo tuorum tibi scelerum veniat in mentem. Potestne tibi ulla spes salutis commoda ostendi, quum recordaris in deos immortales quam impius, quam sceleratus, quam nefarius fueris? Apollinemne tu Delium spoliare ausus es? illine tu templo, tam antiquo, tam sancto, tam religioso, manus impias ac sacrilegas afferre conatus es? Si in pueritia non his artibus ac disciplinis institutus eras ut ea quae literis mandata sunt disceres atque cognosceres, ne postea quidem, quum in ea ipsa loca venisti, potuisti accipere id quod est proditum memoria ac literis, Latonam ex longo errore et fuga gravidam et jam ad pariendum [vicinam] temporibus exactis confugisse Delum atque ibi Apollinem Dianamque peperisse? qua ex opinione hominum illa insula eorum deorum sacra putatur; tantaque ejus auctoritas religionis et est et semper fuit ut ne Persae quidem, quum bellum toti Graeciae, diis hominibusque indixissent, et mille numero navium classem ad Delum appulissent, quidquam conarentur aut violare aut attingere. Hoc tu fanum depopulari, homo improbissime atque amentissime, audebas? Fuit ulla cupiditas tanta quae tantam exstingueret religionem? et si tum haec non cogitabas, ne nunc quidem recordaris nullum esse tantum malum quod non tibi pro sceleribus tuis jamdiu debeatur?

XIX. In Asiam vero postquam venit, quid ego adventus istius

bum;' and 'tam' the same way, Ad Q. Fr. i. 1. c. 5.

veniat in mentem.] See Divin. c. 13.

his artibus] 'iis artibus' Iordan.

proditum memoria &c.] Orelli has 'memoriae;' and both forms are used. But 'literis' appears to be the ablative, and therefore it should be 'memoria.' This sentence, which begins 'Si in pueritia,' is interrogative. Comp. 'Si te . . ne illud quidem,' c. 34.

ne Persae quidem,] The story of the Persians landing at Delos, B.C. 490, is told by Herodotus (vi. 96). Asconius remarks that it was not only because they were enemies that the Persians destroyed the Greek temples, but because they thought that no temples should be erected to the deities (Cic. De Legibus, ii. 10). Herodotus (i. 131) says that the Persians made no statues, temples, or altars; and that they sacrificed to the sun, the moon, the earth, fire, water, and the winds. The Persians were, therefore, temple-destroyers and iconoclasts by profession, as they showed also in their invasion of Egypt under Cambyses, for the destruction of many of the ancient monuments can hardly be attributed to any other than the Persians; I mean, such monuments as we know to have been destroyed before the Roman period. The reason of their sparing the temples in Delos was, as the Scholiast on Aristophanes (Peace, 410) says, who is quoted by Klotz, because the Persians recognized their sun-god in Apollo, and their moon in Artemis. Verres, however, was not the first who plundered Delos; but it was not Cicero's purpose to tell us that fact. Archelaus, the general of Mithridates, violated its sanctity, as appears from Appian, Mithridat., c. 28; Pausanias, Laconica, c. 23, and Strabo, p. 486, ed. Cas., referred to by Zumpt. But there is a difference between what is done in time of war, and robberies, like those of Verres, in a time of peace.

19. *adventus istius*] Klotz makes 'adventus' the accusative, and the words which

prandia, cenas, equos, muneraque commemorem? Nihil cum Verre de quotidianis criminibus acturus sum. Chio per vim signa pulcherrima dico abstulisse: item Erythris, et Halicarnasso. Tenedo, praetereo pecuniam quam eripuit, Tenem ipsum qui apud Tenedios sanctissimus deus habetur, qui urbem illam dicitur condidisse, cujus ex nomine Tenedus nominatur, hunc ipsum, inquam, Tenem, pulcherrime factum, quem quondam in comitio vidistis, abstulit magno cum gemitu civitatis. Illa vero expugnatio fani antiquissimi et nobilissimi Junonis Samiae, quam luctuosa Samiis fuit, quam acerba toti Asiae, quam clara apud omnes, quam nemini vestrum inaudita; de qua expugnatione quum legati ad C. Neronem in Asiam Samo venissent, responsum tulerunt, ejusmodi querimonias quae ad legatum populi Romani pertinerent, non ad praetorem sed Romam deferri oportere. Quas iste tabulas illinc, quae signa sustulit? quae cognovi egomet apud istum in aedibus nuper quum obsignandi gratia venissem. Quae signa nunc, Verres, ubi sunt? illa quaero quae apud te nuper ad omnes columnas, omnibus etiam

follow 'istius' to be explanatory of what was meant by an 'adventus.' He refers for this plural use of 'adventus' to Act. ii. Lib. 2. c. 34, and Lib. 4. c. 14: but see Lib. 1. c. 24, 'adventus sui.' Iordan follows Madvig in placing a comma after 'adventus,' and I suppose that he understands it as Klotz does. 'Adventus' is often used in the plural (De Imp. Cn. Pompeii, c. 5; De Lege Agraria, i. 5; Pro Archia, c. 3). But when Cicero speaks of a single 'adventus' or one person's 'adventus' he uses the singular. See De Imp. Cn. Pompeii, c. 5, and the note. As to the 'equos,' there is no difficulty, though Asconius makes one: he required horses of the people, as well as other services.

quotidianis] 'common.' So the common Interdictum de vi is called Quotidianum (Pro Caecina, c. 31); and Pro Tullio, § 54, "agi quidem usitato jure et quotidiana actione potuit."

in comitio] The Roman 'aediles' sometimes borrowed valuable works of art from the provinces for the embellishment of the public exhibitions, which it was their office to give to the Romans. It seems likely enough that such loans were not always returned, though in the instance of this statue of Tenes it must have been so. Klotz refers to Act. ii. Lib. 3. c. 4, and Lib. 4. c. 3, for further matter as to this mode of decorating the 'comitium.' As to Tenes or Tennes, see Pausanias, x. 14, and Steph. Byzant. v. Τένεδος.

Junonis Samiae,] Herodotus (iii. 60) speaks of the temple of Hera at Samos, as the largest that he had seen. In Strabo's time (p. 637) the Heraeum was a 'pinacotheke,' or 'picture gallery;' and the Hypaethrum was filled with the finest statues. If Cicero means to blame Nero indirectly, there seems no ground for it; for, though the robbery was committed in the province of Asia, of which Nero was governor, Verres was the 'legatus' of Dolabella. Nero told the people that they must carry their complaint to Rome, and we may suppose that he told them the truth, but it was small consolation to the men who were scandalously pillaged.

obsignandi] The passage shows that the prosecutor had the power of putting seals on such things as ought not to be removed pending the trial; an inference from this passage which Asconius, as usual, expresses in other words.

columnas,] These statues were placed at columns, and in the intercolumniations (intercolumnia), or arranged in the planted grounds or 'horti' (silva). These columns may have been in the atrium and the peristyle of Verres' house. The Romans were fond of gardens, which they decorated with statues and works of art. (Hor. Ep. i. 10. 22.) This kind of 'silva' was sometimes called 'viridarium.'

intercolumniis, in silva denique disposita sub divo vidimus. Cur ea, quamdiu alium praetorem cum iis judicibus quos in horum locum sortitus [es] de te in consilium iturum putasti, tamdiu domi fuerunt? posteaquam nostris testibus nos quam horis tuis uti malle vidisti, nullum signum domi reliquisti praeter duo quae in mediis aedibus sunt, quae ipsa Samo sublata sunt? Non putasti me tuis familiarissimis in hanc rem testimonia denuntiaturum qui tuae domi saepe fuissent, ex quibus quaererem, signa scirentne fuisse quae non essent?

XX. Quid tum hos de te judicaturos arbitratus es, quum viderent te jam non contra accusatorem tuum sed contra quaestorem sectoremque pugnare? Qua de re Charidemum Chium testimonium priore actione dicere audistis; sese, quum esset trierarchus et Verrem ex Asia decedentem prosequeretur, jussu Dolabellae fuisse una cum isto Sami; seseque tum scire spoliatum esse fanum Junonis et oppidum Samum; posteaque se causam apud Chios cives suos Samiis accusantibus publice dixisse; eoque se esse absolutum quod planum fecisset, ea quae legati Samiorum dicerent

sortitus [*es*]] Asconius says, that we must understand Cicero to mean Metellus (alium praetorem), and by the 'judices,' those whom Verres expected to put in the place of those who would be incapacitated for sitting in the 'consilium,' if the trial should be deferred to the next year. Orelli has 'subsortiturus eras,' the emendation of Hotmann; and Zumpt has 'sortitus esses,' which is his own. Iordan has the same. All the MSS. cited by Iordan have 'sortitus es' or 'subsortitus es.' I think that Hotmann's is the best conjecture.

tuis] Iordan places this in [ ]. It is omited by A and cod. Urs. On 'nostris testibus quam horis' Asconius remarks, "Usus est enim prima actione Cicero magis testibus suis quam horis, id est, temporibus sibi ad dicendum lege datis."

testimonia denuntiaturum] 'would give them notice to appear as witnesses.' 'Denuntiare' is used, generally, to give a person notice of any kind, as Ad Fam. xi. 25, "expectanti mihi tuas quotidie literas Lupus noster subito denuntiavit ut ad te scriberem, si quid vellem." The legal 'denuntiatio,' as Klotz shows, precedes the 'citatio' or calling of the witnesses in court. 'Denuntiare' means, to give them a legal summons to attend as witnesses; and 'citare,' to call on them in court (Act. ii. Lib. 2. c. 30; Pro Sext. Rosc. c. 38; Pro L. Flacco, c. 6, 15).—'domi semper fuissent:' G1 2 s, Zumpt, Iordan.

20. *quaestorem &c.*] Asconius says, that there is a reading 'quaesitorem;' but that reading does not suit the meaning of the passage. Cicero means to say, that when Verres removed these things, it was an admission of his guilt; he had given up the struggle against his prosecutor, and was now only contending with those whose business it would be to do execution by taking his goods and selling them, the 'quaestor urbanus' and the 'sector.' Zumpt refers to the term as expressed in a fragment of the Lex Servilia: "eum qui ex hac lege condemnatus erit, quaestor praedes facito det de consilii majoris partis sententia quanti ei censuerint: si praedes dati non erunt, bona ejus facito publice possideantur conquiranturque;" and to Livy, xxxviii. 60, "in bona deinde L. Scipionis possessum publice quaestores praetor misit." Those are called 'sectores' who buy property 'publice' (Gaius, iv. 146), and 'publice' refers to such property as was seized on account of the State. The 'sector' bought it in the lump, and the auction transferred to him the ownership; but it said that he took the property with its liabilities. See the use of 'sectio' in Caesar, B. G. ii. 33.

decedentem] Samos was plundered when Verres was leaving Asia; and probably Chios and Tenedus also.

ad Verrem non ad se pertinere. Aspendum vetus oppidum et nobile in Pamphylia scitis esse, plenissimum signorum optimorum. Non dicam illinc hoc signum ablatum esse et illud: hoc dico, nullum te Aspendi signum, Verres, reliquisse; omnia ex fanis, ex locis publicis, palam, spectantibus omnibus plaustris evecta exportataque esse. Atque etiam illum Aspendium citharistam, de quo saepe audistis id quod est Graecis hominibus in proverbio, quem omnia intus canere dicebant, sustulit et in intimis suis aedibus posuit, ut etiam illum ipsum suo artificio superasse videatur. Pergae fanum antiquissimum et sanctissimum Dianae scimus esse: id quoque a te nudatum ac spoliatum esse, ex ipsa Diana quod habebat auri detractum atque ablatum esse dico. Quae, malum, est ista tanta audacia atque amentia? quas enim sociorum atque amicorum urbes adisti legationis jure et nomine, si in eas vi cum exercitu imperioque invasisses, tamen, opinor, quae signa atque ornamenta ex his urbibus sustulisses, haec non in tuam domum neque in suburbana amicorum sed Romam in publicum deportasses.

XXI. Quid ego de M. Marcello loquar, qui Syracusas urbem

Aspendum] Aspendus was on the river Eurymedon in Pamphylia, six or eight miles from the sea. The epigraph ΕΣΤFΕΔΙΙΥΣ occurs on old medals of Aspendus, but the more recent have Ἀσπενδιων.

plaustris] 'plostris' S G2 dtt. Iordan. — 'exportataque:' 'asportataque' Orelli.

omnia intus &c.] Cicero has this expression (In Rullum, ii. 26), "atque hoc carmen hic tribunus plebis non vobis, sed sibi intus canit." The explanation of this passage by Asconius, which Klotz has adopted, is the following:—"There was something in the manner in which this figure was represented as holding the lyre, to which the words 'intus canere' refer. Asconius says that the player on the cithara holds the 'plectrum' in his right hand, which is 'foris canere;' and he has the fingers of the left hand on the strings, which is 'intus canere.' This 'citharista' of Aspendus was represented doing every thing with the left hand, 'intus;' he did not use the right hand at all. The proverbial expression 'intus canere' was also applied to a person who slily looked after his own interest." Asconius adds: 'unde omnes, quotquot fures erant, a Graecis Aspendii citharistae in proverbio dicebantur, quod, ut ille carminis, ita isti furtorum occultatores erant.' But this explanation of Asconius certainly does not explain the proverb. Zumpt gives a different sense to the words 'intus canere,' as applied to the 'citharista:' "the statue was made with such skill, that the 'citharista' seemed to be feeling his music, or 'intus canebat;'" but nobody else, of course, could hear it. He had, then, all his playing to himself. So Verres played for himself alone. Cicero makes a poor play on the word 'intus,' when he says 'in intimis suis aedibus posuit;' and in the words 'suo artificio,' which Asconius explains, "ut interius positus esset qui intus canere consueverat."

Pergae] Perga or Perge was in Pamphylia north of Attaleia, which is on the coast. There are remains of Perge; and on its coins there is the epigraph Περγαιας Αρτεμιδος.

Quae, malum, est ista] This is one of the familiar modes of expression (malum) which the reader must translate as he pleases. Forcellini's version is 'che diavol è.' Comp. Terence, Phormio, v. 7. 55, "Quid vos, malum, ergo me sic ludificamini?"

suburbana] A 'suburbanum' is a villa near the city.

21. *M. Marcello &c.*] Cicero enumerates the Roman generals, who had enriched Italy with the spoils of conquered countries. L. Mummius carried off a rich booty of works of art from Corinth, which were used to embellish Rome, and some of the surrounding cities. (Strabo, p. 381, ed. Cas.)

ornatissimam cepit? quid de L. Scipione, qui bellum in Asia gessit Antiochumque regem potentissimum vicit? quid de T. Flaminino, qui regem Philippum et Macedoniam subegit? quid de L. Paullo, qui regem Persen vi ac virtute superavit? quid de L. Mummio, qui urbem pulcherrimam atque ornatissimam Corinthum, plenissimam rerum omnium, sustulit, urbesque Achaiae Boeotiaeque multas sub imperium populi Romani ditionemque subjunxit? quorum domus quum honore ac virtute florerent, signis et tabulis pictis erant vacuae. At vero urbem totam, templaque deorum omnesque Italiae partes illorum donis ac monumentis exornatas videmus. Vereor ne haec forte cuipiam nimis antiqua et jam obsoleta videantur; ita enim tum aequabiliter omnes erant ejusmodi ut haec laus eximiae virtutis et innocentiae non solum hominum verum etiam temporum illorum esse videatur. P. Servilius, vir clarissimus, maximis rebus gestis adest de te sententiam laturus. Olympum vi, copiis, consilio, virtute cepit, urbem antiquam et omnibus rebus auctam et ornatam. Recens exemplum fortissimi viri profero. Nam postea Servilius imperator populi Romani Olympum, urbem hostium, cepit quam tu in iisdem illis locis legatus quaestorius oppida pacata sociorum atque amicorum diripienda ac vexanda curasti. Tu quae ex fanis religiosissimis per scelus et [per] latrocinium abstulisti, ea nos videre nisi in tuis amicorumque tuorum tectis non possumus: P. Servilius quae signa atque ornamenta ex urbe hostium, vi et virtute capta belli lege atque imperatorio jure sustulit, ea populo Romano apportavit, per triumphum vexit, in tabulas publicas ad aerarium perscribenda curavit. Cognoscite ex literis publicis hominis amplissimi diligentiam. Recita. RATIONES RELATAE P. SERVILII. Non solum numerum signorum sed etiam uniuscujusque magnitudinem, figuram, statum, literis definiri vides. Certe major

At vero] The use of 'at' in the way of making an objection, is very common; and also in making an answer to an objection. De Sen. c. 6, 'non facit ea quae juvenes'—an objection; to which the answer is, 'at vero multo majora et meliora facit.' The interpretation of the text seems to be this: 'The houses of these men, though ennobled by the honours of the State and by virtue, had, it is true, no statues and paintings. But if their houses were without them, the city, &c. was not.'

P. Servilius,] Named Isauricus, who (as proconsul) conducted the war against the pirates on the south coast of Asia Minor, and took several cities, among which was Olympus (Deliktash), on the coast of Lycia. (B.C. 77.) The place is identified by an inscription 'Ὀλυμπηνῶν ἡ βουλὴ καὶ ὁ δῆμος' (Beaufort's Karamania, p. 45). The MSS. of Cicero have 'Olynthum,' a manifest blunder, corrected from Asconius by Manutius.—Servilius was one of the 'judices.'

belli lege &c.] 'Belli lege' must not be rendered by the 'law of war,' in the modern sense of the term. The word would be 'jus' in such case. (Pro Balbo, c. 6, vol. iv.) 'Belli lege' means according to the terms (lex) on which war is carried on, one of which is that the conqueror acquired the property of the conquered, according to ancient usage.

figuram, statum,] "*Status* est circa

est virtutis victoriaeque jucunditas quam ista voluptas quae percipitur ex libidine et cupiditate: multo diligentius habere dico Servilium praedam populi Romani quam te tua furta notata atque perscripta.

XXII. Dices tua quoque signa et tabulas pictas ornamento urbi foroque populi Romani fuisse. Memini: vidi simul cum populo Romano forum comitiumque adornatum, ad speciem magnifico ornatu, ad sensum cogitationemque acerbo et lugubri. Vidi collucere omnia furtis tuis, praeda provinciarum, spoliis sociorum atque amicorum. Quo quidem tempore, judices, iste spem maximam reliquorum quoque peccatorum nactus est. Vidit enim eos qui judiciorum dominos se dici volebant harum cupiditatum esse servos. Socii vero nationesque exterae spem omnium tum primum abjecerunt rerum ac fortunarum suarum; propterea quod casu legati ex Asia atque Achaia plurimi Romae tunc fuerunt, qui deorum simulacra ex suis fanis sublata in foro venerabantur, itemque cetera signa et ornamenta quum cognoscerent alia alio in loco lacrimantes intuebantur. Quorum omnium hunc sermonem tum esse audiebamus: Nihil esse quod quisquam dubitaret de exitio sociorum atque amicorum, quum quidem viderent in foro populi Romani, quo in loco antea qui sociis injurias fecerant accusari et condemnari solebant, ibi esse palam posita ea quae ab sociis per

gestum situmque membrorum; *figura* circa ornatum et habitum vestis, insignium et armorum." (Ascon.) So it stands in Orelli's text of Asconius; but it seems to me that 'status' and 'figura' should change places.

praedam] 'Praeda' was 'that which was taken in war,' and it was properly brought into the 'aerarium,' if it was money, or the produce of what was sold (Liv. ii. 42): if other things, a catalogue was made, and they were sent to Rome. In certain cases, the 'praeda' was given to the soldiers (Liv. vi. 13; x. 20).—'furta notata atque descripta' Orelli; but 'perscribere' is the usual word for writing out something, or making a list or catalogue of things. (See c. 35.)

22. *comitiumque*] "Locus propter senatum, quo coire equitibus Romanis et populo Romano licet." (Ascon.) This definition seems to refer to the 'comitium' as the place where the 'comitia' were held. The 'comitium' was a place so called from the 'comitia curiata' being held there in the early times, when there were no other 'comitia,' and these 'comitia' were also held there after the establishment of the 'comitia centuriata,' which were held in the Campus Martius, and after the establishment of the 'comitia tributa' which were held in the Forum, in its limited sense. The most probable conclusion from all the ancient authorities seems to be that the 'comitium' was the upper part of the Forum Romanum. It was not a building. The matter is discussed by Becker, Handbuch der Röm. Alter. i. p. 273.

judiciorum dominos] An allusion, says Asconius, to Hortensius and the other nobles. Cicero says that their cupidity was inflamed by the sight of the works of art, which Verres had collected in Rome, and he was encouraged to go on with his robberies during his government of Sicily. It is conjectured by Ferracci, quoted by Klotz, that Verres made this display during the time that he was 'praetor urbanus,' in which capacity he had to superintend the 'Ludi Apollinares.'

fecerant—solebant,] These indicatives,

scelus ablata ereptaque essent. Hic ego non arbitror illum negaturum signa se plurima, tabulas pictas innumerabiles habere: sed, ut opinor, solet haec quae rapuit et furatus est nonnunquam dicere se emisse; quoniam quidem in Achaiam, Asiam, Pamphyliam sumptu publico et legationis nomine mercator signorum tabularumque pictarum missus est.

XXIII. Habeo et istius et patris ejus [accepti] tabulas omnes, quas diligentissime legi atque digessi; patris quoad vixit, tuas quoad ais te confecisse. Nam in isto, judices, hoc novum reperietis. Audimus aliquem tabulas nunquam confecisse; quae est opinio hominum de M. Antonio falsa; nam fecit diligentissime. Verum sit hoc genus aliquod minime probandum. Audimus alium non ab initio fecisse, sed ex tempore aliquo confecisse: est aliqua etiam hujusce rei ratio. Hoc vero novum et ridiculum est quod hic nobis respondit quum ab eo tabulas postularemus, usque ad M. Terentium [et] C. Cassium consules confecisse, postea destitisse. Alio loco hoc cujusmodi sit considerabimus; nunc nihil ad me attinet; horum enim temporum in quibus nunc versor habeo tabulas et tuas et patris. Plurima signa pulcherrima, plurimas tabulas optimas deportasse te negare non potes: atque utinam neges. Unum ostende in tabulis aut tuis aut patris tui emptum esse: vicisti. Ne haec quidem duo signa pulcherrima quae nunc ad impluvium tuum stant, quae multos annos ante valvas Junonis

which occur in the reported words of others, are contrary to Roman usage.

quoniam quidem, &c.] This is said ironically. Asconius read 'legationis nomine cum imperio et securibus mercator.'

23. [*accepti*] *tabulas omnes,*] The account-books of Verres and his father, in which all their receipts or acquisitions were entered. For every Roman was expected to keep his accounts, so as to be able to show his receipts and expenditure. The Romans were a book-keeping people, and very precise in all matters of business. With us every tradesman or merchant is expected to keep accounts; but among the Romans every good 'paterfamilias' or 'head of a family' was expected to keep accounts. The allusions to book-keeping, and the terms of book-keeping, occur very frequently in the Roman writers. G 3 Lg. omnes. H. ψ. Mein. have 'accepi,' and omit 'habeo.' It is not said what MSS. have 'accepti.' Asconius says "Legitur et 'Ab eo' et 'accepi.'" All the MSS. omit 'habeo,' except Lg 6, which has 'ab eo.' 'Accepi,' as Iordan supposes, is from some glossator's hand, and was introduced into the text by a copier, and then to make sense of the passage 'accepi' was changed into 'accepti.' This is very probable. Iordan also observes that the Romans describe book-keeping by the term 'accepti et expensi tabulae,' or 'tabulae' simply. 'Accepti' would express only one side of the account-book.

M. Antonio] Asconius says that this is M. Antonius Creticus, an unprincipled fellow, who has been alluded to before (Divinatio, c. 17). But it appears to be his father, the orator, M. Antonius, for Cicero makes him say (De Or. ii. 23), "sed tamen ne tabulas quidem conficere existimor." The codd. have only 'Antonio,' and this would be the orator.

hujusce] 'ejusce' G 2 *s*, a word which is false in form, for 'ce' is only added to the demonstratives 'hic,' 'iste,' 'ille,' and to the adverbs formed from them. G 1 has 'ejusmodi.' Asconius has 'hujusce.'

impluvium] In the roof of the 'atrium'

Samiae steterunt, habes quomodo emeris; haec, inquam, duo, quae in aedibus tuis sola jam sunt, quae sectorem exspectant, relicta ac destituta a ceteris signis.

XXIV. At, credo, in hisce solis rebus indomitas cupiditates atque effrenatas habebat: ceterae libidines ejus ratione aliqua aut modo continebantur. Quam multis istum ingenuis, quam multis matribusfamilias in illa tetra atque impura legatione vim attulisse existimatis? Ecquo in oppido pedem posuit ubi non plura stuprorum flagitiorumque suorum quam adventus sui vestigia reliquerit? Sed ego omnia quae negari poterunt praetermittam; etiam haec quae certissima sunt et clarissima relinquam: unum aliquod de nefariis istius factis eligam, quo facilius ad Siciliam possim aliquando, quae mihi hoc oneris negotiique imposuit, pervenire. Oppidum est in Hellesponto Lampsacum, judices, in primis Asiae provinciae clarum et nobile; homines autem ipsi Lampsaceni quum summe in omnes cives Romanos officiosi, tum praeterea maxime sedati et quieti, prope praeter ceteros ad summum Graecorum otium potius quam ad ullam vim aut tumultum accommodati. Accidit, quum iste a Cn. Dolabella efflagitasset, ut se ad regem Nicomedem regemque Sadalam mitteret, quumque iter hoc sibi magis ad quaestum suum quam ad rei publicae tempus accommodatum depoposcisset, ut illo itinere veniret Lampsacum cum magna calamitate et prope pernicie civitatis. Deducitur iste ad

of a Roman house, there was an opening, called 'compluvium,' towards which the roof sloped, and the rain-water from the roof was thus carried down into the 'impluvium' or cistern in the floor, round which statues were sometimes placed. If a snake, perchance, got on the roof, it might find its way into the 'impluvium;' manifestly a very bad omen (Terence, Phormio, iv. 4. 26).

ante valvas] There is better authority for 'ante' than 'ad;' but 'ad' is also Latin. There was a great temple of Hera (Juno) at Samos, which is mentioned by Herodotus. It was burnt by the Persians, and restored. As to 'valvas,' see Lib. 4. c. 56.

habes quomodo emeris;] The omission of the infinitive after 'habes' need create no difficulty. The word to be supplied is indicated by the verb 'ostende.' The omission of a verb is common in Cicero, when it is easily supplied from the context.

24. *At, credo, &c.*] 'But it will be said, I suppose,' &c. Here 'at' has its ordinary sense (see c. 21), and 'credo' is used ironically; as in the Letter to Q. Fr. i. 1, 2, 'erit, credo, periculum.'—'Cupiditas' is generally the passion for gain, greediness, love of lucre, as we see in many passages of Cicero.

Lampsacum,] The Greek form is 'Lampsacos;' but the neuter is used here, as 'Cyzicum' for 'Cyzicus.' Lamsaki is probably near the site of Lampsacus, which was opposite to Callipolis in the Thracian Chersonesus. This story, like some others, has nothing to do with Cicero's case, for Verres was prosecuted for 'repetundae;' but it is a good example of Cicero's way of stating facts, and so far we are glad to have it.

Nicomedem] Nicomedes III., king of Bithynia, who gave his states by his testament to the Roman people (B.C. 75), as Attalus, of Pergamus, had done before. Sadala was a Thracian king, whom Garatoni conjectures to be the father of Cotys, and the grandfather of Sadala, who is mentioned by Caesar (Bell. Civ. iii. 4).

Janitorem quendam hospitem, comitesque ejus item apud ceteros hospites collocantur. Ut mos erat istius, atque ut eum suae libidines flagitiose facere admonebant, statim negotium dat illis suis comitibus, nequissimis turpissimisque hominibus, uti videant et investigent ecqua virgo sit aut mulier digna quamobrem ipse Lampsaci diutius commoraretur.

XXV. Erat comes ejus Rubrius quidam, homo factus ad istius libidines, qui miro artificio quocunque venerat haec investigare omnia solebat. Is ad eum rem istam defert, Philodamum esse quendam, genere, honore, copiis, existimatione facile principem Lampsacenorum: ejus esse filiam quae cum patre habitaret propterea quod virum non haberet, mulierem eximia pulchritudine, sed eam summa integritate pudicitiaque existimari. Homo ut haec audivit, sic exarsit ad id quod non modo ipse nunquam viderat, sed ne audierat quidem ab eo qui ipse vidisset, ut statim ad Philodamum migrare se diceret velle. Hospes Janitor qui nihil suspicaretur veritus ne quid in ipso se offenderetur, hominem summa vi retinere coepit. Iste qui hospitis relinquendi causam reperire non posset, alia sibi ratione viam munire ad stuprum coepit: Rubrium delicias suas, in omnibus ejusmodi rebus adjutorem suum et conscium, parum laute deversari dicit; ad Philodamum deduci jubet. Quod ubi est Philodamo nuntiatum, tametsi erat ignarus quantum sibi ac liberis

facere admonebant,] There are other examples of 'admonere' with an infinitive (Forcellini). Whether there is another example in Cicero, I do not know. G 2 Ld have 'facere commovebant.'

commoraretur.] Ernesti's correction, 'commoretur,' made on account of the two present tenses which precede, is unnecessary. Zumpt refers to two like instances, Act. ii. Lib. 2. c. 15. 39.

25. *Hospes Janitor qui nihil suspicaretur*] This form, with 'iste qui non . . . posset,' and 'iste qui . . . reperiretur,' are good examples of one of the niceties of the Latin language, which a few pertinent examples explain better than rules. The dependence of these clauses on 'hospes' and 'iste' is obvious. The ordinary explanation is, that these subjunctives express the reason or motive for what is declared by the clause of the indicative, which follows. They might, therefore, be translated, 'the host, because he had no suspicion of the real intention of Verres, fearing,' &c.; and, 'Verres, because he could not invent any excuse for leaving his host.' The next chapter contains another example: 'homo qui . . . existimatus esset.' In all these, and other like cases, the principal predication of the sentence is not contained in the 'qui' and the subjunctive, which clause is quite subordinate. The meaning is this: 'qui nihil suspicaretur' stands in what some grammarians call the attributive relation to the subject. So we might say, 'Janitor, the host, having no suspicion at all;' and the Latin expression is 'nihil suspicans,' 'quum nihil suspicaretur,' or 'qui nihil suspicaretur;' as to which we must observe that 'quum' itself is a form of 'qui;' but 'quum' with the subjunctive is not exactly the same as 'qui,' which marks the subject more distinctly; and 'quum' in this passage would not say all that 'qui' does. An example will explain the difference between 'qui' with an indicative, and with a subjunctive, in a case of this kind: "Hic lictor istius Cornelius, qui cum ejus servis erat a Rubrio quasi in praesidio ad auferendam mulierem collocatus, occiditur . . . : iste qui sua cupiditate tantos tumultus concitatos videret, cupere aliqua evolare si posset" (c. 26).

viam munire] A metaphorical use of 'munire.' See Lib. 3. c. 68.

suis jam tum mali constitueretur, tamen ad istum venit; ostendit munus illud suum non esse; se, quum suae partes essent hospitum recipiendorum, tum ipsos tamen praetores et consules non legatorum asseclas recipere solere. Iste qui una cupiditate raperetur totum illius postulatum causamque neglexit: per vim ad eum qui recipere non debebat Rubrium deduci imperavit.

XXVI. Hic Philodamus posteaquam jus suum obtinere non potuit, ut humanitatem consuetudinemque suam retineret laborabat. Homo qui semper hospitalissimus amicissimusque nostrorum hominum existimatus esset, noluit videri ipsum illum Rubrium invitus [in] domum suam recepisse: magnifice et ornate, ut erat in primis inter suos copiosus, convivium comparat: rogat Rubrium ut quos ei commodum sit invitet, locum sibi soli si videatur relinquat: etiam filium suum, lectissimum adolescentem, foras ad propinquum suum quendam mittit ad cenam. Rubrius istius comites invitat: eos omnes Verres certiores facit quid opus esset. Mature veniunt: discumbitur. Fit sermo inter eos, et invitatio ut Graeco more biberetur. Hortatur hospes: poscunt majoribus poculis: celebratur omnium sermone laetitiaque convivium. Posteaquam

munus] 'duty,' something of a public nature which a man was bound to do.—'quum suae' &c.: 'when it was his turn to receive strangers.'

asseclas] A shortened form of such a word as 'adsecula,' which contains the crude form 'sequu,' or 'secu,' to follow. Forcellini observes, that in some MSS. of Cicero, the reading in the Pro Sestio, c. 64, is 'assecula.'

26. *jus suum &c.*] 'could not maintain his right.'

quos . . . commodum] 'whom he pleased.' See Lib. 5. c. 5.

invitatio ut Graeco more] Asconius explains this by saying that it was the Greek fashion, when a man drank his wine, to address the gods, and then his friends by name. In the Tusculanae Disputationes (i. 40) it is said that Theramenes, on drinking the poison, threw what remained at the bottom out of the cup, so as to make a noise on the floor, we may suppose, and said: "Propino hoc pulcro Critiae, qui in eum fuerat teterrimus: Graeci enim in conviviis solent nominare cui poculum traditori sint." Zumpt explains 'Graeco more' to be the 'propinandi mos,' or the custom of addressing the person to whom you wish well, and offering him a glass to empty, after having first put it to your lips.

poscunt majoribus] 'they call for larger cups:' 'bibere' being supplied, as it is generally explained. In Lib. 3. c. 44, there is 'quum maximis poculis . . ministraretur.' The expression seems to be elliptical, a phrase of ordinary conversation, in which part is omitted of what ought to be said. In Horace (Carm. i. 4) we have in some texts

"Seu poscat agna sive malit haedo,"

which is to be understood by referring to the previous verse. Asconius says, "sunt qui producta scilicet O litera poscunt legunt, quasi saepe potant;" though he does not adopt this interpretation, and it is not likely that any one else will. There does not appear to be a verb 'po-scere,' containing the root 'po,' 'to drink,' though it is a possible form, and there is the noun 'po-sca,' which may be compared with 'e(d)-sca.'

celebratur . . . convivium.] Such sentences as these, so different from our mode of expression, are instances of the extreme difficulty of translating the Latin language. The notion of 'celebrare' is to 'fill,' as in Cicero, De Prov. Cons. c. 9, "cujus literis, &c., celebrantur aures quotidie meae novis nominibus gentium;" "domus nostra celebratur," Pro Murena, c. 34. The meaning here is: 'all the guests were talking and enjoying themselves.'

satis calere res Rubrio visa est, Quaeso, inquit, Philodame, cur ad nos filium tuam non intro vocari jubes? Homo qui et summa gravitate, et jam id aetatis et parens esset, obstupuit hominis improbi dicto. Instare Rubrius. Tum ut aliquid responderet negavit moris esse Graecorum, ut in convivio virorum accumberent mulieres. Hic tum alius ex alia parte: Enimvero ferendum hoc [quidem] non est; vocetur mulier: et simul servis suis Rubrius ut januam clauderent et ipsi ad fores assisterent imperat. Quod ubi ille intellexit id agi atque id parari ut filiae suae vis afferretur, servos suos ad se vocat: his imperat ut se ipsum negligant, filiam defendant; excurrat aliquis qui hoc tantum domestici mali filio nuntiet. Clamor interea fit tota domo inter servos Rubrii atque hospitis. Jactatur domi suae vir primus et homo honestissimus: pro se quisque manus affert: aqua denique ferventi a Rubrio ipso Philodamus perfunditur. Haec ubi filio nuntiata sunt, statim exanimatus ad aedes contendit ut et vitae patris et pudicitiae sororis succurreret. Omnes eodem animo Lampsaceni simul ut hoc audierunt, quod eos quum Philodami dignitas, tum injuriae magnitudo movebat, ad aedes noctu

satis calere res] Hotmann compares Demosthenes περὶ παραπρεσβείας, § 196, Bekk., ὡς δὲ προῄει τὸ πρᾶγμα καὶ διεθερμαίνοντο, &c. But 'calere' and διεθερμαίνοντο are not aptly compared. Forcellini translates the passage thus: 'when Rubrius thought that they were all well heated with wine.' The meaning is what Zumpt says: 'when matters seemed ripe, when all seemed to be going on well.' As to this impudent proposal to call in the young woman, and the answer of Philodamus, compare Herodotus (v. 18), where the Persian ambassadors having well drunk called for the women of their host, the king of Macedonia. The king's reply was: Ὦ Πέρσαι, νόμος μὲν ἡμῖν γέ ἐστι οὐκ οὗτος ἀλλὰ κεχωρίσθαι ἄνδρας γυναικῶν.

id aetatis] 'of such an age' as he was. 'Id' and 'hoc' are often used with genitives. See Lib. 2. c. 37.

Tum ut &c.] 'Tum ille ut' Orelli.

Enimvero] The word 'enim' sometimes stands alone at the beginning of a sentence; and with 'vero' attached to it, very often. It means 'in very deed,' 'in very truth this is not to be endured;' and it is an expression of emotion, and some irritation, as we see in Terence (Phorm. iii. 4. 1), "Enimvero, Antipho, multimodis cum istoc animo es vituperandus;" and in Plautus.

Quod . . . id] "Quod," says Zumpt, "ad orationem continuandam pertinet, fere ut Germ. *was*, cum sine accentu dicitur." But this is no explanation. 'Quod' is the relative, and 'id' is a further exponent; 'now when he observed this, that the object was.' See Lib. 2. c. 26, and the note. So Cicero says, "Quod utinam, Quirites, ego id aut primus aut solus ex hac re publica sustulissem," Pro C. Rabirio, c. 3.

filio nuntiet.] 'filio suo nuntiet' Orelli. —'tota domo, pugna inter:' Orelli, Iordan; but 'pugna' is in no MSS. The authority for it is Rufin. de figg. i. 36. Rau proposes 'pugnatur.' There may be still another proposition, which is to let the text stand as it is in the MSS.

vir primus] Zumpt compares Lib. 2. c. 4. 8; and Lib. 3. c. 71. He omits 'homo,' and Iordan also, following his best MSS., though he gives good reasons for retaining 'homo.' Cicero, he says, often uses both 'vir' and 'homo' together, and generally couples 'honestissimus' with 'homo' and not with 'vir.'

pro se quisque] As in Terence, 'pro se quisque sedulo faciebant,' Haut. i. 1. 70. It is a common Roman expression, and perhaps it means 'every man does his best, without respect to what others are doing.' Comp. c. 35, 'pro sua quaeque parte . . . civitates.'

convenerunt. Hic lictor istius Cornelius, qui cum ejus servis erat a Rubrio quasi in praesidio ad auferendam mulierem collocatus, occiditur, servi nonnulli vulnerantur, ipse Rubrius in turba sauciatur; iste qui sua cupiditate tantos tumultus concitatos videret, cupere aliqua evolare si posset.

XXVII. Postridie homines mane in contionem conveniunt: quaerunt quid optimum factu sit: pro se quisque, ut in quoque erat auctoritatis plurimum, ad populum loquebatur: inventus est nemo cujus non haec et sententia esset et oratio: Non esse metuendum, si istius nefarium scelus Lampsaceni ulti vi manuque essent, ne senatus populusque Romanus in eam civitatem animadvertendum putaret: quod si hoc jure legati populi Romani in socios nationesque exteras uterentur, ut pudicitiam liberorum servare ab eorum libidine tutam non liceret, quidvis esse perpeti satius quam in tanta vi atque acerbitate versari. Haec quum omnes sentirent et quum in eam rationem pro suo quisque sensu ac dolore loqueretur, omnes ad eam domum in qua iste deversabatur profecti sunt; caedere januam saxis, instare ferro, ligna et sarmenta circumdare, ignemque subjicere coeperunt. Tum cives Romani qui Lampsaci negotiabantur concurrunt: orant Lampsacenos ut gravius apud eos nomen legationis quam injuria legati putaretur: sese intelligere hominem illum esse impurum ac nefarium; sed quoniam nec perfecisset quod conatus esset, neque futurus esset Lampsaci postea, levius eorum peccatum fore si homini scelerato pepercissent quam si legato non pepercissent. Sic iste multo sceleratior et nequior quam ille Hadrianus aliquanto etiam felicior fuit. Ille quod ejus avaritiam cives Romani ferre non potuerant Uticae domi suae vivus exustus est: idque illi merito accidisse existimatum est, ut laetarentur omnes neque ulla animadversio constitueretur: hic sociorum ambustus incendio, tamen ex illa flamma periculoque evolavit; neque adhuc causam ullam excogitare potuit quamobrem commiserit aut quid

27. *optimum factu*] 'optimum factum' G 1 2 Lg 29. The variation is common in Latin MSS.

Hadrianus] This C. Fabius Hadrianus was the governor of Africa. The story is told by Valerius Maximus (ix. 10, § 2. Comp. Livy, Epitome, 86, and Orosius, v. 20). Klotz remarks that Cicero does not tell us that the death of this scoundrel was not avenged, mainly because he was opposed to the party of Sulla, which had then the supremacy, and was glad to be rid of him.—'ferre non potuerunt:' Zumpt, Jordan.—'idque ita illi merito:' Orelli.

causam . . . quamobrem] So after 'causa' Cicero often uses 'cur,' a short form of 'qua re,' as in c. 31, 'quae igitur fuit causa cur.' Terence (Hec. iii. 3. 32) has the same expression as Cicero: "Abs te quamobrem haec abierit causam vides," so far as 'causam' and 'quamobrem;' but in this case we have also another clause depending on 'commiserit.' The text means: 'Nor has Verres ever yet been able to invent any excuse founded either on his acts, or on circumstances which will ex-

evenerit ut in tantum periculum veniret. Non enim potest dicere, Quum seditionem sedare vellem, quum frumentum imperarem, quum stipendium cogerem, quum aliquid denique rei publicae causa gererem; quod acrius imperavi, quod animadverti, quod minatus sum. Quae si diceret, tamen ignosci non oporteret, si nimis atrociter imperando sociis in tantum adductus periculum videretur.

XXVIII. Nunc quum ipse causam illius tumultus neque veram dicere neque falsam confingere audeat, homo autem ordinis sui frugalissimus, qui tum accensus C. Neroni fuit, P. Tettius, haec eadem se Lampsaci cognosse dixerit, vir omnibus rebus ornatissimus C. Varro, qui tum in Asia tribunus militum fuit, haec eadem ipsa se ex Philodamo audisse dicat—potestis dubitare quin istum fortuna non tam ex illo periculo eripere voluerit quam ad vestrum judicium reservare? Nisi vero illud dicet quod et in testimonio Tettii priore actione interpellavit Hortensius:—quo tempore quidem signi satis dedit, si quid esset quod posset dicere, se tacere non posse, ut quamdiu tacuit in ceteris testibus scire omnes possemus nihil habuisse quod diceret:—hoc tum dixit, Philodamum et ejus filium a C. Nerone esse damnatos. De quo ne multa disseram, tantum dico, secutum id esse Neronem et ejus consilium, quod Cornelium lictorem occisum esse constaret: putasse non oportere esse cuiquam ne in ulciscenda quidem injuria hominis occidendi potestatem. In quo video Neronis judicio non te absolutum esse improbitatis, sed illos damnatos esse caedis. Verum ista damnatio tamen cujusmodi fuit? Audite, quaeso, judices, et aliquando miseremini sociorum, et ostendite aliquid his in vestra fide praesidii esse oportere.

XXIX. Quod toti Asiae jure occisus videbatur istius ille, verbo lictor, re vera minister improbissimae cupiditatis, pertimuit iste ne Philodamus Neronis judicio liberaretur: rogat et orat Dolabellam ut de sua provincia decedat, ad Neronem proficiscatur; se demon-

plain how he got into such great danger.' It is difficult to translate, and yet the meaning is perfectly clear.

28. *accensus*] 'A summoning officer.' The functions of an 'accensus' appear from the Commentarii Consulares, quoted by Varro (L. L. vi. 88, ed. Müller): "qui exercitum imperaturus erit, accenso dicit hoc: Calpurni, voca in licium omnes Quirites huc ad me," &c. 'Accensi' were also employed in the courts (Ad Q. Fr. 1. c. 4). See 'Accensus,' Forcellini.—The word 'frugalitas' is defined by Cicero (Tusc. Disp. iii. 8): "ejus (frugalitatis) enim videtur esse proprium motus animi appetentes regere et sedare, semperque adversantem libidini moderatam in omni re servare constantiam; cui contrarium vitium nequitia dicitur."

ut quamdiu &c.] 'ut, quamdiu in ceteris rebus tacuerit' Orelli.—'Sed hoc tum dixit' Orelli. 'Sed' is an addition of Lambinus.—'Ne multum disseram' Zumpt, Klotz, and Iordan.

strat incolumem esse non posse, si Philodamo vivere atque aliquando Romam venire licuisset. Commotus est Dolabella: fecit id quod multi reprehenderunt, ut exercitum, provinciam, bellum relinqueret, et in Asiam hominis nequissimi causa in alienam provinciam proficisceretur. Posteaquam ad Neronem venit, contendit ab eo ut Philodami causam cognosceret. Venerat ipse qui esset in consilio et primus sententiam diceret; adduxerat etiam praefectos et tribunos militares suos quos Nero omnes in consilium vocavit; erat in consilio etiam aequissimus judex ipse Verres; erant nonnulli togati creditores Graecorum, quibus ad exigendas pecunias improbissimi cujusque legati plurimum prodest gratia. Ille miser defensorem neminem reperire poterat. Quis enim esset aut togatus qui Dolabellae gratia, aut Graecus qui ejusdem vi et imperio non moveretur? Accusator autem apponitur civis Romanus de creditoribus Lampsacenorum, qui si dixisset quod iste jussisset, per ejusdem istius lictores a populo pecuniam posset exigere. Quum haec omnia tanta contentione, tantis copiis agerentur; quum illum miserum multi accusarent, nemo defenderet; quumque Dolabella cum suis praefectis pugnaret in consilio; Verres fortunas agi suas diceret; idem testimonium diceret, idem esset in consilio, idem accusatorem parasset; haec quum omnia fierent et quum hominem constaret occisum, tamen tanta vis istius injuriae, tanta in isto improbitas putabatur ut de Philodamo AMPLIVS pronuntiaretur.

XXX. Quid ego nunc in altera actione Cn. Dolabellae spiritus, quid hujus lacrimas et concursationes proferam? quid C. Neronis, viri optimi atque innocentissimi, nonnullis in rebus animum nimium timidum atque demissum? qui in illa re quid facere potuerit non habebat, nisi forte, id quod omnes tum desiderabant, ut ageret eam

29. *quod multi reprehenderunt,*] Cicero merely says that many persons found fault with Dolabella for leaving his province under the circumstances. Hotmann's notion that such conduct was punishable, hardly requires a confutation. Klotz, however, has shown that the old commentator was mistaken. A mere personal absence from his province, like this, was not an offence; the governor, who quitted his province for a temporary purpose, left a representative behind him.

togati] Romans: 'equites,' as Asconius says. They may or may not have been 'equites,' though it is most probable that they were. They were 'negotiatores.' 'Togati' is a general name for Roman citizens (Sallust, Jug. c. 21).

amplius] He was not condemned or acquitted, but the case was adjourned: 'causa ampliata est.' See the passage in Gellius (xiv. c. 2), 'juravi mihi non liquere;' and the examples in Forcellini, v. Amplius, &c.

30. *in altera actione*] In the proceedings against Philodamus after the adjournment. "Hinc apparet etiam in ampliatione *alteram* dici quemadmodum in comperendinatione." (Ascon.)

nimium timidum] 'nimis timidum' Orelli.

facere potuerit] Ernesti proposed 'faceret' or 'facere posset.' Jordan says, "h. l. conjunctivus perfecti violat leges sermonis Tulliani." See ii. Lib. 2. c. 21, 'ponerent.'

rem sine Verre et Dolabella. Quidquid esset sine his actum, omnes probarent: tum vero quod pronuntiatum est, non per Neronem judicatum sed per Dolabellam ereptum existimabatur. Condemnatur enim perpaucis sententiis Philodamus et ejus filius. Adest, instat, urget Dolabella ut quamprimum securi feriantur, quo quam minime multi ex illis de istius nefario scelere audire possent. Constituitur in foro Laodiceae spectaculum acerbum et miserum et grave toti Asiae provinciae; grandis natu parens adductus ad supplicium; ex altera parte filius; ille quod pudicitiam liberorum, hic quod vitam patris famamque sororis defenderat. Flebat uterque non de suo supplicio, sed pater de filii morte, de patris filius. Quid lacrimarum ipsum Neronem putatis profudisse? quem fletum totius Asiae fuisse? quem luctum et gemitum Lampsacenorum? securi esse percussos homines innocentes, nobiles, socios populi Romani atque amicos, propter hominis flagitiosissimi singularem nequitiam atque improbissimam cupiditatem? Jam, jam, Dolabella, neque me tui neque tuorum liberum, quos tu miseros in egestate atque in solitudine reliquisti, misereri potest. Verresne tibi tanti fuit ut ejus libidinem hominum innocentium sanguine lui velles? Idcircone exercitum atque hostem relinquebas ut tua vi et crudelitate istius hominis improbissimi pericula sublevares? Quod enim eum tibi quaestoris in loco constitueras, idcirco tibi amicum in perpetuum fore putasti? Nesciebas ab eo Cn. Carbonem consulem, cujus re vera quaestor fuerat, non modo relictum sed etiam spoliatum auxiliis, pecunia, nefarie oppugnatum et proditum? Expertus igitur es istius perfidiam tum quum se ad inimicos

Laodiceae] Cicero does not say which Laodicea he means; but the place appears to be Laodicea ad Lycum, in Phrygia, which was within the limits of Dolabella's government (c. 38). It is now Eski Hissar, or the Old Castle, in the south-west angle of the old province of Phrygia. Under the Roman dominion it was a flourishing commercial city, and one of the earliest Christian communities in Asia Minor.

neque me—misereri potest.] Zumpt compares Cic. Pro Ligar. c. 5, 'cave te fratrum—misereatur.'

lui] 'Luere' means to loose, like 'solucre' (solvere). 'Luere' is used, like 'solvere,' to express the payment of a debt (Act. i. c. 9, note); as in the Twelve Tables (Plin. H. N. xvii. c. 1); and 'luere pignus,' to release a pledge (Julian, Dig. 30. s. 86). The expression 'luere peccata sua' is exactly the same: it means 'to loosen or discharge their offences;' that is, to pay the penalty, and so to remove the offence. Cicero says: 'Was Verres, in your estimation, worth so much, that you would have the guilt of his lustful passion discharged by the blood of innocent men?' It ought to have been discharged by his own blood. It is natural enough that when 'luere' signified to pay the penalty of an offence, as (Ad Attic. iii. 9) 'itaque mei peccati luo poenas,' 'I pay the penalty of my offence,' it should come to be used briefly thus: 'itaque peccatum meum luo.' The loose translation of 'luere' by 'expiate,' and the like words, should be abandoned.

quaestor fuerat,] Zumpt correctly explains 'auxiliis, pecunia,' by 'auxilia quae pecunia continebantur,' as Asconius also does.

tuos contulit, quum in te homo ipse nocens acerrimum testimonium dixit, quum rationes ad aerarium nisi damnato te referre noluit.

XXXI. Tantaene tuae, Verres, libidines erunt ut eas capere ac sustinere non provinciae populi Romani, non nationes exterae possint? Tune quod videris, quod audieris, quod concupieris, quod cogitaris, nisi id ad nutum tuum praesto fuerit, nisi libidini tuae cupiditatique paruerit, immittentur homines, expugnabuntur domus, civitates non modo pacatae, verum etiam sociorum atque amicorum ad vim atque ad arma confugient, ut ab se atque a liberis suis legati populi Romani scelus ac libidinem propulsare possint? Nam quaero abs te circumsessusne sis Lampsaci, coeperitne domum in qua deversabare illa multitudo incendere; voluerintne legatum populi Romani comburere vivum Lampsaceni. Negare non potes. Habeo enim testimonium [tuum] quod apud Neronem dixisti; habeo quas ad eundem literas misisti. Recita hunc ipsum locum de testimonio. TESTIMONIVM C. VERRIS IN ARTEMIDORVM. [Recita ex Verris literis ad Neronem. EX LITERIS C. VERRIS AD C. NERONEM] NON MVLTO POST IN DOMVM. Bellumne populo Romano Lampsacena civitas facere conabatur, deficere ab imperio ac nomine nostro volebat? Video enim et ex iis quae legi et audivi intelligo, in qua civitate non modo legatus populi Romani circumsessus, non modo igni, ferro, manu, copiis oppugnatus, sed aliqua ex parte violatus sit, nisi publice satisfactum sit, ei civitati bellum indici atque inferri solere. Quae fuit igitur causa cur cuncta civitas Lampsacenorum de contione, quemadmodum tute scribis, domum tuam concurrerit? Tu enim neque in literis quas Neroni mittis, neque in testimonio causam tanti tumultus ostendis ullam. Obsessum te dicis, ignem allatum, sarmenta circumdata, lictorem tuum occisum esse dicis, prodeundi tibi in publicum potestatem factam negas: causam hujus tanti terroris occultas. Nam si quam Rubrius injuriam suo nomine ac non impulsu tuo et tua cupiditate fecisset, de tui comitis injuria questum ad te potius quam te oppugnatum venirent. Quum igitur quae causa illius tumultus fuerit testes a nobis producti dixerint, ipse celarit, nonne causam

damnato te] Because Dolabella after his condemnation went into exile, and his evidence could not be received to contradict the accounts of Verres.

31. *Recita ex Verris &c.*] These words, as far as 'C. Neronem,' "fluxerunt ex solius Hotomani opinione, et a Lambino primo temere sunt in ordinem recepta, pro perpetua ejus ac servili obedientia erga illum" (Zumpt). This remark shows Zumpt's opinion of Lambinus as an editor of Cicero. Classen (Pro Cluentio, c. 16, note) gives Lambinus a better character; and I hope that he deserves it.

concurrerit?] 'concurrerent' dtt. Orelli.

hanc quam nos proposuimus quum illorum testimonia tum istius taciturnitas perpetua confirmat?

XXXII. Huic homini parcetis igitur, judices, cujus tanta peccata sunt ut ii quibus injurias fecerit neque legitimum tempus exspectare ad ulciscendum neque vim tantam doloris in posterum differre potuerint? Circumsessus es. A quibus? A Lampsacenis: barbaris hominibus, credo, aut iis qui populi Romani nomen contemnerent. Immo vero ab hominibus et natura et consuetudine et disciplina lenissimis, porro autem populi Romani conditione sociis, fortuna servis, voluntate supplicibus; ut perspicuum sit omnibus, nisi tanta acerbitas injuriae, tanta vis sceleris fuisset, ut Lampsaceni moriendum sibi potius quam perpetiendum putarent, nunquam illos in eum locum progressuros fuisse ut vehementius odio libidinis tuae quam legationis metu moverentur. Nolite, per deos immortales, cogere socios atque exteras nationes hoc uti perfugio quo, nisi vos vindicatis, utentur necessario. Lampsacenos in istum nunquam ulla res mitigasset, nisi eum poenas Romae daturum credidissent. Etsi talem acceperant injuriam quam nulla lege satis digne persequi possent, tamen incommoda sua nostris committere legibus et judiciis quam dolori suo permittere maluerunt. Tu mihi—quum circumsessus a tam illustri civitate sis propter tuum scelus atque flagitium; quum coëgeris homines miseros et calamitosos quasi desperatis nostris legibus et judiciis ad vim, ad manus, ad arma confugere; quum te in oppidis et civitatibus amicorum non legatum populi Romani sed tyrannum libidinosum crudelemque praebueris: quum apud exteras nationes imperii nominisque nostri famam tuis probris flagitiisque violaris; quum te ex ferro amicorum populi Romani eripueris, atque ex flamma sociorum evolaris—hic tibi perfugium speras futurum? Erras. Ut huc incideres non ut hic conquiesceres illi te vivum exire passi sunt.

XXXIII. Et ais judicium esse factum te injuria circumsessum esse Lampsaci, quod Philodamus cum filio condemnatus sit. Quid si doceo, si planum facio, teste homine nequam, verum ad hanc rem tamen idoneo, te ipso, inquam, teste docebo, te hujus circumsessionis

32. *legitimum tempus*] 'the time fixed by the Lex;' for it was only after the expiration of his office that Verres could have been tried at Rome. Garatoni quotes the words of the Lex Servilia: "de hisce dum magistratum aut imperium habebunt judicium non fiet." The praetor, under whom a 'legatus' was, might rescind the acts of his inferior, as in the case mentioned in the Divinatio (c. 17), to which Klotz refers, but he could not try him. He might, however, dismiss him from his office. See Act. ii. Lib. 2. c. 11, referred to by Klotz.

Tu mihi] See Lib. 2. c. 32, note.

33. *teste docebo,*] 'teste doceo,' Orelli, Iordan. 'Doceo' is a correction of Ernesti.

tuae causam et culpam in alios transtulisse, neque in eos quos tu insimularas esse animadversum. Jam nihil te judicium Neronis adjuvat. Recita quas ad Neronem literas misit. EPISTOLA C. VERRIS AD NERONEM. THEMISTAGORAS ET THESSALVS. Themistagoram et Thessalum scribis populum concitasse. Quem populum? Qui te circumsedit, qui te vivum comburere conatus est. Ubi hos persequeris? ubi accusas? ubi defendis jus nomenque legati? In Philodami judicio dices id actum? Cedo mihi ipsius Verris testimonium: videamus quid idem iste juratus dixerit. [Recita.] AB ACCVSATORE ROGATVS RESPONDIT IN HOC IVDICIO NON PERSEQVI: SIBI IN ANIMO ESSE ALIO TEMPORE PERSEQVI. Quid igitur te juvat Neronis judicium, quid Philodami damnatio? Legatus quum esses circumsessus, quumque, quemadmodum tute ad Neronem scripsisti, populo Romano communique causae legatorum facta esset insignis injuria, non es persecutus: dicis tibi in animo esse alio tempore persequi. Quod fuit id tempus? quando es persecutus? Cur imminuisti jus legationis? cur causam populi Romani deseruisti ac prodidisti? cur injurias tuas conjunctas cum publicis reliquisti? Non te ad senatum causam deferre, non de tam atrocibus injuriis conqueri, non eos homines qui populum concitarent consulum literis evocandos curare oportuit? Nuper M. Aurelio Scauro postulante, quod is Ephesi se quaestorem vi prohibitum esse dicebat quo minus e fano Dianae servum suum, qui in illud asylum confugisset,

transtulisse,] Zumpt and Klotz have preferred 'contulisse,' and 'insimularis,' the readings of Asconius, to the MSS. authority. There is no doubt that Asconius found these readings in his MSS. Iordan has 'insimularis.'

ab accusatore rogatus] Verres was produced as a witness in the case of Philodamus, as Asconius says; and Cicero says so too. Asconius adds, "Loqui enim nisi interrogato testi non licebat;" and we can readily believe that too. A witness only answers the questions which are put to him, when he can be kept to his office, which is sometimes difficult to do (Asconius). He also says, "Interrogabatur autem et ab eo contra quem productus est:" a witness was cross-examined: and we know that too.

imminuisti &c.] 'Why have you impaired the rights and privileges of Legati?' He means to say to Verres, 'If your cause was just, why did you not prosecute those who violated the privileges of a Legatus of the Roman people? By acting in this way you have damaged the dignity of a Legatus.' The expression 'minuere,' or 'imminuere,' is also applied to the offence of 'majestas,' that is, the impairing of the integrity of the Roman power; and the conduct of Verres was, in fact, if Cicero's statement were true, a case of 'majestas imminuta.'

reliquisti?] 'neglected.'

populum concitarent] On the authority of the better MSS., Zumpt writes 'concitarent.' Orelli and Iordan have 'concitarant.' It is one of those cases in which either word may stand; but the sense of the passage will vary with the form of this verb. 'Qui concitarant' would be an affirmation by Cicero, that certain persons had stirred up the people to a riot; which Cicero certainly did not mean to admit. 'Qui concitarent' is what Verres says. Zumpt seems to me not consistent in writing 'concitarent' here, and 'quos insimularis' above.

asylum] The practice of criminals taking refuge or seeking asylum in temples, was

abduceret, Pericles Ephesius, homo nobilissimus, Romam evocatus est, quod auctor injuriae illius fuisse argueretur: tu, si te legatum ita Lampsaci tractatum esse senatum docuisses, ut tui comites vulnerarentur, lictor occideretur, ipse circumsessus paene incenderere, ejus autem rei duces et auctores principes fuisse quos scribis Themistagoram et Thessalum, quis non commoveretur? quis non ex injuria quae tibi esset facta sibi provideret? quis non in ea re causam tuam, periculum commune agi arbitraretur? Etenim nomen legati ejusmodi esse debet quod non modo inter sociorum jura sed etiam inter hostium tela incolume versetur.

XXXIV. Magnum hoc Lampsacenum crimen est libidinis atque improbissimae cupiditatis. Accipite nunc avaritiae propemodum in suo genere non levius. Milesios navem poposcit quae cum praesidii causa Myndum prosequeretur. Illi statim myoparonem egregium de sua classe ornatum atque armatum dederunt. Hoc praesidio Myndum profectus est. Nam quid Milesiis lanae publicae

common among the Greeks, of which there is a notable example in the case of Pausanias (Thucydides, i. 134). A passage in Tacitus (Ann. iii. 61) shows that this practice was checked by the Roman Senate in the time of Tiberius. The great temple of Artemis at Ephesus was one of the noblest monuments raised by ancient art, and an asylum, as Cicero says (Strabo, p. 641). But the asylum became a great abuse.—'fuisse arguebatur,' Zumpt, Iordan.—'auctores et principes:' Orelli, Iordan.

sociorum jura] 'The name of Legatus ought to be inviolate, not only in the midst of the rights of the Socii, but even amidst the weapons of enemies.' It is clear enough what Cicero means to say, but to transfer it into another language is not easy; for, if we abandon the Roman form, we lose the force of the expression; and, if we keep to it closely, we produce a version which is hardly English. To express the meaning without regard to Cicero's form, we may say: 'in fact, the name of Legatus ought to be a protection to him who bears it, not only among our Socii, who have rights which the Roman people acknowledge, but also against an enemy in time of war.' 'Jus legatorum,' 'jus legationis' are the privileges of 'legati' (see Divin. c. 20, note on 'jus'). Compare Caesar, B. G. iii. 9, "legatos, quod nomen ad omnes nationes sanctum inviolatumque semper fuisset."

34. *Milesios*] "*a Milesiis* Lg 29, Serv. ad Virg. Georg. iv. 334, quae constructio Ciceroni sane est multo usitatior." (Iordan.)

myoparonem] The μυοπάρων is mentioned by Plutarch (Antonius, c. 35). Compare Appian, Civil War, v. 95. It appears that the Milesians had a fleet which, according to Asconius, they were required to maintain, by virtue of their 'foedus' with the Roman people. See c. 35, and Pro Flacco, c. 12. 'Decem enim naves jussu L. Murenae, &c.—quae cum praesidii causa,' &c.: Zumpt gives other examples of 'is' being used, when the reflective pronoun appears to be the proper word (Cic. De Or. i. 54; Pro Sest. c. 24, "ne noctem quidem consules inter meum discrimen et eorum praedam interesse passi sunt"). See also Act. ii. Lib. 2. c. 62; Lib. 4. c. 39.

Nam quid] The usual form when Cicero does not intend to dwell on a subject.

lanae publicae] Milesian wool (Milesia vellera) is often mentioned. Graevius explains this wool to be that which the city of Miletus derived from the sheep on the public pastures, part of which wool was paid as a contribution to the Romans. But the text says simply 'public;' it says nothing of any part of it being due to the Romans. Lambinus has 'publice.' Miletus was famed for its skill in dyeing wool. Athenaeus, quoting Timaeus, says that the people of Sybaris in Italy wore dresses of Milesian wool, and this commercial connexion made these cities friends (Athen. xii. p. 519, ed. Casaub.).

abstulerit, item de sumptu in adventum, de contumeliis et injuriis in magistratum Milesium, tametsi dici quum vere, tum graviter et vehementer potest, tamen dicere praetermittam, eaque omnia testibus integra reservabo: illud, quod neque taceri ullo modo, neque dici pro dignitate potest, cognoscite. Milites remigesque Miletum Myndo pedibus reverti jubet: ipse myoparonem pulcherrimum de decem Milesiorum navibus electum L. Magio et L. Fannio qui Myndi habitabant vendidit. Hi sunt homines quos nuper senatus in hostium numero habendos censuit: hoc illi navigio ad omnes populi Romani hostes usque ab Dianio quod in Hispania est ad Sinopam quae in Ponto est navigaverunt. O dii immortales, incredibilem avaritiam, singularemque audaciam! Navem tu de classe populi Romani, quam tibi Milesia civitas ut te prosequeretur dedisset, ausus es vendere? Si te magnitudo maleficii, si [te] hominum existimatio non movebat, ne illud quidem cogitabas, hujus improbissimi furti sive adeo nefariae praedae tam illustrem ac tam nobilem civitatem testem futuram? An quia tum Cn. Dolabella in eum, qui ei myoparoni praefuerat Milesiisque rem gestam renuntiarat, animadvertere tuo rogatu conatus est, renuntiationemque ejus quae erat in publicas literas relata illorum legibus tolli jusserat, idcirco te ex hoc crimine elapsum esse arbitrabare?

XXXV. Multum te ista fefellit opinio, et quidem multis in locis.

L. Magio &c.] Asconius observes that these two men, who belonged to the Marian faction, were sent by Mithridates the Great to Sertorius in Spain, to propose the formation of an alliance against the Roman power. The communication between Sertorius and Mithridates is mentioned by Plutarch (Sertorius, c. 23), Appian (Mithridatica, c. 68), and Orosius (vi. 2). Cicero says that they sailed in this very ship from Dianium, a town on the east coast of Spain (Denia), and a colony of Massalia, to Sinope in Pontus, one of the chief towns of Mithridates. The MSS. have 'Sinopam;' but 'Sinopen' would be the regular form. Zumpt's remark, "quid? si negotiatoribus illis civitas Milesiorum debebat, ut pignoris capiendi jus haberent," does not seem to me of any weight. We cannot literally accept all that Cicero says, and Verres may have had some show of right or title to sell the ship; but Cicero says nothing that justifies him. Nor does the sentence, 'An quia tum Cn. Dolabella,' &c., support such a conjecture, as Klotz supposes. As we know nothing except what Cicero tells us, we must take all his evidence. He says that Verres borrowed the ship to protect him on his voyage to Myndus, which was no great distance, for it was near Halicarnassus in Caria. Cicero's words imply that Verres sailed in another vessel, and had the Milesian ship to protect him; and having made use of it, he sold it. The captain of the ship reported the sale, and his report was entered on the public books, which was evidence enough of the irregularity of the proceeding, and confirmed by the fact of the captain being punished by Cn. Dolabella, and of the entry being also erased from the public books at his order. If we take the whole as evidence, the guilt of Verres is established by the fact of the entry in the books being destroyed by Dolabella. Here we learn that 'publicae literae' was a name for public records (see Caesar, B. G. v. 47).

quod in Hispania est . . . quae in Ponto est] Iordan omits these words, yet they are in the MSS. It seems probable from the note of Asconius that they were not in his text of Cicero.

sive adeo] See Divin. c. 21.

Semper enim existimasti et maxime in Sicilia satis cautum tibi ad defensionem fore si aut referri aliquid in literas publicas vetuisses, aut quod relatum esset tolli coëgisses. Hoc quam nihil sit, tametsi ex multis Siciliae civitatibus priore actione didicisti, tamen etiam in hac ipsa civitate cognosce. Sunt illi quidem dicto audientes quamdiu adsunt ii qui imperant: simulac discesserunt, non solum illud perscribunt quod tum prohibiti sunt, sed etiam causam adscribunt cur non tum in literas relatum sit. Manent istae literae Mileti, manent, et dum erit illa civitas manebunt. Decem enim naves jussu L. Murenae populus Milesius ex pecunia vectigali populo Romano fecerat, sicut pro sua quaeque parte Asiae ceterae civitates; quamobrem unam ex decem, non praedonum repentino adventu sed legati latrocinio, non vi tempestatis sed hac horribili tempestate sociorum amissam in literas publicas rettulerunt. Sunt Romae legati Milesii, homines nobilissimi ac principes civitatis, qui tametsi mensem Februarium et consulum designatorum nomen exspectant, tamen hoc tantum facinus non modo negare interrogati, sed ne producti quidem reticere poterunt: dicent, inquam, et religione adducti et domesticarum legum metu, quid illo myoparone factum sit; ostendent C. Verrem in ea classe quae contra piratas aedificata sit piratam ipsum consceleratum fuisse.

XXXVI. C. Malleolo quaestore Cn. Dolabellae occiso duas sibi hereditates venisse arbitratus est; unam quaestoriae procurationis, nam a Dolabella statim pro quaestore jussus est esse; alteram tutelae, nam quum pupilli Malleoli tutor esset, in bona ejus

35. *dicto audientes*] 'obedient to orders,' one of Caesar's expressions (B. G. i. 39).

populo Romano] 'populi Romani' Orelli.

Februarium] In this month the Senate gave audience to ambassadors from the provinces, and from foreign states. Klotz refers to the principal passage on this matter in Cicero's Letters (Ad Fam. i. 4): "Senatus haberi ante Kalendas Febr. per legem Pupiam, id quod scis, non potest: neque mense Febr. toto nisi perfectis aut rejectis legationibus." He also refers to the Epistolae ad Quintum Fr. ii. 3; and to Polybius, vi. 12. In place of 'expectant,' Asconius mentions a reading 'extimescunt,' and he adds that the two words here signify the same thing. The Milesians were of course acquainted with the names of the 'consules designati,' Hortensius and Metellus; and 'expectant' does not therefore refer to the knowledge of their names, but to what they might expect from consuls who bore the names of Hortensius and Metellus. The passage means, "though the Milesians have to wait for February, when they will get their audience, and are yet uncertain what treatment to expect from the 'consules designati,' whose names they know."

religione] 'by their oath:' "qui jurati testes produci solent, non solum ne falsa dicant, verum etiam ne ea quae vera sunt taceant." (Ascon.) Whether this is merely derived from the text or contains an independent fact, we cannot tell, nor do we know the form of a Roman judicial oath. The witnesses, he means, were bound to tell the whole truth.

quid illo] 'quid de illo' dtt. mss.; but 'de illo' is Latin.

36. *pupilli – tutor*] We must suppose that Malleolus by his testament appointed

impetum fecit. Nam Malleolus in provinciam sic copiose profectus erat ut domi prorsus nihil relinqueret; praeterea pecunias occuparat apud populos et syngraphas fecerat; argenti optimi caelati grande pondus secum tulerat; nam ille quoque sodalis istius erat in hoc morbo et cupiditate; grande pondus argenti, familiam magnam, multos artifices, multos formosos homines reliquit. Iste quod argenti placuit invasit; quae mancipia voluit abduxit; vina ceteraque quae in Asia facillime comparantur, quae ille reliquerat, asportavit; reliqua vendidit, pecuniam exegit. Quum [eum] ad HS vicies quinquies redegisse constaret, ut Romam rediit, nullam literam pupillo, nullam matri ejus, nullam tutoribus reddidit;

Verres the tutor of his son, who was 'impubes,' that is, under the age when he could do legal acts; and therefore he required, according to Roman usage, a 'tutor,' for the protection of his property and his interests. The ward was called 'pupillus;' that is, 'pupillus' is the legal name of an 'impubes' whose property is under the care of a 'tutor.'

sic copiose] Ernesti thought that 'copiose' was a gloss, but without any reason. Comp. De Sen. c. 8, 'Sic aride.' Zumpt remarks, '*Sic* hoc modo pro *tam* adhiberi rarum est.' Comp. Act. I. c. 6, 'sic erat humilis . . ut videretur.' 'Sic' is often used in this way; and there is no use in saying that it is used for 'tam.'

occuparat] This means, 'he had laid out,' he employed his money in loans to the 'populi,' the provincials. He went out for the purpose of enriching himself by money-lending and traffic, after Roman fashion. 'Occupare,' in this sense, is explained by the examples in Forcellini; and by Cicero, Pro Flacco, c. 21. As to this practice of money-lending at exorbitant interest, see Cic. Ad Att. v. 21. Asconius says: "Between syngraphae and the other chirographa there is this difference, that in the other it is usual for those things or transactions only to be inserted which have actually occurred; in syngraphae, an agreement (pactio) enters which is even contrary to fact (contra fidem veritatis), and money which has never passed (non numerata), or has not passed to the full amount, is entered according to the pleasure of the parties at the time, in conformity with the usage and practice of the Greeks: other writings (tabulae) are used to be kept of the one part only; syngraphae, signed by the hand of each party, are delivered to each party to keep." The passage of Gaius (iii. § 134) is as follows: "Praeterea litterarum obligatio fieri videtur chirographis et syngraphis, id est, si quis debere se aut daturum se scribat; ita scilicet si eo nomine stipulatio non fiat. Quod genus obligationis proprium peregrinorum est."

This distinction of Asconius between 'syngrapha' and 'chirographum' does not appear to be true. 'Syngrapha,' in the old Greek law, did not denote a particular kind of contract, but is the general name for any written evidence of an agreement, a sense which it had in common with other terms which were occasionally used. (Cicero, Phil. ii. 37, vol. iv.). The Romans found such writings in use in their Greek provinces, and also the rule of law established, that a man might sue upon any written agreement, without regard to its form. 'Chirographum,' in Cicero's time, meant any writing, particularly one in the handwriting of the person whom it specially concerned, but it had no particular reference to legal transactions. In the second century of the Christian aera, the word was generally used to signify an acknowledgment of a debt, but it was not limited to the case of a loan; and the two words, 'syngraphae' and 'chirographa,' were generally used indifferently. So it was in the time of Gaius; and in the provinces a man might sue on a contract contained in any informal writing, which was contrary to the rule of Roman law (Savigny, Vermischte Schriften, vol. i., Literalcontract der Römer).

familiam magnam,] 'Familia' is here taken in its wider sense, which includes a man's slaves. 'Familia et pecunia' comprehended all that a man had. "Familiam pecuniamque tuam endo mandatam tutelam custodelamque meam recipio," &c. Gaius, ii. 104.

nullam literam] Schütz conjectured that 'literam' should be 'libellum;' not

servos artifices pupilli quum haberet domi, circum pedes autem homines formosos et literatos, suos esse dicebat, se emisse. Quum saepius mater et avia pueri postularent, uti, si non redderet pecuniam nec rationem daret, diceret saltem quantum pecuniae Malleoli deportasset, a multis efflagitatus aliquando dixit HS decies: deinde in codicis extrema cera nomen infimum in flagitiosa litura fecit: expensa Chrysogono servo HS sexcenta millia accepta pupillo Malleolo rettulit. Quomodo ex decies HS sexcenta sint facta; quomodo ne eodem modo quadrarint ut illa de Cn. Carbonis pecunia reliqua HS sexcenta facta sint; quomodo Chrysogono expensa lata sint; cur id nomen infimum in lituraque sit vos existimabitis. Tamen HS sexcenta millia quum accepta rettulisset, HS quinquaginta millia soluta non sunt; homines, posteaquam reus factus est, alii redditi, alii etiam nunc retinentur: peculia omnium vicariique retinentur.

an improbable conjecture (Act. ii. Lib. 2. c. 10), if 'literam' is unintelligible. If 'litera' is right, it has reference to 'ratio,' 'accounts,' and means, that he did not give in a single letter of accounts.—'multis efflagitatus:' Orelli. But 'a multis,' which Zumpt has taken from some of the best MSS., seems better; for 'multis,' as Zumpt observes, is 'multis verbis.'

circum pedes] I suppose that this means 'about him,' 'in attendance on him.'

codicis &c.] 'Codex' or 'codices,' or 'codex accepti et expensi,' 'tabulae,' 'domestica ratio,' are names for account-books, which were, it appears, sometimes kept on tablets smeared with wax. At the bottom of the 'codex,' in the lowest part of the 'tabella,' there was an erasure in the last entry (nomen). As to these 'codices,' which every citizen kept who was 'sui juris,' see Pro Rosc. Am. c. 2, 3.

expensa &c.] These are the usual Roman forms. 'Expensum ferre,' or 'referre,' is to make an entry on the credit side in a man's books: 'acceptum ferre,' or 'referre,' is to make an entry of money received, or on the debit side. If a man lent another a sum of money, it would appear in the lender's books as an 'expensum' (Phil. vi. c. 5). Verres entered six hundred thousand as received by him on account of Malleolus, but he also entered the same amount as paid to Chrysogonus. "You may conjecture," says Cicero, "how he reduced the 'decies' (centena millia) to 'sexcenta millia.'" Comp. c. 39, 'Quod minus Dolabella,' &c.; and Lib. 2. c. 70. 'Nam quas pecunias,' &c. It does not appear how Verres could discharge himself by such an entry against Chrysogonus, who was probably his slave. His books showed that he had received the six hundred thousand, and he was answerable for it. But we cannot explain that which Cicero professes himself unable to understand. See c. 38, note on 'his nominibus.'—'sexcenta facta sunt:' Orelli.

quinquaginta millia &c.] The common reading is 'quinque millia,' which Ernesti explains thus: that Verres did not pay even 'quinque millia' to the 'heredes.' But this cannot be the meaning, as Zumpt shows. Verres was bound to pay what his books showed that he had received; but, in some way that is not explained, he contrived to retain 'quinquaginta millia,' as the best MSS. have it.

peculia &c.] The 'peculium' was that property which a 'filiusfamilias,' that is, a son who was in his father's power, or a slave held, with the father's or master's consent; for a 'filiusfamilias,' or a slave, could not strictly hold property. All that a son acquired, with some limitations (castrense peculium), and all that a slave acquired, belonged to the father or master; but, by usage, a slave had a kind of property which was considered his own, and it was called his 'peculium.'

'Vicarii servi' were such slaves as another slave was allowed to hold as part of his 'peculium;' and such slaves were part of the 'peculium' of the slave, who was

XXXVII. Haec est istius praeclara tutela. En cui tuos liberos committas: en memoria mortui sodalis: en metus vivorum existimationis. Quum tibi se tota Asia spoliandam ac vexandam praebuisset, quum tibi exposita esset omnis ad praedandum Pamphylia, contentus his tam opimis rebus non fuisti; manus a tutela, manus a pupillo, manus a sodalis filio abstinere non potuisti? Jam te non Siculi, non aratores, ut dictitas, circumveniunt, non hi qui decretis edictisque tuis in te concitati infestique sunt: Malleolus a me productus est, et mater ejus atque avia, quae miserae, flentes, eversum a te puerum patriis bonis esse dixerunt. Quid exspectas? an dum ab inferis ipse Malleolus exsistat, atque abs te officia tutelae, sodalitatis familiaritatisque flagitet? Ipsum putato adesse. Homo avarissime et spurcissime, redde bona sodalis filio: si non quae abstulisti, at quae confessus es. Cur cogis sodalis filium hanc primum in foro vocem cum dolore et querimonia emittere? cur sodalis uxorem, sodalis socrum, domum denique totam sodalis mortui, contra te testimonium dicere? cur pudentissimas lectissimasque feminas in tantum virorum conventum insolitas invitasque prodire cogis? Recita omnium testimonia. TESTIMONIUM MATRIS ET AVIAE.

XXXVIII. Pro quaestore vero quomodo iste commune Milyadum vexarit, quomodo Lyciam, Pamphyliam, Pisidiam, Phry-

their 'quasi dominos.' Ulpian (Dig. 15. 1. 17) says, "sicut ipsi vicarii sunt in peculio, ita etiam peculia eorum."

37. *en memoria*] Zumpt observes that some MSS., and one of them among the best, have 'en memoriam—en metum;' but he observes that Cicero always uses 'en' with a nominative; and even 'ecce,' except in De Fin. ii. 30, where he proposes to omit 'ecce.'—'vexandam tradidisset' Orelli.

non potuisti?] I have placed a note of interrogation at the end of this sentence, with Orelli, Klotz, and Iordan.—'ille Malleolus' Or.

at] 'At' may be here translated 'at least.' Neither 'sed' nor 'autem' could perform the office of 'at' in this passage. The sense of the passage is this: 'Si non quae abstulisti' means as much as if Verres were to say, 'I won't restore all that I have taken:' to which the answer is, 'Well, we don't expect that; we don't expect all: but let us have what you have charged yourself with receiving.'

38. *commune*] 'Mire commune rem publicam,' Asconius. There is nothing strange in 'commune' being used for a 'community.' It is the same as the Greek τὸ κοινὸν τῶν 'Αχαιῶν, and 'Αθηναίων τὸ κοινὸν, Thucyd. i. 89. The form τὸ κοινὸν occurs in inscriptions. This use of 'commune' is the remote origin of the French 'commune' (Thierry, Lettres sur l'histoire de France, xiii. xiv.). Forcellini does not supply instances; but 'commune Siciliae' occurs (Act. ii. Lib. 2. c. 46, 59), where it ought to be 'commune Siculorum,' to correspond to the Greek expression. This Milyas is a mountainous tract in the south-west part of Asia Minor, bordering on Lycia and Pamphylia. The form corresponding to 'commune Siciliae' would be 'commune Milyados.' Zumpt supposes that Cicero's 'Milyadum' is a shorter form of 'Milyadarum.' The Greek name of the people is Μιλύαι.

Lyciam, &c.] Dolabella is said to have been propraetor of Cilicia (c. 16), but it has been observed that all the crimes of Dolabella and Verres were committed in other parts of Asia, and that he seems never to have reached the country named Cilicia. It is true that Cicero says nothing

giamque totam frumento imperando, aestimando, hac sua quam tum primum excogitavit Siciliensi aestimatione afflixerit, non est necesse demonstrare verbis. Hoc scitote: his nominibus—quae res

of Cilicia; but that is all. It is also said that P. Servilius Isauricus first established a province of Cilicia in B.C. 75 after his conquests in Lycia, Pamphylia, and Isauria, but even this province of Cilicia does not appear to have comprehended more than a very small part of mountainous Cilicia. The real annexation to the Roman empire of the two countries named Cilicia was the work of Cn. Pompeius Magnus in B.C. 67 and 66. The Romans then seem before B.C. 66 to have used the name Cilicia Provincia to indicate their most remote provincial government in Asia, without regard to accuracy, but perhaps with a view to the possession of Cilicia, when they could get it. (Becker, Röm. Alt. iii. 1, p. 164.)

frumento imperando, &c.] 'requiring certain quantities of grain, and then commuting his demand into a money payment.'

his nominibus] 'Nomen' (c. 36) is a word which signifies 'heads' or 'entries' in a book of accounts, which entries would contain the names of persons and other circumstances. Hence 'nomen' is used generally for a head or title of account. Savigny (Vermischte Schriften, i. 213) shows that the Roman expression, 'nomina facere' (Inst. iv. tit. 21; Cic. De Off. iii. 14), signifies the contracting that 'obligatio' which the Romans called the 'obligatio literis' or 'literarum.' If we can ascertain in what form the 'nomina facere' was made, we shall also ascertain in what form the 'obligatio literis' was effected. Many passages show that 'nomina facere' is an entry in a 'codex' or 'tabulae,' without any reference to any other documentary evidence than that which the 'codex' supplies (Verr. Lib. i. c. 36, 39; Ad Att. iv. 18; Seneca, De Benef. iii. c. 15; Cic. Pro Rosc. Com. c. 5). In this last passage Cicero enumerates the three strict forms of contract upon which a 'pecunia certa' could be sued for. He says that it must be either 'pecunia data,' a loan; or 'stipulata,' that is, the claim must be founded on the peculiar Roman contract called 'stipulatio;' or it must be 'expensa lata,' that is, 'expensilatio,' or an entry in the 'codex.' Such an entry was itself the forming of the contract. It is true that 'tabulae,' like other writings, could be used as evidence; but that does not prove that entries might not be the contract itself. A promissory note, or a bill of exchange, in itself expresses an 'obligatio,' whatever other use may be made of it as evidence. This ordinary 'codex accepti et expensi,' which every man was expected to keep, contained the entries, in the order of time, of all a man's receipts and payments, with the matter to which the receipts and payments referred, and the names of the persons from whom the sums were received, or to whom they were paid. Out of such a book or journal a man might make a more formal book, in which his transactions with each individual might be arranged under their several heads; but this would be a different kind of book from the 'codex accepti et expensi.' As to the 'literarum obligatio,' it was the entry of the creditor in his 'codex' (expensilatio) which made the 'obligatio,' and gave to it its name, and not the entry of the debtor in his 'codex' (acceptilatio), which corresponded to the entry of the creditor. The difficulties that are obvious as to the proof of a debt in the case of an 'obligatio literis,' have nothing to do with the nature of the 'obligatio,' which is clearly ascertained. Nor is it supposed that a mere entry by a man in his 'codex' (expensilatio) could make another man his debtor. If debtor and creditor were both honest men, the 'expensilatio' in the books of the one would correspond to the 'acceptilatio' in the books of the other. If they did not, there must be evidence to prove that the 'expensilatio' was properly made. This is certain, that in the 'obligatio literarum' the creditor sued upon the entry in his 'codex,' as the contract; but this is quite a different matter from the evidence that he might have to produce in order to show that the entry was made under such circumstances as would entitle the maker to sue on it. (See Gaius, iii. 132.)

quae res &c.] 'Quae res' refers to 'nomina,' but 'quae' alone would not have expressed Cicero's meaning. It is explanatory of 'nomina,' and the meaning of 'quae' is enlarged by the addition of 'res:' 'on these items or heads, I mean what he did when he required of the cities corn, skins, hair cloth, sacks,' &c. The skins and hair cloths were for the use of the army and navy. As to 'quae res,' comp. 'quibus ego in rebus interfui,' c. 40.

per hunc gestae sunt quum iste civitatibus frumentum, coria, cilicia, saccos imperaret, neque ea sumeret proque his rebus pecuniam exigeret—his nominibus solis Cn. Dolabellae HS ad tricies litem esse aestimatam. Quae omnia etiamsi voluntate Dolabellae fiebant, per istum tamen omnia gerebantur. Consistam in uno nomine: multa enim sunt ex eodem genere. Recita. DE LITIBVS AESTIMATIS CN. DOLABELLAE PR. PECVNIAE REDACTAE. QVOD A COMMVNI MILYADVM. Te haec coëgisse, te aestimasse, tibi pecuniam numeratam esse dico: eademque vi et injuria, quum pecunias maximas cogeres, per omnes partes provinciae te tamquam aliquam calamitosam tempestatem pestemque pervasisse demonstro. Itaque M. Scaurus, qui Cn. Dolabellam accusavit, istum in sua potestate ac ditione tenuit. Homo adolescens quum istius in inquirendo multa furta ac flagitia cognosset, fecit perite et callide: volumen ejus rerum gestarum maximum isti ostendit: ab homine quae voluit in Dolabellam abstulit; istum testem produxit: dixit iste quae velle accusatorem putavit. Quo ex genere mihi testium qui cum isto furati sunt si uti voluissem magna copia fuisset; qui ut se periculo litium conjunctione criminum liberarent, quo ego vellem descensuros pollicebantur. Eorum ego voluntatem omnium repudiavi. Non modo proditori sed ne perfugae quidem locus in meis castris cuiquam fuit. Forsitan meliores illi accusatores habendi sint qui haec omnia fecerunt. Ita est: sed ego defensorem in mea persona, non accusatorem maxime laudari volo. Rationes ad aerarium antequam Dolabella condemnatus est non audet referre: impetrat a senatu ut dies sibi prorogaretur, quod tabulas suas ab accusatoribus Dolabellae obsignatas diceret, proinde quasi exscri-

proque his rebus] Orelli omits 'que,' contrary to the best MSS., and contrary to the usage of the language; for, as Zumpt observes, 'que' is often used for 'sed,' when it is preceded by a negation—'etiamsi voluntate . . tamen omnia:' Cicero generally, in these orations, uses 'tametsi—tamen.'

calamitosam] See Lib. 3. c. 98.

Forsitan—sint] Orelli has 'sunt;' but it appears that Cicero uses 'forsitan' with the subjunctive (Zumpt).

dies—prorogaretur,] 'that the time should be extended.' Thus the Romans said 'prorogatum imperium,' to express the prolongation of a man's 'imperium' (Ad Q. Fr. i. 1. 1): and, in the same sense, Cicero says 'ne provincia nobis prorogetur' (Ad Att. v. 11).

proinde quasi] 'just as if he had not the power of taking copies.' 'Proinde' is often used thus with 'quasi.' (Ter. Haut. i. 1. 13; Sallust, Cat. c. 12.) 'Proinde' is one of the compound forms of 'inde,' of which there are 'exinde,' 'deinde,' 'subinde.' 'Perinde' is perhaps not a genuine form. (See Key's Lat. Gram. 2nd ed.) In the following chapter, Orelli, Zumpt, and Klotz have 'perinde.' Zumpt maintains the existence of 'perinde,' and he attempts to make a distinction between the meaning of the two words. The MSS. are not decisive authority in a matter of this kind, and they give both forms, as in this passage. Analogy is in favour of 'proinde' only.

bendi potestatem non haberet. Solus est hic qui nunquam rationes ad aerarium referat.

XXXIX. Audistis quaestoriam rationem tribus versiculis relatam; legationis non nisi condemnato et ejecto eo qui posset reprehendere; nunc denique praeturae quam ex senatus consulto statim referre debuit usque ad hoc tempus non rettulit. Quaestorem se in senatu exspectare dixit; proinde quasi non, ut quaestor sine praetore possit rationem referre, ut tu Hortensi, ut omnes, eodem modo sine quaestore praetor. Dixit idem Dolabellam impetrasse. Omen magis patribus conscriptis quam causa placuit. Probaverunt. Verum quaestores quoque jampridem venerunt. Cur non rettulisti? Illarum rationum ex ea faece legationis quaestoriaeque tuae procurationis illa sunt nomina, quae Dolabellae necessario sunt aestimata. EX LITIBVS AESTIMATIS DOLABELLAE PR. ET PROPR. Quod minus Dolabella Verri acceptum rettulit quam Verres illi expensum tulerit, HS quingenta triginta quinque millia; et quod plus fecit Dolabella Verrem accepisse quam iste in suis tabulis habuit, HS ducenta triginta duo millia; et quod plus frumenti fecit accepisse istum, HS decies et octingenta millia, quod tu, homo castissimus,

39. *Quaestorem se &c.*] The reading 'quaestores,' of Orelli and Iordan is a correction of Lambinus, according to Zumpt, who explains 'quaestorem' to be 'alterum quaestorem,' one of the Sicilian 'quaestors,' for there were two 'quaestors' for Sicily. But shortly after we have 'verum quaestores—venerunt;' and the correction of Lambinus seems probable enough. It is also the reading of Asconius. Zumpt observes that it was much more usual for a 'quaestor' to give in his accounts without his 'praetor,' than for the 'praetor' without his 'quaestor.' And he proves this by stating that 'praetors' or 'consuls' often stayed more than a year in a province, while the 'quaestors' were changed annually; and so it appears that 'quaestors' generally rendered their accounts without their 'praetor.' But this is very indifferent arguing, though the conclusion may be true. Zumpt asks, if all 'praetors' had done what Cicero says that they could do, give in their accounts without waiting for their 'quaestor,' with what show of right could Verres have said in the senate, that he was waiting for one of his 'quaestors?' The answer is, that it might be with no show of right, but a great show of impudence. Dolabella, said Verres, obtained permission to wait for his 'quaestor,' who was Verres himself. But this is not in favour of Zumpt's argument; for, if Dolabella had this allowed him (impetrarat), it is clear that it was a favour; and, instead of citing the case of Dolabella, Verres should have appealed to the general practice.

Omen] A Roman mode of expression which is very difficult to translate. Verres urged that Dolabella had obtained what he asked for; and Dolabella was afterwards tried and convicted. The senate was better pleased with the instance which Verres cited than with his argument, for they hoped, as Cicero would have us suppose, that the precedent of Dolabella might be made completo by Verres being convicted also.

PR. &c.] 'PR. ET PROPR.,' the reading of most of the MSS., seem to be the abbreviations for 'praetori' and 'propraetori.' Orelli's text is 'pr. p. r. pecuniae redactae.' But 'pecuniae redactae' is not in the MSS.; and, if these words were, 'p. r.' cannot mean 'populo Romano,' as some have supposed; for 'pecuniae redactae,' as Zumpt observes, is the same as 'exactae.'

castissimus,] 'callidissimus,' Zumpt, from one MS. G1.—'quod—aliud:' Er-

aliud in tabulis habebas. Hinc illae extraordinariae pecuniae, quas nullo duce tamen aliqua ex particula investigamus, redundarunt: hinc ratio cum Q. et Cn. Postumis Curtiis multis nominibus quorum in tabulis iste habet nullum: hinc HS quaterdecies P. Tadio numeratum Athenis testibus planum faciam; hinc empta apertissime praetura; nisi forte id etiam dubium est quomodo iste praetor factus sit. Homo scilicet aut industria aut opera probata aut frugalitatis existimatione praeclara, aut denique, id quod levissimum est, assiduitate, qui ante quaesturam cum meretricibus lenonibusque vixisset, quaesturam ita gessisset quemadmodum cognovistis, Romae post quaesturam illam nefariam vix triduum constitisset, absens non in oblivione jacuisset, sed in assidua commemoratione omnibus omnium flagitiorum fuisset, is repente, ut Romam venit, gratis praetor factus est. Alia porro pecunia ne accusaretur data. Cui sit data, nihil ad me, nihil ad rem pertinere arbitror: datam quidem esse tum inter omnes recenti negotio facile constabat. Homo stultissime et amentissime, tabulas quum conficeres, et quum extraordinariae pecuniae crimen subterfugere velles, satis te elapsurum omni suspicione arbitrabare, si quibus pecuniam credebas iis expensum non ferres neque in tuas tabulas ullum nomen referres, quum tot tibi nominibus acceptum Curtii referrent? Quid proderat tibi te expensum illis non tulisse? An tuis solis tabulis te causam dicturum existimasti?

XL. Verum ad illam jam veniamus praeclaram praeturam, criminaque ea quae notiora sunt his qui adsunt quam nobis qui

nesti would alter 'quod' to 'id;' and other alterations have been proposed, all of which are unnecessary. The text is as plain as it can be: 'the which you, most immaculate of men, had entered quite differently in your books.'

extraordinariae] Any money not acquired in the usual way might be called 'extraordinaria;' but probably this term had a technical meaning. That the money was in this case dishonestly acquired appeared from the amount, and from the fact of Verres keeping no account of these large sums, which he paid over to others to keep for him, and to avoid detection. The 'extraordinaria pecunia,' according to Savigny, consists in the omission of an entry which ought to be made, which entry was omitted for the purpose of fraud and concealment (Pro Rosc. Com. c. 1).

numeratum] The old reading 'numerata,' though the reading of all the MSS., as it is said, is not the true reading; for J. F. Gronovius has shown that HS, with a numeral adverb, must be taken as a neuter singular (Zumpt). See Zumpt's Appendix, and 'in ducentis et triciens sestertio,' Pro Fonteio, iii. 4, ed. Nieb.

assiduitate,] This is a term applied to candidates for offices, who showed themselves to the people, and canvassed for votes. Klotz refers to the oration Pro Cn. Plancio, c. 26, and Pro L. Murena, c. 9.

expensum . . acceptum] Verres made no entries of what he had lent, but the Curtii had made entries of what they had received from him. Cicero says that Verres could not escape by having kept no account of this transaction, for others had kept accounts, and their accounts would be produced. The books of Verres and of the Curtii ought to have agreed, if all the transactions were honest.

meditati ad dicendum paratique venimus; in quibus non dubito quin offensionem negligentiae vitare atque effugere non possim. Multi enim ita dicent: De illo nihil dixit, in quo ego interfui: illam injuriam non attigit, quae mihi aut quae amico meo facta est, quibus ego in rebus interfui. His omnibus qui istius injurias norunt, hoc est, populo Romano universo, me vehementer excusatum volo, non negligentia mea fore ut multa praeteream, sed quod alia testibus integra reservari velim, multa autem propter rationem brevitatis ac temporis praetermittenda existimem. Fatebor etiam illud invitus, me prorsus, quum iste punctum temporis nullum vacuum peccato praeterire passus sit, omnia quae ab isto commissa sunt non potuisse cognoscere. Quapropter ita me de praeturae criminibus auditote, ut ex utroque genere et juris dicundi et sartorum tectorum exigendorum ea postuletis, quae maxime digna sunt eo reo cui parvum ac mediocre objici nihil oporteat. Nam ut praetor factus est qui auspicato a Chelidone surrexisset, sortem nactus est urbanae provinciae magis ex sua Chelidonisque quam ex populi Romani voluntate. Qui principio qualis in edicto constituendo fuerit cognoscite.

XLI. P. Annius Asellus mortuus est C. Sacerdote praetore. Is quum haberet unicam filiam neque census esset, quod natura hortabatur, lex nulla prohibebat, fecit ut filiam bonis suis heredem institueret. Heres erat filia. Faciebant omnia cum pupilla,

40. *commissa sunt*] 'commissa sint,' Iordan, on the authority of the better MSS.; but perhaps 'sunt,' the reading of the worse, is better than 'sint.'

ex utroque genere] That is 'criminum,' of which 'et juris dicundi,' &c., is the explanation.

digna sunt] 'sint,' Orelli, Iordan. The MSS. authority is in favour of 'sunt,' a direct affirmation of Cicero.

Chelidone] Asconius observes that Cicero is playing on the word 'Chelidon,' which in Greek means a 'swallow,' and was also the name of the woman who was a favourite of Verres. As a swallow is a city bird, so Verres, who cohabited with Chelidon, had the good luck to get the city praetorship, under the auspices of Chelidon. But the explanation of Zumpt is better. "Verres," he says, "ought to have performed his religious duties in the morning, instead of which he rose from the embraces of Chelidon to go to the 'comitia.'" He adds, that there is an amphibolia in the word 'surgendo,' 'nam sedentes auspicabantur.' The words 'qui . . surrexisset' must be connected with 'factus est:' he was elected 'praetor' as one whose auspices were his having risen from the bed of Chelidon. As to 'provincia' and 'edictum,' see the Excursus iv. 'Edicta Magistratuum;' and Lib. 2. c. 1.

41. *P. Annius*] C. Ann. G12 s al. and Iordan; P. Ann. al. dtt. In Lib. 2. c. 7 he is named C. Annius in Iordan's ed. In c. 42 of this oration he has P. Annius.

neque census esset,] See the Excursus iii. on the 'Voconia Lex.'

heredem institueret.] 'Instituere' was the technical word for making a person 'heres' by a testament. Gaius (ii. 117). "sollemnis autem institutio haec est: Titius heres esto;" and see his remark on the forms 'heredem instituo,' 'heredem facio.' A 'secundus heres,' or, as Cicero here expresses it, "qui erat institutus secundum filiam" (next to, after), was one who was 'institutus' as 'heres,' if the first could not, or did not, take the 'hereditas.' See Gaius (ii. 174), "inter-

legis aequitas, voluntas patris, edicta praetorum, consuetudo juris ejus quod erat tum quum Asellus est mortuus. Iste praetor designatus—utrum admonitus an tentatus, an, qua est ipse sagacitate in his rebus, sine duce ullo, sine indice, pervenerit ad hanc improbitatem nescio; vos tantum hominis audaciam amentiamque cognoscite—appellat heredem L. Annium qui erat institutus secundum filiam; non enim mihi persuadetur istum ab illo prius appellatum: dicit se posse ei condonare edicto hereditatem; docet hominem quid possit fieri. Illi bona res, huic vendibilis videbatur. Iste, tametsi singulari est audacia, tamen ad pupillae matrem submittebat: malebat pecuniam accipere ne quid novi ediceret quam ut hoc edictum tam improbum et [tam] inhumanum interponeret. Tutores pecuniam praetori si pupillae nomine dedissent, grandem praesertim, quemadmodum in rationem inducerent, quemadmodum sine periculo suo dare possent, non videbant: simul et istum fore tam improbum non arbitrabantur. Saepe appellati pernegaverunt. Iste ad arbitrium ejus cui condonabat hereditatem ereptam a liberis, quam aequum edictum conscripserit, quaeso, cognoscite. QUUM INTELLIGAM LEGEM VOCONIAM. . . . Quis unquam crederet mulierum adversarium Verrem futurum? an ideo aliquid contra mulieres fecit ne totum edictum ad Chelidonis arbitrium scriptum videretur? Cupiditati hominum ait se obviam ire. Quis potius non modo his temporibus sed etiam apud majores nostros? quis tam remotus fuit a cupiditate? Dic, quaeso, cetera: delectat enim me hominis

dum duos pluresve gradus heredum facimus hoc modo," &c. In the case of 'liberi impuberes,' who were in the testator's power, he could also substitute other 'heredes,' even if the 'liberi' took the 'hereditas,' provided they died while 'impuberes.'

consuetudo juris &c.] 'the practice or usage about the rule of law which existed at the time of Asellus' death.' The rule of law which prevailed about wills at the time of the testator's death must be applied to the will. See c. 42, 'nihil de testamento,' &c.

appellat] Cicero makes Verres summon the 'heres,' whereas the 'heres' who claimed the 'hereditas' would apply to (appellare) the 'praetor.'—Orelli reads 'qua est iste sagacitate.'

condonare] Here this word seems to mean no more than 'donare.'

submittebat :] Forcellini explains this, and probably correctly, 'privately sent some one to the mother:' and he compares (Act. ii. Lib. 3. c. 28) 'submittebat iste Timarchidem,' &c.

in rationem inducerent,] 'bring it into their accounts.' 'Tutores' were liable to account for the administration of the property of their 'pupillus,' or 'pupilla,' when their functions were at an end; and they could not have justified such a payment.

condonabat] 'condonarat . . . ereptam liberis . . . scripserit' Orelli, but 'condonabat' is the true tense. Verres had not given yet. V has 'liberis;' but 'a liberis' is also used with 'eripere.' V has also 'aecum' for 'aequum;' and 'aecum' may be written just as we write 'cum' and 'quum.' See Lib. 3. c. 31.

Quis potius] This is said ironically. The words 'obviam ire' show what is to be supplied with 'Quis potius,' &c. 'Verres says that he will check men's greediness after lucre. Who more likely than he to do it, I don't say among men of our day, but even among our ancestors?' The 'majores nostri' belonged to the good old times.

gravitas, scientia juris, auctoritas. [Recita.] QVI AB A. POSTVMIO Q. FVLVIO CENSORIBVS POSTVE EA . . . FECIT, FECERIT. Quis unquam edixit isto modo? quis unquam ejus rei fraudem aut periculum proposuit edicto, quae neque post edictum neque ante edictum provideri potuit?

XLII. Jure, legibus, auctoritate omnium qui consulebantur testamentum P. Annius fecerat, non improbum, non inofficiosum, non inhumanum; quod si ita fecisset, tamen post illius mortem nihil de testamento illius novi juris constitui oporteret. Voconia lex te videlicet delectabat? Imitatus esses ipsum illum [Q.] Voconium qui lege sua hereditatem ademit nulli neque virgini neque mulieri: sanxit in posterum, qui post eos censores census esset, ne

auctoritas.] Klotz conjectured 'praetoris auctoritas,' as V has 'P. R. auctoritas.' Jordan has inserted 'praetoris' before 'auctoritas.'

Quis unquam &c.] This passage is obscure; and its meaning could only be fully ascertained if we had the text of the edict, instead of the few words which are cited: 'who ever made an edict after this fashion? who ever by his edict laid a snare or created a hazard, as to a matter which could not be provided against either after or before the publication of the edict?' Instead of 'ejus rei' 'ei rei' is the reading of V, which also has 'neque post edictum, provideri potuit reprehendi neque ante edictum,' out of which Mai made 'quae neque post edictum reprehendi neque ante edictum provideri potuit.' Orelli repeats 'fecit, fecerit?' thus. Zumpt contends that the words 'fecit, fecerit' are not to be taken in connexion with the words 'Qui ab A. Postumio,' &c., but that the chief part of the edict between 'postve ea' and 'fecit, fecerit' is omitted; and in his note, he gives what he supposes to be the substance of the part which is omitted. 'Qui ab A. Postumio,' &c. cannot, as Zumpt remarks, refer to the 'census' of these 'censors' as a time to reckon from; for, if that were so, the form should be 'A. Postumio, Q. Fulvio censoribus;' but the 'censors' were not thus referred to for the purpose of a determination of time. His conclusion is, and probably a just one, that the words which followed 'postve ea' referred to persons being 'censi;' and 'fecit, fecerit' referred to the words 'virginem mulieremve heredem.' The censorship of Postumius and Fulvius was B.C. 174.

42. *testamentum—non improbum,*] Asconius explains 'improbum testamentum' to be a 'testamentum' made 'contra leges;' which, if correctly interpreted, means in violation of some particular 'leges.' But his statement is not worth any thing. 'Improbus' is 'non probus,' 'not honest or upright:' it is joined with 'intestabilis' in a passage in the Twelve Tables quoted by Gellius (xv. 13). Neither 'improbum' nor 'inhumanum' appears to have a technical meaning. 'Inofficiosum' has a technical meaning. A 'testamentum inofficiosum' is a testament made in legal form, 'sed non ex officio pietatis,' 'not as a good man ought to make it.' If a man exheredated his own children, or passed over his parents, or brethren, or sisters, without some sufficient reason, the will, though good in form, might be attacked by these near kinsfolk, who would be his 'heredes' in case of intestacy, in a suit called 'Querela Inofficiosi.' The persons thus passed over, would, of course, be supposed to have merited this mark of the testator's disapprobation; but, if the disapprobation was unmerited, the testator had done them a wrong, and their remedy was to get the will set aside, as made under the influence of passion. The ultimate object of the suit, was the vindication of the character of the complainants; but the direct effect of the suit was to set aside the will and make them 'heredes.' It is not known when this form of action was introduced; and we cannot conclude because Cicero uses the term 'inofficiosum,' that the 'Querela Inofficiosi' existed in his time. —The subject is explained by Savigny, *System des Heut. Röm. Rechts*, ii. 127. See also Dig. 5, tit. 2, De Inofficioso Testamento.

quis heredem virginem neve mulierem faceret. In lege Voconia non est FECIT, FECERIT; neque in ulla praeteritum tempus reprehenditur nisi ejus rei quae sua sponte scelerata et nefaria est ut, etiamsi lex non esset, magno opere vitanda fuerit. Atque in his [ipsis] rebus multa videmus ita sancta esse legibus ut ante facta in judicium non vocentur. Cornelia testamentaria, nummaria, ceterae complures, in quibus non jus aliquod novum populo constituitur, sed sancitur ut, quod semper malum facinus fuerit, ejus quaestio ad populum pertineat ex certo tempore. De jure vero civili si quis novi quid instituerit, is omnia quae ante acta sunt rata esse non patietur? Cedo mihi leges Atinias, Furias, ipsam, ut dixi, Voconiam, omnes praeterea de jure civili: hoc reperies in omnibus statui jus quo post eam legem populus utatur. Qui plurimum tribuunt edicto, praetoris edictum legem annuam dicunt esse. Tu edicto plus amplecteris quam lege. Si finem edicto praetoris afferunt Kalendae Januariae, cur non initium quoque [edicti] nascitur a Kalendis Januariis? An in eum annum progredi nemo poterit edicto quo praetor alius futurus est; in illum quo alius praetor fuit regredietur? Ac si hoc juris non unius hominis causa edixisses, cautius composuisses.

in ulla] That is, 'in ulla lege.' 'Nisi ejus rei' means, 'nor is past time noticed except in a matter which is naturally criminal and wrong.' He means to say, that the moral notions of a people condemn some things, though there may be no 'lex' nor formal enactment on the matter. Those legal rules which exist in the common understanding and consciousness of a people, and have effect given to them by those who are empowered to declare the law, are a part of 'jus,' and are law in the most strict and exact sense of the term.

scelerata] 'tam scelerata' V, Iordan. The reading of V expresses the meaning, but adjectives are often used in Latin in the emphatic sense without 'tam' or 'ita,' and yet followed by 'ut' and a subjunctive mood.

in his [ipsis] rebus] This refers to 'ejus rei,' &c. He means to say, that many rules of law (jus) received a sanction from 'leges,' and yet the 'leges' were so framed as not to apply to past acts. 'Sanctio' is that part of a 'lex' which gives to it its efficacy, such as a penalty or punishment (Inst. Just. ii. tit. 1. s. 10). He instances a Lex Cornelia de Falso (for Cicero means only one Lex Cornelia here) on forged testaments and forged coin, which made these offences a Crimen Publicum and cognizable as such; but the 'lex' did not apply to offences committed before its enactment, as Cicero says. After 'Cornelia—complures' Hotmann understands 'sunt.'—'ejus quaestio ad populum,' &c., means 'it is made the subject of a Judicium Publicum.' See Excursus ii.

De jure . . . civili] Jus Civile here means Jus Privatum as opposed to Jus Publicum, which term Jus Publicum comprehended Criminal Law. Asconius has correctly marked this sense of Jus Civile.

si quis novi &c.] There is a great discrepancy in the form in which this passage is given in the editions, though none in the sense. Zumpt reads 'si quis novi quid instituit . . . rata esse patitur.' Klotz and Iordan read 'instituit . . . is non omnia . . . patietur?'

Furias,] Iordan has 'Furias, Fusias.' 'Furias' is omitted by Lg. 42. I cannot tell if 'Fusias' or some corrupted form of it is in all the MSS. 'Fusias' is perhaps the same word as 'Furias;' and if that is so, 'Fusias' is properly omitted in this passage. At least either 'Furias' or 'Fusias' should be left out. But see Zumpt's note, and also Orelli's Index Legum. As to these Leges, see Dict. of Antiquities, art. Lex.

XLIII. Scribis, SI QVIS HEREDEM FECIT, FECERIT. Quid si plus legarit quam ad heredem heredesve perveniat, quod per legem Voconiam ei qui census non sit licet? cur hoc quum in eodem genere sit non caves? Quia non generis sed hominis causam verbis complecteris, ut facile appareat te pretio esse commotum. Atque hoc si in posterum edixisses, minus esset nefarium, tamen esset improbum; sed tum vituperari posset, in dubium venire non posset; nemo enim committeret. Nunc est ejusmodi edictum ut quivis intelligat non populo esse scriptum sed P. Annii secundis heredibus. Itaque quum abs te caput illud tam multis verbis mercenario prooemio esset ornatum, ecquis est inventus postea praetor qui idem illud ediceret? Non modo nemo edixit, sed ne metuit quidem quisquam ne quis ediceret. Nam post te praetorem multi testamenta eodem modo fecerunt: in his nuper Annaea de multorum propinquorum sententia, pecuniosa mulier, quod censa non erat, testamento fecit heredem filiam. Jam hoc magnum judicium hominum de istius singulari improbitate, quod Verres sua sponte instituisset, id neminem metuisse ne quis reperiretur qui istius institutum sequi vellet. Solus enim tu inventus es cui non satis fuerit corrigere voluntates vivorum, nisi etiam rescinderes mortuorum. Tu ipse ex Siciliensi edicto hoc sustulisti; noluisti ex improviso si quae res natae essent ex urbano edicto decernere.

43. *si quis*] Iordan omits 'si' on the authority of V, and with V writes 'qui.'

Quia non generis &c.] Klotz and Iordan have 'quia non juris, &c. . . . amplecteris . . . te pretio non jure esse commotum.' This alteration is founded solely on V, which some editors prefer to the reading of all the MSS. It is plain that 'generis' refers to 'genere;' and I have no doubt that it is the true reading; and 'jure' has been added to balance the sentence.

committeret.] 'no one would have acted against the edict.' But the complete form would be 'committeret ut .. venire posset.'

Zumpt says, that the "edictum in dubium non venit, verum testamenta;" and he concludes that 'concinnitatis causa' Cicero has written rather carelessly. V, Iordan have 'in discrimen' in place of 'in dubium.'

Annaea] Zumpt prefers 'Annaea,' for which there is good authority, to the common reading 'Annia;' for, if this 'Annia' had been a kinswoman or sister of P. Annius, Cicero would have made that relationship matter for 'novam aliquam invidiam.' In place of 'multi testamenta eodem modo fecerunt,' Klotz and Iordan have 'multi in iisdem causis fuerunt,' from V.

corrigere voluntates] 'you are the only man ever known, who were not satisfied with regulating the wills of living persons, unless you could also rescind the expressed will of the dead.' He was not satisfied with laying down rules of law, which affected a man's future testamentary power, but he must also undo the testamentary dispositions of those who made their wills before his rule was made. 'Corrigere testamenta' Klotz, Iordan. See c. 44, 'voluntatem mortuis.'

noluisti ex improviso &c.] Orelli, Klotz, Zumpt, and Iordan have 'voluisti,' which, as Menard observes, is directly contrary to the meaning. 'Ex improviso' belongs to 'si quae res,' &c., or 'si quae res nata esset,' as Iordan has it. Zumpt and Klotz have a comma after 'improviso,' which Orelli and Iordan have not.

The difference between 'voluisti' and 'noluisti' in a MS., is so trifling, that we cannot depend on the readings, and we must endeavour to determine from the sense which is the true word. Menard observes, that if

Quam postea tu tibi defensionem relinquebas, in ea maxime offendisti, quum tuam auctoritatem tute ipse edicto provinciali repudiabas.

XLIV. Atque ego non dubito quin ut mihi, cui filia maxime cordi est, res haec acerba videatur atque indigna, sic unicuique vestrum qui simili sensu atque indulgentia filiarum commovemini. Quid enim natura nobis jucundius, quid carius esse voluit, quid est dignius in quo omnis nostra diligentia indulgentiaque consumatur? Homo importunissime, cur tantam injuriam P. Annio mortuo fecisti? cur hunc dolorem cineri ejus atque ossibus inussisti, ut liberis ejus bona patria, voluntate patris, jure, legibus tradita eriperes, et cui tibi esset commodum condonares? Quibuscum vivi bona nostra partimur, iis praetor adimere nobis mortuis bona fortunasque poterit? NEC PETITIONEM, inquit, NEC POSSESSIONEM DABO. Eripies igitur pupillae togam praetextam? detrahes ornamenta non solum

Verres had framed his decrees upon the 'urbanum edictum,' it could not be said that the 'urbanum edictum' was repealed by the Siciliense. In the beginning of c. 46, Cicero observes that Verres, as in the case of 'mulierum hereditates,' so in that of 'hereditatum possessiones,' had not transferred the chapters of his 'urbanum edictum' into the 'provinciale' (cur . . . transferre nolueris); and he says nothing of Verres making his 'decreta' as to such matters, under any circumstances, conformably to the 'urbanum,' but he assumes that these chapters were to have no effect at all.

He asks (c. 46), 'Did you think that the inhabitants of the province had a better title than ourselves to the enjoyment of "aequum jus?"' If Cicero had said that Verres intended (voluit) in cases not provided for, if such arose, to make his 'decreta' in conformity to the 'urbanum edictum,' that is, the inequitable chapters of it, he would have been destroying his own argument, which is, that Verres totally rejected these reprehensible chapters of his 'urbanum edictum.' 'Ex improviso' must be explained by reference to 'provideri' at the end of c. 41; and the sense of the passage is this: 'you did not choose in extraordinary cases to apply to your urban edict.' The end of this chapter proves clearly that 'noluisti' must be read, for Cicero says, 'The future defence which you were reserving for yourself, was a matter in which you made the greatest blunder, when by your provincial edict you repudiated your own precedent.' 'Vol' and 'nol' are often confounded.

44. *cui filia*] Cicero alludes to his daughter Tullia, who was probably born B.C. 79 or 78. See c. 58, 'habemus enim liberos,' &c.—'cui mea filia . . . videtur' V, Klotz, and Jordan.

bona fortunasque] See note on 'bona' and 'fortunas,' Divin. c. 20. 'Fortunam' is used in the singular by Scaevola (Dig. 4. 7. 40), "argentarius coactor totam fortunam in nominibus habebat:" he had all his money invested in loans, or out in some way.

petitionem,] The praetor declared that he would not allow her to sue (petere) for the 'hereditas;' for, in the case of an 'in rem actio,' one of the modes of proceeding was 'per formulam petitoriam,' in which the plaintiff (actor) claimed the thing as his property (Gaius, iv. 91, 92), "Petitoria autem formula haec est, qua actor intendit rem suam esse." Nor would the praetor allow her to take possession of the 'hereditas;' which possession would not of itself have conferred a legal title, though the praetor treated 'bonorum possessores' as 'heredes.'

togam praetextam?] The 'toga praetexta' was worn both by males and females; by boys till they assumed the 'toga virilis,' and by girls till they were married. As the 'toga' was the characteristic dress of the Romans, Cicero means to say, that the conduct of Verres was equivalent to depriving the girl of her citizenship, to stripping her even of the signs of her free birth (ingenuitas), treating her as a slave, as a person without rights.

fortunae sed etiam ingenuitatis? Miramur ad arma contra istum hominem Lampsacenos isse? miramur istum de provincia decedentem clam Syracusis profugisse? Nos si alienam vicem pro nostra injuria doleremus, vestigium istius in foro non esset relictum. Pater dat filiae; prohibes: leges sinunt; tamen te interponis. De suis bonis ita dat ut ab jure non abeat. Quid habes quod reprehendas? nihil, opinor. At ego concedo: prohibe si potes; si habes qui te audiat; si potest tibi dicto audiens esse quisquam. Eripias tu voluntatem mortuis, bona vivis, jus omnibus? Hoc populus Romanus non manu vindicasset, nisi te huic tempori atque huic judicio reservasset?

Posteaquam jus praetorium constitutum est, semper hoc jure usi sumus: si tabulae testamenti non proferrentur, tum, uti quemque potissimum heredem esse oporteret, si is intestatus mortuus esset, ita secundum eum possessio daretur. Quare hoc sit aequissimum facile est dicere; sed in re tam usitata satis est ostendere omnes antea jus ita dixisse, et hoc vetus edictum translatitiumque esse. XLV. Cognoscite aliud hominis in re vetere edictum novum; et simul, dum est unde jus civile discatur, adolescentes ei in disci-

pro nostra &c.] 'if we had grieved for another's lot, as if the wrong had been done to ourselves.' Zumpt compares Cic. Pro Rosc. Am. c. 21, 'pro summa solitudine.'

Posteaquam jus praetorium] See Excursus iv. on the Edicta Magistratuum.

The division into chapters is sometimes made in such a way as to obscure the argument. The matter of Annius, the Voconia Lex, concludes with the indignant words, 'huic judicio reservasset;' and the words 'Posteaquam jus praetorium,' &c., introduce the case of Minucius, as to which Cicero briefly states the law first, and then shows how Verres behaved in this matter. This is the remark of Madvig, Opuscula, p. 348, "De locis aliquot Ciceronis Orationum Verrinarum dissertatio critica."

possessio daretur.] It was part of the praetor's office to grant a 'bonorum possessio,' or permission to take possession of the property of a deceased person in many cases, which are mentioned further on, in the notes to this chapter. The case here put is that of the praetor granting a 'bonorum possessio' when no will was produced, though there might be a will, which for some reason was not produced. In such case, he could, as Cicero says, grant a 'bonorum possessio' to those who would be 'heredes' if the deceased had died intestate. But the praetor could not give such persons a legal title; the utmost that he could do was to protect them in the possession which he had allowed them to take. The words 'si is intestatus mortuus esset' are omitted by Orelli, though they are in the MSS., and in all the old editions, in conformity with the opinion of Hotmann that it is a gloss taken from Asconius. Hotmann observes that there is nothing for 'is' to refer to; but this difficulty Zumpt removes, by understanding 'alicui' with 'heredem esse.' But the true reading is probably indicated by the words of the edict quoted by Julian (Dig. 38. 7. 1), "tum quem ei heredem esse oporteret, si intestatus mortuus esset." The text of Cicero however may be explained as it stands. The words 'tabulae testamenti' imply some person whose 'tabulae testamenti' were not produced. 'Is' therefore is 'the person whose Tabulae were not produced.' 'Secundum eum' means 'in favour of him;' as in Act. ii. Lib. 2. c. 17, "de absente secundum praesentem judicare." So 'vindiciae secundum libertatem,' in favour of liberty (Dig. 1. tit. 2. § 24).

facile est dicere;] Orelli has 'docere.'

45. *aliud hominis*] 'hominis aliud' Jordan, who also has 'in disciplinam ei.'

plinam tradite. Mirum est hominis ingenium, mira prudentia. Minucius quidam mortuus est ante istum praetorem: ejus testamentum erat nullum: lege hereditas ad gentem Minuciam veniebat. Si habuisset iste edictum, quod ante istum et postea omnes habuerunt, possessio Minuciae genti esset data: si quis testamento se heredem esse arbitraretur quod tum non exstaret, lege ageret in hereditatem; aut pro praede litis vindiciarum quum satis accepisset, sponsionem faceret; ita de hereditate certaret. Hoc, opinor, jure et majores nostri et nos semper usi sumus. Videte ut hoc iste correxerit. Componit edictum iis verbis ut quivis intelligere possit unius hominis causa conscriptum esse, tantum quod hominem non nominat; causam quidem totam perscribit; jus, consuetudinem,

prudentia.] means ironically 'juris prudentia.'

lege hereditas] Lex, used thus absolutely, means the Lex Duodecim Tabularum, which, if there were no 'sui heredes,' gave the 'hereditas' to the 'agnati;' and, if there were no 'agnati,' the 'lex' gave the 'hereditas' to the 'gentiles,' which is the case that Cicero puts here (Gaius, iii. § 17; Cicero, De Or. i. 39). If Verres had adopted in his 'edictum' (habuisset) that rule of law which all praetors, both before him and since, have adopted, he would have given the 'possessio' to the 'gens.' The Gentilicium Jus, which was in force in the time of Cicero, had fallen into desuetude in the time of the Antonini, when Gaius wrote, "totum gentilicium jus in desuetudinem abiisse." As to 'gens' and 'gentiles,' see Dict. of Antiqs., 'Gens.'

lege ageret] In the time of Gaius there were three forms of procedure in use where either the ownership of a thing was claimed or an 'hereditas.' These three forms were the 'Sacramenti legis actio,' and the two forms of procedure 'per formulas.' The 'Sacramenti legis actio' is expressed in this passage of Cicero by the words 'lege ageret,' and this form of action was before the court of the Centumviri. The other form by which a man proceeded in Cicero's time in the case of an 'hereditas' was 'per sponsionem,' and that also is mentioned here. The third form by the 'formula petitoria' was also known to Cicero, but it was only used in his time where the ownership of a thing, not an 'hereditas,' was in question. Gaius describes the two methods 'per formulas' in the following terms.

If any man thought that he was entitled to the ownership of a thing or to an 'hereditas,' he could either sue directly by the 'formula petitoria,' in which case there must be a 'stipulatio judicatum solvi' on the part of the defendant in possession, by way of 'satisdatio,' or security, to the plaintiff; or the plaintiff would proceed by the 'sponsio,' and there would be, on the part of the defendant in possession, a 'pro praede litis et vindiciarum stipulatio,' which would be a security for the value of the thing (lis), the ownership of which was in dispute, and for the 'mesne' (intermediate) profits (vindiciae), as Gaius explains it (iv. § 91, &c.). The complete expression is 'pro praede litis et vindiciarum;' but Cicero's omission of 'et,' in which he is followed by Asconius, is conformable to Roman usage, as in the expression, 'Patres Conscripti,' 'usus fructus,' and others. Gaius says (iv. 94), "ideo autem appellata est pro praede litis vindiciarum stipulatio, quia in locum praedium successit, qui olim, cum lege agebatur, pro lite et vindiciis, id est pro re et fructibus a possessore petitori dabantur." Iordan says, "Gaius in hac formula semper habet *litis et vind.*" But the 'et' is omitted in this passage of Gaius, and Savigny infers that 'et' is an interpolation. (See Savigny, System, &c., v. § 209; and Beilage ix.; and also Vermischt. Schriften, i. p. 308.)

In the 'formula petitoria,' the plaintiff's claim (intentio) to the thing was expressed, as in Act. ii. Lib. 2. c. 12. In the 'sponsio,' the form of 'stipulatio' was this, "Si homo quo de agitur ex jure Quiritium meus est, sestertios CXXV nummos dare spondes?" And, with reference to this 'stipulatio,' the 'intentio' of the formula was, "Si paret N. N. A. A. SS. CXXV. nummos dare oportere." (Excursus v.)

aequitatem, edicta omnium negligit. EX EDICTO VRBANO. SI DE HEREDITATE AMBIGITVR. . . . SI POSSESSOR SPONSIONEM NON FACIET. Jam quid id ad praetorem uter possessor sit? nonne id quaeri oportet utrum possessorem esse oporteat? Ergo quia possessor est, non moves possessione; si possessor non esset, non dares. Nusquam enim scribis, neque tu aliud quicquam edicto complecteris nisi eam causam pro qua pecuniam acceperas. Jam hoc ridiculum est. SI DE HEREDITATE AMBIGITVR ET TABVLAE TESTAMENTI OBSIGNATAE NON MINVS MVLTIS SIGNIS QVAM E LEGE OPORTET AD ME PROFERENTVR, SECVNDVM TABVLAS TESTAMENTI POTISSIMVM HEREDITATEM DABO: hoc translatitium est: sequi illud oportet, si

si possessor] Klotz reads 'si est possessor,' and Asconius says 'subauditur *est*,' because there is a reading 'si et,' &c.; but it does not seem necessary to read 'si est.' Cicero quotes the words of the edict of Verres, 'if the person in possession shall not make the Sponsio,' &c. Cicero's argument is, Verres says 'si possessor;' but the question is not who is in possession, but who ought to be: according to your edict, because a man is in possession, you don't disturb him; and, for the same reason, if a man was not in possession, you would not give him the possession.

Possession here is to be taken in its proper sense. If two parties disputed about the ownership of a thing, he who is in possession must be the defendant, and he who is not in possession has the burden of proving his title. If therefore it was uncertain who was in possession, or who must be considered 'possessor,' this question must be settled first; and the praetor settled this by a 'possessorial interdict.' When Cicero then says 'uter possessor sit,' he simply means which of the two is in the corporeal possession of the thing; but that does not determine which of the two ought to be considered 'possessor' for the purposes of the suit, for the actual possessor might not be entitled to the possession. Zumpt says, "si quaeris, quod boni ex ista temporaria possessione homini contingere potuerit, unum hoc vetere proverbio respondeo: Beati possidentes." Such an answer however will not satisfy every body. (Excursus v.)

Jam hoc ridiculum est.] This is not more ridiculous than the pointing of Zumpt and others, who place (:) after 'ridiculum est,' and a full stop after 'hereditatem dabo.' There is nothing ridiculous in the 'translatitium edictum,' which Cicero quotes. The 'ridiculum' lies elsewhere. 'Jam hoc' refers to what precedes.

Si de hereditate &c.] Here we have a portion of the edict. The praetor gave the 'bonorum possessio,' (1) when there was no testament (Dig. 38. tit. 6, "si tabulae testamenti nullae extabunt"), that is, a 'possessio' in the case of intestacy, of which there were several cases, determined by the class of persons who in succession were entitled; (2) if there was a testament; and in this case either 'contra tabulas' or 'secundum tabulas.' 'If,' says the edict, 'a will is produced with the proper number of seals, that is, not fewer than seven, I will give the Hereditas according to the terms of the testament.' He ought to say 'possessio,' for the praetor could not make a 'heres' (Gaius, iii. 32); he could only allow a person to take possession of the property: but 'hereditas,' in the sense of 'possessio hereditatis,' may have been used. In c. 47 there is the expression 'possessionem hereditatis,' which Hotmann proposed to read here. Zumpt and Jordan here read 'possessionem' for 'hereditatem,' and this reading is in one MS. (Lg. 29.)

hoc translatitium est: &c.] These are the words of Cicero, who says that this part of the edict of Verres is adopted from former edicts, and is all right. (Comp. Dig. 38. tit. 6, 'si tabulae testamenti nullae,' &c.) If no 'tabulae' were produced, then the terms of the edict ought to be as in c. 44, 'Posteaquam jus praetorium,' &c. Comp. Dig. 38. 7. 1, "Haec verba edicti: Tum quem ei heredem esse oporteret," &c. But Cicero makes Verres say, 'then he will give the Hereditas to him who says that he is Heres,' that is, to a man who affirms that he is Heres by the testament, but does not produce the testament. Klotz supposes that Verres may have said, 'I will give it to him who proves himself to be Heres.' But, if Verres

TABVLAE TESTAMENTI NON PROFERENTVR. Quid ait? Se ei daturum qui se dicat heredem esse. Quid ergo interest proferantur necne? Si protulerit, uno signo ut sit minus quam ex lege oportet, non des possessionem: si omnino tabulas non proferet, dabis. Quid nunc dicam? Neminem unquam hoc postea alium edixisse? Valde sit mirum neminem fuisse qui istius se similem dici vellet. Ipse in Siciliensi edicto hoc non habet; exegerat enim jam mercedem: item ut illo edicto de quo ante dixi, in Sicilia de hereditatum possessionibus dandis edixit idem quod omnes Romae praeter istum: EX EDICTO SICILIENSI: SI DE HEREDITATE AMBIGITVR . . . .

XLVI. Ac per deos immortales quid est quod de hoc dici possit? Iterum enim jam quaero abs te, sicut modo in illo capite Anniano de mulierum hereditatibus, nunc in hoc de hereditatum possessionibus, cur ea capita in edictum provinciale transferre nolueris? Utrum digniores homines existimasti eos qui habitabant in provincia quam nos qui aequo jure uteremur, an aliud Romae aequum est, aliud in Sicilia? Non enim hoc potest hoc loco dici

said this, he would have said right. He who produced a will in which he was made 'heres' (and he could prove himself to be testamentary 'heres' in no other way), was entitled to the 'possessio.' The note of Asconius is unintelligible. The substance of the matter is, that the edict of Verres, according to Cicero, was irregular, and made for a corrupt purpose; but when he got to Sicily, he adopted the usual form, 'in hereditatum possessionibus dandis,' a form which every praetor at Rome used except himself, and which he deviated from for a corrupt purpose. Zumpt writes 'se ei daturum qui dicat,' &c., but 'invitus,' and in obedience to the MSS. Asconius has 'qui se dicat.'

The whole of this matter about the edict of Verres is difficult to understand, for we are confused between what ought to have been the edict of Verres, and what it was. To understand Cicero, we must take his statement as to the edict of Verres to be true; for, if we do not, we cannot see the justice of his conclusions. As Cicero represents the conduct of Verres, the absurdity of his edictal rule is apparent. Whether Cicero stated every thing correctly, is a different matter. But his statements and his conclusions are consistent.

Quid nunc dicam? &c.]. 'What shall I now say? That no other person ever since made this edictal rule? Strange, indeed, if nobody chose to be called like Verres. But Verres himself does not include this rule in his Sicilian edict.' Orelli omits 'hoc' after 'unquam.' Zumpt adds it, 'fide Lag. 29,' and Iordan. 'Strange, indeed,' is said ironically. 'Strange, that nobody chose to be likened to Verres. Why, Verres did not choose to be like himself; for he changed the rule in Sicily.'

46. *Ac*] 'At,' Orelli; but incorrectly, I think.

capite . . . capita] 'Caput,' in this sense, is equivalent to 'title,' or 'chapter;' for 'caput' was used to express one of the divisions of a 'lex,' which we should call a section. Cic. De Lege Agr. ii. 6, "a primo capite legis usque ad extremum;" and also a division or title of the 'edictum;' Cicero, Ad Fam. iii. 8, "Romae composui edictum —diligentissime scriptum caput est quod pertinet ad minuendos sumptus civitatum; quo in capite sunt quaedam nova, salutaria civitatibus."

habitabant] "habitant Lg. 29 p. m., Prisc.;" Iordan, who has 'habitant.'—'uteremur:' 'uterentur' (Orelli), which is the suggestion of Hotmann. But Zumpt says that there is no variation in the MSS., and that the usage of the Latin requires 'uteremur,' to agree with 'nos.' 'Uterentur,' according to Iordan, who accepts it, is from Priscian.

multa esse in provinciis aliter edicenda; non de hereditatum quidem possessionibus, non de mulierum hereditatibus. Nam [in] utroque genere video non modo ceteros sed te ipsum totidem verbis edixisse quot verbis edici Romae solet. Quae Romae magna cum infamia pretio accepto edixeras, ea sola te, ne gratis in provincia male audires, ex edicto Siciliensi sustulisse video. Et quum edictum totum eorum arbitratu, quamdiu fuit designatus, componeret, qui ab isto jus ad utilitatem suam nundinarentur, tum vero in magistratu contra illud ipsum edictum suum sine ulla religione decernebat. Itaque L. Piso multos codices implevit earum rerum in quibus ita intercessit quod iste aliter atque ut edixerat decrevisset. Quod vos oblitos esse non arbitror, quae multitudo, qui ordo ad Pisonis sellam isto praetore solitus sit convenire; quem iste collegam nisi habuisset, lapidibus coopertus esset in foro. Sed eo leviores istius injuriae videbantur quod erat in aequitate prudentiaque Pisonis paratissimum perfugium, quo sine labore, sine molestia, sine impensa, etiam sine patrono homines uterentur. Nam, quaeso, redite in memoriam, judices, quae libido istius in jure dicundo fuerit, quae varietas decretorum, quae nundinatio, quam inanes domus eorum omnium qui de jure civili con-

nundinarentur,] 'Nundinae,' every ninth day, was a kind of market-day. 'Nundinari' is to buy and sell; hence here it signifies to traffic with Verres, who had 'jurisdictio' as 'praetor urbanus.'—'illud ipsum edictum:' 'ipsum' om. Orelli. Zumpt has taken 'ipsum' from Lg. 29.

decernebat.] 'Decernere,' 'decretum,' are the terms applicable to decisions in particular cases. The praetor's decision, of course, ought to be conformable to his 'edictum,' or 'general rules,' and to deviate from this was an offence against 'religio.' Instances of praetors not acting conformably to their 'edictum' were not rare, and a Lex Cornelia was passed B.C. 67, which required the praetors to administer justice conformably to their Edicta Perpetua (Ascon. in Cic. Cornel. p. 58; Dion Cassius, xxxvi. 23). See Excursus iv.

L. Piso] Piso was a colleague of Verres, and probably Praetor Peregrinus. A 'magistratus' of equal or superior rank might be appealed to from the decree of a 'magistratus,' with whose 'decretum' a defendant was dissatisfied. The appeal was called 'appellatio,' and the interposition of the 'magistratus' who was appealed to was called 'intercessio.' The effect of the 'intercessio' was negative. It stopped any thing from being done by virtue of the decree or order which was appealed against, and consequently it was for the protection of the defendant, and not of the plaintiff. The 'tribuni plebis' had also a power of 'intercessio' against the orders even of the praetors and consuls (Pro Quintio, c. 7. 20, 21, vol. ii.; Savigny, System, &c., Appellatio and Provocatio, vi. Beilage xv.).

We learn from this passage, that the 'magistratus' kept a record, or notes, of their proceedings, which would serve to refresh their memory, and as a guide in future cases. They were sometimes called 'commentarii, actorum commentaria.'

Quod vos . . . quae] There is no difficulty about this form of expression. Comp. De Am. c. 15, "Quod Tarquinium dixisse ferunt . . se intellexisse quos fidos amicos haberet," &c.; and "Quod nisi Metellus hoc tam graviter egisset," Lib. 2. c. 66. Also Act. ii. Lib. 1. c. 26, 'quod ubi ille intellexit id agi,' &c.: Lib. 1. c. 39, 'quod tu— aliud;' Terence, Phorm. ii. 1. 5, "Quod utinam ne Phormioni id suadere in mentem incidisset;" and Andr. i. 5. 54, 'Quod te ego,' &c. See also Pro Cluent. c. 9, 'Ita quod,' &c. vol. ii.

redite in memoriam,] Forcellini cites Cicero De Senectute, c. 7, 'in memoriam redeo;' and Pro Quintio, c. 18; and he says that it means, as in this case, 'see that you remember.'

suli solent, quam plena ac referta Chelidonis; a qua muliere quum erat ad eum ventum et in aurem ejus insusurratum, alias revocabat eos inter quos jam decreverat, decretumque mutabat; alias inter alios contrarium sine ulla religione decernebat ac proximis paulo ante decreverat. Hinc illi homines erant qui etiam ridiculi inveniebantur ex dolore; quorum alii, id quod saepe audistis, negabant mirandum esse jus tam nequam esse verrinum; alii etiam frigidiores erant, sed quia stomachabantur ridiculi videbantur esse, quum Sacerdotem exsecrabantur qui verrem tam nequam reliquisset. Quae ego non commemorarem, neque enim perfacete dicta neque porro hac severitate digna sunt, nisi vos illud vellem recordari, istius nequitiam et iniquitatem tum in ore vulgi atque in communibus proverbiis esse versatam.

XLVII. In plebem vero Romanam utrum superbiam prius commemorem an crudelitatem? sine dubio crudelitas gravior est atque atrocior. Oblitosne igitur hos putatis esse quemadmodum sit iste solitus virgis plebem Romanam concidere? Quam rem etiam tribunus plebis in contione egit, quum eum quem virgis iste ceciderat in conspectum populi Romani produxit; cujus rei cognoscendae faciam vobis suo tempore potestatem. Superbia vero qua fuerit quis ignorat? quemadmodum iste tenuissimum quemque contempserit,

inter alios] 'inter aliquos' V, Iordan.—'contrarium . . . ac:' see Lib. 4. c. 6.

ridiculi] This word, which has the termination that is commonly a diminutive, has the sense of 'moving to laughter.' It appears to be used in this passage, in the first instance, in the sense of moving to laughter, by the play on the word 'jus,' coupled with the word 'verrinum,' where the laugh would be at the joke, not at those who uttered it. In the second instance, the speakers were 'frigidiores,' and their frigid joke furnished rather matter for laughing at them than at what they said. See Caesar, B. G. i. 42, 'non irridicule.'—'ut audistis,' Orelli.

jus . . . verrinum;] Cicero loves this joke. "Tu istic te Hateriano jure delectas; ego me hic Hirtiano," Ad Div. ix. 18.

47. *commemorem*] 'commemorem,' Zumpt from Lg. 29. He adds that Cicero very seldom uses 'memorare' for 'commemorare.' He cites as an example, Lib. 4. c. 48. Orelli has 'memorem.'

tribunus plebis] Asconius says that it was M. Lollius Palicanus, who exerted himself in the restoration of the 'tribunicia potestas.' He appears to have been 'tribunus plebis,' B.C. 71 (Zumpt).

contione] "V et sic ubique, quamquam Maius et hic et in aliis locis falsam scripturam *concio* habet" (Halm). This remark may be useful to those who still doubt about the form and origin of this word.

conspectum] Zumpt from Lg. 29. V has 'conspectu.' Orelli has 'prospectum;' 'contra sermonis usum,' as Zumpt remarks, in conjunction with such a word as 'produxit.'—'cognoscendae:' 'recognoscendae' V, Iordan.

suo tempore] As Klotz remarks, and Asconius also, this matter would belong to the fifth book De Suppliciis; but Cicero has said no more about it.

qua fuerit] V Lg. 29, Priscian have 'quae fuerit,' and Iordan writes 'quae.' I suppose that either of the readings may be genuine.

quemadmodum iste] 'quem. iste,' 'Lambinus contra libros' (Zumpt). But Pris. has 'iste,' and V has 'ste,' which means 'iste.' 'Iste' then should be preferred to the old reading 'is,' for Cicero has just said 'iste ceciderat.' The origin of the mistake seems obvious when we observe that the next word begins with 'te.'

despexerit, liberum esse nunquam duxerit? P. Trebonius viros bonos et honestos complures fecit heredes; in his fecit suum libertum. Is A. Trebonium fratrem habuerat proscriptum. Ei quum cautum vellet, scripsit ut heredes jurarent se curaturos ut ex sua cujusque parte ne minus dimidium ad A. Trebonium [fratrem] illum proscriptum perveniret. Libertus jurat: ceteri heredes adeunt ad Verrem: docent non oportere se jurare: facturos esse quod contra legem Corneliam esset quae proscriptum juvari vetaret. Impetrant ut ne jurent: dat his possessionem. Id ego non reprehendo. Etenim

viros bonos &c.] As these 'boni et honesti' refused to perform the will of the testator, Asconius inquires in what sense Cicero could give them these names. Cicero says he made several men of good character his 'heredes.' If they turned out to be knaves, when they were put to the test, there is nothing strange in that. Zumpt explains it thus: "viros bonos, i. e. rei publicae, qualis tum constituta erat, amicos, nobilitatis fautores, ne P. Trebonium ipsum judices Marianarum partium asseclam clandestinum putarent;" and he is probably right, for Cicero's 'viri boni' is often so used in a political sense.—'in his:' Iordan, following V, has 'in iis,' which is not the true form in this case.

se jurare:] Iordan has 'se id jurare facturos esse, quod esset et.'

quae . . . vetaret.] Orelli and Iordan have 'vetat,' which makes the expression 'quae . . . vetat' the remark of Cicero; but Orelli thinks that the words are a gloss. Zumpt has 'vetaret,' an emendation of Ernesti; and we now know that V has VATAIIT, which may be 'vetaret' (Halm).

This Lex Cornelia was one of those passed in the dictatorship of Sulla, a 'lex de proscribendis malis civibus,' an expression which helps to explain Cicero's 'viri boni.' Cicero (Pro Sex. Ros. Am. c. 43) says that he does not know whether this 'lex' should be called Valeria (Valerii Flacci interregis) or Cornelia.

dat his possessionem.] 'Injuste,' 'illegally,' says Asconius, the false, in this instance at least. He says that the testament should either have been declared invalid, as contrary to the Lex Cornelia, or the entire will of the testator should have been observed. But Cicero says 'id ego non reprehendo;' and he could not find fault with this part of the decision of Verres. It does not appear that the 'jusjurandum' was a 'conditio' (suspensive, or precedent) which must be performed before the persons named as 'heredes' could be 'heredes.' If it was, the praetor could excuse the oath (that is, 'remittere conditionem'); but still the 'heredes' might be required to fulfil the 'conditio' in the form of a 'modus,' that is, if it was not illegal. If, however, any party who was named 'heres' chose to take the oath, he could do so, and he might be compelled to perform the 'conditio' as a 'modus.' The following is an example of a 'modus.' A testator might leave his property to a person, and add that he must do some particular thing; for instance, raise a monument to him. In this case the person was made 'heres' absolutely, but still he was bound to do what the testator wished. But if the doing of the thing was in any way impossible, the 'heres' was released from the obligation to do it, and his right and title as 'heres' were not at all impaired. If the thing was illegal, the conclusion was the same. Now in this case the praetor ought to have given the 'possessio' to all, to those who did not take the oath and to him who did. Those who did not take the oath would not be bound by the 'modus,' if the thing was illegal; and he who took the oath, if he performed the 'modus,' would be liable to the penalty of the Lex Cornelia, if the penalty applied to this case. Cicero's statement and arguments are quite correct. As to 'conditio' and 'modus,' see Savigny, System des Heut. Röm. Rechts, vol. iii. § 116—129. Though Cicero could not deny that the proceeding of Verres was legal so far as concerned the other 'heredes,' he adds 'etenim,' &c.: 'and indeed it was not fair,' &c., which is said with a kind of sneer, as being the remark which Verres or his friends might make. To which Cicero replies, 'At ille,' &c. 'Yet the freedman thought that he should do wrong, if,' &c. Klotz, who seems inclined to set Verres in the right as much as he can, says that he did not strictly act illegally in refusing the 'possessio' to the 'libertus.' But Cicero says that he did, and he knew more of Roman law than his German commentator. The 'libertus' pro-

erat iniquum homini proscripto, egenti, de fraternis bonis quidquam dari. At ille libertus, nisi ex testamento patroni jurasset, scelus se facturum arbitrabatur. Itaque ei Verres possessionem hereditatis negat se daturum ne posset patronum suum proscriptum juvare; simul ut esset poena quod alterius patroni testamento obtemperasset. Das possessionem ei qui non juravit. Concedo: praetorium est. Adimis tu ei qui juravit. Quo exemplo? Proscriptum juvat. Lex est; poena est: quid ad eum qui jus dicit? Utrum reprehendis, quod patronum juvabat eum qui tum in miseriis erat; an quod alterius patroni mortui voluntatem conservabat, a quo summum beneficium acceperat? Utrum horum reprehendis? Et hoc tum de sella vir optimus dixit, Equiti Romano tam locupleti libertinus homo sit heres? O modestum ordinem quod illinc vivus surrexerit.

Possum sexcenta decreta proferre in quibus, ut ego pecuniam non dicam intercessisse, ipsa decretorum novitas iniquitasque declarat. Verum ut ex uno de ceteris conjecturam facere possitis, id quod priore actione cognostis audite.

XLVIII. C. Sulpicius Olympus fuit. Is mortuus est C. Sacerdote praetore, nescio an ante quam Verres praeturam petere coeperit. Fecit heredem M. Octavium Ligurem. Ligur hereditatem adiit: possedit Sacerdote praetore sine ulla controversia. Posteaquam Verres magistratum iniit, ex edicto istius, quod edictum Sacerdos non habuerat, Sulpicii patroni filia sextam partem hereditatis ab Ligure petere coepit. Ligur non aderat.

mised to do that which was forbidden by the Lex Cornelia, but that did not deprive him of his title to the share of the inheritance: it only made him liable to the penalty of the 'lex,' if there was any for such a case. And Klotz observes in his note on 'quae . . . vetaret,' that the Lex Cornelia did not apply directly to the case of a testament, so as to invalidate such a gift, but simply forbade any relief to be given to the proscribed, and therefore applied to all persons. If this is so, how can he say that Verres did not act illegally in refusing the 'possessio?' The orator argues better than the commentator.

At ille libertus,] 'At' is a correction of Hotmann, and apparently a true correction. The MSS. have 'et,' but V omits 'et ille,' and Iordan has 'dari: libertus,' &c.

quod . . . surrexerit.] The common reading is 'surrexit.' A careful reader might ask if it should not be 'surrexerit.' Klotz took 'surrexerit' from the Vatican palimpsest, published by Mai, and he did right. The 'ordo' is the 'ordo libertinorum,' whom, as Asconius remarks, Cicero calls people of great self-restraint in letting Verres leave his judgment-seat alive, after receiving such an insult from him.

ut ego &c.] 'ut ego non dicam, pecuniam intercessisse ipsa,' &c. Iordan, on the authority of V, from which he also takes 'didicistis,' instead of 'cognostis.'

48. *C. Sulpicius . . fuit.*] See Divin. c. 17.—'praeturam petere coepit:' Klotz and Iordan, on the authority of V only.

adiit:] 'took possession of the Hereditas,' a usual term. See Pro Q. Roscio Com. c. 18, note, vol. ii.

sextam partem] Olympus was a freedman, and the daughter of his 'patronus' claimed a portion of the property of which he died possessed. This was the case of a 'libertus' making a testament, to which case the law of the Twelve Tables did not apply. Originally, if a freedman made a testament, he could pass over (praeterire)

L. frater ejus causam agebat: aderant amici, propinqui. Dicebat iste, nisi cum muliere decideretur, in possessionem se ire jussurum. L. Gellius causam Liguris defendebat: docebat edictum ejus non oportere ad eas hereditates valere quae ante eum praetorem venissent; si hoc tum fuisset edictum, fortasse Ligurem hereditatem aditurum non fuisse. Aequa postulatio, summa hominum auctoritas pretio superabatur. Venit Romam Ligur: non dubitabat quin, si ipse Verrem convenisset, aequitate causae, [et] auctoritate sua commovere hominem posset. Domum ad eum venit: rem demonstrat: quam pridem sibi hereditas venisset docet: quod facile in causa aequissima homini ingenioso fuit, multa quae quemvis commovere possent dixit: ad extremum petere coepit ne usque eo suam auctoritatem despiceret, gratiamque contemneret, ut se tanta injuria afficeret. Homo Ligurem accusare coepit qui in re adventitia atque hereditaria tam diligens tam attentus esset: debere eum aiebat suam quoque rationem ducere; multa sibi opus esse, multa canibus suis quos circa se haberet. Non possum illa planius commemorare quam ipsum Ligurem pro testimonio dicere audistis. Quid enim, Verres, utrum ne his quidem testibus credetur, an haec

his patron altogether. But according to Ulpian (Frag. Tit. xxix.), in the case of a 'libertus' making a testament and giving nothing or less than half of his property to his patron, the praetor's edict gave the patron the 'bonorum possessio contra tabulas testamenti' of one half, unless the 'libertus' left behind him as a successor a natural, that is, a not adopted child. When the rule as to the one half was introduced, it does not appear (comp. Gaius, iii. 40); but it was before the enactment of the Lex Papia Poppaea, which gave greater advantages to patrons in the case of the richer class of 'liberti.'

aderant] See Lib. 2. c. 29, note.

nisi—decideretur,] 'unless he came to some terms with the woman.' If this allegation against Verres is true, it shows that he was dishonest. He who has to declare the law, cannot impose terms on the parties, and punish either of them who does not comply. It is his business to declare the law and apply it to the facts of the case. 'Decidere,' in the sense of 'coming to terms,' 'settling an affair,' occurs often. See Act. ii. Lib. 2. c. 32, and Lib. 3. c. 48, 'decidere liceret.' And comp. 'decisione,' c. 54 of this oration; and Pro Flacco, c. 36.

ad eas hereditates] Lambinus has 'in' on the authority of Priscian, which Zumpt disapproves; but the Vatican Codex also has 'in,' which Klotz and Iordan adopt. In place of 'venissent' V has 'fuissent.' An 'hereditas' is said 'venire ad aliquem' or 'alicui,' (Lib. 2. c. 7,) and it was also used as it is here without a case after it.

in re adventitia] "Quia ab alienioro hereditas veniebat," says Asconius.

suam quoque rationem &c.] Verres said that 'he must have respect to himself also.' Some read 'sui,' says Lambinus, who thinks however that 'suam' is right. Hotmann cites a like example from Cicero, 'duxi meam rationem,' Ad Att. viii. 11. D. Zumpt says that it is doubtful if 'suam rationem' is Latin. But Cicero did not think so, for he says also (De Off. i. 39), 'habenda ratio non sua solum.' The 'canes' of Verres are his informers, who smelled out what was to their master's profit (c. 51; and Lib. 4. c. 21, &c.).

Quid enim, Verres,] I have removed the note of interrogation, which is absurdly placed after Verres. Klotz and Iordan read 'Quid est, Verres? utrum ne,' &c., after V. They also read 'Non credemus M. Octavio?' and a little farther on 'praetorem urbanum,' in accordance with V. See c. 55, 'Pr. Urbis.' —'hoc juris:' 'a rule of law like this.' See c. 26, 'id aetatis.'

ad rem non pertinent? Non M. Octavio? non L. Liguri? Quis nobis credet? cui nos? quid est, Verres, quod planum fieri testibus possit, si hoc non fit? An id quod dicunt leve est? Nihil levius quam praetorem urbis hoc juris in suo magistratu constituere, omnibus [iis] quibus hereditas venerit coheredem praetorem esse oportere. An vero dubitamus quo ore iste ceteros homines inferiore loco, auctoritate, ordine, quo ore homines rusticanos ex municipiis, quo denique ore quos nunquam liberos putavit libertinos homines solitus sit appellare, qui ob jus dicundum M. Octavium Ligurem, hominem ornatissimum loco, ordine, nomine, virtute, ingenio, copiis, poscere pecuniam non dubitavit?

XLIX. In sartis tectis vero quemadmodum se gesserit quid ego dicam? Dixerunt qui senserunt: sunt alii qui dicant: notae res atque manifestae prolatae sunt et proferentur. Dixit C. Fannius, eques Romanus, frater germanus Q. Titinii, judicis tui, tibi se pecuniam dedisse. RECITA TESTIMONIVM C. FANNII. Nolite C. Fannio dicenti credere: noli, inquam, tu, Q. Titini, C. Fannio fratri tuo credere; dicit enim rem incredibilem: C. Verrem insimulat avaritiae et audaciae, quae vitia videntur in quemvis potius quam in istum convenire. Dixit Q. Tadius, homo familiarissimus patris istius, non alienus a matris ejus genere et nomine: tabulas protulit quibus pecuniam se dedisse ostendit. RECITA NOMINA Q. TADII. RECITA TESTIMONIVM Q. TADII. Ne tabulis quidem Q. Tadii nec testimonio credetur? Quid igitur in judiciis sequemur? quid est aliud omnibus omnia peccata et maleficia concedere nisi hoc, hominum honest[issim]orum testimoniis et virorum bonorum tabulis non credere?

Nam quid ego de quotidiano sermone querimoniaque populi

omnibus [iis]] '*Iis* sustulimus auctoritate Lg. 29.' Zumpt. He will follow Lag. 29 any where except into a 'scrupulosus locus' (Divin. c. 11). V also omits 'iis.'—'inferiore,' 'inferiores' V, Iordan.—'ordine' om. Zumpt.

49. *sartis tectis*] That is, 'sartis et tectis,' the word 'et' being sometimes omitted conformably to usage in these cases. A building which was in perfect repair was 'sartum, tectum integrumque,' c. 60. 'Sarcire' is applied to the mending of clothes or shoes; and also to the repair of buildings. 'Tegere' properly refers to the roof. Zumpt refers to Cic. Ad Div. xiii. 11, 'sarta tecta aedium,' &c. 'Dach und Fach' as the Germans say (Zumpt), or 'les reparations et entretiens' (Menard). See Livy 29, c. 37, "sarta tecta acriter et cum summa fide exegerunt;" and Plautus, Trinum. ii. 3. 17.

C. Fannius, &c.] If the readings are right, and these men were brothers, they must have been the sons of one mother by different fathers. Klotz writes 'Cn. Phaenius' from V in place of 'C. Fannius.'

tabulas protulit Recita nomina] The entries in the books of Q. Tadius were produced as evidence of the sums which he paid (expensilatio); and such entries were called 'nomina.' See c. 38.

Ne tabulis &c.] 'Ne Tadii quidem tabulis nec testimonio credemus?' V and Iordan.

quotidiano] 'cotidiano' V, and so the Romans doubtless wrote at one time in-

Romani loquar? de istius impudentissimo furto seu potius novo ac singulari latrocinio? ausum esse in aede Castoris, celeberrimo clarissimoque monumento, quod templum in oculis quotidianoque adspectu populi Romani positum est, quo saepenumero senatus convocatur, quo maximarum rerum frequentissimae quotidie advocationes fiunt, in eo loco in sermone hominum audaciae suae monumentum aeternum relinquere?

L. Aedem Castoris, judices, P. Junius habuit tuendam de L. Sulla Q. Metello consulibus. Is mortuus est. Reliquit pupillum parvum filium. Quum L. Octavius C. Aurelius consules aedes sacras locavissent neque potuissent omnia sarta tecta exigere, neque ii praetores quibus erat negotium datum C. Sacerdos et M. Caesius, factum est senatusconsultum, quibus de sartis tectis cognitum et judicatum non esset, uti C. Verres P. Caelius praetores cognoscerent et judicarent. Qua potestate isto permissa, ut ex C. Fannio et ex Q. Tadio cognovistis, verumtamen quum esset omnibus in rebus apertissimo impudentissimeque praedatus, hoc voluit clarissimum relinquere indicium latrociniorum suorum de quo non audire aliquando sed videre quotidie possemus. Quaesivit quis aedem Castoris sartam tectam deberet tradere. Junium ipsum

differently 'quotid.' or 'cotid.,' and 'quum' and 'cum;' 'iniquum' and 'inicum,' which last form V has in c. 47. But V has 'quaerimonia.' It is only when o or a follows 'qu' that co or cu was written.

Castoris,] The temple of Castor and Pollux (Act. ii. Lib. 5. c. 72), vowed by the dictator A. Postumius in the Latin war, after the battle near the lake Regillus (B.C. 499), and dedicated by his son (Liv. ii. 20, 42). It was destroyed in the time of the Gallic invasion; but it must have been rebuilt. L. Metellus Dalmaticus, consul B.C. 119, restored or beautified the temple. See c. 59.

advocationes] 'A place which is daily crowded by those who attend there to give their aid in matters of the greatest importance.' He means the 'advocati,' who assisted parties with their advice and aid, or sometimes even a 'magistratus;' 'ii qui advocati sunt' (see Lib. 3. c. 7). They did not make the speech. That was the business of the 'patronus' or orator. Forcellini, who quotes Asconius, takes the word 'advocationes' to mean 'consultatio,' which is a mistake. It has the meaning which it has in Cicero, Ad Fam. vii. 10. 'Advocatio,' says Zumpt, 'coetus est congregatorum.'

50. *Aedem Castoris,*] Orelli reads 'tuendam. L. Sulla, Q. Metello consulibus is mortuus est. Reliquit,' &c. It appears (c. 55) that Junius made the contract with the censors L. Marcius, M. Perperna (B.C. 86). We avoid the apparent contradiction by omitting 'de,' and connecting the man's death with the year of the consuls. But, as Zumpt remarks, the time of the man's death is quite immaterial. Ernesti supposes that the contract, after being made with the censors, was renewed with the consuls L. Sulla and Q. Metellus (B.C. 80), at which time there were no censors. It appears that the consuls L. Octavius, C. Aurelius (B.C. 75) afterwards made the contracts for repairs (aedes locaviment), but had not time to examine if the contracts were performed as to all the buildings (sarta tecta exigere). Finally, a Senatusconsultum empowered Verres and Caelius to examine into the condition of the temples. 'Tuendam' means to maintain and keep in repair.

cognovistis,] "Ante *verum tamen* lacunam esse recte statuit Madv. i. p. 327." (Jordan.) I am not sure of that. Manutius says, "verum tamen dicam, quamquam ex Fannio et Tadio cognovistis."

mortuum esse sciebat: scire volebat ad quem illa res pertineret. Audit pupillum esse filium. Homo qui semper ita palam dictitasset pupillos et pupillas certissimam praedam esse praetoribus, optatum negotium sibi in sinum delatum esse dicebat. Monumentum illa amplitudine, illo opere, quamvis sartum tectum integrumque esset, tamen aliquid se inventurum in quo moliri praedarique posset arbitrabatur. L. Rabonio aedem Castoris tradi oportebat:† is casu pupilli Junii tutor erat testamento patris. Cum eo sine ullo intertrimento convenerat jam quemadmodum traderetur. Iste ad se Rabonium vocat: quaerit ecquid sit quod a pupillo traditum non sit quod exigi debeat. Quum ille, id quod erat, diceret facilem pupillo traditionem esse, signa et dona comparere omnia, ipsum templum omni opere esse integrum, indignum isti videri coepit ex tanta aede tantoque opere se non opimum praeda praesertim a pupillo discedere.

LI. Venit ipse in aedem Castoris: considerat templum: videt undique tectum pulcherrime laqueatum, praeterea cetera nova atque integra. Versat se: quaerit quid agat. Dicit ei quidam ex illis canibus quos iste Liguri dixerat esse circa se multos, Tu, Verres, hic quod moliare nihil habes, nisi forte vis ad perpendiculum columnas exigere. Homo omnium rerum imperitus quaerit quid sit ad perpendiculum. Dicunt ei fere nullam esse columnam quae ad perpendiculum esse possit. Nam mehercule, inquit, sic agamus: columnae ad perpendiculum exigantur. Rabonius qui legem nosset

L. Rabonio] 'L. Habonio,' Klotz, Jordan, from Lg. 29, Prisc. V has sometimes 'Habonius' and sometimes 'Rabonius.'

is casu] Menard affirms that Rabonius was not a 'tutor' or guardian of the property of the youth; and he proposes to write 'Potitius casu,' but this is certainly not the true reading. We find that there were three 'tutores' of this 'pupillus,' and it appears from c. 54 that Rabonius was not a fourth. I think it is certain that something is lost after 'oportebat' such as 'a P. Potitio,' which addition will make 'is casu' intelligible, and 'cum eo' will mean 'cum Potitio.' It is plain that 'cum eo' and 'is' designate the same person, and I think no one will maintain that 'cum eo' means 'Rabonius.'

intertrimentum] The loss occasioned in a substance by rubbing or wear, as in silver or gold (Liv. xxxii. 2). The explanation of the word by Asconius, "intertrimentum vero . . dantis et accipientis," does not seem applicable. Manutius however takes it so, 'sine ullo alterutrius partis damno.' The word 'intertrimento' is used by Terence, Haut. iii. 1. 39. It appears that Rabonius had in some way taken up the contract, and it had been agreed that the edifice should be delivered to him (tradi) in complete repair. According to Cicero, Rabonius was satisfied with the condition of the temple.

51. *Nam mehercule,*] Zumpt properly compares Lib. 2. c. 29, 'nam hercle;' and Lib. 3. c. 85, 'nam speravissem:' and he adds, that it is now generally agreed that 'nam' is to be explained by an ellipsis. But this is not a right explanation. We must recur to the primary meaning of the word, which seems to be akin to 'enim,' another form; and it means 'indeed,' 'well,' or the like. 'Germanice dixeris, *Ja*' (Zumpt).

legem] 'the terms.' This is a usual meaning of 'lex,' but not its proper meaning. See c. 55, 'lex operi faciundo.'

qua in lege numerus tantum columnarum traditur, perpendiculi mentio fit nulla, et qui non putaret sibi expedire ita accipere, ne eodem modo reddendum esset, negat id sibi deberi; negat oportere exigi. Iste Rabonium quiescere jubet, et simul ei nonnullam spem societatis ostendit: hominem modestum et minime pertinacem facile coercet: columnas ita se exacturum esse confirmat. Nova res atque improvisa pupilli calamitas nuntiatur statim C. Mustio, vitrico pupilli, qui nuper est mortuus, M. Junio patruo, P. Potitio tutori, homini frugalissimo. Hi rem ad virum primarium, summo officio ac virtute praeditum, M. Marcellum, qui erat pupilli tutor, deferunt. Venit ad Verrem M. Marcellus: petit ab eo pro sua fide ac diligentia pluribus verbis, ne per summam injuriam pupillum Junium fortunis patriis conetur evertere. Iste qui jam spe atque opinione praedam illam devorasset, neque ulla aequitate orationis neque auctoritate M. Marcelli commotus est. Itaque quemadmodum ostendisset se id exacturum esse respondit. Quum sibi omnes ad istum allegationes difficiles, omnes aditus arduos ac potius interclusos viderent, apud quem non jus, non aequitas, non misericordia, non propinqui oratio, non amici voluntas, non cujusquam auctoritas [pro pretio,] non gratia valeret, statuunt id sibi optimum esse factu, quod cuivis venisset in mentem, petere auxilium a Chelidone quae isto praetore non modo in jure civili privatorumque omnium controversiis populo Romano praefuit, verum etiam in his sartis tectisque dominata est.

LII. Venit ad Chelidonem C. Mustius, eques Romanus, publicanus, homo cum primis honestus: venit M. Junius, patruus pueri, frugalissimus homo et castissimus: venit homo summo [honore,] pudore, [et] summo officio, spectatissimus ordinis sui, P. Potitius tutor. O multis acerbam, O miseram atque indignam praeturam tuam! Ut mittam cetera, quo tandem pudore tales viros, quo dolore meretricis domum venisse arbitramini? qui nulla conditione istam turpitudinem subissent, nisi officii necessitudinisque ratio coëgisset. Veniunt, ut dico, ad Chelidonem. Domus erat plena:

reddendum] 'tradendum,' Zumpt and Iordan, from Priscian and Lg. 29; which, if we judge by the propriety of the terms, and not the MSS. authority, is the better word. Four Lgg. have 'credendum.'

spem societatis] 'hope of partnership' with Verres in his impudent fraud.—'P. Potitio:' 'P. Titio' Iordan. The real name is doubtful.

allegationes] See c. 16, and 'allegatos,' c. 53, and 'allegat,' c. 57. 'Allegatio' is the 'actus allegandi,' as Forcellini says; and 'allegare' means to send to a place or to a person on matters not of a public nature, and generally for the purpose of obtaining something. 'Legare' applies to a public mission.

[*pro pretio,*]] These words are in all the MSS.; Zumpt explains them as meaning 'tantum quantum pretium' or 'pretii loco.'

52. *summo* [*honore,*]] There is a diffi-

nova jura, nova decreta, nova judicia petebantur: Mihi det possessionem: mihi ne adimat: in me judicium ne det: mihi bona addicat.—Alii nummos numerabant, alii tabulas obsignabant: domus erat non meretricio conventu sed praetoria turba referta. Simulac potestas primum data est, adeunt hi quos dixi. Loquitur Mustius: rem demonstrat: petit auxilium: pecuniam pollicetur. Respondit illa ut meretrix non inhumane: libenter ait se esse facturam, et se cum isto diligenter sermocinaturam: reverti jubet. Tum discedunt. Postridie revertuntur. Negat illa posse hominem exorari: permagnam eum dicere ex illa re pecuniam confici posse.

LIII. Vereor ne quis forte de populo, qui priore actione non adfuit, haec, quia propter insignem turpitudinem sunt incredibilia, fingi a me arbitretur: ea vos antea, judices, cognovistis. Dixit juratus P. Potitius, tutor pupilli Junii: dixit M. Junius tutor et patruus: Mustius dixisset si viveret, sed pro Mustio recenti re de Mustio auditum dixit L. Domitius; qui quum sciret me ex Mustio vivo audisse, quod eo sum usus plurimum, (etenim judicium, quod prope omnium fortunarum suarum C. Mustius habuit, me uno defendente vicit,) quum hoc, ut dico, sciret L. Domitius me scire, ad eum res omnes Mustium solitum esse deferre, tamen de Chelidone reticuit quoad potuit: alio responsionem suam derivavit. Tantus in adolescente clarissimo ac principe juventutis pudor fuit ut aliquamdiu, quum a me premeretur, omnia potius responderet

culty about the word 'honore;' for it appears that this Potitius, or Tettius, as Zumpt has it, or Titius, as Iordan has it, was a plebeian. But the man's name is uncertain. Madvig proposes to omit 'honore.'—'mittam:' 'omittam,' V, Iordan.

numerabant,] Cicero represents some as paying down ready money in the house of Chelidon to purchase the interest of the mistress of Verres; others, as sealing writings, by which he seems to mean an obligation to pay.—'alii tabulas,' &c.: 'ab aliis tabellae obsignabantur,' V, Iordan.

ut meretrix] "considering she was a 'meretrix,' she was not unreasonable." Comp. De Sen. c. 14, "multae etiam ut in homine Romano literae." Cicero represents the affair as conducted with the solemnity of an embassy. We must take the narrative as we have it, without being bound to believe it all.—'inhumane:' 'inhumaniter' V, Iordan.

53. *sed pro Mustio*] 'sed recenti re de M. Mustio auditum est: dixit L. Domitius; qui' &c. Iordan, following V. I do not think that either the common text, or the reading of V, is quite right.

de Mustio auditum] L. Domitius gave evidence as to what he heard from Mustius, who was now dead. See c. 10.

judicium,] 'id judicium' Orelli. Ernesti compares 'sponsionem vincere,' Pro Caecina, c. 31, with 'judicium . . vicit.'

derivavit.] 'he turned off his answer to something else:' he avoided the question. Comp. Act. ii. Lib. 2. c. 20, 'culpam derivare in aliquem.' The metaphor is taken from irrigation and draining, by which water was carried in channels (rivi) from one place to another. In our language the word has lost its primary meaning, and particularly in such a word as rivals (rivales), which in Latin means persons who had a common interest in a 'rivus,' or watercourse, as we see from Ulpian, Dig. 43. 19. 1, "si inter rivales, id est qui per eundem rivum aquam ducunt, sit contentio de aquae usu." The Latin word has also our derived sense of 'rival.'

quam Chelidonem nominaret. Primo necessarios istius ad eum allegatos esse dicebat: deinde aliquando coactus Chelidonem nominavit. Non te pudet, Verres, ejus mulieris arbitratu gessisse praeturam, quam L. Domitius ab se nominari vix sibi honestum esse arbitrabatur?

LIV. Rejecti a Chelidone capiunt consilium necessarium ut suscipiant ipsi negotium. Cum Rabonio [tutore], quod erat vix HS quadraginta millium, transigunt HS ducentis millibus. Refert ad istum rem Rabonius, ut sibi videbatur, satis grandem pecuniam et satis impudentem [esse]. Iste qui aliquanto plus cogitasset, male accipit verbis Rabonium: negat eum sibi illa decisione satisfacere posse. Ne multa, locaturum se esse confirmat. Tutores haec nesciunt: quod actum erat cum Rabonio, putant id esse certissimum: nullam majorem pupillo metuunt calamitatem. Iste vero non procrastinat: locare incipit non proscripta neque edicta die, alienissimo tempore, ludis ipsis Romanis, foro ornato. Itaque renuntiat Rabonius illam decisionem tutoribus. Accurrunt tamen ad tempus tutores: digitum tollit Junius patruus: isti color immutatus est: vultus, oratio, mens denique excidit. Quid ageret coepit cogitare. Si opus pupillo redimeretur, si res abiret ab eo mancipe quem ipse apposuisset, sibi nullam praedam esse. Itaque excogitat —quid? Nihil ingeniose, nihil quod quisquam posset dicere, 'improbe verum callide:' nihil ab isto tectum, nihil veteratorium exspec-

54. [*tutore*].] Menard proposes 'tutores.' See c. 50. Rabonius could not be a 'tutor,' for Cicero adds 'Tutores haec nesciunt,' and again 'renuntiat Rabonius . . . tutoribus.'—'refert:' 'defert,' Iordan. It is indifferent.

ut sibi videbatur,] All the MSS. have 'videbatur.' 'Videatur' is Ernesti's correction. The indicative, as Zumpt observes, cannot be tolerated here. If 'videatur' was Cicero's word, it is difficult to understand how every MS. should have 'videbatur.' I think 'videbatur' may be right, if we omit 'esse' at the end of the sentence, the addition of which may be explained without difficulty.

locaturum] Verres affirmed that he would let the contract anew to another undertaker or contractor (conductor, redemptor, manceps). When Rabonius sent the 'tutores' word (renuntiat) that the bargain which they had made with him was at an end, the 'tutores' determined to bid at the letting on behalf of their 'pupillus,' in order that he might have the benefit of the contract, and not have to deal with a public contractor (manceps) who was in the interest of Verres. The letting of these public contracts was by 'auctio,' or public bidding, to which applies the expression 'digitum tollit,' the sign of a bid (comp. Act. ii. Lib. 3. c. 11). It was the object of Verres to prevent the 'tutores' of Junius from taking the contract.

proscripta &c.] The word 'proscripta,' as Zumpt observes, means a notice put up, on a 'tabula,' for instance; and 'edicta' refers to notice given by proclamation, as by a 'praeco.' As to the gender of 'dies,' see Act. i. c. 2.

ornato.] The Forum was decorated for the Ludi.

quod quisquam &c.] 'ut quisquam posset' Zumpt and Iordan from Lg. 29.

tectum,] 'vafrum,' Madvig's conjecture followed by Iordan, who remarks that 'vafer et veterator' sometimes go together. It seems that the texts of Asconius had 'fabrum,' on which Madvig

taveritis: omnia aperta, omnia perspicua reperientur, impudentia, amentia, audacia.—Si pupillo opus redimitur, mihi praeda de manibus eripitur. Quod est igitur remedium? quod? ne liceat pupillo redimere.—Ubi illa consuetudo in bonis, praedibus praediisque vendendis, omnium consulum, censorum, praetorum, quaestorum denique, ut optima conditione sit is cuja res sit, cujum periculum? Excludit eum solum cui prope dicam soli potestatem factam esse oportebat. Quid enim quisquam ad meam pecuniam me invito adspirat, quisquam accedit? Locatur opus id quod ex mea pecunia reficiatur: ego me refecturum [esse] dico: probatio futura est tua qui locas: praedibus et praediis populo cautum est: et si non

has this ingenious remark: "Illud *fabrum* nihil est aliud quam *vafrum* propter Germanicam pronuntiandi rationem corruptum." There is also in Lgg. 5. 27. 29. 42 a reading 'verum.'

bonis, praedibus &c.] This passage has caused some difficulty. Klotz has a long note on it, but I think that he has mistaken the sense of the passage in following Hotmann. The first question is, if 'bonis' is an adjective, as Asconius takes it to be, when he says "bona praedia dicuntur bona stipulationibus obnoxia;" and "praedia sunt res ipsae; praedes homines, id est, fidejussores, quorum res bona praedia [non] suo nomine dicuntur."

But Klotz is right in taking 'bona' to be a substantive, though he takes it in the wrong sense. 'Praedes' are 'fidejussores,' persons who are securities. 'Praedium' is land; 'praedium urbanum' is land in a city, with buildings on it; 'praedium rusticum' is land in the country, with a house on it, a 'villa' (Dig. 50. 16. s. 27, 115, 221). The expression 'bona vendere, praedia vendere,' is common. 'Praedes vendere' occurs in Cicero again (Phil. ii. 31); and the expression must mean, to sell all the property of a 'praes.' Cicero then means to say, that when a sale of this kind is made by consuls, quaestors, or others, to satisfy the demands of the state, the person whose property was thus put up had a preference, if he offered and paid the whole amount; and why should the same not be the case in letting a contract? For, if the temple required repairs, why not let the 'tutores' of the 'pupillus' have the contract, for the repairs must be done at his cost; and the state had the security of his 'praedes' and (their) 'praedia?' 'If you, the praetor, do not think that the Cautio is sufficient, will you put whom you please in possession of my property, and will you not allow me to have the opportunity of protecting my own interests, that is, of having the contract for repairs, which repairs must be done at my cost, and you will have the opportunity of judging if they are properly done?'

Manutius saw the right meaning of the passage, except that he understands 'praedes' to be 'mancipia,' or slaves, an error which Graevius corrects. 'Bonis' means any 'bona' of any person which are sold by the state.

quisquam accedit?] There is hardly any sense in the common reading 'quid accedit?' Klotz and Iordan have 'quisquam accedit?' according to V.

tua qui locas:] The relative is sometimes used this way, and refers to its antecedent implicated in the adjective pronoun. There is a similar expression in a letter of Cato to Cicero (Ad Fam. xv. 5), "ut tuam virtutem . . domi togati, armati foris." 'Probatio' means that the 'locator' will have the power of determining if the contract was properly performed. 'Probare' was the usual word in such a case. The small theatre of Pompeii has the inscription

DVO. VIR. DEC. DECR.
THEATRVM. TECTVM
FAC. LOCAR. EIDEMQ. PROB.

'Locar.' 'prob.' mean 'locarunt,' 'probarunt.' See Pro Fonteio, c. 8.

et si non putas cautum.] Madvig (Opuscula, p. 350) thinks that some words are omitted after 'cautum;' so that the sentence would run thus: 'et si non putas cautum, amplius cavebitur.' He argues that the conclusion by which the injustice of the new edict is to be expressed, is not appropriately connected with one of the

putas cautum, scilicet tu, praetor, in mea bona quos voles immittes, me ad meas fortunas defendendas accedere non sines?

LV. Operae pretium est ipsam legem cognoscere. Dicetis eundem conscripsisse qui illud edictum de hereditate. Recita. LEX OPERI FACIVNDO. QUAE PVPILLI IVNII. Dic, dic, quaeso, clarius. C. VERRES PR. VRBANVS ADDIDIT. Corriguntur leges censoriae. Quid enim video in multis veteribus legibus?: CN. DOMITIVS L.

preceding members by the word 'et;' for that the word 'scilicet,' this vehement interrogation, should stand by itself. But the graver objection, as he considers it, is this, that Cicero does not affirm that which he ought particularly to affirm; he does not say that, if the security was not sufficient, further security would be given; and yet he does not omit to mention the supposition of insufficient security, but he subjoins (in the following words) what would be an answer for Verres, and show that he had acted legally. This is Madvig's argument, as I understand it; for his language is not very easy to understand. He adds, "nam si non satis cautum putabat, qui poterat Junium admittere? Ridicule ergo prorsus interrogatur. Patet, illa: 'et si non putas cautum' ita dici a Cicerone, ut vel hoc extremum effugium Verri occludatur; itaque quemadmodum illa: 'probatio futura est tua' statim (c. 55) hoc modo rejetuntur: 'at erat probatio tua,' sic haec pars sic effertur: 'at erat, et esset amplius, si velles, populo cautum praedibus et praediis.'" He concludes that after 'et si non putas cautum' there should be something corresponding to 'at erat, et esset amplius' &c. in the following chapter.

If there is no objection to the Latinity of the passage, there is certainly none to the argument. The youth is made to say 'there was security sufficient; and if you don't think that there was, you will, forsooth, send just whom you please to invade my property, and you will not let me have the opportunity of protecting my own interests.' This is further explained in the next chapter: 'at erat probatio,' &c. If the security was not sufficient, Verres ought not to have taken advantage of that, and given the contract to another, the consequence of which would be the ruin of the youth, who would be obliged to pay a large sum for repairs, which he could have made at a light cost. The argument is: 'if you don't think the security sufficient, you will, forsooth, take such a step as will ruin me at once, by giving the contract to others.' The argument is perfectly clear, and the words are sufficient. I cannot tell what MSS. have 'cautum, scilicet.' Jordan only says 'putas cauta' Lgg. praeter 42; 'putas caveto' cod. Urs. Parr. Lall. So the error, if there is any, lies in the words between 'putas' and 'tu.' On this passage Halm says "Brunnius writes 'PVTAS C[illegible] (probably CAV) stands at the end of a line; the next begins with AS, quite certain; then four or five letters, perhaps LICET, but the I stands oblique: then TV.'" Accordingly Halm conjectures that we should read 'caveas licet. Tu praetor,' &c. So we come to this, that the error if any lies in 'tum sci.' Halm's suggestion is ingenious, but the word 'cautum' ought to be repeated. I think that the text as it stands is as likely to be genuine as any thing that can be devised.

55. *lex operi*] All the MSS. have 'ex,' which the very learned Antonio Agustin, archbishop of Tarragona, first recommended to be altered to 'lex,' a certain emendation; for this is the usual formula 'Lex,' &c.; and Cicero has just said 'legem cognoscere,' 'listen to the terms.' The corruption 'ex' easily explains the corruption 'opere,' which all the MSS. have except V, which has 'Lex operi.'

Quid enim video &c.] V omits 'video in.' The usual punctuation is 'Quid enim? video in multis,' &c. In Horace, 1 Sat. i. 7, there is 'Quid enim? concurritur,' according to the usual punctuation, where Heindorf remarks that this form of expression is common in Cicero, and he compares it with τί γάρ; in Greek. I do not propose to examine what is there said about τί γάρ; in Greek, for Greek construction does not explain Latin construction. The translation of the text of Cicero is: 'Don't I see in many old forms of letting used by the censors?' and that of Horace: 'Is not a battle fought?' It may also be rendered correctly enough thus: 'Verres is correcting the terms of the censors. Well, what of that? I see it is so in many of the old terms of contract, &c. Verres would do something of the kind.' It is plain that

METELLVS CENSORES ADDIDERVNT, L. CASSIVS CN. SERVILIVS CENSORES ADDIDERVNT. Vult aliquid ejusmodi C. Verres. Dic: quid addidit? [Recita.] QVI DE L. MARCIO M. PERPERNA CENSORIBVS . . . SOCIVM NE ADMITTITO NEVE PARTEM DATO NEVE REDIMITO. Quid ita? ne vitiosum opus fieret? At erat probatio tua. Ne parum locuples esset? At erat et esset amplius, si velles, populo cautum praedibus et praediis. Hic te si res ipsa, si indignitas injuriae tuae non commovebat, si pupilli calamitas, propinquorum lacrimae, D. Bruti cujus praedia subierunt periculum, M. Marcelli tutoris auctoritas apud te ponderis nihil habebat; ne illud quidem animadvertebas, ejusmodi fore hoc peccatum tuum quod tu neque negare posses (in tabulas enim [legem] rettulisti) nec cum defensione aliqua confiteri? Addicitur [id] opus HS IↃLX millibus, quum tutores HS LXXX millibus id opus ad illius iniquissimi hominis arbitrium se effecturos esse clamarent. Etenim quid erat operis? Id quod vos vidistis. Omnes illae columnae, quas dealbatas videtis, machina apposita nulla impensa dejectae

'Quid enim' begins an interrogative formula, and that it requires a verb. But it is also true that, in rapid and impassioned speech, usage often omitted the verb which ought to go with 'Quid enim,' and the speaker completed his meaning by the enunciation of another verb. And this second verb may be enunciated either as an answer to the first verb suppressed, in which case it may be either an affirmation or a negation; or it may be a continuation of the interrogation, in such a form as 'Quid enim, ad amicosne confugiam?' or as in Divin. c. 11, "Quid illa, Caecili, contemnendane tibi videntur," &c. A like remark applies to sentences beginning with 'Quid ergo,' &c., as in the beginning of c. 57.

CN. DOMITIVS &c.] The first two were censors in B.C. 115, and their censorship was distinguished for the great works constructed during their office, and for the strictness with which the censors performed their duty of revising (legendi) the senate. The censorship of Cassius and Servilius belongs to B.C. 125.

QVI DE L. MARCIO &c.] The text, as it stands in the Variorum edition, contains 'redemerit eum' after 'censoribus,' and 'ei' twice after 'neve,' and is thus explained by Manutius and Gruter: "If any person has taken a contract from the censors, L. Marcius M. Perperna, no other person must admit that person as a partner, nor give him a share in a contract, nor undertake the contract for him, or on his behalf." This was done to exclude the 'pupillus,' and to prevent Junius, or any one else bidding for him. Manutius is wrong in supposing 'de' in this passage to be equivalent to 'post;' and his reason for this explanation is, that, according to c. 50, P. Junius had taken the contract from the consuls, Sulla and Metellus, and not from the censors, Marcius and Perperna. But see the note on c. 50. Zumpt says that the text as he gives it, and as it is pointed here, is the reading of all the MSS. and all the old editions; and the emendations (redemerit, &c.) are not necessary. The words of the edict are not quoted in full, for it is plain that the words 'socium ne redimito,' &c., are separated from what precedes by something which is omitted. But the text is right.

propinquorum] 'si propinquorum . . si D. Bruti; . . . si M. Marcelli,' V, Iordan.

subierunt] Klotz and Jordan have 'suberant,' and read 'si D. Bruti, cujus praedia suberant, periculum.' V Lg. 29 A have 'suberant.' Asconius explains the words thus, 'satisdatorem dicit fuisse D. Brutum.' Zumpt has 'subierant.' Klotz gives no example of 'suberant,' used in the sense which he would give to the word in this passage. (See Horace, Epod. i. 3.)

[*legem*] 'legem' V Lg. 29, Iordan.

dealbatas] 'whitened;' but it was more than that. The plaister (tectorium) was taken off, and fresh plaister or cement put

eisdemque lapidibus repositae sunt: hoc tu HS IↃLX millibus locavisti. Atque in illis columnis dico esse quae a tuo redemptore commotae non sint: dico esse ex qua tantum tectorium vetus delitum sit et novum inductum. Quod si tanta pecunia columnas dealbari putassem, certe nunquam aedilitatem petivissem. At ut videatur tamen res agi et non eripi pupillo: SI QVID OPERIS CAVSA RESCIDERIS, REFICITO. LVI. Quid erat quod rescinderet, quum suo quemque loco lapidem reponeret? QUI REDEMERIT SATISDET DAMNI INFECTI EI QVI A VETERE REDEMPTORE ACCEPERIT. Deridet quum sibi ipsum jubet satisdare Rabonium. PECVNIA PRAESENS SOLVETVR. Quibus de bonis? Ejus qui, quod tu HS IↃLX millibus locasti, se HS LXXX millibus effecturum esse clamavit. Quibus de bonis? Pupilli, cujus aetatem et solitudinem, etiamsi tutores non

on. As to 'tectorium,' see the passages quoted in Forcellini. 'If,' says Cicero, 'I had thought that the cost of whitening columns had been so great, I should certainly never have been a candidate for the aedileship.' Cicero (Act. ii. Lib. 5. c. 14) enumerates, among other duties of the aedile, 'sacrarum aedium procurationem.' The treasury (aerarium) supplied the 'aediles' with some money for the costs of their office, but not enough.

In place of 'dejectum,' the common reading, which Zumpt and Iordan retain, P. Manutius put 'delitum,' which Orelli has, and Klotz. V has DE . ECTVM, "litera post DE incerta." Halm. Most of the MSS. have 'delectum,' 'deletum.' 'Deletus' and 'dejectus' are often confounded in the MSS. 'Dejectum' is the reading of Lg. 29, Prisc.

The Romans put stucco (tectorium) on bricks and sometimes on stone also.

Atque] The reading of all the MSS., and of the editions to that of Victorio, which has 'atqui.' 'Male,' says Zumpt. If 'atqui' is properly used to introduce something by way of opposition, it is not the word that is wanted here.

res agi &c.] Zumpt takes 'res agi' in a general sense: "ut aliquid publici negotii actum, et non (id quod res erat) praeda tantum a pupillo quaesita videatur;" 'that the matter might appear to be treated, &c., with regard to the public interests, and not wrested from the pupillus.'

56. QUI REDEMERIT] Another clause in the terms of the letting was: "let the contractor give security for 'damnum infectum' to him who shall have the building delivered up to him from the former contractor." 'Damnum infectum' is damage (damnum) not done to a man's property, but damage which there is good reason to expect, if precautions are not taken (Dig. 39. tit. 2). For instance, if one man's building threatened damage to another man, in consequence of its dilapidated state, the owner of the dilapidated property might be required to repair it, or to give security (cautio) for any damage that might be caused by the state of the building. In this, says Asconius, the new contractor was required to give security to the former contractor, if he caused any damage to the building, 'pro necessitate operis;' that is, while doing the necessary repairs. Cicero says that the effect of this clause was, that Rabonius had to give security to himself; for 'qui redemerit' is Rabonius, and 'ei qui' is Rabonius also, as Manutius shows. Cicero adds, 'he is merely mocking us, when he requires Rabonius to give security to himself.' There is nothing wrong in the formula itself. The 'vetus redemptor' was the original redemptor Junius, who was now represented by his son. Rabonius then took the contract (c. 50, and note), but Verres, not being satisfied with the state in which Junius left the building, intended to make a new contract for doing what he pretended that Junius had left undone, and he declares that the third contractor shall give security to the second that he will not damage any thing that the second had done. But he intended that Rabonius should be the third contractor, and so he would have to give security to himself. Manutius understood it.

ACCEPERIT.] 'accepit' V A, Klotz, Iordan.—'praesens solvetur:' all the MSS. have 'solvitur' (Zumpt); which he takes to be equivalent to 'solvetur,' which is in fact the reading of V. Orelli has 'solvatur.'

essent, defendere praetor debuit. Tutoribus defendentibus non modo patrias ejus fortunas sed etiam bona tutorum ademisti. Hoc OPVS BONVM SVO CVIQVE FACITO. [Quid est SVO CVIQVE?] Lapis aliquis caedendus et apportandus fuit machina sua. Nam illo non saxum, non materies [ulla] advecta est: tantum operis in ista locatione fuit quantum paucae operae fabrorum mercedis tulerunt et manupretium machinae. Utrum existimatis minus operis esse unam columnam efficere ab integro novam nullo lapide redivivo an quatuor illas reponere? Nemo dubitat quin multo majus sit novam facere. Ostendam in aedibus privatis longa difficilique vectura columnas singulas ad impluvium HS quadragenis millibus

Hoc OPVS—FACITO.] After these words, there is, 'Quid est suo cuique?' in V. Manutius reads 'bono suo quoque.' But 'suo cuique' is probably right, and correctly explained by Graevius: 'let him make the work good with what is fit and proper for each part.' "Suo cuique," says Graevius, "est quod suum cuique est, illa materia quae ad quodque requiritur, cuique convenit ut bonum fiat." He compares the expression in Plautus, 'suo sibi victu vivunt,' though, he adds, he is aware that this is explained differently, and 'sibi' is considered to be pleonastic. Menard has the same as Graevius.

Lapis &c.] Orelli reads 'Lapis aliquis &c., fuit? Machina sua: nam illo, &c.;' and he explains it thus: "'Lapis . . apportandus fuit?' Minime. Machina tantum sua apportanda s. apponenda fuit. Nam, &c. Ceterum lego: machina una."—'Lapis aliqui:' Zumpt, from Lg. 29.

This passage is difficult. The words 'Quid est' &c., from V, do not seem to diminish the difficulty. It is true, as Madvig remarks, that Cicero, after citing formal words, often adds a remark upon them. Ernesti placed a note of interrogation after 'machina sua,' which neither Zumpt nor Madvig approves. If 'lapis' and 'saxum' are to be taken as synonymous, which is at least doubtful, Cicero must be understood as speaking ironically, or making a half-interrogation; but then there is a difficulty in explaining 'nam,' &c., in the following sentence. If 'lapis' can be taken in the sense of smaller pieces, as opposed to 'saxum,' there is no difficulty in the passage, and 'nam' has its common sense of introducing something which is so obvious, or so well known, as not to require the speaker to dwell on it. 'Some small matter of stone, it is true, had to be cut and brought in his own machine; for, as to large pieces of stone or timber, none was carried there. In that contract of letting, there was just so much labour required as the hire of a few workmen amounted to, and the cost of the machine.' All the Lgg. have 'mercedes,' but 'mercedis' is required after 'quantum,' for 'paucae operae fabrorum' is the nominative to 'tulerunt.' Besides, 'merces' is properly used in the singular. Madvig writes 'manupretii machina,' that is, 'quantum manupretii,' or 'manupretii machina tulit.' Zumpt and Iordan read 'manupretium machinae,' and Orelli 'manupretium machinae,' and this agrees with the use of 'manupretium' in the oration against Piso (c. 21), 'manupretium . . . perditae civitatis.' 'Manupretium' is rightly explained by Asconius, but more exactly by Gaius (Dig. 50. tit. 16. s. 13). A thing is said to be no longer the same thing when its form is altered: 'quoniam plerumque plus est in manupretio quam in re;' that is, 'the cost of the labour bestowed on a thing is generally more than the value of the original thing itself.'

lapide redivivo] The context explains the term, which means old materials used for new buildings. Verres added, 'rediviva sibi habeto,' 'let the contractor take the old materials;' just as if he were going to use new materials, whereas all that was done to the building was done with old materials.

columnas singulas] This is correctly explained by Manutius. "It is more expensive to set up one new column, than to take down and set up again four such as those in the temple of Castor. Yet new columns, as large as these, brought a long distance, have been agreed for (locatas) at 'quadragena millia,' whereas Verres has allowed 'quingenta sexaginta millia' for a piece of work, which the 'tutores' of the 'pupillus'

non minus magnas locatas. Sed ineptum est de tam perspicua istius impudentia pluribus verbis disputare, praesertim quum iste aperte tota lege omnium sermonem atque existimationem contempserit qui etiam ad extremum adscripserit, REDIVIVA SIBI HABETO. Quasi quidquam redivivi ex opere illo tolleretur ac non totum opus ex redivivis constitueretur.—At enim si pupillo redimi non licebat, non necesse erat rem ad ipsum pervenire: poterat aliquis ad id negotium de populo accedere.—Omnes exclusi sunt non minus aperte quam pupillus. Diem praestituit operi faciundo Kalendas Decembres. Locat circiter Idus Septembres. Angustiis temporis excluduntur omnes.

LVII. Quid ergo Rabonius istam diem quomodo assequitur? Nemo Rabonio molestus est neque Kalendis Decembribus neque Nonis neque Idibus. Denique aliquanto ante in provinciam iste proficiscitur quam opus effectum est. Posteaquam reus factus est, primo negabat se opus in acceptum referre posse. Quum instaret Rabonius, in me causam conferebat quod tum codicem obsignassem. Petit a me Rabonius et amicos allegat. Facile impetrat. Iste quid ageret nesciebat. Si in acceptum non rettulisset, putabat se aliquid defensionis habiturum. Rabonium porro intelligebat rem totam esse patefacturum. Tametsi qui poterat esse apertius quam nunc est? Ut uno minus teste haberet, Rabonio opus in acceptum

say that they could have done for 'octoginta millia.'"

Zumpt asks "why 'ad impluvium?' that is, in the atrium. Perhaps," he says, "because it was more difficult to place them in a house than outside, as in a portico or porch;" and more usual also.

istius] 'ejus' V, Iordan.

At enim—accedere.] "But it may be urged," says Cicero, "that if the 'pupillus' could not have the contract, there was no necessity for the matter to come into the hands of Verres,"—for 'ipsum' means Verres, not Rabonius, as Hotmann supposes. Cicero means to say that Verres was the real person, not Rabonius, who was his tool.—The objector or supposed objector goes on to say: 'some other person, any other person (aliquis . . . de populo), might have undertaken the contract.' No, says Cicero, every body was excluded from undertaking the contract by the short time allowed for doing the work. And we must supply, as Asconius does, that Rabonius was not afraid of those terms, because he was in collusion with Verres. But Asconius incorrectly says that 'At enim . . . accedere' must be taken interrogatively. Rabonius (c. 57) did not complete the work at the time fixed.

57. *assequitur?*] How does he complete the work at the time which was fixed?

in acceptum &c.] This expression signifies the approbation of him who had the duty of seeing that the contract was performed. The expression which is generally used to signify giving a man credit for a payment, is also used to signify that a contract of work is completed to the satisfaction of him who agreed to have it done (locator).—'se opus:' Orelli omits 'se,' which Zumpt supplies from Lg. 29. If 'se' is properly omitted, the true reading may be 'referri.'

tum codicem] Zumpt, Klotz, and Iordan have 'cum codicem;' and Zumpt supposes the 'codex' mentioned in c. 55 to be referred to, which contained the terms of the letting (in tabulas rettulisti).

apertius quam nunc est? Ut &c.] which Orelli reads: 'Tametsi, quid . . apertius quam nunc est, ut uno minus teste haberet? Rabonio opus,' &c. In place of 'quid poterat' Ernesti proposes 'qui po-

rettulit quadriennio post quam diem operi dixerat. Hac conditione, si quis de populo redemptor accessisset, non esset usus. Quum die ceteros redemptores exclusisset, tum in ejus arbitrium ac potestatem venire nolebant qui sibi ereptam praedam arbitraretur. Nunc ne argumentemur quo ista pecunia pervenerit facit ipse indicium. Primum quum vehementius cum eo D. Brutus contenderet, qui de sua pecunia HS ıↄLX millia numeravit, quod jam iste ferre non poterat, opere addicto, praedibus acceptis, de HS ıↄLX millibus remisit D. Bruto HS CX millia. Hoc si aliena res esset, certe facere non potuisset. Deinde nummi numerati sunt Cornificio, quem scribam suum fuisse negare non potest. Postremo ipsius

terat,' which Zumpt has, and the rest of his text is the same as that of Orelli, except that he puts the interrogation after 'Rabonio,' as Klotz also does. Zumpt's explanation of the passage, as Madvig observes, is not admissible. Madvig says (Opuscula, p. 325), "Testes dicit (Zumpt) esse et accusatoris et rei. At rei sunt testes qui ab eo pro sua causa producuntur: qui igitur dici potest, nihilo *apertiorem* fore fraudem, etiamsi *reus* uno minus teste ad se defendendum utatur? Nec Habonio teste Verres usus est, sed ejus silentium, ne a Cicerone produceretur, emit." It is quite clear that the ordinary punctuation gives a sense different from what Cicero means to say. Madvig adds that he has cleared up the passage by a better punctuation in his Ep. ad Orell. p. 89; and Iordan, who follows Madvig, prints the passage thus: 'patefacturum; (tametsi quid poterat esse apertius, quam nunc est?) ut uno minus teste haberet, Habonio opus:' which is in substance the same pointing that I had in the first edition, and I retain it here. Lambinus would read 'haberem,' 'magis proprie enim et convenientius dicat accusator, se habere testes in reum, quam reus se habere testes in se.' The 'lemma' of Asconius is 'ut uno minus teste haberet,' and his explanation is "ut de tot qui contra se sunt testibus unum Rabonium detraheret." The meaning is that which Asconius gives, 'in order that he might get rid of a single witness, he accepted the work from Rabonius,' &c.; so that 'ut uno' begins a new sentence. But how is 'haberet' to be explained? The usages of this word are very numerous. We have 'sic habet,' 'so it is.' In c. 45 we have 'uno signo ut sit minus quam ex lege oportet,' which Zumpt, following I. Fr. Gronovius, compares with this passage. Gronovius also refers to Ovid's 'me minus uno' and 'uno ore minus,' which is 'hoc uno excepto.' Instead of the former explanation of 'haberet,' which I attempted, I propose another, which I think is the true explanation. 'Haberet' refers to 'aliquid defensionis habiturum.' The orator says this: 'If Verres should not accept Rabonius' contract as complete, he thought that he should have some ground of defence on this charge. But then he saw that Rabonius would tell the whole story—and yet he could not make it plainer than it was—however that he might have some defence by having one witness less against him, he accepts Rabonius' contract as completed, but four years after the date which he had fixed for its completion.' This is all consistent, and I believe that it is Cicero's meaning.

Hac conditione, &c.] This sentence is correctly explained by Graevius: no other contractor, if any other had offered himself, would have had such favourable terms as Rabonius had. It is true that Verres excluded all others by fixing the time so short; but, besides that, other persons were not willing to bid against Rabonius, and by taking the contract put themselves in the power of a man (Verres) who would have considered that his prey was taken out of his hands, if any other than Rabonius were the contractor.

Nunc ne &c.] Orelli reads 'Nam quid argumentamur . . . pervenerit? fecit ipse judicium.' 'Nunc ne,' &c. is the reading of Lg. 29.

quod jam iste &c.] 'and he could stand his importunity no longer.' 'Quod' refers to 'primum quum vehementius,' &c. Brutus had paid the money to Rabonius, yet Verres remitted 'centum decem millia,' which he could not have done if Rabonius had been a contractor altogether unconnected with him.

Rabonii tabulae praedam illam istius fuisse clamant. Recita. NOMINA RABONII.

LVIII. Hic etiam priore actione Q. Hortensius pupillum Junium venisse praetextatum in vestrum conspectum et stetisse cum patruo testimonium dicente questus est; et me populariter agere atque invidiam commovere, quod puerum producerem, clamitavit. Quid erat, Hortensi, tandem in illo puero populare? quid invidiosum? Gracchi, credo, aut Saturnini, aut alicujus hominis ejusmodi produxeram filium ut nomine ipso et memoria patris animos imperitae multitudinis concitarem. P. Junii erat hominis de plebe Romana filius, quem pater moriens quum tutoribus et propinquis, tum legibus, tum aequitati magistratuum, tum judiciis vestris commendatum putavit. Hic istius scelerato nefarioque latrocinio bonis patriis fortunisque omnibus spoliatus venit in judicium, si nihil aliud, saltem ut eum cujus opera ipse multos annos est in sordibus paulo tamen obsoletius vestitum videret. Itaque tibi, Hortensi, non illius aetas sed causa, non vestitus sed fortuna, popularis videbatur: neque te tam commovebat, quod ille cum toga praetexta, quam quod sine bulla venerat. Vestitus enim neminem commovebat is quem illi mos et jus ingenuitatis dabat. Quod ornamentum pueritiae pater dederat, indicium atque insigne fortunae, hoc ab isto praedone ereptum esse graviter tum et acerbe homines ferebant.

58. *praetextatum*] He was under age, 'impubes,' and wore the praetexta.

populariter agere &c.] This means to act in a way calculated to gain popular power, to please the many, to seek their favour and good opinion. It is a form of 'ambitio,' in the sense in which Cicero sometimes uses that term. Ad Q. Fr. i. 1. c. 3.

Gracchi, &c.] An allusion to the two 'tribuni plebis' and agitators, Tib. and C. Gracchus, whose lives Plutarch has written; and to another 'tribunus plebis,' L. Appuleius Saturninus, a turbulent fellow, who lost his life in a disturbance, B.C. 100. 'Credo' gives its usual ironical sense to the expression. 'It was a son of Gracchus, I suppose, or of a Saturninus, or of somebody of that kind, whom I brought forward.'—'ejusmodi:' 'hujusmodi' V, Iordan.

commendatum] 'commendandum' Orelli.

obsoletius vestitum] Verres is supposed to be present in a mean dress, for it was the Roman fashion for an accused man to neglect his person, and to put on old worn attire, during the time that he was under prosecution. 'Obsoletus' means 'out of use' literally. Horace (Carm. ii. 10) 'obsoleti sordibus tecti.'—'esset in sordibus' V, Klotz, Iordan.

bulla] The 'bulla' was a circular plate of metal (gold), "suspended," says Asconius, "from the neck of children who were born free (ingenui)." He adds, that 'infantes libertini' wore them of leather (scortea bulla). But the son of a 'libertinus' was 'ingenuus' if he was not born in servitude. See Smith's Dict. of Antiquities, Bulla, where there is a drawing of one in the British Museum. Macrobius (Sat. i. 6) in his chapter De origine ac usu praetextae, says, "Nonnulli credunt ingenuis pueris attributum ut cordis figuram in bulla ante pectus annecterent, quam inspicientes ita demum se homines cogitarent, si corde praestarent." Cicero represents the child as reduced to such poverty as to be deprived of his 'bulla;' an oratorical exaggeration. Cicero or the boy's friends took care that he should appear without it.—'illae lacrimae' V; 'hae lacrimae,' the common reading.

Neque erant illae lacrimae populares magis quam nostrae, quam tuae, Q. Hortensi, quam horum qui sententiam laturi sunt; ideo quod communis est causa, commune periculum, communi praesidio talis improbitas, tamquam aliquod incendium, restinguenda est. Habemus enim liberos parvos; incertum est quam longa cujusque nostrum vita futura sit; consulere vivi ac prospicere debemus ut illorum solitudo et pueritia quam firmissimo praesidio munita sit. Quis est enim qui tueri possit liberum nostrorum pueritiam contra improbitatem magistratuum? Mater, credo. Scilicet magno praesidio fuit Anniae pupillae mater, femina primaria: minus illa deos hominesque implorante iste infanti pupillae fortunas patrias ademit. Tutoresne defenderent? Perfacile vero apud istiusmodi praetorem a quo M. Marcelli tutoris in causa pupilli Junii et oratio et voluntas et auctoritas repudiata est.

LIX. Quaerimus etiam quid iste in ultima Phrygia, quid in extremis Pamphyliae partibus fecerit, qualis in bello praedonum praedo ipse fuerit, qui in foro populi Romani pirata nefarius reperiatur? Dubitamus quid iste in hostium praeda molitus sit, qui manubias sibi tantas ex L. Metelli manubiis fecerit? qui majore pecunia quatuor columnas dealbandas quam ille omnes aedificandas locaverit? Exspectemus quid dicant ex Sicilia testes? Quis unquam templum illud adspexit quin avaritiae tuae, quin injuriae, quin audaciae testis esset? Quis a signo Vertumni in circum maximum

ideo quod] 'Ideo' is 'id' and 'eo,' as we see by comparing the use of 'ideo' with that of 'idcirco' and with the use of 'id' by itself. This 'id' denotes nothing more than the general reference to a proposition, which is afterwards particularly enunciated. The text may be translated: 'now this (id), for that (eo quod) the cause is common, the danger common, such a piece of villainy ('id' refers to 'improbitas') must be treated like a fire, and quenched by the united efforts of all.' Comp. Act. ii. Lib. 4. c. 4, "idcirco nemo superiorum attigit ut hic tolleret? ideo C. Claudius Pulcher retulit ut C. Verres posset auferre?" And Terence, Eunuch. v. 7. 4, "nunc id prodeo ut conveniam Parmenonem;" where 'id' is explained 'propter id;' but 'ideo' is used exactly in the same way in the passage just quoted. It is no objection to this explanation if it does not suit all the passages in which 'ideo' occurs; for words like this, which perform the office of conjunctions or adverbs, are used without strict regard to their original meaning.—'restinguendum' V, Iordan.

59. *bello praedonum*] See Lib. 5.

manubias] The explanation of this word by Asconius, 'praeda imperatoris, pro portione de hostibus capta,' seems to agree well enough with this passage, for L. Metellus Dalmaticus or Delmaticus (Cos. B.C. 119) is said to have decorated the temple with his 'spolia' gained in the Dalmatic war. (See c. 49.) The explanation of 'manubiae' by Gellius (xiii. 24) is different.

Vertumni] It appears that Verres had made a contract for the repair of the street leading from the statue of Vertumnus to the Circus Maximus, and that with his usual dishonesty, according to Cicero, he examined and approved (exegit) the work though it was badly done. Of course it is implied that he sold his approbation for a sum of money. Klotz refers to Act. ii. Lib. 3. c. 3, and Lib. 5. c. 72.—'ejusmodi exegisti' means, as Asconius says, 'sic exegisti.' He also says "exigere viam dicuntur magistratus, cum viciniam cogunt munire quam diligentissime sumptu facto."

venit quin is unoquoque gradu de avaritia tua commoneretur? quam tu viam thensarum atque pompae ejusmodi exegisti ut tu ipse illa ire non audeas. Te putet quisquam, quum ab Italia freto disjunctus esses, sociis temperasse, qui aedem Castoris testem furtorum tuorum esse volueris, quam populus Romanus quotidie, judices etiam tum quum de te sententiam ferrent viderent?

LX. Atque etiam judicium in praetura publicum exercuit; non enim praetereundum est ne id quidem. Petita multa est apud istum praetorem a Q. Opimio, qui adductus est in judicium, verbo quod, quum esset tribunus plebis, intercessisset contra legem Corneliam, re vera quod in tribunatu dixisset contra alicujus hominis nobilis voluntatem. De quo judicio si velim dicere omnia, multi appellandi laedendique sint, id quod mihi non est necesse. Tantum dicam, paucos homines, ut levissime dicam, arrogantes hoc adjutore Q. Opimium per ludum et jocum fortunis omnibus evertisse. Is mihi etiam queritur quod a nobis IX solis diebus prima actio sui

thensarum] 'Thensae' or 'tensae' are the sacred vehicles used in the solemn pomp or procession of the Ludi Circenses, to carry certain deities in. There is a passage in the speech of Cicero Pro Cn. Plancio, c. 34 (referred to by Klotz), which seems to show that Laterensis, one of the accusers of Cn. Plancius, had referred to this passage and those quoted in the preceding note, to ridicule Cicero, who defended Plancius.

sociis temperasse,] 'refrained from injuring,' as the context of course implies. In 'sibi temperare' we have also a dative, but the sense is not the same. Comp. Lib. 2. c. 6, 'si cuiquam,' &c.

ferrent viderent?] 'ferent, videbunt' Iordan. Graevius conjectured 'ferent.' Prisc. and the codd. have 'ferrent.' 'Videbunt' is the reading of Lg. 29 and 'tres alii,' and 'viderunt' of the other MSS. Priscian has 'viderent.'—I think that there is no sense in Iordan's reading. The passage may be some way corrupt.

60. *judicium — publicum*] Ferracci, quoted by Klotz, remarks that Verres, as 'praetor urbanus,' acted quite consistently in presiding at this trial, because it did not belong to any of the special cases (quaestiones) in which the other praetors were commissioned to preside. This is true; but Cicero is not finding fault with his presiding: he is blaming the motives for the prosecution.

intercessisset] One of the 'leges' of Sulla deprived the 'tribuni plebis' of the power of doing mischief, as Cicero expresses it (De Legg. iii. 9), but left them the power 'auxilii ferendi,' that is, the 'intercessio,' under certain limitations, which Opimius by not observing had made himself liable to a penalty.—'re vera' is not in any MS., and rests on the authority of Priscian only. But if there is no authority for 're vera,' except Priscian, why should Orelli follow Hotmann in taking 're,' part of Priscian's reading, and reject the rest?

laedendique sint,] Zumpt, Klotz, and Iordan have 'sunt.' But if the rule for the use of the subjunctive in hypothetical sentences as laid down in Key's Grammar (1213, &c.) is correct, and it appears to be so, this is not a case in which an indicative can be used in the second clause. 'Sint' is Ernesti's correction, which is consistent with usage, for Cicero would only have to call on many, in case he should choose to tell all. The passage of Cicero Pro Flacc. c. 5 (quoted by Zumpt), 'oratio mea potest,' &c., does not appear to be properly compared, for 'potest' expresses a possibility dependent on what is said in the other clause, 'si mihi libeat;' nor is the other passage, which he cites, aptly compared (Tuscul. iv. 31), "si ridere concessum sit, vituperatur tamen cachinnatio;" where Cicero means to say that 'cachinnatio' is in all cases 'vituperanda.'

ut levissime dicam,] 'ut levissime appellem' Zumpt, from Lg. 29.—'apud ipsum:' 'apud istum ipsum,' Prisc., Iordan.

Is mihi] See Lib. 2. c. 42, 'Is mihi,' &c., and also Lib. 2. c. 32.

judicii transacta sit, quum apud ipsum tribus horis Q. Opimius, senator populi Romani, bona, fortunas, ornamenta omnia amiserit? Cujus propter indignitatem judicii saepissime est actum in senatu, ut genus hoc totum multarum atque ejusmodi judiciorum tolleretur. Jam vero in bonis Q. Opimii vendendis quas iste praedas, quam aperte, quam improbe fecerit, longum est dicere Hoc dico: nisi vobis id hominum honestissimorum tabulis planum fecero, fingi a me hoc totum temporis causa putatote. Jam qui ex calamitate senatoris populi Romani, quum praetor judicio ejus praefuisset, spolia domum suam referre et manubias detrahere conatus sit, is ullam ab sese calamitatem poterit deprecari?

LXI. Nam de subsortitione illa Juniana judicum nihil dico. Quid enim, contra tabulas quas tu protulisti audeam dicere? Difficile est: non enim me tua solum et judicum auctoritas, sed etiam annulus aureus scribae tui deterret. Non dicam id quod probare difficile est: hoc dicam quod ostendam, multos ex te viros primarios audisse quum diceres, ignosci tibi oportere quod falsum codicem protuleris; nam qua invidia C. Junius conflagrarit, ea nisi providisses tibi ipsi tum pereundum fuisse. Hoc modo iste sibi et saluti

senator populi Romani,] Klotz observes that, by one of Sulla's laws, no person could be elected tribune before he was a senator; and he refers to Appian (Civil Wars, i. 100), whose statement is obscure, and to Suetonius (Augustus, c. 10, 40).

manubias] Zumpt and Klotz have 'manubias,' a reading which Orelli does not notice, though it is that of Asconius. Orelli has 'manibus.'—'conatus sit' is the reading of Priscian, and of the 'lemma' of Asconius. All the MSS. have 'conatus est.' Zumpt observes that Priscian not only writes 'sit,' but explains the use of the word, 'conjunctivum de re indubitabili ἐνεχείρησεν ἄρα.' It is clear that the MSS. of Priscian had 'conatus sit.' Any person who has read these three orations with care, will not doubt that the true reading is 'sit.' It is much easier to feel the difference between 'est' and 'sit,' than to express it in a grammatical formula, which I do not believe to be practicable. It means: 'Now, a man who could attempt to do such an act as this, is not one who can ask for mercy for himself.'

61. *subsortitione*] This alludes to the trial of Oppianicus, mentioned before. Asconius explains the text, 'Verres, as praetor, had to superintend the appointment of the "judices" at this trial, and, after the "rejectio," the appointment of those who had to supply the place of those who were rejected. Some of these "judices," and Junius himself, the "judex quaestionis," having been prosecuted for corruption in this affair, Verres helped the condemnation, by erasing from his register-books the names of those who were really appointed, and putting other names in their places, in order to give strength to the suspicion that Junius had himself put other "judices" in the place of those who were appointed under the superintendence of Verres.' Klotz refers to Cicero Pro Cluentio, c. 33. This false entry was formally sealed with the ring of the secretary of Verres, by way of giving it the appearance of authenticity. This 'scriba' was probably the person to whom Verres gave a golden ring in Sicily (Lib. 3. c. 80), as Zumpt suggests, following Asconius.—'difficile est,' &c. All this is clearly ironical and sarcastic.

pereundum fuisse.] All the MSS. and Priscian have 'fuisset;' but 'fuisset' is unnecessary, if we read 'conflagrarit.' Klotz and Jordan have 'conflagravit . . . fuisset.' 'Conflagravit' is the reading of 'Lg. 29 p. m. Prisc. Putschii et cod. Monac.' 'Conflagrarit' is the reading of the MSS. The difference between 'conflagravit' and 'con-

suae prospicere didicit, referendo in tabulas et privatas et publicas quod gestum non esset, tollendo quod esset, et semper aliquid demendo, mutando, interpolando. Eo enim usque progreditur ut ne defensionem quidem maleficiorum suorum sine aliis maleficiis reperire possit. Ejusmodi [sub]sortitionem homo amentissimus

flagrarit' is very little in form. If 'nam qua . . . fuisse' is the remark of Verres, as I take it to be, the text must stand as I have it.

demendo, mutando,] Orelli inserts in brackets, after 'mutando,' the words 'curando ne litura appareat,' which is in the old texts. But this passage was read by Nonius Marcellus, quoted by Zumpt, as it stands in the text; and the words 'curando ne litura appareat' are wanting in Lg. 29.

Ejusmodi [sub]sortitionem] The text stands as it does in Klotz, who adds 'suae' after 'quaestionis,' which word 'suae' I have placed in brackets. He also omits the words [erepta .. eorum]. Q. Curtius is evidently the 'judex' of some other 'quaestio,' and not of this, as Asconius supposes; but the word 'suae' does not for that reason seem necessary. The reading of Klotz is founded on V, which has 'suae.' He translates the whole passage thus: 'such a choice by lot the senseless fellow thought that he could accomplish through his comrade, Q. Curtius, the presiding judge of his (that is, his own) court of inquiry; since, if I had not opposed him with the power of the people, and the shouts and cries of the many, he would have taken by lot from the Decuria, in which I ought to have the utmost freedom (of choice), those whom Verres indicated to him, into his own Consilium, without any (sufficient) reason.' The expression 'quos annuerat' is not conformable to the usage of 'annuere.' The passage is very difficult, and apparently corrupted. The reading of Klotz is not altogether satisfactory; but I can propose nothing better. Iordan has the same as Klotz.

Zumpt reads, at the beginning of the sentence, 'Ejusmodi sortitionem.' The 'lemma' of Asconius has 'subsortitionem;' and he adds, "obscurus locus, sed, ut opinor, sensus hic est;" and he then proceeds to explain it. His explanation requires 'subsortitionem;' and if we reject it, which we must do, there is no reason why we should not adopt 'ejusmodi sortitionem,' and refer it to the original choosing by lot, and not to the supplying by lot the places of those who were rejected. Zumpt retains the words 'erepta esset facultas eorum,' though they are not in V. Klotz thinks that they may be a gloss; but, if these words are retained, it is necessary to add something after 'eorum quos;' and Zumpt has added 'quum.'

This Curtius is probably the Q. Postumius Curtius mentioned in c. 39. He was a 'judex quaestionis,' but not in this case of Verres, for Glabrio presided. Being a 'judex quaestionis' in another case, he attempted to help Verres, by getting the 'judices' for the case before him, his own case, out of the 'decuria,' which was to supply the 'judices' for the trial of Verres; and getting them before the 'consilium' was formed for the trial of Verres. His object was to get the honest men away, and leave the rogues for the 'consilium' of Verres.

Madvig has explained this matter of the 'judex quaestionis,' and Zumpt has given a summary of his explanation. The expression 'judex quaestionis' is only used by Cicero, and in two other passages (Dig. 48. 8. 1; and Collatio Legum Mosaicarum et Romanarum, i. 3), both of which passages refer to the Lex Cornelia de Sicariis. There is an inscription in which C. Octavius, the father of Augustus, is named Judex Quaestionum. (See also In Vatin. c. 14, note on Quaesitores, vol. iv.) The praetor did not preside in those cases where there was a 'judex quaestionis.' Before the time of Sulla, several 'quaestiones' had been established (see the Excursus, De Repetundis), and, as Ferracci thinks, more than four. There were then six praetors, one of whom was the Praetor Urbanus, and another the Praetor Peregrinus. If there were not praetors enough for all the 'quaestiones,' the easiest way of supplying presidents, without making more 'magistratus,' was to appoint 'judices quaestionum' to preside in particular cases. Sulla increased the number of praetors to eight; but the 'quaestiones' also were increased in his time to the number of eight, or even nine, as some suppose. The number of praetors, however, would still be insufficient for the 'urbana' and 'peregrina jurisdictio,' and for all the 'quaestiones.' For at this time two 'quaestiones' were not given to one person, nor were both the 'urbana' and 'peregrina jurisdictio' given to the same

suorum quoque judicum fore putavit per sodalem suum, Q. Curtium, judicem quaestionis [suae]; cui ego nisi vi populi et hominum clamore atque convicio restitissem, ex hac decuria vestra, cujus mihi copiam quam largissimam factam oportebat, [erepta esset facultas eorum] quos iste annuerat, in suum consilium sine causa subsortiebatur.

praetor. Accordingly 'judices quaestionum' were appointed for certain 'quaestiones.' It does not appear how they were appointed, though it is probable that it was by the votes of the people. When C. Julius Caesar or Augustus increased the number of the praetors, the 'judices quaestionum' would not be wanted; and this seems to explain, as Madvig says, why we find no mention of them except within that period when they were required on account of the deficient number of praetors.

The words 'desunt multa' are sometimes printed at the end of this oration. But V. affirms that it is complete by the words 'in C. Verrem explicit feliciter;' and Lg. 29 has 'M. Tullii Ciceronis in C. Verrem liber tertius explicit.' Still I doubt if this oration is complete.

III. LEX VOCONIA.

THE Lex Voconia has been the subject of many dissertations, and of many contradictory opinions. The scanty notices of it in the Roman writers make the investigation difficult; but the difference of opinion has mainly arisen from the fact that many critics have been more disposed to make guesses than to accept and examine evidence. The substance of what follows is contained in Savigny's Essay on the Lex Voconia (Vermischte Schriften, i. 407, &c.).

Savigny contends that the Lex was prepared and carried by the Tribunus Plebis, Q. Voconia Saxa, in B.C. 169, in the consulship of Q. Marcius Philippus and Cn. Servilius Caepio (Cic. De Sen. c. 5). The first and principal provision of the Lex was, that no woman should be instituted 'heres' by a testament, if the testator was registered in the census as having a property of 100,000 Sestertii (Cic. In Verr. Act. i. Lib. 1. c. 42; Gaius, ii. 274). According to these passages, which are confirmed by Asconius (In Verr. Lib. 1. 41), and Augustinus (de Civitate Dei, iii. c. 21), no person could make a woman his 'heres,' either sole 'heres,' or 'heres' as to any part of his property[1]. The prohibition, however, did not extend to all testators, but only to those whose property was of the value of 100,000 Sestertii, as we learn from Asconius, whose testimony agrees with that of Dion Cassius (56, c. 10), who fixes the amount at 25,000 Drachmae, by which he means, as usual, Denarii; and this sum is equivalent to 100,000 Sestertii. In the passage of Gaius, the amount of the property is expressed thus: "item mulier quae ab eo qui centum milia aeris census est per legem Voconiam heres institui non potest." In this passage 'aes' does not mean Asses, but Sestertii, as Savigny contends; and perhaps he is right. If Gaius means Asses, the amount of the property which was within the provision of the Lex would be 25,000 Sestertii, for at the time of the enactment of the Lex the Sestertius was equivalent to four of the

[1] Juvenal, i. 55, alludes to the Lex,

"Quum leno accipiat moechi bona, si capiendi
Jus nullum uxori," &c.

reduced Asses. But the smallness of this sum, if we assume the reduced Asses to be meant, is an argument against the correctness of this interpretation; nor can we admit, as one critic at least has assumed, that the As to which the Lex Voconia refers was the old As; for, though the time when the As was reduced to $\frac{1}{12}$ part is uncertain, we know that it was reduced to $\frac{1}{12}$ before the enactment of the Lex Voconia. The Lex would of course not refer to a denomination of money which was no longer in use, but it would refer to the standard of the time, and the amount would be expressed either in the reduced As, or in Sestertii; and the Leges of this period express amounts of money in Sestertii, not in Asses. That 'aes' was often used as a general term for money, and as a legal term, is stated by Ulpian (Dig. 50. 16. 159, "etiam aureos nummos aes dicimus"): and the word 'aes' is perhaps used in this general sense in a passage in the 'De Re Publica' of Cicero (iii. 10). According to the terms of the Lex, the prohibition only applied to a testator who was 'census' (Cic. In Verr. Act. i. Lib. 1. c. 41—44), that is, to one whose property was ascertained by the census to amount to 100,000 Sestertii, if that be the real sum which was named in the Lex. But this does not show what census is meant, whether the last census, or any census after the date of the Lex Voconia[1]. If we interpret the Lex strictly, the prohibition did not apply to a testator who was not 'census,' whether this happened in consequence of his own neglect or because a census had not been held. It may appear somewhat singular that the legal efficacy of the prohibition should depend on an accident, or even that a man might render it inoperative by avoiding or neglecting to be 'census.' But the fact is so, according to our authorities, and we must either reject the evidence because we do not fully understand the meaning of this provision of the Lex, which is an uncritical mode of proceeding, or we must accept it, even though we do not understand it.

In the case of the daughter of P. Annius Asellus, Cicero contends that Annius could make his daughter 'heres,' because he was not 'census;' and he complains of the Edict of Verres (c. 41), because it said nothing of the census, and yet the prohibition of the Lex (c. 42) only applied to the case of a man being 'census.' Cicero also complains that the Edict of Verres applied to the case of testators, who died before the Edict was published, and consequently it had a retrospective effect. In both points Cicero's objections are well founded, though Hotmann, not always a safe authority, attempts to justify Verres.

[1] "*Neque census esset*, nihil amplius, orator dicit, h. e. nunquam ex quo paterfamilias sive sui juris factus est" (Zumpt).

When Cicero mentions the terms of the Lex Voconia, he says nothing of the 100,000 Sestertii; and Asconius, who saw the omission in the text, endeavoured to complete it by stating the amount, and giving an explanation, which is a bad one. He did know, however, that the Lex mentioned 100,000 Sestertii, and, as he could not find this in the text of Cicero, he must have found it somewhere else. Savigny's explanation of the omission of the 100,000 Sestertii by Cicero is satisfactory. The orator's object was not to state minutely the provisions of the Lex. It was enough to show that the Edict of Verres was in opposition to its most important provision. Annius was notoriously rich; every body knew that he was worth more than 100,000 Sestertii. But the amount of his property was immaterial in this case. He was not 'census,' and therefore the Lex could not apply to the property of such a testator. The simple fact is, that if a man was census and had a property of one hundred thousand, he could not make a woman his 'heres.'

The object of the legislator is supposed to have been to prevent women being enriched by testamentary donations, and so to check the influence which is a consequence of wealth; or, in other terms, to prevent the evils which generally follow from great wealth being at the disposal of women. But this explanation, though it may contain some truth, is not sufficient. Cato the Censor spoke in favour of the Lex at the time when it was proposed to the people; and he was one of those who were for keeping women under proper restraint.

Another clause of the Lex referred to legacies (legata). It declared that no legatee (legatarius) should take more under a testament than the amount which should remain to the 'heres' or to the 'heredes' after he or they had paid the legacy; and this provision also applied only to a testator who was 'census' (Cic. In Ver. Act. i. Lib. 1. c. 43; Gaius, ii. 226). Gaius does not mention the provision as to legacies, and for a good reason; the subsequent Lex Falcidia had entirely repealed this part of the Lex Voconia. In speaking of this clause also of the Lex, Cicero does not mention the 100,000 Sestertii, but we may conclude, that he means a person who was 'census' at 100,000 Sestertii. From these passages it appears that this prohibition of the Lex was not limited to legacies to women; and yet the Lex contained something about legacies to women, as appears from Cicero (De Re Publica, iii. 10), 'de mulierum legatis et hereditatibus.' Indeed the Lex would have been a very imperfect thing, if it had only provided for the case of a female 'heres,' and not for the case of a female legatee. A passage in Quintillian (Declamat. No. 264), if we can rely on it, shows that the Lex did not allow a woman to take as legatee more than one-half of the testator's property.

The prohibitions of the Lex Voconia appear to be very singular, and indeed absurd, when we consider how easily they could be evaded. A man who was 'census,' and whose property was 100,000 Sestertii or upwards, could not make a woman his 'heres,' not even an only daughter; yet, if he died intestate, his daughters had a share in the succession equally with their brothers; and a daughter, if she was the only child, would take all. Further, if the testator, who was 'census,' and whose property amounted to 100,000 Sestertii, made (instituit) a daughter 'heres,' the 'institutio' being invalid made the testament invalid, and the consequence was, that the daughter would be 'heres ab intestato,' that is, she would take the property which it was the object of the Lex to prevent her from taking. Two solutions of this difficulty, or apparent contradiction, are proposed; one by Savigny, and one by Hugo; neither of which is perhaps satisfactory. That this contradiction did exist appears from the words of Philus (Cicero, De Re Publica, iii. 10), "cur—P. Crassi filia posset habere, si unica patri esset, aeris milliens, salva lege, mea triciens non posset." Savigny doubtless has given the right explanation of the words, when he says that they refer to a case of intestacy. The daughter of Crassus, if he had only one daughter, might by his dying intestate succeed to his immense property of one hundred millions of Sesterces; but Philus, who had a much smaller property, and several children, could not give his daughter more than the share that she would take by his intestacy; for he could give her nothing as testamentary 'heres.' The Vestal Virgins could make a testament; and the prohibitions of the Lex Voconia did not apply to them. (Cic. De Re Publica, iii. 10; Gell. i. 12.)

But the Lex was perhaps not so inconsequent as it appears at first sight. The Romans were fond of making testaments, as most people are. The case of intestacy therefore, though not provided for by the Lex Voconia, would be comparatively rare. The Lex was a limitation of a man's testamentary power, and this would certainly be disliked. The legislator might be satisfied with limiting this power, without venturing to make any innovation on the rights of those who claimed 'ab intestato.' If a rich father, for instance, wished an only daughter to enjoy a larger portion of his property than the Lex allowed him to give by testament, he must be content to die intestate. If he did make a will, and was 'census,' he must observe the rules of the Lex. He could give his daughter a limited legacy, but not make her 'heres.'

The essay of Savigny was written in 1820; and he has added to it a few remarks written in 1849. Numerous writers have attempted to explain this Lex; and Savigny mentions as one of the best, Hasse (Rhein. Mus. für Jurisprud. 3[tr] Jahrgang, 1829, pp. 182—214). The latest essay which I have seen is by Dr. J. J. Bachofen, Basel, 1843.

Zumpt contends that the Lex Voconia was enacted in the early part of B.C. 174, in the consulship of Sp. Postumius Albinus and Q. Mucius Scaevola, in which same year were elected the censors A. Postumius and Q. Fulvius, who are mentioned in the Edict of Verres (Lib. 1. c. 41). The operation of the Lex of Voconius would accordingly date from that census, and the Edict of Verres was so formed as to operate also from that census. Zumpt explains the passage in the De Re Publica thus:—"Crassus had two daughters, but Philus supposes the case of his having only one; and he says, that if he had only one, he could give her, in the way of legacy, even 'milliens,' provided he gave his 'heres' no less. And yet Philus could not give a daughter by his testament even 'triciens,' which was all that he had; that is, as we must suppose Zumpt to mean, he could not give her even 'triciens' as 'heres.'"

In the article Voconia Lex, under Lex in Smith's Dictionary of Antiquities, there is an inconsistency, or an error, if any one chooses to call it so, in mentioning the date of the Lex Voconia, as fixed by Cicero at B.C. 169, and shortly after speaking of Postumius and Fulvius as the censors of that year; for they were the censors of the year B.C. 174. I did not believe that B.C. 169 was the date of the Lex, notwithstanding what Cicero says; and I understood the words of the Lex as quoted by Cicero (Lib. 1. c. 42) "qui post eos censores," &c., to be explained by the words of the Edict of Verres, "Qui ab A. Postumio, Q. Fulvio censoribus" (c. 41). As the omission of this explanation, which ought to have been inserted, makes a difficulty, I take this opportunity of setting that matter straight. I agree with Zumpt, whose note I had not read then, that the date is B.C. 174. Zumpt has given his reasons for this opinion. In that article I have stated the difficulties of this Lex, without removing them, for I did not understand the matter. I had not then read Savigny's essay. Now, after carefully looking at the subject again, I think that the chief difficulties about this Lex still remain unexplained, and must remain so for want of better evidence than we possess.

IV. EDICTA MAGISTRATUUM.

The development of Roman Law is the most remarkable phaenomenon in the history of civilization. It was the result of free institutions among a people who had a nice sense of justice, and a singular tact for administration; but the mode of its development is unlike any thing else that we know. Various institutions contributed to produce that immense body of law which has had so powerful an influence on the legal systems of all European nations, and forms so large a part of the rules of law under which we all live and exercise our activity. Among these institutions was the office of the Roman Magistratus.

The office of a Roman Magistratus was limited to a fixed period, after the expiration of which he was answerable for misconduct during his administration. There were several Magistratus who exercised the same office at the same time, and each of them could check any misconduct of those who were his colleagues. The administration was also distributed among several classes of Magistratus, each of which had their several independent functions; but, though not subordinate to one another, the Magistratus of the higher class had the power of preventing abuse of power by those of a lower class, or of rendering their acts null. All the Roman institutions were cast in a religious mould, and every Magistratus must discharge his duties in conformity to the will of the gods; the mode of ascertaining which was by the auspices (auspiciis). Thus it is implicitly declared by the Roman system that every Magistratus exercises his power as the minister of heaven: every man employed as a public functionary is an agent of a superior power in the moral government of the world. Magistratus only, consuls and others, could observe the auspices, the observation of which was called Spectio (Cic. Phil. ii. 32); but, according to the old practice, the Magistratus must have an augur with him, whose function was to declare the auspices to be valid (nuntiatio), or to declare them invalid (obnuntiatio), the effect of which was to prevent something being done. "Nothing of a public nature," says Cicero (De Divin. i. 2), "either in peace or war, was done without auspices." Verres, who cared not for religion, did not regard the auspices: he rose from the bed of his mistress Chelidon, to assume his high office,

instead of beginning the day with his religious duties[1]. A Magistratus could take the auspices, either to ascertain the will of the gods, as to what he intended to do himself; or he could take them (de caelo servare) with reference to what other and inferior Magistratus were going to do, and he could prevent their acting by declaring the auspices unfavourable (obnuntiatio).

But every Magistratus had not this power against another Magistratus. The Auspicia were Maxima and Minora. Those who had the Maxima Auspicia were Magistratus Majores, and the rest were Minores. Consuls, Praetors, Censors, and the extraordinary Magistratus, Dictators and Interreges, had the Maxima Auspicia, and could prevent the acts of all other Magistratus who had the Minora Auspicia. Among themselves the Magistratus Majores, who were 'collegae,' could hinder the acts of one another: a Consul could hinder the acts of another Consul; and a Censor of a Censor. But a Consul could not interfere with a Censor, nor a Censor with a Consul, for the Censors were not 'collegae' of the Consuls, nor of the Praetors (Gellius, xiii. 15, on the authority of the augur M. Messala); but the Praetors were 'collegae' of the Consuls. One Tribunus Plebis could declare (obnuntiare) against the act of another, for the Tribuni Plebis were 'collegae.' The Minores Magistratus were Aediles, Tribuni Plebis, Quaestores Aerarii, and some others.

The use of the Auspicia originated in a religious conviction; and it was retained for political reasons after the religious conviction had lost its force. In war, and in the administration of justice, the use of the Auspicia was, in course of time, less regarded; but it was continued for the Comitia. Yet the Auspicia still determined the nature of the power of a Magistratus; and the Imperium and Auspicium went together. The Imperium of a Magistratus was the power by virtue of which he gave effect to his will. Those who were Magistratus had both Imperium and Auspicium: he who had Imperium without Auspicium was only Promagistratu, as a Proconsul or a Propraetor, whose Imperium was prolonged[2] after the expiration of the office during which he had the Auspicium. The Magistratus Minores had the Minora Auspicia, but no Imperium. Whatever a Magistratus Major could do by virtue of his

[1] Act. ii. Lib. 1. 40, "qui auspicato," &c. This passage is probably not quite free from ambiguity to us. It seems not to refer to the conduct of Verres after being chosen Praetor, but immediately before. It comes, however, to nearly the same thing; for Cicero (De Divin. i. 16) says, "nihil fere quondam majoris rei nisi auspicato ne privatim quidem gerebatur." See what one of the best political writers has said on the religion of the Romans: Machiavelli Discorsi sopra le Deche di Tito Livio, i. cap. 11—14.

[2] Cicero, Ad Q. Fr. i. 1. c. 1, "tibi . . prorogatum imperium." De Divin. ii. 36, "Quam multi anni sunt quum bella a proconsulibus et a propraetoribus administrantur, qui auspicia non habent."

Imperium, a Magistratus Minor could not do, because he had not the necessary authority. Each Magistratus, whether he had Imperium or not, had his own functions, which he swore to exercise within the limits of the law; but within these limits there was room for the exercise of his own judgment, which, in many cases, he was bound to follow, with such advice and assistance as he could have from those who were competent to give it. It did not often happen that one Magistratus was checked by another in the exercise of his functions, and least of all in the administration of justice. The praetorship of Verres was an exception to the ordinary practice. His illegal conduct was so scandalous and oppressive that his colleague had often to interpose his authority (In Verr. Lib. 1. c. 46).

The function of a judge is to apply the law to the facts of the case which is brought before him; to give to the general rules of law a living reality by virtue of his particular application of them. The direct effect of the judgment is to decide a particular case; but the decision of a particular case involves the declaration of a rule or rules of law; and if the judge has rightly understood the rule, and applied it right, his decision is a record of what the law is or is supposed to be: it is a precedent which may be followed in a like case. This is the 'auctoritas rerum judicatarum,' as the Romans called it; and such precedents are one of the means by which the law is made known and declared, particularly in doubtful cases; and, the more precedents there are in like cases, the greater is the certainty that the law is clearly understood and established. But it was not in this way that the Roman Magistratus exercised their influence on the development of law; for it was not the ordinary process for the Magistratus to hear and decide a case. The function of the Magistratus was to prepare the questions for the investigation and decision of a Judex: his was the 'officium jus dicentis;' that of the Judex was the 'officium judicis.' There were many cases in which the Praetor did decide or make decrees (decreta, or interdicta), and principally in matters of possession, or quasi-possession. He then acted (principaliter, Gaius, iv. 139, &c.), or in the first instance; but his authority in making decrees is not that part of his functions which we have to explain here.

In the earlier period of Roman law the power of the Magistratus was limited by the forms of procedure. All plaints were made by Legis Actiones, the form of which was fixed by the law, and a complainant must make his demand according to the strict letter of it (Gaius, iv. 11), or at least within the limits which the interpretation of the Jurisprudentes had fixed. The Magistratus had, however, a certain discretionary power. He could determine on what days, besides 'dies fasti,' he would allow parties to apply to him; for besides the 'dies fasti,' which were

appropriated to legal business, and the 'dies nefasti,' on which the courts did not sit, there were some days on which a Magistratus might sit or not, as he pleased. He could also say what persons he would allow to apply to him, or what persons he would allow to act as attorneys for others. This power was necessary in order to maintain the character of the court. We have an example in the Edict (Ulpian, Lib. vi. Ad Edictum, Dig. 3. tit. 1) of the class of persons who were not allowed to apply to him[3]. In cases where sureties were required, the Magistratus had to decide on their sufficiency; and in the case of 'vindicationes,' or actions in which the ownership of property was in question, he had to determine who should have possession provisionally, until the right of ownership was ascertained. He could also require the person whom he pronounced to be in possession to give security for the restoration of the thing, with the intermediate profits (praedes litis et vindiciarum), if it should be decided that the ownership belonged to the other party (Gaius, iv. 16). He had then to determine who must be plaintiff and who must be defendant, for he who claims a thing of which another is in possession must prove that he has a better title than the possessor. A Praetor, however, would not give the possession arbitrarily; he would declare that the person actually in possession must be considered as the possessor, if he had not obtained the possession illegally against the other party, as, for instance, by force; and he would further declare that he would protect him in possession against all violence, until the right was decided. If a person in possession claimed this protection against the attempt of another to disturb his possession, the Magistratus could compel the disturber to make a Sponsio, as it was termed; that is, to acknowledge that he was bound to pay a sum of money if he was guilty of an attempt to disturb the possession. This being done, the possessor could sue upon the Sponsio, and he would declare that the defendant who had entered into the obligation of the Sponsio was indebted to him in the sum of money named in it, inasmuch as the fact of disturbance had taken place. A Judex was then named by the Praetor, whose duty it was to investigate the facts, and, if he found that the disturbance had taken place, he condemned the defendant. (See Excursus V., Sponsiones.) In this way the Magistratus established a new kind of right—the right of possession. This right of possession originated in the general opinion that possession, when not acquired illegally against the claimant of the ownership, must be regarded as a right, and as a right opposed to the still undetermined right of ownership, which might be either in the possessor or the claimant. Out of this notion of the right of possession grew the

[3] Dig. 3. 1. 1, "Hunc titulum Praetor proposuit habendae rationis causa, suaeque dignitatis tuendae et decoris causa, ne sine dedecore passim apud se postuletur."

'interdicta retinendae possessionis;' and, again, out of these grew the 'interdicta recuperandae possessionis.' The determination of the fact of possession determined who should sustain the part of plaintiff, and who should sustain the part of defendant; and in the mean time security was taken, as already observed, that the person out of possession should not be a loser, if his right was ultimately acknowledged. This is a simple and natural explanation of the origin of the Roman right of possession [4]. Cicero argues quite consistently with this, when he finds fault with Verres (Act. ii. Lib. 1. 45): "ergo quia possessor est, non moves possessione: si possessor non esset, non dares." For a man was not to be maintained in the possession simply because he was in possession, for he might have got the possession against his adversary by illegal means; nor ought the Praetor to refuse him the possession, simply because he had it not, for he might be entitled to have it.

The Lex Aebutia, which is of uncertain date, introduced a new mode of procedure, according to which the claims of a party were drawn up by the Praetor in a written formula, the terms of which were independent of the words of any Lex. The Praetor being thus freed from the ancient forms was enabled to grant actions, which could not be founded on the Jus Civile or the strict law (Gaius, iv. 11), and in this way a class of Actiones called Honorariae, from the honor or office of the Praetor, was introduced. To allow a right of action in cases where no such right has existed, is the same thing as to acknowledge a new right; for a right of action implies the existence of a previous right, or the existence of a wrong or legal injury. It is not to be supposed that a Praetor arbitrarily allowed new rights of action. He was merely the organ to declare what already existed in the common understanding of the people,—the consciousness of a want and the necessity of a remedy.

The Praetor in many cases, while he framed his formula with reference to some old-established rule of law, gave it a wider application. He could direct the Judex to decide in a given case as if certain facts existed which did not exist,—a mode of proceeding which might lead to great abuse in unskilful hands, but might be made useful and just when the purpose of the Magistratus was honest and the law was defective. For the Roman Law must not be viewed as modern systems of law may be, which are the results of the experience of past ages. The Romans had to create what they wanted, and all that we have here to consider is the way in which they satisfied their wants. Circumstances might and did occur, for instance, in which a man was not owner of a thing

[4] This is Puchta's view of the matter. Savigny, following Niebuhr, looks for the origin of the Right of Possession in the notion of possession in the case of the Ager Publicus. I think that he is mistaken. (Das Recht des Besitzes, p. 172, &c., 6th edition.)

according to the Jus Civile or strict Roman law, but he was owner so far as concerned the justice of his claim. He might have done all that was necessary to acquire the ownership of a thing, except the observance of some form which the Jus Civile required; and the Praetor might direct the Judex, if he found the facts of the case to be such as stated in the formula, to consider him as owner and decide accordingly, just as if the person had acquired the thing in such a way as would have made him owner by the Jus Civile[1]. This mode of treating a given case, as if it were in all respects conformable to another case, to which certain rules of law are applicable, is what the Romans call Fictio. Some modern writers who have made themselves merry over legal fictions have been more merry than wise. A legal Fiction may be a bad figment or a good one. When it is a good one, it accomplishes its object: it satisfies a want and a necessity. He who by virtue of his office is able to become the interpreter of the common understanding of the people, takes from the people, whose activity is the real generator of law, a material to which his skill gives the proper form and his office the due authority. He legislates in a sense, and he is generally a better legislator than a large body of men called a Legislature. How long a Fiction should be allowed to subsist after it has indicated a social want, and shown how it is to be supplied, is a different question. The direct mode of supplying such a want is by legislation, by the act of a sovereign person, or of a number of persons possessed of sovereign power, or who have power delegated to them for that purpose: this is properly called Legislation, the establishment of new rules of law by Statutes, or by Leges, as the Romans called them.

The Lex Aebutia also gave the Praetor the power of assisting a defendant by means of the formula. The simplest defence is a denial of a plaintiff's claim, who must then prove it. But the claim of the plaintiff in itself may be undeniable, and yet there may be some fact which is sufficient to nullify it. The Praetor in his formula could instruct the Judex to decide in favour of the defendant, not only if the claim of the plaintiff could not be established, but also if the fact or facts, which the defendant alleged as a sufficient answer to the plaintiff's demand, should be established by him. This fact, or these facts, which are an answer to a demand, which otherwise would be a valid demand, are an Exceptio, an answer or plea: and this Exceptio protected the defendant against a demand which was valid by the Jus Civile, whenever the Praetor thought fit to give the Exceptio this effect. Here also the Praetor did not act arbitrarily. He would only allow an Exceptio when common opinion had already pronounced in some way that it

[1] See Gaius, iv. 36, for an instance; and iv. 32—38, on Fictiones.

ought to be allowed, or when the case was such that common opinion could not fail to acquiesce in the rule which had its first distinct expression through the organ of the Praetor. This mode of proceeding, this growth of law out of popular opinion, is neither uncertain nor capricious in those matters which relate to the usual transactions of life. A people will often be bad judges of the logical consequences which flow from an established rule of law; but their sense of justice is clear enough to show them when a new rule of law is wanted, and what it should be. It is the business of one who is expert in Law to give to the rule such a form that it shall be fitted to accomplish its purpose.

Though it is uncertain when the Lex Aebutia was enacted, which led to so great a change, the procedure which originated in consequence of this Lex is much older than Cicero's time, and probably existed a century at least before he was born.

The mode in which a Magistratus made known any new rule that he established, was not by a declaration in a particular case; a mode of proceeding which, however disguised under the form of a declaration of existing law, is an arbitrary mode of proceeding, when it is not really a declaration of law, either in the way of a true deduction from a legal principle or a just interpretation of a Statute (lex), or the recognition of a custom. When a new rule of law is declared in a particular case, which rule has no foundation except in the decision of the court in that case, it is a mode of legislation, the cost of which is borne by one or other of the parties to the suit. It is a mode of legislation imperfect and unjust, because it establishes a rule of law for the first time, and applies it to facts which existed before the rule. Such a mode of making rules of law by establishing what are called precedents has given to the office of judge a character which is quite inconsistent with it.

This was not the mode among the Romans, who had a means of giving publicity to general rules before they were applied. It was an old practice for all the Magistratus to make their will known to the people by official communications, Edicta, which were in writing, and put up in public. The Consuls published Edicta for calling together the assemblies of the people, enrolling troops, and summoning the Senate. The Censors did the same for giving notice of a census and other matters which belonged to their office; and other Magistratus in their several offices did the same. An Edictum might refer either to a single case, as, for instance, an Edictum for the mustering of the army; or it might contain a general rule, according to which the Magistratus declared that he would act in certain cases[1]. Edicta of a general nature

[1] In the Prologue to the Poenulus, Plautus gives a parody on the Edictum in an address to the spectators, about their behaviour during the play. In Livy (xxv. 1)

were published by those Magistratus who had Jurisdictio: they contained the general rules by which they would be guided during their administration. They were written out on a tablet of a white ground (album), and put up in a public place, in such a position that any body could read them (unde de plano recte legi possent). The earliest Edictum that relates to the administration of justice is that of Cn. Flavius Aedilis Curulis in which he published the Dies Fasti. The Edictiones Aedilicine, which related to sales in the open market, are mentioned by Plautus (Captiv. iv. 2. 43)[7]. Cicero mentions the Edict of the Praetors as long in use before his time (In Verr. Act. i. c. 44); and, in another passage (De Invent. ii. 22), where he is describing the nature of custom or usage (consuetudo), he says that custom comprehends many rules of law (jura) which are now certain or fixed by reason of their antiquity. And he adds, "of this kind there are many other rules of law; and by much the largest part of those which the Praetors are accustomed to publish in their edict (edicere)." Cicero here distinctly declares that the Praetor declared by his Edict that which he found established by usage: he gave to usage the form and character of real law. The Praetor Urbanus and Peregrinus published Edicta, which were called Urbana, by way of distinction from the Edicta published by Provincial governors, which were called Provincialia.

It became then the practice at Rome for those who had the Jus Edicendi (Gaius, i. 2. 6), and particularly the Praetors, not merely to publish Edicta during their year of office, as the occasion might arise, but also to publish Edicta upon entering on their office. These Edicta contained general rules, in accordance with which the Praetor declared that he would administer justice during the year. These Edicta were called Perpetua, because they had an enduring force, like the office of him who published them. This word Perpetuum has been the subject of some difference of opinion. It means continuous, uninterrupted; and it may refer both to the continuity of the office of Praetor, and also to the continuity of the Edictum during the year of a Praetor's office; for it seems that we can speak of the Perpetuum Edictum of any particular Praetor. It is at least certain that the term Perpetuum had no reference to the permanence of the rules contained in the Edict, for these rules were only valid during the office of him who declared them (In Verr. Act. ii. Lib. 1. c. 42, 'legem annuam'): they might be adopted or rejected by his successor. If a Praetor made an Edictum for a temporary occasion, it is generally stated that such an Edictum was called

there is an example of an Edict, the first part of which refers to a particular case, and the latter part of which is general.

[7] There is in the Digest a long title on the Aedilicium Edictum, Lib. 21. Tit. 1.

Repentinum, and a passage of Cicero (In Verr. Act. ii. Lib. 3. c. 14) is quoted to prove this; but the passage certainly does not justify the conclusion. It does not appear that Edictum Repentinum occurs as a genuine Roman expression, at least not as a technical expression.

It was the general practice for a Praetor to adopt in his Perpetuum Edictum the rules which had been established by his predecessor. He could not well do otherwise; for a rule when declared in the Edictum was not an arbitrary or capricious rule, as we have seen; it was only an authoritative mode of giving a legal character to something already observed as a rule among the people, or of establishing some rule, the necessity of which was generally felt. A Praetor then could not, consistently with the honest discharge of his office, reject any good rule which was established by his predecessor; but, as he was not bound by his predecessor's practice, he was at liberty to reject that of which he did not approve. If a Praetor had any disposition to declare rules in his Edict which were unjust, he was checked by regard to opinion, and by his responsibility after the expiration of his year of office. It was a ground of complaint against Verres that he made new rules in matters that were already settled by his predecessors, and to which he ought to have made his Edictum conformable (In Verr. Lib. 1. c. 40—47). The general practice of making the new Edictum conformable to what was already established, gave to the Edictum a certain degree of fixedness. Such edictal rules as a Praetor adopted from the Edictum of his predecessor were called Edictum Translatitium (In Verr. Act. ii. Lib. 1. c. 45). By the addition of a new rule, as circumstances called for them, the Edictum was continually enlarged; and old rules which were found to be useless or injurious were dropped. And all this was done before the eyes of a people ever watchful over the conduct of their Magistratus, who were men chosen out of their own body, to which they returned after the expiration of their annual office; and with the advice and assistance of persons learned in the Law (jurisprudentes).

Some Praetors, however, while they escaped the censure of framing a rule for particular occasions, with which Cicero charges Verres, did almost as much mischief in another way. Instead of abiding by their Edictum Perpetuum, they made additions to it from time to time during their year of office, or altered it. But this practice was checked, B.C. 67, by a Cornelia Lex, which required Magistratus to administer justice during their year of office conformably to their Edictum Perpetuum, or the Edict published on entering on their office [a].

[a] Asconius in Cornel. p. 58, ed. Orelli; Dion Cassius, xxxvi. 23. The words of Asconius are: "Aliam deinde legem Cornelius, etsi nemo repugnare ausus est, multis tamen invitis tulit, ut praetores ex edictis suis perpetuis jus dicerent: quae res cunctam gratiam ambitiosis praetoribus, qui varie jus dicere solebant, sustulit."

The Edicta of the Magistratus in course of time formed a considerable body of Law, on which we have the comments of the Jurists contained in the 'excerpta' in Justinian's Digest. That body of Edictal Law which was framed by the Praetors was called Praetorium Jus; and that which was formed by the Edict of the Curule Aediles, Aedilicium Jus. The term Jus Honorarium comprehends both, as the term Honorarium expresses the honor (office) of the Magistratus; though Jus Honorarium is generally used as equivalent to Praetorium Jus. This Honorarium Jus is a part of the Jus Civile Romanorum, or the peculiar law of Rome, for it was formed by Roman Magistratus; it was generally applicable only to Roman institutions and Roman usages, and perhaps originally contained only pure rules of Roman law. But Honorarium Jus may also be viewed as opposed to Jus Civile[a] (the two forming the two great divisions of the whole matter of Roman law), when we look at the Honorarium Jus with reference to its origin in the office of the Magistratus. The Leges and Plebiscita were direct sources of law. "The Praetor on the contrary did not declare in his Edictum what should henceforth be law, to do which he had no authority; but he declared what he would consider and treat as law, so that he merely gave notice of what he should do during his year of office. Accordingly those rules of law which were truly rules of law, were said to exist 'ipso jure,' while the Praetor's rules were said to exist 'jurisdictione, tuitione Praetoris'" (Savigny, *System des Heutigen Römischen Rechts*, i. 117). The Romans formed a clear distinction between the rights which a man had by the strict Jus Civile, to which rights, when they were disputed or infringed, it was the Praetor's duty to give effect; and the rights which he derived simply from the Praetor's Edictum: and this distinction is often expressed in the clearest terms. The Praetor by virtue of his office had the power of giving effect as fully to the rights which were founded on his Edictum, as to the rights which were founded on the strict Jus Civile.

Those who are accustomed to look only to the direct sources of law, to statutes (leges), and who found their narrow notion of law on the definition of a Lex, may have some difficulty in comprehending the Roman system. But we know that a very large part of the Roman law, that which is of most extensive application, was founded on the Edictum, and developed by the Roman jurists. The system in brief was this. There was no continuous and ever active direct legislation among the Romans as to that part of the law which comprehended Privatum Jus. The changes which were from time to time wanted, were made through the organ of an office which was accessible to most of the citizens, and filled by a different person every year. This person,

[a] Jus Civile had several meanings. See the Article Jus, Dict. of Antiqs.

who had no legislative power, had however a power, by virtue of his office, of engaging in the conflict between new opinions and new wants, and old rules of law and old habits, and of establishing by way of experiment, during his year of office, such new rules as he and his advisers considered to be suited to the time. The Praetor's rules were thus tried and tested during his year of office without being put in the rigid form of a statute (lex): whatever was found to be good, was accepted by his successor; and thus in course of time the rules of the Edictum obtained the sanction of usage, and were respected just as much as if they were a statute (lex). Being promulgated in writing, they belong to the division of Written Law (Jus scriptum).

Papinianus describes the character of the Jus Praetorium in these words (Dig. i. 1. 7. § 1): "Jus praetorium est quod praetores introduxerunt adjuvandi vel supplendi vel corrigendi juris gratia propter utilitatem publicam." Instances of the several cases here mentioned are easily found; but one of the most striking is the case in which the Praetor gave the Bonorum Possessio of an 'hereditas' to those who were not entitled by the Jus Civile. After laying down the rules of the Twelve Tables as to the 'intestatorum hereditates,' or the succession to the property of intestates, Gaius adds (iv. 25): "sed hae juris iniquitates edicto Praetoris emendatae sunt," and he proceeds to state in what cases the Praetor gave the Bonorum Possessio to those who were not 'heredes ipso jure,' but who by the Edict of the Praetor 'loco heredum constituuntur.' Thus the claims of persons to the property of intestates were extended to persons who had no claim according to the narrow rules of the old law; and this extension was not effected by a Lex, by the people in their legislative capacity; but it was effected by the popular will through its organ the Praetor, and not in the way of direct legislation, but by gradual steps and in an experimental way.

It has been shown in what manner through the organ of the Praetor the Jus Praetorium was established. The peculiarity of the Jus Praetorium does not however consist in its form only: it is characterized by other matter also. This character has been shown to a certain extent, but its character will be seen more clearly by a short statement of the nature of the Jus Gentium, as conceived by the Romans.

Every nation has something peculiar by which it is distinguished from other nations; and it has something in common with all. This is also the case with its law, which, from originally having a strongly marked individual character, assumes one which is more general and more comprehensive. This change is in a great degree effected by the intercourse amongst different people. The peculiar form which this more general and comprehensive law assumed among the Romans, is the Jus Gentium.

In the early history of Rome treaties were made between the Romans and other people, by which, among other things, were regulated the modes in which Romans and Peregrini, who had dealings with one another, must settle their mutual claims in case of dispute. A foreigner at Rome, or a Roman in a foreign country, must of necessity apply to the courts of the country in which he was at the time. The persons at Rome who settled disputes between a Roman and a Peregrinus were called Recuperatores; and at Rome we must assume that they would be Romans. They had not to apply the rules of Roman law to the cases which came before them, for a Peregrinus could have none of the rights of a Roman citizen, and none of the claims founded on those rights, the possession of which was one of the exclusive characteristics of a citizen of Rome. The functions of the Recuperatores were limited to the decision of such cases as arose out of the dealings between Romans and Peregrini, to which the strict rules of Roman law were not applicable. They must, therefore, decide the cases that came before them according to the general notions of equity, which all men have, or in accordance with such usages as they found established and recognized by Peregrini, or Romans and Peregrini, in their mutual dealings; and though Roman notions of law would generally direct the Recuperatores in their judgments, the notions and usages of foreigners also would exercise some influence on them. A set of rules applicable to the dealings between Romans and Peregrini would thus be formed and confirmed by the frequent application of them. As Romans began to visit other countries more frequently for the purposes of commerce and dealings (mercatores, negotiatores), and Peregrini flocked in greater numbers to Rome, the relations between them would become more numerous and more complicated. This circumstance led to the appointment (B.C. 247) of a Praetor Peregrinus at Rome 'qui inter peregrinos et cives jus diceret,' for the Praetor Urbanus had already sufficient to do; though there are instances, after the appointment of a Praetor Peregrinus, of both functions being exercised by one Praetor (Liv. xxv. 3; xxxvii. 50). Many of these Peregrini were Socii, who stood in some degree of subjection to Rome, and many of them were Provinciales. All these people, though not Roman citizens, were not in the condition of those nations with which Rome had no relations at all[1]. They stood in such a relation to Rome that it was necessary to provide for the administration of justice among them at Rome, between them and Romans. The persons who were appointed by the Praetor to hear and decide on such cases as these may have been generally Recuperatores; but a simple Judex was also sometimes appointed both at Rome and in the provinces.

[1] On the political meaning of these terms, Socii and Peregrini, see Divin. c. 3, note.

Under these circumstances and by these means was formed a body of Roman law applicable both to Peregrini and to Romans. This law is the Roman Jus Gentium in its original sense; a law which arose from a practical necessity, and was adapted to cases of dealings between Peregrini and Romans. As the term implies, this law was not limited in its application to a single Gens, but it was a law of a general character, applicable to many Gentes, and a law which grew up within the Roman territory. It was a law formed for those who, not being Cives Romani, could not be made subjects of the Jus Civile, which was 'proprium Romanorum[1].' This practical notion being established, it was an easy step to view the Jus Gentium as a general law applicable to the Romans and to all people. The Romans, having emerged from the strict and narrow system of their Jus Civile, saw that there was something more general and comprehensive; that besides a 'civilis ratio,' as they termed it, a Roman law founded on Roman notions, there was a 'naturalis ratio;' there was something which was common to all law and to all peoples; and so the Jus Gentium, which was developed without interfering with the Jus Civile, was extended from its original narrow limits to express the idea of law in its more general sense and more extended application. The Jus Gentium did not rise out of any speculative notions; it had a purely practical origin; and when we look at the definitions given of it by the Roman jurists, we must remember that they had attained to this generalizing notion by actually contemplating what had been produced in a practical way[2].

The Jus Gentium received its efficient form from the Edicta of the Magistratus. It became law for Peregrini by the Edictum of the Praetor Peregrinus and by the Provincial Edicta; and law for the Romans by the Edicta of the Praetor Urbanus.

Many rules of law were both Juris Gentium and Juris Civilis. Most of the contracts of daily life, such as buying and selling, letting and hiring, delivery and corresponding possession as a mode of acquiring ownership, were common to the Romans and other nations. But the Romans had many positive institutions which were peculiar to them; marriage, which could only be contracted between Roman citizens; the Patria Potestas, and Agnatio; many of the modes of acquiring ownership (Mancipatio, Usucapio); certain peculiar forms of contract; and all that related to testaments and to succession to intestates. But even these positive institutions contain some general principle,

[1] Thus Gaius (iii. 93) speaks of the Stipulatio as an "obligatio propria civium Romanorum."

[2] "Quod naturalis ratio inter omnes homines constituit, id apud omnes populos peraeque custoditur vocaturque Jus Gentium." Gaius, i. 1. See the Note at the end of this Excursus.

and they appear in other systems of law under another form; for it must be observed that a great part of the peculiar law of all countries is peculiar only in form, not in substance. The Romans in their intercourse with Peregrini were led to recognize that which, in substance, but not in form, agreed with Roman institutions. Thus they recognized a marriage as valid by the Jus Gentium, though it was not a Roman marriage, and could not have the effects of a Roman marriage. They recognized an ownership 'in bonis,' as co-existing with the Roman ownership 'ex jure Quiritium.' They recognized forms of contracts which Peregrini used, and gave to them a legal effect. One of the most striking instances of this recognition of general principles is in the case of ownership 'in bonis.' A Roman might have sold a thing to another, and delivered to him the possession of it; but, if the forms of the Jus Civile had not been observed, the seller was still owner by the Jus Civile, and could recover the thing by action. But the Praetor considered the purchaser as owner: he allowed him a defence (exceptio) against the seller, and even an action for the recovery of the thing against any person who was in possession of it. He treated him as owner, because he was owner according to the universal principles of law, and he gave the purchaser all the advantages of ownership so far as his office could give them.

It is clear, from what has been said, that the Jus Gentium became a body of positive law among the Romans. But it must not be viewed as identical with Jus Honorarium; for the Edicta of the Praetor Urbanus contained many rules of strict Roman law. Nor must we view Jus Civile and Jus Gentium as opposed to one another, and Jus Civile again as subdivided into Jus Civile and Jus Honorarium. For the Provincialia Edicta contained both much of the Jus Gentium and much particular law; and the Edictum of the Praetor Peregrinus also. The Jus Honorarium, or the Edicta of the Praetors, were the organ by which the Roman Law received its more general principles; and the chief part of these general principles are founded on the Jus Gentium. The opposition of Jus Civile and Jus Honorarium is strictly an opposition of form; but to this form we must add the material opposition, which consisted in this, that the matter of the Edicta was derived from another principle than the Jus Civile: it was derived from the 'naturalis aequitas,' the characteristic of the Jus Gentium.

The nature of the Roman mode of establishing law by the office of the Praetor is briefly this: every year new Magistratus were appointed, and it was their duty to ascertain what was defective in the law, and to supply it by the Edictum. The Magistratus were not lawyers, but they had the advice and assistance of men who were learned in the law (jurisconsulti, jurisprudentes). Thus there was

annually a kind of revision made of all that had been effected by the Edicta. What was found good was retained in the new Edictum; and what was wanting was added [4]. We may assume that law had become a study, and received some kind of systematic development, before the Perpetuum Edictum could have much effect; for the lawyers must have assisted in drawing it up, and putting it in its technical form. This mode of making law for all that concerned the ordinary affairs of life, was well suited to a state which originated in a city with a small territory; and it could be continued without inconvenience, for Rome was still the centre of administration, and the rules of law which were established at Rome were introduced by the governors into the provinces, so far as they were applicable; and though many countries and many cities retained their particular laws under the Roman empire, the tendency of their administration was to extend the rules of Roman law to other countries; not the rules of the strict Jus Civile, for many of these were only applicable to Roman citizens, but that more comprehensive law which grew up at Rome under the name of Jus Honorarium.

The length of these remarks must be explained by this, that it seemed necessary to show what the Edictum was; which cannot be done in few words. What is said here will be useful to those who read these orations, and generally to those who read other parts of Cicero. This is that peculiar part of Roman law which the Roman jurists chiefly laboured on: but to explain how they did this is entirely beyond the present purpose. I have made no comparisons between the growth of the Roman and of the English law, as is sometimes done, and done very inaccurately. A student who wishes to see how the English law has grown may read some of the chapters of Mr. Spence's "Equitable Jurisdiction of the Court of Chancery," Vol. i., and particularly chap. ix., "Actions on the Case."

These remarks are founded on Puchta's Cursus der Institutionen, Vol. i. pp. 313—362, and I have adopted, with very slight modifications, all that he has said on the Edicta Magistratuum. I have also used Savigny, System des Heutigen Römischen Rechts, Vol. i.

---

[4] This implies that the drawing up of an Edictum by a Magistratus, before he entered on his office, was a work of some time and labour; and he must have had the assistance of persons learned in the law. And so it was. Cicero says of himself and his Edictum in his government of Cilicia: "Romae composui edictum: nihil addidi nisi quod publicani me rogarunt, quum Samum ad me venissent, ut de tuo edicto totidem verbis transferrem in meum. Diligentissime scriptum caput est quod pertinet ad minuendos sumptus civitatum" (Ad Div. iii. 8).

"Quod naturalis ratio inter omnes homines constituit, id apud omnes populos peraeque custoditur vocaturque Jus Gentium" (Gaius i. 1).

Mr. Austin (An Outline of a Course of Lectures on General Jurisprudence) says, "The Jus Gentium of the earlier Roman lawyers, I shall distinguish from the Jus Naturale or Jus Gentium, which makes so conspicuous a figure in the van of the Institutes and Pandects. I shall show that the Jus Gentium of the earlier Roman lawyers is peculiar to the Roman Law; whilst the latter is equivalent to the Law of Nature, as the terms are commonly understood by modern writers upon jurisprudence. I shall show that the Jus Gentium of the earlier Roman lawyers was a purely *practical* notion: that it arose from the peculiar relations borne by the Urbs Roma to her dependent allies and subject provinces. I shall show that the latter is a purely *speculative* notion: that it was stolen by the jurists styled classical and by them imported into the Roman Law, from certain muddy hypotheses of certain Greek philosophers touching the measure or test of positive law and morality."

The earliest of the extant classical jurists who speaks of 'jus naturale' is Gaius, who wrote in the time of M. Aurelius. He makes two divisions of Law (i. § 1) with respect to its origin, Jus Civile, the peculiar law of any state, and Jus Gentium, the law which prevails among all nations; and this Jus Gentium in his institutional treatise is equivalent to Jus Naturale (ii. 65. 73). This division is that which prevails among the Roman law writers. Ulpian, who died in the reign of Alexander Severus, in the first book of his Institutions makes a threefold division of Law, into Jus Naturale, which is common to men and animals; Jus Gentium, which is common to all peoples; and Jus Civile, which is the law of any particular people, as of the Romans. In the Institutions of Justinian (i. tit. 1, 2) Ulpian's threefold division is adopted, and his definition of Jus Naturale is imported into the Institutiones. Immediately after Ulpian's definition of Jus Naturale Justinian's compilers have placed (i. tit. 2. § 1) the words of Gaius (i. § 1) which make a twofold division of law; and again the compilers in another passage (ii. tit. 1. § 11) have used the words of Gaius, and have added that Jus Naturale is the same as Jus Gentium (quarundam enim rerum dominium nanciscimur jure naturali, quod, sicut diximus, appellatur jus gentium; quarundam jure civili). Certainly the notions of these compilers were very confused, and they did not see clearly what they were doing.

Ulpian's natural law must certainly be excluded altogether from the Roman system; and there remains only the twofold division of Gaius, in which Jus Naturale and Jus Gentium are equivalent, and founded on

the 'naturalis ratio,' as it is defined in the quotation at the beginning of this note. Whatever some of the later Roman law writers, Ulpian, Tryphoninus, and Hermogenianus, may have written or thought of Naturale Jus, what they wrote or thought had no influence on Roman Law, which had been developed practically and independently of any Greek notions. Nor is the opposition between the Jus Gentium of Gaius and that of Cicero's time exactly such as Mr. Austin describes it, for in Cicero Natura and Jus Gentium are sometimes used indifferently. The Romans used the word 'naturalis' in a great many cases as opposed to 'civilis,' as in the 'naturalis obligatio,' which they view as founded on the Jus Gentium. (See Savigny, System, &c., Vol. i., Beilage i.)

These unlucky words 'nature' and 'natural' mislead modern law writers, theologians, and philosophers, who often use them without fixing any clear notion to them. If a man chooses to use them and gives an intelligible meaning to them, and never deviates from that meaning, when he uses them, we cannot blame him, except it be for using words to which some people will give their own inexact meaning.

If any of the Greek schools of philosophy had any influence on Roman Law, it was the Stoic; and it is certain that some of the Roman jurists were Stoics. If they had any philosophy, there was nothing else for a man of sense to take. But nobody, as far as I know, has ever proved that the principles of Roman Law were in any way affected by the Stoical or any other system of philosophy[1]. The compilers of Justinian have certainly shown that they had very obscure notions about the origin of Law; and there may have been law writers, from whom Justinian's workmen compiled, such as Ulpian, who attempted a little philosophy in their Institutional writings. But if we study the Excerpts of Ulpian in the Digest, we shall see that when he is dealing with positive Law, he can write like a man of sense. The Stoic philosophers, whose great practical rule of life was to live according to nature, use that term in a very precise way, and not as it is often used now, in a vague confused sense.

[1] Ritter says (Geschichte der Philosophie, 4ter Th., 2te Aufl. p. 85) that a great number of Stoical principles have been discovered in the doctrine of the Roman Jurists, and it seems that the Stoic Philosophy had an uninterrupted series of teachers and expounders of Roman Law. He refers to J. A. Ortloff's Abhandlung über den Einfluss der Stoischen Philosophie auf die Römische Jurisprudenz, Erlangen 1797; an essay which I have not seen. Ritter prudently adds, that this subject is worth being discussed again by our Jurists; and he remarks, we must admit that the result might be that Philosophy could make only an external impression on such a positive system as Roman Jurisprudence.—All who know any thing of Roman Law will be of the same mind, and I recommend those who maintain the influence of the Stoic Philosophy on Roman Law to prove the fact. Puchta, a much better judge than Ritter, ridicules this as a notion exploded by the best modern Jurists, and he refers to Ratjen's essay, Kiel, 1839, entitled, "Has the Stoic philosophy exercised any important influence on the juristical writings excerpted in Justinian's Pandects?"

V. SPONSIONES.

Stipulationes are a Roman form of contract, made by formal words (verbis obligatio fit). The form is by oral question and answer. He who asks the question is said 'stipulari,' and he who replies to the question is said 'promittere.' 'Stipulatio' and 'promissio' are accordingly correlatives. If the person who thus becomes bound does not perform his promise, the 'stipulatio' gives to the 'stipulator' a right of action. These are 'stipulationes conventionales,' which are founded solely on the agreement of the parties.

There are also 'stipulationes judiciales,' which a Judex could in some cases impose on a defendant; and 'stipulationes praetoriae' (Dig. 45. 1. 5; and Dig. 46. 5, De Stipulationibus Praetoriis), which are of various kinds. One kind was used for processual purposes, and this is the kind which will be explained here. These 'stipulationes' were called 'Sponsiones,' because the 'stipulator' used the word 'spondes?' to which the other party replied, 'spondeo.' This form of 'obligatio' was called Sponsio, and could only take place between Roman citizens (Gaius, iii. 92, &c.)

This Sponsio was employed by the Praetor as the foundation of a process. The matter in dispute was made the object of the Stipulatio. The right of the plaintiff is the condition of the promise of the defendant, who binds himself to something on the condition that the claim of the plaintiff is just. The following is an instance from Cicero (Ad Div. vi. 21), "quum ei dicerem tibi videri sponsionem illam nos sine periculo facere posse, Si bonorum Turpiliae possessionem Q. Caepio Praetor ex Edicto suo mihi dedit." There is another example in the oration Pro P. Quintio, c. 27. The plaintiff could sue on this Sponsio by a Condictio. He declared that the 'conditio' of the Sponsio existed, that is, that he had a right against the defendant. In form it became an action upon the 'obligatio' of the defendant arising out of the Sponsio; but in fact, the foundation of the action was the right of the plaintiff. The action was in form very like the 'actio sacramento,' one of the old 'legis actiones' (Gaius, iv. 11—31). If the object of the Sponsio was merely to give a particular form to the process, it was

called 'Sponsio praejudicialis;' and the defendant, if judgment was given against him, did not pay the amount of the Sponsio. This Sponsio was a pure form; and, as Gaius says (iv. 94), 'propter hoc solum fit ut per eam de re judicetur.' In this case the plaintiff only makes the 'stipulatio.' But the object of the Sponsio might be also to mulct the defendant; and in that case the defendant has a 'restipulatio' against the plaintiff, that is, he can say to him 'spondes?' and require the answer 'spondeo.' This would be a 'sponsio poënalis.'

The 'in rem actio,' as the Romans termed it, was when a man claimed the ownership of a corporeal thing, or when he claimed some right with respect to a corporeal thing, as a 'usus fructus,' or a right of road over a piece of land (Gaius, iv. 3). The claim could be made by the 'formula petitoria,' of which we have an example in Cicero (Verr. Lib. 2. c. 12); and in this case the defendant had to give 'satisdatio judicatum solvi' (Verr. Lib. 1. c. 45; Gaius, iv. 91). Or the claim could be made by the Sponsio, in which case the plaintiff called upon the defendant in such terms as follow: "si homo quo de agitur ex jure Quiritium meus est, sestertios CXXV nummos dare spondes?" With reference to this 'stipulatio,' the Formula contained the following 'intentio,' that is, the demand of the plaintiff, converted into a conditional form: 'si paret N. N. A. A. SS. CXXV nummos dare oportere,' and the defendant gave security, in case the plaintiff's right was established, for the restoration of the property and the intermediate profits; that is, there was a 'stipulatio pro praede litis et vindiciarum.' The object of the security in both cases was to give the plaintiff, if his claim was established, and the thing was not given up to him, or the value of it, a right of action against the defendant or his Sponsores founded on the 'satisdatio.' When a man claimed a thing by the Sponsio, he did not claim it directly, as the Formula shows, but he claimed a certain sum of money as due, the amount mentioned in the Sponsio, if the thing was proved to be his. Thus the 'in rem actio' was in form converted into an 'actio in personam,' that is, an 'actio' founded on contract (Gaius, iv. 2).

Part of this has been said before (Act. ii. Lib. 1. c. 45, note); but the matter will perhaps be better understood after this explanation. Cicero (Lib. 3. c. 57) says, "L. Rubrius Q. Apronium sponsione lacessivit, ni Apronius dictitaret te sibi in decumis esse socium." Here 'sponsione lacessere' is said of him who was the plaintiff. In c. 59, "cum eodem Apronio postea P. Scandilius . . eandem sponsionem fecit—facta est sponsio." P. Scandilius was the actor or plaintiff, as appears from what follows; and 'sponsionem facere' applies to him 'qui stipulatur,' and the expression seems to apply to him more properly than to him 'qui promittit.' But it is certain that 'sponsionem facere' can also be applied to him 'qui promittit' (Lib. 5. c. 54, note; and Keller, Semes-

trium, &c., Vol. i. p. 30). The plaintiff, when he accepted the Sponsio, was said 'sponsionem acceptam facere' (Lib. 3. c. 60)[1].

The expression 'lege ageret' (Lib. 1. c. 45, and the note) is thus explained by Savigny (System, &c., v. p. 30, &c.). Gaius (iv. 95) states that in his time there were two modes of proceeding by the Formulae, the Formula Petitoria, and the Sponsio; and there was also the proceeding before the Centumviri: "Ceterum si apud Centumviros agitur, summam sponsionis non per formulam petimus, sed per legis actionem; sacramento enim reum provocamus." In the passage in Lib. 1. c. 45, we must suppose that Cicero by 'lege ageret' means a proceeding before the Centumviri, which mode of proceeding, and that by the Sponsio, he considered to be the only two forms applicable to a disputed succession. In other actions, where ownership was in dispute, the proceeding might be by the Formula Petitoria, of which Cicero (Lib. 2. c. 12) gives the form, which form agrees precisely with that in Gaius. The history and constitution of the court of Centumviri are a very obscure subject. This court certainly had cognizance of claims to disputed successions, was an old court, and was in existence even as late as the time of Gaius. It is frequently mentioned in the letters of the Younger Pliny. (See the Article CENTUMVIRI, Dict. of Antiqs.) The application of the Formula Petitoria appears in Lib. 2. c. 12. Zumpt, in his note on the passage 'lege ageret' (Lib. 1. c. 45), simply refers to the passage of Gaius (iv. 91): "In rem actio duplex est; aut enim per formulam petitoriam agitur aut per sponsionem," &c. But Savigny's explanation is the true one. 'Lege agere' in this passage refers to a 'legis actio;' for it appears that all the 'legis actiones' were not abolished by the Lex Aebutia. But 'lege agere' is also used in a more general sense, for Cicero says (Lib. 2. c. 16), 'Quis unquam isto praetore Chelidone invita lege agere potuit?' where 'lege agere' is certainly not limited to a 'legis actio;' nor is it in Divin. c. 5.

With respect to the 'beati possidentes' of Zumpt (Act. ii. Lib. 1, note on 'Si possessor'), we may compare the vulgar expression, that possession is nine-tenths of the law. There are in fact legal essays with the title 'beati possidentes,' or 'de commodis possessionis.' The practical advantage of having the possession of a thing is indeed well known. In the case of the disputed ownership of property, he who is in possession has this advantage, that his opponent must prove a title to the property in order to turn him out; and the possessor gains his cause, that is, he remains undisturbed in possession, if no title can be made out by any other person. This is, however, no special beatitude of a possessor, for every person who makes any claim against another must prove it; and

[1] See the note on this passage.

generally, every defendant in any proceeding civil or criminal has the beatitude of not being required to prove any thing.

There were two institutions of Roman Law, Usucapio and Interdicta, which presupposed the existence of possession, and rendered it necessary to determine the legal notion of possession. No other right except these was derived from possession. He who was in possession of a thing under certain conditions had the capacity of acquiring the ownership of the thing in a given time by Usucapio, or uninterrupted enjoyment. And he who was not in possession might have a right to the possession, or, if he was in possession, and his possession was disturbed, a right to protection. To both these cases the Interdicta applied. A man might be in possession, and yet unable to prove his title to the ownership. If he was ejected by another person, and the ejector was then considered to be in possession (in the legal sense), the party who was ejected would have no remedy; for by the supposition he could show no title to the ownership. All 'possessio,' whatever was its origin, was protected, except when the 'possessio' had been obtained against a former possessor 'vi,' 'clam,' or 'precario,' as the Romans expressed it; but these three excepted cases rendered it necessary in many instances to determine which of two claimants must be considered to be in possession, and to be entitled to the protection of the Interdicta. "In a dispute about ownership, the part which the two parties have to act depends on possession: the present possessor has the advantage of being the defendant, and his opponent has the 'onus petitoris.' If both parties make claim to the possession, this matter must be settled first. According to the oldest law there was no particular process for this purpose, and the Praetor decided according to his judgment; but subsequently he gave the Interdictum retinendae possessionis, in consequence of which, the question, Who is possessor? was decided in a separate trial: this, according to Ulpian, was the first occasion for the introduction of these interdicts" (Puchta, Inst. ii. § 225).

The acknowledgment of a right of possession in the Roman law led the Roman jurists to the determination of the nature of that possession, which was the foundation of the right. This subject has been explained by Savigny, 'Das Recht des Besitzes,' which, besides explaining what is peculiarly Roman, contains the fundamental principles of the acquisition and loss of possession; an exact acquaintance with which would materially assist a legal student in analyzing the confused terminology and the vague language employed on this subject by our judges in their judgments and by our law writers in their treatises.

ACTIONIS SECUNDAE

IN C. VERREM

LIBER SECUNDUS.

DE JURISDICTIONE SICILIENSI.

[Meliores codices quibus haec oratio continetur sunt hi:

Lg. 42 p. m. = Lagomarsinianus nr. 42 praestantissimus, qui cum ab initio ex optimo exemplari descriptus esset, postea ab homine imperito ad similitudinem deteriorum codicum corruptus est. Quamobrem *prior manus* accurate ubique commemoratur, quippe quae ad verum inveniendum unice pertineat.

F = Fabricianus. Hujus codicis vetustissimi scripturas a vulgata differentes in libellum relatas ad Lambinum misit Fr. Fabricius Marcoduranus. Eas confirmari duobus codicibus mss. Puteani tradit Lambinus ad initium hujus orationis. Cf. infra ad iii. c. 24 'causa fuit.' Conspirat autem hic codex mirum quantum cum Lg. 42 p. m., ut eos ex eodem codice archetypo descriptos esse liquido appareat. Ubi apud Lamb. vel in textu vel in margine edit. repet. 1584 lectio reperitur ab editione a. 1566 discrepans, cum optima familia codicum, imprimis cum Lg. 42 p. m. concordans, ibi eam ex cod. Fabr. depromptam esse certum est. Ejusmodi lectiones significavimus φ, quo discernerentur ab iis, quibus a Lambino e. c. l. e. veteris codicis Fabriciani auctoritas diserte adscripta est. Ubicunque in libr. ii. et iii. codicis Fabriciani (F. s. φ) mentionem non fecimus, ibi de ejus scriptura nihil constat. Idem valet de Metelliano et Nanniano.

M = Metellianus, cujus varias lectiones a Guilielmo acceptas Gruterus dedit. Hic codex ita cum Fabriciano consentit ut quibusdam non immerito idem esse videatur. Cf. Zumpt. Praef. p. xx. Sed cum ejus variae lectiones tantum usque ad libr. iii. c. 16 pertineant atque iis locis non raro commemorentur, ubi ex Fabriciano, cujus usque ad finem libri iii. mentio fit, nihil enotatur, potest tamen ambiguum aliquo modo videri idemne sit codex an simillimus Fabriciano. Quamobrem ejus varias lectiones noluimus omittere.

N = Nannianus, praestantissimus adnumerandus, ex quo multas (non omnes) varias lectiones enotavit Petr. Nannius. Eas fere omnes recepit Car. Stephanus et in Appendice vol. ii. p. 686 separatim posuit.

Lg. 29 = Lagomarsinianus nr. 29.

A = Parisiensis nr. 4588. Saec. xiii.

B = Parisiensis nr. 7776. Saec. xiii. Hi tres codices, qui ut Lg. 42, diligentissime sunt collati, plerumque conspirant inter se, et ut melioribus sunt adnumerandi, ita superioribus non plane exaequandi.

4 significat consensum codicum Lg. 29 42 A. B.

V = codicis Vaticani fragmenta de quibus vide quae diximus ad lib. i. Sunt ea quidem optima, sed ne his quidem libris (ii. et iii.) tam egregia ut reliquorum codicum optimorum auctoritati, id quod Klotzius (in editione majore) fere fecit, ubique sint praeferenda. —— Sunt autem haec &c.

In deteriorum codicum numero praeter ceteros (Lgg. Huyd. Oxon. φ. Pall. Urs. Hotom. Lannoct. Franc.) etiam referendus est Parisiensis nr. 7786 (C). Pseudo-Asconius desinit c. 13.] (Iordan.)

I. Multa mihi necessario, judices, praetermittenda sunt, ut possim aliquo modo aliquando de iis rebus quae meae fidei commissae sunt dicere. Recepi enim causam Siciliae; ea me ad hoc negotium provincia attraxit. Ego tamen hoc onere suscepto et recepta causa Siciliensi amplexus animo sum aliquanto amplius. Suscepi enim causam totius ordinis; suscepi causam rei publicae; quod putabam tum denique recte judicari posse si non modo reus improbus adduceretur, sed etiam diligens et firmus accusator ad judicium veniret. Quo mihi maturius ad Siciliae causam veniendum est relictis ceteris ejus furtis atque flagitiis, ut et viribus quam integerrimis agere et ad dicendum temporis satis habere possim. Atque [adeo], antequam de incommodis Siciliae dicam, pauca mihi videntur esse de provinciae dignitate, vetustate, utilitate dicenda. Nam quum omnium sociorum provinciarumque rationem diligenter habere debetis, tum praecipue Siciliae, judices, plurimis justissimisque de causis: primum, quod omnium nationum exterarum princeps Sicilia se ad amicitiam fidemque populi Romani applicavit. Prima

The title of this oration is variously given by the old grammarians, and in the MSS. I have here given it as Iordan has. In some editions the title is De Judiciis s. De Praetura Siciliensi. The title is immaterial. Cicero himself speaks of it thus (Orator. c. 62), "ut nos in Accusationis secundo de Siciliae laude diximus."

1. *aliquo modo aliquando*] Cicero now comes to the real matter of the prosecution, the conduct of Verres in Sicily. Comp. Lib. 1. c. 24, "quo facilius ad Siciliam possim aliquando . . pervenire."— 'his rebus:' V, Klotz.

rei publicae;] 4, V. Zumpt has 'populi Romani.' The abbreviations '*p. r.*' and '*r. p.*' are often confounded.

Siciliae dicam,] Zumpt observes: "*antequam* rarissime apud Ciceronem, ne dicam unquam, ubi de instantibus rebus dicitur, cum indicativo praesentis conjungitur." Halm says, 'dicam' is the future.

applicavit.] One might suppose that the subjection of Sicily to Rome was altogether voluntary, if Cicero's words were taken literally; but it was a conquered island. Sicily was the first 'provincia,' that is, the first Roman possession beyond the limits of Italy. Messana first came over to the Romans (Polyb. i. 8, &c.); and Sicily became a province B.C. 241.

The word 'provincia' was doubtless used by the Romans before the conquest of Sicily, but not in the same sense. 'Provincia' is a shortened form of 'providentia,' as Hugo suggested; and we have in some MSS. the form 'provintia.' The term properly designates the particular functions of a magistrate. Thus the Praetor Urbanus at Rome was said to have the 'urbana provincia:' "sortem nactus est urbanae provinciae," Lib. 1. c. 40.

Zumpt maintains that the form 'applicavit,' not 'applicuit,' is that which is used in the MSS. of Cicero, except in one instance (Ep. ad Div. iii. 11). Here 'applicavit' Lg. 42 p. m. φ Arus. M. p. 212: 'applicuit' ctt (Iordan). Orelli has 'ap-

omnium, id quod ornamentum imperii est, provincia est appellata: prima docuit majores nostros quam praeclarum esset exteris gentibus imperare: sola fuit ea fide benevolentiaque erga populum Romanum ut civitates ejus insulae, quae semel in amicitiam nostram venissent, nunquam postea deficerent, pleraeque autem et maxime illustres in amicitia perpetuo manerent. Itaque majoribus nostris in Africam ex hac provincia gradus imperii factus est. Neque enim tam facile opes Karthaginis tantae concidissent, nisi illud et rei frumentariae subsidium et receptaculum classibus nostris pateret.

II. Quare P. Africanus Karthagine deleta Siculorum urbes signis monumentisque pulcherrimis exornavit, ut, quos victoria populi Romani maxime laetari arbitrabatur, apud eos monumenta victoriae plurima collocaret. Denique ille ipse M. Marcellus, cujus in Sicilia virtutem hostes, misericordiam victi, fidem ceteri Siculi perspexerunt, non solum sociis in eo bello consuluit, verum etiam superatis hostibus temperavit. Urbem pulcherrimam Syracusas, quae quum manu munitissima esset, tum loci natura terra ac mari clauderetur, quum vi consilioque cepisset, non solum incolumem passus est esse, sed ita reliquit ornatum ut esset idem monumentum victoriae, mansuetudinis, continentiae, quum homines viderent et quid expugnasset et quibus pepercisset et quae reliquisset. Tantum ille honorem Siciliae habendum putavit ut ne hostium quidem urbem ex sociorum insula tollendam arbitraretur. Itaque ad omnes res Sicilia provincia semper usi sumus ut, quidquid ex sese posset efferre, id non apud eos nasci sed domi nostrae conditum [jam] putaremus. Quando illa frumentum quod deberet non ad diem dedit? quando id quod opus esse putaret non ultro pollicita est?

plicuit.' The word has a technical use, and was applied to one who came to Rome 'in exsilium,' and attached himself (se applicavit) to a 'quasi patronus.' (Cicero, De Or. i. 39.) Macrobius (De Diff. et Soc. Graeci Latinique verbi, De tempore perfecto) says "explico, explicui: sed Cicero pro Tullio 'explicavit' ait."

2. *P. Africanus*] As to P. Africanus, comp. Lib. 4. c. 33.

M. Claudius Marcellus was the conqueror of Sicily (Liv. xxiv. 30; xxv. 23, &c.). His integrity probably could not be called in question, but the Sicilians complained of the severity with which he treated them (Liv. xxvi. 30), and it appears that they had reason to complain. Cicero's 'misericordia' is to be taken 'oratorie,' as the old grammarians would say. The position of Syracuse is described Lib. 4. c. 52, &c.

clauderetur,] Zumpt, Klotz, and Jordan have 'clauderetur;' the reading of Lg. 29 42 p. m. φ A.: 'claudebatur' ett Or. There is nothing unusual in 'quum' with a subjunctive preceding 'tum' with an indicative. Zumpt says: "Conjunctivo intelligimus causam contineri, cur urbem Marcellus vi capere post diuturnam oppugnationem necesse habuerit." Comp. Cicero ad Div. iv. 4, 'consilium tuum' &c.; ad Div. xiii. 16, 'P. Crassum' &c.; ad Div. x. 16, 'quum rebus' &c.

ultro pollicita est?] 'pollicita est' alone would be enough. See the note on the Divin. c. 1. 'Ultro,' 'thitherwards,'

quando id quod imperaretur recusavit? Itaque ille M. Cato Sapiens cellam penariam rei publicae nostrae, nutricem plebis Romanae, Siciliam nominabat. Nos vero experti sumus Italico maximo difficillimoque bello Siciliam nobis non pro penaria cella, sed pro aerario illo majorum vetere ac referto fuisse: nam sine ullo sumptu nostro coriis, tunicis, frumentoque suppeditando maximos exercitus nostros vestivit, aluit, armavit.

III. Quid illa, quae forsitan ne sentiamus quidem, judices, quanta sunt! quod multis locupletioribus civibus utimur, quod habent propinquam, fidelem, fructuosamque provinciam, quo facile excurrant, ubi libenter negotium gerant; quos illa partim mercibus suppeditandis cum quaestu compendioque dimittit, partim retinet ut arare, ut pascere, ut negotiari libeat, ut denique sedes ac domicilium

strengthens the expression. 'Ultro' means towards some point from the subject of the discourse, which point or direction is indicated by the context (see Ovid, Met. iii. 457); consequently it sometimes means 'further,' 'in addition;' and it may be translated here 'did she not even proffer?'

Sapiens] See Divin. c. 15.

cellam penariam] 'Cella' has the form of a diminutive, like 'sella,' and it may be one. It means a store-place. There was the 'cella penaria' for the 'penus,' or year's stock of useful things; the 'cella olearia,' 'vinaria,' and so forth (De Sen. c. 16). The word 'penus' was sometimes the matter of a legacy, and therefore it was necessary for the meaning of it to be fixed. There is a title in the Digest (33. tit. 9), 'De Penu Legata,' in which (s. 3) the various opinions of the Roman lawyers on the meaning of a legacy of 'penus' are given. The term comprehends more than things for eating and drinking. See also Gellius, iv. c. 1. Strabo (p. 273, ed. Cas.) says of Sicily: καὶ δὴ καὶ καλοῦσιν αὐτὴν ταμιεῖον τῆς Ῥώμης. Compare also Livy xxvi. 32.

We see what is meant by Sicily being a 'cella penaria' for Rome. The Romans furnished themselves well at the expense of the cultivators of this fertile island, who gave because they could not help giving. In the Italic or Social War (B.C. 90), we are told that it furnished supplies to the Roman army free of cost,—a circumstance which must have greatly assisted Rome in that terrible struggle for the supremacy in Italy. See Polybius (vi. 39) on the mode of supplying the Roman armies.

In place of 'coriis,' Servius (Ad Aen. i. 5), who quotes the passage, reads 'copiis;' at least so it is in the text of Mascicius. But 'coriis' is the right reading. Prepared skins were used for tents, shields, and other military purposes (Caesar, B. G. iii. 29; Liv. v. 2; Tacit. Ann. iv. 72, xiii. 35).—The common reading is 'frumentoque suppeditato,' which Orelli, Klotz, and Jordan have. 'Suppeditando' is the reading of Lg. 42 p. m. Either reading is Latin.

aerario] See the note on 'fiscos,' Act. i. c. 8. The Roman 'aerarium' was an artificial person. Livy (xxvi. 32) speaks of Syracuse as 'horreum atque aerarium Populi Romani.' Cicero says with more exactness 'pro aerario.' There were three 'aeraria,' or rather three names for the same thing, the names having reference to particular appropriations. The ordinary 'aerarium' received the ordinary taxes and supplied the ordinary expenditure. The 'aerarium sanctius' was supplied from the 'vicesima,' and was called 'sanctius,' because it was only resorted to in the greatest need (Liv. xxvii. 10). The third, or Gallicum, was appropriated for a Gallic war, in case there should be one. The Romans had always before their eyes the dangers of a Gallic invasion. For more than two thousand years Rome has never been safe against the Gaul. P. Manutius (Commentary on Cicero, Ad Att. vii. 15) makes this division into three 'aeraria;' others make only two.

3. *sentiamus*] Lg. 42 p. m. Asc. Orelli has 'sentimus.'

compendioque] 'gain.' See Lib. 3. c. 46; Pro Flacco, c. 3; Caesar, B. G. vii. 43; Tibullus, i. El. 3, v. 39.

domicilium] 'Domicilium' is a man's

collocare. Quod commodum non mediocre rei publicae est, tantum civium [Romanorum] numerum tam prope ab domo, tam bonis fructuosisque rebus detineri. Et quoniam quasi quaedam praedia populi Romani sunt vectigalia nostra atque provinciae, quemadmodum vos propinquis vestris praediis maxime delectamini, sic populo Romano jucunda suburbanitas est hujusce provinciae. Jam vero hominum ipsorum, judices, ea patientia, virtus, frugalitasque est ut proxime ad nostram disciplinam illam veterem, non ad hanc quae nunc increbuit, videantur accedere. Nihil ceterorum simile Graecorum: nulla desidia, nulla luxuries; contra summus labor in publicis privatisque rebus, summa parsimonia, summa diligentia. Sic porro nostros homines diligunt ut his solis neque publicanus neque negotiator odio sit. Magistratuum autem nostrorum injurias ita multorum tulerunt ut nunquam ante hoc tempus ad aram legum praesidiumque vestrum publico consilio confugerint: tametsi et

usual place of residence. The first part of the word is 'domi;' the second part, if the orthography is correct, contains the same root as 'concilium.' If 'consilium' contains the root 'sed,' 'to sit,' which is probable, we might conjecture that 'domisilium' might be the correct form, which would correspond to 'exsilium.' The term occurs in the Lex Plautia, B.C. 89 (Cic. Pro Archia, c. 4), in the sense of a man's fixed residence (sedem omnium rerum ac fortunarum suarum). It was important for many purposes to determine where a man's 'domicilium' was; for instance, if a man was bound to pay a sum of money in Italy, and his 'domicilium' was in a province, he might be sued either in Italy or in the 'provincia' (Dig. 5. 1. 19. § 4). In the Digest (50. 1. 27. § 1) there is a definition of 'domicilium.' In modern law 'domicile' is a title of law of some extent and importance, and some of the principles of this title of law are founded on the Roman rules.

rebus detineri.] Klotz has 'rebus detinere,' merely a blunder of some of those MSS. which are generally good.

increbuit,] It appears from a note of Zumpt (Divin. c. 4), that the authority of the MSS. is rather in favour of 'increbrescere.' He observes that a comparison with 'erub-escere' does not help us in this matter, for the root is 'rub,' as in 'rubere.' His argument is, that 'erub-escere' is derived from the verb 'rubere;' but that in the verbs in 'escere,' from the adjectives 'aeger,' 'miser,' 'piger,' 'scaber,' 'taeter,' the letter 'r' is preserved, though it is true that there are not two 'r's' in these verbs, as 'pigrescere,' &c. He adds, however, that the double 'r' is not so intolerable, for we have 'cribrum' and 'cribrare.'

The notion of some of these verbs in 'escere' being formed from adjectives, and others, as 'erubescere,' from a verb 'rubere,' is a false etymological view. There might be 'rubr-escere' as well as 'rub-escere,' but the reason why there is not is obvious enough. 'Rub' begins with an 'r,' and 'rubrescere' would be as disagreeable to the ear as 'increbrescere.' If the Romans did not say 'rubrescere,' for the same reason they did not say 'increbrescere.' 'Cribrum' is nothing to the purpose, for if the second 'r' was left out we should have an adjective of a neuter form, 'cri-bum,' which would be no word at all. 'Cribrare' may be allowed to Zumpt to support his argument, but he might have added that the diminutive of 'cribrum' is 'cribellum,' not 'cribrellum.' It may be added, that in 'creb-er' the root lies in the part which I have separated from the termination, and the word may be, as Professor Key suggests, another form of 'celeb-er.' (See Lib. 2. c. 66, note.) Nothing therefore of the root is lost by writing 'in-creb-uit.'

aram legum] Hotmann refers to the passage in Aristotle, Rhet. iii. 11: ταὐτὸν εἶναι διαιτητὴν καὶ βωμόν, ἐπ' ἄμφω γὰρ τὸ ἀδικούμενον φεύγειν.

illum annum pertulerant qui sic eos afflixerat ut salvi esse non possent, nisi C. Marcellus quasi aliquo fato venisset, ut bis ex eadem familia salus Siciliae constitueretur; et post [ea] M. Antonii infinitum illud imperium senserant. Sic a majoribus suis acceperant, tanta populi Romani in Siculos esse beneficia ut etiam injurias nostrorum hominum perferendas putarent. In neminem civitates ante hunc testimonium publice dixerunt. Hunc denique ipsum pertulissent, si humano modo, si usitato more, si denique uno aliquo in genere peccasset. Sed quum perferre non possent luxuriem, crudelitatem, avaritiam, superbiam; quum omnia sua commoda, jura, beneficia senatus populique Romani unius scelere ac libidine perdidissent; hoc statuerunt, aut istius injurias per vos ulcisci ac persequi, aut, si vobis indigni essent visi quibus opem auxiliumque ferretis, urbes ac sedes suas relinquere, quandoquidem agros jam ante istius injuriis exagitati reliquissent. IV. Hoc consilio a L. Metello legationes universae petiverunt ut quamprimum isti succederet: hoc animo toties apud patronos de suis miseriis deplorarunt; hoc commoti dolore postulata consulibus, quae non postulata sed in istum crimina viderentur esse, ediderunt.

illum annum] The allusion, as Asconius remarks, is to M. Aemilius Lepidus, who was praetor of Sicily B.C. 80, and consul B.C. 78. He was the father of the Lepidus who was one of the triumviri with Octavianus Caesar and M. Antonius. Lepidus was succeeded in his Sicilian praetorship by C. Marcellus, a great-grandson of the conqueror of Syracuse (Lib. 3. c. 91). He was now one of the 'judices' on the trial of Verres (Divin. c. 4). Cicero, in these orations, often speaks of his honourable administration of the province (Lib. 3. c. 16).

M. Antonii] This is M. Antonius Creticus, the son of the orator Antonius, and the father of M. Antonius, the colleague of Lepidus and Octavianus Caesar in the triumvirate. (See ii. Lib. 1. c. 23, note.) In B.C. 74 he received a commission, with very extensive powers, to carry on the war against the pirates, and he abused his powers. The critics have made a difficulty about the words 'infinitum illud imperium,' for his 'imperium' was limited, as was that which Cn. Pompeius afterwards received by the Manilia Lex, when he was commissioned to clear the Mediterranean of pirates. But Cicero evidently means that his powers were very great, and no more. Ferracci thinks that his 'imperium' was called 'infinitum' because it was not limited by the boundaries of any one province. But there is nothing in this remark. His 'provincia' was the war with the pirates.

relinquere.] Klotz has 'relinquerent;' he has put a colon after 'persequi.'—"*relinquerent* codd. noti, etiam F. Defendit Oudend. ad Ap. T. i. p. 72. Vulgata primum exstat ap. Man. 1540" (Iordan), who has 'relinquere.'

4. *L. Metello*] L. Caecilius Metellus succeeded Verres as praetor of Sicily B.C. 70, and Cicero commends his administration. Yet he and his brothers, Q. Metellus Creticus and M. Metellus, attempted to save Verres in this prosecution (Act. i. c. 8, 9, 10).—'succedere' is to come into the place of another, as one governor is the 'successor' of another. The retiring governor was said 'decedere,' or 'decedere de provincia' (Divin. 1); and he was called 'decessor' (Tacit. Agric. 7).

postulata] 'Postulare' was a forensic term in use in civil actions, but applied also to demands of a public nature. 'Postulare' is defined by Ulpian (Dig. 3. 1. 1): "postulare autem est desiderium suum vel amici sui in jure apud eum qui jurisdictioni praeest exponere, vel alterius desiderio contradicere." The term was also applied to the demands or claims of the Roman provinces before the Roman

Fecerunt etiam ut me, cujus fidem continentiamque cognoverant, prope de vitae meae statu dolore ac lacrimis suis deducerent, ut ego istum accusarem, a quo mea longissime ratio voluntasque abhorrebat: quamquam in hac causa multo plures partes mihi defensionis quam accusationis suscepisse videor: postremo homines ex tota provincia nobilissimi primique publice privatimque venerunt, gravissima atque amplissima quaeque civitas vehementissime suas injurias persecuta est.

At quemadmodum, judices, venerunt? Videor enim mihi jam liberius apud vos pro Siculis loqui debere quam forsitan ipsi velint: saluti enim potius eorum consulam quam voluntati. Ecquem existimatis unquam ulla in provincia reum absentem contra inquisitionem accusatoris tantis opibus, tanta cupiditate esse defensum? Quaestores utriusque provinciae, qui isto praetore fuerant, cum fascibus mihi praesto fuerunt. His porro qui successerunt vehementer istius cupidi, liberaliter ex istius cibariis tractati, non minus acres contra me fuerunt. Videte quid potuerit qui quatuor in una provincia quaestores studiosissimos defensores propugnatoresque habuerit, praetorem vero cohortemque totam sic studiosam, ut facile appareret non tam illis Siciliam, quam inanem offenderant, quam Verrem ipsum qui plenus decesserat provinciam fuisse.

senate (Pro Balbo, c. 15, 'Gaditani .. a senatu de foedere postulaverunt'). See Lib. 2. c. 59.

de . . . statu] See Divin. c. 1.

istum accusarem, a quo] 'A quo' means, as Asconius says, 'a qua re,' which would be the usual Roman expression.

quemadmodum . . . venerunt?] 'Venerint' is the reading of Asconius, and Klotz has adopted it. Orelli, Zumpt, and Iordan have 'venerunt.' There are in Cicero instances of 'quemadmodum' being used in the form of direct interrogative, as in Lib. 2. c. 42, 'At quemadmodum corrupisti?'—'Ecquem existimatis:' most of the MSS. have 'et quem;' but in such cases 'et' and 'ec' are often confounded (Zumpt).

Quaestores utriusque provinciae,] He means the quaestors of the two divisions of Sicily, the quaestor of the division of Syracuse, and the quaestor of the division of Lilybaeum. Two of the former quaestors of Verres are represented by Cicero as appearing before him when he went to Sicily to collect evidence; for 'praesto esse' may imply either for the purpose of hindrance, as in the Pro Caecina, c. 30, quoted by Klotz, or for any other purpose, as in c. 27; and Caesar, B. G. v. 26. Gellius (xiii. 12), quoting Varro, says "ut quaestores et ceteri qui neque lictorem habent neque viatorem." This remark applies to the two Urbani Quaestores. Towards the close of the republican period, the Quaestors in the provinces had a higher station; they had an Imperium, and of course Lictors; yet their Imperium was delegated authority from the Praetor. They had also the 'jurisdictio' of the Curule Aediles (Gaius, i. § 6). Garatoni thinks that Cicero purposely used an ambiguous expression, for he was fond of a joke; "the quaestors were ready to meet me with their fasces;" and a like use of 'praesto' in Q. Curtius (viii. 13) is referred to.

istius cupidi,] 'violent partizans of Verres.'

cibariis] The money paid out of the treasury to magistrates on going to their provinces was called 'cibaria' (Ad Div. v. 20; Ad Att. vi. 3). At the beginning of this sentence Zumpt and Orelli have 'Hi porro;' but 'His porro,' which Klotz and Iordan have from Lg. 29. 42, and other MSS., appears to be the true reading.

Minari Siculis si decrevissent legationem quae contra istum diceret: minari si qui essent profecti: aliis si laudarent benignissime promittere: gravissimos privatarum rerum testes, quibus nos praesentibus denuntiavimus, eos vi custodiisque retinere.

V. Quae quum omnia facta sint, tamen unam solam scitote esse civitatem Mamertinam quae publice legatos qui istum laudarent miserit. Ejus autem legationis principem, civitatis nobilissimum, C. Heium, juratum dicere audistis isti navem onerariam maximam Messanae esse publice coactis operis aedificatam: idemque Mamertinorum legatus, istius laudator, non solum istum bona sua verum etiam sacra deosque penates a majoribus traditos ex aedibus suis eripuisse dixit. Praeclara laudatio, quum duabus in rebus legatorum una opera consumitur, in laudando atque in repetendo. Atque ea ipsa civitas qua ratione isti amica sit dicetur certo loco. Reperietis enim quae causae benevolentiae sint Mamertinis erga istum, eas ipsas causas satis justas esse damnationis. Alia civitas nulla, judices, publico consilio laudat. Vis illa summi imperii tantum potuit apud perpaucos homines, non civitates, ut aut levissimi quidam ex miserrimis desertissimisque oppidis invenirentur qui injussu populi ac senatus proficiscerentur, aut ii qui contra istum legati decreti erant et testimonium publicum mandataque acceperant vi ac metu retinerentur. Quod ego in paucis tamen usu venisse non

si laudarent] See Lib. 5. c. 22, note on 'laudatores.'

5. *nobilissimum,*] 'nobilissimum civem, Lag. 42 p. m. M φ. om. ett' (Iordan), who puts 'civem' in the text, and gives some good reasons against it in his note.

C. Heium,] There is said to be a 'gemma,' or stone, on which the name ΗΕΙΟΥ is cut; and some would take this as evidence that the name on a cammeo was sometimes that of the owner, which is very probable. But the Heius of this gemma may have been an artist. See the note in Creuzer and Moser's edition of this oration, Göttingen, 1847.

coactis operis] 'Operae' has here the sense of 'operarii,' or 'workmen.' The passage means that the ship was built by an impressment of workmen by order of the city. The workmen would be the slaves of individuals, such as were employed in ship-building. Comp. Lib. 1. c. 56, 'paucae operae fabrorum.'

in repetendo.] Cicero ridicules the 'laudatio' of the Mamertini, for, while they came to do honour to Verres, they charged him with an offence which made him liable to be prosecuted for 'repetundae.' They came to bring their public laudations, and at the same time the members of the deputation severally bore testimony to the misdeeds of Verres.—A, B, L have 'repetendo' only, and Iordan omits 'in.' Yet he says in a note on 'ad hanc' (c. 3) "in membris orationis contrariis et ratio et consuetudo Tulliana praepositionem repeti jubet."

injussu populi ac senatus] Cicero uses a form of expression applicable to the Roman constitution; but it was also applicable to these Sicilian cities, which, according to Greek fashion, had a senate (βουλή) and a popular body (δῆμος). The words 'Vis illa,' &c., refer to Metellus, the Sicilian praetor, and his brothers at Rome, one of whom was Praetor Urbanus, and the other Consul, with Hortensius.

vi ac metu] This is a technical expression. See Pro Caecina, c. 15, note; De Imp. Cn. Pomp. c. 9, note, Vol. ii., and the Excursus in this volume on the Formula Octaviana.

usu venisse] Asconius explains by 'contigisse.' It is one of Caesar's expressions:

moleste tuli, quo reliquae tot et tantae et tam graves civitates, tota denique Sicilia plus auctoritatis apud vos haberet, quum videretis nulla vi retineri, nullo periculo prohiberi potuisse quo minus experirentur ecquid apud vos querimoniae valerent antiquissimorum fidelissimorumque sociorum. Nam, quod fortasse non nemo vestrum audierit, istum a Syracusanis publice laudari, id tametsi priore actione ex Heraclii Syracusani testimonio cujusmodi esset cognovistis, tamen vobis alio loco ut se tota res habeat quod ad eam civitatem attinet demonstrabitur. Intelligetis enim nullis hominibus quemquam tanto odio quanto istum Syracusanis et esse et fuisse.

VI. At enim istum Siculi soli persequuntur; cives Romani qui in Sicilia negotiantur defendunt, diligunt, salvum esse cupiunt. Primum, si ita esset, tamen vos in hac quaestione de pecuniis repetundis, quae sociorum causa constituta est, lege judicioque sociali sociorum querimonias audire oporteret. Sed intelligere potuistis priore actione cives Romanos honestissimos ex Sicilia plurimos maximis de rebus et quas ipsi accepissent injurias et quas scirent aliis esse factas pro testimonio dicere. Ego hoc quod intelligo, judices, sic confirmo. Videor mihi gratum fecisse Siculis quod eorum injurias meo labore, inimicitiis, periculo sum persecutus: non minus hoc gratum me nostris civibus intelligo fecisse, qui hoc existimant, juris, libertatis, rerum fortunarumque suarum salutem in istius damnatione consistere. Quapropter de istius praetura Siliensi non recuso quin ita me audiatis ut, si cuiquam generi hominum sive Siculorum sive nostrorum civium, si cuiquam ordini sive aratorum sive pecuariorum sive mercatorum probatus sit, si non horum omnium communis hostis praedoque fuerit, si cuiquam denique ulla in re unquam temperaverit, ut vos quoque ei temperetis.

'haec usu ventura praeceperat' (B. G. vii. 9, 80), and Terence's, Phorm. i. 2. 24; also Cicero, De Sen. c. 3.

6. *si cuiquam ordini*] All the known MSS. have 'sive cuiquam,' which is certainly an error of the copyists.

aratorum] Cicero here enumerates the different classes of persons in Sicily; the 'aratores,' or cultivators, and the 'pecuarii,' or those who pastured their cattle on the public lands, for which they paid a sum of money called 'scriptura.' He then adds the 'mercatores,' or those who went about with their goods, and trafficked with the natives (Caesar, B. G. iv. 3). But his enumeration is incomplete if the 'negotiatores' are omitted, the Roman money-lenders, bankers, and merchants on a large scale. Garatoni accordingly makes a very probable conjecture that the words 'sive negotiatorum' have been omitted by the copyists. Compare c. 77.

The repetition of the 'ut' in 'ut vos quoque ei temperetis,' after many words interposed, is common. Zumpt cites several examples. In Lib. 2. c. 37, 'Sthenius postulat ut . . . ut,' &c. In Lib. 4. c. 23, 'ei negotium dedit ut . . . ut,' &c. There is an example from one of Cicero's later writings, Ad Q. Fr. i. 1. c. 13, 'sed te illud admoneo ut . . . ut,' &c.

Qui simul atque ei sorte provincia Sicilia obvenit, statim Romae et ad urbem antequam proficisceretur quaerere ipse secum et agitare cum suis coepit, quibusnam rebus in ea provincia maximam uno anno pecuniam facere posset. Nolebat in agendo discere, tametsi non provinciae rudis erat et tiro, sed in Siciliam paratus ad praedam meditatusque venire cupiebat. O praeclare conjectum a vulgo in illam provinciam omen communis famae atque sermonis, quum ex nomine istius quid iste in provincia facturus esset perridicule homines augurabantur. Etenim quis dubitare posset quum istius in quaestura fugam et furtum recognosceret, quum in legatione oppidorum fanorumque spoliationes cogitaret, quum videret in foro latrocinia praeturae, qualis iste in quarto actu improbitatis futurus esset? VII. Atque ut intelligatis eum Romae quaesisse non modo genera furandi sed etiam nomina, certissimum accipite argumentum, quo facilius de singulari ejus impudentia existimare possitis. Quo die Siciliam tetigit, videte satisne paratus ex illo omine urbano ad everrendam provinciam venerit, statim Messana literas Halesam mittit, quas ego istum in Italia scripsisse arbitror; nam simul atque e navi egressus est, dedit operam ut Halesinus ad se Dio continuo veniret; se de hereditate velle cognoscere quae ejus filio a propinquo homine Apollodoro Laphirone venisset. Ea erat, judices, pergrandis pecunia. Hic est Dio, judices, nunc beneficio Q. Metelli civis Romanus factus; de quo multis viris primariis testibus multorumque tabulis vobis priore actione satisfactum est, HS decies numeratum esse ut eam causam in qua ne tenuissima

sorte] The praetors determined by lot what provinces they should have after they had discharged their year of office at Rome, as we see from the Ep. ad Attic. (i. 13), and other passages. As to 'ad urbem,' see Act. i. c. 15. 'Ad urbem' is Asconius' reading; all the MSS. have 'ab urbe.'

Nolebat in agendo &c.] The whole passage stands thus in Klotz, 'Nolebat in agendo discere, tametsi non provinciae rudis erat et tiro, sed Siciliae: paratus ad praedam,' &c. M has 'sed Siciliae;' and Lg. 42 p. m. has 'si Siciliae.' Iordan puts 'in Siciliam' in [ ].

ex nomine istius] This miserable pun is explained by the next chapter: "ex illo omine urbano ad everrendam provinciam venerit," where the true reading is 'everrendam,' though most of the MSS. have 'evertendam.' As to the omen from names, see Livy, xxviii. 28.

7. *sed etiam nomina,*] The names of those whom he designed to plunder.

tetigit,] 'attigit, Lg. 42 p. m. φ.' Iordan.

Halesam] A town on the north coast of Sicily, near the river Halesus (Pettineo), on a hill about a mile from the coast. It is mentioned again in Lib. 3. c. 73.

civis Romanus] The Roman 'civitas' was sometimes conferred by a governor; but it does not appear that he could give the 'civitas,' except in conformity to some power which was conferred on him for that purpose. Cn. Pompeius gave the 'civitas' to Cornelius Balbus, pursuant to the provisions of a Lex (Pro Balbo, c. 13). The person on whom the 'civitas' was thus conferred generally seems to have taken the gentile name of his patron, if he was a Greek; thus Dio is called in the next chapter Q. Caecilius Dio. And a Sex. Pompeius Chlorus is mentioned there, also a Greek, who had been made a Roman citizen.

numeratum] 'numerata' F M, 'nume-

quidem dubitatio posset esse isto cognoscente obtineret; praeterea greges nobilissimarum equarum abactos; argenti vestisque stragulae domi quod fuerit esse direptum: ita HS decies Q. Dionem, quod hereditas ei venisset, nullam aliam ob causam perdidisse. Quid haec hereditas, quo praetore Dionis filio venerat? Eodem quo P. Annii senatoris filiae, eodem quo M. Liguri senatori C. Sacerdote [praetore]. Quid tum nemo molestus Dioni fuerat? Non plus quam Liguri Sacerdote praetore. Quid ad Verrem quis detulit? Nemo; nisi forte existimatis ei quadruplatores ad fretum praesto fuisse.

VIII. Ad urbem quum esset, audivit Dioni cuidam Siculo permagnam venisse hereditatem; statuas jussum esse in foro ponere; nisi posuisset, Veneri Erycinae esse multatum. Tametsi positae essent ex testamento, tamen putabat quoniam Veneris nomen esset causam pecuniae se reperturum. Itaque apponit qui petat Veneri Erycinae illam hereditatem: non enim quaestor petit, ut est consuetudo, is qui Erycum montem obtinebat: petit Naevius Turpio

ratam' Lg. 42, a mistake for 'numeratum,' which is the true form.

nobilissimarum equarum] 'nobilissimorum equorum' Lg. 42 p. m. Iordan, and Halm, who says "nobilissimarum equarum codd. rell. et edd.—Idem vitium Lib. i. c. 10. ex eodem cod. corrigendum erat." See the note on Lib. 1. c. 10.

Quid haec hereditas,] The pointing of Zumpt and Iordan is 'Quid? haec hereditas quo praetore . . . venerat?' Our reliance on pointing is one of the causes why we often understand the ancient writers so ill. If we must point in such a case as this, it is easy to see that 'Quid?' &c., is nonsense. The question begins 'Quid haec hereditas.' I do not trouble myself about the grammatical explanation of 'quid' in such a case. It had lost its original meaning. There is a pause after 'hereditas,' and the question is resumed in the words 'quo praetore.' As to the passage 'Quid ad Verrem quis detulit?' I have, as in other cases, put no point after 'Quid.' If the reader does not see that the sense admits a pause there, he may indicate a pause thus: 'Quid, ad Verrem quis detulit?' 'Well, who carried an information to Verres?'

P. Annii] See Lib. 1. c. 41. Iordan has 'C. Annii.'

8. *Veneri Erycinae . . multatum.*] There was a 'poena' or penalty in the testament, which, if the 'heres' did not set up certain statues in the forum, he was bound to pay to the temple of Venus at Eryx. The 'poena' might be the whole 'hereditas,' as it is here implied. It appears that, by the law of Sicily, this temple could take testamentary bequests. See Divin. c. 17 and the notes.—'heredem statuas' Orelli, Klotz.

causam pecuniae] 'some cause or ground for laying hold of the money.' Lg. 42 p. m. M. φ, Iordan, have 'caussam calumniae.'

The words 'Veneris nomen' appear to be an allusion to the Roman game of 'tali,' in which the best throw was called 'Venus.' The sense is, 'As soon as Verres hears the name of Venus, he thinks, like the player, of good luck, and feels sure that he shall make some money out of this affair.' This explanation confirms the reading 'pecuniae' (Creuzer and Moser).

Erycum montem] The old reading is 'Erycinum montem,' which Orelli has. Zumpt contends that the true name is 'Erycus,' as in c. 47. The Greek form is Eryx (Ἔρυξ, Thucyd. vi. 46). "At a little distance to the eastward of Trapani (the ancient Drepanum) is Mount St. Julian, Eryx, on which, at the elevation of 2075 feet, stood a temple dedicated to Venus Erycina. Eryx is at present an abrupt and sterile mountain. There still exist a few granite pillars, and some remains of a Cyclopian wall" (Smyth's Sicily, p. 242). See

quidam, istius excursor et emissarius, homo omnium ex illo conventu quadruplatorum deterrimus, C. Sacerdote praetore condemnatus injuriarum. Etenim erat ejusmodi causa ut ipse praetor, quum quaereret calumniatorem, paulo tamen consideratiorem reperire non posset. Hunc hominem Veneri absolvit, sibi condemnat: maluit videlicet homines peccare quam deos; se potius a Dione quod non licebat quam Venerem quod non debebatur auferre. Quid ego hic nunc Sex. Pompeii Chlori testimonium recitem? qui causam Dionis egit, qui omnibus rebus interfuit, hominis honestissimi, tametsi civis Romanus virtutis causa jamdiu est, tamen omnium Siculorum primi ac nobilissimi: quid ipsius Q. Caecilii Dionis, hominis probatissimi ac pudentissimi? quid L. Caecilii, L. Liguris, T. Manilii, L. Caleni? quorum omnium testimoniis de hac Dionis pecunia confirmatum est. Dixit hoc idem M. Lucullus, se de his Dionis incommodis pro hospitio quod sibi cum eo esset jam ante cognosse. Quid Lucullus, qui tum in Macedonia fuit, melius haec cognovit quam tu, Hortensi, qui Romae fuisti? ad quem Dio confugit, qui de Dionis injuriis gravissime per literas cum Verre questus es? Nova tibi haec sunt, [et] inopinata? nunc primum aures tuae hoc crimen accipiunt? nihil ex Dione, nihil ex socru tua, femina primaria, Servilia, vetere Dionis hospita, audisti? Nonne multa mei testes quae tu scis nesciunt? nonne te mihi testem in hoc crimine eripuit non istius innocentia sed legis exceptio? RECITA TESTIMONIA LVCVLLI, CHLORI, DIONIS.

IX. Satiane vobis magnam pecuniam Venereus homo qui e

Divin. c. 17, note.—'Is qui Erycum montem obtinebat' is the Quaestor Lilybaetanus, as Asconius observes.

excursor et emissarius,] "Sic vocantur conciliatores furtorum quae a magistratibus committuntur atque internuncii" (Ascon.). See Lib. 5. c. 41.

consideratiorem] Though 'consideratus' is passive in form, it seems used to indicate a person of thoughtful and serious demeanour; that is, the 'consideratio' seems to mean the 'consideratio' of him who is called 'consideratus.' Pro Caecin. c. 1, 'illud considerati hominis esse putavit.'

Veneri absolvit,] 'Absolvit' is the technical expression of the formula. See the passage of Gaius cited in the notes to c. 12. The use of the dative seems peculiar, but the sense is plain: 'Verres declared that there was no penalty or forfeiture to the temple of Venus, but he condemned the man to the payment of a sum of money to himself.' 'Hunc hominem' is Dio. It seems strange that there should have been any difficulty about this. See Zumpt's note. Orelli and Klotz have 'Hic hominem.'—'pudentissimi:' Klotz has 'prudentissimi,' from V.

M. Lucullus,] The brother of L. Lucullus, and consul B.C. 73. He probably went to his province, Macedonia, during B.C. 73.

legis exceptio?] The Lex under which Verres was prosecuted excluded a 'patronus' from being a witness. Klotz refers to a similar rule which is laid down in the Digest, 22. 5. 25.

The reading of some of the evidence, as we see, occurs here also in the second Actio, or supposed second Actio, in the middle of the speech. This is also the fashion in the Greek orations.

9. *Venereus homo*] Zumpt and others have 'Venerius.' Orelli writes both. There

Chelidonis sinu in provinciam profectus esset Veneris nomine quaesisse videtur? Accipite aliam in minore pecunia non minus impudentem calumniam. Sosippus et Philocrates fratres sunt Agyrinenses. Horum pater abhinc duo et XX annos est mortuus, in cujus testamento quodam loco si commissum quid esset, multa erat Veneri. Ipsos XX annos, quum tot interea praetores, tot quaestores, tot calumniatores in provincia fuissent, hereditas ab his Veneris nomine petita non est. Verres cognoscit: pecuniam per Volcatium accipit fere HS ccc millia ab duobus fratribus. Multorum testimonia audistis antea. Vicerunt Agyrinenses fratres ita ut egentes inanesque discederent.

X. At enim ad Verrem pecunia ista non pervenit.—Quae est ista defensio? utrum asseveratur in hoc an temptatur? mihi enim nova res est. Verres calumniatores apponebat: Verres adesse jubebat: Verres cognoscebat: Verres judicabat: pecuniae maxi-

is no etymological objection to 'Venereus.' 'Venerei,' as we have seen, is the name of the slaves and freedmen of the temple of Venus Erycina. The note of Asconius is, "Alludit ad nomen, quod hirundo, quam *chelidon* Graeci vocant, veris, id est temporis veris, sit amica." There is no sense in this; but if we adopt the almost certain correction of Creuzer and Moser, 'veri, id est tempori Veneris,' there is sense in the scholium, and probably the true explanation. Such a play on words is quite in Cicero's style. See the note in Creuzer and Moser.

Agyrinenses.] Agyrium was one of the oldest towns of the Siculi, on a hill near the river Cyamosorus, north-east of Henna, and west of Centuripae. The modern city is S. Filippo d'Argirò. It is mentioned again Lib. 3. c. 27. It had the finest theatre in the island, after that of Syracuse (Diod. xvi. 83).

quodam loco . . . commissum] Asconius correctly explains 'commissum' to be something done or omitted to be done contrary to the will of a testator, which commission or omission brought some pecuniary loss on the 'heres.' 'Quodam loco' means 'in a certain passage in the will.'

Ipsos XX *annos,*] The reading of 4, F M and of Asconius is 'ipso vigesimo anno;' and his note is 'praescriptio temporis,' by which he appears to mean that if twenty years had elapsed, any claim of the temple would have been barred by time. But there was no 'praescriptio longi temporis,' either in the time of Cicero, or when the true Asconius wrote. The old editions have 'petita non est' at the end of the sentence; and Zumpt says that he does not know whether the 'non' is omitted in any good MS. But Iordan says, "*petita est* F M, et, ut videtur, Lgg. omnes. *petita non est*, al." The word 'viginti' may be expressed in most of the MSS. by the abbreviation XX. In Lag. 29 it is 'XX°,' but in Lag. 42, '*vigesimo* expressis litteris' (Zumpt).

If 'ipso vicesimo anno' is the true reading, we must read 'petita est.' But the reading of Manutius, which I have adopted, requires 'petita non est:' 'for twenty whole years, though during that time so many praetors, so many quaestors, so many calumniatores had been in the province, the Hereditas was not claimed of them in the name of Venus.' Zumpt, Orelli, Klotz, and Iordan have 'ipso vicesimo anno . . . petita est.'

cognoscit:] 'causam cognoscit' in the common texts; but, as Zumpt observes, 'causam' is often omitted when 'cognoscere' is used.—'ad HS,' the reading of the MSS. except Lg. 42 p. m. M φ. Either reading is Latin.

10. *an temptatur?*] 'is this a serious defence, or is it merely by way of making a show of saying something?' Comp. in this chapter, 'in Verre defensionis temptare rationem.' For the sake of euphony it is certain that the Romans sometimes used the form 'temptatur.' But we must not therefore lose sight of the genuine form, which is 'tenta-re,' and contains the root of 'tend-ere.'

Verres judicabat:] This does not mean

mae dabantur: qui dabant causas obtinebant. Tu mihi ita defendas, "non est ista Verri numerata pecunia." Adjuvo te: mei quoque testes idem dicunt: Volcatio dicunt sese dedisse. Quae vis erat in Volcatio tanta ut HS CCCC millia ab duobus hominibus auferret? Ecquis Volcatio si sua sponte venisset unam libellam dedisset? Veniat nunc: experiatur: tecto recipiet nemo. At ego amplius dico: HS quadringenties cepisse te arguo contra leges: nego tibi ipsi ullum nummum esse numeratum: sed quum ob tua decreta, ob edicta, ob imperia, ob judicia pecuniae dabantur, non erat quaerendum cujus manu numerarentur, sed cujus injuria cogerentur. Comites illi tui delecti manus erant tuae: praefecti, scribae, medici, accensi, haruspices, praecones manus erant tuae: ut quisque te maxime cognatione, affinitate, necessitudine aliqua attingebat, ita maxime manus tua putabatur: cohors tota [tua] illa, quae plus mali dedit Siciliae quam si centum cohortes fugitivorum fuissent, tua manus sine controversia fuit. Quidquid ab horum quopiam captum est, id non modo tibi datum, sed tua manu numeratum judicari necesse est. Nam si hanc defensionem probabitis, "Non accepit ipse," licet omnia de pecuniis repetundis judicia tollatis: nemo unquam reus tam nocens adducetur qui ista defensione non possit uti. Etenim quum Verres utatur, quis erit unquam posthac reus tam perditus qui non ad Q. Mucii innocentiam referatur, si cum isto conferatur? Neque nunc tam mihi isti Verrem defendere videntur quam in Verre defensionis temptare rationem. Qua de re, judices, magno opere vobis providendum est: pertinet hoc ad

that Verres was 'judex.' It was the praetor's function, 'dare judicia' (c. 12), which is expressed formally in the edict, as for instance in the Title De Dolo Malo (Dig. 4. 3. 1), "Quae dolo malo facta esse dicentur, si de his rebus alia actio non erit et justa causa esse videbitur judicium dabo." The praetor was also said 'dare judicem' (c. 12). The word 'judicabat' has caused the commentators some difficulty. Zumpt takes it to be said 'invidiosius:' "significare volebat Verrem judicibus sententia sua praeivisse quid judicarent."

ab duobus hominibus] 'duobus nominibus' Lg. 29 42 p. m. B N, Orelli, Klotz, and Iordan. The other readings are 'duobus hominibus' or 'ab d. h.' *n* and *h* are easily confounded. The money was not taken 'duobus nominibus.' It was taken 'uno nomine,' and from two men. This use of 'hominibus' is quite consistent with Cicero's practice.

cujus manu] See 'tua manu numeratum,' a little further on. It seems that this must be rendered here, 'into whose hand the money was paid.'

fugitivorum] 'Fugitivus' is a runaway slave. The allusion, as Asconius says, is probably to Athenio, who headed the insurgents in Sicily in the second Servile War, and was killed by the consul M'. Aquillius B.C. 101. Comp. Act. ii. Lib. 3. c. 26. 54.

reus tam nocens] Klotz and Iordan have 'nemo unquam tam convictus, tam nocens,' from Lg. 42 p. m.

Q. Mucii] See Divin. c. 17, note. Q. Mucius Scaevola. The Greeks of Asia commemorated his beneficent administration by the institution of a festival day, which they named Mucia. 'Referatur,' with 'ad,' means that the thing spoken of is to be referred to another, as its measure and standard. Cicero says (De Legg. i. 1), "Leges in historia ad veritatem referuntur, in poemate ad delectationem."

ad summam rem publicam] Zumpt shows that this is the genuine expression. The

summam rem publicam et ad existimationem ordinis nostri salutemque sociorum. Si enim innocentes existimari volumus, non solum nos abstinentes sed etiam comites nostros praestare debemus.

XI. Primum omnium opera danda est ut eos nobiscum educamus qui nostrae famae capitique consulant: deinde, si in hominibus eligendis nos spes amicitiae fefellerit, ut vindicemus, missos faciamus, semper ita vivamus ut rationem reddendam nobis arbitremur. Africani est hoc, hominis liberalissimi: verumtamen ea liberalitas est probanda quae sine periculo existimationis est, ut in illo fuit: quum ab eo quidam vetus assectator et ex numero amicorum non impetraret uti se praefectum in Africam duceret et id ferret moleste: Noli, inquit, mirari, si tu a me hoc non impetras: ego jam pridem ab eo cui meam existimationem caram fore arbitror peto ut mecum praefectus proficiscatur, et adhuc impetrare non possum. Etenim re vera multo magis est petendum ab hominibus, si salvi et honesti esse volumus, ut eant nobiscum in provinciam quam hoc illis in beneficii loco deferendum. Sed tu, quum et tuos amicos in provinciam quasi in praedam invitabas et cum iis ac per eos praedabare et eos in contione annulis aureis donabas, non statuebas tibi non solum de tuis sed etiam de illorum factis rationem esse reddendam?

XII. Quum hos sibi quaestus constituisset magnos atque uberes ex his causis, quas ipse instituerat cum consilio, hoc est, cum sua cohorte, cognoscere, tum illud infinitum genus invenerat ad innumerabilem pecuniam corripiendam. Dubium nemini est quin omnes omnium pecuniae positae sint in eorum potestate qui judicia dant et eorum qui judicant: quin nemo vestrum possit aedes suas, nemo

old reading is 'ad summam rei publicae.' He refers to Cicero, Ad Att. i. 16; Pro Cn. Plancio, c. 27; Phil. iii. 15. See c. 61 of this oration. He denies that 'summa rei publicae' is used by the writers of Cicero's time.

sed etiam comites] Cicero said nearly the same thing some time afterwards in a letter to his brother Quintus (i. 1. c. 3), who was then governor of the province of Asia, "circumspiciendum diligenter ut in hac custodia provinciae non te unum sed omnes ministros imperii tui sociis et civibus et rei publicae praestare videare." Compare also the beginning of the following chapter. The 'comites' were, properly, the persons of higher rank immediately about the praetor, who formed his 'cohors.' The inferior personages, 'apparitores,' were 'quasi ex cohorte' (Cic. Ad Q. Fr. i. 1. c. 3, 4).

Iordan writes [abstinentes], meaning, I suppose, that he thinks that the word is not in its place here; and it is omitted by Lg. 42. It may be certainly omitted, as in the example 'te unum . . . praestare,' which I have just quoted.

11. *annulis aureis*] Gold rings were worn at Rome by the senators and equites, and it appears that it became usual for governors of provinces to give gold rings to those whom they delighted to honour. Comp. Lib. 3. c. 76. 80.—'de tuis:' 'de te' Orelli.

12. *qui judicia dant*] Praetors or other magistrates who have the power of granting a 'judicium,' that is, 'judices' for the hearing of a case. 'Qui judicant' are of course the 'judices.'

nemo fundum,] These words are omitted

fundum, nemo bona patria obtinere, si, quum haec a quopiam vestrum petita sint, praetor improbus, cui nemo intercedere possit, det quem velit judicem, judex nequam et levis quod praetor jusserit judicet. Si vero illud quoque accedet ut in ea verba praetor judicium det, ut vel L. Octavius Balbus judex, homo et juris et officii

by Zumpt, without any observation, though they are in Orelli, Klotz, and I suppose in all the old editions, and in the MSS. The omission seems to be an error of the press, which error occurs in the English reprint of Zumpt's edition. 'Obtinere' means 'to maintain his title to.'

nemo intercedere] "In provincia scilicet; nam Romae appellari tribuni possunt contra omnem potestatem." This is a sample of the better part of the Asconian commentary. Compare Cicero, Ad Q. Fr. i. 1. c. 7, where he says of the province of Asia, "ubi nullum auxilium (no appeal to the tribunes), nulla conquestio, nullus Senatus, nulla contio." In a province the governor was not checked by any 'intercessio' of a 'tribunus,' or of any 'magistratus' of equal rank with himself or greater.

L. Balbus judex,] He was one of the 'judices,' and Cicero ingeniously pays him a compliment for his legal knowledge and his integrity; and yet even Balbus, if he had been a 'judex' appointed by Verres, could not have done otherwise than follow the directions contained in the praetor's formula. The words 'Si paret' &c. are taken from the Formulae, examples of which we are now better acquainted with from Gaius; and see Lib. 1. c. 45 and the note: but Savigny remarks that Gaius (iv. § 39—41) does not reckon as part of the Formula the words which always stand at the beginning, as for example, 'L. Octavius judex esto.' The Formula, as it is here supposed by Cicero, is correct in expression, but unjust in the substance. Klotz supposes the Formula to have been perverted by Cicero, but the orator merely gives it as an example of what Verres did or might have done, and what a 'judex' must obey. If, says the Formula, it appears that the land belongs to Servilius, and he does not give it up to Catulus, who was not the owner, then the 'judex' must compel him to do so, or mulct him in damages. This is absurd enough, and palpable injustice; but it is what Cicero represents Verres as doing. Puchta supposes (Inst. ii. § 166) that Catulus was the attorney (procurator) of Servilius; and in such a case, though the 'intentio' or demand is made in the name of the plaintiff, the 'condemnatio' is expressed in favour of the attorney or agent, as in the example in Gaius (iv. 86): "Qui autem alieno nomine agit, intentionem quidem ex persona domini sumit, condemnationem autem in suam personam convertit: nam si verbi gratia Lucius Titius (*pro*) Publio Maevio agat, ita formula concipitur: Si paret N. N. Publio Maevio sestertium x milia dare oportere, judex N. N. Lucio Titio sestertium x milia condemna; si non paret, absolve. In rem quoque si agat, intendit Publii Maevii rem esse ex jure Quiritium et condemnationem in suam personam convertit." Puchta observes that Cicero complains of this Formula of Verres as of something unusual, though there is no doubt that it was of daily application in the case of 'procuratores.' He adds however that Cicero means only its application by a wicked praetor like Verres. But this explanation is quite inconsistent with what follows: 'non necesse erit,' &c., where Cicero says that the 'judex' must compel Servilius, the owner, to give up the land to Catulus. It is singular that most persons have missed the sense of the passage. Cicero takes the usual formula, and shows how Verres applied it in the most extravagant and absurd way; or rather, he supposes a case as extravagant as the one which he puts, a case which we must not suppose to be a real case; but he adds, even a Balbus must have followed the praetor's order. And this extravagant instance is made a kind of sample of the proceedings of Verres in Sicily: 'Ejusdemmodi totum jus praetorium' &c.

On this formula Savigny remarks (System, &c., v. 80, note (*e*)): "Cicero manifestly here selects an established, generally known Formula; and what he remarks thereupon as a crying piece of injustice consists simply in this, that, according to this mode of drawing up the Formula, the restitution of the land (fundus) must be made to another person than the one already designated as owner." Catulus is the plaintiff, Servilius is the owner; and, if the property is proved to belong to Servilius, he must be compelled to give it up to Catulus. This explanation by Voorda

peritissimus, non possit aliter judicare; si judicium sit ejusmodi: L. OCTAVIVS IVDEX ESTO: SI PARET FVNDVM CAPENATEM, QVO DE AGITVR, EX IVRE QVIRITIVM P. SERVILII ESSE NEQVE IS FVNDVS Q. CATVLO RESTITVETVR—non necesse erit L. Octavio judici cogere P. Servilium Q. Catulo fundum restituere, aut condemnare eum quem non oporteat? Ejusdemmodi totum jus praetorium, ejusdemmodi omnis res judiciaria fuit in Sicilia per triennium Verre praetore. Decreta ejusmodi: SI NON ACCIPIT QVOD TE DEBERE DICIS, ACCVSES; SI PETIT, DVCAS. C. Fuficium duci jussit petitorem, L. Suetium, L. Racilium. Judicia hujusmodi: Qui cives Romani erant, si Siculi essent, quum Siculos eorum legibus dari oporteret; qui Siculi, si cives Romani essent.—Verum, ut totum genus amplectamini judiciorum, prius jura Siculorum, deinde istius instituta cognoscite.

(Creuzer and Moser, 5th Excursus), and that of Savigny, are the same as that which I have given. If Servilius did not obey the unjust order, he was to be mulcted in damages. Asconius, though he is Pseudo-Asconius, understood the passage. He says, "Judicio suo fungatur Balbus in Servilium, si constat fundum Capenatem P. Servilii esse, nec restituetur Catulo, cujus non est. Memento omnes judices praesentes esse, quorum nominibus utitur ad exemplum."

si non accipit . . petit,] Klotz reads 'patitur,' which all the MSS. have. Cicero, according to the text, says: 'if he (the creditor) does not receive what you say that you owe, bring a charge against him: if he sues for it, carry him off' as an 'addictus.' Comp. the use of 'duci' in c. 26. This is plain enough: 'if the creditor won't be satisfied with what the debtor admits to be due, bring a charge against him,' says Verres, 'and I will help you: if he should sue for it, I will let you put him in chains.' Manutius understood it correctly. It is merely an extravagant way of showing the iniquity of Verres, who sold his justice. Cicero mentions instances of creditors (petitores) who were treated in this way. 'Patitur,' the MSS. reading, appears to be a corruption of 'petitur,' the reading of some editions, and 'petitur' must be a corruption of 'petit,' if that is the true reading. If 'patitur' is the true reading, the explanation of Asconius is as good as any. He makes 'patitur' equivalent to 'accipit.' But 'duci jussit petitorem' confirms the reading 'petit.'

Theod. Mommsen conjectures 'si non accepit,' i.e. 'si negat se accepisse;' which does not mend the text at all.

Judicia hujusmodi:] This passage stands thus in Klotz's edition: "Judicia hujusmodi: qui cives Romani erant, si Siculi essent, tum si eorum legibus dari oporteret. Qui Siculi, si cives Romani essent." But the reading of this passage is not certain; and I cannot see what is the explanation of the text of Klotz. That which he very confidently gives is opposed to the interpretation of Asconius and of Donatus on Terence (Phormio, ii. 1. 36), whom Klotz, being in a merry mood when he wrote his note, calls a pair of kindred souls.

The explanation of these old commentators, which has been hitherto followed, requires the word 'rei,' or 'partes,' to be supplied in the clauses, 'si Siculi essent,' 'si cives Romani essent,' and Klotz objects to this. In the words 'judicia hujusmodi (fuerunt)' the word 'judices' is implied. The passage may then be translated thus: 'Those who were Roman citizens were (erant) judices, if Siculi were parties, though by their laws Sicilians ought to have been appointed: those who were Sicilians were appointed (judices), if Roman citizens were parties.' Asconius supposes that after 'qui cives Romani erant,' 'addebantur' was to be supplied, in which case 'qui' would be the nominative to 'erant.' But the position of 'erant' and 'essent' is against this interpretation; and 'qui cives Romani' is only a more general form of expression than 'cives Romani.'

XIII. Siculi hoc jure sunt, ut quod civis cum civi agat domi certet suis legibus; quod Siculus cum Siculo non ejusdem civitatis, ut de eo praetor judices ex P. Rupilii decreto, quod is de decem legatorum sententia statuit, quam illi legem Rupiliam vocant, sortiatur. Quod privatus a populo petit, aut populus a privato, senatus ex aliqua civitate qui judicet datur, quum alternae civitates rejectae sunt. Quod civis Romanus a Siculo petit, Siculus judex datur; quod Siculus a civi Romano, civis Romanus datur: ceterarum rerum selecti judices ex civium Romanorum conventu proponi solent. Inter aratores et decumanos lege frumentaria, quam Hieronicam appellant, judicia fiunt. Haec omnia isto praetore non modo perturbata sed plane et Siculis et civibus Romanis erepta sunt: primum suae leges; quod civis cum civi ageret, aut eum judicem quem commodum erat praeconem, haruspicem, medicum suum dabat, aut, si legibus erat judicium constitutum et ad civem suum judicem venerant, libero civi judicare non licebat. Edictum enim hominis cognoscite, quo edicto omnia judicia redegerat in suam potestatem: SI QVI PERPERAM IVDICASSET, SE COGNITVRVM;

13. *P. Rupilii*] P. Rupilius, consul B.C. 132, and proconsul of Sicily, B.C. 131, with the advice of ten commissioners (de decem legatorum sententia) settled the administration of Sicily, and his regulations and ordinances are often spoken of under the term Lex Rupilia; not that his ordinances were a 'lex' in the strict sense, for a 'lex' is that 'quod populus Romanus jubet,' but they were so called as having the substantial character of a 'lex,' though not the formal. There are several instances mentioned of the Romans regulating a conquered country by sending there a commission of Ten (Cic. Ad Att. xiii. Epp. 4, 5, 6; Livy, xxxvii. 55, "Decem legatos more majorum senatum missurum ad res Asiae disceptandas componendasque"). Rupilius was consul with P. Popilius Laenas, and conducted the inquiry which followed the death of Ti. Gracchus (Cic. De Am. c. 11).

Cicero cites mainly such parts of the Lex Rupilia as related to the administration of justice, and we may suppose that Roman institutions were to some extent thus introduced into Sicily. The following chapters of this oration (c. 15. 17, 18), in addition to this chapter, contain some of his rules. See also Lib. 3. c. 10. 12, 13, 14. 28. 40.

alternae civitates] This is somewhat obscure. An individual might have a claim on his own 'civitas' or on another; and a 'civitas' might have a claim on one of its own citizens or on a citizen of another state. The case of a claim by or against a 'civitas' against or by a citizen of that 'civitas' seems to be excluded; and the case proposed is perhaps that of a citizen of one 'civitas' and another 'civitas;' and, if both parties objected to give either of the 'civitates' jurisdiction in the matter, the senate of a third 'civitas' was made 'judex.' Asconius explains the passage thus. If this is not the right explanation, we may take it thus: each party could propose a 'civitas,' and each party could reject the 'civitas' proposed by the other. If this was so, the praetor then named a 'civitas.'

aut, si legibus &c.] 'or if the Judicium (the trial) was constituted legally and the parties had got their proper (suum) Judex,' that is, if the Judex was appointed legally (legibus).

Si qui perperam] The praetor at Rome could himself pronounce judgment in the 'ordinaria judicia,' just as a 'judex' did whom the praetor had named. The praetor also could pronounce judgment in an 'extraordinarium judicium.' There is no evidence that in the republican period there was a regular appeal from one court or 'magistratus' to another for a fresh trial, for such an appeal implies a subor-

QVVM COGNOSSET, ANIMADVERSVRVM: idque quum faciebat, nemo dubitabat quin, quum judex alium de suo judicio putaret judicaturum seque in eo capitis periculum aditurum, voluntatem spectaret ejus quem statim de capite suo putaret judicaturum. Selecti ex conventu aut propositi ex negotiatoribus judices nulli. Haec copia, quam dico, judicum, cohors non Q. Scaevolae, qui tamen de cohorte sua dare non solebat, sed C. Verris. Cujusmodi cohortem putatis hoc principe fuisse? Sicuti videtis edictum: SI QVID PERPERAM IVDICARIT SENATVS. Eum quoque ostendam, si quando sit datus, coactu istius quod non senserit judicasse. Ex lege Rupilia sortitio

dination of one court to another. Now at Rome the 'magistratus,' who possessed the same jurisdiction, were not subordinated one to the other. The praetors had lower rank than the consuls, yet they were entirely independent of them in the exercise of their functions. It might certainly have been supposed that there was an appeal from the judgment of a 'judex' to the superior judgment of the praetor who had appointed him, but there is want of evidence in the republican period to prove this. Cicero reproaches Verres for having reserved to himself by his edict the power of deciding on the judgments of the 'judices' (Savigny, System, &c., vi. § 284).

Selecti ex conventu aut &c.] Cicero has just said that in certain cases 'judices' ought to be selected from the 'conventus' of Roman citizens, that is, from those Romans who used to meet at a certain place at certain times, for the settlement of all legal matters and the transacting of other business, for which the people within a certain district resorted to a fixed place. The word 'conventus,' which literally means 'a coming together,' was used also to denote the place of meeting; the 'forum' (c. 15), to which the inhabitants of a given district must resort (convenire). The word 'conventus' also means the whole district, the inhabitants of which used to meet at a fixed place.

When Cicero says that no 'judices' were selected from the 'conventus' or proposed from the 'negotiatores,' he may mean such 'negotiatores' as were present only accidentally, and were not considered as a part of the 'conventus,' that is, as permanently residing within the district. When he afterwards says 'de conventu ac negotiatoribus,' the two are still distinguished, though spoken of as being together.

There has been much discussion about this passage. The question is, what is the 'conventus' to which 'selecti' applies. The 'conventus civium Romanorum,' says Manutius. Not the 'conventus civium Romanorum,' says Zumpt, but 'Siculorum civitatum;' and he gives his reason for his opinion at some length. 'Conventus' is a general term, and, as already shown, it has several senses. I see no reason why 'conventus' may not be taken in its most general sense here without limiting it to 'cives Romani' or Sicilians. In certain cases, as Cicero has said, 'selecti judices' were taken from the 'civium Romanorum conventus;' in other cases mentioned before, a 'civis Romanus' or a Sicilian might be a 'judex,' and nothing is there said of the 'conventus.' The plain interpretation of the words 'selecti ex conventu aut propositi ex negotiatoribus' requires the 'conventus' and the 'negotiatores' to be considered as two bodies, from which 'judices' might be taken. Why the 'negotiatores' are thus opposed to the 'conventus,' I do not see, any further than I have already suggested; though there is something in Ernesti's remark, that the 'negotiatores' were Roman 'equites,' and are accordingly distinguished from simple 'cives Romani,' as in Paterculus (ii. 110). Creuzer and Moser in their edition give the various commentators' opinions, but not their own very positively,—a mode of commenting which is not satisfactory.

Sicuti videtis] The expression seems a little strange. The question is, 'What kind of a Cohors do you suppose that there was under such a head?' The answer, 'Such a one as you see that his edict is,' &c.

Iordan remarks that this passage is not yet cured. Theod. Mommsen, who was consulted by Halm, proposes this reading, 'fuisse, si uti videtis edictum est, SI QVI PERP. IVDICARIT. Senatum quoque.' I don't think this is an improvement on the text.

coactu istius] An instance of this expression is quoted from the spurious Ep.

nulla, nisi quum nihil intererat istius. Lege Hieronica judicia plurimarum controversiarum sublata uno nomine omnia: de conventu ac negotiatoribus nulli judices. Quantam potestatem habuerit videtis: quas res gesserit cognoscite.

XIV. Heraclius est Hieronis filius, Syracusanus, homo in primis domi suae nobilis, et ante hunc praetorem vel pecuniosissimus Syracusanorum: nunc nulla alia calamitate nisi istius avaritia atque injuria pauperrimus. Huic hereditas ad HS facile tricies venit testamento propinqui sui Heraclii: plena domus caelati argenti optimi, multaeque stragulae vestis, pretiosissimorumque mancipiorum, quibus in rebus istius cupiditates et insanias quis ignorat? Erat in sermone res, magnam Heraclio pecuniam relictam; non solum Heraclium divitem, sed etiam ornatum supellectile, argento, veste, mancipiis futurum. Audit haec etiam Verres, et primo illo suo leviore artificio Heraclium aggredi conatur ut eum roget inspicienda quae non reddat. Deinde a quibusdam Syracusanis admonetur—hi autem quidam erant affines istius, quorum iste uxores nunquam alienas existimavit, Cleomenes et Aeschrio, qui quantum apud istum et quam turpi de causa potuerint ex reliquis criminibus intelligetis—hi, ut dico, hominem admonent rem esse praeclaram, refertam omnibus rebus: ipsum autem Heraclium hominem esse majorem natu, non promptissimum; eum praeter Marcellos patronum quem suo jure adire aut appellare posset habere neminem: esse in eo testamento, quo ille heres esset scriptus, ut statuas in palaestra deberet ponere: faciemus ut palaestritae negent

ad Brut. i. 17, 'coactu tuo.' I call them spurious, notwithstanding a recent attempt to maintain their authority.

Lege Hieronica] The note of Hotmann makes a difficulty where there is none. 'Lege Hieronica judicia' are the 'judicia ex lege H.,' which were 'sublata' by Verres.

14. *stragulae vestis,*] 'Stragula vestis est picta,' says Asconius, whose commentary on the Verrine orations goes no further, as we have it. See Martial, xiv. 147, "stragula purpureis lucent villosa tapetis," &c.; and Pro Sex. Rosc. Am. c. 46.

leviore] 'leniore' Lgg. 42 and 6. These two words are often confounded.

affines] 'Affines' are the cognati of the husband or wife. Cicero calls these two Syracusans 'affines' of Verres, as if Verres were a kinsman of their wives; the kinship being his intimacy with the women.

rem .. refertam omnibus rebus:] Klotz observes that 'res' is first used here in the general sense, and then as comprehending many things (res). It is first spoken of as the 'res hereditaria,' 'hereditas,' or a 'universitas,' and then as comprehending many several things. The conjecture of Lambinus 'domum refertam' is unnecessary.

non promptissimum;] He was old, and not a very active man. 'Promptus' is a man of action, one who is always ready when the occasion arises.

suo jure] 'jure suo,' Orelli, contrary to Roman usage. See v. 1.—'esset, scriptum, ut' &c., Orelli. The reading 'scriptus' is only in Lg. 42 p. m.; but it is the true reading.

palaestritae] The guardians or superintendents of the 'palaestra' or exercise place, such as Greek towns generally had. The 'palaestra' was probably an artificial person, in whose name the 'palaestritae' would claim the 'hereditas,' as forfeited (commissa) by non-compliance with the terms of the testament. In this case the 'palaes-

ex testamento esse positas; petant hereditatem quod eam palaestrae commissam esse dicant. Placuit ratio Verri. Nam hoc animo providebat, quum tanta hereditas in controversiam venisset judicioque peteretur, fieri non posse ut sine praeda ipse discederet. Approbat consilium: auctor est ut quam primum agere incipiant, hominemque id aetatis minime litigiosum quam tumultuosissime adoriantur. Scribitur Heraclio dica.

XV. Primo mirantur omnes improbitatem calumniae: deinde qui istum nossent partim suspicabantur, partim plane videbant adjectum esse oculum hereditati. Interea dies advenit, quo die sese ex instituto ac lege Rupilia dicas sortiturum Syracusis iste edixerat: paratus ad hanc dicam sortiendam venerat. Tum eum docet Heraclius non posse eo die sortiri, quod lex Rupilia vetaret diebus xxx sortiri dicam quibus scripta esset. Dies xxx nondum fuerant. Sperabat Heraclius, si illum diem effugisset, ante alteram sortitionem Q. Arrium, quem provincia tum maxime exspectabat, successurum. Iste omnibus dicis diem distulit, et eam diem constituit ut hanc Heraclii dicam sortiri post dies xxx ex lege posset. Postquam ea dies venit, iste incipit simulare se velle sortiri. Heraclius cum advocatis adit, et postulat ut sibi cum palaestritis, hoc est, cum populo Syracusano, aequo jure disceptare liceat. Adversarii postu-

tra' belonged to the Syracusani (c. 15); and the question was between an individual and the 'civitas.'

dica.] Cicero uses a Greek term to express the formal demand of the 'palaestritae,' as Terence does (Phormio, i. 1. 77), "ego te cognatum dicam, et tibi scribam dicam." In the next chapter there is 'dicas sortiturum,' which means 'sortiri judices,' for that case. Comp. c. 13, at the beginning.

15. *adjectum esse oculum*] 'that he had an eye on the Hereditas.' Cicero has the same expression Pro Lege Agraria (ii. 10), "quum ad omnia vestra pauci homines cupiditatis oculos adjecissent;" and Plautus has (Asin. 4. 1. 21) "Ad eorum ne quem oculos adjiciat suos."

diebus XXX .. *quibus*] The ablative 'diebus' is used in conformity with a general Latin usage, to express a measure of time between two limits, and 'quibus' is put in the same case by a kind of attraction. The meaning is that there could be no 'sortitio' until the thirty days had elapsed — 'ut hanc .. dicam sortiri post dies XXX ex lege posset.' Garatoni observes that when 'diebus' stands without a number, as 'paucis diebus,' it means 'post paucos dies;' but if a number is coupled with it as here, it means 'intra XXX dies,' and that is the old form in legislation, as in the Tab. Herac. (p. 453, ed. Mazochi—"diebus LX proxumeis quibus sciet"). The remark of Garatoni is not quite exact; at least it is not well expressed. The meaning of 'intra,' which he chooses to give in this passage of Cicero, and in the Tab. Herac., depends on the word 'quibus.' A formula of this kind was used in Roman testaments (Gaius, ii. 165), "cernitoque in centum diebus proximis quibus scies poterisque." See c. 26, note.

dicis] Lg. 42 p. m. F M: 'iudiciis' ett.

aequo jure] Verres first declared that he would appoint 'judices' according to the Lex Rupilia on a certain day. Heraclius makes no objection to the mode of appointing the 'judices,' but he claims the benefit of the thirty days fixed by the 'lex,' between the commencement of the suit (dica scripta) and the trial. He hoped by availing himself of this time to put off the trial till a new praetor came. But Verres deferred all the suits, and fixed a day thirty days later for the appointment of 'judices.' Heraclius appeared, and claimed a fair trial (aequo jure) between

lant ut in eam rem judices dentur ex iis civitatibus quae in id forum convenirent, electi qui Verri viderentur. Heraclius contra ut ju-

himself and the 'palaestritae,' that is, the city of Syracuse. He demanded that the 'judices' should be appointed according to the Lex Rupilia. His opponents demanded that they should be appointed in another way. Verres declared that he would not follow the Lex Rupilia (c. 16); and he appointed five 'judices' according to his own pleasure, as Cicero says. For the purpose of understanding the text, it is enough to see that Cicero affirms that Heraclius claimed the appointment of 'judices' according to the Lex Rupilia, and that a selection 'ex iis civitatibus . . . quae,' &c., was not conformable to the Lex Rupilia. Cicero says that the claim against Heraclius was by the 'palaestritae,' and that was the same thing as a claim by the city of Syracuse. The 'judices' then in this case should have been appointed according to the terms mentioned in c. 13, "quod privatus a populo petit—solent." In the note on that chapter I have supposed that the rule 'quod privatus a populo petit' did not apply when a 'civitas' had a claim against one of its own citizens; and Heraclius was a Syracusan. But it is immaterial whether that explanation is correct or not. Cicero founds his statement on the fact of the claim being made by the 'civitas' of Syracuse against a citizen of Syracuse. The citizen appealed to the Lex Rupilia, rightly or wrongly, I know not. Verres appointed five 'judices' at his pleasure. This is all clear; and the real truth of the matter, which we perhaps cannot reach, is perfectly immaterial for the understanding of the passage. Zumpt has a note on the merits of the case, and a very bad one. Heraclius claimed the appointment of 'judices' according to the Lex Rupilia; and, if I understand Cicero right, these would be 'selecti judices ex civium Romanorum conventu.' The 'adversarii' contended that they should be chosen 'ex iis civitatibus quae in id forum convenirent,' that is, from the 'conventus Syracusanus,' but not from Roman citizens. But here comes a difficulty which Madvig has noticed. The common text is 'quae in id forum convenirent. Electi qui Verri viderentur.' The sentence beginning 'adversarii postulant,' expresses the claim of one party. 'Heraclius contra' expresses the claim of Heraclius. If we interpose something about those who were finally chosen, it is obviously out of place. Besides that, the fact of the selection of the 'judices' is mentioned in its proper place at the end of the next chapter. Madvig also says, that if the sentence 'electi,' &c. expresses the fact of selection, it should be 'videbantur,' and not 'viderentur.' Accordingly he removes the 'interpunctio major' before 'electi,' and the sentence will stand as it does in the text; and the word 'electi' must be referred to 'judices dentur.' This is a simple remedy, and the only remedy, unless we expunge the words 'electi . . . viderentur.'

The following explanation of this passage has been suggested to me.—When the day came which Verres had fixed for holding the courts at Syracuse, he intended to name 'judices' for the case of Heraclius. But Heraclius made an objection about the thirty days; the objection was allowed, and Heraclius supposed that his case would stand over to the next 'sortitio.' In the mean time Verres' successor might arrive. It may be supposed that six months might elapse between the praetor's visits for the purpose of holding the courts. But Verres outwitted Heraclius by deferring all the cases, until that of Heraclius could legally be included. When the day came, Heraclius claimed that the trial should proceed 'aequo jure,' that is (c. 13) as 'civis cum civi,' for the Palaestritae were equivalent to the Populus Syracusanus, and the suit could fairly be tried 'suis legibus.' This explanation assumes that 'privatus a populo' (c. 13) applies only to a suit between an individual and another state, in which case there would be no common forms of law between them, and therefore the praetor must assign 'judices' from a third community. The opponents of Heraclius seem to have urged that the 'palaestritae' represented others besides the Populus Syracusanus, inasmuch as other states frequented the public place of Syracuse, and that therefore Verres ought to treat this as a case in which a 'privatus' stood opposed to other states, and ought to appoint 'judices' from such states 'quae in id forum convenirent.' (From Dr. Pears, Head Master of Repton School.)

There may be objections to this explanation, which I leave to others to discover. But as I cannot suggest any other explanation of the passage than that which I originally gave, and as there is some obscurity in Cicero, I think many readers

dicos e lege Rupilia dentur, ut ab institutis superiorum, ab auctoritate senatus, ab jure omnium Siculorum ne recedatur.

XVI. Quid ego istius in jure dicundo libidinem et scelera demonstrem? quis vestrum non ex urbana jurisdictione cognovit? quis unquam isto praetore Chelidone invita lege agere potuit? Non istum ut nonneminem provincia corrupit: idem fuit qui Romae. Quum id quod omnes intelligebant diceret Heraclius, jus esse certum Siculis inter se quo jure certarent, legem esse Rupiliam quam P. Rupilius consul de decem legatorum sententia dedisset; hanc omnes semper in Sicilia consules praetoresque servasse; negavit se lege Rupilia sortiturum: quinque judices quos commodum ipsi fuit dedit. Quid hoc homine facias? quod supplicium dignum libidine ejus invenias? Praescriptum tibi quum esset, homo [deterrime et] impudentissime, quemadmodum judices inter Siculos dares; quum imperatoris populi Romani auctoritas, legatorum decem summorum hominum dignitas, senatus consultum intercederet, cujus consulto P. Rupilius de x legatorum sententia leges in Sicilia constituerat; quum omnes ante te praetorem Rupilias leges et in ceteris rebus et in judiciis maxime servassent; tu ausus es pro nihilo prae tua praeda tot res sanctissimas ducere? tibi nulla lex fuit? nulla religio? nullus existimationis pudor? nullus judicii metus? nullius apud te gravis auctoritas? nullum exemplum quod sequi velles? Verum, ut institui dicere, quinque judicibus nulla lege, nullo instituto, nulla rejectione, nulla sorte, ex libidine istius datis, non qui causam cognoscerent, sed qui quod imperatum esset judicarent, eo die nihil actum est: adesse jubentur postridie.

XVII. Heraclius interea, quum omnes insidias fortunis suis a praetore fieri videret, capit consilium de amicorum et propinquorum sententia non adesse ad judicium: itaque illa nocte Syracusis profugit. Iste postero die mane, quum multo maturius quam unquam

may be glad to see the opinion of another person, who has considered the matter carefully.

convenirent,] Klotz has 'convenerant,' from Lg. 42 p. m. M; and the adoption of this reading renders unnecessary the removal of the full stop after 'convenirent,' as Creuzer and Moser say.

16. *P. Rupilius consul*] The reading 'praetor,' in place of 'consul,' cannot be admitted; for Rupilius was in Sicily as consul, and during his consulship he defeated the insurgent slaves. Garatoni observes that 'praetor' has arisen from a misunderstanding of the letter P (Publius).

hanc omnes] This is the reading of Lg. 42 p. m., which Zumpt has. Orelli has 'hoc omnes,' where 'hoc' must refer to 'jus.'—'negavit se judices e lege,' &c., Orelli; but 'judices e' is not necessary, and is omitted in the MSS., except in Lg. 42 p. m. M. Klotz also has 'judices e lege,' and Iordan.

quod supplicium . . libidine] Orelli has 'libidini,' which is intended for the dative.

servassent;] 'observassent' Orelli.—'nulla rejectione:' 'nulla religione' Orelli.

17. *postero die*] 'postridie' Lg. 42 p. m. Iordan.

antea surrexisset, judices citari jubet. Ubi comperit Heraclium non adesse, cogere incipit eos ut absentem Heraclium condemnent. Illi eum commonefaciunt ut, si ei videatur, utatur instituto suo, nec cogat ante horam decimam de absente secundum praesentem judicare. Impetrant. Interea sane perturbatus et ipse et ejus amici et consiliarii moleste ferre coeperunt Heraclium profugisse: putabant absentis damnationem praesertim tantae pecuniae multo invidiosiorem fore quam si praesens damnatus esset. Eo accedebat quod judices e lege Rupilia dati non erant; multo etiam rem turpiorem [fore] et iniquiorem visum iri intelligebant. Itaque hoc dum corrigere vult, apertior ejus cupiditas improbitasque facta est. Nam illis quinque judicibus uti se negat: jubet, id quod initio lege Rupilia fieri oportuerat, citari Heraclium et eos qui dicam scripserant: ait se judices ex lege velle sortiri. Quod ab eo pridie, quum multis lacrimis oraret [atque obsecraret] Heraclius, impetrare non potuerat, id ei postridie venit in mentem, ex lege Rupilia sortiri dicas oportere. Educit ex urna tres; iis ut absentem Heraclium condemnent imperat: itaque condemnant. Quae, malum, ista fuit amentia? ecquando te rationem factorum tuorum redditurum putasti? ecquando his de rebus tales viros audituros existimasti? Petatur hereditas ea quae nulla debetur in praedam praetoris? interponatur nomen civitatis? imponatur honestae civitati turpissima persona calumniae? neque hoc solum, sed ita res agatur

ut, si ei videatur,] 'ut si sibi videatur' Klotz. M and Lg. 42 p. m. have 'sibi videretur.' But 'ei' is probably right; a case of 'ei' equivalent to 'sibi.' "Grammatica ratio utrumque admittit" (Iordan).

secundum praesentem] 'in favour of the party which appeared.' See Lib. 1. c. 44, 'secundum eum.'

turpiorem] Zumpt and Iordan have 'fore' after 'turpiorem.'

ex lege velle] Klotz has 'lege velle' from V. Either expression is right.

ex urna tres;] This explains the expression 'dicas sortiturum' (c. 16), and 'sortiri dicas.' The 'sortes' were thrown into an 'urna' or vessel; and, after being shaken, the required number of lots was drawn out by the praetor, or by some person (c. 18) who was empowered to draw them out. 'Urna' is a Roman term for a vessel of capacity, but generally for liquids.

quae nulla debetur] 'What, shall an Hereditas be claimed, one too (ea) which is subject to no claim at all, and become booty to the praetor?' Creuzer and Moser compare Cicero (Ad Att. xi. 24), "Philotimus non modo nullus venit, sed" &c. Iordan omits 'ea' with Lg. 42 p. m.

If the reader prefers striking out all the notes of interrogation from this sentence, as Klotz has done, there will be no harm in it, provided he does not read with Klotz 'sed ita res agitur.'

turpissima persona] It is said by Creuzer and Moser, that this is an expression derived from the stage; but this is not a complete view of the matter. 'Persona,' a word of doubtful etymology, is certainly used to signify a mask; and Gabius Bassus (Gell. v. 7) derived it 'a personando.' Whatever may be the original meaning of the word, it had a common use to signify a certain 'status' or condition. A 'person' or 'persona' is not simply a human being, but a human being invested with some particular character, as a husband, father, and the like. There is no histrionic allusion in the passage of Cicero Pro

ut ne simulatio quidem aequitatis ulla adhibeatur? Nam, per deos immortales, quid interest utrum praetor imperet vique cogat aliquem de suis bonis omnibus decedere, an hujuscemodi judicium det, quo judicio indicta causa fortunis omnibus everti necesse sit?

XVIII. Profecto enim negare non potes te ex lege Rupilia sortiri judices debuisse, quum praesertim Heraclius id postularet. Sin illud dices, te Heraclii voluntate ab lege recessisse, ipse te impedies; ipse tua defensione implicabere. Quare enim primum ille adesse noluit, quum ex eo numero judices haberet quos postularet? deinde tu cur post illius fugam judices alios sortitus es, si eos qui erant antea dati utriusque dederas voluntate? deinde ceteras dicas omnes illo foro M. Postumius quaestor sortitus est: hanc solam tu illo conventu reperiere sortitus. Ergo, inquiet aliquis, donavit populo Syracusano illam hereditatem. Primum, si id confiteri velim, tamen istum condemnetis necesse est; neque enim permissum est ut impune nobis liceat quod alicui eripuerimus id alteri tradere. Verum ex ista reperietis hereditate ita istum praedatum ut perpauca occulte fecerit: populum quidem Syracusanum in maximam invidiam sua infamia, alieno praemio pervenisse; paucos Syracusanos, eos qui se nunc publice laudationis causa venisse dicunt, et tunc participes praedae fuisse, et nunc non ad istius

Murena (c. 3) referred to by C. and M., nor in this passage, nor in Cicero De Am. (c. 1), "idonea mihi Laelii persona visa quae de amicitia . . . dissereret." See also Pro Caecina, c. 5; De Leg. Agr. ii. 17, 18; and Phil. vi. 1. This notion of 'persona,' as opposed to 'res,' is the foundation of the division of law by Gaius (Dig. 1. 5. 1), "omne jus quo utimur vel ad personas pertinet vel ad res vel ad actiones."

18. *sortiri judices*] 'sortiri judicium' Orelli; but 'sortiri judices' is the common form, though the other is also correct. A little further on there is 'dicas omnes . . sortitus est.'—'dices:' 'dicis' Iordan.

te Heraclii voluntate &c.] Klotz perversely explains this to mean that Heraclius had at first protested against the 'judices' being appointed according to the Lex Rupilia, though he had afterwards required it. Cicero says nothing of the kind. He says to Verres, 'You can't deny that you ought to have appointed Judices according to the Lex Rupilia, particularly as Heraclius claimed it as his right. If you shall say that you departed from the Lex with the consent of Heraclius, you will involve yourself in a difficulty; for, first, why did he not appear on the day for trial, if he had, as you say, the Judices appointed in the way which he demanded? and, if that answer is not enough for you, will you tell me why you appointed other Judices after he had fled, if those who were first appointed were appointed with the consent of both parties?'

quos postularet?] 'quos postularat' Orelli, Klotz, and Iordan, though his favourite Lg. 42 p. m., which he calls 'optimus codex,' has 'postularet.' Zumpt observes, "Indicativus modus orationis formae hypotheticae non aptus est."

foro . . conventu] "Dixit bis de eadem re, alterum enim loci est, alterum temporis" (Zumpt). The 'conventus,' of course, is the 'temporis,' for the 'forum,' which has a local meaning, cannot be. But Cicero, in fact, has only varied the expression in oratorical fashion. M. Postumius, a quaestor, presided in all the cases tried at this forum, except one. The praetor could delegate certain of his powers to others, as, in this instance, 'jurisdictio' to a quaestor. See Cicero, Ad Q. Fr. i. 1. c. 7.

participes praedae . . . aestimationem]

laudationem sed ad communem litium aestimationem venisse. Posteaquam damnatus est absens, non solum illius hereditatis de qua ambigebatur, quae erat HS tricies, sed omnium bonorum paternorum ipsius Heraclii, quae non minor erat pecunia, palaestrae Syracusanorum, hoc est, Syracusanis, possessio traditur. Quae est ista praetura? Eripis hereditatem quae venerat a propinquo, venerat testamento, venerat legibus; quae bona is qui testamentum fecerat huic Heraclio ante aliquanto quam est mortuus, omnia utenda ac possidenda tradiderat; cujus hereditatis, quum ille aliquanto ante te praetorem esset mortuus, controversia fuerat nulla, mentionem fecerat nemo.

XIX. Verum esto: eripe hereditatem propinquis, da palaestritis; praedare in bonis alienis nomine civitatis; everte leges, testamenta, voluntates mortuorum, jura vivorum: num etiam patriis Heraclium bonis exturbare oportuit? Qui simulac profugit, quam impudenter, quam palam, quam acerbe, di immortales, illa bona direpta sunt! quam illa res calamitosa Heraclio, quaestuosa Verri, turpis Syracusanis, miseranda omnibus videbatur! Nam illud quidem statim curatur ut quidquid caelati argenti fuit in illis bonis ad istum deferatur, quidquid Corinthiorum vasorum, stragulae vestis: haec nemo dubitabat quin non modo ex illa domo capta et oppressa verum ex tota provincia ad istum comportari necesse esset. Mancipia quae voluit abduxit; alia divisit: auctio facta est in qua cohors istius invicta dominata est. Verum illud est praeclarum: Syracusani qui praefuerant his Heraclii bonis, verbo redigendis, re dispertiendis, reddebant eorum negotiorum rationem in senatu: dicebant scyphorum paria complura, hydrias argenteas, pretiosam vestem stragulam, multa mancipia pretiosa Verri data esse: dicebant quantum cuique ejus jussu nummorum esset datum.

'You will find,' says Cicero, 'that the city of Syracuse has incurred the greatest odium in this affair, and that a few of the Syracusani, those who profess that they have been commissioned by the city to uphold the character of Verres, as they were then participators in his crime, so now have they come, not to honour their praetor, as they suppose, but to be present at the assessment of damages, to the payment of which they will have to contribute a part.' The provisions of the Lex Cornelia de Pecuniis Repetundis extended to those to whose hands money came which had been got contrary to the Lex.

bonorum . . quae . . pecunia,] A common Latin formula.—'nulla . . nemo:' a usual position of these emphatic words.

19. *auctio*] The goods were sold by 'auctio,' that is, by public sale, and to the highest bidder. The English auction is in its essentials the same as the Roman 'auctio.' But the 'cohors' of Verres was 'invicta,' was not outbid, for their bidding was only a show, and the real object was to secure every thing for the praetor. Those who will not be called upon to pay can always outbid those who know that they must pay.

dispertiendis,] 'dissipandis' Zumpt and Iordan from Lg. 42 p. m.

Gemebant Syracusani, sed tamen patiebantur. Repente recitatur uno nomine HS CCL millia jussu praetoris data. Fit maximus clamor omnium, non modo optimi cujusque, neque eorum quibus indignum semper visum erat privata bona populi nomine per summam injuriam erepta, verum etiam ipsi illi auctores injuriae et ex aliqua particula socii praedae ac rapinarum clamare coeperunt, sibi ut haberet hereditatem. Tantus in curia clamor factus est ut populus concurreret.

XX. Res ab omni conventu cognita celeriter isti domum nuntiatur. Homo inimicus his qui recitassent, hostis omnibus qui acclamassent, exarsit iracundia ac stomacho. Verumtamen fuit tum sui dissimilis. Nostis os hominis, nostis audaciam: tamen tum rumore et clamore populi et furto manifesto grandis pecuniae perturbatus est. Ubi se collegit, vocat ad se Syracusanos: qui non posset negare ab illis pecuniam datam, non quaesivit procul alicunde, (neque enim probaret,) sed proximum, paene alterum filium, quem illam pecuniam diceret abstulisse: ostendit se reddere coacturum. Qui posteaquam id audivit, habuit et dignitatis et aetatis et nobilitatis suae rationem: verba apud senatum fecit: docuit ad se nihil pertinere: de isto id quod omnes videbant neque ille quidem obscure locutus est. Itaque illi Syracusani statuam postea statuerunt: et is ut primum potuit, istum reliquit de provinciaque decessit. Et tamen aiunt eum queri solere nonnunquam se miserum quod non suis sed suorum peccatis criminibusque prematur. Triennium provinciam obtinuisti: gener electus adolescens unum annum tecum fuit: sodales, viri fortes, legati tui,

privata bona] Klotz has 'privati bona.' Iordan says that Lambinus conjectured 'esse erepta,' and he adds, "vix enim Latine dicitur, indignum visum est bona erepta."

sibi ut haberet] 'even those who were to share in the plunder began to call out that Verres might keep it to himself, they would have none of it.' In c. 31 there is 'habeatis sane . . vobiscum,' perhaps not quite the same thing. But in c. 25, 'sibi habere jussit;' and in Lib. 4. c. 67, 'tibi habe.' See Pro Sulla, c. 9.

20. *celeriter isti*] 'Isti' was added by Zumpt on good authority, and it is wanted.

qui non posset] 'As Verres could not deny that money had been given by them,' that is, by those 'qui praefuerant,' &c. (c. 19), he did not look for strangers, or persons unconnected with him, as the receivers, for he could not have proved that; but he charged his son-in-law with receiving it, and professed that he would make him restore it. The 'proximum, paene alterum filium,' is the son-in-law of Verres. Orelli has 'quia non posset,' a bad reading.

neque ille quidem] 'ne ille quidem' Lg. 42 p. m. Iordan.

sed suorum] Klotz adds 'comitum.'

gener electus] Orelli and Klotz have 'gener electus adolescens.' Zumpt, who has 'lectus,' from Lg. 42 p. m., refers to Divin. c. 9; Lib. 1. c. 37; and Lib. 4. c. 86; but in these cases the superlative is used. Servius Sulpicius (Ad Div. iv. 5) has the expression, 'ex hac juventute generum deligere.' 'Gener electus adolescens' is certainly Latin, and 'gener, lectus adolescens,' Iordan's reading, may be so too.

primo anno te reliquerunt: unus legatus P. Tadius qui erat reliquus non ita multum tecum fuit; qui si semper [tecum] una fuisset, tamen summa cura quum tuae tum multo etiam magis suae famae pepercisset. Quid est quod tu alios accuses? quid est quamobrem putes te tuam culpam non modo derivare in aliquem sed communicare cum altero posse? Numerantur illa HS ducenta quinquaginta Syracusanis. Ea quemadmodum ad istum postea per pseudothyrum revertantur tabulis vobis testibusque, judices, planum faciam.

XXI. Ex hac iniquitate istius et improbitate, judices, quod praeda ex illis bonis ad multos Syracusanos invito populo senatuque Syracusano venerat, et illa scelera, quae per Theomnastum et Aeschrionem et Dionysodorum et Cleomenem invitissima civitate [illa] facta sunt, primum ut urbs tota spoliaretur, qua de re alius mihi locus ad dicendum est constitutus; ut omnia signa iste per eos homines quos nominavi, omne ebur ex aedibus sacris, omnes undique tabulas pictas, deorum denique simulacra quae vellet auferret; deinde ut in curia Syracusis, quem locum illi buleuterion nomine appellant, honestissimo loco et apud illos clarissimo, ubi illius ipsius M. Marcelli, qui eum Syracusanis locum quem eripere belli ac victoriae lege posset conservavit ac reddidit, statua ex aere facta est, ibi inauratam istius et alteram filio statuam ponerent; ut, dum istius hominis memoria maneret, senatus Syracusanus sine lacrimis et gemitu in curia esse non posset. Per eosdem istius furtorum, injuriarum uxorumque socios istius imperio Syracusis Marcellia tolluntur maximo gemitu luctuque civitatis: quem illi

derivare] See Lib. 1. c. 53; and the Excursus on 'non modo.'

per pseudothyrum] Verres paid back the HS CCL millia, but Cicero says that the money returned to him through a false door, a back-door; it was publicly repaid by Verres, and it privately came back to him.

21. *et illa scelera,*] The reading of Klotz, Zumpt, and Jordan is 'et illa scelera.' The reading of Lambinus is 'etiam illa scelera sunt.' The text may be understood if we take 'et' in the sense of 'etiam.' Zumpt takes it so, but refers the 'et' to what follows in the next sentence, 'Per eosdem istius . . . socios;' an explanation which seems to me inadmissible. The sense of the passage appears to be this: 'Of the same kind as this iniquity and improbity of Verres, Judices, in that out of that property of Heraclius a share of the plunder came to many of the Syracusans, contrary to the will of the community and the senate of Syracuse, are these crimes also which were committed with the help of Theomnastus,' &c.; and he then proceeds to enumerate them, 'primum ut urbs,' &c. The emphatic words 'et illa scelera' make the omission of 'sunt' tolerable.—'invitissima civitate [illa]:' 'illa' was added by Zumpt from Lg. 42 p. m. Jordan omits 'illa.'

quem locum] See c. 18, 'quae . . pecunia.'

statuam ponerent;] 'Ponerent' is the reading of Zumpt and Jordan from Lg. 42 p. m. Klotz retains 'posuerint,' the reading of the other MSS.; but, if this reading be accepted, Cicero has deviated from the regular construction which the sentence requires. See Lib. 1. c. 30.

diem festum quum recentibus beneficiis C. Marcelli debitum reddebant, tum generi, nomini, familiae Marcellorum maxima voluntate tribuebant. Mithridates in Asia, quum eam provinciam totam occupasset, Mucia non sustulit. Hostis, et hostis in ceteris rebus nimis ferus et immanis, tamen honorem hominis deorum religione consecratum violare noluit: tu Syracusanos unum diem festum Marcellis impertire noluisti, per quos illi adepti sunt ut ceteros dies festos agitare possent. At vero praeclarum diem illis reposuisti, Verria ut agerent, et ut ad eum diem quae sacris epulisque opus essent in complures annos locarentur. Jam in tanta istius impudentia remittendum aliquid videtur, ne omnia contendamus, ne omnia cum dolore agere videamur. Nam me dies, vox, latera deficiant, si hoc nunc vociferari velim, quam miserum indignumque sit istius nomine apud eos diem festum esse qui sese istius opera funditus exstinctos esse arbitrentur. O Verria praeclara! Quo quaeso, accessisti, quo non attuleris istum tecum diem? Etenim quam tu domum, quam urbem adisti, quod fanum denique quod non eversum atque extersum reliqueris? Quare appellentur sane ista Verria, quae non ex nomine sed ex manibus naturaque tua constituta esse videantur.

XXII. Quam facile serpat injuria et peccandi consuetudo, quam non facile reprimatur videte, judices. Bidis oppidum est, tenue sane, non longe a Syracusis. Hujus longe primus civitatis est Epicrates quidam. Huic hereditas HS quingentorum millium venerat a muliere quadam propinqua, atque ita propinqua ut ea etiamsi intestata esset mortua Epicratem Bidinorum legibus here-

C. Marcelli] This is the C. Marcellus who succeeded Lepidus in the government of Sicily (c. 3). 'Mithridates' is Mithridates Eupator, or the Great, who B.C. 88 was in possession of the province of Asia. The MSS. vary between the forms 'Marcellia' and 'Marcellea.' The Greek termination would be -εια, which seems to have been generally expressed in Latin by -ia.

locarentur.] Verres, in place of the festal day which he abolished, established one in honour of himself, and made provision for letting to contractors the care of providing what was necessary for celebrating the new festival.—'Jam in tanta:' Orelli has 'Sed jam,' &c., but there is little authority for the 'sed.' Zumpt observes that 'sed' would denote an interruption of what the orator is speaking of, and a transition to something else, which is not the case. 'Jam' introduces the conclusion, which is further explained by 'Nam me dies.'

eversum &c.] Here we have again a miserable pun on the name of Verres. To the word '*eversum*' Cicero adds '*extersum*,' 'wiped out;' in illustration of which Garatoni cites Cicero's Paradoxa, v. 2, 'qui tergunt, qui verrunt.' Graevius thinks that there is no allusion in '*eversum*' to the name of Verres, but that Cicero gives the explanation of what he means in the following words: 'ex manibus naturaque,' "quasi is natus et manus ejus factae sint ad omnia evertenda et extergenda."

22. *Bidis*] The Ethnic name is Bidini or Bidenses. The modern church of S. Giovanni di Bidino, not far west from Syracuse, seems to indicate the site of this little place.

dem esse oporteret. Recens Syracusana erat illa res quam ante demonstravi de Heraclio Syracusano, qui bona non perdidisset, nisi ei venisset hereditas. Huic quoque Epicrati venerat, ut dixi, hereditas. Cogitare coeperunt ejus inimici nihilo minus eodem praetore hunc everti bonis posse quo Heraclius esset eversus. Rem occulte instituunt: ad Verrem per ejus interpretes deferunt. Ita causa componitur ut item palaestritae Bidini peterent ab Epicrate hereditatem, quemadmodum palaestritae Syracusani ab Heraclio petivissent. Nunquam vos praetorem tam palaestricum vidistis. Verum ita palaestritas defendebat ut ab illis ipse unctior abiret; qui statim quum praesensisset jubet cuidam amicorum suorum numerari HS LXXX. Res occultari satis non potuit. Per quendam eorum qui interfuerant fit Epicrates certior. Primum contemnere et negligere [coepit], quod causa prorsus quod dubitari posset nihil habebat. Deinde quum de Heraclio cogitaret, et istius libidinem nosset, commodissimum putavit esse de provincia clam abire, itaque fecit: profectus est Rhegium.

XXIII. Quod ubi auditum est, aestuare illi qui pecuniam dederant: putare nihil agi posse absente Epicrate. Nam Heraclius tamen affuerat quum primo sunt dati judices: de hoc, qui ante-

Syracusana] Omitted by Lg. 42 p. m. and Iordan.

everti bonis] As 'eversum,' in the preceding chapter, contains an allusion to the name of Verres, it has been proposed to read 'everri bonis.' But we have in Lib. 1. c. 51, 'fortunis patriis . . evertere;' and 'voluntatem defuncti evertere' is a legal expression, which is used here in c. 19.

quo Heraclius] 'quam Heraclius' V and Guilielmius.

palaestricum] This word, Klotz remarks, expresses better what Cicero means than 'palaestritam,' the reading of Lg. 42 p. m. cod. Urs. and of Zumpt. The word 'unctior' is a manifest allusion to the anointing of the wrestlers; and it also contains a double meaning, for 'unctus' is applied to one who is rich. Comp. Horace, 1 Ep. xvii. 12, and the other examples in Forcellini. Verres gave his protection to the Bidini, but on such terms that he was well paid for it.—'unctior discederet,' Orelli. Comp. Lib. 1. c. 50, 'opimum praeda discedere.'

praesensisset] As soon as Verres got a hint of this new booty, he came upon the Bidini for a sum of money, a kind of fee to be paid beforehand, in consideration of what he was going to do for them. See c. 23, 'aestuare qui illi dederant pecuniam.' The commentators have found a difficulty in this passage, and much has been said upon it. 'Qui statim quod praesens esset' is the reading of Lg. 29 42 p. m. B. cod. Urs. But 'praesens esset' appears to be a corruption of 'praesensisset,' the reading of all the other known MSS. V has 'qui statim quod statim praesensisset.' The explanation of Massé is in substance the same as this, which I have given, except that he incorrectly places a comma after 'statim,' as Iordan also does. "As soon as Verres got notice of this (palaestritas Bidenses litem moturos contra Epicratem), he requires the 'palaestritae' to pay a sum of money to one of his friends (tanquam judicii pretium)."—Verres was acquainted with the whole matter, from the beginning, by his 'interpretes,' who in this and some other passages are not 'interpreters,' but 'agents,' or 'emissaries.'

quod causa] "Quod in caussa prorsus quod disputari posset nihil habebat," Klotz. For 'disputari' there is very good authority, and Iordan has it. But 'in causa' has no authority except V, and it spoils the sense. 'Causa' is the nominative to 'habebat.'

quam in jus aditum esset, antequam mentio denique controversiae facta esset ulla, discessisset, putabant nihil agi posse. Homines Rhegium proficiscuntur: Epicratem conveniunt: demonstrant id quod ille sciebat se HS LXXX dedisse: rogant eum ut sibi id quod ab ipsis abisset pecuniae curet; ab sese caveat quemadmodum velit de illa hereditate cum Epicrate neminem esse acturum. Epicrates homines multis verbis male acceptos ab se dimittit: redeunt illi Rhegio Syracusas: queri cum multis, ut fit, incipiunt sese HS LXXX nummum frustra dedisse. Res percrebuit et in ore atque sermone omnium coepit esse. Verres refert illam suam Syracusanam; ait se velle de illis HS LXXX cognoscere. Advocat multos: dicunt Bidini Volcatio se dedisse: illud non addunt, jussu istius. Volcatium vocat: pecuniam referri jubet. Volcatius animo aequissimo nummos affert qui nihil amitteret: reddit inspectantibus multis: Bidini nummos auferunt. Dicet aliquis, Quid ergo in hoc Verrem reprehendis, qui non modo ipse fur non est, sed ne alium quidem passus est esse? Attendite: jam intelligetis hanc pecuniam, qua via modo visa est exire ab isto, eadem semita revertisse.

23. *in jus aditum*] V has 'aditum postulatum in jus esset,' where 'postulatum' is a manifest interpolation.

curet;] The impudent demand was, that Epicrates should pay, or see that they were paid (curet), the amount which they had given to Verres, and take such security from them (ab sese caveat) as he should think proper, that nobody should raise any question about the 'hereditas.' This use of 'curare' is common in Cicero: 'me cui jussisset curaturum' (Ad Fam. xvi. 9). The MSS. have 'abesset,' and Brunnius thinks that the word in V is rather 'abesset' than 'abisset.' Still 'abisset' is a proper correction.—'velit de' &c.: Iordan has it thus, 'velit: de illa' &c.

ut fit,] Klotz and Iordan from V and Lg. 42 p. m. Zumpt has 'ita ut fit.'

Syracusanam:] 'Verres resorts to his old trick.' There seems no occasion to suppose with Hotmann, that there is any error in the text. Manutius supplies 'malitiam;' and Gruter 'cautilenam.' But the word to be supplied is the universal 'res,' which means any thing. Zumpt refers to a similar omission of 'res' in Cicero, De Nat. Deorum, i. 8, 'sed illa palmaris,' where Davis unnecessarily proposes to read 'sed illud palmare.' Iordan has 'rem refert;' but there is a difference between mentally supplying the word and adding it to Cicero's text. Madvig supposes that we should understand 'fabulam.'

referri jubet.] Zumpt, from Lg. 42 p. m. Orelli and the previous editors have 'imperat,' the reading of the other MSS.

via] The contrast between 'via' and 'semita' is obvious enough. A 'via' was the largest kind of road, a carriage-road, as in the case of a 'servitus,' and its width was fixed by the Twelve Tables (Dig. 8. 3. 8). It is also the term for a public or high road, as Via Appia. Among the various examples cited of the contrast of 'via' and 'semita' is one from Ennius (Cic. De Divin. i. 58):

"Qui sibi semitam non sapiunt alteri monstrant viam."

The old reading is 'qua via . . eadem semita,' the objection to which, as Zumpt states it, is this: "intelligi nequit, quomodo, quae via sit, eadem e contrario semita dici possit." But, as the money was not really repaid by a 'via,' so neither did it return by a 'semita.' It was repaid openly: it was returned privately. If the word 'semita' were omitted, nobody could doubt about the reading; for it is plain that the sentence does not require the relative (qua) to refer to 'pecunia,' but to the antecedent which follows. "Jam intelligetis hanc pecuniam . . revertisse:" "and how did it return? why, in the same directio

Quid enim debuit praetor facere—cum consilio cognita causa quum comperisset suum comitem juris, decreti, judicii corrumpendi causa, qua in re ipsius praetoris caput existimatioque ageretur, pecuniam accepisse, Bidinos autem pecuniam contra praetoris famam ac fortunas dedisse—non et in eum qui accepisset animadvertisse, et in eos qui dedissent? Tu qui institueras in eos animadvertere qui perperam judicassent, quod saepe per imprudentiam fit, hos pateris impune discedere qui ob tuum decretum, ob tuum judicium pecuniam aut dandam aut accipiendam putarant.

XXIV. Volcatius idem apud te postea fuit, eques Romanus, tanta accepta ignominia. Nam quid est turpius ingenuo, quid minus libero dignum quam in conventu maximo cogi a magistratu furtum reddere? qui si eo animo esset quo non modo eques Romanus, sed quivis liber debet esse, aspicere te postea non potuisset; inimicus, hostis esset tanta contumelia accepta, nisi tecum collusisset et tunc potius existimationi servisset quam suae. Qui quam tibi amicus non modo tum fuerit, quamdiu tecum in provincia fuit, verum etiam nunc sit, quum jam a ceteris amicis relictus es, et tu intelligis et nos existimare possumus. An hoc solum argumentum est nihil isto imprudente factum, quod Volcatius ei non succensuit, quod iste nec in Volcatium nec in Bidinos animadvertit? Est magnum argumentum: verum illud maximum, quod illis ipsis Bidinis quibus iratus esse debuit, a quibus comperit, quod jure agere cum Epicrate nihil possent, etiamsi adesset, idcirco suum decretum pecunia esse temptatum; his, inquam, ipsis non modo illam hereditatem quae Epicrati venerat, sed, ut in Heraclio Syracusano, item in hoc, paulo etiam atrocius, quod Epicrates appellatus omnino non erat, bona patria fortunasque ejus Bidinis tradidit. Ostendit enim novo modo, si quis quid ab absente peteret se auditurum. Adeunt

that it went out; but with this difference, that the 'via' became a 'semita.'" The expression in Latin is not so awkward as in a modern version: and it is to me more intelligible than Zumpt's and Iordan's reading: 'quae via . . cum semita,' &c. Hotmann made the alteration first, but he wrote 'quae via . . eandem semita;' but for 'eandem' Zumpt wrote 'eam.' All the MSS. have 'qua,' and all the MSS. 'eadem' except Lg. 42 p. m. which has 'eam.'

Quid enim debuit praetor facere] Orelli omits 'facere.'

animadvertisse,] 'animadvertisset' Lg. 42 p. m. F and Iordan, which of course means 'animadvertere debuit;' and Cicero ought to have written 'animadvertere' if he used the infinitive. But 'animadvertisse' may be right, as it is so far removed from 'debuit.'

ob tuum decretum,] Zumpt omits on the authority of Lg. 42 p. m.; and for 'putarant' he has 'putabant' on the same authority.

24. *quum . . relictus es,*] It does not appear that any MS. has 'es,' except Lg. 42 p. m.; the rest have 'sis.' This is a case somewhat doubtful; but perhaps the indicative is preferable. Orelli has 'sis relictus.'

ab absente &c.] "conj. Angelii: 'de absentem (vel apsentem)' V; 'absente'

Bidini, petunt hereditatem: procuratores postulant ut se ad leges suas rejiciat aut ex lege Rupilia dicam scribi jubeat. Adversarii non audebant contra dicere: exitus nullus reperiebatur. Insimulant hominem fraudandi causa discessisse: postulant ut bona possidere jubeat. Debebat Epicrates nummum nullum nemini: amici, si quis quid peteret, judicio se passuros, judicatum solvi satis-

ett." (Iordan.)—'adeunt Bidini, qui petunt' &c. V.

procuratores postulant] The 'procuratores' of Epicrates; those who represented him and acted for him. See Divin. c. 4. They offered to give security that their principal would comply with the terms of the decision (judicatum solvi satisdaturos).

fraudandi causa] One of the cases in which the praetor's edict permitted possession to be taken of a person's property was that of his concealing himself, or keeping out of the way, for the purpose of defrauding his creditors. Klotz refers to the terms of the edict (Pro P. Quintio, c. 19), "Qui fraudationis causa latitant;" and to the Digest, 42. 4, "quibus ex causis in possessionem eatur." The creditors were said 'in possessionem mitti.' The case resembles that of the English Bankrupt Law of 6 Geo. IV. c. 16, s. 3, by which, if a trader "shall depart from his dwelling-house, or otherwise absent himself, or begin to keep his house, &c., with intent to defeat or delay his creditors, he shall have committed an act of bankruptcy." When the trader has been adjudged to be a bankrupt, the commissioners sign a warrant directed to a person called a messenger, who is empowered to seize the bankrupt's property for the benefit of his creditors.—'possidere liceat' Orelli.

nullum nemini:] An instance of a double negation which does not produce an affirmative. Klotz and Iordan omit 'nullum,' and it is not in V. Keller retains 'nullum' (Sem. i. p. 121, note). If a reader had heard nothing about two negatives producing an affirmative,—an expression which is incapable of any exact meaning,—he would find no difficulty here, and he would translate it: 'Epicrates owed not a sesterce to no man.' The instances in which the Latin writers use such a mode of negation are not common; nor would they use it in a sentence like this, if Cicero had said 'non debebat.' Other cases of a different kind of double negation are not uncommon, as Zumpt shows. After a general negation in the principal sentence, there may be negation of the several parts, as Cicero, Pro Murena, c. 29, "viri non esse neque exorari neque placari," where, in fact, the omission of the 'neque' would give quite a different meaning; also c. 40, "si nemini nec domi nec militiae odio fuit." Zumpt quotes also the following instances from these orations of the use of 'ne—quidem:' Lib. 1. c. 60, "non enim praetereundum est ne id quidem;" and Lib. 3. c. 90, "non fugio ne hos quidem mores." See also Lib. 4. c. 1.

judicio se passuros,] This is the reading of all the MSS., including V, except that Lg. 42 p. m. has 'in judicio.' In place of the MSS. reading 'judicium se passuros,' 'judicio secum agi passuros' have been substituted. Klotz refers to Act. ii. Lib. 3. c. 28, where also he reads 'judicio se passuros,' from Lg. 42 and V. Klotz also refers to Pro P. Quintio, c. 28. Zumpt has it thus: 'si quis quid peteret in judicio, se passuros.'

In the Digest there is 'judicium accipere:' "Qui non cogitur defendere absentem, tamen si judicatum solvi satisdedit defendendi absentis gratia, cogendus procurator judicium accipere, ne decipiatur is qui satis accepit" (Dig. 3. 3. 43). But Cicero also has 'judicium accipere' (Pro P. Quintio, c. 20, vol. ii.); and in the Digest (5. 1. 8) there is 'judicium pati.' Zumpt seems to doubt if 'petere judicio' can be said, and with good reason. It is not a Roman expression, simply because the 'petitor' did not make his claim 'in judicio,' but 'in jure.' The accepting of the 'judicium' was the formal conclusion of the 'Litis Contestatio,' or 'the proceedings of the litigant parties before the praetor,' in which both parties, by their mutual statements, determine the matter in dispute in such way that it is ready to be carried before the 'judex.' These proceedings are the last act 'in jure,' that is to say, of the preliminary proceedings before the praetor: they are contemporaneous with the Formula which is given by the praetor and presupposes the naming of a 'judex,' for his name is mentioned in the formula (Savigny, System des Heut. Röm. Rechts, vi. 9, Litis contestatio). I have allowed

daturos esse dicebant. XXV. Quum omnia consilia frigerent, admonitu istius insimulare coeperunt Epicratem literas publicas corrupisse, a qua suspicione ille aberat plurimum: actionem ejus rei postulant. Amici recusare ne quod judicium neve ipsius cognitio illo absente de existimatione ejus constitueretur: et simul idem illud postulare non desistebant ut se ad leges suas rejiceret. Iste amplam occasionem calumniae nactus, ubi videt esse aliquid quod amici absente Epicrate nollent defendere, asseverat se ejus rei in primis actionem daturum. Quum omnes perspicerent ad istum non modo illos nummos qui per simulationem ab isto exierant revertisse, sed multo etiam plures eum postea nummos abstulisse, amici Epicratem defendere destiterunt: iste Epicratis bona Bidinos omnia possidere et sibi habere jussit. Ad illa HS ↀ millia hereditaria accessit ipsius antiqua HS quindecies pecunia. Utrum res ab initio ita ducta est, an ad extremum ita perducta est, an ita parva est pecunia, an is homo Verres ut haec quae dixi gratis facta esse

'judicio se passuros' to stand, for it may be right, even though Zumpt cannot understand it (quod intelligi nequit). But in his Appendix he says of 'judicio se passuros,' "nescio an verum sit, ut illud ipsum agi serum cogitatione adulatur." Keller (Sem. l. p. 121) says, "vana sunt omnia, quae Klotzius cum de sententia tum de egregia Latinitate ejus formulae 'judicio pati' commentus est." It is certain that 'judicium pati' in the Digest is a genuine expression. But there is so much evidence here, and in Lib. 3. c. 28, and also Pro Quintio, c. 28, that Cicero used 'judicio pati' that we cannot fairly get rid of the form. Th. Mommsen in a communication to Halm says that we ought not to alter a number of passages in which there is such an agreement; and he says right. Further, he thinks that 'judicio pati' can be easily explained, and that 'judicium pati' is a strange expression; but I do not assent to either of these assertions.—This was a case of 'negotiorum gestio,' as the Romans called it (Dig. 3. tit. 5), where a man undertook to defend the interests of an absent person, and thus constituted himself an attorney without any authority. If the self-constituted agent was condemned, there could be no 'actio judicati' against the person whom he represented, and the agent was accordingly required to give security that he would abide by the judgment, 'satisdare judicatum solvi.' The Roman doctrine was 'publice utile est absentes a quibuscunque defendi' (Dig. 3. 3. 33. § 2). A reader would hardly suppose that Horace, when he says 'absentem qui rodit amicum, Qui non defendit,' &c. (1 Sat. iv. 81), was using the legal language of the day, the same that the jurist Ulpian uses two centuries later; 'si amicus quum absentem defenderet.'

25. *Quum omnia consilia frigerent,*] Orelli has 'quum omnia [judicia] frigerent.'

actionem . . postulant.] Cicero also writes in this chapter 'actionem daturum,' and in c. 27, from which it appears that it is equivalent to 'judicem' or 'judicium daturum.' In Pro Caecina, c. 11, Cicero uses the expression 'habere actionem.'—'ne qua ipsius' Orelli, Klotz, Jordan. I do not know the authority for this reading.

ad leges . . rejiceret.] 'refer them to their own laws,' literally. It is a common Latin formula (Lib. 3. c. 60; and ad Div. xiii. 14, "ea res a Volcatio, qui Romae jus dicit, rejecta in Galliam est").

absente Epicrate] Many MSS. have 'absentem Epicratem,' but, as Zumpt observes, a double accusative after 'defendo' cannot be found.

antiqua . . pecunia.] 'his former property,' for that is the meaning of 'antiquus' (ant-icus), which is opposed to 'posticus.' 'Pecunia,' in its proper and larger sense, means a whole property (Gaius, ii. 104).

videantur? Hic nunc de miseria Siculorum, judices, audite. Et Heraclius ille Syracusanus et hic Bidinus Epicrates expulsi bonis omnibus Romam venerunt: sordidati, maxima barba et capillo, Romae biennium prope fuerunt. Quum L. Metellus hinc profectus in provinciam est, tum isti bene commendati cum Metello una proficiscuntur. Metellus simulac advenit Syracusas, utrumque rescidit et de Epicrate et de Heraclio. In utrisque bonis nihil erat quod restitui posset, nisi quod moveri loco non poterat. XXVI. Fecerat haec egregie primo adventu Metellus ut omnes istius injurias quas modo posset rescinderet et irritas faceret. Quod Heraclio restitui jusserat ac non restituebatur, quisquis erat eductus senator Syracusanus ab Heraclio, duci jubebat. Itaque permulti ducti sunt. Epicrates quidem continuo est restitutus. Alia judicia Lilybaei, alia Agrigenti, alia Panhormi restituta sunt. Census qui isto praetore sunt habiti non servaturum se Metellus ostenderat: decumas quas iste contra legem Hieronicam vendiderat seso venditurum Hieronica lege edixerat. Omnia erant

prope fuerunt.] The passage is thus in Klotz and Iordan: 'biennio prope fuerunt, quoad L. Metellus in provinciam profectus est; tum isti,' &c., founded on V, which has 'fuerunt quod ad.' Zumpt, in his Appendix, seems to prefer this reading.

advenit] Lg. 42 p. m. A. φ. 'Venit' Iordan. With a case like 'Syracusas,' or 'in Siciliam,' as in this chapter, 'venire' is the usual word.

rescidit] 'Rescindere' is to undo, to declare null. "Praeses provinciae rescindi venditionem . . jussit" (Dig. 18. 5. 9).

In utrisque bonis] 'V Lg. 42 p. m. fort. recte' (Hahn). I think that he is right. The common reading is 'in utriusque bonis.'—'nisi quod' V. 'nisi si quid' Lg. 29. 42 p. m. B. φ. Iordan.

moveri loco] All was gone except the land and what was attached to the land, as buildings. Cicero's expression has a reference to a natural and legal division of corporeal things into 'res mobiles,' things which can be moved without any alteration in their nature (moveables), and 'res immobiles,' as the ground (solum) and things attached to it (res soli). "Labeo scribit: edictum Aedilium curulium de venditionibus rerum esse tam earum quae soli sint quam earum quae mobiles aut se moventes" (Dig. 21. 1. 1. pr.).—'poterat:' 'potuerat' Lg. 42 p. m. F.

26. *eductus—duci*] Whatever senator Heraclius brought before Metellus (educeret) for non-compliance with the order, Metellus ordered to be taken to prison (duci). 'Quod' is the relative. 'Quod . . . jusserat . . . quisquis,' &c., is a form of expression altogether unlike any thing in English. Nor is there any real difference between this expression and 'Quod erant mihi . . . constitui,' &c., in c. 27.—'Quod Heraclio:' Lg. 42 p. m. M.; 'quod Heraclium' F, Iordan.

judicia . . . restituta] Metellus seems to have proceeded in the case of Epicrates and Heraclius 'extra ordinem,' that is, he decreed the restitution of his property without a new 'judicium.' In other cases he appears after examining the matter (causa cognita) to have instituted a new 'judicium' (judicium restitutum), that is, to have sent the cases before a 'judex' to be heard again in the ordinary way. Comp. Dig. 4. 4. 13. § 1, "potest desiderare interdum adversus possessorem restitui ne rem suam perdat vel re sua careat, et hoc vel cognitione praetoria vel rescissa alienatione dato in rem judicio." See Puchta, Inst. ii. § 177; and Savigny, System, &c., vii. § 315, where the real nature of the doctrine of 'restitutio' is explained, which it would be out of place to examine here.—The reading 'Panhormi' is in conformity to the best MSS., and to the general usage of coins and inscriptions (Zumpt). The coins have also ΠΑΝΟΡΜΙΤΑΝ.

Metelli ejusmodi ut non tam suam praeturam gerere quam istius praeturam retexere videretur. Simul atque ego in Siciliam veni, mutatus est. Venerat ad eum illo biduo Letilius quidam, homo non alienus a literis: itaque eo iste tabellario semper usus est. Is epistolas complures attulerat, in his unam domo quae totum mutarat hominem. Repente coepit dicere se omnia Verris causa velle: sibi cum eo amicitiam cognationemque esse. Mirabantur omnes hoc ei tum denique in mentem venisse, posteaquam tam multis eum factis decretisque jugulasset. Erant qui putarent Letilium legatum a Verre venisse qui gratiam, amicitiam, cognationemque commemoraret. Ex illo tempore a civitatibus laudationes petere, testes non solum deterrere verbis sed etiam vi retinere coepit. Quod ego nisi meo adventu illius conatus aliquantum repressissem, et apud Siculos non Metelli sed Glabrionis literis ac lege pugnassem, tam multos huc evocare non potuissem. XXVII. Verum, quod institui dicere, miserias cognoscite sociorum. Heraclius ille et Epicrates longe mihi obviam cum suis omnibus processerunt: venienti Syracusas egerunt gratias flentes: Romam mecum decedere cupiverunt. Quod erant mihi oppida complura etiam reliqua quae adire vellem, constitui cum hominibus quo die mihi Messanae praesto essent. Eo mihi nuntium miserunt se a praetore retineri. Quibus ego testimonium denuntiavi, quorum nomina edidi Metello, cupidissimi veniendi, maximis injuriis affecti adhuc non venerunt. Hoc jure sunt socii ut iis ne deplorare quidem de suis incommodis liceat.

Jam Heraclii Centuripini optimi nobilissimique adolescentis

illo biduo] 'Biduo ante quam ego adveni,' Zumpt, who compares 'paucis illis diebus' in Lib. 4. c. 18, and De Sen. c. 14, "qui his diebus paucis Pontifex Maximus factus est." See Lib. 2. c. 41, note; and 'brevi illo tempore,' Pro M. Tullio, § 19.

a literis: . . tabellario] A frigid joke. 'Literae' is used for 'letters' or 'literature;' and a 'tabellarius' carries 'literae' or epistles.

Quod ego nisi . . illius conatus] 'Quod' pro 'sed,' says Manutius; and he compares Act. i. Lib. 1. c. 46, 'Quod vos oblitos esse,' &c. But he is mistaken. 'Quod' is the relative, and it relates to the preceding sentence, and 'illius conatus' is its exponent, or epexegesis, or whatever other name may be used. The 'literae' of Glabrio are the written authority from him to summon witnesses and so forth. Zumpt observes on 'Quod nisi ego,' which is his reading and Iordan's: "sic verba collocantur in Lg. 42 p. m. rectius quam vulgo 'quod ego nisi.'" But why 'rectius?' V also has 'nisi ego.' Klotz in this case has 'Quod nisi ego;' but he has (Lib. 1. c. 61) 'cui ego nisi,' where Orelli has 'cui nisi ego.' By way of compensation Orelli has in this passage 'Quod ego nisi.'

27. *constitui cum*] Zumpt has 'tum' from Lg. 42 p. m. Both the dative is used, and the ablative with 'cum.' I do not think that the examples of the use of this word justify Zumpt's remark: "neque *cum aliquo* constituo, quando quid ille facere debeat, *alicui* potius."—'praesto adessent' V, Klotz. Iordan's remark is true: "At *praesto esse* Tullio usitatissimum sexcenties in his orationibus legitur, numquam *praesto adesse*."

Centuripini] Centuripa (Κεντόριπα, Thucyd. vi. 94) was originally a town of

testimonium audistis, a quo HS c millia per calumniam malitiamque petita sunt. Iste poenis compromissisque interpositis HS cccc extorquenda curavit; quodque judicium secundum Heraclium de compromisso factum erat, quum civis Centuripinus inter duos cives judicasset, id irritum jussit esse, cumque judicio falsum judicasse judicavit: in senatu esse, locis commodisque publicis uti vetuit: si quis eum pulsasset, edixit sese judicium injuriarum non daturum: quidquid ab eo peteretur, judicem de sua cohorte daturum, ipsi autem nullius actionem rei se daturum. Quae istius auctoritas tantum valuit ut neque illum pulsaret quisquam, quum praetor in provincia sua verbo permitteret, re hortaretur, neque quisquam ab eo quidquam peteret, quum iste calumniae licentiam sua auctoritate ostendisset: ignominia autem illa gravis tamdiu in illo homine fuit quamdiu iste in provincia mansit. Hoc injecto metu judicibus novo more, nullo exemplo, ecquam rem putatis esse in Sicilia nisi ad nutum istius judicatam? Utrum id solum videtur esse actum, quod est tamen actum, ut haec Heraclio pecunia eriperetur, an etiam illud, in quo praeda erat maxima, ut nomine judiciorum omnium bona atque fortunae in istius unius essent potestate?

the Siculi, on the road from Catina to Panhormus, near the Simaethus, at the foot of Aetna. It is now Centorbi, a place situated on a steep height. It was at this time one of the richest towns in the island, and had a senate and a municipal constitution. The inhabitants carried on an extensive cultivation of corn and trade in corn in various parts of Sicily. See Lib. 2. c. 68; 3. c. 45; 4. c. 23. 50; 5. c. 27.

poenis compromissisque] 'under penalties and terms.' The 'compromissum' is the terms of the agreement of two persons to refer the matter in dispute between them to an arbiter, and in these terms was contained a penalty (poena) if either party did not abide by the award. (Pro Q. Rosc. Com. c. 4.) The terms of the edict were: "Qui arbitrium poena compromissa receperit" (Dig. 4. 8. s. 3. § 2).—Klotz has 'iste ad praesens poenis,' &c., from V.—'de compromisso:' Klotz omits 'de,' with V.—'judicasset:' 'dijudicasset' Iordan, which is bad.—'cumque judicio,' &c.: 'cumque judicem falsum judicasse' Iordan. V has 'iudicio,' according to Iordan; but Halm says '*iudicem* habet V, ut videtur non *iudicium*.' 'Falsum judicasse,' 'gave a false judgment.' 'Eumque judicem,' if that is the true reading, means, 'and that he as Judex.'

civis . . . duos cives] See c. 13.

in senatu esse,] Klotz has 'in senatu ne esset: locis,' &c.

injuriarum] The 'actio,' or 'judicium injuriarum' was for assault and beating, for abusive words, and for other matters (Gaius, iii. 220, &c.). When Verres declared that he would allow any action against the 'judex,' but would not allow him to sue any person, he was putting this innocent man in a worse condition than those who were 'infames' (Dig. 3. tit. 1 and 2). 'Ignominia' is a technical term.

in provincia mansit.] Zumpt omits 'mansit.'—'novo more:' Klotz has 'novo jure,' the reading of V, and perhaps the better word. But either is Latin.

in istius . . essent potestate?] F N have 'potestatem.' This use of 'in' with 'esse' is Ciceronian, and it is remarked on by Gellius (i. 7). There is another example in these orations, Lib. 5. c. 38, 'in eorum potestatem . . futurum.' (See also Phil. xii. 2, and the note; Pro P. Quintio, c. 5, 'res esse in vadimonium coepit;' and Ter. Haut. v. 2. 33, 'quod mi in mentem est.') It seems to have been an old form of expression, but Zumpt is perhaps right in rejecting it in those cases in which the

XXVIII. Jam vero in rerum capitalium quaestionibus quid ego unamquamque rem colligam et causam? Ex multis similibus ea sumam quae maxime improbitate excellere videbuntur. Sopater quidam fuit Halicyensis, homo domi suae cum primis locuples atque honestus. Is ab inimicis suis apud C. Sacerdotem praetorem rei capitalis quum accusatus esset, facile eo judicio est liberatus. Huic eidem Sopatro iidem inimici ad C. Verrem, quum is Sacerdoti successisset, ejusdem rei nomen detulerunt. Res Sopatro facilis videbatur, et quod erat innocens et quod Sacerdotis judicium improbare istum ausurum non arbitrabatur. Citatur reus: causa agitur Syracusis: crimina tractantur ab accusatore ea quae erant antea non solum defensione verum etiam judicio dissoluta. Causam Sopatri defendebat Q. Minucius, eques Romanus in primis splendidus atque honestus, vobisque, judices, non ignotus. Nihil erat in causa quod metuendum aut omnino quod dubitandum videretur. Interea istius libertus et accensus idem Timarchides, qui est, id quod ex plurimis testibus priore actione didicistis, rerum hujuscemodi omnium transactor et administer, ad Sopatrum venit: monet hominem ne nimis judicio Sacerdotis et causae suae confidat; accusatores inimicosque ejus habere in animo pecuniam praetori dare; praetorem tamen ob salutem malle accipere, et simul mallo

MSS. have not preserved it. In the Lex Thoria (Zeitschrift für Geschichtl. Rechtsw. vol. x. by Rudorff), at the beginning of the first chapter, there is "Quei ager poplicus populi Romanei in terram Italiam P. Mucio L. Calpurnio *cos. fuit*." The words '*cos. fuit*' are supplied from conjecture. But a little further, in the same chapter, there is the same passage complete, with the variation 'in terra Italia;' and again in c. 3 and 5, the same; and in other places also. The expression 'quei ager in Africa est' also occurs frequently. It might be concluded that 'in terram Italiam,' which I think occurs once only in this Lex, is a mistake; but that conclusion would not be certain.

28. *Halicyensis,*] Halicyae was a 'libera civitas' (Act. ii. Lib. 3. c. 6), but it appears that the privileges of a 'libera civitas' did not extend to the exclusion of the criminal jurisdiction of the Praetor. Halicyae (Ἁλικύαι, Steph.) lay between Entella and Lilybaeum, and about twenty miles from Lilybaeum, if the modern Salemi is on the site of Halicyae, which is possible, but not certain.

Huic eidem Sopatro] This is the MSS. reading. Such a use of a dative with 'defero' is not common, but it is intelligible. Some grammarians oddly enough call it a dative 'incommodi.' This matter was certainly an 'incommodum' to Sopater. This kind of dative is a dative of frequent use, especially with pronouns. See Pro Caelio, c. 23, "Si hic nemini nomen detulisset."

agitur Syracusis:] Sopater was summoned to Syracuse, where the Praetor 'conventus agebat.' Garatoni cites a passage from Livy (xxxi. 29), "Siculorum civitatibus Syracusas aut Messanam aut Lilybaeum indicitur concilium. Praetor Romanus conventus agit," &c.

dissoluta.] 'settled,' 'entirely cleared away.' Not unlike Horace's

"Solventur risu tabulae, tu missus abibis."

monet hominem] 'he warns the man;' 'hominem' emphatically designates a person. That is all. See c. 29; Pro Q. Quintio, c. 4. It is a common Latin formula.

ob salutem] Lg. 29 A B L. The other readings are 'a salute' and 'absolute.' Orelli has 'ab salute,' which is hardly intelligible. The omission of a final *m* is so

si fieri posset rem judicatam non rescindere. Sopater, quum hoc illi improvisum atque inopinatum accidisset, commotus est sane, neque in praesentia Timarchidi quid responderet habuit nisi se consideraturum quid sibi de ea re esset faciendum: et simul ostendit se in summa difficultate esse nummaria. Post ad amicos rettulit, qui quum ei fuissent auctores redimendae salutis, ad Timarchidem venit: expositis suis difficultatibus hominem ad HS LXXX perducit, eamque ei pecuniam numerat.

XXIX. Posteaquam ad causam dicendam ventum est, tum vero sine metu, sine cura omnes erant qui Sopatrum defendebant. Crimen nullum erat: res [erat] judicata: Verres nummos acceperat. Quis posset dubitare quidnam esset futurum? Res illo die non peroratur: dimittitur judicium. Iterum ad Sopatrum Timarchides venit: ait accusatores ejus multo majorem pecuniam praetori polliceri quam quantam hic dedisset; proinde, si saperet, videret quid sibi esset faciendum. Homo, quamquam erat et Siculus et reus, hoc est, et jure iniquo et tempore adverso, ferre tamen atque audire diutius Timarchidem non potuit: Facite, inquit, quod [vobis] libet, daturus non sum amplius. Idemque hoc amicis ejus et defensoribus videbatur: atque eo etiam magis quod iste, quoquo modo se in ea quaestione praebebat, in consilio tamen habebat homines honestos e conventu Syracusano, qui Sacerdoti quoque in consilio fuerant tum quum est idem hic Sopater absolutus. Hoc rationis habebant, facere eos nullo modo posse ut eodem crimine iisdem testibus Sopatrum condemnarent iidem homines qui antea absolvissent. Itaque hac una spe ad judicium venitur. Quo posteaquam ventum est, quum in consilium frequentes convenissent iidem qui solebant, et hac [una] spe tota defensio Sopatri niteretur, consilii frequentia et dignitate, et quod erant, ut dixi, iidem qui antea Sopatrum eodem illo crimine liberarant, cognoscite hominis apertam ac non modo non ratione sed ne dissimulatione quidem tectam improbitatem et audaciam. M. Petilium, equitem Roma-

common, even in the best MSS., that it is a very small correction to add it, especially as we see that the next word begins with *m.*—'de ea re:' om. Lg. 42 p. m. M, and Iordan.

in praesentia] See Lib. 3. c. 1.

29. *quid sibi esset faciendum.*] Klotz and Iordan omit these words: and they are omitted in Lg. 42 p. m. F M. Garatoni argues that as these words are not in the best MSS., they are not necessary, and that 'proinde, si saperet, videret,' is the best form of expression, and that all caution is contained in the word 'videret.' This is true, but Cicero may still have written the words, and I think that the text is better with them than without them, for they are the very words which Sopater had used, c. 28.

est . . absolutus.] 'esset . . absolutus' Orelli. The imperfect 'absolveretur,' says Zumpt, might be endured, but 'esset . . absolutus' is contrary to the sense. Yet it is the reading except in Lg. 42 p. m. M.

num, quem habebat in consilio, jubet operam dare quod rei privatae judex esset. Petilius recusabat, quod suos amicos quos sibi in consilio esse vellet ipse Verres retineret in consilio. Iste homo liberalis negat se quemquam retinere eorum qui Petilio vellent adesse. Itaque discedunt omnes: nam ceteri quoque impetrant ne retineantur, qui se velle dicebant alterutri eorum qui tum illud judicium habebant adesse. Itaque iste solus cum sua cohorte nequissima relinquitur. Non dubitabat Minucius qui Sopatrum defendebat quin iste, quoniam consilium dimisisset, illo die rem illam quaesiturus non esset, quum repente jubetur dicere. Respondet, Ad quos? Ad me, inquit, si tibi idoneus videor qui de homine Siculo ac Graeculo judicem. Idoneus es, inquit; sed pervellem adessent ii qui affuerant antea causamque cognorant. Dic, inquit: illi adesse non possunt. Nam hercule, inquit Minucius, me quoque Petilius ut sibi in consilio essem rogavit, et simul a subselliis abire coepit. Iste iratus hominem verbis vehementioribus prosequitur, atque ei gravius etiam minari coepit quod in se tantum crimen invidiamque conflaret.

XXX. Minucius qui Syracusis sic negotiaretur ut sui juris dignitatisque meminisset, et qui sciret ita se in provincia rem augere oportere ut ne quid de libertate deperderet, homini quae visa sunt et quae tempus illud tulit et causa respondit: causam sese dimisso atque ablegato consilio defensurum negavit, itaque a subselliis discessit: idemque hoc praeter Siculos ceteri Sopatri amici advocatique fecerunt. Iste quamquam est incredibili importunitate et audacia, tamen subito solus destitutus pertimuit et conturbatus est. Quid ageret, quo se verteret nesciebat. Si dimisisset eo tempore quaestionem, post illis adhibitis in consilium quos ablegaverat absolutum iri Sopatrum videbat: sin autem homi-

operam dare quod] M. Petilius was a 'judex' in a 'privatum judicium' which was pending, and Verres, in order to get rid of him, told him to go and attend to his function of 'judex' in the 'res privata,' or matter in suit between two parties.—'quos sibi in consilio esse vellet:' a 'judex' in a 'res privata' was often assisted by the advice of his friends, but he gave the judgment himself.

alterutri eorum . . adesse.] 'Adesse' is a word of technical use, to accompany a person to court, there to give him your aid and advice. Horace (1 Sat. ix. 38):

"Si me amas, paulum hic ades. Inteream si
Aut valeo stare aut novi civilia jura;"

and Heindorf's note. See Pro Murena, c. 3. A little further on there is 'ut sibi in consilio essem,' where Orelli has 'adessem.' 'Alterutri' is 'either of the two parties;' 'qui illud judicium habebant,' 'who had this suit.' The passage is explained wrong by Orelli, and right by Ernesti.

Nam hercule,] See Lib. 3. c. 85.

verbis . . prosequitur,] See Caesar, B. G. ii. 5, 'liberaliterque oratione prosecutus:' Virg. Aen. vi. 899, 'prosequitur dictis.'

30. *qui . . sic negotiaretur ut*] 'Minucius being one of those who carried on his business at Syracuse without forgetting his rights and his character.'—'augere:' Naugerius. The 'codd. noti' have 'agere.'

nem miserum atque innocentem ita condemnasset, quum ipse praetor sine consilio, reus autem sine patrono atque advocatis fuisset, judiciumque C. Sacerdotis rescidisset, invidiam se sustinere tantam non posse arbitrabatur. Itaque aestuabat dubitatione: versabat se in utramque partem non solum mente verum etiam corpore, ut omnes qui aderant intelligere possent in animo ejus metum cum cupiditate pugnare. Erat hominum conventus maximus, summum silentium, summa exspectatio quonam esset ejus cupiditas eruptura: crebro se accensus demittebat ad aurem Timarchides. Tum iste aliquando, Age, dic, inquit. Reus orare atque obsecrare ut cum consilio cognosceret. Tum repente iste testes citari jubet: dicit unus et alter breviter: nihil interrogatur: praeco Dixisse pronuntiat. Iste quasi metueret ne Petilius privato illo judicio transacto aut dilato cum ceteris in consilium reverteretur, ita properans de sella exsilit: hominem innocentem a C. Sacerdote absolutum, indicta causa de sententia scribae, medici haruspicisque condemnat.

XXXI. Retinete, retinete hominem in civitate, judices: parcite et conservate ut sit qui vobiscum res judicet, qui in senatu sine ulla cupiditate de bello et pace sententiam ferat. Tametsi minus id quidem nobis, minus populo Romano laborandum est, qualis istius in senatu sententia futura sit. Quae enim ejus auctoritas erit? quando iste sententiam dicere audebit aut poterit? quando autem homo tantae luxuriae atque desidiae nisi Februario mense adspi-

ita condemnasset,] Orelli omits 'ita;' of which Zumpt says 'est enim fere pro *tam*.' But it is for what it is, that is 'ita,' 'under such circumstances as are next mentioned.'

exspectatio quonam] A like use of this noun is common in Cicero. See Lib. 5. c. 7.

praeco Dixisse] See Act. i. c. 18.

dilato] 'prolato' Klotz and Jordan; but Jordan says that 'prolato' is Zumpt's conjecture. It means 'adjourned,' whether we read one or the other.

ita properans] 'so hastily.' See Lib. 1. c. 18, note; and with a negative, Lib. 2. c. 20, "non ita multum tecum fuit."—'exsiluit' Orelli and Klotz. 'He hurried from his seat, to take the votes of his consilium.'

31. *sententiam ferat.*] Hotmann observes that 'sententiam ferre,' is said of a 'judex,' but a senator was said 'sententiam dicere' in the senate. Yet the expression 'sententiam ferre' was sometimes used in its most general sense, and applied even to a senator giving his opinion in the Senate. Ernesti refers to Cic. Ad Fam. xi. 21. In the Tab. Herac. (ii. p. 422, ed. Mazochi) both forms occur, as usual in legal language, which, from the time of the Romans to our own, delights in a superfluity of words: "neve sententiam rogato, neve dicere neve ferre jubeto."

Februario mense] See Lib. 1. c. 35. Cicero insinuates that Verres would attend the senate-house (curia) in February, in the hope of getting something from the deputations which came from the provinces. (Cic. Ad Q. Fr. ii. 3.) February was jobbers' month at Rome. There was money stirring then. The envoys of foreign states and kings made presents to senators to get their vote and influence. Cicero is much given to wicked insinuations. But if the consuls had been questioned in the Senate about such practices, might they not have answered as wisely as the English minister, who 'had heard that members of Parliament advocating in-

rubit in curiam? Verum veniat sane: decernat bellum Cretensibus; liberet Byzantios; regem appellet Ptolemaeum; quae vult Hortensius omnia dicat et sentiat: minus haec ad nos, minus ad vitae nostrae discrimen, minus ad fortunarum nostrarum periculum pertinent.

Illud, [illud] est capitale, illud formidolosum, illud optimo cuique metuendum, quod isto si ex hoc judicio aliqua vi se eripuerit, in judicibus sit necesse est, sententiam de capite civis Romani ferat, sit in ejus exercitu signifer qui imperium judiciorum tenere vult. Hoc populus Romanus recusat, hoc ferre non potest: clamat permittitque vobis ut, si istis hominibus delectemini, si ex isto genere splendorem ordini atque ornamentum curiae constituere velitis, habeatis sane istum vobiscum senatorem, etiam de vobis judicem si vultis habeatis: de se homines, si qui extra istum ordinem sunt, quibus ne rejiciundi quidem amplius quam trium judicum praeclarae leges Corneliae faciunt potestatem, hunc hominem tam crudelem, tam sceleratum, tam nefarium nolunt judicare.

XXXII. Etenim si illud est tam flagitiosum quod mihi omnium rerum turpissimum maximeque nefarium videtur ob rem judicandam pecuniam accipere, pretio habere addictam fidem et religionem;

dian claims received presents from native princes, but he did not know that officially?'

Various important matters, which Cicero alludes to, were under discussion at this time. L. Metellus, the colleague of Hortensius (B.C. 69), had declared war against the Cretans, and Byzantium was made a 'libera civitas.' Ptolemaeus is probably Auletes or Ptolemaeus XII., who succeeded Alexander or Ptolemaeus XI. At this time Alexander was king, but he was ejected a few years afterwards, and died at Tyre. Auletes reigned in his stead.—'decernat,' 'liberet,' 'appellet,' mean of course 'let him vote for,' &c.

adspirabit in curiam!] Cicero is fond of this poetic expression. See Divin. c. 16; and Lib. 1. c. 54, 'ad meam pecuniam . . adspirat;' Pro P. Sulla, c. 18. Virgil has it (Aen. xii. 352) with a dative.

quibus ne rejiciundi quidem] It appears that the Lex Cornelia did not allow those who were not senators to challenge more than three 'judices' in a criminal trial; but Verres, as a senator, had the right of challenging more, and had challenged six at least, as Zumpt shows by reference to Act. ii. Lib. 1. c. 7; Lib. 3. c. 41; and Lib. 5. c. 44. The conjecture of Antonio Agustin, that the 'trium judicum rejectio' was enacted only by the Cornelia Lex de Repetundis, will, as Zumpt observes, explain 'si qui extra istum ordinem sunt,' for few except senators were likely, as experience showed, to act in such manner as to come within the penalties of the Lex de Repetundis.

trium judicum] Zumpt refers to his Grammar (§ 661) for four other examples from Cicero of a genitive in the place of an accusative when coupled with a gerund. In Cicero, De Invent. ii. 2, there is "ex majore enim copia nobis quam illi fuit exemplorum eligendi potestas." A reference to the host of critics who have discussed this subject is given in the fifteenth Excursus in Creuzer and Moser's edition of this oration. Compare "Ab his fit initium retinendi Silii atque Velanii," Caesar, B. G. iii. 8, and Schneider's note. In this passage Lg. 29. 42 have 'trium iudicium,' as Halm observes.

32. *tam flagitiosum*] Most of the MSS. have 'tam,' it appears, except Lg. 42 N; and why it should be rejected nobody has yet explained. Orelli thought it should be 'jam.' In the letter of Cicero, Ad Q. Fr. i. 1. 5, Ernesti thinks that 'tam fideles' should be 'jam fideles.' If a man will carefully read these orations, he will easily dispense with this suggestion.

pretio . . addictam] Forcellini explains

quanto illud flagitiosius, improbius, indignius, eum a quo pecuniam ob absolvendum acceperis condemnare, ut ne praedonum quidem praetor in fide retinenda consuetudinem conservaret? Scelus est accipere ab reo: quanto magis ab accusatore? quanto etiam sceleratius ab utroque? Fidem quum proposuisses venalem in provincia, valuit apud te plus is qui pecuniam majorem dedit. Concedo: forsitan aliquis aliquando ejusmodi quidpiam fecerit. Quum vero fidem ac religionem tuam jam alteri addictam pecunia accepta habueris, post eandem adversario tradideris majore pecunia, utrumque falles, et trades cui voles, et ei quem fefelleris ne pecuniam quidem reddes? Quem mihi tu Bulbum, quem Staienum, quod unquam hujuscemodi monstrum aut prodigium audivimus aut vidimus, qui cum reo transigat, post cum accusatore decidat? honestos homines qui causam norint ableget a consilioque dimittat? ipse solus reum absolutum a quo pecuniam acceperit condemnet pecuniamque non reddat? Hunc hominem in judicum numero habebimus? hic alteram decuriam senatoriam judex obtinebit? hic de

it under the head "Translate *addictus* est, obstrictus, devinctus, obnoxius." But this is not the exact meaning. 'Addicere,' in one of its usages, is a word used in selling, and signifies the declaration of him who sells as to the transfer of the thing to the buyer. 'Pretium' is 'price,' that which the buyer gives. The passage means, 'to have his good faith and conscience bargained and sold for money.' There is a use of 'addicere' in Lib. 5. c. 63, which shows the sense of the word; and it is common in the law writers. See also Lib. 3. c. 33.

conservaret?] 'conservet' Lg. 42 p. m. Iordan.

quanto magis] All the 'cod. noti' except Lg. 29, which has 'quanto majus,' which some may prefer.

Quem mihi tu Bulbum, &c.] These were two of the mercenary 'judices' in the trial of Oppianicus. See the oration Pro Cluentio, c. 26. 28, &c. A note of interrogation is usually placed after Stalenus or Staienus (perhaps the true name), which spoils the sentence, for 'Bulbum, Staienum' depend on 'audivimus' and 'vidimus.' Zumpt, who places a note of interrogation after 'Staienum,' supplies 'dicis.' But this artifice will not always answer. The 'mihi tu,' so placed, marks the contrast of the two persons, 'I, Cicero,' and 'you, Verres.' The original form of expression may have had a verb on which 'mihi' would depend, but usage established the formula without the verb, and it means as much as this: 'What Bulbus, tell me if you can, what Staienus, what monster ever of this kind, or what prodigious thing have we heard of or have we seen, that comes to terms with the accused, and then finally compromises with the accuser?' Compare 'Tu mihi, quum circumsessus es,' &c., Act. ii. Lib. 1. c. 32. 'Transigat' and 'decidat' are both forensic words. 'Transigere' is to settle a matter with a person. Dig. 2. tit. 15, De Transactionibus.

in judicum numero] Zumpt has a note on this passage, in which he contends that 'in' is necessary; for the meaning is, as the context shows, 'shall we allow this man to be one of the Judices?' but if 'in' were omitted, then the sense ought to be 'to consider him as a Judex.' Now, if this were the meaning, he contends that it ought to be 'numero judicis.' He cites two examples where the plural is used in this sense, one from the Life of Agesilaus, by Nepos, "mirari se non sacrilegorum numero haberi," 'he wondered that he was not considered a sacrilegious person;' and another from Suetonius (Caesar, c. 11). But he finds no such instance in Cicero, who uses such a phrase as (Ad Q. Fr. i. 1. c. 4) "ascensus sit eo numero quo eum majores nostri esse voluerunt;" or he says 'numero aliquo,' and the like.

decuriam] There were, it is said, three 'decuriae,' each consisting of one hundred senators, out of which the 'judices' were

capite libero judicabit? huic judicialis tabella committetur? quam iste non modo cera verum etiam sanguine, si visum erit, notabit. XXXIII. Quid enim horum se negat fecisse? Illud videlicet unum quod necesse est, pecuniam accepisse. Quidni iste neget? At eques Romanus qui Sopatrum defendit, qui omnibus ejus consiliis rebusque interfuit, Q. Minucius juratus dicit pecuniam datam: juratus dicit Timarchidem dixisse majorem ab accusatoribus pecuniam dari: dicent hoc multi Siculi, dicent omnes Halicyenses, dicet etiam praetextatus Sopatri filius qui ab isto homine crudelissimo patre innocentissimo pecuniaque patria privatus est. Verum, si de pecunia testibus planum facere non possem, illud negare posses aut nunc negabis, te consilio tuo dimisso, viris primariis qui in consilio C. Sacerdoti fuerant tibique esse solebant remotis, de re judicata judicavisse? teque eum quem C. Sacerdos adhibito consilio, causa cognita, absolvisset, eundem remoto consilio, causa incognita, condemnasse? Quum haec confessus eris quae in foro palam Syracusis, in ore atque in oculis provinciae gesta sunt, negato tum sane, si voles, pecuniam accepisse: reperies, credo, aliquem qui, quum haec quae palam gesta sunt videat, quaerat quid tu occulte egeris, aut qui dubitet utrum malit meis testibus an tuis defensoribus credere.

Dixi jam antea me non omnia istius quae in hoc genere essent enumeraturum, sed electurum ea quae maxime excellerent. XXXIV. Accipite nunc aliud ejus facinus nobile et multis locis saepe commemoratum, et ejusmodi ut in uno omnia maleficia inesse videantur. Attendite diligenter; invenietis enim id facinus natum a cupiditate, auctum per stuprum, crudelitate perfectum atque conclusum. Sthenius est, is qui nobis assidet, Thermitanus, antea multis propter summam virtutem summamque nobilitatem, nunc propter suam calamitatem atque istius insignem injuriam omnibus notus. Hujus hospitio Verres quum esset usus, et quum apud eum non solum Thermis saepenumero fuisset sed etiam habitasset, domo ejus omnia abstulit quae paulo magis animum cujuspiam aut oculos

chosen. The 'decuria,' says Gruter, is only another name for the 'album,' as Casaubon showed in his note on Sueton., August. c. 32.

The meaning of the word 'cera' is explained by reference to the coloured tablets mentioned in the Divinatio. Verres would colour his with human blood.

si visum erit,] 'si usus erit,' Klotz; but it is the conjecture of Guilielm. founded on the reading of Lg. 42 p. m. M 'si visus erit,' which may be a corruption of 'si usus erit.'

33. *Quid enim*] 'Enim' merely marks the transition to another part of the subject. 'Now what is there here that he will deny? Why, the one thing which he must deny, for it is his only defence—he will deny that any money has come to his hands. I should indeed be surprised if he did not deny it.' The supposed defence of Verres is, that it could not be proved that he received the money.

possent commovere. Etenim Sthenius ab adolescentia paulo studiosius haec compararat, supellectilem ex aere elegantiorem et Deliacam et Corinthiam, tabulas pictas, etiam argenti bene facti, prout Thermitani hominis facultates ferebant, satis. Quae quum esset in Asia adolescens studiose, ut dixi, compararat, non tam suae delectationis causa quam ad invitationes adventusque nostrorum hominum, suorum amicorum atque hospitum. Quae posteaquam iste omnia abstulit, alia rogando, alia poscendo, alia sumendo, ferebat Sthenius ut poterat; angebatur animi necessario quod domum ejus exornatam et instructam fere jam iste reddiderat nudam atque inanem. Verumtamen dolorem suum nemini impertiebat: praetoris injurias tacite, hospitis placide ferendas arbitrabatur. Interea iste cupiditate illa sua nota atque apud omnes pervagata, quum signa quaedam pulcherrima atque antiquissima Thermis in publico posita vidisset, adamavit; a Sthenio petere coepit ut ad ea tollenda operam suam profiteretur seque adjuvaret. Sthenius vero non solum negavit, sed etiam ostendit fieri id nullo modo posse, ut signa antiquissima monumenta P. Africani ex oppido Thermitanorum incolumi illa civitate imperioque populi Romani tollerentur.

XXXV. Etenim, ut simul Africani quoque humanitatem et aequitatem cognoscatis, oppidum Himeram Karthaginienses quondam ceperunt, quod fuerat in primis Siciliae clarum et ornatum. Scipio, qui hoc dignum populo Romano arbitraretur, bello confecto

34. *supellectilem*] 'Supellex' was frequently the matter of a legacy, and accordingly the word obtained a legal signification (Dig. 33. tit. 10, De Supellectile Legata). Paulus (s. 3) gives a list of what is included in 'supellex,' namely, 'mensae,' 'trapezophora,' 'delphica,' and many other things. But the lawyers do not seem to have been quite agreed as to the extent of the meaning of the term. Alfenus says (s. 6) "supellectilis eas res esse puto quae ad usum communem patrisfamilias paratae essent, quae nomen sui generis separatim non haberent." Alfenus was a contemporary of Cicero, though younger than Cicero. Labeo (s. 7) gives an absurd etymology of the word. The original nominative was 'supellectilis,' and the word means that which lies on the surface (super, lego), and it is the negative of that which is 'solum,' or fixed to the 'solum.' 'Lectilis,' a possible word, differs not in form from 'fictilis.' Originally, perhaps, 'supellex' denoted all the moveables; but, however this may be, it did not, in Cicero's time and later, comprehend things which were included under other names, as 'argentum,' 'vestis.'

Deliacam &c.] Bronze vessels made at Delos and at Corinth, household utensils. As to these Delian and Corinthian bronzes, see Pliny, H. N., Lib. xxxiv. c. 2, &c., ed. Hard., and Cicero, Pro Sex. Roscio, c. 46. Pliny observes, "antiquissima aeris gloria Deliaco fuit, mercatus in Delo concelebrante toto orbe, et ideo cura officinis, tricliniorum pedibus fulcrisque."

prout] This appears an odd juxtaposition of words, but it arose from an elliptical expression, 'pro eo ut.' See Lib. 3. c. 54.

angebatur] "tangebatur tamen animi dolore necessario," Orelli. Zumpt has the same, except that he has 'angebatur;' but in his Appendix he approves of the omission of 'tamen' and 'dolore.' The reading in the text is that of M V.

35. *ceperunt,*] 'ceperant,' Iordan.

arbitraretur,] Zumpt has 'arbitrabatur,' from a single MS. Lg. 42. He says,

socios sua per nostram victoriam recuperare, Siculis omnibus Karthagine capta quae potuit restituenda curavit. Himera deleta, quos cives belli calamitas reliquos fecerat, ii se Thermis collocarant in isdem agri finibus neque longe ab oppido antiquo. Hi se patrum fortunas ac dignitatem recuperare arbitrabantur, quum illa majorum ornamenta in eorum oppido collocabantur. Erant signa ex aere complura, in his eximia pulchritudine ipsa Himera in muliebrem figuram habitumque formata ex oppidi nomine et fluminis. Erat etiam Stesichori poëtae statua senilis, incurva, cum libro, summo,

"neque interest, quomodo dicatur, utrum de Scipionis voluntate an simpliciter narrandi causa;" which does not seem a clear form of expression, though the meaning may be right.

Himera deleta,] Himera, on the north coast of Sicily, near the mouth of the river Himera, was founded by Chalcidians from Zancle or Messana (B.C. 649). But geographers are not agreed about the site of this ancient city. Probably about B.C. 476, after a great civil commotion, it received a large accession of citizens, Dorians and others, from Theron, tyrant of Acragas (Agrigentum), and became a very flourishing place. In B.C. 408 it was destroyed by the Carthaginians, and never rebuilt (Diodorus, xi. 49). After the destruction of the city, the Carthaginians founded a new city at the hot springs (Thermae) in the neighbourhood, on the east side of the river; but the name of the former city was also retained, for the place was called Thermae Himeraeae (Polyb. i. 24). There is also an inscription: HIMERAEORVM THERMIT. The figure of a female, the symbol of Himera, appears on some of the coins of this city. A coin of the Principe of Torremuzza exhibits on one side Himera, the goddess of the river and the city, with a veil on the back part of the head, and with a mural crown; behind the head is a cornucopia. On the other side is the bald-headed, stooping old man, Stesichorus, resting on a strong staff, and reading in a roll. The inscription is ΘΕΡΜΙΤΩΝ ΙΜΕΡΑΙΩΝ. Visconti, Iconographie Grecque, quoted by Creuzer and Moser. Garatoni, quoted by Iordan, refers to Castelli, Num. Sic. p. 33, and adds a remark useful for those to whom it is new: "Nam typi numismatum statuas imitabantur, si quae in urbibus essent artificio praestantes, tum conditorum, tum civium clarorum, tum deorum et fluminum, quorum omnium effigies placebat insculpere." The modern name of Thermae is Termini. "The chalybeate sulphureous spring raises Fahrenheit's thermometer to 121°." Smyth's Sicily, p. 95.

eximia pulchritudine] Orelli has 'mira pulchritudine.' V has 'pulcritudine,' but in the preceding chapter 'pulcherrima.' This is probably one of the numerous words, the orthography of which was unsettled in Cicero's time, as appears from the passage Orat. c. 48: "Quin ego ipse quum scirem ita majores locutos esse ut nusquam nisi in vocali adspiratione uterentur, loquebar sic, ut *pulcros, Cetegos, triumpos, Cartaginem* dicerem: aliquando idque sero convicio aurium quum extorta mihi veritas esset, usum loquendi populo concessi, scientiam mihi reservavi."

Stesichori] One of the oldest Greek lyric poets, was born some time in the seventh century B.C., in Sicily, but the place of his birth is not stated. Stesichorus lived at Himera some part of his life, as Cicero says, and Pausanias (iii. 19): but it is uncertain if it was his birthplace.

The words 'ab eo' make a difficulty. It is clear, as Klotz observes, that they are not to be connected with 'facta,' for 'qui fuit' undoubtedly refers to Stesichorus. Cicero means to connect Stesichorus with Himera in some way, but there is probably some corruption in the text. Klotz finds no difficulty in explaining 'ab eo:' "Cicero says, according to a Latin form of expression, used in common life, the more particular explanation of which we naturally cannot here enter upon—I mean that Stesichorus who resided at Himera," &c. Zumpt omits the words 'ab eo,' though it seems that the MSS., except N φ, have them. There seems no way of explaining 'ab eo.' The attempt of Klotz is ridiculous. The words 'qui fuit' seem in themselves insufficient; we want something more positive; and this which is wanted seems to lie in the corrupted words 'ab eo.' But if we observe that 'qui fuit Himerae' may be connected

ut putant, artificio facta; [ab eo] qui fuit Himerae, sed et est et fuit tota Graecia summo propter ingenium honore et nomine. Haec iste ad insaniam concupiverat. Etiam, quod paene praeterii, capella quaedam est, ea quidem mire—ut etiam nos qui rudes harum rerum sumus intelligere possimus—scite facta et venuste. Haec et alia Scipio non negligenter abjecerat ut homo intelligens Verres auferre posset, sed Thermitanis restituerat: non quo ipse hortos aut suburbanum aut locum omnino ubi ea poneret nullum haberet; sed quod, si domum abstulisset, non diu Scipionis appellarentur sed eorum ad quoscunque illius morte venissent: nunc iis locis posita sunt ut mihi semper Scipionis fore videantur itaque dicantur.

XXXVI. Haec quum iste posceret agereturque ea res in senatu, Sthenius vehementissime restitit, multaque, ut in primis Siculorum in dicendo copiosus est, commemoravit: urbem relinquere Thermitanos esse honestius quam pati tolli ex urbe monumenta majorum, spolia hostium, beneficia clarissimi viri, indicia societatis populi Romani atque amicitiae. Commoti animi sunt omnium: repertus est nemo quin mori diceret satius esse. Itaque hoc adhuc oppidum Verres invenit prope solum in orbe terrarum, unde nihil ejusmodi rerum de publico per vim, nihil occulte, nihil imperio, nihil gratia, nihil precario posset auferre. Verumtamen

with 'summo . . . nomine,' we have only to consider the words interposed as a rapid parenthesis. Rau suggests 'Himerâ,' a good suggestion. See Caesar, B. G. iii. 20. Bake suggests 'qui fuit Himeraeus,' also a good suggestion. But though both are good, Cicero may not have written either.

intelligere possimus] This is Zumpt's reading, who has no note on it; and it is affirmed (Creuzer and Moser) that there is not a single MS. authority in favour of it: but still I keep it. Klotz, Orelli, and Iordan have 'possumus,' though the sense requires 'possimus,' and indeed Halm says that all the Lgg. have 'possimus' except 6, 29, 48. The expression 'mire—scite facta et venuste' has also caused difficulty. But there is none. Cicero stops at 'mire' and introduces a passing remark, and then he resumes by a word, which is not a repetition of 'mire,' but apt enough for the purpose.

sed quod, si] Orelli and Klotz omit 'quod,' which is only in Lg. 42 N φ, but even one MS. is enough, when it supplies what is wanted.

36. *Thermitanos*] 'Thermitanis' Zumpt, Iordan, from Lg. 42 p. m. and φ, a reading to which there is no objection.

quin mori] 'qui non modo' Lg. 42 p. m.; whence Halm suggests that the original had 'qui non mori,' which is an ingenious remark. 'Qui non' would be much more forcible.

nihil precario] Zumpt, Orelli, and Iordan have 'nihil pretio.' Klotz has 'nihil precario' from Lg. 42, 3 codd. Lbi, cod. Hot., and there is some reason for preferring it. Verres wished to get the statues into his possession, but not by purchase. Cicero adds that he found he could not do it either by force, by stealth, or by entreaty in the way of 'precario.' The passage seems to be an allusion to the three 'vitia possessionis,' or wrongful modes of obtaining possession, as in Pro Caecina, c. 32, 'ut nec vi nec clam nec precario possederit;' and Terence, Eunuch. ii. 3. 27, 'hanc tu mihi vel vi vel clam vel precario fac tradas.' Ulpian says (Dig. 43. 26. 1), "habere precario videtur qui possessionem vel corporis vel juris adeptus est ex hac solummodo causa, quod preces adhibuit et impetravit ut sibi possidere aut uti liceat." See Savigny, Das Recht des Besitzes, Interdictum de precario.

hasce ejus cupiditates exponam alio loco: nunc ad Sthenium revertar. Iratus iste vehementer Sthenio et incensus hospitium ei renuntiat: domo ejus [e]migrat atque adeo exit: nam jam ante migrarat. Eum autem inimicissimi Sthenii domum suam statim invitant ut animum ejus in Sthenium inflammarent ementiendo aliquid et criminando. Hi autem erant inimici Agathinus, homo nobilis, et Dorotheus, qui habebat in matrimonio Callidamam, Agathini ejus filiam de qua iste audierat. Itaque ad generum Agathini migrare maluit. Una nox intercesserat quum iste Dorotheum sic diligebat ut diceres omnia inter eos esse communia; Agathinum ita observabat ut aliquem affinem ac propinquum. Contemnere etiam signum illud Himerae jam videbatur, quod eum multo magis figura et lineamenta hospitae delectabant.

XXXVII. Itaque hortari homines coepit ut aliquid Sthenio periculi crearent criminisque confingerent. Dicebant se illi nihil habere quod dicerent. Tum iste his aperte ostendit et confirmavit eos in Sthenium quidquid vellent simul atque ad se detulissent probaturos. Itaque illi non procrastinant: Sthenium statim educunt: aiunt ab eo literas publicas esse corruptas. Sthenius postulat ut—quum secum sui cives agant de literis publicis corruptis, ejusque rei legibus Thermitanorum actio sit; senatusque et populus Romanus Thermitanis, quod semper in amicitia fideque mansissent, urbem, agros, legesque suas reddidisset, Publiusque Rupilius postea leges ita Siculis ex senatus consulto de decem legatorum sententia dedisset ut cives inter sese legibus suis agerent; idemque hoc haberet Verres ipse in edicto—ut de his omnibus causis se

[e]migrat &c.] Cicero corrects the expression '[e]migrat' by the words 'adeo exit.' "Verres moves off from his house with bag and baggage, or rather simply quits it, for he had moved off all his baggage, his plunder, before." Garatoni explains 'migrare' to signify a man's sending his goods from a house which he is going to quit to another house which he is going to inhabit, and this is called 'migrare,' though the man has not yet quitted the house which he intends to leave. Perhaps 'emigrat' ought to be 'migrat,' as in Lg. 42 p. m., for the difference is made by the tense of the verb, and not by the preposition in 'emigrat.' Iordan writes 'emigrat . . . emigrarat.' It is plain that we should read either 'emigrat . . emigrarat,' or 'migrat . . migrarat.' Lg. 42 has 'emigrarat.'

omnia . . communia;] This means more than it seems. It was a complete partnership between Verres and the man. They had put all in a common stock.

affinem &c.] The insinuation is that Verres lay with Callidama, and accordingly looked on her father as an 'affinis,' as if he had become his daughter's husband. Comp. c. 14.

37. *ostendit et confirmavit*] The reading of this passage is doubtful. It stands thus in Klotz: 'tum iste his aperte ostendit et confirmavit eos: in Sthenium quidquid vellent dicerent: simul atque ad se detulissent, probaturos;' which I do not believe to be the genuine text. The word 'dicerent' is not in Lg. 42 F M.

ejusque rei] Half a dozen of the older editors have 'ejusce' for 'ejusque,' and this false reading is in M. Zumpt correctly remarks of 'ejusce'—"verbum ipsum nullum est, nec possis h. l. copula egere."

haberet] So in Lg. 42. Orelli and Klotz have 'habuerit,' which is wrong.

ad leges rejiceret. Iste, homo omnium aequissimus atque a cupiditate remotissimus, se cogniturum esse confirmat: paratum ad causam dicendam venire hora VIIII jubet. Non erat obscurum quid homo improbus ac nefarius cogitaret: neque enim ipse satis occultarat nec mulier tacere potuerat. Intellectum est id istum agere ut, quum Sthenium sine ullo argumento ac sine teste damnasset, tum homo nefarius de homine nobili atque id aetatis suoque hospite virgis supplicium crudelissime sumeret. Quod quum esset perspicuum, de amicorum hospitumque suorum sententia Thermis Sthenius Romam profugit: hiemi sese fluctibusque committere maluit quam non istam communem Siculorum tempestatem calamitatemque vitare.

XXXVIII. Iste homo certus et diligens ad horam VIIII praesto est: Sthenium citari jubet. Quem posteaquam videt non adesse, dolore ardere atque iracundia furere coepit: Venereos domum Sthenii mittere, equis circum agros ejus villasque dimittere. Itaque dum exspectat quidnam sibi certi afferatur, ante horam tertiam noctis de foro non discedit. Postridie mane descendit: Agathinum ad se vocat: jubet eum de literis publicis in absentem Sthenium dicere. Erat ejusmodi causa ut ille ne sine adversario quidem apud inimicum judicem reperire posset quid diceret. Itaque tantum verbo posuit Sacerdote praetore Sthenium literas publicas corrupisse. Vix ille hoc dixerat quum iste pronuntiat, 'Sthenium literas publicas corrupisse videri:' et hoc praeterea addit homo Venereus,

ad leges rejiceret.] Sthenius claimed to be tried by the 'leges' of his own city, which Cicero expresses by a usual formula: he called on Verres to bring the matter to issue in the way provided by law, to refer (rejicere) the decision to a properly constituted court.

a cupiditate] 'a cupiditate omnium remotissimus' Klotz. In place of 'omnium' we may read 'omni,' with Lg. 29 A.

sine ullo argumento] 'nulla ratione, nulla causa,' says P. Manutius, and he compares c. 45, "Quid tandem habuit argumenti," &c. The translation of 'argumentum' by 'argument' will not always do. The use of the word in Lib. 4. c. 56, 'ex ebore . . perfecta argumenta,' is worth notice.

id aetatis] See c. 14, and Act. ii. Lib. 1. c. 26. 'Id temporis' occurs in the next chapter. Comp. Pro Cluentio, c. 51; Ter. Haut. i. 1. 58.

38. *Venereos*] These Venerei were 'viatores' and 'apparitores.'—'equis circum agros,' &c., 'on horseback he sends them in various directions.' The MSS., except Lg. 42 p. m. M, and Orelli have 'equites circum,' &c.

corrupisse videri:] Klotz refers to a note of Hotmann on this word 'videri.' Hotmann refers to Cicero, Academ. ii. 47, "quaeque jurati judices cognovissent, ea non ut esse facta, sed ut videri pronuntiarent." See also In Pisonem, c. 40, 'Fecisse videri.' The form, then, in which the 'judex' pronounced his judgment, and the 'praetor' also, as it appears from this passage, was not 'Fecit,' but 'Fecisse videtur.' The Roman jurists, in giving their 'responsa,' used the word 'videtur,' as in Dig. 15. 3. 16. It was not the Roman fashion either for 'judex' or jurist to pronounce absolutely, but to express opinion; not that the opinion was doubtful, but it was a form of expression considered more suitable to the fallibility of human judgment. It appears from the passage of the 'Academica' just referred to, that a wit-

novo modo, nullo exemplo, 'ob eam rem HS ıɔ Veneri Erycinae de Sthenii bonis exacturum;' bonaque ejus statim coepit vendere, et vendidisset, si tantulum morae fuisset quo minus ei pecunia illa numeraretur. Ea posteaquam numerata est, contentus hac iniquitate iste non fuit: palam de sella ac tribunali pronuntiat, Si quis absentem Sthenium rei capitalis reum facere vellet, sese ejus nomen recepturum:—et simul ut ad causam accederet nomenque deferret Agathinum novum affinem atque hospitem coepit hortari. Tum ille clare omnibus audientibus se id non esse facturum, neque se usque eo Sthenio esse inimicum ut eum rei capitalis affinem esse diceret. Hic tum repente Pacilius quidam homo egens et levis accedit: ait, si liceret, nomen absentis deferre se velle. Iste vero et licere et fieri solere et se recepturum: itaque defertur. Edicit statim ut Kalendis Decembr. adsit Sthenius Syracusis. Hic, qui Romam pervenisset, satisque feliciter anni jam adverso tempore navigasset, omniaque habuisset aequiora et placabiliora quam animum praetoris atque hospitis, rem ad amicos suos detulit; quae, ut erat acerba et indigna, sic videbatur omnibus.

XXXIX. Itaque in senatu continuo Cn. Lentulus et L. Gellius consules faciunt mentionem placere statui, si patribus conscriptis videretur, Ne absentes homines in provinciis rei fierent rerum capitalium. Causam Sthenii totam et istius crudelitatem et iniquitatem senatum docent. Aderat in senatu Verres pater istius, et flens unumquemque senatorem rogabat ut filio suo parceret; neque tamen multum proficiebat: erat enim summa voluntas senatus. Itaque sententiae dicebantur, Quum Sthenius absens reus factus esset, de absente judicium nullum fieri placere, et si quod esset

ness did not affirm absolutely, but used the word 'arbitrari.' Klotz refers also to the oration Pro M. Fonteio, c. 13, "qui primum illud verbum consideratissimum nostrae consuetudinis, Arbitror, quo nos etiam tunc utimur quum ea dicimus jurati quae comperta habemus, quae ipsi vidimus, ex toto testimonio suo sustulit atque omnia se scire dixit." Comp. also Pro A. Caecina, c. 25, and the use of 'videbatur' at the end of this chapter, and 'videretur' in the following chapter.

HS ıɔ] The common reading is 'HS quingenties,' for which Zumpt substituted what stands in the text, 'quingenties' being manifestly too large a sum. Hotmann's conjecture is 'quingenta,' i.e. 'millia,' and so Zumpt intends his symbols to be read, but he preferred giving the symbols, in order that the origin of the corruption may appear.

rei capitalis affinem] 'Affinis' here means 'guilty of,' 'implicated.' Some of the critics have laboured to show that 'affinem' is a blunder in the MSS., but their labour is unnecessary. See In Cat. iv. 3; Pro Tullio, c. 5; Pro Sex. Rosc. Am. c. 7; Pro Cluentio, c. 45; Ter. Haut. i. 3. 1.

quae, ut erat &c.] Orelli has 'erant,' 'videbantur.'

39. *summa voluntas*] This expression means 'hearty good-will or mind towards a purpose,' which, in this case, was to rescind the act of Verres. Hotmann [illegible] another expression of Cicero, '[illegible] accusatoris voluntate.'

factum id ratum esse non placere.—Eo die transigi nihil potuit, quod et id temporis erat, et ille pater istius invenerat homines qui dicendo tempus consumerent. Postea senex Verres defensores atque hospites omnes Sthenii convenit: rogat eos atque orat ne oppugnent filium suum; de Sthenio ne laborent; confirmat his curaturum se esse ne quid ei per filium suum noceretur; se homines certos ejus rei causa in Siciliam [et] terra et mari esse missurum. Et erat spatium dierum fere triginta ante Kalendas Decembr. quo die iste ut Syracusis Sthenius adesset edixerat. Commoventur amici Sthenii; sperant fore ut patris literis nuntiisque filius ab illo furore revocetur. In senatu postea causa non agitur. Veniunt ad istum domestici nuntii, literasque a patre afferunt ante Kalendas Decembres, quum isti etiam tum de Sthenio in integro tota res esset: eodemque [ei] tempore de eadem re literae complures a multis ejus amicis ac necessariis afferuntur.

XL. Hic iste, qui prae cupiditate neque officii sui neque periculi neque pietatis neque humanitatis rationem habuisset unquam, neque in eo quod monebatur auctoritatem patris, neque in eo quod rogabatur voluntatem anteponendam putavit libidini suae, mane Kalendis Decembribus, ut edixerat, Sthenium citari jubet. Si abs te istam rem parens tuus alicujus amici rogatu benignitate aut ambitione adductus petisset, gravissima tamen apud te voluntas patris esse debuisset: quum vero abs te tui capitis causa peteret, hominesque certos domo misisset, hique eo tempore ad te venissent quum tibi in integro tota res esset, ne tum quidem te potuit, si non pietatis, at salutis tuae ratio ad officium sanitatemque reducere? Citat reum: non respondit. Citat accusatorem. Attendite, quaeso,

id temporis] 'so late in the day.' Ernesti misunderstood it. The senate did not sit after sunset, or, at least, did not come to any formal resolution after sunset, as a general rule.

homines certos] 'Certus,' the same as 'cretus,' 'separated,' 'determined,' and so forth, means also 'trusty,' as Ad Att. v. 21. 6; Pro Sex. Rosc. Am. c. 19; Pro P. Quintio, c. 3. Sometimes 'certus' seems to mean the same as 'quidam,' as in Brutus, c. 16; and perhaps Gaius, ii. 152.—'ab illo furore:' all the Lgg. have 'ab incepto furore,' and it is the reading of some other MSS. too.

in integro] 'integra' Orelli, for which also there is good authority. But see the next chapter, and Livy iii. 10.

40. *rogatu benignitate &c.*] Cicero supposes three motives or inducements, the request of a friend, good intention, or a desire to get good-will or good opinion. The word 'ambitio,' which had the original signification of going about, came to signify means of conciliating opinion, popularity, and so forth. A word of the same origin, 'ambitus,' was used to signify the legal offence of getting votes by bribery and improper means. Comp. the use of 'ambitio' in c. 55, and in the letter Ad Q. Fr. i. 1. c. 3.

tui capitis causa] 'out of regard to your own personal interest and danger;' for the acts of Verres made him liable to a prosecution in which his 'caput' or civil 'status' was in peril, not his life. In this chapter Cicero uses the expression 'cum periculo capitis,' at the risk or hazard of life, in a different and not in a technical sense.

judices, quanto opere istius amentiae fortuna ipsa adversata sit, et simul videte qui Sthenii causam casus adjuverit. Citatus accusator M. Pacilius nescio quo casu non respondit; non affuit. Si praesens Sthenius reus esset factus, si manifesto in maleficio teneretur, tamen, quum accusator non adesset, Sthenium condemnari non oporteret. Etenim, si posset reus absente accusatore condemnari, non ego a Vibone Veliam parvulo navigio inter fugitivorum ac praedonum ac tua tela venissem; quo tempore omnis illa mea festinatio fuit cum periculo capitis ob eam causam ne tu ex reis eximerere, si ego ad diem non affuissem. Quod igitur tibi erat in tuo judicio optatissimum, me quum citatus essem non adesse, cur Sthenio non putasti prodesse oportere, quum ejus accusator non affuisset? Ita fecit ut exitus principio simillimus reperiretur: quem absentem reum fecerat, eum absente accusatore condemnat.

XLI. Nuntiabatur illi primis illis temporibus, id quod pater quoque ad eum pluribus verbis scripserat, agitatam rem esse in senatu: etiam in contione tribunum plebis de causa Sthenii M. Palicanum esse questum: postremo me ipsum apud hoc collegium tribunorum plebis, quum eorum omnium edicto non liceret Romae quemquam esse qui rei capitalis condemnatus esset, egisse causam Sthenii: et quum rem ita exposuissem quemadmodum nunc apud vos, docuissemque hanc damnationem duci non oportere, x tribunos plebis hoc statuisse idque de omnium sententia pronuntiatum esse, Non videri Sthenium impediri edicto quo minus ei liceret Romae esse.— Quum haec ad istum afferrentur, pertimuit aliquando et commotus est: vertit stilum in tabulis suis, quo facto causam omnem evertit suam. Nihil enim sibi reliqui fecit quod defendi aliqua ratione

Vibone &c.] The orator is alluding to his return from Sicily, and says that he went in a small vessel from Vibo (Monte Leone) to Velia (Castellamare della Bruca), and ran the risk of being captured by pirates, or assassinated by the emissaries of Verres.

41. *primis illis*] Within the time immediately after the condemnation of Sthenius; like 'paucis illis diebus,' c. 26.—'in contione,' with *t*, 'omnes Lagom.' (Zumpt.) But Lg. 42 p. m. omits 'in.'

edicto non liceret] It appears that the 'tribuni plebis' had the power of making 'edicta' or general orders, as the Praetors and the Aediles Curules had in their several jurisdictions. Cicero here represents himself as defending the cause of Sthenius before the 'collegium' or body of 'tribunes,' which shows that they held a court for matters within their jurisdiction, which were either cases of appeal, or cases in which they had original jurisdiction.

damnationem duci] 'that Sthenius should not be considered as condemned,' says Hotmann, and this seems to be the meaning. See Lib. 5. c. 55, and Caesar, B. G. iv. 30.

vertit stilum] Verres erased with the upper or flat end of the 'stilus' what he had written with the lower or pointed end on his 'tabulae.' "Tollit ex tabulis id quod erat: facit coram esse delatum." Horace has the expression, "Saepe stilum vertas iterum quae digna legi sunt Scripturus" (Hor. 1 Sat. x. 72). There is obviously a play on the words 'vertit' and 'evertit.'

posset. Nam si ita defenderet: recepi nomen absentis; licet hoc fieri in provincia; nulla lex vetat; mala et improba defensione verum aliqua tamen uti videretur. Postremo illo desperatissimo perfugio uti posset, se imprudentem fecisse, existimasse id licere: quamquam haec perditissima defensio est, tamen aliquid dici videretur. Tollit ex tabulis id quod erat, [et] facit coram esse delatum.

XLII. Hic videte in quot se laqueos induerit, quorum ex nullo se unquam expediret. Primum ipse in Sicilia saepe et palam de loco superiore dixerat et in sermone multis idem demonstrarat, licere nomen recipere absentis: se exemplo multorum fecisse quod fecisset. Haec cum dictitasse priore actione et Sex. Pompeius Chlorus dixit, de cujus virtute antea commemoravi, et Cn. Pompeius Theodorus, homo et Cn. Pompeii clarissimi viri judicio plurimis maximisque in rebus probatissimus et omnium existimatione ornatissimus, et Posides Macro Soluntinus, homo summa nobilitate, existimatione, virtute: et hac actione quam voletis multi dicent, et qui ex isto ipso audierunt, viri primarii nostri ordinis, et alii qui interfuerunt quum absentis nomen reciperetur. Deinde Romae, quum haec acta res esset in senatu, omnes istius amici, in his etiam pater ejus hoc defendebat licere fieri; saepe esse factum; isto quod fecisset, aliorum exemplo institutoque fecisse. Dicit praeterea testimonium tota Sicilia, quae in communibus pos-

recepi . . . licet &c.] Lg. 29 V.—'recipi nomen absentis licet: hoc fieri in provincia nulla lex vetat' Iordan, who has here spoiled the text.

Postremo illo] Zumpt adds 'tamen' after 'illo,' from Lg. 42 p. m.

42. *in quot . . . induerit,*] Compare Pro Murena, c. 5, and Caesar, B. G. vii. 73.

expediret.] 'expediet' Klotz, Iordan, from V. Either reading may be explained. Lg. 29 A have 'videri expediret.'

de loco superiore] This may be either the 'rostra,' as when an orator addresses the people, or the tribunal, from which the 'magistratus' declares his will; as in Lib. 4. c. 40, 'de sella ac de loco superiore.' Creuzer and Moser refer to Cic. Ad Fam. iii. 8, 'et ex superiore et ex aequo loco.' In the senate a man spoke 'ex aequo loco.'

idem demonstrarat,] This 'idem' and 'multorum' (exemplo multorum) are from V. Iordan omits 'idem' and 'multorum.'

Soluntinus,] The form in Zumpt's text is 'Soluntinus,' which is not according to analogy, for the name of the place is Solus (Σολόεις, Σολοῦς, Σολοῦντος), like Opus, of which the Latin Ethnic name is Opuntius. From Solus we should have Soluntii. The coins of Solus have the legend Σολοντίνων. The place was on the north coast of Sicily, between Panhormus and Thermae, now Castello di Solanto.

quam voletis multi] 'as many as you please.' This form of expression must be compared with the like uses of 'quamvis.' Also Act. i. c. 8, 'quantam vellent pecuniam;' Lib. 2. c. 58, 'quam volent magnas;' and c. 62, 'quem voles eorum.'—'isto ipso:' 'ipso' om. V.

audierunt . . . interfuerunt] The common reading is 'audierint . . interfuerint.' Zumpt adds "sed ejus conjunctivi vereor ut quis rationem reddere possit, immo si verus esset, oratoris de ea re certitudinem minuere videretur." This points to the true reason for the indicative. Cicero means to make a substantive affirmation. V has 'audierunt.'

tulatis civitatum omnium consulibus edidit, Rogare atquo orare patres conscriptos, ut statuerent ne absentium nomina reciperentur. Qua de re Cn. Lentulum, patronum Siciliae, clarissimum adolescentem, dicere audistis Siculos, quum se causam quae sibi in senatu pro his agenda esset docerent, de Sthenii calamitate questos esse, propterque hanc injuriam quae Sthenio facta esset cos statuisse, ut hoc quod dico postularetur. Quae quum ita essent, tantane amentia praeditus atque audacia fuisti ut in re tam clara, tam testata, tam abs te ipso promulgata, tabulas publicas corrumpere auderes? At quemadmodum corrupisti? nonne ita ut omnibus nobis tacentibus ipsae te tuae tabulae condemnare possent? Cedo, quaeso, codicem: circumfer, ostende. Videtisne hoc totum nomen, coram ubi facit delatum, esse in litura? Quid fuit istic antea scriptum? quod mendum ista litura correxit? Quid a nobis, judices, exspectatis argumenta hujus criminis? Nihil dicimus: tabulae sunt in medio quae se corruptas atque interlitas esse clamant. Ex his etiam tu rebus effugere te posse confidis, quum te nos non opinione dubia sed tuis vestigiis persequamur, quae tu in tabulis publicis expressa ac recentia reliquisti? Is mihi etiam Sthenium literas publicas corrupisse causa incognita judicavit, qui defendere non potuerit se non ex ipsius Sthenii nomine literas publicas corrupisse?

XLIII. Videte porro aliam amentiam: videte ut, dum expedire sese vult, induat. Cognitorem adscribit Sthenio—quem? cognatum

promulgata,] The MSS. have 'pervagata,' except Lg. 42 p. m., which has 'promulgata.' The corruption of 'promulgata' into 'pervulgata,' which Orelli and Iordan have, is very simple. As to 'promulgare,' see c. 71. The word here refers to what Verres had declared, 'saepe et palam de loco superiore.'

Cedo, quaeso, &c.] 'Give me, I pray, the codex.' This word occurs only in the form 'cedo' and the plural 'cette.' 'Cedo' has also the sense of 'dic,' as in c. 43. Cicero addresses some officer of the court in the same manner as the Greek orators often call for the production of some documentary evidence. Demosth. *περὶ παραπρεσβείας*, c. 10: *καί μοι λέγε τὸ ψήφισμα καὶ τὰ γράμματα καὶ τοὺς μάρτυρας κάλει.*

Is mihi etiam Sthenium] As to the position of 'is' and 'mihi,' and the meaning of the sentence, compare Lib. 1. c. 60, 'Is mihi queritur;' and Lib. 2. c. 32. Hotmann injudiciously proposed 'judicabit' in place of 'judicavit.' Zumpt translates the passage thus: "und der hat mir noch einen andern verurtheilt, der sich jetzt selbst nicht hat rechtfertigen können." The English language can no more express the German 'mir' than the Latin 'mihi,' except by several words.

potuerit] 'potuit' Lg. 42 φ Grut. (ex M ?) Iordan.

43. *amentiam:*] The reading of the better MSS. Orelli has 'dementiam.' Zumpt says, "*dementia* mentis repentina perturbatio est, *amentia* perpetua hebetudo et stultitia." These attempts to distinguish Latin words which are near akin are often unsuccessful; and perhaps we attempt sometimes to make distinctions where the Romans themselves would not have found it easy to do so. The law writers sometimes use 'demens' as equivalent to 'furiosus' (Dig. 27. 10. 7), which is the technical term in the Twelve Tables for a person of unsound mind.

Cognitorem adscribit] Verres made an entry in the 'tabulae,' among other false

aliquem aut propinquum? Non. Thermitanum aliquem, honestum hominem ac nobilem? Ne id quidem. At Siculum in quo aliquis splendor dignitasque esset? Neminem. Quid igitur? Civem Romanum. Cui hoc probari potest? Quum esset Sthenius civitatis suae nobilissimus, amplissima cognatione, plurimis amicitiis; quum praeterea tota Sicilia multum auctoritate et gratia posset; invenire neminem Siculum potuit qui pro se cognitor fieret? hoc probabis? An ipse civem Romanum maluit? Cedo, cui Siculo, quum is reus fieret, civis Romanus cognitor factus unquam sit. Omnium praetorum literas qui ante te fuerunt profer, explica: si unum inveneris, ego hoc tibi quemadmodum in tabulis scriptum habes, ita gestum esse concedam. At, credo, Sthenius hoc sibi amplum putavit, eligere e civium Romanorum numero, ex amicorum atque hospitum suorum copia, quem cognitorem daret. Quem delegit? quis in tabulis scriptus est? C. Claudius C. F. Palatina. Non quaero, quis hic sit Claudius, quam splendidus, quam honestus, quam idoneus propter cujus auctoritatem et dignitatem Sthenius ab omnium Siculorum consuetudine discederet et civem Romanum cognitorem daret. Nihil horum quaero. Fortasse enim Sthenius non splendorem hominis sed familiaritatem secutus est. Quid si omnium mortalium nemo Sthenio inimicior quam hic C. Claudius quum semper tum in his ipsis rebus et temporibus fuit, si de literis corruptis contra venit, si contra omni ratione pugnavit, utrum potius pro Sthenio inimicum cognitorem esse factum an te ad Sthenii periculum inimici ejus nomine abusum esse credemus?

entries, after the erasure above mentioned, that he had named a 'cognitor' or attorney to represent Sthenius in his absence. See Divin. 4, 'cognitorem.'

Neminem. Quid igitur?] 'Minime. Quid igitur?' is the common reading; but there is better authority for 'Neminem.'

probabis?] This is clearly the true reading, and not 'probabitis.' 'Probare' means not only to 'approve,' as we say, but to 'prove,' to 'make people accept and believe.' See the use of 'probabilis' Div. c. 20.—'gestum esse concedo' Zumpt.

Palatina.] C. Claudius, Caii Filius, Palatina. The last word is in the ablative case, and is equivalent to 'ex tribu Palatina.' The letters C. F. are the usual Roman form of abbreviation in inscriptions, and in formally describing a person.

contra venit,] This is a judicial expression, as Manutius observes, and he gives other instances. Comp. Pro Q. Rosc. c. 6, "Quid tu, Saturi, qui contra hunc venis, existimas aliter?" and Phil. ii. c. 2. This C. Claudius 'contra venit;' he was the enemy of Sthenius in the matter of the 'literae corruptae,' with which Sthenius was charged.

utrum potius &c.] If all this is so, 'which must we rather believe, that the enemy of Sthenius was made his cognitor, or that you, in the record of his condemnation, falsely inserted the name of his enemy?' Either conclusion is against Verres: we must either believe that the enemy of Sthenius was made his 'cognitor,' or that Verres falsely recorded him as such. Zumpt and Klotz explain 'periculum' in this passage, following Ernesti, to be the record or the register of the fact of condemnation; and they compare the use of 'pericula' in Lib. 3. c. 79, "tabulae publicae periculaque magistratuum." Klotz also refers to Cujas on the Cod. Theod. 7. tit. 44, 'De sententiis ex periculo recitandis.' The common reading is 'in Sthenii periculo.'

XLIV. Ac ne quis forte dubitet cujusmodi hoc totum sit negotium, tametsi jamdudum omnibus istius improbitatem perspicuam esse confido, tamen paulum etiam attendite. Videtis illum subcrispo capillo, nigrum, qui eo vultu nos intuetur ut sibi ipsi peracutus esse videatur, qui tabulas tenet, qui scribit, qui monet, qui proximus est? Is est C. Claudius, qui in Sicilia sequester istius, interpres, confector negotiorum, prope collega Timarchidi numerabatur, nunc obtinet eum locum ut vix Apronio illi de familiaritate concedere videatur, et qui se non Timarchidi sed ipsius Verris collegam et socium esse dicebat. Dubitate etiam, si potestis, quin eum iste potissimum ex omni numero delegerit cui hanc cognitoris falsi improbam personam imponeret, quem et huic inimicissimum et sibi amicissimum esse arbitraretur. Hic vos dubitabitis, judices, tantam istius audaciam, tantam crudelitatem, tantam injuriam vindicare? dubitabitis exemplum judicum illorum sequi qui damnato Cn. Dolabella damnationem Philodami Opuntii resciderunt, quod is non absens reus factus esset, quae res iniquissima atque acerbissima est, sed quum ei legatio jam Romam a suis civibus esset data? Quod illi judices multo in leviore causa statuerunt aequitatem secuti, vos id statuere in gravissima causa praesertim aliorum auctoritate jam confirmatum dubitabitis?

XLV. At quem hominem, C. Verres, tanta, tam insigni injuria affecisti? quem hominem absentem de literis corruptis causa incognita condemnasti? cujus absentis nomen recepisti? quem absentem non modo sine crimine et sine teste verum etiam sine accusatore damnasti? Quem hominem? dii immortales! non dicam amicum tuum, quod apud homines carissimum est, non hospitem, quod sanctissimum est; nihil enim minus libenter de Sthenio comme-

44. *Timarchidi numerabatur, &c.*] 'Timarchidi' is intended for the genitive. See c. 54. Zumpt observes that Garatoni proposes to write 'socium esse dicit,' which shows that he mistook the meaning. Claudius was reckoned (numerabatur) almost a colleague of Timarchides, but he used to call himself a colleague of Verres.

legatio jam Romam] The ambassador or 'legatus' in this case was not absent when he was prosecuted; for, if he had been, his case would have been the same as that of Sthenius; but he had received his commission of ambassador, and during the time of his holding this function he enjoyed protection, even though he had not left his city for Rome. It was a general rule of Roman law that no man could be prosecuted while he was absent on business of the state; to confirm which Klotz refers to Dig. 48. 2. 12. The rule of Roman law, it appears, was applied to the city of Opus.

45. *At quem hominem,*] This is a favourite formula with Cicero (Pro Fonteio, c. 17), for which he had the example of Terence:

> "At quem virum? quem ego optimum in vita viderim."—Phorm. iii. 2. 20.

The ? in this case is of no use.

The words 'quem hominem . . . condemnasti?' are omitted by Orelli, Zumpt, and Iordan. Klotz has admitted them on the authority of Lg. 42 F. Comp. c. 37, 38.

moro, nihil aliud in eo quod reprehendi possit invenio, nisi quod homo frugalissimus atque integerrimus te hominem plenum stupri, flagitii, sceleris, domum suam invitavit, nisi quod, qui C. Marii, Cn. Pompeii, C. Marcelli, L. Sisennae, tui defensoris, ceterorum virorum fortissimorum hospes fuisset atque esset, ad eum numerum clarissimorum hominum tuum quoque nomen adscripsit. Quare de hospitio violato et de tuo isto nefario scelere nihil queror: hoc dico, non iis qui Sthenium norunt, hoc est, nemini eorum qui in Sicilia fuerunt: nemo enim ignorat quo hic in civitate sua splendore, qua apud omnes Siculos dignitate atque existimatione sit: sed ut illi quoque qui in ea provincia non fuerunt intelligere possint, in quo homine [tu] statueris exemplum ejusmodi, quod quum propter iniquitatem rei, tum etiam propter hominis dignitatem, acerbum omnibus atque intolerandum videretur. XLVI. Estne Sthenius is qui omnes honores domi suae facillime quum adeptus esset, amplissime ac magnificentissime gessit? qui oppidum non maximum maximis ex pecunia sua locis communibus monumentisque decoravit? cujus de meritis in rem publicam Thermitanorum Siculosque universos fuit aenea tabula fixa Thermis in curia, in qua publice erat de hujus beneficiis scriptum et incisum; quae tabula tum imperio tuo revulsa nunc a me tamen deportata est, ut omnes hujus honores inter suos et amplitudinem possent cognoscere. Estne hic qui apud Cn. Pompeium clarissimum virum quum accusatus esset, quod propter C. Marii familiaritatem et hospitium contra rem publicam sensisse eum inimici et accusatores ejus

C. Marii, &c.] C. Marius, who was seven times consul; Cn. Pompeius Magnus, who was at this time (B.C. 70) consul; C. Marcellus, who had been 'praetor' of Sicily, and was a 'judex' at this trial; L. Cornelius Sisenna, an orator (Brutus, c. 64).

hoc dico,] 'Id quod subjungitur,' observes Manutius: 'Estne Sthenius is,' &c., c. 46.—'tu statueris:' Zumpt and Iordan omit 'tu.'

46. *Estne Sthenius is &c.*] 'Is not this the Sthenius?' &c. This is the proper translation of 'ne' thus placed with the principal verb; as in Cic. Pro Mil. c. 14, "potuitne, quum domum ac deos penates suos illo oppugnante defenderet, jure se ulcisci?" But, when 'ne' is added to a noun or particle, it is that interrogative form which implies a negative answer; as in Lib. 3. c. 77, "his civitatibus omnisne pecunia . . dissoluta est?" It is also used in sentences which express admiration or surprise, as if a thing were scarcely possible; Lib. 1. c. 18, "Apollinemne tu Delium spoliare ausus es?" (Zumpt.)

aenea tabula] His services were recorded by the order of the town (publice) on a tablet of bronze, which in Italy and Sicily was much used for public records, and for the preservation of 'leges.' The Tabula Heraclea, the fragment of the Lex Servilia, and other 'leges,' have been thus preserved. Ovid, Metam. i. 91:

——— "nec verba minacia fixo
Aere legebantur."

apud Cn. Pompeium] When Cn. Pompeius was sent into Sicily after Carbo, one of the partizans of Marius, whom he put to death. Plutarch, Pomp. c. 10.—'statueret:' the MSS. have 'statuerit,' which Ernesti altered to 'statueret,' which is consistent with 'arbitraretur.'

contra . . . sensisse] This is a usual

dicerent, quumque magis invidioso crimine quam vero arcesseretur, ita a Cn. Pompeio absolutus est ut in eo ipso judicio Pompeius hunc hospitio suo dignissimum statueret? ita porro laudatus defensusque ab omnibus Siculis ut idem Pompeius non ab homine solum sed etiam a provincia tota se hujus absolutione inire gratiam arbitraretur? Postremo estne hic qui et animum in rem publicam habuit ejusmodi et tantum auctoritate apud suos cives potuit, ut perficeret in Sicilia solus te praetore quod non modo Siculus nemo sed ne Sicilia quidem tota potuisset, ut ex oppido Thermis nullum signum, nullum ornamentum, nihil ex sacro, nihil de publico attingeres; quum praesertim et essent multa praeclara et tu omnia concupisses? Denique nunc vide quid inter te, cujus nomine apud Siculos dies festi agitantur et praeclara illa Verria celebrantur, cujus statuae Romae stant inauratae, a communi Siciliae, quemadmodum inscriptum videmus, datae; vide, inquam, quid inter te et hunc Siculum, qui abs te est patrono Siciliae condemnatus, intersit. Hunc civitates ex Sicilia permultae testimonio suo legationibusque ad eam rem missis publice laudant: te omnium Siculorum patronum una Mamertina civitas socia furtorum ac flagitiorum tuorum publice laudat; ita tamen novo more, ut legati laedant, legatio laudet; ceterae quidem civitates publice literis, legationibus, testimoniis accusant, queruntur, arguunt; si tu absolutus sis, funditus eversas se esse arbitrantur.

XLVII. Hoc de homine ac de hujus bonis etiam in Eryco monte monumentum tuorum flagitiorum, furtorum crudelitatisque posuisti, in quo Sthenii Thermitani nomen adscriptum est. Vidi argenteum Cupidinem cum lampade. Quid tandem habuit argumenti aut rationis res quamobrem in eo potissimum Sthenianum prae-

formula. It means 'to have bad sentiments towards the state,' and such as might produce corresponding acts, if the opportunity was given. The act against the state is 'contra rem publicam facere.' See Pro Milone, c. 5, vol. iv.—'crimine . . arcesseretur:' see c. 58.

animum . . . ejusmodi] Zumpt thinks that 'animum ejusmodi' for 'tali animo' is rare. He refers to 'fuit ejusmodi,' c. 57. There is nothing peculiar in this expression, which is the same as 'praerogativam . . . ejusmodi,' &c., Act. i. c. 9, 'ejusmodi literas,' Lib. 2. c. 70, and corresponding to 'ejusmodi,' there is, Lib. 2. c. 75, 'cujusmodi praedo . . fuerit;' Lib. 3. c. 74, 'frumentum ejusmodi . . ut.' A dozen other examples will easily be found in these orations, in some of which 'ejusmodi' is used alone, and in other cases followed by 'ut' or some form of 'qui.'

agitantur] 'aguntur' Lg. 42 p. m., Zumpt. He has also 'cui statuae,' with Orelli. V has 'cujus,' and Iordan.

Romae stant] 'Romae estant' V, which may indicate a reading 'extant,' as Mai has it.

legati laedant, &c.] The embassy was sent to do Verres honour, but the members of whom it was composed still complained of his robberies and acts of violence. See Lib. 4. c. 7, the case of Heius.—'se eversas funditus esse arbitrantur' is the order in V, followed by Klotz. There is no rule to determine such matters as these.

47. *potissimum*] 'Potissimum' in this

mium poneretur? utrum hoc signum cupiditatis tuae an tropaeum necessitudinis atque hospitii an amoris indicium esse voluisti? Faciunt hoc homines quos in summa nequitia non solum libido et voluptas verum etiam ipsius nequitiae fama delectat, ut multis in locis notas ac vestigia suorum flagitiorum relinqui velint. Ardebat amore illius hospitae propter quam hospitii jura violarat. Hoc non solum sciri tum verum etiam commemorari semper volebat. Itaque ex illa ipsa re quam accusante Agathino gesserat, Veneri potissimum deberi praemium statuit, quae illam totam accusationem judiciumque conflarat. Putarem te gratum in deos, si hoc donum Veneri non de Sthenii bonis dedisses sed de tuis; quod facere debuisti, praesertim quum tibi illo ipso anno a Chelidone venisset hereditas. Hic ego si hanc causam non omnium Siculorum rogatu recepissem, si hoc a me muneris non universa provincia poposcisset, si me animus atque amor in rem publicam existimatioque offensa nostri ordinis ac judiciorum non hoc facere coëgisset atque haec una causa fuisset, quod amicum atque hospitem meum Sthenium, quem ego in quaestura mea singulariter dilexissem, de quo optime existimassem, quem in provincia existimationis meae studiosissimum cupidissimumque cognossem, tam crudeliter, scelerate, nefarieque tractasses; tamen digna causa videretur cur inimicitias hominis improbissimi susciperem, ut hospitis salutem fortunasque defenderem. Fecerunt hoc multi apud majores nostros: fecit etiam nuper homo clarissimus Cn. Domitius, qui M. Silanum consularem homi-

position Creuzer and Moser take as an adjective. But it means 'in eo potissimum,' 'in that place before all others.'

sciri tum] 'scribtum' V, 'scriptum' Lg. 42 p. m. These two blunders show what kind of mistakes may be made in copying, and how we should proceed in deducing a true reading from a false reading.

Hic ego si &c.] "Apodosis non respondet principio periodi *Hic ego*, cui aptius esset 'tamen hanc causam dignam existimarem,' si orator accurate componere verba voluisset" (Zumpt). This strange misconception seems to arise solely from the practice of putting a comma after 'ego;' thus, 'hic ego, si.' I suppose that if Cicero had said, which however he would not say, 'hic si ego,' Zumpt's remark would hardly have been made. Compare Lib. 1. c. 61, where however Zumpt has 'cui nisi ego,' instead of 'cui ego nisi.' In Divin. c. 9, there is 'Eum ego si putem, &c., facile intelligo,' where 'facile intelligo' is not necessarily the form, because of the 'eum ego si.' The fact is, that 'hic ego si' is Cicero's general form of expression, and not 'hic si ego;' for, if the 'ego' is used, it ought to come either first in the sentence, or as near the beginning as the claims of another word will allow. Examples are abundant: Divin. c. 8, 'huic ego homini;' 'in quo ego quid,' &c., not 'in quo quid ego;' c. 9, 'hic ego de te;' c. 13, 'cujus ego ingenium.' Act. i. c. 7, 'quae ille si' &c., where a vicious practice places a comma after 'ille,' as if 'ille' belonged to 'dixisset,' whereas it belongs to 'noluisset.'

Creuzer and Moser fall into the same mistake as Zumpt, and Iordan also does. The pointing of Klotz shows that he understood it right.

Cn. Domitius,] See Divin. c. 20.—'Transalpini hominis' Zumpt, from Lg. 42 p. m. only; which reading we might prefer, if it were good criticism simply to take what we like best.

nem accusavit propter Aegritomari Transalpini hospitis injurias. Putarem me idoneum qui exemplum sequerer humanitatis atque officii, proponeremque spem meis hospitibus ac necessariis, quo tutiorem sese vitam meo praesidio victuros esse arbitrarentur. Quum vero in communibus injuriis totius provinciae Sthenii quoque causa contineatur, multique uno tempore a me hospites atque amici publice privatimque defendantur, profecto vereri non debeo ne quis hoc quod facio non existimet me summi officii ratione impulsum coactumque suscepisse. XLVIII. Atque ut aliquando de rebus ab isto cognitis judicatisque et de judiciis datis dicere desistamus, et, quoniam facta istius in his generibus infinita sunt, nos modum aliquem et finem orationi nostrae criminibusque faciamus, pauca ex aliis generibus sumemus.

Audistis ob jus dicendum Q. Varium dicere procuratores suos isti centum triginta millia nummum dedisse: meministis Q. Varii testimonium, remque hanc totam C. Sacerdotis hominis ornatissimi testimonio comprobari: scitis Cn. Sertium, M. Modium, equites Romanos, sexcentos praeterea cives Romanos multosque Siculos dixisse se isti pecuniam ob jus dicendum dedisse. De quo crimine quid ego disputem quum id totum positum sit in testibus? quid porro argumenter qua de re dubitare nemo possit? An hoc dubitabit quisquam omnium quin is venalem in Sicilia jurisdictionem habuerit, qui Romae totum edictum atque omnia decreta vendiderit, et quin is ab Siculis ob decreta interponenda pecunias ceperit, qui M. Octavium Ligurem pecuniam ob jus dicendum poposcerit? Quod enim iste praeterea genus pecuniae cogendae praeteriit? quod non ab omnibus aliis praeteritum excogitavit? Ecqua res apud civitates Siculas expetitur in qua aut honos aliquis sit aut potestas

48. *de judiciis datis*] To prevent a possible mistake, the reader may be reminded that 'judicia dare' is the same as 'judices dare.' Cicero has said before that the fortunes of all persons are in the power of those 'qui judicia dant, et eorum qui judicant.' Lg. 42 p. m. has omitted 'de,' one of many proofs that Lg. 42 p. m. is not infallible.

Cn. Sertium,] 'Sertium,' as Ernesti remarked, is an unknown gentile name. The MSS. have also 'Sergium' and other varieties. Zumpt has 'Sentium,' for which there is no authority.

sexcentos] A usual expression for an indefinite number. Pro Fonteio, c. 3, vol. ii.

ob decreta interponenda] Of which Cicero has given instances in the cases of the 'bonorum possessio' of Heraclius and Epicrates. Gaius says (iv. 139), "Certis igitur ex causis Praetor aut Proconsul principaliter (in the first instance) auctoritatem suam finiendis controversiis praeponit; quod tum maxime facit cum de possessione aut quasi possessione inter aliquos contenditur." In this passage it has been suggested that we should read 'interponit' in place of 'praeponit' (Lachmann, Gaius). The distinction between the Decreta and the Interdicta is given by Gaius (iv. 140), "vocantur autem decreta cum fieri aliquid jubet, &c.; interdicta vero cum prohibet fieri," &c.

aut honos aliquis &c.] Cicero alludes to the universal venality which existed under

aut procuratio quin eam rem tu ad tuum quaestum nundinationemque hominum traduxeris?

XLIX. Dicta sunt priore actione et privatim et publice testimonia: legati Centuripini, Halesini, Catinenses, Panhormitanique dixerunt, multarum praeterea civitatum, jam vero privatim plurimi; quorum ex testimoniis cognoscere potuistis tota Sicilia per triennium neminem ulla in civitate senatorem factum esse gratis, neminem, ut leges eorum sunt, suffragiis, neminem nisi istius imperio aut literis; atque in his omnibus senatoribus cooptandis non modo suffragia nulla fuisse, sed ne genera quidem spectata esse ex quibus in eum ordinem cooptari liceret, neque census neque aetates neque cetera Siculorum jura valuisse: quicunque senator voluerit fieri, quamvis puer, quamvis indignus, quamvis ex eo loco ex quo non liceret, si is pretio apud istum idoneus esset ut vinceret, factum esse semper; non modo Siculorum nihil in hac re valuisse leges, sed ne ab senatu quidem populoque Romano datas. Quas enim leges sociis amicisque dat is qui habet imperium a populo Romano, auctoritatem legum dandarum ab senatu, hae debent et populi Romani et senatus existimari. Halesini pro multis ac magnis suis majorumque suorum in rem publicam nostram meritis atque beneficiis suo jure nuper L. Licinio Q. Mucio consulibus quum haberent inter se controversias de senatu cooptando, leges ab senatu nostro petiverunt. Decrevit senatus honorifico senatus consulto ut his C. Claudius Appii filius Pulcher praetor de senatu cooptando leges con-

the administration of Verres, when every 'honos,' such as the election of a senator; every 'potestas,' such as the office of a magistrate; every 'procuratio,' such as the discharge of any function, was to be bought. Instances are given in the following chapters. See 'curationes,' c. 51, and 'aliquem curatorem praeficere,' c. 58.

49. *cooptandis*] 'Optare,' as already observed, is a word of selection; and 'cooptare' is said of bodies who, by election of the remaining members, supply the places which become vacant by death or otherwise. Cicero, De Divin. ii. 9, says of Caesar, "in eo senatu quem majore ex parte ipse cooptasset."—'atque in iis omnibus senatoribus' Klotz and Iordan from V.

quicunque . . . voluerit] 'voluerat' Lgg. omnes A B V. 'voluerit' cum Naug. Or. (Iordan), who has 'voluerat.' He does not say if any MSS. have 'voluerit,' which I think is the true reading.

si is . . . vinceret,] This, according to Halm, appears to have been the reading of V, and not what Klotz makes it, 'idoneus, et vinceret;' but we are not quite certain what V originally had. But the reading of Lg. 42 may be the best, 'si quis pretio apud istum idoneus inveniretur.' Iordan, following Garatoni, has 'si is pretio . . . idoneus vinceret:' 'fieret idoneus et vinceret,' Orelli.

leges . . . datas.] 'Leges latas,' or 'perlatas,' is the term of Roman legislation, when a 'lex' was enacted in the proper form, on the proposal of some 'magistratus' ('qui tulit ad populum,' or 'qui tulit,' simply): but 'dare leges,' or 'conscribere leges,' is the term used when the Roman people, or those whom they empowered, made a 'lex' for the subject states.

dat is] 'datas' V; a blunder from which something may be learned.

hae debent] 'eae debent' Lg. 29, 'ea debent' A. Some may prefer 'eae' to 'hae.'

scriberet. C. Claudius adhibitis omnibus Marcellis qui tum erant de eorum sententia leges Halesinis dedit; in quibus multa sanxit de aetate hominum Ne qui minor triginta annis natu; de quaestu quem qui fecisset, ne legeretur; de censu, de ceteris rebus. Quae omnia ante istum praetorem et nostrorum magistratuum auctoritate et Halesinorum summa voluntate valuerunt. Ab isto et praeco qui voluit illum ordinem pretio mercatus est, et pueri annorum senum septenumque denum senatorium nomen nundinati sunt: et quod Halesini, antiquissimi et fidelissimi socii atque amici, Romae impetrarant ut apud se ne suffragiis quidem fieri liceret, id pretio ut fieri posset effecit.

L. Agrigentini de senatu cooptando Scipionis leges antiquas habent, in quibus et illa eadem sancta sunt, et hoc amplius: quum Agrigentinorum duo genera sint, unum veterum, alterum colonorum, quos T. Manlius praetor ex senatus consulto de oppidis Siculorum deduxit Agrigentum, cautum est in Scipionis legibus ne plures essent in senatu ex colonorum numero quam ex vetere Agrigentinorum. Iste qui omnia jura pretio exaequasset omniumque rerum delectum atque discrimen pecunia sustulisset, non modo illa quae erant aetatis, ordinis, quaestusque permiscuit, sed etiam in his duobus generibus civium novorum veterumque turbavit. Nam quum esset ex veterum numero quidam senator demortuus, et quum

Ne qui minor &c.] The common reading is 'ne quis.' Lg. 42 p. m. A B have the singular blunder 'iniqui.' The Romans seem to have used both forms in their 'leges.' 'Ne quis' is certainly used in the Lex Thoria. Garatoni proposes to change 'natu' into 'natus,' but Zumpt has proved that this change is not necessary. He says that, in all the cases where 'natus' occurs, the accusative is required. He gives various instances, to which may be added the following from the Lex Thoria: "quaeque ex eis (pequdibus) minus annum gnatae erunt post ea quam gnatae erunt." In such cases 'quam' may be omitted or inserted, as in Livy, 45. c. 32, "quos cum liberis majoribus quam quindecim annos natis praecedere in Italiam placeret." The Romans said 'minor quinque et triginta annis' (Liv. 32. c. 11): and they also often added 'natu,' as in this passage, and in the Praetor's Edict (Dig. 4. 4. 1), "Praetor edicit, quod cum minore quam quinque et viginti annorum natu gestum esse dicetur, uti quaeque res erit, animadvertam." The addition of 'quam' in this instance is no argument against the text of Cicero, for Ulpian adds this remark, "apparet minoribus annis XXV eum opem polliceri." Thus the text of Cicero is fully justified. Klotz has 'natus.' Jordan has 'natu,' and in his critical note "'natus' Lg. 29 42 B [recte; cf. Madvig, Bemerkungen über lat. Sprachl. p. 84]." These rules as to age, occupation, and fortune, were taken from the Roman practice. The limitation as to age and fortune was merely a political disability which time and improved circumstances would remove. That as to the mode of gaining a living (quaestus) was a personal disability which was fixed on those who followed certain occupations, probably 'lenocinium,' and acting on the stage, and the like.

50. *T. Manlius*] Zumpt says that this is the same person who is called in Livy (xxvii. 36) C. Mamilius, and that this colonization took place B.C. 207. He does not however alter the reading of the text. Jordan remarks that 'C. Mamilius' is the conjecture of Pighius.

demortuus,] This word is used when the discourse is of a person or thing that has died or perished, and another is to be

ex utroque genere par numerus reliquus esset, veterem cooptari necesse erat legibus ut is amplior numerus esset. Quae quum ita se res haberet, tamen ad istum emptum venerunt illum locum senatorium non solum veteres verum etiam novi. Fit ut pretio novus vincat literasque a praetore auferat. Agrigentini ad istum legatos mittunt qui eum leges doceant consuetudinemque omnium annorum demonstrent, ut iste intelligeret ei se illum locum vendidisse, cui ne commercium quidem esse oporteret. Quorum oratione iste, quum pretium jam accepisset, ne tantulum quidem commotus est. Idem fecit Heracliae. Nam eo quoque colonos P. Rupilius deduxit, legesque similes de cooptando senatu et de numero veterum ac novorum dedit. Ibi non solum iste ut apud ceteros pecuniam accepit, sed etiam genera veterum ac novorum numerumque permiscuit. LI. Nolite exspectare dum omnes obeam oratione mea civitates. Hoc uno complector omnia, neminem isto praetore senatorem fieri potuisse nisi qui isti pecuniam dedisset. Hoc idem transfero in magistratus, curationes, sacerdotia; quibus in rebus non solum hominum jura sed etiam deorum immortalium religiones omnes repudiavit.

Syracusis lex est de religione quae in annos singulos Jovis sacer-

put in its place; as in an example cited by Forcellini (Dig. 7. 1. 18), "in locum demortuarum arborum aliae substituendae." See Verr. Lib. 4. c. 5; and Mazochi, Tab. Herac. p. 407, and his note on the words 'nisi in demortui damnative locum.' It seems that the Romans did not say 'in mortui locum.' (See Livy, xxiii. 20.) Mazochi's explanation of the reason for using the word 'demortuus' is perhaps more curious than true.

literasque &c.] 'literasque a praetore adferat Agrigentum. Agrigentini,' Klotz and Jordan from V; which reading may by some be preferred. But 'auferat' Lg. 42 is the true word.

commercium] This term is not used by Cicero with strict propriety here. In its legal or political sense it signifies generally the power or capacity to buy and sell, not to buy and sell generally, but the symbolical buying which the Romans called 'mancipatio;' and this strict sense of 'commercium' was extended to other legal transactions. In this case a thing was sold which was not vendible, and Cicero's expression means, that, admitting it to be a purchase, the purchaser was a man who was incapacitated from acquiring.—Klotz has 'cui neque commercium quidem esse oporteret.' But V has 'cui neque . . . esset;' and, if we take that, we may reject 'oporteret.' See Lib. 3. c. 40.

Heracliae.] Zumpt gives 'Heracliae' from Lg. 42 p. m., in place of the common reading 'Heracleae;' and he says that the best MSS. always have 'Heraclienses.' The terminations *-ia* and *-ea* may have been used indifferently by the Romans to represent the Greek *εια*. Heraclia, called also Minoa, was on the south coast of Sicily, near the mouth of the river Halycus (Platani).

51. *Jovis sacerdotem*] Diodorus (xvi. 70) says that "Timoleon, after having made the younger Dionysius retire from Syracuse (B.C. 356), established the annual most honourable office, which the Syracusans call the ministry (ἀμφιπολία) of Zeus Olympius, and the first who was chosen minister of Zeus Olympius was Callimenes, and from this time the Syracusans reckoned their years by these magistrates (ἄρχοντες), until the writing of this history, and the change in their political condition; for, when the Romans made the Siceliots participators of the citizenship, the office of the ministers was lowered, having continued more than three hundred years." It lasted then till

dotem sortito capi jubeat, quod apud illos amplissimum sacerdotium putatur. Quum suffragiis tres ex tribus generibus creati sunt, res revocatur ad sortem. Perfecerat iste imperio ut pro suffragio Theomnastus familiaris suus in tribus illis renuntiaretur: in sorte cui imperare non poterat exspectabant homines quidnam acturus esset. Homo, id quod erat facillimum, primo vetat sortiri: jubet extra sortem Theomnastum renuntiari. Negant id Syracusani per religiones sacrorum ullo modo fieri posse: fas denique negant esse. Jubet iste sibi legem recitari. Recitatur, in qua scriptum erat, Ut quot essent renuntiati, tot in hydriam sortes conjicerentur: cujum nomen exisset ut is haberet id sacerdotium. Iste homo ingeniosus et peracutus, Optime, inquit: nempe scriptum ita est, quot renuntiati erunt. Quot ergo, inquit, sunt renuntiati? Respondent, tres. Numquid igitur oportet nisi tres sortes conjici, unam educi? Nihil. Conjici jubet tres in quibus omnibus esset inscriptum nomen Theomnasti. Fit clamor maximus quum id universis indignum ac nefarium videretur. Ita Jovis illud sacerdotium amplissimum per hanc rationem Theomnasto datur.

LII. Cephalocdi mensis est certus quo mense sacerdotem maximum creari oporteat. Erat ejus honoris cupidus Artemo quidam, Climachias cognomine, homo sane locuples et domi nobilis; sed is fieri nullo modo poterat si Herodotus quidam adesset. Ei locus ille atque honos in illum annum ita deberi putabatur ut ne Climachias quidem contra diceret. Res ad istum defertur et istius more deciditur. Toreumata sane nota ac pretiosa auferuntur. Herodotus Romae erat: satis putabat se ad comitia tempore venturum si pridie venisset. Iste ne aut alio mense ac fas erat comitia haberentur aut Herodoto praesenti honos adimeretur, id quod iste non laborabat, Climachias minime volebat, excogitat—dixi jamdudum,

the Sicilians got the Latinitas or Jus Latii, in B.C. 44 (Ad Att. xiv. 12).

The word 'capere' is a Latin expression applied to the election of the Vestals and ministers of religion. See Gellius, i. 12.—'capi jubebat' was the reading of Gruter, which passed into other editions; but it was, according to Zumpt, a typographical error. Ernesti restored 'jubeat.' Compare 'oportent' at the beginning of the next chapter.

pro suffragio] This means 'in the voting,' as Zumpt observes; and it is like the expression 'pro testimonio.'

per religiones &c.] 'Per religionem' would be the usual form, which Man. and Lamb. have, and also Lg. 6.—'jubet ille' Klotz, from Lg. 42 p. m. V has 'iste.'

52. *Cephaloedi*] Cephaloedium (Κεφαλοίδιον) was a small place, with a port, on the north coast of Sicily, east of Thermae. It is now Cefalù or Cefalò.

Toreumata &c.] 'Toreumata' is explained by 'caelatum argentum,' 'silver chased;' though the toreutic art (τορευτική) appears to have comprehended more than cutting and ornamenting the surface of silver. See Lib. 4. 'Auferuntur,' 'are carried off,' is an invidious mode of saying that Verres was paid for his services in this matter.

non est homo acutior quisquam nec fuit—excogitat, inquam, quemadmodum mense illo legitimo comitia haberentur nec tamen Herodotus adesse posset. Est consuetudo Siculorum ceterorumque Graecorum, quod suos dies mensesque congruere volunt cum solis lunaeque ratione, ut nonnunquam si quid discrepet eximant unum aliquem diem aut summum biduum ex mense, quos illi exaeresimos dies nominant; item nonnunquam uno die longiorem mensem faciunt aut biduo. Quae iste quum cognosset, novus astrologus qui non tam caeli rationem quam caelati argenti duceret, eximi jubet non diem ex mense sed ex anno unum dimidiatumque mensem; hoc modo ut quo die, verbi causa, esse oporteret Idus Januarias, eo die Kalendas Martias proscribi juberet. Itaque fit omnibus recusantibus et plorantibus: dies is erat legitimus comitiis habendis: eo modo sacerdos Climachias renuntiatus est. Herodotus quum Roma revertitur diebus, ut ipse putabat, quindecim ante comitia, offendit eum mensem qui consequitur mensem comitialem, comitiis jam abhinc diebus XXX factis. Tunc Cephaloeditani decrerunt intercalarium XLV dies longum ut reliqui menses in suam rationem reverterentur. Hoc si Romae fieri posset, certe aliqua ratione expugnasset iste ut dies XLV inter binos ludos tollerentur, per quos solos judicium fieri posset.

LIII. Jam vero censores quemadmodum in Sicilia isto praetore

summum] 'at the most:' 'höchstens,' as the Germans say. Zumpt observes, that in the passage of Cicero, Pro Mil. c. 5, vol. iv. instead of 'ad summum quinque,' we must read 'aut summum quinque.'

exaeresimos] 'exereasimos' Lg. 42 p. m., 'exheresimos' cet. Codd. Orelli changed the word into the Greek form ἐξαιρεσίμους. Nothing further is necessary to understand the text of Cicero than what he says himself. The people set the matter right by intercalating forty-five days, or making an 'intercalarium,' which the Greeks called ἐμβόλιμον. Hotmann refers to a like trick of Alexander, but for another purpose (Plutarch, Alex. c. 16).

astrologus] This word generally meant astronomer in our sense of the term, and not astrologer in our sense of that term. So Astrologia (De Divin. ii. 42). See Forcellini.

qui consequitur mensem] Gruter affirms that Lambinus added these words from conjecture, but they are in Lg. 42 p. m. φ. Cicero explains this trickery about the election-day by substituting the Roman for the Greek Calendar, to make it intelligible. And it is easily understood, if the reader will look at it in Cicero's way.

ut dies XLV] See Act. i. c. 10. Cicero means the time between the Ludi Romani and the Ludi Victoriae, which was not forty-five days, though he chooses to call it so. Lg. 42 and φ have XXXV, and also a little before φ has 'intercalarium XXXV,' but this is nothing: Cicero clearly means to say forty-five days. "Hunc numerum (XXXV) si cum Halmio restituas utroque in loco, ratio ita recte constat ut a fine ludorum Romanorum in circo usque ad ludos Victoriae numeres" (Iordan). It is true that XXXV will express the real time between the two 'ludi,' but XXXV would not set the calendar of Cephaloedium right, and the proposed reading is absurd. Would Cicero scruple to affirm that two unequal things were equal, if it suited his purpose?

53. *Jam vero censores quemadmodum &c.*] All the MSS. have 'creati sunt,' but the confusion between 'sunt' and 'sint' in the MSS. is very common. Lambinus made the correction 'sint.' 'Quemadmodum' may be used in a direct inter-

creati sint operae pretium est cognoscere. Ille enim est magistratus apud Siculos qui diligentissime mandatur a populo propter hanc causam, quod omnes Siculi ex censu quotannis tributa conferunt: in censu habendo potestas omnis aestimationis habendae summaeque faciendae censori permittitur. Itaque et populus cui maximam fidem suarum rerum habeat maxima cura deligit; et propter magnitudinem potestatis hic magistratus a populo summa ambitione contenditur. In ea re iste nihil obscure facere voluit, non in sortitione fallere neque dies de fastis eximere: nihil sane vafre nec malitiose facere conatus est: sed, ut studia cupiditatesque honorum atque ambitiones ex omnibus civitatibus tollerentur, quae res evertendae rei publicae solent esse, ostendit sese in omnibus civitatibus censores esse facturum. Tanto mercatu praetoris indicto concurritur undique ad istum Syracusas. Flagrabat domus tota praetoria studio hominum et cupiditate: nec

rogative, as in Lib. 5. c. 47, and other passages. We might then write 'Jam vero censores &c. creati sunt? Operae pretium est cognoscere.'

These 'censores' were provincial 'magistratus,' appointed by the provincials themselves (c. 55). They made a census or rating for the taxation of the towns for municipal purposes, and not for the purpose of giving the produce of the taxes to the Romans. The Romans took for themselves the 'vectigalia,' which consisted of the Decumae, Portorium, and Scriptura. This tax for provincial purposes is called here 'tributum.'

mandatur] 'Mandare' is a word that signifies the entrusting of something to another to perform, with the addition of the proper authority. Accordingly 'mandatum' is that Roman contract which expresses the relation of principal or person empowering and agent or person empowered, but the person empowered (mandatarius) acted gratuitously. The word was therefore applicable enough to the conferring of an office by the people, an office of honour and duties, but of no emolument. Horace uses the word in the same sense as Cicero (1 Sat. vi. 18):

> "Namque esto, populus Laevino mallet honorem
> Quam Decio mandare novo;"

and Liv. iv. 3. The old reading, 'cui mandatur,' needs no refutation, though it is the reading of most of the codd. Lg. 29 42 have 'qui.'

aestimationis habendae &c.] This refers to the censor's rating of each person according to the estimate of his property, and to his fixing the amount that each had to pay (summae faciendae), as Manutius explains it. As to the expression 'cui maximam fidem suarum rerum habeat,' Zumpt is acquainted with one other instance, which is Plautus, Persa, v. 2. 8, "Quia ei fidem non habui argenti, eo mihi eas machinas molitu 'st;" but Creuzer and Moser add another from Caesar, Bell. Gall. i. 19. Compare also B. G. vi. 23, "omniumque iis rerum postea fides derogatur."

omnibus civitatibus] 'hominibus civitatibusque' Lg. 42 p. m. and Zumpt. I now think that the common reading, which Jordan has, ought to be retained.

evertendae rei publicae] A few MSS. add 'causa,' which is the addition of a copyist. Zumpt refers to Cort's Sallust, Cat. c. 6, for this use, which does not occur elsewhere in Cicero, as Zumpt observes. He takes the words to be in the genitive. Garatoni takes them for the dative. In the passage of Sallust the genitive is certainly used, if 'libertatis' is right. In Sall. Cat. 46 'perdundae rei publicae fore' might be the dative.

solent esse,] "postulatur 'solerent esse,' quippe illo praetextu utebatur Verres; alienissimo loco suam sententiam posuisset orator" (Bake, quoted by Halm). I do not agree with the remark 'alienissimo loco' &c., but the learned critic has correctly explained the difference between 'solerent' and 'solent' in this passage.

mirum omnibus comitiis tot civitatum unam in domum revocatis, tantaque ambitione provinciae totius in uno cubiculo inclusa. Exquisitis palam pretiis et licitationibus factis describebat censores binos in singulas civitates Timarchides. Is suo labore suisque accessionibus hujus negotii atque operis molestia consequebatur ut ad istum sine ulla sollicitudine summa pecuniae referretur. Jam hic Timarchides quantam pecuniam fecerit plane adhuc cognoscere non potuistis: verumtamen priore actione quam varie, quam improbe praedatus esset multorum testimoniis cognovistis.

LIV. Sed ne miremini qua ratione hic tantum apud istum libertus potuerit, exponam vobis breviter quid hominis sit, ut et istius nequitiam qui illum secum habuerit eo praesertim numero ac loco et calamitatem provinciae cognoscatis. In mulierum corruptelis et in omni ejusmodi luxuria atque nequitia mirandum in modum reperiebam hunc Timarchidem ad istius flagitiosas libidines singularemque nequitiam natum atque aptum fuisse; investigare, adire, appellare, corrumpere, quidvis facere in ejusmodi rebus, quamvis callide, quamvis audacter, quamvis impudenter; eundem mira quaedam excogitare genera furandi; nam ipsum Verrem tantum avaritia semper hiante atque imminente fuisse, ingenio et cogitatione nulla, ut quidquid sua sponte faciebat, item ut vos Romae cognovistis, eripere potius quam fallere videretur. Haec vero hujus erat ars et malitia miranda, quod acutissime tota provincia, quid cuique accidisset, quid cuique opus esset, indagare et odorari solebat: omnium adversarios, omnium inimicos diligenter

suisque accessionibus] Manutius explains this to mean the personal applications of Timarchides to the individuals who wished to purchase the office of censor. Klotz takes it the other way, to signify the audiences or interviews which Timarchides granted to these persons. The difference is not great, and 'suis' may perhaps be taken either way; but I prefer the interpretation of Manutius.—'Hujus negotii atque operis molestia' must be taken as the explanation of what precedes, 'by the trouble that he took in this affair and business:' he saved Verres all the trouble, and Verres got the money. I am not sure about the meaning of 'accessionibus.' See Lib. 3. c. 49, 50.—'summa pecuniae:' the reading of Lg. 42 p. m. and φ. Orelli has 'summa pecunia.'—'quam varie:' Klotz writes 'quam vafre,' without informing the reader that he has altered the text without any authority.

54. *quid hominis sit,*] Creuzer and Moser compare Terence, Hecyra, iv. 4. 22, 'Quid mulieris;' Hauton. iv. 8. 7, 'Quid hominis es;' Plaut. Rud. i. 2. 60, 'Quid illuc est hominum?' If this be the only instance in Cicero, that is no argument against it. The phrases of common life occur in Terence and Plautus, and Cicero often uses them.

eo praesertim numero &c.] 'especially if we consider in what estimation and rank Verres held this fellow.' 'Numerus' and 'locus,' 'number' and 'place,' mean the confidence which Verres placed in this freedman. See Divin. c. 19, and Phil. iii. 6, 'homo nullo numero.'

nam . . Verrem . . fuisse,] This accusative depends on 'reperiebam,' that is, it is used because a verb in the indicative has been used. I have therefore followed Iordan and improved the pointing.

cognoscere, colloqui, attentare; ex utraque parte causas, voluntates perspicere, facultates et copias; quibus opus esset metum offerre; quibus expediret spem ostendere: accusatorum et quadruplatorum quidquid erat habebat in potestate: quod cuique negotii conflare volebat nullo labore faciebat: istius omnia decreta, imperia, literas peritissime et callidissime venditabat. Ac non solum erat administer istius cupiditatum, verum etiam ipse sui meminerat; neque solum nummos si qui isti exciderant tollere solebat, ex quibus pecuniam maximam fecit, sed etiam voluptatum flagitiorumque istius ipse reliquias colligebat. Itaque in Sicilia non Athenionem, qui nullum oppidum cepit, sed Timarchidem fugitivum omnibus oppidis per triennium scitote regnasse: in Timarchidi potestate sociorum populi Romani antiquissimorum atque amicissimorum liberos, matresfamilias, bona, fortunasque omnes fuisse. Is igitur, ut dico, Timarchides in omnes civitates accepto pretio censores dimisit. Comitia isto praetore censorum ne simulandi quidem causa fuerunt.

LV. Jam hoc impudentissime: palam, licebat enim videlicet legibus, singulis censoribus denarii trecenti ad statuam praetoris imperati sunt. Censores CXXX facti sunt: pecuniam illam ob censuram contra leges clam dederunt; haec denarium XXXIX millia palam salvis legibus contulerunt in statuam. Primum quo tantam pecuniam? Deinde quamobrem censores ad statuam tibi conferebant? Ordo aliqui censorum est, collegium, genus aliquod hominum. Nam aut publice civitates istos honores habent, aut generatim homines, ut aratores, ut mercatores, ut navicularii.

tollere] 'to take up, in order to keep.' See Divin. c. 2, and Heindorf, Horat. 1 Sat. iv. 11.

Athenionem,] See c. 10, and Diodorus, Excerpt. xxxvi.

55. *denarii trecenti*] 'Trecenti' ought to be 'treceni.' But no variation is noted. Compare Act. i. c. 56, "columnas singulas . . quadragenis millibus;" and Divin. c. 10, "in modios singulos duodenos sestertios;" and Lib. 4. c. 26.—After 'impudentissime' Klotz has 'statuam datam,' from Lg. 42 p. m.—Creuzer and Moser follow Klotz, who writes 'in singulis censoribus,' following Lg. 42, and with 'singulis' they understand 'civitatibus,' and make 'censoribus' the dative. I cannot accept this explanation.

salvis legibus] 'without violating the law.'

Ordo aliqui &c.] No note of interrogation is necessary. Cicero says 'I suppose,' but he does not mean to admit that the 'censores' are an 'ordo,' or a 'collegium,' or 'genus hominum:' and this proves that the demand just mentioned was imposed on the several censors, and that 'in' ought to be omitted.

Nam aut publice &c.] 'Why, it is either cities in their capacity of communities that confer such honours, or men according to their classes, as cultivators, as merchants, as masters of ships.' Klotz reads 'aut si generatim, homines ut aratores,' &c. The MSS. have 'aut si,' except Lg. 6. Klotz's explanation of his reading is sufficient to condemn it. See the use of 'generatim' in Caesar, B. G. i. 51.—'navicularii.' A 'navicularius' is the same as a 'nauclerus,' master of a ship (Cod. Just. xi. tit. 1), and Forcellini's Lexicon.

Censores quidem qui magis quam aediles? Ob beneficium? Ergo hoc fatebere abs te haec petita esse; nam empta non audebis dicere: te eos magistratus hominibus beneficii non rei publicae causa permisisse? Hoc quum tute fateare, quisquam dubitabit quin tu istam apud populos provinciae totius invidiam atque offensionem, non ambitionis neque beneficiorum collocandorum, sed pecuniae conciliandae causa susceperis? Itaque illi censores fecerunt idem quod in nostra re publica solent ii qui per largitionem magistratus adepti sunt: dederunt operam ut ita potestatem gererent ut illam lacunam rei familiaris explerent. Sic census habitus est te praetore ut eo censu nullius civitatis res publica posset administrari. Nam locupletissimi cujusque censum extenuarant, tenuissimi auxerant. Itaque in tributis imperandis tantum oneris plebi imponebatur ut, etiamsi homines tacerent, res ipsa illum censum repudiaret: id quod intelligi facillime re ipsa potest.

LVI. Nam L. Metellus qui, posteaquam ego inquirendi causa in Siciliam veni, repente L. Letilii adventu istius non modo amicus verum etiam cognatus factus est; is quod videbat istius censu stari nullo modo posse, eum censum observari jussit qui viro fortissimo atque innocentissimo Sex. Peducaeo praetore habitus esset. Erant enim tum censores legibus facti, delecti a suis civitatibus; quibus si quid commisissent poenae legibus erant constitutae. Te autem praetore, quis censor aut legem metueret qua non tenebatur, quoniam creatus lege non erat, aut animadversionem tuam, quum id quod abs te emerat vendidisset? Teneat jam sane meos testes Metellus; cogat alios laudare sicut in multis conatus est; modo haec faciat quae facit. Quis enim unquam tanta a quoquam contumelia, quis tanta ignominia affectus est? Quinto quoque anno

pecuniae conciliandae &c.] 'for the purpose of getting money.'

Itaque illi] If we picked out of Cicero all his political remarks, there would be a large store of true things said in apt words. The Roman knew men well. Those who get place or office by money will take care, if they can, to repay themselves in some way. They have bought their place, and they will have their money back with interest. All representative assemblies contain such men.

largitionem] This word is peculiarly applied to the offence of 'ambitus,' or the soliciting votes by illegal means. It is a name for bribery. Cic. De Or. ii. 25.

censum extenuarant,] These censors rated the rich too low and the poor too high. They were dishonest men. The rating of people in respect of land, houses, and income, for the purposes of taxation, is faulty in most countries, partly from dishonesty, partly from a bad system.

homines tacerent,] Klotz has 'omnes' from V. These words are often confounded.

56. *censu stari*] The common reading is 'censum stare.' V has 'censu stari.' F M have 'census stari.' The other MSS. have 'censum stare.'

Quinto quoque] There were only three clear years between the census under Peducaeus and that under Verres. But the number 'fifth' is made by enumerating the intermediate years and the two extremes. (Savigny, System, iv. 605.)

Sicilia tota censetur. Erat censa praetore Peducaeo: quintus annus quum in te praetorem incidisset, censa denuo est. Postero anno L. Metellus mentionem tui census fieri vetat: censores dicit de integro sibi creari placere: interea Peducaeanum censum observari jubet. Hoc si tuus inimicus fecisset, tamen, si aequo animo provincia tulisset, inimici judicium grave videretur. Fecit amicus recens et cognatus voluntarius: aliter enim, si provinciam retinere, si salvus ipse in provincia vellet esse, facere non potuit. LVII. Exspectas etiam quid hi judicent? Si tibi magistratum abrogasset, minore ignominia te affecisset quam quum ea quae in magistratu gessisti sustulit atque irrita jussit esse. Neque in hac re sola fuit ejusmodi, sed, antequam ego in Siciliam veni, in maximis rebus ac plurimis: nam et Heraclio Syracusanos tuos illos palaestritas bona restituere jussit, et Epicrati Bidinos, et pupillo Drepanitano A. Claudium: et nisi mature Letilius in Siciliam cum literis venisset, minus XXX diebus Metellus totam triennii praeturam tuam rescidisset.

Et quoniam de ea pecunia quam tibi ad statuam censores contulerunt dixi, non mihi praetermittendum videtur ne illud quidem genus pecuniae conciliatae, quam tu a civitatibus statuarum nomine coëgisti. Video enim ejus pecuniae summam esse pergrandem ad HS tricies: tantum conficitur ex testimoniis et literis civitatum. Et iste hoc concedit, nec potest aliter dicere. Quare cujusmodi

in te praetorem] This is the reading of Klotz and Jordan, and apparently the right reading. Orelli and Zumpt have 'quum te praetore.'

tamen, si . . animo &c.] The common reading is 'tamen etsi' or 'tametsi,' which are the same. Zumpt shows that 'tametsi' is wrong, for it spoils the sense. It would introduce something adversative or opposed to his argument, and it would require to be followed by another 'tamen,' as in Divin. c. 4, "tametsi utrumque esse arbitror perspicuum, tamen de utroque dicam."—'si animo aequo,' &c., 'if the province were pleased with it.' If 'tametsi' is used, the sense must be 'though the province cared not about it;' and few people will venture on such a version. Besides, the text has the authority of 4 V al.

cognatus voluntarius:] Metellus now professed to be a kinsman of Verres, but Cicero means to say that he was not.

57. *magistratum abrogasset,*] 'Abrogare,' a word of Roman legislation, is used to express the repeal of a 'lex,' and also to deprive a 'magistratus' of his office, which it appears could only be done by a proceeding as formal as that by which he was appointed. An instance occurred in the time of Ti. Gracchus, who deprived a colleague of the tribuneship (Plut. Tib. Gracch. c. 12). As to the expression, compare Cic. De Off. iii. 10. 'Magistratum' is the office.

pupillo Drepanitano] Lib. 4. c. 17.

minus XXX diebus] See c. 49, note.

ad HS tricies:] The real amount is immaterial. It was a very large sum, and therefore more than HS CXX millia, or CXXX, as some MSS. have it. There is always confusion in the MSS. in these numerals. One state alone, as Zumpt observes, Centuripa, contributed CCC millia; but perhaps we should read there 'HS CC millia' in c. 58, with V. Zumpt gives his reasons for writing 'triciens.' Garatoni would have 'vicies,' founded on the reading of one MS. (c. 69), which has ∞∞, and that is the same as CIↃ CIↃ, or vicies, that is, a thousand times a thousand repeated, or, in other words, 'decies, decies.'

putamus esse illa quae negat quum haec tam improba sint quae fatetur? Quid enim vis constitui? consumptam esse omnem istam pecuniam in statuis? Fac ita esse: tamen hoc ferendum nullo modo est tantam ab sociis pecuniam auferri ut in omnibus angiportis praedonis improbissimi statua ponatur, qua vix tuto transiri posse videatur.

LVIII. Verum ubi tandem aut in quibus statuis ista tanta pecunia consumpta est? Consumetur, inquies. Scilicet exspectemus legitimum illud quinquennium; si hoc intervallo non consumpserit, tum denique nomen ejus de pecuniis repetundis statuarum nomine deferemus. Reus est maximis plurimisque criminibus in judicium vocatus: HS tricies ex hoc uno genere captum videmus. Si condemnatus eris, non, opinor, id ages ut ista pecunia in quinquennio consumatur in statuis: sin absolutus eris, quis erit tam amens qui te ex tot tantisque criminibus elapsum post quinquennium statuarum nomine arcessat? Ita si neque adhuc consumpta est ista pecunia, et est perspicuum non consumptum iri, licet jam intelligamus inventam esse rationem, quare et iste HS tricies ex hoc uno genere conciliarit et ceperit, et ceteri, si hoc a vobis erit comprobatum, quam volent magnas hoc nomine pecunias capere possint; ut jam videamur non a pecuniis capiundis homines abstinere, sed, quum genera quaedam pecuniarum capiendarum comprobarimus, honesta nomina turpissimis rebus imponere. Etenim, si C. Verres HS cxx millia populum, verbi gratia, Centuripinum poposcisset, eamque ab iis pecuniam abstulisset, non, opinor, esset dubium quin eum quum id planum fieret condemnari necesse esset. Quid si eundem populum HS ccc millia poposcit, eaque

quum haec tam improba sint] The MSS. have 'sunt.' Nobody can doubt which it should be, if he has read so far in these orations with any care. Iordan says 'sint,' Priscian.

58. *legitimum*] We collect from this passage that one of the 'leges de repetundis' allowed a period of five years within which statues in honour of a governor might be erected out of the money raised for that purpose. If this time elapsed, then the legal presumption would be that the statues were merely a pretext for raising money; but we must assume that no governor could be prosecuted 'repetundarum nomine,' in the instance under consideration, 'statuarum nomine,' unless it could be proved that the money raised for statues came to his hands, or to the hands of his agents. As to statues see Ad Q. Fr. i. 1. c. 9; Pro Flacco, c. 25.

arcessat?] This word signifies to 'summon,' to 'send for,' as in Cicero, De Sen. c. 16; and the summoning may be for one thing or for another, to receive an honourable commission, or to answer a charge. As to the form 'arcessere,' see Act. i. c. 9. V and Klotz have 'accersat,' which is not the genuine old form.

neque . . et] 'Neque' and 'et,' and also 'nec' and 'et,' are sometimes thus placed; like *οὔτε* and *τέ*.

ex hoc uno] 'HS viciens ex hoc uno' Klotz, from V. Zumpt has 'triciens uno.'

abstinere,] The common reading and that of V is 'absterrere,' which Halm prefers. Lg. 42 p. m. ϕ have 'abstinere.'

coëgit atque abstulit, num idcirco absolvetur quod adscriptum est, eam pecuniam datam statuarum nomine? non, opinor: nisi forte is agimus non ut magistratibus nostris moram accipiendi sed ut sociis causam dandi afferre videamur. Quod si quem statuae magno opere delectant, et si quis earum honore aut gloria ducitur, is haec tamen constituat necesse est: primum, averti pecuniam domum non placere; deinde, ipsarum statuarum modum quendam esse oportere; deinde illud, certe ab invitis exigi non oportere. LIX. Ac de avertenda pecunia quaero abs te utrum ipsae civitates solitae sint statuas tibi faciundas locare ei cui possent optima conditione [locare], an aliquem curatorem praeficere qui statuis faciundis praeesset, an tibi an cui tu imperasses adnumerare pecuniam. Nam si per eos statuae fiebant a quibus tibi iste honos habebatur, audio: sin Timarchidi pecunia numerabatur, desine, quaeso, simulare te, quum in manifestissimo furto teneare, gloriae studiosum ac monumentorum fuisse.

Quid vero, modum statuarum haberi nullum placet? Atqui habeatur necesse est. Etenim sic considerate. Syracusana civitas, ut eam potissimum nominem, dedit ipsi statuam; est honos: et patri; bella haec pietatis et quaestuosa simulatio: et filio; ferri hoc potest; hunc enim puerum non oderant: verum quoties et quot nominibus a Syracusanis statuas auferes? Ut in foro statuerent abstulisti: ut in curia coëgisti: ut pecuniam conferrent in eas statuas quae Romae ponerentur imperasti: ut iidem darent homines aratorum nomine; dederunt: ut iidem pro parte in commune Siciliae conferrent; etiam id contulerunt. Una civitas quum tot nominibus pecuniam contulerit, idemque hoc civitates ceterae fecerint, nonne res ipsa vos admonet ut putetis modum aliquem huic cupiditati constitui oportere? Quod si hoc voluntate sua nulla

59. *audio*:] See Lib. 5. c. 27, where he has both 'video' and 'audio.' 'Audio' is a common form, to which the reader may easily give a meaning.

in . . furto teneare,] See Lib. 3. c. 64.

non oderant:] Hotmann detected, and perhaps rightly, an odious insinuation in these words.

Ut . . statuerent abstulisti:] 'You extorted from them the placing of a statue in the forum.' The words which follow, 'coëgisti,' &c., make the meaning plain enough. The correction 'statuisti' of a Vir d., recorded by Orelli, is certainly a mistake; yet Lg. 42 p. m. has it: but the same MS. has also 'aut' for 'ut.'

ut putetis] Omitted by Lg. 42, and placed in [ ] by Iordan.

Quod si hoc] Lg. 29 B have 'Quid si hoc;' but Zumpt will not listen to them. '*Quod si* est pro *si vero*,' he says. But 'Quod si' is what it is. The Romans fell into this form of expression when 'quod' lost by use its strict demonstrative meaning; for such it had originally. The true English translation is, 'The which if no state did this of its own free will.' There is no objection now to our writing 'Quodsi,' and taking it for what it corresponds to in our language; 'now if no state did this;' but the origin of the expression should be looked to. 'Quod si quem statuae delectant,' c. 58, is not different from

civitas fecit, si omnes imperio, metu, vi, malo adductae, pecuniam statuarum nomine contulerunt, per deos immortales, num cui dubium esse poterit quin, etiamsi statuerit accipere ad statuas licere, idem tamen statuat eripere certe non licere? Primum igitur in hanc rem testem totam Siciliam citabo, quae mihi una voce statuarum nomine magnam pecuniam per vim coactam esse demonstrat. Nam legationes omnium civitatum in postulatis communibus, quae fere omnia ex tuis injuriis nata sunt, etiam hoc ediderunt, Ut statuas ne cui, nisi quum is de provincia decessisset, pollicerentur. LX. Tot praetores in Sicilia fuerunt, toties apud majores nostros Siculi senatum adierunt, toties hac memoria, tamen hujusce novi postulati genus atque principium tua praetura attulit. Quid enim tam novum, non solum re sed genere ipso postulandi? Nam cetera, quae sunt in iisdem postulatis de injuriis tuis, sunt nova, sed tamen non novo modo postulantur. Rogant et orant Siculi patres conscriptos "ut nostri magistratus posthac decumas lege Hieronica vendant." Tu primus contra vendideras. Audio. "Ne in cellam quod imperatur aestiment." Hoc quoque propter tuos ternos denarios nunc primum postulatur: sed genus ipsum postulandi non est novum. "Ne absentis nomen recipiatur." Ex Sthenii calamitate et tua natum est injuria. Cetera non colligam. Sunt omnia Siculorum postulata ejusmodi ut crimina collecta in unum reum te esse videantur; quae tamen omnia novas injurias habent, sed postulationum formulas usitatas. Hoc postulatum de statuis ridiculum esse videatur ei qui rem sententiamque non perspiciat. Postulant enim non uti ne cogantur statuere. Quid igitur? Ut ipsis ne liceat.—Quid est hoc? petis a me quod

this: 'statuae' explains 'quod.' Ter. And. i. 5. 54, 'Quod ego te,' &c.

vi, malo] The old reading 'modo,' for 'malo,' is nonsense. 'Malo,' thus used absolutely, ought to have some specific meaning, and as it follows 'vi, metu,' Zumpt supposes that it may mean 'plagis ac verberibus;' not that they were actually whipped to make them pay; but there was the fear of the scourge before their eyes. It means some harm generally, as in Lib. 3. c. 41, 'malo dignus judicaretur;' and also in Lib. 3. c. 23; and in c. 60 of this oration, 'metu ac malo coactus.'

postulatis] It was the month of February, as we have already seen, in which the 'legati' of the provincials received an audience of the Roman senate, and brought their 'postulata,' claims or petitions, before them. The 'postulata' appear to have been handed in to the consuls (c. 64), who brought them before the senate.

60. *postulantur. Rogant*] 'postulant, sed rogant,' &c., N Lg. 42, Klotz, which will hardly be preferred to the text.

in cellam &c.] 'That the praetors should not fix a money value on the contributions in kind which were required for the consumption of their household,' that is, should not have the power of demanding a money payment instead of the contributions in kind to which they were entitled for the use of their household. See c. 2. The 'cella' here is the praetor's 'cella.'

ternos denarios] See Divin. c. 10, and Lib. 3. c. 85—87.

Quid est hoc?] 'Quid enim? petis' Lg. 42 p. m. Klotz.—'nihil egero' means,

in tua potestate est ut id tibi facere ne liceat: peto potius ne quis te invitum polliceri aut facere cogat. Nihil egero, inquit: negabunt enim omnes se coëgisse: si me salvum esse vis, mihi impone istam vim ut omnino mihi ne liceat polliceri. Ex tua praetura primum haec est nata postulatio; qua quum utuntur hoc significant atque adeo aperte ostendunt, sese ad statuas tuas pecuniam metu ac malo coactos invitissimos contulisse. Quid, si hoc non dicant, tibi non necesse sit ipsi id confiteri? Vide et perspice qua defensione sis usurus. Jam intelliges hoc tibi de statuis confitendum esse. LXI. Mihi enim renuntiatur ita constitui a tuis patronis hominibus ingeniosis causam tuam, et ita eos abs te institui et doceri: ut quisque ex provincia Sicilia gravior homo atque honestior testimonium vehementius dixerit, sicuti Siculi multi primarii viri multa dixerunt, te statim hoc istis tuis defensoribus dicere—inimicus est propterea quod arator est. Itaque uno genere, opinor, circumscribere habetis in animo genus hoc aratorum, quod eos infenso animo atque inimico venisse dicatis quia fuerit in decumis iste vehementior. Ergo aratores inimici omnes et adversarii sunt: nemo eorum est quin perisse te cupiat. Omnino praeclare te habes, quum is ordo atque id hominum genus, quod optimum atque honestissimum est, a quo uno et summa res publica et illa provincia maxime continetur, tibi est inimicissimum. Verum esto: alio loco de aratorum animo et injuriis videro: nunc quod mihi abs te datur, id accipio, eos tibi esse inimicissimos. Nempe ita dicis, propter

'I shall gain nothing by that.' 'Egero' is the reading of Lg. 29 A B cod. Urs., 'ego rogo' of Lg. 42 p. m., 'rogo' F N, 'ergo' of the dtt.

atque adeo] 'they hint this, and indeed openly show that' &c. 'Adeo' is often used by Cicero and other writers in the sense of 'moreover,' 'further,' 'even,' and the like. Comp. Lib. 1. c. 34, "hujus improbissimi furti sive adeo nefariae praedae;" Lib. 2. c. 65, "ex Sicilia decedendum atque adeo fugiendum;" Lib. 3. c. 61, "si qui pudor in te atque adeo si qui metus fuisset," that is, 'if you had any sense of shame, nay, if you had any fear;' and Lib. 2. c. 35, "adducitur a Venereis atque adeo attrahitur Lollius."

61. *circumscribere*] This word, which signifies to enclose within a circle, has various derived meanings, among which is that of 'limiting and confining.' Hotmann observes on this passage, 'modo significat rejicere et excludere;' but, though this is the result of what Cicero expresses by 'circumscribere,' it is not the true explanation of the term. The meaning of the passage is this: 'Accordingly it is your intention, I suppose, to comprehend the cultivators under one class, by virtue of the assertion (quod dicatis) that they have come to Rome with a hostile and unfriendly disposition;' and, as such, would not be impartial witnesses. Zumpt's explanation is like Hotmann's, and he refers to Lib. 1. c. 16, 'hoc omni, &c., circumscripto.'

Omnino praeclare te habes,] Said sarcastically, 'you are in an excellent plight or condition.' Zumpt compares Cicero, Ad Att. vii. 2, "quamquam videbatur se non graviter habere."—'a quo . . continetur' seems to mean 'by which class is protected,' but a similar example does not appear to be known.

Nempe ita dicis,] Klotz reads 'nempe id sit' from Lg. 42 p. m., and observes that such changes from one person to another, as from addressing Verres (praeclare te habes) to addressing the 'judices' (nempe

decumas. Concedo; non quaero jure an injuria sint inimici. Quid ergo illae sibi statuae equestres inauratae volunt, quae populi Romani oculos animosque maxime offendunt propter aedem Vulcani? Nam inscriptum esse video quandam ex his statuam aratores dedisse. Si honoris causa statuam dederunt, inimici non sunt: credamus testibus; tum enim honori tuo, nunc jam religioni suae consulunt. Sin autem metu coacti dederunt, confiteare necesse est te in provincia pecunias statuarum nomine per vim ac metum coëgisse. Utrum tibi commodum est elige.

LXII. Equidem libenter hoc jam crimen de statuis relinquam ut mihi tu illud concedas, quod tibi honestissimum est, aratores tibi ad statuam honoris tui causa voluntate sua contulisse. Da mihi hoc: jam tibi maximam partem defensionis praecideris. Non enim poteris aratores tibi iratos esse atque inimicos dicere. O causam singularem! O defensionem miseram ac perditam! nolle hoc accipere reum ab accusatore, et eum reum qui praetor in Sicilia fuerit, aratores ei statuam sua voluntate statuisse; aratores de eo bene existimare, amicos esse, salvum esse cupere: metuit ne hoc

id ait), are not uncommon in Cicero. The word 'nempe' generally stands at the beginning of a sentence, but not always. The word apparently is 'nam,' with the addition of 'pe,' as 'quippe;' for the change of 'nam' into 'nem,' after the addition of 'pe,' presents no difficulty, and is in accordance with a law of euphony. It is that use of 'nam' at the beginning of a sentence, by which a thing is introduced to our notice, when there is no intention to dwell upon it; when we intend to affirm or to assume something that cannot be disputed, and requires no argument: 'Well, then, you say it is on account of the tenths.' Horace (1 Sat. x. 1) has an example:

"Nempe incomposito dixi pede currere versus
Lucili."

'It is true, I did say that the verses of Lucilius move with ill-assorted step; but that is all that I said.' Heindorf, on this passage, observes that 'nempe' is always a particle of affirmation, in the form of a half-interrogation. He denies that it is ever used as a word of concession, as one of the scholiasts explains it; wherein he is perhaps not quite correct. As to this word being a compound of 'nam' and 'pe,' this view is confirmed by some of the uses of 'namque' and 'nempe' (Ovid, Met. ii. 474).

Quid ergo &c.] 'Quid ergo illae, quid sibi statuae,' &c. Klotz, from Lg. 42 p. m. M. Creuzer and Moser adopt this reading, and spoil it by their pointing: 'Quid ergo? illae quid,' &c. Jordan's reading and pointing are the same as the text.

aedem Vulcani?] This temple was, according to tradition, founded by Romulus, who there assembled the senate with his partner King Tatius (Plutarch, Quaest. Rom. c. 47). The temple was out of the old city, but became included within it by the extension of the 'pomoerium.' These gilded statues have been mentioned before, c. 46 (Creuzer and Moser, from Garatoni).

62. *relinquam ut*] This use of 'ut' seems to have arisen from the omission of 'ita' before 'relinquam,' for the passage means: 'for my part, I will now willingly give up this charge about the statues, if you will make me this admission, that' &c.

O causam singularem!] Hotmann takes 'causam' in the sense of πρόφασις.

salvum esse cupere:] Klotz and Jordan, on the authority of Lg. 42 p. m., omit 'esse.' As far as concerns the language, we know that it can be omitted, and the Romans could say 'salvum te cupio' or 'volo' (Hor. 1 Sat. i. 81). But it would seem pretty clear that the repetition of 'esse' is emphatic here. The omission of it in a single MS. is a pre-

vos existimetis; obruitur enim aratorum testimoniis. Utar eo quod datur. Certe hoc vobis ita judicandum est eos qui isti inimicissimi sunt, ut ipse existimari vult, ad istius honores atque monumenta pecunias voluntate sua non contulisse. Atque ut hoc totum facillime intelligi possit, quem voles eorum testium quos produxero qui ex Sicilia testes sint sive togatum sive Siculum rogato et eum qui tibi inimicissimus esse videbitur, qui se spoliatum abs te esse dicet, ecquid suo nomine in tuam statuam contulerit. Neminem reperies qui neget; etenim omnes dederunt. Quemquam igitur putas dubitaturum quin is, quem tibi inimicissimum esse oporteat, qui abs te gravissimas injurias acceperit, pecuniam statuae nomine dederit vi atque imperio adductus, non officio ac voluntate? Hujus ego pecuniae, judices, quae permagna est impudentissimeque coacta ab invitis, non habui rationem neque habere potui, quantum ab aratoribus, quantum ab negotiatoribus qui Syracusis, qui Agrigenti, qui Panhormi, qui Lilybaei negotiantur, esset coactum, quoniam intelligitis ipsius quoque confessione ab invitissimis coactam esse.

LXIII. Venio nunc ad civitates Siciliae de quibus facillime judicium fieri voluntatis potest. An etiam Siculi inviti contulerunt? non est probabile. Etenim sic C. Verrem praeturam in Sicilia gessisse constat ut, quum utrisque satisfacere non posset et Siculis et togatis, officii potius in socios quam ambitionis in cives rationem duxerit. Itaque eum non solum PATRONVM illius insulae sed etiam SOTERA inscriptum vidi Syracusis. Hoc quantum est? ita magnum

sumption that the omission is accidental, especially as '*esse*' has just been used. The conclusion is, that the rejection of '*esse*' is a proof of bad judgment in the estimation of evidence and of the force of the passage.

ex Sicilia—sint] Klotz and Iordan have 'sunt,' from Lg. 42 V. It is difficult to lay down a rule in these cases. In the preceding sentence 'eos qui isti inimicissimi sunt' is the better reading, which Zumpt in that case prefers for the following reason: "hoc moneo, esse h. l. aratores intelligendos, non in universum quicunque Verrem persequantur;" and this is a sufficient reason. But in this passage the meaning is: 'ask any of the witnesses you please, among those whom I shall produce, witnesses from Sicily;' not 'the witnesses who are from Sicily.'

togatum] There is also a reading 'civem Romanum,' which may be merely an explanation of 'togatum.' See c. 63, 'et Siculis et togatis;' and c. 65, 'et Siculorum et civium Romanorum.'

Hujus . . pecuniae, &c.] That is, 'hujus pecuniae quantum &c. non habui rationem.' Zumpt and Iordan have 'Et hujus.' V omits 'Et.'

63. *officii . . ambitionis*] This, of course, is said ironically, or assumed for the purpose of the argument. 'Ambitio' means 'popularity-seeking,' as it often does in Cicero.

SOTERA] Klotz says that the Latin 'servator' would not express the force of σωτήρ, for 'servator' would refer to a single act. I don't know if this is true; but there is another reason why 'servator' would not do, for the notion contained in it is different, as Manutius shows, from that contained in 'soter,' for which Cicero only finds an equivalent in 'salus.' The adjective 'salvus,' which contains the same element as 'salus,' had not produced the word 'salvator' in Cicero's time.

inscriptum] Klotz adds 'esse,' from V, which rarely adds superfluous words,

est ut Latine uno verbo exprimi non possit. Is est nimirum soter qui salutem dedit. Hujus nomine etiam dies festi agitantur, pulchra illa Verria, non quasi Marcellia, sed pro Marcelliis, quae illi istius jussu sustulerunt. Hujus fornix in foro Syracusis est in quo nudus filius stat, ipse autem ex equo nudatam ab se provinciam prospicit. Hujus statuae locis omnibus, quae hoc demonstrare videantur propemodum non minus multas statuas istum posuisse Syracusis quam abstulisse. Huic etiam Romae videmus in basi statuarum maximis literis incisum, 'a communi Siciliae datas.' Quamobrem qui hoc probari potest cuiquam tantos honores habitos esse ab invitis? LXIV. Hic tibi etiam multo magis quam paulo ante in aratoribus videndum et considerandum est quid velis. Magna res est. Utrum tibi Siculos publico privatimque amicos an inimicos existimari vis? Si inimicos, quid te futurum est? quo confugies? ubi nitere? Modo aratorum honestissimorum hominum ac locupletissimorum et Siculorum et civium Romanorum maximum numerum abs te abalienasti: nunc de Siculis civitatibus quid ages? Dices tibi Siculos esse amicos? qui poteris? qui quod nullo in homine antea fecerant, ut in eum publice testimonium dicerent, quum praesertim ex ea provincia condemnati sint complures, qui ibi praetores fuerunt, duo soli absoluti, hi nunc veniunt cum literis, veniunt cum mandatis, veniunt cum testimoniis publicis; qui si te publice laudarent, tamen id more potius suo quam merito tuo facere viderentur; hi quum de tuis factis publice conqueruntur, nonne hoc indicant tantas esse injurias ut multo maluerint de suo more decedere quam de tuis moribus non dicere? Confitendum est igitur tibi necessario Siculos inimicos esse qui quidem et in te gravissima postulata con-

though it does sometimes.—'magnum est' V, is better than Zumpt and Iordan's 'magnum' without 'est.'—From V Klotz takes 'Is est enim nimirum,' which has the recommendation of being something uncommon.

fornix] An arch in honour of Verres, like the Fabianus at Rome, which Cicero often mentions. It seems that an equestrian statue of Verres was placed upon the arch, which is the only intelligible explanation of the passage.

a communi . . datas.] Iordan puts this in capitals, as if they were the exact words of the inscription. There might be no more than 'a communi Siciliae.'

Quamobrem qui &c.] The old editors understood this right. The later editors, as Zumpt observes, spoiled the sense by a note of interrogation after 'quamobrem.' The reading of Klotz, from V, is 'quam ob rem qui hoc probare potes' &c.

64. *Magna res &c.*] 'Magna res est, utrum . . existimari velis' Iordan. But this pointing is bad. 'Velis' is the reading of Lg. 42 p. m. and V. The rest have 'vis.'

quid te futurum est?] Compare Lib. 1. c. 16, 'Quid hoc homine faciatis?' and the note.—'ubi nitere? Quomodo? aratorum' &c. Klotz, following V, as if it were infallible.

qui quod . . . hi nunc] V has 'ii' in place of 'hi,' but 'ii' is a false reading. Compare c. 66, 'Tauromenitani . . qui . . hi.' I think 'hi' is generally supposed to be a repetition of 'qui;' but 'qui' is the nominative to 'fecerant.'

sulibus ediderint, et me ut hanc causam salutisque suae defensionem susciperem obsecrarint; qui quum a praetore prohiberentur, a quatuor quaestoribus impedirentur, omnium minas atque omnia pericula prae salute sua levia duxerint; qui priore actione ita testimonia graviter vehementerque dixerint ut Artemonem Centuripinum legatum et publice testem Q. Hortensius accusatorem non testem esse diceret. Etenim ille quum propter virtutem et fidem cum Androne homine honestissimo et certissimo, tum etiam propter eloquentiam, legatus a suis civibus electus est, ut posset multas istius et varias injurias quam apertissime vobis planissimeque explicare.

LXV. Dixerunt Halesini, Catinenses, Tyndaritani, Hennenses, Herbitenses, Agyrinenses, Netinenses, Segestani; enumerare omnes non est necesse. Scitis quam multi et quam multa priore actione dixerint: nunc et illi et reliqui dicent. Omnes denique hoc in hac causa intelligent, hoc animo esse Siculos ut, si in istum animadversum non sit, sibi relinquendas domos ac sedes suas, et ex Sicilia decedendum atque adeo fugiendum esse arbitrentur. Hos homines tu persuadebis ad honorem atque amplitudinem tuam pecunias maximas voluntate sua contulisse? credo, qui te in tua civitate incolumem esse nollent, hi monumenta tuae formae ac nominis in suis civitatibus esse cupiebant. Res declarabit ut cupierint. Jam-

ediderint, &c.] Klotz has 'ediderunt,' 'obsecrarunt,' 'duxerunt,' 'dixerunt.' Iordan, who has also the indicatives, says, "Quattuor his locis cum uterque modus recte admitti possit, codicum auctoritatem potiorem secuti sumus. Similiter variant boni codd. infra c. 55, 'Itaque Rhodii etc.'" Creuzer and Moser, who adopt the indicatives, say, "Cicero urges the *facts* against Verres; he does not urge him to think of the ground or cause of the hatred, and to consider it as in a manner justified by the four clauses 'ediderint,' &c." I think that these editors are mistaken, and that Cicero does not place his positive affirmations in this form in a sentence. His affirmation is 'Siculos inimicos esse,' after which, according to my understanding of his fashion, he drops into the subjunctive, that is, the subjoined, subordinate, dependent form of expression.—'prae salute sua:' 'pro salute sua' Lg. 42 φ, Klotz.

certissimo,] In the sense of 'trustworthy,' 'faithful.' In c. 38 Verres is called 'homo certus,' in a different sense.

65. *Hennenses,*] The Roman coins and the best MSS. have this word with the aspirate. Eckhel, Doctr. Num. i. p. 206, says that there is a very old Greek coin on which the aspirate is marked by a 'littera singularis' (Zumpt).

'Netinenses' is the reading of all the edd. and codd. except Lg. 42, which has 'Nethini.' Iordan has 'Netini,' which may be the true form; but 'Netinenses' is also a legitimate form. Netum, now Noto Vecchio, is on a hill near the source of the Asinarus and s.w. of Syracuse.

'Segestani' is the common orthography, but there is authority for the form 'Egestani' (Eckhel, T. i. p. 236). The Greek word is always without the aspirate in the Greek MSS., but the oldest coins have ΣΕΓΕΣΤΑ.

enumerare] The MSS. appear to have 'numerare,' but this word means to tell, or count a certain number, and hence to pay money. M has 'et numerare,' and we may therefore safely accept 'enumerare,' the conjecture of Lambinus.

ut cupierint.] 'ut certissimum glossema delendum puto' (Garatoni), quoted by Iordan, who however has showed his judgment by keeping the words.

dudum enim mihi nimium tenuiter Siculorum erga te voluntatis argumenta colligere videor, utrum statuas voluerint tibi statuere an coacti sint. De quo homine auditum est unquam, quod tibi accidit, ut ejus in provincia statuae in locis publicis positae, partim etiam in aedibus sacris, per vim et per universam multitudinem dejicerentur? Tot homines in Asia nocentes, tot in Africa, tot in Hispania, Gallia, Sardinia, tot in ipsa Sicilia fuerunt: ecquo de homine hoc unquam audivistis? Novum est, judices; in Siculis quidem et in omnibus Graecis monstri simile. Non crederem hoc de statuis nisi jacentes revulsasque vidissem, propterea quod apud omnes Graecos hic mos est, ut honorem hominibus habitum in monumentis ejusmodi nonnulla religione deorum consecrari arbitrentur. Itaque Rhodii, qui prope soli bellum illud superius cum Mithridate rege gesserunt, omnesque ejus copias acerrimumque impetum moenibus, littoribus, classibusque suis exceperunt, tamen, quum ei regi inimici praeter ceteros essent, statuam ejus, quae erat apud ipsos in celeberrimo urbis loco, ne tum quidem in ipsis urbis periculis attigerunt. Ac forsitan vix convenire videretur quem ipsum hominem cuperent evertere, ejus effigiem simulacrumque servare: sed tamen videbam apud eos quum essem et religionem esse quandam in his rebus a majoribus traditam, et hoc disputari, cum statua se ejus habuisse temporis rationem quo posita esset, cum homine vero quo gereret bellum atque hostis esset.

LXVI. Videtis igitur consuetudinem religionemque Graecorum quae monumenta hostium in bello ipso soleat defendere, eam summa in pace praetoris populi Romani statuis praesidio non fuisse. Tauromenitani, quorum est civitas foederata, homines quietissimi, qui

De quo homine] 'De quo hoc homine' Lg. 42 p. m., Klotz.

monstri simile.] 'Patris similis,' Lib. 3. c. 68; 'sui similes,' Lib. 3. c. 9; and there are other examples.

Rhodii . . . superius] Cicero alludes to the war declared against Mithridates, B.C. 88. In this year the Rhodii bravely defended themselves against Mithridates (Appian, Mithrid. c. 24). In B.C. 87 Sulla was sent into Greece to oppose the generals of Mithridates, and in B.C. 84 he went into Asia and brought the king to terms. This was the 'bellum superius.' In B.C. 74 the war began again, and L. Lucullus had the command against Mithridates. The war was still going on at the time of Verres' trial (B.C. 70).

gesserunt . . . exceperunt,] Lg. 42 has gesserunt;' the rest 'gesserint.' All the codd. have 'exceperint.' 'Exceperunt' is Zumpt's correction.

vero] 'ejus' Lg. 42, Iordan: 'non' plerique codd. 'vero,' alii, Or.

66. *civitas foederata,*] A 'civitas foederata' was a community connected with Rome by the terms of a 'foedus' or treaty. The term was applied to the Italian Socii before B.C. 90 (see Divin. c. 3), whose 'foedus' with Rome implied a kind of political subjection. There were also 'civitates foederatae' out of Italy, as Massilia in Gaul, the city of Tauromenium in Sicily, and others. This matter is further explained Lib. 3. c. 6. As to the various kinds of 'foedera,' see Livy, 34. c. 57.

Tauromenium, which is the genuine orthography, not Taurominium, is now Taormina, on the east coast of Sicily, between Messana and Catina. Naxus, the first

maxime ab injuriis nostrorum magistratuum remoti consuerant esse praesidio foederis, hi tamen istius evertere statuam non dubitaverunt. Qua abjecta basim tamen in foro manere voluerunt; quod gravius in istum fore putabant, si scirent homines statuam ejus a Tauromenitanis esse dejectam, quam si nullam unquam positam esse arbitrarentur. Tyndaritani dejecerunt in foro; et eadem de causa equum inanem reliquerunt. Leontinis, misera in civitate atque inani, tamen istius in gymnasio statua dejecta est. Nam quid ego de Syracusanis loquar, quod non est proprium Syracusanorum, sed et illorum et commune conventus illius ac prope totius provinciae? Quanta illic multitudo, quanta vis hominum convenisse dicebatur tum quum statuae sunt illius dejectae atque eversae? At quo loco? Celeberrimo ac religiosissimo, ante ipsum Serapim in primo aditu vestibuloque templi. Quod nisi Metellus hoc tam graviter egisset atque illam rem imperio edictoque prohibuisset, vestigium statuarum istius in tota Sicilia nullum esset relictum.

Greek colony in Sicily (Thucyd. vi. 3), was founded by the Chalcidians, three miles south of a rock called Taurus. It was destroyed by Dionysius, B.C. 403 (Diodorus, xiv. 15). In B.C. 358 the remnant of the Naxians were settled by Andromachus not on the ruins of the old town, but on the Taurus, which had been already occupied by the Siculi and was called Tauromenium. The place became flourishing and populous, an evidence of which is the magnitude of the theatre, partly cut in the rock, which is nearly entire, and capable of containing many thousand persons.

Leontinis,] This means 'in Leontini,' for 'Leontini' was the name both of the people and of the place, both in the Greek and the Latin writers. The words 'misera in civitate' are explained by Lib. 3. c. 46.

sed et illorum &c.] The reading of this passage is not certain, and various attempts have been made to amend it. The text is that of Zumpt, and it is intelligible. Cicero says, "Why should I speak of the Syracusani in a matter which is not peculiar to them, but is both their affair and common to that 'conventus,' and almost to the whole province?"—'de Syracusis loquar' Zumpt.

illius] codd., 'istius' Iordan; and Cicero ought to have written 'istius.'

Serapim] 'Serapim' is the reading of 4 M φ, Pal. sec. (Iordan.) In the other MSS. it is corrupt. I do not propose to trace the history of this divinity. He got a footing in Egypt, and kept it there till a bold hand demolished his idol. Serapis is said to be an importation into Egypt from Pontus. Whether he came into Greece and Sicily from Egypt, or was imported direct, I do not know. Gibbon, c. 28, has told his story.—A 'celeberrimus locus' is a much-frequented place. See Lib. 1. c. 26, 'celebratur .. convivium.' The following will serve as an instance of the proper meaning of this word:

"Colle sub aprico celeberrimus ilice lucus
Stabat et in ramis multa latebat avis,"
Ovid, Am. iii. 5. 3,

where the poet might have said 'creberrimus,' for he does say it in another passage, 'creber arundinibus tremulis ibi surgere lucus' (Met. xi. 190). Thus the usage of the language confirms the conclusion as to the relationship of 'creber' and 'celebris,' Lib. 2. c. 3.

'Religiosissimo:' Gaius (ii. 1) "sacrae sunt quae Diis superis consecratae sunt; religiosae, quae Diis manibus relictae sunt." A 'locus' could be made 'religiosus' by burying a dead body in it, "si modo ejus mortui funus ad nos pertineat." I doubt if Cicero is using the word here in a technical sense; for, if he were, he seems not to have the right word, which ought to be 'sacer.'

Atque ego hoc non vereor ne quid horum non modo impulsu verum omnino adventu meo factum esse videatur. Omnia ista ante facta sunt non modo quam ego Siciliam verum etiam quam iste Italiam attigit. Dum ego in Sicilia sum, nulla statua dejecta est. Posteaquam illinc discessi, quae sunt gesta cognoscite. LXVII. Centuripinorum senatus decrevit populusque jussit ut, quae statuae C. Verris ipsius et patris ejus et filii essent, eas quaestores demoliendas locarent, dumque ea demolitio fieret senatores ne minus XXX adessent. Videte gravitatem civitatis ac dignitatem. Neque eas in urbe sua statuas esse voluerunt quas inviti per vim atque imperium dedissent; neque ejus hominis in quem ipsi cum gravissimo testimonio publice, quod nunquam antea, Romam mandata legatosque misissent: et id gravius esse putarunt, si publico consilio quam si per vim multitudinis factum esse videretur. Quum hoc consilio statuas Centuripini publice sustulissent, audit Metellus: graviter fert: evocat ad se Centuripinorum magistratus et decemprimos: nisi restituissent statuas, vehementer minatur. Illi ad senatum renuntiant: statuae quae istius causae nihil prodessent reponuntur: decreta Centuripinorum quae de statuis erant facta non tolluntur. Hic ego aliud alii concedo: Metello homini sapienti prorsus non possum ignoscere si quid stulte facit. Quid ille hoc putabat Verri criminosum fore, si ejus statuae essent dejectae, quod saepe vento aut aliquo casu fieri solet? Non erat in hoc neque crimen ullum neque reprehensio. Ex quo igitur crimen atque accusatio nascitur? Ex hominum judicio et voluntate.

quae sunt gesta cognoscite.] 'hear what happened.' If the reading were 'quae gesta sint cognoscite,' we could hardly express the meaning differently from the translation which I have given. But the Latin language has two forms of expression, one of which, the indicative, affirms distinctly that something was done which the speaker is going to mention; the other, the subjunctive mood, indirectly states that something was done, but lays the chief emphasis on the other verb. Both forms may occur in one sentence, and there is no reason to doubt the genuineness of such expressions. Servius says, in a letter to Cicero (Ad Div. iv. 5), "de iis rebus quae hic geruntur quemadmodumque se provincia habeat certiorem faciam." Comp. Lib. 2. c. 72, "tantum mihi licet dicere quantum possum, tantum judici suspicari quantum velit." The better translation of the text would be something like this, 'After I left the island, what happened next, I will tell you.'

67. *populusque jussit*] The term applied to the formal voting of the Roman people. See Gellius, v. 19. Senatus 'decernit,' 'censet,' 'mandat.' Populus 'jubet.'

decemprimos:] The first ten in rank of the Senate or of the 'decuriones,' a body which in a municipal town corresponded to the Senate of Rome. Cicero says, Pro Sex. Roscio Am. c. 9, "itaque decurionum decretum statim fit ut decem primi proficiscantur ad L. Sullam."

aliud alii concedo:] This means, says Hotmann, 'I excuse the Centuripini;' and this may be implied; but it is not said. Cicero says, 'I can make different allowances for different persons. Metellus, who is a man of judgment, I cannot altogether excuse, if he does a foolish thing.'

LXVIII. Ego, si Metellus statuas Centuripinos reponere non coëgisset, haec dicerem: Videte, judices, quantum et quam acerbum dolorem sociorum atque amicorum animis inusserint istius injuriae, quum Centuripinorum amicissima et fidelissima civitas, quae tantis officiis cum populo Romano conjuncta est ut non solum rem publicam nostram sed etiam in quovis homine privato nomen ipsum Romanum semper dilexerit, ea publico consilio atque auctoritate judicarit C. Verris statuas esse in urbe sua non oportere. Recitarem decreta Centuripinorum: laudarem illam civitatem, id quod verissime possem: commemorarem decem millia esse civium Centuripinorum, fortissimorum fidelissimorumque sociorum; eos omnes hoc statuisse, Monumentum istius in sua civitate nullum esse oportere. Haec tum dicerem, si statuas Metellus non reposuisset. Velim quaerere nunc ex ipso Metello quidnam sua vi et auctoritate mihi ex hac oratione praeciderit. Eadem opinor omnia convenire. Neque enim, si maxime statuae dejectae essent, eas ego vobis possem jacentes ostendere. Hoc uno uterer, civitatem tam gravem statuas judicasse C. Verris demoliendas. Hoc mihi Metellus non eripuit: hoc etiam addidit ut quererer, si mihi videretur, tam iniquo jure sociis atque amicis imperari, ut iis ne in suis quidem beneficiis libero judicio uti liceret; ut vos rogarem ut conjecturam faceretis, qualem in iis rebus in me L. Metellum fuisse putaretis, in quibus rebus obesse mihi posset, quum in hac re tam aperta cupiditate fuerit, in qua nihil obfuit. Sed ego Metello non irascor, neque ei suam purgationem eripio qua ille apud omnes utitur, ut nihil malitiose neque consulto fecisse videatur.

LXIX. Jam igitur est ita perspicuum ut negare non possis nullam tibi statuam voluntate cujusquam datam, nullam pecuniam statuarum nomine nisi vi expressam et coactam. Quo quidem in crimine non illud solum intelligi volo, te ad statuas HS tricies coëgisse; sed multo etiam illud magis, quod simul demonstratum

68. *reponere . . coëgisset,*] Comp. c. 59, 'ut in curia coëgisti.' 'Cogere' admits both forms of expression.

ea publico &c.] 'Ea' is not the correlative of 'quae' in 'quae tantis officiis.' It is the repetition of 'civitas,' a long expression being interposed.

si maxime] 'Si maximae' in Zumpt's large edition is a misprint.

ut vos] 'vos' Lg. 42 M, Jordan.

purgationem] The reading of several MSS. is 'vacationem' or 'vagationem.' It is not said what the rest have. 'Purgationem,' apparently an emendation of Naugerius, is very doubtful. Klotz has 'culpae vacationem,' a piece of Latin hardly justified by the genuine Latin expression, 'culpa vacare.' Halm says, "Ac videtur lectio *vacationem* ferri posse; cf. quem locum attulit Klotzius in ed. I. p. xii. Ciceronis apud Nonium p. 436, 19: 'quo (scr. quom) mihi et Philippo vacationem das, bis gaudeo; nam et praeteritis ignoscis et concedis futura.'"

69. HS *tricies*] The usual reading is cxx millia or milia. See c. 67, note.

est, quantum odium aratorum, quantum omnium Siculorum sit et fuerit. In quo quae vestra defensio futura sit conjectura assequi non queo. "Oderunt Siculi; togatorum enim causa multa feci." At hi quidem acerrimi inimicissimique sunt. "Inimicos habeo cives Romanos, quod sociorum commoda ac jura defendi." At socii in hostium numero sese abs te habitos queruntur. "Aratores inimici sunt propter decumas." Quid qui agros immunes liberosque arant, cur oderunt? cur Halesini? cur Centuripini? cur Segestani? cur Halicyenses? Quod genus hominum, quem numerum, quem ordinem proferre possis, qui te non oderit, sive civium Romanorum sive Siculorum? ut etiamsi causam cur te oderint non possim dicere, tamen illud dicendum putem, quem omnes mortales oderint, eum vobis quoque odio esse oportere. An hoc dicere audebis, utrum de te aratores, utrum denique Siculi universi bene existiment [aut quo modo existiment], ad rem id non pertinere? Neque tu hoc dicere audebis, nec si cupias licebit. Eripiunt enim tibi istam orationem contemnendorum Siculorum atque aratorum statuae illae equestres, quas tu paulo ante quam ad urbem venires poni inscribique jussisti, ut omnium inimicorum tuorum animos accusatorumque tardares. Quis enim tibi molestus esset, aut quis appellare te auderet, quum videret statuas ab negotiatoribus, ab aratoribus, a communi Siciliae positas? Quod est aliud in illa provincia genus hominum? Nullum. Ergo ab universa provincia generatimque a singulis ejus partibus non solum diligitur sed etiam ornatur. Quis hunc attingere audeat? Potes igitur dicere nihil tibi obesse oportere aratorum, negotiatorum, Siculorum omnium testimonia, quum eorum nominibus in statuarum inscriptione oppositis omnem te speraris invidiam atque infamiam tuam posse extinguere? an quorum tu auctoritate statuas cohonestare tuas conatus es, eorum

possim] 'possum' 4 V, Iordan. 'possim' dtt. I think that 'possim' is the true reading.

aut quo modo existiment,] 'Primus inseruit e Cd. Nann. Steph.' (Orelli.) Hotmann conjectured 'bene an male existiment.' These words probably ought to be omitted, and they are omitted in all the MSS. except Lg. 42 F N.

nec si cupias] 'nec si cupies' Klotz, from V and other MSS., 'cupias' Lg. 42 φ.

orationem contemnendorum Siculorum] The word 'contemnendorum' seems very doubtful. Ursini says that one MS. has in its place 'negotiatorum.' 'Contemnendorum' has a kind of meaning, if we refer back to the words 'An hoc dicere audebis,' &c.; and it may mean 'these Sicilians, whose opinions you affect to despise.' We must perhaps connect the genitives 'contemnendorum Siculorum' with 'statuae.' But see Lib. 3. c. 44, note.

omnium inimicorum] This reading of V is perhaps preferable to Zumpt's and Iordan's 'iniquorum,' which may however be defended by Lib. 5. c. 69.

appellare te] V. Zumpt and Orelli omit 'te.' 'Appellare' here means 'in jus vocare.' See Cic. De Off. i. c. 25.

quorum tu &c.] This order of the words, adopted by Klotz from V, is recom-

ego dignitate accusationem meam comprobare non potero? Nisi forte quod apud publicanos gratiosus fuisti, in ea re spes te aliqua consolatur. Quae gratia ne quid tibi prodesse posset ego mea diligentia perfeci: ut etiam obesse deberet tu tua sapientia curasti. Etenim rem totam, judices, breviter cognoscite.

LXX. In scriptura Siciliae pro magistro est quidam L. Carpinatius, qui et sui quaestus causa, et fortasse quod sociorum interesse arbitrabatur, bene penitus in istius familiaritatem sese dedit. Is quum praetorem circum omnia fora sectaretur neque ab eo unquam discederet, in eam jam venerat familiaritatem [consuetudinemque] in vendendis istius decretis et judiciis transigendisque negotiis ut prope alter Timarchides numeraretur. Hoc erat etiam capitalior, quod idem pecunias iis qui ab isto aliquid mercabantur

mended by several reasons, and by the following words, 'eorum ego,' &c. Zumpt and Iordan have 'quorum auctoritate tu.'

apud publicanos] V has 'apud adversus publicanos;' one of these words is evidently a gloss of the other, or the copyist had two readings before him, and took both. Though 'apud' is common in such a formula as this, 'adversus' is also used; for 'adversus' is simply 'turned towards,' and may be a friendly or a hostile movement. Klotz has 'adversus.'

70. *scriptura*] The 'scriptura,' one of the oldest sources of Roman revenue, consisted of the payments made by those who pastured their cattle on the public lands. The name is derived from the circumstance of those who pastured their cattle on these lands being required to register (scribere) their names, and the number and kind of their animals, in respect of which they paid a certain sum of money. This source of revenue, like others, was let to the Publicani, who paid the state a sum of money, and collected the payments for themselves.

The Publicani formed 'societates' or partnerships for the farming of this and other sources of revenue; and as the state would often require the money paid at once, the members of these 'societates' took shares in these undertakings, and paid down their money. (Pro Rabirio Post. c. 2; Val. Max. vi. 9, 7; Polyb. vi. 17.) The affairs of such a 'societas' were managed by a 'magister' or 'director' at Rome, and a 'pro magistro' or deputy director in the province or place where the money was to be collected (comp. Cic. Ad Att. xi. 10). A person employed in the collection was said 'operas dare:' "Canuleius .. qui in portu Syracusis operas dabat." In Cicero, Ad Att. xi. 10, "P. Terentius operas in portu et scriptura Asiae pro magistro dedit;" where the 'pro magistro' is said 'operas dare.' A passage of Valerius Maximus (vi. 9, n. 8) is quoted by Garatoni, where 'operas dare' is contrasted with 'publicanum agere:' "P. Rupilius non publicanum in Sicilia egit, sed operas publicanis dedit;" and the note in the edition of Torrenius.

The two following extracts from the Lex Thoria will illustrate the text. Cap. 42, "Mag. prove mag. queive pro eo inperio iudicio suo quae publica Populi Romani in Africa sunt eruntve vectigalia fruenda locabit vendetve," &c.; and "ex lege dicta quam L. Caeci. Cn. Dom. cens. quom eorum agrorum vectigalia fruenda locaverunt legem deixerunt, neive quod in eis agreis pequs pascetur scripturae pecoris legem deicito," &c.

fora sectaretur] A 'forum' is a small community, as Forum Julii in Italy, and others. "'Fora,' 'conciliabula,' 'castella,' were places which in extent and importance stood between towns and villages (vici); they also belonged to the territory of some town, and had corporate rights" (Savigny, System, &c., ii. 251). This is the meaning of 'forum' as a town; but it may mean here all the 'fora,' that is, all the towns in which there were 'fora.'

familiaritatem] M. Lg. 42 omit this word and the 'que' after 'consuetudinem.' Zumpt and Iordan retain the words. Klotz omits them.

capitalior,] Klotz observes, after Zumpt, that 'capitalis,' in the sense of 'perniciosus,' is applied also to persons (Phil. v. 12; De Offic. iii. 21); and he adds, that in this word 'capitalis' Cicero also alludes to the

fenori dabat. Ea autem feneratio erat ejusmodi, judices, ut etiam is quaestus huic cederet. Nam quas pecunias ferebat iis expensas quibuscum contrahebat, eas aut scribae istius aut Timarchidi aut etiam isti ipsi referebat acceptas. Idem praeterea pecunias istius extraordinarias grandes suo nomine fenerabatur. Hic primo Carpinatius, antequam in istius tantam familiaritatem pervenisset, aliquoties ad socios literas de istius injuriis miserat. Canuleius vero, qui in portu Syracusis operas dabat, furta quoque istius permulta nominatim ad socios perscripserat, ea quae sine portorio Syracusis erant exportata: portum autem et scripturam eadem societas habebat. Ita factum est ut essent permulta quae ex

'capita' or capital which Carpinatius employed in money-lending. Such a play on words is quite in Cicero's fashion.

Nam quas &c.] "For the sums which he entered in his books against those with whom he contracted, those very sums he also entered as received either from a 'scriba' of Verres, or from Timarchides, or from Verres himself." See Lib. 1. c. 36. Verres, with the aid of this knave, lent money on interest to those who borrowed it to bribe Verres. This ingenious way of charging a man with an annual payment of interest in respect of money of which he never had the use, is a device that none but a Roman could have hit on.

extraordinarias] Such sums as were not entered in the books of accounts. See Lib. 1. c. 39.

portorio] The 'pro magistro' informed his associates that Verres did not pay the duties on articles exported (portorium); for, adds Cicero, the same 'societas' or company farmed the 'portoria' and the 'scriptura.' Cicero (De Imperio Cn. Pompeii, c. 6) enumerates the three kinds of dues or payments to the state: "Quum hostium copiae non longe absunt, etiam si irruptio facta nulla sit, tamen pecua relinquuntur, agricultura deseritur, mercatorum navigatio conquiescit: ita neque ex portu, neque ex decumis, neque ex scriptura vectigal conservari potest." The 'portoria' were levied at ferries, bridges, and certain barriers, as well as in the ports. Probably they were always levied on goods which passed from one province to another, and they were also claimed sometimes on goods carried from one part of the same province to another, as we see from Cicero (Ad Att. ii. 16; Dion Cass. xxxvi. 51). This oppressive tax was abolished in Italy B.C. 60 (Cic. Ad Q. Frat. i. 1. c. 11); but it was continued in the provinces, and let to the Publicani, and so the Roman Aerarium had the benefit of it. Towns which were 'liberae et immunes' took the 'portoria' for their own use; at least we know that many such towns did. The duties levied in sea-ports seem to us reasonable, because we are accustomed to them; but they were also levied at other places, as I have observed. The 'portitores' or 'collectors' lay in wait for the unfortunate merchant and his goods, and eased him of some of his money before they would let him pass. A twentieth of the value, it appears, was payable at Syracuse (c. 75). In France, before the revolution of '89, the same system of organized plunder existed. On the banks of the Loire, for instance, there was a series of toll-houses, from which the collectors pounced upon the traveller, and took money from him under the name of 'droits de traite' for the use of the state, and 'péages' in the name of communities or some lord (L. Blanc, Hist. de la Révol. Française, i. 513). A collector was 'portitor.' The 'portitor Orci' (Virg. Georg. iv. 502) was a personage with whom a Roman was very familiar in his lifetime.

societas] This is the Roman word for a partnership, the fundamental rules of which are the same in the Roman and in the English law. It was one of those 'obligationes' which were formed 'consensu' (Gaius, iii. 135). Gaius says (iii. 148), "societatem coire solemus aut totorum bonorum aut unius alicujus negotii, veluti mancipiorum emendorum aut vendendorum." Some of the Roman 'societates' were considered as artificial persons, a term not unknown in the English law, and a better term than 'corporations.' Savigny observes, "Also commercial undertakings, in which individuals are united, appear in the form of juristical (artificial) persons, and the general name of such associations is 'societas;' but

societatis literis dicere in istum et proferre possemus. Verum accidit ut Carpinatius, qui jam cum isto summa consuetudine, praeterea re ac ratione conjunctus esset, crebras postea literas ad socios de istius summis officiis in rem communem beneficiisque mitteret. Etenim quum iste omnia quaecunque Carpinatius postulabat facere ac decernere solebat, tum ille etiam plura scribebat ad socios, ut si posset ea quae antea scripserat plane extingueret. Ad extremum vero, quum iste jam decedebat, ejusmodi literas ad eos misit ut huic frequentes obviam prodirent, gratias agerent, facturos se si quid imperasset studiose pollicerentur. Itaque socii fecerunt vetere instituto publicanorum, non quo istum ullo honore dignum arbitrarentur, sed quod sua interesse putabant se memores gratosque existimari: gratias isti egerunt: Carpinatium saepe ad se de ejus officiis literas misisse dixerunt.

LXXI. Iste quum respondisset ea se libenter fecisse operamque Carpinatii magno opere laudasset, dat amico suo cuidam negotium, qui tum magister erat ejus societatis, ut diligenter caveret atque prospiceret ne quid esset in literis sociorum, quod contra caput

most of these had merely a contractual character, produced 'obligationes,' and were subject to be dissolved by notice, and also by the death of a single member. Some of them, however, obtained the powers of corporations, without on that account abandoning the name of 'societates:' to these belonged partnerships for the working of mines, salines, and contracts for farming the taxes." The Romans did not allow all 'societates' to have a 'corpus,' to be incorporated (Dig. 3. 4. 1). Those which were merely of a contractual nature were called 'privatae societates' (Dig. 17. 2. 69). "Paucis admodum in causis concessa sunt hujusmodi corpora; ut ecce vectigalium publicorum sociis permissum est corpus habere, vel auri fodinarum, vel argenti fodinarum, et salinarum. Item collegia (corporations) Romae certa sunt, quorum corpus senatusconsultis atque constitutionibus principalibus conformatum est, veluti pistorum, et quorundam aliorum, et naviculariorum, qui et in provinciis sunt." It appears that the Romans gave facilities for the incorporation of persons who were united in any great commercial undertakings. The Romans knew the value of this privilege, as a mode of making the capitals of individuals efficient by combination, an advantage which the law of England has not given till lately in an equal degree to the industry and capital of its citizens.

The real nature of a corporate body, or of an artificial person, has been obscured and made almost unintelligible by a careless use of words, and the loose language of English law writers. Those who wish to understand what the notion is may read Savigny, System des Heut. Röm. Rechts, Juristische Personen, vol. ii.

non quo . . arbitrarentur,] Zumpt observes that Lambinus, Gruter, Graevius, edited 'non quod,' but the MSS. have 'quo.' Ernesti edited 'non quo,' only because he thought that 'quod' could not go with the subjunctive, of which however we have abundant examples, and also of 'quia' with the subjunctive: "neque enim *quod* solum, sed etiam *quia* in hac structura, ubi, quid non sit, significatur, cum conjunctivo apud Ciceronem ponitur" (Zumpt). It would be strange if 'qui' and 'quum' could go with the subjunctive, and 'quod' and 'quia' could not. In another place, 'non quo . . haberet' is followed by 'quod non . . appellarentur.' To reduce to rules the usages of all the forms of 'quo,' is not easy.

sua interesse] Above, 'sociorum interesse,' which we must consider an elliptical expression. In 'sua interesse,' 'sua' must be the accusative, and there is good reason for taking it to be equivalent to 'suam.' Key's Latin Grammar, § 910.

suum aut existimationem valere posset. Itaque ille multitudine sociorum remota decumanos convocat: rem defert. Statuunt illi atque decernunt ut eae literae quibus existimatio C. Verris laederetur removerentur, operaque daretur ne ea res C. Verri fraudi esse posset. Si ostendo hoc decrevisse decumanos, si planum facio hoc decreto remotas esse literas, quid exspectatis amplius? possumne rem magis judicatam afferre, magis reum condemnatum in judicium adducere? At quorum judicio condemnatum? Nempe eorum quos ii qui severiora judicia desiderant arbitrantur res judicare oportere, publicanorum judicio; quos videlicet nunc populus judices poscit, de quibus, ut eos judices habeamus, legem ab homine non nostri generis, non ex equestri loco profecto, sed nobilissimo promulgatam videmus. Decumani, hoc est, principes et quasi senatores publicanorum, removendas de medio literas censuerunt. Habeo ex iis qui affuerunt, quos producam, quibus hoc committam, homines hones-

71. *decumanos*] Cicero explains the sense in which he uses the word; they were the leading men, the farmers of the 'decumae.' But if the 'decumani' are the farmers of the 'decumae,' as they are (Lib. 3. c. 8), and this 'societas' for which Carpinatius acted, farmed only the 'scriptura et portoria' (c. 70), it may be asked, how did the 'decumani' come to interfere in the matter? The 'magister' of the 'societas' kept the body of his partners out of the way and called a meeting of the 'decumani,' who had a general interest in the affair, and did not wish that any evidence against Verres should appear on the books of the 'publicani.' They could not properly, one may assume, interfere in the affairs of this 'societas;' but the 'magister' got them together for this purpose, and they came to the resolution that the evidence must be destroyed. These fellows were great rascals; but in modern times worse things are done. The Roman system of farming the taxes was bad, but we cannot say whether in those days it would have been better for the Roman state to employ tax collectors; I mean better both for the Roman treasury and for those who paid the taxes. The Publicanus was undoubtedly a terrible scourge in a province. "Ubi Publicanus est, ibi aut jus publicum vanum aut libertatem sociis nullam esse" (Lib. 45. c. 18). The tax-gatherer's face is never pleasant to look on. Sometimes he gets more out of us than we are bound to pay, and it is often cheaper to put up with the loss than to waste your time in trying to get it back.

removerentur,] The meaning of 'removere,' 'to put out of the way,' is clear from this chapter. Cic. Ad Q. Fr. i. 1. c. 12, 'remoto imperio ac vi potestatis et fascium;' and Ulpian (Dig. 14. 3. 11. § 3), 'non in loco remoto sed evidenti.' In this instance 'multitudine sociorum remota' is what we call jobbing. The directors kept the shareholders away while they perpetrated the scandalous job.

legem .. promulgatam] The Lex of L. Aurelius Cotta, the praetor, which was enacted under the name of the Lex Aurelia, was promulgated in this year, B.C. 70. The expression 'legem promulgare,' that is, 'provulgare,' is not quite correct, for 'promulgare' signified to put up notice of a proposed 'lex,' or 'rogatio,' as a 'lex' was called before it was enacted. The correct expression 'rogationem promulgare' is used by Sallust. Festus correctly considers 'promulgare' the same as 'provulgare.'

Cotta was not a patrician, but he was 'nobilis,' for his ancestors long before him had filled curule magistracies. The 'nostri generis' refers to Cicero's equestrian rank.

quibus hoc committam,] These words are omitted in the Variorum edition. (See the note.) Graevius cannot see what they do here; but they are easily explained. Cicero had no evidence for what he affirmed except the 'decumani:' the written evidence was destroyed. Yet he says, 'I will produce men who were present when the order (decretum) for destroying the written evidence was made. I will trust to them for the proof (iis hoc committam), for they will not lie.' Zumpt understood it; he says

tissimos ac locupletissimos, istos ipsos principes equestris ordinis, quorum splendore vel maxime istius qui legem promulgavit oratio et causa nititur. Venient in medium; dicent quid statuerint. Profecto, si recte homines novi, non mentientur: literas enim communes de medio removere potuerunt, fidem suam et religionem removere non possunt. Ergo equites Romani, qui te suo judicio condemnarunt, horum judicio condemnari noluerunt. Vos nunc utrum illorum judicium an voluntatem sequi malitis considerate.

LXXII. Ac vide quid te amicorum tuorum studium, quid tuum consilium, quid sociorum voluntas adjuvet. Dicam paulo promptius: neque enim jam vereor ne quis hoc me magis accusatorie quam libere dixisse arbitretur. Si istas literas non decreto decumanorum magistri removissent, tantum possem in te dicere quantum in literis invenissem: nunc decreto isto facto literisque remotis tantum mihi licet dicere quantum possum; tantum judici suspicari quantum velit. Dico te maximum pondus auri, argenti, eboris, purpurae, plurimam vestem Melitensem, plurimam stragulam, multam Deliacam supellectilem, plurima vasa Corinthia, magnum numerum frumenti, vim mellis maximam Syracusis exportasse: his pro rebus quod portorium non esset datum, literas ad socios misisse L. Canuleium qui in portu operas daret. Satisne magnum crimen hoc videtur? Nullum, opinor, majus. Quid defendet Hortensius? postulabit ut literas Canuleii proferam? crimen ejusmodi, nisi literis confirmetur, inane esse dicet? Clamabo literas remotas esse de medio; decreto sociorum erepta mihi esse istius indicia ac monumenta furtorum. Aut hoc contendat nunquam esse factum, aut omnia tela excipiat necesse est. Negas esse factum? Placet

'quorum religioni rem permittam.' Caesar, B. G. iv. 5, has 'nihil committendum,' exactly in the same sense. See a similar use of 'committere,' De Domo, c. 19; Pro Milone, c. 23.

istius] Schütz proposed 'illius,' on which Iordan says: "Sed cum Cicero, homo senatorius, equestrem ordinem et Aurelium Cottam in causa illa iudiciaria haberet adversarios (?), recte pronomine *iste*, ut alibi de Verre utitur." I suppose that the (?) is Halm's addition. I do not think that Iordan's explanation can be admitted, and I think that 'istius' is the wrong word here.

72. *paulo promptius:*] 'a little more boldly or confidently.' In c. 14, 'Heraclium ... non promptissimum;' and Divin. c. 13, "quo paratior ad usum forensem promptiorque esse possim." 'Accusatorie' is as an accuser, that is, one who has the licence of saying any thing, or may be supposed to say any thing that criminates a defendant.

vestem Melitensem,] See Lib. 4. c. 46.

magnum numerum frumenti,] The form 'magna vis frumenti' also occurs in Tacit. Hist. v. 12.

vim mellis] Honey was one of the products of Sicily; and a branch of rural economy (Virgil, Georg. Lib. iv.).—'qui .. daret:' 'the port-collector.'

Quid defendet] 'Qui id defendet,' Klotz and Iordan from Lg. 42. Zumpt will not have it, because '*defendere crimen* non videtur dici posse.' But, though he is mistaken in this, I think that he is right in reading 'quid defendet,' which means, 'What will Hortensius say in defence?'

omnia tela] 'omnium tela' Lg. 42 p. m. M, Klotz, Iordan.

mihi ista defensio, descendo: aequa enim contentio, aequum certamen proponitur. Producam testes et producam plures eodem tempore: quoniam tum quum actum est una fuerunt, nunc quoque una sint: quum interrogabuntur, obligentur non solum jurisjurandi atque existimationis periculo sed etiam communi inter se conscientia. Si planum fit hoc ita quemadmodum dico esse factum, num poteris dicere, Hortensi, nihil in istis fuisse literis quod Verrem laederet? Non modo id non dices, sed ne illud quidem tibi dicere licebit, tantum quantum ego dicam non fuisse. Ergo hoc vestro consilio et gratia perfecistis ut, quemadmodum paulo ante dixi, et mihi summa facultas ad accusandum daretur et judici libera potestas ad credendum.

LXXIII. Quod quum ita sit, nihil fingam tamen. Meminero me non sumpsisse quem accusarem, sed recepisse quos defenderem; vos ex me causam non a me prolatam sed ad me delatam audire oportere; me Siculis satis esse facturum si, quae cognovi in Sicilia, quae accepi ab ipsis, diligenter exposuero; populo Romano, si nullius vim, nullius potentiam pertimuero; vobis, si facultatem vere atque honeste judicandi fide et diligentia mea fecero; mihimet, si ne minimum quidem de meo curriculo vitae quod mihi semper propositum fuit decessero. Quapropter nihil est quod metuas ne quid in te confingam: etiam quod laetere habes. Multa enim quae scio abs te esse commissa, quod aut nimium turpia aut parum credibilia sunt, praetermittam: tantum agam de hoc toto nomine societatis. Ut jam scire possis, quaeram decretumne sit: quum id invenero, quaeram remotaene sint literae. Quum id quoque constabit, vos jam hoc me tacito intelligetis; si illi, qui hoc istius

descendo:] This is an acceptance of the challenge. 'Your defence is this: well, I accept it. I descend to the contest.' L. Valla (Eleg. v. 36), quoted by Creuzer and Moser, says "*Descendo* in praelium, in forum, in campum dicimus, non quia de loco superiore in inferiorem descendimus, sed quia de loco tuto in locum discriminis."

una sint:] 'una adsint' Lg. 42 p. m., Iordan.

potestas ad credendum.] 'potestas ad decernendum' Klotz, because Lg. 42 p. m. φ have 'ad cernendum,' which seems, as Garatoni suggests, like a blunder for 'credendum.' Iordan says that 'decernendum' is the conjecture of Lambinus. It is a bad one.

73. *nihil fingam tamen.*] 'Though this is so, I will use no invention, all the same as if it were not so.' Examples of 'tamen' placed in a like position occur Lib. 2. c. 41, 'aliqua tamen;' Lib. 4. c. 20, 'testimonium tamen;' Lib. 4. c. 35, 'religionem tamen.' In the present passage it has the same force as the Greek word ὅμως in a like position.

quos defenderem;] "'quos def.' Lg. 42, 'quod def.' ett. codd. noti." (Iordan.)

nullius potentiam] 'nullius potestatem' Klotz from Lg. 42 p. m. Lg. 42 also omits 'nullius vim.'

Ut jam scire possis,] Lg. 42 F M; 'ut eam scire possitis' ett.; and Orelli has this, except that he writes 'jam' for 'eam.' Hake suggests 'ut factum scire possitis.'—'jam hoc me tacito:' Zumpt omits 'hoc.'

causa decreverunt, equites Romani, nunc iidem in eum judices essent, istum sine dubio condemnarent de quo literas eas, quae istius furta indicarent, et ad se missas et suo decreto remotas scirent esse. Quem igitur ab iis equitibus Romanis, qui istius causa cupiunt omnia, qui ab eo benignissime tractati sunt, condemnari necesse esset, is a vobis, judices, ulla vi aut ratione absolvi potest? Ac ne forte ea quae remota de medio atque erepta nobis sunt omnia ita condita fuisse atque ita abdita latuisse videantur ut haec diligentia, quam ego a me exspectari maxime puto, nihil eorum investigare, nihil assequi potuerit, quae consilio aliquo aut ratione inveniri potuerunt, inventa sunt, judices; manifestis in rebus hominem jam teneri videbitis. Nam quod in publicanorum causis vel plurimum aetatis meae versor vehementerque illum ordinem observo, satis commode mihi videor eorum consuetudinem usu tractandoque cognosse.

LXXIV. Itaque ut hoc comperi remotas esse literas societatis, habui rationem eorum annorum per quos iste in Sicilia fuisset: deinde quaesivi, quod erat inventu facillimum, qui per eos annos magistri illius societatis fuissent apud quos tabulae fuissent. Sciebam enim hanc magistrorum qui tabulas haberent consuetudinem esse ut, quum tabulas novo magistro traderent, exempla literarum ipsi habere non nollent. Itaque ad L. Vibium, equitem Romanum, virum primarium, quem reperiebam magistrum fuisse eo ipso anno, qui mihi maxime quaerendus erat, primum veni. Sane homini praeter opinionem improviso incidi. Scrutatus sum quae potui,

in eum judices essent,] I find no MS. variations noted. The text is intelligible. See Act. ii. Lib. 1. c. 7.

qui . . cupiunt &c.] It would be a mistake to make a literal and stiff translation of an expression which is borrowed from the polite formulae of common life; as we see from Horace, 1 Sat. ix. 5, "Suaviter ut nunc est . . et cupio omnia quae vis." See Heindorf's note. Creuzer and Moser quote other examples from Cicero, Ad Fam. x. 19; xiii. 6, 64, and 75.

ulla vi] The old reading is 'nulla vi' without an interrogation. Hotmann saw the feebleness of this, and he made the emendation 'ulla,' which is confirmed by the MSS. since collated. Iordan says nothing about 'ulla.' Ernesti could not understand how 'vis' could be used in the acquittal of Verres; but Zumpt explains it by 'opes adversariorum,' and correctly. To remove the supposed difficulty, Ernesti thought that we should write 'via,' which Lg. 29 has, and Iordan. But we cannot accept it. The origin of the blunder is palpable. Wesenberg argues in favour of 'via.'

ut haec diligentia, &c.] The common reading is 'ut hac diligentia . . . investigari —assequi;' and a reader is rather inclined to expect 'hac diligentia.' But then 'assequi' must have a passive sense; and it does not appear that an example can be found (Zumpt). Lg. 42 p. m. has 'haec,' or rather 'hec.' The other codd. have 'hac.'

74. *apud quos*] 'et apud quos' Lg. 29 A B.—'hanc . . . consuetudinem:' Cicero says 'magistrorum,' and adds 'qui tabulas haberent,' which has the sense of an adjective. Altogether he says, 'I knew this to be the practice of the book-keepers.' It is one of the Roman generalizing forms of expression, like 'qui operas daret' in c. 72, and in the oration Pro Cn. Plancio, c. 27

exempla] 'copies.'—'et quaesivi omnia:' 'et quae vidi omnia' Lg. 42 p. m.

et quaesivi omnia: inveni duos solos libellos a L. Canuleio missos sociis ex portu Syracusis, in quibus erat ratio scripta mensium complurium rerum exportatarum istius nomine sine portorio. Itaque obsignavi statim. Erant haec ex eo genere quod ego maxime genus ex sociorum literis reperire cupiebam; verum tantum inveni, judices, quod apud vos quasi exempli causa proferre possem. Sed tamen quidquid erit in his libellis, quantulumcunque videbitur esse, hoc quidem certe manifestum erit: de ceteris ex hoc conjecturam facere debetis. Recita mihi, quaeso, hunc primum libellum: deinde illum alterum. LIBELLI CANVLEIANI. Non quaero, unde ccc amphoras mellis habueris, unde tantum Melitensium, unde quinquaginta tricliniorum lectos, unde tot candelabra: non, inquam, jam quaero unde haec habueris; sed quo tantum tibi opus fuerit, id quaero. Mitto de melle: sed tantum Melitensium, quasi etiam amicorum uxores—tantum lectorum, quasi omnium istorum villas ornaturus esses.

LXXV. Et quum haec paucorum mensium ratio in his libellis sit, facite ut vobis triennii totius veniat in mentem. Sic contendo; ex his parvis libellis apud unum magistrum societatis repertis vos jam conjectura assequi posse cujusmodi praedo iste in illa provincia

mensium complurium] Zumpt finds a difficulty in deciding if we should write 'mensium' or 'mensum,' for the MSS. have both. He takes no notice of the fact, that 'mensi-s' should regularly have 'mensi-um.' It is true that Ovid has 'mensum' (Met. viii. 500), as the editors write it; but we may make 'mensium' a dissyllable. There are several words of this declension which drop the 'i' in the genitive plural, and 'mensis' may be one of them. See Key's Grammar, 'Remarks on the Third or I Declension;' and the note of Creuzer and Moser, who give seven reasons for 'mensum.'

obsignavi statim.] It appears that the prosecutor had authority to put a seal on such written testimony as he could find, and, as it seems, to carry it off with him; or, at any rate, to call upon the person in whose possession the papers were to produce them with the seals. An excepted case, as to carrying written evidence to Rome, is mentioned at the end of c. 76.

Erant haec &c.] There seems no occasion to adopt the suggestion of Hotmann, 'Nec erant haec.' Cicero found something that he was looking for, but it was not much. It was enough however to serve as a sample. Again, Zumpt would mend 'ex eo genere.' "Vellem *erat aliud ex eodem genere*, sive *erant alia* vel *plura ex eodem genere*." It is singular that a good critic should take such pains to spoil what is so clear. All that the MSS. could justify us in doing is, to change 'eo' into 'eodem,' which seems no improvement. Klotz has 'erant haec ex eodem.' Halm suggests 'erant haec ex eo quidem,' which is better.

amicorum uxores] Cicero suggests that the Malta vests were intended as presents for the wives of those whom Verres honoured with his dubious friendship.—'mitto:' compare Lib. 4. c. 3, 'mitto jam rationem.' Zumpt and Iordan have 'omitto,' from Lg. 42 p. m. On the same authority he omits 'ne' after 'tantum,' but his reason is not worth much. 'Ne' is not however wanted: "I say nothing of the honey: but such a quantity of Malta vests—as if you were going to dress out even your friends' wives—such a number of couches, as if you were going to furnish the 'villae' of all of them." Tacitus has a like use of 'sed' (Ann. i. 10), 'Sane Cassii' &c.; 'sed Pompeium' &c.

75. *ut vobis triennii &c.*] Comp. Lib. 5. c. 70, 'venit mihi in mentem M. Catonis;' and Act. i. c. 18.

fuerit, quam multas cupiditates, quam varias, quam infinitas habuerit; quantam pecuniam non solum numeratam verum etiam hujuscemodi in rebus positam confecerit: quae vobis alio loco planius explicabuntur. Nunc hoc attendite. His exportationibus, quae recitatae sunt, scribit HS LX socios perdidisse ex vicesima portorii Syracusis. Pauculis igitur mensibus, ut hi pusilli et contempti libelli indicant, furta praetoris quae essent HS duodecies ex uno oppido solo exportata sunt. Cogitate nunc, quum illa Sicilia sit, hoc est insula, quae undique exitus maritimos habeat, quid ex ceteris locis exportatum putetis; quid Agrigento, quid Lilybaeo, quid Panhormo, quid Thermis, quid Halesa, quid Catina, quid ex ceteris oppidis; quid vero Messana, quem iste sibi locum maxime tutum esse arbitrabatur, ubi animo semper soluto liberoque erat, quod sibi iste Mamertinos delegerat, ad quos omnia quae aut diligentius servanda aut occultius exportanda erant deportaret. His inventis libellis ceteri remoti et diligentius sunt reconditi: nos tamen, ut omnes intelligant hoc nos sine cupiditate agere, his ipsis libellis contenti sumus.

LXXVI. Nunc ad sociorum tabulas accepti et expensi, quas removere honeste nullo modo potuerunt, et ad amicum tuum Carpinatium revertemur. Inspiciebamus Syracusis a Carpinatio confectas tabulas societatis, quae significabant multis nominibus eos homines versuram a Carpinatio fecisse qui pecunias Verri dedissent. Quod erit vobis luce clarius, judices, tum quum eos ipsos produxero qui dederunt. Intelligetis enim illa tempora per quae quum essent in periculo pretio sese redemerunt cum societatis tabulis non solum consulibus verum etiam mensibus convenire.

hujuscemodi] 'ejuscemodi' Lg. 42; but the editors have not been deceived by this false form.

alio loco] Lib. 4. c. 26.

furta praetoris quae essent] 'things stolen by the praetor to the amount of,' &c. This is the proper translation of 'quae essent.' The HS LX means sixty thousands. Orelli has 'LX millia;' but 'millia' is often omitted. 'HS duodecies' is rightly explained by the addition of 'centena millia,' as appears from the amount of the tax, which was a twentieth of the value. For twenty times sixty thousand make twelve times a hundred thousand. The abbreviation of 'duodecies' in Lg. 42 is $\overline{\infty}$ cc. The horizontal stroke denotes a thousand, but the stroke is often omitted. Klotz has 'HS ∞ cc.'

The export duty was a twentieth. A twentieth on goods was a common charge; and, if they were not valued too high, five per cent. is a more moderate duty than many modern nations have been content with on imported goods. See Thucydides, vii. 28.

sine cupiditate] 'that I am not too eager to press the evidence against him.' See Index, Cupidus.

76. *versuram*] 'Versuram facere' means no more than to borrow in order to pay an old debt. 'Versura solvere,' 'to pay by borrowing,' means that a debt still exists, though the creditor is changed. Cic. Ad Att. v. 21, "Salaminii quum Romae versuram facere vellent;" and Tacit. Ann. vi. 16, 'postremo vetita versura.' See Pro Fonteio, c. 5; Pro Flacco, c. 20.

Quum haec maxime cognosceremus et jam in manibus tabulas haberemus, repente aspicimus lituras ejusmodi, quasi quaedam vulnera tabularum recentia. Statim suspicione offensi ad ea ipsa nomina oculos animumque transtulimus. Erant acceptae pecuniae C. VERRUTIO C. F. sic tamen ut usque ad alterum R literae constarent integrae, reliquae omnes essent in litura. Alterum, tertium, quartum, permulta erant ejusdemmodi nomina. Quum manifesta res [tum] flagitiosa litura tabularum atque insignis turpitudo teneretur, quaerere incepimus de Carpinatio, quisnam is esset Verrutius quicum tantae pecuniae rationem haberet. Haerere homo, versari, rubere. Quod lege excipiuntur tabulae publicanorum quominus Romam deportentur, ut res quam maxime clara ac testata esse posset, in jus ad Metellum Carpinatium voco, tabulasque societatis in forum defero. Fit maximus concursus hominum; et quod erat Carpinatii nota cum isto praetore societas ac feneratio, summe exspectabant omnes quidnam in tabulis teneretur.

LXXVII. Rem ad Metellum defero, me tabulas perspexisse sociorum, in his tabulis magnam rationem C. Verrutii permultis nominibus esse; meque hoc perspicere ex consulum mensiumque ratione hunc Verrutium neque ante adventum C. Verris neque post decessionem quidquam cum Carpinatio rationis habuisse: postulo ut mihi respondeat qui sit iste Verrutius, mercator an negotiator an arator an pecuarius; in Sicilia sit an jam decesserit. Clamare omnes ex conventu neminem unquam in Sicilia fuisse

ejusmodi,] Iordan remarks that this word can hardly be explained here. Halm suggests 'ejusdem modi.' 'Ejusmodi' is explained by 'quasi quaedam' &c. It differs not from 'exemplum ejusmodi, quod' &c. c. 45.

acceptae &c.] Orelli reads 'erant acceptae pecuniae A. C. Verrutio C. F.,' and so does the Variorum edition and Iordan. Zumpt and Klotz omit the preposition, for the full expression is 'alicui acceptum ferre' or 'referre,' where the dative depends on the verb. But it appears from Cicero that the preposition was also used: "una praepositio est *abs*, eaque nunc tantum in accepti tabulis manet, et ne iis quidem omnium: in reliquo sermone mutata est" (Orat. c. 47). See the note in Goeller's edition. In this case the A is omitted by Lg. 42 p. m. This is the only MS. which Iordan cites, and I do not know what the rest have.

[*tum*]] codd. 'cum,' Hotmann, Iordan. Lambinus erased 'tum,' and we know that it is omitted in Lg. 42. If we omit it, all is right. Or we might change 'tum' to 'tam,' as Wyttenbach proposed.

versari,] Most of the MSS. and the older editions have 'aversari,' which is the reading of Orelli and Klotz. Zumpt and Iordan have 'versari,' from M Lg. 42. There is also a reading 'adversari.' 'Versari' is supposed to be equivalent to 'versat se,' Lib. 1. c. 51.

testata] In a passive sense, as we call it; but these forms in 'tus' serve various purposes in Latin, for the language has no active participle except the present: 'testatam rem,' Pro Murena, c. 21. 'Adeptam' is used passively, De Sen. c. 2.

defero.] Lg. 42 p. m. M N have 'defert,' which Klotz has. But there is no sense in this reading unless we also write 'tabulas' without 'que.'

77. *qui sit*] Halm suggests 'quis,' which Iordan has. 'Quis esset,' shortly after.

mercator an negotiator &c.] See Lib. 2. c. 3, 'mercibus suppeditandis,' &c.

Verrutium. Ego instare ut mihi responderet quis esset, ubi esset, unde esset; cur servus societatis qui tabulas conficeret semper in Verrutii nomine certo ex loco mendosus esset. Atque haec postulabam, non quo illum cogi putarem oportere ut ad ea mihi responderet invitus, sed ut omnibus istius furta, illius flagitium, utriusque audacia perspicua esse posset. Itaque illum in jure metu conscientiaque peccati mutum atque exanimatum ac vix vivum relinquo: tabulas in foro summa hominum frequentia exscribo: adhibentur in exscribendo de conventu viri primarii: literae liturae-que omnes assimulatae, expressae, de tabulis in libros transferuntur. Haec omnia summa cura et diligentia recognita et collata et ab hominibus honestissimis obsignata sunt. Si Carpinatius mihi tum respondere noluit, responde mihi nunc tu, Verres, quem esse hunc tuum paene gentilem Verrutium putes. Fieri non potest ut, quem video te praetore in Sicilia fuisse et quem ex ipsa ratione intelligo locupletem fuisse, eum tu in tua provincia non cognoveris. Atque adeo, ne hoc aut longius aut obscurius esse possit, procedite in medium, atque explicate descriptionem imaginemque tabularum, ut omnes mortales istius avaritiae non jam vestigia sed ipsa cubilia videre possint.

LXXVIII. Videtis VERRUTIUM? videtis primas literas integras? videtis extremam partem nominis, caudam illam verrinam tam-

servus] There is no reason why this should not be taken literally to signify a slave who was employed in keeping accounts. Hotmann supposes the 'servus societatis' to be one who 'Syracusis operam dabat societati,' as opposed to the 'magister,' an absurd explanation. Manutius says the same, and adds that the 'servus' is Carpinatius. 'Cave credideris.' —'qui tabulas confecerit' is, according to Jordan, the reading of all the MSS. except *Lg.* 42 p. m., which has 'qui tabulas conficeret.' As both expressions are Latin, and no MSS. evidence is decisive in such a case, we must determine by other reasons which reading we will take, and this is not difficult to do. 'Qui . . confecerit' is the man who kept the accounts, made the entries, the particular entries of which Cicero is speaking. 'Qui . . conficeret' is the book-keeper; and the imperfect consists with the other parts of the sentence.

certo ex loco] 'beginning from a certain place in the entries.' Klotz, from V, has 'certo in loco,' which Creuzer and Moser take to be the true reading. But 'certo ex loco' is quite as consistent with Cicero's statement, and more intelligible. —'ad ea:' 'ad' is from V, and perhaps properly added.

in jure] 'before the praetor.' See Lib. 3. c. 15, note.

in exscribendo] This passage is worthy of note, as showing the way in which documentary evidence was secured when the originals could not be produced at the trial. In this case there was an exception in favour of the 'publicani.' They were not compelled to produce their books. Accordingly copies were made and attested. —'de conventu' seems better than 'ex conventu,' which Klotz has from V.

gentilem] The resemblance between Verres and Verrutius is the foundation of this remark of Cicero, though Verres was not a gentile name.

Atque adeo,] Comp. Lib. 2. c. 1, 'Atque adeo, ante quam' &c.

omnes mortales] See In Pison. c. 31, note, vol. iv.

ipsa cubilia] Creuzer and Moser compare Cicero, In Pisonem, c. 34, 'An vero tu parum putas,' &c.

78. *caudam*] The end of the name of

quam in luto demersam esse in litura? Sic habent se tabulae, judices, ut videtis. Quid exspectatis? quid quaeritis amplius? Tu ipse, Verres, quid sedes? quid moraris? nam aut exhibeas nobis Verrutium necesse est aut te esse Verrutium fateare. Laudantur oratores veteres, Crassi illi et Antonii, quod crimina diluere dilucide, quod copiose reorum causas defendere solerent. Nimirum illi non ingenio solum his patronis sed fortuna etiam praestiterunt. Nemo enim ita tum peccabat ut defensioni locum non relinqueret: nemo ita vivebat ut nulla ejus vitae pars summae turpitudinis esset expers: nemo ita in manifesto peccatu tenebatur ut, quum impudens fuisset in facto, tum impudentior videretur si negaret. Nunc vero quid faciat Hortensius [patronus]? Avaritiaene crimina frugalitatis laudibus deprecetur? At hominem flagitiosissimum, libidinosissimum, nequissimumque defendit. An ab hac ejus infamia,

Verres. There is a delicious note of Hotmann on this passage, which I copy out, for fear that it should be lost: "extremitatem. Sumpta videtur translatio a bestia cujus cauda extra cubile extans index est eam ibi delitescere." Did Hotmann ever see a beast in its 'cubile,' with its tail on the outside, keeping watch instead of the head? Cicero could not refrain from a joke on the name of Verres, on which Nannius acutely remarks: "festive autem Verrem *caudatum* fecit, alludens ad id quod Verres suem significat." There is however an objection to this explanation, for a pig's tail is too short to trail in the mud. But this difficulty may be removed by comparing another passage, in which Verres is a hog wallowing in the mire (Lib. 4. c. 15).

There is a reading 'codam.' The reading of Klotz, 'Verrinam' for 'Verris,' is an improvement, and what is intended in V, the reading of which is 'Verris nam.'

exhibeas] 'Exhibere' is a word of art, which means to produce for various purposes. The title of the Digest (10. 4), Ad exhibendum, is the best comment upon it. The following passage from Gaius (Dig. 10. tit. 4. s. 13) will explain the text: "si liber homo detineri ab aliquo dicatur, interdictum adversus eum qui detinere dicitur de exhibendo eo potest quis habere." The person who detained the free man was obliged to produce him, that the question of freedom might be tried. This 'interdictum' was like the English writ of Habeas Corpus. See also Dig. 48. tit. 3, De Custodia et exhibitione reorum, an instructive title, from which we learn that accused persons could be out on bail, but the bail must produce them or pay (s. 4): "si quis reum criminis, pro quo satisdedit, non exhibuerit, poena pecuniaria plectitur." We have the name 'exhibit' in chancery proceedings, which is the Roman name, but not the thing.

Crassi . . et Antonii,] The orators M. Antonius and L. Licinius Crassus.

crimina diluere dilucide,] 'Diluere' means literally 'to take away by washing.' Cicero adds 'dilucide,' as if there might be some connexion between the two words, but he is merely playing on the sound.

nemo ita vivebat . . . negaret.] These words are quoted by Gellius, xiii. 20, who observes that he found 'peccatu' written 'in uno atque altero antiquissimae fidei libro Tironiano;' and he defends the form 'peccatu' by like instances. 'Peccatu' is also in Lg. 42.

At hominem] This passage is thus quoted by Gellius (vi. 16), "Nunc vero quid faciat Hortensius? Avaritiaene crimina, &c. An hominem . . defendat," which variation may be either owing to the carelessness of Gellius, in not looking further, or to his copyists; for one MS. has 'at.' It is an instance however of the care that we should take in adopting the readings of single passages which are quoted by ancient writers; for they were often misquoted. Here the context disproves the reading in the text of Gellius. As to the omission of 'patronus,' the text of Gellius cannot be decisive; but 'patronus' is only in Lg. 42 p. m.

An ab hac ejus] 'An ab hac illius' Lg. 42 p. m., Klotz, Iordan.

nequitia, vestros animos in aliam partem fortitudinis commemoratione traducat? At homo inertior, ignavior, magis vir inter mulieres, impura inter viros muliercula proferri non potest. At mores commodi. Quis contumacior? quis inhumanior? quis superbior? At haec sine cujusquam malo. Quis acerbior? quis insidiosior? quis crudelior unquam fuit? In hoc homine atque in ejusmodi causa quid facerent omnes Crassi et Antonii? Tantum, opinor, Hortensi: ad causam non accederent neque in alterius impudentia sui pudoris existimationem amitterent. Liberi enim ad causas solutique veniebant, neque committebant ut si impudentes in defendendo esse noluissent ingrati in deserendo existimarentur.

impura] "Lego: 'magis vir inter mulieres, inter viros muliercula;' cetera sine dubitatione librariis adscribo," Garatoni, who gives his reasons for this proposed change. Jordan thinks that his specious argument is not sufficient to induce us to make the change. Nor do I think that it is. Zumpt remarks that 'magis' must also be referred to 'impura.'

in alterius impudentia] The use of the preposition 'in' with the ablative is very extensive, and I have not seen it well explained. The sense can only be reached by carefully looking at the context. Caesar has examples, for instance (B. G. I. 33), 'in tanto imperio,' 'when the Romans had so great an empire;' Cicero, Pro Caelio, c. 19, 'in tantis praemiis eloquentiae,' 'when there are such rewards for eloquence.' The text means 'they would not throw away their own self-respect by defending the shameless conduct of a client.' That is the meaning, but it may be expressed otherwise and perhaps better. Cicero's remark is good, and some wise advocates don't neglect it now. A man may do his best for his client, but he must think of himself too.

Liberi &c.] Klotz observes that this is an allusion to the relationship that subsisted between Verres and Hortensius, who is said to have received from Verres many costly works of art, and he was therefore not 'liber et solutus,' being under obligations to him. He also came within the terms of the Lex Cincia de donis et muneribus, at least if he had received any presents for defending Verres. Among other things, Hortensius is said to have received a sphinx of excellent workmanship, about which a joke of Cicero's is recorded by Plutarch (Cicero, c. 7); Quintilian (Inst. Or. vi. c. 3. § 93); and Pliny (H. N. xxxiv. 18).

In place of 'noluissent' some editions have 'voluissent;' and 'voluissent' is the reading of Lg. 29 42 φ ψ. These two words have sometimes been interchanged in the MSS.; but 'noluissent' is the right reading here. 'These old orators used to come to a case perfectly free and unshackled, and they took care not to act in such a way that, if they did not choose to be shameless in conducting a defence, they could be charged with ingratitude for declining it.'

ACTIONIS SECUNDAE

IN C. VERREM

LIBER TERTIUS.

"De codicibus, quibus lib. iii. continetur, jam supra ad lib. ii. dictum est. Metellianus desinit cap. xvi. Erfurtensis fragmentum continet cap. i.—v. § 12 *deprecati*. Melchioris *Hittorpii* schedae, quae vocantur a Grutero, excerpta sunt codicis Erfurtensis. A codice Lag. 6 abest haec oratio. Codex Vaticanus haec continet fragmenta : ——." (Iordan.)

("Ab hoc inde libro nova collatione Palimpsesti Vaticani ab Henr. Brunnio diligentissime facta nobis uti licuit, quam Halmius munificentia eorum, qui rebus scholasticis in Bavaria praesunt, adjutus faciendam curavit. Quae Brunnius de locis superioribus qui in Palimpsesto supersunt accuratius quam Maius rettulit, in Addendis exhibebimus." Bait.)

I. Omnes qui alterum, judices, nullis impulsi inimicitiis, nulla privatim laesi injuria, nullo praemio adducti, in judicium rei pub-

Frumentum.] This oration is sometimes entitled in the editions 'Frumentaria,' or 'De Frumento.' It treats of the maladministration of Verres with respect to the products of Sicily, which are included under the term 'Frumentum.' In the last chapter of this oration, Cicero enumerates the various kinds of imposts which related to the 'Frumentum' in Sicily: "Quum unae decumae lege et conditione detrahantur, alterae novis institutis propter annonae rationem imperentur, ematur praeterea frumentum quotannis publice, postremo etiam in cellam magistratibus et legatis imperetur." The nature of these several imposts is explained by Cicero (c. 5, &c.). The oration treats (c. 6–69) of the 'Frumentum decumanum;' then (c. 70—80) of the 'Frumentum emptum;' and lastly (c. 81—97) of the 'Frumentum aestimatum.'

The word 'Frumentum' contains the same element as 'fruges' and 'fructus.' A word like this must have had a legal or technical meaning, for it would occur both in testaments and contracts, and accordingly its meaning was settled. Gallus (Dig. 50. 16. 77), quoted by Paulus, explains "*frumentum* id esse quod arista in se teneat: lupinum vero et fabam *fruges* potius dici, quia non arista sed siliqua continentur, quae Servius apud Alfenum in frumento contineri putat." Pliny (H. N. xviii. 7, ed. Harduin) makes 'fruges' a general term, and divides 'fruges' into two kinds: "sunt autem duo prima earum genera: frumenta, ut triticum, hordeum; et legumina, ut faba, cicer. Differentia vero notior quam ut indicari deceat." A legacy of the 'fruges' of land included "tam legumina quam hordeum et triticum" (Paulus, Rec. Sent. iii. 6. 78). The Greek word σῖτος corresponds to 'frumentum;' for under the general term σῖτος is placed

licae causa vocant, providere debent non solum quid oneris in praesentia tollant, sed [etiam] quantum in omnem vitam negotii suscipere conentur. Legem enim sibi ipsi dicunt innocentiae virtutumque omnium qui ab altero rationem vitae reposcunt; atque eo magis, si id, ut ante dixi, faciunt nulla re commoti alia nisi utilitate communi. Nam qui sibi hoc sumpsit ut corrigat mores aliorum ac peccata reprehendat, quis huic ignoscat, si qua in re ipse ab religione officii declinarit? Quapropter hoc etiam magis ab omnibus ejusmodi civis laudandus ac diligendus est, quod non solum ab re publica civem improbum removet, verum etiam se ipsum ejusmodi fore profitetur ac praestat ut sibi non modo communi voluntate virtutis atque officii, sed etiam vi quadam magis necessaria recte sit honesteque vivendum. Itaque hoc, judices, ex homine clarissimo atque eloquentissimo L. Crasso saepe auditum est, quum se nullius rei tam poenitere diceret quam quod C. Carbonem unquam in judicium vocavisset; minus enim liberas omnium rerum voluntates habebat, et vitam suam pluribus quam vellet observari oculis arbitrabatur. Atque ille his praesidiis ingenii fortunaeque munitus tamen hac cura continebatur, quam sibi nondum confirmato consilio sed ineunte aetate susceperat. Quo minus etiam praecipitur eorum virtus et integritas, qui ad

πυροί (wheat) and *κριθαί* (barley), as species. We have no English word which distinctly represents the grasses which contain cereal products. The word 'grain' is perhaps the nearest.

The word 'triticum,' which Cicero often uses in this oration, is 'wheat,' and 'hordeum' is 'barley.' That the 'triticum' is the same as our wheat, and that it has not been essentially changed in the course of many centuries, is proved by the grains which have been found in Egypt in the tombs of Thebes; and there is the same evidence for the permanence of the character of the 'hordeum' or barley. Cicero does not mention any other cerealia in this oration than 'triticum' and 'hordeum.'

1. *in praesentia*] Zumpt refers to Cicero, Ad Fam. ii. 10, for an example of 'in praesenti:' 'hoc ad te in praesenti scripsi,' where the reading may be wrong. 'In praesentia,' 'for the present,' is Latin. See Lib. 2. c. 28; Caesar, B. G. i. 15.—'sed [etiam]:' Lg. 42 p. m. E, V, Iordan omit 'etiam.'—'continentiae virtutumque omnium' Orelli, Klotz, and Iordan. Lg. 42 p. m. E, M, omit 'continentiae.'

hoc .. quod] The common reading is 'qui,' for which Zumpt properly wrote 'quod,' which refers to 'hoc:' 'quod' is the reading of Lg. 42 p. m. E φ.—'ab re publica .. removet:' this use of the preposition with 'removet' is doubtful in Cicero, according to Zumpt. But there is 'removent ab oculis' (De Off. i. 35).

L. Crasso] C. Papirius Carbo was prosecuted for Repetundae B.C. 119, by L. Licinius Crassus, who was then only one-and-twenty. Carbo escaped condemnation by committing suicide. 'Cantharides sumpsisse dicitur,' says Cicero (Ad Fam. ix. 21). The passages relating to the prosecution of Carbo are collected by Meyer, Orat. Rom. Fragm. p. 295, 2nd ed. See the note on Divin. c. 21.

praecipitur] The common reading is 'perspicitur,' which does not suit the sense. An expression of Cicero (De Off. i. 23) helps to explain 'praecipitur.' He says: "illud etiam ingenii magni est, praecipere cogitatione futura," &c. Here he means to say: 'for this reason, it is not so easy to form a conjecture of the integrity of young men who become accusers, for they have not lived long enough to be tried, as to form a conjecture of the integrity of

hanc rem adolescentuli quam qui jam firmata aetate descendunt. Illi enim, antequam potuerunt existimare quanto liberior vita sit eorum qui neminem accusarint, gloriae causa atque ostentationis accusant: nos, qui jam et quid facere et quantulum judicare possemus ostendimus, nisi facile cupiditates nostras teneremus, nunquam ipsimet nobis praecideremus istam licentiam libertatemque vivendi.

II. Atque ego hoc plus oneris habeo quam qui ceteros accusarunt, si onus est id appellandum quod cum laetitia feras ac voluptate, verumtamen ego hoc amplius suscepi quam ceteri, quod ita postulatur ab omnibus ut ab iis abstineant maxime vitiis in quibus alterum reprehenderint. Furem aliquem aut rapacem accusaris: vitanda tibi semper erit omnis avaritiae suspicio. Maleficum quempiam adduxeris aut crudelem: cavendum erit semper ne qua in re asperior aut inhumanior fuisse videare. Corruptorem, adulterum: providendum diligenter ne quod in vita vestigium libidinis appareat. Omnia postremo quae vindicaris in altero tibi ipsi vehementer fugienda sunt. Etenim non modo accusator sed ne objurgator quidem ferendus est is qui quod in altero vitium reprehendit in eo ipse deprehenditur. Ego in uno homine omnia vitia quae possunt in homine perdito nefarioque esse reprehendo; nullum esse dico indicium libidinis, sceleris, audaciae, quod non in istius unius vita perspicere possitis. Ego in isto reo legem hanc mihi, judices, statuo, vivendum ita esse ut isti non modo factis dictisque omnibus sed etiam oris oculorumque illa contumacia ac superbia quam videtis dissimillimus esse ac semper

those who become accusers at a more advanced time of life.' Lg. 42 E, M have 'percipitur.'

et quid facere] "Facere, non ad onus accusandi, sed ad universae vitae rationem refero:" P. Manutius. The meaning of 'quantulum judicare' is not clear, and the commentators say nothing about it. There is a reading 'dicere,' Lg. 42 p. m. N, Iordan. 'Facere,' 'dicere' would then express what Cicero could do, and what he could say. But 'facere' appears to refer to his past life, and, as Hotmann says, probably to his conduct in Sicily as quaestor, under Sex. Peducaeus, his praetor. 'Judicare' then may refer to his judgment or discretion.

2. *Furem . . accusaris:*] It is usual to place a note of interrogation in such cases, as Zumpt here does after 'accusaris,' 'crudelem,' and 'adulterum.' But these notes of interrogation are used much too freely in our Latin texts, and they are not wanted here. It may be rendered, 'suppose you accuse a man of theft or robbery,' for 'rapacem' contains the notion of 'rapina' (Gaius, iii. 209, 'Qui res alienas rapit, tenetur etiam furti,' &c.). In the passage of Terence (Eunuch. ii. 2. 21), quoted by Cicero (De Am. c. 25), 'Negat quis; nego: ait; aio;' it is usual to place a note of interrogation after 'quis' and after 'ait;' but incorrectly. See Seyffert's note in his edition of the De Amicitia.

Ego in isto reo] 'When I undertake to be the prosecutor of this man whom I bring before you, I am imposing these terms on myself.' This use of 'in' with the ablative is best learnt by examples: 'Et in hoc homine,' c. 3. There are many other examples in these orations.

fuisse videar. Patior, non moleste fero, judices, eam vitam, quae mihi sua sponte antea jucunda fuerit, nunc jam mea lege et conditione necessariam quoque futuram.

III. Et in hoc homine saepe a me quaeris, Hortensi, quibus inimicitiis aut qua injuria adductus ad accusandum descenderim. Mitto jam rationem officii mei necessitudinisque Siculorum: de ipsis tibi inimicitiis respondeo. An tu majores ullas inimicitias putas esse quam contrarias hominum sententias ac dissimilitudines studiorum et voluntatum? Fidem sanctissimam in vita qui putat potest ei non inimicus esse, qui quaestor consulem suum consiliis commissis, pecunia tradita, rebus omnibus creditis, spoliare, relinquere, prodere, oppugnare ausus sit? Pudorem ac pudicitiam qui colit potest animo aequo istius quotidiana adulteria, meretriciam disciplinam, domesticum lenocinium videre? Qui religiones deorum immortalium retinere vult, ei qui fana spoliarit omnia, qui ex thensarum orbitis praedari sit ausus, inimicus non esse qui potest? Qui jure aequo omnes putat esse oportere, is tibi non infestissimus sit quum cogitet varietatem libidinemque decretorum tuorum? Qui sociorum injuriis provinciarumque incommodis doleat, is in te non expilatione Asiae, vexatione Pamphyliae, squalore et lacrimis Siciliae concitetur? Qui civium Romanorum jura ac libertatem sanctam apud omnes haberi velit, is non tibi plus etiam quam inimicus esse debeat, quum tua verbera, quum secures, quum cruces ad civium Romanorum supplicia fixas recordetur? An, si qua in re contra rem meam decrevisset aliquid injuria, jure ei me inimicum esse arbitrarere: quum omnia contra omnium bonorum rem, causam, rationem, utilitatem, voluntatemque fecerit, quaeris cur ei sim inimicus cui populus Romanus infestus est? qui praesertim plus etiam quam pars virilis postulat pro voluntate populi Romani oneris ac muneris suscipere debeam?

3. *et voluntatum?*] 'ac voluntatum' Lg. 42 E. "At Cicero *ac* vel *atque*, quod sciam, non ita bis ponit, ut prius duo membra, posterius membri alterius partes copulet. Ubi ejusmodi exempla inveniuntur, codicum auctoritate recte emendantur" (Iordan).

pecunia tradita,] See Lib. 1. c. 13, 'pecunia attributa,' &c.

thensarum orbitis] See Lib. 1. c. 59.

haberi velit.] Most of the MSS. have 'vult.' Lg. 42 E, F, M have 'velit,' which Zumpt and Klotz have. The use of 'qui' with the indicative, 'qui putat,' 'qui colit,' &c., and the transition to the subjunctive form, 'qui doleat,' &c., are intelligible. Cicero begins with speaking of himself, and as he becomes more animated he transfers the same opinion to others; he becomes general. Zumpt's explanation is right: "nimirum conjunctivus cujusvis hominis est, indicativus ad unum Ciceronem pertinet, neque male ab uno ad plures et omnes transitus fit."

pars virilis] Cicero explains this Lib. 4. c. 37, 'est aliqua mea pars virilis,' &c. Here he says, that out of regard to the good wishes of the Roman people towards him, shown by their raising him to the Curule Aedileship, he, as one of those, as

IV. Quid illa quae leviora videntur esse, non cujusvis animum possunt movere, quod ad tuam ipsius amicitiam ceterorumque hominum magnorum atque nobilium faciliorem aditum istius habet nequitia et audacia quam cujusquam nostrum virtus et integritas? Odistis hominum novorum industriam; despicitis eorum frugalitatem; pudorem contemnitis; ingenium vero et virtutem depressam extinctamque cupitis. Verrem amatis. Ita credo: si non virtute, non industria, non innocentia, non pudore, non pudicitia; at sermone, at literis, at humanitate ejus delectamini. Nihil eorum est, contraque sunt omnia cum summo dedecore ac turpitudine, tum singulari stultitia atque inhumanitate oblita. Huic homini si cujus domus patet, utrum ea patere an hiare ac poscere aliquid videtur?

one of the all, who hate Verres, imposes on himself even more than his share of the burden of punishing this scoundrel. Every Roman, every man, must hate him, for he has injured every body (contra omnium bonorum rem, &c.). It is the duty of all to punish him; and Cicero imposes on himself more than his share of this duty. We may now see why, after beginning in the earlier part of this chapter with his own personal dislike of Verres, he then makes all other persons of the same mind as himself (qui doleat, &c.). 'Pars virilis' is well explained by Forcellini, as usual. The law writers make the matter still plainer. Paulus (Recep. Sent. iii. tit. 2) says, "si unius patroni duo sint liberi, alterius quatuor, singuli viriles, id est, aequales portiones habebunt."

4. *nostrum .. hominum novorum*] Cicero is here showing his soreness at the contempt with which the old 'nobiles' looked on the 'novi homines,' of whom he was one. (See Pro Cluentio, c. 40.) The speech of Marius (Sallust, Jug. 63) may serve as a comment on this passage. The precise signification of the term 'novus homo' is well explained by W. A. Becker, in his excellent work, "Handbuch der Röm. Alterthümer" (2er Th. 1ste Abth. p. 225): "he who was the first man of his family to obtain a 'curule' magistracy, was, as Cicero says, 'princeps nobilitatis,' or 'auctor generis;' that is, with him begins the 'nobilitas' of his family. He is the first who has the 'jus imaginis ad posteritatis memoriam prodendae' (Cic. Pro Rab. Post. c. 7; Verr. v. 14); but he has no 'imagines' himself, not even 'suam,' as it is often incorrectly said; for it is natural and certain that his bust would not be set up until after his death (Polyb. vi. 53). He is not yet 'nobilis' in the full sense; it is a 'nova nobilitas;' he himself is and is called 'homo novus,' and thus 'novitas' is placed between 'ignobilitas' and 'nobilitas.' From this it follows that a patrician could never be a 'homo novus,' but only a plebeian, and that L. Sextius, the first plebeian consul, was also the first 'homo novus' (Liv. vii. 1)."

at sermone, &c.] See Lib. 1. c. 37.

humanitate] Gellius (xiv. 16) says: "humanitatem appellaverunt id propemodum quod Graeci παιδείαν vocant; nos eruditionem institutionemque in bonas artes dicimus: quas qui sinceriter cupiunt appetuntque, hi sunt vel maxime humanissimi, &c. Sic igitur eo verbo vel veteres esse usos et cumprimis M. Varronem Marcumque Tullium omnes ferme libri declarant." The juxtaposition of 'literis' assists the explanation of 'humanitas.' In the letter Ad Q. Fr. i. 1. c. 9, Cicero says of the inhabitants of the province of Asia: "quum vero ei generi hominum praesimus, non modo in quo ipsa sit sed etiam a quo ad alios pervenisse putetur humanitas," where the word has the same sense as in this passage. But there are passages in which it seems to be used in the wider sense of the general feeling of good-will to others, which is one of the characteristics of men as distinguished from brutes: "tametsi nullus in te sensus humanitatis, nulla ratio unquam fuit religionis," Lib. 1. c. 18; and in De Am. c. 13: "Quamobrem si cadit in sapientem animi dolor, qui profecto cadit, nisi ex ejus animo extirpatam humanitatem arbitramur," where the word means the natural feelings and affections generally.

poscere aliquid] As if every noble's house were gaping for what it could get from Verres to put into its mouth.

Hunc vestri janitores, hunc cubicularii diligunt: hunc liberti vestri, hunc servi ancillaeque amant: hic cum venit extra ordinem vocatur: hic solus introducitur; ceteri saepe frugalissimi homines excluduntur. Ex quo intelligi potest eos vobis esse carissimos qui ita vixerint ut sine vestro praesidio salvi esse non possint. Quid hoc cuiquam ferendum putas esse, nos ita vivere in pecunia tenui ut prorsus nihil acquirere velimus, ut dignitatem nostram populique Romani beneficia non copiis sed virtute tueamur; istum rebus omnibus undique ereptis impune eludentem circumfluere atque abundare? hujus argento dominia vestra, hujus signis et tabulis forum comitiumque ornari? praesertim quum vos vestro Marte his rebus omnibus abundetis? Verrem esse qui vestras villas suis manubiis ornet? Verrem esse qui cum L. Mummio certet? ut plures hic sociorum urbes quam ille hostium spoliasse videatur; plures hic villas ornamentis fanorum quam ille fana spoliis hostium ornasse; et is erit ob eam rem vobis carior ut ceteri libentius suo periculo vestris cupiditatibus serviant?

V. Verum haec et dicentur alio loco et dicta sunt: nunc proficiscemur ad reliqua, si pauca ante fuerimus a vobis, judices, deprecati. Superiore omni oratione perattentos vestros animos habuimus:

janitores,] 'Door-keepers,' such as we see in some houses now, but perhaps not so well fed. 'Cubicularius' is a chamber-servant, 'cameriere.' Cicero, Ad Att. vi. 2, speaking of his government of his province of Cilicia, says, "Aditus autem ad me minime provincialis. Nihil per cubicularium."—'servi ancillaeque:' 'slaves, male and female;' which remark may not be useless, when we recollect how we are taught to translate 'ancilla.' Gaius (i. 85): "ex diverso ex ancilla et libero poterant liberi nasci: nam ea lege cavetur ut si quis cum aliena ancilla, quam credebat liberam esse, coierit," &c.

extra ordinem] Cicero, it is likely enough, had often made his calls on great men, and had seen those who came after him introduced to the great man's presence before him. Good honest folks, poor it is true,—a thing which cannot always be helped,—had the mortification of seeing a rich rogue called out of his turn by the obsequious slave. Horace gives the right rule (Carm. iii. 14) in another case:

"Si per invisum mora janitorem
Fiet, abito."

dominia vestra,] The common reading is 'domos' or 'domus vestras,' a reading which has apparently arisen from the old copyists not understanding 'dominia.' In the passage of Gellius (ii. 24), "qui Ludis Megalensibus antiquo ritu mutitarent, id est, mutua inter sese dominia agitarent," 'dominia' has been changed into 'convivia' in some editions. Lipsius (Saturn. i. 19. Vol. iii. ed. Vesal. 1675) explains the matter: "Dominus antiquis, Praebitor; et Dominia, Praebitiones hilariores;" and he refers to this passage of Cicero. In Horace, 2 Sat. viii. 92, "si non causas narraret earum et Naturas dominus," 'dominus' is the master of the feast. The passage of Nonius may be easily corrected, for he explains 'dominus' in one of its senses to be 'convivii exhibitor,' and 'dominia' to be 'convivia.' The corrupt text of Nonius is 'Adria argento dominos vestrae,' instead of which it ought to be 'ornari argento dominia vestra.'

vestro Marte . . . manubiis] Cicero is making these plunderers ridiculous. They have all robbed and pilfered; and he sarcastically calls their plunder 'manubiae.' See Lib. 1. c. 59, 60.—'L. Mummii:' see Lib. 1. c. 21.

id fuit nobis gratum admodum. Sed multo erit gratius si reliqua voletis attendere: propterea quod in his omnibus quae antea dicta sunt erat quaedam ex ipsa varietate ac novitate rerum et criminum delectatio. Nunc tractare causam instituimus frumentariam, quae magnitudine injuriae et re [fere] criminibus ceteris antecellit, jucunditatis in agendo et varietatis minus habebit: vestra autem auctoritate et prudentia dignissimum est, judices, in audiendi diligentia non minus religioni tribuere quam voluptati. In hac causa frumentaria cognoscenda haec vobis proponite, judices, vos de rebus fortunisque Siculorum omnium, de civium Romanorum qui arant in Sicilia bonis, de vectigalibus a majoribus traditis, de vita victuque populi Romani cogituros. Quae si magna atque adeo

5. *reliqua—attendere:*] See Lib. 5. c. 57; Divin. c. 15; Lib. 1. c. 10.

[*fere*] *criminibus*] 'et re fere' Lg. 42 p. m. Iordan: 'et re' E, F, M: 'fere' rell. Orell. I doubt if 'et re fere' is genuine.

religioni] To the obligation of their oath, to do justice. There will seldom be any difficulty in translating this word, if the reader will bear in mind that it is said of man when viewed with reference to the gods.

civium Romanorum qui arant] This may be taken as one definition of 'aratores.' On the matter of pointing a remark may be made here. Zumpt, Klotz, and Iordan write 'de civium Romanorum, qui arant in Sicilia, bonis, de' &c. Now this is vicious in the extreme. We first observe that the Romans would generally say 'de civium Romanorum bonis,' as 'de consilii sententia,' and so forth. If these 'civium Romanorum' are to be further defined, it may be done briefly by 'qui arant in Sicilia;' but this is not said with emphasis; it is pronounced as it would be if one word in the genitive plural could represent these four words. It is a qualification, an exposition of the terms 'civium Romanorum,' and the practice of fencing these words in with commas has no other effect than to divert the learner from what he would see clearly if the fences were removed. Cicero abounds in examples of this collocation of words, as in the letter Ad Q. Fr. i. 1. c. 15, "non est tibi his solis utendum existimationibus ac judiciis qui nunc sunt hominum;" and yet even here Orelli has hemmed in with commas the 'qui nunc sunt.' Cicero (Lib. 2. c. 3), when he is speaking of the advantages of Sicily to the Romans, says "quos illa partim retinet ut arare, ut pascere, ut negotiari libeat, ut denique sedes ac domicilium collocare." The 'aratores' of Sicily were the cultivators, who had to pay the 'decumae,' or tenths. The 'arator' is opposed to the 'decumanus,' who farmed the tenths (c. 8. 10. 16, &c.). Some of these 'aratores' were Roman 'equites,' as we see in the case of Q. Lollius (c. 25): "qui—affirmavit se decumanis plus quam deberet non daturum." 'Aratores' was a general name for the cultivators in the Roman provinces, whether the provincials themselves, or Roman citizens. These 'aratores' might either be the owners of land, or the lessees. If the land was let, the owner was distinguished by the term 'dominus,' and the occupier by the term 'arator' (c. 54). In c. 21, one Nympho is mentioned, and he was a Sicilian, who was the lessee of a large extent of land (arationes magnas conductas haberet); and many rich Sicilians were large tenant farmers. In another case, the property of a man's wife was let to a 'colonus;' and this 'colonus' was of course an 'arator' (c. 22). Again (c. 40), "Diocles Panhormitanus—arabat agrum conductum in Segestano;" a man of Panhormus was the lessee of lands in the territory of Segesta, in which it appears that persons who were not Segestani could not acquire the ownership of land. The 'decumani,' as already explained, were those 'publicani' who farmed the 'decumae,' and the chief among the 'publicani' (Lib. 2. c. 71).

maxima vobis videntur, quam varie et quam copiose dicantur exspectare nolite.

Neminem vestrum praeterit, judices, omnem utilitatem opportunitatemque provinciae Siciliae, quae ad commoda populi Romani adjuncta sit, consistere in re frumentaria maxime; nam ceteris rebus adjuvamur ex illa provincia, hac vero alimur ac sustinemur. Ea causa tripertita, judices, erit in accusatione; primum enim de decumano, deinde de empto dicemus frumento, postremo de aestimato.

VI. Inter Siciliam ceterasque provincias, judices, in agrorum vectigalium ratione hoc interest, quod ceteris aut impositum

videntur,] 'videbantur' Lg. 42 p. m. Iordan.

6. *vectigalium*] 'Vectigal' contains the root 'vec,' the same as 'veh,' in 'vehere;' but the reason of 'vectigal' signifying a tax is not clear. So long as Rome had a small territory, there was little public property from which the State could derive a revenue. If any tax was derived in such way, it may have been called Vectigal, as it is asserted (Becker, Handbuch, &c., iii. 2. 122). When Rome began to acquire territory in Italy, the revenue from the public lands would increase. 'Tributum' is the tax which from the time of Servius Tullius was paid by the Roman citizens. It was a sum paid in respect of the estimated value of a man's property; and, inasmuch as property in land was the chief property, it was in substance a land-tax, paid under the form of a general tax on property. Whatever may be the reason of the name, it is certain that from the time of Servius Tullius, it was a tax which was founded on the 'census' or rating of the Roman citizens. It was a property-tax, and it varied according to the necessities of the State, or rather according to the expenditure, like our income-tax. This is not the place to examine the matter fully. The reader may refer to Becker, as above, where he will find the passages cited, and some things said which he will not believe, if he uses his own judgment.

When the treasury was enriched by the Macedonian war, the 'tributum' was abolished, B.C. 167, and it was never afterwards permanently restored in Italy. From this time the chief income of the Roman State consisted of the taxes raised in the provinces, particularly of the produce of the earth, as tenths or tithes. This produce and other taxes were included under the term 'vectigal,' in which Cicero, De Imp. Cn. Pomp. c. 6, includes 'portoria' and 'scriptura.' In the Lex Thoria, cap. 10, we find "neive quid quoi ob eam rem vectigal neive scripturam dare debeto," where both 'vectigal' and 'scriptura' are used, according to the legal superfluity of expression, the object being to exclude any possible payment for the pasturage of cattle, the matter of which this clause in the Lex treats. 'Vectigal,' then, which had a limited meaning, became a general term for a tax, as this passage proves, for Cicero speaks of 'vectigal certum quod stipendiarium dicitur,' by which he means a fixed money payment or land-tax, which money payment is contrasted with the 'censoria locatio,' or the tenths which were let by the censors at Rome, and pursuant to a Lex Sempronia, probably the Agraria Lex of C. Sempronius Gracchus. Under the empire, all the provincial payments were ultimately reduced to a fixed sum of money, the progress towards which we see in the time of Gaius, by his application of the terms 'stipendiaria' and 'tributoria' (ii. 21) to lands in the provinces.

The following passage will serve as a commentary on this chapter: "All the provinces except Sicily," says Cicero (Verr. Lib. 3. c. 6), "pay either a fixed land-tax (vectigal stipendiarium) or variable duties (that is, tenths or other quotae of produce), which last are let in Rome by the censors. Sicily, on the other hand, has the following constitution: two foederate cities and five others are tax-free; a few which have come under the Roman dominion by conquest, lost the ownership of their land, but received it back on condition of paying certain dues, which are let by the censors (that is, they have the same terms as other provinces); all the rest of the land

vectigal est certum, quod stipendiarium dicitur, ut Hispanis et plerisque Poenorum quasi victoriae praemium ac poena belli, aut censoria locatio constituta est, ut Asiae lege Sempronia. Siciliae civitates sic in amicitiam fidemque recepimus ut eodem jure essent quo fuissent, eadem conditione populo Romano parerent qua suis antea paruissent. Perpaucae Siciliae civitates sunt bello a majoribus nostris subactae; quarum ager quum esset publicus populi Romani factus tamen illis est redditus: is ager a censoribus locari

is subject to the payment of tenths (decumae), yet so that the old mode of administration is maintained in conformity to the Lex Hieronica (that is, so that the tenths were let separately in Sicily, and generally let to those who were bound to pay them, and on easy terms). But without any respect to these differences Cicero calls all land in the provinces by the general name of 'agri vectigales,' which consequently was at that time the general name for all land that paid a tax; and it is this liability to taxation which he always considers as the general character of all the provinces, so that only particular towns were exempt from it" (Savigny, Vermischte Schriften, Römische Steuerverfassung, ii. 97). But we must understand that the 'perpaucae civitates,' whose land became 'publicus Populi Romani,' did not recover the ownership of the land. (See the next note.) In the time of Gaius it was the legal doctrine that the 'dominium' or ownership of all provincial land was either in the Roman people or in the Caesar (ii. 7): "in provinciali solo . . dominium populi Romani est vel Caesaris, nos autem possessionem tantum et usumfructum habere videmur."

Zumpt attempts to ascertain the number of these 'perpaucae civitates;' but if his interpretation of this passage is not true, his attempt is a failure.

publicus populi Romani &c.] The following is one interpretation of this passage. These states being conquered by the Romans, their land, according to the rule of war, became the property of the Roman people, but it was restored to these states. They paid a 'vectigal,' which was let at Rome by the censors; and in this respect the occupiers of 'ager redditus' were on the same footing as the inhabitants of those Punic towns which paid tenths of grain, wine, and oil. For when Cicero says 'is ager—locari solet,' he means that the tenths were let, not the land itself. Still these least favoured Sicilian towns, whose tithes were let at Rome by the censors to the 'publicani,' were on the footing of the more favoured Punic towns which were directly subject to the 'imperium' of the Proconsul of Africa; for the other Punic towns, which were under the Proconsul, lost a part of their land, which was made Publicus Populi Romani, and for the rest, which was restored to them, they paid a fixed tax, 'stipendium' or 'vectigal stipendiarium.' They also paid a capitation-tax both for males and females (Appian, Pun. c. 135). This will explain Cicero's expression 'plerisque Poenorum.' Several of the Punic towns, which had sided with the Romans, received a portion of the conquered land, and were 'liberae et immunes,' that is, like those Sicilian towns which Cicero mentions. They were not immediately under the governor's jurisdiction. (See Rudorff, Zeitschrift für Geschichtl. Rechtsw. Das Ackergesetz des Sp. Thorius, vol. x.)

There is still difficulty in this passage. Becker (Handbuch, iii. 1, p. 42) maintains that this land, which Cicero calls 'redditus,' was let to the Sicilians; that the 'locatio' does not apply to the tenths, but that it means a lease of the land itself for certain payments. He observes that the Ager Leontinus was 'ager publicus populi Romani,' and Leontini was therefore one of these few states (Cic. Phil. ii. 17. 39; iii. 9). Now Cicero says that the lands of these conquered states had been restored; but in Verres' time not a single Leontine except one family occupied any land in the Ager Leontinus. The land was, Cicero says, let to eighty-four farmers (aratores), some Sicilians, and others Romans. (Lib. 3. c. 51; and c. 18. 24. 41). Becker concludes from the words 'paternas arationes' (Lib. 3. c. 41), that the leases were transmissible by succession (vererblich); but I have some doubt whether he knew exactly what he meant when he wrote this. If the lease was for a certain number of years,

solet. Foederatae civitates duae sunt quarum decumae venire non soleant, Mamertina et Tauromenitana: quinque praeterea sine foedere immunes ac liberae, Centuripina, Halesina, Segestana, Halicyensis, Panhormitana. Praeterea omnis ager Siciliae civitatum decumanus est, itemque ante imperium populi Romani ipsorum Siculorum voluntate et institutis fuit. Videte nunc majorum sapientiam, qui, quum Siciliam tam opportunum subsidium belli atque pacis ad rem publicam adjunxissent, tanta cura

we can easily suppose that the 'heredes,' or as we should say, the personal representatives of a deceased lessee would be entitled to the remainder of an unexpired lease. But if we admit that the land was leased, this is all. The terms of the leases are unknown. Becker further remarks that the 'decumae' of the Leontine land were not let in Rome, but in Sicily, and conformably to the Lex Hieronica. He concludes that the words 'is ager . . solet' refer to the leasing of these lands by the censors, and this was done every Lustrum, when any of the lands happened to be vacant. Accordingly this Sicilian land was dealt with exactly as the Campanus Ager in Italy was. Finally, he adds, that this explains how the Leontine land, though it was originally given back to the Leontini without sale, gradually came into other hands.

I am inclined to think that Cicero does mean that the lands of these states were let at Rome. But the explanation of 'redditus' is not easy. The restoration would be of course to the former owners, who would be owners no longer, but tenants under a lease. Only one family of Leontini now occupied a farm in the territory, but the fact of one family remaining helps to explain the word 'redditus.' We may suppose that all the rest, for some reason, which is not explained, had ceased to occupy these lands under the Roman State. Cicero's statement, which is obscure to us, may have been clear to his countrymen.

Mamertina] The Civitas Mamertina was Messana, now Messina, on the north-east coast of Sicily, and on the straits, a city whose various fortunes require a separate history (Lib. 2. c. 5). The original town Zancle, or Dankle, as the name appears on the oldest coins, took the name of Messana when it was occupied by Messenians from Rhegium (Thucyd. vi. 5). In B.C. 282 it fell into the hands of the Mamertini (Polyb. i. 7), and hence it is sometimes called Mamertina. Pliny (iii. 8. 14) calls it 'oppidum civium Romanorum;' but it must have been made such after the time of Cicero. In this passage Cicero omits the 'Netina civitas,' which he calls 'foederata' (Lib. 5. c. 51). The Netini had the same grounds for their 'foedus' with Rome as the Mamertini (Lib. 5. c. 22).

immunes ac liberae,] These five cities were 'immunes et liberae.' Their 'libertas' consisted in having magistrates of their own, and being free from the government of the praetor in most matters: the 'immunitas' was an exemption from paying taxes to the Roman State. Cicero says of the 'foederatae civitates'—'quarum decumae venire non soleant,' where 'non soleant' seems by the form of expression to imply that this was incident to a 'foedus.' He says of the five, that they were 'immunes et liberae' without a 'foedus,' meaning apparently that they had the same advantages as the 'foederatae,' though they had no 'foedus.' Becker affirms that the possession of 'libertas' only did not confer freedom from taxation (immunitas), unless this 'immunitas' was expressly granted. I do not know whether this is true or not.

The words 'Praeterea omnis,' &c., seem somewhat ambiguous. Cicero says of the two foederate cities, and we must suppose the same remark to apply to the third, which he does not mention here, that their 'decumae' were not let by the censors. He does not in direct terms say that they paid no 'decumae.' Five cities besides were 'immunes ac liberae,' though they had no 'foedus.' He then says 'Praeterea omnis,' which is explained to mean that all the cities were 'decumanae,' except those to which the 'censoria locatio' applied, and the seven (or eight) cities. If the order of the words were 'Omnis praeterea ager,' the meaning would seem to be more clearly expressed. But the difficulty which I have hinted at may be only imaginary. Caesar writes (B. G. i. 40), 'Quod si praeterea nemo sequatur,' &c.

Siculos tueri ac retinere voluerunt, ut non modo eorum agris vectigal novum nullum imponerent, sed ne legem quidem venditionis decumarum neve vendundi aut tempus aut locum commutarent, ut certo tempore anni, ut ibidem in Sicilia, denique ut lege Hieronica venderent: voluerunt eos in suis rebus ipsos interesse; eorumque animos non modo lege nova sed ne nomine quidem legis novo

lege Hieronica venderent:] This system of taxation was established by Hiero II., who died probably B.C. 216. His land-tax was a tenth of the produce. The letting of the 'vectigalia' in general, as already observed, was managed at Rome by the censors, and the farmers of them were the Societates of Publicani. This 'censoria locatio' applied also, as Cicero says, to a small number of towns in Sicily. But other 'civitates' were under the Lex Hieronica. Their lands were subject to the 'decumae,' which the 'aratores' had to pay; and these 'decumae' were let or sold, which is the Roman expression, to Publicani, who were called Decumani. They were let or sold at Syracuse (c. 64). The expression 'decumas emisse' occurs in c. 12; and in c. 8 we have the equivalent expression, 'in locandis vectigalibus.' To buy the 'decumae' is an ambiguous expression, for it might signify to buy the right of collecting them for ever. But this is not the meaning of the Roman expression. To buy and to sell the 'decumae' expresses a contract for a given time, by which contract the farmers of the revenue gave a sum of money for the tenths for a fixed period. We might doubt whether such a contract was a case of 'emptio et venditio,' or of 'locatio, conductio.' The following passage from the Institutiones of Justinian will explain what is meant: "Adeo autem familiaritatem aliquam inter se habere videntur emptio et venditio, item locatio et conductio ut in quibusdam causis quaeri soleat, utrum emptio et venditio contrahatur an locatio et conductio. Ut ecce de praediis, quae perpetuo quibusdam fruenda traduntur, id est ut quamdiu pensio sive reditus pro his domino praestetur, neque ipsi conductori neque heredi ejus, cuive conductor heresve ejus id praedium vendiderit, aut donaverit, aut dotis nomine dederit aliove quo modo alienaverit, auferre liceat; sed talis contractus quia inter veteres dubitabatur, et a quibusdam locatio, a quibusdam venditio existimabatur, lex Zenoniana lata est, quae emphyteuseos contractui propriam statuit naturam," &c. (Inst. iii. tit. 24, (25)). In the same way, the Romans applied the term 'selling' to the furnishing of the inhabitants of a town with a certain supply of water by those to whom the management of this part of municipal administration was entrusted. The administrators were said to sell this water, though the agreement belongs more to the head of 'locatio, conductio,' than to the head of 'emptio, venditio.' (Zeitschrift für Geschichtl. Rechtsw. vol. xv. p. 311.) Compare τὸν θεάτρων ἀποδόσθαι, Demosth. Adv. Leptin. 48, ed. Wolf, and Wolf's note.

non modo] Cicero clearly means to say that the Romans willed that the Siculi should not be disturbed by a new 'lex,' or even by the change of the name of the old 'lex.' If the 'modo' were omitted, the first 'non' would negative 'lege.' As it stands, the 'non' negatives 'modo lege,' &c. The meaning is plain: they willed that 'not in any degree,' by a new 'lex,' should they be disturbed, and not even by a new name of the 'lex.' It is the Roman fashion to make 'sed' the adversative of 'non,' which we do sometimes. And if we do it here, we must resort to the form of a double negative — not only that they should not be disturbed by a new 'lex,' but not even by the new name of an old 'lex.' But this is not the Roman form of expression, and it leads us to the false supposition of 'non modo' being put for 'non modo non.' Another 'non' after 'modo' is not wanted. Sometimes 'non solum' stands in the first clause, followed by 'ne — quidem,' as in this passage. In both cases there is only a single verb of predication, which is placed in the 'ne — quidem' clause. In a passage in Lib. 2. c. 72, 'non modo id non dices,' &c., some MSS. omit the 'non' before 'dices,' where the copyist may have been misled by the words 'sed ne illud quidem tibi dicere licebit,' which follow. But if the 'non' before 'dices' were omitted, it would make palpable nonsense; for the 'id' refers to what has been mentioned in the preceding sentence, and the 'illud' refers to what Cicero says at the end of this sentence. "It is not all, that you won't be able to deny this (id)—'nihil in istis literis

commoveri. Itaque decumas lege Hieronica semper vendundas censuerunt ut iis jucundior esset muneris illius functio, si ejus regis qui Siculis carissimus fuit non solum instituta commutato imperio, verum etiam nomen maneret. Hoc jure ante Verrem praetorem Siculi semper usi sunt: hic primus instituta omnium, consuetudinem a majoribus traditam, conditionem amicitiae, jus societatis, convellere et commutare ausus est.

VII. Qua in re primum illud reprehendo et accuso, cur in re tam vetere, tam usitata quidquam novi feceris. Ingenio aliquid assecutus es? tot homines sapientissimos et clarissimos qui illam provinciam ante te tenuerunt prudentia consilioque vicisti? Est tuum, est ingenii diligentiaeque tuae. Do hoc tibi et concedo. Scio te Romae, quum praetor esses, edicto tuo possessiones hereditatum a liberis ad alienos, a primis heredibus ad secundos, a legibus ad libidinem tuam transtulisse. Scio te edicta superiorum omnium correxisse, et possessiones hereditatum non secundum eos qui proferrent, sed secundum eos qui dicerent testamentum factum, dedisse; easque res novas abs te prolatas et inventas magno tibi quaestui fuisse scio: eundemque te memini censorias quoque leges in sartis tectis exigendis tollere et commutare, ne is redimeret cuja res esset; ne pupillo tutores propinquique consulerent quo minus fortunis omnibus everteretur: exiguam diem praefinire operi qua ceteros ab negotio excluderes, ipse in tuo redemptore nullam certam diem observares. Quamobrem novam legem te in decumis statuisse non miror, hominem in edictis praetoriis, in censoriis legibus tam prudentem, tam exercitatum: non, inquam, miror te aliquid excogitasse; sed quod tua sponte, injussu populi, sine senatus auctoritate, jura provinciae Siciliae mutaveris, id reprehendo, id accuso. L. Octavio et C. Cottae consulibus senatus permisit ut vini et olei decumas et frugum minutarum, quas ante quaestores in Sicilia vendere consuessent, Romae venderent legemque his rebus quam ipsis videretur dicerent. Quum locatio fieret, publicani postularunt

fuisse'—you won't have the right of affirming as much as this—'tantum quantum ego dicam non fuisse.'"

functio,] 'the performance of that duty,' the payment of the 'decumae.' Zumpt refers to c. 86, 'quid . . . muneris in re publica fungi.' See also c. 16, 'quum tribus decumis pro una defungeretur.'

7. *secundum eos qui dicerent*] See Lib. 1. c. 45. This passage shows that the interpretation of 'se ei daturum,' &c. given in the note, is right. The passage from 'Scio te Romae' to 'diem observares' will cause no difficulty to those who have read Lib. 1. c. 44, &c.

L. Octavio &c.] The consuls of B.C. 75, the year in which Cicero was a quaestor in Sicily. From this passage we collect that there were 'decumae' of wine, oil, and of what Cicero calls 'fruges minutae,' which are explained to be 'legumina.'

quam ipsis videretur] That is, 'videretur dicere.' Zumpt refers to Drakenborch's note on Liv. vi. 26, for examples, of which

quasdam res ut ad legem adderent neque tamen a ceteris censoriis legibus recederent. Contra dixit is qui casu tum Romae fuit, tuus hospes, Verres, hospes, inquam, et familiaris tuus, Sthenius hic Thermitanus. Consules causam cognoverunt, quum viros primarios atque amplissimos civitatis multos in consilium advocassent: de consilii sententia pronuntiarunt se lege Hieronica vendituros.

VIII. Itane vero prudentissimi viri, summa auctoritate praediti, quibus senatus legum dicendarum in locandis vectigalibus omnem potestatem permiserat populusque Romanus jusserat, Siculo uno recusante, cum amplificatione vectigalium nomen Hieronicae legis mutare noluerunt; tu, homo minimi consilii, nullius auctoritatis, injussu populi ac senatus, tota Sicilia recusante, cum maximo detrimento atque adeo exitio vectigalium totam Hieronicam legem sustulisti? At quam legem corrigit, judices, atque adeo totam tollit? acutissime ac diligentissime scriptam, quae lex omnibus custodiis subjectum aratorem decumano tradidit, ut neque in segetibus neque in areis neque in horreis neque in amovendo neque in exportando frumento grano uno posset arator sine maxima poena fraudare decumanum. Scripta lex ita diligenter est ut eum scripsisse appareat qui alia vectigalia non haberet; ita acute ut Siculum; ita severe ut tyrannum; qua lege Siculis tamen arare expediret. Nam ita diligenter constituta sunt jura decumano ut tamen ab invito aratore plus decuma non posset auferri.

Quum haec ita essent constituta, Verres tot annis atque adeo saeculis tot inventus est qui haec non commutaret sed everteret, eaque quae jamdiu ad salutem sociorum utilitatemque rei publicae composita comparataque essent ad suos improbissimos quaestus converteret; qui primum certos instituerit nomine decu-

there is no lack. In Liv. vi. 26, "precibus eventum vestris senatus quem videbitur dabit." In Lib. 2. c. 13, there is 'cum judicem quem commodum erat — dabat.'

neque tamen &c.] The Publicani asked the consuls to add certain things to the terms (legem) of the letting, but yet not so as in other respects to deviate from the terms which the censors observed. The words 'neque tamen,' &c., are added, as Zumpt observes, to show that the Publicani asked for nothing unreasonable, but only for what was observed in letting the 'decumae' of other provinces. But the consuls kept to the Lex Hieronica. The senate however had infringed it by letting these 'decumae' at Rome, the reason for which Cicero does not explain.

8. *Itane vero*] Zumpt, Klotz, and Iordan, as usual, put an interrogation after 'vero.'—'idem jusserat' Iordan; but Lg. 42 p. m. omits 'idem.'

adeo exitio] 'even to the ruin of the Vectigalia.' Another example shortly after follows, 'atque adeo—tollit.' Also in the next section, 'atque adeo saeculis tot.'

amovendo] "'admovendo' V; recte, ut videtur," Halm. I cannot see it.—'exportando:' 'asportando,' Orelli, the wrong word.

commutaret sed everteret, . . . instituerit] There is no doubt of the correctness of

manos, re vera ministros ac satellites cupiditatum suarum; per quos ostendam sic provinciam per triennium vexatam atque vastatam, judices, ut eam multis annis multorum innocentia sapientiaque recreare nequeamus. IX. Eorum [omnium] qui decumani vocabantur princeps erat Q. ille Apronius quem videtis; de cujus improbitate singulari gravissimarum legationum querimonias audistis. Aspicite, judices, vultum hominis et aspectum; et ex ea contumacia quam hic in perditis rebus retinet illos ejus spiritus Siciliensis quos fuisse putetis cogitate ac recordamini. Hic est Apronius, quem in provincia tota Verres, quum undique nequissimos homines conquisisset, et quum ipse secum sui similes duxisset non parum multos, nequitia, luxuria, audacia sui simillimum judicavit. Itaque istos inter se perbrevi tempore non res, non ratio, non commendatio aliqua, sed studiorum turpitudo similitudoque conjunxit. Verris mores improbos impurosque nostis: fingite vobis, si potestis, aliquem qui in omnibus isti rebus par ad omnium flagitiorum nefarias libidines esse possit: is erit Apronius ille, qui, ut ipse non solum vita sed etiam corpore atque ore significat, immensa aliqua vorago est aut gurges vitiorum turpitudinumque omnium. Hunc in omnibus stupris, hunc in fanorum expilationibus, hunc in impuris conviviis principem adhibebat; tantamque habet morum similitudo conjunctionem atque concordiam ut Apronius, qui aliis inhumanus ac barbarus, isti uni commodus ac disertus videretur; ut quem omnes odissent neque videre vellent, sine eo iste esse non posset; ut quum alii ne conviviis quidem iisdem quibus Apronius, hic iisdem etiam poculis uteretur; postremo, ut odor Apronii taeterrimus oris et corporis, quem, ut aiunt, ne bestiae quidem ferre possent, uni isti suavis et jucundus videretur. Ille erat in tribunali proximus, in cubiculo solus, in convivio dominus, ac tum maxime, quum accubante praetextato praetoris filio in convivio saltare nudus coeperat. X. Hunc, uti dicere institui, principem

'commutaret' instead of 'commutarit,' which most of the MSS. have, and the old editions. But a new form is introduced with 'qui primum,' and a careful reader of Cicero will find no difficulty in 'instituerit.' I now find that V has 'instituerit,' and not 'constituerit.'

sed everteret,] Klotz has 'sed verteret,' from V.

9. *Eorum [omnium]*] V omits 'omnium.'—'aspicite:' 'videte' Lg. 29.

cogitate ac] Omitted by V and Klotz. —'et quum ipse:' 'et' om. V. "Recte, opinor, nam *et* posito alterum *cum* abundat" (Halm). I do not think so. The repetition of 'quum' adds emphasis to the expression.—'in omnibus istis rebus' Klotz, which follows e V; hardly right here.

sed etiam] 'sed' Lg. 42 M, Iordan.

disertus] 'Inhumanus' may be explained by contrasting it with 'humanus' (c. 4). 'Barbarus' has its secondary meaning of 'uncultivated,' 'brutish.' 'Commodus' appears to be the antithesis of 'barbarus,' and 'disertus' of 'inhumanus.' 'Disertus' means a man of some taste and accomplishments.

saltare nudus] 'Abest *nudus*, a Lg.

Verres ad fortunas aratorum vexandas diripiendasque esse voluit: hujus audaciae, nequitiae, crudelitati fidelissimos socios optimosque cives scitote hoc praetore traditos, judices, atque addictos fuisse novis institutis et edictis, tota Hieronica lege, quemadmodum ante dixi, rejecta et repudiata.

Primum edictum, judices, audite praeclarum: QVANTVM DECVMANVS EDIDISSET ARATOREM SIBI DECVMAE DARE OPORTERE, VT TANTVM ARATOR DECVMANO DARE COGERETVR. Quomodo? Quantum poposcerit Apronius dato. Quid est hoc? utrum praetoris institutum in socios an in hostes victos insani edictum atque imperium tyranni? Ego tantundem dabo quantum ille poposcerit? poscet omne quantum exaravero. Quid omne? plus immo etiam, inquit, si volet. Quid tum? quid censes? Aut dabis aut contra edictum fecisse damnabere. Per deos immortales quid est hoc? veri enim simile non est. Sic mihi persuadeo, judices, tametsi omnia in istum hominem convenire putetis, tamen hoc vobis falsum videri. Ego enim, quum hoc tota Sicilia diceret, tamen affirmare non auderem, si haec edicta non ex ipsius tabulis totidem verbis recitare possem, sicuti faciam. Da, quaeso, scribae; recitet ex codice. Recita edictum de professione. Negat me recitare totum; nam id significare nutu videtur. Quid praetereo? an illud ubi caves tamen Siculis et miseros respicis aratores? dicis enim te in decumanum, si plus abstulerit quam debitum sit, in octuplum judicium daturum esse. Nihil mihi placet praetermitti. Recita hoc quoque quod postulat, totum. EDICTVM DE IVDICIO IN OCTVPLVM.

XI. Judicio ut arator decumanum persequatur? Miserum atque iniquum ex agro homines traduci in forum, ab aratro ad subsellia, ab usu rerum rusticarum ad insolitam litem atque judicium. Quum omnibus in aliis vectigalibus Asiae, Macedoniae, Hispaniae, Galliae, Africae, Sardiniae, ipsius Italiae quae vectigalia sunt, quum in his,

29 et Paris. A. B.' (Zumpt). He might have omitted 'nudus' out of respect to Lg. 29. 'Nudus' does not necessarily mean stark naked, but Cicero may mean that. If so, the scandal of the affair was aggravated by the presence of the praetor's son, who still wore the 'toga praetexta,' the dress of those who were 'impuberes.'

10. *tantundem dabo*] The reading of V. Zumpt and Iordan have 'tantum dem quantum.'

recitet ex codice.] Klotz and Iordan add 'professionem' from V.

dicis] This is the MSS. reading: 'edicis' is Hotmann's conjecture.—'plus abstulerit:' this reading has better MSS. authority than 'plura sustulerit;' a reading which would be at variance with the sense and the usage of the Latin language.

totum.] 'totum recita' Iordan.

11. *traduci*] 'traducis' 4, V. If we read 'traducis' with Zumpt, we must put a colon after 'iniquum.'

quae vectigalia] That is, the parts of Italy which are 'agri vectigales,' as the Ager Campanus and Stellatis or Stellas, as Orelli writes it. This was the land which the Lex Agraria of Caesar, B.C. 59,

inquam, rebus omnibus publicanus petitor aut pignerator, non ereptor neque possessor soleat esse, tu de optimo, de justissimo, de honestissimo genere hominum, hoc est, de aratoribus ea jura constituebas quae omnibus aliis essent contraria. Utrum est aequius decumanum petere an aratorem repetere? judicium integra re an perdita fieri? eum qui manu quaesiverit, an eum qui digito licitus sit possidere? Quid qui singulis jugis arant, qui ab opere ipsi non recedunt, quo in numero magnus ante te praetorem numerus, magna multitudo Siculorum fuit, quid facient? quum dederint Apronio quod poposcerit, relinquent arationes? relinquent Larem familiarem suum? venient Syracusas ut te praetore videlicet aequo jure Apronium delicias ac vitam tuam judicio recuperatorio

distributed among Roman citizens. After this land was disposed of, and the 'portoria' were abolished in Italy, there was no revenue raised in Italy except the 'vicesima,' from the sale and manumission of slaves (Cic. Ad Att. ii. 16; Dion Cassius, xxxviii. 1, &c., ed. Reimarus).

The Roman 'pignoris capio' or 'captio,' and the English 'distress,' were, in many cases, the same process. Property of the person who owes a duty is seized, and it becomes in the condition of property pledged. The owner must pay the demand, and then he is entitled to have his property back. Klotz absurdly supposes that when the property was seized the owner must proceed by action to recover it, whereas, if he pays the money, he is entitled to have it back. Of course, if it is not given back, he must sue for it. This process was in use, as we see from this passage, in Cicero's time, for the recovery of the 'vectigalia' in the provinces, and also in Italy. In the time of Gaius this practice of distress no longer existed, and the Publicani were required to proceed by action for the recovery of what was due. But the 'intentio' in this case contained a fiction, in which mention was made of the old process: Gaius (iv. 32), "in ea forma, quae publicano proponitur, talis fictio est, ut quanta pecunia olim, si pignus captum esset, id pignus is a quo captum erat luere deberet, tantam pecuniam condemnetur." A Rescript of M. Antoninus and L. Verus declared that the proceedings for the recovery of 'vectigalia' should be against the land (praedia), which thus became liable for arrears in the hands of any person who was in possession of it (Dig. 39. 4. 7).

The 'pignoris capio' was an old Roman institution. (Gaius, iv. 27; Gellius, vii. 10.) Gaius says (iv. 28), "item lege . . . data est pignoris captio publicanis vectigalium publicorum populi Romani adversus eos qui aliqua lege vectigalia deberent." The name of the 'lex' which gave this power is not legible in the Verona MS. except the termination 'toria.' In the time of Gaius, as already observed, this particular 'pignoris capio' no longer existed.

The 'pignoris capio' was also employed by the 'magistratus' to compel obedience to their orders, or to enforce the discharge of some public duty: the thing taken in such a case could only be recovered by the payment of a sum of money. It was also one of the modes of execution, by which a man's goods were seized when he did not satisfy a judgment, and they were sold within two months for the benefit of the creditor; but this process belongs to a period after Cicero's time, and to the reign of Antoninus Pius (Dig. 42. 1. 15, 31).

The nature of 'distress,' in the English system, is well explained in the article "Distress," in the Penny Cyclopaedia.

The MSS. reading is 'petitor ac pignerator,' but Lg. 42 p. m. has 'aut.' There seems no objection to 'ac,' if we suppose that the Publicanus might proceed by action to recover what was due to him, as well as by distress. Iordan has 'ac.'

singulis jugis] The MSS., except Lg. 42 and V, have 'in singulis jugis;' but in c. 51 we have 'minus multis jugis,' where 'jugum' means a pair of beasts. In this passage it means those who plough with a single pair, small cultivators. Orelli has 'in singulis jugis.'

recuperatorio] The 'judices' in such a trial would be 'recuperatores.' See Divin. c. 17, note; and c. 12. 21.

persequantur? Verum esto: reperietur aliqui fortis et experiens arator, qui, quum tantum dederit decumano quantum ille deberi dixerit, judicio repetat et poenam octupli persequatur. Exspecto vim edicti, severitatem praetoris: faveo aratori, cupio octupli damnari Apronium. Quid tandem postulat arator? nihil nisi ex edicto judicium in octuplum. Quid Apronius? non recusat. Quid praetor? jubet recuperatores rejicere. Decurias scribamus. Quas decurias? De cohorte mea rejicies, inquit. Quid ista cohors, quorum hominum est? Volusii haruspicis et Cornelii medici et horum canum quos tribunal meum vides lambere. Nam de conventu nullum unquam judicem nec recuperatorem dedit; iniquos decumanis aiebat omnes esse qui ullam agri glebam possiderent. Veniendum erat ad eos contra Apronium, qui nondum Aproniani convivii crapulam exhalassent. O praeclarum et commemorandum judicium! O severum edictum! O tutum perfugium aratorum!

XII. Atque ut intelligatis cujusmodi ista judicia in octuplum, cujusmodi istius de cohorte recuperatores existimati sint, sic attendite. Ecquem putatis decumanum hac licentia permissa ut tantum ab aratore quantum poposcisset auferret plus quam deberetur poposcisse? Considerate cum vestris animis vosmetipsi ecquem putetis, praesertim quum id non solum avaritia sed etiam imprudentia accidere potuerit. Multos necesse est. At ego omnes dico plus ac multo plus quam decumam abstulisse. Cedo mihi unum ex triennio praeturae tuae qui octupli damnatus sit: damnatus?

experiens arator,] See c. 21, 'experientissimus.'—'aliqui' Lg. 42 V.

Exspecto vim &c.] Some of the hearers are supposed to say this.—'postulat:' Lib. 2. c. 4.

rejicere.] 'To reject or challenge,' that is, to come to the 'rejectio' or challenge, so as to determine who shall be the 'recuperatores,' by rejecting as many out of the whole number as the parties were entitled to reject. Hence it is equivalent to select, as here, and in c. 29 and 59.

Decurias scribamus.] Say the 'aratores.' "Let us put down the 'decuriae' of those who are qualified to act as 'recuperatores.'" "You shall make your challenges out of my 'cohors,'" says Verres; "the 'recuperatores' must be taken from this body, and not from the 'decuriae;' not from the 'conventus,' that is, not from those 'qui in id forum conveniebant.'" See Lib. 2. c. 32. 'Decuria' is properly a body or union of ten persons, and also a 'collegium' generally without respect to the number of members. The expression is also used with reference to the Senate (in Rome and in the towns in the country), and with reference to the 'judices;' but in none of these instances is it of so usual or so universal application as in reference to the 'scribae.' Savigny, System, &c., vol. ii. p. 254, note (c).

12. *istius*] Lg. 42 has 'isti;' but Iordan, who has 'istius,' compares 'de cohorte istius' at the end of this chapter.

Ecquem putatis] The direct form has the indicative; but where the expression depends on another verb, as 'considerate,' we must have the subjunctive. 'Num' is used just in the same way (c. 15, 'quaeritis, num quas . . . ceperit'); and also 'quid' and other words.

plus quam decumam] Lg. 42 V, Zumpt, Iordan. Orelli has 'decumas.' See Index, c. 6.

immo vero in quem judicium ex edicto tuo postulatum sit. Nemo erat videlicet aratorum qui injuriam sibi factam queri posset: nemo decumanorum qui grano amplius sibi quam deberetur deberi professus esset. Immo vero contra, rapiebat et asportabat quantum a quoque volebat Apronius: omnibus autem locis aratores spoliati ac vexati querebantur; neque tamen ullum judicium reperietur. Quid est hoc? tot viri fortes, honesti, gratiosi, tot Siculi, tot equites Romani ab homine nequissimo ac turpissimo laesi, poenam octupli sine ulla dubitatione commissam non persequebantur? quae causa? quae ratio est? una illa, judices, quam videtis, quod ultro etiam illusos se et irrisos ab judicio discessuros videbant. Etenim quod esset judicium, quum ex Verris turpissimo flagitiosissimoque comitatu tres recuperatorum nomine assedissent, asseclae istius, non a patre ei traditi sed a meretricula commendati? Ageret videlicet causam arator: nihil sibi frumenti ab Apronio relictum, bona sua etiam direpta, se pulsatum verberatumque diceret: conferrent viri boni capita, de comissatione loquerentur inter se, ac de mulierculis si quas a praetore abeuntes possent deprehendere: res agi videretur. Surrexisset Apronius, nova dignitas publicani, non ut decumanus, squaloris plenus ac pulveris, sed unguentis oblitus, vino vigiliisque languidus: omnia primo motu ac spiritu suo, vini, unguenti, corporis odore complesset: dixisset haec quae vulgo dicere solebat, non se decumas emisse sed bona fortunasque

Nemo—videlicet] Said ironically, as the words 'immo vero contra' show.

commissam] That is, the penalty was incurred.—'ultro:' either 'ultro' or 'etiam' would seem enough. We may translate 'ultro etiam' 'even further than that.' They would get nothing by their suit, and would be insulted too.

asseclae] Klotz writes 'adseculae,' following Lg. 29 42 B, which is only the same word as 'adseclae,' written in full.

The words 'a patre ei traditi' are not clear. No various reading is noted. Graevius says: "Quis hic patri locus? Franc. 'non a populo Romano ei traditi,' quod verum esse videtur." Cicero says to his brother Quintus, when he was governor of Asia: "atque inter hos, eos quos tibi comites et adjutores negotiorum publicorum dedit ipsa res publica, dumtaxat finibus iis praestabis quos ante praescripsi. Quos vero aut ex domesticis convictionibus aut ex necessariis apparitionibus tecum esse voluisti, qui quasi ex cohorte praetoris appellari solent, horum non modo facta sed etiam dicta omnia praestanda nobis sunt" (i. 1. c. 3). It appears that some of the 'comites,' at least, were given to a governor by the state, and were not appointed by the governor. Others of the inferior class were his own intimates and men of his own choice. These are the men here alluded to. They were recommended by Chelidon: they were not even such as his father had introduced to him; and even they would be none of the best, though certainly the recommendation of a father, even the father of Verres, would be something better than the recommendation of Chelidon. This may be the meaning.

conferrent . . . capita,] Put their heads together, as men do in the jury-box, when they appear to be deliberating. These good men would talk over their last debauch and other delicate matters, and people would think that they were talking of the matter on which they had to give their verdict, 'res agi videretur.' See Lib. 1. c. 55, 'res agi.'

aratorum; non se decumanum esse Apronium sed Verrem alterum, dominum illorum ac tyrannum. Quae quum dixisset, illi viri optimi, de cohorte istius recuperatores, non de absolvendo Apronio deliberarent, sed quaererent ecquo modo petitorem ipsum Apronio condemnare possent.

XIII. Hanc tu licentiam diripiendorum aratorum quum decumanis, hoc est, quum Apronio permisisses, ut quantum vellet posceret, quantum poposcisset auferret, hoc tibi defensionis ad judicium tuum comparabas, habuisse te edictum recuperatores in octuplum daturum? Si mehercule ex omni copia conventus Syracusani, splendidissimorum honestissimorumque hominum, facere potestatem aratori non modo rejiciendi sed etiam sumendi recuperatores, tamen hoc novum genus injuriae ferre nemo posset, te, quum tuos omnes fructus publicano tradidisses et rem de manibus amisisses, tum bona tua repetere ac persequi lite atque judicio. Quum vero verbo judicium sit in edicto, re quidem vera tuorum comitum hominum nequissimorum collusio cum decumanis, sociis tuis atque adeo procuratoribus, tamen audes ullius mentionem judicii facere? praesertim quum id non modo oratione mea sed etiam re ipsa refellatur, quod in tantis incommodis aratorum injuriisque decumanorum nullum ex isto praeclaro edicto non modo factum sed ne postulatum quidem judicium invenitur. Erit tamen in aratores lenior quam videtur. Nam qui in decumanos octupli judicium se daturum edixit, idem habuit in edicto se in aratorem in quadruplum daturum. Quis hunc audet dicere aratoribus infestum aut inimicum fuisse? quanto lenior est quam in publicanum? Edixit ut quod decumanus edidisset sibi dari oportere, id ab aratore magistratus Siculus exigeret. Quid reliqui est judicii quod in aratorem dari possit? Non malum est, inquit, esse istam formidinem, ut, quum exactum sit ab aratore, tamen ne se com-

Apronio condemnare] 'Condemnarent,' some MSS. Lambinus, in his first ed., wrote 'condonarent' (Zumpt): an absurd alteration. Instead of simply refusing the demand of the 'arator,' they would, says Cicero, try if they could not give a verdict against him, which of course they could not do; but Cicero speaks oratorically. The dative 'Apronio' is in conformity to the formula. Gaius (iv. 47), "id judex Numerium Negidium Aulo Agerio condemnato."

13. *Si mehercule*] Klotz has 'me Hercules.' 'Unus (Lg. 42) *mehercules*,' Zumpt. It is not likely that Cicero wrote 'me Hercules.' The expression 'ita me Hercules juvet' had become reduced to the familiar form 'mehercule.'

publicano tradidisses] Verres had let the 'decumae' to the Publicani, and had nothing more to do with them; but Cicero represents him acting as a man who had a direct claim on the 'aratores.'

re quidem vera] Lg. 42 has 're vera quidem,' which Klotz follows. Zumpt says of this reading, "male, nam illo potius modo Cicero solet."

istam formidinem,] By the edictum of Verres, the 'decumanus' could enforce his claim against an 'arator' before a Sicilian 'magistratus.' There were in the several

moveat reliquus metus judicii sit. Si judicio vis a me exigere, remove Siculum magistratum: si hanc vim adhibes, quid opus est judicio? Quis porro erit quin malit decumanis tuis dare quod poposcerint quam ab asseclis tuis quadruplo condemnari?

XIV. Illa vero praeclara est clausula edicti, quod omnium controversiarum quae essent inter aratorem et decumanum, si uter velit, edicit se recuperatores daturum. Primum, quae potest esse controversia, quum is qui petere debet aufert, et quum is non quantum debetur sed quantum commodum est aufert; ille autem unde ablatum est judicio suum recuperare nullo modo potest; deinde in hoc homo luteus etiam callidus ac veterator esse vult, quod ita scribit, Si uter volet, recuperatores dabo. Quam lepide se furari putat! Utrique facit potestatem; sed utrum ita scripserit, Si uter volet, an, Si decumanus volet, nihil interest: arator enim tuos istos recuperatores nunquam volet.

Quid illa cujusmodi sunt quae ex tempore ab Apronio admonitus edixit? Q. Septitio honestissimo equite Romano resistente Apronio, et affirmante se plus decuma non daturum, exoritur peculiare edic-

towns courts for the recovery of the 'decumae,' if they were not paid. The 'decumanus' would declare his demand, and the Sicilian 'magistratus' would enforce it. "What other process remains against the 'arator?'" says Cicero; "this is enough; there is no need of any other." "It is no bad thing," Verres is supposed to say, "that there should be an apprehension of that other process, in which the 'arator' may be sued for fourfold the value of the demand, in order that, though the 'arator' has been compelled to pay, he may have some dread of being sued again by the other process, if he should seem disposed to be restive." Cicero rejoins, on the part of the 'arator:' "if you will get the money from me by this other process, then put this Sicilian 'magistratus' out of the way; or, if you give the Sicilian 'magistratus' power to compel me to pay the demand, what is the use of the other process? Besides, who would not rather give to your 'decumani' what they demand, than be compelled by your route to pay four times the amount?" The object of the supposed 'arator' is to show that the 'judicium in octuplum' against the 'decumani,' which looks very severe, was a farce. For, in the first instance, the 'arator' could be compelled by a Sicilian 'magistratus' to pay whatever was demanded. If he complained, he had before his eyes the fear of a 'judicium in quadruplum,' with the 'recuperatores' of Verres for 'judices;' and if he came before them as a plaintiff, to recover the 'octuplum,' he knew that he should certainly fail.

14. *quod . . . edicit*] Those who call 'quod' a conjunction will find no difficulty here. But it is the relative, and the formula is 'Illa . . edicti, quod . . edicit.'

quae essent] Here we have the subjunctive in one of its general, indeterminate senses. 'In all disputes which might arise' is not an adequate version. Our expression 'in all disputes arising between' is nearer the sense of the Latin.

homo luteus] The old reading, and that of Ernesti, is 'lynceus,' which has no sense. 'Luteus' means, says Zumpt, a worthless fellow. A dirty fellow, perhaps. See Lib. 2. c. 78, 'tamquam in luto;' 'luto volutatum' (Lib. 4. c. 24). 'Luteum negotium' (Lib. 4. c. 14), in a somewhat different sense, perhaps.

Si uter] 'Uter' is here said to be equivalent to 'alteruter' (Zumpt).

Quid illa &c.] Zumpt and Iordan, as usual, 'Quid? illa cujusmodi,' &c., whereas the repetition of the question is in the 'cujusmodi.' The reader may put a comma after 'illa,' if he prefers it, or he may learn to read the passage right without this artificial help.

edictum repentinum,] See Excursus iv.

tum repentinum, 'Ne quis frumentum de area tolleret antequam cum decumano pactus esset.' Ferebat hanc quoque iniquitatem Septitius, et imbri frumentum corrumpi in area patiebatur, quum illud edictum repente uberrimum quaestuosissimumque nascitur, 'ut ante Kalendas Sextiles omnes decumas ad aquam deportatas haberent.' Hoc edicto non Siculi, nam eos quidem superioribus edictis satis perdiderat atque afflixerat, sed isti ipsi equites Romani, qui suum jus retinere se contra Apronium posse erant arbitrati, splendidi homines et aliis praetoribus gratiosi, vincti Apronio traditi sunt. Attendite enim cujusmodi edicta sint: 'Ne tollat,' inquit, 'ex area nisi erit pactus.' Satis haec magna vis est ad inique paciscendum: malo enim plus dare quam non mature ex area tollere. At ista vis Septitium et nonnullos Septitii similes non coercet, qui ita dicunt, Non tollam potius quam paciscar. His hoc opponitur: Deportatum habeas ante Kalendas Sextiles. Deportabo igitur. Nisi pactus eris, non commovebis. Sic deportandi dies praestituta tollere cogebat ex area: prohibitio tollendi, nisi pactus esset, vim adhibebat pactioni non voluntatem.

XV. Jam vero illud non solum contra legem Hieronicam nec solum contra consuetudinem superiorum, sed etiam contra omnia jura Siculorum, quae habent a senatu populoque Romano, ne quis extra suum forum vadimonium promittere cogatur. Statuit iste,

area] An 'area' in a city is a vacant piece of ground (Dig. 50. 16. 27, 115, 211, where other technical words are explained). Here it means the floor on which the grain was trod out, an open place prepared for this purpose. Virgil (Georg. i. 178) gives directions for making one. The 'area' was in the open air, and the corn was spoiled by the rain. Such an 'area' is or was used sometimes in the United States, in a field. The want of a cover for the corn, when it was trod out, as we must infer to have been the case in Sicily, shows a low state of cultivation. The corn must often have been dirty. Arthur Young (Travels in France, vol. i. p. 355, 2nd edition) says of the years 1787—1789, "there is not a plank threshing-floor in France; and no miller can grind corn as he receives it from the farmer, without further cleaning." Virgil's 'area' was made of earth; and Varro, Cato, and Columella give pretty nearly the same instructions for making one.

ad aquam] They were required to carry down the corn to the sea-coast. Dureau de la Malle (Économie Politique des Romains, ii. 427) quotes this passage to prove that, as a general rule, the people had to convey their 'decumae' to the coast. Zumpt thinks that the edict applied to the 'alterae decumae' (see c. 82, 83), which were bought of the Siculi for the use of Rome. And it seems probable that the regular 'decumae' would be delivered to the 'decumani' on the land of each 'arator,' or at some place within a limited distance. Zumpt appears to be right in not joining 'omnes' with 'decumas.'

suum jus retinere] Cicero uses 'obtinere' in the same sense (Lib. 1. c. 26); and see the use of 'obtinemus' (Lib. 3. c. 35).

cujusmodi edicta sint:] Only Lg. 45 A have 'sint.' Klotz has 'Adtendite enim: cujus modi edicta sunt?'

15. *forum vadimonium*] This 'forum' is the place to which the people of a certain district resorted to settle their legal disputes, and for other court business; it is also the court-house of a district, and hence the district itself. In the next sentence most of the MSS. have erroneously 'quod vellet.' But compare c. 20, and c. 34.

'Ut arator decumano quo vellet decumanus vadimonium promitteret;' ut hic quoque Apronio, quum ex Leontino usque [ad] Lily-

'promittunt Herbitenses vadimonium Syracusas.' Shortly after, in this chapter, we have '[ad] Lilybaeum aliquem vadaretur.' Iordan says 'usque ad' Lg. 42.

'Vadimonium' is thus explained by a German writer (Puchta, Inst. ii. § 160, 1st ed.): "When the parties appeared '*in jure*' (that is, before the Praetor or other magistrate who had 'jurisdictio'), as a general rule, the proceedings before the 'magistratus' were by no means ended on the same day, for the plaintiff now declared to the defendant what kind of action he intended to bring (Editio Actionis, Dig. 2. tit. 13), and it was necessary that time should be allowed to the defendant to prepare his defence. Accordingly the parties agreed on a time when they should again appear '*in jure*,' and this engagement is called '*vadimonium*,' and is comprehended under the general expression, '*cautio judicio sisti*:' it refers to a sum of money, as the '*poena desertionis*,' which, in some cases, was equal in amount to the matter in dispute; in other cases, to one-half; but never exceeded one hundred thousand sesterces. The defendant had, as a general rule, to furnish sureties (*vades*) for the amount of the 'vadimonium;' sometimes the sureties were dispensed with (*vadimonium purum*); in other cases, sureties were replaced by the oath, or by an immediate condemnation in the amount of the '*poena*,' by '*recuperatores*,' if the '*vadimonium*' was broken (Gaius, iv. 184–187). Under these circumstances, it was manifestly more convenient for the parties to save themselves the first appearance before the court, and, instead of the '*in jus vocatio*,' to agree from the first about a day for the actual decision of the question, and to secure it by 'vadimonium.' This was, in fact, even in Cicero's time, the usual process; the proper '*in jus vocatio*' was only used in the case of a stubborn and resisting defendant." He refers to the passage in Horace (1 Sat. ix. 74), "casu venit obvius illi Adversarius . . Rapit in jus."

This passage, and another in the same Satire (36),

—— "et casu tum respondere vadato
Debebat, quod ni fecisset, perdere litem,"

may be properly examined here. On the 'rapit in jus,' Orelli remarks, "ad recuperatores vel ad centumvirale judicium;" and then he adds a reference to Plautus, Poen. iii. 5. 45, "priusquam obtorto collo ad praetorem trahas;" so that in the same note he contradicts himself. For 'in jus' is 'before the Praetor or Magistratus,' as Heindorf rightly explains it, and he quotes, to prove what he says, the same passage of Plautus, which Orelli quotes, without perceiving that it contradicts his own explanation. The scholiast on Horace, Porphyrio, understands the passage to mean, that as the man did not appear according to his 'vadimonium,' the 'adversarius' arrested him to drag him before the Praetor, and he quotes the words of the Twelve Tables, "Si in jus vocat, ni it, antestator. Igitur em capito;" but here again there is contradiction, for the 'in jus vocatio' is the first step in a suit. As to the correction of the corrupted text of Porphyrio, see Dirksen, Uebersicht, &c. der Zwölf-Tafel-Fragmente, p. 129. According to the explanation of Orelli, the 'adversarius' in Horace is the 'vadato' mentioned in v. 36. According to Puchta and others, it cannot be this 'vadato,' because the 'in jus vocatio' was the first step in a civil procedure. Bethman-Hollweg (Handbuch des Civilprozesses, i. p. 247, Bonn, 1834), after explaining the 'vadimonium' in the same way as Puchta, adds: "of this 'vadimonium' we accordingly find numerous examples in Cicero; of the 'in jus vocatio' not one; though in the case of such people as the importunate fellow in Horace, or more obstinate persons, it still did good service." He adds, in a note, "force was used to the importunate fellow in Horace, in consequence of the 'vadimonium;' for, if a man did not keep the 'vadimonium,' he had still to apprehend the use of force." I do not believe that this explanation is correct; but it would be out of place to follow up this matter further.

When Hollweg says that no example of the 'in jus vocatio' occurs in Cicero, perhaps he means no example of the violent process mentioned by Horace; for the phrase occurs often. In De Leg. ii. 4, 'A parvis, Quirites, didicimus, Si in jus vocat,' &c.; Verr. Lib. 2. c. 76, 'in jus ad Metellum Carpinatium voco;' Lib. 3. c. 47, 'in jus ipsum eduxi.' A reader would certainly be inclined to conclude that the 'adversarius,' 'qui rapit in jus,' in Horace, is the 'vadato;' and it may be so. But if it is so, we must conclude that Horace is

bacum aliquem vadaretur, ex miseris aratoribus calumniandi quaestus accederet. Quamquam illa fuit ad calumniam singulari consilio reperta ratio quod edixerat, 'Ut aratores jugera sationum suarum profiterentur.' Quae res quum ad pactiones iniquissimas magnam vim habuit, sicut ostendam, neque ad ullam utilitatem rei publicae pertinuit, tum vero ad calumnias in quas omnes inciderent quos vellet Apronius. Ut enim quisque contra voluntatem ejus dixerat, ita in eum judicium de professione jugerum postulabatur, cujus judicii metu magnus a multis frumenti numerus ablatus, magnaeque pecuniae coactae sunt: non quo jugerum numerum vero profiteri esset difficile aut amplius etiam profiteri, quid enim in eo periculi posset esse? sed causa erat judicii postulandi quod ex edicto professus non esset. Judicium autem quod fuerit isto praetore, si quae cohors et qui comitatus fuerit meministis, scire debetis. Quid igitur est quod ex hac iniquitate novorum edictorum intelligi velim, judices? Injuriamne factam sociis? At videtis. Auctoritatem superiorum repudiatam? Non audebit negare. Apronium tantum isto praetore potuisse? Confiteatur necesse est. Sed vos fortasse, quod vos lex commonet, id in hoc loco quaeretis, num quas ex hisce rebus pecunias ceperit? Docebo cepisse maximas, omnesque eas iniquitates, de quibus antea dixi, sui quaestus causa constituisse convincam, si prius illud propugnaculum quo

not a sufficient authority for legal procedure.

The student should form a clear notion of the 'in jus vocatio,' and he must carefully distinguish 'in jure,' 'before the praetor,' from 'in judicio,' 'before a judex' (in civil matters). The passage in Plautus, Persa iv. 9. 8, "S. age, ambula in jus, leno. D. Quid me in jus vocas? S. Illi apud praetorem dicam, sed ego in jus voco. D. Nonne antestaris?" &c., is as good, for the purpose of explanation, as any comment.

The expression 'vadari aliquem' means to require 'vades,' 'sureties,' of a party. It has nothing to do with the verb 'vad-ere,' to go. The corresponding term is 'vadimonium promittere,' which is said of him who gives 'vades.' Bentley's correction of 'vadatus,' for 'vadato,' in the passage of Horace, is against all the MSS. and the general usage of the word; though 'vadatus' is sometimes used passively, as he shows. In place of 'vadari,' Gaius (iv. 187) uses another expression: "quas autem personas sine permissu Praetoris impune in jus vocare non possumus, easdem nec vadimonio invitas obligare possumus, praeterquam si Praetor aditus permittit."

profiterentur.] 'Make a return,' as we say.

quod ex edicto &c.] This is the subject of the sentence, of which is predicated, 'causa erat:' 'but the not making of a return was a ground of proceeding against him.' There is no difficulty here, except what is created by putting a point after 'postulandi,' as Iordan does.

Apronium tantum] 'Apronium tamen' Lg. 42, whence Halm concludes that we should read 'Apronium tantum,' instead of the common reading, 'Tantum Apronium.'

lex commonet,] The Lex de Repetundis, under which the proceeding against Verres was instituted. Cicero often rambles a good deal from the point, but he makes a show now and then of coming back to it. The direct demand against Verres was a certain sum, which he was charged with getting illegally; and it was necessary to prove that the money had come to his hands.

convincam,] 'vincam' Lg. 42 F M. Iordan: 'convincam' Lgg. roll. A B N.

contra omnes meos impetus usurum se putat ex defensione ejus dejecero.

XVI. Magno, inquit, decumas vendidi. Quid ais? an tu decumas, homo audacissime atque amentissime, vendidisti? tu partes eas quas te senatus populusque Romanus voluit an fructus integros atque adeo bona fortunasque aratorum omnes vendidisti? Si palam praeco jusso tuo praedicasset, non decumas frumenti sed dimidias venire partes, et ita emptores accessissent ut ad dimidias partes emendas, si pluris vendidisses tu dimidias quam ceteri decumas, cuinam mirum videretur? Quid vero si praeco decumas pronuntiavit, re vera, hoc est, lege, edicto, conditione plus etiam quam dimidiae venierunt, tamen hoc tibi praeclarum putabis, te pluris quod non licebat quam ceteros quod oportebat vendidisse?—Pluris vendidi decumas quam ceteri.—Quibus rebus id assecutus es? innocentia? Aspice aedem Castoris: deinde, si audes, fac mentionem innocentiae. Diligentia? Codicis lituras tui contemplare in Sthenii Thermitani nomine: deinde aude te dicere diligentem. Ingenio? Qui testes interrogare priore actione nolueris et iis tacitus os tuum praebere malueris, quamvis et te et patronos tuos ingeniosos esse dicito. Qua re igitur id quod ais assecutus es? Magna est enim laus, si superiores consilio vicisti, posterioribus exemplum atque auctoritatem reliquisti. Tibi fortasse idoneus fuit

16. *Quid vero si*] Klotz has 'quid? si praeco decumas pronuntiavit; re vera' &c. The larger stop after 'pronuntiavit' is hardly necessary to prevent a mistake. The 'decumas pronuntiavit,' the declaration of the 'praeco,' that the 'decumae' were going to be sold, is opposed to what in fact (re vera) was done: more than half the produce was really sold, though it was sold under the name of 'decumae.' Zumpt has 'Quid vero,' &c.; but V omits 'vero.'

Pluris vendidi &c.] Zumpt and Iordan have from Lg. 42 φ 'pluris decumas vendidisti.'

lituras tui &c.] Klotz has from V 'codicis lituras tu contemplare;' but I take 'tu' to be a blunder of the copyist.

tacitus os] 'Tacitum os' in the English reprint of Zumpt, and I suppose in the edition from which it was printed. In his large edition Zumpt remarks, "nunquam *tacitum os praebere*, sed quia tacet, ideo os praebet." Terence, Adelph. ii. 2. 7:

"SA. Qui potui melius qui hodie et usque os praebui?"

and in Cicero, Ad Att. (i. 13), "quam dignus qui Palicano, sicut facit, os ad male audiendum quotidie praebeat."

Verres or his advocates are here supposed not to have cross-examined the witnesses against him in the 'prior actio,' which they might have done.

quamvis et te &c.] 'quantum vis et te' B, C, Or. If 'quantum vis' is right, it is certainly not the common form of expression, which is 'quamvis.' It is more usual to place 'quamvis' nearer the word which it qualifies, which is here 'ingeniosos.' Zumpt says that 'quamvis' is said for 'quantum vis,' which I do not believe. It is said for what it is. His note is "*quamvis* secundum originem suam pro *quantumvis* dici, et adverbialiter (non conjunctionaliter) cum aliis Adverbiis vel Adjectivis componi, ut h. l. *quamvis ingeniosos*, non est quod multis doceam." In Lib. 5. c. 6 there is 'expectate facinus quam vultis improbum,' where 'quam' has a reference to a 'tam' suppressed. I can hardly suppose Zumpt to mean that 'tam' and 'quam' are the same as 'tantum' and 'quantum.'

nemo quem imitarere. At te videlicet inventorem rerum optimarum ac principem imitabuntur omnes. Quis arator te praetore decumam dedit? quis duas? quis non maximo se affectum beneficio putavit, quum tribus decumis pro una defungeretur, praeter paucos qui propter societatem furtorum tuorum nihil omnino dederunt? Vide inter importunitatem tuam senatusque bonitatem quid intersit. Senatus quum temporibus rei publicae cogitur ut decernat ut alterae decumae exigantur, ita decernit ut pro his decumis pecunia solvatur aratoribus; ut quod plus sumitur quam debetur, id emi non auferri putetur. Tu, quum tot decumas non senatusconsulto sed novis edictis tuis nefariisque institutis exigeres et eriperes, magnum te fecisse arbitrare, si pluris vendideris quam L. Hortensius, pater istius Q. Hortensii, quam Cn. Pompeius, quam C. Marcellus, qui ab aequitate, ab lege, ab institutis non recesserunt? An tibi unius anni aut biennii ratio fuit habenda, salus provinciae, commoda rei frumentariae, ratio rei publicae in posteritatem fuit negligenda? Quum rem ita constitutam accepisses ut et populo Romano satis frumenti ex Sicilia suppeditaretur, et aratoribus tamen arare atque agros colere expediret, quid effecisti? quid assecutus es? Ut populo Romano nescio quid te praetore ad decumas accederet, deserendas arationes relinquendasque curasti. Successit tibi L. Metellus. Tu innocentior quam Metellus? tu laudis et honoris cupidior? Tibi enim consulatus quaerebatur, Metello paternus honos et avitus negligebatur. Multo minoris vendidit non modo quam tu, sed etiam quam qui ante te vendiderunt. XVII. Quaero, si ipse excogitare non potuerat quemadmodum quam plurimo venderet, ne tua quidem recentia proximi praetoris vestigia persequi poterat, ut tuis praeclaris abs te principe inventis et excogitatis edictis atque institutis uteretur? Ille vero tum se minime Metellum fore putavit si te ulla in re imitatus esset; qui ab urbe Roma, quod nemo

ut pro his decumis pecunia] This is the order of Lg. 42 and V, which Klotz and Iordan have. The common order is 'ut pecunia pro his decumis,' &c. These variations in the order of words easily happen in copying from a common original, and are the most common of variations in the text of Cicero, and of other ancient writers. It is useful now and then to note a few, even though, as in this instance, it may be impossible to decide which is the genuine language of Cicero.

quod plus] Zumpt has 'quo plus,' which I hardly understand, notwithstanding his explanation. Iordan also has 'quo plus,' the reading of Lg. 42 A, B, φ. V ett have 'quod,' which seems more easily explained than the other: 'What is taken over and above what is due, that is to be considered as bought, not as enforced.'

C. Marcellus,] See Lib. 2. c. 3, note.

Tibi enim consulatus &c.] Said ironically: 'you were trying to secure the consulship, I suppose; Metellus was careless about obtaining an office which his father and grandfather had enjoyed. Metellus sold them much lower, not only than you, but lower than your predecessors did.'

unquam post hominum memoriam fecit, quum sibi in provinciam proficiscendum putaret, literas ad Siciliae civitates miserit, per quas hortatur et rogat ut arent, ut serant. In beneficio praetor hoc petit aliquanto ante adventum suum, et simul ostendit se lege Hieronica venditurum, hoc est, in omni ratione decumarum nihil isti simile facturum. Atque haec non cupiditate aliqua scribit inductus ut in alienam provinciam mittat literas ante tempus, sed consilio, ne si tempus sationis praeterisset granum de provincia Sicilia nullum haberemus. Cognoscite Metelli literas. EPISTOLA L. METELLI.

XVIII. Hae literae, judices, L. Metelli, quas audistis, hoc quantum est ex Sicilia frumenti hornotini exaraverunt. Glebam commosset in agro decumano Siciliae nemo, si Metellus hanc epistolam non misisset. Quid Metello divinitus hoc venit in mentem an ab Siculis qui Romam frequentissimi convenerant negotiatoribusque Siciliae doctus est? quorum quanti conventus ad Marcellos, antiquissimos Siciliae patronos, quanti ad Cn. Pompeium consulem designatum, ceterosque illius provinciae necessarios, fieri soliti sint quis ignorat? Quod quidem judicium nullo unquam de homine factum est, ut absens accusaretur ab iis palam quorum in bona liberosque summum imperium potestatemque haberet. Tanta vis erat injuriarum ut homines quidvis perpeti quam non de istius

17. *In beneficio &c.*] Klotz has 'populi Romani' before 'praetor,' which two words V omits. Zumpt and Orelli have 'ut serant in beneficio Populi Romani. Et hoc petit,' &c. Zumpt explains 'in beneficio' thus: "*In* praepositionem omnes libri praeter Nannianum agnoscunt, rectissime, nam beneficium est in agris, quos populus Romanus vi ceperat, Siculisque concesserat, non in serendo." Thus 'in beneficio' is equivalent to 'in agris populi Romani,' an explanation which we cannot accept. Klotz gives the true explanation of the passage. He compares c. 48, "atque hoc in beneficii loco petitum est ab Apronio;" and we have only to suppose 'in beneficio' to be equivalent to 'in beneficii loco.' Cicero tells us the same thing again (c. 22), 'Metellus . . . ut sererent quam plurimum;' but there is nothing in that passage which helps us here.

isti simile] Klotz and Jordan have from V, 'istius simile,' which may be the true reading, though I doubt.—'de provincia' is the reading of V, in place of the common reading, 'ex provincia.'

18. *hornotini*] 'the produce of the year.' The word is a longer form of 'hornus,' an adjective, which signifies 'the produce of the season' (hora). Horace, Epod. ii. 47, has 'Et horna dulci vina promens dolio,' where the scholiast in the note has the expression 'hornotinum vinum.' There is also 'annotinus,' Caesar, B. G. v. 8.

consulem] V has 'tuum consulem,' which means 'tum consulem,' which reading Klotz and Jordan have. In place of 'quod quidem judicium' V has 'quod quidem jud.,' out of which Mai makes 'quod quidem judices;' and this is perhaps the true reading.—At the end of this chapter V has 'relinquerunt,' on which Zumpt remarks, in his Appendix, 'ediditque admirabiliter Maius.' Mai is so fond of his palimpsest, that he does not even object to coin new words out of it. In Lib. 2. c. 58 there is the reading 'non, opinor, esset dubium,' which satisfies ordinary men's judgment. But V has 'resset' for 'esset,' a blunder, the origin of which is palpable; yet Mai takes it under his protection, and becomes the sponsor for a new verb, 'resum.'

improbitate deplorare et conqueri mallent. Quas literas quum ad omnes civitates prope suppliciter misisset Metellus, tamen antiquum modum sationis nulla ex parte assequi potuit: diffugerant enim permulti, id quod ostendam; nec solum arationes sed etiam sedes suas patrias istius injuriis exagitati reliquerant.

Non mehercule augendi criminis causa, judices, dicam: sed quem ipse accepi oculis animoque sensum, hunc vere apud vos et ut potero planissime exponam. Nam quum quadriennio post in Siciliam venissem, sic mihi affecta visa est ut hae terrae solent in quibus bellum acerbum diuturnumque versatum est. Quos ego campos antea collesque nitidissimos viridissimosque vidissem, hos ita vastatos nunc ac desertos videbam ut ager ipse cultorem desiderare ac lugere dominum videretur. Herbitensis ager, Hennensis, Murgentinus, Assorinus, Imacharensis, Agyrinensis, ita relictus erat ex maxima parte ut non solum jugerum sed etiam dominorum multitudinem quaereremus; Aetnensis vero ager qui solebat esse cultissimus, et, quod caput est rei frumentariae, campus Leontinus, cujus antea species haec erat ut, quum obsitum vidisses, annonae caritatem non vererere, sic erat deformis atque horridus ut in uberrima Siciliae parte Siciliam quaereremus. Labefactarat enim vehementer aratores jam superior annus, proximus vero funditus everterat.

hae terrae solent] V has 'eae,' &c., a variation which I note, that the reader may better understand how frequently these two forms, in certain cases, are interchanged or used indifferently.

Murgentinus,] This is the MSS. reading. There are also the forms Μοργάντιον, Μοργαντίνη, Μοργαντῖνοι. The Greek form on the coins is Μοργαν and Μοργαντινα. See Excursus viii. The site of the place is uncertain. Livy (24, c. 27) speaks of it as on the coast. Diodorus seems to place it north-west of the plain of Leontini.

The codd. here have 'Macharensis.' Pliny (iii. c. 8) has 'Imacarenses.' The site of the place is uncertain, but Imachara seems, like the other towns here mentioned, to be in the corn country included between Henna and Aetna, and extending south to Leontini.

jugerum] V. has 'jugorum,' accepted by Klotz and Iordan. The context shows that 'jugerum' is the true word. 'Quaereremus' is equivalent to 'desideraremus,' 'I looked in vain for;' and so it is used again shortly after in this chapter.

campus Leontinus,] This is the extensive plain through which the Lissus flows. This river is described in ancient times as entering a lake, and issuing from it in two branches, one of which was navigable. This is now the lake of Biviere, near Lentini, the site of the ancient Leontini. This lake, "in its greatest winter extent, is about nineteen miles in circumference, but it decreases, as the sun advances, to eight or nine, leaving a feculent bed of mud and marsh on its banks, that, during the summer exhalations, teems with pestilence and death" (Smyth's Sicily, p. 158). Smyth adds that this inconvenience might be easily removed, "as there is a communication by the rivulet of San Leonardo with the sea, which might easily be deepened." This rivulet may be the ancient Terias. (Thucyd. vi. 50.) Swinburne describes the plain along the coast as full of ponds and marshes, which abound with wild fowl. After leaving the fens, he came upon a "noble plain, covered with promising crops of corn, but without a single enclosure, or even tree." Polybius (vii. 6) describes the position of Leontini. The corn plains lie north of the city.

XIX. Tu mihi etiam audes mentionem facere decumarum? Tu in tanta improbitate, [tu] in tanta acerbitate, in tot ac tantis injuriis, quum in arationibus et in earum rerum jure provincia Sicilia consistat, eversis funditus aratoribus, relictis agris, quum in provincia tam locuplete ac referta non modo rem sed ne spem quidem ullam reliquam cuiquam feceris, aliquid te populare putabis habere, quum dicis te pluris quam ceteros decumas vendidisse? Quasi vero aut populus Romanus hoc voluerit, aut senatus tibi hoc mandaverit ut, quum omnes aratorum fortunas decumarum nomine eriperes, in posterum fructu illo commodoque rei frumentariae populum Romanum privares; deinde, si quam partem tuae praedae ad summam decumarum addidisses, bene de re publica, bene de populo Romano meritus viderere.

Atque proinde loquor quasi in eo sit iniquitas ejus reprehendenda, quod propter gloriae cupiditatem, ut aliquos summa frumenti decumani vinceret, acerbiorem legem, duriora edicta interposuerit, omnium superiorum auctoritatem repudiarit. Magno tu decumas vendidisti. Quid si doceo te non minus domum tuam avertisse quam Romam misisse decumarum nomine? quid habet populare oratio tua, quum ex provincia populi Romani aequam partem tu tibi sumpseris ac populo Romano miseris? quid si duabus partibus doceo te amplius frumenti abstulisse quam populo Romano misisse: tamenne putamus patronum tuum in hoc crimine cerviculam jactaturum et populo se ac coronae daturum? Haec vos antea, judices, audistis: verum fortasse ita audistis ut auctorem rumorem haberetis sermonemque omnium. Cognoscite

19. *cuiquam feceris,*] 'cujusquam feceris' Klotz, from Lg. 42. He has also 'cum dicis te,' which seems to be the true reading. Zumpt and Iordan have 'cum dices.'

rei frumentariae &c.] 'frumentariae rei rem publicam privares' Lg. 42.

proinde] 'perinde,' Zumpt, Klotz, and Iordan. No MSS. variation is noticed.

oratio] Zumpt from Lg. 42, which seems, as he says, to be preferable to the common reading 'ratio.' The defence of Verres would be, 'I have sold the decumae at a high price;' but such a declaration would not be calculated to conciliate the good-will of the people; it would not be 'populare.'

cerviculam] An allusion to the theatrical gesture of Hortensius. Klotz refers to the Brutus (c. 88), "motus et gestus etiam plus artis habebat quam erat oratori satis."

The 'corona' is the mass of bystanders, the crowd generally, as in Ovid, Met. lib. xiii. v. 1:

> "Consedere duces, et vulgi stante corona
> Surgit ad hos clypei dominus septemplicis Ajax."

A passage from the oration Pro Flacco (c. 28) is aptly cited here: "a judicibus oratio avertitur, vox in coronam turbamque effunditur." See also Pro Milone, c. 1. Hahn proposes to read here 'ac populi se coronae.'

auctorem &c.] This word is explained in a note to Lib. 5. c. 22. In place of 'omnium' it has been proposed to write 'hominum,' but no MS. variation is noted. The two words 'homines' and 'omnes,' in their several cases, are often confounded.

nunc innumerabilem pecuniam frumentario nomine ereptam, ut simul illam quoque ejus vocem improbam agnoscatis, qui se uno quaestu decumarum omnia sua pericula redempturum esse dicebat.

XX. Audivimus hoc jamdiu, judices: nego quemquam esse vestrum quin saepe audierit socios istius fuisse decumanos. Nihil aliud arbitror falso in istum esse dictum ab iis qui male de isto existimarint nisi hoc. Nam socii putandi sunt quos inter res communicata est. Ego rem totam fortunasque aratorum omnes istius fuisse dico: Apronium, Venereosque servos, quod isto praetore fuit novum genus publicanorum, ceterosque decumanos procuratores istius quaestus et administros rapinarum fuisse dico. Quomodo hoc doces?—Quo modo ex locatione illa columnarum docui istum esse praedatum: opinor, ex eo maxime quod iniquam legem novamque dixisset. Quis enim unquam conatus est jura omnia et consuetudinem omnium commutare cum vituperatione sine quaestu? Pergam atque insequar longius. Iniqua lege vendebas quo pluris venderes. Cur addictis jam et venditis decumis, quum jam ad summam decumarum nihil, ad tuum quaestum multum posset accedere, subito atque ex tempore nova nascebantur edicta? Nam ut vadimonium decumano quocunque is vellet pro-

20. *Nam socii*] Cicero's meaning is this: "You have often heard it said that the 'decumani,' or farmers of the 'decumae,' were his partners. This is, as I think, the only false charge made against Verres by those who have a bad opinion of him: for we must consider those as partners whose stock is made common property, or whose pecuniary interests become a joint interest. But, instead of this partnership existing, I affirm that the whole property and fortunes of the 'aratores' fell into the hands of Verres."

Cicero's language is founded on the legal notion of partnership. 'Quos inter res communicata est' means, that the property of the several partners, if it is a general partnership ('totorum bonorum,' Gaius iii. 148), becomes joint property by virtue of the agreement for a partnership, and no mutual transfer is required. This is the doctrine of the Roman law, and the language is that of Cicero: "in societate omnium bonorum omnes res quae coeuntium sunt continuo communicantur" (Paulus, Dig. 17. 2. 1). See Pro Sext. Rosc. Am. c. 40.

addictis . . et venditis] The contract of buying and selling, in the Roman system, and in all legal systems, is complete as soon as the thing to be sold and the price are agreed on. When this is done, the contract of buying and selling is complete. Delivery (traditio) and taking possession are no part of the contract, but a different transaction. The word 'addictis,' of which examples have occurred before, has, among other significations, that of declaring the highest bidder at a public auction to be the purchaser; and Cicero appropriately says 'addictis et venditis,' for the 'addictio' here is part of the contract, and necessary to its completion. Comp. c. 63, "neque iis voluisse te addicere qui contra Apronium licerentur." A passage of Suetonius (Caesar, c. 60), referred to by Forcellini, shows the proper use of this word: "ei . . . amplissima praedia ex auctionibus hastae minimo addixit," where some editions read 'ei nummo' for 'minimo.' (See the note in Burmann's edition.) It is also used as applied to private bargains (Julian, Dig. 41. 4. 7). See Horace, 2 Sat. v. 109, 'nummo te addicere,' and Heindorf's note; but he says nothing of 'addicere.'

quocunque is vellet] See c. 15, note.

mitteretur, ut ex area nisi pactus esset arator ne tolleret, ut ante Kalendas Sextiles decumas deportatas haberet, haec omnia jam venditis decumis anno tertio te edixisse dico: quae si rei publicae causa faceres, in vendendo essent pronuntiata; quia tua causa faciebas, quod erat imprudentia praetermissum, id quaestu ac tempore admonitus reprehendisti. Illud vero cui probari potest, te sine tuo quaestu ac maximo quaestu tantam tuam infamiam, tantum capitis tui fortunarumque tuarum periculum neglexisse; ut, quum totius Siciliae quotidie gemitus querimoniasque audires, quum, ut ipse dixisti, reum te fore putares, quum hujusce judicii discrimen ab opinione tua non abhorreret, paterere tamen aratores indignissimis injuriis vexari ac diripi? Profecto, quamquam es singulari crudelitate et audacia, tamen abs te totam alienari provinciam, tot homines honestissimos ac locupletissimos tibi inimicissimos fieri nolles, nisi hanc rationem et cogitationem salutis tuae pecuniae cupiditas ac praesens illa praeda superaret. Etenim, quoniam summam ac numerum injuriarum vobis, judices, non possum exponere, singillatim autem de uniuscujusque incommodo dicere infinitum est, genera ipsa injuriarum, quaeso, cognoscite.

XXI. Nympho est Centuripinus, homo navus et industrius, experientissimus ac diligentissimus arator. Is quum arationes magnas conductas haberet, quod homines etiam locupletes, sicut ille est, in Sicilia facere consuerunt, easque magna impensa magnoque instrumento tueretur, tanta ab isto iniquitate oppressus est ut

reprehendisti.] 'you changed or altered.' Compare c. 35, "unum hoc aliquot senatus consultis reprehensum," &c. 'Prehendere' is to lay hold of with the hand, and 'reprehendere' is to lay hold of for the purpose of checking or pulling back. Plautus, Mil. Glor. i. 1. 59, 'quae here pallio me reprehenderunt.' It has also the sense of reconsidering, handling over again, and the like:

——— "pernoscite
Furtumne factum existumetis, an locum
Reprehensum, qui praeteritus negligentia
est."—Ter. Adelph. Prol. 12.

alienari] 'abalienari,' N, V, Iordan.

21. *navus*] The true writing of the word is 'gnavus,' as we see from the compound 'ignavus,' and the corresponding Greek form γενναῖος. But the MSS. have 'navus,' except V, which has 'gnavus.' Cicero says that the practice in his time was to write 'navus;' the orthography had adapted itself to the pronunciation, for we must suppose that the Romans gave up pronouncing the initial 'g' in this and some other words. Cicero's remark is (Orat. c. 47), "*Noti* erant et *navi* et *nari*, quibus quum IN praeponi oporteret, dulcius visum est, *ignoti, ignavi, ignari* dicere quam ut veritas postulabat." He seems to have taken no notice of the Greek forms, which with the Latin compounds explain the true forms of these words. Klotz has 'gnavus.' Should we write the word as it ought to be written, if we look to its origin, or should we write it in the text of Cicero in the way in which he says that he would write it himself? There cannot be any doubt on this point, I think.

instrumento] See c. 50. We may collect from this passage that these 'conductores' (lessees) farmed at their own cost,

non modo arationes relinqueret, sed etiam ex Sicilia profugeret Romamque una cum multis ab isto ejectis veniret. Fecit ut decumanus Nymphonem negaret ex edicto praeclaro, quod nullam ad aliam rem nisi ad hujusmodi quaestus pertinebat, numerum jugerum professum esse. Nympho quum se vellet aequo judicio defendere, dat iste viros optimos recuperatores, eundem illum medicum Cornelium—is est Artemidorus Pergaeus qui in sua patria dux isti quondam et magister ad spoliandum Dianae templum fuit—et haruspicem Volusium, et Valerium praeconem. Nympho antequam plane constitit condemnatur. Quanti fortasse quaeritis. Nulla erat edicti poena certa. Frumenti ejus omnis quod in areis esset. Sic Apronius decumanus non decumam debitam, non frumentum remotum atque celatum, sed tritici septem millia medimnum ex Nymphonis arationibus edicti poena, non redemptionis aliquo jure tollit.

XXII. Xenonis Menaeni, nobilissimi hominis, uxoris fundus

and paid a fixed rent. It was not the métayer system. Cicero speaks of them as rich, and farming 'magna impensa magnoque instrumento,' 'with a great outlay, and a large farming-stock.' 'Conductas' means the contract of 'locatio et conductio,' of which 'merces,' or a money payment, is as essential a part as 'pretium' (price) is in buying and selling. Gaius (iii. 142), "locatio autem et conductio similibus regulis constituuntur: nisi enim merces certa statuta sit, non videtur locatio et conductio contrahi." See also Gaius, Dig. 19. 2. 2.

Artemidorus Pergaeus] It seems that this Artemidorus had been made a Roman citizen, as we may infer from his name, Cornelius. Cicero alludes to this part of the plundering of Verres in Lib. 1. c. 20.

ad spoliandum] V. The common reading is 'ad despoliandum.'

Frumenti] I make this the beginning of a new sentence. It is the answer to 'Quanti fortasse quaeritis.'

non redemptionis &c.] 'not by any right that he had as undertaker.' I prefer using a genuine word, which expresses the meaning well, though with us in England it is now generally applied to one peculiar kind of undertaking. A 'decumanus' was said 'redimere' or 'conducere' the 'decumae' (c. 30); he could also be said 'emere,' the reason of which has been already explained c. 61.

22. *Menaeni,*] The safest orthography seems to be 'Menaeni,' though the MSS. have 'Meneni,' and 'Moneni,' except V, which has 'Menaeni.' But, as Zumpt observes, and the remark is worth noting, to prevent MSS. being cited where the citation is not applicable, in the MSS. very often *ae* diphthongus is represented by simple *e*, especially in foreign names. The form on the coins is ΜΕΝΑΙΝΩΝ. The place is called Μέναινον in Diodorus (xi. 78), but the usual Greek form is Μέναι. The place is now Mineo, west of Leontini.

fundus] A 'fundus' is an estate in land; a piece of land as a whole. A 'fundus' was often designated in Italy by some name, as 'Sempronianus.'

This 'fundus' was the property of Xeno's wife, and was let (locatus) to a 'colonus.' The word 'colonus,' if we explain the term according to Roman usage, means the lessee of a farm. He who lets the use of a thing is 'locator.' He who promises money for the use of a thing (conductor) is 'inquilinus,' if the thing let is a house or lodgings. If it is a piece of cultivable ground, the 'conductor' is called 'colonus.' Gaius, Dig. 19. 2. 25. § 1, "qui fundum fruendum vel habitationem alicui locavit, si aliqua ex causa fundum vel aedes vendat, curare debet ut apud emptorem quoque eadem pactione et colono frui et inquilino habitare liceat; alioquin prohibitus is aget cum eo ex conducto." The annual payment agreed on was 'pensio.' Sometimes there was an agreement for the division of the produce, in which case the 'colonus' was called 'par-

erat colono locatus: colonus quod decumanorum injurias ferre non poterat ex agro profugerat. Verres in Xenonem judicium dabat illud suum damnatorium de jugerum professione. Xeno ad se pertinere negabat: fundum elocatum esse dicebat. Dabat iste judicium, Si paret jugera ejus fundi plura esse quam colonus esset professus, tum uti Xeno damnaretur. Dicebat ille non modo se non arasse, id quod satis erat, sed nec dominum ejus esse fundi nec locatorem: uxoris esse; eam ipsam suum negotium gerere: ipsam locavisse. Defendebat Xenonem homo summo

tiarius.' Gaius, Dig. 19. 2. 25. § 6, "apparet autem de eo nos colono dicere qui ad pecuniam numeratam conduxit; alioquin partiarius colonus quasi societatis jure et damnum et lucrum cum domino fundi partitur." This is the métayer system.

The 'coloni' of the later empire are quite different from these 'coloni' of Cicero's time, who were simply tenant farmers. There are only two passages in the writings of the great Roman jurists in which these later 'coloni' are mentioned. One is an excerpt from Marcian, Dig. 30. s. 112; and the other is a rescript of Alexander Severus, of A.D. 225 (Cod. Just. 8. 52. 1). There are passages in which the 'coloni Caesaris' are mentioned, which, as Savigny observes, may apply as well to the common free tenant farmers, as to 'coloni' in the later sense. Nobody will suppose that the 'colonus aratorque vester' of this oration (c. 23) means any thing more than 'colonus' in its original sense. On the later 'coloni,' see Savigny, Vermischte Schriften, vol. ii., 'Ueber den Römischen Colonat,' a reprint of his essay, with supplementary remarks.

Xeno] The Greek name is *Ξένων*. The best MSS., including V, have 'Xeno' for the nominative. Whether the Romans wrote it so or not, is uncertain. If we write 'Xeno,' we ought to write 'Solo,' and Zumpt observes that it is so in Cicero De Republica, ii. 1. But I find it written 'tum Draco, tum Solon.'

The name 'Xenophon' belongs to a different class, for the crude form is Xenophont.

fundum elocatum] Zumpt says that this is the reading of all his MSS., but that some of the old editions have 'locatum.' He says it makes some difference, that it is not mentioned to whom it was let. If so, we should have presently afterwards 'elocavisse' instead of 'locavisse.'

Dabat iste judicium,] Klotz has 'dat iste,' &c., following V, from which he also adopts the vicious reading 'si pareret' for 'si paret:' 'si pareret' is also the reading of B N. Iordan also has 'pareret.' Lg. 29. 42 F have 'paret.' Garatoni, in his note on Divin. c. 17, doubts about the form 'si paret' here; that is, "possetne atque adeo deberet ipsa formula, quo tempore verbi in actu rerum profertur, etiam in indirecta oratione servari" (Zumpt). I don't see how the remark applies to this passage; and if it did, I conceive that the formula would be given in its proper terms.

The 'condemnatio' in the formula is as extravagant as the instance in Lib. 2. c. 12, and so far helps to explain that chapter. Xeno, who had no interest in the land, for it was his wife's property, was to pay the penalty of the alleged false return of his wife's tenant. And even if he had been the owner, the case would have been as bad, for the occupier of the land, the cultivator, was bound to make the return (profiteri). And this was the defence of Xeno. He had not cultivated the land, which was in itself enough (id quod satis erat); but more than that, he was not the owner (dominus) nor the lessor (locator), by which he means, I suppose, that he had not let it for another, though 'locator' is properly said of him who lets his own. In fact, it was his wife's property, and she was accustomed to look after her own affairs (suum negotium gerere).—V and Lg. 48 have, in place of 'id quod satis,' the corrupt reading 'id quod satum,' a variation hardly worth noticing, except for the fact that an editor could be found to adopt it. Klotz reads 'non arasse id, quod satum erat, sed' &c.; and Halm asks, 'quidni scribitur *quod satum erat* cum optimo V?' I leave the reader to answer this question.

splendore et summa auctoritate praeditus M. Cossutius. Iste nihilominus judicium [HS LXXX] dabat. Ille tametsi recuperatores de cohorte latronum sibi parari videbat, tamen judicium accepturum se esse dicebat. Tum iste maxima voce Venereis imperat ut Xeno audiret, dum res judicetur, hominem ut asservent; quum judicata sit, ad se ut adducant: et illud simul dixit, se non putare illum, si propter divitias poenam damnationis contemneret, etiam virgas contemnere. Hac ille vi et hoc metu adductus tantum decumanis dedit quantum iste imperavit.

XXIII. Polemarchus est Murgentinus, vir bonus atque honestus. Is quum pro jugeribus quinquaginta medimna DCC decumae imperarentur, quod recusabat domum ad istum in jus eductus est, et, quum iste etiam cubaret, in cubiculum introductus est, quod nisi mulieri et decumano patebat alii nemini. Ibi quum pugnis et calcibus concisus esset, qui DCC medimnis decidere noluisset, mille promisit. Eubulidas est Grosphus, Centuripinus, homo quum virtute et nobilitate domi suae, tum etiam pecunia princeps. Huic

judicium [HS LXXX] *dabat.*] The numerals seem to be uncertain. Klotz and Iordan have 'HS ɪↄↄↄ,' and Orelli 'HS LXXX millium.'

ut Xeno audiret,] The reading of Klotz from V is 'ut Xeno adesset, dum res judicaretur: hominem adservent: cum judicata sit,' &c. One would have supposed that the words 'maxima voce' would have prevented the adoption of this reading; though it is true that Klotz has diminished the effect of 'maxima' by writing 'magna.' But 'magna voce' is idle and unmeaning, unless something followed to explain why the governor spoke loud. He spoke loud enough to be heard. The 'ut . . ut' occasions no difficulty. The first 'ut' depends on 'maxima,' the second on 'imperat.' Iordan has 'magna . . . audiret.'

contemnere.] 'contemturum' V, Iordan.

23. *Is quum*] 'Ei quum' V, Iordan.

medimna DCC] 'medimnae ɪↄↄↄ V, atque edidit Maius quod mireris:' Zumpt. But after adopting 'resset' (c. 18), he may be excused this.

ad istum in jus] A Roman 'praetor' could not be 'in jure,' that is, in court in his own house. It seems that, to be 'in jure,' he must be 'in tribunali.' It is no objection to this, that he could do certain acts, not judicial, out of court; as, for instance, give his sanction to the manumission of a slave when he was going to the bath or the theatre (Gaius, i. 20). Ernesti thought the words 'in jus' were improperly added; but this is a strange misunderstanding. Cicero evidently means to say that it was a very irregular affair for the 'praetor' to pretend to be 'in jure' in his bedchamber.

cubaret,] This verb is said to mean a person lying sick; and it often has this meaning. See Heindorf, Hor. 1 Sat. ix. 18:

"Trans Tiberim longe cubat is prope Caesaris hortos;"

but there seems no reason why it may not be used in a general sense, as it certainly is here. Ovid (Heroid. 20, v. 164) opposes it to 'valet:' 'haec cubat, ille valet,' which passage, as it clearly shows what 'cubat' means there, so it might be alleged to show that 'cubat' has this particular sense by virtue of the contrast (valet) rather than in itself. And the same may be said of the passage in Horace, 2 Sat. iii. 289:

"Mater ait pueri menses jam quinque cubantis,
Frigida si puerum quartana reliquerit;"

for here the context gives the word its special meaning. The word occurs in Horace, 2 Ep. ii. 68; and Epod. 3, where it is said of one reclining at a banquet.

homini, judices, honestissimae civitatis honestissimo, non modo frumenti scitote sed etiam vitae et sanguinis tantum relictum esse quantum Apronii libido tulit. Nam vi, malo, plagis adductus est ut frumenti daret non quantum deberet sed quantum cogeretur. Sostratus et Numenius et Nymphodorus ejusdem civitatis quum ex agris tres fratres consortes profugissent, quod iis plus frumenti imperabatur quam quantum exararant, hominibus coactis in eorum arationes Apronius venit, omne instrumentum diripuit, familiam abduxit, pecus abegit. Postea quum ad eum Nymphodorus venisset Aetnam et oraret ut sibi sua restituerentur, hominem corripi ac suspendi jussit in oleastro quodam, quae est arbor, judices,

sed etiam vitae] V omits 'etiam,' and Klotz and Iordan also follow it.

non quantum deberet] Klotz has preferred the reading of V, 'non quantum vellet,' which makes a contrast between 'vellet' and 'cogeretur.' But a man's will could not be the measure of his duty. It is not unjust for a man to be compelled to pay more than he would choose to pay, but it is unjust to be compelled to pay more than he owes. The old reading, which Orelli has, is 'quantum haberet.' But 'deberet' is evidently the true word, as in c. 25, "se decumanis plus quam deberet non daturum."

Sostratus et Numenius] Zumpt and Klotz, in the usual fashion, place a comma after 'civitatis,' which leads a reader to expect another verb to which those names are the nominative. This seems to be a sufficient objection to this pointing, for nouns thus placed before 'quum' are very often the nominatives to the verb which follows 'quum.' It may be said that a reader naturally, that is, according to the organic laws of articulation, would pause after the word 'civitatis,' and that is true; but, as stops are now used in the printed texts of Greek and Latin authors, they are supposed to indicate in some measure the grammatical relations of words, and they should therefore be struck out whenever they are likely to mislead in this matter. But if this punctuation is objectionable, it is still more so to place a colon after 'quantum exararant,' as Zumpt and Klotz do. In whatever way the Germans understand the colon, it is certain that an English reader will misunderstand it. Iordan's pointing is right.

consortes] This is explained by Klotz to signify that the three brothers had inherited a patrimonial estate which they had not divided; they still held it as tenants in common. He refers to Festus, v. Sors, and v. Disertiones; and to Cujacius, Observ. Lib. 6. 10. But see the note on 'colonus aratorque vester.' Horace (Carm. iii. 24) has the expression 'consortem socium.' See also Cicero, Pro Flacco, c. 15.

hominibus coactis] This is the expression used to signify a violent invasion of a man's property. The words are found in the Interdictum de Vi; Cicero, Pro Caecina, c. 21, vol. ii.: "Perge porro hoc idem interdictum sequi: Hominibus Coactis."

familiam] This word seems to mean the slaves only here. In its widest sense it comprehends all that is subjected to the power of a person, a 'paterfamilias,' particularly when the discourse is of the property of a testator considered as a whole; as in the expressions 'familiae erciscundae,' 'familiae emptor' (Gaius, iii. 102, &c.; Cic. De Or. i. 56). Sometimes 'familia' is used to signify all the *persons* who are subjected to the power of a 'paterfamilias,' all, both free and slaves; and it may then be opposed to 'pecunia,' or property, in the sense of things only. Sometimes it signifies all the free persons who are subjected to the power of a 'paterfamilias,' a notion which is also extended to all the 'agnati,' or those whose descent can be traced to one 'paterfamilias.' Sometimes it means the slaves only, as it probably does in this passage, and certainly does in many others. (Pro Caecina, c. 19, "unde tu aut familia aut procurator tuus." Ad Div. xiv. 4.) And sometimes it is used to express things only as the collective name for a property: 'agnatus proximus familiam habeto' (Dig. 50. 16. 195).

Aetnae in foro. Tamdiu pependit in arbore socius amicusque populi Romani in sociorum urbe ac foro, colonus aratorque vester, quamdiu voluntas Apronii tulit.

Genera jamdudum innumerabilium injuriarum, judices, singulis nominibus profero: infinitam multitudinem injuriarum praetermitto. Vos ante oculos animosque vestros tota Sicilia decumanorum hos impetus, aratorum direptiones, hujus importunitatem, Apronii regnum proponite. Contempsit Siculos; non duxit homines: nec ipsos ad persequendum vehementes fore et vos eorum injurias leviter laturos existimavit. XXIV. Esto: falsam de illis habuit opinionem, malam de vobis. Verumtamen quum de Siculis male mereretur, cives Romanos coluit, his indulsit, eorum voluntati et gratiae deditus fuit. Iste cives Romanos? At nullis inimicior aut infestior fuit. Mitto vincla, mitto carcerem, mitto verbera, mitto secures; crucem denique illam praetermitto quam iste civibus Romanis testem humanitatis in eos ac benevolentiae suae voluit esse: mitto, inquam, haec omnia, atque in aliud dicendi tempus rejicio: de decumis, de civium Romanorum conditione in arationibus disputo, qui quemadmodum essent accepti, judices, audistis ex ipsis: bona sibi erepta esse dixerunt. Verum haec, quoniam ejusmodi causa fuit, ferenda sunt; nihil valuisse aequitatem, nihil consuetudinem: damna denique, judices, nulla tanta sunt quae non viri fortes magno ac libero animo affecti ferenda arbitrentur. Quid si equitibus Romanis non obscuris neque ignotis, sed honestis et illustribus, manus ab Apronio isto praetore sine ulla dubitatione afferebantur, quid exspectatis? quid a me amplius dicendum pu-

colonus aratorque vester,] If the lands of these men were in the 'Civitas Centuripina,' then the lands of this 'civitas' must have paid 'decumae,' and yet it was a 'civitas immunis' (c. 6). Cicero says afterwards 'tota Sicilia decumanorum hos impetus,' which, taken literally, proves that all Sicily paid 'decumae.' But 'tota Sicilia' is an oratorical expression, and means every part of Sicilia where the 'decumae' were payable. These three brothers would not pay 'decumae' for lands in the 'Centuripina civitas;' and therefore the lands, in respect of which they were liable, must have been situated elsewhere. It seems probable that they were lessees of the land in question, rather than owners (see c. 21); but, if they were owners, the land must have been out of the limits of the 'Centuripina civitas.' Nymphodorus was not called 'colonus aratorque vester' with strict propriety, any more than the 'ager decumanus' was called properly 'populi Romani;' as in c. 39, where he says of the 'decumae' of the Amestratini, "ut ex agro populi Romani plus frumenti servo Venereo quam populo Romano tribui pateretur."

24. *At nullis &c.*] This is Zumpt's reading. Some MSS. have 'nullus,' which Hotmann corrected. Klotz, following V, has 'an ulli,' on which Zumpt briefly observes 'mendose.' A more signal instance of a depravation of the text cannot be found. 'At' contains the answer to the assumption.

ejusmodi causa] Thus explained by Zumpt: "res ita comparata est, aiebant homines: avaro praetori cedendum." 'Nihil valuisse,' &c., are instances of 'haec.' Klotz, following V, has 'ejusmodi casus.'

tatis? an id agendum ut eo celerius de isto transigamus, quo maturius ad Apronium possimus, id quod ego illi jam in Sicilia pollicitus sum, pervenire? qui C. Matrinium, judices, summa virtute hominem, summa industria, summa gratia, Leontinis in publico biduum tenuit. Quo ab Apronio, judices, homine in dedecore nato, ad turpitudinem educato, ad Verris flagitia libidinesque accommodato, equitem Romanum scitote biduum cibo tectoque prohibitum; biduum Leontinis in foro in custodiis Apronii retentum atque servatum, neque ante dimissum quam ad conditiones ejus depectus est.

XXV. Nam quid ego de Q. Lollio, judices, dicam, equite Romano spectato atque honesto? clara res est quam dicturus sum, tota Sicilia celeberrima atque notissima: qui quum araret in Aetnensi, quumque is ager Apronio cum ceteris agris esset traditus, equestri vetere illa auctoritate et gratia fretus affirmavit se decumanis plus quam deberet non daturum. Refertur ejus sermo ad Apronium. Enimvero iste ridere ac mirari Lollium nihil de Matrinio, nihil de ceteris rebus audisse. Mittit ad hominem Venereos: hoc quoque attendite, apparitores a praetore assignatos habuisse decumanum, si hoc mediocre argumentum videri potest istum decumanorum nomine ad suos quaestus esse abusum: adducitur a Venereis atque adeo attrahitur Lollius commode quum Apronius a palaestra redisset et in triclinio quod in foro Aetnae straverat decubuisset. Statuitur Lollius in illo tempestivo gladiatorum convivio. Non mehercule haec quae loquor crederem, judices, tametsi vulgo audieram, nisi mecum ipse senex, quum mihi atque huic voluntati accusationis meae lacrimans gratias

id agendum] 'Id' does not refer to what goes before. It refers to 'ut eo,' &c. 'Must I take all pains to be the quicker in settling the case of Verres, in order to come sooner to Apronius?' As to 'transigere' see Divin. c. 14.

in publico] This is explained by what follows. 'He was kept two days in the forum without cover and without food.'

Quo ab Apronio,] 'Ab' is omitted by Lgg. except 42, A, B, C, V; but, as Zumpt observes, 'ab' cannot be supplied. Zumpt and Iordan read 'Atque ab Apronio;' but he says '*atque* paret abesse;' and indeed it seems quite out of place. Klotz proposes 'a quo Apronio,' and Madvig, 'a Q. Apronio.'—'ad conditionem ejus depectus est' Klotz, from Lg. 42 V. Zumpt approves of 'depectus est,' in place of the common reading 'depactus est.' Iordan has 'conditionem . . depectus est.'

25. *commode quum*] 'just as Apronius had returned from the palaestra.' Lg. 42 has 'commodo.' Cicero, quoted by Zumpt (Ad Att. ii. 12), says, "emerseram commode ex Antiati quum in me incurrit." V has 'postmodum' in place of 'commode;' and Klotz reads 'Lollius. Postmodum quum Apronius . . recubuisset.' V φ have 'recubuisset.' Iordan has 'commodum' from the margin of Lambinus 1584. 'Commodum' is Latin in this sense. See Plaut. Trinum. 400.

tempestivo] This means an entertainment which began before the usual time of the day. The same expression, in the same sense, occurs in the oration Pro Murena, c. 6, "tempestivi convivii . . comes est extrema saltatio."

ageret, summa cum auctoritate esset locutus. Statuitur, ut dico, eques Romanus, annos prope xc natus, in Apronii convivio, quum interea Apronius caput atque os suum unguento confricaret. Quid est, Lolli? inquit: tu nisi malo coactus recte facere nescis? Homo quid ageret, taceret responderet, quid facere denique illa aetate et auctoritate praeditus nesciebat. Apronius interea coenam ac pocula poscebat. Servi autem ejus, qui et moribus iisdem essent quibus dominus et eodem genere ac loco nati, praeter oculos Lollii haec omnia ferebant. Ridere convivae; cachinnare ipse Apronius: nisi forte existimatis eum in vino atque luxu non risisse, qui nunc in periculo atque exitio suo risum tenere non possit. Ne multa, judices, his contumeliis scitote Q. Lollium coactum ad Apronii leges conditionesque venisse. Lollius aetate et morbo impeditus ad testimonium dicendum venire non potuit. Quid opus est Lollio? nemo hoc nescit: nemo tuorum amicorum, nemo abs te productus, nemo abs te interrogatus nunc se primum hoc diceret audire. M. Lollius, ejus filius, adolescens lectissimus, praesto est: hujus verba audietis. Nam Q. Lollius ejus filius, qui Calidium accusavit, adolescens et bonus et fortis et in primis disertus, quum his injuriis contumeliisque commotus in Siciliam esset profectus, in itinere occisus est: cujus mortis causam fugitivi sustinent; re quidem vera nemo in Sicilia dubitat quin eo sit occisus quod habere clausa non potuerit sua consilia de Verre. Iste porro non dubitabat quin is, qui alium antea studio adductus accusasset, sibi advenienti praesto esset futurus, quum esset parentis injuriis et domestico dolore commotus.

XXVI. Jamne intelligitis, judices, quae pestis, quae immanitas in vestra antiquissima, fidelissima, proximaque provincia versata sit? Jam videtis quam ob causam Sicilia, tot hominum antea furta, rapinas, iniquitates, ignominiasque perpessa hoc non potuerit novum ac singulare atque incredibile genus injuriarum contumeliarumque perferre? Jam omnes intelligunt cur universa provincia defensorem suae salutis eum quaesiverit, cujus iste fidei, diligentiae, perseverantiae, nulla ratione eripi possit. Tot judiciis interfuistis: tot homines nocentes et improbos accusatos et vestra et superiorum memoria scitis esse: ecquem vidistis, ecquem audistis in tantis furtis, in tam apertis, [in] tanta audacia, tanta impudentia

Calidium] See Act. i. c. 13.

fugitivi] He was reported to have been killed by some of the slaves who were then in rebellion in Lower Italy, a circumstance likely enough; but Cicero, after the oratorical fashion of antiquity, without any evidence, as far as we know, makes his death a charge against Verres.

26. [*in*] *tanta*] Schütz erased the 'in,'

esse versatum? Apronius stipatores Venereos secum habebat: ducebat eos circum civitates: publice sibi convivia parari, sterni triclinia, et in foro sterni jubebat: eo vocari homines honestissimos, non solum Siculos sed etiam equites Romanos, ut quicum vivere nemo unquam nisi turpis impurusque voluisset, ad ejus convivium spectatissimi atque honestissimi viri tenerentur. Haec tu, omnium mortalium profligatissime et perditissime, quum scires, quum audires quotidie, quum videres, si sine tuo quaestu maximo fierent, cum tanto tuo periculo fieri paterere atque concederes? Tantum apud te quaestus Apronii, tantum ejus sermo inquinatissimus et blanditiae flagitiosae valuerunt ut nunquam animum tuum cura fortunarum tuarum cogitatioque tangeret? Cernitis, judices, quod et quantum incendium decumanorum impetu non solum per agros sed etiam per reliquas fortunas aratorum, neque solum per bona sed etiam per jura libertatis et civitatis isto praetore pervaserit. Videtis pendere alios ex arbore, pulsari autem alios et verberari, porro alios in publico custodiri, destitui alios in convivio, condemnari alios a medico et praecone praetoris, bona tamen interea nihilominus eorum omnium ex agris auferri ac diripi. Quid est hoc? populi Romani imperium? populi Romani leges? judicia? socii fideles? provincia suburbana? Nonne omnia potius ejusmodi quae, si Athenio vicisset, in Sicilia non fecisset? Non, inquam, judices, esset ullam partem istius nequitiae fugitivorum insolentia consecuta.

XXVII. Privatim hoc modo. Quid publice, civitates tractatae quemadmodum sunt? Audistis permulta, judices, testimonia civitatum, et reliquarum audietis. Ac primum de Agyrinensi populo

but it is in the MSS., and Iordan has also erased it.

triclinia,] In c. 25, Cicero uses the singular, 'triclinium,' a sofa or seat for persons at dinner; though there is no reason for supposing that he there means a single sofa. There might be several 'triclinia,' with their coverlids (strata). In Lib. 2. c. 74, there is the expression 'quinquaginta tricliniorum lectos,' which means the furniture for fifty 'triclinia,' the soft cushions, and the like. Though 'triclinium' is used to signify a room to eat in, as in Cic. Ad Att. xiii. 52, and elsewhere, this is not its original meaning, as the passages in which it occurs, and its etymology, clearly show. The scholiast on Horace, 1 Sat. iv. 86, "saepe tribus lectis videas caenare quaternos," says that a 'triclinium,' or eating-room, was so called, because there were three 'lecti' placed in it, one on each of three sides of the table. But the room took its name from the piece of furniture, and not from the number of the pieces of furniture.

provincia suburbana?] Compare Lib. 2. c. 3.—'Athenio,' Lib. 2. c. 10, note.

27. *Quid publice, .. sunt?*] Klotz and Iordan have the absurd pointing, 'Quid? publice civitates tractatae quem ad modum sunt?' Zumpt, who writes, 'quid publice? civitates' &c., says properly, "Ceterum redii ad veterem ante Lambinum interpungendi rationem *quid publice?* Nam *publice*, si cum *civitatibus* conjungas, abundat, nec habet *privatim*, quod recte opponatur." The sense is, 'In matters concerning private persons, in this way. How as to those concerning the public; the cities, how were they dealt with?'

fideli et illustri breviter cognoscite. Agyrinensis est in primis honesta civitas Siciliae, hominum ante hunc praetorem locupletium summorumque aratorum. Ejus agri decumas quum emisset idem Apronius, Agyrium venit. Qui cum apparitoribus eo et cum vi ac minis venisset, poscere pecuniam grandem coepit, ut accepto lucro discederet: nolle se negotii quidquam habere dicebat, sed accepta pecunia quam primum in aliam civitatem occurrere. Sunt omnes Siculi non contemnendi, si per nostros magistratus liceat, sed homines fortes satis et plane frugi ac sobrii; et in primis haec civitas de qua loquor, judices. Itaque homini improbissimo respondent Agyrinenses sese decumas ei quemadmodum deberent daturos; lucrum, quum ille praesertim magno emisset, non addituros. Apronius certiorem facit istum cuja res erat.

XXVIII. Statim, tamquam conjuratio aliqua Agyrii contra rem publicam facta aut legatus praetoris pulsatus esset, ita Agyrio magistratus et quinqueprimi accitu istius evocantur. Veniunt Syracusas: praesto est Apronius: ait eos ipsos qui venissent contra edictum praetoris fecisse. Quaerebant, quid? respondebat se ad recuperatores esse dicturum. Iste, aequissimus homo, for-

Qui cum . . eo &c.] "'Qui cum appar. eo et cum | agminis venisset' (deest *vi* in fine versus) V; 'qui cum appar. eo cum vi ac minis venisset' A B Lg. 29, et item Lg. 1. 5. 14. 45. 48, nisi quod hi *cum minis ac vi* habent; 'qui cum appar. cum vi ac minis eo venisset' Lg. 12," from all which Halm concludes that we should read 'Qui cum app. eo et cum vi ac minis venisset,' and he explains 'Qui . . venisset' as equivalent to 'quum is venisset,' and he compares Lib. 2. c. 20, 'qui non posset' &c. I think that he has probably restored the genuine text.

in aliam occurrere.] This is the common reading, except that the MSS. have dropped the 'in.' Zumpt and Iordan follow the single MS. Lg. 42, and write 'aliam occupare.' But V supplies the 'in.' This instance shows how unsafe it is sometimes to abandon the common reading. It is true, as Zumpt observes, that 'occurrere,' with an accusative, and without 'in,' is not Latin; but it would have required no great boldness to insert the 'in' before 'aliam;' and it has now good authority.

si per nostros &c.] 'All the Sicilians are not despicable. I say this under the correction of our Sicilian governors.'

quum ille praesertim] This is the order of Zumpt, who follows Lg. 42. V, with the other Codd., places 'praesertim' after 'magno,' but V omits 'quum.' The right place seems to be after 'ille.' See Divin. c. 2, note.—V has 'auditurus' for 'additurus;' and Klotz has not adopted it. The people declared that they would pay what was due, but they would not give any thing. The 'lucrum' was probably not unusual, a kind of fee to the 'decumani,' to keep them in good humour. Cicero himself (Ad Q. Fr. i. 1. c. 12) hints pretty plainly, that it is better to over-pay the 'decumani' than to have any trouble: "Quod si genus ipsum et nomen publicani non iniquo animo sustinebunt, poterunt iis consilio et prudentia tua reliqua videri mitiora. Possunt in pactionibus faciendis non legem spectare censoriam sed potius commoditatem conficiendi negotii et liberationem molestiae." See Lib. 3. c. 57.

facit istum cuja &c.] If we are to have any pointing here, it is best to put the comma after 'facit,' for 'istum cuja res erat' is only a further description. Zumpt, Klotz, and Iordan put the comma after 'istum.'—After 'erat' Orelli has 'quid rei esset,' which seems superfluous, and it is omitted in Lg. 42 and V.

28. *quinqueprimi*] The 'magistratus' and the first five members of the senate (βουλή). See Lib. 2. c. 67, 'magistratus et decemprimos.'

midinem illam suam miseris Agyrinensibus injiciebat: recuperatores se de cohorte sua daturum minabatur. Agyrinenses viri fortissimi judicio se passuros esse dicebant. Ingerebat iste Artemidorum Cornelium medicum et Tlepolemum Cornelium pictorem et ejusmodi recuperatores, quorum civis Romanus nemo erat, sed Graeci sacrilegi, jampridem improbi, repente Cornelii. Videbant Agyrinenses quidquid ad eos recuperatores Apronius attulisset, illum perfacile probaturum: condemnari cum istius invidia infamiaque malebant quam ad ejus conditiones pactionesque accedere. Quaerebant quae in verba recuperatores daret. Respondebat, SI PARET ADVERSVS EDICTVM FECISSE; quam in rem in judicio dicturum esse dicebat. Iniquissimis verbis, improbissimis recuperatoribus, conflictari malebant quam quidquam cum isto sua voluntate decidere. Summittebat iste Timarchidem qui moneret eos, si saperent, ut transigerent. Pernegabant. "Quid ergo? In singulos HS quinquagenis millibus damnari mavultis?" Malle dicebant. Tum iste clare omnibus audientibus, Qui damnatus erit, inquit, virgis ad necem caedetur. Hic illi flentes rogare atque orare coeperunt

judicio se passuros] V and Lg. 42 have 'judicio.' See Lib. 2. c. 24, and the note.

repente Cornelii.] These Greeks were, or affected to be, Roman citizens; but Cicero means to insinuate that they had assumed the name of 'Cornelii' all at once. Sulla made a great number of 'Cornelii' of manumitted slaves (Appian, Civil War, Lib. 1. c. 100. 104); and these men may have been among them; or, as there were so many 'Cornelii,' they may have thought that they might venture on assuming the name. This is one of the passages from which an argument has been derived that Cornelius was the gentile name of Verres, and that these men, being his freedmen, had, as was usual in such cases, taken the gentile name of their 'patronus.' But this conclusion is by no means certain. Cicero gives no indication that they were freedmen of Verres. Cicero calls them 'Graeci sacrilegi' probably in allusion to their having assisted Verres to rob the temples of the Greeks; for Artemidorus is charged (c. 21) with assisting Verres to rob the temple of Diana at Perga. As to 'sacrilegus,' see Lib. 1. c. 3.

quae in verba] That is, what would be the form in which the demand against them should be put? or, in other words, what would be the formula? In place of 'si paret,' the old editions had the usual blunder, 'si pateret.' (See Divin. c. 17, note.) Hotmann made the correction 'si pareret,' which Orelli has. But Lg. 1 29 V φ Franc. have 'paret,' and B has 'parret.' The rest have 'pareret' or 'pateret,' or some other erroneous form. We now know the genuine form, 'si paret,' from Gaius.

Zumpt reads 'quam rem in judicio.' 'Qua re' Lg. 42 N, 'quia re' Lg. 29. 'In qua re' V, 'qua in re' A B, 'quae' Lgg. rell. H and Orelli. Mai conjectures 'de qua re.' Halm prefers the reading of V, 'in qua re,' which he explains 'scil. Agyrinenses adversum edictum fecissent.' Yet 'quam in rem' may be the true reading, and it corresponds to 'quae in verba.' In c. 29 there is 'judicium in aratorem in quadruplum.'

esse dicebat.] N V have 'esse aiebat;' and also Klotz and Iordan. Iordan says that 'aiebat' and 'dicebat' are often confounded, but that 'aiebat' in this passage is 'magis Tullianum,' as Stuerenberg has shown by many examples.

quinquagenis millibus] V has the numerals ſↃↃ without 'millibus.'—'damnari . . dicebant:' V has 'damnari septu mavultis damnari dicebant.' It is difficult to see what the corrupt word 'septu' indicates. —Lg. 42 has 'suas sibi segetes,' which, with Zumpt, I take to be the genuine order. Klotz and Iordan have 'sibi suas.'

ut suas sibi segetes fructusque omnes arationesque vacuas Apronio tradere liceret, ut ipsi sine ignominia molestiaque discederent. Hac lege, judices, decumas vendidit Verres. Dicat licet Hortensius, si volet, magno Verrem vendidisse. XXIX. Haec conditio fuit isto praetore aratorum ut secum praeclare agi arbitrarentur, si vacuos agros Apronio tradere liceret. Multas enim cruces propositas effugere cupiebant. Quantum Apronius edidisset deberi, tantum ex edicto dandum erat. Etiamne si plus edidisset quam quantum natum esset? Etiam. Quomodo? Magistratus ex istius edicto exigere debebant. At arator repetere poterat. Verum, Artemidoro recuperatore. Quid si minus arator dedisset quam poposcisset Apronius? Judicium in aratorem in quadruplum. Ex quo judicum numero? Ex cohorte praetoria praeclara hominum honestissimorum. Quid amplius? Minus te jugerum professum esse dico: recuperatores rejice quod adversus edictum feceris. Ex quo numero? Ex eadem cohorte. Quid erit extremum? Si damnatus eris, atque adeo quum damnatus eris—nam dubitatio damnationis illis recuperatoribus quae poterat esse?—virgis te ad necem caedi necesse erit. His legibus, his conditionibus erit quisquam tam stultus qui decumas venisse arbitretur, qui aratori novem partes reliquas factas esse existimet, qui non intelligat istum sibi quaestui praedaeque habuisse bona, possessiones, fortunasque aratorum? Virgarum metu Agyrinenses quod imperatum esset facturos se esse dixerunt.

XXX. Accipite nunc quid imperarit, et dissimulate, si potestis, vos intelligere ipsum praetorem, id quod tota Sicilia perspexit, redemptorem decumarum atque adeo aratorum dominum ac regem fuisse. Imperat Agyrinensibus ut decumas ipsi publice accipiant,

29. *edidisset . . . edidisset*] V in both cases has 'edixisset,' which Klotz has admitted into his text. As if Apronius could make an 'edictum,' and as if 'ex edicto' the 'edictum' of Verres did not show that 'edidisset' is the true reading. Further, in c. 13, we have the form of the 'edictum' of Verres, 'edixit ut quod decumanus edidisset sibi dari oportere,' which is the very expression of this passage, except that for 'dari oportere' we have the equivalent expression 'deberi;' and Klotz in c. 13 has 'edidisset.'

Verum,] 'Yes, but Artemidorus would be a recuperator.' Iordan has 'Poterat vero Artemidoro recuperatore' from V.

Minus te jugerum] 'Jugerum' is the genitive case. This word is a medley. It seems to be generally of the second declension in the singular; but in the plural the word has the form of the third declension, as gen. 'jugerum,' 'jugeribus.'

quod adversus &c.] It is usual to place a comma after 'rejice.' How the 'quod' is understood by those who use this comma, I don't know. 'Rejice' is here equivalent to 'select,' that is, to determine the 'recuperatores' by challenging the legal number out of the whole number proposed. Cicero says, "select 'judices' for the matter which is to be tried, your violation of the 'edictum.'" The full expression would be 'in id quod . . feceris.'

atque adeo quum damnatus eris—] These words are in V only. It is singular that so expressive a clause should appear only in one MS.; but we can hardly doubt that the words are genuine.

30. *decumas . . publice accipiant,*] Verres required the Agyrinenses to take the 'de-

Apronio lucrum dent. Si magno emerat, quoniam tu es qui pretia diligentissime exquisisti, qui, ut ais, magno vendidisti, quare putabas emptori lucrum addi oportere? Esto: putabas. Quamobrem imperabas ut adderent? Quid est aliud capere et conciliare pecunias, in quo te lex tenet, si hoc non est, vi atque imperio cogere invitos lucrum dare alteri, hoc est, pecuniam dare? Quid tum? Apronio deliciis praetoris lucelli aliquid jussi sunt dare. Putatote Apronio datum, si Apronianum lucellum ac non praetoria praeda vobis videbitur. Imperas ut decumas accipiant; Apronio dent lucri tritici medimnum $\overline{\text{XXXIII}}$. Quid hoc est? una civitas ex uno agro plebis Romanae prope menstrua cibaria praetoris imperio donare Apronio cogitur. Tu magno decumas vendidisti, quum tantum lucri decumano sit datum? Profecto, si pretium exquisisses diligenter tum quum vendebas, $\bar{\text{X}}$ medimnum potius addidissent quam HS $\overline{\text{DC}}$ postea. Magna praeda videtur: audite reliqua, et diligenter

cumae' on the account of the 'civitas' (publice) on the terms which Apronius had given for them, which were too high. Thus they would, in fact, pay more than the 'decumae;' and, besides this, they were to give something to Apronius, who would thus be rid of his bargain, and get a sum of money simply for nothing. The money however was really for Verres, as Cicero says. Apronius was his man of all work. See c. 32. 37.

capere et conciliare] Lg. 42 omits the 'et' between these words, and Zumpt, Klotz, and Iordan follow it. If Cicero were closely adhering to the technical form of the Roman Leges, he would omit the 'et;' and he may have done so here, as in c. 94, 'de pecunia capta conciliata,' where Zumpt notices no variation in the reading. But in that instance the form of expression is such that the 'et' might well be omitted, even if Cicero were not following the technical terms of a 'lex.' In c. 40 Zumpt reads 'pecuniae captae et conciliatae.' As to the Roman legal form of expression, it is well known that the usual formula is to heap words upon one another, as our own legislation does, so as by the fulness of the expression to comprehend all that is intended (see c. 84); and the conjunction 'et' is omitted. Examples are abundant. The following may suffice:

"QVAEQVE AQVA IN OPPIDVM VENAFRORVM IT FLVIT DVCITVR EAM AQVAM DISTRIBVERE DISCRIBERE VENDVNDI CAVSA," &c. (From the Edict of Augustus relating to the Aqueduct at Venafrum, Zeitschrift für Geschichtl. Rechtsw. vol. xv.)

lucri tritici] 'Lucri' is a correction of Hotmann's, confirmed by Lg. 42. The reading of the other MSS. is 'lucrum,' which Orelli has.

Quid hoc est?] Lg. 42. Iordan has 'Quid est hoc?'

ex uno agro] 'Ager' is a name for a territorial division, as 'Ager Sabinus,' 'Ager Romanus;' or a name by which a whole tract of some definite limits is signified. 'Plebis Romanae' is so placed that we may doubt whether it is to be connected with 'agro' or with 'prope menstrua cibaria,' but I think that Cicero means 'plebis . . cibaria.' The 'decumae' were for the supply of Rome, and this was almost as much as would furnish the 'plebs' of Rome for a month. This practice of distributing wheat among the poor citizens of Rome at a low rate, ½ as the modius, was established by the Lex Frumentaria of C. Gracchus. Compare c. 36, 'de populi Romani victu,' &c.

HS $\overline{\text{DC}}$] So it stands in Zumpt; and at the end of this chapter he writes 'HS,' (= sestertii i.e. singuli sest.) instead of 'HS III.' By a comparison of the numbers in this and the following chapter, it appears that there is an error in some of the numerals, for the sum total of the money that was got for approving of the corn which was given as a present, is made $\overline{\text{LX}}$. If the money mentioned as extorted in c. 30 is made HS $\overline{\text{XXXIII}}$, which is the same number of sesterces as of me-

attendite quo minus miremini Siculos re necessaria coactos auxilium a patronis, ab consulibus, ab senatu, ab legibus, ab judiciis petivisse. Ut probaret Apronius hoc triticum quod ei dabatur, imperat Agyrinensibus Verres ut in medimna singula dentur Apronio HS.

XXXI. Quid est hoc? tanto numero frumenti lucri nomine imperato et expresso nummi praeterea exiguntur ut probetur frumentum? An poterat non modo Apronius sed quivis, exercitui si metiendum esset, improbare Siculum frumentum quod illi ex area si vellet admetiri licebat? Frumenti tantus numerus imperio tuo datur et cogitur. Non est satis: nummi praeterea imperantur. Dantur. Parum est. Pro decumis hordei alia pecunia cogitur: jubes HS $\overline{\text{XXX}}$ lucri dari. Ita ab una civitate vi, minis, imperio, injuriaque praetoris eripiuntur tritici medimnum $\overline{\text{XXXIII}}$, et praeterea HS $\overline{\text{LX}}$. At haec obscura sunt, aut si omnes homines velint, obscura esse possunt, quae tu palam egisti, in conventu imperasti, omnibus inspectantibus coëgisti? qua de re Agyrinenses magistratus et quinqueprimi, quos tu tui quaestus causa evocaras, acta et imperia tua domum ad senatum suum renuntiaverunt; quorum renuntiatio legibus illorum literis publicis mandata est; quorum legati, homines nobilissimi, Romae sunt, qui hoc idem pro testimonio dixerunt. Cognoscite Agyrinensium publicas literas: deinde testimonium publicum civitatis. Recita literas publicas, testimonium publicum. Animadvertistis in hoc testimonio, judices, Apollodorum, cui Pyragro cognomen est, principem suae civitatis, lacrimantem testari ac dicere nunquam post populi Romani nomen ab Siculis auditum et cognitum Agyrinenses contra quemquam infimum civem Romanum dixisse aut fecisse quidpiam, qui nunc contra praetorem populi Romani magnis injuriis et magno dolore publice testimonium dicere cogerentur. Uni mehercule huic civitati, Verres, obsistere tua defensio non potest: tanta auctoritas est in eorum hominum

dimna, and if we add to this HS $\overline{\text{XXX}}$, mentioned as extorted in c. 31, we have a total of HS $\overline{\text{LXIII}}$, which comes very near $\overline{\text{LX}}$.

re necessaria coactos] Zumpt compares Caesar, Bell. Civ. i. 40, "necessaria re coactus locum cepit superiorem."

31. *exercitui . . . metiendum*] "Intellexit et diem instare, quo die frumentum militibus metiri oporteret." Caesar, B. G. i. 16.—'illi' Lgg. omnes, 'isti' Or.

Pyragro] The name is uncertain, owing to the variations of the MSS., and it is most immaterial. 'Cogitabam,' says Zumpt, 'de nomine Προῤῥαγής.' Klotz has 'cui Perirrhagi cognomen est,' with the following remark: "Since such 'cognomina' must certainly have a meaning, we write, following the indications of the MSS., 'Perirrhagi.' Apollodorus probably had this cognomen on account of his wide, gaping mouth, a peculiarity which is more fully expressed by [illegible]ῤῥαγὴς τὰ χείλη." There are various modes of commenting on an author, and this may [illegible] to some people's taste.

fidelitate, tantus dolor in injuria, tanta religio in testimonio. Verum non una te [tantum] sed universae similibus afflictae [injuriis et] incommodis civitates legationibus ac testimoniis publicis persequuntur.

XXXII. Etenim deinceps videamus Herbitensis civitas, honesta et antea copiosa, quemadmodum spoliata ab isto ac vexata sit. At quorum hominum? summorum aratorum, remotissimorum a foro, judiciis, controversiis; quibus parcere et consulere, homo impurissime, et quod genus hominum studiosissime conservare debuisti. Primo anno venierunt ejus agri decumae tritici modium $\overline{\text{XVIII}}$. Atidius, istius item minister in decumis, quum emisset, et praefecti nomine quum venisset Herbitam cum Venereis, locusque ei publice

[*injuriis et*]] These words are only in V.

persequuntur.] V has 'persecuntur,' on which Zumpt remarks 'vere quidem.' I suppose he means that Cicero wrote the word so; or I do not understand in what the 'vere' consists. Certainly 'persecuntur' is as good as 'persecutus;' but there is nothing gained by adopting this orthography in a single instance. It will be some time before Roman orthography is settled. The inscription of Venafrum (c. 30), of the time of Augustus, writes CVIVS as the genitive of 'qui;' and the Lex Thoria, which may be considered as belonging to Cicero's early age, writes QVOIVS. It also writes PEQVNIAE, PERSEQVTIO, PEQVDES, and also PECVDES. It also writes QVOI (cui), QVOM ('quum' or 'cum'); but no C appears in it in any form of the word 'quo.' The Romans, as it appears, soon came to write 'cuius' for 'quoius,' as we see in the inscription of Venafrum, which also has CVI (cui) and CVM ('cum,' the conjunction). This letter Q is only followed by V. In this same Thoria Lex we find PECOBIS. This letter Q went out of use in some forms; but it was still retained in a great many, as we may see in any page of a Latin author. See Professor Key's remarks on Q in his work entitled "The Alphabet," &c.

32. *Herbitensis*] The place is Herbita, once a place of some note, and governed by 'tyranni' (Diod. xii. 8). Its site is supposed by some geographers to be near the sources of the Symaethus and N.W. of Agyrium. Zumpt places it in a line between Centuripa and Menae, and about half-way between these two places.

At quorum hominum?] See Lib. 2. c. 45, 'at quem hominem?'

parcere et consulere,] V omits 'et.'

modium $\overline{\text{XVIII}}$.] All these numbers are uncertain. As an instance of the mode of representing the numbers in V, where they agree with this text, we may take 'tritici modium $\overline{\text{XXV}}$ DCC,' which is 25700. In this case V has M. CCIƆƆ CCIƆƆ IƆƆƆ CICCC, where M represents 'modium,' and the rest of the symbols respectively, 10000, 10000, 5000, 800, which is 100 more than this text. In place of HS CIƆ CIƆ V has HS II, and Lg. 42, 48 have ∞ ∞, which is the same thing, 2000.

praefecti nomine] I find no note on this word 'praefecti' in any of the commentaries which I have. Among the various officers in a province, Cicero has already enumerated 'legati,' 'praefecti,' 'tribuni.' The word 'praefectus' is so general in its signification, that it is impossible to assign to it any exact meaning, unless something is added to qualify the term, or unless it be associated with other words which give it a meaning. Where 'tribuni militares et praefecti' go together, we understand of course a military officer. No description is added here, and nothing is said by which we can conjecture what the 'praefectus' was in whose name this man came. But Cicero elsewhere uses the word absolutely (Ad Att. vi. 3): "aut quia praefectus non est, quod ego nemini tribuo negotiatori;" and again (Ad Att. v. 21): "Scaptius ad me in castra venit—praefecturam petivit: negavi me cuiquam negotianti dare:" and "Q. Volusium . . . nisi in Cyprum, ut ibi pauculos dies esset, ne cives Romani, qui illic negotiantur, jus sibi dictum negarent; nam evocari ex insula Cyprios non licet." These 'praefecti' appear to have been persons who were empowered by the governor to administer justice in certain districts. It seems, then,

quo deverteretur datus esset, coguntur Herbitenses ei lucri dare tritici modium XXXVII millia, quum decumae venissent tritici modium $\overline{\text{XVIII}}$. Atque hoc tantum lucri coguntur dare publice tum quum jam privatim aratores ex agris, spoliati atque exagitati decumanorum injuriis, profugissent. Anno secundo quum emisset Apronius decumas tritici modium $\overline{\text{XXV}}$ DCC, et ipse Herbitam cum illa sua praedonum copia manuque venisset, populus publice coactus est ei conferre lucri tritici modium $\overline{\text{XXI}}$ et accessionis HS CIↃCIↃ. De accessione dubito an Apronio ipsi data sit merces operae atque impudentiae; de tritici quidem numero tanto quis potest dubitare quin ad istum praedonem frumentarium, sicut Agyrinense frumentum, pervenerit? Anno tertio vero in hoc agro consuetudine usus est regia. XXXIII. Solere aiunt barbaros reges Persarum ac Syrorum plures uxores habere, his autem uxoribus civitates attribuere hoc modo: haec civitas mulieri in redimiculum praebeat, haec in collum, haec in crines. Ita populos habent universos non solum conscios libidinis suae verum etiam administros. Eandem istius, qui se regem Siculorum esse ducebat, licentiam libidinemque

that Atidius came to Herbita as a 'praefectus juri dicundo' (praefecti nomine); which will explain why a lodging was furnished him by the town. He was both a farmer of the 'decumae' and a 'praefectus.' Cicero tells us, in the passages above cited, that when he was governor of Cilicia, he refused to give a 'praefectura' to any negotiator, lest the sources of justice should be corrupted.

et accessionis] This is the reading of N V φ, and is preferable to the common reading 'accessionem,' for the genitive is of the same form as 'lucri.'

operae &c.] The common reading is 'merces operae pretiumque impudentiae.' The text is that of Lg. 42 V. Zumpt and Iordan have 'anno vero tertio.'

33. *barbaros reges*] By 'Syrorum' Cicero cannot mean the Greek kings of Syria, but he must mean the Assyrians; for the names Syrian and Assyrian are often confounded. Whatever the practice may have been with the barbarian Syrian or Assyrian kings, it was the fashion with the Persians. Klotz quotes the passage of Plato from the first Alcibiades, p. 123; ἐπεί ποτ' ἐγὼ ἤκουσα ἀνδρὸς ἀξιοπίστου, &c. Xenophon, in his Anabasis, mentions certain villages, which the army came to, that were set apart for the girdle of Queen Parysatis (i. 4. 10).

Klotz refers to Böttiger's Sabina to show that these extravagant dames of antiquity could spend the income of a whole community on such ornaments as Cicero alludes to. This may be so; but it seems more reasonable to consider that these donations were made nominally for such and such purpose, not because a woman required the revenue of a whole district to keep her hair or head-gear in order. When Artaxerxes provided royally for the traitor Themistocles (Thucyd. i. 138), by giving him Magnesia as bread, Lampsacus as wine, and so forth, the Greek made something of his bread, for it amounted to fifty talents the year, rather more than he and his household would consume. See Athenaeus also, Lib. i. p. 29, ed. Casaub.

his autem uxoribus] 'iis autem' &c. Klotz.

attribuere] 'to assign.' This word is also used to express a territory and people being placed in a state of dependence on another people. See Caesar, B. G. vii. 9. 76.

mulieri] 'mulierem' V, i. e. 'mulieri in, ut Hotom. egregie emendavit,' Halm. This is a certain emendation, and Halm has acutely confirmed it by his interpretation of the reading of V.

esse ducebat,] 'Sic Nannianus, nostri omnes *dicebat*' (Zumpt). Zumpt has 'ducebat:' Klotz and Iordan have 'dicebat.' We can hardly suppose that Verres called

fuisse cognoscite. Aeschrionis Syracusani uxor est Pipa, cujus nomen istius nequitia tota Sicilia pervagatum et pervulgatum est, de qua muliere versus plurimi supra tribunal et supra praetoris caput scribebantur. Hic Aeschrio, Pipae vir adumbratus, in Herbitensibus decumis novus instituitur publicanus. Herbitenses quum viderent, si ad Aeschrionem pretium recidisset, se ad arbitrium libidinosissimae mulieris spoliatum iri, liciti sunt usque eo quoad se efficere posse arbitrabantur. Suprajecit Aeschrio, neque enim metuebat ne praetore Verre decumana mulier damno affici posset. Addicitur med. $\overline{\text{VIII}}$ c dimidio fere pluris quam superiore anno. Aratores funditus evertebantur, et eo magis quod jam superioribus annis afflicti erant ac paene perditi. Intellexit iste ita magno venisse ut amplius ab Herbitensibus exprimi non posset. Demit de capite medimna DC: jubet in tabulas pro med. $\overline{\text{VIII}}$ c referri $\overline{\text{VII}}$ D.

XXXIV. Hordei decumas ejusdem agri Docimus emerat. Hic est Docimus, ad quem iste deduxerat Tertiam, Isidori mimi filiam, vi abductam ab Rhodio tibicine. Hujus Tertiae plus etiam quam

himself King of Sicily, or that Cicero meant to say that he did.

pervagatum et pervulgatum est,] The reading of V. Zumpt has in his text 'Sicilia pervulgatum est;' and also Iordan. In his Appendix, where he notices the readings of V, Zumpt tells us to read 'Sicilia pervagatum est.' It is perhaps doubtful if we ought to keep both words.

versus plurimi] It seems that Verres could not check the propensity to pasquinades, in which the Romans have always indulged; for we may presume that the 'versus' were Roman rather than Greek, though I would not pretend to decide so important a question. They were written above the seat (tribunal) where the Praetor sat in court. Plutarch tells a like story of words being written on the seat of M. Junius Brutus, for another purpose, when he was Praetor (Brutus, c. 9). But the Sicilians had their songs about Pipa (Lib. 5. c. 31), and a taste for humour (De Or. ii. 54).

adumbratus,] Husband in name. It is a painter's term, but it does not mean to make a mere outline, though originally the word may have meant to take a likeness by means of a shadow. It seems sometimes to be used generally of a picture or likeness. So Aeschrio was the portrait or likeness of Pipa's husband; but he was not the real husband.

recidisset,] Lg. 42 and V have 'resedisset,' which Klotz and Iordan adopt. The common reading of the MSS. is 'redisset.'

liciti sunt] Here we have an instance of a community bidding for the 'decumae.' They went as high as they thought prudent. But Aeschrio, of course, outbid (suprajecit) them, for he knew that his wife's favour with the praetor would save him harmless. —'suprajecit' is the reading of Lg. 42, and probably the true reading. See Zumpt's note. The common reading, and that of V, is 'supra adjecit.'—'et eo magis quod:' 'adeo magis quod,' V.

I have followed Zumpt in the numerals, and they are consistent.

de capite] 'from the total.' 'Caput' is used for any principal sum. Thus it can signify a principal sum of money for which interest is paid: 'quinas hic capiti mercedes exsecat,' Hor. 1 Sat. ii. 14.

34. *Hordei*] It appears that in this instance, at least, the 'decumae' of barley were sold or let separately.

deduxerat] The common reading is 'qui ad istum deduxerat.' This woman is again mentioned (Lib. 5. c. 12. 31), and in the latter chapter as a married woman. Docimus played the part of husband. Klotz has 'adduxerat' from V.

Pipae, plus quam ceterarum, ac prope dicam tantum apud istum in Siciliensi praetura auctoritas potuit quantum in urbana Chelidonis. Veniunt Herbitam duo praetoris aemuli non molesti, muliercularum deterrimarum improbissimi cognitores, incipiunt postulare, poscere, minari. Non poterant tamen quum cuperent imitari Apronium: Siculi Siculos non tam pertimescebant. Quum omni ratione illi tamen calumniarentur, promittunt Herbitenses vadimonium Syracusas. Eo posteaquam ventum est, coguntur Aeschrioni, hoc est, Pipae, tantum dare quantum erat de capite demptum, tritici mod. $\overline{\text{III}}$ DC. Mulierculae publicanae noluit ex decumis nimium lucri dare, ne forte ab nocturno suo quaestu animum ad vectigalia redimenda transferret. Transactum putabant Herbitenses, quum iste, Quid de hordeo, inquit, et de Docimo amiculo meo, quid cogitatis? Atque hoc agebat in cubiculo, judices, atque in lecto suo. Negabant illi quidquam sibi esse mandatum.—Non audio: numerate HS $\overline{\text{XII}}$.—Quid facerent miseri, aut quid recusarent? praesertim quum in lecto decumanae mulieris vestigia viderent recentia quibus illum inflammari ad perseverandum intelligebant? Ita civitas una sociorum atque amicorum duabus deterrimis mulierculis Verre praetore vectigalis fuit. Atque ego nunc eum frumenti numerum et eas publice pecunias decumanis ab Herbitensibus datas esse dico, quo illi frumento et quibus pecuniis tamen ab decumanorum injuriis cives suos non redemerunt. Perditis enim jam et direptis aratorum bonis haec decumanis merces dabatur ut aliquando ex eorum agris atque ex urbibus abirent. Itaque cum Philinus Herbitensis, homo disertus et prudens, et domi nobilis, de calamitate aratorum et de fuga et de reliquorum paucitate publice diceret, animadvertistis, judices, gemitum populi Romani, cujus frequentia huic causae nunquam defuit. Qua de paucitate aratorum alio loco dicam.

XXXV. Nunc illud quod paene praeterii non omnino relinquendum videtur. Nam per deos immortales, quod de capite iste dempsit, quo tandem modo vobis non modo ferendum verum etiam

aemuli non molesti,] This is all to the same effect as what he has hinted in c. 33. Aeschrio and Docimus are the rivals of Verres for the favours of Pipa and Tertia, but rivals who did not give him trouble. Cicero represents them as the agents (cognitores) of their wives, for though the husbands had bought the 'decumae,' it was through the interests of their wives that they had made the bargain. Accordingly Cicero makes the women the principals in the matter. This is said 'oratorie,' or 'accusatorie,' as Cicero sometimes terms it.

Ita . . vectigalis] This is explained by c. 43: "omnes denique agros decumanos per triennium populo Romano ex parte decuma, C. Verri ex omni reliquo vectigales fuisse." They paid their 'decumae,' but that was not all. Verres made them give him money too.

audiendum videtur? Unus adhuc fuit post Romam conditam, dii immortales faxint ne sit alter, cui res publica totam se traderet temporibus et malis coacta domesticis, L. Sulla. Hic tantum potuit ut nemo illo invito nec bona nec patriam nec vitam retinere posset: tantum animi habuit ad audaciam ut dicere in contione non dubitaret, bona civium Romanorum quum venderet, se praedam suam vendere. Ejus omnes res gestas non solum obtinemus, verum etiam propter majorum incommodorum et calamitatum metum publica auctoritate defendimus: unum hoc aliquot senatus consultis reprehensum, decretumque est ut quibus illo de capite dempsisset hi pecunias in aerarium referrent. Statuit senatus hoc, ne illi quidem esse licitum, cui concesserat omnia, a populo factarum quaesitarumque rerum summas imminuere. Illum viris fortissimis judicarunt patres conscripti remittere de summa non potuisse; te mulieri deterrimae recte remisisse senatores judicabunt? Ille, de quo legem populus Romanus jusserat ut ipsius voluntas ei posset esse pro lege, tamen in hoc uno genere veterum religione legum reprehenditur: tu qui omnibus legibus implicatus tenebare libidi-

35. *L. Sulla.*] The dictator, L. Cornelius Sulla, to whose yoke the Romans had submitted in a manner that would appear incredible, if it were not explained by the fact which Cicero points at, that a country which has long been distracted by civil commotion readily yields to a bold usurper. Zachariae has written a Life of Sulla, which is the work now usually referred to; but it is not impartial, nor always discriminating. Plutarch has drawn a picture of this singular compound of sensuality, cruelty, and ability, in his Life of Sulla.

in contione] Klotz refers to Cicero, De Off. ii. 8: "Est enim ausus dicere hasta posita quum bona in foro venderet et bonorum virorum et locupletium et certe civium, praedam se suam vendere." This insolent tyrant treated the property of proscribed Roman citizens as if it were booty taken from an enemy.

obtinemus,] 'maintain all that he did,' in order to maintain tranquillity; for, after a violent revolution, it is unsafe and impossible, all at once at least, to restore a former state of things. Klotz quotes Quintilian (Inst. ix. 1. § 85), who refers to a lost oration of Cicero, De Liberis Proscriptorum, in which the same opinion is expressed: "sed ita legibus Sullae cohaerere statum civitatis affirmat ut his solutis stare ipse non possit." After the assassination of Caesar, the conspirators thought of rescinding his 'acta,' but through fear they did not make the attempt (Sueton. Caesar, c. 82).

de capite] Rightly explained by Zumpt to refer to the purchasers of the property of the proscribed, who, after agreeing to pay for it, prevailed on Sulla to remit the whole or part of the purchase-money. The words 'a populo factarum,' &c., mean that the senate would not consent to diminish the amount of the property which had been got and acquired by the Roman people. The property of the proscribed citizens was declared public, and accordingly the 'aerarium' was entitled to the full value of it.—'aerarium referrent:' Zumpt has 'aerarium deferrent' in his minor edition, and so it is in the English reprint; a singular mistake, but Zumpt candidly acknowledges his error in his larger edition. He took 'deferrent' from Lg. 42. 14. 48, 'propter auctoritatem codicis illius.' 'Referre in aerarium,' 'referre rationes,' and the like, are the usual expressions. 'Deferre' has a different meaning. An instance of 'deferre' occurs in Lib. 2. c. 19, "ut quidquid caelati argenti fuit in illis bonis ad istum deferatur;" and there are various other examples of its use in these orations.

legem . . jusserat] The usual formula: 'populus Romanus jubet,' and 'jubere legem.' Orelli has retained the false reading 'lege,' which might be safely corrected, even if all the MSS. had it.

nem tuam tibi pro lege esse voluisti? In illo reprehenditur quod ex ea pecunia remiserit quam ipse quaesierat; tibi concedetur qui de capite vectigalium populi Romani remisisti?

XXXVI. Atque in hoc genere audaciae multo etiam impudentius in decumis Acestensium versatus est, quas quum addixisset eidem illi Docimo, hoc est, Tertiae, tritici modium $\bar{\text{v}}$ et accessionem adscripsisset HS MIↃ, coëgit Acestenses a Docimo tantundem publice accipere; id quod ex Acestensium publico testimonio cognoscite. Recita testimonium publicum. Audistis quanti decumas acceperit a Docimo civitas, tritici mod. $\bar{\text{v}}$ et accessionem. Cognoscite nunc quanti se vendidisse rettulerit. LEX DECVMIS VENDVNDIS C. VERRE PR. Hoc nomine videtis tritici modium CIↃCIↃCIↃ de capite esse dempta, quae quum de populi Romani victu, de vectigalium nervis, de sanguine detraxisset aerarii, Tertiae mimae condonavit. Utrum impudentius ab sociis abstulit, an turpius meretrici dedit, an improbius populo Romano ademit, an audacius tabulas publicas commutavit? Ex horum severitate te ulla vis eripiet aut ulla largitio? Non eripiet. Sed si eripuerit, non intelligis haec quae jamdudum loquor ad aliam quaestionem atque ad peculatus judicium pertinere? Itaque hoc mihi reservabo genus totum integrum: ad illam quam institui causam frumenti ac decumarum revertar. Qui quum agros maximos ac feracissimos per seipsum, hoc est, per Apronium, Verrem alterum, depopularetur, ad minores civitates habebat alios quos tamquam canes immitteret, nequam homines et improbos, quibus aut frumentum aut pecuniam publice cogebat dari.

XXXVII. A. Valentius est in Sicilia interpres, quo iste interprete non ad linguam Graecam sed ad furta et flagitia uti solebat. Fit interpres hic, homo levis atque egens, repente decumanus: emit agri Liparensis miseri atque jejuni decumas tritici medimnis

36. *Acestensium*] Orelli has 'Segestensium.' No MS. has 'Acestensium,' which is Garatoni's emendation. Pliny (H. N. iii. 14) mentions the Acestaei. 'Segestensium' cannot be right, for the Ethnic name in Cicero is 'Segestani.'

peculatus] See Lib. 1. c. 4 and 5.

Qui quum] It is very common for Cicero to use 'quum' preceded by some form of the relative. Iordan makes a new paragraph begin with 'Qui quum,' the meaning of which should be that the speaker is supposed to pause a little after 'revertar;' and then to begin again 'Qui quum,' 'Now as he,' &c. 'Qui quum' does not refer to what precedes; it refers to the suppressed antecedent which belongs to 'habebat,' and it is a usual Latin formula.

37. *interpres,*] Here the word has its sense of interpreter of languages. An interpreter was one of the 'apparitores' of a governor (Ad Div. xiii. 54). Diognetus is called 'Venereus apparitor,' c. 38. Caesar had interpreters with him in Gaul (B. G. i. 19).

medimnis DC.] There is great confusion in the MSS., as Zumpt observes, between 'modii' and 'medimna,' as the abbrevia-

DC. Liparenses vocantur: ipsi accipere decumas et numerare Valentio coguntur lucri HS XXX millia. Per deos immortales, utrum tibi sumes ad defensionem? tantone minoris te decumas vendidisse ut ad medimna DC HS XXX millia lucri statim sua voluntate civitas adderet, hoc est, tritici medimnum II millia? an, quum magno decumas vendidisses, te expressisse ab invitis Liparensibus hanc pecuniam? Sed quid ego ex te quaero quid defensurus sis potius quam cognoscam ex ipsa civitate quid gestum sit? Recita testimonium publicum Liparensium, deinde quemadmodum nummi Valentio sint dati. TESTIMONIVM PVBLICVM. QVOMODO SOLVTVM SIT, EX LITERIS PVBLICIS. Etiamne haec tam parva civitas, tam procul a manibus tuis atque a conspectu remota, sejuncta a Sicilia, in insula inculta tenuique posita, cumulata aliis tuis majoribus injuriis, in hoc quoque frumentario genere praedae tibi et quaestui fuit? quam tu totam insulam cuidam tuorum sodalium sicut aliquod munusculum condonaras, ab hac etiam haec frumentaria lucra tamquam a mediterraneis exigebantur? Itaque qui tot annis agellos suos ante te praetorem redimere a piratis solebant, iidem seipsos abs te pretio imposito redemerunt.

XXXVIII. Quid vero a Tissensibus, perparva et tenui civitate sed aratoribus laboriosissimis frugalissimisque hominibus, nonne

tions *mod.* *med.* are easily confounded. The true reading here is 'medimnis,' as appears from the value put on the 'medimnum II millia.' See c. 39, 'quum medimnum esset HS XV.' Cicero is clearly speaking of 'medimna' here.

mediterraneis] This use of the word is explained by c. 83, 'Henna est mediterranea maxime;' nearly in the centre of Sicily. See also Lib. 5. c. 27. The application of this word to the Mediterranean Sea was not made by the Roman writers, and could not be made consistently with the meaning of the word.

ante te praetorem] Lg. 42 V have 'te praetore,' which Klotz and Iordan adopt. Zumpt says of 'te praetore:' "quod magnopere placeret, quippe conjunctum cum Verris infamia, si *tot annis* recte dici de tribus videretur posse." This is a mistaken view. The Liparenses, before the time of Verres, had to ransom their property from the pirates. Verres played the part of pirate to them.

Cicero appears to be speaking only of Lipare, now Lipari, the largest and the richest of the group of the Aeolian islands. It is about eighteen miles and a quarter in circuit, and contains at present about 12,000 persons. "The interior of the country forcibly recalls to the memory the 'agri Liparensis, miseri atque jejuni,' of Cicero; for it is singularly rugged and broken, presenting sterile hills of volcanic glass, porphyritic lava, pumice, and other vitrifications; many of which must be more than three thousand years old, and yet exhibit no symptoms whatever of decomposition.—There are also two large but unequal plains; the one to the northward is called Piano Grande, and the other Piano de' Conti: the soil of both is chiefly an argillaceous tufa, mixed with various decompositions; and, as they are well cultivated, they produce fine fruit, cotton, pulse, olives, and other vegetables, besides a three months' supply of corn for the island" (Smyth's Sicily, p. 265). These Aeolian islands would naturally attract pirates, for the people, though poor, had still something, and they could make no great resistance. Captain Smyth adds, that "the people are accounted expert throwers of stones; a valuable talent in an unarmed population, exposed to predatory excursions from pirates." But stones would not keep Verres away.

plus lucri nomine eripitur quam quantum omnino frumenti exararant? ad quos tu decumanum Diognetum Venereum misisti, novum genus publicani. Cur hoc auctore non Romae quoque servi publici ad vectigalia accedunt? Anno secundo Tissenses HS $\overline{\text{XXI}}$ lucri dare coguntur inviti: tertio anno $\overline{\text{XII}}$ mod. tritici lucri Diogneto Venereo dare coacti sunt. Hic Diognetus, qui ex publicis vectigalibus tanta lucra facit, vicarium nullum habet, nihil omnino peculii. Vos etiam nunc dubitate, si potestis, utrum tantum numerum tritici Venereus apparitor istius sibi acceperit an huic exegerit. Atque haec ex publico Tissensium testimonio cognoscite. TESTIMONIVM PVBLICVM TISSENSIVM. Obscure, judices, praetor ipse decumanus est, quum ejus apparitores frumentum a civitatibus exigant, pecunias imperent, aliquanto plus ipsi lucri auferant quam quantum populo Romano decumarum nomine daturi sunt. Haec aequitas in tuo imperio fuit, haec praetoris dignitas, ut servos Venereos Siculorum dominos esse velles. Hic delectus, hoc discrimen te praetore fuit ut aratores in servorum numero essent, servi in publicanorum.

XXXIX. Quid Amestratini miseri impositis ita magnis decumis ut ipsis reliqui nihil fieret, nonne tamen numerare pecunias coacti sunt? Addicuntur decumae M. Caesio, quum adessent legati

38. *accedunt?*] V and others have 'accedant.' 'Hoc auctore' means, when Diognetus sets such an example. 'Accedere ad vectigalia' signifies, to become farmers of the public revenue. The Thermitani (c. 42) gave Venuleius a handsome sum 'ne accedat,' that he should not meddle with the contract. Communities (res publicae) often owned slaves, who were 'servi publici;' and the Venerei were of this class.

Tissenses] The city is Tissae (Τίσσαι or Τίσσα), from which the Roman Ethnic name is regularly formed. The site of this little place does not appear to be certain. Zumpt, in his map, places it west of Tauromenium, on the river Onobalas, which flows on the north-eastern base of Aetna. But the site is unknown. Ptolemy places it about Aetna. V has 'Atheniensibus,' another proof that it cannot always be followed.

vicarium] This expression and 'peculium' are explained Lib. 1. c. 36. Cicero means to say that Diognetus was a slave, and one even of the lower kind, who had no 'vicarius' and no 'peculium.'

39. *Amestratini*] The name of the place is Amestratus. The name occurs also in Stephanus, but no where else. The position of Mistretta, where there are some ruins, in the interior south of Halesa, may be the site. But there is no evidence at all for this supposition except the resemblance of name. The fact of the Calactini being required to deliver their grain at Amestratus (c. 43) is no evidence of those two places being near to one another, for the Siculi were often required by Verres to deliver their corn in places remote from their residence. There are coins of Amestratus.

A name Mytistratus occurs in Stephanus, Diodorus (23. c. 9), Polybius, and Zonaras. Pliny has the Ethnic name Mutustratini. The site of Mytistratus is entirely unknown, and it is a probable conjecture that Mytistratus and Amestratus are the same place. I am not aware that there are any coins of Mytistratus. The difference of name between Amestratus and Mytistratus is slight; and if Stephanus is the only author who mentions both names, that is a very small argument against the identity.

Amestratini: statim cogitur Heraclius legatus numerare HS $\overline{\text{XXII}}$. Quid hoc est? quae est ista praeda? quae vis? quae direptio sociorum? Si erat Heraclio ab senatu mandatum ut emeret, emisset: si non erat, qui poterat sua sponte pecuniam numerare? Caesio renuntiat se dedisse. Cognoscite renuntiationem ex literis publicis. LITERAE PVBLICAE. Quo senatus consulto erat hoc legato permissum? nullo. Cur fecit? coactus est. Quis hoc dicit? tota civitas. Recita testimonium publicum. TESTIMONIVM PVBLICVM. Ab hac eadem civitate anno secundo simili ratione extortam esse pecuniam et Sex. Vennonio datam ex eodem testimonio cognovistis. At Amestratinos, homines tenues, quum eorum decumas medimnis DCCC vendidisses Banobali Venereo, cognoscite nomina publicanorum, cogis eos plus lucri addere quam quanti venierant, quum magno venissent. Dant Banobali medimna DCCCL, HS MD. Profecto nunquam iste tam amens fuisset ut ex agro populi Romani plus frumenti servo Venereo quam populo Romano tribui pateretur, nisi omnis ea praeda servi nomine ad istum ipsum perveniret. Petrini, quum eorum decumae magno addictae essent, tamen invitissimi P. Naevio Turpioni, homini improbissimo, qui injuriarum Sacerdote praetore damnatus est, HS $\overline{\text{LII}}$ dare coacti sunt. Itane dissolute decumas vendidisti ut, quum esset medimnum HS XV, venissent autem decumae medimnum $\overline{\text{III}}$, hoc est, HS $\overline{\text{XXXXV}}$, ut lucri decumano HS $\overline{\text{LII}}$ darentur? At permagno decumas ejus agri vendidisti. Videlicet gloriatur non Turpioni lucrum datum esse sed Petrinis pecuniam ereptam.

XL. Quid Halicyenses, quorum incolae decumas dant, ipsi agros immunes habent, nonne huic eidem Turpioni, quum decumae C med. venissent, HS $\overline{\text{XV}}$ dare coacti sunt? Si id quod maxime vis posses probare, haec ad decumanos lucra venisse, nihil te attigisse,

mandatum] 'if he had received instructions, he would have bought.' He was the agent or representative of the Amestratini, and Cicero uses the Roman word 'mandare,' which expresses the relation between principal and agent. The construction of the verb is with a dative, 'Quum autem is cui recte mandaverim,' &c. (Gaius, iii. 161); and further (§ 162), "in summa sciendum (*est, quoties faciendum*) aliquid gratis dederim, quo nomine, si mercedem statuissem, locatio et conductio contraheretur, mandati esse actionem; veluti si fulloni polienda curandave vestimenta aut sarcinatori sarcienda (*dederim*)."

Banobali] 'Hariobali' Iordan.

ipsum perveniret.] Klotz has 'pervenerit,' from Lg. 42.

Petrini,] The name of the town is Petra, which may be a Greek name and significant of a rocky position. There is no certain evidence about its position.

40. *Halicyenses,*] See Lib. 2. c. 28. Halicyae was an 'immunis civitas' (c. 6). He says that 'incolae' of Halicyae 'dant decumas,' but that their lands were 'immunes;' by which he seems to mean that the Halicyenses would pay 'decumae' for any land, liable to 'decumae,' which they cultivated elsewhere, but not for the lands of their own 'civitas.' Or 'incolae' may mean foreign cultivators in Halicyae.

tamen hae pecuniae per vim atque injuriam tuam captae et conciliatae tibi fraudi et damnationi esse deberent: quum vero hoc nemini persuadere possis te tam amentem fuisse ut Apronium et Turpionem servos homines tuo liberumque tuorum periculo divites fieri velles, dubitaturum quemquam existimas quin illis emissariis haec tibi omnis pecunia quaesita sit? Segestam item ad immunem civitatem Venereus Symmachus decumanus immittitur. Is ab isto literas affert ut sibi contra omnia senatus consulta, contra omnia jura, contraque legem Rupiliam, extra forum vadimonium promittant aratores. Audite literas quas ad Segestanos miserit. LITERAE C. VERRIS. Hic Venereus quemadmodum aratores eluserit ex una pactione hominis honesti gratiosique cognoscite; in eodem enim genere sunt cetera. Diocles est Panhormitanus, Phimes cognomine, homo illustris ac nobilis. Arabat is agrum conductum in Segestano; nam commercium in eo agro nemini est; conductum

Segestam] Another 'civitas immunis.' See the note, Lib. 4. c. 33.

eluserit] 'luserit' Lg. 29 A B.

commercium] The meaning of Cicero may be collected from his words. Diocles was the lessee of lands in the 'ager Segestanus' (conductum habebat), and he belonged to Panhormus. He could not hold land as owner in the territory of Segesta, 'nam commercium in eo agro nemini est;' that is, the law of Segesta did not allow the citizens of other places to be the owners of land in the territory of Segesta. Becker (Handbuch, &c. iii. 1, p. 245) quoting this passage says "that in Sicily also most of the states had no 'commercium' among themselves;" and he adds that "the Centuripini only (c. 45) had the capacity for acquiring land in other states." But his first remark is a much larger conclusion than Cicero's text allows us to make; and the second is not consistent with the first. He also assumes that this limitation was a Roman rule, like that in the case of Macedonia, which will presently be mentioned; but I do not admit that to be certain. It may have been an old rule of law among the Segestani to allow none but citizens to acquire the ownership of land in their territory.

Cicero uses a Roman word (commercium) which had a technical meaning. It is fully explained by Savigny: "'Commercium' primarily signifies the legal capacity to buy and sell; this technical expression, however, does not refer to the usual selling of daily life, but to the symbolical sale, which the Romans call Mancipatio (Ulpian, tit. 19, § 4, 5). But as Mancipatio has only a significant meaning as the oldest and most usual form of alienation of Roman ownership, the capacity to have this most complete kind of ownership is properly indicated by this term; consequently, also, it indicates the capacity of the In jure cessio, of Usucapio, and of the strict Vindicatio. Further developed, however, this technical expression comprises also the capacity to have Servitutes, which capacity, as well as ownership, is Juris Quiritium; further, the capacity to contract many kinds of obligations (Gaius, iii. 93, 94); finally, and most especially, the Testamenti Factio, that is, the fundamental condition of the capacity to make a testament or a codicil, to be named 'heres,' 'legatee,' or 'fidei commissarius,' and to be a witness to a testament" (System, &c., ii. 27). This incapacity for any person not a Segestan to hold land in the territory of Segesta may, as I have said, not have been a rule made by the Romans, but a custom of this particular state. The Romans sometimes imposed these terms on conquered people, with the view of keeping them isolated and weak communities, or, at any rate, of preventing any close union among them. In Livy (8. c. 14) we read, "Ceteris Latinis populis connubia, commerciaque et concilia inter se ademerunt." The object was, to break the national unity of the Latini. Macedonia, after the Roman conquest (B.C. 168), was divided into four regions: "pronuntiavit deinde neque connubium neque commercium agrorum aedificiorumque inter se placere cuiquam extra fines regi-

habebat HS sex millibus. Pro decuma, quum pulsatus a Venereo esset, decidit HS XVI millibus et medimnis DCLIII. Id ex tabulis ipsius cognoscite. NOMEN DIOCLIS PANHORMITANI. Huic eidem

onis suae esse" (Liv. 45. c. 29). The effect was, that no inhabitant of one 'regio' could contract a lawful marriage with an inhabitant of another 'regio;' if a union was formed in the nature of marriage, it would not have the effect of a legal marriage. Further, no inhabitant of one region could in any way acquire the ownership of land or houses in another 'regio,' a provision which would be partly effected by the prohibition as to marriage; at least, in case of intestacy, there could be no claim by the children of such a prohibited marriage, for they would not be recognized as the offspring of a legal marriage. Such acquisition of land or houses also could not be obtained under a testament, or by purchase; if we interpret this provision, as we perhaps ought to do, according to the strict meaning of the Roman term 'commercium.' Thus Macedonia was split up into four parts, completely disunited. It by no means follows that the inhabitants of one 'regio' could not live in another 'regio,' and carry on traffic; and perhaps they might hold land as occupiers or tenants, but not as owners.

'Commercium' is poorly explained in Forcellini, where explanations are generally very good and complete. As to the English Lexicons, the reader may judge for himself by looking at them.

There are some remarks on this passage by Zumpt and Klotz which seem to me worth noticing; not that the remarks are of any value, but they suggest the question as to the right method of interpretation and commenting. Zumpt observes that Cicero takes pains (laborat) to show that Diocles had no other reason for hiring the land, except that he could not buy it; but Zumpt is of opinion that the hiring was simulated on account of the legal impediments, and that there was a 'vera possessio agri maximi,' which I will not venture to translate. Now Cicero does not take any particular pains to prove that this man hired the land because he could not buy it. If he was so anxious to buy, why did he not go where he could buy? The man wanted to farm; and we may suppose that he preferred the land of Segesta to buying or hiring land elsewhere. This is however of no great importance. But the assumption that he had bought in evasion of the law, contrary to the law, and contrary to what Cicero says, is a monstrous absurdity to broach, when we know nothing about the matter except what Cicero tells us; and he tells us that he had not bought the land, and could not buy it. If he bought it, we must assume that he paid for it; that he bought land, the title to which he could never maintain, even against the man who had sold it. Possibly, too, if the law was what it ought to be, in order to secure its object, the transfer might be valid against the seller, but the land would be forfeited to the 'civitas' as soon as it came into the ownership of a person who could not hold it. But there is no end of the objections that may be urged to Zumpt's assumption, which is sufficiently answered by saying that it must be considered false till he can prove it to be true. Klotz says that he is of a different mind from Zumpt; he thinks that Diocles was merely a tenant; and we may observe that there is great weight in this remark, for this is precisely Cicero's statement, and we know no more about the thing than what he tells us. However, Klotz has a little secret of his own also. He says that Cicero merely gave this explanation, that no one might suppose that the words 'homo illustris et nobilis' were not to be taken in their strict sense, if Diocles was merely the tenant of the land. But why should Cicero be so anxious to save this gentleman's character for respectability, when he was only doing what other rich men did in Sicily? "Is quum arationes magnas conductas haberet, quod homines etiam locupletes, sicut ille est, in Sicilia facere consuerunt" (c. 21). But why did Cicero make the remark then? I can't tell. He might have omitted it, and then all we should have known was, that this man was a tenant-farmer, like many other rich Sicilians; and neither Zumpt, nor Klotz, nor I, should have made a note on this part of the passage. However, Cicero has told us something worth knowing, though it has no direct bearing on the subject in hand; and nothing is so common as for a man to do this who has abundance of matter in him.

Id ex tabulis &c.] 'Id ex ipsius tabulis' Klotz and Jordan from Lg. 42. There is no rule to determine which is the genuine order. If the emphasis is placed on 'ipsius,' it should come first.

Symmacho C. Annaeus Brocchus, senator, homo eo splendore, ea virtute qua omnes existimatis, nummos praeter frumentum coactus est dare. Venereone servo te praetore talis vir, senator populi Romani, quaestui fuit?

XLI. Hunc ordinem si dignitate antecellere non existimabas, ne hoc quidem sciebas, judicare? Antea quum equester ordo judicaret, improbi et rapaces magistratus in provinciis inserviebant publicanis: ornabant eos qui in operis erant: quemcunque equitem Romanum in provincia viderant, beneficiis ac liberalitate prosequebantur: neque tantum illa res nocentibus proderat quantum obfuit multis, quum aliquid contra utilitatem ejus ordinis voluntatemque fecissent. Retinebatur hoc tum nescio quomodo quasi communi consilio ab illis diligenter, ut, qui unum equitem Romanum contumelia dignum putasset, ab universo ordine malo dignus judicaretur: tu sic ordinem senatorium despexisti, sic ad libidines injuriasque tuas omnia coaequasti, sic habuisti statutum cum animo ac deliberatum, omnes qui habitarent in Sicilia aut qui Siciliam te praetore attigissent judices rejicere, ut illud non cogitares tamen ad ejusdem

41. *equester . . judicaret,*] See Excursus on the Judicia.—'beneficiis . . prosequebantur:' this is a usual form of expression, but we have nothing like it. Cicero means 'the Magistratus treated them favourably and liberally,' or something of that kind. The force of the phrase is in the nouns. Compare Caesar, B. G. ii. 5.

in operis] The governors paid great attention to those who were employed in the provinces (in operis erant, or 'operas dabant,' Lib. 2. c. 70) by the Publicani to collect their dues; and Cicero explains why. The collection of the 'vectigalia' in the provinces employed a great number of people, and gave a large patronage to the Publicani at Rome. To get a good place under them in the provinces, was like a good office under the powerful body which levied contributions on so large a part of Hindustan. Cicero (Pro Plancio, c. 19) says: "Jam ut ego doceo, gratiosum esse in sua tribu Plancium quod . . in operas plurimos patris auctoritate et gratia miserit." Plancius got employment for many of his 'tribules' in the provinces, through his father, who was a leading man among the Publicani. These persons showed their gratitude by voting for Cn. Plancius, when he was a candidate for the aedileship. Thus they helped one another for a consideration: the world went as it does now. Terence says it all in a few words, 'Tradunt operas mutuas' (Ter. Phorm. ii. 3. 37).

quasi communi consilio] Cicero gives us an example of the conduct of men who are bound together by some common interest. All of them become the enemies of every man who touches their interests in the person of any member of their body. Thus in modern states the interests of a whole community are often sacrificed to the greediness of a few men, who are closely united by the common purpose of making their profit out of the loss of others.

qui habitarent] Lg. 42 N φ have '*haberent*, quod Garatonius perite defendit' (Zumpt). The objection made to 'habitarent' is, that very few Roman senators could have dwelt (habitasse) in Sicily. But Cicero says 'aut . . attigissent,' leaving his hearers to apply 'habitarent' to as many or as few as they pleased. Further, it is said, it is probable that many senators might have held lands there (*habuisse* agros vel praedia); but the reasons for the probability are not stated. The assertion that it is improbable is quite as good. Finally, 'haberent in Sicilia' is an odd phrase to express ownership of land in Sicily, and requires confirmation. It is not exactly like 'habet in nummis' (c. 86).

tamen ad ejusdem] Klotz: 'tamen ad ejusdem ordinis homines: te ad judices'

ordinis homines te ad judices esse venturum, in quibus, si ex ipsorum domestico incommodo nullus dolor insideret, tamen esset illa cogitatio, in alterius injuria sese despectos dignitatemque ordinis contemptam et abjectam? Quod mehercule, judices, mihi non mediocriter ferendum videtur. Habet enim quendam aculeum contumelia quem pati pudentes ac viri boni difficillime possunt. Spoliasti Siculos; solent enim muti esse in injuriis suis. Vexasti negotiatores; inviti enim Romam raroque decedunt. Equites Romanos ad Apronii injurias dedisti; quid enim jam nocere possunt quibus non licet judicare? Quid, quum senatores summis injuriis afficis, quid aliud dicis nisi hoc?—cedo mihi etiam istum senatorem, ut hoc amplissimum nomen senatorium non modo ad invidiam imperitorum sed etiam ad contumeliam improborum natum esse videatur. Neque hoc in uno fecit Annaeo sed in omnibus senatoribus, ut ordinis nomen non tantum ad honorem quantum ad ignominiam valeret. In C. Cassio, clarissimo et fortissimo viro, quum is eo ipso tempore primo istius anno consul esset, tanta improbitate usus est ut, quum ejus uxor femina primaria paternas arationes haberet in Leontino, frumentum omne decumanos auferre jusserit. Hunc tu in hac causa testem, Verres, habebis, quoniam judicem ne haberes providisti. Vos autem, judices, putare debetis esse quiddam nobis inter nos commune atque conjunctum. Multa sunt imposita huic ordini munera, multi labores, multa pericula non solum legum ac judiciorum sed etiam rumorum ac temporum. Sic est hic ordo quasi propositus atque editus in altum ut ab omnibus ventis invidiae circumflari posse videatur. In hac tam misera atque iniqua conditione vitae, ne hoc quidem retinebimus, judices, ut magistratibus nostris in obtinendo jure nostro ne contemptissimi ac despicatissimi esse videamur?

XLII. Thermitani miserunt qui decumas emerent agri sui.

&c. The 'ad' before 'judices' is from Lg. 42. Iordan omits it.

domestico incommodo] 'any loss or damage which affected themselves.' Caesar often uses 'incommodum.'

ad . . injurias dedisti;] Forcellini gives another example like this from the Pro Cluentio, c. 61: "mulieri crudelissimae servum fidelissimum non in quaestionem tulit, sed plane ad supplicium dedit."

Quid, quum senatores] 'qui cum,' &c. Zumpt from Lg. 42. The old reading is better.

C. Cassio,] One of the consuls of the year B.C. 73, the first year of the government of Verres. It is not said what was the kind of title to these 'paternae arationes' (see Lib. 3. c. 6, note). Cassius could be a witness, because he was not a 'judex.'

42. *qui . . emerent*] Another instance of a community proposing to purchase the 'decumae' of their territory. The 'civitas' would then collect the 'decumae' from their cultivators, and would deliver as much corn as they agreed to give for the 'decumae,' or pay its value in money; but they would have no further trouble, and would thus escape the rapacity of the agents of Verres.

Magni sua putabant interesse publice potius quamvis magno emi quam in aliquem istius emissarium incidere. Appositus erat Venuleius quidam qui emeret. Is liceri non destitit. Illi quoad videbatur ferri aliquo modo posse contenderunt: postremo liceri destiterunt: addicitur Venuleio tritici medimnum VIII millibus. Legatus Pasidorus renuntiat. Quum omnibus hoc intolerandum videretur, tamen Venuleio dantur ne accedat tritici mod. $\overline{\text{VII}}$ et praeterea HS $\overline{\text{II}}$. Ex quo facile apparet quae merces decumani, quae praetoris praeda esse videatur. Cedo Thermitanorum mihi literas et testimonium. TABVLAE THERMITANORVM ET TESTIMONIVM. Imacharenses jam omni frumento ablato, jam omnibus injuriis tuis exinanitos, tributum facere miseros ac perditos coëgisti, ut Apronio darent HS XX millia. Recita decretum de tributis et publicum testimonium. SENATVS CONSVLTVM DE TRIBVTO CONFERENDO. TESTIMONIVM IMACHARENSIVM. Hennenses, quum decumae venissent agri Hennensis medimnum $\overline{\text{VIII}}$ CC, Apronio coacti sunt dare tritici modium $\overline{\text{XVIII}}$ et HS III millia. Quaeso, attendite, quantus numerus frumenti cogatur ex omni agro decumano. Nam per omnes civitates quae decumas debent percurrit oratio mea, et in hoc genere nunc, judices, versor, non in quo singillatim aratores eversi bonis omnibus sint, sed quae publice decumanis lucra data sint, ut aliquando ex eorum agris atque urbibus expleti atque saturati cum hoc cumulo quaestus decederent.

XLIII. Calactinis quamobrem imperasti anno tertio ut decumas agri sui, quas Calactae dare consueverant, Amestrati M. Caesio decumano darent, quod neque ante te praetorem illi fecerant neque tu ipse hoc ita statueras antea per biennium? Theomnastus Syracusanus in agrum Mutycensem cur abs te immissus est? qui

Pasidorus] The common reading is 'Possidorus.' Zumpt thinks that 'Pasidorus' may be the man's name, and adds this remark: "sed quis tandem, ut dubitare desinamus, Lexicon Graecorum nominum conficiet, ad historiae fidem et grammaticam rationem necessarium." A diligent German, Dr. W. Pape, has responded to the wish of his countryman by publishing a Dictionary of Greek proper names; but, unluckily, I can't find in it either Pasidorus, or Posidorus, or Possidorus; nor the illustrious Perirrhagus of Klotz (c. 31); nor yet Pyragrus: from which we may perhaps conclude that there is no sure authority for any of these names. We cannot expect to find every Sicilian name in extant Greek authors.

43. *Calactae*] Klotz and Iordan write 'Calacte.' The MS. readings vary, as usual in proper names of rare occurrence. The word appears to be formed by the union of the two words καλὴ ἀκτή, the name of a pleasant tract on the north coast of Sicily (Herod. vi. 22), east of Halesa. The Ethnic name 'Calactini' is certain (Diod. xii. 29). But some MSS. of Cicero have 'Calatini.' The town Calacte is supposed to be on the site of Caronia.

Mutycensem] Besides the common reading 'Muticensem,' there are the variations 'Mutyensem' and 'Mutiensem.' Mutyca may be the place called Mutyca or Motyca, between Syracuse and Camarina, now Modica. If we read 'Mutyensem,' the place intended by Cicero may be

aratores ita vexavit ut illi in alteras decumas, id quod in aliis quoque civitatibus ostendam, triticum emere necessario propter inopiam cogerentur. Jam vero ex Hyblensium pactionibus intelligetis quae factae sunt cum decumano Cn. Sergio sexies tantum quam quantum satum sit ablatum esse ab aratoribus. Recita sationes ex literis publicis. Cognoscite pactiones Menaenorum cum Venereo servo. Recita ex literis publicis professiones sationum et pactiones Menaenorum. Patiemini, judices, ab sociis, ab aratoribus populi Romani, ab iis qui vobis laborant, vobis serviunt, qui ita plebem Romanam ab sese ali volunt ut sibi ac liberis suis tantum supersit quo ipsi ali possint, ab his per summam injuriam, per acerbissimas contumelias, plus aliquanto ablatum esse quam satum sit? Sentio, judices, moderandum mihi esse jam orationi meae fugiendamque vestram satietatem: non versabor in uno genere diutius, et ita cetera de oratione mea tollam ut tamen in causa relinquam. Audietis Agrigentinorum, fortissimorum viro-

Motya (Μοτύη), a considerable place near Lilybaeum, on a small island connected with the main land by a dyke (Diod. xiv. 48), now Isola di Mezzo, an old Phoenician settlement (Thucyd. vi. 2). But there are several reasons for supposing that this is not the place. Himilco removed the inhabitants of Motya (B.C. 396) to the site of Lilybaeum, and from that time we hear no more of it. Besides, such a place could hardly have a territory. It was a mere commercial post and stronghold; and in fact Motya was lost in Lilybaeum (now Marsala). There can then be no doubt that Mutyca is Modica. "The contéa of Modica is a county of about eighty thousand inhabitants, and possessing nearly a hundred and twenty thousand acres of land."—There is "a superior spirit of activity and industry among the natives, attended by greater affluence and comfort than any other agricultural part of Sicily displays, although it is not naturally so fertile as the rest" (Smyth's Sicily, p. 191).

ex Hyblensium pactionibus] The place is Hybla Major, so called to distinguish it from two other places of the same name in Sicily. Hybla Major was on the southern slope of Aetna, on the Symaethus; now Paternò on the Giaretta, according to some authorities.

sexies tantum] 'sexiens tanto' Lg. 42 ('Recte, ut videtur;' Halm, who refers to 'quinquies tanto,' c. 97).

qui ita . . volunt] This is a most extravagant way of showing the fidelity and attachment of the Sicilians to Rome. There is great difficulty in translating it, which I remark for the benefit of those who may not discover the difficulty. 'Volunt' expresses 'will,' 'purpose,' and the like, not 'wish.' 'Ita' is related to 'ut,' but this relation is very difficult to express in English. The meaning is: 'the Sicilians have a hearty good-will to maintain the Roman Plebs, and they ask for no better terms than to have enough left for the support of themselves and their children.' It is ludicrous to us for an orator to represent these laborious cultivators of Sicily as working with hearty good-will to support the lazy population of Rome, and content if they could only have enough left to give them strength to go on working. Cicero is here alluding to the provisioning of Rome, which had long been a settled part of Roman policy. The state provided the grain, and sold it for less than the cost, at least to the poor. The produce of the 'decumae' cost nothing, except probably the transport from the coast to Rome; and as the state got this corn cheap, they could sell it cheap. Corn was also bought, as we learn from this oration, when there was scarcity. The distribution of corn gratis did not begin until after the date of this oration, as it is said; and the tribune Clodius has the credit of introducing this pestilent measure (B.C. 58). See the note c. 70.

rum, diligentissimorum aratorum querimonias; cognoscetis Entellinorum, hominum summi laboris summaeque industriae, dolorem et injurias: Heracliensium, Gelensium, Soluntinorum incommoda proferentur: Catinensium, locupletissimorum hominum amicissimorumque, agros vexatos ab Apronio cognoscetis: Tyndaritanam, nobilissimam civitatem, Cephaloeditanam, Haluntinam, Apolloniensem, Enguinam, Capitinam perditas esse hac iniquitate decumarum intelligetis: Inensibus, Murgentinis, Assorinis, Elorinis, Ietinis nihil omnino relictum: Cetarinos, Acherinos, parvarum civitatum homines, omnino abjectos esse ac perditos: omnes denique agros decumanos per triennium populo Romano ex parte decuma, C. Verri ex omni reliquo vectigales fuisse, et plerisque aratoribus nihil omnino superfuisse; si cui quid aut relictum aut remissum sit, id fuisse tantum quantum ex eo quo istius avaritia contenta fuit redundarit.

XLIV. Duarum mihi civitatum reliquos feci agros, judices, fere optimos ac nobilissimos, Aetnensem et Leontinum. Horum ego

Entellinorum,] Entella was situated on the east side of the river Hypsas, in the interior, between Panhormus and Selinus.

Catinensium,] The place is Catina. I have followed Zumpt in writing Catina, which appears to be the more usual Roman form of the name, though the Greek form is always Κατάνη. Catina was an ancient Chalcidian colony on the south side of Aetna and on the coast. It was founded about B.C. 730, by the people of the neighbouring city of Naxos. It is now Catania, a large city, which has often suffered from its vicinity to the great volcanic mountain.

Apolloniensem,] Apollonia is probably Pollina, a place near the north coast, about eight miles east of Cephaloedium, Cefalù.

Enguinam,] The Greek name of the place is Ἔγγυον or Ἐγγύιον. The authority of the MSS. is in favour of representing the γγ by *gg*, which may have been the Roman fashion sometimes. But it is conformable to the doctrine of the grammarians to write 'Enguina.' Engyum was an old town of the Siculi, south of Halesa, with a famous temple of the Magna Mater. The remains are said to be near Gangi Vetere, south of the supposed site of Apollonia.

Capitinam] This is the Capitium of Ptolemy (iii. 4), supposed to be Capizzi, in the highest part of the valley of the Symaethus.

Inensibus,] Garatoni's correction, I believe.—'Mensibus' Lg. 42, om. rell. 'Mensibus' may be intended for 'Inensibus.' Ptolemy (iii. 4) enumerates Ina among the inland towns of Sicily.

Elorinis,] The Greek form is Ἔλωρον or Ἔλωρος, whence we should expect the Latin form 'Helorus.' This town was near the mouth of the river Helorus, in a delightful country called 'Heloria Tempe' (Ovid, Fast. iv. 477). A road ran from Syracusae to Elorus.

Ietinis] Graevius, 'Letinis' codd. But there are no Letini, and Graevius supposed that the Ietini are meant whom Pliny calls Ietenses. The Ethnic name is Ἰετῖνοι, and the place is Ἰεταί (Thucyd. vii. 2, so the name should be read, perhaps: see Goeller; and Steph. Byz. Ἰεταί, who makes the Ethnic name Ἰεταῖος).

Cetarinos,] 'Citarinos' Zumpt. The name is uncertain.—'Acherinos:' 'Getherinos' Lg. 42. 'Scherinos' has been suggested.

redundarit.] 'redundaret' Lg. 42. Halm prefers this reading.

44. *Aetnensem*] Hiero I. (B.C. 476) transplanted the inhabitants of Catina to Leontini, and settled five thousand Syracusans and as many Peloponnesians at Catina (Diod. xi. 49). He also gave to Catina the name of Aetna. (Pind. Pyth. i.) After Hiero's death the new settlers

agrorum missos faciam quaestus triennii: unum annum eligam quo facilius id quod institui explicare possim. Sumam annum tertium, quod et recentissimus est et ab isto ita administratus ut, quum se certe decessurum videret, non laboraret si aratorem in Sicilia nullum omnino esset relicturus. Agri Aetnensis et Leontini decumas agemus. Attendite, judices, diligenter. Agri sunt feraces: annus tertius: decumanus Apronius. De Aetnensibus perpauca dicam; dixerunt enim ipsi priore actione publice. Memoria tenetis Artemidorum Aetnensem legationis principem publice dicere Apronium venisse Aetnam cum Venereis; vocasse ad se magistratus; imperasse ut in medio foro sibi lecti sternerentur; quotidie solitum esse non modo in publico sed etiam de publico convivari; quum in eis conviviis symphonia caneret maximisque poculis ministraretur, retineri solitos esse aratores atque ab eis non modo per injuriam sed etiam per contumeliam tantum exprimi frumenti quantum Apronius imperasset. Audistis haec, judices, quae nunc ego omnia praetereo et relinquo. Nihil de luxuria Apronii loquor, nihil de insolentia, nihil de singulari nequitia ac turpitudine: tantum de quaestu ac lucro dicam unius anni et unius agri, quo facilius vos conjecturam de triennio et de tota Sicilia facere possitis. Sed mihi Aetnensium brevis est ratio. Ipsi enim venerunt, ipsi

were driven out of Catina by the combined Siceli and Syracusans (Diod. xi. 76; Strabo, p. 268), and they founded, about twelve miles north of Catina, a new city Aetna, which before this time was called Inessa. The old inhabitants of Catina finally got their city again (B.C. 461) and restored to it the old name of Catina. The new town of Aetna kept its name, and it is the place which Cicero means. The site is uncertain.

decumas agemus.] Zumpt takes this to mean the same as 'de' with its case, but he finds no other like expression with the active form of 'ago.' It seems however, as he observes, to express the same as the passive form 'aguntur decumae;' and he refers to 'aguntur injuriae sociorum,' Lib. 4. c. 51; and to 'aguntur vectigalia populi Romani,' De Imp. Cn. Pompeii, c. 2.

ad se magistratus;] The MSS., except Lg. 42, have 'magistratum;' but the Sicilian towns had more than one 'magistratus.' Zumpt refers to c. 28, as proving that Agyrium had only one; but I don't see how that appears.

symphonia] This dissolute fellow had a band of music at his feast. 'Symphonia' is the nominative to 'caneret.' Cicero (Ad Div. xvi. 9) apparently alludes to Tiro having been at a merry meeting where there was music: 'symphoniam Lysonis vellem vitasses.' This word 'symphonia' was naturalized among the Romans (Pro M. Caelio, c. 15, 'cantus, symphonias'). There was a Collegium, or association of Symphoniaci, as we see from the following inscription found at Rome in 1847, in a Columbarium:

DIS MANIBVS
COLLEGIO SYMPHONIA
CORVM QVI SACRIS PVB
LICIS PRAESTV SVNT QVIBVS
SENATVS C.C.C. PERMISIT E
LEGE IVLIA EX AVCTORITATE
AVG LVDORVM CAVSA.

See the Zeitschrift für Geschicht. Rechtsw. xv. Römische Urkunden von Mommsen, and the learned author's remarks.

de insolentia,] After which Klotz adds 'nihil de permissa ab isto licentia' from Lg. 29, A, B, cod. Urs.

brevis est ratio.] Compare the beginning of c. 46, which would be sufficient to show that the old reading 'oratio,' which Orelli and Klotz have, is not the true

publicas literas deportaverunt: docuerunt vos quid lucelli fecerit homo non malus, familiaris praetoris, Apronius. Id, quaeso, ex ipsorum testimonio cognoscite. Recita testimonium Aetnensium. XLV. Quid ais? dic, dic, quaeso, clarius ut populus Romanus de suis vectigalibus, de suis aratoribus, de suis sociis atque amicis audiat. 'L̄. med., HS L̄.' Per deos immortales, unus ager uno anno trecenta millia modium tritici et praeterea HS L̄ lucri dat Apronio! Tantone minoris decumae venierunt quam fuerunt, an, quum satis magno venissent, hic tantus tamen frumenti pecuniaeque numerus ab aratoribus per vim ablatus est? Utrum enim horum dixeris, in eo culpa et crimen haerebit. Nam illud quidem non dices, quod utinam dicas, ad Apronium non pervenisse tantum. Ita te non modo publicis tenebo sed etiam privatis aratorum pactionibus ac literis, ut intelligas non te diligentiorem in faciundis fuisse furtis quam me in deprehendendis. Hoc tu feres? hoc quisquam defendet? hoc hi, si aliter de te statuere voluerint, sustinebunt? Uno adventu ex uno agro Q. Apronium praeter eam quam dixi pecuniam numeratam ccc millia modium tritici lucri nomine sustulisse? Quid hoc Aetnenses soli dicunt? immo etiam Centuripini qui agri Aetnensis multo maximam partem possident; quorum legatis,

reading. But Lg. 42 has 'ratio.' Klotz translates his text thus: 'I can be brief in what I say about the Aetnenses;' and adds, it is only necessary to rightly understand the genitive, which depends on 'oratio.' He compares Lib. 2. c. 69: "Eripiunt tibi istam orationem contemnendorum Siculorum atque aratorum statuae illae equestres," which, of course, he would explain in the same way. Zumpt says of the reading 'Sed mihi . . oratio,'—"quae dicendi ratio vix Latina potest haberi, *Aetnensium* pro *de Aetnensibus*." Klotz observes that a grammarian like Zumpt should not have allowed such a remark to escape him. Klotz may be right, and Zumpt wrong, for what I know, but I should like to have seen other instances produced besides the only one that Klotz refers to in Lib. 2. c. 69.

homo non malus,] Divin. c. 14, 'homini minime malo.'

45. *me in deprehendendis.*] All the MSS. and the older editions have 'reprehendendis.' The things opposed are 'committing theft,' and 'detecting;' and the word for detection is 'deprehendere.' Zumpt observes, "nam dicitur h. l. non de corrigendo, sed de inveniendo."

partem possident;] We cannot tell what technical signification 'possident' here has; whether these men were owners or tenants. He means to say that the largest part of the 'Aetnensis ager' was cultivated by Centuripini. They were the great farmers of Sicily, as this chapter shows: 'Arant enim tota Sicilia fere Centuripini.' He adds, 'quod in omnium fere finibus possessiones habent;' which may mean that these enterprising agriculturists held land as owners in many parts of Sicily. There is no difficulty about giving 'possessiones' this meaning (c. 46). They certainly farmed as tenants, c. 21. See the note on Commercium, c. 40, and the reference to Becker.

Rudorff (Gromat. ii. 306) says that the Centuripini had the capacity of owning landed property in all the other Sicilian states, and that all these states had no 'commercium agrorum' among them, and consequently the inhabitants of these several states could only be tenant farmers in the states to which they did not belong; and thus gradually the ownership of the land must come into the hands of Centuripini. He refers to iii. 40, 45, and to iv. 23, as evidence for his assertion. This is one of the most monstrous perversions of evidence that I have seen in a philological

hominibus nobilissimis, Androni et Artemoni, senatus ea mandata dedit, quae publice ad civitatem ipsorum pertinebant; de iis injuriis, quas cives Centuripini non in suis sed in aliorum finibus acceperunt, senatus et populus Centuripinus legatos noluit mittere: ipsi aratores Centuripini, qui numerus est in Sicilia maximus hominum honestissimorum et locupletissimorum, tres legatos cives suos delegerunt, ut eorum testimonio non unius agri, sed prope totius Siciliae calamitates cognosceretis. Arant enim tota Sicilia fere Centuripini: et hoc in te graviores certioresque testes sunt, quod ceterae civitates suis solum incommodis commoventur, Centuripini, quod in omnium fere finibus possessiones habent, etiam ceterarum civitatum damna ac detrimenta senserunt.

XLVI. Verum, uti dixi, ratio certa est Aetnensium et publicis et privatis literis consignata. Meae diligentiae pensum magis in Leontino agro est exigendum propter hanc causam quod ipsi Leontini publice non sane multum me adjuverunt: neque enim eos isto praetore hae decumanorum injuriae laeserunt; potius etiam, judices, adjuverunt. Mirum fortasse hoc vobis aut incredibile videatur in tantis aratorum incommodis Leontinos qui principes rei frumentariae fuerint expertes incommodorum atque injuriarum fuisse. Hoc causae est, judices, quod in agro Leontino praeter unam Mnasistrati familiam glebam Leontinorum possidet nemo. Itaque Mnasistrati, hominis honestissimi atque optimi viri testimonium, judices, audistis: ceteros Leontinos, quibus non modo Apronius in agris sed ne tempestas quidem ulla nocere potuit, exspectare nolite. Etenim non modo incommodi nihil ceperunt, sed etiam in Apronianis illis rapinis in quaestu sunt compendioque versati. Quapropter, quoniam me Leontina civitas atque legatio propter eam quam dixi causam defecit, mihimet ineunda ratio et via reperiunda est, qua ad Apronii quaestum sive adeo qua ad istius ingentem immanemque praedam possim pervenire. Agri Leontini decumae tertio anno venierunt tritici medimnum $\overline{\text{XXXVI}}$, hoc est, tritici modium CC et

treatise; and such perversions are not rare.

46. *qui principes . . fuerint*] "Conjunctivum *fuerint* admodum multi codices, interque eos, cui soli plus paene tribuo quam ceteris omnibus, Lag. 42, habent pro vulg. *fuerunt*" (Zumpt). 'Alii multi' have 'fuerint' (Jordan). Klotz and Jordan have 'fuerint.' Orelli has 'fuerunt.' I have no doubt that 'fuerint' is right. It is easier to feel convinced of this than to explain the reason.

audistis:] Lg. 42 φ, 'audietis' rell. and Orelli. It is immaterial which we take. We cannot tell whether Cicero meant to say that the evidence had been given or would be given. There is the same discrepancy of readings in other places.

compendioque versati.] Compare Lib. 2, c. 3, "quos illa . . . cum quaestu compendioque dimittit," and the note.

anno venierunt] 'anno veneunt,' Lg. 42.

XVI millibus. Magno, judices, magno; neque enim hoc possum negare. Itaque necesse est aut damnum aut certe non magnum lucrum fecisse decumanos. Hoc enim solet usu venire iis qui magno redemerunt. Quid si ostendo in hac una emptione lucri fieri tritici modium C? quid si CC? quid si CCC? quid si CCC millia? dubitabitis etiam cui ista tanta praeda quaesita sit? Iniquum me esse quispiam dicet qui ex lucri magnitudine conjecturam capiam furti atque praedae. Quid si doceo, judices, eos qui CCCC mod. lucri faciunt damnum facturos fuisse, si tua iniquitas, si tui ex cohorte recuperatores non intercederent, num quis poterit in tanto lucro tantaque iniquitate dubitare quin propter improbitatem tam magnos quaestus feceris, propter magnitudinem quaestus improbus esse volueris?

XLVII. Quomodo igitur hoc assequar, judices, ut sciam quantum lucri factum sit? non ex Apronii tabulis quas ego quum conquirerem non inveni, et quum in jus ipsum eduxi, expressi ut conficere se tabulas negaret. Si mentiebatur, quamobrem removebat si hae tabulae nihil tibi erant offuturae? Si omnino nullas confecerat literas, ne id quidem satis significat illum non suum negotium gessisse? Ea est enim ratio decumanorum ut sine plurimis literis confici non possit: singula enim nomina aratorum et cum singulis pactiones decumanorum literis persequi et conficere necesse est. Jugera professi sunt omnes aratores imperio atque instituto tuo: non opinor quemquam minus esse professum quam quantum arasset, quum tot cruces, tot supplicia, tot ex cohorte recuperatores proponerentur. In jugero Leontini agri medimnum fere tritici seritur perpetua atque aequabili satione. Ager efficit

usu venire] 'to happen.' Caesar, B. G. vii. 9, 'usu ventura,' and Pro Q. Rosc. Com. c. 11.—'conject. faciam,' Orelli.

47. *pactiones*] 'Pactum,' 'pactio,' is the general Roman term for any agreement; and 'agreement' is the general and non-technical English word for any agreement, though the lawyers have tried to torture it into a technical word. The curious may see how they have done it, in Wain and Warlters, 5 East, 10. 'Pactio,' or 'pactum,' is also not a technical term. Many 'pacta' did not produce 'obligationes' in the Roman sense. "Pactum autem a pactione dicitur . . Est autem pactio duorum pluriumve in idem placitum consensus:" Ulpian, Dig. 2. 14. 1.

The German 'Vertrag' is another instance of a general word for 'agreement.' The 'pactiones' are the agreements made between the 'aratores' and the 'decumani.' All that the 'decumani' could demand was the 'decumae;' but many arrangements might be made between the payers and receivers for mutual convenience, or rather, mainly for the convenience of the receivers, for one seldom hears of any tax-paying arrangement made for the special case of the payer. See c. 27, and the passage quoted from Cicero's letter to his brother Quintus. Instances of these 'pactiones' we have in Lib. 3. c. 14 and 57.

In jugero] 'In jugere,' the reading of Orelli, is bad. See c. 29.

As to the Roman 'jugerum,' and the 'medimnum,' see Excursus vi.; and also as to the produce raised on the land.

efficit cum octavo &c.] 'with a pro-

cum octavo bene ut agatur; verum ut omnes dii adjuvent, cum decumo: quod si quando accidit, tum fit ut tantum decumae sit quantum severis, hoc est, ut quot jugera sint sata totidem medimna decumae debeantur. Hoc quum ita esset, primum illud dico, pluribus millibus medimnum venisse decumas agri Leontini quam quot millia jugerum sata essent in agro Leontino. Quodsi fieri non poterat ut plus quam decem medimna ex jugero exararent, medimnum autem ex jugero decumano dari oportebat, quum ager, id quod perraro evenit, cum decumo extulisset, quae erat ratio decumanis, si quidem decumae ac non bona venibant aratorum, ut pluribus aliquanto medimnis decumas emerent quam jugera erant sata? In Leontino jugerum subscriptio ac professio non est plus $\overline{\text{XXX}}$.

XLVIII. Decumae $\overline{\text{XXXVI}}$ medimnum venierunt. Erravit aut potius insanivit Apronius? Immo tum insanisset, si aratoribus id quod deberent licitum esset, et non quod Apronius imperasset necesse fuisset dare. Si ostendam minus tribus medimnis in jugerum neminem dedisse decumae, concedes, opinor, ut cum decumo fructus arationis perceptus sit, neminem minus tribus decumis

duce of eight medimna the land does well; but a produce of ten is an especial favour of heaven.' Shortly after occurs the expression 'cum decumo extulisset.' In the next chapter, "ut cum decumo fructus arationis perceptus sit," 'the crop got in with ten for one.' The expression of Columella is the same: "nam frumenta majore quidem parte Italiae quando cum quarto responderint vix meminisse possumus" (iii. 3).

dari oportebat,] The true reading, furnished by Lg. 42, may be noticed, as Orelli has 'poterat,' which is obviously a blunder that has arisen from the proximity of the other 'poterat.'

venibant] The MSS. are not consistent in this form, for Zumpt observes that both here, and in c. 50, all have 'veniebant.' But it is now generally agreed that 'venibant' is the form for which there is best authority.

subscriptio &c.] Lg. 42 has 'subscriptio professio,' which is specious, but probably not true. The omission of the 'et' in formulary language has been remarked on above, c. 30.—In place of 'plus $\overline{\text{XXX}}$,' Klotz has 'plus XXX milium,' which is the same thing.

48. *Decumae* $\overline{\text{XXXVI}}$] Cicero states his case clearly. There were 30,000 'jugera' returned as sown with corn. This was the 'professio' or return, which return the 'aratores' were obliged to make: "jugera professi sunt aratores imperio atque instituto tuo." The 'subscriptio' probably means the signature to the return, which signature shows by whom it was made, as a man signs his return to the Income Tax. The produce of the 'decumae' could not, in the most favourable seasons, be more than $\overline{\text{XXX}}$; but Apronius bought the 'decumae' for $\overline{\text{XXXVI}}$. He would therefore lose $\overline{\text{VI}}$ at least by his bargain, if the people had paid no more than what was due. However, Apronius made his bargain profitable, for he allowed poor people, as a special favour, to compound (decidere), by paying three 'medimna' for each 'jugerum;' so that, if the produce was ten 'medimna,' they paid three 'decumae,' three-tenths, in place of one. If it was less, so much the worse for them, as they paid three 'medimna' out of a smaller amount. But even this, as it appears, was not the worst, for this rascal claimed as much as five 'medimna' for each 'jugerum.'

'Ut cum decumo .. perceptus sit' means as above explained, 'though the produce should have been ten for one.'

Erravit aut] 'Aut' is found only in Lg. 42; but Zumpt, Klotz, and Iordan have preferred it. Orelli, who had not the collations of the Lg. MSS., has 'erravit an potius.' There is a difference; for 'an' is a part of the disjunctive form 'utrum

dedisse. Atque hoc in beneficii loco petitum est ab Apronio ut in jugera singula ternis medimnis decidere liceret. Nam quum a multis quaterna etiam quina exigerentur, multis autem non modo granum nullum sed ne paleae quidem ex omni fructu atque ex annuo labore relinquerentur, tum aratores Centuripini, qui numerus in agro Leontino maximus est, unum in locum convenerunt; hominem suae civitatis in primis honestum ac nobilem, Andronem Centuripinum, legarunt ad Apronium, eundem quem hoc tempore ad hoc judicium legatum et testem Centuripina civitas misit, ut is apud eum causam aratorum ageret ab eoque peteret ut ab aratoribus Centuripinis ne amplius in jugera singula quam terna medimna exigeret. Hoc vix ab Apronio in summo beneficio pro iis qui etiam tum incolumes erant impetratum est. Id quum impetrabatur, hoc videlicet impetrabatur ut pro singulis decumis ternas decumas dare liceret. Quodsi tua res non ageretur, a te potius postularent ne amplius quam singulas quam ab Apronio ut ne plus quam ternas decumas darent. Nunc, ut hoc tempore ea quae regie seu potius tyrannice statuit in aratores Apronius praetermittam neque eos appellem a quibus omne frumentum eripuit, et quibus nihil non modo de fructu sed ne de bonis quidem suis reliqui fecit, ex hisce ternis medimnis, quod beneficii gratiaeque causa concessit, quid fiat cognoscite.

XLIX. Professio est agri Leontini ad jugerum $\overline{\text{XXX}}$. Haec sunt ad tritici medimnum $\overline{\text{XC}}$, id est, mod. DXL: deductis tritici mod. CCXVI, quanti decumae venierunt, reliqua sunt tritici $\overline{\text{CCCXXIV}}$. Adde totius summae DXL millium modium tres quinquagesimas; fit tritici mod. $\overline{\text{XXXII}}$ CCCC: ab omnibus enim ternae praeterea quinquagesimae exigebantur: sunt haec jam ad $\overline{\text{CCCLX}}$ mod. tritici. At ego $\overline{\text{CCCC}}$ lucri facta esse dixeram: non enim duco in hac ratione eos quibus ternis medimnis non est licitum decidere. Verum ut hac ipsa ratione summam mei promissi compleam, ad singula medimna multi HS binos, multi HS singulos semis accessionis

. . an,' which would here signify 'Which was it? Did he make a mistake, or was he mad?' But Cicero's form of expression does not leave it in doubt; the answer must be 'he was mad,' that is, 'he would have been mad, if' &c.

non modo granum nullum] Some MSS. have 'ullum,' contrary to usage. Zumpt refers to Lib. 4. c. 22, 'non modo oppidum nullum' &c. It is certain that 'nullum' might be omitted. It is doubtful if 'ullum' would do. The 'nullum' is a kind of case of reduplicated or emphatic negation.

49. *Professio*] If we write $\overline{\text{CCCLVI}}$ CCCC, the reckoning is clear.

multi HS binos, &c.] The old reading, and that of Orelli, is 'multi HS duo, multi HS quinque accessionis,' &c., to which there are two objections. First, the orator is clearly proceeding from the highest number, 'two,' to the lowest, 'one' (singulos nummos); and therefore 'one and a fraction' of some kind should intervene. Se-

cogebantur dare; qui minimum, singulos nummos. Minimum ut sequamur, quoniam $\overline{\text{xc}}$ med. duximus, accedant eo novo pessimoque exemplo HS xc millia. Hic mihi etiam dicere audebit magno se decumas vendidisse, quum ex eodem agro dimidio ipse plus abstulerit quam populo Romano miserit? $\overline{\text{ccxvi}}$ agri Leontini decumas vendidisti: si ex lege, magno; si ut lex esset libido tua, parvo; si ut quae dimidiae essent decumae vocarentur, parvo vendidisti: multo enim pluris fructus annui Siciliae venire potuerunt, si id te senatus aut populus Romanus facere voluisset. Etenim saepe decumae tanti venierunt, quum lege Hieronica venirent, quanti nunc lege Verria venierunt. Cedo mihi C. Norbani decumas venditas. C. NORBANI DECVMAE VENDITAE AGRI LEONTINI. Atqui tum neque judicium de modo jugerum dabatur, neque erat Artemidorus Cornelius recuperator, neque ab aratore magistratus Siculus tantum exigebat quantum decumanus ediderat; nec beneficium petebatur ab decumano ut in jugera singula ternis medimnis decidere liceret; nec nummorum accessionem cogebatur arator dare nec ternas quinquagesimas frumenti addere: et tamen populo Romano magnus frumenti numerus mittebatur. L. Quid vero istae sibi quinquagesimae, quid porro nummorum accessiones volunt? quo id jure atque adeo quo id potius more fecisti? Nummos dabat arator. Quomodo? aut unde? qui si largissimus esse vellet, cumulatiore mensura uteretur, ut antea solebant facere in decumis, quum aequa lege et conditione venibant. Is nummum dabat. Unde? de frumento? quasi habuisset te praetore quod venderet. De vivo igitur aliquid erat resecandum ut esset unde Apronio ad illos fructus arationum hoc corollarium nummorum

condly, the distributive 'binos' should be used with 'singula;' at least, that is the usage of Cicero, I believe. I have noticed one instance (Lib. 2. c. 55), where, as the text stands, this is not the case. Lg. 42 φ have 'HS binos multi HS singulos semis,' but φ has 'et semiss.' i.e. 'et semisses.' Zumpt says, "solet *semis* numeralibus, sine conjunctione postponi, quemadmodum significavimus in Gramm. § 87." 'Semis' is indeclinable.

50. *De vivo &c.*] The 'arator' could not make a present out of the corn which was left after he had paid his (nominal) 'decumae,' for he had nothing left. 'Something must be carved out of the very life of him, in order to enable him to make a present to Apronius, after giving up his produce.' There is a use of 'resecare' akin to this in Cicero, De Amicit. c. 5: "sed hoc primum sentio nisi in bonis amicitiam esse non posse; neque id ad vivum reseco, ut illi qui haec subtilius disserunt," &c. Zumpt compares Cicero, Pro Flacc. c. 37, 'dat de lucro, nihil detrahit de vivo.'

This expression is most apt; for, to take from a man a large part of his earnings as soon as he has got them, cuts to the very life of a people, and, in the end, checks industry.

corollarium] From 'corolla,' a diminutive of 'corona,' there is formed 'corollarium,' which Pliny defines to be small 'coronae,' made of thin plates of copper, gilt or silvered. Here it signifies something given to a man over that which is due. Comp. Lib. 4. c. 22.

adderetur. Jam id porro utrum libentes an inviti dabant? Libentes? amabant, credo, Apronium. Inviti? qua re nisi vi et malo cogebantur? Jam iste homo amentissimus in vendundis decumis nummorum faciebat accessiones ad singulas decumas; neque multum; bina aut terna millia nummum addebat: fiunt per triennium HS D millia fortasse. Hoc neque exemplo cujusquam neque jure ullo fecit, neque eam pecuniam rettulit, neque hoc parvum crimen quemadmodum defensurus sit homo quisquam unquam excogitavit.

Quod quum ita sit, audes dicere te magno decumas vendidisse, quum sit perspicuum te bona fortunasque aratorum non populi Romani sed tui quaestus causa vendidisse? Ut si qui villicus ex eo fundo qui sestertia dena meritasset, excisis arboribus ac venditis, demptis tegulis, instrumento, pecore abalienato, domino XX

neque multum;] These words seem to refer to what he has just said; and 'no great amount,' 'that was not much,' ironically. For he goes on to say 'bina aut terna millia nummum addebat.'

HS D *millia fortasse.*] 'Fortasse' is so placed by Lg. 42. The common reading is 'fortasse HS,' &c. Zumpt cannot explain how Cicero made out this sum. 'Fortasse' must be taken to signify 'about.' P. Manutius explains it thus. There were seventy-two cities in Sicily, as Pliny says; and if he took 2000 from each for three years, that will make 432,000; and he took from some not 2000, but 3000, which will bring up the sum to a larger amount. But this, as Zumpt observes, is manifestly a false explanation, for many of the cities were 'vectigales,' not 'decumanae;' and some were 'immunes.' Cicero says (c. 51) 'ager decumanus .. desertus est.' The 'decumanae,' so far as appears from Cicero's enumeration, were only thirty-four. It seems to me that the words 'ad singulas decumas' may refer to all the 'decumae' which the 'civitates' paid, and not to the several regular 'decumae' of the several 'civitates;' though, as Zumpt observes, these 'alterae decumae' are treated of afterwards.

audes dicere te] "Lag. 29, Paris. A. B., *audes te dicere*, collocatione verborum admodum eleganti" (Zumpt); but he does not adopt the order; Klotz does.

villicus] Written 'vilicus' by Iordan. The word clearly contains the same root as 'villa,' which may perhaps only be entitled to one 'L.' A 'villicus' was an overseer or manager of an estate, who was sometimes a slave, perhaps generally (Forcellini). The use of 'villicus' explains 'meritasset,' a term which might refer to the 'merces' or rent, but here it means, which had brought in, or 'earned,' as we might say, 'sestertia dena.' Zumpt observes that the reading of Lg. 42 is not 'HS dena,' but 'sestertia dena,' which, as he observes, is very seldom found in prose writers; and he only knows one other example in Cicero (Paradox. vi. 3), where 'sexcena sestertia' is the true reading, not 'sexcenta sestertia.'

instrumento,] This word occurs several times in these orations. Among the Romans it had a fixed legal meaning, for 'instrumentum' was often the subject of a legacy (Dig. 33. tit. 7, 'De instructo vel instrumento legato'). Ulpian (Dig. 33. 7, 8) says: "in instrumento fundi ea esse quae fructus quaerendi, cogendi, conservandi gratia parata sint, Sabinus libris ad Vitellium evidenter enumerat;" and he then proceeds to explain the definition. The term, in its widest extent, might comprehend all the stock of the farm, slaves included. In some parts (quibusdam in regionibus) it had a wider meaning than in others; and the interpretation of the word was determined among the Romans by what we call the custom of the country. It may be observed that *κατασκευὴ* is used in the same, or nearly the same sense, as the Roman 'instrumentum;' but whether it has a strictly technical meaning, as 'instrumentum' had in Latin, I don't know.

millia nummum pro x miserit, sibi alia praeterea centum confecerit, primo dominus ignarus incommodi sui gaudeat, villicoque delectetur quod tanto plus sibi mercedis ex fundo refectum sit; deinde, quum audierit eas res quibus fundi fructus et cultura continetur amotas et venditas, summo supplicio villicum afficiat et secum male actum putet: item populus Romanus, quum audit pluris decumas vendidisse C. Verrem quam innocentissimum hominem cui iste successit, C. Sacerdotem, putat se bonum in arationibus fructibusque suis habuisse custodem ac villicum; quum senserit istum omne instrumentum aratorum, omnia subsidia vectigalium vendidisse, omnem spem posteritatis avaritia sua sustulisse, arationes et agros vectigales vastasse atque exinanisse, ipsum maximos quaestus praedasque fecisse, intelliget secum actum esse pessime, istum autem summo supplicio dignum existimabit.

LI. Unde ergo hoc intelligi potest? Ex hoc maximo quod ager decumanus provinciae Siciliae propter istius avaritiam desertus est. Neque id solum accidit uti minus multis jugis ararent si qui in agris remanserunt, sed etiam ut permulti locupletes homines, magni et navi aratores, agros latos ac fertiles desererent totasque arationes derelinquerent. Id adeo sciri facillime potest ex literis publicis civitatum, propterea quod lege Hieronica numerus aratorum quotannis apud magistratus publice subscribitur. Recita tandem quot acceperit aratores agri Leontini Verres; LXXXIIII: quot anno tertio profiteantur; XXXII. Duo et quinquaginta aratores ita video dejectos ut his ne vicarii quidem successerint. Quot aratores adveniente te fuerunt agri Mutycensis? videamus ex literis publicis. CLXXXVII. Quid anno tertio? LXXXVI. Centum et

refectum sit;] Lg. 42 has 'receptum sit,' which does not appear to be the right word. Zumpt quotes a like use of 'reficiatur' from Paradoxa, vi. 1.

posteritatis] 'all hope for the future,' like 'in posteritatem,' c. 65.

secum actum esse pessime,] A common formula, which may be rendered somewhat differently according to its application. Here it means 'the Roman people well know that they have been treated most scandalously.' Compare Pro P. Sestio, c. 23.

51. *derelinquerent.*] 'relinquerent' Lg. 42.

agri Leontini] The arable land of the ager Leontinus was 30,000 jugera (c. 49). When Verres came to Sicily, it was cultivated by eighty-four 'aratores,' and consequently these cultivators had about 351 jugera apiece. Among them there was only one Leontine. Fifty-two of these eighty-four were ruined, and their lands were left uncultivated. It has already been said that the better opinion is that this Leontine land was Roman land, and that it was leased to tenants, the land, not the 'decumae' (c. 6, note on 'immunes et liberas').

vicarii] This word here simply means one who takes the place of another, as in Lib. 4. c. 37, 'succedam ego vicarius tuo muneri.' Compare Horace, 3 Carm. xxiv. 15:

"Defunctumque laboribus
Aequali recreat sorte vicarius."

unum aratores unus ager istius injuria desiderat, atque adeo res publica, quoniam illa populi Romani vectigalia sunt, hunc tot patrumfamilias numerum desiderat et reposcit. Ager Herbitensis primo anno habuit aratores CCLII, tertio CXX: hinc CXXXII patresfamilias extorres profugerunt. Agyrinensis ager, quorum hominum! quam honestorum! quam locupletium! CCL aratores habuit primo anno praeturae tuae. Quid tertio anno? LXXX, quemadmodum legatos Agyrinenses recitare ex literis publicis audistis.

LII. Pro dii immortales, si ex provincia tota CLXX ejecisses, possesne severis judicibus salvus esse? Unus ager Agyrinensis CLXX aratoribus inanior quum sit, vos conjecturam totius provinciae nonne facietis? Atque hoc peraeque in omni agro decumano reperietis: quibus aliquid tamen reliqui fuerit ex magno patrimonio, eos in agris minore instrumento, minus multis jugis, remansisse, quod metuebant, si discessissent, ne reliquas fortunas omnes amitterent; quibus autem iste nihil reliqui quod perderent fecerat, eos plane non solum ex agris verum ex civitatibus suis profugisse. Illi ipsi qui remanserant, vix decuma pars aratorum, relicturi agros omnes erant, nisi ad eos Metellus Roma literas misisset, se decumas lege Hieronica venditurum, et nisi ab iis hoc petivisset ut sererent quam plurimum; quod illi semper sui causa fecerant, quum eos nemo rogaret, quamdiu intelligebant sese sibi et populo Romano, non Verri et Apronio serere, impendere, laborare. Jam vero, judices, si Siculorum fortunas negligitis, si quemadmodum socii populi Romani a magistratibus nostris tractentur non laboratis, at vos communem populi Romani causam suscipite atque defendite. Ejectos aratores esse dico, agros vectigales vexatos atque exinanitos a Verre, populatam vastatamque provinciam; haec omnia doceo literis civitatum, ostendo testimoniis et publicis honestissimarum civitatum et privatis primariorum virorum. Quid vultis amplius? LIII. Num exspectatis dum L. Metellus, is qui multos in istum testes imperio et potestate deterruit, idem absens de istius scelere, improbitate, audacia testimonium dicat? Non opinor.—At is optime qui successit isti potuit cognoscere.—Ita est: verum amicitia impeditur.—At debet vos certiores facere quo pacto se habeat provincia.—Debet: verumtamen non cogitur. Num quis in Ver-

52. *nonne facietis?*] 'Non facietis,' Orelli. But this is not the form of interrogation in this part of a sentence. Zumpt says: "Vulgo *non facietis*, quae interrogandi forma in indignatione locum habet: in apodosi num habeat ignoro et dubito." He refers to Lib. 2. c. 59, and Lib. 5. c. 32. —'si discessissent,' from Lg. 42 only. The common reading is 'recessissent.'

sui causa] There is the better authority for this. Orelli has 'sua causa.'

rem L. Metelli testimonium requirit? Nemo. Num quis postulat? Non opinor. Quid, si testimonio L. Metelli ac literis haec omnia vera esse docebo, quid dicetis? utrum Metellum falsum scribere an amicum laedendi esse cupidum? an praetorem quemadmodum provincia afflicta sit nesciro? Recita literas L. Metelli quas ad Cn. Pompeium et M. Crassum consules, quas ad M. Mummium praetorem, quas ad quaestores urbis misit. EPISTOLA L. METELLI. 'Decumas frumenti lege Hieronica vendidi.' Quum scribit se lege Hieronica vendidisse, quid scribit? ita se vendidisse ut omnes praeter Verrem. Quum scribit se lege Hieronica vendidisse, quid scribit? se per istum erepta Siculis majorum nostrorum beneficia, jus ipsorum, conditionem societatis, amicitiae, foederum, reddidisse. Dicit quanti cujusque agri decumas vendiderit: deinde quid scribit? 'Summa vi data est a me opera ut quam plurimo decumas venderem.' Cur igitur, Metelle, non ita magno vendidisti? quia desertas arationes, inanes agros, provinciam miseram perditamque offendisti. Quid id ipsum quod satum est, qua ratione quisquam qui sereret inventus est? Recita. Literas ait se misisse et confirmasse, suam se interposuisse auctoritatem: tantummodo aratoribus Metellus obsides non dedit se in nulla re Verri similem futurum. At quid est tandem in quo se laborasse dicit? Recita. 'Ut aratores qui reliqui erant quamplurimum sererent.' Qui 'reliqui?' quid hoc est 'reliqui?' quo ex bello? qua ex vastitate? Quaenam in Sicilia tanta clades, aut quod bellum tam diuturnum, tam calamitosum te praetore versatum est ut is qui tibi successerit reliquos aratores collegisse et recreasse videatur?

LIV. Quum bellis Carthaginiensibus Sicilia vexata est, et post nostra patrumque memoria quum bis in ea provincia magnae fugitivorum copiae versatae sunt, tamen aratorum interitio facta nulla est. Tum sementi prohibita aut messe amissa fructus annuus interibat; tamen incolumis numerus manebat dominorum atque

53. *quaestores urbis*] 'Quaestores urbanos' Klotz, which N only has, but in the unusual order, 'urbanos quaestores.'

tantummodo] This is the reading of Lg. 42 only, which Zumpt, Klotz, and Jordan have preferred, and apparently for good reasons. The common reading is 'tantum quod aratoribus,' &c. It is true that 'tantum quod . . non' occurs in Lib. 1. c. 45, but it is not used in the same way that 'tantum quod' must be understood here.

laborasse dicit?] 'Laborasse dicat' Orelli. Lg. 42 has 'dicit.' The meaning of the two forms is not the same. Cicero asks, 'What is that in which he says that he used his endeavours?' (Comp. 'laboratis,' c. 53.) The other would mean, 'What is there in which he says that he,' &c.? In Divin. c. 3, we have this form, "quid est . . in quo ego rei publicae plus hoc tempore prodesse possim?" See Lib. 4. c. 20, note on 'quid erat quod' &c.

54. *sementi*] 'Sementi' is in Lg. 42 only; the other MSS. have 'semente.' The form 'sementi,' Zumpt observes, is used in Columella. Caesar, B. G. i. 3, has the plural 'sementes.'

aratorum: tum, qui M. Laevino aut P. Rupilio aut M'. Aquillio praetores in eam provinciam successerant, aratores reliquos non colligebant. Tantone plus Verres cum Apronio provinciae Siciliae calamitatis importavit quam aut Hasdrubal cum Poenorum exercitu, aut Athenio cum fugitivorum maximis copiis, ut temporibus illis simul atque hostis superatus esset ager araretur omnis, neque aratori praetor per literas supplicaret neque eum praesens oraret ut quam plurimum sereret, nunc autem ne post abitum quidem hujus importunissimae pestis quisquam reperiretur qui sua voluntate araret, pauci essent reliqui qui L. Metelli auctoritate in agros atque ad suum larem familiarem redirent? His te literis, homo audacissime atque amentissime, jugulatum esse non sentis? non vides, quum is qui tibi successit aratores reliquos appellet, hoc eum diserte scribere, reliquos hos esse non ex bello neque ex aliqua hujusmodi calamitate, sed ex tuo scelere, importunitate, avaritia, crudelitate? Recita cetera. 'Tamen pro eo ut temporis difficultas aratorumque penuria tulit.' 'Aratorum,' inquit, 'penuria.' Si ego accusator toties de re eadem dicerem, vererer ne animos vestros offenderem, judices. Clamat Metellus, 'Nisi literas misissem:' non est satis: 'Nisi praesens confirmassem:' ne id quidem satis est: 'Reliquos,' inquit, 'aratores.' Reliquos! prope lugubri verbo calamitatem provinciae Siciliae significat: addit, 'Aratorum penuria.'

LV. Exspectate etiam, judices, exspectate, si potestis, auctoritatem accusationis meae. Dico aratores istius avaritia ejectos: scribit Metellus 'reliquos' ab se esse confirmatos. Dico agros relictos arationesque desertas esse: scribit Metellus aratorum esse 'penuriam.' Hoc quum scribit, illud ostendit, dejectos, ejectos,

praetores] The old reading is 'praetoribus;' but the three men who have been named were either Consuls or Proconsuls in Sicily. The reading 'praetoribus' is merely a misinterpretation of the abbreviation *Pr.*, and Lg. 42 has 'praetores' at full length. Zumpt suggests it as a matter of consideration, whether 'in eam provinciam' should be changed into 'in ea provincia.'

As to M. Valerius Laevinus, see Livy, Lib. 26. c. 40, and Lib. 27. c. 5. He was in Sicily, as consul, B.C. 210, and tranquillized the island after the capture of Agrigentum.

The inscription in Gruter (150. 7), and in Orelli's Inscrip. Lat. Sel. ii. 71, referred to by Klotz, begins thus: M. AQVILIVS M. F. GALLVS. PROC. . . ET EIDEM PRAETOR IN SICILIA, &c. But it is hard to say what is the value of this inscription. Klotz says that he was Proconsul, and accordingly he calls himself so, for this inscription professes to be made by himself, but he appears, with reference to his administration of Sicily, to have called himself Praetor. Klotz refers to the case of Bibulus (Cic. Ad Div. ii. 17), who is called Praetor of Syria, though he had been Consul. See the note of P. Manutius on this passage of Cicero, and Ernesti, Clavis Cic.

pro eo ut] Servius Sulpicius, in a letter to Cicero (Ad Div. iv. 5), has the expression 'pro eo ac debui.' See Lib. 2. c. 34.

55. *auctoritatem*] 'the evidence.' See the Index, 'auctor.'

ejectos:] Zumpt and Iordan omit 'ejectos' on the authority of Lg. 42 F.—'ani-

fortunis omnibus expulsos esse populi Romani socios atque amicos. Quibus si qua calamitas propter istum salvis vectigalibus nostris accidisset, animadvertere tamen in eum vos oportebat; praesertim quum ea lege judicaretis quae sociorum causa esset constituta: quum vero perditis profligatisque sociis vectigalia populi Romani sint deminuta, res frumentaria, commeatus, copiae, salus urbis atque exercituum nostrorum in posteritatem istius avaritia interierit, saltem populi Romani commoda respicite, si sociis fidelissimis prospicere non laboratis. Atque ut intelligatis ab isto prae lucro praedaque praesenti nec vectigalium nec posteritatis habitam esse rationem, cognoscite quid ad extremum scribat Metellus. 'In reliquum tamen tempus vectigalibus prospexi.' In reliquum tempus ait se vectigalibus prospexisse. Non scriberet se vectigalibus prospexisse, nisi hoc vellet ostendere te vectigalia perdidisse. Quid enim erat quod vectigalibus prospiceret Metellus in decumis et in tota re frumentaria, si iste non vectigalia populi Romani quaestu suo pervertisset? Atque ipse Metellus, qui vectigalibus prospicit, qui reliquos aratores colligit, quid assequitur nisi hoc, ut arent si qui possunt quibus aratrum saltem aliquod satelles istius Apronius reliquum fecit, qui tamen in agris spe atque exspectatione Metelli remanserunt? Quid ceteri Siculi? quid ille maximus numerus aratorum, qui non modo ex agris ejecti sunt, sed etiam ex civitatibus suis, ex provincia denique bonis fortunisque omnibus ereptis profugerunt, qua ratione ii revocabuntur? quot praetorum innocentia sapientiaque opus est ut illa aratorum multitudo aliquando in suis agris ac sedibus collocetur? LVI. Ac ne miremini tantam multitudinem profugisse quantam ex literis publicis aratorumque professionibus cognovistis, scitote tantam acerbitatem

mum advertere,' Lg. 42. Both 'animum advertere' and 'animadvertere' occur in the MSS. The form, I suppose, was originally 'animum advertere.'

deminuta,] "'diminuta' Lgg. praeter 49" (Iordan). Zumpt assents to Oudendorp's remark (Ad Suetonii Caesarem, c. 5), that there is both 'deminuere' and 'diminuere;' and this may be readily admitted, for we have 'describere,' 'discribere;" 'dejicere,' 'disjicere;' and many other like pairs. 'Deminuere,' according to Oudendorp, applies to a thing from which something is taken; 'diminuere,' to a thing that is destroyed by the dissolution of the parts. If this is so, we ought perhaps to say 'deminutio capitis,' and not 'diminutio capitis;' but this matter is still unsettled. Savigny observes, "in the MSS. there occur two modes of writing this word, 'deminutio' and 'diminutio.' Hugo is decidedly in favour of the latter." Savigny is of opinion that the Romans wrote the word both ways (System, &c. ii. p. 61, note).

saltem . . si] Whatever 'saltem' may mean, Cicero often expresses the same notion that he has here by the formula 'si—at,' as in c. 52, 'Si Siculorum . . : at vos,' &c. Further on in this chapter, 'quibus aratrum saltem,' 'saltem' is used there as Cicero often uses 'tamen.'

quaestu suo] Zumpt and Iordan have 'suo quaestu,' from Lg. 42, which some may prefer.—'aratores collegit' A B Lg. 29, Klotz.

istius, tantum scelus in aratores fuisse,—incredibile dictu est, judices, sed et factum et tota Sicilia pervulgatum,—ut homines propter injurias licentiamque decumanorum mortem sibi ipsi consciverint. Centuripinum Dioclem hominem locupletem suspendisse se constat, quo die sit ei nuntiatum Apronium decumas redemisse. Tyracinum principem civitatis eadem ratione mortem oppetisse dixit apud vos homo nobilissimus Archonidas Helorinus, quum audisset tantum decumanum professum esse ex edicto istius sibi deberi quantum ille bonis suis omnibus efficere non posset.

Haec tu, tametsi omnium hominum dissolutissimus crudelissimusque semper fuisti, tamen nunquam perpeterere, propterea quod ille gemitus luctusque provinciae ad tui capitis periculum pertinebat; non, inquam, perpeterere ut homines injuriae tuae remedium morte ac suspendio quaererent, nisi ea res ad quaestum et ad praedam tuam pertineret. Quid illud perpeterere? Attendite, judices; omnibus enim nervis mihi contendendum est, atque in hoc elaborandum ut omnes intelligant quam improbam, quam manifestam, quam confessam rem pecunia redimere conetur. Grave crimen est hoc et vehemens et post hominum memoriam judiciaque de pecuniis repetundis constituta gravissimum, praetorem socios habuisse decumanos. LVII. Non hoc nunc primum audit privatus de inimico, reus ab accusatore: jam antea in sella sedens praetor, quum provinciam Siciliam obtineret, quum ab omnibus non solum id quod commune est propter imperium, sed etiam id quod istius praecipuum est propter crudelitatem metueretur, millies audivit,

56. *pervulgatum,*] Zumpt, Klotz, and Jordan write 'pervagatum,' on the authority of Lg. 42 only. Zumpt says that it is not Latin to apply 'pervulgata,' or hardly Latin ('verum *pervulgata* Latine non fere dicuntur'), to things which are known to all, but to things that are practised by or are in use by all; "nec pervulgamus notitiae causa, sed ut alii vulgo utantur." "Therefore," he says, "if we read 'pervulgatum,' we must understand that the 'aratores' hanged themselves all over Sicily." Cicero hardly means to say this: he means to say, that the thing was notorious all over Sicily. Zumpt even thinks that 'cupiditate illa . . pervagata' (Lib. 2. c. 34) may also be understood of the notoriety of the greediness of Verres; an explanation, I think, which will not generally be received. He refers to 'pervagatum est' in Lib. 4. c. 28. In Lib. 2. c. 42, I have followed Zumpt in writing 'promulgata' for 'pervulgata;' but in that passage 'promulgata' is the appropriate word. But one may doubt whether the difference of meaning between 'pervulgata' and 'provulgata,' or 'promulgata,' is so great as Zumpt makes it.

Quid illud perpeterere?] 'Quid? illud paterere?' Zumpt. He says of 'paterere:' "ex Lg. 42, pro *perpeterere*, quod nimis propinquum est, edidimus."

contendendum &c.] This word is from V. Zumpt has 'mihi nervis connitendum.' —'elaborandum,' in place of 'laborandum,' is also from V.

confessam rem] This is one of the so-called deponent verbs, of which the participles are sometimes used in a passive sense. See Lib. 2. c. 76, note on 'testata.'

57. *privatus de inimico, &c.*] This means 'from his enemy.' But Cicero uses 'ab accusatore,' as if, as Zumpt remarks, 'ab' expressed a more direct purpose in him who speaks, and 'de' a less direct or formal communication.

quum ejus animum ad persequendum non negligentia tardaret, sed conscientia sceleris avaritiaeque suae refrenaret. Loquebantur enim decumani palam, et praeter ceteros is qui apud istum plurimum poterat maximosque agros populabatur, Apronius, perparvum ex illis magnis lucris ad se pervenire; praetorem esse socium. Hoc quum palam decumani tota provincia loquerentur tuumque nomen in re tam turpi nefariaque interponerent, nihilne tibi venit in mentem existimationi tuae consulere, nihil denique capiti ac fortunis tuis providere? quum tui nominis terror in auribus animisque aratorum versaretur, quum decumani aratoribus ad pactiones faciendas non suam vim sed tuum scelus ac nomen opponerent. Ecquod judicium Romae tam dissolutum, tam perditum, tam nummarium fore putasti, quo ex judicio te ulla Salus servare posset, quum planum fieret decumis contra instituta, leges, consuetudinemque omnium venditis, in aratorum bonis fortunisque diripiendis decumanos dictitasse tuas esse partes, tuam rem, tuam praedam, idque te tacuisse, et, quum dissimulare non posses, potuisse tamen perpeti et perferre, quod magnitudo lucri obscuraret periculi magnitudinem, plusque aliquanto apud te pecuniae cupiditas quam judicii metus posset? Esto: cetera negare non potes: ne illud quidem tibi reliquum fecisti ut hoc posses dicere, nihil te eorum audisse, nihil ad tuas aures de infamia tua pervenisse. Querebantur cum luctu et gemitu aratores: tu id nesciebas? Fremebat tota provincia: nemo id tibi renuntiabat? Romae querimoniae de tuis injuriis conventusque habebantur: ignorabas haec? ignorabas haec omnia? Quid quum palam Syracusis te audiente maximo conventu L. Rubrius Q. Apronium sponsione lacessivit, Ni Apronius dictitaret te sibi in decumis esse socium, haec te vox non perculit? non perturbavit? non ut capiti et fortunis tuis prospiceres excitavit? Tacuisti: sedasti etiam lites illorum, et sponsio illa ne fieret laborasti.

LVIII. Pro dii immortales, hoc aut innocens homo perpeti potuisset, aut quamvis nocens, qui modo judicia Romae fore puta-

nummarium] 'Corrupt,' 'accessible to bribes.' Cicero has the expression (Ad Att. i. 16) 'nummariis judicibus.'

ulla Salus] Salus was a goddess, and she had a temple (Liv. ix. 43; x. 1). The similar passage in Terence is referred to by Hotmann:

——— "ipsa si cupiat Salus,
Servare prorsus non potest hanc familiam."
Adelph. iv. 7. 43.

See also Pro Fonteio, c. 10; Pro Murena, c. 13. Salus is also represented on many Roman medals (Ant. Agostini, Dialoghi, &c., Salus).

Ni . . dictitaret . . socium,] Klotz and Iordan write these words in capitals, as if they were the words of the Sponsio. See Excursus v. and Lib. 5. c. 54, note.

ret, non aliqua simulatione existimationi se hominum venditasset? Quid est hoc? Sponsio fit de capite ac fortunis tuis: tu sedes et quiescis? non persequeris? non perseveras? non perquiris cui dixerit Apronius, quis audierit, unde hoc natum, quemadmodum prolatum sit? Si tibi aliquis ad aurem accessisset et dixisset, Apronium dictitare te sibi esse socium, commoveri te oportuit, evocare Apronium, nec illum ante tibi satisfacere quam tu omnium existimationi satisfecisses. Quum vero in foro celeberrimo tanta frequentia hoc verbo ac simulatione Apronio, re vera tibi objectum esset, tu unquam tantam plagam tacitus accipere potuisses, nisi hoc ita statuisses in re tam manifesta quidquid dixisses te deterius esse facturum? Quaestores, legatos, praefectos, tribunos suos multi missos fecerunt et de provincia decedere jusserunt, quod illorum culpa se minus commode audire arbitrarentur aut quod peccare ipsos aliqua in re judicarent; tu Apronium, hominem vix liberum, contaminatum, perditum, flagitiosum, qui non modo animum integrum sed ne animam quidem puram conservare potuissset, eum in

58. *non aliqua &c.*] "Codd. *non aliqua re simul. populi Rom. existimationi se hominum*, item sic editiones veteres, et praeterea *vendicasset s. vindicasset.* Victor." (Zumpt.) Manutius struck out 'populi Rom.;' but he kept 'vindicasset.' Gruter first gave the text as it stands in Zumpt's edition and in this. The reading is very uncertain. Iordan says nothing about it. 'Venditare se' is explained by Forcellini as equivalent to 'ostentare,' 'to make a show or display.' The text means "simulata aliqua virtute studere efficere ut homines bene de te existiment" (Graevius).

tu sedes &c.] If the reader will omit the notes of interrogation after 'quiescis' and the other words in this sentence, he will not miss them.

prolatum sit?] Here the word is used in its ordinary sense, 'to bring forward.' See Lib. 2. c. 30, where Klotz has 'prolato' for 'dilato' in a sense in which 'prolato' can also be used: Pro Muren. c. 13, 'prolatis rebus;' and Ad Att. xiv. 5, 'res prolatas.'

tribunos suos] He means 'tribuni militum.' See Pro P. Sestio, c. 3, note on 'abstinentia.'—'missos fecerunt:' similar to 'reliquum fecerunt' c. 57, and other like usages of 'facere' (c. 60). In other languages also we observe that some particular words are made to do a great deal of work. The Italian 'fare,' and particularly the French 'faire,' are worked harder than their Latin parent.

minus commode audire] The good report of the governor of a province, his good name, was a matter that concerned him nearly. Cicero says to his brother, when he was governor of Asia (Ad Q. Fr. i. 1), "ac si te ipse vehementius ad omnes partes bene audiendi excitaris." It appears from this passage that a governor could send away his 'quaestors' and others from the province.—'illorum culpa,' adopted by Zumpt from the better MSS. Orelli's reading is 'eorum culpa;' and 'eorum' is the proper word simply to express a reference to persons; but Cicero means to speak of 'these persons' emphatically. Again, Orelli has 'peccare illos;' but the best MSS. have 'peccare ipsos,' where 'ipsos' refers specially to the 'illos.' These are not slight matters in the text of Latin authors. The right use of the pronouns is one of the great niceties of the language.

animam] This scandalous abuse is in the style of the Roman orators. It is an unsavoury allusion to the foul breath of Apronius. 'Animus,' the intellectual and moral existence, is here contrasted with the breath, as in Juvenal (xv. 148) with the life:

—— "indulsit communis conditor illis
Tantum animas, nobis animum quoque."

tanto tuo dedecore profecto ne verbo quidem graviore appellasses, neque apud te tam sancta religio societatis fuisset ut tui capitis periculum negligeres, nisi rem tam notam esse omnibus et tam manifestam videres.

LIX. Cum eodem Apronio postea P. Scandilius, eques Romanus, quem vos omnes nostis, eandem sponsionem de societate fecit quam Rubrius facere voluerat. Institit, oppressit, non remisit: facta est sponsio HS $\bar{\text{v}}$: coepit Scandilius recuperatores aut judicem postulare. Satisne vobis praetori improbo circumdati cancelli videntur in sua provincia, immo vero in sella ac tribunali, ut aut de suo capite judicium fieri patiatur praesens ac sedens aut confiteatur se omnibus judiciis convinci necesse esse? Sponsio est, NI TE APRONIUS SOCIUM IN DECUMIS ESSE DICAT. Provincia tua est:

ne verbo quidem &c.] 'Locus difficilis,' says Zumpt. Manutius thought that 'non' should be inserted before 'profecto,' and Ernesti did it. 'Appellare asperius,' or 'verbo graviore,' is 'to reprove.' Zumpt says that the sense of the text is this: 'Now, with respect to you and Apronius, &c., you would not, in a matter so discreditable to yourself, have been satisfied even with giving him a reproof, nor &c.;—you would not have spoken to him at all, not even in words of reproof; you would have sent him away.' Still there is something very awkward in this sentence, and it is possible that there is error in the text. The position of 'tu Apronium' is one of the contrasts which are common in Latin.

59. *oppressit,*] 'he kept close to him, he held him fast (oppressit), he would not let the man go.'

HS $\bar{\text{v}}$:] Most of the MSS. have 'HS v.' The horizontal line, which denotes thousands, is often omitted. The full expression is 'sestertium quinque millium.' See Lib. 5. c. 54.

cancelli] 'Cancelli' (in Greek κιγκλίδες, δρύφακτοι) is an enclosure of wood, or a railing, or any thing of the kind, by which a place is enclosed and protected (Forcellini). The word occurs in Pro P. Quintio, c. 10, Pro Sestio, c. 58. Salmasius, who has a prodigious long note on 'Cancellarii' and 'Cancelli' (*Hist. Aug.* p. 483, ed. Paris, 1620), says: "sic κιγκλίδες sunt proprie cancelli: οἱ ἐπὶ κιγκλίδων, cancellarii: κιγκλίδα Graeci τὴν τοῦ δικαστηρίου θύραν passim interpretantur. Latini tamen cancellos non tantum fores τοῦ δικαστηρίου, sed etiam omne conseptum appellant. Graeci quoque δρύφακτον et κιγκλίδα saepe confundunt, et δρυφάκτους, καγγέλλους passim exponunt: nam δρύφακτοι, ut dixi, proprie sunt septa judicialium secretorum: hinc *cancellorum septa* vocat Ammianus Marcellinus, Lib. xxx. de advocatis: 'cum intra cancellorum venerint septa et agi coeperint alicujus fortuna vel salus.'" This will explain what the 'cancelli' are. 'Cancellarii' were door-keepers, who stood at the outer bounds or limits of the court (cancelli), in the later empire (Bethmann-Hollweg, Handbuch des Civilprozesses, &c., p. 190). Those who are curious may trace this name of Cancellarius from his humble duties of a door-keeper to his higher duties of Chancellor in modern times.

Cicero says, "Don't you think that a wicked praetor was shut up close enough in his own province, I would say, on his judgment-seat and tribunal, when he must either in his own presence, and while sitting there, allow a matter to be heard, in which his own character was implicated, or must confess that he must of necessity be convicted in every trial?" or 'in the judgment of all;' which may be the meaning of 'omnibus jud.'

It is a metaphor, says Hotmann (circumdati cancelli), taken from wild beasts shut up in enclosures so that they cannot escape. But the metaphor is not wanted. Verres was so hemmed in, even in his own court, that a man would suppose he must do either one or the other thing. But Verres did neither.

provincia,] 'provintia' Lg. 42; which is worth noting as the genuine form, and the abbreviation of 'providentia,' which appears also in the shape 'prudentia.'

NI TE &c.] See Lib. 5. c. 54, and the note.

ades: abs te judicium postulatur. Quid facis? quid decernis? Recuperatores dicis te daturum. Bene agis: tametsi qui tantis erunt cervicibus recuperatores qui audeant in provincia, quum praetor adsit, non solum contra voluntatem ejus sed etiam contra fortunas judicare? Verum esto: manifesta res est: nemo est quin audisse se liquido diceret: locupletissimus quisque ac certissimus testis esset: nemo erat Sicilia tota quin sciret decumas esse praetoris; nemo quin audisset id Apronium dictitasse: praeterea conventus honestus Syracusis, multi equites Romani, viri primarii, ex qua copia recuperatores rejici oporteret qui aliter judicare nullo modo possent. Instat Scandilius poscere recuperatores. Tum iste homo innocens qui illam suspicionem levare atque ab se removere cuperet recuperatores dicit se de cohorte sua daturum.

LX. Pro deùm hominumque fidem, quem ego accuso? in quo meam industriam ac diligentiam spectari volo? quid est quod ego dicendo aut cogitando efficere aut assequi debeam? Teneo, teneo, inquam, in mediis vectigalibus populi Romani, in ipsis fructibus provinciae Siciliae furem manifesto avertentem rem frumentariam omnem, pecuniam maximam: teneo, inquam, ita ut negare non possit. Nam quid hic dicet? Sponsio facta est cum cognitore tuo Apronio de fortunis tuis omnibus, ni socium te sibi in decumis esse dictitaret. Exspectant omnes quantae tibi ea res curae sit, quemadmodum hominum existimationi te atque innocentiam tuam probari velis. Hic tu medicum et haruspicem et praeconem tuum recuperatores dabis, aut etiam illum ipsum quem tu in cohorte tua Cassianum judicem habebas, si qua res major esset, Papirium Potamonem, hominem severum ex vetere illa equestri disciplina? Scandilius postulare de conventu recuperatores. Tum iste negat

tantis . . cervicibus] 'with necks strong enough.' The expression occurs again in Lib. 5. c. 42; and Pro Sestio, c. 41.

locupletissimus] This word is sometimes applied to 'testes' and 'cognitores,' as an honourable epithet. Cicero says (Topic. c. 2): "quum lex assiduo vindicem assiduum esse jubeat, locupletem jubet locupleti: locuples enim est assiduus, ut ait Aelius, appellatus ab asse dando." 'Locuples' has accordingly a signification which implies some means or wealth; which is more clearly shown by another passage (Orat. Part. c. 34): "atque etiam si obscuri testes erunt aut tenues, dicendum erit non esse ex fortuna fidem ponderandam, et eos esse cujusque locupletissimos testes qui id de quo agatur facillime scire possint." See also Cic. De Re Pub. ii. 22: "ut suffragia non in multitudinis sed in locupletium potestate essent." Comp. Verr. Lib. 2. c. 55, "locupletissimi cujusque censum extenuarant, tenuissimi auxerant;" and Pro Flacco, c. 17.

qui aliter] means that they could not decide differently from what was commonly reported and known, 'decumas esse praetoris.'—'rejici,' as explained in another place, is here equivalent to 'selected.'

60. *avertentem*] 'Averrentem,' the reading of N, and a bad reading.

cognitore] He calls Apronius the 'cognitor' of Verres, though he was not really his 'cognitor.' But it is a way of saying that Verres was the principal, and Apronius was his agent.

Cassianum judicem] See c. 62.

se de existimatione sua cuiquam nisi suis commissurum. Negotiatores sibi putant esse turpe id forum sibi iniquum ejurare ubi negotientur: praetor provinciam suam sibi totam iniquam ejurat. Impudentiam singularem! Hic postulat se Romae absolvi qui in sua provincia judicavit absolvi se nullo modo posse, qui plus existimet apud lectissimos senatores pecuniam quam apud tres negotiatores metum valere? Scandilius vero negat sese apud Artemidorum recuperatorem verbum esse facturum, et tamen auget atque onerat te bonis conditionibus, si [tu] uti velis: si ex provincia Sicilia tota statuas idoneum judicem aut recuperatorem nullum posse reperiri, postulat abs te ut Romam rem rejicias. Hic enimvero tu exclamas, hominem improbum! qui postulet ibi de tua existimatione judicium fieri, ubi te invidiosum esse intelligat: negas te Romam rejecturum; negas de conventu recuperatores daturum: cohortem tuam proponis. Scandilius rem se totam relicturum dicit et suo tempore esse rediturum. Quid tu ibi tum? quid facis? Scandilium cogis—quid? sponsionem acceptam facere?

iniquum ejurare] The plaintiff proposed a Judex (judicem tulit), and the Magistratus appointed him, if the defendant did not object. If he did object, it was in this form, 'ejuro, iniquus est' (Cic. De Or. ii. 70). The Romans also said 'ejurare iniquum,' 'to reject a judex as a partial man' (Philipp. xii. 7). If the defendant accepted the 'judex,' this was 'sumere judicem.' The 'rejectio,' it is said, applied when the Praetor named a certain number of persons, out of whom each party could reject or challenge a certain number; and the 'judices,' or 'recuperatores,' were named by the Praetor out of those who had not been challenged.

The 'negotiatores,' says Cicero, think that it is a scandalous matter to refuse the jurisdiction of the forum, in which they carry on their business; but Verres refuses even the whole province. The number of 'recuperatores' at a trial, at least in Sicily, seems to have been three at this time.

Hic postulat] V has 'id postulat.' 'Id' is probably intended for 'is,' which Klotz has.

provincia judicarit] Zumpt and Iordan have 'judicarit,' because Lg. 42 has 'judicaret.' V and all the rest 'judicavit,' which is probably the true reading. Zumpt says 'conjunctivum requirit quod sequitur *existimet*;' but that is not so. If our MSS. may be trusted, Cicero uses subjunctives and indicatives in the same sentence, though the meaning of the two is not the same. The distinction is a nice one, easier felt than defined. Zumpt makes no difficulty about 'qui se ipse . . . existimari vult, qui . . . appellatus sit,' at the end of c. 62. In c. 65 we have, 'Atque Metellus, qui vectigalibus prospicit, . . quid assequitur,' &c.; and in c. 59, "Tum iste homo innocens qui illam suspicionem levare . . cuperet."

idoneum judicem] Zumpt inserts 'alium,' from Lg. 42, before 'judicem.' V omits 'alium.' If Verres could not find any 'judices' in Sicily whom he was satisfied with, he was asked to remit or refer the matter to Rome (ut Romam rem rejicias). See Lib. 2. c. 25.

esse intelligat:] 'Intelligat' is Ernesti's emendation for 'intelligebat,' which is confirmed by Lg. 42 φ. V has 'intelligit,' manifestly a false reading, but Klotz takes it.

sponsionem acceptam facere?] 'Acceptam facere,' like 'missos facere' (c. 58) in form. But 'acceptum' or 'accepto facere' also means to acknowledge that a man has received a thing, as in Ulpian (Dig. 46. 4. 7), 'accepta facis decem? ille respondit, facio.' Accordingly Zumpt explains the passage thus: "profiteri se pecuniam, de qua sponsio fuerit, accepisse, itaque omittere quidem causam, vicisse tamen. Qua re hominum expectationem de rebus in judicio audiendis

Impudenter tollis exspectatum existimationis tuae judicium: non facis? Quid ergo? Apronio permittis ut quos velit de cohorte sumat recuperatores? Indignum uni potius ex iniquis sumendi quam utrisque ex aequis rejiciendi fieri potestatem. Neutrum facis eorum. Quid ergo? estne aliquid quod improbius fieri possit? Est. Cogit enim Scandilium quinque illa millia nummum dare atque annumerare Apronio.

clusisset." If Verres had done this, he would have avoided the trial, it is true; but if the money had been paid by Apronius, or acknowledged to be received by Scandilius, this would have been a clear admission that Apronius said what he was charged with saying; and the guilt of Verres would have been as clear as it could have been made by the evidence of Apronius. The meaning of 'sponsionem acceptam facere' cannot be what Zumpt says. See the Excursus on SPONSIONES.

But there is another objection to this interpretation of Zumpt. Cicero says that Verres did not compel Apronius 'sponsionem acceptam facere;' and, by not doing this, he impudently disappointed the expectations of those in court, who were waiting to hear this curious affair. If then Verres had compelled Apronius 'sponsionem acceptam facere,' the expectation would not have been disappointed; the matter would have been heard. Therefore 'sponsionem acceptam facere' is something which, if done, would have been followed by a trial, and would have satisfied people's expectations.

The interpretation of P. Manutius is right, which Forcellini (v. Acceptus) warns us against accepting. "Facere," says Manutius, "pro persequi. Quod, inquit, non facis: in quo tollis exspectatum existimationis tuae judicium; quia scire homines cupiebant quid de tua existimatione decerneretur. Hoc igitur est in quo primum peccas, quod Scandilium non cogis litem persequi: alterum quod Apronio non permittis ut quos velit de tua cohorte recuperatores sumat." The meaning of 'sponsionem facere' is carefully examined by Keller, Semestr. i. p. 30, &c.

The explanation of Zumpt, which must be rejected by virtue of the very form of Cicero's argument, assumes that 'sponsionem' here means the money; and it may be admitted that 'sponsio' can have this meaning. But Cicero has used the word 'sponsio' before in the ordinary sense. Gaius (iv. 93), when he speaks of the 'sponsio,' terms the money the 'summa sponsionis.' But I do not rely on this, for, as already observed, 'sponsio' can be used in the sense of the money, which is the subject of the 'sponsio.'

utrisque] This word makes a difficulty, for it is supposed that it should be 'utrique.' Zumpt says that this is the only passage in Cicero where two persons are called 'utrique' in the plural number. He cites from Livy, xxx. 8, 'utraque cornua;' and xlii. 54, 'utraque oppida;' and some instances from other writers. In Lib. 4. c. 14 there is 'binos . . . utrosque,' where I take 'binos' to mean 'two,' a pair. But in this passage φ and V have 'utrique,' which Iordan has printed.

Cogit enim Scandilium] Klotz has a note on this passage, in which he acts the part of the defender of Verres, and shows his legal skill: "Since Scandilius would not accept the 'recuperatores' from among the Roman citizens, who had come with Verres into the province, whom Verres ('negat se de existumatione sua cuiquam nisi suis commissurum,' and 'cohortem proponis') expressly chose to name, it was quite equitable that he lost his wager, and was compelled to pay to Apronius the amount placed on the hazard. It is true that, with respect to that declaration, Scandilius may not have been so much in the wrong, but, according to strict law, he must lose his cause if he had not confidence enough to have the matter investigated before the 'judices' of Verres." Can any man in his senses suppose that Cicero would state a case against Verres in such terms that the obvious and only conclusion must be that Verres was quite in the right? It makes no matter that this speech was not delivered. Cicero was not so dull as to state a thing which he intended to be for him, in such a way that a modern commentator can declare that the statement is direct against him. Scandilius claimed the appointment of 'recuperatores' from the 'conventus,' in which he may have been right or wrong. Let it be either way. Verres would only appoint from his own 'cohors;' he would not trust his reputation to any other persons

LXI. Quid potuit elegantius facere praetor cupidus existimationis bonae, qui ab se omnem suspicionem propulsare, qui se eripere ex infamia cuperet? Adductus erat in sermonem, invidiam, vituperationem: dictitarat homo improbus atque impurus Apronius socium esse praetorem: venerat res in judicium atque discrimen:

than those about him; not to a single man in all Sicily. We do not know enough probably of the mode of appointing 'recuperatores' to understand the whole matter; but we know that there was a 'rejectio' or challenge allowed of a certain number among those who were proposed. Whether Verres could legally propose his own 'cohors,' I don't know. Perhaps he could legally do this (c. 61, at the end), but it was not the practice of good governors at least. If then the 'praetor' acted according to strict law, he did not act conformably to the notion of right, for the question should have been tried by impartial persons. Scandilius, says Cicero, positively refused to have the matter tried by the 'recuperatores' of Verres. He resisted the authority of the court. Perhaps he was wrong in that. What then? What is the next step? He had in effect refused to exercise his challenge; we may even allow that he refused to have any thing to do with the appointment of the 'recuperatores.' Did that justify Verres in pronouncing against him? Can the German editor prove, that because he refused to acknowledge the 'recuperatores,' he must therefore be condemned by Verres, who, it must be remembered, had nothing to do with the matter beyond the appointment of the 'recuperatores?' Verres ought to have appointed the 'recuperatores,' or allowed them to be named by Apronius; that is, he ought to have appointed the 'recuperatores' in the way which he declared to be the proper way, whatever way that was; and the trial ought to have proceeded before these 'recuperatores.' We are not bound to assume or admit that the 'recuperatores' were knaves; they might have turned out honest men; they might have decided for Scandilius, whether they were honest or dishonest; for who could tell what they would do until they had done it? It was their duty to pronounce the judgment; not the office of Verres. It was the office of Verres to see that the trial proceeded in due form; and he would not let the trial proceed (sponsiones . . ab ipso prohibitas judicari). It did not proceed in due form. Verres delivered judgment, which was not his function. All this is clearly stated or implied in Cicero. The proceeding of Verres was neither equitable nor legal; and the defence of it is altogether absurd.

As authority goes further with some people than reason, I quote the following brief exposition from a learned jurist (Rudorff, Zeitschrift für Geschichtliche Rechtsw. xii. p. 153): "It was well known, by the statements of Apronius himself, that he was in partnership with Verres, and shared with him the unjust gains, for the getting of which Verres had lent him his official authority. Already, under the administration of Verres, this connexion between him and Apronius was talked about. P. Rubrius, and after him Scandilius, had challenged Apronius to a 'sponsio' upon this alleged partnership. Scandilius had compelled him to enter into a 'sponsio,' and Verres had only contrived to save himself from the damage with which he was threatened by this matter being brought to a bearing, by compelling Scandilius, without judgment, and wrongfully, to pay the amount of the 'restipulatio,' instead of appointing a 'judex' or impartial 'recuperatores,' or remitting the case to Rome." Keller also says on the words "'Cogit . . . Apronio,' hoc est, opinor, restipulationis summam Scandilium condemnat."

Cicero says (c. 62), "attuli sponsiones ipso praesente factas de decumarum societate, ab ipso prohibitas judicari;" where 'de societate decumarum,' as in c. 61, means the alleged partnership of Apronius and Verres.

The truth of Cicero's statement is immaterial for the understanding of this passage. He means to tell us that Verres committed a monstrous act of illegality. It is almost inconceivable how some modern critics misunderstand what they read. They are so much occupied with their own notions, which are foreign to the matter, that they are quite unable to understand what their author says. Their object is that which is well described by one of the Delphin editors in his preface: to illustrate themselves first, and then their author.

61. *elegantius*] Compare Divin. c. 17: said ironically here.

potestas erat isti homini integro atque innocenti data ut, in Apronium quum animadvertisset, sese gravissima levaret infamia. Quid excogitat poenae? quid animadversionis in Apronium? Cogit Scandilium Apronio ob singularem improbitatem atque audaciam praedicationemque nefariae societatis HS $\bar{v}$ mercedis ac praemii [nomine] dare. Quid interfuit, homo audacissime, utrum hoc decerneres an id quod Apronius dictitabat tute de te confiterere ac dictitares? quem hominem, si qui pudor in te atque adeo si qui metus fuisset, sine supplicio dimittere non debuisti, hunc abs te sine praemio discedere noluisti. Omnia simul intelligere potestis, judices, ex hoc uno crimine Scandiliano: primum, hoc non esse Romae natum de societate decumarum, non ab accusatore fictum, non, ut solemus interdum in defensionibus dicere, crimen domesticum ac vernaculum, non ex tempore periculi tui constitutum, sed vetus, agitatum jam et te praetore jactatum, et non ab inimicis Romae compositum, sed Romam ex provincia deportatum. Simul illud intelligi potest istius in Apronium studium, Apronii de isto non modo confessio verum etiam commemoratio. Eodem accedit quod hoc quoque intelligere potestis, istum statuisse in provincia sua existimationis suae judicium extra cohortem suam committendum fuisse nemini.

LXII. Ecquis est judex cui non ab initio decumani criminis persuasum sit istum in aratorum bona fortunasque impetum fecisse? Quis hoc non ex eo statim judicavit quod ostendi istum decumas nova lege atque adeo nulla lege contra omnium consuetudinem atque instituta vendidisse? Verum ut istos ego judices tam severos, tam diligentes, tam religiosos non haberem, ecquis est

HS $\bar{v}$] "Vulgo v millia, sed 'millia' in quatuor melioribus non est, proque eo in Paris. A. lineola inducta numero" (Zumpt). Klotz has from V 'HS ΙↃↃ mercedis ac praemi nomine.' It might be supposed from what Cicero says, that this five thousand (HS ΙↃↃ) was a different sum, because he adds 'mercedis ac praemi nomine,' but this appears to be only an oratorical embellishment.

confiterere] The reading of V. Zumpt and Iordan have 'profiterere.'—'hunc abs te:' Maius and Brunnius say that V has 'nunc abs te,' and Halm thinks that 'nunc' is an excellent emendation, if we place a colon before 'nunc.'—The reading 'ex hoc uno crimine' of V seems better than 'uno crimine,' which Zumpt has.

crimen domesticum &c.] This appears to have been a common expression to signify some charge against another got up by a man in his own house, not founded on evidence.

ex . . . deportatum.] The reading of V. Zumpt has 'de' and 'apportatum,' from Lg. 42. The MSS. generally have 'exportatum.' There is a great variety in the readings wherever 'asportare,' 'deportare,' 'exportare,' 'apportare,' come in question. One does not always see why one word is preferable to the other. 'Deportatum' seems the right word here, notwithstanding Zumpt's explanation of the difference between 'deportatum' and 'exportatum.'

provincia sua] 'Sua' is from V. Zumpt omits it, but remarks in the Appendix, 'Vat. ut vulgo fit addit *sua*.' Lg. 42 omits 'sua.'

62. *non haberem,*] 'Non habeam,' Zumpt and Iordan from Lg. 42 ϕ et V

ex injuriarum magnitudine, improbitate decretorum, judiciorum iniquitate, qui hoc non jamdudum statuerit ac judicarit? Etiam sane sit aliquis dissolutior in judicando, legum, officii, rei publicae, sociorum atque amicorum negligentior; quid, is possitne de istius improbitate dubitare, quum tanta lucra facta, tam iniquas pactiones vi et metu expressas cognoverit, [quum] tanta praemia civitates vi et imperio, virgarum ac mortis metu, non modo Apronio atque ejus similibus verum etiam Venereis servis dare coactas? Quod si quis sociorum incommodis minus commovetur; si quem aratorum fugae, calamitates, exsilia, suspendia denique non permovent; non possum dubitare quin is tamen, quum vastatam Siciliam, relictos agros, ex civitatum literis et epistola L. Metelli cognoverit, statuat fieri non posse ut de isto non severissime judicetur. Erit aliquis etiam qui haec omnia dissimulare ac negligere possit. Attuli sponsiones ipso praesente factas de decumarum societate, ab ipso prohibitas judicari: quid est quod possit quisquam manifestius hoc desiderare? Non dubito quin vobis satisfecerim, judices; verumtamen progrediar longius, non mehercule quo vobis magis hoc persuadeatur quam jam persuasum esse confido, sed ut ille aliquando impudentiae suae finem faciat, aliquando desinat ea se putare [posse] emere, quae ipse semper habuit venalia, fidem, jusjurandum, veritatem, officium, religionem, desinant amici ejus ea dictitare, quae detrimento, maculae, invidiae, infamiae nobis omnibus esse possint. At qui amici! O miserum atque invidiosum offensumque paucorum culpa atque indignitate ordinem senatorium! Albam Aemilium sedentem in faucibus macelli loqui palam vicisse Verrem, emptos habere

(Br.). Cicero generally says 'hos judices.'

similibus] V 'militibus,' which I only note to prove that no MS. can always be followed.

Quod si quis] V has 'qui' for 'quis.' There is no consistency in these matters. Zumpt writes 'Quodsi quis,' which is a most vicious way of writing, as if 'si' were to be attached to 'quod;' whereas there is an emphasis on 'si.' Klotz writes 'Quod si qui sociorum,' &c.

Erit aliquis] This is equivalent to a supposition: 'Suppose there shall still be some one who can disregard and pay no attention to all these facts.' This form is more common with the second than the first future. To this supposed case, Cicero replies, 'I have brought the Sponsiones.' He has evidence to which even such a careless person, as he supposes, must attend. Iordan unnecessarily places a ? after 'possit.'

[posse] emere,] "'*posse emere*' Victorius et sqq.: '*emere*' codices noti. Vide tamen, ne codicum scriptura aliquam defensionem habeat ex simili locutione '*sperare mihi videor*' = sperare posse mihi videor, de qua cf. Zumpt. ad Act. i. c. 17 (quod sperare mihi videor)." Seyffert ad Lael. § 15 (Iordan).

offensumque] 'O wretched senatorian order, that has incurred all this odium and disgrace through the fault and unworthiness of a few.' (Comp. Pro Cluentio, c. 58.) The whole order is represented as stumbling and floundering through the misconduct of some of its members. Compare Divin. c. 22, "si tantulum offensum titubatumque sit."

Albam Aemilium] P. Manutius collects from the preceding words that he was a senator. He certainly bore a great name.

in faucibus macelli] Cicero (Pro P.

judices, alium HS cccc millibus, alium HS D, quem minimo, ccc. Atque ei quum responsum esset fieri non posse, multos testes esse dicturos, me praeterea causae non defuturum: Licet hercle, inquit, omnes omnia dicant: in illo, nisi ita res manifesta erit allata ut responderi nihil possit, vicimus.—Bene agis, Alba: ad tuam veniam conditionem. Nihil putas valere in judiciis conjecturam, nihil suspicionem, nihil ante actae vitae existimationem, nihil bonorum virorum testimonia, nihil civitatum auctoritates ac literas: res manifestas quaeris. Non quaero judices Cassianos; veterem judiciorum severitatem non requiro; vestram in hac re fidem, dignitatem, religionem in judicando non imploro: Albam habebo judicem, eum hominem, qui se ipse scurram improbissimum existimari

Quintio, c. 6) has the same expression: "tum Naevius pueros circum amicos dimittit: ipse suos necessarios ab atriis Liciniis et a faucibus macelli corrogat." Heindorf, in his notes on the line of Horace, "Cum scurris fartor, cum Velabro omne Macellum" (2 Sat. iii. 229), quotes Varro (De L. L. v. 147). Varro, after speaking of the 'forum boarium, olitorium,' and others, adds, "haec omnia posteaquam contracta in unum locum quae ad victum pertinebant, et aedificatus locus, appellatum Macellum." Here all kinds of 'obsonia,' fish and flesh, were sold. (Comp. Plaut. Aulul. ii. 8. 3, 'Venio ad Macellum: rogito pisces. Indicant caros,' &c.) We may suppose then that Aemilius was fond of good living, and a constant visitor to the Macellum, to see how prices were going, and what dainties were in the market. Juvenal says, Sat. xi. 9:

"Multos porro vides quos saepe elusus ad ipsum
Creditor introitum solet expectare macelli."

Heinrich (Juvenal, v. 94) has a good note on Macellum. This great market was surrounded by a wall (maceria), and hence the name 'macellum.' Here all kinds of eatables were sold—the raw material, as well as things prepared by the Restaurateurs. It was a place where a man might dine (Ter. Eunuch. ii. 2. 25; Sueton. Caesar, c. 26). The word is accordingly used as a general name for the provision market, as in Suetonius (Tib. c. 34), "annonamque macelli senatus arbitrio quotannis temperandam;" the prices of provisions in the Macellum were to be regulated. There were Macella in other places besides Rome. Cicero applies the term 'fauces' to places situated in some narrow space, as to Corinth, on the isthmus (Forcellini, v. Fauces). The word 'faucibus' seems to refer to the position of this Macellum between higher grounds. Martial (ii. 17, ed. Schneid.) says:

"Tonstrix Suburae faucibus sedet primis."

The old Subura was in such a spot. Becker, Handbuch, &c., i. 521; and p. 543, on the Macellum.

A bronze medal of Nero contains on the reverse the legend MAC AVG placed above a building, the front of which has one range of pillars resting on another range. Agostini, Dialoghi, &c., p. 136, has some remarks on the Mac. Aug. He observes that MAC is sometimes read MAG, meaning the Domus Aurea Neronis. But this is a very improbable interpretation.

Licet &c.] Zumpt reads 'Licet hercle, inquit, omnes omnia dicant in illum: nisi' &c. Orelli has the same. Hotmann altered 'in illo' into 'in illum,' from an old MS., as he says. All Zumpt's MSS., and the old editions, have 'in illo;' Lg. 42 has only 'illo.' I have kept the old reading, which Klotz and Iordan have.

Bene agis,] 'Bene ais' Orelli; but the best MSS. have 'agis.' 'Ais' is not so likely to have been changed into 'agis,' as 'agis' into 'ais.'—'ante actae:' Zumpt omits 'ante,' on the authority of Lg. 42 only.

judices Cassianos;] Act. i. c. 10, "L. Cassius ex familia quum ad ceteras res tum ad judicandum severissima." Pro Sex. Roscio Amer. c. 30, "L. Cassius ille quem populus Romanus verissimum et sapientissimum judicem putabat."

scurram] Heindorf, in his notes on Horace (1 Sat. v. 52), observes—'scur-

vult, qui a scurris semper potius gladiator quam scurra appellatus *sit*; afferam rem ejusmodi in decumis ut Alba fateatur istum in re frumentaria et in bonis aratorum aperte palamque esse praedatum.

LXIII. Decumas agri Leontini magno dicis te vendidisse. Ostendi jam illud initio, non existimandum magno vendidisse eum qui verbo decumas vendiderit, re et conditione et lege et edicto et licentia decumanorum decumas aratoribus nullas reliquas fecerit. Etiam illud ostendi, vendidisse alios magno decumas agri Leontini ceterorumque agrorum, et lege Hieronica vendidisse, et pluris etiam quam te vendidisse, nec aratorem quemquam esse questum; nec enim fuit quod quisquam queri posset quum lege aequissime scripta venderent, neque illud unquam aratoris interfuit quanti decumae venirent. Non enim ita est ut, si magno venierint, plus arator debeat; si parvo, minus: ut frumenta nata sunt, ita decumae veneunt: aratoris autem interest ita se frumenta habere ut decumae quam plurimo venire possint: dum arator ne plus decumam det, expedit ei decumam esse quam maximam. Verum hoc, ut opinor, esse vis caput defensionis tuae, magno te decumas vendidisse,

rae' were persons who, after an old Italian fashion, made it a profession to bandy jokes and sarcasms against one another at the tables of their rich fellow-citizens. A personage of exactly the same kind is the γελωτοποιὸς Philippus, who appears in this character in the Symposium of Xenophon. Yet the 'scurrae' originally may have been merely poor Roman citizens, without any landed property (Plaut. Trinum. i. 2. 165, 'urbani assidui cives quos scurras vocant'), who attached themselves to richer people, and were maintained by them.—Horace, in the Satire above referred to, gives a sample of the 'scurrilitas' of a 'scurra.' This Alba was a very prince of 'scurrae.' His fellows called him a 'gladiator.' He was a man with whom you would not readily engage in a war of words. Finally, he patronized Verres in his difficulties. Probably he had eaten some of his dinners.

appellatus sit;] 'appellatus est' Iordan, following Halm; 'appellatus sit' codd. I see no reason why it should be 'sit;' nor yet any reason why all the MSS. should have changed 'est' into 'sit.'

63. *dicis te*] From Lg. 42 φ. Orelli has 'dicit se.'

scripta venderent,] I have followed Iordan in taking 'venderent' instead of the former reading 'venirent.' There is a reading 'viderent,' which is evidently false.

plus decumam] 'Plus decuma' Orelli. Lg. 42 has 'decumam.' Compare 'minus annum' Lib. 2. c. 49, note.

decumas vendidisse, agri vero Leontini] After 'vendidisse' Zumpt has 'atque aliorum quidem agrorum pro portione magno decumas vendidisse.' These words are in the second edition of Lambinus, and Zumpt has adopted them, and also Iordan. Lambinus says that he has inserted them from an old MS. But he is evidently unworthy of credit, for he said in his first edition that the passage was mutilated, and that he had restored it according to the authority of an old MS.; and yet the first edition does not contain these words. In his second edition he makes the same remark about the mutilated state of the passage, and about the authority of this old MS., and then says that these words have been accidentally omitted by a copyist, who passed from one 'vendidisse' to the other, without noticing what lay between.' His carelessness, as Zumpt observes, makes it impossible to know whether these words were in a MS. or not. They are hardly his own, I think. Iordan now says that these words are in Lg. 45 F, but omitted in the other MSS. There seems indeed to be something wanted, for the words 'agri

agri vero Leontini qui plurimum efficit tritici modium CCXVI millibus. Si doceo pluris aliquanto potuisse vendere neque iis voluisse te addicere qui contra Apronium licerentur, et Apronio multo minoris quam aliis potueris vendere tradidisse, si hoc doceo, poteritne te ipse Alba, tuus antiquissimus non solum amicus verum etiam amator, absolvere?

LXIV. Dico equitem Romanum, hominem in primis honestum, Q. Minucium cum sui similibus ad decumas agri Leontini tritici modium non mille, non duo, non tria millia, sed ad unas unius agri decumas tritici modium triginta voluisse addere; ei potestatem emendi non esse factam ne res abiret ab Apronio. Negare hoc, nisi forte negare omnia constituisti, nullo modo potes: palam res gesta est, maximo conventu, Syracusis: testis est tota provincia propterea quod undique ad emendas decumas solent eo convenire. Quod sive fateris sive convinceris, quot et quam manifestis in rebus teneare non vides? Primum tuam rem illam et praedam fuisse: nam, ni ita esset, cur tu Apronium malebas, quem omnes tuum procuratorem [esse] in decumis, tuum negotium agere loquebantur, quam Minucium decumas agri Leontini sumere? Deinde immensum atque infinitum lucrum esse factum: nam si $\overline{\text{XXX}}$ tu commotus non esses, certe hoc idem lucri Minucius Apronio libenter dedisset, si ille accipere voluisset. Quantam igitur illi spem praedae propositam arbitramur fuisse, qui tantum praesens lucrum nulla opera insumpta contempserit atque despexerit? deinde ipse Minucius nunquam tanti habere voluisset, si decumas tu lege Hieronica venderes; sed quia tuis novis edictis et iniquissimis institutis plus aliquanto se quam decumas ablaturum videbat, idcirco longius progressus est. At Apronio semper plus etiam multo abs te permissum est quam quod edixeras. Quantum igitur quaestum puta-

vero Leontini' have a tacit reference to other 'agri.' We might read, in Cicero's own words above, 'decumas vendidisse ceterorum agrorum, agri vero Leontini;' but if we look back only a few lines, to the words 'vendidisse alios magno decumas agri Leontini ceterorumque agrorum,' it will appear that perhaps nothing has been omitted.

As to the words 'pro portione,' Zumpt refers to a like use in Lib. 4. c. 21; Lib. 5. c. 21.

64. *modium triginta*] 'Modium $\overline{\text{XXX}}$' Klotz. The same thing is meant by the text, which is that of Lg. 42 N.

manifestis in rebus] Lg. 42 F omit 'in.' Zumpt says, "*teneri*, quum significat *convictum* esse, peccatum addita praepositione *in* secum habet." He refers to Lib. 1. c. 1, 'in rebus turpissimis,' &c.; Lib. 2. c. 59, 'quum in manifestissimo furto teneare;' and to some other passages. But in Lib. 3. c. 89, he has 'cum manifestis flagitiis tenebitur,' which he explains thus, "cum ita tenebitur ut flagitia ejus manifesta sint." I have no belief in many of these small distinctions.

tuum procuratorem] 'Tuum procurare in decumis negotium loquebantur;' the common reading and that of Orelli. The reading 'tuum procuratorem esse in decumis, tuum negotium agere' is from Lg. 42 φ: but Lg. 42 omits '*esse*.' I think that the old reading is quite as good as the new one.

mus factum esse per eum cui quidvis licitum sit, quum tantum lucri voluerit addere is cui, si decumas emisset, idem non liceret? Postremo illa quidem certe tibi praecisa est defensio, in qua tu semper omnia tua furta atque flagitia latere posse arbitratus es, magno te decumas vendidisse, plebi Romanae consuluisse, annonae prospexisse. Non potest hoc dicere is qui negare non potest se unius agri decumas xxx millibus modium minoris quam potuerit vendidisse; ut—etiam si tibi hoc concedam, Minucio te ideo non tradidisse quod jam addixisses Apronio, (aiunt enim te ita dictitare, quod ego exspecto cupioque te ita illud defendere) verum ut ita sit,—tamen non potes hoc quasi praeclarum aliquid praedicare, magno te decumas vendidisse, quum fuisse fateare qui multo pluris voluerint emere.

LXV. Tenetur igitur jam, judices, et manifesto tenetur avaritia, cupiditas hominis, scelus, improbitas, audacia. Quid si haec quae dico ipsius amici defensoresque judicarunt? quid vultis amplius? Adventu L. Metelli praetoris, quum omnes ejus comites iste sibi

annonae] 'Annona,' a word formed from 'annus,' is the current year's produce, the general measure of plenty or scarcity; for, if the current year fails in any country, there is never so large a supply on hand as to make up the deficiency and prevent prices rising. 'Annona' often occurs in these orations and in the Latin writers in various senses, all of which are easily connected with the primary sense. In Lib. 3. c. 98, it has its common sense of 'produce,' or 'the year's produce:' "Annona porro pretium nisi in calamitate fructuum non habet." It is sometimes used for the price of the necessaries of life, and particularly grain, as in the passage of Suetonius referred to (c. 62).

vendidisse; ut—etiam si] I set no great value on pointing; but if it has a use, it should help to the meaning and not obstruct the discovery of it. Zumpt and Klotz may understand this as I do; but if I pointed it as they have done, most English readers would misunderstand it. The pointing which I have made will show that I connect 'etiam si' and 'tamen,' as in Lib. 1. c. 38, "quae omnia etiamsi . . . per istum tamen," &c. The first 'ut' is resumed in 'verum ita ut sit,' 'but though it be so.'

Klotz here steps in again, like another Alba Aemilius, to help his friend Verres. In reference to the words 'ut—etiam si—addixisses Apronio,' he observes, that the main blow from his adversary fails through the effect of these words, and yet the orator contrived to give the matter such a turn, that a false appearance, even though this admission is made, might easily fall on Verres if a hearer was rather inattentive.—This is something like the meaning of what he says; but it is hard to express. He adds, "one thing only is true, that on this occasion some one was willing to offer more." This is a complete falsification of the text; and a reader can scarcely be so inattentive as to let this false appearance deceive him. Cicero says that Verres sold the 'decumae' for less by xxx than he could have done. He does not admit that the 'decumae' had been 'knocked down' (addictae) to Apronius when this offer was made; and he adds, that even if he should admit that they had been adjudicated to Apronius, Verres cannot deny that an offer was made (palam res gesta est) to give xxx more than Apronius had given. And that would be a good proof that Verres had acted like a knave.

praedicare,] Naugerius. The MSS. have 'praedicere,' 'dicere,' and 'praestare.'—'voluerint:' 'voluerit' Lg. 42, Zumpt, Iordan.

65. *L. Metelli*] This was the Praetor at Rome in B.C. 71, who gave the 'judicium' in the action of M. Tullius. See the speech for M. Tullius, § 39, Vol. ii.

suo illo panchresto medicamento amicos reddidisset, aditum est ad Metellum: eductus est Apronius: eduxit vir primarius C. Gallus senator: postulavit ab L. Metello ut ex edicto suo judicium daret in Apronium, QVOD PER VIM ET METVM ABSTVLISSET, quam formulam Octavianam et Romae Metellus habuerat et habebat in provincia. Non impetrat, quum hoc diceret Metellus, praejudicium se de capite C. Verris per hoc judicium nolle fieri. Tota Metelli cohors hominum non ingratorum aderat Apronio. C. Gallus, homo vestri ordinis, a suo familiarissimo L. Metello judicium ex edicto non potest impetrare. Non reprehendo Metellum: pepercit homini amico, et, quemadmodum ipsum dicere audivi, necessario: non reprehendo, inquam, Metellum; sed hoc miror, quomodo de quo homine praejudicium noluerit fieri per recuperatores, de hoc ipse non modo praejudicarit, verum gravissime ac vehementissime judicarit. Primum enim, si Apronium absolutum iri putaret, nihil erat quod ullum praejudicium vereretur: deinde, si condemnato Apronio conjunctam cum eo Verris causam omnes erant existimaturi, Metellus quidem certe jam hoc judicabat eorum rem causamque esse conjunctam, qui statueret Apronio condemnato de isto praejudicium futurum: et simul una res utrique rei est argumento et aratores vi et metu coactos Apronio multo plus quam debuerint dedisse, et Apronium istius rem suo nomine egisse, quum L. Metellus statuerit non posse Apronium condemnari quin simul de istius scelere atque improbitate judicaretur.

panchresto] 'With his panacea' as we say sometimes, his universal drug, his gold. Cicero goes to the apothecary sometimes for his metaphors, or to the paint-box, as in Ad Att. i. 14: "Totum hunc locum quem ego varie meis orationibus, quarum tu Aristarchus es, soleo pingere, de flamma, de ferro—nosti illas ληκύθους—valde graviter pertexuit."

ET METVM] The old reading is 'aut metum,' which Iordan retains. Yet V has 'et metum,' which Halm justly pronounces to be the true word. The legal expression is 'vis et metus,' or 'vi metusve causa' (Dig. 4. 2. 1). See Excursus vii.

formulam Octavianam] See Excursus vii.

praejudicium se] Zumpt and Iordan have 'praejudicium a se.' Zumpt observes, "abest praepositio a MSS. praeter Nannianum et Lag. 42 omnibus;" and he seems to think that the preposition is better omitted, as to which there can be no doubt. See the note Divin. c. 4, on 'praejudicium.'

vestri ordinis,] The reading of V and of the MSS., except Lg. 42 N, which have 'nostri ordinis.' It is a matter of indifference; but it seems more appropriate for Cicero to address the 'judices' as senators, than to include himself in the 'ordo.'

absolutum iri] This so-called passive future is really a form which does not differ from 'Cur te is perditum' (Ter. Andr. i. 1. 107). The word 'absolutum' (a supine) corresponds to 'perditum,' and depends on the 'iri,' which is used impersonally, as it is termed: that is, the whole phrase means, "if he thought that the 'recuperatores' were going to acquit Apronius."

qui statueret] Zumpt observes "recte Lag. 42 *statueret*, et miror Ernestium in ejusmodi rebus acutissimum vulg. *statuerit* tulisse, cum praecesserit *judicabat*, non *judicarit*." V has 'statuerat.' Iordan has at the beginning of the sentence 'si . . putabat.' V has 'putabant.'

LXVI. Venio nunc ad epistolam Timarchidi, liberti istius et accensi, de qua quum dixero totum hoc crimen decumanum peroraro. Haec epistola est, judices, quam nos Syracusis in aedibus Apronii, quum literas conquireremus, invenimus. Missa est, ut ipsa significat, ex itinere, quum Verres jam de provincia decessisset, Timarchidi manu scripta. Recita epistolam. 'Timarchides Verris accensus Apronio salutem dicit.' Jam hoc quidem non reprehendo quod adscribit 'accensus:' cur enim sibi hoc scribae soli sumant?—L. Papirius scriba.—Volo ego hoc esse commune accensorum, lictorum, viatorum. 'Fac diligentiam adhibeas quod ad praetoris existimationem attinet.' Commendat Apronio Verrem, et hortatur ut inimicis ejus resistat. Bono praesidio munitur existimatio tua, si quidem in Apronii constituitur diligentia atque auctoritate. 'Habes virtutem, [atque] eloquentiam.' Quam copiose laudatur Apronius a Timarchide! quam magnifice! Cui ego illum non putem placere oportere qui tanto opere Timarchidi probatus sit? 'Habes sumptum unde facias.' Necesse est quod redundarit de vestro frumentario quaestu ad illum potissimum per quem agebatis defluxisse. 'Scribas, apparitores recentes arripe: cum L. Volteio, qui plurimum potest, caede, concide.' Videte quam valde malitiae suae confidat Timarchides qui etiam Apronio improbitatis praecepta det. Jam hoc 'caede, concide;' nonne

66. *Timarchidi,*] "Timarchidis codd. praeter φ, in quo est Timarchidi" (Iordan). Cicero may have written either indifferently. Klotz has 'perorabo,' which is the reading of the MSS., except Lg. 42 N. Cicero says, as Zumpt observes, that when he shall have spoken about this letter, he will have finished with this part of the subject; and it is so, for he passes to another part of his subject without a 'peroratio,' which 'perorabo' promises.

ex itinere,] 'on the road,' as in Caesar, B. G. ii. 6: "id ex itinere magno impetu Belgae oppugnare coeperunt." The expression is simple enough in the Latin language, which uses prepositions very significantly and clearly. Cicero says of himself (Topica 1), in addressing Trebatius: "itaque haec . . . in ipsa navigatione conscripsi tibique ex itinere misi."

quod adscribit] 'quom scribat' V, Klotz; 'quod adscripsit' Orelli; the common reading—'scribae soli assumant,' Zumpt and Iordan from Lg. 42. V has 'sumant.' I suppose either will do. Cicero says (Divin. c. 4), 'verum id mihi non sumo.' Klotz omits the words 'Apronio salutem dicit.'

Cicero is ridiculing the addition of his title 'accensus.' He then says, 'Why should Scribae alone assume to add their title?' for instance, 'L. Papirius' might add 'scriba' if he were addressing any one: he might say 'L. Papirius Scriba.' This is said in derision of L. Papirius Potamo, that upright man who is mentioned in c. 60. It does not appear that any letter of Papirius of this kind had been produced; and the words 'L. Papirius scriba' are perhaps somewhat difficult to explain. Zumpt writes '*L. Papirius scriba!* volo ego,' &c., where the (!), I suppose, is significant. But Zumpt's italics and the capitals of Klotz and Iordan make the words part of the letter of Timarchides. If the words are genuine, they seem to be the words of Cicero.

Volo ego hoc] Cicero says, 'I would have all these important functionaries sign their title of office,' even a 'lictor,' and a 'viator.'

quod redundarit] 'si quid redundarit' Iordan. V has 'si quit redundarit.'

caede, concide;] 'In conjunction with

vobis verba domo patroni depromere videtur ad omne genus nequitiae accommodata? 'Volo, mi frater, fraterculo tuo credas'— consorti quidem in lucris atque furtis, gemino et simillimo nequitia, improbitate, audacia. 'In cohorte carus haberis.' Quid est hoc 'in cohorte?' quo pertinet? Apronium doces? quid, in vestram cohortem te monitore an sua sponte pervenerat? 'Quod cuique opus est oppone.' Qua impudentia putatis [eum] in dominatione fuisse qui in fuga tam improbus sit? ait omnia pecunia effici posse; dare, profundere oportere, si velis vincere. Non hoc mihi tam molestum est Apronio suadere Timarchidem, quam quod hoc idem patrono suo praecipit. 'Te postulante omnes vincere solent.' Verre quidem praetore, non Sacerdote, non Peducaeo, non hoc ipso Metello. LXVII. 'Scis Metellum sapientem esse.' Hoc vero ferri jam non potest, irrideri viri optimi L. Metelli ingenium et contemni ac despici a fugitivo Timarchide. 'Si Volteium habebis, omnia ludibundus conficies.' Hic vehementer errat Timarchides qui aut Volteium corrumpi pecunia putet posse aut Metellum unius arbitratu gerere praeturam, sed errat conjectura domestica: quia multos et per se et per alios multa [ludibundos] libidinosa apud Verrem effecisse vidit, ad omnes eosdem patere

L. Volteius, who is all-powerful, cut and slash away:' expressions derived from the gladiatorial fights, says Klotz, when a successful gladiator was encouraged to cut down his adversary. It may be so. He gives no proof, and I know none. Timarchides means that Apronius must lay about him, as we say, and vigorously. "De obsceno sensu, qui inest in verbis *caedere*, *concidere*, cf. quae laudat Gruterus et Forcellinus in lexico: sed hoc tamen loco gladiatorium potius est" (Zumpt). We will hope so.

carus haberis.] From V. Zumpt and Iordan have 'carus habebere.'

oppone.] Explained by Zumpt to mean in this passage 'obtendere, ante oculos ponere (vorhalten), ut aliquid consequare, non ut impedias.' 'Hold out to every man the inducement that will win him.' Zumpt refers to c. 57, "quum decumani .. tuum scelus ac nomen opponerent." '*Appone* cod. Hot. edd. vett.' Orelli remarks that this 'verbum tricliniare' is suited to the genius and style of Timarchides, and that not being understood, it was altered to 'oppone.' But V has 'oppone.'—Klotz has 'quod cuique opus sit, oppone,'

67. *Scis Metellum &c.*] Cicero puts his own interpretation on these words; but it does not follow that it is the true interpretation. Timarchides, according to Cicero, was speaking ironically: he did not think Metellus very clever. Zumpt, in explaining 'et contemni,' which words are not in Lg. 42, supposes that these rascals were laughing at Metellus for devoting himself to some branch of Greek learning rather than to the business of his office. This is far-fetched.

ludibundus] 'As easy as play,' with no trouble. Comp. Lib. 5. c. 70: "ut ad istos honores pervenirent, ad quos vos per ludum et negligentiam pervenistis;" and Ad Div. xvi. 9: "Inde austro lenissimo, coelo sereno, nocte illa et die postero in Italiam ad Hydruntum ludibundi pervenimus:" the voyage was easy.

libidinosa] From V. The reading of the other MSS. is 'libidinose,' which Zumpt and Iordan place thus [libidinose] in their text. V omits 'ludibundos,' and as the word 'ludibundos' can be got rid of on good authority, it will be an improvement to strike it out. It occurs shortly after in the right place. The words 'domestica conjectura' will perhaps hardly make a difficulty. Cicero says, 'Herein Timarchides is greatly mistaken, &c.; but he is mistaken in forming this opinion from his

aditus arbitratur. Facilius vos efficiebatis ludibundi quae volebatis a Verre, quod multa ejus ludorum genera noratis. 'Inculcatum est Metello et Volteio te aratores evertisse.' Quis istuc Apronio attribuebat, quum aratorem aliquem everterat? aut Timarchidi quum ob judicandum aut decernendum aut imperandum aliquid aut remittendum pecuniam acceperat? aut Sextio lictori quum aliquem innocentem securi percusserat? Nemo: omnes enim ei tunc attribuebant quem nunc condemnari volunt. 'Obtuderunt aures te socium praetoris fuisse.' Vides hoc quam clarum sit et fuerit, quum etiam Timarchides hoc metuat. Concedesne hoc crimen in te nos non confingere sed jampridem ad crimen aliquam defensionem libertum quaerere? Libertus et accensus tuus, et tibi ac liberis tuis omnibus in rebus conjunctus ac proximus, ad Apronium scribit, vulgo esse ab omnibus ita demonstratum Metello, tibi Apronium in decumis socium fuisse. 'Fac sciat improbitatem aratorum: ipsi sudabunt, si dii volent.' Quid istuc, per deos immortales, aut qua de causa excitatum esse dicamus in aratores tam infestum odium atque tantum? quantam injuriam fecerunt Verri aratores ut eos etiam libertus et accensus ejus tam irato animo ac literis insequatur?

LXVIII. Neque ego hujus fugitivi vobis, judices, epistolam recitassem, nisi ut ex ea totius familiae praecepta et instituta et disciplinam cognosceretis. Videtis ut moneat Apronium quibus rebus ac muneribus se insinuet in familiaritatem Metelli, Volteium corrumpat, scribas accensumque pretio deleniat: ea praecipit quae vidit; ea monet alienum hominem quae domi didicit ipse: verum in hoc errat uno quod existimat easdem vias ad omnium familiaritates esse munitas. Quamquam merito sum iratus Metello, tamen haec

experience in the household of Verres.' Compare c. 68, 'verum in hoc errat uno quod,' &c.

Obtuderunt aures] 'Obtuderunt ejus aures' Zumpt and Iordan; but V omits 'ejus.'—'Videsne hoc' Zumpt, Iordan. 'Vides hoc' V φ.

Concedesne . . confingere] From V.

si dii volent.] V has 'si dolunt,' which means probably 'si di volunt,' which Klotz and Iordan have.—'Quod istuc' Zumpt, Iordan.

68. *nisi ut ex ea*] "Vulgo *nisi ut ex ea* (Lag. 42, *nisi uti ex ea*) quod miror adhuc toleratum esse. Neque enim constat vel sententia vel constructio verborum, nisi aut *recitari* corrigas aut *ut* tollas" (Zumpt: who omits 'ut'). V has '*si ut* superscr. *ni*.' But the 'ut' seems to be necessary for the meaning; and I do not see the force of Zumpt's note.

se insinuet] 'Se' is from Lg. 42 N; though there are passages in Cicero, which Zumpt refers to, which show that 'insinuare' is used absolutely. See Phil. v. c. 8.

vias . . munitas.] 'that the same roads are made to the intimacy of all persons.' 'Munire' is a road-making word, and the proper word for this purpose, as in the inscription which records the construction of the military road through the Alps, planned by Drusus, and made by the Emperor Claudius his son: "viam Claudiam Augustam quam Drusus pater Alpibus bello patefactis derivavit munit." (Cited

quae vera sunt dicam. Apronius ipsum Metellum non pretio ut Verrem, non convivio, non muliere, non sermone impuro atque improbo posset corrumpere, quibus rebus non sensim atque moderate ad istius amicitiam adrepserat, sed brevi tempore totum hominem totamque ejus praeturam possederat. Cohortem autem Metelli quam vocat, quid erat quod corrumperet, ex qua recuperatores in aratorem nulli dabantur? Nam quod scribit 'Metelli filium puerum esse,' vehementer errat: non enim ad omnes praetorum filios iidem aditus sunt. O Timarchide, Metelli est filius in provincia, non puer, sed adolescens bonus ac pudens, dignus illo loco ac nomine. Vester iste puer praetextatus in provincia quemadmodum fuisset non dicerem, si pueri esse illam culpam ac non patris existimarem. Tune, quum te ac tuam vitam nosses, in Siciliam tecum grandem praetextatum filium ducebas ut, etiamsi natura puerum a paternis vitiis atque a generis similitudine abduceret, consuetudo tamen eum et disciplina degenerare non sineret? Fac enim fuisse in eo C. Laelii aut M. Catonis materiem atque indolem, quid ex eo boni sperari atque effici potest qui in patris luxurie sic vixerit ut nullum unquam pudicum neque sobrium convivium viderit? qui in epulis quotidianis adulta aetate per triennium inter impudicas mulieres et intemperantes viros versatus sit? nihil unquam audierit a patre quo pudentior aut melior esset? nihil unquam patrem facere viderit, quod quum imitatus esset, non, id quod turpissimum est, patris similis putaretur? LXIX. Quibus in rebus non solum filio, Verres, sed etiam rei publicae fecisti injuriam. Susceperas enim liberos non solum tibi sed etiam patriae, qui non modo tibi voluptati sed etiam qui aliquando usui rei publicae possent esse. Eos instituere atque erudire ad majorum instituta atque civitatis disciplinam, non ad tua flagitia neque ad

by Orelli, Horace, Carm. iv. 4.) Comp. Pro S. Rosc. Amer. c. 48; Pro Fonteio, c. 8; Pro Murena, c. 10.

Vester iste puer] The reading of Lg. 42, instead of 'vester ille,' &c.

C. Laelii] This is the C. Laelius, the principal speaker in the treatise De Amicitia. Hotmann, by an odd blunder, supposes that M. Cato is Cato of Utica; but it is, as Manutius says, Cato the Censor. The word 'materiem' was suspected by Lambinus, who says, "quid si legamus *naturam atque indolem?*" but 'materiem' appears to be the reading of all the MSS. 'Materies' is 'stuff' generally, often 'timber.' As Cicero says, Pro Caelio, "si quis hoc robore animi atque hac indole virtutis &c. fuit;" so he might join together 'materies et indoles,' as it seems.

patris similis] The reading of the better MSS. The others have 'patri similis.' The genitive seems to express more of the complete likeness,—'a copy of his father,' as we might say; the other form, 'patri similis,' expressing merely the general external resemblance. See Lib. 5. c. 12. In the next chapter is 'mei similis,' and 'Verris similis;' where Orelli has the common reading, 'Verri similis,' and it may be the right reading.

69. *atque civitatis*] 'ad civitatis' Lg. 42, Iordan.

tuas turpitudines debuisti. Esset ex inerti et improbo et impuro parente navus et pudens et probus filius, haberet aliquid res publica abs te muneris. Nunc pro te Verrem substituisti alterum civitati, nisi forte hoc deteriorem, si fieri potest, quod tu ejusmodi evasisti non in hominis luxuriosi sed tantum in furis atque divisoris disciplina educatus. Quid isto fore festivius arbitramur, si est tuus natura filius, consuetudine discipulus, voluntate similis? Quem ego, judices, quamvis bonum fortemque facile paterer evadere; non enim me inimicitiae commovent, si quae mihi cum isto futurae sunt; nam si in omnibus rebus innocens fuero meique similis, quid mihi istius inimicitiae nocebunt? sin aliqua in re Verris similis fuero, non magis mihi deerit inimicus quam Verri defuit. Etenim, judices, ejusmodi res publica debet esse et erit veritate judiciorum constituta, ut inimicus neque deesse nocenti possit neque obesse innocenti. Quapropter nulla res est quamobrem ego istum nolim ex paternis probris ac vitiis emergere: id quod tametsi isti difficile est, tamen haud scio an fieri possit: praesertim si, ut nunc fit, custodes amicorum cum sectabuntur,

Esset . . haberet] 'If from a lazy and an unprincipled and a filthy father there had sprung an active, and modest, and honest son, the state would have had some service from you.' The form 'esset' in the conditional expression without 'si,' is not common.

furis atque divisoris] A plain-spoken allusion to the father of C. Verres. He calls his father a thief, and a manager of bribes at elections (Divin. c. 8, note). Cicero considers such a bribe-monger worse than a thief. That is the Roman doctrine.

festivius] This is said ironically, for 'festivus' means that which gives pleasure and delight. Cicero says (Ad Att. i. 12): "Puer festivus anagnostes noster Sositheus decesserat, meque plus quam servi mors debere videbatur commoverat." Here he says: 'What youth do we suppose will ever turn out more charming than this of yours; if he is yours by blood, by intercourse your disciple, by inclination your veritable copy?'

si quae . . futurae sunt;] Zumpt seems to suppose that 'sint' might do, though it would give a somewhat different sense. The best MSS. have 'sunt,' which I believe to be the true reading.

ejusmodi . . innocenti.] This is a sound remark. In a well-constituted state there should be no difficulty about prosecuting a guilty administrator. There is not much danger for one who is innocent. A small number had the political power at Rome, and it was difficult to convict a guilty administrator, for he belonged to a powerful body, who protected him, and out of this body at the time of Verres' trial the jury was taken. A guilty or incapable administrator is screened from punishment in modern constitutional states by many circumstances, the risk of attacking a man who is protected by the class to which he belongs, the cost of collecting evidence, and the infinite formal obstacles which those who for the time hold power are able to interpose between a guilty public servant and a private person who should impeach him of mal-administration. A body called by a popular name, which among other functions is supposed to redress public grievances, may be made in skilful and unprincipled hands a means of protecting the guilty. Thus at Rome the tribunes, who were the protectors of the people, often became either mere factious brawlers, and so lost all credit, or were gained over by the powerful and well-combined nobility. See Vol. iii. Pro P. Sestio, c. 65, note.

haud scio an—possit:] Cicero's usual formula for expressing a possibility; not however very strongly expressed, but still it affirms.

quoniam pater tam negligens ac dissolutus est. Verum huc longius quam voluntas fuit ab epistola Timarchidi digressa est oratio mea, qua recitata conclusurum me esse crimen decumanum dixeram; ex quo intellexistis innumerabilem frumenti numerum per triennium aversum a re publica esse ereptumque aratoribus.

LXX. Sequitur ut de frumento empto vos, judices, doceam, maximo atque impudentissimo furto; de quo dum certa et pauca et magna dicam breviter attendite. Frumentum in Sicilia emere debuit Verres ex senatusconsulto et ex lege Terentia et Cassia frumentaria. Emendi duo genera fuerunt; unum decumarum; alterum, quod praeterea civitatibus aequaliter esset distributum:

crimen decumanum] This is an emendation of Lambinus. The MSS. have 'crimen decumarum,' which is an error. See c. 66, 77.

70. *Terentia et Cassia*] This was one of the Leges Frumentariae, the object of which was the securing a supply of grain for Rome. The Lex Terentia Cassia was enacted in B.C. 73. It is mentioned again c. 75 and Lib. 5. c. 21. The purpose of the 'lex,' it is said, was to give authority for the purchasing of corn with the public money, and for the retailing it at a fixed price at Rome. There is little information about the provisions of this 'lex.' The passages relating to it are collected in Orelli's edition of Cicero, Index Legum.

The passage in the Fragments of Sallust (p. 974, ed. Cort.), "Nisi forte repentina ista frumentaria lege munia vestra pensantur, qua tamen quinis modiis libertatem omnium aestimavere, qui profecto non amplius possunt alimentis carceris," is supposed to refer to this 'lex;' but there is nothing in the passage which shows that it does. The passage seems to imply that the corn there spoken of, the five 'modii' (a month), was a gift; for it is spoken of as the price of liberty. Yet it is stated that the corn was not given under the provisions of any Lex, before that of Clodius, but was sold at the price of 6⅓ asses for each 'modius.' (Ascon. in Pis. c. iv. p. 9, ed. Or.; Schol. Bob. Pro Sest. c. 25; but see Livy, Ep. 60, 'semisse et triente.') The corn mentioned in the text was purchased in accordance with the provisions of the 'lex Terentia et Cassia;' but the senate gave the order for each purchase.

This system of buying corn at the public cost led to miserable results. The market at Rome was unsteady: scarcity was often feared, and sometimes felt. The Romans compelled the Sicilians to sell grain at the price which the Romans gave, and so far the Roman state was better off than a modern state would be, which would be compelled to give the market price if it became a purchaser. But this practice must have raised the price of grain in other parts of Italy, and indeed to all persons who were not fed by the state. Arthur Young (Travels in France, 1787—9, p. 490) has some instructive remarks on Neckar's corn-purchases during his administration. The effect of his giving notice that he had made an immense purchase in corn, on the public account, was to raise the price immediately. A 'senatusconsultum' for the purchasing of a quantity of corn for Rome was an announcement of scarcity, necessarily followed by a rise of price. The National Assembly of France followed Neckar's example. They watched over the subsistence of the people, and so made or aggravated scarcity. Even now (1861) the price of bread is fixed at Paris.

unum decumarum;] The reading of the MSS. is either 'unum ceterarum decumarum,' or 'unum certarum decumarum.' 'Ceterarum' may be right: the other certainly not. Neither word is in Lg. 42 N. Hotmann writes 'unum alterarum decumarum.' Klotz has 'unum ceterarum decumarum.' The 'alterae decumae' are meant. Zumpt thinks that we should perhaps read 'decumanum' for 'decumarum,' which is probable. After 'hujus imperati' some MSS. have 'in annos singulos;' and also Jordan.

distributum:] This word is supposed to be equivalent to 'imperatum;' but Ernesti says that a like use of the word cannot be found in Cicero. This 'emptum frumentum' consisted of a second 'decumae' which was paid for; and of 'imperatum frumentum,' an amount required of

illius decumani tantum quantum ex primis decumis fuisset; hujus imperati tritici modium DCCC millia: pretium autem constitutum decumano in modios singulos HS III, imperato HS IIIS. Ita in frumentum imperatum HS duodetricies in annos singulos Verri decernebatur quod aratoribus solveret, in alteras decumas fere ad nonagies. Sic per triennium ad hanc frumenti emptionem Siciliensem prope centies et vicies erogatum est. Hanc pecuniam tantam, datam tibi ex aerario inopi atque exhausto, datam ad frumentum, hoc est, ad necessitatem salutis ac vitae, datam, ut Siculis, ut aratoribus, quibus tanta onera res publica imponeret, solveretur, abs te sic laceratam esse dico ut possim illud probare, si velim, omnem te hanc pecuniam domum tuam avertisse. Etenim sic hanc rem totam administrasti ut hoc, quod dico, probari aequissimo judici possit. Sed ego habebo rationem auctoritatis meae; meminero quo animo et quo consilio ad causam publicam accesserim. Non agam tecum accusatorie; nihil fingam; nihil cuiquam probari volo me dicente quod non ante mihimet ipsi probatum sit. In hac pecunia publica, judices, haec insunt tria genera furtorum: primum quum posita esset pecunia apud eas societates unde erat attributa, binis centesimis feneratus est: deinde permultis civitatibus pro

all the states equally, which was paid for one 'semis' dearer. The words 'emendi duo genera,' 'two kinds of purchase,' explain 'alterum,' which of course means 'the other mode of purchase,' which purchase was to be equally distributed over the different states; as if he had said, the money was to be distributed among the states equally, or proportionately to what was taken of them, as in c. 73, "pecunias quas civitatibus distribuere debeat." There seems no necessity to explain 'distributum' as equivalent to 'imperatum.'

HS III,] The MSS. have 'ternos' by error instead of 'terni,' except Lg. 42, which has the numerals III. The MSS. reading in place of 'HS IIIS' is 'HS IIII,' or half an 'as' more. Zumpt has written 'HS IIIS,' and thus the 800,000 modii, and the sum total 'duodetricies,' are in harmony. And this agrees with c. 75, where the price of a 'medimnum' or six 'modii' is stated at HS XXI.

During these years the sum of nearly twelve millions of 'sestertii' was annually laid out in Sicily only, for the supply of Rome; an enormous sum, when we consider the price of grain, and that the outlay was made for a single city.

societates . . . attributa,] He has just spoken of the money being paid to Verres out of the Aerarium. Here he speaks of the 'societates' or companies of Publicani, on whom Verres received an order for payment (unde erat attributa). But it comes to the same thing. The 'societates' were bound to pay into the Aerarium their rent for the 'vectigalia,' which they farmed, at least such 'vectigalia' as were not derived from grain: but it was the same thing if they paid to Verres such amounts as they were ordered to do; for to such amount they would be discharged. Money paid out of the Aerarium is 'pecunia erogata' (c. 71). Money for which Verres had an order on the 'societates' is 'pecunia attributa.' (See Ernesti, Clavis Cic.) Verres lent this money, or some of it; and, as it appears (c. 71), to the 'societates.' They paid at the rate of twenty-four per cent. per annum for it, 'binae centesimae,' or two hundredths per month, a rate of interest almost incredible; for though in modern times and in some countries such interest has been paid, it has been under peculiar circumstances of great scarcity of money, rash speculation, and the foolish legal limitation of the rate of interest. These Romans must have had large profits by their contracts, to make it worth their

frumento nihil solvit omnino: postremo, si cui civitati solvit, tantum detraxit quantum commodum fuit, nulli quod debitum est reddidit.

LXXI. Ac primum hoc ex te quaero: tu, cui publicani ex Carpinatii literis gratias egerunt, pecunia publica ex aerario erogata, ex vectigalibus populi Romani ad emendum frumentum attributa, fueritne tibi quaestui, pensitaritne tibi binas centesimas? Credo te negaturum; turpis enim est et periculosa confessio. Mihi autem hoc perarduum est demonstrare. Quibus enim testibus? publicanis? Tractati honorifice sunt; tacebunt. Literis eorum? decreto decumanorum remotae sunt. Quo me igitur vertam? Rem tam improbam, crimen tantae audaciae tantaeque impudentiae propter inopiam testium ac literarum praetermittam? Non faciam, judices: utar teste—quo? P. Vettio Chilone, homine equestris ordinis honestissimo atque ornatissimo, qui isti ita et amicus et necessarius est ut, etiamsi vir bonus non esset, tamen quod contra istum diceret grave videretur; ita vir bonus est ut, etiamsi inimicissimus isti esset, tamen ejus testimonio credi oporteret. Admiratur et exspectat quidnam Vettius dicturus sit. Nihil dicet ex tempore, nihil ex sua voluntate, nihil, quum utrumvis licuisse videatur. Misit literas in Siciliam ad Carpinatium, quum esset magister scripturae et sex publicorum, quas ego Syracusis apud Carpinatium

while to pay so much *for* keeping the money for a time. 'Ponere' is a word used for putting money out at interest.

"Haec ubi locutus fenerator Alphius,—
Omnem redegit Idibus pecuniam,
Quaerit Kalendis ponere."
Horat. Epod. ii. 67.

71. *Ac primum*] The old reading is 'At,' which is out of place here. The orator is continuing his subject.—The 'tu' stands alone without any grammatical connexion with the sentence; but that is no reason for omitting it, as Ernesti did. If a man were reading straight on, without troubling himself about grammatical canons, he might hardly observe the irregularity. Graevius quotes an example from Livy, ii. 13: "Quum C. Mucius adolescens, cui indignum videbatur . . . itaque eam indignitatem vindicandam ratus . . . constituit."

ex tempore,] 'Ex tempore' means 'to suit an occasion,' that which is temporary, not permanent; and accordingly it is almost the same as 'fictum,' as Hotmann explains it correctly. See Divin. c. 2.

et sex publicorum,] The editions up to that of Lambinus have 'sex publicanorum.' Lambinus made it 'et societatis publicanorum.' F. Ursini says, "legitur in manuscripto 'ejus societatis publicanorum' sine conjunctionis nota, quae est in vulgatis." "Abest *sex* a Lg. 14, *publicorum* habent omnes Lgg. praeter unum 5" (Jordan). Zumpt supposes that 'publica' may mean 'vectigalia;' and so it means in a passage of Cicero, where he says, 'publicis male redemptis;' and he adds, "quorum cum varia genera fuerint, etiam *sex publica* quasi conjuncta poterant esse a societate illa conducta: certe *eandem societatem portum et scripturam habuisse* cognovimus Lib. 2. c. 70." Klotz observes (Vorrede, p. 13): "we have with Zumpt explained *sex publica* to be six companies for farming the revenues;" but Zumpt seems to speak of six different kinds of 'vectigalia' farmed by one company. Cicero says, 'scripturae et sex publicorum,'—which seems to mean the 'scriptura,' and six other branches of the 'vectigalia,' for 'publicorum' appears to be equivalent to 'vectigalium.' There was the 'portorium,'

in literarum allatarum libris, Romae in literarum missarum apud magistrum L. Tullium, familiarem tuum, inveni; quibus ex literis impudentiam feneratoris, quaeso, cognoscite. LITERAE MISSAE P. VETTII P. SERVILII C. ANTISTII MAGISTRORVM. Praesto ait se tibi futurum Vettius et observaturum quemadmodum rationes ad aerarium referas, ut, si hanc ex fenore pecuniam populo non rettuleris, reddas societati. Possumus hoc teste, possumus P. Servilii et C. Antistii magistrorum literis, primorum hominum atque honestissimorum, possumus auctoritate societatis, cujus literis utimur, quod dicimus obtinere, an aliqua firmiora aut graviora quaerenda sunt?

LXXII. Vettius, tuus familiarissimus, Vettius, tuus affinis, cujus sororem habes in matrimonio, tuae uxoris frater, Vettius, frater tui quaestoris, testatur literis tuum impudentissimum furtum certissimumque peculatum; nam quo alio nomine pecuniae publicae feneratio est appellanda? Scribam tuum dicit, Verres, hujus perscriptorem fenerationis fuisse: ei quoque magistri minantur in literis, et casu scribae tum duo magistri fuerunt cum Vettio.

the vectigal of wheat, of barley, which was let separately in Sicily, of wine, oil, and of the 'fruges minutae,'—all mentioned by Cicero, and these make exactly six. Klotz is delighted to be able to defend 'sex publica' by a pertinent example from Valerius Maximus, vi. 9, § 7: "T. Aufidius cum Asiatici publici exiguam admodum particulam habuisset, postea Asiam proconsulari imperio obtinuit." See the passage from Gaius cited in the note to c. 72; and the note in Torrenius' edition of Valerius Maximus. There are numerous examples in which 'publica' and 'publicum' mean something which belongs to the 'populus,' and some kind of public revenue (Ovid, Fast. v. 283; Horace, 1 Ep. i. 77; Seneca, Ep. 101, 119. See De Imp. Cn. Pomp. c. 7, and the note).

feneratoris,] 'fenerationis' Or.; but there is no MSS. authority for it.

quod dicimus obtinere,] 'Maintain, support, that is, prove what I say.'

72. *peculatum;*] 'Peculatus' was the offence of embezzling public property (pecunia publica), whether the offence was committed by a private person, or by one who held some public office. According to the Romans, the word was derived from 'pecus;' and as fines were paid originally not in money, but in cattle, it was properly the embezzlement of what was so paid as a fine to the state. The explanation is hardly satisfactory. When the offence of 'peculatus' became common, it was the subject of particular enactments (leges); and finally, at some time not ascertained, there was established a 'quaestio perpetua de peculatu,' or a court for the trial of the offenders in this matter. Cases of 'peculatus' appear to have become more common when the Romans began their conquering career, and generals were tempted to appropriate some of the booty. The 'quaestio' existed before this time (B.C. 70). The chief 'lex' on this subject is a Lex Julia, of the time either of the Dictator Caesar or Augustus. (Rein, Das Criminalrecht der Römer, p. 672, &c.)

perscriptorem] He was the man who made all the entries in the books relating to these transactions. The sense of 'perscribere' is explained by other passages (Lib. 5. c. 19): "multas pecunias isti erogatas in operum locationes falsas atque inanes esse perscriptas." Lib. 2. c. 70, "furta quoque istius permulta nominatim ad socios perscripserat." As to the various meanings of 'perscriptio' and 'perscribere,' see Ernesti, Clavis.

scribae] "And it happened that two 'scribae' were at that time 'magistri' together with Vettius." Difficulties have been made about this. It is usual to speak of only one 'magister.' Here three are

Binas centesimas ab sese ablatas ferendum non putant; et recte non putant. Quis enim hoc fecit unquam? quis denique conatus est facere aut posse fieri cogitavit, ut, quum senatus usura publicanos saepe juvisset, magistratus a publicanis pecuniam pro usura auderet auferre? Certe huic homini spes nulla salutis esset, si publicani, hoc est, si equites Romani judicarent. Minor esse nunc, judices, vobis disceptantibus debet, et tanto minor quanto est honestius alienis injuriis quam re sua commoveri. Quid ad haec respondere cogitas? Utrum factum negabis an tibi hoc licitum esse defendes? Negare qui potes? an ut tanta auctoritate literarum, tot testibus publicanis convincare? Licuisse vero qui? Si mehercule te tuam pecuniam praetorem in provincia feneratum docerem, tamen effugere non posses; sed publicam, sed ob frumentum decretam, sed a publicanis fenore accepto, hoc licuisse cuiquam probabis? quo non modo ceteri, sed tu ipse nihil audacius improbiusque fecisti. Non mehercule hoc, quod omnibus singulare videtur, de quo mihi deinceps dicendum est, possum, judices, dicere

mentioned, and two of them 'scribae,' who were more inclined to interfere in this matter, because a 'scriba,' one of their 'ordo,' was acting as the tool of Verres. They may have wished to keep up the character of their 'ordo.' This may have been one motive for their acting in this matter. As to 'scribae,' see c. 78. Ernesti put 'scribae' in the critical stocks thus [scribae]. "Temere factum, nisi hoc potuit ostendere, scribas non fuisse publicanos et publicanorum magistros. Sed cum multi scribae equites Rom. fuerint, quidni etiam publicani?" Zumpt.

usura . . juvisset,] Helped them, not by the loan of money, but by allowing them to have the use of money which was due. 'Usurae' is the term for interest. The senate had often not called for the money from the Publicani so soon as it was due. Hotmann quotes the passage of Cicero, Tusc. Disp. i. c. 39, "Natura dedit usuram vitae tamquam pecuniae, nulla praestituta die," &c. Comp. also Pro Sulla, c. 32. Zumpt observes that 'usurae' is always 'money,' and 'usura' is also 'facultas utendi.'—'pro usura,' Lg. 42 V, except that Lg. 42 has 'quod' instead of 'pro:' 'pro usuris' ett. Or.

disceptantibus] 'Disceptare' is a word applied to judicial investigations and determinations. See c. 79, and Lib. 5. c. 71, "disceptante populo Romano." Cicero (Orat. Part. c. 3) says, "Disceptator rei sententiaeque moderator," and in the De Re Publica (v. 2), "nec vero quisquam privatus erat disceptator aut arbiter litis, sed omnia conficiebantur judiciis regiis." Compare Livy, 43. c. 10, "placuit ut disceptaret coram purgaretque sese," and 38. c. 35; also Caesar, B. G. vii. 37. Cicero, Pro Flacco, c. 38, De Leg. Agr. i. 7.

an ut tanta] This must be explained by looking back to what has been just said. "As to denying it, how can you do that? or will you deny it in order that you may be completely convicted by the evidence of so many documents, and of so many 'publicani?'"

effugere non posses;] We might infer from this that a 'magistratus' could not carry on the trade of money-lending in his province. At any rate this was the law in later times, for a rescript of Gordian states that there had been previous rescripts to this effect (Cod. Just. 3. tit. 2. s. 3, referred to by Zumpt after Hotmann).

fenore accepto,] om. Lg. 42; 'fenore acceptam,' V and Klotz; but he does not say how he understands it. Compare Lib. 2. c. 74, near the end, as to this use of 'sed.'

The following definition of Publicanus may be worth noting: "Eum qui vectigal populi Romani conductum habet, publicanum appellamus. Nam publici appellatio in compluribus causis ad populum Romanum respicit: civitates enim privatorum loco habentur" (Gaius, Dig. 50. 16. 16).

audacius esse aut impudentius quod permultis civitatibus pro frumento nihil solvit omnino: major haec praeda fortasse est: sed illa impudentia certe non minor. Et quoniam de illa feneratione satis dictum est, nunc de hac tota pecunia aversa, quaeso, cognoscite.

LXXIII. Siciliae civitates multae sunt, judices, ornatae atque honestae, ex quibus in primis numeranda est civitas Halesina: nullam enim reperietis aut officiis fideliorem aut copiis locupletiorem aut auctoritate graviorem. Huic iste in annos singulos quum sexagena millia tritici modium imperavisset, pro tritico nummos abstulit quanti erat in Sicilia triticum; quos de publico nummos acceperat, retinuit omnes. Obstupui, judices, quum hoc mihi primum Halesae demonstravit in senatu Halesinorum homo summo ingenio, summa prudentia, summa auctoritate praeditus, Halesinus Aeneas, cui senatus dederat publice causam ut mihi fratrique meo gratias ageret, et simul qui nos ea quae ad judicium pertinerent doceret. Demonstravit hanc istius consuetudinem ac rationem fuisse; quod quum omnis frumenti copia decumarum

73. *Halesina:*] V almost always has this word with the diphthong, 'Halaesa;' but it has also 'Halesa.' It is Ἄλαισα in Strabo, in Diodorus, and on the coins. Halesa was on the north coast, east of Cephaloedium, and near a river Halesus or Alaesus, supposed to be the Pettineo. Halesa being Immunis was free from the regular imposts, but not from the liability to furnish 'frumentum emptum.'

sexagena . . . tritici] "*Sexagena* pro vulg. *sexaginta* scripsi, quia sic liquido testatur Nannius in suo libro se invenisse" (Zumpt). But he thinks that 'sexaginta' also would do. I doubt that; at least, the usual form is 'sexagena' when connected with 'singuli.' See Lib. 2. c. 55, note. Klotz here writes 'LX. M. tritici modium.' The copyists seem to have preferred the numerals to the numerical words; and probably Cicero himself would generally use them in writing to save trouble. We may therefore owe 'sexaginta,' in this case, solely to the copyists; and it may be, that the Romans themselves were not consistent in the use of the forms 'sexagena' and 'sexaginta.'

quanti erat &c.] He took money instead of wheat, and at the price at which wheat then was in Sicily; that is, for every 'modius' he took the money value.

Obstupui,] Or 'obstipui,' for both forms are used, though I see no reason for preferring 'obstipui.' It is a common word to express the surprise which almost takes away utterance.

—"uxor tibi ducenda est, Pamphile, hodie, inquit, para,
Abi domum: id mi visus est dicere,
Abi cito et suspende te.
Obstipui. Censen' me verbum potuisse ullum proloqui?"
Ter. Andr. i. 5. 19.

dederat publice causam] Iordan follows Lg. 42 V in writing 'dederat publicam causam.' The expression is unusual either way. Cicero means to say, that he was empowered or commissioned by the 'civitas.' Cicero's 'frater' is his cousin, L. Tullius Cicero, who accompanied him when he went to Sicily to collect evidence against Verres. Such a 'cognatus' was called 'frater patruelis,' or simply 'frater.' When Cicero speaks of the death of this L. Tullius (Ad Att. i. 5), he calls him 'frater' on that occasion also.

Demonstravit] From V. Orelli, Zumpt, and Iordan have 'demonstrat.'

quod quum omnis] 'Quod omnis' is the reading of Lg. 42 V. All the rest of the MSS. have 'quod cum omnis.' The editors since Naugerius have omitted the 'quod,' and kept the 'quum' (Zumpt). Zumpt, Klotz, and Iordan omit the 'quum,' and retain the 'quod.' I have kept them both, for I think that this usage of 'quod' is often misunderstood in Cicero, and that it is rightly placed here.

nomine penes istum esset redacta, solitum esse istum pecuniam cogere a civitatibus, frumentum improbare, quantum frumenti esset Romam mittendum, tantum de suo quaestu ac de sua copia frumenti mittere. Posco rationes: inspicio literas: video frumenti granum Halesinos, quibus sexagena millia modium imperata erant, nullum dedisse; pecuniam Volcatio, Timarchidi, scribae dedisse: reperio genus hujusmodi, judices, praedae ut praetor, qui frumentum emere debeat, non emat sed vendat; pecunias, quas civitatibus distribuere debeat, eas omnes avertat atque auferat. Non mihi jam furtum sed monstrum ac prodigium videbatur civitatum frumentum improbare, suum probare; quum suum [frumento] probasset, pretium ei frumento constituere; quod constituisset, id a civitatibus auferre; quod a populo Romano accepisset, tenere.

LXXIV. Quot vultis esse in uno furto peccatorum gradus ut, si singulis insistere velim, progredi iste non possit? Improbas frumentum Siculorum. Quid, ipse quod mittis? peculiarem habes aliquam Siciliam quae tibi ex alio genere frumentum suppeditare possit? Quum senatus decernit ut ematur in Sicilia frumentum, aut quum populus jubet, hoc, ut opinor, intelligit, ex Sicilia Siculum frumentum apportari oportere. Tu, quum civitatum Siciliae vulgo omne frumentum improbas, num ex Aegypto aut Syria frumentum

pecuniam Volcatio, &c.] Klotz follows V in writing 'pecuniam Timarchidi et Volcatio scribae.' Zumpt refers to the end of c. 75, where three persons are mentioned; and the 'scriba' appears to be Maevius. Halm prefers the reading of V, 'nam vulgatam vitiosam esse oratio ipsa docet.'

suum probare;] "N et, ut videtur, B: om. V. rell. item Lgg. omnes" (Iordan). These words, it appears, are wanting in the old editions, and in most of the MSS., as well as the words 'quum suum . . . probasset:' 'quod quum constituisset' is the reading of N: 'civitatibus auferre,' Orelli; but in these orations the verb is nearly always used with the preposition 'ab,' as Zumpt observes.

74. *Quot vultis &c.*] Zumpt, Klotz, and Iordan place the ? after 'gradus.' Zumpt himself considers the passage clear enough, though it has plagued the commentators; and yet he mistakes it. He supposes 'tot sunt' to be the answer to the question; that is, 'tot sunt ut si singulis,' &c. Ernesti thought the text should be altered thus,—'Tot videtis esse in uno furto,' &c. But if there is no difficulty with 'Tot videtis,' &c., why should there be any difficulty with the words 'Quot vultis,' &c., which manifestly are connected with 'ut?' 'How many degrees of offence would you have in one single act of fraud, that is, how many do you think will be enough, if I should insist on them severally, to bring the matter to a point where he can go no further?' The meaning is plain and certain, if the passage is not obscured by bad punctuation. Compare Lib. 3. c. 94: "in quo primum injuriae gradu resistere incipiet severitas judicis, quotus erit iste denarius qui non sit ferendus," &c.; where Cicero asks a question to the same effect, and in a like form to this in c. 74: "at what degree of wrong will the strictness of the 'judex' begin to resist; to what number of 'denarii' must that demand of yours be carried, before the amount is considered intolerable?"

peculiarem] 'A Sicily of his own;' a word derived from the use of 'peculium.' See Lib. 1. c. 36, note on Peculium.

Romam missurus es? Improbas Halesinum, Thermitanum, Cephaloeditanum, Amestratinum, Tyndaritanum, Herbitense, multarum praeterea civitatum. Quid accidit tandem ut horum populorum agri frumentum ejusmodi te praetore ferrent, ut neque tibi neque populo Romano posset probari, praesertim quum ex iisdem agris ejusdem anni frumentum ex decumis Romam mancipes advexissent? quid acciderat ut ex eodem horreo decumanum probaretur, emptum improbaretur? Dubiumne est quin ista omnis improbatio cogendae pecuniae causa nata sit? Esto: improbas Halesinum; habes ab alio populo quod probes: eme illud quod placet; missos fac eos quorum frumentum improbasti. Sed ab his quos repudias exigis tantum pecuniae quantum ad eum numerum frumenti satis sit quem ei civitati imperas emendum. [Dubium est quid egeris.] In medimna singula video ex literis publicis tibi Halesinos HS quinos denos dedisse. Ostendam ex tabulis locupletissimorum aratorum eodem tempore neminem in Sicilia pluris frumentum vendidisse.

LXXV. Quae est ergo ista ratio, aut quae potius ista amentia, frumentum improbare id quod ex eo loco sit, ex quo senatus et populus Romanus emi voluerit, et ex eo acervo ex quo partem tu idem decumarum nomine probaris; deinde a civitatibus pecuniam ad emendum frumentum cogere, quum ex aerario acceperis? Utrum enim te lex Terentia Siculorum pecunia frumentum emere an populi Romani pecunia frumentum a Siculis emere jussit? Jam vero ab isto omnem illam ex aerario pecuniam quam his oportuit civitatibus pro frumento dari lucri factam videtis. Accipis enim HS xv pro medimno; tanti enim est illo tempore medimnum: retines HS xxi; tanti enim est frumentum Siciliense ex lege aestimatum. Quid interest utrum hoc feceris an frumentum [Siciliense] non improbaris, sed frumento probato et accepto pecuniam publicam tenueris omnem neque quidquam ulli dissolveris civitati, quum

ferrent, ut neque] 'Ferrent, quod numquam antea, quod neque tibi,' &c., is the reading of Klotz and Iordan. The words 'quod numquam antea' look like an interpolation, and they are not in Lg. 42, though they are in V, and in the other MSS., I suppose.

Esto: improbas] Zumpt has 'improbes' from Lg. 42, a reading which is certainly not so good as the common reading, 'improbas,' which V also has.

[*Dubium est &c.*]] Klotz places a note of interrogation after 'egeris.' But it is not an interrogative sentence in form, though in the enunciation it may be made very nearly so. It is better without the ?. Lg. 42 F V omit 'Dubium . . . egeris.'

75. *quae potius ista &c.*] V omits 'ista.'—'Utrum enim te' V φ, 'utrum enim' Lg. 42, 'utrum te' rell. Or. It might be argued that the Lex Terentia did not empower Verres to make the particular purchase. The senate gave orders for the particular purchases, and pursuant to the general terms of the Lex.

Accipis enim HS xv] See c. 70.

aestimatio legis ejusmodi sit ut ceteris temporibus tolerabilis Siculis, te praetore etiam grata esse debuerit? Est enim modius lege HS IIIS aestimatus: fuit autem te praetore, ut tu in multis epistolis ad amicos tuos gloriaris, HS II. Sed fuerit HS IIS, quoniam tantum a civitatibus in modios singulos exegisti. Quum, si solveres Siculis tantum quantum populus Romanus jusserat, aratoribus fieri gratissimum posset, tu non modo eos accipere quod oportebat noluisti, sed etiam dare quod non debebant coëgisti. Atque haec ita gesta esse, judices, cognoscite et ex literis publicis civitatum et ex testimoniis publicis, in quibus nihil fictum, nihil ad tempus accommodatum intelligitis. Omnia quae dicimus rationibus populorum non interpositis neque perturbatis neque repentinis, sed certis, institutis, ordine relata atque confecta sunt. Recita rationes Halesinorum. Cui pecuniam datam dicit? Dic, dic etiam clarius: VOLCATIO, TIMARCHIDI, MAEVIO.

LXXVI. Quid est, Verres? ne illam quidem tibi defensionem reliquam fecisti, mancipes in istis rebus esse versatos? mancipes frumentum improbasse? mancipes pretio cum civitatibus decidisse, et eosdem abs te illarum civitatum nomine pecunias abstulisse, deinde ipsos sibi frumentum coëmisse; nihil haec ad te pertinere? Mala mehercule ac misera defensio praetorem hoc dicere, Ego frumentum neque attigi neque inspexi; mancipibus potestatem probandi improbandique permisi; mancipes a civitatibus pecunias extorserunt; ego autem quam pecuniam populis dare debui mancipibus dedi. Mala est haec quidem, ut dixi, defensio, ac potius perdita maximorum peccatorum, hujus autem et iniquitatis et inertiae confessio, non defensio criminis; sed tamen hac ipsa tibi,

publicis civitatum] The reading of V in this instance, 'civitatium,' may be worth noting, as a variety. Klotz adopts it here for conformity's sake; but in c. 74 he writes 'civitatum.' The faulty reading of V, 'nihil a to fictum,' may perhaps have induced him to write as he does, 'nihil esse fictum.' Zumpt and Iordan have 'intelligetis.'

non interpositis] This word was taken to be equivalent to 'interpolatis' by Ernesti and Garatoni, on which Zumpt observes, "non credo sic dici posse *interposita*, quibus quid interpositum sit." The meaning of the word seems to be deducible from that with which it is contrasted, 'certis.' All that Cicero affirms was entered (relata), and recorded in the records of the cities. Zumpt supposes, as it seems, that 'rationes' cannot be said of parts of the 'rationes;' or, at any rate, he takes 'rationibus' to mean the whole 'rationes.' I don't see why Hotmann's explanation may not serve, that 'rationes non interpositas' may mean 'rationes' (entries) not foisted in, where they ought not to be.

76. *mancipes*] See Divin. c. 10.

inspexi;] Nannius says that this is the reading in his old codex; and it is the reading of Lg. 42. The other reading is 'adspexi,' which Iordan has. This is one of those cases where we may leave readers to choose that which seems to suit the sense best. 'Inspicere' is a word that expresses a minuter examination. 'Neque adspexi' would mean, that he did not even look at it; and some may prefer this.

si uti cupias, non licet: vetat te Volcatius, tuae tuorumque deliciae, mentionem mancipis facere. Timarchides autem, columen familiae vestrae, premit fauces defensionis tuae, cui simul et Volcatio pecunia a civitate numerata est. Jam vero scriba tuus annulo aureo suo, quem ex his rebus invenit, ista te ratione uti non sinet. Quid igitur est reliquum nisi uti fateare te Romam frumentum emptum Siculorum pecunia misisse, publicam pecuniam domum tuam convertisse? O consuetudo peccandi, quantam habes jucunditatem in improbis et audacibus, quum poena abfuit et licentia consecuta est! Iste in hoc genere peculatus non nunc primum invenitur, sed nunc demum tenetur. Vidimus huic ab aerario pecuniam numerari quaestori ad sumptum exercitus consularis: vidimus paucis post mensibus et exercitum et consulem spoliatum. Illa omnis pecunia latuit in illa caligine ac tenebris quae totam rem publicam tum occuparant. Iterum gessit hereditariam quaesturam cum Dolabella: magnam pecuniam avertit, sed ejus rationem cum damnatione Dolabellae permiscuit. Commissa est pecunia tanta praetori: non reperietis hominem timide nec leviter haec improbissima lucra liguríentem; devorare omnem pecuniam publicam non dubitavit. Ita serpit illud insitum natura malum consue-

columen] Thus in Terence, Phormio, ii. 3. 57:

"Bone custos, salve, columen vero familiae."

annulo aureo] "Quo utebatur ad obsignandas tabulas," says Manutius. His own seal would be evidence.

in improbis] Zumpt omits 'in' "fide meliorum librum, quaeritur enim, *cui* habeat, non *in quo* jucunditatem." Y also and Iordan omit 'in.' But I think it doubtful if Zumpt and Iordan are right.

Vidimus huic] As to this allusion see Lib. 1. c. 13, &c.

hereditariam quaesturam] This is explained by Lib. 1. c. 36: "C. Malleolo quaestore Cn. Dolabellae occiso duas sibi hereditates venisse arbitratus est."

cum Dolabella:] 'quaesturam, cum a Dolabella' Lg. 42 N, Iordan.

ligurrientem;] Zumpt writes the word with 'rr.' There is a dispute about the 'rr.' Zumpt refers to Faernus and Bentley (Ter. Eunuch. v. 4. 14), and to the editors of Horace, 1 Sat. iii. 81, on the line—

"Semesos pisces tepidumve ligurierit jus."

On which Heindorf remarks, that Manutius and Victorius have preferred 'rr' on the authority of the MSS.; and also Bentley in the passage, and in the passage of Terence, though the derivation from *lingere*, and the analogy of *scaturire* are in favour of the single 'r.'—The derivation has nothing to do with the matter. The root is 'lig,' our 'lick.' Whether the termination is to be 'urire' or 'urrire' is a different question. As other words of this form have 'urire,' I write this so also.

Cicero is not sparing of any kind of metaphor for the purpose of abuse. The meaning of this word is explained by its radical signification, and its contrast with 'devorare.' Hotmann also refers to the well-known passage in the Eunuchus, v. 4. 14:—

"Quae cum amatore suo quum coenant, liguriunt.
Harum videre ingluviem, sordes, inopiam,
Quam inhonestae solae sint domi, atque avidae cibi," &c.

insitum natura] 'Insitum in natura' all the MSS., except Lg. 42, which omits the preposition. Zumpt observes, "difficile est statuere de praepos. in aut addenda aut abjicienda, cum praecesserit littera m," the meaning of which any one will know,

tudine peccandi libera, finem audaciae ut statuere ipse sibi non possit. Tenetur igitur aliquando, et in rebus quum maximis tum manifestis tenetur. Atque in eam fraudem videtur mihi divinitus incidisse, non solum ut eas poenas quas proxime meruisset solveret, sed ut illa etiam scelera ejus in Carbonem et in Dolabellam vindicarentur.

LXXVII. Etenim nova quoque alia res, judices, extitit in hoc crimine quae tollat omnem dubitationem superioris illius decumani criminis. Nam ut illud missum faciam, permultos aratores in alteras decumas et in haec octingenta millia modium quod emptum populo Romano darent non habuisse, et a tuo procuratore, hoc est, ab Apronio, emisse, ex quo intelligi potest nihil te aratoribus reliqui fecisse: ut hoc praeteream, quod multorum est testimoniis expositum, potest illo quidquam esse certius, in tua potestate atque in tuis horreis omne frumentum Siciliae per triennium atque omnes fructus agri decumani fuisse? Quum enim a civitatibus pro frumento pecuniam exigebas, unde erat frumentum quod Romam mitteres, si tu id non omne clausum et compressum possidebas? Ita in eo frumento primus tibi ille quaestus erat ipsum frumentum quod erat ereptum ab aratoribus: alter, quod [id] frumentum improbissime per triennium partum non semel sed bis, neque uno sed duobus pretiis, unum et idem frumentum vendidisti: semel civitatibus HS xv in medimnum, iterum populo Romano, a quo HS xxi in medimna pro eodem illo frumento abstulisti.—At enim frumentum Centuripinorum et Agrigentinorum et nonnullorum

who has been accustomed to observe handwriting. I take 'natura' to be used generally, and not to mean the 'natura' of Verres only. Zumpt is inclined, on second thoughts, to think that 'natura' is not said absolutely. The form of the first part of the sentence leads us to expect a general remark, but the end presents us with a special application, if 'ipse' must be applied to Verres. It seems doubtful if all is right. Klotz has 'insitum in,' and also 'ipse sibi non possit.' Zumpt and Iordan omit 'sibi,' which is not in the best MSS., and Zumpt says that it is not wanted, because you can easily understand 'suae' after 'audaciae.' There is not much in the second reason for the omission of 'sibi.'

Cicero has a use of 'serpit' in the De Amicitia (c. 12) which may be compared with this.

77. *et a tuo*] 'Sed a tuo,' the common reading. Zumpt has 'et a tuo,' from the better MSS.; and adds, that 'et' has the signification of 'sed' after a negative. There is no doubt that 'et' is the better reading. Both 'et' and 'que' often come after such a negative clause, and by reading a man acquires a kind of feeling of their propriety in certain cases. As to reducing such a thing to rule, by saying that 'et' is sometimes put for 'sed,' that is saying nothing at all. Cicero says (Ad Q. Fr. i. 1. c. 1), "nere te obrui tamquam fluctu sic magnitudine negotii sinas: contraque eriges ac resistas," &c. And in this oration, c. 4, "nihil eorum est; contraque sunt omnia," &c.

HS xv *in medimnum*,] Ernesti expresses some surprise that we have first 'in medimnum,' and then 'in medimna.' The variation in the expression seems so easy and natural, that a reader might not have observed it, if a critic had not pointed it out. It wants no explanation.

fortasse praeterea probasti, et his populis pecuniam dissolvisti.—Sint sane aliquae civitates in eo numero quarum frumentum improbare nolueris. Quid tandem his civitatibus omnisne pecunia quae pro frumento debita est dissoluta est? Unum mihi reperi, non populum sed aratorem: vide, quaere, circumspice, si quis forte est ex ea provincia in qua tu triennium praefuisti qui te nolit perisse: unum, inquam, da mihi ex illis aratoribus, qui tibi ad statuas pecuniam contulerunt, qui sibi dicat omne esse pro frumento quod oportuerit solutum. Confirmo, judices, neminem esse dicturum.

LXXVIII. Ex omni pecunia quam aratoribus solvere debuisti certis nominibus deductiones fieri solebant: primum pro spectatione et collybo; deinde pro nescio quo cerario. Haec omnia, judices, non rerum certarum sed furtorum improbissimorum sunt vocabula. Nam collybus esse qui potest quum utuntur omnes uno genere nummorum? Cerarium vero quid vocas? quomodo hoc nomen ad rationes magistratus, quomodo ad pecuniam publicam allatum est? Nam illud genus tertium deductionis erat ejusmodi, quasi non modo liceret sed etiam oporteret, nec solum oporteret sed plane necesse esset. Scribae nomine de tota pecunia binae quinquagesimae detrahebantur. Quis hoc tibi concessit? quae lex? quae senatus auctoritas? quae porro aequitas, ut tantam pecuniam scriba tuus auferret sive de aratorum bonis sive de populi Romani vectigalibus? Nam si potest ista pecunia sine aratorum injuria detrahi, populus Romanus habeat, tantis praesertim aerarii angustiis: sin autem et populus Romanus voluit et aequum est ita

dissolvisti.] This is a word of payment, but 'solvere' is sufficient. It is the loosening of the 'obligatio' (see Lib. 1. c. 30, note). For instances of 'dissolvere' in this sense, see Forcellini. The verb 'solvere' and its derivatives have many meanings, easily deducible from the primary sense.

statuas pecuniam] 'statuas pecunias' Lg. 42 Jordan.

78. *deductiones*] These official gentlemen contrived under the name 'deductiones' to get some of the money which passed through their hands and was intended for other people (comp. Pro Rabir. Post. c. 11, note). First, under the head of 'spectatio,' or proving the money to be good, which of course was a mere pretence. Next, for the exchange of one kind of money for another, 'aggio,' as Forcellini says, using an Italian word. 'Collybus' occurs, Ad Att. xii. 6; Sueton. Oct. 4. Then comes the 'cerarium,' or wax money. Nobody knows what that is. We may be consoled for our ignorance by considering that the Sicilians themselves did not know. It was merely the name under which a sum of money was paid. I conjecture that we have something like it. There is or was one Chafe-wax (sometimes called Chaff-wax), thus described: "an officer in chancery, that fitteth the wax for sealing of the writs, commissions, and such other instruments as are there made to be issued out." The wax in the two cases may be used in a very different way; but it comes to the same end. It produces money.

The third 'deductio' was monstrous; two fiftieths, or one twenty-fifth, or four per cent., deducted under the head of 'scriba.' This is worse than chafe-wax. 'Scriba' was paid, as it appears, by the Populus Romanus, small wages (parva merces), and he helped himself to more, as usual in such cases.

solvi aratoribus, tuus apparitor parva mercede populi conductus de aratorum bonis praedabitur? et in hac causa scribarum ordinem in me concitabit Hortensius, et eorum commoda a me labefactari atque oppugnari jura dicet? Quasi vero hoc scribis ullo exemplo aut ullo jure sit concessum. Quid ego vetera repetam? aut quid eorum scribarum mentionem faciam quos constat sanctissimos homines atque innocentissimos fuisse? Non me fugit, judices, vetera exempla pro fictis fabulis jam audiri atque haberi: in his temporibus versabor miseris ac perditis. Nuper, Hortensi, quaestor fuisti. Quid tui scribae fecerint tu potes dicere: ego de meis hoc dico, quum in eadem ista Sicilia pro frumento civitatibus pecuniam solverem, et mecum duos frugalissimos homines scribas haberem L. Mamilium et L. Sergium, non modo istas duas quinquagesimas sed omnino nummum nullum cuiquam esse deductum. LXXIX. Dicerem hoc mihi totum esse attribuendum, judices, si illi unquam hoc a me postulassent, si omnino unquam cogitassent. Quamobrem enim scriba deducat et non potius mulio qui advexit, tabellarius cujus adventu certiores facti petiverunt, praeco qui adire jussit, viator aut Venereus qui fiscum sustulit? Quae pars operae aut opportunitatis in scriba est cur ei non modo merces tanta detur, sed cur cum eo tantae pecuniae partitio fiat?—Ordo est honestus.—Quis

79. *attribuendum,*] He means to say that he should have taken all the blame to himself, if his 'scribae' had ever made such a demand. In Lib. 5. c. 41 there is, "ut aut aliis causam calamitatis attribueret." But the word may be used without an accusative, and the context will explain it.

et non potius] 'non mulio potius qui advexerit' Klotz, which is the reading of V, except that it has 'plus' for 'potius.'—'non tabell.' V.

petiverunt,] The Siculi receive news of the arrival of the money by the letter-carrier, and then go to ask for their money, the payment for their corn. When they came, they would be called in order by the 'praeco,' and then they would go up to the place where the 'scribae' were sitting, and get their money, after the 'deductiones' were made.

viator aut Venereus] See Act. I. c. 8. It would not be making a very bold conjecture to suppose that all these distinguished functionaries received a piece of coin for their services, from the 'aratores.'

operae] 'quae pars operis' Klotz from V; a matter of indifference.

Ordo est honestus.] Cicero calls the 'scribae' an 'ordo,' a class. He applies to them the same name as to the 'Senatorius ordo,' 'Equestris ordo.' The subordinate functionaries attached to the magistrates formed a kind of corporate bodies, or guilds, and therefore belong to the class of artificial persons. The 'scribae' were a class who rose in number and importance with the extension of the Roman empire. They were employed in all branches of the public service; and also, like notaries on the continent, they did various kinds of business for private persons. The functions of a French notary were probably very like those of a Roman 'scriba,' so far as concerns his employment by private persons. Persons of this class are mentioned under various names,—'librarii,' 'fiscales,' 'censuales;' but the name 'scribae' is the most general. They were divided into 'decuriae;' and, though this is a general term, it came to signify, when used absolutely, even in the Republican period, the body of 'scribae;' and it certainly has this meaning in the Imperial period. The members of the 'decuriae' were called 'decuriati;' later, 'decuriales.' These 'decuriae' had no doubt distinct names. There were 'scribae quaestorii,' 'aedilicii,' 'praetorii,' and others. They existed in the other towns

negat, aut quid ea res ad hanc rem pertinet? Est vero honestus, quod eorum hominum fidei tabulae publicae periculaque magistratuum committuntur. Itaque ex his scribis qui digni sunt illo ordine, patribus familias, viris bonis atque honestis, percontamini, quid sibi istae quinquagesimae velint. Jam omnes intelligetis

besides Rome (Sueton. Claud. c. 1). Horace (1 Sat. v. 34) met with one at Fundi, a self-sufficient fool. These guilds of 'scribae' obtained great privileges at Rome, and subsequently at Constantinople.

The principal passages in the Roman writers about 'scribae,' are this chapter; Cicero Ad Q. Fr. ii. 2; Tacit. Ann. xiii. 27; Suetonius, *August.* 57; *Claudius*, 1. Among modern writers, Niebuhr, Roman History, iii. 298, &c. English translation; Savigny, System, &c., ii. 253, &c., and Becker, Handbuch, &c. ii. 2, p. 372, may be consulted.

This class of men, who now aspired to the rank of an 'ordo' in the state, took an active part in political matters, and in times of political excitement appeared in the public places with the clubs (sodalitates), and threatened the peace of Rome. Cicero mentions an occasion on which the Senate made a Consultum, which required these turbulent fellows (sodalitates decuriatique) to disperse, under pain of coming under the laws De Vi. The 'scribae' belonged to the class of 'libertini;' they were all 'libertini,' as Niebuhr affirms, that is, not the sons of free-born Romans. It appears that admission into these 'decuriae,' or some of them, was purchased. Admission was also obtained in other ways, as, for instance, by the nomination of a 'magistratus.' There is a note on the Decuriae and the Scribae by the learned Henri de Valois, in which note he informs us, that Salmasius (Claude de Saumaise) stole the substance of it. (Ammianus Marcellinus, Lib. xxviii. c. 6, ed. J. Gronov.) Horace (Life in the editions of Suetonius) is said to have got, perhaps bought (scriptum quaestorium comparavit) at Rome, a 'writer's' place in the office of the 'quaestor.' The writings of Horace show more familiarity with many legal and technical terms than one would expect from a poet and an indolent man; and he may have picked up some of this learning when he was in the 'quaestor's' office.

It would be instructive to trace the history of guilds and companies, which have made so large a figure in modern towns, to their Roman originals; for they are undoubtedly of Roman origin. The ancient guilds at Rome were nine in number, as Niebuhr remarks; but there were more than the ancient nine of Numa's institution (Plutarch, Numa, c. 17). Niebuhr mentions bankers, merchants, watermen of the river, and butchers. (Comp. these orations, Lib. ii. c. 55, 'Nam aut publice,' &c.) But it is probable that all the trades had their guilds in the later periods, both at Rome and in other towns of Italy. The 'fullones,' for instance, were a numerous guild at Rome. There is a remark of Niebuhr which contains the germ for large inquiries, and which will be appreciated by those who know that Roman history is more than the history of battles and of conquest: "if, according to the view of a clear-sighted jurist, which seems to me to carry conviction with it as soon as it is uttered, the notaries preserved the Roman law in Italy, the manes of the heroes and lawgivers of Rome owe it for the most part to a guild, in which they saw, not unjustly, a germ which might produce the destruction of the old noble institutions—and the pretensions of which rendered them indignant—that a late posterity is enabled to know and admire these institutions, and their development."

The English name 'scrivener' reminds us of the Roman name 'scriba;' and his practice, so far as I can make it out, bore some resemblance to the private business of a 'scriba.' The race is said to have expired in the person of Jack Ellis, who is mentioned in Boswell's Life of Johnson, iii. 20. (Tomlins, Law Dict.)

patribus familias,] V Lg. 29 F V have 'patribus familiis,' which one might suppose to be a blunder. But Zumpt (in his larger edition), Klotz, and Iordan have it. Zumpt observes, that Priscian (p. 679, Putsch.), after speaking of the old genitive of the first declension in *-as*, says, "We may, however, write 'patrem familiae,' 'patres familiae,' and 'familiarum' and 'familiis;'" and to prove it he quotes this passage. —'percontamini:' Klotz writes 'percunctamini' with V.—'novam rem totam:' the order of V. Zumpt and Iordan have 'rem novam totam.'

novam rem totam atque indignam videri. Ad eos me scribas revoca, si placet: noli hos colligere, qui nummulis corrogatis de nepotum bonis ac de scenicorum corollariis, quum decuriam emerunt, ex primo ordine explosorum in secundum ordinem civitatis se venisse dicunt. Eos scribas tecum disceptatores hujus criminis habebo qui istos scribas moleste ferunt esse. Tametsi, quum in eo ordine videamus esse multos non idoneos, qui ordo industriae propositus est et dignitati, quid mirabimur turpes esse aliquos quo cuivis pretio licet pervenire?

LXXX. Tu ex pecunia publica HS terdecies scribam tuum permissu tuo quum abstulisse fateare, reliquam tibi ullam defen-

de nepotum bonis] Zumpt says, "Vetustiores libri scripti editique omnes *bonis*:" but he writes *donis*, for which his reasons seem very insufficient. Cicero says that they had picked up their money from spendthrifts (nepotes), and from the pay, perhaps (corollariis), of actors (scenicorum). Manutius explains 'scenicorum' to be 'spectantium scenicos ludos;' but I know of no case in which 'scenici,' used thus absolutely, means any thing except actors. The learned commentator, no doubt, saw a difficulty in the words 'de nepotum,' &c.; for if these men got their money partly from the 'bona' or 'dona' of extravagant people, and partly from the 'corollaria' of 'scenici,' then the 'scenici' and 'nepotes' are co-ordinated as two classes of persons, out of whom these men got the means of buying a 'decuria.' This is a difficulty which cannot be got rid of, nor explained by those who, like Zumpt and many others, consider the men of whom Cicero speaks to be 'scenici,' or actors. Whatever then be the sense of 'de scenicorum corollariis,' it signifies a source of gain, which Cicero puts on the same footing as 'de nepotum bonis.' There is another difficulty in 'ex primo ordine explosorum.' 'Explosorum' is taken to be the genitive plural of the passive participle, and to signify that these men, originally actors, and poor actors, in the first class of those who were hissed off the stage, after buying a 'decuria,' think that they have attained the second 'ordo' in the state, or have attained equestrian rank. But, if my explanation so far is right, this cannot be the meaning of 'explosorum,' which I take to be the genitive plural of 'explosor,' though I find no other example of the noun. The sense of 'explosus' is well known. Horat. 1 Sat. x. 76:—

"Nam satis est equitem mihi plaudere, ut audax
Contemptis aliis explosa Arbuscula dixit."

These men were 'explosores' at the theatre, noise-makers, hissers, and so forth; and perhaps the 'scenici' paid them to keep quiet. The 'corollaria' were crowns or chaplets given to the actors, originally of flowers, it is said; afterwards, crowns of thin metal, silvered or gilded, were given them; and afterwards the word seems to have got the meaning of money (crown money), for it is nothing unusual to disguise a money payment under another name. Zumpt's remark on the passage seems to be quite wide of the mark; he takes the people to be actors. Klotz takes them not to be actors; and I suppose that he takes 'explosorum' to be a noun; for he says: "diese Leute, meint nun Cicero, hätten sich in die Decurie eingekauft und wären somit von dem Stande der gemeinen Schmarotzer (ex primo ordine explosorum) in den zweiten Stand (in secundum ordinem civitatis), also in den Ritterstand übergegangen." This passage presents considerable difficulties; and with this explanation I recommend it to others who may be more successful than I have been.

For 'explosorum' V has 'expilosoporum,' which seems to be purely a blunder, and to promise nothing for the pains of looking into it. (See Lib. 4. c. 16, note.)

quid mirabimur] V, Klotz. The usual reading is 'mirabimur.'

80. *terdecies*] There is good authority for 'terdecies' or 'terdeciens,' though most of the MSS. have 'tredecies.' Hotmann says that 'terdecies' is the same as 'tricies,' which, as Zumpt observes, requires to be proved. Lambinus would write 'quattuordecies,' because one twenty-fifth

Lipara
Hiera or Vulcania
Fretum
Tauromenium
Naxus
Acis R.
Catina
Leontini
Megara
Thapsus
SYRACUSAE
Ortygia
Plemmyrium
Helorus
Pachynus Prom.
Camarina
Gela
Agrigentum
Heraclea Minoa
Herbessus
Selinus
Mazara
Motya
Lilybaeum
Segesta
Drepanum
Panhormus
Solus or Soluntum
Himera
Thermae
Cephaloedium
Agyrium
Centuripa
Acrae
Netum

sionem putas esse? hoc ferre quemquam posse? hoc quemquam denique nunc tuorum advocatorum animo aequo audire arbitrare, qua in civitate C. Catoni, consulari homini, clarissimo viro, HS VIII millibus lis aestimata sit, in eadem civitate apparitori tuo esse concessum ut HS uno nomine terdecies auferret? Hinc ille est annulus aureus quo tu istum in contione donasti; quae tua donatio singulari impudentia [praedita] nova Siculis omnibus, mihi vero etiam incredibilis videbatur. Saepe enim nostri imperatores superatis hostibus, optime re publica gesta, scribas suos annulis aureis in contione donarunt: tu vero quibus rebus gestis, quo hoste superato contionem donandi causa advocare ausus es? Neque enim solum scribam tuum annulo, sed etiam virum fortissimum ac tui dissimillimum, Q. Rubrium, excellentem virtute, auctoritate, copiis, corona et phaleris et torque donasti, M. Cossutium, sanctissimum virum atque honestissimum, M. Castricium, summo splendore, ingenio, gratia praeditum. Quid haec sibi horum civium Romanorum dona voluerunt? Siculos praeterea potentissimos nobilissimosque donasti, qui non, quemadmodum sperasti, tardiores fuerunt, sed ornatiores tuo judicio ad testimonia dicenda venerunt. Quibus ex hostium spoliis, de qua victoria, qua ex praeda aut manubiis haec abs te donatio constituta est? an quod te praetore paucorum adventu myoparonum classis pulcherrima, Siciliae praesidium propugnaculumque provinciae, piratarum manibus incensa est? an quod ager Syracusanus praedonum incendiis te praetore vastatus est? an quod forum Syracusanum navarchorum sanguine redundavit? an quod in portu Syracusano piraticus myoparo navigavit? Nihil possum reperire quamobrem te in istam amentiam incidisse arbitrer; nisi forte id egisti ut hominibus ne oblivisci quidem rerum tuarum [male gestarum] liceret. Annulo [est] aureo

of the sum mentioned in c. 70, is 'quattuordecies,' and a few thousands more; but the sum in c. 70 is not given as absolutely the true sum, for Cicero says (c. 70), 'in alteras decumas fere ad nonagies.'

C. Catoni,] See Lib. 4. c. 10.

impudentia [*praedita*]] 'Praedita' is in V. It is not in Lg. 42; and Zumpt and Iordan omit it. See Lib. 5. c. 42.

annulus aureus] According to Klotz, or rather according to the German edition of Adam's Roman Antiquities, which Klotz quotes, the presentation of the ring was a formal declaration of the reception of the receiver into the equestrian 'ordo.' Becker, Handbuch, ii. 1, p. 277, has some remarks on this passage. This is further explained by the following words, 'ut esset unde scriba tuus . . . tueretur,' which Klotz explains to mean, 'that he might have the requisite census for the equestrian rank, to which you had raised him.'

Crowns (coronae), ornaments of metal ('phalerae,' Lib. 4. c. 12), and ornaments worn round the neck (torques), were presented to men who distinguished themselves in military service; cheap rewards, like the cross of the Legion of Honour, not so costly as pensions.

M. Castricium,] See Pro Flacco, c. 30, note.

horum civium] 'horum trium civium' Zumpt, Iordan. V omits 'trium.'

[*male gestarum*]] om. Lg. 42 F.

scriba donatus et ad eam donationem contio est advocata. Quod erat os tuum, quum videbas in contione eos homines, quorum ex bonis istum annulo aureo donabas, qui ipsi annulos aureos posuerant liberisque suis detraxerant, ut esset unde scriba tuus hoc tuum munus ac beneficium tueretur? quae porro tua praefatio donationis fuit? Illa scilicet vetus atque imperatoria, 'quandoque tu quid in proelio, in bello, in re militari'—cujus ne mentio quidem te praetore ulla facta est: an illa, 'quandoque tu nulla unquam mihi in cupiditate ac turpitudine defuisti, omnibusque in iisdem flagitiis mecum et in legatione et in praetura et hic in Sicilia versatus es, ob hasce res, quoniam te re locupletavi, hoc annulo aureo dono.' Vera haec fuisset oratio. Neque enim iste annulus aureus abs te datus istum virum fortem sed hominem locupletem esse declarat. Ita eundem annulum ab alio datum testem virtutis duceremus; abs te donatum comitem pecuniae judicamus.

LXXXI. Dictum, judices, est de decumano frumento: dictum de empto: extremum et reliquum est de aestimato, quod quum

videbas in contione] Zumpt omits 'in contione,' on the authority of Lg. 42, 'quoniam parum confert ad rem.' I think most readers will have no objection to 'in contione,' and will think that it 'multum confert ad rem,' for it was not merely seeing, but seeing in the 'contio.'

quandoque tu] This was one of the old Roman precise 'formulae,' which was retained for solemn occasions. No people stuck more closely to the remembrance of the past. Zumpt refers to Livy (ix. 10), and the reading of Gronovius there in support of 'Quandoque tu,' instead of 'Quando tu,' the reading of Zumpt's MSS., except the four better, which have 'Quandoque tu.' Klotz refers to the Pro Caecina, c. 19, 'Quandoque te in jure conspicio.' The Variorum edition, the text of which is often very bad, has 'Quanto tu quidem,' which may be an error of the press; for presently after it reads 'Quandoquidem tu,' &c.

ob hasce res,] 'ob eas res' Zumpt, from Lg. 42. The 're' after 'te' is only found in Lg. 42; but Zumpt and Klotz accept it, and it is hard to reject it.

81. *aestimato,*] Cicero explains what he has to say. The 'praetor' had a sum of money allowed him by the State for his household, and the price was fixed at which he must buy from the provincials. If grain was cheap, he might be able to save out of his allowance (c. 84); but, if it was dear, he still had the grain at a fixed price, and was sure of a sufficient supply, for the money was doubtless a competent allowance. We must suppose that the number of 'modii,' which the governor would want, was estimated, for he had four 'sestertii' allowed for a 'modius' of wheat, and two for a 'modius' of barley; but Cicero says, 'numero ad summam tritici adjecto;' that is, Verres claimed the right of taking a larger number of 'modii' than the number allowed him (c. 79). The price of barley is here stated at half the price of wheat, which, according to Dureau de la Malle (Économie Politique des Romains, i. 104), was the proportion at Athens also in the time of Demosthenes. Verres indeed took money from the 'aratores' instead of grain; and Cicero finds no fault with Verres for doing this; for many good governors, instead of taking from the 'aratores' the grain which they might have taken, and paying for it, allowed the 'aratores' to compound for a sum of money, which the 'aratores' might be willing to do in order to save themselves trouble: and so the governor would get something under the head of 'frumentum aestimatum,' in addition to the sum that he had for his allowance. If the price was higher than the sum allowed by the State to the governor, the 'aratores' might, without loss to themselves, give him a sum of money, instead of selling corn for less than the market price; and the governor would no doubt take care that he was not a loser by the transaction. Verres, who put no

magnitudine pecuniae, tum injuriae genere quemvis debet commovere; tum vero eo magis quod ad hoc crimen non ingeniosa aliqua defensio sed improbissima confessio comparatur. Nam quum ex senatusconsulto et ex legibus frumentum in cellam ei sumere liceret, idque frumentum senatus ita aestimasset, quaternis HS tritici modium, binis hordei, iste numero ad summam tritici adjecto tritici modios singulos cum aratoribus ternis denariis aestimavit. Non est in hoc crimen, Hortensi, ne forte ad hoc meditere, multos saepe viros bonos fortes et innocentes cum aratoribus et cum civitatibus frumentum in cellam quod sumi oporteret aestimasse, et pecuniam pro frumento abstulisse. Scio quid soleat fieri: scio quid liceat. Nihil quod ante fuerit in consuetudine bonorum nunc in istius facto reprehenditur. Hoc reprehendo, quod, quum in Sicilia HS binis tritici modius esset, ut istius epistola ad te missa declarat, summum HS ternis, id quod et testimoniis omnium et tabulis aratorum planum factum antea est, tum isto pro tritici modiis singulis denarios ternos ab aratoribus exegit.

LXXXII. Hoc crimen est, ut intelligas non ex aestimatione neque ex ternis denariis pendere crimen, sed ex conjunctione

bounds to his illegal conduct, extorted, as it appears, for every 'modius' which he was entitled to buy, three 'denarii,' or twelve 'sesterces,' that is, he got all this money for nothing; and he got it in respect of a much larger number of 'modii' than he was entitled to demand. But compare what Cicero says, c. 85, 87.

in cellam quod] Zumpt places a comma after 'frumentum,' and another after 'oporteret;' and he says: "conjunximus (in cellam quod), mutata interpunctione, nam *sumi* per se nihil est. De postposito pronomine relativo, vid. ad cap. 95." His remark on c. 95 is on 'idem qui fecerint.' If we must have pointing, no doubt the point must be before 'in cellam;' but I cannot understand how any person who has attended to the order of Latin will be helped by this pair of commas. On the contrary, a person who is accustomed to read Latin straight forward, as he does a modern language, and to consider that it stands in the right order, a fact which I suppose nobody will dispute, will feel these points rather a hindrance than a help.

82. *conjunctione*] There is no dispute about the meaning of this passage. The offence of Verres did not consist simply in the fact that he took money instead of corn, or simply in the fact that he took three 'denarii' for each 'modius;' but it consisted in the combined fact of the state of the harvest, or the price of grain (annona), and the sum that he received. All the MSS. have 'conjunctione' except Lg. 42, which has 'conjectione;' "perpetua eorum verborum confusione" (Zumpt). Klotz has 'conjectione,' and he explains the passage in the same way as Zumpt, with this remark: "that the joint consideration of the then price of grain, and of the valuation of the Praetor, is a 'conjectio annonae atque aestimationis,' is of itself manifest to the intelligent reader, and we have no occasion to spend more words in defence of this reading of the best MS., which, however, Zumpt has rejected." It may be true that 'conjectio' can be thus used, but Klotz might have given us a few examples, if there are any, of 'conjectio' thus used with reference to two things.

Orelli's reading and the common reading is 'ex conunctione,' which according to Zumpt first appears in the edition of Victorius, and he does not know whether it is not a typographical error. Whatever is the origin of it, the reading has been perpetuated, and the word 'conunctio' is put in the lexicons. Thus it appears in the excellent lexicon of Forcellini, where there is an attempt to explain it. The passage, even in the German edition of Furlanetto's Forcellini, is read thus: 'ex conunctione annonae atque

annonae atque aestimationis. Etenim haec aestimatio nata est initio, judices, non ex praetorum aut consulum sed ex aratorum et civitatum commodo. Nemo enim fuit initio tam impudens qui, quum frumentum deberetur, pecuniam posceret. Certe hoc ab aratore primum est profectum aut ab ea civitate cui imperabatur: quum aut frumentum vendidisset aut servare vellet aut in eum locum quo imperabatur portare nollet, petivit in beneficii loco et gratiae ut sibi pro frumento quanti frumentum esset dare liceret. Ex hujusmodi principio atque ex liberalitate et accommodatione magistratuum consuetudo aestimationis introducta est. Secuti sunt avariores magistratus, qui tamen in avaritia sua non solum viam quaestus invenerunt verum etiam exitum ac rationem defensionis. Instituerunt semper in ultima ac difficillima ad portandum loca frumentum imperare, ut vecturae difficultate ad quam vellent aestimationem pervenirent. In hoc genere facilior est existimatio quam reprehensio, ideo quod eum qui hoc facit avarum possumus existimare, crimen in eo constituere non tam facile possumus; quod videtur concedendum magistratibus nostris esse, ut iis quo loco velint frumentum accipere liceat. Itaque hoc est quod multi fortasse fecerunt, et ita multi ut ii quos innocentissimos meminimus aut audivimus non fecerint.

LXXXIII. Quaero abs te nunc, Hortensi, cum utris tandem istius factum collaturus es? cum iis, credo, qui benignitate adducti per beneficium et gratiam civitatibus concesserunt ut nummos pro frumento darent. Ita credo petisse ab isto aratores ut, quum HS ternis tritici modium vendere non possent, pro singulis modiis ternos denarios dare liceret. An quoniam hoc non audes dicere, illuc confugies, vecturae difficultate adductos ternos denarios dare maluisse? Cujus vecturae? quo ex loco in quem locum ne portarent? Philomelione Ephesum? Video quid inter annonam inter-

existimationis;' two blunders in five words. 'Existimationis' seems to be a typographical error. Iordan retains the MSS. reading 'conjunctione.'

et ita multi] "*i. e.* et ita quidem, ut *ita* sit minuentis, quod satis me explicavisse puto. Gram. Lat. § 281. Qua re fit ut *et* positum videatur pro *sed*, quod Manutius corrigi voluit. De *et—quidem* cum objectione sermonem continuantis vide Goerenz. ad Lib. iii. de Legg. c. 10. p. 217, et ad 1 de Fin. 10, § 35" (Zumpt). The proposed correction of Manutius, 'malim pro sententia, *sed ita multi*,' is unnecessary. Zumpt's explanation of 'ita' is true. The reader can hardly misunderstand the passage; but the best way of translating 'ita' is not so plain.

83. *cum utris*] 'cum utrisne' Klotz; which is the reading of A B Lg 29 V and Iordan.

Ita credo] 'Hoc credo' Klotz from V.

quo ex loco . . Ephesum?] As some persons may doubt about the right pointing of this passage, I give that of Klotz, which differs from the text, which is that of Zumpt and Iordan, 'Quo ex loco? in quem locum? ne portarent Philomelio Ephesum?' V has 'Philomelo' without 'ne.' The name of the place is Philomelium, a town of Phrygia, and of course at some distance from Ephesus. The site has been fixed

esse soleat: video quot dierum via sit: video Philomeliensibus expedire, quanti Ephesi sit frumentum, [tantum] dare potius in Phrygia quam Ephesum portare aut ad emendum frumentum Ephesum pecuniam et legatos mittere. In Sicilia vero quid ejusmodi est? Henna mediterranea est maxime. Coge ut ad aquam tibi, id quod summi juris est, frumentum Hennenses metiantur vel Phintiam vel Halesam vel Catinam, loca inter se maxime diversa: eodem die quo jusseris deportabunt. Tametsi ne vectura quidem est opus. Nam totus quaestus hic, judices, aestimationis ex annonae natus est varietate. Hoc enim magistratus in provincia assequi potest, ut ibi accipiat ubi est carissimum. Ideo valet ista ratio aestimationis in Asia; valet in Hispania; valet in his provinciis in quibus unum pretium frumento esse non solet. In Sicilia vero quid cujusquam intererat quo loco daret? neque enim portandum erat; et quo quisque vehere jussus esset, ibi tanti frumentum emeret quanti domi vendidisset. Quamobrem si vis, Hortensi, docere aliquid ab isto simile in aestimatione atque a ceteris esse factum, doceas oportebit aliquo in loco Siciliae praetore Verre ternis denariis tritici modium fuisse.

LXXXIV. Vide quam tibi defensionem patefecerim, quam iniquam in socios, quam remotam ab utilitate rei publicae, quam sejunctam a voluntate ac sententia legis. Tu, quum tibi ego

at various places by various geographers. Akshehr, where there are ruins and inscriptions, is supposed by some of the most recent authorities to be the place. (Hamilton, Researches in Asia Minor, i. 472, ii. 184.) Cicero takes an instance from the province of Asia, where Ephesus was the head-quarters of the Roman governor. We collect from this chapter and elsewhere that the governor could require the corn to be delivered at any place, and of course at the place of his residence. It might then, as Cicero says, be for the interest of the Philomelienses to pay in Phrygia the price of corn at Ephesus, rather than convey the corn all the way there, and only receive the governor's price. This monstrous abuse of the Roman governors is without any excuse, and yet we learn from Cicero that it was tolerated. The governor had his money allowance for corn, and might have bought with it all that he wanted at Ephesus (for instance), for we are to suppose that there was plenty in the market there, or Cicero would not have added 'aut ad emendum frumentum . . mittere.' Cicero admits that if Hortensius could name a place in Sicily where corn was three 'denarii' the 'modius,' Verres would only have acted like other governors, in Asia and Spain, for example, in receiving three 'denarii' for every 'modius.'

dare] "'dare' V et Lg 29 42, 'tantum dare,' rell et edd." (Iordan); in whose text 'tantum' is omitted.—'metiantur:' 'admetiantur' V, Iordan.

Phintiam] Phintia, or Phintias, as Diodorus writes it, was at the mouth of the Himera, the larger river of that name, on the southern side of the island. The distances from Henna to Phintia (now Alicata, at the mouth of the river Salso), Halesa, and Catina, would not be quite the longest distance that corn would have to be carried from the interior to any good port. If Cicero means to say that they could carry it down in a single day, he speaks oratorically, for the distance from Henna (Castro Giovanni) to Catina is about forty miles in a direct line. In summer the roads might be good, even if they were only the natural roads, not 'munitae.' But in the wet season so rapid a transport is only an oratorical possibility.

tanti frumentum] This is the reading of V. Zumpt and Iordan have 'tantidem.'

frumentum in meis agris atque in mea civitate, denique in iis locis in quibus versaris, rem geris, provinciam administras, paratus sim dare, angulum mihi aliquem eligas provinciae reconditum ac derelictum? jubeas ibi me metiri quo portare non expediat, ubi emere non possum? Improbum facinus, judices, non ferendum, nemini lege concessum, sed fortasse adhuc in nullo etiam vindicatum. Tamen ego hoc, quod ferri nego posse, Verri concedo, judices, et largior. Si ullo in loco ejus provinciae frumentum tanti fuit quanti iste aestimavit, hoc crimen in istum reum valere oportere non arbitror. Verum enimvero quum esset HS binis aut etiam ternis quibusvis in locis provinciae, duodenos sestertios exegisti. Si mihi tecum neque de annona neque de aestimatione tua potest esse controversia, quid sedes, quid exspectas, quid defendis? Utrum tibi pecuniae coactae conciliatae videntur adversus leges, adversus rem publicam, cum maxima sociorum injuria; an vero id ratione, ordine, e re publica, sine cujusquam injuria factum esse defendis? Quum tibi senatus ex aerario pecuniam prompsisset et singulos tibi denarios adnumerasset, quos tu pro singulis modiis aratoribus solveres, quid facere debuisti? Si, quod L. Piso ille Frugi, qui legem de pecuniis repetundis primus tulit, quum emisses quanti esset, quod superaret pecuniae rettulisses: si ut ambitiosi homines aut benigni, quum pluris senatus aestimasset quam quanti esset annona, ex senatus aestimatione non ex annonae ratione solvisses: sin, ut plerique faciunt, in quo erat aliqui quaestus sed is honestus atque concessus, frumentum, quoniam vilius erat, ne emisses,

84. *in quibus versaris,*] 'in quibus es, versaris,' is the common reading. Zumpt says "quorum verborum discrimen, si quis explicarit, Lag. 42 ego fidem deseram, qui *es* proscribit." Iordan retains 'es.' But the editors say "[Recte Zumptius glossam ineptam sustulit]."—'emere non possum:' all the MSS. have 'possum,' which Lambinus altered to 'possim.' The ground of the correction is that there is the same reason for 'possim' that there is for 'expediat.' But 'possum' may be the original.

quid exspectas, quid defendis?] 'Quid defendis' here and a little further on is the reading of Lg. 42. The common reading in both cases is 'defendes.' By 'quid sedes,' &c., Cicero means to say, 'Why do you stay here, being already convicted?'

coactae conciliatae] The word 'coactae' is only in Lg. 42 φ; but the word is genuine. The terms of the Lex Servilia (c. 5), cited by Zumpt, are still more complete, "ablatum captum coactum conciliatum aversumve." See Lib. 2. c. 57.—'ratione, ordine,' &c.: 'ratione' is only in Lg. 42. The common reading is 'recte.' These two words are often interchanged, and Zumpt has done right in preferring 'ratione.' Iordan has 'recte.'—'aratoribus solveres:' 'aratoribus persolveres' Klotz from V.

L. Piso—Frugi,] See the Excursus on 'Repetundae.' Piso was consul B.C. 133, with P. Mucius Scaevola, and was sent into Sicily against the revolted slaves. He was succeeded in the command by P. Rupilius (Orosius, v. 9). It was probably during his stay in Sicily that he behaved in the manner which Cicero mentions. He returned to the treasury so much of his allowance as he had not expended, a rare instance of disregard of money in a Roman.

quoniam vilius erat, &c.] When corn was at a less price the 'modius' than the senate had allowed for, Verres might have declined buying, that is, requiring the people

sumpsisses id nummorum, quod tibi senatus cellae nomine concesserat.

LXXXV. Hoc vero quid est? quam habet rationem non quaero aequitatis sed ipsius improbitatis atque impudentiae? Neque enim est fere quidquam quod homines palam facere audeant in magistratu quamvis improbe, quin ejus facti si non bonam, at aliquam rationem afferre soleant. Hoc quid est? Venit praetor: frumentum, inquit, me abs te emere oportet. Optime. Modium denario. Benigne ac liberaliter: nam ego ternis HS non possum vendere. Mihi frumentum non opus est: nummos volo. Nam sperabam, inquit arator, me ad denarios perventurum: sed, si ita necesse est, quanti frumentum sit considera. Video esse binis HS. Quid ergo a me tibi nummorum dari potest, quum senatus tibi quaternos HS dederit? Quid possit attendite; et vos quaeso, judices, simul aequitatem praetoris attendite. Quaternos HS, quos mihi senatus decrevit et ex aerario dedit, ego habebo et in cistam transferam de fisco. Quid postea? quid? Pro singulis modiis, quos tibi impero, tu mihi octonos HS dato. Qua ratione? Quid quaeris rationem? non

to furnish him with so much corn; for if he had bought in this way, and paid only the market price, he would not have paid the amount which it may be presumed he was expected to pay. However, he was not bound to require grain 'cellae nomine.' He could keep the money, and supply his wants in the market at a low price, like any other purchaser.

85. *Benigne*] A word of courtesy and politeness. 'I must buy corn of you,' says the Praetor. 'Very good,' replies the Arator. 'A denarius the modius,' continues the Praetor. 'Much obliged,' says the man, 'and your price is fair.' Cicero is using the words of common life, as Horace does, 1 Ep. vii. 15:—

"Vescere sodes.—
Jam satis est—At tu quantumvis tolle—
Benigne."

Mihi frumentum] The reading of Lg. 42 φ. The common reading is 'mihi frumento.'

Nam sperabam,] The old reading is 'non,' which Naugerius corrected, and his emendation, which is certain, is confirmed by Lg. 42 'et φ, ut videtur.' Zumpt compares this use of 'nam' with the Greek, ἀλλὰ γάρ, and the German, *ja—doch*. Several instances have occurred before, Lib. 2. c. 29, &c. Zumpt says, "significat homo se assentiri, et intelligere quid rei sit, sed sibi tamen non placere."

Quid possit attendite;] "Codd. et edd. vet. *possit*. Victorius dedit *poscit*, quod et est in Lag. 42. *Poscat* correxit Lambinus et vulgo receptum est" (Zumpt); who reads 'poscat.' Klotz has 'quid poscit? attendite,' and Iordan also. Orelli has the same as Zumpt. The evidence of Lg. 42 is against 'poscat;' and the amount of difference between 'poscit' and 'possit' is not enough to make us sure that 'poscit' is not an error of the copyist. I see no reason for any change, and good reason against it. The question, 'Quin ergo, &c., dari potest?' &c., has very little meaning, unless we read 'Quid possit,' which is the usual form of answer. It is strange that a thing so plain should have been overlooked. "What money, then, can be had from me?" says the 'arator,' "when the Senate has allowed you four 'sestertii' the 'modius?'" "What can be had?" says Cicero: "attend; and you will soon hear." Compare Terence, Adel. ii. 3. 8, '*Sy.* Quid est? Ct. Quid sit?' and Hec. iv. 4. 93; Andria, v. 4. 12; Phormio, i. 2. 71; Plautus, Miles Gloriosus, ii. 6. 16. Perhaps the pointing should be thus, 'Quid possit? attendite; et vos' &c. But however we point it, 'possit' is the genuine reading.

cistam] The 'praetor's' private purse. As to 'de fisco,' see Act. i. c. 8, note.

Quid postea?] 'quid praeterea?' Lg. 42 and Klotz and Iordan.

tantam rationem res habet quantam utilitatem atque praedam. Dic, dic, inquit ille, planius. Senatus te voluit mihi nummos, me tibi frumentum dare: tu eos nummos, quos mihi senatus dare voluit, ipse habes; a me, cui singulos denarios dari oportuit, binos aufers et huic praedae ac direptioni cellae nomen imponis. Haec deerat injuria et haec calamitas aratoribus te praetore, qua reliquis fortunis omnibus everterentur. Nam quid esse reliqui poterat ei qui per hanc injuriam non modo fructum omnem amitteret, sed etiam instrumentum vendere cogeretur? Quonam se verteret? ex quo fructu nummos quos tibi daret inveniret? Decumarum nomine tantum erat ablatum quantum voluntas tulerat Apronii: pro alteris decumis emptoque frumento aut nihil datum, aut tantum datum quantum reliqui scriba fecerat, aut ultro etiam, id quod didicistis, ablatum. LXXXVI. Cogantur etiam nummi ab aratore? quo modo? quo jure? quo exemplo? Nam, quum fructus diripiebantur aratorum atque omni lacerabantur injuria, videbatur id perdere arator quod aratro ipse quaesisset, in quo elaborasset, quod agri segetesque extulissent. Quibus injuriis gravissimis tamen illud erat miserum solatium, quod id perdere videbatur, quod alio praetore eodem ex agro reparare posset. Nummos vero ut daret arator quos non exararat, quos non aratro ac manu quaerit, boves et aratrum ipsum atque omne instrumentum vendat necesse est. Non enim debetis hoc cogitare: habet idem in nummis, habet idem in urbanis praediis. Nam quum aratori aliquid imponitur, non hominis

quantum reliqui &c.] After deducting the 'binae quinquagesimae,' mentioned in c. 78. Manutius explains 'ultro' by 'nullo nomine, nulla causa, pro Verris ipsius libidine.' Nannius says that we ought to read 'aut ultro etiam id, quod dedistis, ablatum,' which he explains thus: "aut nihil datum aut parum datum aut hoc ipsum quod ultro dederit ab aratore revulsum." But the text appears to be right. At any rate, we have no authority for altering it; and the meaning is not obscure. "For the second 'decumae,' &c., either nothing at all was given, or only so much as remained after the 'scriba' had made his deductions, or, more than that (ultro), money was even taken from the 'aratores,' as you have been informed." Cicero has just told us that the 'arator,' instead of getting a 'denarius' for each 'modius,' received nothing at all, and had to pay two 'denarii.' He then resumes, indignantly, 'Cogantur etiam nummi,' &c. "What! shall money even be wrested from the 'arator?'"

86. *daret . . exararat,*] The reading of V. Zumpt and Iordan have 'det . . exarat.' —Zumpt reads 'omnia instrumenta,' from Lg. 42 only, and observes, "ne hoc quidem sine causa, nam *omnia* valent *cetera omnia*, quum jam duo sint nominata, quae omni instrumento comprehenduntur." But 'instrumentum' is the word. Cicero only uses 'instrumenta' once, in these orations at least (c. 97). He mentions the oxen, the plough, and he adds, 'all the stock,' after mentioning part.

habet idem &c.] Zumpt and Iordan omit the second 'idem' after the second 'habet.' V seems to have it.

aliquid imponitur,] The common reading is 'onus aliquid imponitur;' but Lg. 42, 'et Lamb. in margine' (Zumpt), omit 'onus.' Klotz conjectures 'munus aliquod imponitur.' V has 'jus aliquod imponitur.'

si quae sunt praeterea facultates, sed arationis ipsius vis ac ratio consideranda est, quid ea sustinere, quid pati, quid efficere possit ac debeat. Quamquam illi quoque homines sunt ab isto omni ratione exinaniti ac perditi, tamen hoc vobis est statuendum, quid aratorem ipsum arationis nomine muneris in rem publicam fungi ac sustinere velitis. Imponitis decumas; patiuntur: alteras; temporibus vestris serviendum putant: [dent] emptum praeterea; dabunt si voletis. Haec quam sint gravia et quid his rebus detractis possit ad dominos puri ac reliqui pervenire, credo vos ex vestris rebus rusticis conjectura assequi posse. Addite nunc eodem istius edicta, instituta, injurias: addite Apronii Venereorumque servorum in agro decumano regna ac rapinas. Quamquam haec omitto: de cella loquor. Placet[ne] vobis in cellam magistratibus vestris frumentum Siculos dare gratis? Quid hoc indignius? quid hoc iniquius? Atqui hoc scitote aratoribus Verre praetore optandum ac petendum fuisse.

LXXXVII. Sositheus est Entellinus, homo cum primis prudens et domi nobilis, cujus verba audietis, qui ad hoc judicium legatus publice cum Artemone et Menisco primariis viris missus est. Is quum in senatu Entellino multa mecum de istius injuriis ageret, hoc dixit: si hoc de cella atque hac aestimatione concederetur, velle Siculos senatui polliceri frumentum in cellam gratis, ne posthac tantas pecunias magistratibus nostris decerneremus. Perspicere vos certe scio Siculis quanto opere hoc expediat non ad aequitatem conditionis sed ad minima malorum eligenda. Nam qui mille mod. Verri suae partis in cellam gratis dedisset, duo millia nummum aut summum tria dedisset, idem nunc pro eodem numero frumenti HIS VIII millia dare coactus est. Hoc arator assequi per triennium certe fructu suo non potuit: vendiderit

in rem publicam] Lg. 29 has 'in re publica.' The reading of V is doubtful.—'dent emptum,' &c.: V omits 'dent.' If we omit 'dent,' we must supply 'imponitis,' as Halm observes.—"ex vestris impensis, ex vestris rebus," Klotz from V.

Atqui] Whether the reading should be 'atqui' (Zumpt) or 'atque' (Klotz), it is hard to say. Some of the best MSS. have 'atque.'

87. *audietis,*] Klotz has 'audistis;' but Zumpt refers to c. 43.

ad aequitatem] V has 'aequitate condicionis;' but the form of the sentence is against this reading.

mille mod.] This is so left by Zumpt and Iordan. A man may read it 'modios' or 'modiorum,' as he pleases. V has 'modium,' that is, 'modiorum.' 'Suae partis' means 'for his share of the contribution:' 'pro eo quod ad ipsum attinet' (Manutius). 'In that case he would have given only two thousand sesterces, or at most (summum) three thousand.'

certe fructu suo] The reading of Manutius was 'certo,' for which he proposed 'certe.' All the editions have 'certo,' till the time of Lambinus. All Zumpt's MSS. have 'certe.' Hotmann explained 'certo' in his way, but Lambinus could not understand it; nor can any body else. 'Certe,' 'certainly,' is often equivalent to our

instrumentum necesse est. Quod si hoc munus et hoc vectigal arator tolerare, hoc est, Sicilia ferre ac pati potest, populo Romano ferat potius quam nostris magistratibus. Magna est enim pecunia, magnum praeclarumque vectigal, si modo id salva provincia, si sine injuria sociorum percipere possumus. Nihil detraho magistratibus: tantundem detur in cellam quantum semper datum est: quod praeterea Verres imperat, id si facere non possunt recusent; si possunt, populi Romani potius hoc sit vectigal quam praeda praetoria. Deinde cur in isto genere solo frumenti ista aestimatio constituatur? Si est aequa et ferenda, debet populo Romano Sicilia decumas, det pro singulis modiis tritici ternos x: sibi habeat frumentum. Data tibi est pecunia, Verres, una qua frumentum tibi emeres in cellam, altera qua frumentum emeres a civitatibus quod Romam mitteres: tibi datam pecuniam domi retines, et praeterea pecuniam permagnam tuo nomine aufers. Fac idem in eo frumento quod ad populum Romanum pertinet; exige eadem aestimatione pecuniam a civitatibus, et refer quam accepisti: jam refertius erit aerarium populi Romani quam unquam fuit.—At enim istam rem in publico frumento Sicilia non ferret: hanc rem in meo frumento tulit.—Proinde quasi aut aequior sit ista aestimatio in tuo quam in populi Romani commodo, aut ea res quam ego dico, et ea quam tu fecisti, inter se genere injuriae, non magnitudine pecuniae differat. Verum istam ipsam cellam ferre nullo modo possunt: ut omnia remittantur, ut omnibus injuriis et calamitatibus quas te praetore tulerunt in

phrase 'at least.' The 'arator' could not make such a payment out of his produce, at least; he must have sold his farming stock to raise the money.

instrumentum] Lg. 42 has again the false reading 'instrumenta.'

Nihil detraho] The ordinary punctuation 'nihil detraho: magistratibus,' &c., is properly rejected by Zumpt; but Klotz has it.

constituatur?] The common reading is 'constituitur.' "Delector conjunctivo, quem praebuit Lag. 42" (Zumpt). His delight must have been complete when he found that V has 'constituatur' (Zumpt, Appendix). 'Why should this be the rule?' &c. The pointing of this passage seems to be doubtful. It might stand thus: 'Deinde cur . . . constituatur, si est aequa et ferenda? Debet populo,' &c. If the common reading is right, 'debet,' &c., comes in very awkwardly after 'si est,' &c.; though it is quite intelligible if it be read rapidly as a parenthesis. The old editions omit 'debet' and have 'decumas det' &c., which was hard to explain. 'Debet' is from Lg. 29 42 F V.

jam refertius] 'tum refertius' Klotz from V: but we now learn that the word is not legible in V. Between 'jam' and 'tum,' ill-written, the difference is small. I prefer 'jam.'

At enim istam—hanc rem] I copy Garatoni's note, quoted by Zumpt, not that this passage has any difficulty, but to show that a good Italian scholar is fully aware of the meaning of 'iste:' "quam tu dicis, deinde *hanc rem*, quam ego feci." A note of a distinguished scholar (F. A. Wolf, Demosthenis oratio adversus Leptinem, p. 222) may not be out of place here: "nimirum in Graecis oratoribus pronomen οὗτος notat et judicem et clientem et adversarium, quum Latine *iste* dicatur de adversario, *hic* de cliente et judice. Vid. Aesch. et Demosth. Orr. De Corona, Ciceron. pro Rosc. Amer. et alibi passim:" as in these Verrine orations for instance.

posterum liberentur, istam se cellam atque istam aestimationem negant se ullo modo ferre posse.

LXXXVIII. Multa Sophocles Agrigentinus apud Cn. Pompeium consulem nuper, homo disertissimus et omni doctrina et virtute ornatissimus, pro tota Sicilia de aratorum miseriis graviter et copiose dixisse ac deplorasse dicitur; ex quibus hoc iis qui aderant, nam magno conventu acta res est, indignissimum videbatur, qua in re senatus optime ac benignissime cum aratoribus egisset, large liberaliterque aestimasset, in ea re praedari praetorem, bonis everti aratores, et id non modo fieri, sed ita fieri quasi liceat concessumque sit.

Quid ad haec Hortensius? Falsum esse crimen? Hoc nunquam dicet. Non magnam hac ratione pecuniam captam? Ne id quidem dicet. Non injuriam factam Siculis atque aratoribus? Qui poterit dicere? Quid igitur dicet? Fecisse alios. Quid est hoc? Utrum crimini defensio an comitatus exsilio quaeritur? Tu in hac re publica atque in hac hominum libidine, et, ut adhuc se habuit status judiciorum, etiam licentia, non ex jure, non ex aequitate, non ex lege, non ex eo quod oportuerit, non ex eo quod licuerit, sed ex eo quod aliquis fecerit, id quod reprehenditur recte factum esse defendes? Fecerunt alii. Quid, alia quam multa? Cur in hoc uno

istam se cellam—negant se ullo &c.] In both cases V omits 'se;' and in both cases Klotz follows it. Iordan omits 'se' after 'negant.'

88. *Sophocles Agrigentinus*] V has 'Sosippus.' The reading is uncertain, for Lg. 42 has 'Sotiis Agrigentis,' which Zumpt, perhaps correctly, takes to be for Sosis, which is a Greek name. When this Sophocles or Sosippus addressed Cn. Pompeius, one of the 'consuls' of this year, he addressed him probably as a 'legatus,' and presented to him the 'postulata' of his 'civitas,' as was usual on such occasions.

non modo—sed ita] When 'non modo' may be rendered 'not only,' that is, when the thing mentioned in the clause 'non modo' is affirmed, and something is added to it, 'sed' is followed by 'etiam,' generally, though not always. 'Ita' seems to perform the function of 'etiam' here.

comitatus exsilio] This clearly implies that 'exsilium' was a consequence of a conviction under the 'lex' under which Verres was tried. The condemned must leave Rome, and no doubt a limit was fixed within which he must not approach the city.

non ex jure, . . aequitate,] om. Lg. 42.

Fecerunt alii, &c.] Zumpt observes that most of the MSS. and the old editions have 'aliqui alia,' &c. The common reading now is that which Nannius says is the reading of his old MS., 'alii alia.' But Lg. 42 has 'alii quidem.' Zumpt accordingly reads, 'Fecerunt alii quidem alia quam multa;' and he explains 'quam multa' to be the same as 'quamvis multa,' but adds, that it does not occur elsewhere in Cicero, though it does in other Latin writers; and he refers to Spalding, Ad Quintil. x. 7, 7. Iordan has the same reading as Zumpt. V ϕ have 'alii, quid?' out of which Klotz has made 'Fecerunt alii quid? alia quam multa?' But in his collation at the foot of the page he has, 'Fecerunt alii. Quid? alia quam multa.' His book is not remarkable for typographical accuracy. Cicero has already said, 'Fecisse alios. Quid est hoc?' The supposed defence of Verres was that others had done the same thing, which Cicero says is no defence, 'Utrum crimini,' &c. He now resumes the 'Fecisse' in the form 'Fecerunt.' 'Fecerunt alii.' The excuse of others having done the same thing has been disposed of. He is now

crimine isto genere defensionis uteris? Sunt quaedam omnino in te singularia, quae in nullum hominem alium dici neque convenire possint; quaedam tibi cum multis communia. Ergo, ut omittam tuos peculatus, ut ob jus dicendum pecunias acceptas, ut ejusmodi cetera quae forsitan alii quoque etiam fecerint; illud, in quo te gravissime accusavi, quod ob judicandam rem pecuniam accepisses, eadem ista ratione defendes, fecisse alios? Ut ego assentiar orationi, defensionem tamen non probabo. Potius enim te damnato ceteris angustior locus improbitatis defendendae relinquetur, quam te absoluto alii quod audacissime fecerunt recte fecisse existimentur.

LXXXIX. Lugent omnes provinciae: queruntur omnes liberi populi: regna denique omnia de nostris cupiditatibus et injuriis expostulant: locus intra oceanum jam nullus est neque tam longinquus neque tam reconditus, quo non per haec tempora nostrorum hominum libido iniquitasque pervaserit. Sustinere jam populus Romanus omnium nationum, non vim, non arma, non bellum, sed luctus, lacrimas, querimonias non potest. In ejusmodi re ac mori-

going to speak of the supposed defence of others having done other things; for the words 'Cur in hoc uno,' &c., imply that Verres is going to defend what he did, by saying that others had done other things. Cicero accordingly says in reply to 'Fecerunt alii,' 'Quid, alia quam multa?' 'Well, others have done other things, and how many?' which would mean a great many. He then continues, 'Why do you adopt this mode of defence in the case of this one particular charge against you?' V has 'cur in hoc crimine.'

There still remains another mode of explaining this passage. If we omit the 'quid,' we may write 'Fecerunt alii aliquam multa,' 'others have done a good many things;' or 'Fecerunt alii. Quid, aliquam multa?' 'others have done so. Well, suppose they have done a good many things.' See Lib. 4. c. 25, on 'aliquam multa.' As to the argument 'Fecisse alios,' &c., Lambinus refers to a passage in the oration of Demosthenes against Androtion (c. 2), where Demosthenes is handling similar matter: *φήσει τοίνυν ἀνδρας . . . ὥσπερ γάρ, εἴ τις ἐκείνων προῄκατο, σὺ ταῦτ' οὐκ ἂν ἔγραψας, οὕτως, ἂν σὺ νῦν δίκην δῷς, ἄλλος οὐ γράψει.* He contrasts the condensed and subtle style of the Athenian with the copiousness and fulness of the Roman. The matter of the two passages is the same, and one might almost suppose that there is something of imitation in Cicero, particularly if we compare the concluding words of the Greek with the last sentence of this chapter. The manner of the two orators is very different. Each has his merits; but the severer taste will prefer the Athenian. Lambinus also compares a passage from the Busiridis Encomium of Isocrates (c. 18), *ἐπεὶ τόν γε λόγον ὃν συνέγραψας, οὐκ ἀπολογίαν ὑπὲρ Βουσίριδος ἀλλὰ ὁμολογίαν τῶν ἐγκαλουμένων δικαίως ἄν τις εἶναι νομίσειεν*, &c. The style of Isocrates here is not unlike that of Cicero in this passage, full and flowing, but less vigorous than that of the Roman.

89. *denique*] 'denique etiam' V and Klotz.

intra oceanum] This means on this side of the 'oceanus,' from the straits of Gibraltar eastwards; within the habitable or known world. Juvenal expresses the same notion in other words, Sat. x. 1:

"Omnibus in terris quae sunt a Gadibus usque
Auroram et Gangem."

In another passage Cicero expresses himself still more clearly, De Imp. Cn. Pomp. c. 12, "nunc nullam intra Oceani ostium praedonum navem esse."

luctus,] Only in Lg. 42. V and the rest have 'luctum.'—'manifestis in flagitiis,' V. This 'in' is a difficulty. Zumpt omits

bus, si is qui erit adductus in judicium, quum manifestis flagitiis tenebitur, alios eadem fecisse dicet, illi exempla non deerunt, rei publicae salus deerit, si improborum exemplis improbi judicio ac periculo liberabuntur. Placent vobis hominum mores? placet ita geri magistratus ut geruntur? placet socios sic tractari quod restat ut per haec tempora tractatos videtis? cur haec a me opera consumitur? quid sedetis? cur non in media oratione mea consurgitis atque disceditis? Vultis autem istorum audaciam atque libidines aliqua ex parte resecare? Desinite dubitare utrum sit utilius propter multos improbos uni parcere, an unius improbi supplicio multorum improbitatem coërcere.

XC. Tametsi quae ista sunt exempla multorum? Nam quum in tanta causa, quum in crimine maximo dici a defensore coeptum est factitatum esse aliquid, exspectant ii qui audiunt exempla ex vetere memoria, ex monumentis ac literis, plena dignitatis, plena antiquitatis. Haec enim plurimum solent et auctoritatis habere ad probandum et jucunditatis ad audiendum. Africanos mihi et Catones et Laelios commemorabis, et eos idem fecisse dices? Quamvis res mihi non placeat, tamen contra hominum auctoritatem pugnare non potero. An, quum eos non poteris, proferes hos recentes, Q. Catulum patrem, C. Marium, Q. Scaevolam, M. Scaurum, Q. Metellum? qui omnes provincias habuerunt et frumentum cellae nomine imperaverunt. Magna est hominum auctoritas, et tanta ut etiam delicti suspicionem tegere possit. Non habes ne ex his quidem hominibus qui nuper fuerunt ullum auctorem istius aestimationis. Quo me igitur aut ad quae me exempla revocas? Ab illis hominibus, qui tum versati sunt in re publica quum et optimi mores erant et hominum existimatio gravis habebatur et judicia severa fiebant, ad hanc hominum libidinem ac licentiam me abducis, et in quos aliquid exempli populus Romanus statui putat oportere, ab iis tu defensionis exempla quaeris? Non fugio ne hos quidem

it and refers to c. 64. See the note there.

quod restat] means 'in posterum,' as Manutius correctly explains it.

quid sedetis?] Cicero addresses the 'judices.' 'If such are your opinions, why do you sit here? why don't you rise up all at once in the midst of my address, and be gone?' If such are your opinions, what is the use of a trial?—'audaciam ac libidines' V. Zumpt and Iordan have 'audacias,' &c.

90. *Q. Scaevolam,*] There were two of the name, as Zumpt remarks, well-known men. Probably the Pontifex is meant. See Divin. c. 17. The Metelli were many. Metellus Numidicus may be meant, as Zumpt suggests, consul B.C. 100.

ullum auctorem] 'any one who set the example of such a fixing of the price as you have adopted.'

ad quae me exempla] 'ad quae me exempla' Lg. 42; but Zumpt has not accepted the 'me.'—'et judicia severa fiebant:' Zumpt suspects that these words are an interpolation.

mores, dummodo ex his ea quae probat populus Romanus exempla, non ea quae condemnat, sequamur. Non circumspiciam, non quaeram foris: habeo judices tecum principes civitatis, P. Servilium et Q. Catulum, qui tanta auctoritate sunt, tantis rebus gestis, ut in illo antiquissimorum clarissimorumque hominum de quibus antea dixi numero reponantur. Exempla quaerimus et ea non antiqua. Modo uterque horum exercitum habuit. Quaere, Hortensi, quoniam te recentia exempla delectant, quid fecerint. Itane vero Q. Catulus frumento est usus, pecuniam non coëgit? P. Servilius quinquennium exercitui quum praeesset et ista ratione innumerabilem pecuniam facere quum posset, non statuit sibi quidquam licere quod non patrem suum, non avum Q. Metellum, clarissimum hominem, facere vidisset: C. Verres reperietur, qui quidquid expediat id licere dicat? quod nemo nisi improbus fecerit, id aliorum exemplo se fecisse defendat?

XCI. At in Sicilia factitatum est.—Quae est ista conditio Siciliae? cur quae optimo jure propter vetustatem, fidelitatem, propinquitatemque esse debet, huic praecipua lex injuriae definitur? Sed in ista ipsa Sicilia non quaeram exemplum foris: hoc ipso ex consilio utar exemplis. C. Marcelle, te appello. Siciliae provinciae quum esses pro consule praefuisti. Num quae in tuo imperio

habeo judices tecum] 'Habeo' is the reading of Lg. 29 42 φ. Cicero says, "Here we have the very 'judices' who are trying you. You and I have persons to whose conduct we may appeal: let us see how they have conducted themselves." Cicero has mentioned Servilius before, Lib. 1. c. 21. He mentions Catulus again, Lib. 4. c. 21; and C. Marcellus, Lib. 4. c. 42.

Itane vero] The current punctuation is this: 'Itane vero? Q. Catulus . . . coëgit.' Another instance of this form occurs in Lib. 3. c. 8, 'Itane vero . . . sustulisti?' the true form of which it is not easy to mistake.

quinquennium] From his consulship, B.C. 79, to his triumph, B.C. 75, P. Servilius held a command for five years. He took Olympus (Lib. 1. c. 21), and Phaselis (Lib. 4. c. 10), destroyed Corycus, was the first Roman who led an army through the Taurus, and he reduced the Isauri, whence he had the name Isauricus. He was the son of a daughter of Q. Metellus Macedonicus (Zumpt).

91. *optimo jure*] 'Optimo jure' is a legal phrase, which signifies 'on the best or most favourable terms.' Akin to this is the expression used in the terms of contract for selling a piece of land, 'uti optimus maximusque est,' which means free from all claims and incumbrances. The following passage will explain the expression, Paulus, Dig. 50. 16. 169, "non tantum in traditionibus sed et in emptionibus et stipulationibus et testamentis adjectio haec 'ut optimus maximusque est,' hoc significat ut liberum praestetur praedium, non ut etiam servitutes ei debeantur." It means that the land owes no 'servitus,' but it does not mean that any other land is servient to it.

huic praecipua] Hotmann says that 'huic praecipue' would be 'apertius,' by which I suppose he means 'clearer.' His explanation of 'lex,' in the sense of a 'lex' proper, or a 'privilegium,' is not correct, which is proved by the word 'injuriae.' We could not say in Latin, 'lex injuriae,' in the sense of a 'lex' proper. 'Lex' means 'terms.'

pro consule] A 'praetor' was often invested with the title and power of 'proconsul.' There is a note on this matter by Oudendorp on the Bellum Africanum, c. 80. 'Pro consule' is said of him who has 'pro-

pecuniae cellae nomine coactae sunt? Neque ego hoc in tua laude pono: alia sunt tua facta atque consilia, summa laude digna, quibus illam tu provinciam afflictam et perditam erexisti atque recreasti; nam hoc de cella ne Lepidus quidem fecerat cui tu successisti. Quae sunt tibi igitur exempla ex Sicilia cellae, si hoc crimen non modo Marcelli facto sed ne Lepidi quidem potes defendere? An me ad M. Antonii aestimationem frumenti exactionemque pecuniae revocaturus es? Ita, inquit, ad M. Antonium: hoc enim mihi significasse et annuisse visus est. Ex omnibus igitur populi Romani praetoribus, consulibus, imperatoribus, M. Antonium delegisti, et ejus unum improbissimum factum quod imitarere. Et hic utrum mihi difficile est dicere an his existimare ita se in isto infinito imperio M. Antonium gessisse ut multo isti perniciosius sit dicere se in re improbissima voluisse Antonium imitari, quam si posset defendere nihil in vita se M. Antonii simile fecisse? Homines in judiciis ad crimen defendendum non quid fecerit quispiam proferre solent, sed quid probarit. Antonium, quum multa contra sociorum salutem, multa contra utilitatem provinciarum et faceret et cogitaret, in mediis injuriis ejus et cupiditatibus mors oppressit. Tu mihi, quasi omnia ejus facta atque consilia senatus populusque

consulare imperium,' though he may be only 'pro praetore.' See also his note on Bell. Civil. i. 12.

ex Sicilia] V: 'in Sic.' Zumpt.

Ita, inquit, ad M. Antonium:] See Lib. 2. c. 3. He was in Sicily, B.C. 74, when Sacerdos was 'praetor' there, and apparently also in B.C. 73 (Divin. c. 17), when Verres was 'praetor.' Klotz reads 'Ita, inquit, ad Antonii: hoc,' &c., from V.

M. Antonii simile] The use of 'simile' with a genitive is not exactly like some of the instances that have occurred. No variation of the MSS. is noted.

ad crimen defendendum] Zumpt has observed in a note on another passage (Lib. 2. c. 72), that 'crimen defendere' is not Latin; but I suppose he changed his mind when he came to this passage, for he makes no objection to it. 'Crimen defendere' does not differ from 'bellum defendere' (Caesar, B. G. i. 44). 'Quid probarit' means what he has made good, or satisfied the 'judices' to be right and proper. This sense of the word is not uncommon in these orations. All the MSS. except V have 'probarint,' the sense of which is the same; but the word would refer to 'homines.' Hotmann had conjectured 'probarit.'

mors oppressit.] This is a common use of 'oppressit.' 'Death surprised him,' came upon him suddenly. So in Divin. c. 14, 'nunquam ille me opprimet consilio.'

Tu mihi,] The juxtaposition of pronouns is common in Cicero, and some instances have been noticed. We can feel what it means. But persons may differ as to the mode in which they will express it. Virgil has an example:

"Tu mihi seu magni superas jam saxa
Timavi."—Ecl. viii. 6.

The words 'Tu mihi' are properly connected with 'superas,' and not with the more remote verb 'accipe' (v. 11), as some would have it.—'Quasi' and 'ita' sometimes stand thus; and the meaning is clear, if we observe that 'quasi' contains a form of the relative, and 'ita' is a form of 'is,' so that there is nothing different in this expression from the ordinary position, 'qui—is,' 'quem—eum,' and the like.

Most of the MSS. and the old editions have 'S. P. que R. judices,' that is, 'Senatus Populusque Romanus judices,' a reading which some editions have kept: others have 'Senatus Populique Romani judices,'

Romanus judices comprobarint, ita M. Antonii exemplo istius audaciam defendis.

XCII. At idem fecit Sacerdos.—Hominem innocentem et summa prudentia praeditum nominas; sed tum idem fecisse erit existimandus si eodem consilio fecerit. Nam genus aestimationis ipsum a me nunquam est reprehensum; sed ejus aequitas aratorum commodo et voluntate perpenditur. Non potest reprehendi ulla aestimatio quae aratori non modo incommoda non est sed etiam grata est. Sacerdos, ut in provinciam venit, frumentum in cellam imperavit. Quum esset ante novum tritici modius denariis v, petiverunt ab eo civitates ut aestimaret. Remissior aliquanto ejus fuit aestimatio quam annona; nam aestimavit denariis III. Vides eandem aestimationem propter temporis dissimilitudinem in illo laudis causam habere, in te criminis, in illo beneficii, in te injuriae. Eodem tempore praetor Antonius denariis III aestimavit post messem, summa in vilitate, quum aratores frumentum dare gratis mallent. Et aiebat se tantidem aestimasse quanti Sacerdotem, neque mentiebatur; sed eadem aestimatione alter sublevarat aratores, alter everterat. Quod nisi omnis frumenti ratio ex temporibus esset et annona, non ex numero neque ex summa consideranda, nunquam tam grati hi sesquimodii, Q. Hortensi, fuissent, quos tu

which, as Zumpt observes, we cannot admit. Zumpt, following Lg. 42, reads 'senatus, populus, judices comprobarint,' and he adds, "ut tres potestates in rep. ἀσυνδέτως nominentur." But this explanation is not satisfactory. Klotz settles the difficulty by omitting 'judices' as V was supposed to do. But Brunnius thinks that V has

SENATVS POPVLVS IVD. CONPROBARINT.

If the text is right, 'judices' must be either the vocative or the nominative. The vocative 'judices' would seem out of place. Manutius observes that it is not the vocative, but the nominative: "judices enim appellat senatum populumque Romanum." This explanation seems to me sufficient: for 'judices comprobarint' perhaps may be said in the same sense as 'judicio suo comprobarint.'

92. *ante novum*] That is, as Manutius explains it, 'frumentum.' Before the new corn came in, the 'modius' of wheat sold for five 'denarii,' or twenty 'sesterces,' which is a high price. There is nothing improbable in wheat rising before the harvest, especially if the produce should be uncertain: after the harvest (post messem) it was lower. This being the case, the Sicilians asked Sacerdos to set an 'aestimatio.' He might, we presume, have demanded wheat at four 'sestertii' the 'modius;' which would have been a loss of sixteen to the farmer. Instead of this he took money, fixing the value of a 'modius' nominally at three 'denarii,' which amount he seems to have received: for the 'aestimatio' was not the sum paid to the farmer, but the sum that the 'praetor' was to receive. We will hope that he did not take the money in respect of a larger number of 'modii' than he was entitled to. The x, which occurs sometimes both in the MSS. and in the editions, is the symbol of the 'denarius.'

sesquimodii,] Which he distributed as 'quaestor,' Manutius says. It alludes to a gratuitous distribution of corn, as we may collect. 'Describere,' says Hotmann, is 'distribuere, dispertiri,' and there is no doubt that the word here must mean that. But it ought to be 'discripsisses.' 'Discribere, distribuere,' go together in the inscription of Venafrum (Lib. 2. c. 30). The MS. of the De Re Publica (ii. 22) has

quum ad mensurae tam exiguam rationem populo Romano in capita discripsisses, gratissimum omnibus fecisti. Caritas enim annonae faciebat ut istuc, quod re parvum videtur, tempore magnum videretur. Idem istuc si in vilitate populo Romano largiri voluisses, derisum tuum beneficium esset atque contemptum.

XCIII. Noli igitur dicere istum idem fecisse quod Sacerdotem, quoniam non eodem tempore neque simili fecit annona. Dicito potius, quoniam habes auctorem idoneum, quod Antonius uno adventu et vix menstruis cibariis fecerit, id istum per triennium fecisse, et istius innocentiam M. Antonii facto atque auctoritate defendito. Nam de Sex. quidem Peducaeo, fortissimo atque innocentissimo viro, quid dicetis? de quo quis unquam arator questus est? aut quis non ad hoc tempus innocentissimam omnium diligentissimamque praeturam illius hominis existimat? Biennium provinciam obtinuit, quum alter annus in vilitate, alter in summa caritate fuerit. Num aut in vilitate nummum arator quisquam dedit, aut in caritate de aestimatione frumenti questus est?—At uberiora cibaria facta sunt caritate.—Credo; neque id est novum neque reprehendendum. Modo C. Sentium vidimus, hominem vetere illa ac singulari innocentia praeditum, propter caritatem frumenti quae fuerat in Macedonia permagnam ex cibariis pecuniam deportare. Quamobrem non ego invideo commodis tuis, si quae ad te lege venerunt: injuriam queror, improbitatem coarguo, avaritiam in crimen et in judicium voco.

XCIV. Quod si suspiciones injicere velitis, ad plures homines, ad plures provincias crimen hoc pertinere, non ego istam defen-

'reliquum populum distribuit in quinque classis . . . eosque ita disparavit. . . . Quae discriptio,' &c.; where the word 'discriptio' refers to 'distribuere.' This word 'discribere' has long been proscribed by editors and lexicographers, but it must be restored to the texts and to the lexicons.

93. *auctorem idoneum.*] This is Antonius. Cicero is speaking sarcastically. You have the example or authority of Antonius, which you think sufficient. What he did for a month's allowance, Verres did for three years. The 'istius innocentiam' is the 'innocentia' of Verres, which of course is said ironically.

At uberiora] The supposed objection of the defenders of Verres: "the 'cibaria' of Peducaeus were made more productive to him in consequence of the high price." Cicero admits this, but it was no novelty. Manutius explains it thus: "He either received the value of the 'frumentum,' or he received the 'frumentum' itself, and by selling it raised more money than when it was cheap; which also C. Sentius did." If he received money from the 'aratores,' when corn was dear, and kept the money which the Senate allowed him, he would gain, if the two sums put together enabled him to buy what he wanted for his household, and left something over. The result might be the same, if he gave for the corn the price which the Senate set on it, and, having more than he wanted, sold the surplus at the high current price. Cicero shows by an instance one of the ways in which a fortune might be acquired by a governor. That which he admits to be a proceeding free from blame, seems to us a monstrous abuse. This 'cellae nomine' was a fruitful source of gain even to an honest governor.

sionem vestram pertimescam, sed me omnium provinciarum defensorem esse profitebor. Etenim hoc dico, et magna voce dico: ubicunque hoc factum est, improbe factum est; quicunque hoc fecit, supplicio dignus est. Nam per deos immortales videte, judices, et prospicite animis quid futurum sit. Multi magnas pecunias ab invitis civitatibus atque ab invitis aratoribus ista ratione cellae nomine coëgerunt: omnino ego neminem video praeter istum, sed do hoc vobis et concedo esse multos: in hoc homine rem adductam in judicium videtis. Quid facere potestis? Utrum, quum judices sitis de pecunia capta conciliata, tantam pecuniam captam negligere, an, quum lex sociorum causa rogata sit, sociorum querimonias non audire? Verum hoc quoque vobis remitto: negligite praeterita, si vultis, sed ne reliquas spes turbetis atque omnes provincias evertatis; id providete ne avaritiae, quae antehac occultis itineribus atque angustis uti solebat, auctoritate vestra viam patefaciatis illustrem atque latam. Nam si hoc probatis et si licere pecunias isto nomine capi judicatis, certe hoc, quod adhuc nemo nisi improbissimus fecit, posthac nemo nisi stultissimus non faciet. Improbi sunt qui pecunias contra leges cogunt; stulti qui quod licere judicatum est praetermittunt. Deinde, judices, videte quam infinitam istis hominibus licentiam pecuniarum eripiendarum daturi sitis. Si ternos denarios qui coegit erit absolutus, quaternos, quinos, denos denique aut vicenos coget alius. Quae erit reprehensio, in quo primum injuriae gradu resistere incipiet severitas judicis, quotus erit iste denarius qui non sit ferendus, et in quo primum aestimationis iniquitas atque improbitas reprehendatur? Non enim a vobis summa sed genus aestimationis erit comprobatum: neque hoc potestis judicare, ternis denariis aestimare licere, denis non licere. Ubi enim semel ab annonae ratione et ab aratorum voluntate res ad praetoris libidinem translata est, non est jam in lege neque in officio sed in voluntate hominum atque avaritia positus modus aestimandi. XCV. Quapropter si vos semel in judicando

94. *evertatis*] Orelli placed (;) after 'evertatis.' Iordan, following Madvig, I believe, points it thus, 'evertatis, id providete, ne' &c.

istis hominibus . . daturi sitis.] The reading of Lg. 42. The other reading is 'sitis hominibus . . . daturi.'

injuriae gradu] 'at what degree of wrong shall the severity of the Judex begin to make resistance?' Horace (C. i. 3) has 'Quem mortis timuit gradum?'

ternis denariis] V has 'tribus denariis,' which Klotz also has; and yet he writes 'denis non licere.' Lg. 42 has 'tuis.'

ad praetoris libidinem] 'ad praetorum libidinem' V and Klotz.

neque in officio] 'Editi omnes *atque in officio*' (Zumpt). '*Neque* V, 7 Lagg., alii: *que* Lg. 42; *atque*, Or.' (Iordan). Zumpt doubts if 'atque' is admissible in such a case as this, for there is first a negative (non), and 'lege . . . officio' are separated by a repetition of the preposition.

finem aequitatis et legis transieritis, scitote vos nullum ceteris in aestimando finem improbitatis et avaritiae reliquisse. Videte igitur quam multa simul a vobis postulentur. Absolvite eum qui se fateatur maximas pecunias cum summa sociorum injuria cepisse. Non est satis. Sunt alii quoque complures qui idem fecerint. Absolvite etiam illos si qui sunt, ut uno judicio quam plurimos improbos liberetis. Ne id quidem satis est. Facite ut ceteris posthac idem liceat. Licebit. Adhuc parum est. Permittite ut liceat quanti quisque velit [tanti] aestimet: aestimabit. Videtis jam profecto, judices, hac aestimatione a vobis comprobata neque modum posthac avaritiae cujusquam neque poenam improbitatis futuram. Quam ob rem quid agis, Hortensi? Consul es designatus: provinciam sortitus es: de aestimatione frumenti quum dices, sic te audiemus quasi id quod ab isto recte factum esse defendes te facturum profiteare, et quasi quod isti licitum esse dices vehementer cupias tibi licere. Atqui si id licebit, nihil est quod putetis quemquam posthac commissurum ut de pecuniis repetundis condemnari possit. Quantam enim quisque concupierit pecuniam, tantam licebit per cellae nomen aestimationis magnitudine consequatur.

XCVI. At enim est quiddam quod, etiamsi palam in defendendo non dicet Hortensius, tamen ita dicet ut vos id suspicari et cogitare

95. *Absolvite eum*] '*Eum* etiam V (non *illum* ut legit Maius)' (Iordan). As there is no authority, I suppose, for 'illum,' I now take 'eum' instead of 'illum,' which, if there were authority for it, might be defended, for we may suppose Cicero to dwell with emphasis on it. Shortly after there is 'absolvite illos.'

qui idem] Zumpt prefers '*idem qui* eleganter Lg. 42;' and he gives examples where a word precedes 'qui,' which belongs to the same clause, as Lib. 4. c. 4, 'omnia qui regna coerceret.' There is no difficulty in collecting many instances; but this is not a case in which the ear prefers the elegance of Lg. 42. Iordan has 'idem qui.'

Adhuc parum est.] This, I think, is the true reading, and not 'At hoc,' which Zumpt and Orelli have. V has 'adhuc,' and Klotz and Iordan.

tanti . . aestimabit.] "'*tanti aestimabit* (med. om.) codd. vulgares (*aestimabitis* Lg. 29); *tanti aestimet. Aestimabit*' edd. post Crat." (Iordan). The readings of Lg. 42 and V show that something has been lost in this passage. Iordan has in the text 'tanti aestimare; † permissum est: stultissimus quisque posthac minimo aestimabit.'

Quam ob rem] Zumpt properly (Appendix) rejects his reading 'Quas ob res,' for that of V, 'Quam ob rem.' But his pointing spoils the sense, 'Quam ob rem, quid agis, Hortensi?' as if two questions were asked, though I do not suppose that he takes it so. Cicero often places 'quam ob rem' at the beginning of a sentence, not as an interrogative, but as a word of reference. It is as if he were to say, 'now for all these reasons, Hortensius, consider what you are doing.'

provinciam sortitus] The consular provinces were fixed by the Senate before the election, pursuant to a 'lex Sempronia,' B.C. 123; and the consuls determined by lot which of the two provinces assigned to them each should take. Hortensius got Crete, but he gave it up to his colleague, Q. Metellus, who earned the name of Creticus. Hortensius remained at Rome. See De Provinciis Consularibus, Introd. vol. iv. Sallust, Jug. c. 27.

Atqui si id] 'Atque' &c., Lg. 42. V omits 'atqui;' and Klotz also.

96. *non dicet—tamen ita dicet*] Klotz has the future 'dicet' in both cases from

possitis, pertinere hoc ad commodum senatorium, pertinere ad utilitatem eorum qui judicent, qui in provinciis cum potestate aut cum legatione se futuros aliquando arbitrentur. Praeclaros vero existimas judices nos habere, quos alienis peccatis concessuros putes quo facilius ipsis peccare liceat. Ergo id volumus populum Romanum, id provincias, [id] socios nationesque exteras existimare, si senatores judicent, hoc certe unum genus infinitae pecuniae per summam injuriam cogendae nullo modo posse reprehendi? Quod si ita est, quid possumus contra illum praetorem dicere qui quotidie templum tenet, qui rem publicam sistere negat posse nisi ad equestrem ordinem judicia referantur? Quod si ille hoc unum agitare coeperit, esse aliquod genus cogendae pecuniae senatorum commune et jam prope concessum ordini, quo genere ab sociis maxima pecunia per summam injuriam auferatur, neque id ullo modo senatoriis judiciis reprehendi posse, idque dum equester ordo judicaret nunquam esse commissum, quis obsistet, quis erit tam cupidus vestrum, tam fautor ordinis, qui de transferendis judiciis possit recusare?

XCVII. Atque utinam posset aliqua ratione hoc crimen quamvis falsa modo humana atque usitata defendere: minore periculo vestro, minore periculo provinciarum omnium judicaretis. Negaret hac aestimatione se usum; vos id homini credidisse, non factum

V; which reading is at least consistent with the future tenses in the preceding chapter, where Zumpt however has 'defendis . . dicis;' and here 'dicit . . dicit.'

templum tenet,] The Praetor is L. Aurelius Cotta, who was now agitating about the Lex Aurelia de Judiciis, which was enacted in this year (Lib. 5. c. 69). Cotta was daily addressing the people about his proposed Lex, before the Rostra. The Templum means a place chosen by the Augurs, for the observation of the 'auspicia' (Livy, i. 4). Cicero (De Divin. i. 20) quotes a line from Ennius:—

> "Quamquam multa manus ad caeli caerula templa
> Tendebam lacrimans."

Every inaugurated place was a Templum; as the Rostra in this passage, and in the oration In Vatin. c. 10, "in Rostris, in illo inquam inaugurato templo ac loco." The word Templum is explained by Varro, De L. L. vii. 7—9: "quaqua intuitus erat oculi, a tuendo primum templum dictum. Quocirca caelum qua attuimur dictum templum.—Ejus templi partes quattuor dicuntur, sinistra ab oriente, dextra ab occasu, antica ad meridiem, postica ad septentrionem." This applies to the ethereal 'templum.' He says further: "in terris dictum templum locus augurii aut auspicii causa quibusdam conceptis verbis finitus." See the remarks on Auspicia, Becker, Handbuch der Röm. Alterthümer, ii. 3, p. 68.

sistere] Manutius would prefer '*stare*.' N Lg. 42 have 'subsistere;' but 'sistere' is used sometimes in an intransitive sense. The metaphor seems to be taken from a thing which is falling, and its downward course cannot be stopped.

judicaret] 'iudicauit V, ut Brunnio videtur, idque optime' (Iordan); but he retains 'judicaret' in his text.

97. *Negaret*] This means 'if he should deny.' Lambinus conjectured that 'si' should be prefixed to 'negaret,' which is unnecessary. Orelli incorrectly puts a note of interrogation after 'usum,' which spoils the phrase. See Lib. 3. c. 2, note. Zumpt refers to Lib. 5. c. 65.

vos id homini &c.] This is the text of Zumpt, and of codd. plerique, except that

comprobasse videremini. Nullo modo negare potest: urgetur a tota Sicilia: nemo est ex tanto numero aratorum a quo pecunia cellae nomine non sit exacta. Vellem etiam hoc posset dicere, nihil ad se istam rationem pertinere; per quaestores rem frumentariam esse administratam. Ne id quidem ei licet dicere propterea quod ipsius literae recitantur ad civitates de ternis denariis missae. Quae est igitur defensio? "Feci quod arguis: coëgi pecunias maximas cellae nomine: sed hoc mihi licuit; vobis si prospicitis licebit." Periculosum provinciis genus injuriae confirmari judicio; perniciosum nostro ordini populum Romanum existimare non posse eos homines qui ipsi legibus teneantur leges in judicando religiose defendere. Atque isto praetore, judices, non solum aestimandi frumenti modus non fuit sed ne imperandi quidem. Neque enim id quod debebatur, sed quantum commodum fuit imperavit. Summam faciam vobis ex literis publicis ac testimoniis civitatum frumenti in cellam imperati: reperietis quinquies tanto, judices, amplius istum quam quantum in cellam sumere [ei] licitum sit civitatibus imperasse. Quid ad hanc impudentiam addi potest, si et aestimavit tanti ut homines ferre non possent, et tanto plus quam erat ei concessum legibus imperavit?

Quapropter cognita tota re frumentaria, judices, jam facillime perspicere potestis amissam esse populo Romano Siciliam, fructuosissimam atque opportunissimam provinciam, nisi eam vos istius damnatione recuperatis. Quid est enim Sicilia, si agri cultionem sustuleris, et si aratorum numerum ac nomen extinxeris? Quid autem potest esse in calamitate residui quod non ad miseros aratores isto praetore per summam injuriam ignominiamque pervenerit? quibus quum decumas dare deberent vix

the order is "vos id credidisse homini,' but 'homini' should come first. V and Iordan have 'vos id credidissetis: homini credidisse,' &c., which is capable of being explained in several ways. Klotz prints, 'vos id credidissetis: credidisse homini, non factum' &c. Lg. 42 F have 'hominibus credidisse,' where 'hominibus' is a mistake for 'homini.'

de ternis denariis] 'de tribus denaris' V.

si prospicitis] If you look forward, if you take care, that is, if you acquit me; as Verres is supposed to say.

vos homines] The Senators, for only 'magistratus' came within the provisions of the Lex de Repetundis, as the first part of the Lex Servilia shows. Compare Pro Rabirio Post. c. 5 (Zumpt). Manutius gives the same explanation.

quinquies tanto,] See Lib. 3. c. 43, note.

potestis] 'poteritis' Lg. 42, Iordan.

si agri cultionem] The common reading is 'si ei agri cultionem,' &c. Klotz and Iordan omit 'ei,' following Lg. 42. Zumpt observes, "neque dativum magnopere desidero, immo malo abesse. Cf. ad Lib. iv. 12 extr." But still he keeps the 'ei.' It is better omitted. The omission of the pronouns in Latin, where they are not required to make the sense clear, is one of the nicetics of the language, which by careful reading we appreciate.

residui] Lg. 42 has 'reliqui.'

quibus quum decumas &c.] Zumpt has a curious note on this passage: "conjunge *quibus ipsis*, et facile senties, quam

ipsis decumae relictae sunt; quum pecunia deberetur, soluta non est; quum optima aestimatione senatus frumentum eos in cellam dare voluisset, etiam instrumenta agrorum vendere coacti sunt. XCVIII. Dixi jam antea, judices, ut has omnes injurias tollatis, tamen ipsam rationem arandi spe magis et jucunditate quadam quam fructu atque emolumento teneri. Etenim ad incertum casum et eventum certus quotannis labor et certus sumptus impenditur. Annona porro pretium nisi in calamitate fructuum non habet: si autem ubertas in percipiendis fructibus fuit, consequitur vilitas in vendendis; ut aut male vendendum intelligas, si bene processit, aut male perceptos fructus, si recte licet vendere. Totae autem res rusticae ejusmodi sunt ut eas non ratio neque labor, sed res incertissimae venti tempestatesque moderentur. Hinc quum unae decumae lege et conditione detrahantur, alterae novis institutis propter annonae rationem imperentur, ematur praeterea frumentum quotannis publice, postremo etiam in cellam magistratibus et legatis imperetur; quid aut quantum praeterea est quod aut liberum possit habere ille arator ac dominus in potestate suorum fructuum aut in ipsis fructibus solutum? Quod si haec ferunt omnia, si potius vobis ac rei publicae quam sibi et suis commodis opera, sumptu, labore deserviunt, etiamne haec nova debent edicta et imperia praetorum, et Apronii dominationem, et Venereorum servorum furta rapinasque ferre? etiamne frumentum pro empto gratis dare? etiamne in cellam quum cupiant gratis dare, ultro pecuniam grandem addere? etiamne

hoc praestet conjecturae Lambini *ipsae*." Instead of which say, "read the passage straight forward, and you will find no difficulty in 'ipsis,' and you will reject the 'ipsae,' which Lambinus proposes."

instrumenta] Here we have the plural with 'agrorum.' See c. 86.

98. *pretium*] Abundance and low prices; a failure of crops and high prices. No chance of high prices with good crops. A man only sells at a good price ('recte' opposed to 'male') when the harvest is bad. 'Recte,' says Manutius, as the farmer would say, because he likes a short crop and high prices, better than a good crop and low prices. Cicero's remarks on the risks of the farmer are true. He may sometimes lose all his labour. He is not however the only person who sometimes labours without profit. This is a calamity which is incident to all labour.

calamitate fructuum] A damage of the crops. The word occurs in another sense in Lib. 1. c. 16. The old grammarians define a 'calamitas' to be a fall of hail, or a tempest, which damages the crops (see Forcellini, Calamitas); and, after their fashion, they derived the word from 'calamus,' because the 'culmus' was injured; which is absurd every way. If I am not mistaken, Professor Key has suggested that 'calamitas' contains the root 'cad' to fall, which fits the meaning well. The interchange of *d* and *l* is not unusual.

Totae autem &c.] The reading of Lg. 42 is 'Totae autem res hujusmodi rusticae,' &c.; and 'ventus tempestasque.'—Lg. 42 N have 'lege et consuetudine,' which Klotz and Jordan have. But this is not a case of 'consuetudo:' Cicero joins with 'lege' a word of like import, a 'conditio' or terms of submission to Rome. Zumpt refers to the passage, c. 6, 'ut eadem conditione,' &c.

rapinasque ferre?] Lg. 42. Perhaps better than the other reading 'perferre;' for 'perferre' occurs afterwards, and the orator seeks to magnify the wrong as he proceeds.

ultro] 'Ultro,' says Zumpt, belongs to

haec tot detrimenta atque damna cum maximis injuriis contumeliisque perferre? Itaque haec, judices, quae pati nullo modo potuerunt non pertulerunt. Arationes omnes tota Sicilia desertas atque ab omnibus relictas esse cognostis; neque quidquam aliud agitur hoc judicio nisi ut antiquissimi socii et fidelissimi Siculi, coloni populi Romani atque aratores, vestra severitate et diligentia, me duce atque auctore in agros atque in sedes suas revertantur.

'pecuniam addere,' about which there can be no dispute. But his remark is not useless, for he observes that it is usually so pointed as to be connected with 'gratis dare;' and Orelli has it so: 'gratis dare ultro, pecuniam,' &c. 'Ultro' means 'besides.'

ab omnibus relictas] Zumpt and Jordan have 'a dominis relictas;' but this is not consistent with the facts, for all the 'aratores' were not 'domini.' Klotz has 'a dominis omnes relictas;' to which there is the same objection; and this besides, that Cicero has already said 'omnes.' 'ad dominis omnis rel.' Lg. 42 p. m.; 'ab do- no minis omnibus r.' sec. m.; 'ab omni relictas' sic V (Jordan). I conclude that the true reading is either 'ab omnibus relictas' or 'omnino relictas.'

VI.

Lib. 3. c. 47: "In jugero Leontini agri," &c.

Cicero informs us that the produce of wheat on the plains of Leontini was ten for one in very favourable years; but that eight for one was a good produce. The quantity sown on a 'jugerum' was a 'medimnum' as a general rule, 'in jugero Leontini agri medimnum fere tritici seritur perpetua atque aequabili satione;' which does not mean that the land was sown every year, but that the uninterrupted and regular practice was to sow a 'medimnum' on each 'jugerum.'

Dureau de la Malle (Économie Politique des Romains, vol. ii. chap. 11) has discussed the subject of the proportion between the seed and the produce in Roman cultivation. The first passage that he quotes is from Varro (De Re Rustica, i. c. 44), the substance of which is this: There are sown on a 'jugerum' four 'modii' of beans, five of wheat, six of barley, ten of far or spelter; but sometimes more or less, according to the locality and the soil: the same grain produces here ten for one, in other places fifteen for one, as in Etruria and some parts of Italy: it is even said, that in the territory of Sybaris in the South of Italy, in Syria near Garada, and in Byzacium in Africa, they get a hundred 'modii' for one; he adds, that it is important to distinguish in sowing between new land, and land which is sown every year (which is called *restibilis*), and land which rests sometimes.

This produce of a hundred for one is given by Varro merely as a report; and it does not appear whether he believes it or not. Pliny, indeed (H. N. xviii. 10, ed. Harduin), says that some land in the territory of Leontini produced a hundred for one; but Cicero's testimony is clear and precise, that ten for one is an extraordinary produce for the lands of Leontini. The produce is still the same in the plains of Catania, which term comprises the former Leontini; eight for one in good years: ten for one in years of extraordinary fertility. Probably the mode of cultivation and the agricultural instruments have changed very little in Sicily since the time of Cicero.

There is a passage in Strabo (vii. p. 311), in which he says that the grain produce of the level and fertile part of the Taurica Chersonesus (Crimea) was thirty for one.

Columella (iii. 3, 4) gives four for one as rather above the produce of wheat lands in the larger part of Italy; and this is stated to be the mean produce at the present day in Piedmont. It appears then that fifteen for one, or ten for one, which Varro speaks of, was an unusual produce

in Italy. According to the observations of Professor Symonds, printed in Arthur Young's Travels in Italy, some lands on the great plains of Apulia (La Puglia) produced in 1767 twelve, fifteen, and even eighteen bushels for one. Some other parts of Italy produce ten or twelve for one; but these are exceptions. The Agro Romano is said to give thirteen for one.

So small a return as four for one would not pay in all countries. This low produce is explained by the particular circumstances. Dureau de la Malle observes: "Count Prospero Balbo and M. Charles Pictet, in their Mémoires on the agriculture of Piedmont, give the proportions between the seed and the produce, which perfectly agree with those which Columella has transmitted to us. Their observations at the same time explain the phenomenon of a large population, with a bad rotation of crops, and a comparatively unskilful agriculture. The proportion between the seed and the produce of wheat, is, according to Count Balbo, in Piedmont, as one to four, and that of rye as one to nine: there are no fallows; and they get two crops in a year. They lay little manure on the ground, considering this uninterrupted production: but almost all the meadows are fertilized by irrigation, and produce three crops of hay. The leaves of trees are used for feeding cattle. It is especially the excellent construction of the Piedmontese plough, which is managed by two oxen and a man; the four or five workings which they give the land with this plough for the cultivation of wheat, the repeated diggings for the maize and leguminous vegetables, which, according to M. Pictet, are the principal cause of this abundance of gross products. All the land is let at half-produce, when it grows wheat, maize, rye, rice, and silk: the meadows alone are let at a fixed rent, which is one-half of the net produce. The proprietor pays the taxes: the métayer (massaro) furnishes the animals and the implements for ploughing: yet the proportion of the crop of wheat to the seed, is, I must repeat, only four for one. Thus in Piedmont the cultivated land at present returns, as it did during the first six centuries of the Roman Republic, only a very small net produce; but it gives a very large gross produce, which supports a very great population."

The author concludes by adding, that the mean product of wheat in France was estimated at five to six for one, in 1780, by Necker and Lavoisier; but that it is now from seven to eight, owing to the improvement in cultivation. Arthur Young (Travels in France in 1787—9, 2nd edit. p. 352) also gives the average produce of France before the Revolution at six for one; and the average produce of wheat and rye at eighteen bushels the English acre. The produce of some districts is stated at only four for one. That of the fertile Limagne of Auvergne is stated by him at from seven to ten for wheat. The smallness of wheat produce compared with the great fertility of the soil was partly explained by the

fact of the ground being too rich for that grain (p. 332); for which reason they sowed rye on the best soils and wheat on the worst. The Limagne at that time never rested in a fallow; and the cultivation was very bad. Young estimated the average produce of wheat in England at twenty-four bushels the acre, "which," he says, "forms a vast superiority to eighteen, the produce of France, amounting to twelve for one of the seed, instead of six for one; but the superiority is greater than is apparent in the proportion of those two numbers; for the corn of England, as far as respects dressing, that is, cleaning from dirt, chaff, seeds of weeds, &c., is as much better than that of France, as would make the difference at least twenty-five, instead of twenty-four, to eighteen; and I am inclined to think even more."

The average produce of wheat in England, or perhaps in the United Kingdom, is still said to be twenty-four bushels; but one would expect that the average should be higher now than when Young wrote.

I am informed on the authority of an experienced agriculturist[1], that on good land in England, of the kind suited for the growth of wheat, and fairly farmed, such as that of the Vale of White Horse in Berkshire, the average quantity of wheat sown on a statute acre is 2·25 bushels, and that the average produce is 36 bushels. On such land a smaller quantity of seed would be sufficient, especially if dibbled. It is stated, however, by the same authority, that there have been instances of 60 and even 65 bushels of wheat being produced on an acre of ground in England; and in the years 1835 and 1844 many thousands of acres gave an average produce of 48 bushels[2]. The average produce of an acre in England is usually estimated at 24 bushels.

The Roman 'jugerum' was a measure of surface, 240 feet in length and 120 in breadth, and accordingly contained 28,800 square feet (Roman). The 'jugerum' is estimated at nearly five-eighths of the English acre. The 'modius' is estimated at 1 gallon 7·36 pints; and, as the 'medimnum' contained 6 'modii' (Lib. 3. c. 45, 46), the capacity of the 'medimnum' is 11·52 gallons. The comparative produce will stand thus:—

Seed sown on a statute acre of Leontine land in the time of Cicero	2·3	bushels.
Produce at 8 for 1	18·4	„
„ at 10 for 1	23·	„
Seed sown on an English statute acre of good land	2·25	„
Produce	36·	„

[1] The following facts were furnished me through the Rev. G. Cotterill by T. S. Woolley, junr., South Collingham, near Newark.

[2] I have heard of a crop of ten quarters of barley the acre on a six acre field near Chichester.—In 1861 Mr. F. F. Hallett grew 57 bushels of wheat the acre on a ten acre field. The straw was 140 trusses, 36lbs. each. The seed was one peck the acre; and so one bushel of seed produced 228 bushels. (See p. 428.)

The average weight of an English bushel of wheat on the land here referred to would be 62lbs. I am not aware that there is any authority for the weight of a bushel of Sicilian corn; but it would probably be the same that it is now, and I suppose that the hard corn of the south of Europe weighs heavier than English grain. The gross produce on the best Sicilian land, according to Cicero's statement, in the most favourable years, was only equal to the average of the English produce. On the poor lands we must assume it to be only one-half.

The following facts are from the same authority that I have referred to:—In 1845, six pieces of land, measuring half an acre each, were sown with one bushel each, of six different kinds of wheat. The following was the result, as given by Mr. C. Hillyard, who tried the experiment to determine the most productive kind of wheat.

No.	Bushels per half-acre.	Bushels per acre.	Weight per bushel.
1	20	40	64lbs.
2	18	36	64
3	20	40	63·5
4	19½	39	63
5	22½	45	63
6	18	36	60

The large amount of produce raised by the best farmers in Scotland under what is called high farming, appears from an article in Blackwood's Magazine, 1850, p. 94. The cost of getting a large produce is not a matter that comes into question here. But it may be well to observe, for the benefit of those who look only to results, without considering how they are produced, that a smaller crop in some countries may be more profitable to the grower than a larger crop in other countries. The larger crop may cost so much as to bring its net value to the grower below the net value of the smaller crop.

In the rich lands of North America a crop of corn is produced at small cost after the land is cleared. An old traveller, Michaux[1] (1802), speaks of 25 to 30 bushels the acre in Kentucky, weighing 60lbs. the bushel, raised with no application of manure and little tillage. Near Wheeling, on the Ohio, he speaks of 15 to 20 bushels the acre, when the land is cleared; but no manure is used, there is little tillage, and the soil is never idle. In Alabama, in 33 N. lat., the wheat is generally sown on inferior land, and put in with very little care. It is reaped early in May, about which time wheat is also cut in some parts of Sicily. Ten, fifteen, twenty bushels are considered a good average. In 1853, in one case reported to me, some land in Alabama produced from 20 to 25 bushels the acre. On the prairie and hill lands of Illinois, one of the

[1] A traveller in the United States sixty years ago is an old traveller. I assume that Michaux uses the English statute acre.

largest corn-growing states, the average produce of wheat is about 25 bushels the English acre (1860). On a good soil with little labour they get in America what pays them, though it is not much. When it will pay to get more, they can have it by more labour.

Mr. F. F. Hallett, of Kemp Town, Brighton, is attempting to increase the productiveness of our corn-fields on the same principle by which we have improved our breeds of cattle, by a repeated selection of the finest ears of wheat, which possess the properties of tillering well and producing large ears. But after selection of seed it is also necessary to give the plants the opportunity of growing, and he does this by allowing each grain sufficient room to grow in. He thus makes a great saving in seed and secures a larger crop. He informs me that there are instances in England where so much seed is used for sowing and the soil is so poor, that the proportion between the seed and the produce is not larger than that mentioned above in the case of Piedmont. Such an extreme result may be rare, but the general proportion in England between the seed sown and the produce is very different from the result of his experiments.

On twenty-three acres of land, very much exhausted, he sowed five gallons the acre, dibbled, but not in single grains. The crop was 736 bushels or 51 fold.

On one acre he sowed five pints of seed; the grains were planted separately, and twelve inches apart every way. This crop was planted much too late, and was greatly injured by wireworm. The produce was 40 bushels or 500 fold.

On 698 square feet, planted with 'Hallett's pedigree nursery wheat,' the grains planted singly nine inches apart every way, the crop was 1·75 bushels or 80¼ fold.

Mr. Hallett's principle is briefly this. A grain of wheat, like other grains and seeds, requires a certain area to grow in and develope itself according to its nature. Wheat cannot do this if it is sown or planted thick. I have seen one of Mr. Hallett's wheat plants of this year (1861), which has the enormous number of 52 stems from one root and one grain, each stem bearing a full long ear something like double the length of ordinary ears. By selecting good seed and planting the grains wide apart he obtains a strong plant with many stems and large heads. His field may contain no more stems than other people find on their fields when they have sowed two bushels or more of seed; but his plants are stronger, less liable to be laid, and he gains in the length of the ear. Every plant requires a certain horizontal area for its proper growth; but its growth in the vertical direction, in the ear, is independent of the other condition.

VII.

The Formula Octaviana. Lib. 3. c. 65.

The Roman 'praetor' gave relief to persons who had under compulsion done any act which was against their interests, and it was a more complete relief than was given in the case of other Restitutiones. The injured person received fourfold the amount of the loss or damage which he had sustained; and not only was the wrong-doer liable to make this reparation, but every person who had derived a profit from the compulsory act, either directly or indirectly, was also liable to make reparation. The remedy was by the 'Actio quod metus causa' (Dig. 4. tit. 2); and its origin must be explained, according to Rudorff, by a reference to the history of Repetundae. The Leges which relate to Repetundae are enumerated in Excursus I.

The proceeding under the Lex Calpurnia (B.C. 149) was, in its material part, a 'condictio,' that is, an action for the recovery of what was claimed by the injured party or parties; but the 'litis aestimatio,' or assessment of the damage, was limited to the simple amount of what had been wrongfully taken. But, though the proceeding was substantially a 'condictio,' it was not conducted by a Legis Actio per Condictionem, for this had been abolished by the Lex Aebutia. The proceeding was in the form of a Sacramenti Actio before the Praetor Peregrinus. The Sacramentum contained a penalty for the illegal act; whereas the 'litis aestimatio,' which followed after judgment against the defendant, gave to the complainant satisfaction only to the amount of the loss which he had sustained by the illegal act. The penalty in the Sacramentum, it is assumed, came to the State, and, not like the 'Sponsionis summa,' to the successful party. The proceeding by the Sacramentum was preserved in the Lex Junia, and also in the Servilia, according to the restored text[1] (l. 72—74). It also appears that if a man was condemned or acquitted in a Sacramenti Actio, there could be no proceeding against him under the Servilia Lex; but the Lex excluded a man who had been condemned in the Sacramenti Actio from acting as a 'judex.' The Sacramenti Actio of the Lex Calpurnia, and of the Lex Junia, was

[1] Thus in the restored text of the Lex Servilia, line 23: "quei de pecunia capta condemnatus fuerit aut quod cum eo lege Calpurnia aut lege Junia sacramento actum siet, aut quod h. l. nomen delatum siet."

not a Privatum Judicium, like the Condictiones, or actions brought by a single injured party: it was a proceeding in the name of a whole province, conducted by a prosecutor, before a body of sworn Judices. Yet the indemnification of the injured parties was still the main object. The Servilia gave to the proceedings another character. The 'nominis delatio,' the public prosecution before the Praetor Quaesitor, or the Judex Quaestionis, was the principal thing: the Petitio and the Litis Aestimatio occupy a secondary place. If the defendant was condemned, he did not escape the Litis Aestimatio. "In this, however, the Litis Aestimatio is independent of the result of the public prosecution, that it affects even one who has been acquitted, and is applied to him who has pleaded guilty, without presupposing a condemnation of the defendant by a body of Judices [1]." The Servilia raised the amount of damages to double of the loss sustained; but only one-half of this sum, or the amount of loss, went to the injured parties; the rest went to the treasury (aerarium). But the proceedings were not confined to the guilty person; they extended to his 'heredes,' or representatives, and to the 'heredes' of the 'heredes.' Even innocent third persons, who might have been enriched, that is, have got some profit, in consequence of the illegal acts of the defendant, were liable to be proceeded against before a body of 'judices;' they came under the general terms 'quo ea pecunia quam is ceperit qui damnatus sit pervenerit.' The condemnation of a third person, however, relieved the defendant from payment of damages. It is generally said that the Lex Cornelia of the Dictator Sulla raised the Litis Aestimatio to quadruple the amount of the real damage. But there is no direct evidence for this. This Lex retained the chapter 'Quo pervenerit,' as we see from the oration Pro Cluentio, c. 41, which was delivered when the Lex Cornelia was in force. The last Lex de Repetundis was the Lex Julia, passed in Caesar's first consulship.

It appears that all the Leges de Repetundis applied only to abuse of their office by Magistratus; but the principle of these Leges was extended to the acts of private persons, which were of a like character with those acts that came within the provisions of those Leges de Repetundis. To this class of private actions, formed in imitation of the proceedings under the Leges de Repetundis, belong the 'in factum actio,' on the ground of 'calumnia' [2] (Dig. 3. 6. 1), and the 'Actio quod metus causa,' which we are now considering.

[1] I don't understand this. If a man pleaded guilty, that was as good as if he was found guilty. But, if he was acquitted on the charge of Repetundae, I don't see how he could be liable to pay any thing in respect of a charge which had not been proved.

[2] "In eum qui, ut calumniae causa negotium faceret vel non faceret, pecuniam accepisse dicetur, intra annum in quadruplum ejus pecuniae quam accepisse dicetur, post annum simpli in factum actio competit."

The introduction of the 'Actio quod metus causa' is attributed by Cicero to a Praetor Octavius, who is conjectured to be the L. Octavius who was consul B.C. 75. If this was the man, he was probably 'praetor' about four years earlier, or B.C. 79. Accordingly, the introduction of this Actio would belong to the year B.C. 79, two years after the enactment of the Lex Cornelia de Repetundis, and two years before the introduction of the 'Actio Vi bonorum raptorum,' by the praetor M. Lucullus. This confirms Rudorff's opinion, which he establishes on other grounds, that the action 'Quod metus causa' was not founded on, or derived from, the 'Actio Vi bonorum raptorum,' as some have supposed. After Sulla's death, B.C. 78, this 'Actio quod metus' was applied to compel persons to make restitution, who during the time of Sulla had by violent means got possession of other persons' property. Cicero appears to allude to this application of the Actio by that active and excellent Praetor, C. Octavius, the father of him who was afterwards the emperor Augustus: "cogebantur Sullani homines quae per vim et metum abstulerant reddere" (Ad Qu. Fr. i. 1. c. 7). The edict into which the Octaviana Formula was received, applied to the case of agreements (Cicero, De Off. iii. 24; Dig. 2. 14. 7. § 7), to cases where Restitutio was claimed, in consequence of a man having sustained loss by having been prevented from doing something (Dig. 4. 6. 1. § 1); and, lastly, to cases where Restitutio was claimed, in consequence of a man's rights having been impaired by acts done under compulsion. The clause applicable to the last case ran thus: "Quod metus causa gestum erit, ratum non habebo;" but the original form was, "Quod vi metusve causa" (Dig. 4. 2. 1). Under this head, Octavius declared that he would allow an action for fourfold the amount of the loss sustained by this compulsion; and an action, not only against the person who had been guilty of the violence, but also against any innocent person who had got direct pecuniary profit in consequence of the act of violence.

This measure of Octavius was caused by the circumstances of the times. During the tyranny of the Dictator Sulla, acts of violence had become so common, and so many persons had been deprived of their property by threats, and other illegal proceedings, that a stronger remedy seemed to be required than a simple action (condictio), to which however a person might still have recourse. After the publication of the new Formula, the two remedies subsisted together. As citizens now practised with respect to other citizens the same unlawful means that Roman 'magistratus' practised against provincials, there was a reason for applying what Cicero calls the principles of the Lex Socialis, the Lex de Repetundis (Divin. c. 5), to the case of Roman citizens oppressing their fellow-citizens. The Formula of Octavius having been introduced

into the Edictum Urbanum, was thence transferred to the Provinciale; for Cicero tells us (Lib. 3. c. 65), that L. Caecilius Metellus, the successor of Verres, had admitted the Formula into his edict at Rome, and also into his provincial edict. The claim of C. Gallus before Metellus was, that pursuant to his edict the 'praetor' should grant him an action against Apronius, in respect of "quod per vim et metum—abstulisset." Cicero, in speaking of the exactions of this scoundrel, uses the words which brought his acts within the terms of the edict; 'iniquas pactiones vi et metu expressas'—'civitates virgarum ac mortis metu'—'aratores vi et metu coactos Apronio multo plus quam debuerint dedisse.' There was sufficient reason to allow the action against Apronius, but Metellus refused it, because he wished to keep back what would have appeared to the prejudice of Verres in the trial at Rome. Verres was, indeed, the real culprit, for Apronius only acted as his tool; but Apronius was at least liable for whatever had come to his hands. Now Metellus saw, that if Apronius had been condemned to restore fourfold to C. Gallus, this would have been indirectly a condemnation of Verres in the matter of the Repetundae. It was, however, a principle of law, that when the condemnation of a defendant by Recuperatores, in a civil matter, preceded the trial for a matter that affected a man's 'caput' (causa capitalis), the accused had the advantage of an exception in this form, 'extra quam si in reum capitis praejudicium fiat,' which means, that the result of this trial was not to prejudice him in the future trial (Cicero, De Invent. ii. 20: "non enim oportet in recuperatorio judicio ejus maleficii, de quo inter sicarios quaeritur, praejudicium fieri" &c. Paulus, Dig. 5. 1. 54: "per minorem causam majori cognitioni praejudicium fieri non oportet; major enim" &c.: and Dig. 47. 10. 7. § 1). This was precisely the case before Metellus. The 'Actio quod metus causa' against Apronius would have been decided in the province, and Verres would have to be tried by a body of senators at Rome on the charge of Repetundae. Metellus did not wish the judgment in Sicily, which would certainly have been obtained against Apronius, to prejudice Verres at Rome in any way: 'praejudicium se . . . nolle fieri' (c. 65). Cicero expresses his surprise that Metellus did not perceive that he was in effect passing judgment on Verres, by refusing to allow this action: 'sed hoc miror . . . judicarit' (c. 65).

It has been urged that the words 'quod per vim et metum abstulisset' cannot have been the words of the Formula, which may be true to a certain degree. Neither the word 'quod,' nor the subjunctive 'abstulisset,' would appear in the Formula; but the words 'per vim et metum abstulisse,' so often repeated by Cicero, can only be referred to the Formula as their source. The words 'ablata pecunia' are also one of the expressions used in the Lex Servilia to designate one of the

offences to which that Lex applied; and this, which is an argument in favour of the analogy between the Octaviana Formula and the Lex de Repetundis, is also in favour of some form of the word 'auferre' being contained in the Formula. Repetundae comprehended both the offence of receiving money as a gift—a bribe, for instance—aud also the getting of money by force and threats. The 'Actio quod metus causa' could have no reference to gifts, because a gift from one private person to another is a trausaction which does not come under the head of things forbidden; but the obtaiuing of money, or any thing valuable from another by threats and force, is precisely the act to which the Formula Octaviana applied.

The position of the defendant in the 'Actio quod metus causa' shows also that this 'actio' is framed after the model of the proceedings in the case of Repetundae. The principle of the action is not only to punish the man who has used 'vis et metus,' but to restore the injured party to all his rights. Accordingly the 'Actio quod metus' could be maintained even against artificial persons, though they are not capable of committing a delict (Dig. 4. 2. 9. § 1. 3); also against the 'heredes' of the person who had used 'vis et metus,' though they had taken no personal share in the compulsion; against third persons who had derived some direct advantage from the application of the 'vis et metus,' though as a general rule third persons are not affected by the acts of others. It also holds against those who have acquired by singular succession, if they have got the profit which the person who used compulsion derived from the act (Dig. 4. 2. 14. § 5), though as a general rule personal plaints do not pass from one defendant to another. But these persons, who may become liable to the plaintiff, are only liable so far as the advantage derived from the 'metus et vis' has come to their hands (quantum ad eos pervenit), and at the time of the commencement of the action is still a part of their property (Dig. 4. 2. 20). The principle was that the gain which had accrued from the unlawful act could be recovered from any person to whom it could be traced. If the thing was consumed, neither the wrong-doer nor his 'heres' was released; the 'actio' is 'perpetua.' If it has perished, a third person in whose hands it was, is released; but if such person has parted with the thing, which was originally wrongfully gotten, he is still liable; for the thing having been exchanged for money, or any thing else, he must be considered to have been a gainer, even if that thing afterwards perish or is consumed.

The object of the 'Actio quod metus' is clearly then, in the case of private wrong-doers, the same as that of the proceedings for Repetundae in the case of Magistratus. The object of the clause 'quo ea pecunia pervenerit,' and the extension of the action to third persons, is to give

the injured party complete compensation, and to take from third persons a profit or advantage, which they have got without good grounds, and at the cost of him who has suffered 'vis et metus.' The ignorance in a third party of the unlawful act was not a necessary condition of the plaintiff's right of action. The principle was the same as that applied to stolen goods, where the ownership still remained unchanged, into whatever hands the stolen thing came. Accordingly, a 'bonae fidei emptor,' that is, a man who believed that the seller had a good title, if he bought things from a person who had got them 'vi et metu,' or if he received such things as a gift, or as a legacy, was still liable to this action for restitution (Dig. 4. 2. 14. § 5).

The Octaviana Formula further agrees with the Litis Aestimatio as to the fourfold value to be recovered; whether this fourfold value first appeared in the Lex Julia, and was thence transferred to the Formula, or whether it was in the Lex Cornelia, and was thence transferred into the Formula at its original formation, as in the case of the 'actio vi bonorum,' where the 'quadruplum' was a part of the original Formula[1].

The object of the 'quadruplum' seems to have been rather an indirect means of compelling 'restitutio' than the proper object of the 'Actio quod metus causa;' and accordingly the right to demand the 'quadruplum' was extinguished if the complainant had obtained satisfaction by the immediate aid of the 'praetor,' by the 'exceptio metus,' or by the 'actio doli.' For if this 'Actio quod metus' had been a mixed penal action, the claim for the 'triplum' would still have remained, after the 'simplum' was made good[2]. If one of several persons who has used 'metus et vis,' or one of several persons to whose hands the thing had come, either has restored the thing before judgment pronounced against him, or has paid the 'quadruplum' pursuant to a judgment, the demand against the rest is extinguished: the solidarity which is a characteristic of penal actions does not hold here[3]. This rule as to the 'Actio quod

[1] Dig. 47. 8. 2: "Praetor ait: Si cui dolo malo hominibus coactis damni quid factum esse dicetur, sive cujus bona rapta esse dicentur, in eum qui id fecisse dicetur intra annum quo primum de ea re experiundi potestas fuerit in quadruplum, post annum in simplum judicium dabo."

[2] Savigny, System, &c. v. 232, 233. In all cases of this kind the second action can be prosecuted, although the first has been prosecuted and a judgment obtained for the plaintiff. Thus the 'Actio vi bonorum raptorum' had for its object simple recovery of the value, and also three times the value as a penalty.

[3] "If several persons steal at the same time, each of them is guilty of the whole act of theft, and the circumstance that others help a man in the act of theft neither alters nor diminishes the penal character of his act. Accordingly the 'furti actio' is maintainable against each for the full penalty, even though the rest have already paid their penalty, because the punishment of each of the several delicts is a separate and distinct object." Savigny, System, &c. v. 234.

metus causa' is expressed as follows by Ulpian (Dig. 4. 2. 14. § 15): "Si plures metum adhibuerint et unus fuerit conventus, siquidem sponte rem ante sententiam restituerit, omnes liberati sunt. Sed etsi id non fecerit, sed ex sententia quadruplum restituerit, verius est etiam sic perimi adversus ceteros quod metus causa actionem."

Finally, the Edict gave a man the opportunity of avoiding the 'quadruplum' by restitution (Dig. 4. 2. 14. § 1, 'Si quis non restituat, in quadruplum in eum judicium pollicetur,' &c.). He had the power of making restitution at any time before the sentence was pronounced.

The Formula Octaviana only related to the action of the party who had been wronged: for Formula is only another name for Actio. If the injured party was sued upon some promise obtained by 'vis et metus,' or any cause of action, the foundation of which was in 'vis et metus,' his defence or answer was by the 'metus exceptio,' or the plea of constraint. This 'exceptio' was 'in rem,' that is, general, and consequently it was an answer not only to the 'heres' of the person who had used the 'vis et metus,' and to any person who had purchased from him, but also to any third person ('enimvero metus causa exceptio in rem scripta est: Si in ea re nihil metus causa factum est; ut non inspiciamus an is qui agit metus causa fecerit aliquid sed an omnino metus causa factum sit in hac re a quocunque, non tantum ab eo qui agit:' Dig. 44. 4. 4. § 33).

I have given as well as I can the substance of Rudorff's essay in the Zeitschrift für Geschichtliche Rechtswissenschaft (xii. 131); but it is not easy to compress an essay of forty pages and to treat the matter properly. If this is considered too technical an exposition, the fault is with the subject, and it cannot be helped. Those who will read with care may understand it pretty well; and they will see what pains the Romans took to protect persons who had been constrained by force or threats to do any act by which their pecuniary interests were damaged, or who had been by like means prevented from doing some act, the omission of which was injurious to their interests. The 'condictiones' of the Jus Civile applied to many cases; and, among others, they enabled a man to recover what had been got from him by force or threats; and Cicero alludes to this process in the Divinatio (c. 5), 'Civibus quum sunt ereptae pecuniae,' &c. But the 'condictio' could only be maintained against the original wrong-doer (Dig. 12. 6. 40); and the thing itself (a sum of money, for instance), or the simple amount of the loss or damage only could be recovered.

It was remarked that the Edict ran originally 'Quod vi metusque causa,' and that afterwards the word 'vi' was omitted, and properly omitted. It is properly 'vis,' when the person to whom 'vis' is applied is overpowered by physical force; for instance, if money is taken from

his pocket in spite of his resistance, or if he is prevented by physical force from doing something which he wishes to do, voting at an election, making his testament, or the like. If no force is used, but the will is operated on by threats, that is, by producing fear, this is 'metus.' Savigny observes (System, &c., iii. p. 101, note (*a*)), that the opposition between 'vis' and 'metus' appears most clearly in the case of the loss of possession; for possession may be lost either through physical force or through threats. If a man is forcibly ejected, that is Dejectio, and to this case applied the 'Interdictum de vi' (Dig. 43. 16. 5). If a man gives up possession through threats, that is compulsive Traditio (delivery), and the 'Actio quod metus causa' applies (Dig. 4. 2. 9). The Romans did not consider that fear produced by threats took away the free exercise of the will. The cases to which the 'Actio quod metus' applies are not those where physical force was used, but where fear was produced by threats; they were cases in which the person had chosen to act in obedience to the threat rather than submit to the consequences of refusal. Such are the numerous cases mentioned in these orations, where persons had through fear, and some through pain, consented to comply with the demands of Verres or his agents. The Romans were right in saying that threats do not exclude the freedom of the will; and accordingly they did not consider acts done under the influence of this kind of fear to be void. But they gave a remedy to the person who had acted under the influence of the motive of fear caused by threats; and the ground was this, that means to induce him to consent had been applied, which were immoral, just as it is immoral to tempt a woman's chastity by money; and only one degree less immoral than to violate it by force. Wherever then immoral means are applied to induce consent, the consenting party is entitled to restitution or reparation as far as it is possible. What means are immoral is a matter that may be safely left to the 'communis sensus,' the moral notions of all people who are not immediately interested in the decision of any particular case. This subject is discussed by Savigny, System, Vol. iii., Zwang und Irrthum.

It is possible that some things in this Excursus may not be quite consistent with some things that occur elsewhere in this book. The explanation is this: there are great difficulties in some of the subjects discussed in this volume, and certain differences of opinion about them.

ACTIONIS SECUNDAE

IN C. VERREM

LIBER QUARTUS.

DE SIGNIS.

"Codices Meliores libr. iv. et V:

R = Regius Parisiensis nr. 7774 A—[Cum Iordano, quamquam tot codicis optimi collationes ei ad manus erant, tamen haud paucis locis dubitatio de vera codicis lectione relicta fuerit, a familiari meo Car. Bursiano petivi ut codicem denuo excuteret, cujus opera diligentissima tandem factum est ut verum codicis lectionem ubique repraesentare possemus. HALM.]

G 1 2 = Guelferbytani duo, de quibus vide ad Divinat.

Ld = Leidensis (i. e. P. Francii in Perizonianis nr. 12. teste Bakio), cujus collationem a Bakio diligentissime confectam ad me misit Baiterus.

R 3 significat consensum codicum R G 1 2 Ld.

G 3 consensum codicum G 1 2 Ld.

λ = vetus codex Lambini in marg. 1584.

C = Cujacianus Guilielmii apud Gruterum.

V = Vaticanus qui haec habet fragmenta &c.

E = Erfurtensis, ex quo Melch. Hittorpii schedae excerptae sunt. Ejus autem fragmenta supersunt haec &c.

Lg. 29 = Lagomarsinianus nr. 29, qui quamquam melioribus est annumerandus, tamen optimis paulo inferior est.

Ad Deteriores Codices referendi sunt ceteri septem Lagomarsiniani (nam in libr. iv. et v. Lg. 42 in deteriorum numero est), Palatini, Francianus, Gruterianus, Oxoniensis ψ, Huydecoperanus, Sangallensis.

Quamquam codices meliores, quos supra commemoravimus, praeter Vaticanum omnes ejusdem familiae sunt [immo codd. G 1 2 Ld et λ, ut mihi quidem persuasum est, ex nullo alio codice nisi ex ipso Regio originem duxerunt. HALM], Regius tamen ita ceteris praestat ut ejus auctoritati fere ubique obtemperandum sit. Quae cum hujus codicis sit praestantia, omnes fere varias lectiones, quas ex eo enotatas habemus, in annotationes criticas transtulimus; paucula quaedam menda, quorum commemoratio ad nullam rem utilis esse videbatur, omisimus. In rebus autem levioribus, in quibus dijudicandis plus valere debet librorum MSS. auctoritas quam ratio et iudicium (id quod saepissime usu venit in verborum collocatione) codicis Regii potius quam Vati-

cani fidem secuti sumus. Nam etsi Vaticanus optimae notae est, tamen non est cur Regio praeponatur; et cum pauca tantum in his duobus libris supersint ejus fragmenta, Regius (praeter lacunam in libro V) integer sit servatus, hujus auctoritatem in rebus levioribus ambiguique judicii potiorem habere consentaneum erat. Propter codicis autem Regii praestantiam eas quoque varias lectiones, quae ad orthographiae rationem pertinent, suis locis afferendas putavimus." (Iordan.)

I. Venio nunc ad istius quemadmodum ipse appellat studium; ut amici ejus, morbum et insaniam; ut Siculi, latrocinium. Ego quo nomine appellem nescio: rem vobis proponam: vos eam suo non nominis pondere penditote. Genus ipsum prius cognoscite, judices; deinde fortasse non magno opere quaeretis quo id nomine appellandum putetis. Nego in Sicilia tota, tam locupleti, tam vetere provincia, tot oppidis, tot familiis tam copiosis, ullum argenteum vas, ullum Corinthium aut Deliacum fuisse, ullam gemmam aut margaritam, quidquam ex auro aut ebore factum, signum ullum aeneum, marmoreum, eburneum; nego ullam picturam neque in tabula neque in textili, quin conquisierit, inspexerit, quod placitum sit abstulerit. Magnum videor dicere: attendite etiam quemadmodum dicam. Non enim verbi neque criminis augendi causa complector omnia: quum dico nihil istum ejusmodi rerum in tota provincia reliquisse, Latine me scitote, non accusatorie loqui. Etiam

1. *studium;*] Zumpt refers to Cicero, De Invent. i. 25, for a definition of 'studium:' "studium est animi assidua et vehemens ad aliquam rem applicata magna cum voluntate occupatio, ut philosophiae, poeticae, geometriae, literarum."

Corinthium &c.] See Lib. 2. c. 34.

gemmam] 'Gemmae' are precious stones, as 'adamas, smaragdus, beryllus, opalus,' and many others, which Pliny, in his multifarious work (H. N. xxxvii. 4), describes. They were used in many ways. They were set in gold, and worn in a ring. They were used for adorning drinking-cups (Juv. v. 43), and for the gem-cutter to exercise his art upon. See also c. 27.

margaritam,] 'Margarita,' or 'margaritum,' is the pearl. It is mentioned (μαργαρίτης) by Arrian (Indic. c. 8) as being found in the Indian seas in a shell-fish; and he adds, that the name is Indian, as we might suppose (τὸν μαργαρίτην δὴ τὸν θαλάσσιον, οὕτω τῇ Ἰνδῶν γλώσσῃ καλεόμενον). Pliny (H. N. ix. c. 35) treats of pearls, an article on which immense sums of money were spent in his time. He says that he once saw Lollia Paullina covered with pearls and emeralds; she wore them all over her head, in her hair, in her ears, on her neck, and her fingers. The value of these costly ornaments was 'quadringenties H.S.'

tabula] The Romans sometimes used 'tabula' absolutely for 'pictura;' sometimes they added 'picta.' 'Pictura' is the painting; and 'tabula' is the material, which was 'wood.' The word 'textili' is used as a noun, and means 'cloth' or 'canvas.' Cicero however does not mean a painting on canvas, but a work made by the needle, or possibly woven. 'Picta vestis,' 'picta toga,' mean a dress ornamented with needlework.

> "Non ego praetulerim Babylonica picta superbae
> Texta Semiramia quae variantur acu."
> Martial, viii. 28.

According to Pliny (H. N. xxxv. 33), canvas was not used to paint on till the time of Nero. On ancient painting, the reader may consult the useful article Pictura, in Smith's Dictionary of Antiquities. The great shawl, or 'peplus,' which was carried in the Panathenaic festival at Athens, contained a representation of the battle of the gods and the giants.

Latine] That is, 'simply,' 'plainly,' 'literally,' 'in plain English,' as we should say, "Ut ii qui plane et Latine loquuntur"

planius: nihil in aedibus cujusquam, ne in oppidis quidem; nihil in locis communibus, ne in fanis quidem; nihil apud Siculum, nihil apud civem Romanum; denique nihil istum quod ad oculos animumque acciderit, neque privati neque publici, neque profani neque sacri tota in Sicilia reliquisse.

Unde igitur potius incipiam quam ab ea civitate, quae tibi una in amore atque in deliciis fuit, aut ex quo potius numero quam ex ipsis laudatoribus tuis? Facilius enim perspicietur qualis apud eos fueris, qui te oderunt, qui accusant, qui persequuntur, quum apud tuos Mamertinos inveniare improbissima ratione esse praedatus. II. C. Heius est Mamertinus, omnes hoc mihi qui Messanam accesserunt facile concedunt, omnibus rebus illa in civitate ornatissimus. Hujus domus est vel optima Messanae, notissima quidem certe et nostris hominibus apertissima maximeque hospitalis. Ea domus ante istius adventum ornata sic fuit ut urbi quoque esset ornamento. Nam ipsa Messana, quae situ, moenibus portuque ornata sit, ab his rebus quibus iste delectatur sane vacua atque nuda est. Erat apud Heium sacrarium magna cum dignitate in aedibus, a majoribus traditum, perantiquum, in quo signa pulcherrima quatuor, summo artificio, summa nobilitate, quae non modo istum hominem ingeniosum et intelligentem, verum etiam quemvis nostrum, quos iste idiotas appellat, delectare possent:

(Phil. vii. 6; Pro Caecina, c. 21). So we find 'Il m'a parlé français,' or 'bon français,' 'Er hat Deutsch mit mir gesprochen,' in the same sense. Martial says (Epigr. Lib. i. Ad Lectorem Epistola), "si quis tamen tam ambitiose tristis est ut apud illum in nulla pagina Latine loqui fas sit, potest epistola vel potius titulo contentus esse." This is Martial's excuse for obscenity. 'Accusatorie' means with the licence which an accuser takes, that is, falsely. He often has the expression: Lib. 3. c. 70, and elsewhere.

nihil . . neque] See Lib. 2. c. 24, on the negative.—'Mamertinos:' see Lib. 3. c. 6, note.

quae tibi una] 'which especially of all others.'

2. *C. Heius*] See Pro Cluentio, c. 39. It was a Roman gentile name.

quae situ, . . . portuque] 'i.e. licet ornata sit,' as Zumpt correctly explains it; and adds, that he is surprised that Ernesti, 'alioquin diligentissimus conjunctivi observator,' could think of correcting the passage. It means, 'For as to Messana, though it is a city embellished by situation, walls, and harbour, it is' &c.

The port of Messana "is one of the most picturesque, commodious, and safe that can be imagined" (Smyth's Sicily, p. 113). The old name of Zancle was derived from its curved or hooked form (Lib. 3. c. 6).

"Quique locus curvae nomina falcis habet."
Ovid, Fast. iv. 474.

The mouth of the harbour is seven hundred yards wide. The old coins represent the form of the harbour, with a Pharos upon it. There is a view of Messana in Swinburne's Travels, 'as in 1777.'

ab his rebus] "ab *iis rebus* malim; in G 1, 2 est *hiis*, ut semper" (Iordan). But 'his' is the true word here.

sacrarium] A little chapel, in which Heius almost daily performed a religious service (c. 8). Cicero has translated the Greek term by a Roman equivalent. Familiae, both among the Greeks and the Romans, had their family rites; and the maintenance of the private 'sacra' was a part of the Roman religious system.

idiotas] Cicero uses a term familiar to the Greeks (*ἰδιώτης*), which, as its etymology shows, is a person in a private capacity, as opposed to one who has a

unum Cupidinis marmoreum Praxiteli—Nimirum didici etiam, dum in istum inquiro, artificum nomina. Idem, opinor, artifex ejusdemmodi Cupidinem fecit illum qui est Thespiis, propter quem Thespiae

public function. It was also used generally to signify a person who is ignorant of any particular science or art, as opposed to one who is versed in it. Demosthenes (adv. Leptin. 73, ed. Wolf) says, ἵν᾽ εἷς ᾖ περὶ τῶν ὄντων ἑκάστου νόμος καὶ μὴ τοὺς ἰδιώτας αὐτὸ τοῦτο ταράττῃ καὶ ποιῇ τῶν ἅπαντας εἰδότων τοὺς νόμους ἔλαττον ἔχειν. See Thucydides ii. 47. Cicero here uses a rhetorical artifice, pretending to be almost unacquainted even with the names of the Greek artists. But he was fond of works of art even at this time, and he spent more money on them than he could afford: "nam in eo genere sic studio efferimur ut abs te adjuvandi, ab aliis prope reprehendendi simus" (Ad Att. i. 8; and i. 5. 11). He had when he wrote this letter (B.C. 67), only three years after the supposed delivery of this speech, a 'studium' (see c. 1). In Lib. 4. c. 6 again he declares that he sets no great value on such things: 'Ego vero ad meam rationem,' &c.; but this is said oratorically.

Praxiteli] The Romans sometimes used this form of the genitive for many of the Greek nouns in -*es*. 'Timarchidi' has occurred before, Lib. 2. c. 44, &c. As to Praxiteles and his works, see Plin. H. N. xxxiv. c. 8; and the article Praxiteles in Sillig's Catalogus. The birth-place of Praxiteles is unknown. His period is the first part of the fourth century B.C. This artist made statues of deities, heroes, and women; but his great glory was the statue of Aphrodite. Cnidus possessed his naked Aphrodite which strangers came from far to see. (Lucian, Ἔρωτες, ii. 397, Hemst.) Cos had the draped Aphrodite. It is probable that Praxiteles fixed the type which became the usual mode of representing the goddess. We have now the Medicean Venus, a naked figure, and the Venus of Milo, partially draped. The Medicean may be a copy of the naked Aphrodite. Our lady of Milo is worthy to be an original of the great artist.

Nimirum] See c. 57.

Cupidinem] Eros (Ἔρως) was worshipped at Thespiae, a place in Boeotia, chief of all the gods. The oldest statue of Eros was a rude stone. Lysippus made a bronze Eros for the Thespians, and Praxiteles had previously made one of Pentelic marble. This appears to be the statue which Phryne got from him (Pausan. i. 20). Strabo (p. 410) says that Thespiae was visited by people to see the Eros of Praxiteles, which the courtezan Glycera, a Thespian woman, gave to her townsmen, having received it as a present from the artist; and 'in former times people used to go to Thespiae to see it.' Strabo is mistaken in the name of the lady. All the other authorities agree that the donor was Phryne, of whom there was at Thespiae a statue, also the work of her lover Praxiteles. We might infer from Strabo's words that the statue of Eros was not at Thespiae in his time, though this inference is not necessary. But, according to the other authorities, the statue was still at Thespiae in Strabo's time, for Strabo did not live to the reign of Caligula, and the emperor Caius (that is, Caligula) first removed it from Thespiae. Claudius gave it back; but Nero, the universal plunderer, carried it off again, and it was destroyed at Rome in a fire, in the time of Titus, A.D. 80. (Dion Cassius, Lib. lxvi. c. 24, ed. Reimarus; Pausanias, ix. 27.) The Thespians still clung to their divinity; for Menodorus, an Athenian, made them a copy of the statue of Praxiteles, and this was the figure which Pausanias saw at Thespiae, in the second century of our aera (Pausan. ix. 27; and i. 20).

Pliny (H. N. xxxvi. c. 5, ed. Hard.) says of Praxiteles: "Ejusdem est et Cupido objectus a Cicerone Verri, ille propter quem Thespiae visebantur, nunc in Octaviae scholis positus." Pliny also mentions another Cupido by Praxiteles, at Parium, on the Propontis; and he speaks of this Cupido as being at Parium when he wrote. Pliny's text is either corrupt, or this is an instance of his carelessness; for he clearly says that the Cupido which Verres was charged with taking, was the Cupido which people used to go to Thespiae to see, and which in his time was in the Scholae of Octavia. But the Cupido of Heius was not that of Thespiae. It was either the statue from Parium, or a third work of Praxiteles, or what is more likely than either supposition, a copy of one of the Cupids of the great master. Sillig (Catalogus Artificum) supposes that the Cupido of Heius was the Parian statue, which he conjectures had been carried off by some Roman proconsul, and had come to the hands of Heius. He adds, that Pliny's authority remains in-

visuntur; nam alia visendi causa nulla est. Atque ille L. Mummius, quum Thespiadas quae ad aedem Felicitatis sunt, ceteraque profana ex illo oppido signa tolleret, hunc marmoreum Cupidinem quod erat consecratus non attigit. III. Verum ut ad illud sacrarium redeam, signum erat hoc quod dico Cupidinis e marmore: ex altera parte Hercules egregie factus ex aere. Is dicebatur esse Myronis, ut opinor; et certe. Item ante hos deos erant arulae quae cuivis religionem sacrarii significare possent. Erant aenea duo praeterea signa, non maxima, verum eximia venustate, virginali habitu atque vestitu, quae manibus sublatis sacra quaedam more Atheniensium virginum reposita in capitibus sustinebant. Canephoroe ipsae vocabantur. Sed earum artificem, quem? quemnam?

tact, and he is only mistaken in saying that the statue of Heius was the statue of Thespiae; not a small mistake however. He further adds, that this explains why he considered the other statue to be still at Parium; that is, one blunder explains another. For, if Sillig is right in supposing that the statue of Heius was the Parian statue, Pliny was quite wrong in saying that it was still at Parium. He must have made the assertion without making inquiry. The Thespian was at Rome; he knew that: and yet he did not know how it came there, though Nero brought it, and he was living when it came.

L. Mummius,] See Lib. 1. c. 21.

Thespiadas] The Greek accusative. These were the figures of the Musae, mentioned by Pliny (H. N. xxxiv. c. 8, ed. Harduin.): "signa quae ante aedem Felicitatis fuere, Veneremque, quae cum ipsa aede incendio cremata est Claudii principatu, marmoreae illi suae per terras inclytae parem." This Venus and the Thespiades were bronze figures. See c. 57, note on the temple of Felicitas.

profana] The meaning is explained by the contrast with 'consecratus,' that which is devoted to religious purposes.

3. *Myronis,*] A skilful artist in bronze (Pliny, H. N. xxxi. 8, ed. Hard.), was a Boeotian, born about B.C. 480. The famous Hercules of Myron was at Samos, and there was another at Rome. This of Heius may have been by Myron; or, what came to the same thing, it was said to be by Myron. In ancient times, as in modern, there was often more than one original. It was not a colossal statue, like the Hercules of Samos (Strabo, p. 637, ed. Casaub.).

arulae] Small altars. The inferior MSS., and the old editions, have 'tabulae.'

Canephoroe] This word represents the Greek κανηφόροι, the carriers of the κανοῦν, or basket. Cicero accurately describes the composition of these figures, not like an 'idiotes,' but like a man of taste. Pliny (H. N. xxxvi. c. 5, ed. Hard.) mentions Canephoroe by Scopas, but not by Praxiteles. Canephoroe walked in processions at Athens at great festivals (Thucyd. vi. 56). They are described by Ovid (Metam. ii. 713):—

> "Illa forte die castae de more puellae
> Vertice supposito festas in Palladis arces
> Pura coronatis portabant sacra canistris."

An 'antefixa' in the British Museum represents two 'canephoroe' approaching a 'candelabrum;' one arm supports the basket on the head, and the other slightly raises the dress. The Caryatid figures, as to the origin of which Vitruvius gives so absurd a story, belong to the same style as the Canephoroe. They were employed in the temple of Pandrosos, on the Acropolis, in supporting the architrave of the southern portico. These stately figures, walking with solemn pace in religious processions, are probably alluded to by Horace, 1 Sat. iii. 10:

> —"persaepe velut qui
> Junonis sacra ferret,"

and 2 Sat. viii. 13, and Heindorf's notes. A 'canephoros' of Artemis is mentioned (Theocr. ii. 66).

Sed earum artificem, . . . Polyclitum] 'Polyclitum' appears to be the usual Latin form, as Zumpt shows, not 'Polycletum.' Cicero here uses an artifice, which he probably borrowed from the Athenian orators.

Recte admones: Polyclitum esse dicebant. Messanam ut quisque nostrum venerat, haec visere solebat: omnibus haec ad visendum patebant quotidie: domus erat non domino magis ornamento quam civitati. C. Claudius, cujus aedilitatem magnificentissimam scimus fuisse, usus est hoc Cupidine tamdiu dum forum diis immortalibus populoque Romano habuit ornatum: et quum esset hospes Heiorum, Mamertini autem populi patronus, ut illis benignis usus est ad commodandum, sic ipse diligens fuit ad reportandum. Nuper homines nobiles hujusmodi, judices, et quid dico nuper, immo vero modo ac plane paulo ante vidimus, qui forum ac basilicas non

He gives an air of reality, or of a spoken discourse, to that which was only written; as Demosthenes and other Athenians did, for they wrote out and polished their speeches after the delivery, which does not exclude the supposition of their being written also before delivery. Wolf (adv. Leptin. 68) compares with this passage of Cicero the following passage of Demosthenes: Λάβε δὴ καὶ τὸ Χαβρίᾳ ψήφισμα ψηφισθέν. ὅρα δὴ καὶ σκόπει· δεῖ γὰρ αὐτὸ ἐνταῦθα εἶναί που. See the note of Wolf, who refers to Quintil. Inst. Or. ix. 2. 61. Pliny, the younger, in a letter to Tacitus (i. 20), also quotes this passage: "ideo in optima quaque mille figuras extemporales invenimus: in his etiam quas tantum editas scimus, ut in Verrem, Artificem, quem? quemnam?" &c.

Polycletus was either a native of Sicyon or Argos. There is some difficulty about the matter (Sillig. Catalogus). There were at least two sculptors of the name. Cicero may mean the elder and more illustrious, who was a great artist. His Doryphorus, which appears to be the same as the Canon, or model statue, was the example which Lysippus studied.

C. Claudius,] Pulcher, Aedilis Curulis, B.C. 99, who, as Pliny says (H. N. viii. 7, ed. Hard.), was the first who ornamented the 'scena' with paintings. (See Valerius Max. ii. c. 4. 6.) This practice of decorating the Forum is mentioned by Livy (ix. 40), and he attempts to assign the origin of the practice. See Lib. 1. c. 22.

Zumpt says that this is an oblique attack on Hortensius, who made a magnificent display in his aedileship (B.C. 75), but was suspected of having received money and presents for this purpose, from persons who had been guilty of irregularities like Verres (De Off. ii. 16. Brut. c. 92).

basilicas] This is a Greek word, signifying a royal building of some sort. The Basilicae of Rome were large buildings, designed for public business, particularly mercantile business. They were afterwards also used, or part of them, as courts of justice. A Basilica was a roofed building supported by columns, so arranged as to form a portico all round the interior of it. The 'tribunal' was at one end of the building, on a raised platform. Vitruvius (v. 1) explains the plan and uses of this kind of building. These 'basilicae' were the originals of the modern exchange or bourse. The best representations of them are the early Christian churches in Rome, and some of them exhibit many of the characteristics of the Roman Basilicae. There are twelve churches in Rome now which are called Basilicae. The most perfect Basilica of antiquity is that of Pompeii, which agrees very well with the description of Vitruvius. The plan of the building is 220 feet by 80.

Livy (xxvi. 27) says that in B.C. 210 there was no Basilica at Rome. M. Porcius Cato, when Censor, was the first who erected a Basilica, B.C. 185; and it was named Porcia. It was close to the Curia and the Comitium. It was burnt B.C. 51, and there is no account of its having been rebuilt. The second Basilica was built (B.C. 180) in the censorship of Aemilius Lepidus and M. Fulvius Nobilior. This was called Basilica Aemilia et Fulvia (Varro, L. L. vi. 2); but it is commonly called Aemilia. The next was the Basilica Julia, built in the midst of the Forum. A Sempronia, built by the censor, T. Sempronius Gracchus (B.C. 170), is also mentioned.

On the Roman Basilicae see Becker's Handbuch, i. p. 300; and the article Basilicae in the Penny Cyclopaedia. It would be out of place to say more of these Basilicae, or to discuss their position in Rome. Those who have paid any attention to the Topography of Ancient Rome, know the

spoliis provinciarum sed ornamentis amicorum, commodis hospitum non furtis nocentium ornarent; qui tamen signa atque ornamenta sua cuique reddebant, non ablata ex urbibus sociorum atque amicorum quatridui causa per simulationem aedilitatis domum deinde atque ad suas villas auferebant. Haec omnia quae dixi signa, judices, ab Heio e sacrario Verres abstulit. Nullum, inquam, horum reliquit, neque aliud ullum tamen praeter unum pervetus ligneum Bonae Fortunae, ut opinor: eam iste habere domi suae noluit.

'Beschreibung der Stadt Rom,' and the work of W. A. Becker, 'Handbuch der Römischen Alterthümer.' There are also three pamphlets which are connected with these two works: 'Die Römische Topographie in Rom, eine Warnung,' by W. A. Becker: 'Römische Topographie in Leipzig, ein Anhang zur Beschreibung der Stadt Rom,' by L. Urlichs: and 'Zur Römischen Topographie Antwort an Herrn Urlichs,' by W. A. Becker.

commodis] Cicero has just used 'ad commodandum;' and he here uses 'commodis,' in the sense of 'loans.' When things which are determined by weight, number, or measure, were the subjects of a loan, such as pieces of coin, wine, oil, corn, brass, silver, gold, these things became the property of the borrower, who was not bound to return the same things, but only things of the same value. This is a loan of things which in their nature are consumed in the use, and was called 'mutuum' (Gaius, iii. 90). If things were lent, which were not consumed in the use, and were lent for a specific purpose, without any pay for the lending, and on the terms of being restored to the lender after being used, the contract was named 'commodatum' (Dig. 13. tit. 6. Inst. Just. Lib. iii. tit. 14. s. 2). This use of 'commodis' seems something peculiar. Zumpt observes: "praeter communem vocabuli usum dicuntur res, quae ab hospitibus ad tempus concessae sunt sive commodatae;" and he quotes after Graevius, Isidorus, Orig. v. 25: "Commodum est id quod nostri juris est et ad alium temporaliter translatum est cum commodo temporis, quamdiu apud eum sit, unde commodum dictum." But the thing lent cannot be called 'commodum;' its name is 'commodatum.' Gaius, iii. 206, says of him 'cui rem commodavimus:' "hic quoque utendo commodum percipiendo similiter necesse habet custodiam praestare:" he is bound to take due care of the thing from which he derives 'commodum.'

sociorum] V adds 'atque amicorum.'—'quatridui causa:' Lambinus wished to get rid of the 'quatridui.' He says, "*quatridui causa* genus loquendi inusitatum;" and the conclusion is, that because it is 'inusitatum' it is wrong. It means 'for the purpose of the few days of the exhibition.' Cicero calls it four, but it may have been more. Iordan writes 'quadridui,' following R 3 V.

e sacrario] 'de sacrario' V.

neque aliud ullum tamen] 'not one of them, I say, he left;' but he partly corrects himself, only to give more effect to what he had said—not another, at least, except one very old one, of wood. "Nam *tamen* non raro poni pro *certe*, ut Germanice *doch* pro *wenigstens* satis constat" (Zumpt).—'Bonae Fortunae' V ?. 'Bonam Fortunam' is the common reading.

The oldest statues of Greece were of wood. The Greek name is ξόανον. Pausanias (2. 19. 3) says of the temple of Apollo Lycius (Ἀπόλλωνος ἱερὸν Λυκίου, ed. Bek.), 'originally both the temple and the ξόανον were a dedication of Danaus; for I am convinced, that at that time all statues were ξόανα, and particularly Egyptian statues.' He says in another place (8. 17. 2): "of old, as far as I have been able to learn, these were the woods of which ξόανα were made, ebony, cypress, cedar, oak, smilax, lotus." To this list may be added olive-wood (Herod. v. 82). Pausanias mentions a statue of Hermes, made of θύον (citrus ?), about eight feet high. We know that the Egyptians also made wooden statues. The small figures of sycamore-wood are still common. Belzoni found two wooden figures of fine workmanship, about seven feet high, in the tombs of the kings at Thebes. The Greek artist finally overlaid the wooden statue with ivory and gold, and made a wonder of art out of a kernel of wood.

IV. Pro deum hominumque fidem, quid hoc est? quae haec causa est? quae ista impudentia est? Quae dico signa, antequam abs te sublata sunt, Messanam cum imperio nemo venit quin viderit. Tot praetores, tot consules in Sicilia, quum in pace tum etiam in bello fuerunt; tot homines cujusque modi—non loquor de integris, innocentibus, religiosis; tot cupidi, tot improbi, tot audaces, quorum nemo sibi tam vehemens, tam potens, tam nobilis visus est qui ex illo sacrario quidquam poscere aut tollere aut attingere auderet. Verres quod ubique erit pulcherrimum auferet? nihil habere praeterea cuiquam licebit? tot domus locupletissimas domus istius una capiet? Idcirco nemo superiorum attigit ut hic tolleret? ideo C. Claudius Pulcher rettulit ut C. Verres posset auferre? At non requirebat ille Cupido lenonis domum ac meretriciam disciplinam: facile illo sacrario patrio continebatur: Heio se a majoribus relictum esse sciebat in hereditate sacrorum: non quaerebat meretricis heredem.

V. Sed quid ego tam vehementer invehor? Verbo uno repellar: Emi, inquit. O dii immortales, praeclaram defensionem! Mercatorem in provinciam cum imperio ac securibus misimus, omnia qui signa, tabulas pictas, omne argentum, aurum, ebur, gemmas coëmeret, nihil cuiquam relinqueret. Haec enim mihi ad omnia defensio patefieri videtur, Emisse. Primum, si id quod vis tibi ego concedam, ut emeris, quoniam in toto hoc genere hac una defensione usurus es, quaero cujusmodi tu judicia Romae putaris esse, si tibi hoc quemquam concessurum putasti, te in praetura

4. *viderit.*] Perhaps it should be 'viserit,' as Baiter suggests.

ut hic tolleret!] The common reading is 'iste;' "sed hic, qui nunc est, opponitur aetate superioribus" (Zumpt).

in hereditate sacrorum:] "*Sacra* h. l. non sunt sacrificia, sed ipsa signa sacrata" (Zumpt). Halm says the same, and he refers to 'sacra majorum,' c. 8. But this is not the correct interpretation. Cicero is speaking after Roman fashion; for, among the Romans, the 'sacra,' or sacred rites, which a family had to perform, were a part of the 'hereditas' or succession. It is no objection that this might not be a rule of Sicilian law; Cicero speaks of it as if it were: "In the Roman religious system there was a kind of divine worship, which was required from mere private persons, as a duty, and like every other, was under the superintendence of the Pontifices: 'sacra privata.' If, for instance, a Roman vowed certain offerings, and the Pontifices approved of them, he was for ever bound to this duty. Nay, this duty did not cease with his life, but, so far as was possible, it must have perpetual continuance. For this reason the Pontifices assumed, that the obligation did not rest so much on the person as on the property, and passed with this property after the death to other persons" (Savigny, Vermischte Schriften, i. p. 152, 'Ueber die Juristische Behandlung der Sacra Privata bei den Römern'). The 'signa' were of course included in the 'hereditas sacrorum.' Hotmann understood the passage right.

meretricis] An allusion to Chelidon (Lib. 1. c. 40). As to 'leno,' see Index.

5. *cum imperio ac securibus*] See Lib. 1. c. 22, where the text of Asconius had these words, which may have been borrowed from this passage.

atque imperio tot res, tam pretiosas, omnes denique res quae alicujus pretii fuerint tota ex provincia coëmisse. Videte majorum diligentiam qui nihildum etiam istiusmodi suspicabantur; verumtamen ea quae parvis in rebus accidere poterant providebant. Neminem qui cum potestate aut legatione in provinciam esset profectus, tam amentem fore putaverunt ut emeret argentum; dabatur enim de publico: ut vestem; praebebatur enim legibus: mancipium putaverunt, quo et omnes utimur et non praebetur a populo. Sanxerunt, Ne quis emeret nisi in demortui locum. Si qui Romae esset demortuus? Immo, si quis ibidem. Non enim te instruere domum tuam voluerunt in provincia, sed illum usum provinciae supplere. Quae fuit causa cur tam diligenter nos in provinciis ab emptionibus removerent? Haec, judices, quod putabant ereptionem esse non emptionem, quum venditori suo arbitratu vendere non liceret. In

argentum; dabatur enim] Comp. In Pison. c. 35, "quasi vasarii nomine . . . ex aerario tibi attributum." 'Argentum' is plate.

vestem;] We have no corresponding word. 'Vestis' had a fixed meaning, as we see by the definition of what passed to a legatee by a legacy of 'vestis:' "veste legata ea cedunt quae ex lana et lino texta sunt; item serica et bombycina, quae tamen induendi, operiendi, cingendi, sternendi, injiciendique causa parata sunt: pelles quoque indutoriae continebantur." (Paulus, Rec. Sent. iii. 6, 79.)

Ne quis emeret] After 'emeret' is found in most MSS. 'mancipium,' but Zumpt observes, that it seems better omitted, so that the transition to the masculine gender is easier. He refers to Lib. 2. c. 32, "Quod unquam hujusmodi monstrum . . . qui;" and to Liv. xxxviii. c. 34, "tum uti quae servitia tyranni liberassent, ea magna multitudo erat, ante diem certam abirent: qui ibi mansissent," &c.

Hotmann refers to Dig. 18. 1. 46 and 62, which show that there were imperial constitutions, which prevented a governor from trafficking; and these constitutions were founded on old rules: "Non licet ex officio, quod administrat quis, emere quid vel per se vel per aliam personam; alioquin non tantum rem amittit, sed et in quadruplum convenitur secundum constitutionem Severi et Antonini;" that is, Septimius Severus, and his son, Antoninus Caracalla.

Athenaeus (vi. 273, ed. Cas., on the authority of Polybius and Posidonius) tells a story of Scipio Africanus taking only five slaves with him when he went abroad on a public mission, and one of those having died on the road, he wrote to his friends to buy another in his place, and send him. There is also a curious passage in the Life of Alexander Severus, by Lampridius, c. 42, on the allowance to governors of provinces, in which he seems to refer to this passage of Cicero: so many pounds of silver, so many cups, mules, and so forth. They had one cook allowed; "et si uxores non haberent, singulas concubinas quod sine his esse non possent: reddituri deposita administratione, mulas, mulos, equos, muliones et coquos; caetera sibi habituri si bene egissent; in quadruplum reddituri, si male, praeter condemnationem aut peculatus aut repetundarum."

illum usum] The whole passage from 'sanxerunt' means this: 'They made a rule that no governor should buy a slave, except in the place of one who died. What, if one should die at Rome? No; if one died in the place where the governor was. For they did not intend that you should stock your household in the province, but that you should supply your provincial wants.'

ereptionem esse non emptionem,] This, as Zumpt observes, is the figure 'annominatio,' which is described in the Lib. ad Herennium, iv. 21. Some people are, perhaps, not aware of the obscure diligence with which the ancient writers on rhetoric tortured language into rules and figures. It is instructive as a warning against trifling. "Annominatio est quum ad idem verbum et ad idem nomen acceditur commutatione unius literae aut literarum, aut ad res dissimiles similia verba accommo-

provinciis intelligebant, si is qui esset cum imperio ac potestate quod apud quemque esset emere vellet, idque ei liceret, fore uti quod quisque vellet, sive esset venale sive non esset, quanti vellet auferret. Dicet aliquis, Noli isto modo agere cum Verre: noli ejus facta ad antiquae religionis rationem exquirere: concede ut impune emerit, modo ut bona ratione emerit, nihil pro potestate, nihil ab invito, nihil per injuriam. Sic agam. Si quid venale habuit Heius, si id quanti aestimabat tanti vendidit, desino quaerere cur emeris.

VI. Quid igitur nobis faciendum est? num argumentis utendum in re ejusmodi? Quaerendum credo est Heius iste num aes alienum habuerit, num auctionem fecerit: si fecit, num tanta difficultas eum rei nummariae tenuerit, tanta egestas, tanta vis presserit ut sacrarium suum spoliaret, ut deos patrios venderet. At hominem video auctionem fecisse nullam; vendidisse praeter fructus suos nihil unquam; non modo in aere alieno nullo, sed in suis nummis multis esse et semper fuisse; si haec contra ac dico essent omnia, tamen illum haec quae tot annos in familia sacrarioque majorum fuissent venditurum non fuisse. Quid si magnitudine pecuniae persuasum est? Verisimile non est ut ille homo tam locuples, tam honestus, religioni suae monumentisque majorum pecuniam anteponeret. Sunt ista; verumtamen abducuntur homines nonnunquam etiam ab institutis suis magnitudine pecuniae. Videamus quanta ista pecunia fuerit quae potuerit Heium, hominem maxime

dantur" (iv. 21). In Lib. 1. c. 1, there is "ut ad audiendum projectus, sic paratus ad audiendum." There is a good, or a bad example of 'annominatio,' whichever way the reader chooses to take it, in Phil. ii. c. 11: "qui me non solum meis laudibus ornarent, sed etiam onerarent alienis." Zumpt observes, that Cicero, though he indulges in this figure to some extent, takes more delight in contrasting things by means of the prepositions, as when he opposes 'deportare' to 'asportare' (Lib. 1. c. 4).

cum imperio ac potestate] See c. 20.

modo ut . . emerit,] The whole expression (concede ut, &c.) means this; "allow that he made this purchase without incurring the penalty of the 'lex,' if he only made it on fair terms," &c.: for this seems to be the meaning of 'bona ratione.' 'Modo ut' occurs in Terence, Andria (ii. 4. 6), 'Modo ut possim,' 'if I only can,' which is there as much as to say, 'I wish I may be able.'

6. *presserit*] The reading of B 3, which is preferable to 'oppresserit,' the reading of Orelli. For this use of 'premere' Zumpt refers to Pro Rosc. Am. c. 34.

in aere] Compare Hor. 2 Ep. ii. 12; Pro Rosc. Com. c. 8, 'in suis nummis versabatur.' 'Aes' is a general term for money: 'etiam aureos nummos aes dicimus' (Ulp. Dig. 50. 16. 159). Again: "Aes alienum est quod nos aliis debemus; aes suum est quod alii nobis debent" (Ulp. Dig. 50. 16. 213).

contra ac] See Pro Balbo, c. 3; In Pison. c. 8. Also 'contra atque,' In Cat. iii. 8. Cicero uses 'contra quam,' Ad Q. Fr. 1. 1. c. 1, "factum est enim mea culpa contra quam tu mecum . . . egeras."

persuasum est?] Zumpt and others omit 'ei' before 'persuasum.' Orelli keeps 'ei.'

Verisimile . . ut] Zumpt compares a like passage in the oration Pro Sulla, c. 20.

locupletem, minime avarum, ab humanitate, a pietate, a religione deducere. Ita jussisti, opinor, ipsum in tabulas referre: Haec omnia signa Praxiteli, Myronis, Polycliti HS VI millibus et D Verri vendita. Sic rettulit. Recita ex tabulis. Juvat me haec praeclara nomina artificum, quae isti ad coelum ferunt, Verris aestimatione sic concidisse. Cupidinem Praxiteli HS CIↃDC. Profecto hinc natum est, Malo emere quam rogare.

VII. Dicit aliquis, Quid tu ista permagno aestimas? Ego vero ad meam rationem usumque meum non aestimo: verumtamen a vobis ita arbitror spectari oportere quanti haec eorum judicio, qui studiosi sunt harum rerum, aestimentur, quanti venire soleant, quanti haec ipsa si palam libereque venirent venire possent, denique ipse Verres quanti aestimet. Nunquam si X. CCCC Cupidinem illum putasset, commisisset ut propter eum in sermonem hominum atque in tantam vituperationem veniret. Quis vestrum igitur nescit quanti haec aestimentur? In auctione signum aeneum non maximum HS XL millibus venire non vidimus? Quid si velim nominare homines, qui aut non minoris aut etiam pluris emerint, nonne possum? Etenim qui modus est in his rebus cupiditatis, idem est

vendita.] 'vendita esse,' Madvig, Jordan. The word 'rettulit' is omitted in all the Lgg. except Lg. 29. V has VERRI VENDITA SIC RETV . . . || REC . . . EX TABVLIS. This is plainly intended for 'sic rettulit;' and so Halm has printed it. There are also the readings 'vendita; sed' R 3, and 'vendita sic' dett. Jordan does not say what is the authority for 'vendita sunt,' which was the former reading in this edition.

HS CIↃDC.] This reading agrees with the X. CCCC or 400 'denarii' of the following chapter, for a 'denarius' was equivalent to four 'sestertii.'

7. *commisisset ut*] 'would have acted in such a way as,' or 'would have made such a mistake as' &c. Comp. Lib. 1. c. 43, 'nemo enim committeret.'

qui modus] The passion for works of art among the wealthy Romans began with the conquest of Magna Graecia and Greece Proper. We find in Horace many allusions to the large sums of money expended on such objects, and particularly on such as were of supposed high antiquity. Horat. 2 Sat. iii. 20:

—— "Olim nam quaerere amabam
Quo vafer ille pedes lavasset Sisyphus aere," &c.

and Heindorf's notes.

Martial ridicules the passion for these antiques:—

"Argenti furiosa sui cum stemmata narrat
Garrulus et verbis mucida vina facit —
'Hoc cratere ferox commisit praelia Rhoecus
Cum Lapithis: pugna debile cernis opus,'" &c.—Martial, viii. 6.

Heindorf observes that 'signum' is said of every work of the class of sculpture, also of busts and rilievi; on the contrary, 'statua' is said of a figure that is cast, or worked with the chisel, of the complete human form, and of the size of life. In c. 34, a full-length figure of Diana, of more than the natural size, is called 'signum;' and in c. 33 it is mentioned under the more general term 'simulacrum.' The word 'signum' is very general, and applied to any work on which the chisel was used; and, as it seems, also to works cast in metal. 'Statua' seems to be properly applied to a full-length figure, from its being adapted to be set up in public. An equestrian figure was called 'statua,' not 'signum' (c. 40, &c.). Ovid, Heroid. Phyllis to Demophoon, has:—

"Inter et Aegidas media statuaris in urbe,
Magnificus titulis stet pater ante tuis."

aestimationis: difficile est enim finem facere pretio si non libidini feceris. Video igitur Heium neque voluntate neque difficultate aliqua temporis nec magnitudine pecuniae adductum esse ut haec signa venderet, teque ista simulatione emptionis vi, metu, imperio, fascibus, ab homine eo, quem una cum ceteris sociis non solum potestati tuae sed etiam fidei populus Romanus commiserat, eripuisse atque abstulisse. Quid mihi tam optandum, judices, potest esse in hoc crimine quam ut haec eadem dicat ipse Heius? Nihil profecto: sed ne difficilia optemus. Heius est Mamertinus: Mamertina civitas istum publice communi consilio sola laudat: omnibus iste ceteris Siculis odio est; ab his solis amatur: ejus autem legationis quae ad istum laudandum missa est princeps est Heius, etenim est primus civitatis, ne forte, dum publicis mandatis serviat, de privatis injuriis reticeat. Haec quum scirem et cogitarem, commisi tamen, judices, Heio: produxi [eum] prima actione; neque id tamen ullo periculo feci. Quid enim poterat Heius respondere, si esset improbus, si sui dissimilis? Esse illa signa domi

Any full-length figure placed any where may be a 'statua' (Pomponius, Dig. 50. 16. 245), "statuae affixae basibus structilibus," &c., where there is a good rule as to the law of fixtures.

Sillig, in his Catalogus, speaks of bronze-casters as 'statuarii,' and makers of marble statues as 'sculptores.' The word 'sculptor' seems to be the appropriate word for a worker in marble, and 'scalptor' to denote a cutter of stones, or 'gemmae.' The two verbs 'sculpere' and 'scalpere,' which are really the same word, are often confounded in the MSS.; but yet it is possible that usage may have assigned one to express sculpture, and the other to express gem-cutting. A gem or stone-cutter was sometimes called δακτυλιογλύφοι by the Greeks. There is apparently no difference between γλύφω and γλάφω. 'Caelator' (Sillig, Preface) properly signifies one who employed metal for the making of smaller things, as cups, metal vases, and the like; but it was also applied to workers in other material, so as to comprehend all who made 'bassi rilievi,' whether in metal or marble. But, as work in marble was the sculptor's province, Sillig limits 'caelator' to workers in metal, who were sometimes called 'vascularii,' of whom Mentor is an example. Quintilian (Inst. ii. 21. 8) limits 'caelatura' to the working on gold, silver, bronze, and iron; but he makes 'sculptura' to comprehend all that 'caelatura' does, and also working on wood, ivory, marble, glass, and 'gemmae.' The Greek word τορευτική expresses the art of the 'caelator;' but 'toreutic' was also applied to those colossal statues which Phidias made, called Chryselephantine, which were of wood, overlaid with gold and ivory. Müller, Handbuch der Archaelogie der Kunst, will supply references both to ancient and modern authorities.

temporis] Cicero often uses this word to express something transitory, a temporary difficulty, a temporary motive, a matter of immediate self-interest, and the like.

sola laudat:] See c. 65, "Ut laudatio quae C. Verri decreta esset tolleretur."

ne forte, &c.] Hotmann says that something is wanting. Lambinus changed 'serviat' to 'servit.' Zumpt adopts Beck's incorrect explanation, 'omissa terendi notione.' P. Manutius, one of the best of the interpreters of Cicero, says correctly: "Joci genus, quasi civitas id spectaverit, cum legatum misit: quod ei certe propositum non fuit; ipse tamen utrumque fecit, et faciet."

commisi tamen,] The word 'me,' which is usually added, is properly omitted by Zumpt. It is not 'me,' but 'rem,' as in Lib. 3. c. 71, 'quibus hoc committam.' But the 'rem' can be omitted, as in De Leg. Agr. ii. 8, 'universo populo neque ipse committit,' &c., cited by Madvig. Lib. 3. c. 60, 'negat se . . . commissurum.'

suae, non esse apud Verrem? Qui poterat quidquam ejusmodi dicere? Ut homo turpissimus esset impudentissimeque mentiretur, hoc diceret, illa se habuisse venalia, eaque sese quanti voluerit vendidisse. Homo domi suae nobilissimus, qui vos de religione sua ac dignitate vere existimare maxime vellet, primo dixit se istum publice laudare, quod sibi ita mandatum esset: deinde neque se illa habuisse venalia neque ulla conditione, si utrum vellet liceret, adduci unquam potuisse ut venderet illa, quae in sacrario fuissent a majoribus suis relicta et tradita.

VIII. Quid sedes, Verres? quid exspectas? quid te a Centuripina civitate, a Catinensi, ab Halesina, Tyndaritana, Hennensi, Agyrinensi, ceterisque Siciliae civitatibus circumveniri atque opprimi dicis? tua te altera patria, quemadmodum dicere solebas, Messana circumvenit; tua, inquam, Messana, tuorum adjutrix scelerum, libidinum testis, praedarum ac furtorum receptrix. Adest enim vir amplissimus ejus civitatis, legatus hujus judicii causa domo missus, princeps laudationis tuae, qui te publice laudat: ita enim mandatum atque imperatum est—tametsi rogatus de cybaea, tenetis memoria quid responderit: aedificatam publicis operis, publice coactis, eique aedificandae publice Mamertinum senatorem praefuisse—idem ad vos privatim, judices, confugit: utitur hac lege qua judicium est, communi arce sociorum. Tametsi lex est de

8. *Tyndaritana,*] 'a Tyndaritana' V.

cybaea,] See Lib. 5. c. 17, from which it appears that it was a ship for the conveyance of goods, a merchant ship, built at the cost of Messana.

The commentators suppose the word to be formed from *κύπη*, a kind of ship: Κύπαι, εἶδός τι νεώς (Hesych.). Salmasius, in Jul. Capitol. Maxim. Duo, c. 22, p. 253, has a long note on the phrase 'ponte itaque cupis facto,' where the word means 'tubs' or 'casks.' From this meaning of 'cupa,' a containing vessel, he derives 'cybaea.' Casaubon (In Capitol. Not. p. 186) quotes Lucan, iv. 420:

"Namque ratem vacuae sustentant undique cupae."

It seems that we may conclude that a Cybaea was a big-bellied ship, adapted to hold a good deal. Hotmann would derive the word from *κύβος*; and he says, that accordingly it means a square ship, or, as he further says, 'quae in omnes partes aeque patent.' One would suppose that this would be a round ship. It is hardly possible that Hotmann can have seen a ship. Upon this Graevius acutely remarks, that square ships were not known to the ancients. From Hotmann's note on square ships, I glean the following reference to Juvenal, Sat. viii. 105:—

"Inde Dolabella est, atque hinc Antonius; inde
Sacrilegus Verres; referebant navibus altis
Occulta spolia et plures de pace triumphos."

publicis . . . coactis,] See Lib. 2. c. 5, note.

qua judicium est,] One might be tempted to think that something is omitted after 'est,' such as 'constitutum:' but the passage from 'qua' to 'sociorum' stands thus in the old editions. Compare Lib. 5 c. 1, 'quum judicium certa lege sit.' The reading which has obtained since the Juntina Veneta is 'est communis et privatae rei sociorum.' Zumpt refers to Divin. c. 5, 'hanc habent arcem,' that is, the Lex de Repetundis.

pecuniis repetundis, ille se negat pecuniam repetere quam ereptam non tanto opere desiderat: sacra se majorum suorum repetere abs te dicit: deos penates te patrios reposcit. Ecqui pudor est? ecquae religio, Verres? ecqui metus? Habitasti apud Heium Messanae: res illum divinas apud eos deos in suo sacrario prope quotidiano facere vidisti: non movetur pecunia: denique quae ornamenti causa fuerunt non requirit: tibi habe Canephoros: deorum simulacra restitue. Quae quia dixit, quia tempore dato modeste apud vos socius amicusque populi Romani questus est, quia religioni suae non modo in diis patriis repetendis sed etiam in ipso testimonio ac jurejurando proximus fuit, hominem missum ab isto scitote esse Messanam de legatis unum, illum ipsum qui navi istius aedificandae publice praefuit, qui a senatu peteret ut Heius afficeretur ignominia. IX. Homo amentissime, quid putasti, impetraturum te? quanti is a civibus suis fieret, quanti auctoritas ejus haberetur ignorabas? Verum fac te impetravisse; fac aliquid gravius in Heium statuisse Mamertinos: quam putas auctoritatem laudationis eorum futuram, si in eum quem constet verum pro testimonio dixisse poenam constituerint?

Tametsi quae est ista laudatio, quum laudator interrogatus laedat necesse est? Quid isti laudatores tui, nonne testes mei sunt? Heius est laudator: laesit gravissime. Producam ceteros: retice-

quotidiano] Or 'cotidiano,' as Zumpt writes it, which mode of writing, even if it has the best MSS. authority, I should not choose to follow until we agree to write 'cotus' and 'cot.' The common reading is 'quotidie.' Similar usages of 'crastinus,' 'vespertinus,' 'matutinus,' &c., are compared with this by Madvig, Epist. ad Orell. p. 60, referred to by Zumpt.

'Res divinas facere,' or 'rem divinam,' is a common phrase for a religious ceremonial. (Ter. Hec. i. 2. 109.) 'Facere' alone is so used, as in Virgil, Bucol. iii. 77, 'Quum faciam vitula.'

tibi habe] There is good authority for 'tibi,' and it is necessary: "*sibi enim habere* jubemus, cum possidere patimur et jus nostrum relinquimus" (Zumpt). See Lib. 2. c. 19. Gruter omitted 'tibi,' and so it stands in the text of the Variorum ed. 'habe Canephoros,' and in Orelli.

religioni . . proximus] 'was true to his Religio.' The following explanation of 'proximus' may not be quite useless: "proximus est quem nemo antecedit, supremus est quem nemo sequitur" (Paulus, Dig. 50. 16. 92).

ignominia.] The word is a Roman term, which perhaps comes near to the Greek ἀτιμία. 'Ignominia' occurs in the praetor's edict (De his qui notantur infamia, Dig. 3. tit. 2): "Infamia notantur qui ab exercitu ignominiae causa ab imperatore eove cui de ea re statuendi potestas fuerit dimissus erit." Ulpian remarks: "ignominiosa autem missio toties est quoties is qui mittit addidit nominatim, ignominiae causa se mittere; semper enim debet addere cur miles mittatur." A man who was sent on a public mission, had of course to account for his conduct, and was liable to some punishment if he had neglected his duty. Malversation on an embassy is the παραπρεσβεία of the Greeks.

9. *quid putasti, impetraturum te?*] R, V, Jordan. The common reading is 'qui putasti,' &c. There does not seem much reason for preferring one to the other; but perhaps 'quid' &c. is the better.—'pro testimonio dixisse:' a common form. See In Vatin. c. i. vol. iv.

bunt quae poterunt libenter: dicent quae necesse erit ingratis. Negent isti onerariam navem maximam aedificatam esse Messanae? negent si possunt. Negent ei navi senatorem Mamertinum publice praefuisse? utinam negent. Sunt etiam cetera quae malo integra reservare, ut quam minimum sit illis temporis ad meditandum confirmandumque perjurium. Haec tibi laudatio procedat in numerum: hi te homines auctoritate sua sublevent, qui te neque debent adjuvare si possint, neque possunt si velint; quibus tu privatim injurias plurimas contumeliasque imposuisti; quo in oppido multas familias totas in perpetuum infames tuis stupris flagitiisque fecisti.—At publice commodasti.—Non sine magno quidem rei publicae provinciaeque Siciliae detrimento. Tritici modium LX millia empta populo Romano dare debebant et solebant: abs te solo remissum est. Res publica detrimentum fecit quod per te imperii jus in una civitate imminutum est; Siculi, quod ipsum non de summa frumenti detractum est, sed translatum in Centuripinos et Halesinos, immunes populos, et hoc plus impositum quam ferre possent. Navem imperare debuisti ex foedere: remisisti in triennium: militem nullum unquam poposcisti per tot annos. Fecisti item ut praedones solent, qui quum hostes communes sint omnium, tamen aliquos sibi instituunt amicos quibus non modo parcant, verum etiam praeda quos augeant, et eos maxime qui habent oppidum

ingratis.] Zumpt writes 'ingratiis' in his smaller edition, and so it stands in the English reprint. In his larger edition he comes to the conclusion that 'ingratis' is the proper form; for, as the prose writers say 'gratis,' so we should expect them to say 'ingratis.' He observes that Plautus and Terence write 'ingratiis,' but then they have only the form 'gratiis.' (Bentley, Ad Terent. Adelph. iv. 7. 26.) R 3, V have 'ingratis.'

si possunt.] This is the better reading. 'Si possint' is the common reading, but the words are wanting in Lagg. Zumpt prefers 'si possunt,' but for a bad reason: "hanc ob causam quod *si possint* tempore excidit remque in futurum removet."—'sit' G 3; 'dem' Lagg. Iordan; 'idem' R, which means 'dem.'

procedat in numerum:] "Ex animi tui sententia. Sumptum, opinor, ab histrionibus numerum in motu servantibus" (P. Manutius). He refers to the Paradoxa, iii., "Histrio si paulo se movit extra numerum," &c. Hotmann completely misunderstood the passage.

publice commodasti.] 'Beneficio eos affecisti' (P. Manutius), that is 'the state.' Comp. Ter. Hec. v. 1. 34.

Siculi, quod ipsum] That is, 'Siculi detrimentum fecerunt quod ipsum.' 'The Sicilians sustained damage in this, that this very amount was not subtracted from the sum total, but it was made a burden on the Centuripini and Halesini.' This 'quod ipsum' shows how 'quod' is to be taken in the first part of the sentence. If 'quod' is considered as a conjunction, it is misunderstood.

From this it appears that a 'foederata civitas' was bound to supply 'frumentum emptum.' It would seem strange if a 'foederata civitas' owed this duty, and the 'immunes populi' did not; a conclusion which some may be inclined to derive from these words. But it is not a necessary conclusion; and we learn from other passages that all Sicily was bound to supply 'frumentum emptum' or 'imperatum.' (See Lib. 3. c. 73, v. c. 21.)

Navem . . foedere:] The 'foedus' with Messana dated from B.C. 264. Compare Lib. 1. c. 34, 35, as to the Milesii. We there learn how the Romans maintained a fleet.

opportuno loco, quo saepe adeundum sit navibus, nonnunquam etiam necessario.

X. Phaselis illa, quam cepit P. Servilius, non fuerat urbs antea Cilicum atque praedonum: Lycii illam, Graeci homines, incolebant. Sed quod erat ejusmodi loco atque ita projecta in altum, ut et exeuntes e Cilicia praedones saepe ad eam necessario devenirent, et quum se ex hisce locis reciperent eodem deferrentur, asciverunt sibi illud oppidum piratae primo commercio, deinde etiam societate. Mamertina civitas improba antea non erat: etiam erat inimica improborum, quae C. Catonis, illius qui consul fuit, impedimenta retinuit. At cujus hominis? clarissimi potentissimique; qui tamen quum consul fuisset, condemnatus est, [ita] C. Cato, duorum hominum clarissimorum nepos, L. Pauli et M. Catonis, et P. Africani sororis filius; quo damnato tum quum judicia fiebant, HS IIII mil-

10. *Phaselis &c.*] 'Antea' means 'originally.' Phaselis, now Tekrova, was a Lycian town on the coast, on a small peninsula at the foot of Toktalu, the ancient Solyma, the bare summit of which rises 7800 feet above the sea. It had three ports, and there was a lake on the isthmus which joined to the main land the peninsula on which Phaselis stood. Its position is well described by Livy (Lib. 37. c. 23). The flat top of the peninsula is covered with ruins, and the identity of the place is proved by Greek inscriptions: ΦΑΣΗΛΕΙΤΩΝΗΒΟΥΛΗΚΑΙΟΔΗΜΟΣ, &c. There is a description of Phaselis in Beaufort's Karamania.

These Lycii were Greeks, as Cicero observes; and we have an account of their political constitution in Strabo (p. 664, ed. Cas.). The Lycii of Homer appear in the war of Troy.

C. Catonis,] See Lib. 3. c. 80. C. Cato, consul B.C. 114, a grandson of the Censor. He had Macedonia for his province, where he got money by illegal means, was tried, convicted, and fined. As to the 'impedimenta retinuit,' I find no further information.—'At cujus hominis?' see Lib. 2. c. 45.

[*ita*] *C. Cato,*] Zumpt has followed Ernesti in placing these words, 'ita C. Cato .. sororis filius,' in [ ]. He supposes them to have been transferred into the text from a marginal note; and he adds, "Auctor, a quo petita videntur, in promptu est, Velleius, Lib. ii. 8: Mandetur deinde memoriae severitas judiciorum, quippe C. Cato consularis, M. Catonis nepos, Africani sororis filius (*nepos igitur L. Aemilii Paulli*) repetundarum ex Macedonia damnatus est cum lis ejus IIII aestimaretur." The precise sum is uncertain, owing to the diversity in the MSS. See Lib. 3. c. 80. Klotz (Vorrede, p. 13) contends that the passage is right. He points the disputed part thus, 'condemnatus est: ita C. Cato duorum .. filius;' and explains it thus, 'Yes, C. Cato, &c., was condemned.' He makes 'ita' correspond to the German 'ja, so ist es.' I am not acquainted with this peculiar use of 'ita,' and Klotz is not accustomed to support his explanations by instances. I think, however, that he is right in rejecting Zumpt's supposition that these words have been interpolated from Paterculus. The words are undoubtedly genuine, but there seems to be something wrong in the connexion between 'condemnatus est' and what follows. The blunder appears to be in the 'ita;' and if it is omitted, perhaps the difficulty is removed. Though I cannot accept Klotz's explanation, I leave the words standing, as genuine; and having enclosed 'ita' in the critical [ ], I commend the passage to the consideration of the learned. Iordan has included in [ ] the words 'ita C. Cato . . . aestimata est.'

quum judicia fiebant,] Zumpt has 'quum severa judicia fiebant,' and yet he says that 'severa' is wanting in all the better MSS. But it may be omitted. Iordan only notes it as wanting in R 3, λ. Compare Lib. 5. c. 50, 'quum judicia fiebant;' and c. 12, 'non jus dici, non judicia fieri.' Klotz omits it in this passage. See Lib. 3. c. 80. note on 'ad quae exempla.'

libus lis aestimata est. Huic Mamertini irati fuerunt, qui majorem sumptum quam quanti Catonis lis aestimata est in Timarchidi prandium saepe fecerunt. Verum haec civitas isti praedoni ac piratae Siciliensi Phaselis fuit. Huc omnia undique deferebantur; apud istos relinquebantur: quod celari opus erat, habebant sepositum ac reconditum: per istos quae volebat clam imponenda, occulte exportanda curabat: navem denique maximam quam onustam furtis in Italiam mitteret apud istos faciendam [aedificandamque] curavit: pro hisce rebus vacatio data est ab isto sumptus, laboris, militiae, rerum denique omnium: per triennium soli non modo in Sicilia, verum, ut opinio mea fert, his quidem temporibus in omni orbe terrarum, vacui, expertes, soluti ac liberi fuerunt ab omni sumptu, molestia, munere. Hinc illa Verria nata sunt, quod in convivium Sex. Cominium protrahi jussit, in quem scyphum de manu jacere conatus est, quem obtorta gula de convivio in vincla atque in tenebras abripi jussit. Hinc illa crux, in quam iste civem Romanum multis inspectantibus sustulit; quam non ausus est usquam defigere nisi apud eos quibuscum omnia scelera sua ac latrocinia communicavit.

XI. Laudatum etiam vos quemquam venitis? qua auctoritate? utrum quam apud senatum an quam apud populum Romanum habere debetis? Ecquae civitas est, non in provinciis nostris verum in ultimis nationibus, aut tam potens aut tam libera aut etiam tam immanis ac barbara; rex denique ecquis est qui senatorem populi Romani tecto ac domo non invitet? qui honos non homini solum habetur, sed primum populo Romano, cujus beneficio nos in

deferebantur;] R 3 λ, Zumpt, in his larger edition, Klotz, and Iordan. The common reading is 'deportabantur.' On 'clam imponenda' Zumpt observes, "omisi quae vulgo praemittuntur verba *in navem* propterea quod absunt a Lambini duobus, et Regio Graevii, nec in Guelff. inveniuntur." 'Imponere' can be thus used absolutely; and, as a matter of taste, 'in navem' is better omitted.

vacatio] A release or excuse from a duty. The verb occurs in the same sense in De Sen. c. 11, 'ergo . . vacat aetas nostra muneribus,' &c. With a noun, the construction is with the genitive, as in the excerpt from Scaevola (Dig. 50. 5. 3): "His qui naves marinas fabricaverunt . . . muneris publici vacatio praestatur ob naves."

quod in convivium] These words refer to 'Verria,' to the banquet which accompanied this festival in honour of Verres. The drunken governor, we may suppose, threw a cup at Cominius:

"Natis in usum laetitiae scyphis
Pugnare Thracum est."
Horat. I Carm. xxvii.

communicavit.] 'communicavisset' dett.; 'communicasset' Lg. 29 48.

11. *Ecquae civitas*] Zumpt says that it is difficult to decide if we should write 'ecquae' or 'ecqua,' for there is the authority of the poets for both. Klotz and Iordan have 'ecqua.'

domo non invitet?] Lambinus says 'forte *in tectum ac domum*,' on which Graevius says 'pessime.' He explains 'invitare' to be the same as 'excipere,' and refers to Justin. i. 6, 'eosdem apparatis epulis invitat.' Zumpt refers to Cic. Phil. xii. 9, 'hospitio invitabit.' See Graevius, note on Justin.

populo Romano, cujus beneficio] A man

hunc ordinem venimus, deinde ordinis auctoritati, quae nisi gravis erit apud socios et exteras nationes, ubi erit imperii nomen et dignitas? Mamertini me publice non invitarunt. Me quum dico, leve est: senatorem populi Romani si non invitarunt, honorem debitum detraxerunt non homini sed ordini. Nam ipsi Tullio patebat domus locupletissima et amplissima Cn. Pompeii Basilisci, quo etiamsi esset invitatus a vobis tamen devertisset: erat etiam Perenniorum, qui nunc item Pompeii sunt, domus honestissima, quo L. frater meus summa illorum voluntate devertit. Senator populi Romani, quod in vobis fuit, in vestro oppido jacuit et pernoctavit in publico. Nulla hoc civitas unquam alia commisit.—Amicum enim nostrum in judicium vocabas.—Tu quid ego privatim negotii geram interpretabere imminuendo honore senatorio? Verum haec tum queremur, si quid de vobis per eum ordinem agetur, qui ordo a vobis adhuc solis contemptus est. In populi Romani quidem conspectum quo ore vos commisistis, nec prius illam crucem, quae

became admissible to the senate after being a quaestor, and as he was elected to a quaestorship by the people, their vote indirectly placed him in the senate. See Pro Sestio, c. 65, and the note on the Roman senate.—'publice:' 'on behalf of the state.' See c. 9, and Caesar, B. G. i. 16. Also Verr. ii. 1. c. 25, where Philodamus admits his liability to entertain praetors and consuls on behalf of his town.

exteras nationes,] 'Socii et externae nationes' comprise all people with whom the Romans had any dealings of any kind. Madvig (quoted by Klotz) says that the 'externae nationes' are those whom the Romans had subdued and made tributary. This is manifestly a mistake. All who were not 'socii' were 'externae nationes,' and the 'provinciales' were included among 'socii' (Lib. 1. c. 31, 'non provinciae,' &c.). There were nations which were not 'socii,' nor yet conquered, with whom the Romans had relations of some kind. Thus Caesar (B. G. i. 43) speaks of Ariovistus having been addressed by the title of king, and friend of the Roman senate. Certainly he was not a 'socius' like the Aedui, nor did he pay a tribute. He belonged to the 'externae gentes.'—'et amplissima' Zumpt and Iordan omit.

nunc item Pompeii] They also were now 'Pompeii,' Roman citizens, who had obtained the 'civitas' through the favour of Cn. Pompeius.

L. frater] His 'frater patruelis,' or cousin Lucius, who accompanied him to Sicily on this occasion. See Introd. to this volume. His death is mentioned (Ad Att. i. 5. A.U.C. 686).

Tu quid &c.] Here Cicero supposes some one to have said 'Amicum enim,' &c. 'Well, it was because you were bringing our friend to trial.' (See Lib. 1. 9, 'causam enim.') Cicero answers, 'Tu quid ego privatim,' &c. Hotmann explains 'privatim' to mean 'as a single person,' as opposed to the senatorian 'ordo;' for he says 'publice quidem Cicero negotium hoc gerebat.'—'Imminuendo honore' is the better reading, which Graevius established in place of 'in minuendo honore.' The translation of 'interpretabere' is difficult. Hotmann's explanation of 'privatim' is right. Cicero is contrasting himself and his 'ordo;' and what he means to say is this: 'Will you disparage the honour that is due to a senator, in order to show your opinion of my conduct as a private individual?' for Cicero, though a senator, was not sent to Sicily as a senator, but as a private individual who had undertaken to prosecute Verres. This is what he means to say here, but it may not be consistent with what he has said elsewhere. (Lib. 1. c. 6.)

si quid . . agetur,] That is, if the senate shall call you to account for your behaviour in this matter.

vos commisistis,] 'presented yourselves before,' 'trusted yourselves.' See Pro Sestio, c. 54.

etiam nunc civis Romani sanguine redundat, quae fixa est ad portum urbemque vestram, revellistis neque in profundum abjecistis locumque illum omnem expiastis, quam Romam atque in horum conventum adiretis? In Mamertinorum solo foederato atque pacato monumentum istius crudelitatis constitutum est. Vestrane urbs electa est ad quam quum adirent ex Italia crucem civis Romani prius quam quemquam amicum populi Romani viderent? quam vos Rheginis, quorum civitati invidetis, itemque incolis vestris civibus Romanis ostendere soletis, quo minus sibi arrogent minusque vos despiciant, quum videant jus civitatis illo supplicio esse mactatum.

XII. Verum haec emisse te dicis. Quid illa Attalica tota Sicilia nominata ab eodem Heio peripetasmata emere oblitus es? Licuit eodem modo ut signa. Quid enim actum est? an literis pepercisti? Verum hominem amentem hoc fugit; minus clarum putavit fore quod de armario quam quod de sacrario esset ablatum. At quomodo abstulit? non possum dicere planius quam ipse apud vos dixit Heius. Quum quaesissem numquid aliud de bonis ejus pervenisset ad Verrem, respondit istum ad se misisse ut sibi mitteret Agrigentum peripetasmata. Quaesivi an misisset: respondit, id quod necesse erat scilicet, dicto audientem fuisse praetori; misisse. Rogavi pervenissentne Agrigentum: dixit pervenisse. Quaesivi quemadmodum revertissent: negavit adhuc revertisse. Risus populi atque admiratio omnium vestrum facta est. Hic tibi in mentem non venit jubere ut haec quoque referret HS VI millibus D

crucem, . . civis Romani] See Lib. 5. c. 66.

Rheginis, quorum] The Rhegini were Roman citizens since the enactment of the Julia Lex, B.C. 90. 'Reginis' is the reading of R. The oldest form of the Ethnic name on the Greek coins is PECINON. Rhegium is Reggio, at the southern extremity of Italy and nearly opposite to Messana, and about six miles distant from it in a direct line.—'incolis:' see c. 58.

12. *Verum haec &c.*] 'But you say you bought these things. Well, did you forget to buy those other matters?' &c. Zumpt joins 'nominata ab eodem Heio.' It seems to me that 'nominata' must be connected with 'Sicilia.' He says that 'nominata,' in the sense of 'celebrata,' cannot be said; but the sense of this passage requires it.

'Attalica peripetasmata' were draperies embroidered with gold, which one of the Attali of Pergamum introduced; or he encouraged the manufacture. Plin. H. N. viii. c. 48, ed. Hard. Those who worked at such decorations were ποικιλταί, mentioned by Plutarch, Pericles, c. 12.

peripetasmata. . . pervenissentne Agrigentum:] "om. R3. Cum in optimis codd. totus hic locus omissus sit, jure suspecta est particula *an*, quam dett. codd. habent. Cf. Madv. Op. ii. p. 164. Itaque Halmius edidit 'num misisset' " (Iordan), who suggests 'cane misisset.'

Some editors place the comma after 'erat' and others after 'scilicet.' "*Respondit, id quod necesse erat, se dicto* ex Hotom. conj. Halm.;" which we might prefer, if it were good criticism to remove a difficulty by altering a text. But we cannot explain how 'scilicet' came into the text, if Cicero did not write it. Perhaps it is not placed in the sentence where it should be.

se tibi vendidisse? metuisti ne aes alienum tibi cresceret, si HS VI millibus D tibi constarent ea quae tu facile posses vendere HS ducentis millibus? Fuit tanti, mihi crede: haberes quod defenderes: nemo quaereret quanti illa res esset: si modo te posses docere emisse, facile cui velles tuam causam et factum probares: nunc de peripetasmatis quemadmodum te expedias non habes.

Quid a Phylarcho Centuripino, homine locuplete ac nobili, phaleras pulcherrime factas, quae regis Hieronis fuisse dicuntur, utrum tandem abstulisti an emisti? In Sicilia quidem quum essem,—sic a Centuripinis, sic a ceteris audiebam, non enim parum res erat clara,—tum te has phaleras a Phylarcho Centuripino abstulisse dicebant quam alias item nobiles ab Aristo Panhormitano, quam tertias a Cratippo Tyndaritano. Etenim si Phylarchus vendidisset, non ei posteaquam reus factus es redditurum te promisisses. Quod quia vidisti plures scire, cogitasti si ei reddidisses te minus habiturum, rem nihilominus testatam futuram: non reddidisti. Dixit Phylarchus pro testimonio, se quod nosset tuum istum morbum, ut amici tui appellant, cupisse te celare de phaleris: quum abs te appellatus esset, negasse habere sese: apud alium quoque eas habuisse depositas, ne qua invenirentur: tuam tantam fuisse sagacitatem ut eas per illum ipsum inspiceres ubi erant depositae: tum se deprehensum negare non potuisse: ita ab se invito phaleras ablatas gratis.

XIII. Jam ut haec omnia reperire ac perscrutari solitus sit, judices, est operae pretium cognoscere. Cibyratae sunt fratres quidam, Tlepolemus et Hiero, quorum alterum fingere opinor e cera solitum esse, alterum esse pictorem. Hosce opinor, Cibyrae

Fuit tanti,] 'It was worth your while,' as we say. 'Est tanti,' c. 20. See Pro Rosc. Com. c. 8.

phaleras] 'Equorum ornamenta' (Manutius).

alias] Halm compares Caesar, B. G. i. 1: "Gallia est omnis divisa in partes tres, quarum unam incolunt Belgae, aliam Aquitani, tertiam" &c.

minus habiturum,] In the old editions it was 'minus invidiae habiturum,' but 'invidiae' spoils the sense. Zumpt supposes that Manutius first corrected the passage. The explanation of Manutius shows that he did not admit 'invidiae.' He says 'phaleras ipsas non habiturum.' 'Invidiae' is not in the best MSS. (Zumpt); but it is in Lagg. except 29.

illum ipsum . . ubi] The adverbs 'ubi,' 'quo,' 'unde' are often thus used in place of some form of the relative, which here would be 'apud quos.' Halm refers to 'apud eos quo,' c. 18, and other instances.

ablatas gratis.] The inferior MSS. have 'ablatas,' and the better have 'sublatas,' which reading Zumpt had in his minor edition. But in his larger edition he prefers 'ablatas' as the proper word to be used when we take a thing from a person who is in possession of it (qui possidet). In c. 13 we have 'ab sese . . abstulisset' and 'a se esset ablatum.'

13. *fingere . . e cera*] He was a modeller in wax, an art which the Greeks practised. It must have been common at Rome after it became the fashion to make wax busts or 'imagines.' Lib. 5. c. 14.

Cibyra] Cibyra Magna, which Cicero probably means, was the chief city of the Cibyratis, a district between Lycia and Pisidia. Cibyra was situated at Horzoom, on a branch of the Dalaman Tchy or

quum in suspicionem venissent suis civibus fanum expilasse Apollinis, veritos poenam judicii ac legis domo profugisse. Quod Verrem artificii sui cupidum cognoverant tum quum iste, id quod ex testibus didicistis, Cibyram cum inanibus syngraphis venerat, domo fugientes ad eum se exules quum iste esset in Asia contulerunt. Habuit eos secum ab illo tempore, et in legationis praedis atque furtis multum illorum opera consilioque usus est. Hi sunt illi quibus in tabulis refert sese Q. Tadius dedisse jussu istius Graecis pictoribus. Eos jam bene cognitos et re probatos secum in Siciliam duxit. Quo posteaquam venerunt, mirandum in modum canes venaticos diceres, ita odorabantur omnia et pervestigabant ut ubi quidque esset aliqua ratione invenirent. Aliud minando, aliud pollicendo, aliud per servos, aliud per liberos, per amicum aliud, aliud per inimicum inveniebant: quidquid illis placuerat perdendum erat. Nihil aliud optabant quorum poscebatur argentum nisi ut [id] Hieroni et Tlepolemo displiceret.

XIV. Verum mehercule hoc, judices, dicam. Memini Pamphilum Lilybaetanum, amicum et hospitem meum, nobilem hominem, mihi narrare, quum iste ab sese hydriam Boëthi manu factam, praeclaro opere et grandi pondere, per potestatem abstulisset, se sane tristem et conturbatum domum revertisse, quod vas ejusmodi, quod sibi a patre et majoribus esset relictum, quo solitus esset uti ad festos dies, ad hospitum adventus, a se esset ablatum. Quum

Indus (Spratt's Lycia), about 37° 10′ N. lat. The site is determined by inscriptions found on the spot. There are many remains. Under the Romans Cibyra was the seat of a Conventus Juridicus. The inhabitants were skilled in the working of iron with a cutting tool (Strabo, p. 630).

inanibus syngraphis] See Lib. 1. c. 36. It is difficult to conjecture why these 'syngraphae' are called 'inanes.' Zumpt supposes that this is an allusion to the affair of Malleolus (Lib. 1. c. 36), and that they were forms of agreement with blanks for the names of the parties, the blanks to be filled up with the name of Verres and the names of the debtors of Malleolus. Cicero is alluding to some act of knavery, but his meaning is doubtful.

Q. Tadius] See Lib. 1. c. 49.

quidque esset] P. Manutius corrected the old reading 'quicquid esset.' R, G 1 have 'quicque.'

14. *mehercule*] There is a reading 'mehercules,' but Zumpt observes that Cicero prefers 'mehercule.' Orat. 47, "impetratum est a consuetudine ut peccare suavitatis causa liceret; et *pomeridianas quadrigas* quam *postmeridianas* libentius dixerim; et *mehercule* quam *mehercules*;" a passage which I had not observed when I made the note on 'mehercule,' Lib. 3. c. 13. Cicero says also 'medius fidius,' Pro Sext. Rosc. Am. c. 34.

Boëthi manu] Plinius (H. N., Lib. 33. c. 5, ed. Hard.) names him in conjunction with Acragas and Mys. He was a 'caelator,' or worker in silver. Pausanias (v. 17) calls him a Carthaginian: Βοηθὸς δὲ *ἐτόρευσεν αὐτὸ Καρχηδόνιος*. But it is suggested by Müller that we should read Καλχηδόνιος, which is likely enough. The word *ἐτόρευσε* shows that he practised the toreutic art: he was a *τορευτής* or 'caelator.' He was also a 'statuarius.'

A 'hydria' was a general name for any vessel adapted to hold a liquid.

adventus,] R, G 2, Lg. 29. The common reading is 'adventum.' As to 'adventus,' see Lib. 1. c. 19, note.

sederem, inquit, domi tristis, accurrit Venereus: jubet me scyphos sigillatos ad praetorem statim afferre. Permotus sum, inquit; binos habebam; jubeo promi utrosque ne quid plus mali nasceretur, et mecum ad praetoris domum ferri. Eo quum venio, praetor quiescebat: fratres illi Cibyratae inambulabant. Qui me ubi viderunt, Ubi sunt, Pamphile, inquiunt, scyphi? Ostendo tristis. Laudant. Incipio queri me nihil habiturum quod alicujus esset pretii, si etiam scyphi essent ablati. Tum illi, ubi me conturbatum vident, Quid vis nobis dare ut isti abs te ne auferantur? Ne multa, sestertios CIↃ me, inquit, poposcerunt: dixi me daturum. Vocat interea praetor: poscit scyphos. Tum illos coepisse praetori dicere putasse se id quod audissent alicujus pretii scyphos esse Pamphili; luteum negotium esse; non dignum quod in suo argento Verres haberet. Ait ille idem sibi videri. Ita Pamphilus scyphos optimos aufert. Et mehercule ego antea, tametsi hoc nescio quid

scyphi sigillati] These were cups with figures on them, for 'sigillum' is a diminutive of 'signum.' The term may be applied to figures cut or formed on the material itself, as on marble. Cicero (Ad Att. i. 10) purchased 'putealia sigillata.' If the figures are separate things, and attached to the vessel, they are expressed by the Greek term 'emblemata,' figures inlaid (c. 17). In c. 21, Cicero speaks of a 'patella' on which there were 'sigilla,' and Verres took off the 'sigilla,' and returned the vessel; and in another instance (c. 21) he pulled off the 'emblema,' and returned the 'turibulum' without the figures. Juvenal (Sat. i. 76):

"Argentum vetus et stantem extra pocula caprum;"

on which Heinrich remarks that the Romans had no name for 'emblema.' The word was used by Lucilius to indicate a kind of Mosaic work, or inlaying of small pieces of various shapes and colours; and, metaphorically, it is applied to a style of writing (Cicero, Orat. c. 44):

"Quam lepide lexeis compostae, ut tesserulae omnes
Arte pavimento atque emblemate vermiculato."

binos habebam;] 'I had a pair.' In reference to which he uses 'utrosque.' Halm says that it means two pairs. I think it is one pair. See Lib. 3. c. 60, note on 'utrisque.' Pseudo-Ascon. ad Act. ii. Lib. 2. c. 8, "Is qui Erycum montem obtinebat] Lilybaetanus scilicet quaestor, non Syracusanus. Nam hos binos quaestores annuos habuit Sicilia." Sallust (Cat. c. 6) writes, "Annua imperia binosque imperatores sibi fecere," where he means the two consuls annually chosen. But these two examples may not be conclusive, because in both cases it is a pair chosen annually. In Lib. 2. c. 19 Cicero says 'scyphorum paria complura,' and if he meant two pairs of cups here, he would have said 'scyphorum paria duo.' If he meant simply two, and not a pair, he would have said 'duos,' as he says 'duo pocula' c. 22.

luteum negotium] See Lib. 3. c. 14. It means here, as the context shows, that the cups were a poor affair, not fit to have a place in the plate (argentum) of Verres.

aufert.] 'carries off,' 'saves.' Comp. Pro P. Quintio, c. 5. Pro Cluentio, c. 24.

Et mehercule &c.] Graevius says that either 'hoc' or 'ista' is superfluous, in which he is entirely mistaken. It is usual with Cicero to place 'hoc' thus, and then to explain what he means, as in Lib. 1. c. 4, "Nam quis hoc non intelliget istum absolutum," &c.; Lib. 3. c. 65, "Metellus quidem certe jam hoc judicabat eorum rem causamque esse conjunctam." Graevius quite misunderstands the whole passage, the sense of which appears from the following sentence, 'Tum primum intellexi,' &c. Cicero says, 'In truth, for my part, before I heard of this affair, though I knew that it (hoc) was but a trifling matter to be a judge of such works of art, yet I used to wonder that Verres had any understanding

nugatorium sciebam esse ista intelligere, tamen mirari solebam istum in his ipsis rebus aliquem sensum habere, quem scirem nulla in re quidquam simile hominis habere. XV. Tum primum intellexi ad eam rem istos fratres Cibyratas fuisse ut iste in furando manibus suis, oculis illorum uteretur. At ita studiosus est hujus praeclarae existimationis ut putetur in hisce rebus intelligens esse, ut nuper, videte hominis amentiam, posteaquam est comperendinatus, quum jam pro damnato mortuoque esset, ludis Circensibus mane apud L. Sisennam, virum primarium, quum essent triclinia strata argentumque expositum in aedibus, quum pro dignitate L. Sisennae domus esset plena hominum honestissimorum, accessit ad argentum, contemplari unumquidque otiose et considerare coepit. Mirari stultitiam alii quod in ipso judicio ejus ipsius cupiditatis cujus insimularetur suspicionem augeret; alii amentiam, cui comperendinato, quum tam multi testes dixissent, quidquam illorum venisset in mentem: pueri autem Sisennae, credo, qui audissent quae in istum testimonia dicta essent, oculos de isto nusquam dejicere, neque ab argento digitum discedere. Est boni judicis parvis ex rebus conjecturam facere uniuscujusque [et] cupiditatis et incontinentiae. Qui reus, et reus lege comperendinatus, re et opinione hominum paene damnatus, temperare non potuerit maximo conventu quin L. Sisennae argentum tractaret et consideraret,

in these particular things, when I knew that in no one thing had he any resemblance to a human being. Then, for the first time, I learned,' &c. 'Ista intelligere' is explained by 'in hisce rebus intelligens esse' (c. 15).

15. *comperendinatus,*] See Index. Cicero writes as if the second Actio was going on after the adjournment on account of the Ludi of Pompeius and the Circenses or Ludi Romani (Introd. to the Orations).

L. Sisennam,] Ernesti conjectures that L. Cornelius Sisenna was 'curule aedile' in this year. If Sisenna was 'curule aedile' he would have to look after the Circenses. Sisenna was 'praetor' in B.C. 67, and served under Cn. Pompeius in the Mithridatic war (Appian, Mithrid. c. 95). It seems almost a necessary conclusion from this chapter that he filled some public office. He was an orator and an historian (Krause, Vitae et Frag., &c., p. 300). He is mentioned Lib. 2. c. 45, and Lib. 4. c. 20.

accessit . . coepit.] The form of the sentence requires 'accesserit . . . coeperit,' which Orelli has. But the indicative appears to be the reading of the MSS. If Cicero wrote thus, we need not be surprised, for, owing to the words interposed after 'ut nuper,' a reader might easily fail to observe the irregularity of the sentence.

venisset] Zumpt and Klotz prefer this to 'veniret.' Iordan has 'veniret.'

pueri] 'the slaves,' as Horace often uses 'puer.' This is its ordinary sense when thus used absolutely. We have a definition of 'puer' by Alfenus, a contemporary of Cicero (Paulus, Lib. 2. Epitom. Alfeni, Dig. 50. 16. 204): "pueri appellatio tres significationes habet: unam, quum omnes servos pueros appellaremus, alteram, quum puerum contrario nomine puellae diceremus, tertiam, quum aetatem puerilem demonstraremus."

et incontinentiae.] R, G 2, Iordan have 'et continentiae,' Ld. om., 'et' om. G 1, 'et incontinentiae' rell. Madvig proposes to erase 'cupiditatis et.' I do not think that 'cupiditatis et continentiae' can be the true reading.

hunc praetorem in provincia quisquam putabit a Siculorum argento cupiditatem aut manus abstinere potuisse?

XVI. Verum uti Lilybaeum unde digressa est oratio revertatur, Diocles est, Pamphili gener illius, a quo hydria ablata est, Popillius cognomine. Ab hoc abaci vasa omnia ut exposita fuerant abstulit. Dicat se licet emisse: etenim hic propter magnitudinem furti sunt, ut opinor, literae factae. Jussit Timarchidem aestimare argentum. Quo modo? Quo qui unquam tenuissime in donatione[m] histrionum aestimavit. Tametsi jamdudum ego erro qui tam multa de tuis emptionibus verba faciam, et quaeram utrum emeris necne, et quomodo et quanti emeris; quod verbo transigere possum. Ede

16. *oratio revertatur,*] The reading of the English reprint of Zumpt, and, I suppose, of his minor edition. In his larger he has 'oratio, revertamur.' '*Revertamur* G 3, codd. Lamb.; *revertantur* R; *revertatur*, dett' (Iordan, who has 'revertamur').

abaci] An 'abacus' is a board, or slab of marble, or any thing of the kind on which plate could be arranged, as we often put it on a sideboard. Verres took it all off, just as it was laid out on the 'abacus.' See Lib. 4. c. 59, 'mensas Delphicas,' and Juv. iii. 204, 'ornamentum abaci.'

exposita fuerant] 'exposita fuerunt' Klotz, Iordan.

literae factae.] Entries were made; that is, the transaction was entered in account-books in the usual way.

in donatione[m] histrionum] 'in donationem' Klotz, Iordan. Iordan says 'in donatione,' dett. I suppose we must conclude that the 'meliores' have 'in donationem.' Cicero says that Timarchides valued the things very low, as low as any man ever did in the case of a donation or present to the 'histriones' or actors. Zumpt's explanation is this, that they were allowed to keep the 'corollae' which they had worn (deorum honoris causa), on paying a small estimated value. He refers to Pliny (H. N., Lib. 21. c. 3) as to these 'corollae;' and Klotz says it appears that a present of fixed value was given to the actors who were approved of; and, if it was intended to give more, the present was valued below its real value, to avoid breaking the rule. This explanation, I believe, is merely a guess; there is nothing added to give credibility to it. I neither accept it nor reject it. There is a short note on 'corollarium' (Plin. H. N. ix. 35, ed. Hard.): "corollarium apud Ciceronem non semel, et apud Tranquillum, pro munusculo sumitur, ultra legitima praemia exhibito, et quidem quasi additamento debitae mercedis. Unde corollarium hic pro re leviore et appendicula usurpatur." This does not help us much; but the expression 'ultra legitima praemia' may point to the truth: 'legitimus' always means that which is determined by a 'lex.' Manutius says, "Locus hic ostendit bona histriones argento donari solitos." I suppose 'histriones' in those days, as well as now, did not live on nothing, nor act simply to please spectators. They must have been paid some way. Manutius adds, "aestimationi tamen locum esse non video;" but Cicero did, and that is the matter which wants explanation. There may have been some rule of law as to these 'donationes.' There is a remark in Smyth's Sicily that strikes me as applicable to these gifts or 'corollaria,' for I believe that the 'corollaria' is money. He says of the Sicilian actors: "there is little encouragement given to the profession, and at their benefits they are obliged to submit to the degrading habit of going round and presenting a plate to each of the spectators to receive a contribution" (p. 48). I don't quote this for the purpose of explaining the language of the text; I merely observe that the practice of the spectators putting something in the hat or plate for the 'histriones' may have existed at Rome, and that would be a 'donatio.' Halm quotes a passage from Varro (de L. L. v. 178): "corollarium si (quid) additum praeter quam quod debitum ejus, vocabulum fictum a corollis, quod eas, cum placuerant actores, in scena dare solitae." This agrees with Pliny (ix. 35). Crassus Dives, as Pliny says (xxi. c. 3), was the first who gave 'coronae' of gold and silver at his Ludi.

mihi scriptum quid argenti in provincia Sicilia pararis, unde quidque aut quanti emeris. Quid fit? Quamquam non debebam ego abs te has literas poscere; me enim tabulas tuas habere et proferre oportebat. Verum negas te horum annorum aliquid confecisse. Compone hoc quod postulo de argento; de reliquo videro. 'Nec scriptum habeo nec possum edere.' Quid futurum igitur est? Quid existimas hos judices facere posse? Domus plena signorum pulcherrimorum jam ante praeturam: multa ad villas tuas posita, multa deposita apud amicos, multa aliis data atque donata: tabulae nullum indicant emptum. Omne argentum ablatum ex Sicilia est; nihil cuiquam quod suum dici vellet relictum. Fingitur improba defensio, praetorem omne id argentum coëmisse; tamen id ipsum tabulis demonstrari non potest. Si quas tabulas profers, in his quae habes quomodo habeas scriptum non est, horum autem temporum quum te plurimas res emisse dicis tabulas omnino nullas profers, nonne te et prolatis et non prolatis tabulis condemnari necesse est?

XVII. Tu a M. Coelio, equite Romano, lectissimo adolescente, quae voluisti Lilybaei abstulisti: tu C. Cacurii, prompti hominis et

transigere] 'settle by a single word.' See Divin. c. 14.

argenti] om. Lg. 29.

Quid fit?] "Cur mihi quod postulo scriptum non edis?" (P. Manutius.) This seems to be the meaning. 'However,' continues Cicero, 'I ought not to demand of you these accounts; for I ought to have your books, and to produce them;' for he was empowered to take possession of such evidence. But it is all explained by what follows. Verres had no account-books of this date; he had kept no accounts (aliquid confecisse). Manutius explains 'horum annorum' by reference to Lib. 1. c. 23, since the consulship of M. Terentius and C. Cassius. Cicero says 'compone hoc,' &c.: 'make up for me an account about this matter of the silver; I will look after the rest.'

aliquid] G 3, 'aliquit' R, 'aliquot' dett. and Iordan. If 'aliquid' is the right reading, the genitives 'horum annorum' depend on it.

deposita] Deposited for safe keeping, and to prevent all his treasures from being seen. 'Deposita' in this sense is a technical term, and 'depositum' is one of the Roman contracts which were made 're' (Inst. Just. iii. tit. 14). He who accepted the deposit was bound to take care of it as he would of his own property. "Depositum est quod custodiendum alicui datum est." (Ulpian, Dig. 16. 3. 1 pr.)

Si quas tabulas] I cannot accept Zumpt's punctuation and interpretation of this passage. He has a full stop after 'nullas profers,' and he makes 'nonne' begin a new sentence; whereas it is the apt conclusion after the two premises 'si quas,' &c., and 'horum autem,' &c. He places a semicolon after 'habes,' and he says, "tu subintellige ex iis quae sequuntur *perscripta sunt*." 'Quae habes' appears to be the true reading. The common reading is 'quid habeas,' which Victorius introduced, but from conjecture, as Zumpt supposes. Klotz takes the passage as I do, for the colon which he places after 'nullas profers' is, if I understand it right, merely a German way of pointing. But Klotz places a comma after 'temporum,' and writes 'cum . . . dicas;' but 'quum . . . dicis' must be connected with 'horum temporum,' and 'quum' is equivalent to 'per quae,' if that be Latin. The pointing, or the absence of pointing, shows that I consider 'horum temporum' and 'tabulas' in the relation of a noun and its genitive, as Zumpt also does.

in his] 'in iis' Iordan; but 'in his,' the reading of R, is the true word here.—'condemnari:' 'condempnari' R.

experientis et in primis gratiosi, supellectilem omnem auferre non dubitasti: tu maximam et pulcherrimam mensam citream a Q. Lutatio Diodoro, qui Q. Catuli beneficio ab L. Sulla civis Romanus factus est, omnibus scientibus Lilybaei abstulisti. Non tibi objicio quod hominem dignissimum tuis moribus, Apollonium, Niconis filium, Drepanitanum, qui nunc A. Clodius vocatur, omni argento optime facto spoliasti ac depeculatus es. Taceo. Non enim putat ille sibi injuriam factam, propterea quod homini jam perdito et collum in laqueum inserenti subvenisti, quum pupillis Drepanitanis bona patria erepta cum illo partitus es. Gaudeo etiam si quid ab eo abstulisti, et abs te nihil rectius factum esse dico. Ab Lysone vero Lilybaetano, primo homine, apud quem deversatus es, Apollinis signum ablatum certe non oportuit. Dices te emisse. Scio: HS CIↃ: ita opinor. Scio, inquam: proferam literas: tamen id factum non oportuit. A pupillo Heio, cui C. Marcellus tutor est, a quo pecuniam grandem eripueras, scaphia cum emblematis Lilybaei utrum empta esse dicis an confiteris erepta? Sed quid ego istius in ejusmodi rebus mediocres injurias colligo, quae tantummodo in furtis istius et damnis eorum a quibus auferebat versatae esse videantur? Accipite, si vultis, judices, rem ejusmodi ut amen-

17. *experientis*] See Hor. 1 Ep. 17. 41.

mensam citream] A table of the wood of the 'citrus,' probably a kind of cypress. Tables were an article of Roman luxury. Pliny (H. N., Lib. xiii. c. 15, ed. Harduin) treats of these tables. He mentions one that Cicero himself bought for HS x, which numerals his editor (Harduin) makes to be 'decies,' a sum which is incredible. Harduin says that the 'citrus' is the same as the Greek θυόs (see c. 3, and the note on ξόανα). It was an African wood from the Atlas and the country of the Mauri, and was used for making these tables. Pliny mentions one made of two large pieces of wood, each half a circle, which were so cunningly fitted together that the juncture was not apparent. These are the round tables which Martial (ix. 22) calls 'orbes,' and describes as supported by ivory feet:—

"Ut Mauri Libycis centum stent dentibus orbes,
Et crepet in nostris aurea lamna toris."

And again:—

"Gemmantes prima fulgent testudine lecti
Et Maurusiaci pondera rara citri."
(xii. 66.)

Catuli beneficio] See the note on 'beneficium,' Lib. 1. c. 5, and Lib. 4. c. 11; and Caesar, B. G. vii. 65, 'C. Valerio Donotauro.' Here we have other instances of Greeks being made Roman citizens. Diodorus, as usual, took the Gentile name of his benefactor, Q. Lutatius Catulus, and the Praenomen also.—'depeculatus es:' R 3 C λ have 'depecuniatus es.'

Drepanitanum,] Of Drepana or Drepanum, now Trapani, situated on a peninsula near Mons Eryx.—'pupillis Drepanitanis:' see Lib. 2. c. 57, where Cicero speaks of only one 'pupillus.'

deversatus es,] The reading before the edition of Lambinus was 'diversatus es.' Zumpt affirms that 'deversatus' is the true form. But we may doubt.

scaphia] Said to be drinking vessels. As to 'emblematis' see c. 14.

versatae] Zumpt and Klotz have 'versata.' "Sic omnes libri et olim editi et manu scripti" (Zumpt), except Lg. 45, which has 'versatae.' The omission of an *e* at the end may be easily explained, as the next word begins with an *e*. Though 'quae . . . versata' is intelligible, as Zumpt explains it, 'quae' being 'ea sive talia *quae*,' it seems pretty clear that in that case 'videantur' should be 'videntur.' 'Quae versatae esse videantur' is too closely connected with 'injurias,' to leave any doubt of the true reading.

tiam singularem et furorem, non jam cupiditatem ejus perspicere possitis.

XVIII. Melitensis Diodorus est, qui apud vos antea testimonium dixit. Is Lilybaei multos jam annos habitat, homo et domi nobilis et apud eos quo se contulit propter virtutem splendidus et gratiosus. De hoc Verri dicitur habere eum perbona toreumata; in his pocula quaedam, quae Thericlia nominantur Mentoris manu summo artificio facta. Quod iste ubi audivit, sic cupiditate inflammatus est non solum inspiciendi verum etiam auferendi ut Diodorum ad se vocaret ac posceret. Ille qui illa non invitus haberet respondet Lilybaei se non habere, Melitae apud quendam propinquum suum reliquisse. Tum iste continuo mittit homines certos Melitam: scribit ad quosdam Melitenses ut ea vasa perquirant: rogat Diodorum ut ad illum propinquum suum det literas: nihil ei longius videbatur quam dum illud videret argentum. Diodorus, homo frugi ac diligens, qui sua servare vellet, ad propinquum suum scribit ut iis qui a Verre venissent responderet illud argen-

non jam cupiditatem] Klotz and Iordan have 'et furorem jam, non cupiditatem,' which seems a wrong position of 'jam;' but it is the common reading. Zumpt observes, '*non jam esse non amplius* notum est.' The readings are 'jam non' R, Lagg., 'non jam' G 1 Ld λ, 'non nim' G 2.

18. *De hoc . . . eum*] A good example of the use of these pronouns. He has just used 'is' in the usual way to refer to Diodorus. If he had said 'De eo Verri,' this second reference might have appeared rather too remote. He must repeat the word 'Diodoro,' or use a pronoun which more directly points to the person; the 'hoc.' But 'eum' comes again, having the same relation to the 'hoc' that the 'is' has to Diodorus.

Thericlia] R C G 1 2. The common reading is 'Heraclea.' This Thericles was a maker of earthen vessels, and lived in the time of Aristophanes, according to Bentley (Dissertation on the Epistles of Phalaris). "The name Thericlia was given to cups made in imitation of those of Thericles; in imitation of the style, of course, for they were made in other material, wood, silver, and glass. Welcker denies the existence of an artist Thericles, and maintains that these cups were so called from the figures of animals (θῆρια), with which they were adorned; but this explanation will hardly be received (Art. Thericles, in Smith's Dictionary of Biography).

Mentor was a worker in silver, and the most celebrated of all the Greek artists of his class. His period is fixed to some extent by Pliny's statement (H. N., Lib. 33. c. 12, ed. Hard.), that his works perished either in the conflagration of the temple of Diana, or in that of the Roman capitol. Whatever the fact may be, Pliny supposes that Mentor must have produced his great works before the burning of the temple of Diana, B.C. 356: see also Pliny (H. N., Lib. 7. c. 39). Though the great works of Mentor may have been destroyed, his name survived, and works passed current as his in Martial's time (iii. 41):—

"Inserta phialae Mentoris manu ducta
Lacerta vivit et timetur argentum;"

and Juv. viii. 104:—

"—— rarae sine Mentore mensae."

qui illa non invitus] This is only a rhetorical way of saying what he says shortly after, 'qui sua servare vellet.'

nihil ei longius] This means 'he was impatient to see.' Comp. Phil. 5. c. 1. vol. iv.

ad propinquum . . scribit] Zumpt's reading and Iordan's. The common reading is 'propinquo suo scribit.' Both expressions are Latin. Zumpt observes, that when 'scribere' is equivalent to sending a letter, it is used with the accusative; when it signifies to inform by letter, it has generally a dative. There may be some truth

tum se paucis illis diebus misisse Lilybaeum. Ipse interea recedit: abesse a domo paulisper maluit quam praesens illud optime factum argentum amittere. Quod ubi iste audivit, usque eo commotus est ut sine ulla dubitatione insanire omnibus ac furere videretur. Quia non potuerat eripere argentum, ipse a Diodoro erepta sibi vasa optime facta dicebat; minitari absenti Diodoro, vociferari palam, lacrimas interdum vix tenere. Eriphylam accepimus in fabulis ea cupiditate ut quum vidisset monile, ut opinor, ex auro et gemmis, pulchritudine ejus incensa salutem viri proderet. Similis istius cupiditas: hoc etiam acrior atque insanior, quod illa cupiebat id quod viderat; hujus libidines non solum oculis sed etiam auribus excitabantur.

XIX. Conquiri Diodorum tota provincia jubet. Ille ex Sicilia jam castra commoverat et vasa collegerat. Homo ut aliquo modo in provinciam illum revocaret, hanc excogitat rationem, si haec ratio potius quam amentia nominanda est. Apponit de suis canibus quendam qui dicat se Diodorum Melitensem rei capitalis reum velle facere. Primo mirum omnibus videri Diodorum reum, hominem quietissimum, ab omni non modo facinoris verum etiam minimi errati suspicione remotissimum: deinde esse perspicuum fieri omnia illa propter argentum. Iste non dubitat jubere nomen deferri; et tum primum opinor istum absentis nomen recepisse. Res clara Sicilia tota propter caelati argenti cupiditatem reos fieri rerum

in this distinction. Cicero says, for instance (Ad Div. xiv. 8), "nam mihi et scriptum et nuntiatum est te in febrim subito incidisse."

paucis illis diebus] 'in those few days which preceded the arrival of the letter.' See Lib. 2. c. 26; and Pro Cluentio, c. 39; Phil. i. c. 13. See the Index. The poets also use this form:—

"In thalamos venere Procae. Proca natus in illis
Praeda recens avium quinque diebus erat."—Ovid, Fasti, vi. 143.

Eriphylam] The story is of a woman who sold her husband, Amphiaraus, for a chain of gold:—

Μαῖράν τε Κλυμένην τε ἴδον στυγερήν τ' Ἐριφύλην
ἣ χρυσὸν φίλου ἀνδρὸς ἐδέξατο τιμήεντα.
Od. xi. 326.

The story is told by Diodorus (iv. 65), and Apollodorus, iii. 6. Compare also Sophocles, Electra, 837:—

οἶδα γὰρ ἄνακτ' Ἀμφιάρεων χρυσοδέτοις, &c.

19. *vasa collegerat.*] 'had packed up his baggage.' 'Vasa' are the moveables of an army, or of a man on a journey; the same as the Greek *σκεύη*. See Caesar, Bell. Civ. i. 66. Cicero uses 'vasa' in a double sense here.

Homo] 'The man,' Verres. This is an emphatic way of writing, often used by the Romans; but it is merely 'emphatic.' 'Homo' itself expresses neither praise nor blame. See Quum Senatui, c. 9, vol. iii.

nomen deferri;] See Index.

opinor] 'ut opinor' R 3, E, Iordan, and Klotz. I do not know how they explain 'ut opinor.' Halm says that it is a form of Anakoluth. Cicero says that this, he believes, is the first instance of Verres allowing a prosecution to be commenced against a man in his absence. The rule of law was that a man must have notice of such a proceeding and the opportunity of defending himself. See Lib. 2. c. 39. 42.

capitalium, neque solum reos fieri sed etiam absentes. Diodorus Romae sordidatus circum patronos atque hospites cursare, rem omnibus narrare. Literae mittuntur isti a patre vehementes, ab amicis item—videret quid ageret de Diodoro, quo progrederetur: rem claram esse et invidiosam; insanire hominem; periturum hoc uno crimine nisi cavisset. Iste etiamtum patrem, si non in parentis, at in hominum numero putabat: ad judicium nondum se satis instruxerat: primus annus erat provinciae; non ut in Sthenio jam refertus pecunia. Itaque furor ejus paululum non pudore sed metu ac timore repressus est. Condemnare Diodorum non audet absentem: de reis eximit. Diodorus interea praetore isto prope triennium provincia domoque caruit. Ceteri non solum Siculi sed etiam cives Romani hoc statuerant, quoniam iste tantum cupiditate progrederetur, nihil esse quod quisquam putaret se quod isti paulo magis placeret conservare aut domi retinere posse. Postea vero quam intellexerunt isti virum fortem, quem summe provincia exspectabat, Q. Arrium non succedere, statuerunt nihil se tam clausum neque tam reconditum posse habere quod non istius cupiditati apertissimum promptissimumque esset.

XX. Tum iste ab equite Romano splendido et gratioso, Cn. Calidio, cujus filium sciebat senatorem populi Romani et judicem esse, equuleos argenteos nobiles qui Q. Maximi fuerant aufert. Imprudens huc incidi, judices: emit enim, non abstulit: nollem

in Sthenio] See Lib. 2. c. 36, &c.

metu ac timore] See Vol. iii. In Cat. iii. c. 4, and the note on 'metus,' 'timor.'

non audet absentem:] The punctuation of Klotz. Zumpt has the common punctuation, 'non audet: absentem de reis eximit.' I think that the punctuation of Klotz shows the true meaning. Iordan has it also.

20. *judicem esse,*] He was in the 'decuriae' of the 'judices.'—'equuleos' or 'eculeos.' Manutius supposes that they were silver vessels, which may be inferred from the words, 'Vende mihi vasa caelata.' The vessels had probably figures of horses on them, or horses' heads. The Q. Maximus may be Q. Fabius Maximus, the conqueror of the Allobroges, as Manutius supposes. Gulielmius, following Priscian, who quotes these words, conjectures that we should read, 'quique maximi fuerant,' where he explains 'maximi' as equivalent to 'plurimi,' 'of the highest value.' Graevius adopted this reading from R, and it stands in the Variorum edition; but R has 'quique maxime.' G 3 have the reading 'quique maximi.' Zumpt thinks that if this is the sense of the passage, 'fuerant' ought to be 'erant.' And so it ought. Klotz and Iordan have the reading 'quique maximi fuerant.' I suppose that, if Cicero meant to speak of the value, he would have said 'plurimi,' and not 'maximi;' and the addition of a word of price after 'nobiles' can hardly be what Cicero meant. Their real value would have been enhanced by having belonged to a Q. Maximus, who was a man of taste. 'Qui Q. Maximi' is the reading of Lagg. except Lg. 42, which omits 'Q.'

Orelli quoted by Halm has the following note on 'equuleos:' "Memini me videre ejusmodi eculeum aureum, qui ante haec tria saecula in equitum Melitensium epulis adhibebatur, cujus in dorsum perforatum vinum infundebatur, epotabatur per cannam e pectore prominentem. Eam poculi formam ex antiquitate artifex quisquis fuit retinuisse videtur."

nollem dixisse:] The reading of the

dixisse: jactabit se et in his equitabit equuleis. 'Emi: pecuniam solvi.' Credo, etiam tabulae proferentur. Est tanti: cedo tabulas: dilue sane crimen hoc Calidianum, dum ego tabulas aspicere possim. Verumtamen quid erat quod Calidius Romae quereretur se, quum tot annos in Sicilia negotiaretur, abs te solo ita esse contemptum, ita despectum, ut etiam una cum ceteris Siculis despoliaretur? Si emeras, quid erat quod confirmabat se abs te argentum esse repetiturum, si id tibi sua voluntate vendiderat; tu porro posses facere ut Cn. Calidio non redderes, praesertim quum is L. Sisenna defensore tuo tam familiariter uteretur, et quum ceteris familiaribus Sisennae reddidisses? Denique non opinor negaturum esse te homini honesto, sed non gratiosiori quam Cn. Calidius est, L. Curidio te argentum per Potamonem amicum tuum reddidisse. Qui quidem ceterorum causam apud te difficiliorem fecit. Nam quum te confirmasses compluribus redditurum, posteaquam Curidius pro testimonio dixit te sibi reddidisse, finem reddendi fecisti, quod intellexisti praeda te de manibus emissa testimonium tamen effugere non posse. Cn. Calidio, equiti Romano, per omnes alios praetores licuit habere argentum bene factum; licuit posse domesticis copiis, quum magistratum aut aliquem superiorem invitasset, ornare et apparare convivium. Multi domi Cn. Calidii cum potestate atque

codd. Hahn and Iordan have 'nollem dixissem,' the usual Latin form. But I do not see why 'nollem dixisse' is not Latin.

Est tanti:] 'It is worth your while:' as before. It is worth your while to produce the books, and clear yourself of this charge. It is hardly 'tanti,' perhaps, to remark that Hotmann misunderstood what is so plain: he says, 'tanti sunt venditi.'

despoliaretur!] In the old editions 'spoliaretur,' for which Naugerius wrote 'dispoliaretur,' the reading of E G1 2 dett. Ernesti was of opinion that 'dispoliaretur' is the genuine form in Cicero (Clavis Cic. v. Dispoliare). One does not see the objection to 'despoliare;' but it is a matter to be decided by evidence. It is singular that Ernesti, who is so zealous about 'dispoliare,' should not have taken up the claims of 'discribere' in some of the passages which he has under Describere (Clavis, v. Describere).

quid erat quod confirmabat] They who place a comma after 'erat' (Zumpt and some others) have, as far as they could, prevented a reader from understanding the text. It means: 'if you had bought it, what did he mean when he affirmed that he would bring an action against you for the recovery of the plate, if he had sold it to you of his own free will; and you, on your part, what was there that you could do to prevent your delivering it back to Cn. Calidius?' 'Quid erat quod' must be supplied between 'porro' and 'posses facere.' Here we have 'quid erat quod,' in two different constructions, but also in two different senses. The sense with the subjunctive is shown by numerous instances, as in Lib. 3. c. 55, "quid enim erat quod vectigalibus prospiceret Metellus?" &c. See also Lib. 3. c. 63, and note on 'laborasse dicit.'

emissa] See Pro Caelio, c. 27, note on 'amiserunt.'

apparare] Perhaps an ordinary word in such cases. Horace (1 Carm. xxxviii.) has 'Persicos odi, puer, apparatus.' 'Conviviis apparatis,' In Cat. ii. 9.

Multi . . cum potestate atque imperio] Governors or others, who had all the powers which the Roman people could confer on a consul, or praetor, or proconsul. The expression often occurs in Cicero, as in Lib. 5. c. 40. The common reading in this passage is 'cum imperio ac potestate;' but Zumpt observes, that the order in the text is the more usual order, 'nam antecedit

imperio fuerunt: nemo inventus est tam amens qui illud argentum tam praeclarum ac tam nobile eriperet, nemo tam audax qui posceret, nemo tam impudens qui postularet ut venderet. Superbum est enim, judices, et non ferendum, dicere praetorem in provincia homini honesto, locupleti, splendido, Vende mihi vasa caelata. Hoc est enim dicere, Non es dignus tu qui habeas quae tam bene facta sunt: meae dignitatis ista sunt. Tu dignior, Verres, quam Calidius qui—ut non conferam vitam neque existimationem tuam cum illius; neque enim est conferenda; hoc ipsum conferam quo tu te superiorem fingis, quod HS ccc millia divisoribus ut praetor renuntiarere dedisti, trecenta accusatori ne tibi odiosus esset, ea re contemnis equestrem ordinem ac despicis?—ea re tibi indignum visum est quidquam quod tibi placeret Calidium potius habere quam te? XXI. Jactat se jamdudum de Calidio: narrat omnibus emisse se. Num etiam de L. Papinio, viro primario, locupleti honestoque equite Romano, turibulum emisti? qui pro testimonio dixit te, quum inspiciendum poposcisses, evulso emblemate remisisse; ut intelligatis in homine intelligentiam esse, non avaritiam, artificii cupidum non argenti fuisse. Nec solum in Papinio fuit hac abstinentia: tenuit hoc institutum in turibulis omnibus quaecunque in Sicilia fuerunt. Incredibile est autem quam multa et quam praeclara fuerint. Credo tum quum Sicilia florebat opibus et copiis magna artificia fuisse in ea insula; nam domus erat ante istum

potestas, insuper datur imperium.' See Lib. 3. c. 57, 'quum ab omnibus . . propter imperium,' &c. But in Lib. 3. c. 18, Zumpt has 'summum imperium potestatemque haberet:' and in this same book, c. 22, 'pro imperio et potestate.' The matter is not worth notice, except to show the uselessness of these minute canons.

quae tam bene facta sunt:] The question is between 'sunt' and 'sint,' says Zumpt, who decides for 'sunt' on sufficient reasons. Nobody can doubt, who has studied Cicero with any care. He means *the* 'vasa' of Calidius.

qui—ut non conferam &c.] Does 'qui' refer to 'Tu—Verres,' and is it to be connected with 'contemnis?' Or does it refer to Calidius, and is the sentence interrupted at 'qui,' and a new form given to it? Or what is the true explanation? By looking back we may see what is meant. 'Non es dignus tu qui habeas—meae dignitatis ista sunt.' Cicero then says, 'Tu dignior, Verres, quam Calidius, qui —;' and he would have added 'habeas:' but he breaks off, and says, 'ut non conferam . . . tuam,' &c., where the 'tuam' seems to show that the 'qui' must be referred to 'Tu.' He proceeds to 'ac despicis,' with which words he closes these sarcastically assumed reasons of the greater worthiness of Verres to possess. But, instead of continuing the regular construction, 'qui habeas,' which he had rendered impossible by the words interposed, he resumes with a new form of expression, 'ea re tibi indignum,' &c. I have endeavoured to point it as I understand it. The pointing of the editors is unintelligible; at least to me.

divisoribus] See Index.—'trecenta:' " codd.: LXXX de Garat. conj. Zumpt. Kl. In numeris aliquo modo turbatum est, sed incertum quo" (Iordan). 'Ne tibi odiosus esset' means 'that he should give you no trouble.'

21. *artificia*] The word means the 'arts,' a conclusion that Zumpt has come to, though at first he says that he was inclined to take it for 'officinas caelatorum.' Comp. Pro S. Rosc. Amer. c. 46, where

praetorem nulla paulo locupletior qua in domo haec non essent, etiamsi praeterea nihil esset argenti, patella grandis cum sigillis ac simulacris deorum, patera qua mulieres ad res divinas uterentur, turibulum. Haec autem omnia antiquo opere et summo artificio facta, ut hoc liceret suspicari fuisse aliquando apud Siculos peraeque pro portione cetera, sed quibus multa fortuna ademisset, tamen apud eos remansisse ea quae religio retinuisset. Dixi, judices, multa fuisse fere apud omnes Siculos: ego idem confirmo nunc ne unum quidem esse. Quid hoc est? quod hoc monstrum, quod prodigium in provinciam misimus? Nonne vobis id egisse videtur ut non unius libidinem, non suos oculos, sed omnium cupidissimorum insanias quum Romam revertisset expleret? Qui simul atque in oppidum quodpiam venerat, immittebantur illi continuo Cibyratici canes, qui investigabant et perscrutabantur omnia. Si quod erat grande vas et majus opus inventum, laeti afferebant: si minus ejusmodi quidpiam venari potuerant, illa quidem certe pro lepusculis capiebantur, patellae, paterae, turibula. Hic quos putatis fletus mulierum, quas lamentationes fieri solitas esse in hisce rebus? quae forsitan vobis parvae esse videantur, sed magnum et acerbum dolorem commovent mulierculis praesertim, quum eripiuntur e manibus ea quibus ad res divinas uti consuerunt, quae a suis acceperunt, quae in familia semper fuerunt.

XXII. Hic nolite exspectare dum ego haec crimina agam ostia-

the meaning is plain. Sicily must have had great artists, and the people great taste for the arts, as we may see from the coins of the island. Every family, it appears, of the moderately wealthy class had its few articles of plate for religious services: a 'patella,' or large open vessel or dish; a 'patera,' or saucer-formed vessel; and a 'turibulum,' or incense holder. In place of 'patella' R 3 have 'patina,' which Zumpt objects to, because the 'patina' was not used for religious purposes. 'Patella' is a diminutive form of 'patera,' and 'patina' contains the same root as 'patera.' Manutius thought 'patella' and 'grandis' were contradictory; and he would prefer 'patera grandis,' and then write 'patella' for 'patera.'

sigillis ac simulacris] Orelli explains 'sigilla' to mean small figures forming a group (gruppo di figurine), and 'simulacra' to mean single figures cut on 'patellae.'

peraeque pro portione] The true text is doubtful. Lg. 29, codd. Lambini have 'peraequa proportione.' Adr. Turnebus suggested 'peraeque pro portione.' See Lib. 3. c. 63, and Lib. 5. c. 21.

quod hoc monstrum, &c.] Zumpt, in his later edition, added this 'hoc' on the authority of R 3 E. It must be translated, 'What is this monster that we have sent into the province?' which is an ordinary Greek form of expression as well as Latin.

Qui simul &c.] This sentence, and the concluding sentence of this chapter, contain examples of the indicative mood, all of which are consistent with Cicero's usage, when he states particular facts. The 'Cibyratici canes' of Verres (c. 13) went a hunting for their master, and were content to get small game (lepusculi) when they could find nothing better. Verres kept a pack of such hounds (Lib. 1. c. 48). All this is plain; but Hotmann goes out of his way to compare the passage, in a letter of Caelius to Cicero (Ad Div. viii. 4), where Caelius says, "item de pantheris, ut Cibyratas arcessas curesque ut mi vehantur."

22. *ostiatim,*] It occurs again in c. 24:

tim, ab Æschylo Tyndaritano istum pateram abstulisse, a Thrasone item Tyndaritano patellam, a Nymphodoro Agrigentino turibulum. Quum testes ex Sicilia dabo, quem volet ille eligat quem ego interrogem de patellis, pateris, turibulis: non modo oppidum nullum, sed ne domus quidem ulla paulo locupletior expers hujus injuriae reperietur. Qui quum in convivium venisset, si quidquam caelati aspexerat, manus abstinere, judices, non poterat. Cn. Pompeius est Philo, qui fuit Tyndaritanus. Is coenam isti dabat apud villam in Tyndaritano. Fecit quod Siculi non audebant; ille, civis Romanus quod erat, impunius id se facturum putavit: apposuit patellam in qua sigilla erant egregia. Iste continuo ut vidit, non dubitavit illud insigne penatium hospitaliumque deorum ex hospitali mensa tollere; sed tamen, quod ante de istius abstinentia dixeram, sigillis avulsis reliquum argentum sine ulla avaritia reddidit. Quid, Eupolemo Calactino, homini nobili, Lucullorum hospiti ac perfamiliari, qui nunc apud exercitum cum L. Lucullo est, non idem fecit? Coenabat apud eum. Argentum ille ceterum purum apposuerat, ne purus ipse relinqueretur; duo pocula non magna, verumtamen cum emblematis. Hic tamquam festivum acroama, ne sine

'from house to house,' as we say; or 'from door to door.'

Quum testes . . dabo,] He writes as if other witnesses were still to be produced. See p. 84.

quem volet ille] R 3, E λ have 'ille;' the dett. omit it. Orelli inclusit [ ].

apud villam] Zumpt quotes Nonius (cap. 12. nr. 19), who has a note on this use of 'apud' in Cicero, of which this is said to be the only instance in Cicero: "error consuetudinis *apud* pro *in* utitur. Itaque vitiose dicimus, cum nos *in foro* fuisse dicamus, *apud forum* fuisse, cum *apud* juxta significat." Nonius also cites the passage of Terence (Andria ii. 1. 2): "apud forum modo e Davo audivi."

Captain Smyth, speaking of the neighbourhood of Tyndaris, says, "a picturesque path, lined with trees, conducts the traveller to a gentle eminence, on which stands the baronial palace of Scalaproto, where there are some sculptures, vases, and stelae from the neighbouring ruins. The beauty of the situation, with the antiquity of the cisterns, and several local indications, lead me to imagine this to be the site of the villa of Pompeius Philo, from whose dish Verres plucked the fine cameos" (Sicily, p. 102). The 'sigilla' however were not cammeos; they were silver.

apud . . L. Lucullo] Comp. Caesar, B. G. i. 39, "reliquisque qui ex urbe amicitiae causa Caesarem secuti" &c. Eupolemus was with the army. Lucullus was at this time engaged in the war against Mithridates.

Argentum ille &c.] Hotmann, who had the reading 'illi,' found the passage difficult; but he saw that 'illi' must be 'ille,' that is, Eupolemus. The use of 'ille' is obvious, for 'ille' is contrasted with 'hic' (Verres). Manutius also suggested 'ille' for 'illi.'

'Purum' means without any workmanship, plain, as in c. 23, where the plate is called 'purum,' when the ornamental part had been taken off.—'emblemate' R 3, Lordan, 'emblate' E, 'emblematis' dett. If 'emblemate' is right, we must take it in a collective sense.

acroama,] Literally, 'a hearing' (ἀκρόαμα), was used to signify a pleasant story, and the like; and also a person who told a merry tale, or pleased his hearers in some such way. So Verres, as if he had amused the company, thought that he ought to get something for his trouble, and he helped himself to the ornamental work on the plate. As to 'corollarium,' see Lib. 3. c. 79; and the note on Sueton. Vespas. c. 19 (ed. Burmann); where another passage from Cicero is quoted: 'ipse non solum

corollario de convivio discederet, ibidem convivis spectantibus emblemata evellenda curavit. Neque ego nunc istius facta omnia enumerare conor, neque opus est, neque fieri ullo modo potest: tantum uniuscujusque de varia improbitate generis indicia apud vos et exempla profero. Neque enim ita se gessit in his rebus, tamquam rationem aliquando esset redditurus, sed prorsus ita quasi aut reus nunquam esset futurus, aut quo plura abstulisset eo minore periculo in judicium venturus esset; qui haec quae dico jam non occulte, non per amicos atque interpretes, sed palam de loco superiore ageret pro imperio et potestate.

XXIII. Catinam quum venisset, oppidum locuples, honestum, copiosum, Dionysiarchum ad se proagorum, hoc est, summum magistratum, vocari jubet: ei palam imperat ut omne argentum quod apud quemque esset Catinae conquirendum curaret et ad se afferendum. Phylarchum Centuripinum, primum hominem genere, virtute, pecunia, non hoc idem juratum dicere audistis, sibi istum negotium dedisse atque imperasse ut Centuripinis, in civitate totius Siciliae multo maxima et locupletissima, omne argentum conquireret et ad se comportari juberet? Agyrio similiter istius imperio vasa

spectator, sed actor et acroama fuit.'—'spectantibus:' 'inspectantibus' is the common reading.

tantum uniuscujusque] 'Tantum,' or 'tantummodo,' is the true reading.—'de loco superiore.' Becker, Handbuch, ii. 2. p. 51, contends that 'de loco superiore' always means 'tribunal.' Accordingly he rejects the explanation of this expression that is given in Lib. 1. c. 5 (note). There is no doubt that it often does mean the 'tribunal,' as in Lib. 2. c. 42; Lib. 4. c. 40; with which he compares Lib. 2. c. 38, and Lib. 3. c. 59, where 'sella ac tribunal' correspond to 'sella ac locus superior,' in Lib. 4. c. 40. That it does mean 'tribunal' in these passages, is quite clear, for the context shows that. It may perhaps mean 'tribunal' here; but there seems no reason in restricting the signification of the words, when they are not restricted by the context. The passage in Cicero, Ad Att. ii. 24, "postero autem die Caesar, is qui olim quum praetor esset Q. Catulum ex inferiore loco jusserat dicere, Vettium in rostra produxit," which seems to show, as I have no doubt that it does, that 'rostra' is contrasted with an 'inferior locus,' Becker explains thus: since Caesar was Praetor, the 'ex inferiore loco' is to be considered as said in opposition to the 'tribunal.' This is a most forced explanation. Becker indeed shows, that when Cicero means the 'rostra,' as he does in another passage where he does not use the word, he adopts a different form of expression, and does not use 'locus superior.' The passage is Act. i. c. 12, "quod agam ex eo loco, ex quo me Populus Romanus secum agere," &c. I think that Becker is wrong in thus limiting the sense of 'locus superior.'

23. *proagorum,*] Lg. 29 G 1. The reading of the editions before that of Hervagius (1534), and that of Manutius (1559), was 'Pardiorum.' The correct word occurs again in c. 39. F. Ursini quotes a bronze tablet of the Agrigentini, in his own possession, in which occurs προαγοροῦντος διοκλέους τοῦ διοκλέους. See Gruter, Inscript. p. 401.

primum hominem] The middle-age editors, as Zumpt remarks, altered 'primum' into 'primarium.' Zumpt refers to Lib. 1. c. 26; and Lib. 5. c. 63. See Lib. 1. c. 26.

Centuripinis,] 'codd. noti. *Centuripis,* St. L. Or.' (Iordan.) It might be supposed that the reading should either be 'in Centuripinis,' or 'Centuripis:' but Cicero (Lib. 2. c. 66) writes 'Leontinis, misera in civitate.' Leontini is the name both of the people and the town.

Corinthia per Apollodorum, quem testem audistis, Syracusas deportata sunt. Illa vero optima est, quod, quum Haluntium venisset praetor laboriosus et diligens, ipse in oppidum noluit accedere, quod erat difficili ascensu atque arduo; Archagathum Haluntinum, hominem non solum domi sed tota Sicilia in primis nobilem, vocari jussit: ei negotium dedit ut, quidquid Halunti esset argenti caelati, aut si quid etiam Corinthiorum, ut omne statim ad mare ex oppido deportaretur. Ascendit in oppidum Archagathus. Homo nobilis qui a suis et amari et diligi vellet ferebat graviter illam sibi ab isto provinciam datam, nec quid faceret habebat. Pronuntiat quid sibi imperatum esset: jubet omnes proferre quod haberent. Metus erat summus. Ipse enim tyrannus non discedebat longius: Archagathum et argentum in lectica cubans ad mare infra oppidum exspectabat. Quem concursum in oppido factum putatis, quem clamorem, quem porro fletum mulierum? qui videret, equum Trojanum introductum, urbem captam diceret. Efferri sine thecis vasa, extorqueri alia de manibus mulierum, effringi multorum fores, revelli claustra. Quid enim putatis? Scuta si quando conquiruntur a privatis in bello ac tumultu, tamen homines inviti dant, etsi ad salutem communem dari sentiunt; ne quem putetis sine maximo dolore argentum caelatum domo quod alter eriperet protulisse. Omnia deferuntur. Cibyratae fratres vocantur: pauca improbant: quae probarant, iis crustae aut emblemata detrahebantur. Sic Haluntini excussis deliciis cum argento puro domum revertuntur.

Illa vero optima est,] 'Intelligo res' (Zumpt). See Lib. 2. c. 23, and the note. —'optima est' codd. noti. Iordan omits 'est.'

Haluntium] Mentioned in Lib. 3. c. 43. The form of the name on a Greek coin is Alont. See Excursus VIII. The text says that it was near the sea. It is conjectured that the site is San Marco on the north coast of Sicily, east of Calacte, and on a hill of difficult ascent about three miles from the sea. If the inscription τὸ Μουνικίειον τῶν 'Αλοντίνων was found at San Marco, we may conclude that it is the site of Haluntium or Aluntium (Dict. Geog. art. Aluntium).

Ascendit] *escendit* (with *a* written over the *e*), sic R. The *a* over the *e* is by another hand, in a different ink and in a different form. Therefore the reading of R is 'escendit.' 'Ascendere' and 'escendere' are often confounded.

illam . . provinciam] 'That business.' This is not an improper use of the word 'provincia,' but it is its primary signification (Lib. 2. c. 1, note). Terence (Phormio, i. 2. 24) has a like use:—

> "D. O Geta, provinciam
> Cepisti duram."

—'nec . . habebat:' the uses of 'habeo' in Latin, and ἔχω, are numerous and varied. A reader learns them as he does other things, by use. Virgil has, Eclog. ii. 2,

> "—— nec quid speraret habebat."

cubans] See Lib. 3. c. 23, note on 'cubaret.'—'qui videret:' 'a spectator.'

tumultu,] Cicero speaks of a requisition for arms made upon private persons in an emergency, a war, or a 'tumultus.' The word 'tumultus' means a sudden rising, or hostile demonstration, several instances of which are mentioned in Livy, who uses the word. (Lib. 34. c. 56, for instance.) Cicero in some passages limits the meaning of 'tumultus' to a rising in Italy or Cisalpine Gallia (In Cat. iii. c. 2; Pro Sext. Rosc. Am. c. 6; Phil. viii. c. 1).

crustae] The passages in Forcellini

XXIV. Quod unquam, judices, hujuscemodi everriculum ulla in provincia fuit? Avertere aliquid de publico quam obscurissime per magistratum solebant; etiam quum aliquid a privato nonnunquam, occulte auferebant: et ii tamen condemnabantur. Et si quaeritis, ut ipse de me detraham, illos ego accusatores puto fuisse, qui hujusmodi hominum furta odore aut aliquo leviter presso vestigio persequebantur. Nam nos quidem quid facimus in Verre, quem in luto volutatum totius corporis vestigiis invenimus? Permagnum est in eum dicere aliquid, qui praeteriens lectica paulisper deposita non per praestigias, sed palam per potestatem uno imperio ostiatim totum oppidum compilaverit. Ac tamen ut posset dicere se emisse, Archagatho imperat ut illis aliquid, quorum argentum fuerat, nummulorum dicis causa daret. Invenit Archagathus paucos qui vellent accipere: his dedit. Eos nummos tamen iste Archagatho non reddidit. Voluit Romae repetere Archagathus; Cn. Lentulus Marcellinus dissuasit, sicut ipsum dicere audistis. Recita Archagathi et Lentuli testimonium.

Et ne forte hominem existimetis hanc tantam vim emblematum sine causa coacervare voluisse, videte quanti vos, quanti existimationem populi Romani, quanti leges et judicia, quanti testes Siculos, negotiatores[que] fecerit. Posteaquam tantam multitudinem collegerat emblematum ut ne unum quidem cuiquam reliquisset, instituit officinam Syracusis in regia maximam: palam artifices omnes, caelatores ac vascularios, convocari jubet; et ipse suos complures habebat. Eo concludit magnam hominum multitudinem. Menses octo continuos his opus non defuit, quum vas nullum fieret nisi

show the meaning of 'crusta,' which is the hard outward covering of a thing. Many of these vessels which Verres laid his hands on were not solid metal, but they had a case or covering of metal. This he took off, and if there were 'emblemata,' or figures attached to the surface, he took them. Cicero's expression (aut) shows that 'crustae' and 'emblemata' were different things.

24. *Avertere . . solebant;*] The sentence seems awkward without a nominative to 'solebant,' but it may be supplied from the context, 'hujusmodi hominum.' Cicero says that the accusers of such offenders had to track their petty thefts by the scent or by light foot-marks: he compares them to dogs. When he says this, it is the same as disparaging his own merits as an accuser (ut ipse de me detraham); for he found the print of the whole body of this hog where he had wallowed in the mud. 'Permagnum est' is said ironically.

dicis causa] 'For form's sake;' to give the transaction the show of a purchase; as in the form of testament 'per aes et libram' (Gaius, ii. 103), "nunc vero alius heres testamento instituitur a quo etiam legata relinquuntur, alius dicis gratia propter veteris juris imitationem familiae emptor adhibetur." The word often occurs in Cicero. Forcellini places it under 'dica,' a word which the Romans seem to have borrowed from the Greek (δίκη), and he considers 'dicis' equivalent to δίκης; an explanation which does not seem quite satisfactory. Halm says that 'dicis' is from an unused nominative 'dix,' which contains the same root as 'dic-ere.'

vascularios,] See c. 7, note.

Eo concludit] 'eos' R 3, E, 3 codd. Lamb. Iordan; 'eo' dett. Orelli. I think 'eo' is the true reading. It refers to 'regia.'

aureum. Tum illa, ex patellis et turibulis quae evellerat, ita scite in aureis poculis illigabat, ita apto in scaphiis aureis concludebat ut ea ad illam rem nata esse diceres: ipse tamen praetor, qui sua vigilantia pacem in Sicilia dicit fuisse, in hac officina majorem partem diei cum tunica pulla sedere solebat et pallio. XXV. Haec ego, judices, non auderem proferre, ni vererer ne forte plura de isto ab aliis in sermone quam a me in judicio vos audisse diceretis. Quis enim est qui de hac officina, qui de vasis aureis, qui de istius pallio non audierit? Quem voles e conventu Syracusano virum bonum nominato: producam: nemo erit quin hoc se audisse aut vidisse dicat. O tempora, O mores! Nihil nimium vetus proferam. Sunt vestrum aliquammulti, qui L. Pisonem norunt, hujus L. Pisonis qui praetor fuit patrem. Ei, quum esset in Hispania praetor, qua in provincia occisus est, nescio quo pacto dum armis exercetur annulus aureus quem habebat fractus et comminutus est. Quum vellet sibi annulum facere, aurificem jussit vocari in forum ad sellam Cordubae et palam appendit aurum: hominem in foro jubet sellam ponere et facere annulum omnibus praesentibus. Nimium fortasse dicet aliquis hunc diligentem. Hactenus reprehendet si qui volet: nihil amplius. Verum fuit ei concedendum, filius enim L. Pisonis erat, ejus qui primus de pecuniis repetundis legem tulit. Ridiculum est me nunc de Verre dicere, quum de Pisone Frugi dixerim: verum tamen quantum intersit videte. Iste quum aliquot abacorum faceret vasa aurea, non

scaphiis aureis] The common reading is 'scyphis aureis.' 'Scaphis' is the reading of the best MSS., and 'scafis' of the older Guelf., and accordingly Gulielmius proposed 'scaphiis' (see c. 17).—'concludebat' R 3 E C, 'includebat' dtt. Or.

tunica pulla . . et pallio.] 'He used to sit among his workmen in the common dark-coloured Tunica, which the common Romans wore; and with the Pallium on, or cloak, a Greek article of dress.' Hotmann explains the passage fully. He quotes from the oration In Vatinium, "ut in epulo Q. Arrii familiaris mei cum toga pulla accumberes" (c. 12). And again, "Quis unquam coenarit atratus?"

25. *aliquammulti,*] Zumpt observes that this expression occurs in no other writer except Appuleius, who was however an imitator of the rarer forms of expression in the ancient writers. Lagg. have 'aliquam multi,' R 3 codd. Lamb. 'alii quam multi.' 'Aliquam multi' must mean, as Zumpt says, 'satis multi,' for those who knew this Piso could not be many. The grandfather was L. Piso, consul B.C. 133, 'qui primus de repetundis legem tulit' (B.C. 149). His son, of whom this story is told, was praetor of Spain, B.C. 112, and he was killed perhaps in that year. Two-and-forty years had therefore elapsed between his death and the time of this trial. This Piso was the father of the Piso then living, who had been a colleague of Verres (B.C. 74) (Lib. 1. c. 46).

norunt] G 2 Ld, 'gnorunt' G 1, 'gonrit' R, 'cognoverint' Lg. 29 et 5 alii, 'cognoverunt' Lg. 27 42. Halm suggests 'noriat,' and that may be right.

Cordubae] Cordoba on the Baetis or Guadalquivir, at the head of water navigation, a Roman settlement, founded by C. Claudius Marcellus B.C. 152. It was afterwards the chief city of a 'conventus' or civil division of Baetica, and the largest town in these parts after Gades (Cadiz).

aliquot abacorum &c.] 'Faceret vasa,' says Graevius, is 'colligeret, conquireret, ut *facere rem, exercitum*.' He was col-

laboravit quid non modo in Sicilia verum etiam Romae in judicio audiret; ille in auri semuncia totam Hispaniam scire voluit unde praetori annulus fieret. Nimirum ut hic nomen suum comprobavit, sic ille cognomen.

XXVI. Nullo modo possum omnia istius facta aut memoria consequi aut oratione complecti. Genera ipsa cupio breviter attingere, ut hic modo me commonuit Pisonis annulus, quod totum effluxerat. Quam multis istum putatis hominibus honestis de digitis annulos abstulisse? nunquam dubitavit, quotiescunque alicujus aut gemma aut annulo delectatus est. Incredibile dicam, sed ita clarum ut ipsum negaturum non arbitrer. Quum Valentio ejus interpreti epistola Agrigento allata esset, casu signum iste animadvertit in cretula. Placuit ei. Quaesivit unde esset epistola: respondit, Agrigento. Iste ad quos solebat literas misit, ut is annulus ad se primo quoque tempore afferretur. Ita literis istius patrifamilias, L. Titio, civi Romano, annulus de digito detractus est. Illa vero ejus cupiditas incredibilis est. Nam ut in singula conclavia, quae iste non modo Romae sed in omnibus villis habet, tricenos lectos optime stratos cum ceteris ornamentis convivii quaereret, nimium multa comparare videretur. Nulla domus in Sicilia locuples fuit ubi iste non textrinum instituerit. Mulier est Segestana, perdives et nobilis, Lamia nomine: per triennium isti plena domo telarum stragulam vestem confecit, nihil nisi conchylio tinctum. Attalus, homo pecuniosus, Neti; Lyso Lilybaei; Critolaus Aetnae; Syracusis Aeschrio, Cleomenes, Theomnastus; Helori

lecting gold vessels enough to load several sideboards.

26. *ut hic modo*] This passage is quoted by Quintilian, Inst. Or. ix. 2. 61. The passage in Quintilian has 'annulos aureos,' but 'aureos' is wanting in R 3, λ, and Lambinus thought that it ought to be rejected, for, as Zumpt observes, it was the workmanship of the stone, not the metal, which attracted the cupidity of Verres.

cretula.] The Romans used wax to seal their letters with. The Greeks used a kind of earth for this purpose (cretula), on which they made a stamp with their seal; hence it is called 'cretula anularia' (Plin. H. N. xxxv. 27). Herodotus (ii. 38) has the expression γῆ σημαντρίς. In the oration Pro Flacco, c. 16, Cicero says: "Haec quae est a nobis prolata laudatio obsignata erat creta illa Asiatica, quae fere est omnibus nota nobis" (Zumpt).

Iste . . . literas] The order of G 3. Iordan has 'iste literas ad quos' &c.

tricenos] Halm suggests 'ternos,' as Iordan says. In his ed. of 1859 he suggests 'trinos.'

textrinum] A weaving establishment. Zumpt compares the form 'pistrinum,' but remarks that there is also 'tonstrina' and 'sutrina.'

conchylio] Cicero shortly after uses 'purpuram' exactly in the same sense. In this chapter then he takes 'conchylium' and 'purpura' to be the same. 'Conchylium' is a shell-fish, and also the juice of a shell-fish used for dyeing.

Aetnae;] Perhaps the true name. Zumpt has 'Hennae,' but the best MSS., though some of the readings are corrupt, indicate 'Aetnae.'—'Helori' is a correction of F. Ursini for 'Pelori,' the reading of the MSS.; but Pelorus (Lib. 5. c. 34) was not a town. 'Archonidas' (Lib. 3. c. 56) is no doubt the genuine form, and not 'Archonides.' It was a Sicilian-Greek name (Thucyd. vii. 1).

Archonidas—dies me citius defecerit quam nomina.—Ipse dabat purpuram tantum, operam amici.—Credo: jam enim non libet omnia criminari: quasi hoc mihi non satis sit ad crimen, habuisse tam multum quod daret; voluisse deportare tam multa; hoc denique quod concedit, amicorum operis esse in hujuscemodi rebus usum. Jam vero lectos aeratos et candelabra aenea, num cui practer istum Syracusis per triennium facta esse existimatis?—Emebat.—Credo: sed tantum vos certiores, judices, facio, quid iste in provincia praetor egerit, ne cui forte negligens nimium fuisse videatur, neque se satis quum potestatem habuerit instruxisse et ornasse.

XXVII. Venio nunc non jam ad furtum, non ad avaritiam, non ad cupiditatem, sed [ad] ejusmodi facinus in quo omnia nefaria contineri mihi atque inesse videantur; in quo dii immortales violati, existimatio atque auctoritas nominis populi Romani imminuta, hospitium spoliatum ac proditum, abalienati scelere istius a nobis omnes reges amicissimi nationesque quae in eorum regno ac ditione sunt. Nam reges Syriae, regis Antiochi filios pueros, scitis

dies] R 3, A, 'vox' dett.

purpuram] Zumpt points 'Ipse dabat purpuram, tantum operam amici.' Perhaps a Roman could tell how this was to be taken without the aid of points. If he could not, his language would be uncertain. But I think that the form of the sentence requires the pause after 'tantum.' Klotz, Iordan, and Halm put the point after 'purpuram.'—'Ipse dabat' &c. may be supposed to be said by a friend of Verres: 'he only gave the purpura, his friends did the work;' which was worth more than the material. 'I suppose so,' says Cicero, 'but it is charge enough against him that he had so much to give; and besides it is an admission that he made use of his friends to supply the labour.' It was no criminal offence for a man's friends to work for him, if they did it voluntarily; and all these fine things were produced, as the defender of Verres would say, by the voluntary work of his friends on the material which Verres furnished. Halm explains it: 'he furnished the material, they only the work;' and he takes 'tantum operam' to be an ironical expression, as if the labour were a trifle. But he has placed 'Ipse . . . amici' within inverted commas, as if somebody said this to Cicero, and said it ironically, which is nonsense: and the answer 'credo' makes it greater nonsense. Shortly after the same friend of Verres says 'Emebat,' to which Cicero replies with a 'Credo.' If the pause is rightly placed after 'purpuram,' there is an emphasis on 'Ipse,' and the meaning is, 'Verres supplied the stuff, his friends only the labour;' as if the labour were a small matter and the stuff were every thing. But it is a serious defence, not irony.—There are some remarks on this shell-fish dye in Smyth's Sicily, p. 24, and in Swinburne's Travels in the Two Sicilies, i. p. 239.

lectos aeratos] Couches decorated with metal. The feet and legs were of metal, and perhaps they used to make the frame of couches altogether of metal sometimes, as we make bedsteads now.

27. *reges Syriae,*] Zumpt has a note on this passage, the substance of which is as follows. These kings were Antiochus and Seleucus, the sons of Antiochus Eusebes, who was now dead. The elder of these two, Antiochus Asiaticus, was afterwards deprived of the Syrian throne by Cn. Pompeius Magnus. They were in possession of Syria, as Cicero observes, so far as their claim was undisputed, for their competitors, the sons of Antiochus Grypus, seem to have been dead; but Tigranes, the son-in-law of Mithridates, was actually in possession of Syria, to which country the Syrians themselves had invited him (B.C. 83), being weary of the contentions among the native princes. Zumpt says that Cicero suppressed this fact, that these kings might not appear

Romae nuper fuisse; qui venerant non propter Syriae regnum, nam id sine controversia obtinebant ut a patre et a majoribus acceperant; sed regnum Aegypti ad se et ad Selenen matrem suam pertinere arbitrabantur. Hi [ipsi] posteaquam temporibus rei publicae exclusi per senatum agere quae voluerant non potuerunt, in Syriam, in regnum patrium profecti sunt. Eorum alter, qui Antiochus vocatur, iter per Siciliam facere voluit. Itaque isto praetore venit Syracusas. Hic Verres hereditatem sibi venisse arbitratus est, quod in ejus regnum ac manus venerat is quem iste et audierat multa secum praeclara habere et suspicabatur. Mittit homini munera satis large haec ad usum domesticum, olei, vini, quod visum est; etiam tritici quod satis esset de suis decumis. Deinde ipsum regem ad coenam vocavit: exornat ample magnificeque triclinium: exponit ea quibus abundabat plurima et pulcherrima vasa argentea: nam haec aurea nondum fecerat: omnibus curat rebus instructum et paratum ut sit convivium. Quid multa? Rex ita discessit ut et istum copiose ornatum et se honorifice acceptum arbitraretur. Vocat ad coenam deinde ipse praetorem: exponit suas copias omnes, multum argentum, non pauca etiam pocula ex auro, quae, ut mos est regius et maxime in Syria, gemmis erant distincta clarissimis. Erat etiam vas vinarium ex una gemma pergrandi, trulla excavata manubrio aureo, de qua satis, credo, idoneum, satis gravem testem, Q. Minucium dicere audistis. Iste unumquodque vas in manus sumere, laudare, mirari. Rex gaudere praetori populi Romani satis jucundum et gratum illud esse convivium. Posteaquam inde discessum est, cogitare nihil iste aliud, quod ipsa res declaravit, nisi quemadmodum regem ex provincia spoliatum expilatumque dimitteret. Mittit rogatum vasa ea quae pulcherrima apud eum viderat: ait se suis caelatoribus velle osten-

poor and contemptible personages; and, as Lucullus was now vigorously carrying on the war against Tigranes, the Syrian kings might have some reasonable hopes of being restored, and indeed may have come to Rome on this business. Their mother, Selene, was the daughter of Ptolemaeus Physcon, king of Egypt, and the sister of Ptolemaeus Lathyrus, who had been killed, as well as his only legitimate daughter, Berenice; and the throne of Egypt was claimed by Ptolemaeus XI. Auletes, an illegitimate son of Lathyrus. There is great confusion about the marriages of this Selene; but that is immaterial for the present purpose. See Clinton, Fasti, Kings of Syria.

temporibus rei publicae] The commentators are not agreed about these 'tempora;' but there seems no other explanation than that suggested by Zumpt. Cicero alludes to the Servile war in Italy, which was going on while Verres was praetor, in B.C. 73, 72. The war of Mithridates was too distant to be alluded to in this manner, and the same may be said of the war with Sertorius in Spain. The king's visit was not in the last part of the praetorship of Verres, for Cicero says, 'nam haec aurea nondum fecerat.'—'coenam:' 'cenam' R.

trulla] This word seems to be a diminutive of 'trua,' and to signify a drinking vessel. See the article Trulla, in Forcellini.

dere. Rex qui illum non nosset sine ulla suspicione libentissime dedit. Mittit etiam trullam gemmeam rogatum; velle se eam diligentius considerare. Ea quoque ei mittitur.

XXVIII. Nunc reliquum, judices, attendite, de quo et vos audistis, et populus Romanus non nunc primum audiet, et in exteris nationibus usque ad ultimas terras pervagatum est. Candelabrum e gemmis clarissimis, opere mirabili perfectum, reges hi quos dico Romam quum attulissent, ut in Capitolio ponerent, quod nondum perfectum templum offenderant, neque ponere potuerunt, neque vulgo ostendere ac proferre voluerunt, ut et magnificentius videretur, quum suo tempore in cella Jovis Optimi Maximi poneretur, et clarius, quum pulchritudo ejus recens ad oculos hominum atque integra perveniret, statuerunt id secum in Syriam reportare; ut, quum audissent simulacrum Jovis Optimi Maximi dedicatum, legatos mitterent qui cum ceteris rebus illud quoque eximium atque pulcherrimum donum in Capitolium afferrent. Pervenit res ad istius aures, nescio quomodo; nam rex celatum voluerat, non quo quidquam metueret aut suspicaretur, sed ut ne multi illud ante perciperent oculis quam populus Romanus. Iste petit a rege et

28. *pervagatum est.*] Klotz has 'pervulgatum est,' the reading of R 3 E. Zumpt defends 'pervagatum.' It may be right or wrong. I don't know. See Lib. 3. c. 56.

Candelabrum] The 'candelabrum' was only ornamented with the 'gemmae,' for the material was gold (c. 32), 'e gemmis auroque perfectum.' Candelabra of a large size were made for temples and public buildings. Some of the bronze candelabra of the ancients, which have been found, consist of a long slender bronze stand, resting on three legs—goat's legs or legs of other animals. On the top is a cup or open vessel to contain the oil. The ancient candelabra were of varied forms, often very elegant: they were both useful and ornamental. There is a marble candelabrum in the Townley Gallery, British Museum, about seven feet high, with the representation of a flame at the top. Sometimes the stand was a representation of a human figure, holding in one hand the lamp or cup for the oil. The candelabrum was one of those household articles in which the artists of antiquity displayed their taste.

"Si non aurea sunt juvenum simulacra per aedes,
Lampadas igniferas manibus retinentia dextris,
Lumina nocturnis epulis ut suppeditentur."—Lucretius, ii. 24.

There are two candelabra represented on the reverse of a coin of Cyzicus, with a flame at the summit, and a snake twisting round each. A low altar, with a flame on it, stands between the candelabra. The legend is Κυζικηνων Νεοκορων.

nondum perfectum] The temple of Jupiter Capitolinus was accidentally burnt B.C. 83, in the consulship of L. Cornelius Scipio and C. Norbanus. Sulla began its restoration, but he did not live to see it completed, the only instance in which his good fortune failed him. It was dedicated by Q. Lutatius Catulus B.C. 69 (Zumpt). Liv. Ep. 98.

statuerunt] Zumpt, Klotz, Iordan, and Halm have 'integra perveniret. Statuerunt id secum,' &c. But 'statuerunt' begins the latter member of the sentence, which is only confused by the parenthetical matter, 'quod nondum . . perveniret.'

perciperent] 'praeciperent' R E Ld. Lg. 29, Iordan; 'perciperent' rell. It is difficult to determine which is the true reading even in some MSS. in consequence

eum pluribus verbis rogat ut id ad se mittat; cupere se dicit inspicere, neque se aliis videndi potestatem esse facturum. Antiochus qui animo et puerili esset et regio nihil de istius improbitate suspicatus est: imperat suis ut id in praetorium involutum quam occultissime deferrent. Quo posteaquam attulerunt involucrisque rejectis constituerunt, clamare iste coepit dignam rem esse regno Syriae, dignam regio munere, dignam Capitolio. Etenim erat eo splendore qui ex clarissimis et pulcherrimis gemmis esse debebat: ea varietate operum ut ars certare videretur cum copia: ea magnitudine ut intelligi posset non ad hominum apparatum sed ad amplissimi templi ornatum esse factum. Quum satis jam perspexisse videretur, tollere incipiunt ut referrent. Iste ait se velle illud etiam atque etiam considerare: nequaquam se esse satiatum: jubet illos discedere et candelabrum relinquere. Sic illi tum inanes ad Antiochum revertuntur.

XXIX. Rex primo nihil metuere, nihil suspicari: dies unus, alter, plures: non referri. Tum mittit, si videatur, ut reddat. Jubet iste posterius ad se reverti. Mirum illi videri: mittit iterum. Non redditur. Ipse hominem appellat: rogat ut reddat. Os hominis insignemque impudentiam cognoscite. Quod sciret, quod ex ipso rege audisset in Capitolio esse ponendum, quod Jovi Optimo Maximo, quod populo Romano servari videret, id sibi ut donaret rogare et vehementissime petere coepit. Quum ille se et religione Jovis Capitolini et hominum existimatione impediri

of the very minute difference between the abbreviations of 'per' and 'prae.'

regio] "*religio* sic R. quod mutavit sec. manus in *religioso* ut est in G 3 E λ" (Iordan).

ad . . . templi ornatum] R 3 E. The common reading is 'ornamentum.' 'Secundum deteriores, meliores *ornatum*' (Zumpt). Though 'ornamentum' by its form indicates a thing and not a purpose, there seems no reason why it may not signify for the purpose of ornament. Zumpt himself refers to an instance in c. 8, 'ornamenti causa.' Again, in c. 33 we have 'omniaque quae ornamento urbi esse possent,' where 'ornamento' is not a thing, a 'res,' but means 'all things suitable to the decoration of the city.' And in c. 54, 'quae ornamento urbi esse possent.' Also in Lib. 1. c. 22. But it seems that 'ornamentum,' when so used, is followed by a dative. 'Ornatus' seems to be followed by a genitive, as in Lib. 4. c. 54, 'in ornatu urbis habuit victoriae rationem.' Perhaps then 'ad templi ornamentum' is hardly Latin, and Zumpt and others have done right in preferring 'ornatum.'

The skill of the workmanship, says Cicero, vied with the richness and variety of the materials, which Ovid (Met. ii. 5) expresses in another way, 'Materiem superabat opus.'

29. *Ipse . . appellat:*] 'The king himself applies to the man.' It is a word used when a creditor demands payment of his debtor. See Pro P. Quintio, c. 11.

Quod sciret,] 'Quod . . id.' 'Though he knew, though he had heard from the king himself that this candelabrum was to be placed in the Capitol &c., still he began to ask the king to give to him.' But in this version the 'quod' loses its place at the head of the sentence, and so the effect is spoiled. The Latin language can both place the 'quod' where it ought to be, and by the subjunctive form can express what we must do in another way.

diceret, quod multae nationes testes essent illius operis ac muneris, iste homini minari acerrime coepit. Ubi videt eum nihilo magis minis quam precibus removeri, repente hominem de provincia jubet ante noctem decedere: ait se comperisse ex ejus regno piratas ad Siciliam esse venturos. Rex maximo conventu Syracusis in foro, ne quis forte me in crimine obscuro versari atque affingere aliquid suspicione hominum arbitretur, in foro, inquam, Syracusis flens atque deos hominesque contestans clamare coepit candelabrum factum e gemmis quod in Capitolium missurus esset, quod in templo clarissimo populo Romano monumentum suae societatis amicitiaeque esse voluisset, id sibi C. Verrem abstulisse: de ceteris operibus ex auro et gemmis quae sua penes illum essent se non laborare: hoc sibi eripi miserum esse et indignum. Id etsi antea jam mente et cogitatione sua fratrisque sui consecratum esset, tamen tum se in illo conventu civium Romanorum dare, donare, dicare, consecrare Jovi Optimo Maximo, testemque ipsum Jovem suae voluntatis ac religionis adhibere.

XXX. Quae vox, quae latera, quae vires hujus unius criminis querimoniam possunt sustinere? Rex Antiochus qui Romae ante oculos omnium nostrum biennium fere comitatu regio atque ornatu fuisset, is quum amicus et socius populi Romani esset, amicissimo patre, avo, majoribus, antiquissimis et clarissimis regibus, opulentissimo et maximo regno, praeceps provincia populi Romani exturbatus est. Quemadmodum hoc accepturas nationes exteras, quemadmodum hujus tui facti famam in regna aliorum atque in ultimas terras perventuram putasti, quum audirent a praetore populi Romani in provincia violatum regem, spoliatum hospitem, ejectum socium populi Romani atque amicum? Nomen vestrum populique Romani odio atque acerbitati scitote nationibus exteris, judices,

removeri,] R 3 λ, 'permoveri' E (?) dett. Or. If 'removeri' is the word, the sense is 'moved from his refusal.'

suspicione hominum] Lambinus altered 'suspicione' into 'suspicioni.' E has 'suspitioni.' The ablative is easily explained: 'that no one may suppose that I am adding any invention founded on men's suspicions.' Zumpt quotes Tuscul. iii. 23, "qui nihil opinione affingat assumatque ad aegritudinem."

30. *latera,*] 'What lungs,' as we might say. Comp. De Sen. c. 9. So he also says, De Sen. c. 5, 'magna voce et bonis lateribus,' 'with a loud voice and sound wind.'

amicus et socius] There are many instances of kings on whom the senate condescended to confer the title of 'amicus et socius.' Cicero afterwards speaks of 'nationes exterae,' a term which clearly meant countries which were neither Roman provinces nor countries in friendship and alliance with Rome. The term 'socius' was evidently used in an enlarged sense, compared with its early application to the Italian Socii (Divin. c. 3); for it is applied both to provincials, and to people not provincials, who were in friendship and alliance with Rome. See c. 11, note.

quum audirent] The common reading is 'audierint,' which is inconsistent with 'putasti.' R 3 E 5 Parr. have 'audirent.'

futurum, si istius haec tanta injuria impunita discesserit. Sic omnes arbitrabuntur, praesertim quum haec fama de nostrorum hominum avaritia et cupiditate percrebuerit, non istius solius hoc esse facinus sed eorum etiam qui approbarint. Multi reges, multae liberae civitates, multi privati opulenti ac potentes habent profecto in animo Capitolium sic ornare ut templi dignitas imperiique nostri nomen desiderat; qui si intellexerint interverso hoc regali dono graviter vos tulisse, grata fore vobis populoque Romano sua studia ac dona arbitrabuntur. Sin hoc vos in rege tam nobili, [in] re tam eximia, [in] injuria tam acerba neglexisse audierint, non erunt tam amentes ut operam, curam, pecuniam impendant in eas res quas vobis gratas fore non arbitrentur.

XXXI. Hoc loco, Q. Catule, te appello, loquor enim de tuo clarissimo pulcherrimoque monumento; non judicis solum severitatem in hoc crimine sed prope inimici atque accusatoris vim suscipere debes. Tuus [est] enim honos in illo templo senatus populique Romani beneficio: tui nominis aeterna memoria simul cum templo illo consecratur: tibi haec cura suscipienda, tibi haec opera sumenda est, ut Capitolium, quemadmodum magnificentius est restitutum, sic copiosius ornatum sit quam fuit; ut illa flamma divinitus extitisse videatur, non quae deleret Jovis Optimi Maximi templum, sed quae praeclarius magnificentiusque deposceret. Audisti Q. Minucium dicere domi suae deversatum esse Antiochum regem Syracusis: se illud scire ad istum esse delatum: se scire non redditum: audisti et audies omni e conventu Syracusano qui ita dicant sese audientibus illud Jovi Optimo Maximo dicatum esse ab rege Antiocho et consecratum. Si judex non esses et haec ad te delata res esset, te potissimum hoc persequi, te petere, te agere oporteret. Quare non dubito quo animo judex hujus criminis esse debeas, qui apud alium judicem multo acrior quam ego sum actor accusatorque esse deberes.

percrebuerit,] R G 2 Ld., 'percrebruerit' 2 Parr. G 1 Lg. 29.

habent . . in animo . . sic ornare] Cicero also uses 'habere' alone in this manner. 'De re publica nihil habeo ad te scribere' (Ad Att. ii. 22), like *οὐκ ἔχω εἰπεῖν*.

interverso] The word is not easy to render, but the meaning is plain, as appears from the following passage of Scaevola (Dig. 43. 20. 8, referred to by Forcellini): "cui per fundum iter aquae debetur, quacunque vult in eo rivum faciat licet, dum ne aquaeductum intervertat;" but he must not divert the water from the course that is once fixed. There is also (Dig. 16. 3. 22) "si duo heredes rem apud defunctum depositam dolo interverterint," 'if two Heredes have fraudulently appropriated a thing that has been deposited with the deceased.' Cicero, Phil. ii. c. 32, "ille promissum et receptum intervertit ad seque transtulit."

[in] re tam eximia, [in] injuria] Klotz and Jordan omit 'in' twice.

31. *Q. Catule,*] One of the 'judices,' as he says below.—'Capitolium:' see c. 28.

actor accusatorque] See Divin. c. 1, note.

XXXII. Vobis autem, judices, quid hoc indignius aut quid minus ferendum videri potest? Verresne habebit domi suae candelabrum Jovis e gemmis auroque perfectum? Cujus fulgore collucere atque illustrari Jovis Optimi Maximi templum oportebat, id apud istum in ejusmodi conviviis constituetur quae domesticis stupris flagitiisque flagrabunt? In istius lenonis turpissimi domo simul cum ceteris Chelidonis hereditariis ornamentis Capitolii ornamenta ponentur? Quid huic sacri unquam fore aut quid religiosi fuisse putatis qui nunc tanto scelere se obstrictum esse non sentiat? qui in judicium veniat, ubi ne precari quidem Jovem Optimum Maximum atque ab eo auxilium petere more omnium possit? a quo etiam dii immortales sua repetunt in eo judicio quod hominibus ad suas res repetendas est constitutum. Miramur Athenis Minervam, Deli Apollinem, Junonem Sami, Pergae Dianam, multos praeterea ab isto deos tota Asia Graeciaque violatos, qui a Capitolio manus abstinere non potuerit? Quod privati homines de suis pecuniis ornant ornaturique sunt, id C. Verres ab regibus ornari non passus est. Itaque hoc nefario scelere concepto nihil postea tota in Sicilia neque sacri neque religiosi duxit esse: ita sese in ea provincia per triennium gessit ut ab isto non solum hominibus verum etiam diis immortalibus bellum indictum putaretur.

XXXIII. Segesta est oppidum pervetus in Sicilia, judices, quod

32. *repetunt . . repetendas*] A play on the title of the Lex de Repetundis, under which Verres was tried.—'Miramur Athenis' &c.: see Lib. 1. c. 17, &c.

neque sacri . . duxit esse:] There is the same use of 'duxit' in Lib. 5. c. 55.—'sacri . . religiosi' refer to the Roman division of things. The first division is into things 'divini juris' and 'humani juris,' things appropriated to the gods and things appropriated to man. The things 'divini juris' were divided into 'sacrae' and 'religiosae:' "Sacrae sunt quae diis superis consecratae sunt: religiosae quae diis manibus relictae sunt" (Gaius, ii. 3. 4).

33. *Segesta*] One of the 'civitates liberae' (Lib. 3. c. 6). Cicero here adopts the popular notion of Aeneas having come from Troy to Italy, and he makes him found Segesta on his way. There was certainly a tradition that the place was founded by Asiatic colonists. Thucydides (vi. 2) says, that some of the Trojans having fled from the Achaei upon the capture of Troy sailed to Sicily, and settled close to the Sicani, the old inhabitants of the island, and the two peoples got the common name of Elymi, and their cities were Eryx and Egesta. The Roman form of the name is always Segesta, as it appears. The Greek form on the older coins is Segesta, and on the later coins and in our Greek MSS. it is Egesta. It was the Roman tradition that Acestes, who gave his name to the city, and was born in Sicily of a Trojan mother, was assisted by Aeneas in the founding of the city. There was a temple of Aeneas at Segesta (Dion. Halic. i. 53). The Romans, after their usual fashion, were politic enough to encourage, or to invent the supposed relationship during their contest with the Carthaginians in Sicily; and the Duilian column (B.C. 264) contains the official recognition of this relationship in the words, 'Ecestanos cocnatos popli Romani' (P. Ciacconii in Columm. Rostrat. Inscriptionem, Graevii Thes. Rom. Antiq. iv. 1810; and in Duker's Florus). Nicias, as he is represented speaking by Thucydides, calls the Egestaei 'barbari,' not Hellenes. It was a part of the old story in Thucydides (vi. 2), that certain Phocis of those who had been at

ab Aenea fugiente a Troja atque in haec loca veniente conditum esse demonstrant. Itaque Segestani non solum perpetua societate atque amicitia verum etiam cognatione se cum populo Romano conjunctos esse arbitrantur. Hoc quondam oppidum, quum illa civitas cum Poenis suo nomine ac sua sponte bellaret, a Karthaginiensibus vi captum atque deletum est, omniaque quae ornamento urbi esse possent Karthaginem sunt ex illo loco deportata. Fuit apud Segestanos ex aere Dianae simulacrum, quum summa atque antiquissima praeditum religione, tum singulari opere artificioque perfectum. Hoc translatum Karthaginem locum tantum hominesque mutarat; religionem quidem pristinam servabat, nam propter eximiam pulchritudinem etiam hostibus digna quam sanctissime colerent videbatur. Aliquot saeculis post P. Scipio bello Punico tertio Karthaginem cepit; qua in victoria—videte hominis virtutem et diligentiam, ut et domesticis praeclarissimae virtutis exemplis gaudeatis et eo majore odio dignam istius incredibilem audaciam judicetis—convocatis Siculis omnibus, quod diutissime saepissimeque Siciliam vexatam a Karthaginiensibus esse cognorat, jubet omnia conquiri: pollicetur sibi magnae curae fore ut omnia civitatibus quae cujusque fuissent restituerentur. Tum illa quae quondam erant Himera

the siege of Troy, came to dwell near the Egestaei, being driven by stress of weather to Libya first, and thence to Sicily. It was probably a motley population, in which the Greek part at last prevailed.

The remains of Segesta are about six miles from Castellamare, in the north-west angle of Sicily. There is a Doric temple, and vestiges of an ancient theatre. The remains "stand in a bleak, deserted, sterile situation, to the eastward of the boundary of the ancient city; and the only resting-place for the traveller is the shade of a neighbouring tree, where there is a good spring of fresh water; the scenery and stillness, however, make it appear wild, grand, and impressive." "The temple is somewhat peculiar, probably was never finished, for the 'cella' is wanting; but it is nearly entire" (Smyth's Sicily, 671). There are twelve Doric unfluted pillars on each side, without reckoning those at the angles; and six at each end, reckoning those at the angles; thirty-six pillars in all. Swinburne (Travels in the Two Sicilies, ii. 232) gives the name of Barbara to the site of Egesta. Castellamare was the port of Egesta. Swinburne describes the position of the city as very good, "upon a ridge of hills gently sloping towards the northern aspect, sheltered on the southern and eastern quarters by high rocky eminences, at the foot of which two roaring brooks winded their course, and embraced the city." Swinburne describes plainly and clearly what he sees. These two brooks may be the Simois and Scamandrus of Strabo (p. 608). Diodorus also (xx. 71) mentions the Scamandrus. The united stream flows to the sea at Castellamare. The names Simois and Scamandrus remind us of the rivers of the Troad, whence, according to the tradition, the settlers of Segesta came. There is a description of the temple of Segesta in Goethe's Italiänische Reise.

captum atque deletum] The destruction of Segesta by the Carthaginians is not mentioned elsewhere; and, if there is no evidence except this passage, Cicero may have misstated the fact. Agathocles, B.C. 307 or 306, destroyed a large part of the inhabitants with circumstances of the greatest cruelty, in order to get their money. He sold the women and children, and gave the city a new name, Dicaeopolis, and a fresh population (Diod. xx. 71). After his death the remnant of the old inhabitants returned, and the city resumed its former name.

sublata, de quibus antea dixi, Thermitanis sunt reddita: tum alia Gelensibus, alia Agrigentinis; in quibus etiam ille nobilis taurus quem crudelissimus omnium tyrannorum Phalaris habuisse dicitur, quo vivos supplicii causa demittere homines et subjicere flammam solebat. Quem taurum quum Scipio redderet Agrigentinis, dixisse dicitur, aequum esse illos cogitare utrum esset Agrigentinis utilius, suisne servire anne populo Romano obtemperare, quum idem monumentum et domesticae crudelitatis et nostrae mansuetudinis haberent.

XXXIV. Illo tempore Segestanis maxima cum cura haec ipsa Diana de qua dicimus redditur: reportatur Segestam: in suis antiquis sedibus summa cum gratulatione civium et laetitia reponitur. Haec erat posita Segestae sane excelsa in basi, in qua

antea dixi,] Lib. 2. c. 36.

Gelensibus,] The people of Gela (Γέλα), one of the old Greek settlements in Sicily, founded by Rhodians from Lindus, and Cretans. It was on the south coast of Sicily, between Agrigentum and Camarina. The name Gela is from the name of the river near the city; and we observe that several Sicilian towns have the name of the river on which they were situated. This once flourishing place, the parent city of Agrigentum, was a ruin before the age of Cicero. Dionysius destroyed the old aristocratical constitution by massacring the chief inhabitants (B.C. 406), and the place was afterwards plundered by the Carthaginians (Diod. xiii. 108). It was again plundered by Agathocles (B.C. 311); and finally, it is said, that the remnant of the inhabitants were transferred by Phintias, tyrant of Agrigentum, to his new town of Phintias (Diodorus, Lib. 22. c. 2). But the town of Gela could not have been entirely destroyed, nor all the inhabitants removed, if Cicero's story is true about the restoration of the statues. Besides this, he mentions the Gelenses (Lib. 3. c. 43) as a still existing community. The site of the place, it is generally agreed, is Terra Nuova, where there is, or was not long ago, the fragment of a Doric column, the last remnant of a great city. Swinburne in his Travels gives a sketch of it.

Agrigentinis;] This city, called by the Greeks Acragas, once the largest city in Sicily, requires a history. From its Roman name Agrigentum, is formed the modern corruption Girgenti. It never recovered from the damage which it sustained from the Carthaginians (B.C. 406: Diod. xiii. 90). It finally came under the dominion of Rome about B.C. 207, and the Romans gave it a kind of new constitution (Lib. 2. c. 50; Lib. 4. c. 43). The ruins of the colossal temple of Olympian Zeus, the temple of Concord, as it is now commonly called, which is nearly complete except part of the entablature and the roof, and other remains, make this the most interesting historical town in Sicily. The greater part of the old city appears to have been in the valley. The modern stands on the height once occupied by the ancient citadel.

The period of Phalaris is not quite certain. If his reign commenced B.C. 570, as Eusebius in one passage states, he was a contemporary of Croesus, king of Lydia. This story of a brazen bull, made by Perillus, on whom the tyrant made the first experiment with it, by roasting him in the inside, is told by several writers of antiquity (Diodorus, xiii. 90; Polybius, xii. 25, ed. Bekker). Here Cicero mentions a bull as recovered from the Carthaginians. There seems no reason to doubt the fact of such a work of art existing, but whether it was the bull of Phalaris, or another that was called the bull of Phalaris, may be doubted. Sillig (Catalogus) refers to Göller, De Situ et Origine Syracusarum, and to Böttiger, Kunstmythologie, i. 380, for further information about this bull.

utrum . . . suisne . . . anne] "*Anne* pro vulg. *an* e vet. cod. Lambini et reliquis melioribus scripsimus: Guelf. cum vulgaribus facit" (Zumpt). 'Anne' is the reading of R A E G 2 Ld., 'an' of G 1 and dett. Zumpt compares Orat. c. 6, "quaerendum utrum una species et longitudo sit earum anne plures." There is 'utrumne . . . an' Hor. Epod. 1.

grandibus literis P. Africani nomen erat incisum, eumque Karthagine capta restituisse perscriptum. Colebatur a civibus: ab omnibus advenis visebatur: quum quaestor essem, nihil mihi ab illis est demonstratum prius. Erat admodum amplum et excelsum signum cum stola; verumtamen inerat in illa magnitudine aetas atque habitus virginalis. Sagittae pendebant ab humero; sinistra manu retinebat arcum; dextra ardentem facem praeferebat. Hanc quum iste sacrorum omnium et religionum hostis praedoque vidisset, quasi illa ipsa face percussus esset, ita flagrare cupiditate atque amentia coepit. Imperat magistratibus ut eam demoliantur et sibi dent: nihil sibi gratius ostendit futurum. Illi vero dicere sibi id nefas esse; seque quum summa religione tum summo metu legum et judiciorum teneri. Iste tum petere ab eis, tum minari, tum spem, tum metum ostendere. Opponebant illi nomen interdum P. Africani: populi Romani illud esse dicebant: nihil se in eo potestatis habere quod imperator clarissimus urbe hostium capta monumentum victoriae populi Romani esse voluisset. Quum iste nihilo remissius atque etiam multo vehementius instaret quotidie, res agitur in senatu. Vehementer ab omnibus reclamatur. Itaque illo tempore ac primo istius adventu pernegatur. Postea quidquid erat oneris in nautis remigibusque exigendis, in frumento imperando, Segestanis praeter ceteros imponebat aliquanto amplius quam ferre possent. Praeterea magistratus eorum evocabat: opti-

34. *amplum et excelsum*] This description of the statue is another instance of Cicero's own language belying his assertions. He had a taste for art, as we have already seen (c. 3, note); and he takes some pains to show that he was not one of those whom Verres called 'idiotae.'

He describes this Diana (Ἄρτεμις) as a colossal figure, with the characteristics of a young unmarried female, with long drapery reaching to the feet, as in the statues of the old style, and not with the short frock, as she was afterwards represented. The quiver and the arrows were suspended from her shoulder; and in her left hand she held a bow, and in the right hand a blazing torch. So Sophocles, Oed. Tyr. 201, represents her:

> τάς τε πυρφόρους
> Ἀρτέμιδος αἴγλας ξὺν αἷς
> Λύκι' ὄρεα διάσσει.

Sometimes she was represented with a torch in each hand, and the bow and quiver hung over her shoulders. Pausanias (x. 37, 1) describes an Artemis at Anticyra in Phocis, the work of Praxiteles. She held a torch in her right hand, she had a quiver on her shoulders, and a dog was standing by her on the left. The size of the figure was above that of the largest woman. There is in the Louvre a figure of Diane à la Biche, as it is called, because a fawn is running by her on the left side. She holds the bow in her left hand downwards; with the right she is taking an arrow from the quiver on her shoulder. Her legs are bare, and she has richly ornamented sandals. The representations of the goddess were numerous, and varied according to the different characters in which she was supposed to act. See Müller, Handbuch der Archäologie der Kunst.—'humero:' 'umero' R.

nautis remigibusque] From this and other passages we collect that the provincials were liable to requisitions of men for the navy, as well as bound to supply ships in some cases (Lib. 1. c. 34). Segesta was 'immunis ac libera' (Lib. 3. c. 6; Lib. 5. c. 47).

mum quemque et nobilissimum ad se arcessebat: circum omnia provinciae fora rapiebat: singillatim unicuique calamitati fore se denuntiabat: universis se funditus eversurum esse illam civitatem minabatur. Itaque aliquando multis malis magnoque metu victi Segestani praetoris imperio parendum esse decreverunt. Magno cum luctu et gemitu totius civitatis, multis cum lacrimis et lamentationibus virorum mulierumque omnium, simulacrum Dianae tollendum locatur.

XXXV. Videte quanta religio fuerit apud Segestanos. Repertum esse, judices, scitote neminem, neque liberum neque servum, neque civem neque peregrinum, qui illud signum auderet attingere. Barbaros quosdam Lilybaeo scitote adductos esse operarios. Hi denique illud ignari totius negotii ac religionis mercede accepta sustulerunt; quod quum ex oppido exportabatur, quem conventum mulierum factum esse arbitramini, quem fletum majorum natu, quorum nonnulli etiam illum diem memoria tenebant, quum illa eadem Diana Segestam Karthagine revecta victoriam populi Romani reditu suo nuntiasset. Quam dissimilis hic dies illi tempori videbatur! Tum imperator populi Romani, vir clarissimus, deos patrios reportabat Segestanis ex urbe hostium recuperatos: nunc ex urbe sociorum praetor ejusdem populi turpissimus atque impurissimus eosdem illos deos nefario scelere auferebat. Quid hoc tota Sicilia est clarius quam omnes Segestae matronas et virgines convenisse quum Diana exportaretur ex oppido, unxisse unguentis, complesse coronis et floribus, ture odoribus incensis usque ad agri

provinciae fora] The 'fora' were the places where the courts or 'conventus' were held; but there may have been more 'fora' than those in the chief cities of the island. He hurried them, says Manutius, about the province, to their great inconvenience, wherever he was going to hold his courts ('conventus agere,' Lib. 5. c. 11); that is, if they had any court business, he made them follow him, instead of hearing their cases at more convenient places.

tollendum locatur.] The Segestani made a contract with somebody for the removal of the statue, or rather gave notice that there was a job to be done, that a 'redemptor' or 'conductor' was wanted to remove the statue. Such contracts, and all other matters relating to public business, were entered in the books (publicae literae) of the town (c. 35). As to like entries, see Lib. 1. c. 34, and Lib. 4. c. 42, 'publicae literae sunt,' &c.

35. *Videte quanta &c.*] The old reading, 'Videte quanta religione fuerit: apud Segestanos,' &c., is faulty. The better MSS. have 'religio.'

Barbaros quosdam] These barbarians, from Lilybaeum, may have been Sicani, the old inhabitants of the island (Thucyd. vi. 2), for it appears that they were not all expelled by the invasion of the Siculi. Some of the very old inhabitants of Segesta might remember the restoration of their favourite statue after the destruction of Carthage, B.C. 146.

quod quum . . exportabatur,] The common reading is 'quod quum . . exportaretur,' of which Zumpt says, "quod non condemno—verum indicativus . . nihilo deterior, immo describendae rei aptior est." A little further on there is 'quum Diana exportaretur.'

Quid hoc . . clarius quam] Zumpt, following Scheller, refers to three other examples of 'hoc' and 'quam;' Ad Att. iv. 8; De Orat. i. 37; and De Divin. i. 39.

fines prosecutas esse? Hanc tu tantam religionem si tum in imperio propter cupiditatem atque audaciam non pertimescebas, ne nunc quidem in tanto tuo tuorumque liberorum periculo perhorrescis? Quem tibi aut hominem invitis diis immortalibus aut vero deum tantis eorum religionibus violatis auxilio futurum putas? Tibi illa Diana in pace atque in otio religionem nullam attulit? quae quum duas urbes in quibus locata fuerat captas incensasque vidisset, bis ex duorum bellorum flamma ferroque servata est; quae Karthaginiensium victoria loco mutato religionem tamen non amisit, P. Africani virtute religionem simul cum loco recuperavit. Quo quidem scelere suscepto quum inanis esset basis et in ea P. Africani nomen incisum, res indigna atque intoleranda videbatur omnibus, non solum religiones esse violatas verum etiam P. Africani, viri fortissimi, rerum gestarum gloriam, memoriam virtutis, monumenta victoriae C. Verrem sustulisse. Quod quum isti renuntiaretur de basi ac literis, existimavit homines in oblivionem totius negotii esse venturos, si etiam basim tamquam indicem sui sceleris sustulisset. Itaque tollendam istius imperio locaverunt; quae vobis locatio ex publicis literis Segestanorum priore actione recitata est.

XXXVI. Te nunc, P. Scipio, te, inquam, lectissimum ornatissimumque adolescentem appello: abs te officium tuum debitum generi et nomini requiro et flagito. Cur pro isto qui laudem honoremque tuum familiaeque tuae depeculatus est pugnas? cur eum defensum esse vis? cur ego tuas partes suscipio? cur tuum munus sustineo? Cur M. Tullius P. Africani monumenta requirit, P. Scipio eum qui illa sustulit defendit? Quum mos a majoribus traditus sit, ut monumenta majorum ita suorum quisque defendat ut ne ornari quidem nomine aliorum sinat, tu isti aderis qui non obstruxit aliqua ex parte monumentum P. Scipionis, sed [id] fundi-

36. *P. Scipio,*] P. Cornelius Scipio Nasica, a son of a father of the same name, who was praetor B.C. 94. He was adopted by the testament of Q. Metellus Pius, probably after the date of this oration. He was consul B.C. 52, and the father of Cornelia, the last wife of Cn. Pompeius Magnus. He killed himself after the battle of Thapsus, B.C. 46. Scipio was one of the advocates of Verres.

tuum familiaeque tuae] "Sic olim notatur a Fulvio Ursino et a Lambino inventum esse in codicibus suis, nosque in Guelferbytanis invenimus. Havn. coll. silet" (Zumpt). The common reading, which Klotz and Iordan have, is 'qui laudem honoremque familiae vestrae depeculatus est;' but Zumpt objects to 'vestrae,' since Cicero is addressing Scipio only. Yet there is in c. 37, "quamobrem si suscipis . . de vestris monumentis." 'Tuum' is in G 1 2. In place of 'tuae,' the reading of λ G 3 cod. Urs., there is 'vestrae' in R. Lgg.

aliorum] R G 3 Lg. 29, 'alieno' dett. Or. Klotz.

tu isti aderis] 'Will you give your assistance to this defendant,' &c. See the note on 'adesse,' Lib. 2. c. 29.

obstruxit] The old reading is 'obtru-

tua doluit ac sustulit? Quisnam igitur, per deos immortales, tuebitur P. Scipionis memoriam mortui? quis monumenta atque indicia virtutis, si tu ea relinques aut deseres? nec solum spoliata illa patieris, sed etiam eorum spoliatorem vexatoremque defendes? Adsunt Segestani, clientes tui, socii populi Romani atque amici: certiorem te faciunt P. Africanum Karthagine deleta simulacrum Dianae majoribus suis restituisse, idque apud Segestanos ejus imperatoris nomine positum ac dedicatum fuisse; hoc Verrem demoliendum et asportandum nomenque omnino P. Scipionis delendum tollendumque curasse: orant te atque obsecrant ut sibi religionem, generi tuo laudem gloriamque restituas, ut quod per P. Africanum ex urbe hostium recuperarint id per te ex praedonis domo conservare possint.

XXXVII. Quid aut tu his respondere honeste potes aut illi facere nisi ut te ac fidem tuam implorent? Adsunt et implorant. Potes domesticae laudis amplitudinem, Scipio, tueri, potes: omnia sunt in te quae aut fortuna hominibus aut natura largitur. Non praecerpo fructum officii tui: non alienam mihi laudem appeto: non est pudoris mei P. Scipione, florentissimo adolescente, vivo et incolumi me propugnatorem P. Scipionis defensoremque profiteri. Quamobrem si suscipis domesticae laudis patrocinium, me non solum silere de vestris monumentis oportebit, sed etiam laetari P. Africani ejusmodi fortunam esse mortui, ut ejus honos ab iis qui ex eadem familia sunt defendatur neque ullum adventitium auxilium requiratur. Sin istius amicitia te impedit, si hoc quod ego abs te postulo minus ad officium tuum pertinere arbitrabere, succedam ego vicarius tuo muneri, suscipiam partes quas alienas esse arbitrabar. Deinde ista praeclara nobilitas desinat queri popu-

sit,' which Manutius attempts to explain, but not satisfactorily. R 3 C A Lg. 29 have 'obstruxit.' This word has the sense of stopping up a passage, as a road or a river, by some structure or building, and is followed by the accusative. Zumpt observes that in this passage we must take it to mean the building of something which would prevent a thing from being seen, or would obstruct the approach to it. But in this sense he is inclined to think that the verb would require a dative, as in the expression 'luminibus obstruere,' which means to build up something which interferes with your neighbour's lights, or, as it is otherwise expressed, 'luminibus officere' (Dig. 8. 2. 17, 23). But there seems to be a difference between 'luminibus obstruere' and 'monumentum obstruere,' which may very well mean to build it up, surround it with other buildings, as 'portas obstruere' means 'to build up, stop up, gateways' (Caesar, B. G. vii. 41). *Monumentū* (sic R), *monumentū* G 3, *monumenta* dett. R 3 have also 'sed id.' The evidence seems to be in favour of the text, as I have now made it, though we cannot be quite certain that we have the true reading. Iordan has 'monumento.'

37. *familia sunt*] R Ld. 7 Lagg. have 'familia sint,' and Iordan.

vicarius] See Index.

Deinde ista praeclara] Zumpt gives his reasons for this reading instead of the old reading, 'Nae ista,' &c., which he had in

lum Romanum hominibus novis industriis libenter honores mandare semperque mandasse. Non est querendum in hac civitate quae propter virtutem omnibus nationibus imperat virtutem plurimum posse. Sit apud alios imago P. Africani; ornentur alii mortui virtute ac nomine: talis ille vir fuit, ita de populo Romano meritus est, ut non uni familiae sed universae civitati commendatus esse debeat. Est aliqua mea pars virilis, quod ejus civitatis sum quam ille amplam, illustrem, claramque, reddidit; praecipue quod in his rebus pro mea parte versor quarum ille princeps fuit, aequitate, industria, temperantia, defensione miserorum, odio improborum: quae cognatio studiorum et artium propemodum non minus est conjuncta quam ista qua vos delectamini generis et nominis.

XXXVIII. Repeto abs te, Verres, monumentum P. Africani: causam Siculorum quam suscepi relinquo; judicium de pecuniis repetundis ne sit hoc tempore; Segestanorum injuriae negligantur: basis P. Scipionis restituatur; nomen invicti imperatoris incidatur, signum pulcherrimum Karthagine captum reponatur. Haec abs te non Siculorum defensor, non tuus accusator, non Segestani postulant; sed is qui laudem gloriamque P. Africani tuendam conservandamque suscepit. Non vereor ne hoc officium meum P. Servilio judici non probem, qui quum res maximas gesserit, monumentaque

his first edition. Most of the MSS. have 'Ne ista,' which caused some of the older commentators a difficulty, as they did not perceive that 'ne' is an adverb of affirmation, which we now distinguish from the dehortatory 'ne,' by writing it with a diphthong. It is doubtful if we should write 'nae.' Klotz reads 'Aliquando ista praeclara,' which in his Preface he maintains to be the true reading, as deduced from the indications of the MSS. Lg. 29 has 'deinde,' and it now appears that the reading of R also means 'deinde.'

hominibus novis] Cicero means himself and others like himself. He was a 'homo novus.' See Lib. 3. c. 4.

in hac civitate quae] The common reading is 'in ea,' &c. It is clear to those who have attended to the use of the pronouns, that 'in hac civitate quae . . imperat,' the demonstrative 'hac' is required, and R λ G 2 Ld. have 'hac.' The dett. have 'ea.' If Cicero meant to say 'in a city that rules,' meaning any city, he would say, or could say, 'in ea civitate quae . . imperet,' and I now find that Lg. 29 has 'imperet,' a 'lectio notabilis,' which Zumpt had not noticed.

imago] 'Let others have the bust or effigies of P. Scipio.' The word 'imago' (εἰκών) is explained by Polybius, vi. 53. 'Imagines' were masks of wax. See the note Lib. 5. c. 14.

Est aliqua mea] The glory and name of P. Scipio belonged to the Roman people; but Cicero says, 'I have some share in it, a full share or portion, because I belong to a state which he made great, illustrious, and renowned; particularly because I take my full share in those things in which he was a model, in equity, painstaking, self-restraint, and the defence of the unfortunate.' As to 'pars virilis' see Lib. 3. c. 3.

in his rebus] 'in his' codd., but Iordan writes 'in iis.' 'Rebus' is the reading of R 3. The dett. have 'artibus.'

conjuncta] 'i. e. arta' (Zumpt), who refers to a like use of 'conjunctus,' in the Ep. ad Div. iii. 10. He also refers to the speech of Iphicrates to the Athenians, about the descendants of Harmodius (Aristotle, Rhet. ii. 23, ed. Bekker). The reader however will not find much for the trouble of seeking the passage.

suarum rerum gestarum quum maxime constituat atque in iis elaboret, profecto volet haec non solum suis posteris verum etiam omnibus viris fortibus et bonis civibus defendenda non spolianda improbis tradere. Non vereor ne tibi, Q. Catule, displiceat, cujus amplissimum in orbe terrarum clarissimumque monumentum est, quam plurimos esse custodes monumentorum et putare omnes bonos alienae gloriae defensionem ad officium suum pertinere. Equidem ceteris istius furtis atque flagitiis ita moveor ut ea reprehendenda tantum putem: hic vero tanto dolore afficior ut nihil mihi indignius, nihil minus ferendum esse videatur. Verres Africani monumentis domum suam, plenam stupri, plenam flagitii, plenam dedecoris, ornabit? Verres temperantissimi sanctissimique viri monumentum,

38. *suarum . . . quum maxime*] Zumpt says that it ought to be 'rerum suarum,' &c., and Ernesti adopted this order, though there is no MS. authority for it. The pronouns, 'meus,' 'tuus,' may either stand before their noun or after; and the place of 'meus,' 'tuus,' &c., is determined by the sense.

'Quum maxime,' or 'cummaxime,' as Zumpt has it, is a genuine form; nor is it necessary to erase 'quum,' or to write with G 1 'quam maxime.' 'Quummaxime,' says Zumpt, when used adverbially, marks either present time, or time indefinitely; and when it particularly signifies present time, it requires the addition of 'nunc,' as 'nunc quum maxime:' as to time past, we say 'tum maxime.' He refers to Drakenborch, Liv. xxvii. 4, and particularly to the learned note of Duker on Florus, ii. 16. 3 (ed. 1744), which is worth reading. Some of the editors have been disposed to get rid of the form 'tum maxime,' and change it into 'quum maxime;' but the distinction between them seems clear.

In Cicero (Ad Div. ix. 23) there is "expecta igitur hospitem quum minime edacem tum inimicum coenis sumptuosis." But here the form of the sentence is different, for 'quum' is followed by 'tum;' and this passage cannot be compared with that in the text. In Terence, Phormio, ii. 3. 11, there is—

"Quamobrem omnes quum secundae res sunt maxime, tum maxime
Meditari secum oportet," &c.,

where 'tum' marks the time already expressed by 'quum.' I see no reason why the 'quum' in this passage of Cicero should not be taken in the same sense as the 'quum' in 'quum res maximas gesserit,' and not 'adverbialiter' with 'maxime.' The use of 'quam,' and 'quum' and 'tum,' still waits for fuller explanation.

elaboret,] '*laboret*' G 3 Lg. 29. The distinction between the two words is generally observed. Zumpt says that '*laborare* ob aliquam rem' is 'laborem habere,' 'to be troubled, perplexed,' and so forth. But there are instances of 'laborare' followed by 'ut,' where it is used like 'elaborare;' and Zumpt has in his edition one instance, at least (Lib. 3. c. 56), "atque in hoc laborandum ut omnes intelligant:" but the true reading there is probably 'elaborandum.' In Lib. 3. c. 57, "sedasti etiam lites illorum, et sponsio illa ne fieret laborasti."

in orbe] 'orbi' R 3 Iordan; 'in orbe' dett. Or. Halm observes that Charisius confirms the use of the ablative form 'orbi' in Cicero, and adds "frequenter antiquos ita locutos Plinius eodem libro vi. notat." I do not doubt that forms like 'orbi' were used, but they mean 'in a place,' and 'orbi terrarum' does not seem a proper example. In this chapter I should have written 'Karthagini captum,' if any MSS. authority were cited for 'Karthagini,' for I do not explain it as Halm does, 'taken from Carthage,' nor is it the same as 'Karthagine tollere.'

Equidem] The reading of the old editions, and of the dett. is 'et quidem.' The best MSS. have 'equidem,' and the sense requires it. Drakenborch (Liv. vi. 54) shows how frequently the two forms are confounded, even in good MSS.

temperantissimi] R, 'temperatissimi' G 3 Lgg. In the Pro Fonteio, c. 17, there is 'homo sanctissimus ac temperantissimus.' The Romans perhaps used both 'temperantissimus' and 'temperatissimus.'

Dianae simulacrum virginis in ea domo collocabit in qua semper meretricum lenonumque flagitia versantur?

XXXIX. At hoc solum Africani monumentum violasti. Quid, a Tyndaritanis non ejusdem Scipionis beneficio positum simulacrum Mercurii pulcherrime factum sustulisti? At quemadmodum, dii immortales, quam audacter! quam libidinose! quam impudenter! Audistis nuper dicere legatos Tyndaritanos, homines honestissimos ac principes civitatis, Mercurium qui sacris anniversariis apud eos ac summa religione coleretur, quem P. Africanus Karthagine capta Tyndaritanis non solum suae victoriae sed etiam illorum fidei societatisque monumentum atque indicium dedisset, hujus vi, scelere, imperioque esse sublatum. Qui ut primum in illud oppidum venit, statim, tamquam ita fieri non solum oporteret sed etiam necesse esset, tamquam hoc senatus mandasset, populus Romanus jussisset, ita continuo signum ut demolirentur et Messanam deportarent imperavit. Quod quum illis qui aderant indignum, qui audiebant incredibile videretur, non est ab isto primo illo adventu perseveratum. Discedens mandat proagoro Sopatro, cujus verba audistis, ut demoliatur: quum recusaret, vehementer minatur et statim ex illo oppido proficiscitur. Refert rem ille ad senatum: vehementer undique reclamatur. Ne multa: iterum iste ad illos aliquanto post venit, quaerit continuo de signo. Respondetur ei senatum non permittere; poenam capitis constitutam si injussu senatus quisquam attigisset: simul religio commemoratur. Tum

39. *violasti.*] Iordan writes 'violasti?' but the ? is not wanted.

Tyndaritanis] The place is Tyndaris (Τυνδαρίς), or Tyndarium, on the north coast of Sicily, in the modern gulf of Patti. It was founded by some Greeks, under the elder Dionysius, B. C. 395, close to the promontory of the same name (Diod. xiv. 78), and it became a place of some importance. "A fine plain leads from the Marina of Patti, to a pass among the hills called the 'Scala di Tindari,' on the summit of which stood the city of Tyndaris. Numerous ruins attest the once flourishing state of this town, in a situation combining every advantage of health, strength, and beauty" (Smyth's Sicily, p. 101). It seems probable that excavations would lead to valuable discoveries. Smyth adds, that "two colossal statues, and some columns, were cut up to decorate the chapel of the Madonna and Child."

qui . . apud eos] This is a case where a man, who should now attempt to write Latin, might find a difficulty; and it seems that the Romans found it sometimes, for there is no absolute rule as to the use of the reflective 'se,' in a sentence where two persons, or sets of persons, are mentioned. If Cicero had here used 'se' for 'eos,' his meaning would have been equally clear; but 'se' would not harmonize with the rest of the sentence, 'non suae . . . sed illorum;' and 'eos' is necessary. Comp. Lib. 2. c. 17, note, 'ut si ei videatur.'

Refert rem ille] It is the proper word in this case. He laid the matter before the Senate for deliberation. The consuls at Rome are said, in like cases, 'referre ad senatum.' Shortly after, 'rem defert,' where 'rem' is added by Zumpt from the better MSS. G 2 Ld. have 'refert rem;' but 'defert' is the right word in this second instance; for the sense is, 'that he simply informed the Senate.' So in c. 45, 'rem ad magistratus deferunt.'

iste: Quam mihi religionem narras? quam poenam? quem senatum? vivum te non relinquam: moriere virgis nisi mihi signum traditur. Sopater iterum flens ad senatum rem defert, istius cupiditatem minasque demonstrat. Senatus Sopatro responsum nullum dat, sed commotus perturbatusque discedit. Ille praetoris arcessitus nuntio rem demonstrat; negat ullo modo fieri posse. XL. Atque haec, nihil enim praetermittendum de istius impudentia videtur, agebantur in conventu, palam, de sella ac de loco superiore. Erat hiems summa, tempestas, ut ipsum Sopatrum dicere audistis, perfrigida, imber maximus, quum iste imperat lictoribus ut Sopatrum de porticu, in qua ipse sedebat, praecipitem in forum dejiciant nudumque constituant. Vix erat hoc plane imperatum quum illum spoliatum stipatumque lictoribus videres. Omnes id fore putabant ut miser atque innocens virgis caederetur: fefellit haec homines opinio. Virgis iste caederet sine causa socium populi Romani atque amicum? Non usque eo est improbus: non omnia sunt in uno vitia: nunquam fuit crudelis. Leniter hominem clementerque accepit. Equestres sunt medio in foro Marcellorum statuae, sicuti fere ceteris in oppidis Siciliae; ex quibus iste C. Marcelli statuam delegit, cujus officia in illam civitatem totamque provinciam recentissima erant et maxima. In ea Sopatrum, hominem quum domi nobilem, tum summo magistratu praeditum, divaricari ac deligari jubet. Quo cruciatu sit affectus venire in mentem necesse est omnibus, quum esset vinctus nudus in aere, in imbri, in frigore. Neque tamen finis huic injuriae crudelitatique fiebat, donec populus atque universa multitudo, atrocitate rei misericordiaque

Quam mihi] There are many instances of this position of 'mihi:' 'What religious difficulties are you talking about to me,' or rather to keep the emphatic position of 'mihi' as nearly as we can, 'What is it to me this religion that you talk about?'

arcessitus] 'accersitus' dett. 'Accersitus,' though some editors of Latin books adopt the form, is a mistake, and one that may easily arise in copying. But it is very likely that this corrupt form was used sometimes.

40. *de sella*] See Lib. 2. c. 42. This was done 'in conventu,' in full court, in the presence of all the people, 'qui in id forum convenerant.' The 'praetor' was sitting 'in portica,' under a covered place. —'hiemus:' 'hiemps' R.

Equestres . . statuae,] See Lib. 2. c. 21; and Livy, xxvi. c. 32: and as to C. Marcellus, Lib. 2. c. 3. Verres ordered Sopater to be placed astride the statue (divaricari), and to be fastened down.

It has been doubted if we should write 'in aëre,' as it is in the English reprint of Zumpt, and in Iordan, or 'in aere,' as in his larger edition. The MSS. are of no use here. Cicero means to say, on the 'bronze' or 'metal;' for, as Zumpt observes, it was not the least part of the torture, that he sat on metal, which is colder than stone or wood. Stone, indeed, would be cold enough; but the barbarity of the act was aggravated by seating the man on metal, which is a rapid conductor of heat. One has heard of soldiers being seated astride a cannon by way of punishment. Besides this, an equestrian statue placed in the open air would not be of marble.

commota, senatum clamore coëgit ut isti simulacrum illud Mercurii polliceretur. Clamabant fore ut ipsi se dii immortales ulciscerentur: hominem interea perire innocentem non oportere. Tum frequens senatus ad istum venit: pollicetur signum. Ita Sopater de statua C. Marcelli, quum jam paene obriguisset, vix vivus aufertur.

XLI. Non possum disposite istum accusare, si cupiam: opus est non solum ingenio verum etiam artificio quodam singulari. Unum hoc crimen videtur esse, et a me pro uno ponitur, de Mercurio Tyndaritano: plura sunt, sed ea quo pacto distinguere ac separare possim nescio. Est pecuniarum captarum, quod signum a sociis pecuniae magnae sustulit. Est peculatus, quod publicum populi Romani signum, de praeda hostium captum, positum imperatoris nostri nomine, non dubitavit auferre. Est majestatis, quod imperii nostri gloriae rerumque gestarum monumenta evertere atque asportare ausus est. Est sceleris, quod religiones maximas violavit. Est crudelitatis, quod innocentem in hominem, in socium vestrum atque amicum, novum ac singulare supplicii genus excogitavit. Illud vero quid sit jam non queo dicere, quo nomine appellem nescio, quod in C. Marcelli statua. Quid est hoc? Patronusne quod erat? Quid tum? quo id spectat? Utrum ea res ad opem an ad calamitatem clientium atque hospitum valere debebat? an ut hoc ostenderes, contra vim tuam in patronis praesidii nihil esse? Quis non hoc intelligeret in improbi praesentis imperio majorem esse vim quam in bonorum absentium patrocinio? An vero ex hoc illa tua singularis significatur insolentia, superbia, contumacia? Detrahere videlicet aliquid te de amplitudine Marcellorum putasti. Itaque nunc Siculorum Marcelli non sunt patroni: Verres in eorum locum substitutus est. Quam in te tantam virtutem esse aut dignitatem arbitratus es ut conarere clientelam tam splendidae, tam illustris provinciae traducere ad te, auferre a certissimis antiquissimisque patronis? Tu ista stultitia, nequitia, inertia non modo totius Siciliae sed unius tenuissimi Siculi clientelam tueri potes? Tibi

41. *disposite*] The words 'ordo' and 'dispositio' sometimes come together in Cicero. He partly explains what he means by 'disposite' by the following words: 'distinguere ac separare.' He says, 'I cannot distinctly separate his crimes, were I ever so desirous to do it.' For this affair of Tyndaris, which seems to be one offence, contains, says Cicero, several distinct offences or grounds of accusation.

pecuniarum captarum,] That is, 'crimen,' or the offence of Repetundae. The orator proceeds to explain how many offences are comprehended in this one act of taking the Mercury. 'Pecuniae magnae' means 'of great value.' See Lib. 5. c. 7; and also Pro Sex. Rosc. c. 37, Vol. ii.

ad opem] 'Whether ought the circumstance of Marcellus being their Patronus to have secured the protection, or to have brought misfortune on his clients?'

Marcelli statua pro patibulo in clientes Marcellorum fuit? tu ex illius honore in eos ipsos qui honorem habuerant supplicia quaerebas? Quid postea, quid tandem tuis statuis fore arbitrabare? An vero quod accidit? Nam Tyndaritani statuam istius quam sibi propter Marcellos altiore etiam basi poni jusserat, deturbarunt simulac successum isti audierunt.

XLII. Dedit igitur tibi nunc fortuna Siculorum C. Marcellum judicem, ut cujus ad statuam Siculi te praetore alligabantur, ejus religione te isti devinctum adstrictumque dedamus. Ac primo, judices, hoc signum Mercurii dicebat iste Tyndaritanos M. Marcello huic Aesernino vendidisse, atque hoc sua causa etiam M. Marcellum ipsum sperabat esse dicturum; quod mihi nunquam verisimile visum est, adolescentem illo loco natum, patronum Siciliae, nomen suum isti ad translationem criminis commodaturum. Verumtamen ita mihi res tota provisa atque praecauta est ut, si maxime esset inventus qui in se suscipere istius culpam crimenque cuperet, tamen is proficere nihil posset. Eos enim deduxi testes et eas literas deportavi ut de istius facto dubium esse nemini posset. Publicae literae sunt deportatum Mercurium esse Messanam sumptu publico. Dicent quanti. Praefuisse huic negotio publice legatum Poleam. Quid is, ubi est? Praesto est: testis est. Proagori Sopatri jussu. Quis est hic? Qui ad statuam adstrictus est. Quid

qui honorem habuerant] The pronoun 'illi' is generally added after 'honorem;' but Zumpt has omitted it on the authority of C 3 λ. R has it. It was probably added by some one who wished to explain the meaning. Cicero asks, 'did you seek to turn the statue of Marcellus into a means of punishing those, who had raised the statue to his honour?' See Lib. 1. c. 15, 'habuit honorem,' &c.

42. *religione te isti devinctum &c.*] 'religione te isti devinctum adscriptumque' &c. R 3 ('devictum' G 3); 'religioni te eundem vinctum adstrictumque' dett. Or. Madvig would write 'istic,' i. e. 'in subsellio ubi reus sedes,' and 'videamus' for 'dedamus.' Zumpt writes 'istis,' and makes it refer to the Siculi present at the trial. If we read 'istis,' we must explain it so. Halm has changed 'isti' into 'ipsi.' It would be easy to take the reading 'religioni te' and to omit 'isti,' but 'isti' is in R 3. The conclusion is that there is something wrong, and we cannot with certainty discover what the original was.

Aesernino] He is mentioned in the Brutus, c. 35, where Meyer remarks that M. Claudius Marcellus, the father of Aeserninus, distinguished himself in the war with the Teutones, as a 'legatus' of Marius, B.C. 102. In the Marsic war, after the defeat of the consul L. Julius Caesar, B.C. 90, he fled to the colony Aesernia, and was compelled by famine to surrender to the Samnites (Liv. Ep. 73). His son was called Aeserninus from this ignominious circumstance.

posset.] 'possit' Lg. 29, Halm.

Publicae literae sunt &c.] 'There is evidence in the public records that the Mercury was taken.' Cicero sometimes uses this form, which is a short way of saying, 'Ex publicis literis constat,' or something of the kind.

Quid is, ubi est?] Cicero first says, 'Quis est hic?' 'Who is he?' 'The man who was fastened to the statue.' Then, 'Well, the man who was fastened to the statue, where is he? You have seen him, you have heard what he said.' Zumpt, Klotz, and Jordan have 'Quid? is ubi est?' I have noticed this absurd mode of pointing several times, but not too often, if it can be got rid of.

is, ubi est? Vidistis hominem, et verba ejus audistis. Demoliendum curavit Demetrius gymnasiarchus, quod is ei loco praeerat. Quid, hoc nos dicimus? Immo vero ipse praesens. Romae nuper ipsum istum esse pollicitum sese id signum legatis [esse] redditurum, si ejus rei testificatio tolleretur cautumque esset eos testimonium non esse dicturos: dixit hoc apud vos Zosippus et Ismenias, homines nobilissimi et principes Tyndaritanae civitatis.

XLIII. Quid Agrigento, nonne ejusdem P. Scipionis monumentum, signum Apollinis pulcherrimum, cujus in femore literis minutis argenteis nomen Myronis erat inscriptum, ex Aesculapii religiosissimo fano sustulisti? Quod quidem, judices, quum iste clam fecisset, quum ad suum scelus illud furtumque nefarium quosdam homines improbos duces atque adjutores adhibuisset, vehementer commota civitas est. Uno enim tempore Agrigentini beneficium Africani, religionem domesticam, ornamentum urbis, indicium victoriae, testimonium societatis requirebant. Itaque ab iis qui principes in ea civitate erant praecipitur et negotium datur quaestoribus et aedilibus, ut noctu vigilias agerent ad aedes sacras. Etenim iste Agrigenti—credo propter multitudinem illorum hominum atque virtutem, et quod cives Romani viri fortes atque honesti permulti in illo oppido conjunctissimo animo cum ipsis Agrigentinis vivunt ac negotiantur—non audebat palam poscere aut tollere quae placebant. Herculis templum est apud Agrigentinos, non longe a

ei loco] Demetrius was director of the gymnasium, which word is in substance referred to by the words 'ei loco,' for no place has been mentioned. The statue of Mercury would be appropriately placed in the gymnasium.

Romae nuper &c.] I have followed Jordan in the punctuation, which used to be 'immo vero ipse praesens Romae' &c.

dixit .. Zosippus et Ismenias,] Zumpt cites some other similar instances. One is from De Orat. i. 62, 'dubitare visus est Sulpicius et Cotta.'

43. *Agrigento,*] Ernesti altered this to Agrigenti, as Zumpt says, because 'ex fano' follows. But it ought to be the ablative, whether there is 'ex fano' or not. See c. 50. Zumpt compares Caesar, Bell. Civ. iii. 105, "T. Ampium conatum esse tollere pecunias Epheso, ex fano Dianae;" where there is no various reading. See Lib. 1. c. 19, for various examples of the ablative; and Lib. 5. c. 72, 'Henna ex sua sede . . . sustulerit.'

femore] 'Femine' in the English reprint, and in Zumpt's original edition. In his second edition he has adopted this reading from R 3 A. Zumpt admits that in the plural number the forms 'femina,' 'feminum,' 'feminibus,' are much more common. It is not likely that this interchange between *s* and *r* is due solely to the copyists. It is probable that the Romans used both forms.

minutis] The name of Myron was put on the thigh of the statue, in small letters of silver, let into the bronze. Zumpt refers to Suetonius, Aug. c. 7, "nactus puerilem imagunculam ejus aeream veterem, ferreis ac paene jam exolescentibus literis, hoc nomine inscriptam." Here the figure was of bronze, and the letters of iron, if the readings are right. See Burmann's edition, and the notes. D'Anville (Notice de la Gaule, Forum Segusianorum) quotes the historian of the Forez, who mentions a Roman copper weight, found I suppose at Feur in the Forez, which had on it in silver letters the inscription DEAE. SEG. F.

Herculis templum] One of the great

foro, sane sanctum apud illos et religiosum. Ibi est ex aere simulacrum ipsius Herculis, quo non facile dixerim quidquam me vidisse pulchrius, tametsi non tam multum in istis rebus intelligo quam multa vidi, usque eo, judices, ut rictum ejus ac mentum paulo sit attritius, quod in precibus et gratulationibus non solum id venerari verum etiam osculari solent. Ad hoc templum, quum esset iste Agrigenti, duce Timarchide repente nocte intempesta servorum armatorum fit concursus atque impetus. Clamor a vigilibus fanique custodibus tollitur, qui primo quum obsistere ac defendere conarentur, male mulcati clavis ac fustibus repelluntur. Postea convulsis repagulis effractisque valvis demoliri signum ac vectibus labefactare conantur. Interea ex clamore fama tota urbe percrebuit expugnari deos patrios non hostium adventu necopinato neque repentino praedonum impetu, sed ex domo atque ex cohorte praetoria manum fugitivorum instructam armatamque venisse. Nemo Agrigenti neque aetate tam affecta neque viribus tam infirmis

monuments of Agrigentum, which some remains are supposed to represent.

'Rictum' is the neuter. It means the mouth or lips, as this passage of Lucretius shows, v. 1063:—

> "Mollia ricta fremunt duros nudantia dentes:"

and another passage in Lib. vi. 1193.

Though 'rictum' does not occur elsewhere in Cicero, we have the authority of Nonius Marcellus in support of 'rictum,' who says, 'rictum neutrius generis;' and refers to 'Marc. Tull. De Signis.' R 3 E C also have 'rictum.' The touching of the chin was one of the forms of supplication among the Greeks. Hotmann quotes the Iliad, i. 501, and refers to Pliny (H. N. xi. 45), "Antiquis Graeciae in supplicando mentum attingere mos erat." Hotmann also cites a passage to the same effect from Arnobius, Contra Gent. Lib. 6. There are other passages which show that to touch the chin was the act of a suppliant; as Polyxena (Eurip. Hecub. 347) says, addressing Ulysses:

> —— καὶ πρόσωπον ἔμπαλιν
> στρέφοντα μή σου προσθίγω γενειάδος.

The statue could not be of colossal size, if the devotees could kiss the mouth and chin, unless it were reclining, which is not the usual attitude of the statues of Hercules. But the god was represented in several forms; as the ideal of strength and endurance, in a standing posture; and also in a reclining posture, as the hero who rests from his labours, and is received into heaven. See Muller's Handbuch &c. —'usque eo,' &c. These words refer to 'pulchrius;' and the translation will be 'so beautiful, Judices, that the lips and chin are a little worn, because in their prayers and thanksgivings they are wont not only to worship, but even to kiss it.' We may perhaps conclude from this, that it was a statue of Hercules 'rejuvenescent,' after the close of his earthly labours.

nocte intempesta] Phil. i. c. 3, and the note.

mulcati] This is said to be the true form of the word, when blows and stripes are spoken of, as in Livy xxiv. 9, "Legatis prius indignum in modum mulcatis." In this passage the old editions have 'mulctati' (Zumpt). See Forcellini, v. Mulco. Whether there are two words 'mulcare' and 'mulctare,' or 'multare,' or there is only one, of which the orthography was unsettled, seems to be disputed. A comparison of the usages of these words appears to lead to the conclusion that there is one verb, of which the root is 'mulc.' 'Morte . . . multatus' occurs Lib. 1. c. 5.

repagulis] This passage is cited by Festus, v. Repagula, which word is thus explained: "quae patefaciendi gratia ita figuntur, ut ex contrario quae oppanguntur;" so the passage is read in the Delphin edition, but apparently it is corrupt.

percrebuit] R E G 2 Lagg. See Index.

fuit qui non illa nocte eo nuntio excitatus surrexerit, telumque quod cuique fors offerebat arripuerit. Itaque brevi tempore ad fanum ex urbe tota concurritur. Horam amplius jam in demoliendo signo permulti homines moliebantur: illud interea nulla lababat ex parte, quum alii vectibus subjectis conarentur commovere, alii deligatum omnibus membris rapere ad se funibus. Ac repente Agrigentini concurrunt: fit magna lapidatio: dant sese in fugam istius praeclari imperatoris nocturni milites: duo tamen sigilla perparvula tollunt, ne omnino inanes ad istum praedonem religionum revertantur. Nunquam tam male est Siculis quin aliquid facete et commode dicant; velut in hac re aiebant in labores Herculis non minus hunc immanissimum verrem quam illum aprum Erymanthium referri oportere.

XLIV. Hanc virtutem Agrigentinorum imitati sunt Assorini postea, viri fortes et fideles, sed nequaquam ex tam ampla neque tam ex nobili civitate. Chrysas est amnis qui per Assorinorum agros fluit. Is apud illos habetur deus et religione maxima colitur. Fanum ejus est in agro propter ipsam viam qua Assoro itur Hennam. In eo Chrysae simulacrum est praeclare factum e marmore. Id iste poscere Assorinos propter singularem ejus fani religionem non ausus est: Tlepolemo dat et Hieroni negotium. Illi noctu facta manu armataque veniunt: fores aedis effringunt: aeditui cus-

Horam amplius] I have now taken this, the reading of R E Ld. Lg. 29. It means 'an hour and even more.' 'Hora amplius' is also Latin.

tam male . . Siculis] A usual Latin formula: 'it is never so ill with the Siculi that they cannot make a joke.' See Lib. 3. c. 33. A like piece of Sicilian wit is mentioned by Quintilian, Inst. Or. vi. 3. 41.

44. *Assorus*] The town keeps its name, hardly altered, Asaro. It was about half-way between Agyrium and Henna. (Diod. xiv. 58. 78.) The river is the Dittaino, a branch of the Symaethus, now the Giaretta. Zumpt observes, that Guelf. 1 has 'Crisas' without the aspirate, and that the name without the aspirate also occurs on an ancient coin, Eckhel, Doct. Num. Vet. I. p. 198. F. Ursini speaks of a coin in his possession, which has on one side the head of a beardless youth, bound with a fillet, and with long hair, with the legend 'Assoru' for 'Assori,' as 'Menandru' for 'Menandri.' On the other side is the river god, which Cicero describes, with a pitcher in his right hand, and a 'cornucopiae' in his left, and the legend 'Crysas' without the aspirate. I have a cast of a coin which corresponds with this description. The legend ASSORV is plain; and on the other face CRYSAS.

facta . . armataque] The reading of the MSS. There is no authority for 'armatique.' 'Facere manum,' to collect a body of men, is explained by Zumpt by reference to the oration Pro Caecina, c. 12; and to these orations, Lib. 5. c. 30, 'si aliquam manum . . . facere,' &c.

aeditui] The keepers of the 'aedes.' All the MSS. have 'aeditui;' but Gellius, xii. 10, says: "In Verrem M. Tullii in exemplaribus fidelissimis ita inveni scriptum, 'Aeditumi custodesque mature sentiunt.' In libris autem hoc vulgariis 'Aeditui' scriptum est" (ed. Gronov.). Gellius compares 'aeditimus' with 'finitimus,' 'legitimus.' He adds, that 'aeditimus' is the old form, but that 'aedituus' was generally used when he wrote. He calls 'aedituus' a new usage, 'quasi a tuendis aedibus appellatus.'

Varro, De L. L. vii. 12 (ed. Müller) says: "Ut cum dicimus *Bellum* furor et *terri*

todesque mature sentiunt: signum quod erat notum vicinitati bucina datur: homines ex agris concurrunt: ejicitur fugaturque Tlepolemus; neque quidquam ex fano Chrysae praeter unum perparvulum signum ex aere desideratum est.

Matris magnae fanum apud Enguinos est: jam enim non modo breviter mihi de unoquoque dicendum, sed etiam praetereunda videntur esse permulta ut ad majora istius et illustriora in hoc genere furta et scelera veniamus: in hoc fano loricas galeasque aeneas caelatas opere Corinthio, hydriasque grandes simili in genere atque eadem arte perfectas, idem ille Scipio, vir omnibus rebus praecellentissimus, posuerat et suum nomen inscripserat. Quid jam de isto plura dicam aut querar? omnia illa, judices, abstulit: nihil in religiosissimo fano praeter vestigia violatae religionis nomenque P. Scipionis reliquit: hostium spolia, monumenta imperatorum, decora atque ornamenta fanorum posthac his praeclaris nominibus amissis in instrumento atque in supellectile Verris nominabuntur. Tu videlicet solus vasis Corinthiis delectaris: tu illius aeris temperationem, tu operum lineamenta sollertissime perspicis. Haec Scipio ille non intelligebat, homo doctissimus atque humanissimus: tu sine ulla bona arte, sine humanitate, sine ingenio, sine literis intelligis et judicas. Vide ne ille non solum temperantia, sed etiam intelligentia te atque istos, qui se elegantes dici volunt, vicerit. Nam quia quam pulchra essent intelligebat, idcirco existimabat ea non ad hominum luxuriem, sed ad ornatum fanorum

villam, a quo etiam quidam dicunt illum qui curat aedes sacras, aeditumum, non aeditomum." 'Aeditomum' is the reading of the MSS. of Varro, except one, which has 'editumum;' but the word that is meant is 'aeditimum' or 'aeditumum,' as appears from Gellius. In the treatise De R. R. i. 2. 1, Varro says: "Sementivis feriis in aedem Telluris veneram rogatus ab aeditimo, ut dicere didicimus a patribus nostris, ut corrigimur a recentibus urbanis, ab aedituo." These passages are cited by Hotmann. Klotz has 'aeditumi.'

bucina] See the word in Forcellini and Varro, De R. R. ii. 4. 20. In Ovid, Met. i. 335, it is Triton's shell. The better orthography seems to be with the one *c*, as R has it; for the word perhaps contains the same root as 'bu-cula;' and may have meant originally a cow's horn. (Virg. Aen. vii. 512, 519.) There is the form 'tibicina.'

Matris magnae] The 'Mater Magna' was Cybele. But it was the temple of the *θεῶν μητέρων*, according to Diodorus, iv. 79. The Matres were the Cretan women who nursed Zeus, and hid him from his father Cronus. They were rewarded with a place in heaven, *καὶ καταστερισθείσας ἄρκτους προσαγορευθῆναι*. These goddesses had a large temple at Enguion; and the temple had great possessions: "even a little before my time," says Diodorus, "the goddesses had three thousand sacred cows, and land enough to produce a large income." Plutarch (Marcellus, c. 20) mentions the armour in this temple. As the worship of these divinities came from Crete, it seems probable that Enguion was a Cretan colony, or received Cretan colonists, as Diodorus says. See Lib. 3. c. 43.

posthac] 'post haec' R 3 E λ.

humanissimus:] See Lib. 3. c. 4, note; to which add the following from Gellius, xiii. 16: "Praxiteles qui propter artificium egregium nemini est paulum modo humaniori ignotus."

atque oppidorum esse facta, ut posteris nostris monumenta religiosa esse videantur.

XLV. Audite etiam singularem ejus, judices, cupiditatem, audaciam, amentiam in his praesertim sacris polluendis quae non modo manibus attingi sed ne cogitatione quidem violari fas fuit. Sacrarium Cereris est apud Catinenses eadem religione qua Romae, qua in ceteris locis, qua prope in toto orbe terrarum. In eo sacrario intimo signum fuit Cereris perantiquum, quod viri non modo cujusmodi esset sed ne esse quidem sciebant: aditus enim in id sacrarium non est viris; sacra per mulieres ac virgines confici solent. Hoc signum noctu clam istius servi ex illo religiosissimo atque antiquissimo loco sustulerunt. Postridie sacerdotes Cereris atque illius fani antistitae, majores natu, probatae ac nobiles mulieres, rem ad magistratus suos deferunt. Omnibus acerbum, indignum, luctuosum denique videbatur. Tum iste permotus illa atrocitate negotii ut ab se sceleris illius suspicio demoveretur, dat hospiti suo cuidam negotium ut aliquem reperiret quem illud fecisse insimularet, daretque operam ut is eo crimine damnaretur, ne ipse esset in crimine. Res non procrastinatur. Nam quum iste Catina profectus esset, servi cujusdam nomen defertur. Is accusatur: ficti testes in eum dantur. Rem cunctus senatus Catinensium legibus judicabat. Sacerdotes vocantur: ex his quaeritur secreto in curia quid esse factum arbitrarentur, quemadmodum signum esset ablatum. Respondent illae praetoris in eo loco servos esse visos. Res quae esset jam antea non obscura sacerdotum testimonio perspicua esse coepit. Itur in consilium: servus ille innocens omnibus sententiis absolvitur, quo facilius vos hunc omnibus sententiis condemnare possitis. Quid enim postulas, Verres? quid speras? quid exspectas? quem tibi aut deum aut hominem auxilio futurum putas? Eone tu servos ad spoliandum fanum immittere ausus es, quo liberos adire ne orandi quidem causa fas erat? Hisne rebus manus

45. *in his*] 'in iis' L, 'in his' R, cett. Iordan has 'in iis.' He seldom allows 'his' to stand.

antistitae,] There is the authority of Gellius (xiii. 20) for this form; and also the authority of Priscian (v. 4. p. 560, Putsch.; 183, Krehl, referred to by Zumpt). The MSS. have both 'antistitae' and 'antistites.' In c. 50 there is 'antistites,' but it applies to all the 'cives.'

demoveretur,] "Codd. vulgares et edd. veteres *removeretur*" (Zumpt).

judicabat.] The senate formed a court for the investigation and trial of this affair; and this was according to the laws of Catina.

arbitrarentur,] See Lib. 2. c. 38, and the note.

Itur in consilium:] 'They deliberate on the verdict.' This is the Roman form of expression applied to a body of men who are acting as judges of a fact. In Lib. 1. c. 9, there is the similar phrase, 'mittam in consilium,' the meaning of which is explained by the context.

afferre non dubitasti, a quibus etiam oculos cohibere te religionum jura cogebant? Tametsi ne oculis quidem captus in hanc fraudem tam sceleratam ac tam nefariam decidisti, nam id concupisti quod nunquam videras; id, inquam, adamasti quod antea non aspexeras. Auribus tu tantam cupiditatem concepisti ut eam non metus, non religio, non deorum vis, non hominum existimatio contineret. At ex bono viro credo audieras et bono auctore. Qui id potes qui ne ex viro quidem audire potueris? Audisti igitur ex muliere, quoniam id viri neque vidisse neque nosse poterant. Qualem porro illam feminam fuisse putatis, judices, quam pudicam quae cum Verre loqueretur? quam religiosam quae sacrarii spoliandi rationem ostenderet? An minime mirum quae sacra per summam castimoniam virorum ac mulierum fiant, eadem per istius stuprum ac flagitium esse violata?

XLVI. Quid ergo hoc solum auditione expetere coepit, quum id ipse non vidisset? Immo vero alia complura: ex quibus eligam spoliationem nobilissimi atque antiquissimi fani, de qua priore actione testes dicere audistis: nunc eadem illa, quaeso, audite, et diligenter sicut adhuc fecistis attendite. Insula est Melita, judices,

religionum jura] The rules of law which concern matters relating to religion. See Divin. c. 20. This word (jus, jura) has a very extensive use. It is necessary to distinguish when it has the sense of the rules which relate to a thing, and the rights which persons may have; in fact, between a rule of law and a right which a person claims by virtue of such rule. Poets and prose writers use the word freely, as Ovid:

"Ne tamen ignores variorum jura dierum"
(Fasti, i. 45);

where he means the particular character, religious or other, which usage assigned to the several days of the Calendar. Again he says (Fasti, i. 252):

"Nullus erat justis reddere jura labor;"

where 'reddere jura' expresses the office of him who declares the law, and establishes the rights of the parties who have come before him. Cicero (De Sen. c. 4) has the expression 'qui mortuis tam religiose jura tribuerunt,' which refers to the law of interment and sepulchres.

oculis . . captus] Cicero explains his meaning. It was not by the effect produced on his eyes that Verres fell in love with this statue. The expression sometimes has a larger meaning, and signifies one who is so affected in the eyes as to be blind; as in Ovid (Fasti, vi. 204) it is said of Appius:

"Multum animo vidit: lumine captus
erat."

Comp. Lib. 5. c. 25, and In Cat. iii. c. 9.

bono auctore.] See the note Lib. 5. c. 22.

An minime mirum] 'At' in the English reprint of Zumpt, of course without the note of interrogation at the end of the sentence. 'An' R 3, 'ac' Lg. 29, 'at' dett. Madvig maintains that the reading 'at' cannot be admitted; but Zumpt is not convinced of the truth of his remark.

The words 'castimoniam virorum' have caused a difficulty. Zumpt, after rejecting Ernesti's explanation, adds, "malim intelligere quod a consuetudine mulierum (viri) abstinent, quibus sacra facienda sunt;" which may be the true explanation.

46. *complura:*] 'compluria' Klotz, following the authority of Priscian, who quotes 'immo vero compluria' from this oration of Cicero, with the remark that 'complura' occurs in some MSS. But all the extant MSS. have 'complura.'

Melita,] The island of Malta. Diodorus (v. 12) describes it as being about eight hundred stadia from Syracuse. It has se-

satis lato a Sicilia mari periculosoque disjuncta, in qua est eodem nomine oppidum quo iste nunquam accessit; quod tamen isti textrinum per triennium ad muliebrem vestem conficiendam fuit. Ab eo oppido non longe in promontorio fanum est Junonis antiquum, quod tanta religione semper fuit ut non modo illis Punicis bellis, quae in his fere locis navali copia gesta atque versata sunt, sed etiam hac praedonum multitudine semper inviolatum sanctumque fuerit. Quin etiam hoc memoriae proditum est, classe quondam Masinissae regis ad eum locum appulsa praefectum regium dentes eburneos incredibili magnitudine e fano sustulisse, et eos in Africam portasse Masinissaeque donasse. Regem primo delectatum esse munere; post ubi audisset unde essent, statim certos homines in quinqueremi misisse qui eos dentes reponerent. Itaque in his scriptum literis Punicis fuit, Regem Masinissam imprudentem accepisse, re cognita reportandos curasse. Erat praeterea magna vis eboris, multa ornamenta, in quibus eburneae Victoriae antiquo opere ac summa arte perfectae. Haec iste omnia, ne multis morer, uno impetu atque uno nuntio per servos Venereos, quos ejus rei causa miserat, tollenda atque asportanda curavit.

XLVII. Pro dii immortales, quem ego hominem accuso, quem legibus aut judiciali jure persequor, de quo vos sententiam per

veral good harbours; the inhabitants are rich, for it contains all kinds of artizans, but the best are those who make linen cloth (ὀθόνια), which is remarkable for fineness and softness. The direct distance from Syracuse to the nearest point of Malta is about ninety English miles. Diodorus adds that the island was settled by the Phoenicians, who brought with them the useful arts from their native country. Tyre was noted for its manufactures. Ezekiel (xxvii. 7) speaks of "fine linen with broidered work from Egypt," and of the Syrian merchants (v. 16): "they occupied in thy fairs with emeralds, purple, and broidered work, and fine linen, and coral, and agate." This seems somewhat ambiguous in the English version. But we may conclude that the Tyrians became skilled in many of the arts, and carried them into their colonies. Greeks also settled in Malta, which we infer from the fact of Greek inscriptions having been found in Malta and coins with the Greek legend ΜΕΛΙΤΑΙΩΝ.

promontorio] "'promunturio' R, 'promuntorio' Lg. 29 et 5 alii" (Iordan). See Caesar, B. G. iii. 12, and the note, ed. Long. In I. Vossius' edition of Mela, i. 19, the word is written 'promuntoria.'

hac praedonum] Cicero contrasts the robberies of the pirates, who scoured the Mediterranean in his time, with the state of affairs in the now somewhat remote period of the Punic wars (illis). He alludes to the 'piratae' in the following chapter. R Ld. Iordan have 'hac' instead of 'in hac,' the former reading. This ablative denotes a state or condition of things. Compare Caesar, B. G. i. 18, 'imperio populi Romani,' and ii. 12, 'summaque erat vasto atque aperto mari . . . difficultas navigandi.'

certos homines] 'Sure, trusty men,' as Graevius rightly explains it.

eburneae] Ivory was one of the articles of commerce which reached Tyre (Ezekiel, xxvii. 15), and it was no doubt used as a material for the skill of the carver, and to decorate articles of furniture. There were probably small figures carved in ivory, a branch of art in which we see in modern times some excellent specimens. The colossal statue of Ceres (c. 49) held in the hand a figure of Victory. We often see such representations on coins.

47. *judiciali jure*] Lambinus found a difficulty in 'judiciali,' and he proposed to omit it, or to transpose the word and make

tabellam feretis? Dicunt legati Melitenses publice spoliatum templum esse Junonis; nihil istum in religiosissimo fano reliquisse, quem in locum classes hostium saepe accesserint, ubi piratae fere quotannis hiemare soleant; quod neque praedo violaverit ante, neque unquam hostis attigerit, id ab uno isto sic spoliatum esse ut nihil omnino sit relictum. Hic nunc iste reus, aut ego accusator, aut hoc judicium appellabitur? Criminibus enim coarguitur aut suspicionibus in judicium vocatur. Dii ablati, fana vexata, nudatae urbes reperiuntur: earum autem rerum nullam sibi iste neque infitiandi rationem neque defendendi facultatem reliquit: omnibus in rebus coarguitur a me, convincitur a testibus, urgetur confessione sua, manifestis in maleficiis tenetur, et manet etiam ac tacitus facta mecum sua recognoscit.

Nimium mihi diu videor in uno genere versari criminum. Sentio, judices, occurrendum esse satietati aurium animorumque vestrorum. Quamobrem multa praetermittam: ad ea autem, quae dicturus sum, reficite vos, quaeso, judices, per deos immortales eos ipsos de quorum religione jamdiu dicimus, dum id ejus facinus commemoro et profero quo provincia tota commota est. De quo si paulo altius ordiri ac repetere memoriam religionis videbor, ignoscite: rei magnitudo me breviter perstringere atrocitatem criminis non sinit.

XLVIII. Vetus est haec opinio, judices, quae constat ex antiquissimis Graecorum literis ac monumentis, insulam Siciliam totam esse Cereri et Liberae consecratam. Hoc quum ceterae gentes sic arbitrantur, tum ipsis Siculis ita persuasum est ut in animis eorum insitum atque innatum esse videatur. Nam et natas esse has in iis

it agree with 'tabellam' (see Divin. c. 7). Zumpt thinks the text is right, for there is, he says, another *jus* according to which Cicero thinks that such a plunderer should be treated, the *jus belli*, to which is opposed that *judiciale jus* which is displayed in Judicia. Halm has taken Cobet's emendation 'sociali,' and he refers to 'judicio sociali,' Lib. 2. c. 6. There is no reason why a Roman could not say 'judiciale jus,' as he said 'Pontificium jus' and other like things.

aut suspicionibus] 'haud suspicionibus' Franc., which Graevius accepted and so spoiled the sense. Cicero is speaking ironically in this sentence. After the question 'Hic nunc . . appellabitur?' he adds, 'Why I suppose he is convicted on (bare) charges, or brought to trial on suspicion (only).' But he adds, 'Deities carried off, temples attacked, cities stripped are proven facts.'

earum autem . . . infitiandi rationem] Halm says that the genitive depends not on 'infitiandi,' but on 'infitiandi rationem,' which stands for 'infitiatio.' It certainly would not depend on 'infitiandi' if 'rationem' were not there, nor would 'infitiandi' be where it is without 'rationem' or some equivalent word. But it is a bad explanation to say that two words stand for one, which does not express what the two express. See Caesar (B. G. iii. 8), "Ab his fit initium retinendi Silii atque Velanii," and Schneider's note.

48. *Liberae*] Hotmann refers to the passage of Cicero, De Natura Deorum (ii. 26), "Terrena autem vis omnis atque natura Diti patri dedicata est," &c.

has in iis] Here Jordan has 'has in

locis deas et fruges in ea terra primum repertas arbitrantur, et raptam esse Liberam, quam eandem Proserpinam vocant, ex Hennensium nemore, qui locus, quod in media est insula situs, umbilicus Siciliae nominatur. Quam quum investigare et conquirere Ceres vellet, dicitur inflammasse taedas iis ignibus qui ex Aetnae vertice erumpunt, quas sibi quum ipsa praeferret, orbem omnium peragrasse terrarum. Henna autem, ubi ea quae dico gesta esse

his,' contrary to his practice; and incorrectly.

fruges . . repertas]

"Prima Ceres docuit turgescere semen in agris,
Falce coloratas subsecuitque comas.
Prima jugo tauros supponere colla coegit,
Et veterem curvo dente revellit humum."—Ovid, Am. iii. El. 10.

And again,

"Prima Ceres homini ad meliora alimenta vocato
Mutavit glandes utiliore cibo."
Fasti, iv. 401.

There is a paper in the Journal of the Royal Agricultural Society of England, 1854, by M. Esprit Fabre of Agde, in which he reports his experiments on the cultivation of the Aegilops ovata, the grains of which even in its wild state gave rise to the variety called Triticoides. Professor Duval in a note at the end of the paper says: "The necessary inference is that some if not all cultivated Tritica are peculiar forms of Aegilops, and ought to be regarded as races of this species. If this be admitted, it is easy to reconcile the accounts given of the origin of wheat. It has been said both in ancient and in modern times that wheat was wild in Babylonia, Persia, and Sicily. In all these countries Aegilops is common, and it is not surprising that some of its species may have accidentally acquired a wheat-like form, and have afterwards been improved and propagated by cultivation."

umbilicus] So the Greeks used the word ὀμφαλός, and applied it to Delphi, Eurip. Med. v. 666:

τί δ' ὀμφαλὸν γῆς θεσπιῳδὸν ἐστάλης;

iis ignibus]

"Alta jacet vasti super ora Typhoeos Aetne,
Cujus anhelatis ignibus ardet humus.
Illic accendit geminas pro lampade pinus:
Hinc Cereris sacris nunc quoque taeda datur."—Ovid, Fasti, iv. 491.

quas sibi quum . . peragrasse] This passage may perhaps be compared with the passage 'Siculos sane . . non venisse.' (See the note, Act. i. c. 9.) It is an instance of the use of 'qui . . quum,' which is very different from the usage of our language. It differs from other passages in which 'qui . . quum' occur, in this, that 'dicitur inflammasse' is connected with 'peragrasse,' and the usage of the Latin language in this case neither requires nor admits the conjunction 'and' between the two infinitive verbs. See c. 58.

Henna] Cicero's descriptions of places are generally very clear. He had an exact eye. He marks the site of Henna in such a way that it cannot be mistaken. (Comp. Livy, 24. c. 37.) Strabo (vi. p. 272, ed. Cas.) speaks of the flowers about Henna, and the legend of the girl who was plucking them when she was carried off by 'gloomy Dis.' The place is described, and the story is told by a great master in this kind (Ovid, Met. v. 385, &c.):

"Haud procul Hennaeis locus est a moenibus altae,
Nomine Pergus, aquae—
Silva coronat aquas, cingens latus omne, suisque
Frondibus ut velo Phoebeos submovet ictus.
Frigora dant rami, Tyrios humus humida flores.
Perpetuum ver est. Quo dum Proserpina luco
Ludit, et aut violas aut candida lilia carpit," &c.

He has also the story in his Fasti (iv. 419, &c.) of the rape of Proserpine, told in a way that a painter might picture, if he were a master of his art, as the poet is. An ancient artist has represented the rape of Proserpine. The god has his bride in the chariot, and is already at the entrance of the chasm which leads to his subterranean kingdom. Mercury leads the horses, which are well represented as moving with equal speed. But the artist also represents the wheels as seen obliquely and therefore as

memorantur, est loco perexcelso atque edito, quo in summo est aequata agri planities et aquae perennes; tota vero ab omni aditu circumcisa atque directa est: quam circa lacus lucique sunt plurimi atque laetissimi flores omni tempore anni, locus ut ipse raptum illum virginis quem jam a pueris accepimus declarare videatur. Etenim prope est spelunca quaedam conversa ad aquilonem, infinita altitudine, qua Ditem patrem ferunt repente cum curru exstitisse, abreptamque ex eo loco virginem secum asportasse, et subito non longe a Syracusis penetrasse sub terras, lacumque in eo loco repente exstitisse; ubi usque ad hoc tempus Syracusani festos dies anniversarios agunt celeberrimo virorum mulierumque conventu.

XLIX. Propter hujus opinionis vetustatem, quod horum in his locis vestigia ac prope incunabula reperiuntur deorum, mira quaedam tota Sicilia privatim ac publice religio est Cereris Hennensis. Etenim multa saepe prodigia vim ejus numenque declarant: multis saepe in difficillimis rebus praesens auxilium ejus oblatum est, ut haec insula ab ea non solum diligi sed etiam incoli custodirique videatur. Nec solum Siculi, verum etiam ceterae gentes nationesque Hennensem Cererem maxime colunt. Etenim si Atheniensium sacra summa cupiditate expetuntur, ad quos Ceres in illo errore venisse dicitur frugesque attulisse, quantam esse religionem convenit eorum apud quos eam natam esse et fruges invenisse constat? Itaque apud patres nostros atroci ac difficili rei publicae

of oval form, and by also placing them a little out of the perpendicular he has suggested the notion of falling, and consequently of movement (Lessing).

circumcisa atque directa] 'Circumcisus' is used by Cicero, De Re Pub. ii. 6, and by Caesar, B. G. vii. 36. 'Directa' is the reading of R 3, λ, Lg. 29. The dett. have 'direpta.' There is no authority for 'dirempta.' Zumpt compares Caesar, B. C. i. 45, "praeruptus locus erat omni ex parte directus;" and the description of Henna by Diodorus (v. 3), who was a native of Sicily. He says that "the place at the summit is level and perfectly well watered, but all round lofty and on every side abrupt with precipices; and it is supposed to lie in the middle of the whole island, wherefore it is called the navel of Sicily by some." The passage by which father Dis ascended to carry off his flower-gathering bride, is a large cave, with an opening into the earth turned to the north. There is a very particular description of the spot in the "Lexicon Topographicum Siculum . . studio et labore S. T. D. D. Vitim. Amico et Statella ordinis S. Benedicti, &c. Panormi M.DCC.LVII." From the north side of the plateau of Henna there is a view of Aetna.

The place where the god descended with his prize is the fountain Cyane near Syracuse, "at which," says Diodorus (v. 4), "the Syracusans annually celebrate a splendid festival."

49. *horum in his*] 'horum in iis' Klotz, Halm, a variation that is perpetually recurring.

Atheniensium sacra] The ceremonies of Ceres, and more particularly the 'mysteria' of Eleusis. The Athenians received Ceres very kindly when she was traversing the world in search of her lost daughter, and they were rewarded with the precious gift of corn next after the Sicilians (Diod. v. 4).

tempore, quum Ti. Graccho occiso magnorum periculorum metus ex ostentis portenderetur, P. Mucio L. Calpurnio consulibus aditum est ad libros Sibyllinos, ex quibus inventum est Cererem antiquissimam placari oportere. Tum ex amplissimo collegio decemvirali sacerdotes populi Romani, quum esset in urbe nostra Cereris pulcherrimum et magnificentissimum templum, tamen usque Hennam profecti sunt. Tanta enim erat auctoritas et vetustas illius religionis ut, quum illuc irent, non ad aedem Cereris sed ad ipsam Cererem proficisci viderentur. Non obtundam diutius; et enim jamdudum vereor, ne oratio mea aliena ab judiciorum ratione et a quotidiana dicendi consuetudine esse videatur. Hoc dico, hanc ipsam Cererem, antiquissimam, religiosissimam, principem omnium sacrorum quae apud omnes gentes nationesque fiunt, a C. Verre ex suis templis ac sedibus esse sublatam. Qui accessistis Hennam vidistis simulacrum Cereris e marmore et in altero templo Liberae. Sunt ea perampla atque praeclara, sed non ita antiqua. Ex aere fuit quoddam modica amplitudine ac singulari opere, cum facibus, perantiquum, omnium illorum quae sunt in eo fano multo antiquissimum. Id sustulit; ac tamen eo contentus non fuit. Ante aedem Cereris in aperto ac propatulo loco signa duo sunt, Cereris unum, alterum Triptolemi, pulcherrima ac perampla. His pulchritudo periculo, amplitudo saluti fuit, quod eorum demolitio atque asportatio perdifficilis videbatur. Insistebat in manu Cereris dextra simulacrum pulcherrime factum Victoriae. Hoc iste e signo Cereris avellendum asportandumque curavit.

Ti. Graccho] The tribune Ti. Gracchus, who lost his life at Rome, B.C. 133, in a riot, or whatever name we ought to give to the tumult, led by P. Scipio Nasica. Plutarch (Ti. Gracchus, c. 19) tells the story; but he says nothing of the Sibylline books and of the mission to Henna.

collegio decemvirali] This is the 'collegium' entitled 'decemviri sacris faciundis,' who had the care of the Libri Sibyllini and the power of interpreting them. The technical expressions are 'adire' or 'adire ad libros Sibyllinos' or 'inspicere.' The keepers of the books were originally two, then ten, and then fifteen. The increase from ten to fifteen is said to have been the Dictator Sulla's work.

Non obtundam diutius;] The old editions and the inferior MSS. and even Lg. 29 add 'aures vestras.' In Lib. 3. c. 67 there is 'obtuderunt aures,' in the letter of Timarchides. Zumpt says that 'obtundere,' in other passages of Cicero, does not occur without its accusative, which fact is in favour of the words being kept. The word is used absolutely in Terence. As to the excuse, Zumpt compares Pro Arch. c. 2.

non ita antiqua.] See Lib. 1. c. 18.

dextra simulacrum] In his larger edition Zumpt has 'grande' between 'dextra' and 'simulacrum,' on the authority of 'Guelff. et Harn. coll.' Klotz also and Iordan have 'grande.' Iordan says that the codd. dett. omit 'grande,' and they have done right. The objection to 'grande' is obvious, and is hardly removed by the consideration that the statue of Ceres was colossal. Most probably the statue of Ceres was in a sitting posture. The size of the figure in the hand would depend on the position of the hand, whether it was outstretched, or rested on the lap. But the usual attitude probably was that of the outstretched hand, in which case the figure

L. Qui tandem istius animus est nunc in recordatione scelerum suorum, quum ego ipse in commemoratione eorum non solum animo commovear verum etiam corpore perhorrescam? Venit enim mihi fani, loci, religionis illius in mentem: versantur ante oculos omnia: dies ille, quo ego Hennam quum venissem, praesto mihi sacerdotes Cereris cum infulis ac verbenis fuerunt: contio conventusque civium, in quo ego quum loquerer, tanti gemitus fletusque fiebant ut acerbissimus tota urbe luctus versari videretur. Non illi decumarum imperia, non bonorum direptiones, non iniqua judicia, non importunas istius libidines, non vim, non contumelias quibus vexati oppressique erant conquerebantur: Cereris nomen, sacrorum vetustatem, fani religionem istius sceleratissimi atque audacissimi supplicio expiari volebant: omnia se cetera pati ac negligere dicebant. Hic dolor erat tantus ut Verres alter Orcus venisse Hennam et non Proserpinam asportasse sed ipsam abripuisse Cererem videretur. Etenim urbs illa non urbs videtur sed fanum Cereris esse: habitare apud sese Cererem Hennenses arbitrantur; ut mihi non cives illius civitatis, sed omnes sacerdotes, omnes accolae atque antistites Cereris esse videantur. Henna tu simulacrum Cereris tollere audebas? Henna tu de manu Cereris Victoriam deripere et deam deae detrahere conatus es? quorum nihil violare, nihil attingere ausi sunt, in quibus erant omnia quae sceleri propiora sunt quam religioni. Tenuerunt enim P. Popillio P. Rupilio consulibus illum locum servi, fugitivi, barbari, hostes: sed neque tam

held in it could not be large. On a medal of Nerva, which has the legend ROMA RENASCENS, there is a female figure seated in a chair, with the right arm stretched out, and holding a small figure in the hand. On a medal of Vespasian, with the legend ANNONA AVG, there is a standing figure, with a cornucopiae in the left hand, and a small figure in the right hand, the arm of the right hand being stretched out from the elbow. The statue of Triptolemus was also colossal. 'Twas he who first ploughed the Rharian plain, and transmitted to his countrymen the 'Cerealia dona' (Ovid, Fasti, iv. 549; Pausanias, i. 14 and 38).

50. *Venit enim mihi fani,*] See Divin. c. 13.

contio] R. Orelli has the false form 'concio.'

vexati oppressique] *Vulgo, operti oppressique* (Zumpt). R 3 A have 'vexati' in place of 'operti.'

Henna tu] In both places the reading was 'Hennae' until Ernesti changed it to 'Henna' in the first instance; but he retained 'Hennae' in the second place; and Klotz does also. See c. 43. The reading is 'Henna' in both places R 3 A: "*Ennae*, dett. [sine *tu*, ut videtur]" (Iordan).

deripere] 'eripere' R 3, codd. Lbi. Iordan.

P. Popillio &c.] They were the consuls of B.C. 132, during the first Servile war in Sicily. The second Servile war was terminated by M'. Aquillius, B.C. 99. (See Lib. 5.) In the first Servile war, the slaves held Tauromenium and Henna (Orosius, v. 9). The history of their leader Eunus is told by Diodorus (Excerpt. Phot. Lib. 34). These slaves had good reason for rising, and they showed their character in a better way than by respect to Ceres. They protected the daughter of the tyrant master Damophilus of Henna and of his infamous wife Megallis; and, while they punished the master and mistress according to their merits, they sent the innocent young woman safe to Catina. (See also Strabo, p. 272).

servi illi dominorum quam tu libidinum; neque tam fugitivi illi a dominis quam tu ab jure et ab legibus; neque tam barbari lingua et natione illi quam tu natura et moribus; neque tam illi hostes hominibus quam tu diis immortalibus. Quae deprecatio est igitur ei reliqua qui indignitate servos, temeritate fugitivos, scelere barbaros, crudelitate hostes vicerit?

LI. Audistis Theodorum et Numenium et Nicasionem legatos Hennenses publice dicere sese a suis civibus haec habere mandata, ut Verrem adirent et eum simulacrum Cereris et Victoriae reposcerent: id si impetrassent, tum ut morem veterem Hennensium conservarent, publice in eum, tametsi vexasset Siciliam, tamen quoniam haec a majoribus instituta accepissent testimonium ne quod dicerent: sin autem ea non reddidisset, tum ut in judicio adessent, tum ut de ejus injuriis judices docerent, sed maxime de religione quererentur. Quas illorum querimonias nolite, per deos immortales, aspernari; nolite contemnere ac negligere, judices. Aguntur injuriae sociorum: agitur vis legum: agitur existimatio veritasque judiciorum. Quae sunt omnia permagna, verum illud maximum: tanta religione obstricta tota provincia est, tanta superstitio ex istius facto mentes omnium Siculorum occupavit, ut quae-

51. *instituta*] The common reading is 'constituta,' which Hotmann would have altered to 'instituta' if he could have found MS. authority. But R 3, λ, Lg. 29 have 'instituta,' and it is the word used in such cases. The old reading 'judicio adessent,' which Orelli has retained, was corrected by Lambinus. 'Adesse' with a dative means 'to be present as a helper.' See Lib. 2. c. 29; Lib. 4. c. 36.

Aguntur injuriae] This word 'agere' is a word of the most general use in the Latin language. It means here 'the wrongs of the allies are in question.' There is a like passage in Horace, 1 Ep. xviii. 84:

"Nam tua res agitur paries quum proximus ardet."

Zumpt observes that 'aguntur injuriae' may create a difficulty; and he adds "nam quantum scio, *agi* dicitur id, quod ne pereat periculum est." The old editions have 'jus legum.' (See De Domo, c. 15, note, Vol. iii.) The difference between 'uis' and 'ius' is so slight, that such a mistake in the MSS. may easily happen. Zumpt is inclined to write 'severitas' in place of 'veritas;' and he refers to Act. i. c. 1, where he has written 'religionem severitatemque,' according to the conjecture of Manutius, but against all the MSS. except one. In this passage however he retains 'veritas,' and in Lib. 3. c. 69 he has 'veritate judiciorum.' There seems no doubt that 'veritas judiciorum' is Latin. In the passage in Act. i. c. 1 there is more excuse for conjecture, as the words 'severe ac religione' are used in the first part of the sentence.

superstitio] Cicero has defined the word (De Nat. Deorum, i. 42): "Nisi forte Diagoram aut Theodorum, qui omnino deos esse negabant, censes superstitiosos esse potuisse. Ego ne Protagoram quidem; cui neutrum licuerit nec esse deos nec non esse. Horum enim sententiae omnium non modo superstitionem tollunt, in qua inest timor inanis deorum, sed etiam religionem quae deorum pio cultu continetur," &c.

The Romans distinguished 'superstitio' from 'religio' (De Nat. Deorum, ii. 28): "non enim philosophi solum verum etiam majores nostri superstitionem a religione separaverunt." The word manifestly contains the same elements as 'superstes,' of which the crude form is 'superstit.' [illegible] Cicero assigns an absurd reason for the application of the word. Lactantius (iv. 28), quoted by Forcellini, gives a better reason, though it may not be the true one. Every

cunque accidant publice privatimque incommoda propter eam causam sceleris istius evenire videantur. Audistis Centuripinos, Agyrinenses, Catinenses, Aetnenses, Herbitenses, compluresque alios publice dicere, quae solitudo in agris esset, quae vastitas, quae fuga aratorum, quam deserta, quam inculta, quam relicta omnia. Ea tametsi multis istius et variis injuriis acciderunt, tamen haec una causa in opinione Siculorum plurimum valet, quod Cerere violata omnes cultus fructusque Cereris in his locis interisse arbitrantur. Medemini religioni sociorum, judices: conservate vestram. Neque enim haec externa vobis est religio neque aliena. Quod si esset, si suscipere eam nolletis, tamen in eo qui violasset sancire vos velle oporteret. Nunc vero in communi omnium gentium religione, inque his sacris, quae majores nostri ab exteris nationibus ascita atque arcessita coluerunt, quae sacra, ut erant re vera, sic appellari Graeca voluerunt, negligentes ac dissoluti, si cupiamus esse, qui possumus?

LII. Unius etiam urbis, omnium pulcherrimae atque ornatissimae, Syracusarum direptionem commemorabo et in medium pro-

nation does not distinguish superstition from religion; for the distinction implies a cultivated understanding and an exercise of the reason. Those who distinguish superstition and religion may call the religion of those who do not make the distinction by the name of superstition; but they cannot properly call the religion of those who do make the distinction by the name of superstition. We cannot translate the Latin word 'religio' by the English word 'superstition,' even if we think that the Roman 'religio' was superstition. Lucretius may have used 'religio' as we would use superstition now, when he said (i. 63):

"Humana ante oculos foede quum vita jaceret
In terris oppressa gravi sub religione;"

for he made no distinction between religion and superstition.

publice privatimque] In his minor edition Zumpt has 'publice vel privatim,' which is the common reading. The objection to it is that a single 'vel' is not used in this manner by Cicero, but is used for the purpose of giving more emphasis to a word, or with the addition of 'potius,' or 'dicam,' or 'verius dicam,' for the purpose of correcting something that has been said, or stating it more explicitly (Zumpt).

propter eam causam &c.] The common reading, says Zumpt, hitherto has been 'propter eam causam scelere istius.' There is obviously something wrong in this, and it has been proposed to omit 'scelere istius,' or to omit 'propter eam causam.' But the reading in the text removes all difficulty, and has the authority of R 3, λ. The literal translation is 'on account of that matter of his wickedness,' but the meaning is 'through his crime, which is the cause.' This use of 'causa' with a genitive is defended by Zumpt and Madvig; but it needs no defence, for those who have read Latin authors with care may find plenty of examples. In Lib. 5. c. 9 there is 'sine causa quaestus,' which means 'unless he had the motive or object of gain;' though the word 'causa' has not the same sense as here. In this last passage 'causa' denotes the end or object of an act, a thing future. Here it refers to a thing past, as the antecedent of another thing. The word has both these senses in legal language, and is explained by Unterholzner, Lehre des Römischen Rechts von Schuldverhältnissen, i. p. 67.

inque his sacris,] 'inque iis sacris' Klotz.

sic appellari Graeca] Cicero says the same in the oration Pro Balbo, c. 24, where he is speaking of the 'Sacra Cereris:' "Quae quum essent assumpta de Graecia, et per Graecas curata semper sunt sacerdotes et Graeca omnia nominata."

feram, judices, ut aliquando totam hujus generis orationem concludam atque definiam. Nemo fere vestrum est quin, quemadmodum captae sint a M. Marcello Syracusae, saepe audierit, nonnunquam etiam in annalibus legerit. Conferte hanc pacem cum illo bello, hujus praetoris adventum cum illius imperatoris victoria, hujus cohortem impuram cum illius exercitu invicto, hujus libidines cum illius continentia; ab illo qui cepit conditas, ab hoc qui constitutas accepit, captas dicetis Syracusas. Ac jam illa omitto quae disperse a me multis in locis dicentur ac dicta sunt, forum Syracusanorum, quod introitu Marcelli purum caede servatum est, id adventu Verris Siculorum innocentium sanguine redundasse; portum Syracusanorum qui tum et nostris classibus et Karthaginiensium clausus fuisset, eum isto praetore Cilicum myoparoni praedonibusque patuisse. Mitto adhibitam vim ingenuis, matresfamilias violatas, quae tum in urbe capta commissa non sunt neque odio hostili neque licentia militari neque more belli neque jure victoriae: mitto, inquam, haec omnia, quae ab isto per triennium perfecta sunt: ea quae conjuncta cum illis rebus sunt de quibus antea dixi cognoscite. Urbem Syracusas maximam esse Graecarum,

52. *M. Marcello*] See Lib. 2. c. 2, and Livy 25. c. 31, 26. c. 30, &c.; and also Plutarch, Marcellus, c. 19.

annalibus] Cicero refers to the Roman historians who wrote Annales, which treated of Roman affairs. The oldest of these Roman prose writers were Q. Fabius Pictor and L. Cincius Alimentus. Livy refers to these old writers in the same terms that Cicero uses. He has (iv. 7) the expression 'in annalibus priscis;' and (vii. 9) 'in vetustioribus annalibus;' and (iii. 23) 'apud vetustiores scriptores.' Some of these old writers treated of Roman affairs from the origin of the city to their own time. Others treated of particular periods, as, for instance, P. Sempronius Asellio, who served under Scipio Africanus, wrote the history of what he saw (Gellius, ii. 13). The Roman literature was rich in this class of writing. When Cicero refers to the Annales of the conquest of Syracuse, he may perhaps refer to writers contemporary with those events. He would not probably speak of the historical works of any of his contemporaries as Annales. Thus he speaks of L. Cornelius Sisenna, one of the friends of Verres (Lib. 2. c. 45), as a writer of Historia (Brutus, c. 64): "hujus omnis facultas ex historia ipsius perspici potest, quae quum facile omnes vincat superiores, tum indicat tamen, quantum absit a summo, quamque genus hoc scriptionis nondum sit satis Latinis literis illustratum."

Conferte hanc pacem] Cicero (Orat. 50, §167) refers to this passage when he is speaking of 'numerus:' "nos etiam in hoc genere frequentes ut illa sunt in quarto accusationis: Conferte," &c. This, and another passage already referred to (Lib. 2. c. 1), show that Cicero merely numbered the books of his Accusatio. The titles, De Signis, and so forth, are due to somebody else.

adventu Verris] The whole of this passage is laboured 'oratorie,' with more regard to effect than to truth. It was not on the first occasion of Verres entering the city that all this happened, but in the third year of his government. Nor is it true, Zumpt observes, that the Carthaginian fleet did not enter the port, for it went in and out in spite of the Romans (Liv. xxv. c. 25).

Karthaginiensium] 'Kartaginensium' R, which ought to be the form.

Syracusas] The ancient descriptions of Syracuse are in Livy, xxv. 24; Strabo, 270; Thucydides, Lib. vi.; and this passage of Cicero. The best modern description is Leake's Plan of Syracuse and Topographical and Historical Notes on Syracuse, Transactions of the Royal Society of Literature, Second Series, vol. iii., 1850. The

pulcherrimam omnium, saepe audistis. Est, judices, ita ut dicitur. Nam et situ est quum munito, tum ex omni aditu vel terra vel mari praeclaro ad aspectum: et portus habet prope in aedificatione aspectuque urbis inclusos, qui quum diversos inter se aditus habeant, in exitu conjunguntur et confluunt. Eorum conjunctione pars oppidi, quae appellatur Insula, mari disjuncta angusto, ponte rursus adjungitur et continetur.

LIII. Ea tanta est urbs ut ex quatuor urbibus maximis constare dicatur: quarum una est ea quam dixi Insula, quae duobus portubus cincta in utriusque portus ostium aditumque projecta est; in qua domus est quae Hieronis regis fuit, qua praetores uti solent. In ea sunt aedes sacrae complures, sed duae quae longe ceteris antecellunt, una Dianae, et altera, quae fuit ante istius adventum ornatissima, Minervae. In hac insula extrema est fons aquae dulcis, cui nomen Arethusa est, incredibili magnitudine, plenissi-

topography of the place has nothing to do with Cicero's case, and the passage may be considered merely an embellishment.

The common reading is 'pulcherrimamque,' which, as Zumpt observes, would limit the superiority of Syracuse in beauty to the Greek cities. But, if Syracuse was the finest of Greek cities, we may suppose that it was the finest of all cities then existing. Rome certainly, in Cicero's time, could not be compared with it. However, there is good authority for omitting the 'que,' and the remark will then be general, as it is at the beginning of c. 52. Hotmann thought that 'Graecarum urbium' ought to be placed, in c. 52, between the words 'omnium' and 'pulcherrimae.' Zumpt settles the matter by a quotation from the De Re Publica, iii. 31: "Urbs illa praeclara, quam ait Timaeus Graecarum maximam, omnium autem esse pulcherrimam."

ex omni aditu] 'on whatever side you approach.' See Caesar, B. G. ii. 29, 'ex omnibus in circuitu partibus.'

53. *Insula,*] The island is Ortygia, the original city. Cicero speaks of the two ports, the larger and the smaller, which may be considered as united in the more remote part (exitu) from the sea by the narrow channel which separated the island from the main land. In the time of Thucydides the island was united to the main land by a mole. Afterwards the mole was cut through, and a bridge was thrown across; and so it was when Strabo saw it (p. 270, ed. Cas.). The channel was again filled up, and modern Syracuse stands on the island and on the isthmus.

quae . . . antecellunt,] Zumpt, Klotz, and Iordan have 'antecellant.' Zumpt remarks on 'antecellant:' "sic prorsus Erfurt. Lag. 29. Havn. coll. nec multum absunt Leid. et Guelf. 2. *antecedant*, alter autem 1 *antecedunt*. Sed hoc verbum male positum hoc sensu non placet. Conjunctivum autem nemo opinor abjiciet a libris oblatum, quoniam inest judicii significatio. Vulgo *antecellunt*." If Cicero means to say that these two temples surpassed all others, there is no other way of expressing it except by the indicative. The remark of Zumpt seems to me founded on a complete misconception. If he meant to say 'two temples, being superior to all the rest,' or 'because they are superior to all the rest, are held in the greatest honour,' he would say 'duae quae longe ceteris antecellant maximo sunt in honore,' as he does in other like cases. I should reject 'antecellant' with perfect confidence, if every MS. had it. But we cannot trust every collator's eyes for distinguishing between *a* and *u*, nor trust every copyist. "'Antecellant' R E Lg. 29; 'antecedant' G 2 Ld; 'antecedunt' G 1; 'antecellunt' dett. Or." (Iordan.)

Minervae.] "The columns of this temple are Doric, with cyathiform capitals; the intercolumniations have been walled up, an overloaded façade has been added, and it is now become the cathedral; having thus been a place of public worship upwards of two thousand five hundred years" (Smyth's Sicily, p. 170).

Arethusa] On the margin of this island (in hac insula extrema) was the noted foun-

mus piscium, qui fluctu totus operiretur, nisi munitione ac mole lapidum disjunctus esset a mari. Altera autem est urbs Syracusis, cui nomen Achradina est; in qua forum maximum, pulcherrimae porticus, ornatissimum prytanium, amplissima est curia, templumque egregium Jovis Olympii: ceterae urbis partes una lata via

tain of Arethusa, now a much diminished source, in which the nymphs of modern Syracuse wash their dirty linen. Pietro della Valle (Let. 15, P. iii.) saw them at work, and others have seen them.

The Greeks had a legend for every striking natural phenomenon, and they told how the nymph Arethusa, being pursued by the Alpheus, was changed into a fountain by Diana, to save her from the amorous river-god (Ovid, Met. v. 639):

"Delia rumpit humum. Caecis ego mersa cavernis
Advehor Ortygiam; quae me cognomine divae
Grata meae superas eduxit prima sub auras."

The nymph changed into a fountain, plunged into the cavern, and emerged from the sea in the island of Ortygia.

Diodorus (v. 4) speaks of this fountain, and of its sacred fish, which were protected even to his time, the reign of Augustus. He observes that persons who had eaten of these fish, in times when the city was surrounded by an enemy, suffered from the deity for their daring irreverence. Strabo speaks of the Arethusa as "flowing into the sea, a very river at its source." It is much less copious now. Strabo refutes the story of the river Alpheus flowing under the sea, by serious arguments.

"At the distance of about eighty feet from this fountain (Arethusa), a copious spring, called L'Occhio della Zilica, and probably derived from the same source, rises from the bottom of the harbour (distinguishable only on very calm days) with such force, that it does not intermingle with the salt water until it gains the surface" (Smyth's Sicily, p. 171).

"Sic tibi quum fluctus subter labere Sicanos,
Doris amara suam non intermisceat undam."—Virg. Eclog. x. 4.

Perhaps some readers may not see the exact signification of 'extrema,' which I have explained by the translation. The same form occurs a little further on: 'quam ad summam,' 'on the top of which;' an expression that few readers will be liable to mistake. The other, 'in insula extrema,' 'on the outer side or margin,' is sometimes mistaken. The Greek has the same form in ἔσχατος, which contains the root ἐκ or ἐξ:

ἔστιν πόλις Κάνωβος ἐσχάτη χθονός.
Aesch. Prom. 848.

Canobus, on the margin of the sea.

prytanium,] The Greek πρυτανεῖον, a word of perhaps doubtful origin. Herodotus (vii. 197) observes that the Achaeans called their Prytaneium by the term Leiton (λήϊτον), which is as much as to say Publicum: but we have no modern equivalent. The Romans kept their perpetual fire burning in the temple of Vesta; the Greeks in their Prytaneium. But a Prytaneium was used, at Athens at least, for other purposes besides the conservation of the ever-burning fire: it was used for public entertainments to foreign ambassadors; and it appears that a regular table was kept there for those to whom the state granted free commons.

Zumpt quotes Livy (xli. 20): "Cyzici in prytaneum, id est penetrale urbis, ubi publice quibus is honos datus est vescuntur;" and he refers to the note of Casaubon, Athenaeus, xv. c. 60, p. 700.

Cicero has not translated Prytaneium, for the Romans had not the thing. The Roman word Curia is the translation of the Greek βουλευτήριον, for it appears from c. 61, that it was the meeting-place of what he calls the Senatus (βουλή) of Syracuse. The official title of a Greek community was ἡ βουλὴ καὶ ὁ δῆμος, as of Rome it was Senatus Populusque Romanus (Lib. 4. c. 10).

Jovis Olympii: ceterae] The passage stands thus in Zumpt: 'Jovis Olympii, ceteraeque urbis partes, quae una," &c. He has added 'quae' from the best MSS., but it is not easy to explain. Zumpt, observes, if we retain the common reading, that is, if we do not accept the 'quae,' we cannot tell what to do with the 'que.' I cannot tell; and I have struck it out, and thus all becomes plain: 'the remaining parts of the city being divided by one broad continuous street, and many cross streets are occupied by private buildings.'—cae-

perpetua multisque transversis divisae privatis aedificiis continentur. Tertia est urbs quae, quod in ea parte Fortunae fanum antiquum fuit, Tycha nominata est, in qua gymnasium amplissimum est et complures aedes sacrae; coliturque ea pars et habitatur frequentissime. Quarta autem est quae, quia postrema coaedificata est, Neapolis nominatur; quam ad summam theatrum est maximum: praeterea duo templa sunt egregia, Cereris unum, alterum Liberae, signumque Apollinis, qui Temenites vocatur, pulcherrimum et maximum, quod iste si portare potuisset, non dubitasset auferre.

LIV. Nunc ad Marcellum revertar, ne haec a me sine causa commemorata esse videantur. Qui quum tam praeclaram urbem vi copiisque cepisset, non putavit ad laudem populi Romani hoc pertinere, hanc pulchritudinem ex qua praesertim periculi nihil ostenderetur delere et extinguere. Itaque aedificiis omnibus, publicis privatis, sacris profanis, sic pepercit quasi ad ea defendenda cum exercitu, non expugnanda venisset. In ornatu urbis habuit victoriae rationem, habuit humanitatis. Victoriae putabat esse multa Romam deportare quae ornamento urbi esse possent; humanitatis, non plane exspoliare urbem praesertim quam conservare voluisset. In hac partitione ornatus non plus victoria Marcelli populo Romano appetivit quam humanitas Syracusanis reservavit.

teraeque' R, 'partes quae' R 3 E λ. The dett. omit 'quae.' As to the meaning of 'perpetua,' see Act. i. c. 11, note.

Quarta autem est] 'Quarta autem est urbs' Orelli. '*Urbs* abest a bonis omnibus' (Zumpt).

Temenites] The name appears to be corrupted in all the MSS., but P. Manutius suggested that the corrupt reading 'Thesmotes' should be changed to 'Temenites.' The truth of the correction cannot be doubted, and R Lg. 29 have 'Temnites.' This very statue, Apollo Temenites, was brought to Rome in the time of Tiberius, to be placed in the library of a new temple (Sueton. Tiber. c. 74). Stephan. Byz. v. Τέμενος τόπος Σικελίας ὑπὸ ταῖς Ἐπιπολαῖς πρὸς ταῖς Συρακούσαις, οὗ οἰκήτωρ Τεμενίτης. Lambinus was the first who printed Temenites, and in a note he complains of the learned Adrian Tournebœuf (Turnebus) publishing the emendation as his own in his Adversaria. Finding this and other valuable discoveries appropriated by said Tournebœuf, Lambinus set about detecting the theft, and he discovered that the bibliopole used to send this Tournebœuf the sheets of Lambinus as they were printed. This bit of history is not out of place in the oration De Signis. I do not know if this distinguished scholar was also a thief. I give the story as Lambinus tells it. See Zumpt's note; and A. Turnebi Adversaria, p. 256, and In Pison. c. 39, note, Vol. iv.

54. *publicis privatis, &c.*] The passage was corrupted, as Graevius remarks, by those who inserted 'et' between 'publicis privatis,' and between 'sacris profanis.' Cicero, with his usual fulness of expression, makes a complete enumeration of all edifices, according to the Roman notion, 'public and private,' which is one division of 'res;' devoted to religion, and not devoted to religion, which is another division of 'res' (see Gaius, ii. 1, and Justin. Inst. i. tit. 1). See c. 32.

expugnanda] 'oppugnanda' Ld. Jordan. 'exoppugnanda,' R.

urbi] 'urbis' R 3 et codd. rel. noti.—In a fragment of Polybius, ix. 10, it is said that the Romans determined to carry all the most costly things from Syracuse to Rome, and to leave nothing.

Romam quae apportata sunt ad aedem Honoris et Virtutis itemque aliis in locis videmus. Nihil in aedibus, nihil in hortis posuit, nihil in suburbano: putavit, si urbis ornamenta domum suam non contulisset, domum suam ornamento urbi futuram. Syracusis autem permulta atque egregia reliquit: deum vero nullum violavit, nullum attigit. Conferte Verrem; non ut hominem cum homine comparetis, ne qua tali viro mortuo fiat injuria sed ut pacem cum bello, leges cum vi, forum et jurisdictionem cum ferro et armis, adventum et comitatum cum exercitu et victoria conferatis.

LV. Aedis Minervae est in Insula de qua ante dixi; quam Marcellus non attigit, quam plenam atque ornatam reliquit, quae ab isto sic spoliata atque direpta est non ut ab hoste aliquo, qui tamen in bello religionum et consuetudinis jura retineret, sed ut a barbaris praedonibus vexata esse videatur. Pugna erat equestris Agathocli regis in tabulis picta; his autem tabulis interiores templi parietes vestiebantur. Nihil erat ea pictura nobilius, nihil Syracusis quod magis visendum putaretur. Has tabulas M. Marcellus quum omnia victoria illa sua profana fecisset, tamen religione impeditus non attigit: iste, quum illa jam propter diuturnam

aedem Honoris &c.] An 'aedes' of Honor was outside the Porta Collina (Cic. De Leg. ii. 23). Cicero mentions both temples in the De Natura Deorum (ii. 23): "vides Virtutis templum, vides Honoris a M. Marcello renovatum, quod multis ante annis erat bello Ligustico a Q. Maximo dedicatum." There seems to be an error in 'Porta Collina.' See c. 55.

suburbano:] 'a residence near Rome.' The Romans used the word as a noun.

putavit, si urbis] Rightly explained by Hotmann: the absence of decoration in the house of Marcellus would be a proof of his integrity; and the character of the man would be an honour to the state.

adventum] This is a kind of technical word, or at least a word which, like many Roman words of common use, obtained also a particular signification. It is the 'advent,' or coming of the governor here (see Lib. 1. c. 19). The word appears in a like sense on Roman Imperial medals, as on one of Hadrianus, which has the legend ADVENTVS AVG. This medal belongs to the second year of Hadrian, or at least his second consulship, and commemorates his arrival at Rome from the East, where he was when Trajan died.

55. *Aedis*] Zumpt in his larger edition has 'aedis,' perhaps the genuine form of the nominative. 'Aedis' R, G 1 2.

quae ab isto . . videatur.] This is quoted by Gellius, ii. 6.

retineret,] Zumpt admires that all the better MSS. have 'contineret.' Klotz has 'contineret.' We must follow the worse here. Gellius has 'retineret.'

Agathocli] See the note on c. 2.

The history of this adventurer, who made himself a king, is chiefly told by Diodorus and Polybius. This picture appears to have been on panels of wood. There are many coins of Agathocles. One of them, a common bronze coin, has a female head with the legend ΣΩΤΕΙΡΑ, and on the reverse ΑΓΑΘΟΚΛΕΟΣ ΒΑΣΙΛΕΟΣ.

profana fecisset.] By the law of war they had become the property of the conquerors, and lost their sacred quality. See Macrob. Sat. iii. 9, on the 'evocatio.'

illa jam] 'Illa' refers to 'has tabulas.' Verres, by virtue of the long peace and fidelity of the Syracusans, had [illegible] these works of art as things consecrated to the service of religion. [illegible] has 'accepisset:' R 3 'cepisset,' which is a mistake.

pacem fidelitatemque populi Syracusani sacra religiosaque accepisset, omnes eas tabulas abstulit; parietes quorum ornatus tot saecula manserat, tot bella effugerat, nudos ac deformatos reliquit. Et Marcellus, qui si Syracusas cepisset duo templa se Romae dedicaturum voverat, id quod erat aedificaturus his rebus ornare quas ceperat noluit: Verres, qui non Honori neque Virtuti, quemadmodum ille, sed Veneri et Cupidini vota deberet, is Minervae templum spoliare conatus est. Ille deos deorum spoliis ornare noluit: hic ornamenta Minervae virginis in meretriciam domum transtulit. Viginti et septem praeterea tabulas pulcherrime pictas ex eadem aede sustulit, in quibus erant imagines Siciliae regum ac tyrannorum, quae non solum pictorum artificio delectabant sed etiam commemoratione hominum et cognitione formarum. Ac videte quanto taetrior hic tyrannus Syracusanis fuerit quam quisquam superiorum; quia illi tamen ornarunt templa deorum immortalium, hic etiam illorum monumenta atque ornamenta sustulit.

LVI. Jam vero quid ego de valvis illius templi commemorem? Vereor ne haec qui non viderint omnia me nimis augere atque

manserat, . . effugerat,] All the good MSS. have 'manserant . . . effugerant,' and of course 'ornatus' must then be taken for the plural.

voverat,] These temples of Honor and Virtus, built by Marcellus, before the Porta Capena, were adorned with the spoils of Syracuse, as Livy (xxv. 40) says. Zumpt observes, that he has not seen it remarked that Cicero has made a mistake, in saying that Marcellus made this vow during the siege of Syracuse; for Livy (xxvii. 25) says that he made this vow in his first consulship, B.C. 222, during the Gallic war, when he was before Clastidium. But P. Manutius has remarked on this discrepancy between Cicero and Livy. Becker, Handbuch, i. p. 509, has collected the passages which relate to these temples, which stood close together, but were separate buildings.

id] 'is id' R λ E G 1 2, and Iordan; 'id' G 1 et dett. 'Is' occurs in the second member of the sentence: 'Verres, qui . . . is,' and we might therefore conclude that it ought to stand in the first member also.

ornare . . noluit:] 'ornari—noluit' R E L.

Viginti et septem] We do not know the names of so many kings and tyrants of Syracuse; for Cicero seems to mean Syracuse, though he says 'of Sicily.' Syracuse had many political revolutions, and probably more kings and tyrants than have been recorded—

"sed ignotis perierunt mortibus."

quia] 'cum' Lagg. 'quam' R E, 'qui' Ld, 'quia' G 1 2 λ. Iordan has 'cum illi . . . ornarint.' E Lg. 29 have 'ornarent,' and G 2 Ld. 'ornaverunt.'

illorum monumenta] 'Illorum' refers to 'illi,' and is the reading of all the good MSS. The common reading is 'deorum' (Zumpt).—"*sustulit* libri meliores omnes inde a Stephaniano vetere" (Zumpt). The common reading is 'quum illi tamen ornarint—sustulerit.' Klotz has 'quum illi tamen ornarint . ., hic etiam deorum . . sustulit.' I prefer the reading of Zumpt. As to 'illorum,' it is obviously the reading which the sense requires. The tyrants (illi) ornamented the temples of the gods, but Verres took away even the memorials and decorations of the tyrants (illorum). As to the remainder of the sentence, I am not sure that Zumpt's reading is better than the common reading.

56. *non viderint*] G 1, Zumpt, 'viderunt' R, ett. Iordan has 'viderint.' The common reading is 'viderunt.' Zumpt observes, that as it is not certain persons, who had not seen these things, but all persons are meant who had not seen them, he considers the subjunctive to be necessary.

ornare arbitrentur; quod tamen nemo suspicari debet tam esse me cupidum ut tot viros primarios velim, praesertim ex judicum numero qui Syracusis fuerint, qui haec viderint, esse temeritati et mendacio meo conscios. Confirmare hoc liquido, judices, possum, valvas magnificentiores, ex auro atque ebore perfectiores, nullas unquam ullo [in] templo fuisse. Incredibile dictu est quam multi Graeci de harum valvarum pulchritudine scriptum reliquerint. Nimium forsitan haec illi mirentur atque efferant: esto; verumtamen honestius est rei publicae nostrae, judices, ea quae illis pulchra esse videantur imperatorem nostrum in bello reliquisse quam praetorem in pace abstulisse. Ex ebore diligentissime perfecta argumenta erant in valvis: ea detrahenda curavit omnia. Gorgonis os pulcherrimum cinctum anguibus revellit atque abstulit; et tamen indicavit se non solum artificio sed etiam pretio quaestuque duci. Nam bullas aureas omnes ex his valvis, quae

cupidum] This word means eager or passionate in any matter. Zumpt compares the expression 'cupidi testes' in the oration Pro Flacco, c. 8. Gruter refers to the Pro Caecina, c. 3. See also Phil. vi. 6. Graevius says of Lambinus, who started a difficulty about 'cupidum,' 'hallucinatur;' he quotes Cicero, Pro Fonteio, c. 6: "Potest igitur testibus judex non credere? Cupidis et iratis . . . non solum potest, sed etiam debet." Again, in a letter to Tiro (Ad Div. xvi. 11), "Nos agimus nihil cupide." In Lib. 3. c. 61, we have the phrase 'praetor cupidus existimationis bonae.' Poor Lambinus is overwhelmed with evidence against his hallucination.

'Quod tamen nemo,' &c. Cicero very frequently uses 'id,' 'illud,' 'hoc,' with reference to something that he is going to say. He uses 'quod' just in the same way, 'quod' being in fact a demonstrative in its original. No person can take 'quod' for what they call a conjunction here. 'Tamen' forbids that. Examples of this form of expression are common.

fuerint, . . viderint,] 'fuerunt . . . viderunt' G 2 Ld.

valvas . . auro &c.] 'Valvae' are doors which open inwards, as Garatoni explains by reference to Isidorus, xiii. 7; and 'fores' are those which open outwards (foras). I do not take this to be a true explanation.

A doorway and a door are things on which an architect can show his taste, and an artist his skill. Some of the great works of art, both of ancient and modern times, are doors and gates. Cicero says that many had written about these doors, and yet he does not mention the names of the artists. The 'argumenta' or 'subjects' were in gold and ivory. 'Argumentum' in this sense occurs in Lib. 2. c. 57. The word is used in the same sense by Virgil, Aen. vii. 791, where he describes the armour of Turnus:—

"Argumentum ingens et custos virginis Argus."

Servius, in his note on this passage of Virgil, quotes this passage of Cicero.

The palace of the sun had a splendid door of the same kind, Ovid, Met. ii. 4:—

"Argenti bifores radiabant lumine valvae.
Materiem superabat opus: nam Mulciber illic
Aequora caelarat medias cingentia terras
Signaque sex foribus dextris, totidemque sinistris."

But here Ovid calls the two parts of the doors 'fores.'

bullas] The heads of the nails, or fastenings, as Hotmann supposes, so called because they were like 'bullae' (see Lib. 2. c. 58, note). He refers to a passage in the Asinaria of Plautus, ii. 4. 20:

"Jussin' in splendorem dari bullas has foribus nostris."

There is a medal of Nero, on the reverse of which is the door of the temple of Janus, as we may conclude from the legend:—PACE · PR · TERRA · MARIQ · PARTA · IANVM CLVSIT. The door is divided into six panels by a vertical band in the middle, and

erant multae et graves, non dubitavit auferre; quarum iste non opere delectabatur sed pondere. Itaque ejusmodi valvas reliquit ut, quae olim ad ornandum templum erant maxime, nunc tantum ad claudendum factae esse videantur. Etiamne gramineas hastas —vidi enim vos in hoc nomine quum testis diceret commoveri, quod erat ejusmodi ut semel vidisse satis esset; in quibus neque manu factum quidquam, neque pulchritudo erat ulla, sed tantum magnitudo incredibilis, de qua vel audire satis esset, nimium videre plus quam semel—etiam id concupisti?

LVII. Nam Sappho, quae sublata de prytanio est, dat tibi

two transverse bands. In the vertical band there are two large 'bullae,' placed respectively at the height of the two cross bands; and in each panel there is a smaller 'bulla.' In the upper part of each of the central panels, which are larger than the panels above and below, and right above the 'bullae' of these central panels, there is the head of an animal, or whatever it may be, which seems to correspond to a door-handle, or the 'Gorgonis os' which Cicero describes.

gramineas hastas] Here the old commentators were entirely at fault, partly from an imperfect notion of the meaning of 'gramen,' partly from want of that kind of knowledge in which we have an advantage over them. Hotmann would have 'fraxineas.' The spear of Achilles was 'fraxinea.' As if there could be any thing surprising in the size of 'fraxinea hasta.' We might make one of a whole tree, if we chose. In this instance, Lambinus, whom Zumpt charges with being a servile follower of Hotmann, does not follow him; but he does not explain 'gramineus.' Graevius makes an absurd attempt at explanation. The reading is certain; and Servius (Aen. v. 287) refers to the passage: "Cicero de Hastis: *Bene etiamne gramineas hastas:* quia gramineum est ex gramine." So the passage stands in the edition of Virgil, by Masvicius; but the word 'Bene' is the remark of Servius, and should not be in italics. Hotmann, who quotes Servius, has it 'Cicero de signis,' &c., which is manifestly false; for Servius means to say that Cicero applies Virgil's word 'gramineum' (Gramineum in campum) to 'hastae.' But it does not appear that Servius knew what the passage in Cicero meant. Garatoni has explained the mystery. The 'gramineae hastae' are bamboos, a genus of grasses, as botanists term them. Some are thirty feet long, and even more; and as thick as a man's body for some height from the base. They are well known now, and there is no difficulty in the passage. These 'hastae' or canes must have been brought from India, or parts further East. I find no mention of African bamboos, technically so called; but it is probable enough that large canes may occur in some parts of North Africa; and there are also large reeds in Sicily. These great Indian canes were known to Ctesias (p. 248, ed. Bähr): *ὅτι ὁ Ἰνδὸς ποταμὸς ῥέων διὰ πεδίων καὶ δι' ὀρέων ῥεῖ· ἐν οἷς καὶ ὁ λεγόμενος Ἰνδικὸς κάλαμος φύεται. πάχος μὲν ὅσον δύο ἄνδρε περιοργυιωμένοι μόλις περιλάβοιεν· τὸ δὲ ὕψος ὅσον μυριοφόρου νεὼς ἱστός.* Ctesias has generally a foundation of truth, and a superstructure of lies. He adds, there are both larger and smaller, with the absurd remark, *οἵους εἰκὸς νὲ ὄρει μεγάλῳ.* Zumpt refers to Pliny (H. N. xvi. 65, ed. Harduin.), who says among other things: "arundini quidem Indicae arborea amplitudo: qualem vulgo in templis videmus." He also cites L. Ampelius, Liber Memorialis, c. 8 (Miracula Mundi), who says of the Minerva of Athens: "ipsa autem dea habet hastam de gramine." These 'hastae' were simply canes, for Cicero says, 'neque manu factum quidquam.' They were merely wondrous things, which a man may be satisfied with hearing of; to see them more than once would be too often. Nobody, except the stupid, go more than once to look at things simply because they are bigger than usual.

'Quod erant' Zumpt. The old editions and R 3, Lg. 29, have 'erat;' and also Klotz. 'Erat' agrees better with 'id concupisti.' Iordan has 'erant,' and says 'agitur autem de hastis gramineis.' The common reading is 'etiamne id concupisti;' but Zumpt observes that the omission of the 'ne' is usual in a continued interrogation, where the particle has once been used. He refers to Lib. 5. c. 47, and 58, near the beginning.

justam excusationem, prope ut concedendum atque ignoscendum esse videatur. Silanionis opus tam perfectum, tam elegans, tam elaboratum, quisquam non modo privatus sed populus potius haberet quam homo elegantissimus atque eruditissimus Verres? Nimirum contra dici nihil potest. Nostrum enim unusquisque, qui tam beati quam iste est non sumus, tam delicati esse non possumus, si quando aliquid istiusmodi videre volet, eat ad aedem Felicitatis, ad monumentum Catuli, in porticum Metelli; det operam ut admittatur in alicujus istorum Tusculanum; spectet forum ornatum, si quid iste suorum aedilibus commodarit: Verres haec habeat domi; Verres ornamentis fanorum atque oppidorum habeat plenam domum, villas refertas. Etiamne hujus operarii studia ac delicias, judices,

57. *Silanionis*] He was an Athenian artist of the age of Lysippus. (Plin. H. N. xxxiv. 8.) He made also a dying Jocasta and a statue of Corinna.

Verres, says Cicero, was almost excusable for taking the Sappho. It was a perfect work; and, besides, it was a woman.

Nimirum contra] This is the sarcastic answer to the question, the purport of which is, that nobody is fit to have such fine works as Verres. 'To be sure,' says Cicero, 'it is so, it can't be contradicted. Verres is the only man who ought to have such things.' 'Nimirum' means 'strange if it were not so.' Terence sometimes says 'Mirum ni,' &c. Andria, iii. 4, 19.

ad aedem Felicitatis,] See c. 2. This temple was built by L. Licinius Lucullus to commemorate his success in his Celtiberian campaign, B.C. 151, 150. But his campaign was a failure, and he ought to have been punished. After the end of the Achaean war (B.C. 146) Lucullus asked L. Mummius to lend him some of the statues which he had brought from Greece. Lucullus said he only wanted to decorate his temple with them till it was consecrated, and he would then return them. But Lucullus dedicated the statues with the temple, and then told Mummius that he might take them away if he chose. As the statues had become sacred things (res sacrae) by the consecration, Mummius could not take them back, unless, we may suppose, the college of Pontifices, which was the supreme court in matters of religion, should give him permission. But Mummius took no notice of the dirty trick, and so he got more credit than Lucullus who had dedicated the temple. (Strabo, viii. 381.)

The noble works of Praxiteles in this temple perished in a fire in the time of Claudius. (Pliny, H. N. xxxiv. 8. s. 19.) Fire has devoured of the great works of the Greeks more than time and barbarians have destroyed.

monumentum Catuli,] Not the Capitol, as Zumpt properly reminds us, but the temple of Fortuna which Catulus vowed in the Cimbric war (Plut. Marius, c. 26). Pliny (H. N. xxxiv. 19) speaks of it.

porticum Metelli;] Of Q. Metellus Macedonicus in the ninth 'regio' of the city (Plin. H. N. xxxiv. 14). It was built after his triumph over Macedonia, B.C. 146. On the place see Becker, Handbuch der Röm. Alterthüm. i. p. 608. Pliny says that the Porticus contained the statue of Cornelia, the mother of the Gracchi. Plutarch mentions a statue of Cornelia (C. Gracch. c. 4).

Tusculanum;] Some of the wealthy Romans had 'villae' at Tusculum (Frascati) adorned with sculptures. Cicero himself had one a few years later, which he embellished at great cost. He could hardly have had one now, or he would not here have used this expression. His progress in wealth, or expenditure, at least, was rapid, for a few years after this date he was spending at a great rate in adorning his Tusculanum. Strabo has a passage on Tusculum (p. 239, ed. Casaub.): he says that "Tusculum is adorned with plantations about it and houses, and particularly in the part that is turned towards Rome; for in these parts Tusculum is a fertile eminence, and well watered, and suitable for the most splendid palatial structures."

operarii] An 'operarius' is one of the class of 'operae,' the men with rough hands, those who do the real work of a country. It is explained by what follows. Verres was more fit to be a porter than the possessor of such treasures. The governor of

perferetis? qui ita natus, ita educatus est, ita factus et animo et corpore, ut multo appositior ad ferenda quam ad auferenda signa esse videatur. Atque haec Sappho sublata quantum desiderium sui reliquerit dici vix potest. Nam quum ipsa fuit egregie facta, tum epigramma Graecum pernobile incisum est in basi, quod iste eruditus homo et Graeculus, qui haec subtiliter judicat, qui solus intelligit, si unam literam Graecam scisset, certe non sustu-

Sicily, we may infer, was a strong-built, brawny fellow, and that is enough for Cicero's sarcasm. He was a thief and a fellow of no principle; but he had taste: that is clear.

The common reading is 'ad deferenda,' which does not express what Cicero means to say. Besides this, R 3 have 'ad ferenda,' which does express Cicero's meaning. 'Ferenda' expresses what has been expressed before by 'portare,' c. 53, 'si portare potuisset.'

epigramma Graecum] The word 'epigramma' is well understood in the Greek sense. It is something in verse, short and pertinent, which tells us in few words a great deal. The Greeks excelled in this style of composition, the highest style of all; for to express well in few words something that is worth remembering is a work of art. The term is as old as Herodotus, and the example is the simplest possible (Lib. vi. 58):

Ἀμφιτρύων μ' ἀνέθηκε νέων ἀπὸ Τηλεβοάων.

Herodotus (vii. 228) has other examples. The best is that on the Spartans who died at Thermopylae, which Cicero has translated, Tuscul. Disput. i. 42. There are many 'epigrammata' on Sappho. Why that of Plato should be selected as the one alluded to here (Zumpt), I don't know. It is in the Antholog. Brunck. 1. 171, and of Brodaeus, p. 135, and is the best of the set; if for no other reason, because it is the shortest:

Ἐννέα τὰς μούσας φασίν τινες· ὡς ὀλιγώρως·
Ἠνίδε καὶ Σαπφὼ Λεσβόθεν ἡ δεκάτη.

I conjecture that the 'epigramma' of the text was something more than this.

non sustulisset.] This is the common reading, and the MSS. and the editions offer no help, says Zumpt. All the MSS. have 'non sustulisset' (Iordan). Klotz keeps the common reading. Zumpt says of this 'non,' 'sententiam prorsus evertit,' and he must descend to conjecture. His conjecture, or rather that of Herelius, is 'una,' which he adopts, and Iordan also. Garatoni would simply strike out the 'non' One of the two things must be done, he says. Let us see if there is not a third. Let it stand, and see what it means. I don't take 'quod' to be governed, as they call it, by 'sustulisset.' That is the origin of the blunder. 'Quod' is used as it often is; it refers to 'unam literam Graecam.' Cicero might have simply said 'quod si iste unam . . . scisset;' and in fact he does say it, for he has only interposed certain words between 'quod' and 'si,' and instead of placing 'quod si' together, as he often does, he has separated them; but that does not alter the meaning. Cicero says this: 'The statue of Sappho was of excellent workmanship, and there was a very famous inscription cut on the pedestal; now this inscription, this scholar of yours and ape of the Greeks, he who is so excellent a judge of these matters, in fact the only judge, if he had understood a single Greek letter, he would not have carried off the statue. For now what is written on the bare pedestal tells us what was there, and shows that it has been taken away.' I admit that the objection against 'non' is very specious; almost convincing on the first impression. The inscription contained something which showed that there ought to be a statue above it. The inscription and the statue were parts of one whole. If then Verres had carried off the two together, there would have been the statue and the inscription entire; the integrity of the work would have been preserved. But if Verres kept the work entire, statue and inscription, he would have been betrayed; for the thing and the inscription, I assume, were appropriate to the place. At any rate, it was notorious where it had been; and, if kept entire, the evidence of the theft would have been perpetuated by the integrity of the work. Well; but he might have kept the statue and removed or destroyed the basis, as he did in another case (c. 35). True; he might have done so; nor does Cicero deny it. He simply says that, if he had under-

lisset. Nunc enim quod scriptum est inani in basi declarat quid fuerit, et id ablatum indicat.

Quid, signum Paeanis ex aede Aesculapii praeclare factum, sacrum ac religiosum, non sustulisti? quod omnes propter pulchritudinem visere, propter religionem colere solebant. Quid, ex aede Liberi simulacrum Aristaei non tuo imperio palam ablatum est? Quid, ex aede Jovis religiosissimum simulacrum Jovis Imperatoris, quem Graeci Urion nominant, pulcherrime factum, nonne abstulisti? Quid, ex aede Liberae parvum caput illud pulcherrimum, quod visere solebamus, num dubitasti tollere? Atque ille Paean sacrificiis anniversariis simul cum Aesculapio apud illos

stood the inscription on the basis, he would not have taken the statue. He does not say that he would not have taken both of them. That was nothing to his purpose. He did take the statue and he left the basis; and he certainly would not have done this, says Cicero, if he had understood a single Greek character. Zumpt has corrupted the text through misunderstanding what Cicero meant to say. Zumpt refers to the case in c. 35, as confirmatory of his emendation. In that case Verres carried off the statue and afterwards had the basis removed, because he knew what was on it. If he had known what was on this basis, he might have removed this basis also, or have destroyed the inscription; but he did not destroy it, and that fact furnished Cicero with his argument, such as it is. It is worth noting that Cicero speaks (c. 35) of removing the basis (tollendam locaverunt). The words 'tollere' and 'sustulisset' are properly applied to removing a basis; but if Zumpt's interpretation of this passage (c. 57) is right, 'sustulisset' would apply to the 'epigramma.' I do not deny that we might say 'tollere epigramma;' but if Cicero meant to speak of simply destroying it, he would perhaps have used another word; and if he meant to speak of removing the basis, as in c. 35, he would have said 'basim sustulisset.' Klotz retains 'non,' and says that nobody would misunderstand the passage if it stood thus, 'quod (epigramma) iste eruditus homo . . . si intellexisset, certe non sustulisset (signum poetriae).' Certainly nobody could misunderstand this, but it is not what Cicero wrote. Klotz has not understood the use of 'quod,' but still he makes 'non sustulisset' apply to the statue, and not to the 'epigramma.' See c. 66, note on 'quod.'

58. *Jovis Imperatoris,*] This name occurs three times in this chapter without any variation in the MSS.; and this is sufficient, as Zumpt observes, to deter all attempts at correction. It has been proposed to correct the word Imperator, not because of any doubt about a Jupiter Imperator (Livy, vi. 29; Plin. Panegyr. c. 5, ed. G. H. Schaefer, and the notes), but because of his being made the same with Jupiter Urius, that is, the Zeus of favourable winds. The proposed corrections of Imperator, in order to make it suit the meaning of Urius, are not worth recording. Cicero says that there were three statues of Jupiter Imperator, which were great works of art. There might be more than three, but there were three which were most conspicuous; one was the Macedonian, which, says Cicero, we have seen in the capitol; a second was at the entrance of the Euxine, that is, at the eastern end of the channel of Constantinople, on the Asiatic side; and the third was at Syracuse. No Roman statue is mentioned; and that which was formerly in the capitol must be the Macedonian statue. It all comes to this then, that the Macedonian statue, to which the Greeks gave the name of Ζεὺς Οὔριος, the Romans called by the name of Imperator; and it is a mistake to attempt to force out of Imperator, as Zumpt does, by a false etymology, a meaning which should correspond to that of Urius.

parvum] "'Parinum' R. 4 Parr. Lall. G 2, Lagg. omnes corrupte: 'parnum' C. 'parvum' G 1, 'Parium' Ld et Or." (Jordan.)—'num dubitasti' ed. Ascens. 1511; 'non dub.' R 3, 'dubitasti' dett. Or.

Paean] Paean got a place in the temple of Aesculapius, and received honours with his landlord. Paean is mentioned by Homer (Il. v. 401 and 899).

colebatur: Aristaeus, qui, ut Graeci ferunt, [Liberi filius,] inventor olei esse dicitur, una cum Libero patre apud illos eodem erat in templo consecratus. Jovem autem Imperatorem quanto honore in suo templo fuisse arbitramini? Conjicere potestis, si recordari volueritis, quanta religione fuerit eadem specie atque forma signum illud, quod ex Macedonia captum in Capitolio posuerat Flamininus. LVIII. Etenim tria ferebantur in orbe terrarum signa Jovis Imperatoris uno in genere pulcherrime facta; unum illud Macedonicum, quod in Capitolio vidimus; alterum in Ponti ore et angustiis: tertium, quod Syracusis ante Verrem praetorem fuit. Illud Fla-

Aristaeus,] The words 'ut Graeci ferunt, Liberi filius' cause a difficulty, for Aristaeus was the son of Apollo, as Cicero himself calls him (De Nat. Deorum, iii. 18). The words 'Libero patre' mean simply 'father Liber;' and these words almost decisively prove that the words 'Liberi filius' are spurious. Virgil (Georg. iv. 317) has told the story of Aristaeus and his bees. Aristaeus has the credit of having first made cheese and oil, and also of having kept bees (Justin xiii. 7). His useful inventions gave him a claim to be in company with father Liber.

Flamininus.] 'Fuerit' and 'posuerat' imply that the statue did not exist when Cicero wrote this, and it doubtless perished in the conflagration of the capitol, B.C. 84. This statue of Jupiter Imperator however, according to Livy (vi. 29), was brought from Praeneste, B.C. 379, by the Dictator, T. Quinctius Cincinnatus. Cicero, we must suppose, is speaking of the same statue; and he says that T. Quinctius Flamininus, consul B.C. 197, who defeated king Philip at Cynoscephalae, in Thessaly, brought it to Rome. Zumpt concludes that one of the two is mistaken, which is quite certain, if they are speaking of the same statue. He fixes the blunder on Cicero, and suggests that the sameness of the name T. Quinctius, may have deceived him; a most insufficient explanation, which is not however his own, for it was suggested by Graevius, or rather by Lipsius, who thinks that the blunder arose from the inscription on the statue being T. Quinctii only, and some referring it to one T. Quinctius, and some to the other. But it could not in Cicero's time be a matter of doubt, whether Flamininus brought a statue to Rome from Macedonia, a statue which was a great work of art. Zumpt objects, that it is certain that Flamininus did not penetrate into any part of Macedonia with his army, and accordingly it is not clear where the statue came from. In answer to this we have this passage. I conclude that Flamininus certainly brought from the Macedonian war a statue, which in excellence might vie with that of Syracuse. As to the Praenestine statue, we cannot suppose that this was one of the finest statues in the world, though it may have been a Jupiter. It is clear enough that there were two, one from Praeneste, if Livy is right; and another, certainly from Macedonia, for Cicero, who does make mistakes sometimes, would hardly have published so notorious a blunder, if the fact were that Flamininus did not bring a Jupiter to Rome. Another thing is clear, that the Romans gave Jupiter the epithet Imperator, without respect to the Greek name. Manutius and Graevius saw this. Graevius says: "Latinos autem Jovem, quem Graeci dixerunt *οὔριον*, Imperatorem appellasse, nulla habita ratione Graecae vocis, constat non modo ex sequentibus, uti Jovis Imperatoris signum, quod in Capitolio fuit, ex Macedonia adportatum est, quod tamen Livius Lib. vi. Praeneste advectum scribit, sed et ex Plinii Panegyrico c. 5, et P. Victore ut ibi Lipsius docet."

58. *vidimus;*] "edit. Mediol. Asc., 'videmus' codd." (Iordan.)

in Ponti ore] This statue belonged to a temple on the Bosporus, on the Asiatic side, at the point where the channel opens to the Euxine (Mela, i. 19). Here was the temple of Ζεὺς Οὔριος, and a statue of the god. See Demosthen. adv. Leptin. ed. Wolff, § 29, and his note. An inscription belonging to this statue was discovered by Wheler and Spon, and printed in Chishull's Antiqq. Asiatic., p. 61, and frequently since. The inscription is now in the British Museum.

mininus ita ex aede sua sustulit ut in Capitolio, hoc est, in terrestri domicilio Jovis poneret. Quod autem est ad introitum Ponti, id, quum tam multa ex illo mari bella emerserint, tam multa porro in Pontum invecta sint, usque ad hanc diem integrum inviolatumque servatum est. Hoc tertium, quod erat Syracusis, quod M. Marcellus armatus et victor viderat, quod religioni concesserat, quod cives atque incolae Syracusani colere, advenae non solum visere, verum etiam venerari solebant, id C. Verres ex templo Jovis sustulit. Ut saepius ad M. Marcellum revertar, judices, sic habetote, plures esse a Syracusanis istius adventu deos quam victoria Marcelli homines desideratos. Etenim ille requisisse etiam dicitur Archimedem illum, summo ingenio hominem ac disciplina, quem quum audisset interfectum, permoleste tulisse: iste omnia quae requisivit, non ut conservaret, verum ut asportaret requisivit. Jam illa quae leviora videbuntur ideo praeteribo, quod mensas Delphicas e marmore, crateras ex aere pulcherrimas, vim maximam vasorum Corinthio-

ita . . ut] There are various ways of translating this form (see Pro Plancio, c. 2. Vol. iv.), but it can seldom be translated literally. It means here 'Flamininus it is true took that statue out of its temple, but he placed it in the Capitol.' See c. 67, 'ita tamen laudent,' &c.

cives atque incolae] "Qui cives non sunt, incolae dicuntur," P. Manutius. He refers to Lib. 3. c. 40, "Quid Halicyenses, quorum incolae decumas dant, ipsi agros immunes habent." See also Lib. 4. c. 11, "itemque incolis vestris civibus Romanis;" that is, Roman citizens resident at Rhegium.

Archimedem] He was killed by a Roman soldier, as it is said, at the capture of Syracuse by Marcellus, B.C. 212 (Liv. xxv. 31; Plutarch, Marcellus, c. 19). Cicero (Tusc. Disp. v. 23) tells us that he discovered the tomb of the great geometrician, when he was 'quaestor' in Sicily.

'Quem quum audisset' R 3. The common reading is 'eumque quum audisset interfectum,' of which Zumpt says, 'satis perspicua interpolatorum vestigia prodit.' I suppose he means to say that the 'interpolatores' tried to mend the passage; but why, it is hard to say. The reading in the text is preferable to the common reading. Zumpt adds, that Garatoni cites a similar passage from Act. i. 9. He means the passage 'qui quamobrem,' on which there is a note. I don't know why an ordinary construction of the Latin language should cause a difficulty, or require to be defended. See Lib. 4. c. 48, 'quas sibi quum . . . peragrasse,' and the note; also Pro Plancio, c. 38, 'qui quoniam' &c.

Delphicas] A Delphica was a slab of marble, resting on some support; sometimes used as an 'abacus,' as Martial (xii. 66, ed. Schneidew.) shows:—

"Argentum atque aurum non simplex Delphica portat."

So called, says Zumpt, from the resemblance to the 'mensa,' on which the Pythia sat when she delivered her oracles. The passage of Pliny (H. N. xxxiv. c. 3) is: "ex aere factitavere et cortinas, tripodum nomine Delphicas, quoniam donis maxime Apollinis Delphici dicabantur." These were of bronze, whatever the form might be, and supported on legs. It seems however that Delphica was used among the Romans to signify a marble table (Juv. Sat. iii. 204; and the Scholiast). Probably some of them were tables made of different specimens of stone. Plutarch (Ti. Gracch. c. 2) has the expression, δελφῖνας ἀργυροῦς, which has been altered to δέλφικας ἀργυροῦς by Coraes (ed. Sintenis); but it is said that all the MSS. have δελφῖνας. I suppose that the editors who adopt the correction δέλφικας, mean to give it the sense of 'Delphicas' here; but it ought to be δελφικὰς ἀργυρᾶς.

'Crateras:' the form 'cratera' is not limited to the poets, as Zumpt shows. Ernesti's proposal to write 'pulcherrimos' is therefore unnecessary.

rum ex omnibus aedibus sacris abstulit Syracusis. Itaque, judices, ii qui hospites ad ea quae visenda sunt solent ducere et unumquidque ostendere, quos illi mystagogos vocant, conversam jam habent demonstrationem suam. Nam ut ante demonstrabant quid ubique esset, item nunc quid undique ablatum sit ostendunt.

LIX. Quid tum, mediocrine tandem dolore eos affectos esse arbitramini? Non ita est, judices: primum, quod omnes religione moventur, et deos patrios quos a majoribus acceperunt colendos sibi diligenter et retinendos esse arbitrantur: deinde hic ornatus, haec opera atque artificia, signa, tabulae pictae, Graecos homines nimio opere delectant. Itaque ex illorum querimoniis intelligere possumus, haec illis acerbissima videri quae forsitan nobis levia et contemnenda esse videantur. Mihi credite, judices, tametsi vosmetipsos haec eadem audire certo scio, quum multas acceperint per hosce annos socii atque exterae nationes calamitates et injurias, nullas Graeci homines gravius ferunt ac tulerunt quam hujusmodi spoliationes fanorum atque oppidorum. Licet iste dicat emisse se, sicuti solet dicere: credite hoc mihi, judices; nulla unquam civitas tota Asia et Graecia signum ullum, tabulam pictam, ullum denique ornamentum urbis sua voluntate cuiquam vendidit. Nisi forte existimatis, posteaquam judicia severa Romae fieri desierunt, Graecos homines haec venditare coepisse, quae tum non modo non venditabant, quum judicia fiebant, verum etiam coëmebant: aut nisi arbitramini L. Crasso, Q. Scaevolae, C. Claudio, potentissimis hominibus, quorum aedilitates ornatissimas vidimus, commercium

mystagogos] He gives the Greek word. If their business was only to show strangers the wonders, we know exactly what they were. The race still exists.

59. *desierunt*,] R S λ; 'desierint' dett.

quum judicia fiebant,] That is, 'severa.' 'Post judiciorum dissolutionem' means the same as 'postquam . . . severa fieri desierunt.'

'Nisi forte existimatis' implies a negation, as Manutius remarks. It is a form of expression which has the purport of a negation. The argument is this. During the time that the 'judicia' were strict at Rome, the Greeks were so far from being ready to sell their works of art, that they were even purchasers of such things. It is not likely that they would be ready to sell when the 'judicia' ceased to be severe. If they were so fond of these things as to refuse to part with them, when, if they sold them at all, they could command their own price, they would not be ready to sell them when they might be forced by a governor to part with them at his price. Or, he says, can you suppose that L. Crassus, Q. Scaevola, and C. Claudius, who exhibited such splendour in their 'aedileship,' and among other objects of display there would be statues (Lib. 1. c. 22), could not trade with the Greeks for such things; and that those who have been 'aediles' since could trade with them? He does not mean that these three men had 'commercium,' though Manutius takes it so. Cicero means to say, you must not suppose that they could not, and that others could. He means that nobody could. Manutius has mistaken the meaning of 'commercium.' The explanation of Lambinus is nearer the mark.

As to L. Crassus and the others, see De Offic. Lib. ii. 16; and this oration, c. 3, 4.

istarum rerum cum Graecis hominibus non fuisse, his qui post judiciorum dissolutionem aediles facti sunt fuisse.

LX. Acerbiorem etiam scitote esse civitatibus falsam istam et simulatam emptionem quam si qui clam surripiat aut eripiat palam atque auferat. Nam turpitudinem summam esse arbitrantur referri in tabulas publicas, pretio adductam civitatem et pretio parvo ea quae accepisset a majoribus vendidisse atque abalienasse. Etenim mirandum in modum Graeci rebus istis quas contemnimus delectantur. Itaque majores nostri facile patiebantur haec esse apud illos quam plurima, ut imperio nostro quam ornatissimi florentissimique essent; apud eos autem, quos vectigales aut stipendiarios fecerant, tamen haec relinquebant, ut illi quibus haec jucunda sunt, quae nobis levia videntur, haberent haec oblectamenta et solatia servitutis. Quid arbitramini Rheginos, qui jam cives Romani sunt, merere velle ut ab iis marmorea Venus illa auferatur? quid Taren-

60. *abalienasse.*] 'Alienasse' the common reading; and that of Klotz: but the better MSS. have 'abalienasse,' of which Zumpt says, 'ad augendam rei indignitatem appositius.' This is an idle remark. 'Abalienatio' is a technical word: "abalienatio est ejus rei quae mancipi est aut traditio alteri nexu aut in jure cessio inter quos ea jure civili fieri possunt" (Cic. Top. c. 5). Comp. 'pecore abalienato,' Lib. 3. c. 50; and Gaius, i. 119.

quas contemnimus] 'Vulgo *nos* contemnimus' (Zumpt). Cicero did not despise them. His own language in these orations shows that he did not, and the passion for sculpture that he afterwards indulged in. A man, like Cicero, humanized by the literature of the Greeks, could not fail to admire their taste and artistic skill, the great and enduring legacy which they have left to all nations. But his hearers, or many of them, either cared not for these things, or knew nothing about them. The mission of the Roman was conquest and civil administration; and it seems as if the arts do not find their home in a nation which is busy in getting money, and subduing the world. Virgil, who was himself not deficient in taste, claims no great amount of it for his countrymen:—

"Excudent alii spirantia mollius aera,
Credo equidem, vivos ducent de marmore vultus—
Tu regere imperio populos, Romane, memento."—Aen. vi. 848.

quam plurima, ut &c.] Klotz and Iordan have 'quam plurima: apud socios, ut' &c. 'Apud socios' is found in Guelf. Leid. Havn. Coll.—"'apud illos' R3: om. codd. rell. et O. virgula post 'socios' posita" (Iordan). It is possible then that 'apud illos' and 'apud socios' are not both genuine. Zumpt omits 'apud socios;' perhaps rightly. For the 'illos' are the Greeks, who are opposed to the 'vectigales aut stipendiarios,' who were under more severe terms of obedience to Rome. It is probable then that 'apud socios' is an interpolation, made for the purpose of explaining the text. But, as Zumpt remarks, the 'vectigales et stipendiarii' are also called 'socii,' as we see in the case of Sicily, for Cicero sometimes calls all the Sicilians 'socii.' Zumpt adds, that the phrase which is opposed to 'socii' in the larger sense, is 'Liberi populi,' such as most of the Greek states were, the Cyziceni, Rhodii, Athenienses, Rhegini. But the Rhegini were Roman citizens now.

Rheginos, . . cives Romani] See c. 11.

merere velle] 'What do you think that the Rhegini would take for their marble statue of Venus?' The word is wrongly explained by Manutius. It means to earn as wages, or receive as pay. It follows that the old readings 'ut—ne auferatur,' 'ut ne—amittant' are wrong; and these readings have since been corrected from the better MSS. The word 'meritasset' is used in a similar sense, Lib. 3. c. 50. Zumpt quotes Cicero, De Natura Deorum, i. 24, "quid enim mereas ut Epicureus esse desinas?" and De Fin. ii. 22, "quid mereas igitur ut te dicas in eo magistratu

tinos, ut Europam in tauro amittant, ut Satyrum qui apud illos in aede Vestae est, ut cetera? quid Thespienses, ut Cupidinis signum propter quod unum visuntur Thespiae? quid Cnidios, ut Venerem marmoream? quid, ut pictam, Coos? quid Ephesios, ut Alexan-

omnia voluptatis causa facturum esse?" (ed. Orelli.) See also Phil. i. c. 14.

Europam in tauro] After which the cold. dett. and Orelli add the idle word 'sedentem.' The old stories of the Greeks and their art were inseparable. The real elements of art existed in the minds of the people, and the artist had only to embody them. It is different with us, among whom the idea does not exist, and consequently either cannot be embodied, or if a man arises who has the idea and the power to give it form, there are few who understand what he has done. He has given a form to an idea which does not exist in the mind of the people.

A modern artist has placed a naked Ariadne on a leopard's back, which people admire, or affect to admire, though it is, to most who see it, a naked woman in marble seated on a beast, and no more. If we admit the mechanical skill of the sculptor, we must still condemn his taste. Ovid has the story of Europa (Met. ii. 850):

"Induitur tauri faciem."

Ovid has materials for an artist who can use them. There is a large folio Dutch translation of the Metamorphoses, by Vondel, 'with beautiful copper-plates' (Amsterdam, 1703). Some of them are not bad. They show what a man of genius might do, if he took Ovid for his master.

If we may put a woman on a beast, it should be an animal on which she can sit, and a bull's back will answer the purpose. It will also be consistent with the heavy nature of this beast that he should be at rest, or have very little action. If a Greek placed a woman on a leopard or such an animal, he would make the beast in motion, and he would not make the woman naked. In a beautiful coin of Sybrita in Creto we see a woman seated on the back of a sculptor's leopard. She has one hand on the animal's neck, and in the other a thyrsus. She sits upright bare to the waist; the drapery is well fixed about her hips and hangs down leaving her feet free. The beast is galloping at a great rate, but the woman will not come off. She sits firm.

Satyrum] Satyrus, says Zumpt, was the native deity of the Tarentini. Hence Saturum Tarentum (Virg. Georg. ii. 197) is explained, though Servius supposes a town, Saturum or Satureium, near Tarentum; and also Steph. Byzant. v. Σατύριον. Heindorf also adopts this explanation of the scholiast on the line of Horace, 1 Sat. vi. 60:

"Me Satureiano vectari rura caballo."

Cupidinis signum propter &c.] The words 'propter . . . Thespiae' are out of place here. See c. 2.

Cnidios,] See c. 2, note on Praxiteles, and add to the references Lucian, Imag. 6.

Coos?] The people of Cos had also a Venus of Praxiteles, a draped statue, inferior to the naked figure of the Cnidii. (Plin. H. N. 34, 8; 36, 5, ed. Hard.) But the pride of Cos was the Aphrodite Anadyomene of Apelles, in the temple of Aesculapius, Venus rising from the waves, and pressing from her hair the water which dripped from her like a transparent veil. Ovid (Trist. ii. 527), who had seen the picture and could paint much in few words, has preserved the characteristics:

"Sic madidos digitis siccat Venus uda capillos,
Et modo maternis tecta videtur aquis."

The model of the Anadyomene was the beautiful Campaspe or Pancaste, the favorite mistress of Alexander, who ordered Apelles to paint her naked. The painter fell in love with Pancaste, and the king generously made him a present of the woman, and contented himself, we must suppose, with the picture. Another story says (Athenaeus, xiii. 590) that Apelles copied his Aphrodite Anadyomene from Phryne, when she entered the sea naked at Eleusis at the festival Posidonia, in the presence of all the people. But there may be some chronological objections to Athenaeus' story. The picture was carried to Rome in the time of Augustus, who took it in lieu of certain demands which the Romans had on the people of Cos. It was placed in the temple of the Divus Julius. The picture was damaged on the voyage, and was in such a bad state in the time of Nero, that a copy of it was made by Dorotheus. It is not known what became of it.

drum? quid Cyzicenos, ut Ajacem aut Medeam? quid Rhodios, ut Ialysum? quid Athenienses, ut ex marmore Iacchum, aut Paralum pictum, aut ex aere Myronis buculam? Longum est et non necessarium commemorare quae apud quosque visenda sunt tota Asia et Graecia; verum illud est quamobrem haec commemorem, quod existimare vos hoc volo, mirum quendam dolorem accipere eos ex quorum urbibus haec auferantur.

LXI. Atque ut ceteros omittamus, de ipsis Syracusanis cognoscite. Ad quos ego quum venissem, sic primum existimabam, ut Romae ex istius amicis acceperam, civitatem Syracusanam propter Heraclii hereditatem non minus esse isti amicam quam Mamertinam propter praedarum ac furtorum omnium societatem: simul et verebar ne mulierum nobilium et formosarum gratia, quarum iste arbitrio per triennium praeturam gesserat, virorumque quibuscum illae nuptae erant nimia in istum non modo lenitudine sed etiam liberalitate oppugnarer, si quid ex literis Syracusanorum conquirerem. Itaque Syracusis cum civibus Romanis eram: eorum tabulas exquirebam, injurias cognoscebam. Quum diutius in negotio

The Alexander, in the temple of Diana of Ephesus, was another picture of Apelles, the Ceraunophorus, or lightning-darter. Apelles, like most great painters, was a master in portrait. (Plin. H. N. xxxv. 10. Strabo, xiv. p. 657.) The fingers seemed to project, and the lightning to stand out of the picture. The Ceraunophorus was a great painting, but the criticism of the sculptor Lysippus was just. Lysippus blamed Apelles for putting lightning in the king's hand. The bronze statue of Alexander by Lysippus held a spear.

Cyzicenos,] The dictator Caesar is said to have bought two pictures by Timomachus, a Medea and an Ajax, for eighty talents (Plin. vii. 38), for the purpose of placing them in the temple of Venus Genetrix. Zumpt makes a difficulty about what Pliny says in another place (xxxv. 11), that Timomachus painted these pictures in the time (aetate) of Caesar. But there seem no grounds for fixing the birth of Timomachus with any accuracy; and we know that his period came at least near enough to the time of Caesar to allow Pliny to use this expression. Caesar did not buy the pictures from Timomachus, for Cicero here speaks of them (B.C. 70) being in possession of the Cyziceni.

Ialysum?] The Ialysus and Paralus were the work of Protogenes. The Ialysus was taken to Rome and placed in the temple of Pax (Plin. xxxv. 10). It is not known what Iacchus is meant.

Myronis buculam?] This cow or heifer of Myro (c. 3), one of the great works of the class of mere imitative art, was, as it here appears, at Athens. Ausonius (58–68) has eleven epigrams on it, and there are others in the Anthology. Propertius (ii. 31, 7) mentions four 'Myronis . . . boves.'

dolorem &c.] 'Dolorem accidere eis,' the common reading, but Zumpt doubts if the expression can be found elsewhere.

61. *Heraclii*] See Lib. 2. c. 14.

non modo lenitudine] "'Illae' et deinde 'modo' om. Legg. praeter 29" (Iordan). Zumpt observes that all the passages of Cicero at least cited by Garatoni here and in his notes on Lib. 3. c. 1, and on Agr. ii. 16, and those which Duker defends (Florus, ii. 2. 20), where *modo* is omitted when *sed etiam* follows, are not only doubtful, but ought not to be produced.

ex literis Syracusanorum] He means the 'literae publicae,' the books, the records of the town.—'tabulas exquirebam:' 'was engaged' in examining.' Manutius has 'exscribebam' (ed. 1540), a conjecture; the inferior MSS. have 'scribebam,' both false readings.

Quum . . fueram, . . revertebar,] There is no variation noted here. Cicero does

curaque fueram, ut requiescerem curamque animi remitterem, ad Carpinatii praeclaras tabulas revertebar, ubi cum equitibus Romanis, hominibus ex illo conventu honestissimis, illos Verrutios, de quibus ante dixi, explicabam: a Syracusanis prorsus nihil adjumenti neque publice neque privatim exspectabam, neque erat in animo postulare. Quum haec agerem, repente ad me venit Heraclius, is qui tum magistratum Syracusis habebat, homo nobilis qui sacerdos Jovis fuisset, qui honos est apud Syracusanos amplissimus. Agit mecum et cum fratre meo ut, si nobis videretur, adiremus ad eorum senatum: frequentes esse in curia: se jussu senatus a nobis petere ut veniremus. LXII. Primo nobis fuit dubium quid ageremus: deinde cito venit in mentem non esse vitandum illum nobis conventum et locum; itaque in curiam venimus. Honorifice sane consurgitur: nos rogatu magistratus assedimus. Incipit is loqui qui et auctoritate et aetate et, ut mihi visum est, usu rerum antecedebat, Diodorus Timarchidi; cujus omnis oratio hanc habuit primo sententiam: senatum et populum Syracusanum moleste graviterque ferre, quod ego quum in ceteris Siciliae civitatibus senatum populumque docuissem quid iis utilitatis, quid salutis afferrem, et quum ab omnibus mandata, legatos, literas, testimoniaque sumpsissem, in illa civitate nihil ejusmodi facerem. Respondi neque Romae in conventu Siculorum, quum a me auxilium communi omnium legationum consilio petebatur causaque totius provinciae ad me deferebatur, legatos Syracusanorum affuisse, neque me postulare ut quidquam contra C. Verrem decerneretur in ea

not say 'fuissem,' and perhaps 'fuissem' would not express his meaning. He says 'When I had been a long time . . I began to look again' &c.

*Romanis, *hominibus*] Zumpt added 'hominibus' in his larger edition, on good authority; but he does not accept 'illius Verrutios,' which the same authority offers in place of 'illos Verrucios.' Klotz and Jordan have 'illius Verrucios' (see Lib. 2. c. 70, 76). Zumpt approves of the orthography 'Verrucios;' and he says "quippe cum nomine *verruca* derivandum videretur."

qui sacerdos . . fuisset,] 'Homo nobilis qui,' &c. Cicero could of course say 'fuit,' which is the reading of the inferior MSS. But he means to say that he was a man distinguished for having held this high office (Lib. 2. c. 51).

fratre meo] R 3 have 'Q. fratre meo;' but it was his cousin Lucius (c. 65). We might perhaps insert the true praenomen L. here in place of Q., as Zumpt remarks.

esse in curia:] 'esse in curiam' R G 1 2. See the note on Lib. 2. c. 27.

62. *Diodorus Timarchidi;*] This is the true reading, and not 'Diodorus Timarchides,' as Zumpt shows. The Greeks mentioned in these orations have more than one name only when they are Romanized Greeks, and then they retain their Greek name with Roman 'praenomina' and 'nomina.' But it is consistent with Greek usage to designate a man by the addition of his father's name. It is an honourable way of mention, to say that the man has a father, and to give his name. (See Lib. 2. c. 42.)

Respondi . . quum . . petebatur] I suppose that this is a case in which we should have 'peteretur,' as the words are the reported words of Cicero. But he reports them himself.

curia in qua inauratam C. Verris statuam viderem. Quod posteaquam dixi, tantus est gemitus factus aspectu statuae et commemoratione ut illud in curia positum monumentum scelerum non beneficiorum videretur. Tum pro se quisque, quantum dicendo assequi poterat, docere me coepit ea quae paulo ante commemoravi, spoliatam urbem, fana direpta: de Heraclii hereditate, quam palaestritis concessisset, multo maximam partem ipsum abstulisse; neque postulandum fuisse ut ille palaestritas diligeret, qui etiam inventorem olei deum sustulisset; neque illam statuam esse ex pecunia publica neque publice datam, sed eos qui hereditatis diripiendae participes fuissent faciendam statuendamque curasse; eosdem Romae fuisse legatos, illius adjutores improbitatis, socios furtorum, conscios flagitiorum; eo minus mirari me oportere si illi communi legatorum voluntati et saluti Siciliae defuissent.

LXIII. Ubi eorum dolorem ex istius injuriis non modo non minorem sed prope majorem quam ceterorum Siculorum esse cognovi, tum meum animum in illos, tum mei consilii negotiique totius suscepti causam rationemque proposui; tum eos hortatus sum ut causae communi salutique ne deessent; ut illam laudationem quam se vi ac metu coactos paucis illis diebus decresse dicebant tollerent. Itaque, judices, Syracusani haec faciunt, istius clientes atque amici. Primum mihi literas publicas quas in aerario sanctiore conditas habebant proferunt, in quibus ostendunt omnia quae dixi ablata esse perscripta, et plura etiam quam ego potui dicere: perscripta autem hoc modo, Quod ex aede Minervae hoc et illud abesset, quod ex aede Jovis, quod ex aede Liberi. Ut quisque iis rebus tuendis praefuerat, ita perscriptum erat, quum rationem ex lege redderent

quantum dicendo] I think Hotmann is right in explaining this to mean that the Sicilians tried to express themselves in Latin, a language which the Greeks had no great liking for, and generally spoke ill. Cicero afterwards spoke Greek in the senate, which was beneath the dignity of a Roman. But the words may mean, as Halm says, 'as forcibly as he could.'

olei deum] See c. 58.

63. *paucis illis diebus*]. The expression has been explained. It means in the few days before Cicero's arrival; and is in fact explained by the words at the end of the chapter: 'posteaquam meus adventus appropinquaret, imperasse eum,' &c.; that is, L. Metellus, then the governor, forced them to this 'laudatio' just before Cicero arrived; a most scandalous affair for Metellus. If it is true, he was as bad as Verres.

aerario sanctiore] Cicero uses a Roman term, not in the Roman sense. He simply means that these documents were kept in the most secure place in the Aerarium. The Roman 'aerarium sanctius' contained a reserve of money for dangerous times (Livy, xxvii. 10).

Ut quisque..ita perscriptum erat,] 'As to every person who had been set over these things to take care of them, there was the following entry: when they were giving in their accounts pursuant to the law, and were bound to deliver up all that they had received, they prayed that they might be excused as to the deficiency in these things to which I have already referred.'

The old readings, 'redderet'—'acceperat'—'deberet,' were changed by Zumpt into the plural, on good authority as to 'redderent'—'deberent;' but R has 'ac-

et quae acceperant tradere deberent, petisse ut sibi quod hae res abessent ignosceretur: itaque omnes liberatos discessisse, et esse ignotum omnibus: quas ego literas obsignandas publico signo deportandasque curavi. De laudatione autem ratio sic mihi reddita est: primum quum a C. Verre literae aliquanto ante adventum meum de laudatione venissent, nihil esse decretum: deinde, quum quidam ex illius amicis commonerent oportere decerni, maximo clamore esse et convicio repudiatos: posteaquam meus adventus appropinquaret, imperasse eum qui summam potestatem haberet ut decernerent: decretum ita esse ut multo plus illi laudatio mali quam boni posset afferre. Id adeo, judices, ut mihi ab illis demonstratum est, sic vos ex me cognoscite.

ceperat,' which we must take to be a blunder of the copyist. It is no objection to the plural that Cicero does not use 'quisque,' 'unusquisque,' with the plural; on which Zumpt has a note (Act. i. c. 14; Lib. 2. c. 39).

Zumpt writes 'e lege' in place of 'ex lege.' He is not quite certain whether there is any difference between 'e lege' and 'ex lege.' On this matter 'subdubitat,' and he refers to his note on Lib. 2. c. 17, where he has 'e lege,' 'lege,' 'ex lege,' all in the same chapter. It may be doubtful whether Cicero wrote 'e lege' or 'ex lege,' though not doubtful that the Romans generally would write it both ways. But Cicero was particular in such matters, and may have preferred one form to the other, though I do not recollect if he has any where, among his multifarious communications, given us his opinion on this matter. The supposition of any difference in meaning between 'e lege' and 'ex lege' is rather too trifling to be discussed.

But there is another matter here that requires notice. G 2 Ld. have 'lege' only; and Zumpt thinks that 'lege' by itself is not good Latin; and he recollects no instance of it, except in the common formula 'lege agere.' He has apparently forgotten 'lege Rupilia,' in Lib. 2. c. 17; for if we can say 'ex lege Rupilia,' 'e lege Rupilia,' 'lege Rupilia,' and 'ex lege,' we may perhaps say 'lege' simply. Again, he has in a note on Lib. 5. c. 5, the following passage from Quintilian (Inst. v. 7. 9, &c.): "duo genera sunt testium aut voluntariorum aut eorum quibus in judiciis lege denuntiari solet." Zumpt was a good critic, and a sensible man, but his memory was not strong. I have no confidence in many of his minor canons. That 'lege' can be so used is certain. (See Lib. 2, c. 17, note.) As 'lex,' in its proper sense, means *a* 'lex,' it is usual to join the name to it, as 'Julia,' and so forth; but when the 'lex' has been mentioned, or it is clearly understood what 'lex' is meant, the qualifying name may be omitted. Zumpt takes 'ex lege' here to be the same in sense as in Lib. 1. c. 54, 'Habonius qui legem nosset:' the terms of the contract. I am inclined to think that he means a law proper, under which the care of these things was given to certain people, and they were bound to give them up as they received them. The 'lex,' in fact, contained the terms by which they were bound; but it was not here 'id quod contractum Icti vocant,' as Zumpt says. In this passage Ernesti would make 'lege' equivalent to 'inventario,' which is a mistake.

obsignandis publico signo] Cicero carried off these entries, and had their authenticity attested by the seal of the city. Thus we see that in those days, artificial persons, as cities, and Res Publicae of various kinds, had their seal as the evidence of the act of the artificial person. The practice has been transmitted to our own days. Compare Pro Flacco, c. 15.

appropinquaret,] The reading of Zumpt, in his larger edition, in place of 'appropinquarit.' Halm proposes to write 'postea cum' for 'posteaquam,' "ut et asyndeton vitetur et conjunctivus imperfecti recte se habeat" (Jordan).

Id adeo,] Zumpt gives to these words the meaning which he has explained in his Grammar, § 349, 'ut fere *potius* sit.' Let the reader substitute 'potius' for 'adeo,' and see if he can understand it. Zumpt perhaps relies on such examples as occur in Lib. 2. c. 60, &c., where the meaning of

LXIV. Mos est Syracusis ut, si qua de re ad senatum referatur, dicat sententiam qui velit: nominatim nemo rogatur; et tamen, ut quisque aetate et honore antecedit, ita primus solet sua sponte dicere, idque a ceteris ei conceditur: sin aliquando tacent omnes, tum sortito coguntur dicere. Quum hic mos esset, refertur ad senatum de laudatione Verris. In quo primum, ut aliquid esset morae multi interpellant: de Sex. Peducaeo, qui de illa civitate totaque provincia optime meritus esset, sese antea quum audissent ei negotium facessitum, quumque eum publice pro plurimis ejus et maximis meritis laudare cuperent, a C. Verre prohibitos esse: iniquum esse, tametsi Peducaeus eorum laudatione jam non uteretur, tamen non id prius decernere quod aliquando voluissent quam quod tunc cogerentur. Conclamant omnes et approbant ita fieri oportere. Refertur de Peducaeo. Ut quisque aetate et honore antecedebat, ita sententiam dixit ex ordine. Id adeo ex ipso senatus consulto cognoscite; nam principum sententiae perscribi solent. Recita. 'Quod verba facta sunt de Sex. Peducaeo.' Dicit qui

'adeo' seems plain, and is consistent with its etymon 'ad' and 'eo' the pronoun. It is used in the clause which strengthens and exemplifies what has been said before. 'Id adeo' occurs in the next chapter (c. 64), where it may mean 'accordingly,' and here too. See also Lib. 5. c. 4. We read in Terence, Phorm. iv. 3. 40, 'Quod dixi adeo ei:' 'That is exactly what I said to him.'

64. *Mos est Syracusis*] Cicero explains this because the Roman fashion was different. The Roman senators were called on according to a certain rule. If there were 'consules designati,' they spoke first. If there were no 'consules designati,' the consuls called on the 'princeps senatus,' and then on such persons as he thought proper, but yet in such wise as to call on a 'consularis' before a 'praetorius,' and so on. See Becker, Handbuch, ii. 2, p. 425.

idque a ceteris] 'Itaque a ceteris' R 3, Klotz, Iordan.—'sin . . tacent:' 'sin . . taceant' in the reprint of Zumpt, and I suppose in his minor edition. In his larger one he has properly taken the better reading, 'sin . . tacent,' which Klotz also has.

ut aliquid esset morae] 'Ut eum diem interpellatione eximerent,' Hotmann. This was done by some who were the friends of Verres, or the tools of Metellus. There were some; for he says, c. 65, 'prope cunctis sententiis.' He does not say all.

negotium facessitum,] 'Reum esse factum' (Manutius). He quotes a letter of Cicero to Appius, in which the same expression occurs. In Divin. c. 14, the expression is 'ne innocenti periculum facesseris.' Peducaeus did not want their testimonial now, for either he had escaped a prosecution or had been acquitted.

de Peducaeo.] He was praetor of Sicily in the years B.C. 76, 75, in the second of which years Cicero was quaestor under him. Zumpt supposes him to be the man who is mentioned De Fin. ii. 18. He had two sons, one of whom is called Sextus, and is often named in Cicero's letters. C. Sacerdos was praetor of Sicily in B.C. 74; Verres in the years B.C. 73, 72, 71; and now, B.C. 70, L. Metellus was praetor.

Quod verba &c.] This was the Roman formula for expressing the subject in debate, and it was followed by the decision or resolution as in the passage of Frontinus De aquae duct. c. 100 (cited by Halm): "Quod Q. Aelius Tubero Paullus Fabius Maximus coss. verba fecerunt de etc. de ea re quid fieri placeret, de ea re ita censuerunt placere huic ordini" &c. There are other examples in Frontinus De aquae duct. See also c. 66, 'quod . . verba fecissem.'

In Gellius (xv. 11) there is the Senatusconsultum 'De philosophis et de rhetoribus Latinis,' of which this is the form: "M. Pomponius praetor senatum consuluit. Quod verba facta [sunt] de philosophis et

primi suaserint. Decernitur. Refertur deinde de Verre. Dic, quaeso, quomodo. 'Quod verba facta sunt de C. Verre.' Quid postea scriptum est? 'Quum surgeret nemo neque sententiam diceret'—Quid est hoc? 'sors ducitur.' Quamobrem? nemo erat voluntarius laudator praeturae tuae, defensor periculorum, praesertim quum inire a praetore gratiam posset? Nemo. Illi ipsi tui convivae, consiliarii, conscii, socii, verbum facere non audent. In qua curia statua tua stabat et nuda filii, in ea nemo fuit quem ne nudus quidem filius [et] nudata provincia commoveret. Atque etiam hoc me docent, ejusmodi senatus consultum fuisse [laudationem] ut omnes intelligere possent non laudationem, sed potius irrisionem esse illam, quae commonefaceret istius turpem calamitosamque praeturam: etenim scriptum esse ita, 'Quod is virgis neminem cecidisset;' a quo cognostis nobilissimos homines atque innocentissimos securi esse percussos: 'Quod vigilanter provinciam administrasset;' cujus omnes vigilias in stupris constat esse consumptas: hoc vero scriptum esse quod proferre non auderet reus, accusator recitare non desineret, 'Quod praedones procul ab insula Sicilia prohibuisset Verres;' quos etiam intra Syracusanam insulam recepisset. LXV. Haec posteaquam ex illis cognovi, discessi cum fratre e curia ut nobis absentibus si quid vellent decernerent.

de rhetoribus, de ea re ita censuerunt," &c. The same S. C. is in Suetonius, De Claris Rhetoribus.

nuda filii, . . ne nudus quidem] Hotmann entirely mistook the meaning of this. It is an ungenerous insinuation against the son of Verres, repeated for the fourth time. Hotmann discovered it before. Lib. 2. c. 59.—All the MSS. have 'ne quem' (Zumpt), which Klotz and Iordan have, with ? after 'commoveret.' R omits 'et' before 'nudata,' and perhaps it should be omitted. If we write 'ne quem nudus quidem,' it must mean 'not even one,' and the emphasis will be on 'quem.' But then we have two words between 'ne' and 'quidem,' and there is plainly an emphasis on 'nudus' also. I know that we may have two words between 'ne' and 'quidem,' but I do not know an example like 'ne quem nudus quidem.'

senatus consultum fuisse [laudationem]] The common reading is 'senatus consulto esse fecisse laudationem.' Iordan says that all the MSS. have 'fecisse,' but that if we accept 'fecisse,' we can hardly omit 'se' before 'fecisse.' The dett. have 'sese fecisse.' Graevius denies that 'facere laudationem' is Latin. He proposes to write 'ejusmodi senatusconsulti fuisse laudationem.' Zumpt observes that 'fecisse' and 'fuisse' are sometimes confounded. He writes 'ejusmodi senatusconsultum fuisse laudationis;' and Iordan has the same except that he retains 'fecisse.' In some of the MSS. we have for 'senatusconsultum' the abbreviation S. C.; but, in place of this, some of the inferior MSS. have 'Siciliam' or 'in Sicilia.' Iordan only mentions the readings 'laudationes' and 'laudationem;' but it seems clear from what follows, that the singular is intended. I think that it is doubtful if the first 'laudationem' is genuine.

esse consumptas:] The passage stands thus in Klotz: 'esse consumptas: cujus modi, constat: hoc autem scriptum esse,' &c. Zumpt says of these words, "sine sensu e prioribus mendose, opinor, repetita." But R 3 has 'cujusmodi constat hoc.'

65. *Haec posteaquam*] The reading of the dett. is 'Quae posteaquam;' a matter of indifference.

Decernunt statim, primum, Ut cum Lucio fratre hospitium publice fieret, quod is eandem voluntatem erga Syracusanos suscepisset quam ego semper habuissem. Id non modo tum scripserunt, verum etiam in aere incisum nobis tradiderunt. Valde hercule te Syracusani tui quos crebro commemorare soles diligunt, qui cum accusatore tuo satis justam causam conjungendae necessitudinis putant, quod te accusaturus sit et quod inquisitum in te venerit. Postea decernitur, ac non varie sed prope cunctis sententiis, Ut laudatio quae C. Verri decreta esset tolleretur. In eo, quum jam non solum discessio facta esset sed etiam perscriptum atque in tabulas relatum, praetor appellatur. At quis appellat? Magistratus aliquis? Nemo. Senator? Ne id quidem. Syracusanorum aliquis? Minime. Quis igitur praetorem appellat? Qui quaestor istius fuerat P. Caesetius. O rem ridiculam! o desertum hominem! desperatum, relictum a magistratu Siculo! Ne senatus consul-

in aere incisum] 'Hospitii publici tesseram significat,' Hotmann. Graevius explains by several inscriptions what 'hospitium facere' is. One inscription contains the words 'tesseram hospitalem cum eo fecerunt.' Another is 'Senatus Populusque Thiniligensis hospitium fecerunt cum C. Silio C. F. Aviola, &c., eumque posterosque ejus sibi posterisque suis patronum ceperunt.' That these 'tabulae hospitales' were on bronze, appears from the termination of one of them in these terms: 'tabula hospitali incisa hoc decreto in domo sua posita permittat censuere.' Graevius says that there are other examples in Tomasinus, cap. 2, de tesseris hospitalitatis.

cunctis] "Vulgo legebatur *conjunctis sententiis* ex deterrimis codicibus" (Zumpt). See the note on 'cunctus,' Divin. c. 1.

In eo,] 'At vero' is the common reading. The inferior MSS. have 'an eo,' which is certainly wrong. R 3 λ Lg. 29 have 'in eo.' Lambinus edited from conjecture, 'Cum jam in id non solum,' &c., where 'in id' is rightly connected with 'discessio;' but it is only a conjecture. 'In eo' must be connected with 'appellatur;' 'hereupon the praetor is appealed to.' (See c. 66, 'in quo praetor appellatus esset.')

But this reading (in eo) does not set all right. For if the passage stands as it does here, we must translate it 'therein (in eo), in respect to that matter, though the division had not only taken place, but (something) had been drawn up and entered on the records.' The 'something' is the 'senatus consultum;' and Hotmann's conjecture, that the usual abbreviation S. C. has been omitted by the copyists, is a reasonable conjecture. If this is not so, we must supply 'id,' derived from the 'eo.' The 'in eo' seems to be well explained by the words 'illud S. C. in quo' (c. 66).

discessio] The word applied to a division in the Roman senate for the purpose of ascertaining the votes (Gellius, xiv. 7). Sallust says (Cat. 55) 'senatus in Catonis sententiam discessit.' See Phil. iii. c. 9, and the note.

aliquis?] 'aliqui' R 3, and Jordan.

P. Caesetius.] The common reading in the editions is 'Caecilius,' which can be by no means endured, says Zumpt, as Garatoni has shown; and one of his arguments settles the matter—that Caecilius had long ago left the province, had opposed Cicero in the matter of the choice of a prosecutor, that he had failed, and thereupon Cicero had gone to Sicily to collect his evidence. All which we know already; and it is not the slightest presumption against this Caecilius being in Sicily again, for he could go as well as Cicero. The real argument is, that the MSS. have a different reading, 'Caesecius,' 'Cesetius,' and 'Cesellius.' P. Caesetius is mentioned in Lib. 5. c. 25. Halm thinks that the passage in Lib. 1. c. 38, refers to this Caesetius, 'Quaestorem se in senatu expectare dicit.'

relictum] Zumpt rightly rejects Madvig's proposed full stop after 'relictum.' Madvig would connect 'a magistratu Siculo' with 'quis igitur praetorem appellat.' This distinguished scholar sometimes does

tum Siculi homines facere possent, ne suum jus suis moribus, suis legibus obtinere possent, non amicus istius, non hospes, non denique aliquis Siculus, sed quaestor [P. R.] praetorem appellat. Quis hoc vidit? quis audivit? Praetor aequus et sapiens dimitti jubet senatum. Concurrit ad me maxima multitudo. Primum senatores clamare sibi eripi jus, eripi libertatem: populus senatum laudare, gratias agere: cives Romani a me nusquam discedere. Quo quidem die nihil aegrius factum est multo labore meo quam ut manus ab illo appellatore abstinerentur. Quum ad praetorem in jus adissemus, excogitat sane acute quid decernat. Nam antequam verbum facerem, de sella surrexit atque abiit. Itaque tum de foro, quum jam advesperasceret, discessimus.

LXVI. Postridie mane ab eo postulo ut Syracusanis liceret senatus consultum quod pridie fecissent mihi reddere. Ille enimvero negat, et ait indignum facinus esse quod ego in senatu Graeco verba fecissem; quod quidem apud Graecos Graece locutus essem, id ferri nullo modo posse. Respondi homini, ut potui, ut debui, ut volui. Quum multa, tum etiam hoc me memini dicere, facile esse perspicuum quantum inter hunc et illum Numidicum, verum ac germanum Metellum, interesset: illum noluisse sua laudatione juvare L. Lucullum, sororis virum, quicum optime convenisset; hunc homini alienissimo a civitatibus laudationes per vim et metum comparare. Quod ubi intellexi multum apud illum recentes nuntios, multum tabellas non commendaticias sed tributarias valuisse, ad-

good service to the ancient texts, but he is not always right. It is unnecessary to show reasons against his proposed punctuation. Any one who will read the chapter attentively will find them. The text of Klotz and Iordan stands thus: 'o desertum hominem, desperatum, relictum. A magistratu Siculo, ne' &c. It is not denied that this is Latin; it is proved by the oration Pro Quintio, c. 20, 'a praetore tribunos appellare,' and other passages. There is also no objection to 'relictum' thus used absolutely. In c. 51 there is 'quam deserta, quam inculta, quam relicta omnia.' Manutius, so far as I can collect from his commentary, for I have not his edition, made the words 'A magistratu' begin a sentence, and explained it as Madvig does.

66. *Postridie mane*] See Lib. 1. c. 27, and Lib. 2. c. 38.

in senatu Graeco] Hotmann quotes a passage from Valerius Maximus (ii. 2, 2): "magistratus vero prisci quanto opere suam Populique Romani majestatem retinentes se gesserint, hinc cognosci potest; quod inter cetera obtinendae gravitatis indicia, illud quoque magna cum perseverantia custodiebant, ne Graecis unquam nisi Latine responsa darent," &c. See Livy, 45. c. 29.

Numidicum,] Q. Caecilius Metellus Numidicus, who commanded in the war against Jugurtha, consul B.C. 109. His sister married L. Lucullus, the father of the L. Lucullus who was now (B.C. 70) carrying on the war against Mithridates. This L. Lucullus, the father, was prosecuted by the augur Q. Servilius for peculation (κλοπῇ), and convicted (Plutarch, Lucullus, c. 1). It appears that Metellus refused to make a laudatory speech, or to give evidence in favour of his brother-in-law.

Quod ubi intellexi] '*Quod* pro *sed*,' says Manutius, for the second time; and he refers to two other instances, one of which is Lib. 1. c. 46, 'quod vos oblitos esse,' &c. See ii. 2. c. 26. The use of 'quod' misleads many critics.

tabellas] Zumpt, in his larger edition, prefers 'tabellas' to the common reading

monitu Syracusanorum ipsorum impetum in eas tabulas facio in quibus S. C. perscripserant. Ecce autem nova turba atque rixa, ne tamen istum omnino Syracusis sine amicis, sine hospitibus, plane nudum esse ac desertum putetis. Retinere incipit tabulas Theomnastus quidam, homo ridicule insanus, quem Syracusani Theoractum vocant, qui illic ejusmodi est ut eum pueri sectentur, ut omnes quum loqui coepit irrideant. Hujus tamen insania, quae ridicula est aliis, mihi tum molesta sane fuit: nam quum spumas ageret in ore, oculis arderet, voce maxima vim me sibi afferre clamaret, copulati in jus pervenimus. Hic ego postulare coepi ut mihi tabulas obsignare ac deportare liceret. Ille contra dicere: negare esse illud S. C. in quo praetor appellatus esset; negare id mihi tradi oportere. Ego legem recitare, omnium mihi tabularum et literarum fieri potestatem. Ille furiosus urgere nihil ad se nostras leges pertinere. Praetor intelligens negare sibi placere, quod senatus consultum ratum esse non deberet, id me Romam deportare. Quid multa? nisi vehementius homini minatus essem, nisi legis sanctionem poenamque recitassem, tabularum mihi potestas facta non esset. Ille autem insanus, qui pro isto vehementissime contra me declamasset, postquam non impetravit, credo, ut in gratiam mecum rediret, libellum mihi dat in quo istius furta Syracusana perscripta erant; quae ego antea jam ab illis cognoram et acceperam.

LXVII. Laudent te jam sane Mamertini quoniam ex tota pro-

'tabulas;' whether with good reason, I hardly know. As to these letters, see Lib. 2. c. 26. The 'literae commendaticiae,' or letters of recommendation to the governor, were common. Many are extant in the collection of Cicero's letters. Hotmann explains 'tabellae tributariae,' as if there were such things. He says they were 'tabellae' which were sent 'si quando provincialibus aliquod tributum sit imperandum;' to which explanation the objections are very numerous. One is enough. It does not explain the text at all; and so Hotmann saw, for he adds, that by 'translata significatione,' they here mean letters 'quae praetori tribuerent et promitterent;' that is, they mean something quite different from the explanation that he has just given. Forcellini, v. Tributarius, refers to Lib. 4. c. 26.

S. C. perscripserant.] R A G 1; 'S. C. perscripserunt' G 2 Ld. As we have this authority, we can justly prefer this to the former reading 'S. C. perscripta erant.'

Theoractum] Theomnastus had a nickname, which among the Greeks was no unusual thing; or Cicero, to enliven his speech, invents one for him, and fathers it on the Syracusans. This 'quidam' is the man who was elected priest of Zeus in such an extraordinary way (Lib. 2. c. 51). To indicate his rabid temper, Cicero calls him Theoractus, or god-struck. Cicero represents himself as seizing the 'tabulae,' and Theomnastus as laying hold of them too. Thus they came 'in jus' before the praetor. 'copulati,' as if fastened together by a 'copula.' Cicero makes as ridiculous a figure as the madman.

legem] The Lex Cornelia, under the authority of which Cicero was collecting evidence. See Lib. 2. c. 74. Cicero speaks of the 'legis sanctionem poenamque.' The 'poena,' or penalty, was in fact the 'sanctio.' (Just. Inst. ii. tit. 1. s. 10: "ideo et legum eas partes quibus poenas constituimus adversus eos qui contra leges fecerint sanctiones vocamus.")

impetravit,] 'impetravisset' R 3. Klotz has 'impetravisset,' undoubtedly a false reading.

vincia soli sunt qui te salvum velint; ita tamen laudent ut Heius qui princeps legationis est adsit; ita laudent ut ad ea quae rogati erunt mihi parati sint respondere. Ac ne subito a me opprimantur haec sum rogaturus: Navem populo Romano debeantne? fatebuntur. Praebuerintne praetore C. Verre? negabunt. Aedificarintne navem onerariam maximam publice quam Verri dederunt? negare non poterunt. Frumentum ab iis sumpseritne C. Verres quod populo Romano mitteret, sicuti superiores? negabunt. Quid militum aut nautarum per triennium dederint? nullum datum dicent. Fuisse Messanam omnium istius furtorum ac praedarum receptricem negare non poterunt: permulta multis navibus illinc exportata: hanc navem denique maximam a Mamertinis datam onustam cum isto profectam fatebuntur. Quamobrem tibi habe sane istam laudationem Mamertinorum: Syracusanam quidem civitatem, ut abs te affecta est, ita in te esse animatam videmus, apud quos etiam Verria illa flagitiosa sublata sunt. Etenim minime conveniebat ei deorum honores haberi qui simulacra deorum abstulisset. Etiam hercule illud in Syracusanis merito reprehenderetur, si, quum diem festum ludorum de fastis suis sustulissent celeberrimum et sanctissimum, quod eo ipso die Syracusae a Marcello captae esse dicuntur, iidem diem festum Verris nomine agerent, quum iste a Syracusanis quae ille calamitosus dies reliquerat ademisset. At videte hominis impudentiam atque arrogantiam, judices, qui non solum Verria haec turpia ac ridicula ex Heraclii pecunia constituerit, verum etiam Marcellia tolli imperarit, ut ei sacra facerent quotannis, cujus opera omnium annorum sacra deosque patrios amiserant; ejus autem familiae dies festos tollerent per quam ceteros quoque festos dies recuperarant.

67. *salvum velint;*] A usual form, as in Lib. 2. c. 60, 'si me salvum esse vis;' and Horace, 1 Sat. 1. v. 84, 'non uxor salvum te vult.'

quam Verri dederunt?] Ernesti thought that the Latin idiom requires 'dederint.' Zumpt is of a different opinion: "nam aedificandi consilium si Cicero exprimere voluisset, scripsisset, opinor, *quam Verri darent*, si conjunctam actionem, *eamque Verri dederint*. Intellige igitur *eam, quam Verri dederunt*." (See Lib. 5. c. 17.) I follow Zumpt and the MSS. Iordan also has 'dederunt.'

si, quum diem festum . . iidem] I find no variation noted here; but it may be observed that 'iidem' ought to have something to correspond to it in the former part of the sentence, and this would be 'qui.' 'Si, qui diem,' &c., would express exactly the same meaning as the text, and it would have the advantage of a word which correlates with 'iidem.'

celeberrimum] See Index.

ACTIONIS SECUNDAE

IN C. VERREM

LIBER QUINTUS.

DE SUPPLICIIS.

Liber Quintus Verrinarum iisdem codicibus continetur quos ad librum quartum commemoravimus. Palimpsesti Vaticani haec extant fragmenta' &c. (Iordan.)

I. Nemini video dubium esse, judices, quin apertissime C. Verres in Sicilia sacra profanaque omnia et privatim et publice spoliarit versatusque sit sine ulla non modo religione verum etiam dissimulatione in omni genere furandi atque praedandi. Sed quaedam mihi magnifica et praeclara defensio ejus ostenditur, cui quemadmodum resistam multo mihi ante est, judices, providendum. Ita enim causa constituitur, provinciam Siciliam virtute istius et vigilantia singulari dubiis formidolosisque temporibus a fugitivis atque a belli periculis tutam esse servatam. Quid agam, judices? quo accusationis meae rationem conferam? quo me vertam? ad omnes enim meos impetus quasi murus quidam boni nomen imperatoris opponitur. Novi locum; video ubi se jactaturus sit Hortensius. Belli pericula, tempora rei publicae, imperatorum penuriam commemorabit: tum deprecabitur a vobis, tum etiam pro suo jure contendet, ne patiamini talem imperatorem populo Romano Siculorum

1. *Novi locum;*] 'I am familiar with the topic.' 'Ubi' refers to 'locum.' It is a topic on which Hortensius will make a great display. It will supply him with matter. Cicero (Top. 2) defines a 'locus' after Aristotle: "Sic enim appellatae ab Aristotele sunt hae quasi sedes e quibus argumenta promuntur. Itaque licet definire, locum esse argumenti sedem, argumentum autem quae rei dubiae faciat fidem." See also De Or. ii. 72.

pro suo jure] 'As consul,' as Zumpt remarks, who refers to the oratio Pro Murena, c. 37. But this interpretation is not correct. Manutius says "eo quod is quasi dominari soleret in judiciis," which appears to be the meaning. Compare 'pro meo jure' (De Or. ii. 72), and this oration, c. 8; also Verr. ii. 2, 14; Pro Sestio, c. 23; Pro Caecina, c. 29; De Amic. c. 9; Terence, Ad. i. 1, 26.

testimoniis eripi, ne[ve] obteri laudem imperatoriam criminibus avaritiae velitis. Non possum dissimulare, judices: timeo ne C. Verres propter hanc eximiam virtutem in re militari omnia quae fecit impune fecerit. Venit enim mihi in mentem in judicio M'. Aquillii quantum auctoritatis, quantum momenti oratio M. Antonii habuisse existimata sit; qui, ut erat in dicendo non solum sapiens, sed etiam fortis, causa prope perorata ipse arripuit M'. Aquillium constituitque in conspectu omnium tunicamque ejus a pectore abscidit, ut cicatrices populus Romanus judicesque aspicerent adverso corpore exceptas: simul et de illo vulnere quod ille in capite ab hostium duce acceperat multa dixit, eoque adduxit eos qui erant judicaturi vehementer ut vererentur, ne, quem virum fortuna ex hostium telis eripuisset, quum sibi ipse non pepercisset, hic non ad populi Romani laudem sed ad judicum crudelitatem videretur esse servatus. Eadem nunc ab illis defensionis ratio viaque temptatur: idem quaeritur. Sit fur, sit sacrilegus, sit flagitiorum omnium vitiorumque princeps. At est bonus imperator, at felix et ad dubia rei publicae tempora reservandus. Non agam summo jure tecum:

ne[ve] obteri] 'ne obteri' R 3, Orelli, who prefers the ἀσύνδετον, and Iordan.

M'. Aquillii] He was tried (B.C. 98) for Repetundae. (Pro Flacco, c. 39.) His offence was committed in Sicily, where he put an end to the Servile war (B.C. 101). Whether we should write 'Aquillius' or 'Aquilius' is doubtful. Here R and Lagg. have 'Aquilii.' The MS. of Gaius has 'Aquilia lex.'

M. Antonius is the great orator, who perished in the Marian proscription. He is introduced by Cicero (De Orat. ii. 47) speaking of the artifice which he employed on this occasion. Antonius was one of the greatest masters in his profession that has ever lived. See his remarks on his way of dealing with a case (De Or. ii. 72).

exceptas:] 'acceptas' Lg. 29.—'temptatur' R.—'fortuna.' 'Fortuna' is the subject of a reflexion by Caesar, B. G. vi. 30; and see Cicero, Cat. i. c. 6, and the note.

felix] 'Felix' means 'fortunate.' Sulla took the name of Felix. Good fortune was part of a general's recommendation, as we see from the encomium on Cn. Pompeius (De Imp. Cn. Pomp. c. 16).

summo jure] 'I will not insist on the utmost rigour of law,' if 'jure' is here to be taken in what some people call its objective sense. But it may mean 'I will not insist on my strict right in this prosecution,' which right would be, inasmuch as Verres was tried under a particular lex (certa lege) and for a particular offence (repetundae), not to allow him to urge in his defence that which, if true, was no answer to this charge.

The old editions and the inferior MSS. have 'constitutum' after 'sit.' See Lib. 4. c. 8, note. But it appears to be rightly omitted on MSS. authority. Ernesti says that 'judicium constitutum' is rather said of the first establishment of a kind of trial by a new 'lex,' than of the several trials which take place according to that 'lex.' Madvig has a remark to the same effect: "nam judicium *constitui* dicitur aut quum lege lata aut edicto, ut de re aliqua judicio agi possit, efficitur; aut quum praetor judice dato rem certa ratione agi jubet. Hoc a nostro loco alienum est; illud minus h. l. commode dicitur de prima constitutione judicii;" for, as he adds, Cicero is speaking of a case as tried under a certain 'lex.' I have in this and a few other instances quoted a Latin note, either because the meaning was not quite clear to me, or for some other reason that seemed to me sufficient. If I understand this right, 'judicium constitutum certa lege' is taken to mean a kind or form of trial established by a 'lex;' that is, a general form applicable to all the cases to which it applies. Whether, if 'constitutum' is used, 'certa

non dicam id quod debeam forsitan obtinere, quum judicium certa lege sit, non quid in re militari fortiter feceris, sed quemadmodum manus ab alienis pecuniis abstinueris, abs te doceri oportere: non, inquam, sic agam; sed ita quaeram, quemadmodum te velle intelligo, quae tua opera et quanta fuerit in bello.

II. Quid dicis? an bello fugitivorum Siciliam virtute tua liberatam? Magna laus et honesta oratio; sed tamen quo bello? Nos enim post illud bellum quod M'. Aquillius confecit sic accepimus, nullum in Sicilia fugitivorum bellum fuisse. At in Italia fuit. Fateor, et magnum quidem ac vehemens. Num igitur ex eo bello partem aliquam laudis appetere conaris? num tibi illius victoriae gloriam cum M. Crasso aut Cn. Pompeio communicatam putas? Non arbitror hoc etiam tuae deesse impudentiae, ut quidquam ejusmodi dicere audeas. Obstitisti videlicet ne ex Italia transire in Siciliam fugitivorum copiae possent. Ubi? quando? qua ex parte? quum aut ratibus aut navibus conarentur accedere. Nos enim nihil unquam prorsus audivimus; et illud audivimus, M. Crassi, fortissimi viri, virtute consilioque factum ne ratibus conjunctis freto fugitivi ad Messanam transire possent; a quo illi conatu non tanto opere prohibendi fuissent, si ulla praesidia in Sicilia ad illorum adventum opposita putarentur. At quum esset in Italia bellum tam

lege' is properly used without 'e' or 'ex,' I am not quite sure; but I think that it is. The words 'certa lege' imply a special case, and if 'constitutum' can be used with 'certa lege,' it follows that 'constitutum' may apply to a special case. Who would ever say that a 'judicium' (general), a general form of trial or procedure, was established by a 'certa lex?' It seems that 'constitutum' may apply either to a general rule (Lib. 1. c. 9), or to what is arranged and ordered in a particular case. (Divin. c. 15, 'si tu *eris* actor constitutus.')

2. *At in Italia*] This was the war which Spartacus stirred up B.C. 73, and it cost the Romans some trouble to put down this vigorous rebel and his bands. L. Crassus at last succeeded in breaking the force of Spartacus; and Cn. Pompeius, on his return from Spain (B.C. 71), got more credit for destroying a remnant of them than he deserved. Plutarch (Crassus, c. 11, and Pompeius, c. 21) has told the story.

tuae deesse] Ernesti found a difficulty here, and thought that we should write 'esse.' That which caused a difficulty to him, may cause a difficulty to others. 'I don't suppose that you would carry your impudence so far as to venture to say this,' would express the meaning pretty nearly; but this form of expression is not exactly that of Cicero, which is this: 'I don't think that your impudence requires this also to complete it.'

Obstitisti] That Cicero as a prosecutor exaggerated things is shown by a fragment of Sallust's Hist. iv. 31, ed. Kritz: "C. Verres litora Italiae propinqua firmavit." (Halm.)

conarentur accedere.] The editions place a note of interrogation after 'accedere,' as if a question were contained in 'quum . . . accedere,' which is manifestly a mistake.

et illud] Ernesti proposed to write 'at' for 'et;' and Halm 'sed' for 'et.' I do not think that any change should be made.

ratibus conjunctis] This can only mean 'by making rafts.' In Caesar, B. G. i. 8, I think 'navibus junctis' means 'by bridges of boats.'

At quum esset] This is supposed to be urged on the side of Verres, to which 'Quid mirum?' is the answer.

prope a Sicilia, tamen in Sicilia non fuit. Quid mirum? ne quum in Sicilia quidem fuit eodem intervallo pars ejus belli in Italiam ulla pervasit. III. Etenim propinquitas locorum ad utram partem hoc loco profertur? utrum aditum facilem hostibus an contagionem imitandi belli periculosam fuisse? Aditus omnis hominibus sine ulla facultate navium non modo disjunctus sed etiam clausus est, ut illis quibus Siciliam propinquam fuisse dicis facilius fuerit ad Oceanum pervenire quam ad Peloridem accedere. Contagio autem ista servilis belli cur abs te potius quam ab iis omnibus, qui ceteras provincias obtinuerunt, praedicatur? An quod in Sicilia jam ante bella fugitivorum fuerunt? At ea ipsa causa est cur ista provincia minimo in periculo sit et fuerit. Nam posteaquam illinc M'. Aquillius decessit, omnium instituta atque edicta praetorum fuerunt ejusmodi ut ne quis cum telo servus esset. Vetus est quod dicam, et propter severitatem exempli nemini fortasse vestrum inauditum; L. Domitium praetorem in Sicilia, quum aper ingens allatus esset ad eum, admiratum requisisse quis eum percussisset: quum audisset pastorem cujusdam fuisse, eum ad se vocari jussisse: illum cupide ad praetorem quasi ad laudem atque praemium accurrisse: quaesisse Domitium qui tantam bestiam percussisset: illum respondisse venabulo: statim deinde jussu praetoris in crucem esse sublatum. Durum hoc fortasse videatur neque ego ullam in partem disputo: tantum intelligo maluisse Domitium crudelem in animadvertendo quam in praetermittendo dissolutum videri.

IV. Ergo his institutis provinciae jam tum quum bello sociorum

3. *ne quis cum telo*] 'Esse cum telo,' to go about with a 'telum' (Pro Milone, c. 4). 'Telum' is defined by Gaius (Dig. 50. 16. 233). Sallust (Cat. 27) has the expression 'ipse cum telo esse.' Cicero (Lib. 5. c. 16) writes 'quum esses cum tunica pulla et pallio.'

L. Domitium] His praetorship belongs to a period after the retirement of M'. Aquillius from Sicily, and before the Social war, B.C. 91, 90. It was probably B.C. 96. —'Vetus' is explained by Orelli: "pervagatum exemplum, saepe commemoratum."

in crucem . . sublatum.] 'Sublatus' is one of the terms applied to crucifixion. 'Suffigere' (Hor. 1 Sat. iii. 82) is another. Our word 'cross' does not fully render 'crux,' for the 'crux' was of various forms. It might be in the form of the trunk of a tree, or upright post, or it might have cross-pieces to fasten the hands to. It is called 'arbor infelix' (Livy, i. 26), and was an ancient mode of punishment even for free men. In Cicero's time it was peculiarly a mode of punishing slaves; but under the emperors, at least, it was sometimes also the punishment of free men. Lipsius has a treatise De Cruce (J. Lipsii Opera, iii. p. 1141, ed. Vesal. 1675). In c. 6, 'ad palum alligati' might seem equivalent to 'in crucem sublati;' but it may not be.

ullam in partem] Compare 'utram in partem' in this chapter. 'In nullam partem disputare' means 'to dispute or question in no way.'

4. *bello sociorum*] The reading of R 3 λ. The dett. have 'fugitivorum,' and it was the common reading. After the establishment of tranquillity in Sicily by M'. Aquillius, the Social war, or Marsic war, as it is often called, broke out in Italy. The Italian Socii were dissatisfied with the Roman supremacy, which brought with it heavy requisitions for the army, and they attempted to establish a kind of federal system of their own. During this commotion Sicily was

tota Italia arderet, homo non acerrimus nec fortissimus, C. Norbanus, in summo otio fuit; perfacile enim sese Sicilia jam tuebatur ut ne quod ex ipsa bellum posset exsistere. Etenim quum nihil tam conjunctum sit quam negotiatores nostri cum Siculis usu, re, ratione, concordia, et quum ipsi Siculi res suas ita constitutas habeant ut iis pacem expediat esse, imperium autem populi Romani sic diligant ut id imminui aut commutari minime velint, quumque haec a servorum bello pericula et praetorum institutis et dominorum disciplina provisa sint, nullum est malum domesticum quod ex ipsa provincia nasci possit. Quid igitur, nulline motus in Sicilia servorum Verre praetore, nullaene consensiones factae esse dicuntur? Nihil sane quod ad senatum populumque Romanum pervenerit; nihil quod iste publice Romam scripserit: et tamen coeptum esse in Sicilia moveri aliquot locis servitium suspicor. Id adeo non tam ex re quam ex istius factis decretisque cognosco.

V. Ac videte quam non inimico animo sim acturus: ego ipse haec quae iste quaerit, quae adhuc nunquam audistis, commemorabo et proferam. In Triocalino, quem locum fugitivi jam ante tenuerunt, Leonidae cujusdam Siculi familia in suspicionem est vocata conjurationis. Res delata ad istum. Statim, ut par fuit, jussu ejus homines qui fuerant nominati comprehensi sunt adductique Lilybaeum: domino denuntiatum est: causa dicta: damnati. Quid deinde? quid censetis? Furtum fortasse aut praedam exspectatis aliquam. Nolite usquequaque idem quaerere. In metu

quiet: the slaves had just felt the Roman scourge, and were not willing to provoke it again. The Sicilian praetorship of C. Norbanus must have preceded that of Sex. Peducaeus (B.C. 76, 75), and was therefore before the Servile war in Italy, which coincided with the praetorship of Verres (B.C. 73—71). The praetorship of Norbanus must belong to B.C. 91 or 90, the time during which the Social war was raging. Zumpt supposes Norbanus to be the Tribunus Plebis, B.C. 95, who was accused of Majestas by P. Sulpicius Rufus, and defended by M. Antonius, as Cicero mentions in several passages of the De Oratore, Lib. 2. c. 25, 47—50. See Meyer, Or. Fr.

Romam scripserit:] The common reading is 'conscripserit,' contrary to the usage in such cases, which is 'scripserit.' Orelli has 'conscripserit,' which, he says, means 'de consilii sententia scripserit.' He adds that this reading is one of those in which the 'vulgares codices' have preserved the genuine hand of Cicero. It is true that the 'vulgares' are sometimes the better, but it is not so here.

5. *quaerit.*] 'What is he looking for.' I will supply him with some facts in proof of there being some movement of the slaves in Sicily.

Triocalino.] The place is Triocala, or Tricala, or Tricalon (Steph. Byz. ed. Meineke). It was situated between Selinus and Heraclea, but in the interior, and at a place now called Troccoli. Diodorus (36. Exc. Phot.) says that Trypho, a rebel slave, made this place his head-quarters in the second Servile war.

denuntiatum] 'Ut adesset' is generally added after 'denuntiatum,' but it is not in the better MSS., though it is meant, for it is added shortly after, 'denuntavit ut adesset.' 'Denuntiatum' means that notice was given to the owner to appear and defend his slaves.

causa dicta: damnati.] I have followed Orelli's text here. Zumpt has 'causa dicta damnati.' But 'causa dicta' is the nominative, and so Iordan has it.

belli furandi locus qui potest esse? etiam si qua fuit in hac re occasio, praetermissa est. Tum potuit a Leonida nummorum aliquid auferre quum denuntiavit ut adesset. Fuit nundinatio aliqua et isti non nova, ne causam diceret: etiam alter locus, ut absolverentur. Damnatis quidem servis quae praedandi potest esse ratio? produci ad supplicium necesse est. Testes enim sunt qui in consilio fuerunt: testes publicae tabulae: testes splendidissima civitas Lilybaetana: testis honestissimus maximusque conventus civium Romanorum. Fieri nihil potest: producendi sunt. Itaque producuntur et ad palum alligantur. Etiam nunc mihi exspectare videmini, judices, quid deinde factum sit, quod iste nihil unquam fecit sine aliquo quaestu atque praeda. Quid in ejusmodi re fieri potuit? Quod commodum est exspectate, facinus quam vultis improbum: vincam tamen exspectationem omnium. Homines sceleris conjurationisque damnati, ad supplicium traditi, ad palum alligati, repente multis millibus hominum inspectantibus soluti sunt et Triocalino illi domino redditi. Quid hoc loco potes dicere, homo amentissime, nisi id quod ego non quaero,—quod denique in re tam nefaria, tametsi dubitari non potest, tamen, ne si dubitetur quidem, quaeri oporteat—quid aut quantum aut quomodo acceperis? Remitto tibi hoc totum, atque ista te cura libero. Neque enim metuo ne hoc cuiquam persuadeatur ut ad quod facinus nemo praeter te ulla pecunia adduci potuerit, id tu gratis suscipere conatus sis.

ne causam diceret: . . . absolverentur.] Graevius says that his Reg. has 'dicerent,' and that this reading is confirmed by 'ut absolverentur.' Quite the contrary. The slaves could not be said 'dicere causam.' The slaves were tried and condemned, and what followed then? Cicero intends to surprise us by the termination of the affair. 'Verres might have got some money from Leonidas at the time when he summoned him. There was room for some bargaining—no new thing to Verres—that Leonidas should not be called on to defend the case; there was even another subject-matter for a bargain, their acquittal.' But they were already convicted, and after conviction comes execution. Klotz has 'diceret' in his text, but he has a note in favour of 'dicerent,' a reading which is not to be rejected solely because 'dicere causam' cannot properly be said of a slave; for it may mean here simply 'that they should not be tried.' But I take 'diceret' to be the genuine text, though, according to Jordan, it is the reading of the dett.

qui in consilio] See Divin. c. 4.

Fieri nihil potest:] Orelli omits 'fieri,' following the 'vulgares,' as the conservators of the genuine text. In this way the 'vulgares' have a chance of becoming the 'meliores.'

Quod commodum est &c.] Zumpt has 'quod commodum est? Exspectate' &c. We may feel surprised that he found no difficulty in 'quod commodum est?' 'Quod commodum est' is the answer, and means 'just what you please.' (Pro Tullio, § 17; Pro Cluentio, c. 35; Pro Flacco, c. 9; Ter. Phorm. i. 2, 81.) Madvig set this right, and Orelli and Jordan follow him. Orelli's text is 'Quod commodum est exspectato facinus quam vultis improbum.' The answer is 'Quod commodum est exspectate,' and then a pause, followed by the further explanation, 'facinus quam vultis improbum.'

inspectantibus] Perhaps we should write 'spectantibus,' as Cicero certainly sometimes does in like cases.

Verum de ista furandi praedandique ratione nihil dico: de hac imperatoria jam tua laude disputo.

VI. Quid ais, bone custos defensorque provinciae? Tu quos servos arma capere ac bellum facere in Sicilia voluisse cognoras et de consilii sententia judicaras, hos ad supplicium jam more majorum traditos, et ad palum alligatos, ex media morte eripere ac liberare ausus es, ut quam damnatis crucem servis fixeras, hanc indemnatis videlicet civibus Romanis reservares? Perditae civitates desperatis jam omnibus rebus hos solent exitus exitiales habere, ut damnati in integrum restituantur, vincti solvantur, exules reducantur, res judicatae rescindantur. Quae quum accidunt, nemo est quin intelligat ruere illam rem publicam: haec ubi eveniunt, nemo est qui ullam spem salutis reliquam esse arbitretur. Atque haec sicubi facta sunt, facta sunt ut homines populares aut nobiles supplicio aut exilio levarentur: at non ab iis ipsis qui judicassent; at non statim; at non eorum facinorum damnati quae ad vitam et ad fortunas omnium pertinerent. Hoc vero novum et ejusmodi est ut magis propter reum quam propter rem ipsam credibile videatur, ut homines servos, ut ipse qui judicarat, ut statim e medio supplicio

6. *Quid ais, &c.*] A sarcastic address, such as a man would use in ordinary life. So Terence says, 'bone custos, salve, columen vero familiae' (Phormio, ii. 3, 57).

more majorum] A usual phrase. See Caesar, B. G. vi. 44; Sueton. Nero, 49. The 'mos majorum' was different in different cases; for slaves it was flogging first and then crucifixion. See c. 9, "tot supplicia in improbos more majorum constituta."

et ad palum alligatos,] Zumpt omits these words in his larger edition; and Iordan also, who says that they are only in the dett. They have been used above. Cicero might repeat them for the purpose of effect. The men were tied to be flogged perhaps. See c. 3.—'indemnatis:' see c. 61.

exitus exitiales] Klotz cites a passage from De Leg. Agr. ii. 4: "qui civitatum afflictarum perditis jam rebus extremi exitiorum solent esse exitus;" but Orelli thinks that this passage is corrupt.

in integrum restituantur, . . rescindantur.] See the Index.

populares aut nobiles] The term 'nobiles' is explained elsewhere. 'Populares' is a common Roman term to express the leaders of the 'populus' in the sense which the word had in Cicero's time, or those who affected to consult the interests of the many as opposed to the interests of the few, of the 'nobiles.' In this passage the 'nobiles' and the 'populares' are put in opposition, as the two rival parties in a state, but Cicero generally contrasts 'populares' with 'optimates,' the best people in the state, as they called themselves, the conservative party, which consisted of the senate, the rest of the nobility, and the Equites; in fact, all who attached themselves to the party. Yet as 'popularis' is one who favours the 'populus,' of whatever rank he might be, it often happened that one of the 'nobiles' chose the popular side, as the best means of promoting his own interests; and thus, though a 'nobilis,' he would not be one of the 'optimates,' but a 'popularis.' Cicero on several occasions explains the terms 'optimates' and 'populares,' and gives to each the complexion which suits his purpose (Pro Sestio, c. 45, 65; Pro Cluentio, c. 34; De leg. Agr. ii. c. 4). Thus his 'popularis homo' is sometimes the same as 'turbulentus.' Machiavelli (Istor. Fiorent. iii.) uses the same terms, 'gli uomini Popolari e i Nobili,' and characterizes them with his usual precision.

Iordan following R 3 reads 'populares ac nobiles,' and he says "opponuntur *homines populares ac nobiles* (i. e. qui iidem sunt nobiles) *hominibus servis*, i. e. homines nobili loco nati et apud populum gratiosi hominibus infimae condicionis," &c.

dimiserit, ut ejus facinoris damnatos servos quod ad omnium liberorum caput et sanguinem pertineret. O praeclarum imperatorem nec jam cum M'. Aquillio, fortissimo viro, sed vero cum Paullis, Scipionibus, Mariis conferendum! Tantumne vidisse in metu periculoque provinciae! Quum servitiorum animos in Sicilia suspensos propter bellum Italiae fugitivorum videret, ne quis se commovere auderet quantum terroris injecit! Comprehendi jussit: quis non pertimescat? causam dicere dominos: quid servis tam formidolosum? 'Fecisse videri' pronuntiat: exortam videtur flammam paucorum dolore ac morte restinxisse. Quid deinde sequitur? Verbera atque ignes et illa extrema ad supplicium damnatorum, metum ceterorum, et cruciatus et crux. Hisce omnibus suppliciis sunt liberati. Quis dubitet quin servorum animos summa formidine oppresserit, quum viderent ea facilitate praetorem ut ab eo [servorum] sceleris conjurationisque damnatorum vita vel ipso carnifice internuntio redimeretur?

VII. Quid, hoc in Apolloniensi Aristodamo? quid, in Leonte Imacharensi non idem fecisti? Quid, iste motus servorum bellique subita suspicio, utrum tibi tandem diligentiam custodiendae provinciae an novam rationem improbissimi quaestus attulit? Halicyensis Eumenidae, nobilis hominis et honesti, magnae pecuniae, villicus quum impulsu tuo insimulatus esset, HS $\overline{\text{LX}}$ a domino accepisti, quod nuper ipse juratus docuit quemadmodum gestum esset. Ab equite Romano C. Matrinio absente, quum is esset Romae, quod ejus villicos pastoresque tibi in suspicionem venisse dixeras, HS $\overline{\text{DC}}$ abstulisti. Dixit hoc L. Flavius, qui tibi eam pecuniam

sed vero] Orelli remarks that 'sed' and 'vero' are seldom united in Cicero, so that 'vero' retains its original signification. Pro Cluentio, c. 6.

servis] '*servo*' Iordan; 'servis' dett.—'Fecisse videri:' see Lib. 2. c. 38, note.

7. *servorum*] 'Servitiorum' R 3 λ; Orelli, 'exquisitius quam *servorum*.' Iordan has 'servitiorum.'

magnae pecuniae,] Ernesti prefixed 'et' to these words solely from conjecture. Zumpt properly ejected 'et;' but he connects 'magnae pecuniae' with 'villicus,' and explains it to be a 'villicus' of great value. Klotz follows him. There is no doubt of the value of a good 'villicus,' and a master might gladly pay a large sum to save him. But the value of the 'villicus' was not so important here as the wealth of the master. Zumpt gives no instance to show that 'magnae pecuniae' can be taken in his sense. The instance which he quotes from Sallust (Bell. Jug. c. 85), to show the opinion of C. Marius of the relative value of a 'cook' and a 'villicus,' does not help us in the explanation. Iordan has 'magnae pecuniae vilicus,' and he explains it 'a valuable vilicus.' He compares Lib. 4. c. 41, 'signum magnae pecuniae.' There is also De leg. Agr. ii. c. 14, 'via . . magnae pecuniae,' and Pro S. Rosc. Amer. c. 37. However I take 'magnae pecuniae' to be the same as 'pecuniosus,' which occurs in this chapter, and in Lib. 4. c. 25. Orelli, who understands the passage right, observes that some interpreters have connected 'magnae pecuniae' with 'insimulatus:' 'qua servitia concitare posset.' But he observes that 'insimulari' occurs in c. 41 without any case.

numeravit, procurator C. Matrinii: dixit ipse C. Matrinius: dicet vir clarissimus Cn. Lentulus censor, qui Matrinii honoris causa recenti negotio ad te literas misit mittendasque curavit. Quid, de Apollonio, Diocli filio, Panhormitano, cui Gemino cognomen est, praeteriri potest? Ecquid hoc tota Sicilia clarius? ecquid indignius? ecquid manifestius proferri potest? Quem ut Panhormum venit ad se vocari et de tribunali citari jussit concursu magno frequentiaque conventus. Homines statim loqui: 'mirabar quod Apollonius, homo pecuniosus, tamdiu ab isto maneret integer: excogitavit, nescio quid attulit: profecto homo dives repente a Verre non sine causa citatur.' Exspectatio summa hominum quidnam id esset, quum exanimatus subito ipse accurrit cum adolescente filio; nam pater grandis natu jam diu lecto tenebatur. Nominat iste servum quem magistrum pecoris esse diceret: eum dicit conjurasse et familias concitasse. Is omnino servus in familia non erat. Eum statim exhiberi jubet. Apollonius affirmare se omnino nomine illo servum habere neminem. Iste hominem abripi a tribunali et in carcerem conjici jubet. Clamare ille quum raperetur nihil se miserum fecisse, nihil commisisse, pecuniam sibi esse in nominibus, numeratam in praesentia non habere. Haec quum maxime summa

honoris causa] 'Out of regard to Matrinius,' as Zumpt correctly explains it, or 'to show his respect to Matrinius.' Ernesti thought that 'Matrinii causa' would be sufficient, and so it might be; but Cicero did not think so. Zumpt cites Caesar (Bell. Gall. ii. 15), 'Caesar honoris Divitiaci . . causa;' Cicero, Pro Rosc. Am. c. 35; Ad Attic. xv. 14. Also Livy, 32. c. 34. 'Honoris causa' also occurs on the inscription of C. Poblicius beneath the capitol in Trajan's Forum: C. POBLICIO. L. F. BIBVLO. AED. PL. HONORIS. VIRTVTISQVE. CAVSSA. . . . &c.

mirabar] Better than the common reading 'mirari,' which would not agree with the fact. 'I was wondering,' says one of the by-standers, 'that Apollonius remained so long safe from the attacks of Verres.' See Ter. Phorm. iii. 5, 6. He was no longer safe. Compare 'nam sperabam, inquit,' &c., Lib. 3. c. 85.—'excogitavit nescio quid: attulit:' Schuetz. I have followed Zumpt and Orelli.

Exspectatio . . quidnam] This is the same as if he had said 'exspectabant omnes quidnam;' the noun in a manner performs the office of a verb. There are other instances in Cicero where this is still clearer, as where 'scientia' is followed by 'quid' (Act. i. c. 18), "scientiam quid agatur memoriamque quid a quoque dictum sit." In c. 14, "habeo rationem quid a populo Romano acceperim;" but in c. 28, "habebant rationem omnes quotidie piratarum qui securi ferirentur." The following passages may also be compared: Cic. Ad Att. i. 17, 'affectus admiratione quidnam accidisset;' Pro Cluentio, c. 28; Pro P. Sulla, c. 1. The use of accusatives neuter, both in Greek and Latin, is much more loose or free than in the case of other words.

hominum] I have now taken 'hominum,' the reading of R 3 λ, instead of 'omnium,' the reading of dett. 'Hominum' is more emphatic in this passage. Zumpt and Iordan have also the reading 'hominum.' It is often very difficult to decide between these two words.

magistrum pecoris] A 'magister pecoris' was a flockmaster, chief of all the shepherds (Varro, De R. R. ii. 10, 2, cited by Hahn).

exhiberi] 'To be produced.' See Lib. 2, c. 78, note.

in nominibus,] He had money due to him, which in the next chapter is called 'pecuniis creditis.' See the explanation of 'nomina' Lib. 1. c. 38. 'Pecunia numerata' is money in coin (Pro Flacco, c. 22). If he had it, he meant to say, he was ready to give it to the praetor.

hominum frequentia testificaretur, ut quivis intelligere posset eum quod pecuniam non dedisset, idcirco illa tam acerba injuria affici; quum maxime, ut dico, hoc de pecunia clamaret, in vincula conjectus est.

VIII. Videte constantiam praetoris, et ejus praetoris qui in iis rebus non ita defendatur ut mediocris praetor, sed ita laudetur ut optimus imperator. Quum servorum bellum metueretur, quo supplicio dominos indemnatos afficiebat, hoc servos damnatos liberabat: Apollonium, hominem locupletissimum, qui si fugitivi bellum in Sicilia facerent amplissimas fortunas amitteret, belli fugitivorum nomine indicta causa in vincla conjecit: servos quos ipse cum consilio belli faciendi causa consensisse judicavit, eos sine consilii sententia sua sponte omni supplicio liberavit. Quid, si aliquid ab Apollonio commissum est quamobrem in eum jure animadverteretur, tamenne hanc rem sic agemus ut crimini aut invidiae reo putemus esse oportere, si quo de homine severius judicaverit? Non agam tam acerbe: non utar ista accusatoria consuetudine, si quid est factum clementer, ut dissolute factum criminer; si quid vindicatum est severe, ut ex eo crudelitatis invidiam colligam. Non agam ista ratione; tua sequar judicia; tuam defendam auctoritatem, quoad tu voles: simul ac tute coeperis tua judicia rescindere, mihi succensere desinito: meo jure enim contendam eum qui suo judicio damnatus sit juratorum judicum sententiis damnari oportere. Non defendam Apollonii causam, amici atque hospitis mei, ne tuum judicium videar rescindere; nihil de hominis frugalitate, virtute, diligentia dicam; praetermittam illud etiam, de quo antea dixi, fortunas ejus ita constitutas fuisse familia, pecore, villis, pecuniis creditis, ut nemini minus expediret ullum in Sicilia tumultum aut bellum commoveri: non dicam ne illud quidem, si maxime in culpa fuerit Apollonius, tamen in hominem honestissimae civitatis honestissimum tam graviter animadverti causa indicta non oportuisse. Nullam in te invidiam ne ex illis quidem rebus concitabo, quum esset talis vir in carcere, in tenebris, in

8. *sed ita laudetur*] 'Sed ita laudatur' R 3, L. St., Orelli, which can also be explained.

cum consilio] 'Boni Codd. omnes *de consilio*' (Zumpt), that is, R 3 λ (Iordan). I suppose that the 'mali' have 'cum consilio;' and they may be right. Lambinus suspects that Cicero wrote 'de consilii sententia.' This was a criminal affair, and was tried by the praetor and a body of 'judices,' his 'consilium.' In c. 9 there is 'sententia sine consilio.' I suppose then we may say 'cum consilio.' Klotz, who has 'de consilio,' applies it to the slaves in the sense of 'purposely,' 'designedly.' If this is the explanation, it is an additional argument against the reading.

succensere] 'suscensere' R, Iordan; and this may be the true form.—'meo jure:' see c. 1, note.

squalore, in sordibus, tyrannicis interdictis tuis patri exacta aetate et adolescenti filio adeundi ad illum miserum potestatem nunquam esse factam. Etiam illud praeteribo, quotiescunque Panhormum veneris illo anno et sex mensibus, nam tamdiu fuit Apollonius in carcere, toties te senatum Panhormitanum adisse supplicem cum magistratibus sacerdotibusque publicis orantem atque obsecrantem ut aliquando ille miser atque innocens calamitate illa liberaretur. Relinquo haec omnia; quae si velim persequi, facile ostendam tua crudelitate in alios omnes tibi aditus misericordiae judicum jampridem esse praeclusos. IX. Omnia tibi ista concedam et remittam. Praevideo enim quid sit defensurus Hortensius: fatebitur apud istum neque senectutem patris neque adolescentiam filii neque lacrimas utriusque plus valuisse quam utilitatem salutemque provinciae: dicet rem publicam administrari sine metu ac severitate non posse: quaeret quamobrem fasces praetoribus praeferantur, cur secures datae, cur carcer aedificatus, cur tot supplicia sint in improbos more majorum constituta? Quae quum omnia graviter severeque dixerit, quaeram cur hunc eundem Apollonium Verres idem repente nulla re nova allata, nulla defensione, sine causa de carcere emitti jusserit: tantumque in hoc crimine suspicionis esse affirmabo ut jam ipsis judicibus sine mea argumentatione conjecturam facere permittam, quod hoc genus praedandi, quam improbum quam indignum, quamque ad magnitudinem quaestus immensum infinitumque esse videatur. Nam quae iste in Apollonio fecit, ea primum breviter cognoscite quot et quanta sint; deinde haec expendite atque aestimate pecunia: reperietis idcirco haec in uno homine pecunioso tot constituta, ut ceteris formidines similium incommodorum atque exempla periculorum proponeret. Primum insimulatio est repentina capitalis atque invidiosi criminis: sta-

aditus misericordiae judicum] "Qui aliquem sermonis aditum causamque amicitiae cum Caesare habebant," Caesar, B. G. v. 41. The use of the Latin genitive is peculiar. Besides writing 'aditus misericordiae' Cicero adds 'judicum.'

9. *Praevideo*] 'Provideo' R 3 λ, alii, Iordan; 'praevideo' Lg. 48.

fasces praetoribus] In the provinces 'lictors' carried six 'fasces' before a 'propraetor,' at the extremity of which were the axes. Cicero makes an apt allusion to these symbols of authority in his letter to his brother Quintus (i. 1. c. 4), when he was governor of Asia, "majorque praeferant fasces illi ac secures dignitatis insignia quam potestatis."

quod hoc genus] 'What kind of plundering this must be considered.'

criminis:] Rein (Das Criminalrecht der Römer, p. 93) discusses the various meanings of 'crimen.' The first and most usual meaning is 'charge,' 'formal accusation.' But a legal 'charge' must be founded on some violation of law, and accordingly 'crimen' has also the meaning of 'illegal act,' and 'crime.' In some passages it seems doubtful which of these two senses is the meaning. In this passage Rein gives this second meaning to 'crimen.' Wesenberg, quoted by Halm, gives to it the first meaning.

tuite quanti hoc putetis et quam multos redemisse: deinde crimen sine accusatore, sententia sine consilio, damnatio sine defensione: aestimate harum omnium rerum pretia, et cogitate in his iniquitatibus unum haesisse Apollonium, ceteros profecto multos ex his incommodis pecunia se liberasse: postremo tenebrae, vincula, carcer, inclusum supplicium, a conspectu parentum ac liberûm, denique a libero spiritu atque a communi luce seclusum: haec vero, quae vel vita redimi recte possint, aestimare pecunia non queo. Haec omnia sero redemit Apollonius jam maerore ac miseriis perditus; sed tamen ceteros docuit ante istius avaritiae ac sceleri occurrere: nisi vero existimatis hominem pecuniosissimum sine causa quaestus electum ad tam incredibile crimen, aut sine eadem causa repente e carcere emissum, aut hoc praedandi genus ab isto in illo uno adhibitum et temptatum, et non per illum omnibus pecuniosis Siculis metum propositum et injectum.

X. Cupio mihi ab illo, judices, subjici, quoniam de militari ejus gloria dico, si quid forte praetereo. Nam mihi videor jam de omnibus rebus ejus gestis dixisse quae quidem ad belli fugitivorum suspicionem pertinerent: certe nihil sciens praetermisi. Habetis hominis consilia, diligentiam, vigilantiam, custodiam defensionemque provinciae. Summa illuc pertinet ut sciatis, quoniam plura genera sunt imperatorum, ex quo genere iste sit. Ne diutius in tanta penuria virorum fortium talem imperatorem ignorare possitis—non ad Q. Maximi sapientiam neque ad illius superioris Africani in

haesisse] A metaphor taken from snares, says Hotmann. Apollonius was caught: the rest took warning by his example.

inclusum supplicium,] Gruter would be glad to know what these words mean here. Graevius thinks that they ought to be erased. Perhaps the expression is unusual. The punishment was imprisonment. That is all that is meant.—'aque conspectu' Orelli; 'atque conspectu' R, Iordan.

vel vita] That is, it would be better to die than suffer such punishment.—'recte possunt' is the common reading, and Iordan's. Either may do. Zumpt considers the conjunctive more elegant. 'Possint' G 1 2; 'possent' Ld.

occurrere:] 'to anticipate,' 'prevent.' See Lib. 4. c. 47, 'occurrendum esse satietati.'

sine causa quaestus] 'Sine aliqua causa quaestus,' the common reading; but all the good MSS. omit 'aliqua' (Zumpt). As to 'causa,' see Lib. 4. c. 51.

10. *non ad Q. Maximi*] Zumpt, Klotz, Orelli, and Iordan have made this the beginning of a new sentence. The words 'ne diutius' have generally been made the beginning of the sentence, but these editors have attached them to the end of the preceding sentence.

Zumpt also reads 'ne quis diutius . . possit.' R 3 have 'ne qui,' but G 'ne quis.' R has 'possit,' G 3 'posset,' and the dett. have 'possitis.' Zumpt also reads 'sed aliud genus imperatoris;' but the words 'plura genera . . ex quo genere sit' are against this reading. 'Imperatorum' is the reading of some old eds., as Iordan observes. The sense then of the first sentence is this: 'The sum of the matter results in this; you must learn, since there are several kinds of Imperatores, what kind Verres belongs to.'

Klotz says that the construction of the sentence 'non ad' &c., appears somewhat abrupt, and that we must supply a 'qui accedat' in the first member.

The text of Orelli and Klotz is the same

re gerunda celeritatem, neque ad hujus qui postea fuit singulare consilium, neque ad Paulli rationem ac disciplinam, neque ad C. Marii vim atque virtutem, sed ad aliud genus imperatorum sane diligenter retinendum et conservandum—quaeso, cognoscite. Itinerum primum laborem qui vel maximus est in re militari, judices, et in Sicilia maxime necessarius, accipite quam facilem sibi iste et jucundum ratione consilioque reddiderit. Primum temporibus hibernis ad magnitudinem frigorum et ad tempestatum vim ac fluminum praeclarum hoc sibi remedium compararat. Urbem Syracusas elegerat; cujus hic situs atque haec natura esse loci coelique dicitur ut nullus unquam dies tam magna ac turbulenta tempestate fuerit quin aliquo tempore ejus diei solem homines viderint. Hic ita vivebat iste bonus imperator hibernis mensibus ut eum non facile non modo extra tectum, sed ne extra lectum quidem quisquam videret: ita diei brevitas conviviis, longitudo noctis stupris et flagitiis conterebatur. Quum autem ver esse coeperat, cujus

as Zumpt's, except that they have 'ne qui diutius,' &c. But these editors don't agree about the interpretation. The 'ad,' according to Graevius and Orelli, means 'in comparison with' (im Vergleich—mit); and the passages Pro Deiot. 8, 'Veteres credo,' &c.; and De Or. ii. 6, 'nihil ad Persium,' are quoted. Zumpt objects to this: his explanation is the following: "Cognoscite eum, qualis fuerit, non ut Maximum aliquem aut Scipionem aut Marium sed ut aliud quoddam novum genus imperatoris in civitate diligenter retineatis." This, I think, is nearer the meaning, and it is unimportant whether the 'ad' before 'aliud' is added or omitted. I prefer keeping it. There only then remains the difference between 'imperatoris' and 'imperatorum;' and the question whether the sentence begins with 'ne diutius,' or 'ne quis diutius,' and 'non ad.' I have adopted the reading of Orelli's larger edition, with the punctuation slightly altered. The meaning is this: 'That in such a dearth of brave men, you may no longer be strangers to such an Imperator—I pray you, make yourselves acquainted with him.' The words 'non ad Q. Maximi . . retinendum et conservandum' are thrown in parenthetically, and I explain them as Zumpt does.—'hujus' is the younger Africanus.

fluminum] The rains in Sicily are often very heavy in the winter, and owing to the hilly nature of the country and their short course the streams become very impetuous and difficult to pass. The regular rains do not commence till November, between which month and March they fall often in heavy torrents. "The violent rains that deluge the island at this season swell the rivers, damage the roads, and set the Fiumare running: these are torrents, occasioned by the waters descending from the mountains into deep ravines, through which they rush with impetuosity into the sea, carrying every thing before them.—The boisterous force of the Fiumare while flowing, the badness of the roads, and the want of bridges, render travelling in the winter dangerous, and at times wholly impracticable" (Smyth's Sicily, p. 7). Swinburne (Travels in the Two Sicilies, ii. 266) describes the curious way in which he crossed the Halycus (Platani) when it was swollen by the winter rains.

solem] This happy climate, where the sun is seen every day in the year, is also attributed to Rhodes by Pliny (ii. 62), and to Alexandria by Ammianus Marcellinus (xxii. 16). Seneca, in the consolation to Marcia (c. 17), says the same of Syracuse, but he gives a bad account of the summer climate. Compare Livy, xxv. 25.—'quis . . viderent' is the common reading and that of Ernesti. Zumpt wonders that he did not see that it ought to be 'viderint.' Madvig, quoted by Orelli, remarks: "nulla est hic temporum historica, quam dicunt, consecutio, sed absolute unam certam definitamque rem omnino factam dicit."

conterebatur.] 'continebatur' Klotz, Iordan; 'conterebatur' dett.

initium iste non a Favonio neque ab aliquo astro notabat, sed quum rosam viderat, tum incipere ver arbitrabatur, dabat se labori atque itineribus, in quibus eo usque se praebebat patientem atque impigrum ut eum nemo unquam in equo sedentem viderit. XI. Nam, ut mos fuit Bithyniae regibus, lectica octophoro ferebatur, in qua pulvinus erat perlucidus Melitensis, rosa fartus: ipse autem coronam habebat unam in capite, alteram in collo, reticulumque ad nares sibi admovebat, tenuissimo lino, minutis maculis, plenum rosae. Sic confecto itinere, quum ad aliquod oppidum venerat, eadem lectica usque in cubiculum deferebatur. Eo veniebant Siculorum magistratus, veniebant equites Romani, id quod ex multis juratis audistis: controversiae secreto deferebantur, paulo post palam decreta auferebantur. Deinde ubi paulisper in cubiculo pretio, non aequitate, jura descripserat, Veneri jam et Libero reliquum tempus deberi arbitrabatur. Quo loco non mihi praetermittenda videtur praeclari imperatoris egregia ac singularis dili-

Favonio]

"Solvitur acris hiems grata vice veris et Favoni."—Hor. 1 Carm. iv.

Verres waited for the blooming of the roses. He did not reckon the commencement of spring in the usual way. Varro (De R. R. 1. 28), quoted by Hotmann, says 'dies primus est veris in Aquario,' &c. Zumpt refers to Pliny, H. N. xxi. 11.

sedentem viderit.] 'Videret' is the common reading; but R 3 Lg. 29 have 'viderit.' These forms are often confounded. Madvig remarks that 'videret' is a universal negation, and is not much more than 'videre soleret;' the perfect, with the addition of 'nemo unquam,' signifies that it did not take place even once.

11. *octophoro*] He was carried in a litter or palankeen by eight men. His cushion was of the fine linen of Malta (Lib. 2. c. 72), stuffed with rose-leaves. He had a small bag of the finest thread, 'a bag of fine gauze or netted work, such as is still used to enclose scents;' as I am reminded by the Rev. R. Blackburn. In the former edition I took 'maculis' to mean 'spots;' but Mr. Blackburn remarks that the word 'reticulum' evidently points to the sense of 'meshes.' See Forcellini.

Travelling in a lettiga (lectica) is still used in Sicily. The lettiga is a kind of narrow chaise, with room for two persons to sit opposite to each other, mounted on two long poles, and carried by mules at the average rate of three miles and a half an hour (Smyth's Sicily, p. 8). But this is not a Roman 'lectica,' which was intended for reclining. The 'sella' was for sitting, a kind of sedan.

Klotz refers to Böttiger's Sabina, Th. ii. p. 181, 204, 212. He adds that at a later period the Roman ladies generally used such 'lecticae,' and that the practice was derived from Asia, whence they also got chair-bearers (lecticarii). The use of these 'lecticae' was not confined to luxurious persons, for Servius Sulpicius used one (Cicero, Ep. ad Div. iv. 12). His health was probably not good. Lipsius (Elect. i. c. 19. Vol. i. ed. Vesal.) has, as usual, all the learning in this matter. The 'lectica' was not common in Italy about the time of C. Gracchus, as an extract from one of his speeches shows (Gellius, x. 3). The Bithynian origin of the 'lectica' seems hinted at by Catullus, or at least Bithynia was a country where a man might supply himself with porters for his 'lectica:'

"At certe tamen, inquiunt, quod illic
Natum dicitur esse, comparasti
Ad lecticam homines."
Catull. x. ed. Sillig.

jura descripserat,] There is no notice of 'discripserat' in the readings, and yet I believe that it is the right word here, and Halm has so written it on his authority, I believe, as I have done sometimes, and any body may do here, if he likes. See Lib. 3. c. 92, note; and Cicero, De Off. i. 34, 'jura describere,' according to the common reading.

gentia. Nam scitote oppidum esse in Sicilia nullum ex iis oppidis in quibus consistere praetores et conventum agere solent, quo in oppido non isti ex aliqua familia non ignobili delecta ad libidinem mulier esset. Itaque nonnullae ex eo numero in convivium adhibebantur palam; si quae castiores erant, ad tempus veniebant, lucem conventumque vitabant. Erant autem convivia non illo silentio praetorum populi Romani atque imperatorum, neque eo pudore qui in magistratuum conviviis versari solet, sed cum maximo clamore atque convicio: nonnunquam etiam res ad pugnam atque ad manus vocabatur. Iste enim praetor severus ac diligens qui populi Romani legibus nunquam paruisset, illis legibus quae in poculis ponebantur diligenter obtemperabat. Itaque erant exitus ejusmodi ut alius inter manus e convivio tamquam e proelio auferretur, alius tamquam occisus relinqueretur, plerique fusi sine mente ac sine ullo sensu jacerent, ut quivis quum aspexisset non se praetoris convivium sed ut Cannensem pugnam nequitiae videre arbitraretur.

XII. Quum vero aestas summa esse coeperat, quod tempus omnes semper Siciliae praetores in itineribus consumere consuerunt, propterea quod tum putant obeundam esse maxime provinciam quum in areis frumenta sunt, quod et familiae congregantur et

solent,] Zumpt has 'soleant' from R 3. The dett. have 'solent.' Of 'soleant' he says, "prorsus e consuetudine scriptoris, ubi ambitus rei accuratius definiendus est." I don't clearly understand him; but the indicative is admissible here. And we have the form in this chapter 'qui . . versari solet.' Madvig says '*solent* non improbandum per se est,' which is rather an unmeaning expression; however, he gives a reason for preferring 'soleant.' I believe either form will do, but with the indicative it expresses 'the towns in which the praetors are accustomed to hold a Conventus,' and there was a limited number. With the subjunctive it would mean 'any towns in which,' &c. A little further Orelli and Iordan have 'qui in magistratuum . . soleat;' and they have 'soleant' here.

Zumpt concludes from Lib. 2. c. 26, that the four cities in which the 'conventus' were held were Syracusae, Agrigentum, Lilybaeum, and Panhormus; and it may be so. But we cannot with certainty conclude from that chapter that there were not others. These four cities were conveniently placed for the division of the island into four 'conventus;' for the term 'conventus' was also applied to the district of which the people 'conveniebant in quemdam locum.' Thus Pliny says (H. N. iv. 22) of Lusitania: "Universa provincia dividitur in conventus tres, Emeritensem, Pacensem, Scalabitanum."

'Conventum' or 'conventus agere' means to hold the meetings and to do all that was usual at such meetings; one part of which was to hear and determine causes. See Caesar, B. G. i. 54, and the note, Long's edit. Cicero also uses 'forum agere' in the same sense (Ad Att. v. 16).

vocabatur.] The common reading is 'veniebat.'—'quae in poculis.' See De Senectute, c. 14, "me vero et magisteria delectant a majoribus instituta," &c.

inter manus] Carried off by the attendants or others, as Graevius shows, and he compares Phaedrus, Fab. v. 7:

"Inter manus sublatus et multum gemens
Domum fertur."

—'fusi:' 'ut fusi' R 3, Iordan.

12. *omnes semper*] If this is the genuine order, the expression may perhaps be compared with the Greek *οἱ ἀεὶ στρατηγοί*. Orelli has 'omnes Siciliae semper,' and Iordan. 'Novi semper scriptores' occurs in Livy, Praef.

magnitudo servitii perspicitur, et labor operis maxime offendit, frumenti copia commonet, tempus anni non impedit; tum, inquam, quum concursant ceteri praetores, iste novo quodam [ex] genere imperator pulcherrimo Syracusarum loco stativa sibi castra faciebat. Nam in ipso aditu atque ore portus, ubi primum ex alto sinus ab littore ad urbem inflectitur, tabernacula carbaseis intenta velis collocabat. Huc ex illa domo praetoria, quae regis Hieronis fuit, sic emigrabat ut eum per illos dies nemo extra illum locum videre

servitii] The number of slaves. This is a collective term, as in c. 4, 'moveri aliquot locis servitium suspicor.'

offendit,] Some of the old editions have 'ostenditur,' a conjecture. Naugerius restored the reading of the dett., 'offenditur;' but Hervagius, having got a MS. of a better family, wrote 'offendit.' R 3, codd. Lamb. have 'offendit,' and Jordan. Klotz and Orelli, who have 'offendit,' adopt Madvig's explanation, that 'servos' is to be supplied, and we are to consider that Cicero is speaking of the season in which the slaves, on account of the oppressive labour, are most easily excited to rebellion. Zumpt, following the opinion of Lambinus, takes 'offenditur' to be the true reading, and to have the sense of 'deprehenditur.' But, as Madvig observes, Zumpt cannot produce an instance of this use of 'offenditur.' Madvig considers all the passage, down to 'non impedit,' to refer to the slaves, and that Cicero enumerates all those things which at this season of the year could chiefly excite the slaves to a rising. This passage is difficult, and, as opinions may differ about it, I give Madvig's full interpretation: "Scilicet haec omnia ad servos referenda sunt, enumeranturque ea, quae servos ad bellum hoc potissimum anni tempore concitare possunt; quod ne oriatur, ideo praetor provinciam obire tum solet: aestate familiae congregabantur; itaque occultae conjurationis occasio erat; magnitudo servitii perspiciebatur; ergo vires fiduciam dabant; labor messis gravissimus erat; itaque animi offensi et irati, ad arma proni; frumenti copia parata bellantibus, tempus anni rebus gerendis aptum." Zumpt has 'et frumenti,' but 'et' is omitted by the best MSS.; and the omission makes the sense plainer. Cicero says that it is the custom of the praetors to travel through Sicily particularly at the time when all the corn is collected at the threshing-floors (tum . . . quum . . . frumenta sunt); when the harvest is over, and the grain is to be got out. So far is plain. He then adds a number of circumstances which would be concurrent with this period, and they are alleged as reasons ('quod et,' &c.) for the circuit being made at this season. I think that 'frumenti . . . impedit' apply to the praetor. The words 'familiae . . . perspicitur' of course apply to the slaves: they are collected at the 'areae,' and their numbers can be seen; they may be counted, if necessary. There remains 'labor . . . offendit.' If it is supposed that this applies to the slaves, we may observe that the getting out of the corn is not so laborious as cutting it; unless we suppose that the slaves threshed it in some way, and I know no evidence that they did. I don't see why the sight of the corn should suggest insurrection. If the slaves rose, they could not carry the corn with them. Nor do I see that the time of the year was seasonable for insurrection. If the slaves of each estate were at the threshing-floor, those of one estate would not see those of another estate, and as the slaves of each estate were in one place, they would be watched and all their movements would be seen. The danger of insurrection would be greatest when the slaves had little to do. If the summer was favourable for an insurrection, it was also favourable for suppressing it, by bringing together all the force that the island had. The winter would be the best time for the slaves to rise, when the communications were difficult for every body, but still practicable for men resolved to make a rising. I do not believe that Madvig's interpretation of 'labor operis maxime offendit' is true. But it is very difficult to suggest what is meant.

concursant] See c. 31.

carbaseis] Plin. H. N. (xix. 1). 'Carbasus' was made of flax: "Et Hispania citerior habet splendorem lini praecipuum, torrentis in quo politur natura, qui alluit Tarraconem. Et tenuitas mira, ibi primum carbasis repertis." See Servius ad Aeneid. iii. 357.

posset. In eum autem ipsum locum aditus erat nemini, nisi qui aut socius aut minister libidinis esse posset. Huc omnes mulieres quibuscum iste consuerat conveniebant, quarum incredibile est quanta multitudo fuerit Syracusis: huc homines digni istius amicitia, digni vita illa conviviisque veniebant. Inter ejusmodi viros ac mulieres adulta aetate filius versabatur, ut eum, etiamsi natura a parentis similitudine abriperet, consuetudo tamen ac disciplina patris similem esse cogeret. Huc Tertia illa perducta per dolum atque insidias ab Rhodio tibicine maximas in istius castris effecisse dicitur turbas, quum indigne pateretur uxor Cleomenis Syracusani, nobilis mulier, itemque uxor Aeschrionis, honesto loco nata, in conventum suum mimi Isidori filiam venisse. Iste autem Hannibal qui in suis castris virtute putaret oportere non genere certari, sic hanc Tertiam dilexit ut eam secum ex provincia deportaret. Ac per hos dies quum iste cum pallio purpureo talarique tunica versaretur in conviviis muliebribus, non offendebantur homines, neque moleste ferebant abesse a foro magistratum, non jus dici, non judicia fieri: locum illum littoris percrepare totum mulierum vocibus cantuque symphoniae, in foro silentium esse summum causarum atque juris non ferebant homines moleste; non enim jus abesse videbatur a foro neque judicia, sed vis et crudelitas et bonorum acerba et indigna direptio.

XIII. Hunc tu igitur imperatorem esse defendis, Hortensi? hujus furta, rapinas, cupiditatem, crudelitatem, superbiam, scelus, audaciam rerum gestarum magnitudine atque imperatoriis laudibus tegere conaris? Hic scilicet est metuendum ne ad exitum defensionis tuae vetus illa Antoniana dicendi ratio atque auctoritas proferatur; ne excitetur Verres, ne denudetur a pectore, ne cicatrices populus Romanus aspiciat ex mulierum morsu vestigia

Tertia] Lib. 3. c. 34.

Hannibal] The allusion is, as Manutius supposes, to the expression of Hannibal, as we have it in Ennius (p. 100, ed. Hessel):

"Hostem qui feriet mihi erit Carthaginiensis
Quisquis erit."

talarique] The MSS. have 'parique,' in which there is no sense. The text is an emendation of Naugerius, founded on the expression in c. 33. There is 'manicatis et talaribus tunicis,' In Cat. ii. c. 10.

The 'pallium' was a Greek garment, or rather the Roman name for it. The 'tunica talaris' was a woman's dress, as Gellius (vii. 12) informs us: "feminisque solis vestem longe lateque diffusam decoram existimaverunt ad ulnas cruraque adversus oculos protegenda."

Horace (1 Sat. ii. 25) describes the two extremes of the tunicated vest:

"Malthinus tunicis demissis ambulat: est qui
Inguen ad obscenum subductis usque facetus."

13. *excitetur*] 'roused from his seat.' 'Excitare' means 'to raise up.' Caesar, B. G. iii. 14; Frontinus, Aquaeduct. 7; Virgil, Georg. iv. 549.

libidinis atque nequitiae. Dii faciant ut rei militaris, ut belli mentionem facere audeas. Cognoscentur enim omnia istius aera illa vetera, ut non solum in imperio verum etiam in stipendiis qualis fuerit intelligatis. Renovabitur prima illa militia, quum iste e foro abduci, non, ut ipse praedicat, perduci solebat: aleatoris Placentini castra commemorabuntur, in quibus quum frequens fuisset, tamen aere dirutus est: multa ejus in stipendiis damna proferentur quae ab isto aetatis fructu dissoluta et compensata sunt. Jam vero quum in ejusmodi patientia turpitudinis aliena non sua satietate obduruisset, qui vir fuerit, quot praesidia, quam munita pudoris et pudicitiae vi et audacia ceperit, quid me attinet dicere aut conjungere cum istius flagitio cujusquam praeterea dedecus? Non faciam, judices: omnia vetera praetermittam: duo sola recentia sine cujusquam infamia ponam, ex quibus conjecturam facere de omnibus possitis: unum illud, quod ita fuit illustre notumque omnibus ut nemo tam rusticanus homo L. Lucullo [et] M. Cotta consulibus Romam ex ullo municipio vadimonii causa venerit quin sciret jura omnia praetoris urbani nutu atque arbitrio Chelidonis meretriculae gubernari: alterum, quod, quum paludatus exisset votaque pro

aera illa vetera,] His old campaigns, the 'aera' being the soldiers' pay. Here 'aera' is equivalent to 'stipendia.'

abduci,] This is a foul allusion. The sense of 'perduci' is not so clear. 'Ad meretrices,' says Manutius, as Verres would have it, to avoid a worse imputation. Graevius has a note on the passage. He takes 'perduci' in the ordinary sense, like 'duci,' not in the sense in which 'perductores' occurs in Lib. 1. c. 12, and elsewhere. He says that 'perduci' here means "in forum duci, ut solebant nobiles pueri quum primum praetextam deponerent." Klotz takes 'abduci' in the same sense that others do; as to 'perduci,' he says that it means 'in forum,' and adds that the expression 'perduci in forum' is sufficiently known. His translation of the passage is 'wo er sich vom Forum entführen, als Knabe zu schändlichem Dienste, nicht hinführen liess, um daselbst sich zu unterrichten.' Orelli's remark is "*abduci*, a creditore aliquo propter aes alienum: *perduci*, ad amatorem a lenone." But Orelli's explanation of 'abduci' is false. His translation of 'perduci' is probably right.

frequens] Halm compares Paulus Festi, p. 112: "infrequens appellatur miles qui abest afuitque a signis."

aere dirutus] Explained by Festus and others. Festus: "Dirutum aere militem dicebant antiqui, cui stipendium ignominiae causa non erat datum, quod aes diruebatur in fiscum, non in militis sacculum." Festus should have said 'in aerarium.' Verres is compared to a soldier who lost his pay through misconduct in his campaigns (in stipendiis)—"sed eandem diminutionem pecuniae Verres cum sensisset, quod nimis frequens in istis castris aleatoriis esset, detrimentum resarsit pudicitia prodenda," as Zumpt explains it. G 3 have 'aere direptus.'

dissoluta] 'cleared off and made good (compensata).' See Lib. 3. c. 77, note on 'dissolvisti.'

aut conjungere] 'ac conj.' Jordan.

Romam . . vadimonii causa] See Lib. 3. c. 15. The year of these consuls was the year of the praetorship of Verres at Rome, B.C. 74.

praetoris urbani] 'Populi R.,' the common codices and the old editions. Orelli also has it. But R 3 codd. Lambini have 'praetoris urbani.' Orelli says that 'jura omnia praetoris urbani' is an expression of which there is no other instance. Here it must be taken as equivalent to 'omne jus praetorium.' "Solita confusio notarum *pr.* et *p. r.* et *r. p.* turbas h. l. dedit" (Zumpt).

paludatus] When a consul or praetor

imperio suo communique re publica nuncupasset, noctu stupri causa lectica in urbem introferri solitus est ad mulierem, nuptam uni, propositam omnibus, contra fas, contra auspicia, contra omnes divinas atque humanas religiones.

XIV. O dii immortales, quid interest inter mentes hominum et cogitationes? Ita mihi meam voluntatem spemque reliquae vitae vestra populique Romani existimatio comprobet, ut ego quos adhuc mihi magistratus populus Romanus mandavit, sic eos accepi ut me omnium officiorum obstringi religione arbitrarer. Ita quaestor sum factus ut mihi illum honorem tum non solum datum sed etiam creditum et commissum putarem: sic obtinui quaesturam in Sicilia provincia ut omnium oculos in me [unum] conjectos esse arbitrarer, ut me quaesturamque meam quasi in aliquo terrarum orbis theatro versari existimarem; ut semper omnia, quae jucunda esse videntur, ea non modo his extraordinariis cupiditatibus sed etiam ipsi naturae ac necessitati denegarem. Nunc sum designatus aedilis:

went forth with 'imperium,' he put on the 'paludamentum.' (De Prov. Cons. c. 15.) "Paludamenta (Varro, De L. L. vii. 37, ed. Müller) insignia et ornamenta militaria." He gives an absurd etymology of the word. The exercise of the 'militare imperium,' which was conferred on a consul or a praetor, "began from the moment when the consul or the praetor, after making the solemn vows in the capitol, left the city preceded by the lictors, 'secundum vota in Capitolio nuncupata paludatus cum lictoribus proficiscebatur,' or 'in provinciam ibat;' and it ended as soon as he returned and crossed the 'pomoerium,' or if he had a triumph, as soon as it was over" (Becker, Handbuch, &c., 2ter Th. p. 65). Verres therefore acted against the law in entering the city in this manner.

Some of the passages in Livy, as to the 'votorum nuncupatio' and the 'paludamentum,' are the following: xxi. 63; xxxi. 14; xlii. 49; xlv. 39.

communique re publica] 'Communique populi Romani,' the common reading. Orelli observes, "exempla hujus formulae collegit Gronov. Obs. 1, 12, p. 83."

14. *datum . . creditum &c.*] Zumpt says "*damus* simpliciter, *credimus* quod grave putamus, *committimus* quod carum habemus." No doubt Cicero means to strengthen his expression. But these distinctions which critics make are not worth much. 'Credere' is properly said of something that is to be restored, whence we have the correlatives 'creditor' and 'debitor,' which indeed comprehend any case in which one person has a claim on another, and that other owes to him a duty. See De Prov. Cons. c. 4, note. Cicero in another place (Ad Q. Fr. i. 1. c. 8) expresses the notion of a thing entrusted which is to be restored, by qualifying 'datum' thus: "quonam modo retinendi sunt iis quibus imperium ita datum est ut redderent." 'Committere' is often applied to cases where we entrust something which is dear to us to a person's good faith.

in me [unum]] 'unum' om. G 3 λ (not R). Iordan has it. I would rather omit it. Compare the passage in the Pro Plancio about Cicero's Sicilian quaestorship.

theatro] Cicero has the same form of expression in a corrupted passage in the letter Ad Q. Fr. i. 1. c. 14, "Quare quoniam ejusmodi theatrum est," &c.

extraordinariis] See Lib. 1. c. 39, and the note.

designatus aedilis:] He was 'aedilis curulis.' The duties of the 'aediles' are fully discussed in Becker's Handbuch, &c., 2ter Th. 2te Abth. p. 291. Cicero (Pro Murena, c. 19) mentions his superintendence of the Ludi Cereales, the Floralia, and the Ludi Romani. (See the Didascalia to Terence's Phormio: 'Acta Ludis Romanis L. Postumio Albino L. Cornelio Merula Aedilibus Curulibus.') The words 'Cereri, Libero Liberaeque' must be referred to the Cerealia. Orelli compares

habeo rationem quid a populo Romano acceperim: mihi ludos sanctissimos maxima cum cura et caerimonia Cereri, Libero Liberaeque faciendos, mihi Floram matrem populo plebique Romanae ludorum celebritate placandam, mihi ludos antiquissimos, qui primi Romani appellati sunt, cum dignitate maxima et religione Jovi, Junoni, Minervaeque esse faciundos, mihi sacrarum aedium procurationem, mihi totam urbem tuendam esse commissam: ob earum rerum laborem et sollicitudinem fructus illos datos, antiquiorem in senatu sententiae dicendae locum, togam praetextam, sellam curulem, jus imaginis ad memoriam posteritatemque pro-

Tacit. Ann. ii. 49, 'Libero Liberaeque et Cereri.' These three deities had a common temple near the Circus Maximus. The superintendence of the temples is here mentioned as within the province of the 'aediles' (sacrarum aedium procuratio), which is explained to mean, that they had to see that the temples and other public buildings were maintained in good condition, and were not used improperly by private persons, or injured. See the Tab. Heracl. 1. v. 68, QVAE LOCA PVBLICA, &c. They had also the general superintendence of police, and of matters which concerned the public health (totam urbem . . . commissam). Their duties were indeed multifarious.

Among other privileges Cicero mentions 'antiquiorem . . . locum.' He would have a prior rank (antiquior) or precedence in giving his opinion in the senate, next to those of higher rank than himself, 'consulares' and 'praetorii.' The 'sella curulis' was the official seat or chair of the 'aedilis curulis,' and of the 'magistratus' who were above the 'aediles curules.' The seat, 'sella,' a diminutive from the form 'sedi,' as if it were 'sedula,' was ornamented with ivory, whence the expression 'curule ebur.' It is most usually spoken of with reference to the 'praetor,' and is often simply called 'sella,' as in these orations. The etymology which Gellius gives (iii. 18, after Gabius Bassus) from 'currus' is incorrect, nor can the derivation from 'curia' be accepted. In Sueton. Augustus, c. 22, there is however the expression 'Curulis triumphus.'

Plutarch (Marius, c. 5) derives 'curulis' from the curved form of the chair, or rather the legs, so that it would contain the crude form 'curvo:' *δύο γάρ εἰσι τάξεις ἀγορανομιῶν, ἡ μὲν ἀπὸ τῶν δίφρων τῶν ἀγκυλοπόδων ἐφ' ὧν καθεζόμενοι χρηματίζουσιν ἔχουσα τοὔνομα τῆς ἀρχῆς.* This corresponds with the form of the legs in what are supposed to be representations of the 'sella curulis,' as they are given in Smith's Dict. of Antiqus.

populo plebique] Comp. Pro Murena, c. 1.

jus imaginis] See Lib. 3. c. 4. In this passage G 3 omit 'ius.' "*imaginis*, R pr. m., dett. Non. p. 363. 541: *imagines* R m. sec. G 3.—*prodendae* J. Fr. Gronovius (Observv. 1. 12): *prodendam* codd. Cic. et Nonii" (Iordan). The expression in the oration Pro Rabirio Post. c. 7 is 'imago ipsa ad posteritatis memoriam prodita.' The form in which this passage is given, Lib. 3. c. 4, note, is a quotation from Bekker, which of course I did not alter. Zumpt has here altered the text to 'prodendae,' as he does not think that 'prodendam' is capable of explanation. Orelli also and Iordan have 'prodendae.' If 'posteritatemque' were omitted, there would be no difficulty. We have 'ut . . . memoriam proderet,' Caesar, B. G. i. 13; and 'ad prodendam virtutis memoriam,' Tacit. Agric. c. 1. The 'jus imaginis' would be for the purpose of transmitting a memorial of the person. 'Posteritas' is the state or condition of 'posteri,' and is generally used by Latin writers precisely as our word 'posterity' is. But there is perhaps no reason against its being taken in the sense of a 'futurity' generally, 'an after existence,' or something of the kind. There is a passage in Cicero in which it seems to have a sense very near this, Tusc. 1. 15, "quum optimus quisque posteritati maxime serviat," which Forcellini explains to mean 'famae apud posteros.' Klotz defends 'prodendam,' and maintains that 'posteritas' can have the sense of our 'futurity;' and he considers 'ad memoriam posteritatemque' to be equivalent to 'ad memoriam posteritatis,' a phrase which Quintilian uses (Inst. Or. x. 1, 41). There

dendam. Ex his ego rebus omnibus, judices, ita mihi omnes deos propitios velim, etiamsi mihi jucundissimus est honos populi, tamen nequaquam capio tantum voluptatis quantum et sollicitudinis et laboris, ut haec ipsa aedilitas, non quia necesse fuerit, alicui candidato data, sed quia sic oportuerit, recte collocata et judicio populi in loco posita esse videatur.

XV. Tu, quum esses praetor renuntiatus quoquo modo—mitto enim et praetereo quid tum sit actum—sed quum esses renuntiatus, ut dixi, non ipsa praeconis voce excitatus es, qui te toties seniorum

is a use of 'posteritas' in Lib. 3. c. 50 and 55, which seems to help a little to the understanding of 'posteritas' in this passage. The alteration 'prodendae' seems to me a corruption of the text.

The two principal passages as to the 'imagines' are Polybius (vi. 53) and Pliny (H. N. xxxv. 2). These 'imagines' or masks of wax (expressi cera vultus) were made to represent the person both in features and complexion; and they were placed in wooden boxes or niches (armaria) on the walls of the Atrium. The 'tituli' of the deceased, the titles of honour which he had gained in his life, were written near the receptacle of the 'imago;' and the 'imagines' were so arranged and connected by lines (lineae) as to show the degrees of consanguinity of the several persons. This arrangement of the figures by lines made what the Romans called a 'stemma.' Probably the arrangement was something like our fashion of drawing up a pedigree. Pliny says "stemmata vero lineis discurrebant ad imagines pictas." The allusions to this practice are numerous in the Roman writers (Juvenal, viii. 1). It appears from a passage of Isidorus (Orig. ix. 6)—"stemmata dicuntur ramusculi, quos advocati faciunt in genere, cum gradus cognationis partiuntur,"—that the lawyers adopted this practice of drawing up degrees of consanguinity, as we see in the table of consanguinity in any of the ordinary editions of the Institutes of Justinian. These 'imagines' were not made until after death. Of course a 'novus homo,' like Cicero, could have no 'imagines;' and he could only transmit his own 'imago' to his descendants. The 'imagines' of a family were taken out of their cases on funeral occasions, and carried in the funeral procession (Tacit. Ann. iv. 9). The effigies of ancestors with their 'tituli' were placed in the Atria, that their descendants might not only see the records of their virtues, but imitate them also (Val. Max. v. 8. 3). Polybius considered this practice conducive to a spirit of emulation. Whether a modern portrait gallery in a large house has this effect or not, I do not know. Becker, Handbuch ii. 1, p. 220, has collected the passages concerning the 'imagines.'

ita mihi . . deos] See Divin. c. 13, where the better order is 'ita mihi deos,' instead of 'ita deos mihi,' and see the beginning of this chapter.

in loco] 'i.e. suo et idoneo,' Zumpt. And we do not require the addition of 'digno,' which is in some old editions.

15. *toties seniorum &c.*] A 'praeco' proclaimed the result of the votes; probably there were many 'praecones' (Cic. De Leg. Agr. ii. 2, 'neque singulae voces praeconum'). Zumpt asks how often proclaimed; and he answers, at least 97 times, for all the 'centuriae' are 193, of which 97 make a majority.

On the voting see Becker, Handbuch ii. 3, p. 100, &c.; and on the reform of the Comitia Centuriata, ii. 3, p. 1, &c. Becker (p. 9) considers the following points as established. 1. The Centuriae of Servius' constitution are represented as independent of the division into Tribus, but the Centuriae of the reformed constitution stand in a definite relation to the Tribus: every Centuria is a part of a Tribus. 2. On the other hand the classes of the census still remained under the reformed constitution, and the number of the classes was not changed. The voting was by Centuriae which were still distributed into Centuriae Juniorum and Seniorum, and the Centuriae were called to vote according to their Classes. 3. There still remained the Centuriae of the Equites, and perhaps also the Centuria of the Fabri.—This being established, says Becker, the inquiry is reduced to two questions, First, what was the number of the centuries in the new ar-

juniorumque centuriis illo honore affici pronuntiavit, ut hoc putares aliquam rei publicae partem tibi creditam? annum tibi illum unum domo carendum esse meretricia? Quum tibi sorte obtigisset uti jus diceres, quantum negotii, quid oneris haberes nunquam cogitasti? neque illud rationis habuisti, si forte expergefacere te posses, eam provinciam, quam tueri singulari sapientia atque integritate difficile esset, ad summam stultitiam nequitiamque venisse? Itaque non modo a domo tua Chelidonem in praetura excludere noluisti, sed in Chelidonis domum praeturam totam detulisti. Secuta provincia est, in qua nunquam tibi venit in mentem, non tibi idcirco fasces ac secures et tantam imperii vim tantamque ornamentorum omnium dignitatem datam, ut earum rerum vi et auctoritate omnia repagula pudoris officiique perfringeres, ut omnium bona praedam tuam duceres, ut nullius res tuta, nullius domus clausa, nullius vita septa, nullius pudicitia munita contra tuam cupiditatem et audaciam posset esse; in qua tu te ita gessisti ut omnibus quum teneare rebus ad bellum fugitivorum confugias; ex quo jam intelligis non modo nullam tibi defensionem sed maximam vim criminum exortam; nisi forte Italici fugitivorum belli reliquias atque illud Tempsanum incommodum proferes, ad quod recens quum te peropportune fortuna attulisset si quid in te virtutis aut industriae habuisses, idem qui semper fueras inventus es.

XVI. Quum ad te Valentini venissent et pro his homo disertus ac nobilis, M. Marius, loqueretur ut negotium susciperes, ut, quum

rangement, and in what relation did they stand to the Tribus? Second, What change was made in the order of voting?

This explanation may so far be useful. The subject is so difficult that it cannot be discussed in the compass of a note, nor is it very closely connected with the meaning of this passage of Cicero. It is enough for the understanding of the text to know that the voting and the declaration of the votes would be continued until a majority of Centuriae was obtained.

eam provinciam,] That is 'juris dictio,' which is said properly of the Praetor Urbanus et Peregrinus only. 'Jus diceres' expresses here the office of the Praetor. Cicero first uses 'provincia' in the general sense, the office of the praetor, and then in the sense of his administration of Sicily (secuta provincia est).

ad summam stultitiam &c.] "Ad te omnium stultissimum ac nequissimum," Manutius. Hotmann misunderstood the passage, and thought it was corrupted.—'praeturam tuam totam' dett. Orelli.

Tempsanum] The place is Temesa or Tempsa, on the west coast of the Bruttii, and north of Vibo. It is mentioned by Homer, as it seems (Od. i. 184); and by Strabo (p. 255). From this we may collect that it was seized by some of the bands of Spartacus at the close of the Servile war, for Verres at this time was returning to Rome from Sicily.

16. *Valentini*] The Valentini were the inhabitants of Vibo, or Vibo Valentia, as it was sometimes called, in the Bruttii. Its original name was Hippo and Hipponium. It is now Monte Leone, on the west coast of Italy, and the name is preserved in Bivona, the name of the port. Cicero calls it a 'municipium;' but Livy (xxxv. 40) and Paterculus call it a colony. The difference at this time was unimportant, for after the passing of the Lex Julia the inhabitants were Roman citizens.

pence te praetorium nomen esset, ad illam parvam manum extinguendam ducem te principemque praeberes, non modo id refugisti, sed eo ipso tempore quum esses in littore, Tertia illa tua quam tu tecum deportaras erat in omnium conspectu; ipsis autem Valentinis ex tam illustri nobilique municipio tantis de rebus responsum dedisti quum esses cum tunica pulla et pallio. Quid hunc proficiscentem, quid in ipsa provincia fecisse existimatis, qui quum jam ex provincia non ad triumphum, sed ad judicium decederet, ne illam quidem infamiam fugerit quam sine ulla voluptate capiebat? O divina senatus frequentis in aede Bellonae admurmuratio! Memoria tenetis, judices, quum advesperasceret et paulo ante esset de hoc Tempsano incommodo nuntiatum, quum inveniretur nemo qui in illa loca cum imperio mitteretur, dixisse quendam Verrem esse non longe a Tempsa. Quam valde universi admurmuraverunt, quam palam principes dixerunt contra? Et his tot criminibus testimoniisque convictus in eorum tabella spem sibi aliquam proponit, quorum omnium palam causa incognita voce damnatus est?

XVII. Esto, nihil ex fugitivorum bello aut suspicione belli laudis adeptus est, quod neque bellum ejusmodi neque belli periculum fuit in Sicilia neque ab isto provisum est ne quod esset. At vero contra bellum praedonum classem habuit ornatam diligentiamque in eo singularem; itaque ab isto praeclare defensa provincia est. Sic de bello praedonum, sic de classe Siciliensi, judices, dicam ut hoc jam ante confirmem, in hoc uno genere omnes inesse culpas istius maximas, avaritiae, majestatis, dementiae, libidinis, crudeli-

praetorium nomen] 'Praetorium imperium ac nomen' dett. Orelli.

responsum] 'responsum' G 2 Ld., 'responsum nullum' dett. Or. Zumpt also has 'nullum.' Madvig properly asks, what is the meaning of its being said, what dress he wore, not when he did something, but when he did nothing? The scandal was, that he gave his answer on such an occasion to such people in such a dress.

esses cum . . . pallio.] Comp. c. 3, note. Verres wore a dark-coloured 'tunica,' the dress of slaves and of the lowest class, and the 'pallium,' or Greek upper vest, instead of the Roman light-coloured 'tunica' and the 'toga' with the insignia of a senator on them.

proficiscentem,] Ernesti refers this to the time when Verres was leaving Rome for his province. Zumpt to his being in the province, or, as he expresses it, 'proficiscentem in provincia,' and refers to c. 11.

dixerunt contra?] G 2 Ld.—'tabella:' see Index, Tabellae.

17. *bellum ejusmodi*] 'Nor was there any such war,' a common use of 'ejusmodi' in these orations.—'neque ab isto provisum.' Manutius observes "potius opera data est ut aliquod esset liberatis post condemnationem Leonidae servis." He understands it to be said ironically, but it may be understood in its plain sense. 'Well, it may be said that be got no glory from a servile war, or from the alarm of a servile war, because there was not any war of the kind, nor danger of a war in Sicily, nor did he take any precautions against there being a war. But, on the other hand, to oppose a piratical war he had a well-equipped fleet, and showed in that matter unusual activity; accordingly the province was well defended by this governor now before you.'

majestatis,] that is 'minutae.' See Divin. c. 21, note; and Lib. 5. c. 20, note.

tatis. Haec dum breviter expono, quaeso, ut fecistis adhuc, diligenter attendite.

Rem navalem primum ita dico esse administratam non uti provincia defenderetur sed uti classis nomine pecunia quaereretur. Superiorum praetorum consuetudo quum haec fuisset, ut naves civitatibus certusque numerus nautarum militumque imperaretur, maximae et locupletissimae civitati Mamertinae nihil horum imperavisti. Ob hanc rem quid tibi Mamertini clam dederint pecuniae, post si videbitur ex ipsorum literis testibusque quaeremus. Navem vero cybacam maximam, triremis instar, pulcherrimam atque ornatissimam, palam aedificatam sumptu publico, sciente tota Sicilia, per magistratum senatumque Mamertinum tibi datam donatamque esse dico. Haec navis onusta praeda Siciliensi, quum ipsa quoque esset ex praeda, simul quum ipse decederet appulsa Veliam est cum plurimis rebus et iis quas iste Romam mittere cum ceteris furtis noluit, quod erant carissimae maximeque eum delectabant. Eam navem nuper egomet vidi Veliae multique alii viderunt, pulcherrimam atque ornatissimam, judices; quae quidem omnibus qui eam aspexerant prospectare jam exilium atque explorare fugam domini videbatur.

XVIII. Quid mihi hoc loco respondebis, nisi forte id quod tametsi probari nullo modo potest, tamen dici quidem in judicio de pecuniis repetundis necesse est, de tua pecunia aedificatam esse navem? Aude hoc saltem dicere, quod necesse est. Noli metuere, Hortensi, ne quaeram qui licuerit aedificare navem senatori. Anti-

naves . . imperaretur,] See Lib. 1. c. 34. As to 'cybaeam,' Lib. 4. c. 8.

cybaeam] Jordan put the first 'cybaeam' in [ ], and he has 'ornatissimam cybaeam,' which is the reading of R G 1. It is probable that the word should not stand in both places.

instar,] Is a noun not declined, and means 'magnitude,' 'size,' and the like, as appears from c. 34. It is used by Ulpian (*Dig.* 39. 1. 21) thus, "instar quoddam operis et quasi facies quaedam facti operis;" and Caesar, B. G. ii. 17, "effecerunt ut instar muri hae sepes munimentum praeberet."

palam aedificatam &c.] If we accept the reading of R 3, cod. Urs., we shall have 'palam aedificatam sumptu publico, tuo nomine, publice.' Zumpt and Orelli agree that some of these words are a gloss, but they differ as to which must be ejected. Orelli writes 'aedificatam tuo nomine, publice,' for he says that 'sumptu publico' is the gloss of 'publice.' Zumpt thinks that 'tuo nomine publice' have been taken in from the margin. I see no objection to all the words; and Jordan has them all. Zumpt omits 'senatumque,' and has 'magistratumque;' and Jordan has the same. 'Per magistratumque' is the reading of R 3. The dett. have 'per magistratum senatumque.' Zumpt explains his text thus: "senatus populusque Mamertinus dedit *per* magistratum suum quem unum habebant." Other instances of a single 'magistratus,' a 'proagorus,' in Sicilian towns are mentioned in Lib. 1. c. 17, 34; Lib. 2. c. 67; Lib. 3. c. 38; Lib. 4. c. 23. For these reasons and for the MSS. authority, 'magistratum' is preferable to the reading 'magistratus' of Graevius.

Veliam] Velia was on the west coast of Lucania, south of Paestum.

18. *aedificare navem*] Cicero alludes,

quae sunt istae leges, et mortuae, quemadmodum tu soles dicere, quae vetant. Fuit ista res publica quondam, fuit ista severitas in judiciis, ut istam rem accusator in magnis criminibus objiciendam putaret. Quid enim tibi navi? qui si quo publice proficisceris, praesidii et vecturae causa sumptu publico navigia praebentur, privatim autem nec proficisci quoquam potes nec arcessere res transmarinas ex iis locis in quibus te habere nihil licet. Deinde cur quidquam contra leges parasti? Valeret hoc crimen in illa vetere severitate ac dignitate rei publicae. Nunc non modo te hoc crimine non arguo, sed ne illa quidem communi vituperatione reprehendo: tu tibi hoc nunquam turpe, nunquam criminosum, nunquam invidiosum fore putasti, celeberrimo loco palam tibi aedificari onerariam navem in ea provincia quam tu cum imperio obtinebas? Quid eos loqui qui videbant, quid existimare eos qui audiebant arbitrabare? inanem te navem esse illam in Italiam deducturum? navicularium quum Romam venisses esse facturum? Ne illud quidem quisquam poterat suspicari te in Italia maritimum habere fundum et ad

as it seems, to a Lex Claudia, B.C. 218 or 219 (Liv. xxi. 63): "ne quis senator cuive senator pater fuisset maritimam navem quae plus quam trecentarum amphorarum esset haberet. Id satis habitum ad fructus ex agris vectandos: quaestus omnis patribus indecorus visus est." A rule of this kind was applied by the Romans in their legislation for other places, as in the case of Halesa, Lib. 2. c. 49. Cicero speaks of these 'leges' as 'antiquae et mortuae,' as having fallen into desuetude. It is a principle of Roman law, that custom (consuetudo) was efficient to abolish a 'lex,' and substitute for it a different rule of law, or to abolish it simply. This is distinctly expressed by Julian (Dig. 1. 3. 32. § 1): "quare rectissime etiam illud receptum est, ut leges non solum suffragio legislatoris, sed etiam tacito consensu omnium per desuetudinem abrogentur" (Savigny, System, &c., i. p. 152). The English system does not acknowledge this principle.

Quid enim tibi &c.] "Vulgo *quid enim tibi nave opus fuit*, sed omittunt *opus fuit* boni omnes," Zumpt. These same MSS. have 'navi,' except one, which has 'navim.' The text is intelligible, for it is the Roman fashion in such a case to omit the verb. Iordan quotes Cicero, Ad Att. xv. 1 a, 1, "Quid mihi iam medico? aut si opus est, tanta inopia est?"

qui si quo] Lambinus changed 'qui' into 'cui.' There is no doubt that 'cui' or 'quoi' and 'qui' have often been confounded by the copyists; but 'qui' is right here. All the MSS. have 'qui si;' and 'qui' is the nominative to 'proficisceris.' The position of 'qui' in such cases is common, though all the instances are not the same. In Lib. 2. c. 6 there is "Qui simul atque ei sorte provincia Cilicia obvenit, statim Romae . . . coepit," which there is no reason for correcting.

te habere nihil licet.] R 3 codd. Lamb. The common reading is 'tibi habere mercari nihil licet.' Zumpt shows that there is no objection to the 'te,' for it is so used, the dative being understood, as in c. 32 and 59. 'Mercari' has been added from the dett. Lambinus erased 'habere' and allowed 'mercari' to stand. A senator by the old law might have been forbidden to have (habere) lands out of Italy. To forbid him 'mercari,' to be a 'mercator,' would hardly be necessary. It had long been settled that a senator could not be a trader. Graevius affirms that senators had and were allowed to have land in the provinces; but he gives no evidence. Orelli has 'in quibus te habere, mercari nihil licet.'

navicularium . . facturum?] 'To carry on the business of navicularius,' a 'ship-carrier.' So the Romans said 'argentariam (rem) facere.' Graevius mistook the meaning of this passage.

maritimum . . fundum] An estate near

fructus deportandos onerariam navem comparare. Ejusmodi voluisti de te sermonem esse omnium palam ut loquerentur te illam navem parare quae praedam ex Sicilia deportaret et ad ea furta quae reliquisses commearet? Verum haec omnia, si doces navem de tua pecunia aedificatam, remitto atque concedo. Sed hoc, homo amentissime, non intelligis priore actione ab istis ipsis Mamertinis, tuis laudatoribus, esse sublatum? Nam dixit Heius, princeps istius legationis quae ad tuam laudationem missa est, navem tibi operis publicis Mamertinorum esse factam eique faciendae senatorem Mamertinum publice praefuisse. Reliqua est materies. Hanc Rheginis, ut ipsi dicunt, tametsi tu negare non potes, publice, quod Mamertini materiem non habent, imperavisti.

XIX. Si et ex quo fit navis et qui faciunt, imperio tibi tuo, non pretio, praesto fuerunt, ubi tandem istuc latet quod tu de tua pecunia dicis impensum?—At Mamertini in tabulis nihil habent.—Primum video potuisse fieri ut ex aerario nihil darent: etenim vel Capitolium, sicut apud majores nostros factum est, publice coactis fabris operisque imperatis gratis exaedificari atque effici potuit: deinde id quod perspicio et quod ostendam, quum ipsos produxero, ipsorum ex literis, multas pecunias isti erogatas in operum locationes falsas atque inanes esse perscriptas. Nam illud minime mirum est Mamertinos, a quo summum beneficium acceperant, quem sibi amiciorem esse quam populo Romano cognoverant, ejus capiti literis suis pepercisse. Sed si argumento est Mamertinos tibi pecuniam non dedisse, quia scriptum non habent, sit argumento tibi gratis stare navem quia quid emeris aut quid locaveris scriptum

the coast.—Iordan and Halm omit the ? after 'commearet.'

princeps istius] 'Princeps civitatis, princeps istius legationis' dett. Orelli.

materiem] R G 1 Ld (om. G 2), 'materiam' Lg. 29; 'materies' dett.

19. *Capitolium*,] The old story was, that Tarquinius impressed people of the 'plebes' to work at the capitol (Livy, i. 56). This is 'publice coactis,' &c.

deinde id quod &c.] This is the MSS. reading, which Zumpt has altered on very slight grounds, and Orelli follows him. Zumpt's reading is 'deinde perspicio, id quod ostendam,' which seems easier to understand, but we cannot alter the text simply to make it clearer. Madvig defends the vulgate with this remark: "optime Cicero, quum Verres rem confectam putaret tabulis Mamertinorum, opponit, etiamsi in illis tabulis nihil sit, videre se, id est, ex rei natura intelligere, *fieri potuisse* aliquid, quod deinde *factum quoque esse* dicat se perspicere ex certis vestigiis literarum. Tantum illa quae sequuntur (*multas pecunias*, &c.) conjungenda sunt cum verbis proximis, *perspicio et ostendam*."

erogatas . . perscriptas.] Sums of money paid to Verres (erogatae) were entered (perscriptae) as expended on the undertakings of works which were never really done. False entries were made as to expenditure in order to conceal the real objects of the expenditure, a usual and vulgar trick of knaves who have the management of other people's money. See Lib. 3. c. 72.

Nam] 'iam' R 3 Lg. 29, 'nam' dett. Iordan has 'iam.'

quid emeris aut quid locaveris] 'Because you cannot show any written evidence of what you have bought or what

proferre non potes. At enim idcirco navem Mamertinis non imperasti quod sunt foederati. Dii approbent: habemus hominem in fetialium manibus educatum, unum praeter ceteros in publicis

you have contracted for building.' 'Emere' (to purchase) is one way of getting a thing. 'Locare' (to agree to give so much for a piece of work to be done) is the only other usual way of getting a thing. There remain two other ways, by gift, and by fraud or theft. Verres must have either bought the ship (emere), or he must have furnished materials and engaged (locare) some person to build it for him; or he must have got it in some irregular way.

Dii approbent:] Said sarcastically. 'We have a man brought up among the fetiales:' so expert is he in the Jus Fetiale. Varro, De L. L. iv. 15: "Fetiales fidei publicae inter populos praeerant. Per hos enim fiebat ut justum conciperetur bellum et ut foedere fides constitueretur." The Jus Fetiale was that branch of law, improperly so called, which had reference to treaties, the declaring of war and peace, the condition of ambassadors, and so forth; the original of that kind of law which we call the Law of Nations, or International Law.

The Romans had a short way and a good way of dealing with a Roman who violated the Jus Fetiale, or in fact dealt with an enemy in any way that they did not like. They gave him up (dederunt) to the enemy, and so eased themselves of him. Here we learn that some places, by the terms of their 'foedus,' were relieved from the contribution of ships, or ship-money. The following passage of Varro is quoted by Nonius: "si cujus legati violati essent, qui id fecissent, quamvis nobiles essent, uti dederentur civitati statuerunt, fetialesque viginti qui de his rebus cognoscerent, judicarent, statuerent, constituerunt."

These foreign dependencies of Rome were not solely protected at the expense of Rome. They were required to supply means for their own protection, and they also furnished contributions to the ruling state. So different is the modern system, and particularly the English system. The English acquire foreign possessions by conquest and by making colonies, the protection of which is paid for mainly by the taxes levied on the people at home. The whole sum paid by all the colonies for the soldiers stationed in them is about $\frac{1}{16}$ of the whole military cost. Even the wages of labour, when they reach above a certain amount, are taxed (1851—61), in order to supply, among other things, the means of defending foreign possessions which make no direct contribution to the ruling state. The management of the extensive Indian dominions is an exception, and is conducted after the Roman fashion. The subjects pay every thing, and get little in return. For instance, from 1830 to 1834, the gross revenue from salt alone, in the three presidencies of India, averaged 2,184,415*l.* annually. This salt is manufactured by the Indian government, and the government is the only salt-maker. Salt is also imported, and the duty brings in a large sum. For the year ending April 30th, 1861, the gross receipts on Salt are estimated at 3,391,630*l.*, exclusive of Customs' duty on salt imported. The anticipated receipts on salt for 1861-2 are 3,990,000*l.*, and on the Customs' duty for salt 1,255,000*l.* An increase of near 600,000*l.* in the Salt Revenue is expected to arise from a small increase in the duty. In a rich country like England an increased revenue is got by a reduction of duties on articles of common use; for the consumption increases in a greater ratio than the duty is reduced; more is consumed, and consequently more persons get what they want, or the same number get more of what they want. In a poor country like India, more money may be raised by a tax, though no more of the taxed article may be consumed; but then the people pay the increased tax out of their earnings, and have so much less left for other necessary purposes. Those who are curious to see how and how much money is raised by the Indian government and how it is spent, may turn to East India Finance and Revenue Accounts 15th May, 1861. There is no oppression in India such as Verres practised, but I doubt if the Romans would have got as much out of India as the Indian government does. If we look to the expenditure of this large revenue of about 40,000,000*l.*, we see how many British subjects are maintained by the labour of a poor country. Great Britain as a state gets nothing from India. It is not unlikely that India may some day be a cost to Great Britain, while many of our people are living on the produce of Indian taxation. But when that time shall come, if it ever shall come, the empire of British India will end, or India must be ruled at less cost.

religionibus foederum sanctum ac diligentem. Omnes qui ante te fuerunt praetores dedantur Mamertinis, quod iis navem contra pactionem foederis imperarint. Sed tamen tu, sancte homo ac religiose, cur Tauromenitanis item foederatis navem imperasti? An hoc probabis in aequa causa populorum sine pretio varium jus et disparem conditionem fuisse? Quid si ejusmodi esse haec duo foedera duorum populorum, judices, doceo, ut Tauromenitanis nominatim cautum et exceptum sit foedere, ne navem dare debeant; Mamertinis in ipso foedere sanctum atque praescriptum sit, ut navem dare necesse sit; istum autem contra foedus et Tauromenitanis imperasse et Mamertinis remisisse? numquid dubium poterit esse quin Verre praetore plus Mamertinis cybaea quam Tauromenitanis foedus opitulatum sit? Recitentur foedera.

XX. Isto igitur tuo quemadmodum ipse praedicas beneficio, ut res indicat, pretio atque mercede, minuisti majestatem rei publicae, minuisti auxilia populi Romani, minuisti copias majorum virtute ac sapientia comparatas, sustulisti jus imperii, conditionem sociorum, memoriam foederis. Qui ex foedere ipso navem vel usque ad Oceanum, si imperassemus, sumptu periculoque suo armatam atque ornatam mittere debuerunt, ii ne in freto ante sua tecta et domos navigarent, ne sua moenia portusque defenderent, pretio abs te jus foederis et imperii conditionem redemerunt. Quid censetis in hoc foedere faciundo voluisse Mamertinos impendere laboris, operae, pecuniae, ne haec biremis adscriberetur, si id ullo modo possent a nostris majoribus impetrare? Nam, quum hoc munus imponebatur tam grave civitati, inerat nescio quo modo in illo foedere societatis quasi quaedam nota servitutis. Quod tum recentibus suis officiis, integra re, nullis populi Romani difficultatibus, a majoribus nostris foedere assequi non potuerunt, id nunc, nullo officio suo, tot annis

cybaea] See Lib. 4. c. 8.

20. *majestatem*] See Lib. 4. c. 41, 'est majestatis,' &c. Cicero (De Invent. ii. 17) has a formal definition of 'majestatem minuere:' "Majestatem minuere est de dignitate aut amplitudine aut potestate populi aut eorum quibus potestatem dedit, aliquid derogare." This definition not only comprehends the case in this chapter—a direct attack on the 'majestas' of the Roman people, but also any attack on the authority or dignity of those who are the representatives of the people, such as the higher 'magistratus.' The passages relating to 'majestas,' in the Republican period, are collected by Becker, Handbuch, ii. 2, p. 69. The 'majestas' of the Imperial period is a different thing.

jus foederis] 'Jus' means here the duty which the 'foedus' imposed on them. The term comprehends a demand on the side of Rome and a duty on the part of the Mamertini. The 'imperii conditionem' is the terms on which Rome rules her subjects.

recentibus . . officiis,] He seems to allude to the time when the Mamertini first joined the Romans, B.C. 264 (Polybius, i. 7, &c.). Dett. and Orelli have 'nullo novo officio.' 'Integra re:' while the treaty was still under consideration, before it was made.

post, jure imperii nostri quotannis usurpatum ac semper retentum, summa in difficultate navium a C. Verre pretio assecuti sunt, ac non hoc solum assecuti ne navem darent: ecquem nautam, ecquem militem, qui aut in classe aut in praesidio esset, te praetore, per triennium Mamertini dederunt?

XXI. Denique quum ex senatus consulto, itemque ex lege Terentia et Cassia frumentum aequabiliter emi ab omnibus Siciliae civitatibus oporteret, id quoque munus leve atque commune Mamertinis remisisti. Dices frumentum Mamertinos non debere. Quomodo non debere? an ut ne venderent? non enim erat hoc genus frumenti ex eo genere quod exigeretur, sed ex eo quod emeretur. Te igitur auctore et interprete ne foro quidem et commeatu Mamertini populum Romanum juvare debuerunt. Quae tandem civitas fuit quae deberet? Qui publicos agros arant certum est quid e lege censoria debeant: cur his quidquam praeterea ex alio genere imperasti? Quid decumani, num quid praeter singulas decumas ex

usurpatum . . retentum,] A better reading than the old reading, 'usurpato . . retento.' 'Id . . usurpatum' means 'retained by constant use:' there was no intermission of the usage. 'Usurpare,' which is supposed to be compounded of 'usu' and 'rap,' is rather a difficult word to explain in all its senses. One common meaning, and the meaning here, is to exercise a right without interruption (Lib. 5. c. 62). But 'usurpatio' has another sense, 'usucapionis interruptio,' which will not apply here (Dig. 41. 3. 2).

ac non . . solum] The old editions have 'at non solum,' which makes these words the defence of Verres, and at the same time nonsense, for they contain a fresh charge. Lambinus corrected the passage by simply omitting 'non;' and then the meaning would be, 'but you will say, this is all they got from Verres, not to supply a ship.' R G 1 2 have 'ac non,' the true reading. It is a continuation of what has been said; but, as Halm remarks, if Cicero had written in the usual way, he would have added 'sed ne nautam quidem dederunt,' but he gives the sentence a new and more expressive turn.

21. *Terentia et Cassia*] See Lib. 3. c. 70.

omnibus . . . civitatibus] This chapter shows that all the Sicilian 'civitates' were liable to furnish corn at a price (frumentum emptum). See Lib. 3. c. 6. The argument in this chapter is liable to be misunderstood. Cicero says that all the 'civitates' were liable to furnish the 'frumentum emptum.' If any one 'civitas' obtained a remission, the deficiency would have to be supplied by further demands on the rest. Cicero says 'Neque hoc dico ceteris non recte imperatum; sed Mamertinis,' &c. The Mamertini ought to have supplied their share. The two modes of purchasing are mentioned in Lib. 3. c. 70, 'emendi duo genera fuerunt.' From the 'decumani' were bought the 'alterae decumae,' and this was properly called 'emptum.' There was also the 'emptum' which was distributed equally among all the 'civitates,' and this was properly called 'imperatum.' It appears then that the 'decumani' were liable both to the 'emptum' and the 'imperatum,' for Cicero says of the 'imperatum,' that it was required of all alike. This 'imperatum,' which was required from all alike, is called by Cicero indifferently 'emptum' and 'imperatum.'

Quae tandem civitas] These words are to be explained by a reference to 'debuerunt.' If the Mamertini were not bound to supply 'frumentum emptum,' what state was there which owed this duty? The demands on the 'aratores' of the 'ager publicus' were fixed; the demands on the 'decumani' were fixed; they owed 'singulae decumae.' The 'immunes' owed nothing in the shape of tax. Yet Verres called on them for 'frumentum emptum,' without calling on the Mamertini. That was his offence. As to 'publicos agros,' see Lib. 3. c. 6, note.

lege Hieronica debent? cur his quoque statuisti quantum ex hoc genere frumenti empti darent? Quid immunes, hi certe nihil debent. At eis non modo imperasti, verum etiam quo plus darent quam poterant, haec sexagena millia modium quae Mamertinis remiseras addidisti. Neque hoc dico ceteris non recte imperatum; sed Mamertinis, qui erant in eadem causa, et quibus superiores omnes [praetores] item ut ceteris imperarant pecuniamque ex senatus consulto et ex lege dissolverant, his dico non recte remissum. Et ut hoc beneficium, quemadmodum dicitur, trabali clavo figeret, cum consilio causam Mamertinorum cognoscit, et de consilii sententia Mamertinis se frumentum non imperare pronuntiat. Audite decretum mercenarii praetoris ex ipsius commentario, et cognoscite quanta in scribendo gravitas, quanta in constituendo jure sit auctoritas. Recita commentarium D.C.S. 'Libenter' ait se facere,

omnes [praetores]] 'omnes' R 3 Lg. 29, 'omnes praetores' dett. Or. Orelli says "ego retinui cum G. Facile scil. excidit compendium PR."

trabali claro] This seems to be a proverb (quemadmodum dicitur): 'to clench the matter,' as we say, to fix it, and make it sure. Horace, 1 Carm. xxxv., has adopted this ordinary expression:

"Te semper anteit saeva Necessitas
Clavos trabales et cuneos manu
Gestans ahena."

But in Carm. iii. 24 he has, as Zumpt observes, the more poetic form, or the form further removed from ordinary language, 'clavos adamantinos.'

ex ipsius commentario,] 'from his own note-book,' or his notes. 'Commentarii,' the plural being generally used, are books in which something is entered for the purpose of being remembered and used when the occasion may arise. Accordingly 'commentarii' may mean 'tabulae acceptorum et expensorum,' the 'tabulae censoriae,' and among other things 'mémoires pour servir,' for which we have no name, such as Caesar's Commentarii. See also Cic. Ad Fam. v. 12.

D.C.S.] "D.C.S. (i.e. *de consilii sententia*) de Zumptii conjectura; qui tamen titulum esse voluit; rectius Halmius, id quod sequentia docent, commentarii verba esse statuit: C.S. R 3; R.C. dett." (Iordan.) Accordingly Iordan and Halm write 'D.C.S. *libenter* ait *se facere*.' It is possible that these letters are spurious; and it is possible that Hervagius' conjecture R.D. i.e. 'rerum decretarum' may be right. But if D.C.S. must stand, Halm's pointing is wrong. 'Se facere' has also been incorrectly made part of the Decretum; but 'libenter' is the only word quoted here. D.C.S. was the title of the Decretum, and was followed according to Roman fashion by the names of those who composed the 'consilium.' 'Itaque perscribit' means 'and accordingly he draws up the Decretum,' as the Romans said 'perscribere senatusconsultum' (Lib. 4. c. 66). The following words, 'ac de consilii sententia,' no more support Halm's opinion than the preceding words, 'de consilii sententia Mamertinis,' &c. If the words D.C.S. were omitted, 'de consilii sententia,' which is a quotation like 'libenter,' would be explained by the words 'cum consilio cognoscit,' &c.

In the first edition I said that 'consilium' had evidently two meanings in this chapter. It means both the body of advisers, and the thing which was done with their advice.

The difficulty in this passage lies in the word 'consilium.' The Romans used 'recitare' when they spoke of publicly reading something written, as a letter to the Senate, a 'senatusconsultum,' and the like. Also they said 'recitare testimonia,' 'to read the evidence of witnesses which had been taken down in writing,' where 'testimonium' comprehends both the names of the witnesses and what they said. But the Romans could also say 'recitare senatum,' and 'testamento heres recitatus est,' 'a man's name is read out of the testament in which he is named Heres.' Accordingly in this passage 'recitari consilium' might mean simply 'to read the names of the

itaque perscribit. Quid, si hoc verbo non esses usus, 'libenter,' nos videlicet invitum te quaestum facere putaremus? Ac 'de consilii sententia.' Praeclarum recitari consilium, judices, audistis. Utrum vobis consilium tandem praetoris recitari videbatur quum audiebatis nomina, an praedonis improbissimi societas atque comitatus? En foederum interpretes, societatis pactores, religionis auctores. Nunquam in Sicilia frumentum publice est emptum quin Mamertinis pro portione imperaretur, antequam hoc delectum praeclarumque consilium iste dedit, ut ab his nummos acciperet ac sui similis esset. Itaque tantum valuit istius decreti auctoritas quantum debuit ejus hominis, qui a quibus frumentum emere debuisset iis decretum vendidisset. Nam statim L. Metellus ut isti successit, ex C. Sacerdotis et Sex. Peducaei instituto ac literis frumentum Mamertinis imperavit. XXII. Tum illi intellexerunt se id quod a malo auctore emissent diutius obtinere non posse. Age

Consilium;' though as 'consilium' has certainly the double sense both of the body, 'qui in consilio sunt,' and of 'advice, deliberation,' and so forth, 'recitari consilium' is not exactly like 'recitare senatum' and 'testamento heres recitatus est.' Cicero is fond of using words in a double sense, and I think he gives two meanings to 'consilium;' for when the names were read on this occasion, and they certainly were read, it was not merely the names which showed the villainy of the act, for Cicero says nothing directly against the men, but it was the 'decretum' which showed what was done; and the word 'societas,' 'partnership,' has no meaning unless it shows what the partnership was. Cicero adds 'comitatus,' which indicates the 'men' who were in this 'societas.'

There is a further difficulty in the words 'consilium dedit.' Hahn takes this to be like the expression 'judices dare,' but I know no example of 'consilium dare' in this sense. Suetonius has 'consilia sortiri.' I think that 'consilium dedit' does not mean only those 'qui in consilio erant,' but the whole thing, the names of the men and what was done by them, in a word the 'decretum.' In the word 'consilium' the two senses are sometimes mixed together, for those who form a 'consilium' (qui in consilio sunt) are said 'ire in consilium,' where we hardly know how to separate the 'consilium,' 'the persons,' from their 'consilium' or 'deliberation:' and the presiding magistrate is said 'mittere in consilium' the 'judices,' who are already called the 'consilium,' before the magistrate sends them 'in consilium.' But we have something else here. Cicero says 'consilium dedit ut ab his nummos acciperet,' where 'consilium' has the plain sense of 'he gave advice to get money.'

This, I believe, is the only sense in which the words 'consilium dare' can be used, but it is very easy to give these words the further meaning of 'consilium constituit' in connexion with the whole matter, though 'consilium dedit' simply by itself would not mean 'consilium constituit.'

As to the words 'delectum praeclarumque consilium,' Orelli remarks that 'consilium' in this passage cannot mean 'consilii sententia,' as appears from the word 'delectum.' Orelli also remarks that 'dare consilium,' for 'consilium constituisse,' is a strange expression; and he suggests the emendation, '*isti dedit* scil. facultatem, or permisit, concessit, ut cet.;' a suggestion which is quite useless.

pactores,] "Ἅπαξ λεγόμενον, servatum a G., in R. L. corruptum in *partiones.*" Orelli. 'pactiones' R 3 (Iordan).

pro portione] See Lib. 3. c. 63, note.

22. *malo auctore*] 'They then saw that they could not keep (obtinere) any longer that which they had bought from a man who had no title to sell.' A seller is sometimes called 'auctor,' as (Dig. 21. 2. 28) "sed si ex utriusque persona, et auctoris et emptoris" (and Pro Tullio, § 17; Pro Caecina, c. 10). The seller seems to have been so called with reference to his obligation to the buyer, in case the buyer should be evicted from his purchase. If the seller gave a 'fidejussor' or surety in

porro, tu, qui tam religiosum existimari te voluisti interpretem foederum, cur Tauromenitanis frumentum, cur Netinis imperasti, quarum civitatum utraque foederata est? Ac Netini quidem sibi non defuerunt, ac simul pronuntiasti libenter te Mamertinis remittere, te adierunt et eandem suam causam foederis esse docuerunt. Tu aliter decernere eadem in causa non potuisti. Pronuntias Netinos frumentum dare non debere, et ab his tamen exigis. Cedo mihi ejusdem praetoris literas et rerum decretarum et frumenti imperati. LITERAE RERUM DECRETARUM. Quid potius in hac tanta et tam turpi inconstantia suspicari possumus, judices,

case of eviction, the surety was commonly called 'auctor secundus' (Dig. 21. 2. 4).

The uses of 'auctor' and 'auctoritas,' in the Roman writers, are so copious, and so closely connected with technical matters, that a full explanation of them would go beyond the limits of a note. 'Auctor' contains the root 'aug,' to cause to wax or grow, to strengthen, confirm, and so forth. One of the most common uses of 'auctor' and 'auctoritas' appears in the case of 'pupilli,' for many of the acts of 'pupilli' were not valid without the knowledge and consent of a 'tutor' whose experience and years were intended to supply the defects in the experience and years of the 'pupillus' (Inst. i. 21): "tutor autem statim in ipso negotio praesens debet auctor fieri, si hoc pupillo prodesse existimaverit." The doctrine is contained in the following words (Dig. 41. 2. 32. § 2): "infans possidere recte potest, si tutore auctore coepit, nam judicium infantis suppletur auctoritate tutoris;" and in the following passage of Paulus (Dig. 26. 8. 3): "etiamsi non interrogatus tutor auctor fiat, valet auctoritas ejus quum se probare dicit id quod agitur: hoc est enim auctorem fieri."

Generally then 'auctoritas' is that which gives to a thing its efficiency or completeness, according to the nature of the case. There is 'auctoritas' in what a man of good character says and does. There is 'auctoritas' in him who holds a public office, and he has it by virtue of his office. A trustworthy person, one on whose evidence we can rely, is 'auctor idoneus.' Livy calls Polybius 'auctor non spernendus,' a man whose evidence and statements may be relied on. Compare Lib. 4. c. 45, 'bono auctore.' So we have as an 'auctor' one who sets an example, as 'unum cedo auctorem tui facti' (c. 26, and elsewhere). In c. 50, 'auctores testesque produco.'

There are other technical significations of 'auctor' and 'auctoritas,' the explanation of which would be foreign to the matter which is explained in this note; but a reference to them may be useful. The phrase 'patres auctores' (Livy, i. 17, 22, 32, and elsewhere) is explained by Becker, Handbuch, ii. 1, p. 314, &c. The difficulty lies in the application of the term; but, in order to understand it, we must recur to the sense of 'auctor,' which has been already explained.

The meaning of 'auctoritas' follows that of 'auctor,' for he who is 'auctor' gives his 'auctoritas.' Thus, in the old Roman legislation, the vote of the 'centuriae' and the 'auctoritas patrum' made a complete act. The voting of a 'lex,' or the choice of a person at an election, was made complete by the 'auctoritas patrum.' The equivalence of the expressions 'auctor fieri' and 'fieri pati' appears from Gaius (i. 99): "quia et is qui adoptat rogatur, id est, interrogatur, an velit eum quem adoptaturus sit, justum sibi filium esse; et is qui adoptatur rogatur, an id fieri patiatur," where he is speaking of 'adrogatio.' In the oration De Domo, c. 29, occurs the expression 'auctorne esses,' which was the old formula, in the same sense in which Gaius says 'an id fieri patiatur.' Compare also Gellius (v. 19).

As to the 'auctoritates' of the Senatus, see Becker, Handbuch, ii. 2, p. 441. The extreme difficulty of finding adequate expressions for the word 'auctor' will appear from a passage in this oration, c. 67, "senatores . . . legum et judiciorum et juris auctores." He who can give an adequate translation of these words has learned something of the Latin language, and of Roman affairs.

Ac Netini] 'At Netini' G 1 Zumpt. I now think that 'Ac Netini' (Iordan) is the true reading. As to 'Netini' see Lib. 3. c. 6.

ab his . . . exigis.] 'from the Netini.'

quam id quod necesse est, aut isti a Netinis pecuniam quum posceret non datam, aut id esse actum ut intelligerent Mamertini bene se apud istum tam multa pretia ac munera collocasse, quum idem alii juris ex eadem causa non obtinerent? Hic mihi etiam audebit mentionem facere Mamertinae laudationis, in qua quam multa sint vulnera, quis est vestrûm, judices, quin intelligat? Primum, ut in judiciis, qui decem laudatores dare non potest, honestius est ei nullum dare quam illum quasi legitimum numerum consuetudinis non explere. Tot in Sicilia civitates sunt quibus tu per triennium praefuisti: arguunt ceterae: paucae et parvae et metu repressae silent: una laudat. Hoc quid est nisi intelligere quid habeat utilitatis vera laudatio, sed tamen ita provinciae praefuisse ut hac utilitate necessario sit carendum? Deinde, quod alio loco antea dixi, quae est ista tandem laudatio cujus laudationis legati principes et publice tibi navem aedificatam et privatim se ipsos abs te spoliatos expilatosque esse dixerunt? Postremo quid aliud isti faciunt quum te soli ex Sicilia laudant, nisi testimonio nobis sunt omnia te sibi esse largitum quae tu rei publicae nostrae detraxeris? Quae colonia est in Italia tam bono jure, quod tam immune municipium, quod per hosce annos tam commoda vacatione omnium rerum sit usum quam Mamertina civitas per triennium? Soli ex foedere quod debuerunt non dederunt; soli isto praetore omnium

ut in judiciis,] This 'ut' has caused a difficulty. I doubt if any of the commentators have explained it right. Zumpt's explanation is not clear to me. It is a mode of expression which is perhaps elliptical. It seems like the case mentioned in Lib. 1. c. 52, 'ut meretrix.' So this means: 'First of all, considering it the case of a trial.' Klotz says that Cicero intended to proceed with a 'sic' or 'ita,' in order to show how the case was with Verres, but he gave the sentence a new turn, by which the expression is rendered more animated. He adds, "this slight anacoluthie has been already set in a true light by the interpretors." But the interpreters don't agree. Iordan says 'nos cum Manutio aliisque *ut* uncis inclusimus.' Garatoni explains it thus, 'ut in judiciis fit, more judiciorum.' Madvig finds the passage difficult, and suspects that there is some error in 'ut in judiciis.' Rau suspects that all the words 'ut in judiciis . . . explere' are spurious. But he is a very suspicious critic.

'Laudatores' were persons who came forward to give the defendant a character, such as we see sometimes called to support a lame defence. Ten, it seems, was the number at Rome; not required by any law (legitimus), but by custom, which had the semblance of a positive institution (quasi legitimus). Compare Lib. 4. c. 66, "illum noluisse sua laudatione juvare;" and Cic. Ad Div. ix. 1, "Quum Pompeius ut laudaret P. Sextium introisset in urbem."

Tot . . civitates] See Lib. 2. c. 55, where it is said that there were 130 censores in the Sicilian 'civitates,' two for each 'civitas.' But we cannot be certain that we thence deduce correctly the number of 'civitates.'

cujus] 'quoius' R.

rei publicae] 're publica,' Iordan following the dett. here. R G 2 Ld. have 're publ.' G 1, 'rei publ.'

colonia . . . municipium,] A 'colonia' was either a Romana or Latina colonia. A 'municipium' was an Italian town in a political relationship to Rome. The distinction between the two is unimportant at this time, as to those parts of Italy which had received the Roman 'civitas.'

rerum immunes fuerunt; soli in istius imperio ea conditione vixerunt ut populo Romano nihil darent, Verri nihil denegarent.

XXIII. Verum ut ad classem quo ex loco sum digressus revertar, accepisti a Mamertinis navem contra leges; remisisti contra foedera: ita in una civitate bis improbus fuisti, quum et remisisti quod non oportebat et accepisti quod non licebat. Exigere te oportuit navem quae contra praedones, non quae cum praeda navigaret; quae defenderet ne provincia spoliaretur, non quae spolia provinciae portaret. Mamertini tibi et urbem quo furta undique deportares et navem in qua exportares praebuerunt. Illud tibi oppidum receptaculum praedae fuit: illi homines testes custodesque furtorum: illi tibi et locum furtis et furtorum vehiculum comparaverunt. Itaque ne tum quidem quum classem avaritia ac nequitia tua perdidisti Mamertinis navem imperare ausus es, quo tempore in tanta inopia navium tantaque calamitate provinciae, etiamsi precario essent rogandi, tamen ab iis impetraretur. Reprimebat enim tibi et imperandi vim et rogandi conatum praeclara illa non populo Romano reddita biremis sed praetori donata cybaea. Ea fuit merces imperii, auxilii, juris, consuetudinis, foederis.

XXIV. Habetis unius civitatis firmum auxilium amissum ac venditum pretio: cognoscite nunc novam praedandi rationem ab hoc primum excogitatam. Sumptum omnem in classem frumento, stipendio ceterisque rebus suo quaeque navarcho civitas semper dare solebat. Is neque ut accusaretur a nautis committere audebat, et civibus suis rationes referre debebat, et in omni illo negotio

denegarent.] "Vulgo editur *nihil denegarent*, fortiore verbo, sed ob hanc ipsam, opinor, causam minus apto" (Zumpt). Orelli observes that the copyists more frequently err in substituting the simple for the compound, than the other way. He also thinks that 'darent . . . denegarent' make a better opposition by both beginning with the same letter, and having the same termination. There is some weight in this remark.—'denegarent' dett. (Iordan), who has 'negarent.'

23. *contra leges;*] The better MSS. R 3 λ have 'leges,' as before, c. 18, though only one 'lex' is meant. So he says 'foedera,' though only one 'foedus' is meant.

precario . . impetraretur.] There is no doubt that 'precario' can go with 'rogari;' but the conjecture of Graevius, that it is out of place, and should go with 'impetraretur,' thus, 'precario tamen impetraretur,' seems a probable conjecture. 'Impetraretur,' says Zumpt, is for 'esset impetranda.'—'precario . . . rogandi:' see Lib. 2. c. 36, and to the references there add Gaius, ii. 60, "si neque conduxerit eam rem a creditore debitor neque precario rogaverit ut eam rem possidere liceret." Garatoni defends the passive form, 'precario . . rogandi,' by this example, against Ernesti, who encloses 'precario' in the damnatory [ ]. As 'precario rogare' is Latin, there seems no reason why 'precario . . . rogandi' is not.

reddita] 'paid,' as a debt, as a duty which they owed to the Roman state.

24. *rationes referre*] Zumpt has 'rationes ferre,' and says "sic Regius et Guelff. Vulgo *rationem referre*." 'Rationes referre' is the common expression in these

non modo labore sed etiam periculo suo versabatur. Erat hoc, ut dico, factitatum semper nec solum in Sicilia sed in omnibus provinciis; etiam in sociorum et Latinorum stipendio ac sumptu tum quum illorum auxiliis uti solebamus. Verres post imperium constitutum primus imperavit ut ea pecunia omnis a civitatibus sibi adnumeraretur, ut is eam pecuniam tractaret quem ipse praefecisset. Cui potest esse dubium quamobrem et omnium consuetudinem veterem primus immutaris, et tantam utilitatem per alios tractandae pecuniae neglexeris, et tantam difficultatem cum crimine, molestiam cum suspicione susceperis? Deinde alii quaestus instituuntur ex uno genere navali, videte quam multi: accipere a civitatibus pecuniam ne nautas darent; pretio certo missos facere nautas; missorum omne stipendium lucrari; reliquis quod deberet non dare. Haec omnia ex civitatum testimoniis cognoscite. Recita testimonia civitatum. Huncine hominem! hancine impudentiam, judices! hanc audaciam! civitatibus pro numero militum pecuniarum summas discribere; certum pretium, sexcenos nummos, nautarum missionis constituere; quos qui dederat, commeatum totius aestatis abstulerat, iste quod ejus nautae nomine pro stipendio frumentoque acceperat lucrabatur. Ita quaestus duplex unius missionis fiebat. Atque haec homo amentissimus in tanto

orations (Lib. 1. c. 14), but 'rationem referre' also occurs.

et in omni illo] 'Et in illo omni' (Zumpt), following Stephanus and Lambinus. We now know that R has 'et in.' It is a small matter in itself, the omission or insertion of 'et,' but not unimportant, if it is a question of Cicero's Latinity. Orelli prefers the ἀσύνδετον. Besides, he observes that 'neque' having been followed by 'et,' the addition of another 'et' seems inappropriate. As there is now authority for this 'et,' I accept it.

sociorum et Latinorum] Cicero is speaking of the Italian Socii and the Latini before the enactment of the Julia Lex, B.C. 90. He says 'tum quum illorum,' &c. See Divin. c. 3, note. Ernesti entirely mistook this passage, and erased the 'et' in opposition to all the MSS.; a blunder that is unpardonable. Zumpt corrects it. But Ernesti made a blunder of the same kind in the De Am. c. 3, where, instead of the true reading, 'Populo Romano, sociis et Latinis,' he wrote 'Populi Romani sociis et Latinis.'

post imperium constitutum] Like 'post urbem conditam,' 'since the establishment of the Roman Imperium, Verres is the first man who,' &c.

suspicione] 'suspitione' R, a false form of writing which Halm follows.

Huncine] So Zumpt writes it in his larger edition. He says that in this passage all the MSS., as far as he knows, have the word with one *c*.—'discribere:' in the first edition I had 'describere,' with the remark that I suspected that it should be 'discribere:' and so it is in R 'discribere R pr. m.' Yet Iordan keeps 'describere.' So hard it is to banish some errors. Halm has 'discribere.' See Index, 'Discribere.'

sexcenos] 'sescenos' R, Iordan. Lg. 14 29 have 'sexcentos,' the wrong form; and G 1 Legg. alii 'sexcentenos,' a mixture of two readings, which sometimes is found.

commeatum .. abstulerat,] The 'nauta' got leave of absence, and Verres pocketed the money. This sense of 'abstulerat,' 'carried off' or 'got,' is common in these orations. Manutius has mistaken the meaning of this passage, though it is not doubtful.

praedonum impetu tantoque periculo provinciae sic palam faciebat ut et ipsi praedones scirent et tota provincia testis esset.

XXV. Quum propter istius hanc avaritiam nomine classis esset in Sicilia, re quidem vera naves inanes, quae praedam praetori, non quae praedonibus metum afferrent, tamen quum P. Caesetius et P. Tadius decem navibus suis semiplenis navigarent, navem quandam piratarum, praeda refertam, non ceperunt sed abduxerunt, onere suo plane captam atque depressam. Erat ea navis plena juventutis formosissimae, plena argenti facti atque signati, multa cum stragula veste. Haec una navis a classe nostra non capta est sed inventa ad Megaridem, qui locus est non longe a Syracusis. Quod ubi isti nuntiatum est, tametsi in acta cum mulierculis jacebat ebrius, erexit se tamen, et statim quaestori legatoque suo custodes misit complures ut omnia sibi integra quam primum exhiberentur. Appellitur navis Syracusas: exspectatur ab omnibus supplicium. Iste quasi praeda sibi advecta, non praedonibus captis, si qui senes aut deformes erant, eos in hostium numero ducit; qui aliquid formae, aetatis, artificiique habebant, abducit omnes; nonnullos scribis [suis], filio cohortique distribuit; symphoniacos sex cuidam amico suo Romam muneri misit. Nox illa tota in exinaniunda navi consumitur. Archipiratam ipsum videt nemo, de quo supplicium sumi oportuit; hodieque omnes sic habent, (quid

25. *abduxerunt,*] R 3 Lg. 27 29 have 'adduxerunt.' Iordan refers to Lib. 4. c. 6, and Non. p. 253. In Lib. 4. c. 6, in place of 'abducuntur' G 2 Ld. have 'adducuntur,' and Iordan there remarks that these words are often confounded in these MSS.

onere . . captam] 'It was overloaded.' As to the use of 'captus,' see Forcellini; and Lib. 4. c. 45, note. Cicero is playing on the words 'non ceperunt sed abduxerunt' and 'onere . . . captam.'

argenti facti &c.] 'Argentum factum' is silver vessels. 'Argentum signatum' is money.

Megaridem,] He appears to mean Megara Hyblaea, near Syracuse.

in acta] "Sic codices meliores—Vulgares *noctu*, crassa haud dubie Minerva" (Zumpt). '*Noctu* Lagg. praeter 29' (Iordan). 'In acta' occurs afterwards (c. 31). Manutius defends 'noctu,' for Verres did not remove his quarters to the 'acta' till after the capture of this ship (c. 31). Verres heard of the news at night, as appears from the words 'nox illa,' &c. I don't think that it would prove a man to be 'crassa Minerva,' if he should prefer 'noctu.' Still 'acta' may be right. See Pro Caelio, c. 15; and Virg. Aen. v. 613.

in hostium numero ducit;] 'He puts them to death,' as we are told in c. 28. This is the Roman way of saying that prisoners are put to death. Caesar (B. G. i. 28) has the same form. He put to the sword six thousand Helvetii who had tried to make their escape after surrendering. Compare Cic. In Cat. iii. c. 10; Suetonius, Nero, c. 2. Xenophon has a like form, *ὡς πολεμίοις ἐχρῶντο* (Cyrop. vii. 5. 27).

symphoniacos] Orelli and Iordan add 'homines;' G 3 omit it.

hodieque] dett., 'hodie' R 3 Iordan.

sic habent,] 'Persuasum' is generally added after 'habent;' but it is not in the best MSS. It is also not Cicero's mode of expression, as Zumpt says; for Cicero writes 'persuasum mihi est.' 'Sic habent,' in the sense of 'existimant,' is common. Orelli quotes Cato, De Re Rustica, c. 1, 'majores nostri sic habuerunt;' and Graevius from the Pro Caelio, c. 2, "quibus . . non aeque est cognitus, hi sic habeant."—Manutius explains 'quid ejus sit' by examples from Terence, one of the best sources for explaining Cicero's ordinary language. It

ejus sit vos conjectura assequi debetis,) istum clam a piratis ob hunc archipiratam pecuniam accepisse. XXVI. Conjectura est.—Judex esse bonus nemo potest qui suspicione certa non movetur. Hominem nostis; consuetudinem omnium tenetis, qui ducem praedonum aut hostium ceperit, quam libenter eam palam ante oculos omnium esse patiatur. Hominem in tanto conventu Syracusis vidi neminem, judices, qui archipiratam captum sese vidisse diceret, quum omnes, ut mos est, ut solet fieri, concurrerent, quaererent, videre cuperent. Quid accidit cur tanto opere iste homo occultaretur ut eum ne casu quidem quisquam aspicere posset? Homines maritimi Syracusis qui saepe istius ducis nomen audissent, saepe timuissent, quum ejus cruciatu atque supplicio pascere oculos animumque exsaturare vellent, potestas aspiciendi nemini facta est. Unus plures praedonum duces vivos cepit P. Servilius quam omnes antea. Ecquando igitur isto fructu quisquam caruit ut videre piratam captum non liceret? At contra, quacumque iter fecit, hoc jucundissimum spectaculum omnibus vinctorum captorumque hostium praebebat. Itaque ei concursus fiebant undique, ut non modo ex his oppidis qua ducebantur sed etiam ex finitimis visendi causa convenirent. Ipse autem triumphus quamobrem omnium triumphorum gratissimus populo Romano fuit et jucundissimus? Quia nihil est victoria dulcius, nullum est autem testimonium victoriae certius quam quos saepe metueris eos te vinctos ad supplicium duci videre. Hoc tu quamobrem non fecisti? quamobrem ita pirata iste occultatus est quasi eum aspici nefas esset? quamobrem supplicium non sumpsisti? quam ob causam hominem reservasti? ecquem scis in Sicilia

means, 'how much truth there is in it you must judge from conjecture.' 'Conjectura est' means, 'it is only a conjecture, I admit.' Orelli takes it to be the remark of a friend of Verres, which comes to the same. Caesar, B. G. i. 21, writes 'quid sui consilii sit ostendit.' See also B. G. vi. 7, and vii. 77.

26. *maritimi*] Opposed to 'mediterranei,' a term which Cicero applies to the Centuripini (c. 27), an inland people. Lagg. have the false reading 'Mamertini.'—'cruciatu . . pascere:' Cicero's language, in compliance with the notions of his time, is cruel. The men were to be tortured, to please those who had once feared them. It is just that a pirate should die as soon as he is caught, but that is enough.

P. Servilius] Lib. 3. c. 90. Zumpt has 'victorum captorumque,' the reading of A Ld. He says of the common reading, '*ὑστερολογία* est vix ferenda.' He adds, that the examples which he has collected (Divin. c. 2) in the note on the words 'meum factum aut consilium,' are not to be compared with this; and yet he calls them examples of *ὑστερολογία*, or, as the grammarians sometimes name it, 'hysteron proteron.' He cites from Terence, Hauton. iii. 1. 21, 'valet atque vivit:' Liv. xxiii. 33, 'incendere ac diripere urbes.' An enemy cannot be 'captus,' he says, before he is 'victus.' He seems not to have thought of the possible case that he may become 'victus' by being 'captus,' and not before. We may argue that Cicero would mention, as the striking object of the spectacle, men in chains (vincti), which at once suggests the notion of 'capti.' I prefer 'vinctorum,' which Orelli also has, and Iordan.

fiebant] 'fiebat,' Iordan.—'ex his:' cold.

antea captum archipiratam qui non securi percussus sit? Unum cedo auctorem tui facti: unius profer exemplum. Vivum tu archipiratam servabas, quem per triumphum, credo, quem ante currum tuum duceres; neque enim quidquam erat reliquum nisi uti classe populi Romani pulcherrima amissa provinciaque lacerata triumphus tibi navalis decerneretur.

XXVII. Age porro, custodiri ducem praedonum novo more quam securi feriri omnium exemplo magis placuit.—Quae sunt istae custodiae? apud quos homines? quemadmodum est asservatus? Lautumias Syracusanas omnes audistis, plerique nostis. Opus est ingens, magnificum, regum ac tyrannorum: totum est e saxo in mirandam altitudinem depresso et multorum operis penitus exciso: nihil tam clausum ad exitum, nihil tam septum undique, nihil tam tutum ad custodiam nec fieri nec cogitari potest. In has lautumias, si qui publice custodiendi sunt, etiam ex ceteris oppidis Siciliae deduci imperantur. Eo quod multos captivos cives Romanos conjecerat, [et] quod eodem ceteros piratas condi imperarat, intellexit, si hunc subditivum archipiratam in eandem custodiam dedisset, fore ut a multis in lautumiis verus ille dux quaereretur. Itaque hominem huic optimae tutissimaeque custodiae non audet committere: denique Syracusas totas timet: amandat hominem—quo?

servabas, quem &c.] I have followed the 'vulgata.' Zumpt has 'servabas: quam ob rem? per triumphum, credo,' &c., the reading of G 1. Iordan, 'servabas: quo? Per triumphum, credo,' &c., the reading of R, which Madvig approves. This is an instance in which the genuine hand of Cicero is uncertain. 'Per triumphum ducere' occurs in c. 30.

erat reliquum] 'Tibi erat reliquum' G 1, Zumpt. But 'tibi' spoils the sense, as Orelli remarks. It would mean 'you had no hope left except,' &c. Caesar (B. G. ii. 26) has 'nihil ad celeritatem sibi reliqui fecerunt.'

27. *Lautumias*] They are described in Smyth's Sicily, p. 167. Cicero cannot have supposed, as Zumpt imagines, that these quarries were mainly made for prisons; nor do his words imply that. He must have known what every body knew. The common reading is 'depressum .. excisum,' and perhaps as good as the text.

imperantur.] Halm compares Horace, Ep. i. 5. v. 21, 'procurare imperor.'

subditivum] The common reading is 'subdititium' or 'subditicium,' a form which may be compared with 'dedititius.' The form in 'ivus' certainly occurs, as in Horace, Epod. ii. 19, 'Ut gaudet insitiva decerpens pyra.' R G 1 2 Lg. 29 42 have 'subditivum' here. Most of the inferior MSS. have 'subditum' or 'subditum,' which is a possible form; but Zumpt takes it merely as a tendency (tendere) towards 'subditiuum.' Cicero means that the real archpirate was let loose and a false man put in his place. He calls him shortly after 'ille suppositus.'

quo? Lilybaeum fortasse.] Cicero's imaginary dialogue is not very clear. It is not easy at first to distinguish between what he says himself and what he supposes others to say. I see no way of explaining how I understand the passage except by translating it: 'he sends the man off. But whither? To Lilybaeum perhaps. I see what you mean; you still suppose that he is not altogether afraid of a maritime people. But he does not send him there, Judices. To Panhormus then? I hear what you say: though, as he was captured in the Syracusan territory, Syracuse would have been the proper place for his custody, if not for his punishment. But he did not send him even to Panhormus. Where did he send him then? Where do you think,' &c.

Lilybaeum fortasse. Video: tamen homines maritimos non plane reformidat. Minime, judices. Panhormum igitur? Audio: quamquam Syracusis, quoniam in Syracusano captus erat, maxime, si minus supplicio affici, at custodiri oportebat. Ne Panhormum quidem. Quo igitur? quo putatis? Ad homines a piratarum metu et suspicione alienissimos, a navigando rebusque maritimis remotissimos, ad Centuripinos, homines maxime mediterraneos, summos aratores, qui nomen nunquam timuissent maritimi praedonis, unum te praetore horruissent Apronium, terrestrem archipiratam. Et ut quivis facile perspiceret id ab isto actum esse ut ille suppositus facile et libenter se illum qui non erat esse simularet, imperat Centuripinis ut is victu ceterisque rebus quam liberalissime commodissimeque adhiberetur.

XXVIII. Interea Syracusani, homines periti et humani, qui non modo ea quae perspicua essent videre, verum etiam occulta suspicari possent, habebant rationem omnes quotidie piratarum qui securi ferirentur; quam multos esse oporteret ex ipso navigio quod erat captum et ex remorum numero conjiciebant. Iste, quod omnes qui artificii aliquid habuerant aut formae [removerat atque] abduxerat, reliquos si, ut consuetudo est, universos ad palum alligasset, clamorem populi fore suspicabatur, quum tanto plures abducti essent quam relicti. Propter hanc causam, quum instituisset alios alio tempore producere, tamen in tanto conventu nemo erat qui non rationem numerumque haberet, et reliquos non desideraret solum, sed etiam posceret et flagitaret. Quum magnus numerus deesset, tum iste homo nefarius in eorum locum, quos domum suam de piratis abduxerat, substituere et supponere coepit cives Romanos

Video . . Audio:] See Lib. 2. c. 60, note on 'audio,' which is misplaced under c. 59. Compare also Pro S. Rosc. Am. c. 18, and c. 21.

mediterraneos,] Yet these Mediterranean men, 'summi aratores,' supplied a ship, c. 33.

adhiberetur.] R S λ. Lg. 29 has 'haberetur.' 'Adhiberetur' is thus used by Cicero, Ad Att. x. 12; Ad Q. Fr. i. 1. c. 5, 'quos ego universos adhiberi liberaliter' &c. (Zumpt.) Graevius 'negat se ferre posse' the 'adhibere' in Cic. Ad Att. x. 12; but he must put up with it, whether he will or not. Orelli follows Zumpt, but 'invitus paene.'

28. *periti et humani,*] Experienced, clever people: 'non barbari et indocti.' Manutius.

[removerat atque]] Omitted by R S.

tanto plures] Hotmann thinks 'tanto plures,' 'so many more,' won't do. But it is one of the most ordinary things in the Latin language to use 'tanto,' 'tam,' 'ita,' in this way to express a great degree, without 'quanto,' 'quam,' or 'ut' following. In c. 29 'tanto post.' The objection in this chapter is perhaps merely founded on the comparative 'plures' being joined with 'tanto;' but the objection is not the stronger for that reason.

nemo erat qui non] R V have 'quin' for 'qui non.' V also omits 'et flagitaret' at the end of the sentence.—V has 'quos cervos in carcerem;' and Mai, who believes his codex to be infallible, or nearly so, writes 'quos certos,' which I don't believe to be Latin or sense.

quos in carcerem antea conjecerat: quorum alios Sertorianos milites fuisse insimulabat et ex Hispania fugientes ad Siciliam appulsos esse dicebat: alios qui a praedonibus erant capti, quum mercaturas facerent aut aliquam ob causam navigarent, sua voluntate cum piratis fuisse arguebat. Itaque alii cives Romani ne cognoscerentur capitibus obvolutis e carcere ad palum atque ad necem rapiebantur: alii, quum a multis civibus Romanis cognoscerentur, ab omnibus defenderentur, securi feriebantur. Quorum ego de acerbissima morte crudelissimoque cruciatu dicam, quum eum locum tractare coepero, et ita dicam, ut, si me in ea querimonia, quam sum habiturus de istius crudelitate et de civium Romanorum indignissima morte, non modo vires verum etiam vita deficiat, id mihi praeclarum et jucundum putem. Haec igitur est gesta res, haec victoria praeclara: myoparone piratico capto dux liberatus, symphoniaci Romam missi: formosi homines et adolescentes et artifices domum abducti: in eorum locum et ad eorum numerum cives Romani hostilem in modum cruciati et necati: omnis vestis ablata, omne aurum et argentum ablatum et aversum.

XXIX. At quemadmodum ipse se induit priore actione? Qui tot dies tacuisset, repente in M. Annii, hominis splendidissimi, testimonio, quum is civem Romanum dixisset, archipiratam negasset securi esse percussum, exsiluit: conscientia sceleris et furore ex maleficiis concepto excitatus dixit se, quod sciret sibi crimini datum iri pecuniam accepisse neque de vero archipirata sumpsisse supplicium, ideo se securi non percussisse: domi esse apud sese archipiratas dixit duos. O clementiam populi Romani, seu potius patientiam miram ac singularem! Civem Romanum securi esse percussum M. Annius, eques Romanus, dicit; taces: archipiratam negat; fateris. Fit gemitus omnium et clamor, quum tamen a

Sertorianos] The men who were dispersed after the assassination of Sertorius in Spain, B.C. 72.

civibus Romanis cognoscerentur,] The reading of the better MSS., instead of which we have in some editions, as in the Variorum, 'civ. Rom. recognoscerentur,' the reading of G 1. Zumpt refers to various critics who show that 'cognoscere' is used in the sense of 'agnoscere.' But perhaps something more is meant than 'agnoscere.' In Lib. 5. c. 65, 'neque semper cum cognitoribus esse possunt' occurs, and 'cognosceret hominem.' It seems to mean the recognition of a man by another who is himself well known, and a sufficient voucher for the character of another.

ego] om. Lg. 29.

in eorum . . et ad . . numerum] These are two uses of these prepositions. 'In' expresses 'instead of,' and 'ad' 'to the amount of.' Caesar (B. G. i. 5) writes 'oppida . . . . numero ad duodecim.'—'hostilem in modum:' 'like enemies.' Compare 'in hostium numero,' c. 25. —'aversum:' 'wrongly appropriated by Verres.'

29. *se induit*] 'Entangled himself,' as in Lib. 2. c. 42, 'hic videte in quos se laqueos induerit;' and Lib. 5. c. 64, 'sua confessione induatur,' &c. Caesar (B. G. vii. 73) writes, 'se ipsi acutissimis vallis induebant.' See also vii. 82.

praesenti supplicio tuo continuit populus Romanus se et repressit, et salutis suae rationem judicum severitati reservavit. Quid, sciebas tibi crimini datum iri? Quamobrem sciebas? quamobrem etiam suspicabare? Inimicum habebas neminem: si haberes, tamen non ita vixeras ut metum judicii propositum habere deberes. An te, id quod fieri solet, conscientia timidum suspiciosumque faciebat? Qui igitur quum esses cum imperio jam tum judicium et crimen horrueris, is quum tot testibus coarguare, potes de damnatione dubitare? Verum si crimen hoc metuebas, ne quis suppositum abs te esse diceret qui pro archipirata securi feriretur, utrum tandem tibi ad defensionem firmius fore putasti, in judicio coactu atque efflagitatu meo producere ad ignotos tanto post eum quem archipiratam esse diceres, an recenti re, Syracusis, apud notos, inspectante Sicilia paena tota, securi ferire? Vide quid intersit utrum faciendum fuerit. In illo reprehensio nulla esse potuit; hic defensio nulla est. Itaque illud semper omnes fecerunt: hoc quis ante te, quis praeter te fecerit, quaero. Piratam vivum tenuisti. Quem ad finem?—Dum cum imperio fuisti.—Quam ob causam? quo exemplo? cur tamdiu? cur, inquam, civibus Romanis, quos piratae ceperant, securi statim percussis, ipsis piratis lucis usuram tam diuturnam dedisti? Verum esto; sit tibi illud liberum omne tempus quod cum imperio fuisti: etiamne privatus, etiamne reus,

salutis suae] This is the reading of R 3. The dett. have 'tuae.' Zumpt says that nothing is more manifest than 'suae.' Madvig is of the same mind. Orelli and Bake stand up for 'tuae.' Zumpt's sarcastic argument against 'tuae' is, "scilicet populus saluti Verris consultum voluit," which is not worth answering. Cicero could say that the Roman people checked themselves, and reserved the consideration of 'your judgment' (tuae) for the strictness of the 'judices.' Bake refers to Lib. 1. c. 28, 'istum fortuna non tam,' &c.

Inimicum habebas &c.] Said ironically.

Qui igitur . . . dubitare?] I have let this passage stand as it is in Zumpt, without being convinced of the correctness of his settlement of the text. It stands thus in the Variorum ed.: 'Qui igitur, cum esses in imperio, jam tum judicium et crimen horrebas: reus cum tot testibus arguare, potes de damnatione dubitare?' The old editions have 'quid igitur,' &c. There is good authority for 'horrueris,' but I believe that 'horrebas' (dett.) is the true reading. 'Reus' is only in S. 'Is' is an addition by Zumpt. H ϕ 7 Lgg. have 'hic cum.' Lg. 29 has 'his cum,' and Halm suggests that this should be altered to 'is cum,' saying "nam is post *horrueris* facile in bona familia excidere potuit." 'In imperio,' the reading of dett., will do; but 'cum imperio' is perhaps better here. It is impossible to say what is the genuine text. Orelli has 'Qui igitur . . crimen et judicium horrebas: reus quum . . . coarguare,' &c.

ad ignotos] 'To those who do not know him;' a common use of the word. 'Notis' (Pro Caelio, c. 2) means 'to those who know him,' and it is opposed to 'quibus . . non est cognitus.'

Quem ad finem?] 'How long?' Compare Cic. Cat. i. 1, "Quem ad finem sese effrenata jactabit audacia;" and Pro Caelio, c. 5.

quod cum imperio] 'Quoad' is the reading of R 3 & Lg. 29. Dett. have 'quod.' Zumpt has the remark from Garatoni, that "*quod*, si ad tempus referatur, posse servari, sed praestare *quoad*." What else can 'quod' refer to except 'tempus?' 'Quoad,' which occurs shortly afterwards, has a different sense: it means up to the time when

etiamne paene damnatus hostium duces privata in domo retinuisti? Unum, alterum mensem, prope annum denique domi tuae piratae, a quo tempore capti sunt, quoad per me licitum est, fuerunt; hoc est, quoad per M'. Glabrionem licitum est, qui postulante me produci atque in carcerem condi imperavit. XXX. Quod est hujusce rei jus, quae consuetudo, quod exemplum? Hostem acerrimum atque infestissimum populi Romani, seu potius communem hostem gentium nationumque omnium, quisquam omnium mortalium privatus intra moenia domi suae retinere poterit? Quid, si pridie quam a me tu coactus es confiteri civibus Romanis securi percussis praedonum ducem vivere, habitare apud te, si, inquam, pridie domo tua profugisset, si aliquam manum contra populum Romanum facere potuisset, quid diceres? 'Apud me habitavit: mecum fuit: ego illum ad judicium meum, quo facilius crimen inimicorum diluere possem, vivum atque incolumem reservavi.' Itane vero tu tua pericula communi periculo defendes? tu supplicia quae debentur hostibus victis ad tuum non ad rei publicae tempus conferes? populi Romani hostis privati hominis custodiis asservabitur? At etiam qui triumphant, eoque diutius vivos hostium duces reservant ut his per triumphum ductis pulcherrimum spectaculum fructumque victoriae populus Romanus percipere possit, tamen, quum de foro in Capitolium currus flectere incipiunt, illos duci in carcerem jubent, idemque dies et victoribus imperii et victis vitae finem facit.

my intervention took them out of your house. In this passage either 'quod' or 'quoad' may be explained. Zumpt, Orelli, and Jordan have 'quoad.' See the remarks of Gellius on 'quoad,' Lib. 7. c. 21.

postulante] See Index, 'Postulare.'

30. *mecum fuit:*] Klotz remarks that 'esse cum aliquo' not only means to live with a person, but to have confidential communication with him. He refers to the passage in the Tusculan Disp. iii. 34.

Itane vero] 'Itane vero?' Zumpt, thus always, I think; and Jordan. I may have left the (?) after 'vero' in one or two instances. 'Itane vero?' may indeed be a sentence, that is, an incomplete sentence.

vivos . . reservant] Ernesti defends 'reservant' against the common reading 'servant;' but he says that 'vivos' should be removed. Nobody can tell why. 'Reservare' is 'servare' for some particular purpose. Caesar (B. G. vii. 89) says, "Reservatis Aeduis atque Arvernis si per eos civitates recuperare posset." Zumpt has already given his opinion of Lambinus. This is his judgment of Ernesti: "fuit omnino Ernestius, prout animus ferebat, inconstantior in probando et improbando, sed semper paratus ad tuendam lectionem vulgatam, si quis alius reprehendisset."

currus] R 3 A, 'currum' dett. If these captives were put to death in the Tullianum, the place of execution was near the point where the procession turned off to the capitol. See Sallust, Cat. c. 55, and Plutarch, Cato, c. 55.

victis vitae finem] This passage is authority with others for one of the shameful parts of Roman history, the execution of the conquered generals. Cicero here writes as a Roman. The story of Jugurtha's strangulation, after appearing in the triumph, is told by Plutarch (Marius, c. 12; and Cato, c. 55). Zumpt refers to the death of Simon, the leader in the Jewish war, who was strangled after appearing in the triumph of Vespasian and Titus (Josephus, Bell. Jud. vii. 5). The Gaul Vercingetorix, who surrendered to Caesar at Alesia in B.C. 52, was kept in prison till Caesar's triumph in B.C. 46, and then put to death.

Et nunc cuiquam credo esse dubium quin tu id commissurus non fueris, praesertim quum statuisses, ut ais, tibi causam esse dicendam, ut ille archipirata non potius securi feriretur, quam, quod erat ante oculos positum, tuo periculo viveret.—Si enim esset mortuus, tu qui crimen ais te metuisse, quaero, cui probares? quum constaret istum Syracusis a nullo visum esse archipiratam, ab omnibus desideratum; quum dubitaret nemo quin abs te pecunia liberatus esset; quum vulgo loquerentur suppositum in ejus locum quem pro illo probare velles; quum tu te fassus esses id crimen tanto ante metuisse; si eum diceres esse mortuum, quis te audiret? Nunc quum vivum nescio quem istum producis, tamen te derideri vides: quid, si aufugisset, si vincla rupisset ita ut Nico ille, nobilissimus pirata, fecit, quem P. Servilius, qua felicitate ceperat, eadem recuperavit, quid diceres?—Verum hoc erat: si ille semel verus pirata securi percussus esset, pecuniam illam non haberes: si hic falsus esset mortuus aut profugisset, non esset difficile alium in suppositi locum supponere. Plura dixi quam volui de illo archipirata, et tamen ea quae certissima sunt hujus criminis argumenta praetermisi. Volo enim esse totum mihi crimen hoc integrum. Est certus locus, certa lex, certum tribunal, quo hoc reservetur.

Et nunc cuiquam &c.] This is the reading of R 3 A. The common reading is 'Et non credo esse dubium.' 'Credo' generally stands alone in this form of expression, as in Lib. 1. c. 24, 'At, credo, in hisce solis rebus;' but it may be joined with the infinitive also. Manutius, who read 'Est nunc, credo, cuiquam dubium,' calls this 'implicata sententia;' but he saw the meaning, which is, 'you would not have kept this archpirate in your house with so much danger before your eyes (quod erat ante oculos positum):' the danger was a trial for 'majestas,' which is again mentioned at the end of this chapter. But the sentence is incomplete: 'you would not have run this risk unless you had got something by it.' He has not however pointed out the real connexion of the parts of this confused passage. Cicero, after 'tuo periculo viveret,' instead of finishing his sentence, passes to the supposed case of the man having died while he was in the custody of Verres, or having escaped, and to the consequence of such a contingency; and he resumes 'Verum hoc erat,' 'but the real truth is this,' which must be connected with the sentence that ends with 'tuo periculo viveret.'

tamen te derideri vides:] This is the reading of all the MSS. except G 1, which has 'tantum' for 'tamen;' and Zumpt adopts 'tantum,' in which he is followed by Orelli. But 'tamen,' as Madvig explains it, appears to be the true reading: 'Now when you do produce alive some prisoner or other of yours, still you see that you are ridiculed;' that is, nobody believes. 'What would you have said if he had escaped?' This is all consistent and clear. Zumpt explains 'tantum' thus: "nunc nihil aliud nisi derideris, sed si aufugisset ille et ad socios rediisset, gravissimam culpam subires."

Nico] "*Nico* ab editore Cratandrino conjectura inventus est, codd. (etiam cod. Havn.) *is eo*" (Zumpt).

crimen hoc integrum.] See Lib. 1. c. 5. Zumpt thinks that Cicero would have failed in this 'majestatis judicio,' unless he could have produced some better proof of the archpirate being released for a sum of money; for all that is proved is, that Verres kept him at his house after he left the province. Would not that be enough? He ought to have executed him. Besides, Cicero does not admit that this was the real man. Verres would have to prove that. He was bound to show what became

XXXI. Hac tanta praeda auctus, mancipiis, argento, veste locupletatus, nihilo diligentior ad classem ornandam, milites revocandos alendosque esse coepit, quum ea res non solum provinciae saluti verum etiam ipsi praedae posset esse. Nam aestate summa, quo tempore ceteri praetores obire provinciam et concursare consuerunt, aut etiam in tanto praedonum metu et periculo ipsi navigare, eo tempore ad luxuriem libidinesque suas domo sua regia, quae regis Hieronis fuit, qua praetores uti solent, contentus non fuit: tabernacula, quemadmodum consuerat temporibus aestivis, quod antea demonstravi, carbaseis intenta velis collocari jussit in littore, quod est littus in Insula Syracusis post Arethusae fontem, propter ipsum introitum atque ostium portus, amoeno sane et ab arbitris remoto loco. Hic dies aestivos praetor populi Romani, custos defensorque provinciae, sic vixit ut muliebria quotidie convivia essent, vir accumberet nemo praeter ipsum et praetextatum filium; tametsi recte sine exceptione dixeram virum quum isti essent neminem fuisse: nonnunquam etiam libertus Timarchides adhibebatur; mulieres autem nuptae nobiles praeter unam mimi Isidori

of this piratical captain. This is a sample of the idle way of talking about things which in no way concern the explanation of the text. I would not have it supposed that I believe all that Cicero says. I am very ready to disbelieve him often. But when we know no more of a thing than what Cicero tells us, we must take it as he tells it, and see whether it is for his case or against him. The Roman orator is a match for any number of commentators in handling his matter. Klotz approves of Zumpt's remark. He knows more than he is told by his author.

31. *concursare*] Cicero uses this word to express being active and busy, as in c. 12; and so he uses 'concurrere' in Pro Quint. c. 16, as Graevius remarks. In c. 35, 'concursabat . . multitudo' is not the meeting of the multitude, but the running to and fro of all the persons. So Caesar (B. G. i. 47) says 'Ariovistus . . . conclamavit:' and Cic. In Cat. iv. 8, 'lenonem quendam . . . concursare circum tabernas.'

quae regis &c.] These words have occurred before, see Lib. 4. c. 53; but this is not a sufficient reason for supposing that they are not the genuine words of Cicero here. Klotz observes that each of these books is complete in itself, and that they were at first published separately, though he does not state the evidence for this. It is however common for a man to repeat the same expression when he is speaking a second time of the same thing, and to do it without thinking of what he has said before. Klotz refers to what Cicero says of Thespiae (Lib. 4. c. 2 and 60); and he also compares Lib. 2. c. 8, and Lib. 5. c. 41.

contentus] 'contemptus' R.

arbitris] 'In a pleasant spot, and one safe against all intruders;' visitors, comers. For 'arbiter' is one who comes to a place, from 'ar' (ad), and the root 'bit,' to 'come' or 'go.'

tametsi] Zumpt and Iordan read 'etsi,' following R S λ. Zumpt says, though 'quamquam' is the proper word when a man is thus correcting what he has said, yet 'tametsi' and 'etsi' can be used for it. If so, we gain nothing by this alteration. In Lib. 1. c. 2 there is 'tametsi de absolutione,' which is Zumpt's reading; and he says in his note, 'Guelff. *etsi*, quod non sane contemno.' Here he prefers it. 'Tametsi' is very generally followed by 'tamen' in these orations. But if we take the cases where a word of this meaning stands at the beginning of a sentence, and is not followed by 'tamen,' we find that 'tametsi' is the usual word, and not 'etsi,' in these orations. In c. 34 there is 'etsi in hac quadriremi.' Here V (Br.) drtt. have 'tametsi.'

filiam, quam iste propter amorem ab Rhodio tibicine abduxerat; Pipa quaedam, uxor Aeschrionis Syracusani, de qua muliere plurimi versus qui in istius cupiditatem facti sunt tota Sicilia percelebrantur. Erat Nice, facie eximia, ut praedicatur, uxor Cleomenis [Syracusani]. Hanc Cleomenes vir amabat, verumtamen hujus libidini adversari nec poterat nec audebat; et simul ab isto donis beneficiisque multis devinciebatur. Illo autem tempore iste, tametsi ea est hominis impudentia quam nostis, ipse tamen quum vir esset Syracusis, uxorem ejus parum poterat animo soluto ac libero tot in acta dies secum habere. Itaque excogitat rem singularem: naves quibus legatus praefuerat Cleomeni tradit; classi populi Romani Cleomenem Syracusanum praeesse jubet atque imperare. Hoc eo facit ut ille non solum abesset a domo tum quum navigaret, sed etiam libenter cum magno honore beneficioque abesset, ipse autem remoto atque ablegato viro non liberius quam antea—quis enim unquam istius libidini obstitit?—sed paulo solutiore tamen animo secum illam haberet, si non tamquam virum, at tamquam aemulum removisset. Accipit naves sociorum atque amicorum Cleomenes Syracusanus.

XXXII. Quid primum aut accusem aut querar? Siculone

abduxerat; Pipa] 'abduxerat et Pipa' V (etiam teste Br.): 'abduxerat. Erat Pipa,' the conjecture of Schütz.

Erat Nice,] Zumpt's former reading was 'Erat et Nice;' but he struck out 'et' in his larger edition, and it is in no MS. There is probably some error here. The preceding sentence begins: 'There were, besides, certain married women, women of rank, except one, the daughter of the mimus Isidorus, whom Verres had taken away from the Rhodian flute-player;' and then we come to the enumeration of these noble ladies, of whom Pipa is first; and then the sentence is interrupted. The verb which is to be supplied with 'mulieres,' &c., is 'adhibebantur.'

Cleomenis] G 1 V (Br.) dett. 'Cleomeni Syr.' R G 2 Ld.

ipse tamen] Zumpt observes that it is wonderful (mirum) that, in all the editions after P. Manutius, a point is put after 'tamen,' as if 'tamen' and 'ipse vir' were purposely separated, though all the 'sententiae vis' and 'constructionis ratio' depend on the connexion of these words. I don't know what his smaller edition has, but the English reprint, which labours under a most vicious punctuation, puts a comma after 'tamen.' Zumpt observes, that by frequent punctuation, not following reason, but custom, we separate things which go together, as is often the case with this particle.—'tum quum:' Zumpt and Jordan have 'dum,' the reading of V; 'tum dum' R 3; 'tum cum' dett.

si non tamquam virum, at &c.] So this stands in the English reprint, and I suppose in the smaller edition of Zumpt. In the larger edition he follows Madvig, who writes 'sed tamquam aemulum,' following R 3. But there is no doubt that 'at' is conformable to the usage of Cicero; and it is the reading of V. Zumpt says that 'si' belongs to 'removisset,' and the opposition is this, 'non virum' and 'sed aemulum.' There is no doubt that 'si' belongs to 'removisset;' there is nothing else for it to belong to. It is true too that 'non—sed' are often opposed, and so are 'si non—at.' Zumpt says that 'at' would do if it were in this form: "ut eam secum haberet, si non tamquam uxorem, at tamquam amicam." But in Lib. 3. c. 4, there is "si non virtute, &c., at sermone . . . ejus delectamini;" and in Lib. 4. c. 19, "si non in parentis, at in hominum numero putabat." 'At' is the true word here, and 'sed' spoils the sense.—'accipit:' 'accepit' V.

homini legati, quaestoris, praetoris denique potestatem, honorem, auctoritatem dari? Si te impediebat ista conviviorum mulierumque occupatio, ubi quaestores? ubi legati? ubi ternis denariis aestimatum frumentum? ubi muli? ubi tabernacula? ubi tot tantaque ornamenta magistratibus et legatis a senatu populoque Romano permissa et data? denique ubi praefecti, ubi tribuni tui? Si civis Romanus dignus isto negotio nemo fuit; quid civitates quae in amicitia fideque populi Romani perpetuo manserant? ubi Segestana? ubi Centuripina civitas? quae quum officiis, fide, vetustate, tum etiam cognatione populum Romanum attingunt. O dii immortales! Quid, si harum ipsarum civitatum militibus, navibus, navarchis Syracusanus Cleomenes jussus est imperare, nonne omnis honos ab isto dignitatis, aequitatis, officiique sublatus est? Ecquod in Sicilia bellum gessimus quin Centuripinis sociis, Syracusanis hostibus uteremur? Atque haec ego ad memoriam vetustatis, non ad contumeliam civitatis referri volo. Itaque ille vir clarissimus summusque imperator, M. Marcellus, cujus virtute captae, misericordia conservatae sunt Syracusae, habitare in ea parte urbis quae insula est Syracusanorum neminem voluit. Hodie, inquam, in ea parte Syracusanum habitare non licet. Est enim locus quem vel pauci possent defendere. Committere igitur eum non fidelissimis hominibus noluit, simul quod ab illa parte urbis navibus aditus ex alto est. Quamobrem qui nostros exercitus saepe excluserant, iis claustra loci committenda non existimavit. Vide quid intersit inter tuam libidinem majorumque auctoritatem, inter amorem furoremque

32. *ubi quaestores? ubi legati?*] He then asks where is the 'frumentum,' estimated at three denarii the modius, and the mules, and the tents, &c.; that is, where are all the means which the Roman state put at your command for defending the island. Hotmann quotes (Liv. xlii. 1): "Ante hunc consulem nemo unquam sociis in ulla re sumptui aut oneri fuit: ideo magistratus mulis tabernaculisque et omni alio instrumento militari ornabantur, ne quid tale imperarent sociis." Compare Lib. 4. c. 5, note. "If your 'quaestores' and 'legati' could not take the command," Cicero continues, "where were your 'praefecti' and 'tribuni,' who were under the immediate orders of the 'praetor?'"

populum Romanum] 'pop. Rom.' R 3 (R has 'P. R.'). 'P. R. nomen' V; 'populi R. nomen' dett. Zumpt explains the text to mean that these people deserve to be called almost Romans, as they are so intimately connected with the Romans by good faith and blood. The word 'cognatione' refers to the alleged kinship of the Romans and the Segestani. See Lib. 4. c. 33, note.

nonne omnis] "Sic unum Guelff. 1. fateor, sed tamen in apodosi vix aliter videtur esse. Vulgo non" (Zumpt). He refers to Lib. 2. c. 59, and Lib. 3. c. 62, where he made the same change, on the authority of the best MSS. See Lib. 3. c. 52, and the note. Orelli and Iordan have 'non omnis.'—'quin:' 'quoin' V.

quae insula est] 'quae in insula est' V, not to be followed here; but Iordan has 'in insula.' R 3, dett. om. 'in.' See Lib. 4. c. 53, and Lib. 5. c. 38.—'Syracusanorum neminem:' R 3 A. 'Syracusanum neminem' is the reading of V and dett., which Halm prefers.—'quem vel pauci possent:' 'possunt' is the reading of the inferior MSS., and 'possint' a conjecture of Ernesti.

libidinem] 'your caprice or pleasure.'

tuum et illorum consilium atque prudentiam. Illi aditum littoris Syracusanis ademerunt: tu imperium maritimum concessisti. Illi habitare in eo loco Syracusanum qua naves accedere possent noluerunt: tu classi et navibus Syracusanum praeesse voluisti. Quibus illi urbis suae partem ademerunt, iis tu nostri imperii partem dedisti: et quorum sociorum opera Syracusani nobis dicto audientes sunt, eos Syracusanis dicto audientes esse jussisti.

XXXIII. Egreditur in Centuripina quadriremi Cleomenes e portu: sequitur Segestana navis, Tyndaritana, Herbitensis, Heracliensis, Apolloniensis, Haluntina: praeclara classis in speciem, sed inops et infirma propter dimissionem propugnatorum atque remigum. Tamdiu in imperio suo classem iste praetor diligens vidit, quamdiu convivium ejus flagitiosissimum praetervecta est: ipse autem qui visus multis diebus non esset tum se tamen in conspectum nautis paulisper dedit. Stetit soleatus praetor populi Romani cum pallio purpureo tunicaque talari muliercula nixus in littore. Jam hoc istum vestitu Siculi civesque Romani permulti saepe viderunt. Posteaquam paulum provecta classis est et Pachynum quinto die denique appulsa, nautae coacti fame radices palmarum agrestium, quarum erat in illis locis, sicut in magna parte Siciliae, multitudo, colligebant, et his miseri perditique alebantur. Cleomenes autem, qui alterum se Verrem quum luxuria ac nequitia tum etiam imperio putaret, similiter totos dies in litore tabernaculo posito perpotabat. XXXIV. Ecce autem repente ebrio Cleomene, esurientibus ceteris, nuntiatur naves esse piratarum in portu Odyssese, nam ita is locus nominatur; nostra autem classis erat in portu

This is merely remarked to prevent any one taking it to mean any thing else here. —'Syracusano' R λ G 2 Ld., and Iordan; om G 1. 'Syracusanis' dett.

dicto audientes] Caesar also has this, B. G. i. 39.

33. *in speciem,*] 'specie' Ld. Iordan; 'in specie' R G 1 2 Lagg.; 'in speciem' al. (Iordan.)

soleatus] See Quintil. Inst. Or. viii. 3. 64, referred to by Zumpt. Hotmann refers to Gellius (xiii. 21) as to this wearing of 'soleae,' mere coverings for the soles of the feet: "omnia enim ferme id genus quibus plantarum calces tantum infimae teguntur, cetera prope nuda et teretibus habenis vincta sunt, soleas dixerunt, nonnumquam voce Graeca crepidulas." Comp. In Pison. c. 6.

palmarum] Zumpt stumbled at 'radices,' and thought that 'spadices' might be the word; because Gellius (iii. 9) says "palmae termes ex arbore cum fructu avulsus spadix dicitur." But 'botanice' taught him that it was the root of the 'Chamaerops humilis' of Linnaeus. This instance shows that we should not be in too great a hurry to make alterations in old texts. The port of Pachynus is supposed by Smyth to be the modern Passaro, where "the sailors were compelled by hunger to devour the roots of the dwarf palm, a plant that still flourishes in prodigious quantity" (Sicily, p. 181). Swinburne (ii. 246) says that the dwarf palm is also plentiful about Selinus. Comp. Virg. Aen. iii. 705.

his miseri] 'iis miseri' R, Iordan.

34. *Odyssese,*] The small map shows the position of this place. It seems to be the shallow bay of La Marza (Smyth's Sicily, p. 186).

Pachyni. Cleomenes autem, quod erat terrestre praesidium non re, sed nomine, speravit iis militibus quos ex eo loco deduxisset explere se numerum nautarum et remigum posse. Reperta est eadem istius hominis avarissimi ratio in praesidiis quae in classibus; nam erant perpauci reliqui, ceteri dimissi. Princeps Cleomenes in quadriremi Centuripina malum erigi, vela fieri, praecidi ancoras imperavit, et simul ut se ceteri sequerentur signum dari jussit. Haec Centuripina navis erat incredibili celeritate velis; nam scire isto praetore nemo poterat quid quaeque navis remis facere posset; etsi in hac quadriremi propter honorem et gratiam Cleomenis minime multi remiges et milites deerant. Evolarat jam e conspectu fere fugiens quadriremis quum etiam tum ceterae naves uno in loco moliebantur. Erat animus in reliquis. Quamquam erant pauci, quoquo modo res se habebat, pugnare tamen se velle clamabant, et quod reliquum vitae viriumque fames fecerat, id ferro potissimum reddere volebant. Quod si Cleomenes non tanto ante fugisset, aliqua tamen ad resistendum ratio fuisset. Erat enim sola illa navis constrata et ita magna ut propugnaculo ceteris posset esse, quae si in praedonum pugna versaretur, urbis instar habere inter illos piraticos myoparones videretur: sed tum inopes relicti ab duce praefectoque classis eundem necessario cursum tenere coeperunt. Helorum versus ut ipse Cleomenes ita ceteri navigabant; neque hi tam praedonum impetum fugiebant quam imperatorem sequebantur. Tum ut quisque in fuga postremus, ita in periculo princeps erat; postremam enim quamque navem piratae primam adoriebantur. Ita prima Haluntinorum navis capitur cui praeerat Haluntinus, homo nobilis, Phylarchus, quem ab illis praedonibus Locrenses postea publice redemerunt; ex quo vos priore actione jurato rem omnem causamque cognostis. Deinde Apolloniensis navis capitur et ejus praefectus Anthropinus occiditur.

XXXV. Haec dum aguntur, interea Cleomenes jam ad Helori littus pervenerat; jam sese in terram e navi ejecerat quadrirememque fluctuantem in salo reliquerat. Reliqui praefecti navium, quum in terram imperator exisset, quum ipsi neque repugnare

moliebantur.] They were busy in making ready for flight, and had some trouble about it.

navis constrata] 'A decked vessel,' as appears from c. 40. 'Navis constrata' is opposed to 'navis aperta.' It is the Greek word κατάφρακτος.

Helorum] This is a conjecture of Antonio Agostini, communicated to F. Ursini. When Agostini was in Sicily, he saw that 'Pelorum,' the MSS. reading, could not be the true one. The same blunder occurs twice in the next chapter. This is a case which criticism can safely deal with. There is the same mistake in Lib. 4. c. 26, in the name 'Helori,' where the MSS. have 'Pelori.'

neque mari effugere ullo modo possent, appulsis ad Helorum navibus Cleomenem persecuti sunt. Tum praedonum dux Heracleo, repente praeter spem non sua virtute sed istius avaritia nequitiaque victor, classem pulcherrimam populi Romani in littus expulsam et ejectam, quum primum invesperasceret, inflammari incendique jussit. O tempus miserum atque acerbum provinciae Siciliae! o casum illum multis innocentibus calamitosum atque funestum! o istius nequitiam ac turpitudinem singularem! Una atque eadem nox erat qua praetor amoris turpissimi flamma, classis populi Romani praedonum incendio conflagrabat. Affertur nocte intempesta gravis hujusce mali nuntius Syracusas: curritur ad praetorium quo istum ex illo praeclaro convivio reduxerant paulo ante mulieres cum cantu atque symphonia. Cleomenes, quamquam nox erat, tamen in publico esse non audet: includit se domi, neque aderat uxor quae consolari hominem in malis posset. Hujus autem praeclari imperatoris ita erat severa domi disciplina ut in re tanta et tam gravi nuntio nemo admitteretur, nemo esset qui auderet aut dormientem excitare aut interpellare vigilantem. Jam vero re ab omnibus cognita concursabat urbe tota maxima multitudo; non enim, sicut erat nuper consuetudo, praedonum adventum significabat ignis e specula sublatus aut tumulo, sed flamma ex ipso incendio navium et calamitatem acceptam et periculum reliquum nuntiabat.

XXXVI. Quum praetor quaereretur et constaret neminem ei nuntiasse, fit ad domum ejus cum clamore concursus atque impetus. Tum iste excitatus audit rem omnem ex Timarchide: sagum sumit. Lucebat jam fere: procedit in medium vini, somni, stupri plenus. Excipitur ab omnibus ejusmodi clamore ut ei Lampsaceni periculi similitudo versaretur ante oculos. Hoc etiam majus videbatur quod in odio simili multitudo hominum haec erat maxima. Tum istius acta commemorabatur; tum flagitiosa illa convivia; tum appellabantur a multitudine mulieres nominatim; tum quaerebant ex ipso palam, tot dies continuos, per quos nunquam visus esset, ubi fuisset, quid egisset? tum imperator ab isto praepositus Cleomenes

35. *invesperasceret,*] The reading of R λ G 2 Ld. Lg. 29, which I have now taken instead of 'advesperasceret' G 1 dett.

ignis e specula] A beacon light on some eminence. The Greek is φρυκτώριον: and φρυκτοί are torches or other combustibles lighted for signals. Compare Thucydides (iii. 22), φρυκτοὶ . . . πολέμιοι: and Aeschylus, Agamem. v. 30, ὡς ὁ φρυκτὸς ἀγγέλλων πρέπει. R pr. m. has 'et specula,' Lg. 29 'e spelunca;' samples of the blunders which occur in MSS.

36. *Lampsaceni*] Lib. 1. c. 27, where Hadrianus is mentioned.—'acta commemorabatur:' the MSS. reading and that of V also is 'acta commemorabantur,' but the allusion is to the 'acta,' where Verres had been spending his time in debauchery. This is an emendation of Hotmann, as he says; of Eric Memmius, as Lambinus says.

flagitabatur, neque quidquam propius est factum quam ut illud Uticense exemplum de Hadriano transferretur Syracusas, ut duo sepulchra duorum praetorum improborum duabus in provinciis constituerentur. Verum habita est a multitudine ratio temporis, habita [est] tumultus, habita etiam dignitatis existimationisque communis, quod is est conventus Syracusis civium Romanorum ut non modo illa provincia verum hac etiam re publica dignissimus existimetur. Confirmant ipsi se quum hic etiam tum semisomnus stuperet: arma capiunt: totum forum atque Insulam quae est urbis magna pars complent. Unam illam noctem solam praedones ad Helorum commorati, quum fumantes etiam nostras naves reliquissent, accedere incipiunt ad Syracusas. Qui videlicet saepe audissent nihil esse pulchrius quam Syracusarum moenia ac portus, statuerant se, si ea Verre praetore non vidissent, nunquam esse visuros. XXXVII. Ac primo ad illa aestiva praetoris accedunt, ipsam illam ad partem littoris, ubi iste per eos dies tabernaculis positis castra luxuriae collocarat. Quem posteaquam inanem locum offenderunt et praetorem commosse ex eo loco castra senserunt, statim sine ullo metu in ipsum portum penetrare coeperunt. Quum in portum dico, judices, explanandum est enim diligentius eorum causa qui locum ignorant, in urbem dico atque in urbis intimam partem venisse piratas. Non enim portu illud oppidum clauditur, sed urbe portus ipse cingitur et continetur, ut non alluantur mari moenia extrema sed ipse influat in urbis sinum portus. Hic te praetore Heracleo pirata cum quatuor myoparonibus parvis ad arbitrium suum navigavit. Pro dii immortales! piraticus myoparo, quum imperii populi Romani nomen ac fasces essent Syracusis,

semisomnus] R V, Lg. 27 29. The common reading is 'semisomnis,' which is a genuine Latin word, but a poetical form, as it is said. There is 'insomnis.' V has 'semisomnus stupri plenus stuperet.'

Unam illam] V has 'nam illam.'—'accedere . . . ad Syracusas:' but R 3 A omit 'ad.' V (Br.) has 'ad.' Zumpt keeps 'ad' in c. 37, 'ad omnes crepidines urbis accessit;' and in c. 40 he has 'ad Heracliam . . accederem.' It seems that the 'ad' can be omitted, as it is in some passages, if the readings are right.

37. *portu . . clauditur,*] The piratical captain entered the large port, which is bounded on one side by the island of Ortygia, and on the other by the peninsula Plemmyrium. 'Claudi' has the sense of 'terminated' or 'bounded' in this passage. Graevius has a long note on the word, and cites various instances. One will suffice (Liv. xxi. 43), 'dextra laevaque duo maria claudunt.'—'cingitur et concluditur' is the common reading. See Smyth's Sicily, Appendix, p. xv, on the approach to Syracuse and its fine harbour. The position of the port is such that it may be said to be contained within the city, for an enemy, when inside the port, was within Ortygia; but it is a great exaggeration to say that the whole port was surrounded by the city, for it was only the island Ortygia and a small part of the city which bordered on the bay.

Heracleo] Orosius (vi. 3) briefly tells this story; but the name of the piratical captain is Pyrganio in the text of Orosius, ed. Havercamp.

imperii] The editions have generally 'imperium;' but 'imperii' is the reading

usque ad forum Syracusanorum et ad omnes crepidines urbis accessit, quo neque Karthaginiensium gloriosissimae classes quum mari plurimum poterant, multis bellis saepe conatae, unquam aspirare potuerunt, neque populi Romani invicta ante te praetorem gloria illa navalis unquam tot Punicis Siciliensibusque bellis penetrare potuit; qui locus ejusmodi est ut ante Syracusani in moenibus suis, in urbe, in foro hostem armatum ac victorem quam in portu ullam hostium navem viderint. Hic te praetore praedonum naviculae pervagatae sunt, quo Atheniensium classis sola post hominum memoriam CCC navibus vi ac multitudine invasit, quae in eo ipso portu loci ipsius natura victa atque superata est. Hic primum opes illius civitatis comminutae depressaeque sunt: in hoc portu Atheniensium nobilitatis, imperii, gloriae naufragium factum existimatur. XXXVIII. Eone pirata penetravit, quo simulatque adisset non modo a latere sed etiam a tergo magnam partem urbis relinqueret? Insulam totam praetervectus est, quae est urbs Syracusis suo nomine ac moenibus, quo in loco majores, ut ante dixi, Syracusanum habitare vetuerunt, quod qui illam partem urbis tenerent, in eorum potestatem portum futurum intelligebant. At quemadmodum est pervagatus? Radices palmarum agrestium quas in nostris navibus invenerant jactabant, ut omnes istius improbitatem et calamitatem Siciliae possent cognoscere. Siculosne milites, aratorumne liberos, quorum patres tantum labore suo frumenti exarabant ut populo Romano totique Italiae suppeditare possent, eosne in insula Cereris natos, ubi primum fruges inventae esse dicuntur, eo cibo esse usos a quo majores eorum ceteros quoque frugibus inventis removerunt?

of all the good MSS. (Zumpt.)—'ad forum Syracusanum' V (Br.).

crepidines] These are the artificial works, moles, sea-walls, and the like, by which the port was strengthened or made more convenient. The word appears to have been taken from the Greek *κρηπίς*, and not to be a genuine Latin word. It often signifies 'foundations,' the substructure on which something rests. The scholiast on Juvenal (v. 8) attempts absurdly to derive it from 'concrepitare,' and gives an explanation which does not suit the passage which he professes to explain; for there it means the basement or steps of a house or any public building.

Atheniensium classis] In the battle which was fought in the great port, Thucydides (vii. 70) says that the whole number of the two fleets, Athenian and Syracusan, was not quite two hundred. The Athenian ships were eighty-six, and the Syracusan seventy-six (Thucyd. vii. 52). It is, as Orelli calls it, an 'immanis hyperbole.' Iordan has 'loci ipsius portusque natura:' V omits 'portusque.'

38. *Eone . . relinqueret?*] Perhaps the reader may not observe that 'quo . . . adisset' cannot be expressed in English. 'Did the pirate penetrate so far into the port as to leave a large part of the city not only on his flank but also in his rear?' is the whole meaning. If the reader will translate 'quo . . . adisset,' he must not make use of any form of the relative.

Syracusanum] 'Quemquam' is generally added after 'Syracusanum,' but it is omitted by Zumpt and Iordan on the authority of the best MSS.

potestatem] This is the reading of the better MSS.: 'potestate' Lagg. praeter 29 42. V has 'potestatem.' See the remark, Lib. 2. c. 27, note.

Te praetore Siculi milites palmarum stirpibus, piratae Siculo frumento alebantur. O spectaculum miserum atque acerbum! ludibrio esse urbis gloriam! populi Romani nomen! hominum conventum atque multitudinem! piratico myoparone in portu Syracusano de classe populi Romani triumphum agere piratam, quum praetoris nequissimi inertissimique oculos praedonum remi respergerent! Posteaquam e portu piratae non metu aliquo affecti sed satietate exierunt, tum coeperunt quaerere homines causam illius tantae calamitatis. Dicere omnes et palam disputare, minime esse mirandum si remigibus militibusque dimissis, reliquis egestate et fame perditis, praetore tot dies cum mulierculis perpotante, tanta ignominia et calamitas esset accepta. Haec autem istius vituperatio atque infamia confirmabatur eorum sermone qui a suis civitatibus illis navibus praepositi fuerant, qui ex illo numero reliqui Syracusas classe amissa refugerant. Dicebant quot ex sua quisque nave missos sciret esse. Res erat clara, neque solum argumentis sed etiam certis testibus istius audacia tenebatur.

XXXIX. Homo certior fit agi nihil in foro et conventu tota die nisi hoc quaeri ex navarchis, quemadmodum classis sit amissa: illos respondere et docere unumquemque missione remigum, fame reliquorum, Cleomenis timore et fuga. Quod posteaquam iste cognovit, hanc rationem habere coepit. Causam sibi dicendam esse statuerat jam ante quam hoc usu venit, ita ut ipsum priore actione dicere audistis. Videbat illis navarchis testibus tantum hoc crimen sustinere se nullo modo posse. Consilium capit primo stultum, verumtamen clemens. Navarchos ad se vocari jubet. Veniunt.

populi Romani &c.] The passage stands as follows in Orelli, who follows Madvig: "populi Romani nomen in hominum conventu atque multitudine piratico myoparoni; in portu" &c. I don't believe that Zumpt's reading is all right, though I follow it; nor do I think that the genuine text of Cicero can be established. See Zumpt's note. Iordan has 'atque multitudinem piratico myoparoni! in portu' &c.

fuerant, qui] 'fuerant. Qui . . . dicebant' Iordan, following Orelli's pointing. The old reading 'quos ex sua' should perhaps be 'quot ex sua,' as Iordan has it. 'Quod' R 3, 'quos' dett.

39. *tota die*] G 1 2, Lg. 29. R has 'toto die.'

ante quam &c.] 'Before it turned out, in fact, to be so.' Comp. Pro Q. Roscio, c. 11, and Caesar, B. G. vii. 9. The older readings, 'venerit' and 'veniret,' are properly rejected by Zumpt, who has 'venit.' Madvig observes that a certain time is named, before which time Verres came to this conclusion. The subjunctive after 'ante quam,' he adds, is not used, if we follow the MSS. in the direct form of expression, except when a future thing is spoken of, and a thing which is the object of deliberation, hope, or fear. Accordingly, if 'veniret' were written, the meaning would be, not that Verres had come to this conclusion before (hoc constituisse), but had come to the conclusion that he would have to defend himself before this happened (ante quam hoc eveniret). But in that case we may ask what would the 'hoc' mean?

audistis.] 'vidistis' R 3, that is, the copyist mistook 'audistis' for 'uidistis,' a mistake which might easily be made.

Accusat eos quod ejusmodi sermones de se habuerint: rogat ut [id facere desistant, et] in sua quisque dicat navi se tantum habuisse nautarum quantum oportuerit, neque quemquam esse dimissum. Illi enimvero se ostendunt quod vellet esse facturos. Iste non procrastinat: advocat amicos statim: quaerit ex iis singillatim quot quisque nautas habuerit: respondit unusquisque ut erat praeceptum. Iste in tabulas refert: obsignat signis amicorum providens homo, ut contra hoc crimen si quando opus esset hac videlicet testificatione uteretur. Derisum esse credo hominem amentem a suis consiliariis et admonitum hasce ei tabulas nihil profuturas; etiam plus ex nimia praetoris diligentia suspicionis in eo crimine futurum. Jam iste erat hac stultitia multis in rebus usus ut publice quoque quae vellet in literas civitatum [et tolli et] referri juberet; quae omnia nunc intelligit sibi nihil prodesse, posteaquam certis literis, testibus auctoritatibusque convincitur.

XL. Ubi hoc videt, illorum confessionem, testificationem suam, tabellas sibi nullo adjumento futuras, init consilium non improbi praetoris, nam id quidem esset ferendum, sed importuni atque amentis tyranni. Statuit, si hoc crimen extenuari vellet, nam omnino tolli posse non arbitrabatur, navarchos omnes, testes sui sceleris, vita esse privandos. Occurrebat illa ratio; quid de Cleomene fiet? poterone animadvertere in eos quos dicto audientes esse jussi, missum facere eum cui potestatem imperiumque permisi? poterone eos afficere supplicio qui Cleomenem secuti sunt, ignoscere Cleomeni qui secum fugere et se consequi jussit? poterone esse in eos vehemens qui naves non modo inanes habuerunt sed etiam apertas, in eum dissolutus qui solus habuerit constratam navem et minus exinanitam? pereat Cleomenes una.—Ubi fides? ubi exsecrationes? ubi dexterae complexusque? ubi illud contubernium muliebris militiae in illo delicatissimo littore?—Fieri nullo modo poterat

[*id . . desistant, et*]] These words are wanting in the better MSS.

ex iis] "*ex his* R S, quod tolerari non potest, cum sic ad *amicos* referendum sit; *ex illis* s (i.e. cod. Reg. apud Steph.) habere dicitur, quod quidem est aptissimum huic loco" (Iordan).

in literas] 'in litteras' R 3, 'in litteris' Lg. 29; 'in civitatum literis' dett. The dett. have also 'et tolli;' and R 3 have 'tolli' (but 'toli' in R). Zumpt thinks that 'et tolli et' is an interpolation, for the question was not about erasure, but about making entries.

40. *quid de Cleomene fiet?*] The reading of G 3. Orelli and Iordan have 'quid Cleomene fiet?' the reading of R λ. Both are Latin, but perhaps there is some little difference in meaning. Orelli makes this distinction in meaning: 'quid Cleomene fiet?' 'what will become of Cleomenes?' 'quid de Cleomene fiet?' 'what will be done with Cleomenes?' There is also the Latin expression 'quid Cleomeni fiet?' 'what will happen to Cleomenes?'

exsecrationes?] The word means oaths by which parties bound themselves to fidelity, one form of oath being an imprecation, if a man should prove faithless.

quin Cleomeni parceretur. Vocat Cleomenem: dicit ei se statuisse animadvertere in omnes navarchos; ita sui periculi rationes ferre ac postulare—tibi uni parcam, et potius istius culpae crimen vituperationemque inconstantiae suscipiam quam aut in te sim crudelis, aut tot tam graves testes vivos incolumesque esse patiar.—Agit gratias Cleomenes, approbat consilium: dicit ita fieri oportere. Admonet tamen illud quod istum fugerat, in Phalacrum Centuripinum navarchum non posse animadverti propterea quod secum una fuisset in Centuripina quadriremi.—Quid ergo, iste homo ex ejusmodi civitate, adolescens nobilissimus, testis relinquetur?—In praesentia, inquit Cleomenes, quoniam ita necesse est; sed post aliquid videbimus ne iste nobis obstare possit.

XLI. Haec posteaquam acta et constituta sunt, procedit iste repente e praetorio, inflammatus scelere, furore, crudelitate: in forum venit: navarchos ad se vocari jubet. Qui nihil metuerent, nihil suspicarentur, statim accurrunt. Iste hominibus miseris innocentibus injici catenas imperat. Implorare illi fidem praetoris, et quare id faceret rogare. Tum iste hoc causae dicit, quod classem praedonibus prodidissent. Fit clamor et admiratio populi tantam esse in homine impudentiam atque audaciam ut aut aliis causam calamitatis attribueret quae omnis propter avaritiam ipsius accidisset, aut, quum ipse praedonum socius putaretur, aliis proditionis crimen inferret: deinde hoc quintodecimo die crimen esse natum postquam classis esset amissa. Quum haec ita fierent, quaerebatur ubi esset Cleomenes; non quo illum ipsum, cujusmodi est, quisquam

aut in te sim] 'Ut in te sim' Graevius, from R. But the double 'aut' seems to be required; and Zumpt refers to Drakenborch (Liv. xxxvii. 37), who shows that after 'prius,' 'citius,' 'potius quam,' the 'ut' may be omitted or not.

41. *ad se vocari jubet.*] V (*ad se* om. codd. rell. et edd.), Iordan.—'innocentibus' R 3 V; 'innocentibusque' dett.

hoc causae] See c. 47, note. 'Hoc causae' means 'this as a reason,' 'so much reason as this.'

admiratio] V has 'admurmuratio;' also Orelli.

putaretur,] V (Br.) Lgg. omnes. It being now certain that V has 'putaretur,' there is sufficient reason for preferring 'putaretur' to the former reading 'arbitraretur,' R 3 codd. Lamb. Gruter refers to a passive use of 'arbitrari,' Pro Murena, c. 16, and Zumpt to another instance, Ad Att. i. 11, if it is one.

cujusmodi est,] According to Hotmann this is for 'cujuscunque modi.' Madvig would prefer 'cujuscujusmodi,' but one can hardly suppose that Cicero would use such an intolerably awkward form, unless perchance 'cujus' was simply pronounced 'coos,' as a monosyllable. Zumpt writes in his second edition 'cuicuimodi,' which according to Priscian was for 'cujuscujusmodi.' But I would not compare this form with 'nulli' for 'nullius,' as Zumpt does, but rather take it as representing the crude form of 'quisquis.' There is no authority, as it appears, for 'cuicuimodi' in this passage, except "Cledonius, p. 1098. Pompeius, p. 252. Lind." (Iordan.) R has 'cuimodi.' V has 'quicuiusmodi.' Bake, in his edition of Cicero De Legibus, ii. c. 12, has "neque in populo lex, cuicuimodi fuerat illa," and the following remark: "*cuicuimodi* habent optimi mei: quare accedat hoc testimonium ei, quod Madvigius de Codd. MSS. excitavit ad Fam. iii. 9, 30." See 'cuicuimodi sint' Cic. Ad

supplicio propter illud incommodum dignum putaret: nam quid Cleomenes facere potuit? non enim possum quemquam insimulare falso: quid, inquam, magno opere potuit Cleomenes facere istius avaritia navibus exinanitis? Atque eum vident sedere ad latus praetoris et ad aurem familiariter ut solitus erat insusurrare. Tum vero omnibus indignissimum visum est homines honestissimos, electos e suis civitatibus, in ferrum atque in vincula conjectos, Cleomenem propter flagitiorum ac turpitudinum societatem familiarissimum esse praetori. Apponitur iis tamen accusator Naevius Turpio quidam, qui C. Sacerdote praetore injuriarum damnatus est, homo bene appositus ad istius audaciam, quem iste in decumis, in rebus capitalibus, in omni calumnia, praecursorem habere solebat et emissarium.

XLII. Veniunt Syracusas parentes propinquique miserorum adolescentium hoc repentino calamitatis suae commoti nuntio: vinctos aspiciunt catenis liberos suos, quum istius avaritiae poenam collo et cervicibus suis sustinerent: adsunt, defendunt, proclamant, fidem tuam quae nusquam erat neque umquam fuerat implorant. Pater aderat Dexo Tyndaritanus, homo nobilissimus, hospes tuus, cujus tu domi fueras, quem hospitem appellaras. Eum quum illa auctoritate miseria videres praeditum, non te ejus lacrimae, non senectus, non hospitii jus atque nomen a scelere aliquam ad partem humanitatis revocare potuit? Sed quid ego hospitii jura in hac immani bellua commemoro? Qui Sthenium Thermitanum, hospitem suum, cujus domum per hospitium exhausit et exinanivit,

Att. iii. 22, ed. Or.; Pro S. Roscio Am. c. 34; Pro Flacco, c. 17, note; and Key's Latin Grammar. In 'illum ipsum,' Zumpt omits 'illum.'

Apponitur] A word which Cicero uses in such cases, as Manutius shows (Lib. 2. c. 8), "apponit qui petat Veneri Erycinae illam hereditatem;" this same Naevius Turpio.—'tum accusator:' Zumpt, who has this note: "*Tum* dedi e Guelff. Vulgo *tamen* notarum confusione. Nam *tamen* dici, cum antea iam catenae iniectae sint hominibus, quo pertinet?" 'Tum' is the reading of G 3 only. Orelli prefers 'tamen' for this reason: "Verres does not put them to death immediately without being tried; but that there still (tamen) might be the appearance of a lawful trial, he appoints a prosecutor." This may seem a trifling matter, but the decision of it involves the question of a nice perception of the author's meaning. The reading that I have adopted shows which opinion I prefer. As to 'Naevius Turpio,' see Lib. 2. c. 8. As to 'injuriarum,' see Lib. 2. c. 27; and Index, Calumnia.

42. *cervicibus*] Comp. Lib. 3. c. 59.

illa auctoritate] The common reading is 'illa auctoritate et miseria.' Zumpt thinks the connexion of 'auctoritas' and 'miseria' singular. 'Et' however does not occur in R 3 V. We may therefore read the text as it stands here, and refer 'illa auctoritate' to the rank and condition of the man, though Zumpt doubts if we can say of a man 'illa auctoritate.' He observes however that 'auctoritate' is so abbreviated in the MSS., that it may easily be confounded with 'aetate;' and if we must have a correction, his is the best that can be made. But it is not necessary. There is no difficulty about 'praeditus' being connected with 'miseria.' Zumpt refers to Tusc. v. 41, 'metu praeditus.'

Sthenium] See Lib. 2. c. 34.—'bellua:' 'belua' R V Lg. 29.

absentem in reos rettulerit, causa indicta capite damnarit, ab eo nunc hospitiorum jura atque officia quaeramus? cum homine enim crudeli nobis res est an cum fera atque immani bellua? Te patris lacrimae de innocentis filii periculo non movebant: quum patrem domi reliquisses, filium tecum haberes, te neque praesens filius de liberorum caritate neque absens pater de indulgentia patria commonebat. Catenas habebat hospes tuus Aristeus, Dexonis filius. Quid ita? Prodiderat classem. Quod ob praemium? Deseruerat [exercitum]. Quid Cleomenes? Ignavus fuerat. At eum tu ob virtutem corona ante donaras. Dimiserat nautas. Ab omnibus tu mercedem missionis acceperas. Alter parens ex altera parte erat Herbitensis Eubulida, homo domi suae clarus et nobilis, qui quia Cleomenem in defendendo filio laeserat, nudus paene est destitutus. Quid erat autem quod quisquam diceret aut defenderet? Cleomenem nominare non licet. At causa cogit. Moriere, si appellaris: nunquam enim iste cuiquam est mediocriter minatus. At remiges non erant. Praetorem tu accusas? frange cervices. Si neque praetorem neque praetoris aemulum appellare licebit, quum in his duobus tota causa sit, quid futurum est?

XLIII. Dicit etiam causam Heraclius Segestanus, homo domi suae nobilissimo loco natus. Audite, ut vestra humanitas postulat, judices: audietis enim de magnis incommodis injuriisque sociorum. Hunc scitote fuisse Heraclium in ea causa qui propter gravem morbum oculorum tum non navigarit et jussu ejus qui potestatem habuit in commeatu Syracusis remanserit. Is certe neque classem prodidit neque metu perterritus fugit neque exercitum deseruit. Etenim tunc esset hoc animadversum, quum classis Syracusis proficiscebatur. Is tamen in eadem causa fuit, quasi esset in aliquo manifesto scelere deprehensus, in quem ne falsi quidem causa

Deseruerat] 'Exercitum' om. R 3 C, Zumpt, and Iordan. 'Intellige *classem*' (Iordan).

ante] Lg. 5 14 27 have 'aurea;' R has 'aute;' and plerique dett. 'antea.'

nudus . . destitutus.] Compare Lib. 2. c. 26, 'solus destitutus;' Lib. 3. c. 26, 'destitui alios in convivio;' Lib. 4. c. 40, 'nudumque destituunt.'

At . . erant.] 'ad remiges noncrant' R. This kind of blunder is instructive.

43. *Heraclius*] The Greek is 'Ἡράκλειος. The MSS. have often the form 'Heracleus.'

nobilissimo] R 3. The dett. have 'summo.' ; has 'homo domi suae nobilis, summo loco natus,' on which Iordan remarks, 'quod per se non spernendum est;' and that is quite true. We cannot tell whether such variations as this are due to the hand of the author, or to his copyists. Caesar (B. G. v. 25) writes 'summo loco natus.'

in ea causa qui] This is easy to understand, difficult to express. It is in form like 'ejusmodi' followed by 'ut,' which 'ut' is a form of 'qui.' 'You must know that the case of Heraclius was this, that he did not join the fleet,' &c. He had 'leave of absence.' The MSS. reading is 'in commeatu,' though 'cum commeatu' is in some editions. Both modes of expression are used. Orelli refers to Livy, 7. c. 39, for the expression 'in commeatus mittere.'

criminis conferri potuit. Fuit in illis navarchis Heracliensis quidam Furius, nam habent illi nonnulla hujuscemodi Latina nomina, homo, quamdiu vixit, domi suae, post mortem tota Sicilia clarus et nobilis. In quo homine tantum animi fuit non solum ut istum libere laederet,—nam id quidem, quoniam moriendum videbat, sine periculo se facere intelligebat—verum morte proposita, quum lacrimans in carcere mater noctes diesque assideret, defensionem causae suae scripsit; quam nunc nemo est in Sicilia quin habeat, quin legat, quin tui sceleris et crudelitatis ex illa oratione commonefiat. In qua docet quot a civitate sua nautas acceperit, quot et quanti quemque dimiserit, quot secum habuerit; item de ceteris navibus dicit: quae quum apud te diceret, virgis oculi verberabantur. Ille morte proposita facile dolorem corporis patiebatur: clamabat, id quod scriptum reliquit, 'Facinus esse indignum, plus impudicissimae mulieris apud te de Cleomenis salute quam de sua vita lacrimas matris valere.' Deinde etiam illud video esse dictum, quod, si recte vos populus Romanus cognovit, non falso ille de vobis jam in morte ipsa praedicavit: 'Non posse Verrem testes interficiendo [crimina sua] extinguere: graviorem apud sapientes judices se fore ab inferis testem quam si vivus in judicium produceretur: tum avaritiae solum si viveret, nunc quum ita esset necatus, sceleris, audaciae, crudelitatis testem fore.' Jam illa praeclara, 'Non tes-

domi suae,] Zumpt has settled this passage as Lallemand did, but he is not satisfied with it: 'non domi suae solum, post mortem' &c., which Iordan also has. The editions generally have 'domi suae non solum post' &c. I have followed Graevius, who suggests that 'non solum' may have been introduced into our texts from what follows 'non solum ut istum.' We cannot be certain that the omission of 'non solum' gives us the genuine text, but it gives us what Cicero might have written. Manutius omits 'non' and keeps 'solum,' and says "aperta et magnifica sententia; quod si legas, *domi suae non solum*, quis erit sensus?"

causae suae scripsit;] The reading of all the MSS. It is easy to conjecture that we should have 'scripserit,' as Lambinus and Ernesti proposed; but it is not necessary.

[*crimina sua*]] 'nos' R G Ld. Iordan; 'vos' G 1; 'crimina sua' dett. The words 'crimina sua' seem to be an interpolation; for 'crimina' does not properly mean 'crimes' in Cicero, nor in other prose writers of his age, but the charges made against a man. It may however perhaps be used here in the sense in which 'metu criminibus' is used in Livy (xxxv. 19), to signify the things with which a man is charged. Madvig suspects that the true reading lurks under 'vos;' and he conjectures 'voces,' but with no great confidence. Kiehl, followed by Halm, writes 'ius' for 'nos;' a specious emendation because it is so near 'nos' or 'vos' in form; but the emendation is false, for it is entirely beside the meaning. Cicero makes the man say, that Verres could not get rid of 'something,' whatever it was, by killing witnesses, for that he though dead would be a weightier witness against Verres than if he were alive. There would then be sense if this 'something' were omitted, and the sense would be, Verres 'could not destroy witnesses by killing them, for' &c. I conclude that the 'something,' if it is genuine, relates in some way to witnesses; and as Wesenberg would omit the 'nos,' I suppose that he understands the passage in the way in which I say that it can be understood. But I think that the true reading may be 'eos extinguere.'

tium modo catervas, quum tua res ageretur, sed ab diis manibus innocentium poenas scelerumque furias in tuum judicium esse venturas: sese ideo leviorem suum casum fingere, quod jam ante aciem securium tuarum Sextiique tui carnificis vultum et manum vidisset, quum in conventu civium Romanorum jussu tuo securi cives Romani ferirentur.' Ne multa, judices, libertate quam vos sociis dedistis, hac ille in acerbissimo supplicio miserrimae servitutis abusus est. XLIV. Condemnat omnes de consilii sententia: tamen neque iste in tanta re, tot hominum causa, T. Vettium ad se arcessit, quaestorem suum, cujus consilio uteretur, neque P. Cervium, talem virum, legatum, qui, quia legatus isto praetore in Sicilia fuit, primus ab isto judex rejectus est, sed de latronum, hoc est, de comitum suorum sententia, condemnat omnes. Hic cuncti Siculi, fidelissimi atque antiquissimi socii, plurimis affecti beneficiis a majoribus nostris, graviter commoventur et de suis periculis fortunisque omnibus pertimescunt. Indigne ferunt illam clementiam mansuetudinemque nostri imperii tantam in crudelitatem inhumanitatemque esse conversam: condemnari tot homines uno tempore, nullo crimine; defensionem suorum furtorum praetorem improbum ex indignissima morte innocentium quaerere. Nihil addi jam videtur, judices, ad hanc improbitatem, amentiam, crudelitatemque posse: et recte nihil videtur. Nam si cum aliorum improbitate certet, longe omnes multumque superavit. Secum ipse certat: id agit ut semper superius suum facinus novo scelere vincat. Phalacrum Centuripinum dixeram exceptum esse a Cleomene, quod in ejus quadriremi Cleomenes vectus esset; tamen quia pertimuerat adolescens, quod eandem suam causam videbat esse quam illorum qui innocentes peribant, accedit ad hominem Timarchides: a securi negat esse ei periculum; virgis ne caederetur monet ut caveat. Ne multa, ipsum dicere adolescentem audistis se ob hunc metum

abusus est.] It must not be rendered 'abused.' It is, as Hotmann says, 'ad extremum usus, ut nihil reliqui fecerit.' See Lib. 1. c. 9, note.

44. *T. Vettium*] 'P. Vettium' Zumpt, Orelli. But Madvig shows, by referring to Lib. 3. c. 71, 72, that the brother of the 'quaestor' was named P. Vettius, and therefore the 'quaestor' had another name. And this is confirmed by R pr. m., which has 'tot hominum. t. veccium' (T. Vettium). The word 'causa' is placed in brackets by Orelli, and perhaps it ought to be omitted. Iordan omits it.

Indigne ferunt illam] 'Indigne ferunt' from V; 'indigni ferunt' R 3. Zumpt omits 'indigne ferunt,' as being the addition of some person who wanted to explain the use of the infinitive, and yet did not explain it right. People view the same things in different ways. I believe that the words are genuine. Orelli follows Zumpt. Next we have Ernesti quarrelling with the words 'et recte nihil videtur,' which Zumpt defends. Madvig compares Lib. 3. c. 72, 'et recte non putant.' See also Lib. 1. c. 5, 'et recte putat,' and the note.

Secum] V; 'sed cum' R3; 'sed secum' dett., which are certainly the worse here.

pecuniam Timarchidi numerasse. Levia haec sunt in hoc reo. Metum virgarum navarchus nobilissimae civitatis pretio redemit; humanum est: alius ne condemnaretur pecuniam dedit; usitatum est. Non vult populus Romanus obsoletis criminibus accusari Verrem: nova postulat, inaudita desiderat: non de praetore Siciliae sed de nefario tyranno fieri judicium arbitratur.

XLV. Includuntur in carcerem condemnati: supplicium constituitur in illos; sumitur de miseris parentibus [navarchorum]: prohibentur adire ad filios: prohibentur liberis suis cibum vestitumque ferre. Patres hi quos videtis jacebant in limine, matresque miserae pernoctabant ad ostium carceris ab extremo conspectu liberum exclusae, quae nihil aliud orabant nisi ut filiorum suorum postremum spiritum ore excipere liceret. Aderat janitor carceris, carnifex praetoris, mors terrorque sociorum et civium Romanorum, lictor Sextius, cui ex omni gemitu doloreque certa merces comparabatur. —Ut adeas, tantum dabis: ut tibi cibum [vestitumque] intro ferre liceat, tantum.—Nemo recusabat.—Quid, ut uno ictu securis afferam mortem filio tuo, quid dabis? ne diu crucietur? ne saepius feriatur? ne cum sensu doloris aliquo spiritus auferatur?—Etiam ob hanc causam pecunia dabatur. O magnum atque intolerandum dolorem! O gravem acerbamque fortunam! Non vitam liberum sed mortis celeritatem pretio redimere cogebantur parentes. Atque ipsi etiam adolescentes cum Sextio suo de plaga et de uno illo ictu loque-

humanum est:] This passage is cited by Quintilian, Inst. Or. viii. 4, 19. 'Humanum' here means such a thing as may happen in the usual course of human affairs.—'ne condemnaretur:' Quintilian has 'ne securi feriretur.' We cannot always trust quotations made either by ancient or by modern writers.

obsoletis] 'Obsoletus' means that which has become common by use; ordinary, and the like. Here it is opposed to 'nova.'

45. *sumitur*] 'supplicium sumitur de . . . parentibus,' for they were not allowed to see their sons. It is, as Hotmann says, 'vehemens amplificatio.' I think Memmius is right in condemning 'navarchorum.' This word is superfluous, and feeble.

conspectu] R 3 V; 'complexu' dett.—'filiorum suorum:' 'suorum' added by Zumpt and Orelli; omitted in the older texts.

ore excipere liceret.] Quintilian, Inst. Or. ix. 4, 108, quotes these words, and he must have found 'ore' in his MSS., for his remark on the passage turns mainly on the word 'ore.' Yet 'ore' is omitted in G 2 Ld. et Lagg.—'tibi cibum vestitumque' V (Br.); 'cibum tibi' &c. dett. Quintilian, ix. 4, 71, and Iordan omit 'tibi.'

dabatur.] V has 'lictori datur.' R 3 has only 'dabatur,' the dett. 'lictori dabatur.' Zumpt, who omits 'lictori,' says "nam in diligentissimo hoc verborum delectu quicquid supervacuum est aut secure repetitur, ferri non potest." It is not easy to see the force of this remark. One might so easily make an argument in favour of 'lictori' and the present 'datur.'

Sextio suo] The common reading is 'cum Sextio de eadem plaga.' 'Eadem' is an idle word. As to the addition of 'suo,' though it is found in R 3 C, I doubt. Zumpt approves of it "cum pertinere videatur ad custodiam carceris, cui praepositus ille fuit." It must rather be taken as a word of endearment; they called him their good Sextius, if he would only release them from their fears by one stroke of his axe.

bantur, idque postremum parentes suos liberi orabant ut levandi cruciatus sui causa lictori pecunia daretur. Multi et graves dolores inventi parentibus, et propinquis multi: verumtamen mors sit extrema. Non erit. Estne aliquid ultra quo progredi crudelitas possit? Reperietur. Nam illorum quum erunt securi percussi ac necati corpora feris objicientur. Hoc si luctuosum est parentibus, redimant pretio sepeliendi potestatem. Onasum Segestanum, hominem nobilem, dicere audistis se ob sepulturam Heraclii navarchi pecuniam Timarchidi numerasse, ne hoc posses dicere, 'Patres enim veniunt amissis filiis irati:' vir primarius, homo nobilissimus, dicit, neque de filio dicit. Jam hoc quis tum fuit Syracusis quin audierit, quin sciat, has Timarchidi pactiones sepulturae cum vivis etiam illis esse factas? Non palam cum Timarchide loquebantur? non omnes omnium propinqui adhibebantur? non palam vivorum funera locabantur? Quibus omnibus rebus actis atque decisis producuntur e carcere, deligantur ad palum. XLVI. Quis tam fuit illo tempore ferreus, quis tam inhumanus praeter unum te, qui non illorum aetate, nobilitate, miseria commoveretur? ecquis fuit quin lacrimaretur, quin ita calamitatem illam putaret illorum, ut fortunam tamen non alienam, periculum autem commune arbitraretur? Feriuntur securi. Laetaris tu in omnium gemitu et triumphas, testes avaritiae tuae gaudes esse sublatos. Errabas, Verres, et vehementer errabas, quum te maculas furtorum et flagitiorum tuorum sociorum innocentium sanguine eluere arbitrabare: praeceps amentia ferebare qui te existimares avaritiae vulnera crudeli-

et propinquis multi:] Quintilian, Inst. Or. ix. 3. 34, reads the passage thus: "Respondent primis et ultima: 'Multi et graves dolores inventi parentibus, et propinquis multi.'" Zumpt says, 'fallitur;' and he and Orelli have 'propinquis: multi.' Iordan also puts a point after 'propinquis.' I follow the Roman.

ne hoc posses] The reading of the dett. 'numerasse. Hoc (ne possis dicere . . . irati) vir primarius . . . dicit;' which may perhaps appear to some readers to express the meaning of the passage more clearly. The fact of a man paying money for the interment of another, who was not his son, stops Verres from saying by way of objection to the veracity of the witnesses, 'Yes, but there are fathers who come, who have lost their sons, men under the influence of passion.'

funera locabantur?] These words must be explained by 'redimant pretio sepeliendi potestatem;' for though the words literally mean 'agreements were made for their interment while they were still alive,' we must, as Hotmann remarks, explain this to mean 'sepeliendi potestatem.'

deligantur ad palum.] 'Ad palum' omitted by R 3 V, and Iordan. Zumpt observes "quanta vis sit in hac ipsa articulatim dicendi forma, nemo non sentit admonitus." I do not perceive it. Those who do may erase 'ad palum.' Madvig and Orelli approve of omitting 'ad palum.'

46. *lacrimaretur,*] V has 'lacrumarumet,' and Lg. 29 has 'lacrimaret.' Diomedes the grammarian (p. 377, Putsch., quoted by Zumpt) says "*lacrymo, lacrymas:* nec quisquam esse *lacrymor* credat, quamvis Ovidius (Fast. i. 339) dixerit: lacrymatas cortice myrras."

avaritiae . . . sanare.] An insipid unmeaning bit of rhetoric.—'vivunt et adsunt:' V omits 'et.'

tatis remediis posse sanare. Etenim quamquam illi sunt mortui sceleris tui testes, tamen eorum propinqui neque tibi neque illis desunt, tamen ex ipso illo numero navarchorum aliqui vivunt et adsunt; quos, ut mihi videtur, ad illorum innocentium poenas fortuna et ad hanc causam reservavit. Adest Phylarchus Haluntinus, qui quia cum Cleomene non fugit, oppressus a praedonibus et captus est: cui calamitas saluti fuit: qui nisi captus a piratis esset, in hunc praedonem sociorum incidisset. Dicit is pro testimonio de missione nautarum, de fame, de Cleomenis fuga. Adest Centuripinus Phalacrus, in amplissima civitate amplissimo loco natus: eadem dicit; nulla in re discrepat.

XLVII. Per deos immortales, quo tandem animo sedetis, judices, aut haec quemadmodum audistis? Utrum ego desipio et plus quam satis est doleo tanta calamitate miseriaque sociorum, an vos quoque hic acerbissimus innocentium cruciatus et maeror pari sensu doloris afficit? Ego enim quum Herbitensem, quum Heracliensem securi percussum esse dico, versatur mihi ante oculos indignitas calamitatis. Eorumne populorum cives, eorum agrorum alumnos, ex quibus maxima vis frumenti quotannis plebi Romanae illorum operis ac laboribus quaeritur, qui a parentibus spe nostri imperii nostraeque aequitatis suscepti educatique sunt, ad C. Verris nefariam immanitatem et ad ejus funestam securim esse servatos? Quum mihi Tyndaritani illius venit in mentem, quum Segestani, tum jura simul civitatum atque officia considero. Quas urbes P. Africanus etiam ornandas esse spoliis hostium arbitratus est, eas C. Verres non solum illis ornamentis sed etiam viris nobilissimis nefario scelere privavit. En quod Tyndaritani libenter praedicent: 'Nos in septemdecim populis Siciliae numeramur: nos semper

ad illorum .. reservavit.] The common reading is 'ab illorum innocentium poena fortuna ad hanc causam reservavit.' The reading in the text, which is Zumpt's, is that of R 3 V Lg. 29. 'Poenae innocentium' is explained by Zumpt to mean 'ut illis innocentibus poenas dares crudelitatis.'

47. *plus quam satis est doleo*] 'Plus quam satis doleo,' V. 'Nec tamen moveor' (Zumpt). I state the fact, that others may see whether they are moved or not.

alumnos,] 'Colonos' the reading of dett.

suscepti] Graevius has a note on this passage, written in the style of some of those old commentators whose knowledge was limited to books. What he really means to say is well enough; that in times of prosperity and security there are more marriages, and more children are raised; and as the exposure of children seems to have been not uncommon among the Greeks and Romans, we may assume that more children were exposed in unprosperous than in prosperous times.

P. Africanus] See Lib. 2. c. 2, and Lib. 4. c. 33.

septemdecim .. numeramur:] 'Non eramus' or 'noveramus,' the reading of the dett., is properly rejected by the editors for 'numeramur.' Manutius, in his note on Lib. 3. c. 6, 'perpaucae Siciliae civitates,' observes that Cicero well knew the number of these 'civitates,' for he says (Lib. 5. c. 47) that they were seventeen; and that now he

omnibus Punicis Siciliensibusque bellis amicitiam fidemque populi Romani secuti sumus: a nobis [omnia] populo Romano semper et belli adjumenta et pacis ornamenta ministrata sunt.' Multum vero haec iis jura profuerunt in istius imperio ac potestate. Vestros quondam nautas contra Karthaginem Scipio duxit: at nunc navem contra praedones paene inanem Cleomenes ducit. Vobiscum Africanus hostium spolia et praemia laudis communicavit: at nunc per hunc spoliati nave a praedonibus abducta ipsi in hostium loco numeroque ducimini. Quid vero illa Segestanorum non solum literis tradita neque commemorata verbis, sed multis officiis illorum usurpata et comprobata cognatio quos tandem fructus hujusce necessitudinis in istius imperio tulit? Nempe hoc jure fuit, judices, ut ex sinu patriae nobilissimus adolescens istius carnifici Sextio dederetur. Cui civitati majores nostri maximos agros atque optimos concesserunt, quam immunem esse voluerunt, haec apud te cognationis, fidelitatis, vetustatis, auctoritatis ne hoc quidem juris

magnifies the services of the Tyndaritani by showing that, though so many states opposed the Romans, the Tyndaritani did not join them. Of course it will be seen that he read 'non eramus.' But the negative presents a difficulty, which is obvious. It would seem strange that the Tyndaritani should begin their own eulogium by a negation. The Variorum edition is in this instance a sample of the confusion that reigns there between the notes and the text. In the text the reading is 'numeramur;' and the note that is at the foot of the page, one from Hotmann, is adapted to explain the reading 'non eramus.'

Zumpt shows that these seventeen cities were the cities which had been faithful to Rome in the wars; and this is consistent. The Tyndaritani claim the merit of having always been among the cities friendly to Rome. A passage from Diodorus (iv. 83) makes all clear. He is speaking of the temple at Eryx and the favour shown to it by the Romans: ἥ τε σύγκλητος τῶν Ῥωμαίων εἰς τὰς τῆς θεοῦ τιμὰς φιλοτιμηθεῖσα τὰς μὲν πιστοτάτας τῶν κατὰ τὴν Σικελίαν πόλεων οὔσας ἑπτακαίδεκα χρυσοφορεῖν ἐδογμάτισε τῇ Ἀφροδίτῃ καὶ στρατιώτας διακοσίους τηρεῖν τὸ ἱερόν.

a nobis [omnia]] R 3 omit 'omnia.'

Vestros quondam &c.] Hotmann says "Verba sunt Verris Siculorum orationem irridentis, unde deesse quiddam suspicari licet in quibus Verrem hoc modo respondere orator admonebat." Hotmann read 'at nunc per me' in the next sentence, as Zumpt does. But V has 'at nunc per hunc,' and the meaning must be what Halm says: Cicero addresses himself to the deputies of Tyndaris.—'ipsi . . . ducimini:' see c. 25, note. Cicero as usual is playing on the meaning of 'ducere,' when he uses 'duxit,' 'ducit,' 'ducimini.' V has 'spoliata nave a praedonibus ipsi,' which ought not to be preferred.

The common reading is 'naves . . inanes,' instead of the singular.

illa Segestanorum] See Lib. 4. c. 33.

patriae] R λ G 1, 'patre' G 2 Ld., 'patrio' V (Hr.), 'patris' dett. The dett. and V have also 'adolescens et e complexu matris ereptus innocens filius istius;' but V omits 'filius.' Zumpt and Orelli make objections to the general form of the expression 'ex sinu patris nobilissimus adolescens et e complexu . . filius;' but experience teaches us to give no great weight to such remarks. The reading of V may be genuine, but it is difficult to understand how the words have been omitted in the best MSS.

ne hoc quidem juris] Zumpt has 'ne hoc quidem jus.' 'Juris' is correctly explained by Orelli "ne hanc quidem minimam juris sui partem." He compares 'hoc causae' c. 41. It is a common form of expression, 'neque illud rationis habuisti,' &c. (Lib. 4. c. 15); 'homo qui . . . jam id aetatis esset' (Lib. 1. c. 26); 'ac si hoc juris . . . edixisses' (Lib. 1. c. 42); and in the same chapter there is 'hoc jus,' perhaps not quite in the same sense.

obtinuit ut unius honestissimi atque innocentissimi civis mortem ac sanguinem deprecaretur.

XLVIII. Quo confugient socii, quem implorabunt, qua spe denique ut vivere velint tenebuntur, si vos eos deseretis? Ad senatumne venient? Quid ut de Verre supplicium sumat? non est usitatum, non est senatorium. Ad populum Romanum confugient? Facilis est populi causa; legem enim se sociorum causa jussisse et vos ei legi custodes ac vindices praeposuisse dicet. Hic locus igitur est unus quo perfugiant, hic portus, haec arx, haec ara sociorum; quo quidem nunc non ita confugiunt, ut antea in suis repetundis rebus solebant. Non aurum, non argentum, non vestem, non mancipia repetunt; non ornamenta quae ex urbibus fanisque erepta sunt: metuunt homines imperiti ne jam haec populus Romanus concedat et ita fieri velit. Patimur enim multos jam annos et silemus, quum videamus ad paucos homines omnes omnium nationum pecunias pervenisse. Quod eo magis ferre animo aequo et concedere videmur, quia nemo istorum dissimulat, nemo laborat ut obscura sua cupiditas esse videatur. In urbe nostra pulcherrima atque ornatissima quod signum, quae tabula picta est quae non ab hostibus victis capta atque deportata sit? At istorum villae sociorum fidelissimorum plurimis et pulcherrimis spoliis ornatae refertaeque sunt. Ubi pecunias exterarum nationum esse arbitramini quae nunc omnes egent, quum Athenas, Pergamum, Cyzicum, Miletum, Chium, Samum, totamque Asiam, Achaiam, Graeciam,

Gruter says "vocula *juris* abest Cujaciano, neque sane requiritur." Iordan merely says that G 1 has 'ius.' But 'juris' is wanted. Cicero has said 'Nempe hoc jure fuit;' and he adds 'cognationis . . ne hoc quidem juris obtinuit ut,' 'could not from their relationship, &c. maintain even so much of their rights or claims' as to save one innocent person's life.

48. *deseretis?*] The common reading is 'deseritis.' Cicero does sometimes use the present thus, in careless writing, as we may suppose. But 'deseretis,' for which there is the authority of R G 1 V, is the correct form.—'ad senatumne:' V and Orelli. Zumpt and Iordan omit 'ne.'

sumat?] dett., 'sumant' V R 3. If we take 'sumant,' we must supply 'socii,' as Iordan observes.

senatorium.] The common reading is 'senatorium.' If we write 'senatorum,' the reading of V (Br.), the meaning is intelligible, and 'senatores' must be supplied with the verb 'sumant.' Orelli remarks on Zumpt's reading 'non senatorum,' "solita in talibus *imperatorium*, *augurium* (jus), *oratorium* corruptela." There is an instance in the De Sen. c. 4, where in place of 'juris augurii,' the true reading, some MSS. have 'juris et augurii.' See Vol. iii., De Domo, c. 13, note.

haec arx,] Zumpt omits these words; but they are in V, and perhaps genuine, though V has 'ara.'—'omnes omnium nationum:' V, Orelli. Zumpt omits 'omnes.'—'pervenisse:' R 3, Zumpt, and Iordan have 'pervenire;' but the true reading is 'pervenisse.'

quae nunc omnes] "Editi adhuc *quibus*, in qua scriptura difficile jam esset omnes ad ceteras nationes referre" (Zumpt). R V G 1 2 have 'quae.'

Achaiam,] See Divin. c. 20, note on P. Gabinius; and Pro Flacco, c. 26, note, and c. 27, where Cicero says 'Achaia cuncta' and 'Graecia cuncta,' and In Pison. c. 16, where he writes 'omnis Achaia . . . cuncta Graecia.' It is impossible to say what Cicero means by Achaia and Graecia; he has used these terms very loosely.

Siciliam tam in paucis villis inclusas esse videatis? Sed haec, ut dico, omnia jam socii vestri relinquunt et negligunt, judices. Ne publice a populo Romano spoliarentur officiis ac fide providerunt: paucorum cupiditati tum quum obsistere non poterant, tamen sufficere aliquo modo poterant: nunc vero jam adempta est non modo resistendi verum etiam suppeditandi facultas. Itaque res suas negligunt: pecunias, quo nomine judicium hoc appellatur, non repetunt, relinquunt. Hoc jam ornatu ad vos confugiunt. Aspicite, aspicite, judices, squalorem sordesque sociorum.

XLIX. Sthenius hic Thermitanus cum hoc capillo atque veste domo sua tota expilata mentionem tuorum furtorum non facit; sese ipsum abs te repetit, nihil amplius: totum enim tua libidine et scelere ex sua patria, in qua multis virtutibus ac beneficiis princeps fuit, sustulisti. Dexo hic quem videtis, non quae publice Tyndaride, non quae privatim sibi eripuisti, sed unicum miser abs te filium optimum atque innocentissimum flagitat. Non ex litibus aestimatis tuis pecuniam domum, sed ex tua calamitate cineri atque ossibus filii sui solatium vult aliquod reportare. Hic tam grandis natu Eubulida hoc tantum exacta aetate laboris itinerisque suscepit, non ut aliquid de suis bonis recuperaret, sed ut quibus oculis cruentas cervices filii sui viderat isdem te condemnatum videret. Si per L. Metellum licitum esset, judices, matres illorum miserorum, [uxores,] sororesque veniebant: quarum una, quum ego

relinquunt] 'relinquont' R pr. m., 'relincunt' V.

49. *princeps fuit,*] The 'vulgata' is 'princeps floruit,' which Zumpt does not allow to be Latin: nor does Madvig, who observes that we can say 'florere beneficiis,' and 'princeps esse,' but not 'florere princeps.'

isdem te condemnatum] V, Zumpt, and Iordan have 'iis te.'

Si . . licitum esset, . . veniebant :] As to L. Metellus see Lib. 2. c. 4, 'praetorem . . minari Siculis,' &c. Zumpt has a note on this passage. "Ceterum *veniebant* pro *venissent* historicorum more, id quod olim negavi in Gramm. § 619 fieri a Cicerone nisi per partem aliquam. Verum concedo nunc, quoniam *licitum esset* vere Plusquamperf. esse (non Imperfectum) intelligo e locis a Schellero in lexico allatis, quorum duo sunt harum oratt. iii. 48, Init. et Epist. xiv. 4" (Zumpt). He adds a like example, Epist. xii. 10, "praeclare viceramus nisi Lepidus recepisset Antonium." I don't perfectly comprehend all this note, and I give it as it is. I am not aware that there is any difficulty about the form of expression. There is one in Lib. 3. c. 52, which will serve, "Illi ipsi, &c., relicturi agros omnes erant, nisi ad eos Metellus Roma literas misisset." Both of these examples are used by Professor Key (Gramm. 1214, 5, ed. 1) in his remarks on hypothetical sentences. He translates this: 'Their mothers, wives, sisters, were coming (and would actually have come), if Metellus had permitted.' This is the meaning, but I prefer the version without the parenthetical matter. Cicero represents them as coming (which was not the fact) if they had not been prevented. The object of this form is to give greater animation to the expression, which is effected by the indicative, though the strict expression in a case like this would require the subjunctive in both clauses. There are many sentences in which the indicative might stand in place of the subjunctive in the clause which corresponds to the hypothetical clause; and these sentences, instead of being examples of ordinary construction, would then resemble the present instance, in which Cicero could

ad Heracliam noctu accederem, cum omnibus matronis ejus civitatis et cum multis facibus mihi obviam venit, et ita, me suam salutem appellans, te suum carnificem nominans, filii nomen implorans, mihi ad pedes misera jacuit quasi ego ejus excitare ab inferis filium possem. Faciebant hoc idem ceteris in civitatibus grandes natu matres et item parvi liberi miserorum, quorum utrorumque aetas laborem et industriam meam, fidem et misericordiam vestram requirebat. Itaque ad me, judices, hanc querimoniam praeter ceteras Sicilia detulit: lacrimis ego huc, non gloria inductus accessi, ne falsa damnatio, ne carcer, ne catenae, ne verbera, ne secures, ne cruciatus sociorum, ne sanguis innocentium, ne denique etiam exsanguia corpora mortuorum, ne maeror parentum ac propinquorum magistratibus nostris quaestui posset esse. Hunc ego si metum Siciliae damnatione istius per vestram fidem et severitatem dejecero, judices, satis officio meo, satis illorum voluntati qui a me hoc petiverunt factum esse arbitrabor.

L. Quapropter si quem forte inveneris qui hoc navale crimen conetur defendere, is ita defendat: illa communia quae ad causam nihil pertinent praetermittat; me culpae fortunam assignare, calamitatem crimini dare; me amissionem classis objicere, quum multi viri fortes in communi incertoque periculo belli et terra et mari saepe offenderint. Nullam tibi objicio fortunam: nihil est quod

have used 'venissent' in place of 'veniebant.'

The following is another example (Lib. 1. c. 47), "at ille libertus, nisi ex testamento patroni jurasset, scelus se facturum arbitrabatur:" 'but that freedman was thinking that he should commit a crime if he did not swear to observe the testament of his Patronus.' If this case should not be admitted to be exactly of the same kind as those above, as I think it is, it will not be denied that a subjunctive might stand in the place of 'arbitrabatur.'

On the matter of hypothetical sentences, the reader may consult Key's Grammar.—The following are also examples: Ovidii Epig. in Metam. Libr.; Cic. Ad Att. iii. 22; Horace, Carm. ii. 17; De Imp. Cn. Pomp. c. 17. The French sometimes use the same form, an imperfect indicative after a clause which contains 'if.'

utrorumque] 'utrumque' R 3 V, which is supposed to be a shortened form of 'utrorumque.'

exsanguia corpora] V supplies the true reading 'exsanguia,' in place of 'exsanguium,' but it is corruptly written 'exangula' in V.

60. *is ita*] R 3 V, cod. Mureti. 'Ista' dett., which is a false reading, arising out of 'is ita' being mixed together. Hotman conjectured 'is ita defendat ut illa' &c., which is a specious correction, though not necessary. Manutius read 'ista,' and explains it "quae ego objicio, quae proxime nominavi, falsam damnationem, carcerem, catenas." But he saw that the 'illa communia,' which Cicero tells Verres to omit, are such excuses as Cicero first answers, 'Nullam tibi objicio,' &c., and that we must look to c. 51, 'Quapropter si mihi respondere voles,' &c., for the only answer which Verres ought to make: 'is ita defendat.'

culpae fortunam] The reading of V and Iordan. The reading of Zumpt is 'culpam fortunae,' which he attempts to explain. The meaning of the text is clear: 'culpae assignare' corresponds to 'crimini dare,' and means to 'make fortune, or man's ill luck, a cause of blame.' Cicero says shortly after, 'nullam tibi objicio fortunam.' 'Sceleri assignare' occurs in Cicero (Ad Quint. Fr. i. Ep. 4, quoted by Orelli).

ceterorum res minus commode gestas proferas: nihil est quod multorum naufragia fortunae colligas. Ego naves inanes fuisse dico, remiges nautasque dimissos, reliquos stirpibus vixisse palmarum, praefuisse classi populi Romani Siculum, perpetuo sociis atque amicis Syracusanum; te illo tempore ipso superioribusque diebus omnibus in littore cum mulierculis perpotasse dico: harum rerum omnium auctores testesque produco. Num tibi insultare in calamitate, num intercludere perfugia fortunae, num casus bellicos exprobrare aut objicere videor? tametsi solent ii fortunam sibi objici nolle qui se fortunae commiserunt, qui in ejus periculis sunt ac varietate versati. Istius quidem calamitatis tuae fortuna particeps non fuit. Homines enim in proeliis, non in conviviis, belli fortunam periclitari solent: in illa autem calamitate non Martem fuisse communem sed Venerem possumus dicere. Quod si fortunam tibi objici non oportet, cur tu fortunae illorum innocentium veniam ac locum non dedisti? Etiam illud praecidas licet, te quod supplicium more majorum sumpseris securique percusseris, idcirco a me in crimen et in invidiam vocari. Non in supplicio crimen meum vertitur: non ego nego securi quemquam feriri oportere: non ego metum ex re militari, non severitatem imperii, non poenam flagitii tolli dico oportere. Fateor non modo in socios sed etiam in cives militesque nostros persaepe esse severe ac vehementer vindicatum. Qua re haec quoque praetermittas licet. LI. Ego culpam non in navarchis sed in te fuisse demonstro: te pretio remiges militesque dimisisse arguo. Hoc navarchi reliqui dicunt: hoc Netinorum foederata civitas publice dicit: hoc Amestratini, hoc Herbitenses, hoc Hennenses, Agyrinenses, Tyndaritani publice dicunt: tuus denique testis, tuus imperator, tuus aemulus, tuus hospes Cleo-

perpetuo] "'perpetuo' codd. praeter V, in quo 'perpetum sociisque amicis' legitur" (Jordan). If 'perpetuo' is right, we must connect it with 'sociis atque amicis,' 'uninterruptedly allies and friends;' for Syracuse had made the stoutest resistance to Rome, while other Sicilian states had always been friendly. Orelli writes from conjecture 'praepositum,' referring to c. 38, "qui a suis civitatibus illis navibus praepositi fuerant." He adds "totus autem error inde natus, quod notae P.P. significant et *Praepositus* et *Perpetuus*: (Vid. Indicem I. Inscrip. mesr. Lat. T. 2. p. 467.)"

perfugia fortunae,] R 3 λ Lg. 29. The 'perfugia fortunae' are the excuse which a man makes by alleging his ill luck, a thing which may befall any one.

Martem . . communem] See Pro Milone, c. 21, "Adde casus, adde incertos exitus pugnae, Martemque communem;" where 'Mars communis' explains or is explained by the rest of the sentence. See also Pro Sestio, c. 5, and the note. 'Venerem communem' is an allusion to Verres' intrigues with other men's wives.

praecidas licet, te quod] I have followed Orelli's text. Zumpt has 'praecidas licet, de his quod.' 'Te' seems to be wanting, and it is in λ Lg. 29 V.—'feriri oportere' Zumpt, from V; 'feriri delere' Orelli.

ex re] 'in re' V, and Halm.

51. *Hennenses,*] Lgg. plerique, 'Ennenses' V, 'Ethnenses' alii. Out of the last reading Halm has made 'Aetnenses,' which may be right. But I see no reason why

menes hoc dicit, sese in terram esse egressum ut Pachyno e terrestri praesidio milites colligeret quos in navibus collocaret, quod certe non fecisset, si suum numerum naves haberent; ea est enim ratio instructarum ornatarumque navium ut non modo plures sed ne singuli quidem possint accedere. Dico praeterea illos ipsos reliquos nautas fame atque inopia rerum omnium confectos fuisse ac perditos. Dico aut omnes extra culpam fuisse, aut, si uni attribuenda culpa sit, in eo maximam fuisse qui optimam navem, plurimos nautas haberet, summum imperium obtineret, aut, si omnes in culpa fuerint, non oportuisse Cleomenem constitui spectatorem illorum mortis atque cruciatus. Dico etiam in ipso supplicio mercedem lacrimarum, mercedem vulneris atque plagae, mercedem funeris ac sepulturae constitui nefas fuisse. Quapropter si mihi respondere voles, haec dicito: classem instructam atque ornatam fuisse, nullum propugnatorem abfuisse, nullum vacuum tractum esse remum, rem frumentariam esse suppeditatam, mentiri navarchos, mentiri tot et tam graves civitates, mentiri etiam Siciliam totam; proditum esse te a Cleomene qui se dixerit exisse in terram ut Pachyno deduceret milites; animum illis non copias defuisse; Cleomenem acerrime pugnantem ab iis relictum esse atque desertum: nummum ob sepulturam datum nemini. Quae si dices, tenebere: sin alia dices, ea quae a me dicta sunt non refutabis.

LII. Hic tu etiam dicere audebis, 'Est in judicibus ille familiaris meus, est paternus amicus ille?' Non, ut quisque maxime est quicum tibi aliquid sit, ita te in hujuscemodi crimine maxime ejus pudet? 'Paternus amicus est.' Ipse pater si judicaret, per deos immortales, quid facere posset. Quum tibi haec diceret: Tu in pro-

'Hennenses' may not be the reading. They were inland people, it is true; but so were the Centuripini, c. 33.

vacuum tractum esse] This is the reading of R 3, rightly restored by Zumpt in place of the corruptions of conjecture. V omits 'remum.' A 'vacuus remus' is one which has no man to work it; and it may be said to be 'tractus' when it is attached to its place and dragged, instead of being worked by the hand of the rower. Scheffer, an authority in such matters, so explains the text; and he refers to Ovid, Met. xi. 475:

"Obvertit lateri pendentes navita remos;"

and Statius, Theb. v. 422; Valerius Flaccus, Argon. iii. 34.

52. *ita te . . maxime ejus pudet?*] Verres is supposed to say, "There is among the 'judices' that intimate of mine; there is a friend of my father there." To which Cicero replies, "Just in proportion to your intimacy with any one, ought you not, when charged with an offence of this kind, to be filled with shame before him?" As to this use of 'pudet,' Madvig compares Cicero, Phil. ii. 25, "si te municipiorum non pudebat, ne veterani quidem exercitus?" There is also Phil. xii. 3, 'Pudet hujus legionis' &c.; and Terence, Haut. ii. 3. 19. Orelli gives the instance of the German form: 'sich vor einem schämen.'

posset. Quum &c.] I have now followed Iordan's pointing, which is Madvig's.

vincia populi Romani praetor, quum tibi maritimum bellum esset administrandum, Mamertinis ex foedere quam deberent navem per triennium remisisti: tibi apud eosdem privata navis oneraria maxima publice est aedificata: tu a civitatibus pecunias classis nomine coëgisti: tu pretio remiges dimisisti: tu, navis quum esset ab legato et quaestore capta praedonum, archipiratam ab oculis omnium removisti: tu, qui cives Romani esse dicerentur, qui a multis cognoscerentur, securi ferire potuisti: tu tuam domum piratas abducere, in judicium archipiratam domo producere ausus es: tu in provincia tam splendida, tu apud socios fidelissimos, cives Romanos honestissimos, in metu periculoque provinciae dies continuos complures in littore conviviisque jacuisti: te per eos dies nemo tuae domi convenire, nemo in foro videre potuit: tu sociorum atque amicorum ad ea convivia matresfamilias adhibuisti: tu inter ejusmodi mulieres praetextatum tuum filium, nepotem meum, collocavisti ut aetati maxime lubricae atque incertae exempla nequitiae parentis vita praeberet: tu praetor in provincia cum tunica pallioque purpureo visus es: tu propter amorem libidinemque tuam imperium navium legato populi Romani ademisti, Syracusano tradidisti: tui milites in provincia Sicilia frugibus frumentoque caruerunt: tua luxuria atque avaritia classis populi Romani a praedonibus capta et incensa est: post Syracusas conditas quem in portum nunquam hostis accesserat, in eo te praetore primum piratae navigaverunt: neque haec tot et tanta dedecora dissimulatione tua neque oblivione hominum ac taciturnitate tegere voluisti, sed etiam navium praefectos sine ulla causa de complexu parentum suorum, hospitum tuorum, ad mortem cruciatumque rapuisti, neque te in parentum luctu atque lacrimis mei nominis commemoratio mitigavit: tibi hominum innocentium sanguis non modo voluptati sed etiam quaestui fuit—haec si tibi tuus parens diceret, posses ab eo veniam petere? posses ut tibi ignosceret postulare?

LIII. Satis est factum Siculis, satis officio ac necessitudini, judices, satis promisso nostro ac recepto. Reliqua est ea causa, Judices, quae jam non recepta sed innata, neque delata ad me sed in animo sensuque meo penitus affixa atque insita est; quae non ad sociorum salutem, sed ad civium Romanorum, hoc est, ad uniuscujusque nostrûm vitam et sanguinem pertinet. In qua nolite a

cognoscerentur,] See 'cognoscerent,' c. 59.

53. *jam non*] R S λ, 'non iam' dett. Or. 'Jam non' is the right order, for the sense is 'non recepta,' and it is opposed to 'innata.' For 'innata' R has 'inta' and G 3 'ita.' Mistakes of this kind are instructive for those who occupy themselves with the restoration of corrupt texts.

me, quasi dubium sit aliquid, argumenta, judices, exspectare: omnia quae dicam sic erunt illustria ut ad ea probanda totam Siciliam testem adhibere possem. Furor enim quidam, sceleris et audaciae comes, istius effrenatum animum importunamque naturam tanta oppressit amentia ut nunquam dubitaret in conventu palam supplicia, quae in convictos maleficii servos constituta sunt, ea in cives Romanos expromere. Virgis quam multos ceciderit, quid ego commemorem? Tantum brevissime, judices, dico: nullum fuit omnino civitatis isto praetore in hoc genere discrimen. Itaque jam consuetudine ad corpora civium Romanorum etiam sine istius nutu ferebatur manus ipsa lictoris.

LIV. Num potes hoc negare, Verres, in foro Lilybaei maximo conventu C. Servilium, civem Romanum e conventu Panhormitano, veterem negotiatorem, ad tribunal ante pedes tuos ad terram virgis et verberibus abjectum? Aude hoc primum negare, si potes. Nemo Lilybaei fuit quin viderit, nemo in Sicilia quin audierit. Plagis confectum dico a lictoribus tuis civem Romanum ante oculos tuos concidisse. At quam ob causam, dii immortales! Tametsi injuriam facio communi causae et juri civitatis: quasi enim ulla possit esse causa cur hoc cuiquam civi Romano jure accidat, ita quaero quae in Servilio causa fuerit. Ignoscite in hoc uno, judices: in ceteris enim non magno opere causas requiram. Locutus erat liberius de istius improbitate atque nequitia. Quod isti simulac renuntiatum est, hominem jubet Lilybaeum vadimonium Venereo servo promittere. Promittit. Lilybaeum venitur. Cogere eum coepit, quum ageret nemo, nemo postularet, sponsionem [II millium num-

54. *At quam ob causam,*] The common reading is 'quam ob causam,' but Zumpt added the 'at' on the authority of R 3. The 'at' could be omitted, but it is Cicero's fashion to use it in such a case. He says 'Plagis confectum' &c.; and then, to give greater emphasis to what he has said, he adds, 'at quam ob causam,' 'and for what reason?' Thus in the beginning of c. 66, 'At quae erat ista libido,' &c.; and in the same chapter, 'At quae causa tum subjiciebatur,' &c.

Ignoscite in hoc uno,] 'Excuse me if I ask for a reason in this one case; for I shall not seek much for reasons in the other cases.'

Lilybaeum vadimonium . . . promittere.] See Lib. 3. c. 15.

sponsionem . . facere] Here 'sponsionem facere' is said of him who answers (spondet) and promises (promittit) to him 'qui sponsione lacessit,' as Keller shows, Semestrium ad M. Tullium Ciceronem Libri Sex, i. p. 31. It has also this sense in the Pro Caecina, c. 28, "Aebutius . . necesse est male fecerit sponsionem." In the Pro Quintio, c. 8, 9, Quintius 'qui reus' is said 'sponsionem facere;' and in c. 14, Naevius 'qui spondet ac promittit' is also said 'sponsionem facere.' So in Lib. 1. c. 45, of these orations, 'sponsionem faceret,' and 'si possessor sponsionem non faciet,' are used the same way. To this may be added the Lex Galliae Cisalpinae, c. 21, "si is ibi de ea re in jure non responderit, neque de ea re sponsionem faciet, neque judicio uti oportebit se defendet;" and in another passage, "qui se sponsione judiciove uti oportebit non defenderit."

Instances where the 'stipulator' is said 'sponsionem facere,' occur in Lib. 3. c. 57, and in Cicero, Ad Fam. vii. 21. These re-

mum] facere cum lictore suo, Ni furtis quaestum faceret. Recuperatores se de cohorte sua dicebat daturum. Servilius et recusare et deprecari, ne iniquis judicibus nullo adversario judicium capitis in se constitueretur. Haec quum maxime loqueretur, sex lictores circumsistunt valentissimi et ad pulsandos verberandosque homines exercitatissimi: caedunt acerrime virgis: denique proximus lictor,

marks will serve as a supplement to what has been said before on this expression. (Excursus, Sponsiones.)

sponsionem [*II millium nummum*]] "'spons. millium nummum' R 3. hinc Zumpt: coni. *spons.* II. *millium nummum*; *H S. duobus milibus sponsionem* inde a Naug. Or., sed qua fide codicum haec scriptura nitatur prorsus incertum est. [Nulla, ut videtur; codd. quidem Lagg. nihil habent nisi, *H S. sponsionem* omisso numero.]" (Iordan.)

Ni furtis] Servilius, it must be supposed, had talked of the thefts of Verres; and Verres, in order to punish him, resolved to charge Servilius with theft. Nobody had any demand upon Servilius, and no charge to make against him (quum ageret nemo, nemo postularet). Verres compelled him to make a 'sponsio' with his own 'lictor,' the effect of which was to try the question whether Servilius was a thief or not; rather a singular way of dealing with a man's character, when there was no charge against him. The form of the 'sponsio,' in this case, as Rost explains it, would be this: "Servus or Lictor: *Spondesne, Servili, HS duo millia, si tu* (quod ego affirmo et tu negas) *furtis quaestum facis?* Servilius: *Spondeo, si* &c. Tum Servilius, *Tu vero, lictor, spondesne, si* &c. Lictor: *Spondeo, si*" &c. This explanation of Rost's is adopted by Orelli, but his adoption of it adds nothing to the authority.

But we must distinguish between the direct form of the 'sponsio,' and the form in which it is quoted. In Gaius (iv. 93) we have an example of the direct form: "provocamus adversarium tali sponsione: Si homo quo de agitur ex jure Quiritium meus est, sestertios XXV nummos dare spondes?" The answer would be 'Spondeo.' The corresponding direct form in the passage of Cicero would be this challenge to Servilius, "Si furtis quaestum facis, II millia nummum dare spondes?" Servilius would not say 'Spondeo,' but Verres tried to compel him to answer (sponsionem facere). If the form in the direct 'sponsio' was 'si . . . non' with the indicative, it was in the indirect 'si . . . non' with the subjunctive (Pro Quintio, c. 8. 27). But in affirmative 'sponsiones,' when reported indirectly, the form 'ni' is always used, and not 'si.' Huschke, quoted by Keller (Semestr. i. p. 38), gives a reason for it. The words in legal formulae must not be measured by the ordinary rules of the Latin language. They are often antiquated modes of expression, which differ from the forms in daily use. I take 'ni' in this formula to mean what Keller suggests (ob nicht): and the simple translation of the text will be: 'he compels him to make a Sponsio to the amount of, &c.— If he was not enriching himself by theft.' The question raised was, If he was not a thief; or, Whether he was not a thief: just as if the form had been 'Furtisne quaestum faceret.' This explanation is equally applicable to the passage in Lib. 3. c. 60, where 'sponsionem facere' applies to the 'stipulator.' The 'sponsio' being made, it may be generally referred to as containing the matter, 'If so and so is not the case.' Thus Cicero says (c. 60), 'Sponsio est, ni te' &c.: the 'sponsio,' that is, the question to which 'spondeo' had been answered, involved the question, 'If Apronius did not say that you are his partner in the Decumae?' So in another passage Cicero writes, "Sponsione me, Ni Esquilina introisset, homo promptus lacessivit," In Pison. c. 23.

See Excursus viii., where there are further remarks on this chapter.

judicium capitis] Because a 'condemnatio' in this 'actio' would be followed by 'infamia' (Excursus viii.).

proximus lictor,] As the 'lictors' walked in a line before the 'magistratus,' the nearest 'lictor' would be 'proximus,' as the story in Livy (xxiv. 44) shows; and this appears to be the 'lictor' who was most about the 'magistratus' (Sallust, Jug. c. 12). The term occurs on two inscriptions cited by Orelli, but in the order 'Lictor proximus.' Zumpt refers to a passage in Valerius Maximus (ii. 2, 4), "ne quis se inter consulem et proximum lictorem . . . interponeret;" and Cicero, De Divin. i. 26. Cicero (Ad Q. Fr. i. 1. c. 7) has the ex-

de quo jam saepe dixi, Sextius converso baculo oculos misero tundere vehementissime coepit. Itaque ille, quum sanguis os oculosque complesset, concidit, quum illi nihilo minus jacenti latera tunderentur ut aliquando spondere se diceret. Sic ille affectus illinc tum pro mortuo sublatus perbrevi postea est mortuus. Iste autem homo Venereus, affluens omni lepore ac venustate, de bonis illius in aede Veneris argenteum Cupidinem posuit. Sic etiam fortunis hominum abutebatur ad nocturna vota cupiditatum suarum.

LV. Nam quid ego de ceteris civium Romanorum suppliciis singillatim potius quam generatim atque universe loquar? Carcer ille qui est a crudelissimo tyranno Dionysio factus Syracusis, quae lautumiae vocantur, in istius imperio domicilium civium Romanorum fuit. Ut quisque istius animum aut oculos offenderat, in lautumias statim conjiciebatur. Indignum hoc video videri omnibus, judices, et id jam priore actione quum haec testes dicerent intellexi; retineri enim putatis oportere jura libertatis non modo hic, ubi tribuni plebis sunt, ubi ceteri magistratus, ubi forum plenum judiciorum, ubi senatus auctoritas, ubi existimatio populi Romani et frequentia, sed ubicumque terrarum et gentium violatum jus civium Romanorum sit, statuitis id pertinere ad communem causam libertatis et dignitatis. In externorum hominum maleficorum sceleratorumque, in praedonum hostiumque custodias tu tantum numerum civium Romanorum includere ausus es? Nunquamne tibi judicii, nunquam contionis, nunquam hujus tantae frequentiae, quae nunc animo te iniquissimo infestissimoque intuetur, venit in mentem? nunquam tibi populi Romani absentis dignitas, nunquam species ipsa hujusce multitudinis in oculis animoque versata est? nunquam te in horum conspectum rediturum, nunquam in forum populi Romani venturum, nunquam sub legum et judiciorum potestatem casurum esse duxisti?

pression 'primus lictor,' which Lipsius (Op. vol. i. Elect. p. 727, ed. 1675) explains to mean the 'lictor' who walks first and clears the way, 'qui submovet.' Halm says that the 'proximus lictor' was in rank 'primus;' and that may be so too.

55. *tyranno Dionysio*] This was the elder Dionysius, as he is called, a successful usurper who governed Syracuse till his death in B.C. 367.

ubi tribuni plebis sunt.] Compare with this a passage in the Ep. ad Q. Fr. i. 1. c. 7, 'Quod si haec lenitas grata' &c.

sit,] The codd. have 'sit,' which Halm has changed to 'est.' Iordan says that it is a 'probabilis, sed non necessaria conjectura.' I do not think that it is 'probabilis,' if he uses 'probabilis' in the Roman sense.

judicii, . . venit in mentem?] See Divin. c. 13.—'contionis:' a public meeting, before which the Tribuni pl. could charge a magistrate after his term of office had expired.

esse duxisti?] R S. λ, 'putasti' dett. Orelli observes that the change into 'pe-

LVI. At quae erat ista libido crudelitatis exercendae, quae tot scelerum suscipiendorum causa? Nulla, judices, praeter praedandi novam singularemque rationem. Nam ut illi, quos a poëtis accepimus, qui sinus quosdam obsedisse maritimos aut aliqua promontoria aut praerupta saxa tenuisse dicuntur, ut eos qui essent appulsi navigiis interficere possent, sic iste in omnia maria infestus ex omnibus Siciliae partibus imminebat. Quaecunque navis ex Asia, quae ex Syria, quae Tyro, quae Alexandria venerat, statim certis indicibus et custodibus tenebatur: vectores omnes in lautumias conjiciebantur: onera atque merces in praetoriam domum deferebantur. Versabatur in Sicilia longo intervallo alter, non Dionysius ille nec Phalaris, tulit enim illa quondam insula multos et crudeles tyrannos, sed quoddam novum monstrum ex vetere illa immanitate quae in iisdem locis versata esse dicitur. Non enim Charybdim tam infestam neque Scyllam nautis quam istum in eodem freto fuisse arbitror: hoc etiam iste infestior quod multo se pluribus et immanioribus canibus succinxerat. Cyclops alter multo importunior: hic enim totam insulam obsidebat; ille Aetnam solam et eam Siciliae partem tenuisse dicitur. At quae causa tum subjiciebatur ab ipso, judices, hujus tam nefariae crudelitatis? Eadem quae nunc in defensione commemorabitur. Quicunque accesserant ad Siciliam paulo pleniores, eos Sertorianos milites esse atque a Dianio fugere dicebat. Illi ad deprecandum periculum proferebant, alii purpuram Tyriam, tus alii atque odores vestemque linteam, gemmas alii et margaritas, vina nonnulli Graeca venalesque Asiaticos, ut intelligeretur ex mercibus quibus ex locis navigarent. Non providerant eas ipsas sibi causas esse periculi, quibus argumentis se ad salutem uti arbitrabantur. Iste enim haec eos ex piratarum societate adeptos esse dicebat: ipsos in lautumias abduci imperabat: naves eorum atque onera diligenter asservanda curabat.

tasti' was made by those who did not like 'esse duxisti' (Lib. 3. c. 23).

56. *illi,*] The great robbers of antiquity, Sinis, Procrustes, and other worthies.

promontoria] 'promuntoria' R Lg. 29. —'vectores:' 'passengers,' as in Phil. vii. c. 9.

non Dionysius ille] Zumpt observes that this passage is quoted by Quintilian, Inst. Or. viii. 6. 72, as an instance of hyperbole, but it is quoted with some variations.

canibus succinxerat.] The word properly applies, as Zumpt observes, to Scylla, who appeared surrounded by barking monsters, when the waves withdrew, and displayed the monster: "Illa feris atram canibus succingitur alvum," Ovid, Met. xiii. 732; and Lucret. v. 802. The hounds of Verres have often been mentioned by Cicero.—'immanioribus:' de Meumii conj. L.; 'inmaioribus' R codd. Lamb.; 'maioribus' G 3 dett. (Iordan.)

Cyclops] Homer, Od. Lib. ix.—'obsidebat:' 'obtinebat' dett., Orelli.

Dianio] See Lib. 1. c. 34, and Strabo, p. 159.

LVII. His institutis quum completus jam mercatorum carcer esset, tum illa fiebant quae L. Suetium, equitem Romanum, lectissimum virum, dicere audistis, et quae ceteros audietis. Cervices in carcere frangebantur indignissime civium Romanorum ut jam illa vox et imploratio, Civis Romanus sum, quae saepe multis in ultimis terris opem inter barbaros et salutem tulit, ea mortem illis acerbiorem et supplicium maturius ferret. Quid est, Verres? quid ad haec cogitas respondere? num mentiri me, num fingere aliquid, num augere crimen, num quid horum dicere istis tuis defensoribus audes? Cedo mihi, quaeso, ex ipsius sinu literas Syracusanorum quas iste ad arbitrium suum confectas esse arbitratur: cedo rationem carceris quae diligentissime conficitur, quo quisque die datus in custodiam, quo mortuus, quo necatus sit. LITERAE SYRACUSANORUM. Videtis cives Romanos gregatim conjectos in lautumias: videtis indignissimo in loco coacervatam multitudinem vestrorum civium. Quaerite nunc vestigia quibus exitus eorum ex illo loco compareant. Nulla sunt. Omnesne mortui? Si ita posset defendere, tamen fides huic defensioni non haberetur. Sed scriptum extat in iisdem literis, quod iste homo barbarus ac dissolutus neque attendere unquam neque intelligere potuit: ΕΔΙΚΑΙΩΘΗΣΑΝ, inquit, hoc est, ut Siculi loquuntur, supplicio affecti ac necati sunt.

LVIII. Si qui rex, si qua civitas exterarum gentium, si qua natio fecisset aliquid in cives Romanos ejusmodi, nonne publice vindicaremus? non bello persequeremur? possemus hanc injuriam ignominiamque nominis Romani inultam impunitamque dimittere? Quot bella majores nostros et quanta suscepisse arbitramini, quod cives Romani injuria affecti, quod navicularii retenti, quod mercatores spoliati dicerentur? At ego jam retentos non queror; spoliatos ferendum puto: navibus, mancipiis, mercibus ademptis in vincula

57. *istis tuis &c.*] "Sic Guelferbytani, et solent illa verba conjungi" (Zumpt). Orelli and Iordan follow the vulgate 'istis defensoribus tuis audes.' Or. observes that the other reading makes an hexameter ending, which Cicero studiously avoids 'in clausularum fine.' But there are examples in Cicero of this hexametral ending.

ipsius sinu] The 'sinus' of Verres. He had a copy of the prison rolls (ratio carceris) with him.

attendere] See Lib. 3. c. 5.—*ἐδικαιώθησαν*: Cicero seems to say that this is a Sicilian use, not known to the other Greeks, who would use some other form of expression to convey the notion of capital punishment; or he may simply mean, this is the word which the Sicilians used, and Verres did not understand it. Hotmann refers to a use of *δικαιοῦν* in Herodotus (i. 100), where the word however simply means 'be punished;' and so it may mean here, 'they were punished;' but usage had affixed a meaning to the word. See Suidas, *δικαιούμενοι: κολαζόμενοι, δίκην τυγχάνων*.

58. *non bello*] This is preferred by Zumpt and Orelli to the reading 'nonne bello,' for it appears to be Cicero's fashion, after using 'nonne' once, to use the simple 'non.' See Lib. 4. c. 56, note. But B 3 Lg. 29 have 'nonne,' and Iordan also.

mercatores esse conjectos et in vinculis cives Romanos necatos esse arguo. Si haec apud Scythas dicerem, non hic in tanta multitudine civium Romanorum, non apud senatores lectissimos civitatis, non in foro populi Romani de tot et tam acerbis suppliciis civium Romanorum, tamen animos etiam barbarorum hominum permoverem. Tanta enim hujus imperii amplitudo, tanta nominis Romani dignitas est apud omnes nationes ut ista in nostros homines crudelitas nemini concessa esse videatur. Nunc tibi ego ullam salutem, ullum perfugium putem, quum te implicatum severitate judicum, circumretitum frequentia populi Romani esse videam? Si mehercule, id quod fieri non posse intelligo, ex his te laqueis exueris ac te aliqua via ac ratione explicaris, in illas tibi majores plagas incidendum est in quibus te ab eodem me superiore ex loco confici et concidi necesse est. Cui si etiam id quod defendit velim concedere, tamen ipsa illa falsa defensio non minus esse ei perniciosa quam mea vera accusatio debeat. Quid enim defendit? Ex Hispania fugientes se excepisse et supplicio affecisse dicit. Quis tibi id permisit? quo jure fecisti? quis idem fecit? qui tibi facere licuit? Forum plenum et basilicas istorum hominum videmus, et animo aequo videmus. Civilis enim dissensionis et sive amentiae seu fati seu calamitatis non est iste molestus exitus, in quo reliquos saltem cives incolumes licet conservare. Verres, ille vetus proditor consulis, translator quaesturae, aversor pecuniae publicae, tantum

te laqueis exueris] In the opposite sense he has used 'induere' (Lib. 2. c. 42).—'to . . . explicaris:' comp. Pro Caelio, c. 28, 'qui se nunquam . . explicabunt.'

superiore ex loco] "E Rostris in quibus aedilis accusabo te de majestate" (P. Manutius). This is the right explanation, and this passage must be added to the list of passages in refutation of Becker's opinion that 'superior locus' always means the 'tribunal.' Orelli quotes Fronto, p. 148, ed. Rom.: "locuturum inde nobiscum de loco superiore; nec tantulo superiore quanto Rostra foro et comitio excelsiora sunt." Compare with this passage Lib. 1. c. 6.

istorum hominum] The public places of Rome were crowded with men who had been the partizans of Marius and Sertorius; but they were allowed to return home, and remain unmolested. Cicero adds: 'For as to civil dissension and madness, if you so choose to call it, or give it the name of fate or misfortune that has befallen us, you cannot find fault with a termination which allows us to save at least the remnant of our citizens.' He means to say that, after all the calamities of the civil wars, the Romans may be well satisfied that tranquillity is at last restored, and that those who have survived are allowed to remain unmolested. The impudent defence of Verres was, that those whom he put to death were men who had escaped from the Spanish war, partizans of Sertorius; but these very men were allowed to remain quiet at Rome. Besides, Verres had no authority for punishing them, if they fell into his hands. Orelli and Zumpt place ';' after 'exitus.' Orelli understands the passage right. Ernesti misunderstood it, and tried to correct it; and Zumpt also misunderstood it, as the following note shows: "Tu institutа cum Beckio paulo graviore interpunctione (the ';' after 'exitus'), qua hoc membrum a praegresso discernatur, subintellige '*sed is est*.'"

et sive] dett., 'etsi' R 3, which no doubt means 'et seu,' which Iordan has.

translator quaesturae,] These words

sibi auctoritatis in re publica suscepit ut, quibus hominibus per senatum, per populum Romanum, per omnes magistratus, in foro, in suffragiis, in hac urbe, in re publica versari liceret, iis omnibus mortem acerbam crudelemque proponeret, si fortuna eos ad aliquam partem Siciliae detulisset. Ad Cn. Pompeium, clarissimum virum et fortissimum, occiso Perperna permulti ex illo Sertoriano numero militum confugerunt. Quem non ille summo cum studio salvum incolumemque servavit? cui civi supplici non illa dextera invicta fidem porrexit et spem salutis ostendit? Itane vero quibus fuit portus apud eum quem contra arma tulerant, iis apud te cujus nullum in re publica momentum unquam fuit mors et cruciatus erat constitutus? Vide quam commodam defensionem excogitaris. LIX. Malo mehercule id quod tu defendis his judicibus populoque Romano quam id quod ego insimulo probari: malo, inquam, te isti generi hominum quam mercatoribus et naviculariis inimicum atque infestum putari. Meum enim crimen avaritiae te nimiae coarguit: tua defensio furoris cujusdam et immanitatis et inauditae crudelitatis et paene novae proscriptionis. Sed non licet me isto tanto bono, judices, uti: non licet. Adsunt enim Puteoli toti: frequen-

have caused difficulty to some of the commentators. Cicero describes Verres as a traitor to his consul Cn. Papirius Carbo (Lib. 1. c. 12, &c.). He was the 'quaestor' of Carbo, and in this capacity he deserted him: he transferred his 'quaestorship' to the other party, to Sulla. There seems nothing more strange in calling Verres 'translator quaesturae' than 'aversor pecuniae publicae.'

in suffragiis,] Not access to the 'magistratus,' however, says P. Manutius, for a 'lex' which was passed (B.C. 81) after the victory of Sulla deprived the sons of the proscribed of the capacity of filling 'magistratus.' Cicero (In Pison. c. 2) opposed the repeal of this unjust lex. Compare Velleius, ii. 28; Sallust, Cat. c. 37.

Perperna] M. Perperna, who belonged to the faction of M. Aemilius Lepidus, joined Sertorius in Spain, and afterwards assassinated him (Plutarch, Sertorius, c. 27). Cn. Pompeius, who was then conducting the war in Spain, caught Perperna and put him to death (B.C. 72); but he burnt all the papers of Sertorius without reading them, or letting any one else read them; "and he immediately put Perperna to death, through fear that there might be defection and disturbance if the names were communicated to others" (Plutarch). — 'permulti occiso Perperna ex illo:' Orelli, Iordan. — 'Itane vero? quibus:' Zumpt, Orelli, Iordan, as usual.

59. *isto tanto bono,*] The defence of Verres was, that he had caught and put to death the partizans of Sertorius. Cicero's charge is, that they were 'mercatores' whom he had plundered. This was the 'crimen avaritiae.' Cicero would have had no objection, if Verres could have proved his case, that they were partizans of Sertorius whom he had punished; for Verres would then have proved that he almost made a new proscription. But Cicero goes on to say that he cannot avail himself of this advantage; he cannot have the opportunity of letting Verres prove himself to be merely a bloodthirsty villain, for the evidence of many persons established the fact that these were 'mercatores' whom he plundered of their goods.

Puteoli] This town, now Pozzuoli, was a great place of resort for merchants from Asia and Egypt; and Verres had intercepted many of those who were bound to this port, plundered them of their wares, and put them to death. The ancient navigation required more stoppages than ours, and these vessels had called at Syracuse, probably for water and other conveniences. When St. Paul left Malta after his shipwreck, he sailed in a vessel of Alexandria, which stayed three days at Syracuse. The

tissimi venerunt ad hoc judicium mercatores, homines locupletes atque honesti, qui partim socios suos, partim libertos, ab isto spoliatos, in vincula conjectos, partim in vinculis necatos, partim securi percussos esse dicunt. Hic vide quam me sis usurus aequo. Quum ego P. Granium testem produxero qui suos libertos abs te securi percussos esse dicat, qui abs te navem suam mercesque repetat, refellito, si poteris; meum testem deseram, tibi favebo: te, inquam, adjuvabo: ostendito illos cum Sertorio fuisse, a Dianio fugientes ad Siciliam esse delatos. Nihil est quod te mallem probare: nullum enim facinus quod majore supplicio dignum sit reperiri neque proferri potest. Reducam iterum equitem Romanum, L. Flavium, si voles; quoniam priore actione, ut patroni tui dictitant, nova quadam sapientia, ut omnes intelligunt, conscientia tua atque auctoritate meorum testium testem nullum interrogasti. Interrogetur Flavius, si voles, quinam fuerit T. Herennius, is quem ille argentariam Lepti

vessel then came to Rhegium, and thence on the second day to Puteoli, where St. Paul landed (Acts, xxviii. 11—14). Madvig, quoted by Zumpt, refers to several passages, which show that Puteoli was a place of great trade at this time. Suetonius (Aug. c. 98) speaks of an Alexandrian ship saluting Augustus as he was sailing past the harbour of Puteoli. See also Strabo, p. 793, ed. Cas.

Cicero's allusion (De Fin. ii. 26) to the 'Puteolis granaria' seems to show that it was a depôt for corn.

ab isto spoliatos,] dett. 'partim colibertos spoliatos' R 3, Iordan. I believe that the words 'partim colibertos' are spurious. The words 'partim in vinculis necatos' are omitted by R 3, cod. Lamb.

mallem] 'malim' dett.

argentariam] 'Argentariam facere' (Pro Caecina, c. 4), 'naviculariam facere,' and the like, signify to carry on the business of an 'argentarius' or 'navicularius.' Herennius is called a 'negotiator' (Lib. 1. c. 5). He carried on his business at Leptis in Africa, from which it was a short cut to Sicily, whither his affairs, we may suppose, occasionally took him. Cicero's Leptis may be Leptis Minor, now Lempta, which was in the Byzacium, and south of Hadrumetum. Halm says that Cicero means Leptis Magna, now Lebda, on the coast between the Syrtes. There is nothing which can determine which of the two places Cicero means, but it is more probable that he means the city which is nearer to Sicily. The business of an 'argentarius' was to exchange various kinds of money for merchants and others, as is now done by money-changers. He probably also received deposits, and advanced money on security, as we see in the case mentioned by Gaius (iv. 64), where accounts between the 'argentarius' and Titius are spoken of. Ernesti has a dissertation on the 'negotiatores.' They are easily distinguished from 'mercatores,' who are dealers in wares; and from 'aratores' and cattle-feeders (Verr. Lib. 2. c. 3). The general term 'negotiator' appears to include 'argentarius.' The Roman capitalists used to resort to the provinces, in order to turn their money to account. The least laborious way of making a capital profitable in a new settlement, or in a country where money is scarce, is to lend on security, and get a high rate of interest. It does not appear that a Roman 'negotiator' made any other venture in the provinces than that of placing out his money at interest; and he was not restrained by any rules of law as to the rate of interest that he could demand. If he employed his capital in any other way, he was not a 'negotiator,' except, as it seems, the 'negotiatores' sometimes made large purchases of grain, and probably other articles, for a venture to Rome; or, which is quite as likely, produce and other articles, on which they had made advances, would sometimes fall into their hands from the inability of their debtors to pay what had been advanced.

fecisse dicit: qui cum amplius centum cives Romanos haberet ex conventu Syracusano qui eum non solum cognoscerent, sed etiam lacrimantes ac te implorantes defenderent, tamen inspectantibus omnibus Syracusanis securi percussus est. Hunc quoque testem meum refelli, et illum Herennium Sertorianum fuisse abs te demonstrari et probari volo.

LX. Quid de illa multitudine dicemus eorum qui capitibus involutis in piratarum captivorum[que] numero producebantur ut securi ferirentur? Quae ista nova diligentia, quam ob causam abs te excogitata? An te L. Flavii ceterorumque de T. Herennio vociferatio commovebat? an M. Annii, gravissimi atque honestissimi viri, summa auctoritas paulo diligentiorem timidioremque fecerat? qui nuper pro testimonio non advenam nescio quem nec alienum, sed eum civem Romanum qui omnibus in illo conventu notus, qui Syracusis natus esset, abs te securi percussum esse dixit. Post hanc illorum vociferationem, post hanc communem famam atque querimoniam, non mitior in supplicio sed diligentior esse coepit. Capitibus involutis cives Romanos ad necem producere instituit, quos tamen idcirco necabat palam, quod homines in conventu, id quod antea dixi, nimium diligenter praedonum numerum requirebant. Haeccine plebi Romanae te praetore est constituta conditio? haec negotii gerendi spes? hoc capitis vitaeque discrimen? Parumne multa mercatoribus sunt necessario pericula subeunda fortunae, nisi etiam hac formidines ab nostris magistratibus atque in nostris provinciis impendebunt? Ad eamne rem fuit haec suburbana ac fidelis Sicilia, plena optimorum sociorum honestissimorumque civium, quae cives Romanos omnes suis ipsa sedibus libentissime semper accepit, ut, qui usque ex ultima Syria atque Aegypto navigarent, qui apud barbaros propter togae nomen in honore aliquo fuissent, qui ex praedonum insidiis, qui ex tempestatum periculis profugissent, in Sicilia securi ferirentur, quum se jam domum venisse arbitrarentur?

LXI. Nam quid ego de P. Gavio, Consano municipe, dicam,

amplius centum] See Lib. 1. c. 5.

60. *haec suburbana*] Compare Lib. 2. c. 3, "sic populo Romano jucunda suburbanitas est hujusce provinciae."

togae nomen] Accordingly Roman citizens were called 'togati.'

61. *Consano*] There is the best authority for 'Consano,' but there is also authority for 'Cossano' and 'Cosano.' Cosa is an Etruscan town. Compsa, now Conza, is in the territory of the Hirpini, and is supposed to be the place that is meant. The form 'Consano,' from 'Compsa,' is certainly not what we should expect; but 'Compsanus' may have been corrupted into 'Consanus.' In Livy, xxiii. 1. there is 'Compsa' and 'Compsanus' in the editions. Orelli refers to c. 66, which seems to show, as he thinks, that the home of Gavius was in Southern Italy; but this is

judices? aut qua vi vocis, qua gravitate verborum, quo dolore animi dicam? tametsi dolor non deficit: ut cetera mihi in dicendo digna re, digna dolore meo suppetant, magis laborandum est. Quod crimen ejusmodi est ut, quum primum ad me delatum est, usurum me illo non putarem; tametsi enim verissimum esse intelligebam, tamen credibile fore non arbitrabar. Coactus lacrimis omnium civium Romanorum qui in Sicilia negotiantur, adductus Valentinorum hominum honestissimorum omniumque Rheginorum testimoniis multorumque equitum Romanorum qui casu tum Messanae fuerunt, dedi tantum priore actione testium res ut nemini dubia esse posset. Quid nunc agam? Quum jam tot horas de uno genere ac de istius nefaria crudelitate dicam, quum prope omnem vim verborum ejusmodi quae scelere istius digna sint aliis in rebus consumpserim neque hoc providerim ut varietate criminum vos attentos tenerem, quemadmodum de tanta re dicam? Opinor, unus modus atque una ratio est. Rem in medio ponam, quae tantum habet ipsa gravitatis ut neque mea, quae nulla est, neque cujusquam ad inflammandos vestros animos eloquentia requiratur. Gavius hic, quem dico, Consanus, quum in illo numero civium Romanorum ab isto in vincula conjectus esset et nescio qua ratione clam e lautumiis profugisset Messanamque venisset, qui tam prope jam Italiam et moenia Rheginorum videret et ex illo metu mortis ac tenebris quasi luce libertatis et odore aliquo legum recreatus revixisset, loqui Messanae et queri coepit se civem Romanum in vincula conjectum, sibi recta iter esse Romam, Verri se praesto advenienti futurum.

LXII. Non intelligebat miser nihil interesse utrum haec Messanae an apud istum in praetorio loqueretur. Nam, ut antea vos docui, hanc sibi iste urbem delegerat quam haberet adjutricem scelerum, furtorum receptricem, flagitiorum omnium consciam. Itaque ad magistratum Mamertinum statim deducitur Gavius, eoque ipso die casu Messanam Verres venit. Res ad eum defertur: esse civem Romanum qui se Syracusis in lautumiis fuisse quereretur; quem jam ingredientem [in] navem et Verri nimis atrociter

an absurd argument. He could see no more of one place than of the other; and of the two places, Cosa or Cossa, which is on the coast, is the place that one would prefer.—'dolor me non:' Orelli, who says '*dolor non* nescio unde Zumpt.' 'dolore non' R, which probably means 'dolor me non;' 'dolor non,' G 1 2.—'laborandum:' R 3 Lg. 29, Iordan. I have now taken this reading instead of the former reading 'elaborandum.'

praesto] See Lib. 2. c. 4, note on 'quaestores.'

62. *istum*] R 3 Lg. 29, and therefore we ought to take it. If we could choose what we like, there is no objection to 'ipsum,' the reading of the dett.

ingredientem] 'Ingredientem in' R 3 λ, Iordan.

minitantem a se retractum esse et asservatum, ut ipse in eum statueret quod videretur. Agit hominibus gratias et eorum benevolentiam erga se diligentiamque collaudat: ipse inflammatus scelere et furore in forum venit. Ardebant oculi: toto ex ore crudelitas eminebat. Exspectabant omnes quo tandem progressurus aut quidnam acturus esset, quum repente hominem proripi atque in foro medio nudari ac deligari et virgas expediri jubet. Clamabat ille miser se civem esse Romanum, municipem Consanum: meruisse cum L. Precio, splendidissimo equite Romano, qui Panhormi negotiaretur, ex quo haec Verres scire posset. Tum iste se comperisse [ait] eum speculandi causa in Siciliam a ducibus fugitivorum esse missum; cujus rei neque index neque vestigium aliquod neque suspicio cuiquam esset ulla: deinde jubet undique hominem vehementissime verberari. Caedebatur virgis in medio foro Messanae civis Romanus, judices, quum interea nullus gemitus, nulla vox alia illius miseri inter dolorem crepitumque plagarum audiebatur nisi haec, Civis Romanus sum. Hac se commemoratione civitatis omnia verbera depulsurum cruciatumque a corpore dejecturum arbitrabatur. Is non modo hoc non perfecit ut virgarum vim deprecaretur, sed quum imploraret saepius usurparetque nomen civitatis, crux, crux, inquam, infelici et aerumnoso, qui nunquam istam potestatem viderat, comparabatur.

LXIII. O nomen dulce libertatis! O jus eximium nostrae civitatis! O lex Porcia legesque Semproniae! O graviter desiderata

eminebat.] This passage is cited by Gellius, x. 3, and by Quintilian, Inst. Or. ix. 2. 40, though some editions of Quintilian have 'emicabat.' But the true reading in Quintilian is 'eminebat' (Zumpt).

meruisse] He had served in the army with L. Precius: his comrade therefore would be able to testify who he was.

crepitumque] "*strepitumque* codd. nonnulli Gellii coll. Mart. Cap. p. 426 quod haud scio an rectius sit" (Iordan).

usurpare] This word has here the sense of continuous use of a thing, as in c. 64, 'usurpatione civitatis.'

potestatem] Zumpt has 'pestem,' and he is followed by Orelli and Iordan. There is no authority for 'pestem,' except Lg. 29, which we might accept if it removed the difficulty. Zumpt observes that Verres is frequently called 'pestis,' and other bad men like him; and we have, in Lib. 3. c. 64, 'importunissima pestis.' But if 'pestem' is Verres, there is no point in the remark, 'qui nunquam istam pestem viderat.' Besides, it is very unlikely that Gavius had never seen Verres. Nor is the explanation better if we take 'pestem' to be the cross; for what is the sense of saying that Gavius had never seen the cross; even if we admit that he had never seen it? But if he had never seen a cross, he had not seen that which Cicero speaks of as a thing which every body knew. Manutius explains 'potestatem' thus: 'in crucem agendi cives Romanos,' which may be the meaning. Zumpt observes upon 'potestas:' "neque enim illa *potestas* fuit, sed minime ferendus potestatis abusus;" but there is no weight in that. Of the two readings, 'potestatem' appears more capable of explanation; and the authority for 'pestem' is small.

63. *lex Porcia* &c.] Livy (x. 9) speaks of a Porcia Lex: "Porcia tamen Lex sola pro tergo civium lata videtur, quod gravi poena si quis verberasset necassetve civem Romanum sanxit;" and Sallust (Cat. c. 51). Cicero (De Re Publica, ii. 31) speaks

et aliquando reddita plebi Romanae tribunicia potestas! Huccine tandem omnia reciderunt ut civis Romanus in provincia populi Romani, in oppido foederatorum, ab eo qui beneficio populi Romani fasces et secures haberet deligatus in foro virgis caederetur? Quid quum ignes candentesque laminae ceterique cruciatus admovebantur, si te illius acerba imploratio et vox miserabilis non inhibebat, ne civium quidem Romanorum qui tum aderant fletu et gemitu maximo commovebare? In crucem tu agere ausus es quemquam qui se civem Romanum esse diceret? Nolui tam vehementer agere hoc prima actione, judices, nolui; vidistis enim ut animi multitudinis in istum dolore et odio et communis periculi metu concitarentur. Statui egomet mihi tum modum et orationi meae, et C. Numitorio, equiti Romano, primo homini, testi meo; et Glabrionem, id quod sapientissime fecit, facere laetatus sum ut repente consilio in medio testem dimitteret. Etenim verebatur ne populus Romanus ab isto eas poenas vi repetisse videretur, quas

of three Leges Porciae, "Leges Porciae quae tres sunt trium Porciorum." It is supposed that the last 'lex' was one proposed by P. Porcius Laeca, B.C. 197, of whom there is extant a 'denarius,' with the inscription, P . LAECA . PROVOCO. Zumpt observes, that as there appears to have been nothing about the 'provocatio' or appeal in the Porcia Lex, it is probable that it was a 'lex' proposed by M. Porcius Cato, the censor, who, according to Festus, made a speech 'pro scapulis.' Festus says, "Pro scapulis cum dicit Cato, significat pro injuria verberum. Nam complures leges erant in cives rogatae, quibus sanciebatur poena verberum: his significat prohibuisse multos suos cives in ea oratione quae est contra M. Caelium." It is the opinion of most critics that P. Porcius Laeca proposed the 'lex,' and that M. Porcius Cato spoke in favour of it (suasit). The 'lex' seems to have given an appeal to a Roman citizen in the provinces against the governor, and Gavius accordingly is represented as making his appeal, by declaring that he was a Roman citizen (Meyer, Orat. Rom. Fragm. p. 21, 2nd ed.).

There appears to have been only one Lex Sempronia on this matter, a 'lex' of C. Sempronius Gracchus, B.C. 123. Cicero says (Pro Rabirio, c. 4): "C. Gracchus legem tulit ne de capite civium Romanorum injussu vestro judicaretur."

reddita . . tribunicia] See Divin. c. 3.

reciderunt] "*recciderunt*, Gellii cod. C ex apparatu Hertzii" (Iordan). 'Recciderunt' is certainly a genuine form, like 'reppulerunt.'

consilio in medio testem] This is the MSS. reading. There is no variation. Zumpt cannot explain it, and is driven to adopt Hotmann's conjecture, 'consilium in medio testimonio dimitteret.' Orelli and Iordan follow Zumpt. Hotmann observes that every body knows that the 'praetor' might dismiss the 'consilium' or 'judices,' that is, adjourn the court, when he pleased. I suppose that a 'praetor' might 'consilium dimittere,' when he saw a reason for it, but if he could do so, that is no evidence that he did so here. The MSS. reading makes Glabrio send away the witness, which I suppose that he could also do. The difficulty is in the words 'consilio in medio,' which cannot mean when the Judices 'missi sunt in consilium.' If the reading is right, it means in the midst of the proceedings, and I do not see why the sitting of the court could not be called 'consilium,' as well as the body of 'judices,' who were certainly so called from sitting together. Manutius explains 'consilio in medio' by saying 'judicum,' and if I understand him, he means that 'the Praetor in the midst of the Consilium of the Judices sent away the witness,' to prevent any popular outbreak and to remove all blame on this head from himself and the 'consilium.' Whatever the true explanation may be, I prefer a text, which is supported by all the evidence, to a conjecture for which there is none.

veritus esset ne iste legibus et vestro judicio non esset persoluturus. Nunc quoniam exploratum est omnibus quo loco causa tua sit et quid de te futurum sit, sic tecum agam. Gavium istum, quem repentinum speculatorem fuisse dicis, ostendam in lautumias Syracusis a te esse conjectum, neque id solum ex literis ostendam Syracusanorum, ne possis dicere me, quia sit aliquis in literis Gavius, hoc fingere et eligere nomen, ut hunc illum esse possim dicere; sed ad arbitrium tuum testes dabo qui istum ipsum Syracusis abs te in lautumias conjectum esse dicant. Producam etiam Consanos, municipes illius ac necessarios, qui te nunc sero doceant, judices non sero, illum P. Gavium quem tu in crucem egisti, civem Romanum et municipem Consanum, non speculatorem fugitivorum fuisse. LXIV. Quum haec omnia quae polliceor cumulate tuis proximis plana fecero, tum istuc ipsum tenebo quod abs te mihi datur: eo contentum me esse dicam. Quid enim nuper tu ipse, quum populi Romani clamore atque impetu perturbatus exsiluisti, quid, inquam, locutus es? Illum quod moram supplicio quaereret, ideo clamitasse se esse civem Romanum, sed speculatorem fuisse. Jam mei testes veri sunt. Quid enim dicit aliud C. Numitorius? quid M. et P. Cottii, nobilissimi homines, ex agro Tauromenitano? quid Q. Lucceius qui argentariam Rhegii maximam fecit? quid ceteri? Adhuc enim testes ex eo genere a me sunt dati, non qui novisse Gavium sed se vidisse dicerent, quum is qui se civem Romanum esse clamaret in crucem ageretur. Hoc tu, Verres, idem dicis: hoc tu confiteris illum clamitasse, se civem esse Romanum: apud te nomen civitatis ne tantum quidem valuisse ut dubitationem aliquam, ut crudelissimi taeterrimique supplicii aliquam parvam moram saltem posset afferre. Hoc teneo, hic haereo, judices, hoc sum contentus uno: omitto ac negligo cetera: sua confessione induatur ac juguletur necesse est. Qui esset ignorabas: speculatorem esse suspicabare: non quaero qua suspicione; tua te accuso oratione. Civem Romanum se esse dicebat. Si tu apud Persas aut in extrema India deprehensus, Verres, ad supplicium ducerere, quid

repentinum speculatorem] Who was all at once declared to be a spy, no suspicion of the kind having ever existed before, as Hotmann explains it.

ad arbitrium tuum] 'As many as you choose,' is the meaning. Comp. c. 37, 'ad arbitrium suum.' Halm observes that this is the classical expression for the modern Latin 'ad libitum.' Horace (Carm. iii. 6. v. 40) has 'matris ad arbitrium.'

64. *tuis proximis*] The advocates and friends of Verres, who were about him and the nearest to him. Comp. Lib. 2. c. 44. It is singular that any body should have found a difficulty here.

dubitationem aliquam] Lg. 29 Nang. add 'crucis;' and Jordan has 'crucis' in his text.—'sua confessione induatur:' 'by his own confession he must be caught.' 'Induatur' seems to be used absolutely here. See c. 29.

aliud clamitares nisi te civem esse Romanum? et si tibi ignoto apud ignotos, apud barbaros, apud homines in extremis atque ultimis gentibus positos, nobile et illustre apud omnes nomen tuae civitatis profuisset, ille quisquis erat quem tu in crucem rapiebas, qui tibi esset ignotus, quum civem se Romanum esse diceret, apud te praetorem, si non effugium, ne moram quidem mortis mentione atque usurpatione civitatis assequi potuit?

LXV. Homines tenues, obscuro loco nati, navigant; adeunt ad ea loca quae nunquam antea viderunt, ubi neque noti esse iis quo venerunt neque semper cum cognitoribus esse possunt. Hac una tamen fiducia civitatis non modo apud nostros magistratus qui et legum et existimationis periculo continentur, neque apud cives solum Romanos qui et sermonis et juris et multarum rerum societate juncti sunt, fore se tutos arbitrantur; sed quocunque venerint, hanc sibi rem praesidio sperant esse futuram. Tolle hanc spem, tolle hoc praesidium civibus Romanis; constitue nihil esse opis in hac voce, 'Civis Romanus sum;' posse impune praetorem aut alium quemlibet supplicium quod velit in eum constituere qui se civem Romanum esse dicat, quod quis ignoret; jam omnes provincias, jam omnia regna, jam omnes liberas civitates, jam omnem orbem terrarum qui semper nostris hominibus maxime patuit, civibus

65. *cognitoribus*] This word is explained by the rest of the chapter. It means persons who knew them and could vouch for them.

Hac . . fiducia civitatis] 'Relying solely on this citizenship.' He says, c. 68, 'tua fiducia,' 'in reliance on you.'

esse futuram.] 'Futurum' Orelli, on the authority of Gellius (i. 7), who quotes this passage, "Homines tenues . . sibi rem praesidio sperant futurum." In place of 'viderunt,' the text of Gellius has 'adierant.' Gellius prefaces the extract with this remark: "In oratione Ciceronis Quinta in Verrem, in libro spectatae fidei Tironiana cura atque disciplina facto, ita scriptum fuit." He observes that many people thought that 'futurum' was a blunder; but a friend of his, who was well versed in the old books, observed: "nullum esse in eo verbo neque mendum neque vitium: Ciceronem probe ac venuste locutum; nam *futurum*, inquit, non refertur ad *rem*, sicut legentibus temere et incuriose videretur; neque pro participio positum est; sed verbum est indefinitum quod Graeci appellant ἀπαρέμφατον, neque numeris neque generibus praeserviens, sed liberum undique et impromiscuum est." Gellius cites other instances from C. Gracchus, Claudius Quadrigarius, and other old writers, where 'dicturum,' 'facturum,' &c., are used in cases where 'dicturos,' 'facturos,' would be the later usage. Zumpt admits that this infinitive future was often so used by the old writers; but he asks how it happens that we have only this single instance cited from Cicero. It is not easy to answer this objection. 'Esse futuram' is the reading of Lg. 29 et 4 alii. "*futurum* Lg. 27 45 48 et Gellius (in Lg. 48, item in Lg. 14 locus Gellii citatur): *esse futurum* Lg. 42" (Iordan). In Sallust (Jug. c. 100) some editions have the reading "non tam diffidentia futurum quae imperavisset." Orelli objects to 'esse futurum' in this passage of Cicero as being at variance with the fundamental laws of oratorical number, which do not allow the use of the hexametral termination, not even at the end of a clause. It seems as if he established his rule by destroying all the instances which contradict it.

quod quis ignoret;] Zumpt and Iordan have 'quod cum quis ignoret,' from Lg. 29 only: "sine qua sententia obscura, oratio abrupta est." This is the cod. which Zumpt once calls 'minime fidelis.'

Romanis ista defensione praecluseris. Quid si L. Precium, equitem Romanum, qui tum in Sicilia erat, nominabat, etiamne id magnum fuit Panhormum literas mittere? Asservasses hominem, custodiis Mamertinorum tuorum vinctum clausum habuisses, dum Panhormo Precius veniret. Cognosceret hominem; aliquid de summo supplicio remitteres: si ignoraret, tum si ita tibi videretur, hoc juris in omnes constitueres ut, qui neque tibi notus esset neque cognitorem locupletem daret, quamvis civis Romanus esset, in crucem tolleretur.

LXVI. Sed quid ego plura de Gavio? quasi tu Gavio tum fueris infestus, ac non nomini, generi, juri civium hostis. Non illi, inquam, homini sed causae communi libertatis inimicus fuisti. Quid enim attinuit, quum Mamertini more atque instituto suo crucem fixissent post urbem in via Pompeia, te jubere in ea parte figere quae ad fretum spectaret, et hoc addere, quod negare nullo modo potes, quod omnibus audientibus dixisti palam, te idcirco illum locum deligere ut ille, quoniam se civem Romanum esse diceret, ex cruce Italiam cernere ac domum suam prospicere posset? Itaque illa crux sola, judices, post conditam Messanam illo in loco fixa est. Italiae conspectus ad eam rem ab isto delectus est ut ille in dolore cruciatuque moriens perangusto fretu divisa servitutis ac libertatis jura cognosceret, Italia autem alumnum suum servitutis extremo summoque supplicio affixum videret. Facinus est vincire civem

qui tum in Sicilia &c.] 'Qui tum in Sicilia negotiabatur, nominabat?' Orelli. Zumpt observes that all the MSS. whose collations we are acquainted with, except Lg. 29, have 'qui tum in Sicilia nominabatur.' Lg. 29 has 'erat' and 'nominabat.' The reading of the passage is very doubtful.

Cognosceret hominem;] Lambinus prefixed 'si' to 'cognosceret,' as Zumpt observes, 'liberius quam decet;' but he might have said 'impudentissime.' What business has an editor to corrupt the text by his insertions and omissions? This use of the conditional without 'si' is common. P. Manutius proposed to omit the 'si' before 'ignoraret;' but it is in the MSS. Orelli can see a distinction between the clause 'cognosceret' and 'si ignoraret;' but I cannot.

66. *more*] All the MSS. have 'nomine,' says Zumpt; but Naugerius corrected it. The MS. abbreviation of 'nomine' is 'noie.' Whether 'more' is abbreviated, I don't know. Here is a case where correction is permitted; for first we see how the blunder may have originated: next, we have the formula 'more atque instituto' to guide us. 'Nomine atque instituto' would have no meaning.

fretu] On the authority of Gellius (xiii. 20). But the MSS. of Cicero have 'freto,' except Lg. 42, which has 'fretu.' There is also the authority of the grammarian Charisius (p. 103, Putsch.) for 'fretu' in Cicero (Zumpt). See Pro Sestio, c. 3.

Cicero means to say that the straits, the boundary of Italy and Sicily, separated the freedom of Italy from the servitude of Sicily. If Gavius was a Roman citizen, he was equally entitled to protection against Verres in Italy and Sicily; but he happened to be in Sicily, which was a province, where there was a governor with no power on the spot to control him. See c. 65, note on 'ubi tribuni plebis sunt.'

affixum] "'defixum' Lg. 29, 'ac fixum' Vindob. nr. 64, 'ea fixum' rell., 'fixum' Non. p. 242, 'affectum' Hervag." (Iordan.) 'Supplicio' is the ablative, and means 'by' or 'with.' 'Affixum' therefore, if it is right, means 'fastened to the cross.'

Romanum; scelus verberare; prope parricidium necare: quid dicam in crucem tollere? verbo satis digno tam nefaria res appellari nullo modo potest. Non fuit his omnibus iste contentus. Spectet, inquit, patriam; in conspectu legum libertatisque moriatur. Non tu hoc loco Gavium, non unum hominem nescio quem, [civem Romanum,] sed communem libertatis et civitatis causam in illum cruciatum et crucem egisti. Jam vero videte hominis audaciam. Nonne eum graviter tulisse arbitramini quod illam civibus Romanis crucem non posset in foro, non in comitio, non in rostris defigere? Quod enim his locis in provincia sua, celebritate simillimum, regione proximum potuit, elegit: monumentum sceleris audaciaeque suae voluit esse in conspectu Italiae, vestibulo Siciliae, praetervectione omnium qui ultro citroque navigarent.

LXVII. Si haec non ad cives Romanos, non ad aliquos amicos nostrae civitatis, non ad eos qui populi Romani nomen audissent;

vincire . . verberare; . . necare: . . tollere?] It is singular that the MSS., except Lg. 29, should have the passive forms in the first three words, and keep the active 'tollere.' It seems clear that the active forms are required, and Quintilian cites the passage so (Inst. viii. 4. 4).

prope parricidium] That is 'murder.' It does not appear that the Romans had any name for murder except 'parricidium;' for 'homicidium' seems not to have come into use before the imperial period. Cicero means murder in this passage. The common explanation of this word is, that it is equivalent to 'patricidium;' but it is difficult to see why the genuine form should not have been kept as in 'patrimonium.' It was the opinion of antiquity, that the word meant literally 'parricide,' or the killing of a father by a son. Plutarch (Romulus, c. 22) says that Romulus named all homicide *πατροκτονία*, a statement that has of course no historical value; but it shows how Plutarch understood the word 'parricidium.' Paulus Diaconus, v. Parrici Quaestores, p. 221, Müller, says: "Nam parricida non utique is qui parentem occidisset dicebatur, sed qualemcunque hominem indemnatum. Ita fuisse indicat lex Numae Pompilii regis his composita verbis: Si qui hominem liberum dolo sciens morti duit, parricidas esto." This is explained to mean that all malicious homicide was to be treated as parricide, and tried before the same court.

Besides the derivation of 'parricidium' from 'patri' and 'cid' (caed-ere), it has been proposed to consider it as a shorter form of 'parenticidium;' and also, as formed of 'par' and 'cid,' the killing of one's equal. The latest and the worst attempt is that of E. Osenbrüggen (Das Alt-Römische Parricidium, Kiel, 1841), who derives it ultimately from the Sanscrit 'para,' signifying, as he explains it, 'cunning,' 'perverted;' and so he would explain 'parricidium' to be death caused by treachery or malice (dolo sciens), and it would signify what we call murder, and not the death of a father. From this original signification he supposes that murder in later times was distributed into various kinds, 'homicidium,' 'veneficium,' and 'parricidium' in the narrower sense. But the passages of Roman authors show that parricide in our sense is the original signification of 'parricidium,' and that is a sufficient answer to Osenbrüggen. This subject is one of considerable difficulty; but the explanation most consistent with the use of 'parricidium' by the Roman writers, is that it does properly signify 'parricide,' and that the name became generally applied to any atrocious murder. In this sense we can understand 'parricida patriae,' or 'rei publicae.' In this passage Cicero says 'prope parricidium.' It was not therefore quite 'parricidium.' There is a title in the Dig. 48. 9, 'De Lege Pompeia de Parricidiis.' This subject is discussed by Osenbrüggen, and in Rein, Das Criminal-recht der Römer, p. 401, 449, &c.

[*civem Romanum,*]] "om. Sever. l. 1. et glossatoris inepti manum haec vv. perspicue produnt" (Iordan).

denique, si non ad homines verum ad bestias; aut etiam, ut longius progrediar, si in aliqua desertissima solitudine ad saxa et ad scopulos haec conqueri ac deplorare vellem; tamen omnia muta atque inanimata tanta et tam indigna rerum acerbitate commoverentur. Nunc vero quum loquar apud senatores populi Romani, legum et judiciorum et juris auctores, timere non debeo ne non unus iste civis Romanus illa cruce dignus, ceteri omnes simili periculo indignissimi judicentur. Paulo ante, judices, lacrimas in morte misera atque indigna navarchorum non tenebamus, et recte ac merito sociorum innocentium miseria commovebamur; quid nunc in nostro sanguine tandem facere debemus? Nam civium Romanorum omnium sanguis conjunctus existimandus est, quoniam et salutis omnium ratio et veritas postulat. Omnes hoc loco cives Romani, et qui adsunt et qui ubique sunt, vestram severitatem desiderant, vestram fidem implorant, vestrum auxilium requirunt: omnia sua jura, commoda, auxilia, totam denique libertatem in vestris sententiis versari arbitrantur. A me tametsi satis habent, tamen, si res aliter acciderit, plus habebunt fortasse quam postulant. Nam si qua vis istum de vestra severitate eripuerit, id quod neque metuo, judices, neque ullo modo fieri posse video; sed si in hoc me ratio fefellerit, Siculi causam suam perisse querentur, et mecum pariter moleste ferent; populus quidem Romanus brevi, quoniam mihi potestatem apud se agendi dedit, jus suum me agente suis suffragiis ante Kalendas Februarias recuperabit. Ac si de mea gloria atque amplitudine quaeritis, judices, non est alienum meis rationibus istum mihi ex hoc judicio ereptum ad illud populi Romani judicium reservari. Splendida est illa causa, probabilis mihi et facilis, populo grata atque jucunda. Denique si videor hic, quod ego non quaesivi, de uno isto voluisse crescere, isto absoluto, quod sine multorum scelere fieri non potest, de multis mihi crescere licebit.

67. *inanimata*] 'Inanima' Orelli.—'acerbitate' R 3, codd. Lamb. Sever.; 'atrocitate' dett.

ne non unus] F. C. Wolff proposed to omit 'non,' and Madvig approves of the omission. It seems that they take 'iste civis' to be Gavius, whereas he is Verres. Zumpt and Orelli defend the 'non,' and Jordan keeps it. It is not a clear form of expression; but Cicero's meaning appears to be this: he says that when speaking before Roman senators, 'I ought not to have any apprehension that this one citizen of yours will not be judged worthy of that punishment of the cross, and all the rest will be considered most undeserving of a like danger.' The senators of course would consider the cross an unfit punishment for Roman citizens. But Cicero says, that when they form this judgment, they will not at the same time think that Verres does not deserve it.

quoniam et] 'quoniam id et' dett.—'vestram severitatem desiderant' om. R 3.

Kalendas] Before he has been a month in office as Curule aedile. Compare Act. I. c. 12, and Lib. 1. c. 6, and c. 42, at the end.—'probabilis:' see Divin. c. 21.

de uno . . crescere,] Rightly explained by Graevius, to get power, wealth, or the

LXVIII. Sed mehercule vestra reique publicae causa, judices, nolo in hoc delecto consilio tantum flagitium esse commissum: nolo eos judices quos ego probarim atque delegerim, sic in hac urbe notatos isto absoluto ambulare ut non cera sed caeno obliti esse videantur. Quamobrem te quoque, Hortensi, si qui monendi locus ex hoc loco est, moneo: videas etiam atque etiam et consideres, quid agas, quo progrediare, quem hominem et qua ratione defendas. Neque de illo tibi quidquam praefinio quo minus ingenio mecum atque omni dicendi facultate contendas. Cetera si qua putas te occultius extra judicium quae ad judicium pertineant facere posse; si quid artificio, consilio, potentia, gratia, copiis istius moliri cogitas; magno opere censeo desistas, et illa quae temptata jam et coepta sunt ab isto, a me autem pervestigata et cognita, moneo ut extinguas et longius progredi ne sinas. Magno tuo periculo peccabitur in hoc judicio, majore quam putas. Quod enim te liberatum jam existimationis metu, defunctum honoribus, designatum consulem cogites, mihi crede, ornamenta ista et beneficia populi Romani non minore negotio retinentur quam comparantur. Tulit haec civitas, quoad potuit, quoad necesse fuit, regiam istam vestram dominationem in judiciis et omni re publica; tulit: sed quo die populo Romano tribuni plebis restituti sunt, omnia ista vobis, si forte nondum intelligitis, adempta atque erepta sunt.

like, to the detriment of some other person. Compare Pro S. Rosc. Amer. c. 30, 'ex quibus possem crescere,' and Pro Cluentio, c. 28. Caesar (B. G. i. 20) has 'per se crevisset.'

68. *delecto consilio*] See Excursus ii. 'Judicia,' p. 51.—'probarim:' he had not challenged them (p. 6), and so he says that he chose them (delegerim).

cera] This is explained by Divin. c. 7; Act. 1. c. 6, and 13.

ex hoc loco] That is, from the equal ground from which he now addresses the court. Cicero gives Hortensius a little advice now, if he is wise enough to take it, before Cicero speaks in a different tone when he has entered on his office, and will address the people from a 'superior locus.' In the words 'si qui locus,' the word 'locus' has a different meaning; but we can preserve the double sense by saying 'if there is any place for giving you advice from this place.'

quae temptata] 'quem temptata' R.

ne sinas.] codd. plerique; 'non sinas' Lg.

Quod . . . cogites,] Orelli, following Lambinus, has 'cogitas.' Cicero apparently does not mean to say that Hortensius 'cogitat.' He seems to express himself in this form: 'for as to the opinion that you may entertain, that you are now released from all fear about your character,' &c. Zumpt observes "sed *quod* cum alias facta non opiniones exprimat, h. l. fere *si* valet." It may be translated, 'For if you consider,' &c.

defunctum honoribus,] Hortensius being now 'designatus consul,' had attained the highest rank; he had run through the career of Roman 'honores,' for though he had not yet entered on the discharge of his duty, his office was secured.

vestram dominationem] Cicero uses 'vestram,' though he is only addressing Hortensius. He means Hortensius and his partizans, the nobility, who were in favour of the policy of Sulla. Cicero afterwards says 'omnia ista vobis . . . adempta atque erepta sunt,' by the restoration of the power of the tribunes.

plebis] G 1 dett.; R G 2 Ld., Iordan, have 'plebi.'

Omnium nunc oculi conjecti sunt hoc ipso tempore in unumquemque nostrûm, qua fide ego accusem, qua religione hi judicent, qua tu ratione defendas. De omnibus nobis, si quis tantulum de recta regione deflexerit, non illa tacita existimatio quam antea contemnere solebatis, sed vehemens ac liberum populi Romani judicium consequetur. Nulla tibi, Quinte, cum isto cognatio [est], nulla necessitudo; quibus excusationibus antea nimium in aliquo judicio studium tuum defendere solebas, earum habere in hoc homine nullam potes. Quae iste in provincia palam dictitabat, quum ea quae faciebat tua se fiducia facere dicebat, ea ne vera putentur tibi maxime est providendum.

LXIX. Ego mei rationem jam officii confido esse omnibus iniquissimis meis persolutam: nam istum paucis horis primae actionis omnium mortalium sententiis condemnavi. Reliquum judicium jam non de mea fide quae perspecta est, nec de istius vita quae damnata est, sed de judicibus, et, vere ut dicam, de te futurum est. At quo tempore futurum est?—nam id maxime providendum est, etenim quum omnibus in rebus, tum in re publica permagni momenti est ratio atque inclinatio temporum—nempe eo quum populus Romanus aliud genus hominum atque alium ordinem ad res judicandas requirit; nempe lege de judiciis judicibusque novis promulgata, quam non is promulgavit quo nomine proscriptam videtis, sed hic reus; hic, inquam, sua spe atque opinione quam de vobis

recta regione] "Ant. Augustinus, eruditus olim Italus, pro *regione* scribendum censuit aut *ratione* aut *religione*." But Zumpt refers to 'regio' at the end of c. 70. It is also an expression of Lucretius (iv. 1268), 'recta regione viaque.' This very learned prelate has been mentioned before in these notes. But Agostini was a Spaniard. 'Recta regione' means 'the straight direction,' 'the straight line,' as in Caesar, B. G. vi. 25.

in aliquo judicio] Zumpt refers to Divin. c. 7. The word 'Quinte' shows intimacy between Cicero and Hortensius, or at least Cicero treats him as a friend to whom he is giving some good advice.

69. *rationem . . . officii*] He means to say that he is confident that he has now paid the debt of his duty, even to those who are the most unreasonable of his creditors. He might have said 'officium' only, as in c. 71; but he uses a word (ratio) from common life, a word of reckoning and account.

quo nomine] The reading of R 3. The dett. have 'cujus.' The vulgate 'cujus nomine' may be merely an explanation of 'quo nomine,' which is intelligible, though it seems rather a singular kind of expression. Madvig compares Lib. 4. c. 9, "hi te homines sublevent . . . quo in oppido." The text, he observes, is the same in sense as if it were 'non is, qui id nomen habet, quo' &c. He also compares Lib. 1. c. 38, "his nominibus, quae res per eum gestae sunt," and he explains it thus: 'id est, his nominibus rationum, quae ad eas res pertinent, quae' &c. I don't take this to be a good explanation, no more than the like explanation which he gives of the following passage of Caesar (Bell. Civ. i. 8), "reliquo sermone confecto, cujus rei causa venerat," which means, says Madvig, 'de ea re cujus.' There is, Pro Quintio, c. 4, "Quum aeris alieni aliquantulum esset relictum, quibus nominibus."

The 'lex' is the Aurelia of Cotta, which was now promulgated in the Roman sense, that is, put up in public, that the proposed 'lex' might be well known. Cicero says that the real promulgator is Verres, for the fear of Verres escaping was the immediate motive for the 'lex' being proposed.

habet, legem illam scribendam promulgandamque curavit. Itaque quum primo agere coepimus, lex non erat promulgata; quum iste vestra severitate permotus multa signa dederat quamobrem responsurus non videretur, mentio de lege nulla fiebat: posteaquam iste recreari et confirmari visus est, lex statim promulgata est. Cui legi quum vestra dignitas vehementer adversetur, istius spes falsa et insignis impudentia maxime suffragatur. Hic si quid erit commissum a quoquam vestrûm quod reprehendatur, aut populus Romanus judicabit de eo homine quem jam antea judiciis indignum putavit, aut ii qui propter offensionem judiciorum de veteribus judicibus lege nova novi judices erunt constituti.

LXX. Mihi porro, ut ego non dicam, quis omnium mortalium non intelligit quam longe progredi sit necesse? Potero silere, Hortensi, potero dissimulare, quum tantum res publica vulnus acceperit, ut expilatae provinciae, vexati socii, dii immortales spoliati, cives Romani cruciati et necati impune me actore esse videantur? potero ego hoc onus tantum aut in hoc judicio deponere aut tacitus sustinere? Non agitanda res erit? non in medium proferenda? non populi Romani fides imploranda? non omnes qui tanto se scelere obstrinxerint ut aut fidem suam corrumpi paterentur, aut judicium corrumperent, in discrimen aut judicium vocandi? Quaeret aliquis fortasse, Tantumne igitur laborem, tantas inimicitias tot hominum suscepturus es? Non studio quidem hercule ullo, neque voluntate; sed non idem licet mihi, quod iis qui nobili genere nati sunt quibus omnia populi Romani beneficia dormientibus deferuntur;

de eo homine] Zumpt has 'de eodem homine.' It matters little which we take. The man is Verres. If Verres is not convicted, says Cicero, either the Roman people will pass judgment on him, whom already they have considered unworthy of a trial (c. 63), or those will pass judgment, who, on account of the misconduct of the courts, will be appointed by a new 'lex' new 'judices' to sit in judgment on the former 'judices.' Zumpt remarks that the parts of this sentence do not correspond, at least in position, for there is nothing to correspond to 'de eo.' He observes that, if the words were in this order, 'aut de veteribus judicibus ii qui,' every thing would be in harmony. But this would hardly be an improvement, for 'de veteribus judicibus' cannot well be separated from the words which follow.

putavit,] "*putaret* R. hinc coni. Or. 2. *putarat;* Halm, *putarit*" (Jordan), who has 'putavit.' I think there is no doubt that 'putavit' is the true form here.

70. *longe progredi*] This is correctly explained by P. Manutius. Every body knows that, if Verres is acquitted, I cannot remain quiet; I must prosecute this affair, and bring Verres before the Populus Romanus.

expilatae provinciae,] 'expilata prov.' R 3 λ, Jordan; 'expilatae provinciae' dett. (sed est deinde in R *vexati*).

aut tacitus] Orelli has 'aut diutius tacitus.' But the best MSS. omit 'diutius,' and it seems better omitted. Orelli says that this is one of the kind of omissions which appear in the best MSS., or, as in this instance, is caused by the 'similes literarum ductus.' I suppose he means that 'diutius' and 'tacitus' have a certain resemblance in the forms of the letters. But it is as easy to suppose that the word 'diutius' has arisen from 'tacitus' being repeated.

dormientibus] Cicero alludes to the

longe alia mihi lege in hac civitate et conditione vivendum est. Venit mihi in mentem M. Catonis, hominis sapientissimi et vigilantissimi, qui quum se virtute, non genere, populo Romano commendari putaret, quum ipse sui generis initium ac nominis ab se gigni et propagari vellet, hominum potentissimorum suscepit inimicitias et maximis in laboribus usque ad summam senectutem summa cum gloria vixit. Postea Q. Pompeius, humili atque obscuro loco natus, nonne plurimis inimicitiis, maximisque suis periculis ac laboribus amplissimos honores est adeptus? Modo C. Fimbriam, C. Marium, C. Caelium vidimus non mediocribus inimicitiis ac laboribus contendere ut ad istos honores pervenirent, ad quos vos per ludum et per negligentiam pervenistis. Haec eadem est nostrae rationis regio et via: horum nos hominum sectam atque instituta persequimur.

LXXI. Videmus quanta sit in invidia quantoque in odio apud quosdam nobiles homines novorum hominum virtus et industria; si tantulum oculos dejecerimus, praesto esse insidias; si ullum locum aperuerimus suspicioni aut crimini, accipiendum statim vulnus esse; semper nobis vigilandum, semper laborandum videmus. Inimicitiae

difficulties which a man of mean origin had in attaining the honours of the state, the 'populi Romani beneficia,' compared with the facilities of those of noble family. Rome contained a compact and powerful aristocratic class, who, in spite of any rivalry among themselves, agreed to keep down their plebeian opponents and to secure to themselves all the high offices. So it is in every country in which such an aristocratic class exists. The members of it are thrust into places without an effort of their own; they may sleep and yawn, and still have their pockets filled with money and their pride gratified by distinction, while the laborious plebeian must work his way upwards without help and against opposition. A countryman of Cicero, C. Marius, a native of Arpinum, is represented by Sallust (Bell. Jug. c. 85, &c.) complaining in similar terms of the arrogance of the nobility, who attempted to engross all the honours of the state, and of the difficulty which the plebeian had in attaining them, whatever might be his merit: "queis nobilitas freta, ipsa dissimilis moribus, nos illorum aemulos contemnit; et omnes honores non ex merito sed quasi debitos a vobis repetit." Comp. Cic. Ad Attic. i. 2; and De leg. Agr. ii. c. 1, 2.

M. Catonis,] Cato the Censor, whom Cicero has immortalized in his treatise De Senectute. He was a native of the municipium Tusculum, and the first of his family who raised himself to the ranks of the Roman nobility.

Q. Pompeius,] Cicero proceeds to mention other Romans who raised themselves from a mean condition to the highest 'honores.' Q. Pompeius Rufus was consul B.C. 141, with Cn. Servilius Caepio. He is commemorated by Cicero as an orator of some distinction (Brutus, c. 25): "qui summos honores homo per se cognitus sine ulla commendatione majorum est adeptus."

Cicero next speaks of those whom he had seen himself. C. Flavius Fimbria, consul B.C. 104, with C. Marius, who was then consul for the fourth time. He is mentioned by Cicero (Brutus, c. 34) among the Roman orators as 'truculentus, asper, maledicus.'

This C. Caelius was C. Caelius Caldus, consul B.C. 94, the first of his family who attained this honour. He was also an orator, though of no great distinction. 'Caelius' and other words of the kind are variously written. The inferior MSS. have 'Celius.' The coins have 'Coelius' or 'Coilius.'

per ludum] Or, as Cicero elsewhere expresses it, 'quasi ludibundi.'

regio et via:] 'direction and road.' See c. 68.

71. *Inimicitiae sunt;*] It is usual to place

sunt; subeantur: labor; suscipiatur. Etenim tacitae magis et occultae inimicitiae timendae sunt quam indictae atque apertae. Hominum nobilium non fere quisquam nostrae industriae favet: nullis nostris officiis benevolentiam illorum allicere possumus: quasi natura et genere disjuncti sint, ita dissident a nobis animo et voluntate. Quare quid habent eorum inimicitiae periculi, quorum animos jam ante habueris inimicos et invidos quam ullas inimicitias susceperis? Quamobrem mihi, judices, optatum est illud, in hoc reo finem accusandi facere, quum et populo Romano satis factum et receptum officium Siculis necessariis meis erit persolutum: deliberatum est autem, si res opinionem meam quam de vobis habeo fefellerit, non modo eos persequi, ad quos maxime culpa corrupti judicii, sed etiam illos ad quos conscientiae contagio pertinebit. Proinde si qui sunt qui in hoc reo aut potentes aut audaces aut artifices ad corrumpendum judicium velint esse, ita sint parati ut disceptante populo Romano mecum sibi rem videant futuram: et, si me in hoc reo quem mihi inimicum Siculi dederunt, satis vehementem, satis perseverantem, satis vigilantem esse cognorunt, existiment in his hominibus, quorum ego inimicitias populi Romani salutis causa suscepero, multo graviorem atque acriorem futurum.

LXXII. Nunc te, Jupiter Optime Maxime, cujus iste donum regale, dignum tuo pulcherrimo templo, dignum Capitolio atque ista arce omnium nationum, dignum regio munere, tibi factum ab regibus, tibi dicatum atque promissum, per nefarium scelus de manibus regiis extorsit, cujusque sanctissimum et pulcherrimum simulacrum Syracusis sustulit: teque, Juno Regina, cujus duo fana duabus in insulis posita sociorum, Melitae et Sami, sanctissima et antiquissima, simili scelere idem iste omnibus donis ornamentisque nudavit: teque, Minerva, quam item [iste] duobus in clarissimis et religiosissimis templis expilavit, Athenis, quum auri grande pondus, Syracusis, quum omnia praeter tectum et parietes abstulit: teque, Latona et Apollo et Diana, quorum iste Deli non fanum, sed, ut

a note of interrogation after 'sunt' and 'labor;' but it is better omitted.

corrupti judicii,] The common reading is 'corrumpendi,' for which Zumpt has 'corrupti,' the reading of R 3 A Lg. 29. On 'corrumpendi' Madvig remarks: "est autem perpetua haec apud bonos scriptores ratio illius participii sive gerundivi, ut praesentis temporis sit, praeteriti vix unquam. Itaque in iis, qui judicium corruperunt, corrupti judicii culpa est, non corrumpendi."

disceptante] See Lib. 3. c. 72, as to the meaning of this word.

his] R; 'iis' L, Jordan.

72. *Nunc te,*] Cicero in this address to the gods recapitulates the sacrilegious acts of Verres, which he has already mentioned in various parts of these orations.

Juno Regina,] Zumpt refers to Livy, v. 22, 23, 31, 52, where it is said that Juno Regina was brought from Veii, and had a temple erected on the Aventine.

hominum opinio et religio fert, sedem antiquam divinumque domicilium nocturno latrocinio atque impetu compilavit: etiam te, Apollo, quem iste Chio sustulit: teque etiam atque etiam, Diana, quam Pergae spoliavit, cujus simulacrum sanctissimum Segestae bis apud Segestanos consecratum, semel ipsorum religione, iterum P. Africani victoria, tollendum asportandumque curavit: teque, Mercuri, quem Verres in domo et in privata aliqua palaestra posuit, P. Africanus in urbe sociorum et in gymnasio Tyndaritanorum juventutis illorum custodem ac praesidem voluit esse: teque, Hercules, quem iste Agrigenti nocte intempesta servorum instructa et comparata manu convellere ex suis sedibus atque auferre conatus est: teque, sanctissima mater Idaea, quam apud Enguinos augustissimo et religiosissimo templo sic spoliatam reliquit ut nunc nomen modo Africani et vestigia violatae religionis maneant, monumenta victoriae fanique ornamenta non extent: vosque, omnium rerum forensium, consiliorum maximorum, legum judiciorumque arbitri et testes, celeberrimo in loco populi Romani locati, Castor et Pollux, quorum e templo quaestum iste sibi et praedam improbissimam comparavit: omnesque dii, qui vehiculis tensarum sollemnes coetus ludorum initis, quorum iter iste ad suum quaestum, non ad religionum dignitatem, faciendum exigendumque curavit: teque, Ceres et Libera, quarum sacra, sicut opiniones hominum ac religiones ferunt, longe maximis atque occultissimis caerimoniis continentur, a quibus initia vitae atque victus, morum, legum, mansuetudinis, humanitatis hominibus et civitatibus data ac dispertita esse dicuntur; quarum sacra populus Romanus a Graecis adscita et accepta tanta religione et publice et privatim tuetur, non ut ab illis huc allata, sed ut ceteris hinc tradita esse videantur; quae ab isto uno sic polluta ac violata sunt ut simulacrum Cereris unum, quod a viro non modo tangi, sed ne aspici quidem fas fuit, e sacrario Catinae convellendum auferendumque curaverit, alterum autem Henna ex sua sede ac domo sustulerit; quod erat tale ut homines quum viderent, aut ipsam videre se Cererem, aut effigiem Cereris

Segestae bis] It is usual to place a (,) after 'Segestae,' which is a mistake. If we make a pause after 'Segestae,' it should be 'Segesta,' that is, 'Segesta . . tollendum . . curavit;' as 'Chio sustulit,' and a little further on 'Henna . . sustulerit.'

tensarum] See Lib. 1. c. 59, and Lib. 3. c. 3. In the former of these two passages the word is printed 'thensae.' R has 'thensarum' here. Zumpt says that it is 'a tendendo.' This may be so.

Catinae] dett. Or., 'Catina' Iordan. I think 'Catinae' may be right. The ablative 'Catina' can also be used, if we translate the text 'from the chapel, from Catina.' With the genitive the meaning is 'from the chapel at Catina.' But if the ablative is used, the order perhaps should be 'Catina e sacrario,' as he writes 'Henna ex sua sede,' 'from Henna, from its own place.'

non humana manu factam sed de coelo lapsam, arbitrarentur: vos etiam atque etiam imploro et appello, sanctissimae deae, quae illos Hennenses lacus lucosque incolitis, cunctaeque Siciliae, quae mihi defendenda tradita est, praesidetis; a quibus inventis frugibus et in orbem terrarum distributis omnes gentes ac nationes vestri religione numinis continentur: ceteros item deos deasque omnes imploro et obtestor, quorum templis et religionibus iste nefario quodam furore et audacia instinctus bellum sacrilegum semper impiumque habuit indictum, ut si in hoc reo atque in hac causa omnia mea consilia ad salutem sociorum, dignitatem populi Romani, fidem meam spectaverunt, si nullam ad rem nisi ad officium et virtutem omnes meae curae, vigiliae, cogitationesque elaborarunt, quae mea mens in suscipienda causa fuit, fides in agenda, eadem vestra sit in judicanda; deinde uti C. Verrem, si ejus omnia sunt inaudita et singularia facinora sceleris, audaciae, perfidiae, libidinis, avaritiae, crudelitatis, dignus exitus ejusmodi vita atque factis vestro judicio consequatur, utique res publica meaque fides una hac accusatione mea contenta sit, mihique posthac bonos potius defendere liceat quam improbos accusare necesse sit.

de coelo &c.] 'De coelo delapsam,' the common reading and Orelli.—'lucosque colitis:' Orelli, following Garatoni, who remarks that 'colere' is the ordinary word in such a case; and this appears to be so. But R 3 λ have 'incolitis.'

continentur: ceteros] Zumpt points it 'continentur. Ceteros' &c.; but, as Orelli remarks, this is a continuation of the long sentence which begins 'Nunc te, Jupiter,' &c.

VIII.

On Lib. 5. c. 54.

Halm has an Excursus on the words 'vadimonium promittere—sponsionem facere.' The Excursus was communicated to him by Professor Theodor Mommsen.

After explaining what the Vadimonium was, and that in ordinary cases 'is qui vadatur' and 'is qui agit' (the plaintiff) are the same person, Mommsen says that in this passage the case was manifestly different. If the 'sponsio' was merely the regular commencement of the 'actio,' notice of which was given at the time of the 'vadimonium,' Cicero could not possibly have said 'quum ageret nemo;' and the identity of the 'Venerius servus' and of the lictor with whom C. Servilius was required to make a 'sponsio,' is more than doubtful. Accordingly it appears that Verres set up a pretended claim of the temple of Venus at Eryx, which was within the conventus of Lilybaeum, and commanded Servilius to make a 'vadimonium' to appear at that place. Servilius appeared, but the suit of which notice had been given had no foundation and could not be prosecuted; and, as was always the case, when the defendant appeared and the plaintiff did not appear, the plaintiff lost his cause. In this case the plaintiff did not appear; but Verres devised a new plaint, at least a new plaint in form, for it is most probable that an alleged illegal act with respect to the property of the temple was the foundation both of the first 'vadimonium' and of the 'sponsio,' which the lictor proposed to Servilius. The 'Venerius servus' had evidently served the purpose of furnishing some reason for bringing Servilius from the 'conventus Panhormitanus' before the court of another 'conventus.' For as the temple of Venus Erycina made a demand, it would appear equitable to summon Servilius to the 'conventus' in which Eryx was included, to Lilybaeum.

Mommsen then explains what a 'sponsio' was; and continues thus. The 'vadimonium' is given up; C. Servilius, against whom there is neither a civil action nor a criminal charge, is entirely free. Then a lictor of Verres comes forward and challenges Servilius to the suit, undertaking to prove to him that he, Servilius, was enriching himself by means of 'furtum,' that is, by knavery and fraudulent means (probably

in matters relating to the property of the temple especially). Servilius refuses to accept the 'sponsio,' because there was no proper legal compulsion; because he, the great merchant of Panhormus, was required to submit to the decision of 'judices,' not of his own 'conventus,' and also partial 'judices;' because the loss of the suit, though it would bind him only directly to the payment of a small sum of money, would still be ruinous to him, for if he was 'convictus furti,' he would thereby become 'infamis' and lose his chief civil rights. However, Verres compelled Servilius to make the 'sponsio.' The rest of Mommsen's Excursus is immaterial for the present purpose.

The whole story of this affair, as Cicero tells it, is contained in the few words 'Locutus erat . . . constitueretur.' Servilius had spoken freely about the knavery of Verres, who hears of what Servilius had said and compels him to give the usual security (vadimonium promittere) to a 'Venerius servus.' Servilius promises the 'vadimonium,' and he goes to Lilybaeum conformably to his 'vadimonium.' Now Servilius could not promise a 'vadimonium' without having been already summoned 'in jus,' and being made acquainted with the action which the plaintiff intended to bring (Lib. 3. c. 15, and the note on 'vadimonium'); unless Verres, whose conduct all through this affair was illegal, compelled Servilius to promise the 'vadimonium' in an irregular way, without the previous legal forms. If Cicero's stories about Verres are true, he would have done any thing, and scarcely sought to cover his iniquities with the forms of law. Cicero also says that Servilius promised a 'vadimonium' to a slave, but we know that a slave could not be a plaintiff or defendant in an action. Besides this, we know from Cicero (Lib. 2. c. 8) that it was the office of the quaestor of Lilybaeum to sue for any thing that was due to the temple of Eryx. Verres on a former occasion refused to let the quaestor sue, and he employed Naevius Turpio, one of his tools, to sue on behalf of the temple. But Turpio was a Roman. Accordingly we are stopped by an insuperable difficulty in the beginning of the story.

As soon as Servilius came to Lilybaeum, Verres urged him to make a 'sponsio' with one of his lictors. We do not know who the lictor was, but it is certain that he was not a 'Venerius servus,' because only Roman citizens could use the formal words 'Dari spondes,' and 'spondeo' (Gaius, iii. 93); unless to make the same remark again, Verres behaved as illegally in the matter of the 'sponsio' as he had done in the matter of the 'vadimonium.' If he did, the lictor might be the 'Venerius servus,' to whom the 'vadimonium' had been promised, or he might be any other slave, or any body whom Verres pleased to name.

Though a slave could not be a plaintiff, Cicero says that Servilius made a 'vadimonium' to a slave, and came to Lilybaeum pursuant

to his engagement. When he came, there was no plaintiff (quum ageret nemo), not even the fellow to whom Servilius had given 'vadimonium.' The only way to understand the story is to take Cicero's statements, and to add nothing to them. There was no 'actor' or plaintiff, we are told, when Servilius came to Lilybaeum, and yet Verres forced Servilius to make a 'sponsio' with one of his lictors, as if the matter of the action was already known, and as if the lictor was the man who had commenced the action. Or the case was this, Verres finding that he had Servilius in his hands, simply at once ordered him to make a 'sponsio' with his lictor about a charge of 'furtum,' without any preliminary proceedings, and without any respect to the matter of the 'vadimonium.' It makes no matter which way it was. Either way the act of Verres was irregular. Servilius refused to make the 'sponsio' on the ground that there was no 'adversarius,' no plaintiff in the action in respect of which he had given the 'vadimonium:' and that was true for two reasons, first, because a 'Venerius servus' could not maintain an action against any body, and second, because he had failed to make his appearance, as we must assume, if Servilius on reaching Lilybaeum found no plaintiff there. Verres' next step was to order his lictors to beat Servilius till he cried out 'spondeo.' This proceeding was just as legal or as illegal as all the rest. Servilius died soon after, and Verres, I suppose, took his property, or some of it.

Can any thing be plainer than this, that the whole proceeding from the beginning to the end, which was the murder of Servilius, had not even a show of legal procedure in it, though some legal terms and forms were used? The 'praetor' contrived to bring Servilius to Lilybaeum as a defendant in an impossible suit, and there he murdered him.

If Cicero has told us all the facts, there is no other explanation than this which I give. If he has not told all, it is useless to attempt to find out what he has not told us, and to give something of a legal character to a transaction which was altogether contrary to law and not conformable even to the simplest legal principles.

After this I need hardly remark that Mommsen's explanation is of no value. It is faulty both in respect to what it contains and in respect to what it omits.

IX.

SICILY.

Plinius, Nat. Hist. Lib. iii. c. 8, ed. Harduin.

Verum ante omnes claritate Sicilia, Sicania Thucydidi dicta, Trinacria pluribus, aut Triquetra a triangula specie: circuitu patens, ut auctor est Agrippa, DCXVIII. M. pass. quondam Brutio agro cohaerens, mox interfuso mari avulsa XV. M. in longitudinem freto, in latitudinem autem M. D. pass. juxta columnam Rhegiam. Ab hoc dehiscendi argumento Rhegium Graeci nomen dedere oppido in margine Italiae sito. In eo freto est scopulus Scylla; item Charybdis mare vorticosum: ambo clara saevitia. Ipsius Triquetrae, ut diximus, promontorium Pelorus vocatur adversus Scyllam vergens in Italiam: Pachynum in Graeciam, CCCCXL. M. ab eo distante Peloponneso: Lilybaeum in Africam CLXXX. M. intervallo a Mercurii promontorio: et a Caralitano Sardiniae CXC. M. Inter se autem haec promontoria ac latera distant his spatiis. Terreno itinere a Peloro Pachynum CLXXXXI. M. pass. Inde Lilybaeum, CC. M., inde Pelorum, CLXX. Coloniae ibi quinque: urbes ac civitates LXIII. A Peloro mare Ionium ora spectante, oppidum Messana civium Romanorum, qui Mamertini vocantur. Promontorium Drepanum: colonia Tauromenium, quae antea Naxos, flumen Asines: mons Aetna nocturnis mirus incendiis. Crater ejus patet ambitu stad. XX. Favilla Tauromenium et Catinam usque pervenit fervens: fragor vero ad Maronem et Gemellos colles. Scopuli tres Cyclopum, portus Ulyssis, colonia Catina. Flumina: Symaethum, Terias. Intus Laestrygonii campi. Oppida: Leontini, Megaris: amnis Pantagies. Colonia Syracusae cum fonte Arethusa. Quamquam et Temenitis et Archidemia et Magaea et Cyane et Milichie fontes in Syracusano potantur agro. Portus Naustathmus, flumen Elorum, promontorium Pachynum: a qua fronte Siciliae flumen Hirminium, oppidum Camarina, fluvius Gelas, oppidum Acragas, quod Agrigentum nostri dixere. Thermae colonia: amnes Achates, Mazara, Hypsa. Selinus oppidum. Lilybaeum ab eo promontorium, Drepana, mons Eryx. Oppida: Panhormum, Solus, Himera cum fluvio, Cephaloedis, Aluntium, Agathyrnum, Tyndaris colonia, oppidum Mylae, et unde coepimus Pelorus.

Intus, Latinae conditionis Centuripini, Netini, Segestani. Stipendiarii Assorini, Aetnenses, Agyrini, Acestaei, Acrenses, Bidini, Cetarini,

Cacyrini, Drepanitani, Ergetini, Echetlienses, Erycini, Entellini, Etini, Enguini, Gelani, Galatini, Halesini, Hennenses, Hyblenses, Herbitenses, Herbessenses, Herbulenses, Halicyenses, Hadranitani, Imacarenses, Ichanenses, Ietenses, Mutustratini, Magellini, Murgentini, Mutycenses, Menanini, Naxii, Noaeni, Petrini, Paropini, Phtinthienses, Semellitani, Scherini, Selinuntii, Symaethii, Talarenses, Tissinenses, Triocalini, Tiracienses, Zanclaei Messeniorum in Siculo Freto.

Coloniae] The five coloniae are Tauromenium, Catina, Syracusae, Thermae, and Tyndaris. Diodorus says that there were sixty-eight cities in Sicily, which number agrees with that of the five colonies and sixty-three cities in this text of Pliny. P. Manutius (Lib. 3. c. 50, note) says that there were seventy-two cities in Sicily, according to Pliny. I suppose that he found this number in his text of Pliny.

Messana] It was made a colonia of Roman citizens after Cicero's time, but the date of the establishment is not known. It is stated that the coins struck under Augustus have the legend 'Messenion' in Roman characters, which indicates that the people were then Cives Romani.

Tauromenium] Naxos, the first Greek settlement in the island (Thucyd. vi. 3), was destroyed before Cicero's time, and Tauromenium was built near the site of Naxos (Diodor. xvi. 7). It was made a Roman colony by Augustus, as it seems.

Asines] Harduin in his note assumes this to be the Assinarus of Thucydides (vii. 84), which is a mistake. The Asines, or whatever its true name may be, is placed by Pliny near Tauromenium; but the Assinarus was south of Syracuse. This Asines appears to be the Acesines of Thucydides (iv. 25), and apparently the same that Appian (Bell. Civ. v. 109) calls Onobalas.

Catina] This is said to be the reading of all the MSS. The Greek name is always Κατάνη, of which the Romans made Catina, as they made Massilia of Μασσαλία. The Roman colony sent to Catina is mentioned by Strabo (p. 268, ed. Cas.).

Leontini] This town was in the rich corn country north of Syracuse. In Cicero's time it was a poor place.

Megaris] The genuine name appears to be Megara, a town near the coast between the Terias and the Anapus. This Megara (Steph. Byz. v. Μέγαρα) was originally named Hybla. There were three cities in Sicily named Hybla. This was the Little Hybla, as Stephanus (v. Ὕβλα) calls it, and he names the people Ὑβλαῖοι Γαλεῶται Μεγαρεῖς.

Syracusae] This place received a Roman colony in the time of Augustus, as we learn from Strabo (p. 270) and Dion Cassius (Lib. 54. c. 7).

Elorum] This word was probably written both without the aspirate and with it, like Enna and Henna. Pliny mentions only the river, but there was a town Helorum or Helorus on the river.

Camarina] This town is not mentioned by Cicero. It was decayed long before his time. When Pliny and Ptolemy speak of it, they cannot mean more than to say that there was once a town on the site.

Gelas] The name occurs on an old coin <ΕΛΑΣ, which bears a human head bearded attached to the fore part of a bull. Gela was founded by Rhodian and Cretan colonists (Thucyd. vi. 4).

Thermae] Thermae Selinuntiae. This place was the hot springs, near the coast, between Heraclea and Selinus, and now called Sciacca. It has been suggested that Pliny has made a mistake in calling this Thermae a colonia, and that he should have named Himera on the north coast, which was a colonia.

Selinus] An old Greek coin has the legend ΣΕΛΙΝΟΣ, which is equivalent to Σελινοῦς.

Panhormum] So it stands in Harduin's text, with the 'h.' This, of course, was the Roman mode of writing. The Greek coins have the legend ΠΑΝΟΡΜΙΤΑΝ.

Solus] This word is in form like Selinus, and as the Romans said Hydruntum for Hydrus, so they sometimes said Soluntum.

Himera] This is the city and river mentioned by Cicero, Lib. 2. c. 35. There is a coin with the legend HIMERA, in Roman characters, for the R appears plain. The face, on which the legend is, contains the figure of a cock.

Cephaloedis] There is a Greek coin, apparently of this place, with ΚΕΦ or ΚΕΦΑ legible on it.

Aluntium] A Greek coin, of which I have a cast, has the name ΑΛΟΝΤΙΝ so far legible. Perhaps Haluntium was also the Roman fashion of writing this name.

Tyndaris] It is not known when Tyndaris became a colonia. There is a Greek coin of Tyndaris with the head of a horse on one of the faces.

Latinae conditionis] Pliny mentions Centuripa or Centuripae, Netum, and Segesta, as 'Latinae conditionis,' that is, as possessing the Jus Latinum or Jus Latium, which denoted a condition intermediate between that of Cives Romani and Peregrini. The nature of this political condition is explained by Savigny (Entstehung der Latinität, Vermischte Schriften, vol. i.). But Cicero (Ad Att. xiv. 12) states that the Jus Latium, or, as he terms it, Latinitas, was given to all the Sicilians by the Dictator Caesar. Cicero's words are 'Multa illis Caesar neque me invito, etsi Latinitas erat non ferenda;' the conclusion from which, I think, ought to be that Sicily did receive the Latinitas from Caesar. If then Pliny means to limit the Latinitas to these three towns, his statement is unintelligible. Cicero further remarks, that after Caesar's death M. Antonius set up (fixit) a Lex, as passed in Caesar's lifetime, which gave the Roman civitas to the Sicilians; but his words imply that it was a forgery. However, Diodorus (xiii. 35) speaks of all the Sicilians being made Roman citizens, for such is the meaning of his words: πάντες οἱ Σικελιῶται τῆς Ῥωμαίων πολιτείας ἠξιώθησαν. How all this is to be reconciled, I don't see.

Centuripini] The legend on the Greek coins is ΚΕΝΤΟΡΙΠΙΝΩΝ. Though the Greek name of Segesta is Ἔγεστα, the Greek coins have also ΣΕΓΕΣΤΑ.

Stipendiarii] The meaning of this term in Cicero has been explained. Its meaning in Pliny may be the same; but the condition of being Stipendiarii is inconsistent with having the Roman civitas. Further, if all these states had become Stipendiarii, their condition had been changed since Cicero's time (Lib. 3. c. 6, note).

Assorini] Harduin says that the legend on the coins of Assorus (apud Parutam) is ΑΣΟΡΥ. ΧΡΥΣΑΣ. The coin that I have already referred to has the Roman legend ASSORV and CRYSAS.

Agyrini] The Agyrinenses of Cicero (Lib. 3. c. 52). Pliny uses a Greek form. The coins appear to have ΑΓΥΡΙΝΑΙΩΝ.

Acestaei] The Acestenses of the present text of Cicero (Lib. 3. c. 36).

Acrenses] They are not mentioned by Cicero. Their town was Acrae, on a lofty hill about twenty miles west of Syracuse. It is now Acremonte, near Palazzolo. There is a description of the place in the Museum of Classical Antiquities by John Hogg.

Cetarini] See Cicero, Lib. 3. c. 43.

Cacyrini] The name Cacyrum appears in Ptolemaeus also; and no where else.

Ergetini] The name Ergetium occurs in Stephanus, and he gives Ergetini as the Ethnic name. The name also occurs in Ptolemy with the aspirate, Sergentium, a common variation in the names of these Sicilian towns.

Echetlienses] Echetla is mentioned by Polybius (i. 15) and by Diodorus (xx. 32).

Etini] 'MSS. Edini' (Harduin). He does not say why he does not follow the MSS.

Gelani] This Ethnic name does not agree either with Cicero's form Gelenses, nor with the Greek form Geloi. But Gelani may be a corrupted word.

Galatini] Supposed by Harduin to be the same as the Calactini of Cicero (Lib. 3. c. 43), in which he may be right. The Ethnic name Calactini occurs also in Diodorus (xii. 29).

Halesini] This is another of the words which was probably written both with the aspirate and without.

Hennenses] I have before remarked on the forms Enna and Henna. The Greeks seem to have sometimes prefixed the mark of aspiration, for an ancient coin of Henna has the legend HENNAION.

Herbulenses] The same probably as the Arbelaei of Stephanus (v. 'Αρβέλη).

Hadranitani] The coins are said to have AΔPANITAN without the aspirate, and so it appears to be on the cast of a Sicilian coin which I have, but the legend is hardly legible.

Ichanenses] The name occurs in Stephanus (v. Ἴχανα), who gives the Ethnic name Ἰχανῖνος.

Ietenses] The name of the place occurs in Stephanus (v. Ἰεταί), who gives the Ethnic name Ἰεταῖος. The Ethnic name is IAITIN on a Greek coin. The remainder of the word, which is not legible on the specimen that I have, is probably ΩN. The reading Ietini appears then to be rightly restored in Cicero (Lib. 3. c. 43).

Mutustratini] This may be the Amestratus of Stephanus and of Cicero (Lib. 3. c. 39, and the note; also c. 43). A Greek coin has the first part of the legend AM quite clear; the rest not so legible. In a passage in the Excerpta of Diodorus (Lib. 23) the name is written Mustratus, which is still nearer to Amestratus.

Magellini] The name of the place is Μάκελλα in Polybius (i. 24) and elsewhere.

Murgentini] The Greek orthography appears to be Morgantini. Harduin says 'in nummis MOPΓAN.' A Greek coin has the legend MOPΓANTINA very legible, and on the face of the coin an ear of corn, probably to denote that it was a wheat-growing place.

Mutycenses] The people of Motyca or Mutyca, now Modica, as Harduin rightly says. See Cicero, Lib. 3. c. 43, 51. All the MSS. of Pliny are said to have Mutycenses. There seems to be no doubt that Mutyca is meant by Cicero (Lib. 3. c. 43, 51), and not Motya. There is a Greek coin of Motya, with the legend MOTTAION and the figure of a greyhound on it.

Menanini] 'In nummis apud Parutam MENANINΩN and MHNANINΩN' (Harduin). If this is so, the place was called Menanum or Μέναινον, as in Diod. xi. 78. The Ethnic name in Cicero (Lib. 3. c. 22, 43) is Menaeni, and so it is on a Greek coin legibly MENAINΩN.

Naxii] Naxos was destroyed by Dionysius B.C. 403. In B.C. 358 the scattered inhabitants were collected by Andromachus, and settled on the neighbouring site of Tauromenium (Diodorus, xiv. 15; xvi. 7). Pliny has already mentioned Tauromenium as a colonia, and has incorrectly said that it was originally Naxos; but it was a different place. Here he speaks of the Naxii as a political community at the time when he wrote, and as 'stipendiarii,' though they no longer existed.

Noaeni] Νέαι is mentioned by Stephanus, who makes the Ethnic name Νεαῖος.

Paropini] Paropus (Πάρωπος) is mentioned by Polybius (i. 24) as in the neighbourhood of Thermae; and probably it was between Thermae and Panhormus.

Phthinthienses] Phintia is meant, or Phintias, as Diodorus calls it, near the mouth of the southern Himera. It was founded by Phintias, tyrant of Agrigentum (Diod. xxii. Exc.). There is a Greek coin with the legend BAΣIΛEOΣ ΦINTIA, and the figure of a wild boar running. On the other face is a fine head.

Semellitani] Probably a corrupt name. I can find nothing about it.

Scherini] Schera is also mentioned by Ptolemaeus. The name Acherini in Cicero (Lib. 3. c. 43), though the reading of all the MSS. except one, may be doubted. Probably it should be Scherini.

Symaethii] There was a river Symaethus, but no town of the name is mentioned by any ancient writer, so far as I know.

Talarenses] Stephanus mentions Talaria as a Sicilian city, and the Ethnic name Talarini.

Tissinenses] As the name is Tissa or Tissae, Tissinenses is incorrect, and the true Roman name is Tissenses, as in Cicero. Stephanus calls it χωρίον, which agrees with Cicero's 'perparva et tenuis civitas' (Lib. 3. c. 38).

Triocalini] Tricalini in Stephanus. Cicero (Lib. 5. c. 4) has the same form as Pliny.

Tiracienses] Stephanus gives the name Τυρακῖνοι, and Diodorus (xii. 29) Τρινακία. Harduin says that the MSS. of Pliny have the reading Triracinses.

Zanclaei] Here Pliny mentions Zanclaei Messeniorum as Stipendiarii, and a person might suppose that a different city is meant from that which he has already called Messana, and 'oppidum civium Romanorum.' So much carelessness and inaccuracy may be perhaps charged on our present text, rather than on the compiler. If the text is right, it is difficult to say what Pliny means by the 'Zanclaei Messeniorum in Siculo Freto,' for this is an appropriate description of the position of Messana, which he has already mentioned.

Neither Cicero nor Pliny mentions all the places in Sicily; nor do the texts of these two authors agree entirely. This is not the place for a memoir on the ancient geography of Sicily, nor have I the materials for it. The extract from Pliny, and the remarks on it, may not be altogether useless for the illustration of the text of Cicero. Those who seek information on the architectural remains of Sicily, and the medals of the towns, some of them among the best specimens of Grecian art, will have no difficulty in finding further illustration of some parts of these orations in various works which have been specially devoted to the ancient monuments of Sicily.

The following is Zumpt's classification of the Sicilian towns, including the island Lipara:—

Civitates Foederatae.—Messana, Netum, Tauromenium.

Immunes ac Liberae.—Centuripae, Halesa, Halicyae, Panhormus, Segesta.

Decumanae.—Abacaenum, Aetna, Agathyrnum, Agyrium, Amestratus, Apollonia, Assorus, Bidis, Calacte, Capitium, Catina, Cephaloedium, Cetaria, Enguium, Entella, Gela, Hadranum, Haluntium, Helorus, Henna, Heraclea, Herbessus, Herbita, Hybla, Hyccara, Ietae, Imachara, Ina, Leontini, Lipara, Menae, Murgentia, Mutyca, Mylae, Petra, Schera, Solus or Soluntum, Syracusae, Thermae, Thermae Selinuntiae, Tissa, Tyndaris.

Censoriae.—Acrae, Agrigentum, Camarina, Drepanum, Hybla Heraea, Lilybaeum, Macella, Mazara, Megaris, Motya, Phintia, Selinus, Triocala.

This list is drawn up from the names on the small map attached to Zumpt's edition. On this map he has indicated by marks the cities which belong to the four several classes above mentioned. The map in this volume may be of some little use to refer to in reading these orations. It has no other pretensions.

X.

SICILY A ROMAN PROVINCE.

I SHALL here attempt to explain briefly the condition of Sicily as a Roman province in the time of Cicero.

Hiero II., king of Syracuse, the friend and the ally of the Romans, died about B.C. 216, leaving that part of the island which was under his government well organized in its civil administration. He was succeeded by a youth, his grandson Hieronymus, who deserted the Roman for the Carthaginian alliance. Hieronymus was murdered in B C. 215, and in the next year the Roman senate sent the consul M. Claudius Marcellus to Sicily, who laid siege to Syracuse, and took the city B.C. 212. Marcellus remained in Sicily until the following year; and though he did not terminate the war in the island, he did something towards the settlement of affairs. Scipio Africanus was in Sicily as consul B.C. 205, and as proconsul in B.C. 204; and it appears from Cicero that he had time to do something towards settling the island. He regulated for the Agrigentini the mode of filling up vacancies in their senate (Lib. 2. c. 50), as Rupilius afterwards did for Heraclia. Cicero speaks of these 'leges' of Scipio as 'antiquae;' and it appears from the chapter referred to, that he means the elder Africanus. He informs us in another place (Lib. 2. c. 2; Lib. 4. c. 33, &c.) that P. Africanus (the younger), after the destruction of Carthage B.C. 146, was in Sicily, and that he restored to the Sicilians all the works of art which the Carthaginians had carried off, and which fell into the hands of the Romans on the capture of Carthage. Though Sicily had for some time been a Roman province, the administration does not appear to have been finally settled until B.C. 131, when the proconsul P. Rupilius, after suppressing the revolt of the slaves, and with the assistance of ten commissioners appointed by the senate, made those regulations which subsisted at the time when Cicero delivered his orations against Verres (Lib. 2. c. 13). The regulations of Rupilius were called the Lex Rupilia.

The condition of Sicily and of its towns under the Roman government was not uniform, but the difference had mainly, though not entirely, reference to taxation. The Sicilian towns had a senate, and a commonalty or body of citizens, who had still some power; for Cicero,

speaking of the order made by the Centuripini (Lib. 2. c. 67) for the demolition of the statues of Verres, says "Centuripinorum senatus decrevit populusque jussit." But even in Cicero's time it appears that the Sicilian towns applied to the Roman senate about their internal administration, if a great difficulty arose. In B.C. 95 the Halesini could not agree among themselves about the mode of filling up vacancies in their senate, and they addressed themselves to the senate at Rome. The senate empowered C. Claudius Pulcher to draw up for them a code of rules (leges dare, conscribere) as to the qualifications and the election of senators, which he did with the assistance of all the Marcelli, whom he invited to aid him in this matter (Lib. 2. c. 49). The Romans did not touch the constitution of the Sicilian towns, or, if they did make any alterations, such a practice was the exception and not the rule. The Sicilian towns retained their senate, their chief magistrate, one or more, the various public functionaries, and their priestly offices. The temples retained their property, as we see in the case of Eryx; and the high priesthood of the temple of Jupiter at Syracuse (Lib. 2. c. 51), an honourable, and probably a lucrative office, gave the citizens annually the excitement of an election, like the Roman 'comitia' (Lib. 2. c. 51, 52). Many of these Sicilian temples had large possessions, which were increased by the gifts of pious persons. They could also take gifts by testament, either directly or by virtue of a resolutive condition (Lib. 2. c. 8), or a penalty. Several of the rich temples of Sicily are mentioned by Cicero.

In addition to the property which some at least of the Sicilian towns possessed, they must have required taxes to defray the expenses of the local administration. These taxes (tributa) were levied upon the rated value of property, and the assessment was made every fifth year. Each 'civitas' elected two 'censores' by popular vote, and the office, which we should consider somewhat an invidious one, was an object of great competition 'propter magnitudinem potestatis,' as Cicero says (Lib. 2. c. 53): but there was probably some pecuniary advantage derived from it, indirectly perhaps, or we can hardly understand why the candidates paid money to Verres for the office, when he illegally interfered in the elections. On this occasion at least, according to the orator, the censors abused the office which they had scandalously got; for they made an unfair rating, and threw the burden on the poorer sort. The number of 'civitates' which had censors during the administration of Verres was sixty-five, for the whole number of censors appointed by Verres was a hundred and thirty. The towns could also take property under a testament. The legal notion of an artificial person, as these town communities were for the purpose of holding property, which is indeed the only purpose for which this fiction exists, was fully developed in Sicily,

as it was in the legal system of the Romans, and as it is in modern Europe.

The Lex Rupilia (Lib. 2. c. 13) made regulations for the constitution of the courts by which civil questions were to be tried. In the system of Greek colonization every city had its own constitution and laws: each was a perfect, independent community. The Greek towns of Sicily, which were of various origin, had a great diversity of customs, and most of these customs were retained under Roman dominion. Thus Cicero remarks of the Thermitani (Lib. 2. c. 37), that in consideration of their fidelity to the Romans, the senate and the Roman people restored to them their city, lands, and laws (leges). This favour was probably granted on the conquest of the island, and confirmed by the Lex Rupilia. Sthenius of Thermae was charged with falsifying the public records (de literis publicis corruptis), which was a criminal offence; and yet even in this case he maintained that the Roman praetor had no authority, and he claimed to be tried by the law of his own city. The 'procuratores' of Epicrates of Bidis, a small town, in the case of his title to a succession (hereditas) being disputed by the 'palaestritae' of Bidis, claimed to have the matter tried according to their own law (leges suae), or at any rate according to the Lex Rupilia. Cicero (Lib. 2. c. 13) has explained the general rules applicable to suits between Sicilians, and between Sicilians and Romans. He says that between two Sicilians of the same 'civitas' the matter was decided according to the law of the place; and a citizen of the place was 'judex' (Lib. 2. c. 27). If the parties to the suit were of different states, the praetor appointed (sortitus est) 'judices' pursuant to the Lex Rupilia. Cicero does not say more of this matter than his purpose required. The Lex Rupilia, as he informs us, fixed the constitution of the court which was to try a matter between citizens of different states; and it probably also contained some regulations as to the rules of law applicable to such cases; for as these states had their several laws, it would be necessary to determine in some general way at least what rules of law should prevail when there was a conflict between those of different states. Other cases, which are provided for, are mentioned by Cicero (Lib. 2. c. 13). All disputes between the 'aratores' or cultivators and the 'decumani' or Publicani, who farmed the 'decumae,' were to be settled according to the regulations of King Hiero II. (Lex Hieronica.)

For the purposes of administration Sicily was divided into 'conventus' or districts, so called from the people of a given district meeting at a fixed place for the purpose of having their suits heard and determined, and for the transaction of other business which required the authority of the praetor. Sicily appears to have been divided into four 'conventus' at least (Lib. 2. c. 30; Lib. 5. c. 11), those of Syracuse, Lilybaeum, Pan-

hormus, and Agrigentum. Pliny's remarks on the 'conventus' of the Spanish Peninsula (Lib. 3. c. 1) will explain this. Hispania Baetica was divided into four 'juridici conventus,' or circuits for the administration of justice. The province of Citerior Hispania was divided into seven 'conventus.' In speaking of the 'conventus Carthaginiensis,' Pliny uses the expression 'Carthaginem conveniunt populi LXV:' and in another place he speaks of certain Celtici as belonging to the 'Hispalensis conventus,' or circuit of Seville; and of the Turduli as those 'qui jura Cordubam petunt:' all which are only different modes of expressing the same thing. The governor made his circuits through the island, and he probably visited not only the chief place in each 'conventus,' but other towns also (Lib. 2. c. 70). Among the Comites, or those who formed the body of functionaries attached to the praetor, 'praefecti' are mentioned (Lib. 2. c. 10); and the 'praefecti' appear to have been employed in the administration of justice (Lib. 3. c. 32, and the note on 'praefecti nomine').

There were two quaestors for the island, one for the western part, or the district of Lilybaeum ('is qui Erycum montem obtinebat:' Lib. 2. c. 8); and one for the eastern division, or that of Syracuse. The functions of the quaestors were the same in Sicily as in other provinces. It is stated in one passage (Lib. 2. c. 8) that it was the practice of the quaestor of Lilybaeum to sue for any thing that became due to the temple of Eryx. (See also Divin. c. 17.)

Cicero's statement is, that the Sicilian towns (Lib. 3. c. 6) were subject to Rome on the same terms on which they had been governed before the island became a province. The statement may be correct so far as concerns the towns which were under Hiero's government, but it is rather deficient in precision, if we apply his language to all the towns of the island, for Hiero's kingdom comprised only a part of Sicily. However, as a general remark, the statement is intelligible enough. Seventeen cities are mentioned (Lib. 5. c. 47) as having been faithful to the Romans in all the Punic and Sicilian wars. One of these was Tyndaris, which however is not mentioned among either the Civitates Foederatae or the Immunes ac Liberae. The number of Sicilian cities, says Cicero, which were subdued by the Romans, was very small (Lib. 3. c. 6). The lands of these cities became the property of the Roman people by conquest; but the lands were restored, subject to the payment of certain dues, which dues were let to farm by the censors at Rome (censoria locatio[1]). These are the Censoriae Civitates of Zumpt's list, which is printed at the end of Excursus IX.; but I do not vouch for the accuracy of the list. None of the cities of Sicily paid a fixed land-

[1] This matter is examined in the note on Lib. 3. c. 6, 'ager . . publicus populi Romani.'

tax (vectigal stipendiarium), as was the case in Spain and with most of the Punic towns. Their payment was a variable duty, a tenth or other quota of produce. Three cities, Messana, Tauromenium, and Netum, had a Foedus with Rome, the effect of which is described by Cicero, when he is speaking of the Tauromenitani, in these words (Lib. 2. c. 66), "qui maxime ab injuriis nostrorum magistratuum remoti consuerant esse praesidio foederis." The terms of these 'foedera' were not the same; for the Tauromenitani were excused from supplying a ship of war for the defence of Sicily, and the Mamertini (Messenii) were bound by their Foedus to supply one (Lib. 5. c. 19; Lib. 4. c. 9). Verres is charged by Cicero with releasing the Mamertini from their obligation to supply and equip a vessel, and with requiring a vessel from the Tauromenitani. The 'decumae' of these foederate towns were not let, or sold, as Cicero expresses it; in other words, they paid no taxes (vectigal) to the Romans. Five towns, Centuripa, Halesa, Segesta, Halicyae, and Panhormus, were 'liberae ac immunes' (Lib. 3. c. 6). They paid no 'decumae.' In reply to the supposed argument of the advocates of Verres, that the 'aratores' were his enemies on account of the 'decumae,' Cicero says (Lib. 3. c. 69), "Well, those who cultivate lands which are 'immunes liberique,' why should they be your enemies? why should the Halesini, why the Centuripini, why the Segestani, why the Halicyenses?" A passage in Lib. 3. c. 40, appears to create a difficulty: "quid Halicyenses, quorum incolae decumas dant, ipsi agros immunes habent;" Cicero then mentions that the 'decumae' of Halicyae were sold to Turpio at 'C. Med.' The passage is explained by ascertaining the meaning of 'incolae,' which signifies persons domiciliated at Halicyae, not 'cives' of Halicyae. 'Quorum incolae' means those persons, not citizens of Halicyae, who were domiciliated at Halicyae, and cultivated lands in Halicyae[1]. These lands were only tax-free when cultivated by 'cives.' One Diocles of Panhormus (Lib. 3. c. 40) was the lessee of lands in the territory of Segesta, for no person except a citizen could own land in this territory. Diocles was therefore obliged to hire it; and if he made Segesta his usual residence, he was an 'incola;' and it appears that he paid 'decumae' for the lands which he farmed in the territory of Segesta. (See also Lib. 3. c. 23, note.) All the rest of the cities of Sicily, except the three classes which have been mentioned, paid 'decumae,' or tenths, in respect of their lands; and all the land that was liable to payments to the Roman state was included under the general name of 'agri vectigales.' The 'decumae' were let pub-

[1] See Lib. 3. c. 40, and the note on Halicyenses. As to 'incolae' see Cod. Just. 10. 39. 7; Dig. 50. 16. 239; and Savigny, System des Heut. Röm. Rechts, Vol. viii. Origo und Domicilium. 'Incolae' are persons domiciliated in a community of which they are not 'cives.' See Lib. 4. c. 11, 'incolis vestris civibus Romanis.'

licly in Sicily, or, according to the more common Roman expression, were sold, at a fixed period, and pursuant to the terms of the Lex Hieronica, which terms were so carefully drawn up, that the cultivator (arator) could not defraud the farmer of the 'decumae' (decumanus), nor could the 'decumanus' get more than his due (Lib. 3. c. 8). These 'decumae' were generally let to the Roman Publicani, but sometimes a 'civitas' would bid for the 'decumae' of its district. Cicero (Lib. 3. c. 42) mentions an instance of the Thermitani bidding for their 'decumae.' These 'decumae' consisted of a tenth of wheat and barley, the only two kinds of grain which Cicero mentions; and it seems that sometimes at least the tenths of wheat and barley were let separately (Lib. 3. c. 34). The 'decumae' also comprised the 'fruges minutae,' pulse and the like, and oil and wine (Lib. 3. c. 7, and c. 71, note).

The price at which the 'decumae' were sold was not estimated in money, but by quantity (Lib. 3. c. 47, &c.). The probable amount of the 'decumae' was estimated upon the 'professio' or declaration by the cultivators of the quantity of land which they cultivated (Lib. 3. c. 22. 47. 49). It seems that the inhabitants of a district were required to deliver their 'decumae' at the chief place of the district, and it was an irregular thing for Verres to require them to be delivered at another place (Lib. 3. c. 43). The order of Verres, that the 'aratores' should carry their corn down to the coast, where it could be embarked from Rome, only applied to the 'alterae decumae,' or it was at least an irregular order (Lib. 3. c. 14, note on 'ad aquam'). Dureau de la Malle (ii. 427) concludes from this passage that the cultivators were obliged to carry their 'decumae' to the coast; but this conclusion is not necessary, and it is contradicted by another passage (Lib. 3. c. 43). He says in another place (ii. 353), that "the lands which enjoyed immunity were compelled to sell and to take every year to Rome, and at their own cost, 800,000 modii of wheat, the price of which was four sestertii the modius." But there is no authority for asserting that they were required to take the wheat to Rome, and the thing is altogether improbable.

There were small proprietors and cultivators in Sicily, but there were also many large cultivators, both owners and lessees of land, who employed a large capital on it (Lib. 3. c. 21). The 'aratores' were both Sicilians and Romans, who found profitable employment for their capital in the fertile island of Sicily: it was to the rich men of Rome what a colony is to some British capitalists, or what Ireland may become to the agricultural capitalists of England, when all the lands which are unprofitable in the hands of insolvent owners have been transferred to those who can make better use of them: "quid illa, quae forsitan ne sentiamus quidem, judices, quanta sunt! quod multis locupletioribus civibus utimur, quod habent propinquam, fidelem, fructuosamque provinciam, quo facile

excurrant, ubi libenter negotium gerant; quos illa partim mercibus suppeditandis cum quaestu compendioque dimittit, partim retinet ut arare, ut pascere, ut negotiari libeat, ut denique sedes ac domicilium collocare" (Lib. 2. c. 3). Under these circumstances Sicily was probably the best cultivated country in Europe in the time of Cicero. The amount of produce raised on the fertile lands of Leontini has already been discussed (Excursus VI.).

Cicero says nothing of the 'pecuarii' in these orations beyond mentioning them as one of the industrious classes in Sicily. The pasture lands were probably nearly all Roman property; and the 'pecuarii' paid a sum of money (scriptura) for the pasturage of their flocks. The 'scriptura' in Italy and in the provinces was let by the censors at Rome. This cannot be considered as a tax, but as a rent, like the money paid in some of the Australian colonies of England for pasture licences. "In Australia the flock-owners hold immense tracts on lease from the government at a trifling sum, and a tax of so much a head on sheep and cattle." The 'scriptura' was one of the oldest sources of Roman revenue. Sicily produced a great amount of wool and skins; and in the Italic or Marsic war it fed, clothed, and armed the troops of Rome (Lib. 2. c. 2). The 'scriptura' was farmed by Publicani, and in the time of Verres it happened that the same company (societas) farmed both the 'scriptura' and the 'portoria' (Lib. 2. c. 70). "The censors let also for pasture, forests, coppice, osier-beds, such as those of the Silva Scantia or Sila, the osier-beds of Minturnae; and the tooth of the flocks is the remote cause of the almost general denudation of the Apennines, which at the present day is so painful to look on, and which must have produced on the Italian peninsula hygrometric or thermometric changes which have been appreciable for a period of two thousand three hundred years" (Dureau de la Malle, ii. 445[1]).

The 'portorium' or charge upon articles exported was a 'vicesima' or twentieth, probably of their declared value. Cicero had no occasion to speak of import duties in Sicily; but perhaps we may assume that they were equal to those on exports. Verres defrauded the Publicani by exporting his plunder largely from Sicily (Lib. 2. c. 74, 75); among which there was honey, sofas for dining-rooms, and cloth of Malta, all which ought to have paid duty.

[1] This remark applies of course to Italy. I give it simply as it is, without comment. —It is said (Statistique du Département de la Vienne, An X. p. 58) that one of the most active causes of the rapid destruction of the forests in France was the great quantity of goats kept by the country people. Goats increased prodigiously after the revolution. Those mischievous animals browsed not only on the hedges and the forests, but also devoured the buds of the young plants, and soon killed them. The same complaint is made in the Statistique du Département de l'Allier, An X.

Besides the 'decumae' payable by the cultivators in the 'decumanae civitates,' and, as we have seen also, by the cultivators who were domiciliated within the limits of the states which were free from this charge, there were other demands made on the Sicilians. Cicero has summed them up thus: "quum unae decumae lege et conditione detrahantur, alterae novis institutis propter annonae rationem imperentur, ematur praeterea frumentum quotannis publice, postremo etiam in cellam magistratibus et legatis imperetur; quid aut quantum praeterea est quod aut liberum possit habere ille arator ac dominus in potestate suorum fructuum aut in ipsis fructibus solutum" (Lib. 3. c. 98).

The 'unae decumae' are the tenths of which we have already spoken. There were, says Cicero (Lib. 3. c. 70), two modes of purchasing corn when the necessities of Rome required a larger supply than the 'unae decumae.' A second tenth (alterae decumae) was bought from the Decumanae civitates. The price paid for the 'alterae decumae' was three sestertii the modius. This was 'frumentum emptum.' Corn was also required from the other 'civitates,' and the demand was imposed on all, in proportion to the produce of their territory, as we may suppose. This corn was paid for by the Roman state somewhat higher, three and a half sestertii the modius, if the reading is right: this was the 'frumentum imperatum.' The amount of the 'emptum' was of course equal to that of the 'unae decumae' or regular tenths. The amount of the 'imperatum,' while Verres was praetor, was eight hundred thousand modii of wheat. The 'imperatum' was imposed on all the 'civitates,' as the words of Cicero show, and the example of Halesa (Lib. 3. c. 73), which was one of the 'immunes ac liberae.' Cicero makes it a charge against Verres, that he did not require from the Mamertini (Messana) the portion of 'frumentum imperatum,' which they were bound to supply. He adds, that corn had never been purchased in Sicily on the public account without the Mamertini being required to furnish their proportion, until Verres, from corrupt motives, relieved them of this comparatively light imposition (Lib. 5. c. 21). Messana was one of the Foederatae civitates.

Cicero's words taken literally mean that besides the 'alterae decumae' which were bought from the Decumanae civitates, these states were liable to the 'imperatum:' "emendi duo genera fuerunt; unum decumarum; alterum, quod praeterea civitatibus aequaliter esset distributum;" and I have understood the passage so (Lib. 5. c. 21, note). I am not quite sure that this is Cicero's meaning, but I think that it is.

This commission to purchase corn in Sicily became under the administration of Verres a means of gross oppression, which Cicero has explained (Lib. 3. c. 70—80).

The 'frumentum aestimatum' (Lib. 3. c. 81) was the corn, wheat and

barley, which the governor was empowered to demand of the Sicilians for the use of his household (in cellam). The amount that he could demand was fixed; he was furnished by the Roman state with money to pay for it; and the price that he had to pay was fixed. Here Cicero informs us of a monstrous abuse which was established as a regular practice. A governor could require the grain for his use to be delivered at any place that he named within the province. If the cultivator had no corn to sell, or if he did not wish to sell his corn at the price that he would receive, or if he wished to avoid the expense of carrying it to the place named by the governor, he prayed as a favour that he might be allowed, instead of delivering the corn which was required of him, to pay a sum of money equal to its value. This monstrous abuse is lightly touched by Cicero, for the 'judices' in the case of Verres were men who would have a fellow-feeling with the accused. The charge against Verres was that he got more money out of the Sicilians under the head of 'frumentum aestimatum' than other governors; more than he would have got, if he had done as other governors did and were allowed to do. They were greedy. Verres was greedier. (Lib. 3. c. 81.)

The administration of Verres lasted three years, during which the island was ruined by his oppression. Cicero may have exaggerated the vices of Verres when he speaks of him in general terms, but it is hardly possible that the numerous charges against him, which he states with so much precision, can be far from the truth. Such a system of oppression for three years in a country within a few days' sail of Rome is a foul stain on the character of the Roman senate, who held the administration in their hands. Nothing but a consciousness that they were as guilty as Verres could have prevented the senate from visiting this scoundrel with speedy and well-merited punishment. The administration of Sicily under Verres gives us a just measure of the corruption of the Roman nobles, and prepares us for the advent of the imperial system, the only possible government if the empire was to subsist.

One of the many modes of raising money which Verres resorted to remains to be mentioned. He got money from the Sicilians under the pretext of applying it to the erection of statues of himself; and in fact there were statues of Verres, his son, and his father, erected in Sicily during his administration at the expense of the Sicilians; and statues of Verres even in Rome. But statues were also made a pretext for getting money, which Verres kept; and the law was so considerate, that it allowed a period of five years to elapse before a governor could be called to account for not appropriating the money to the purposes for which it was given or extorted (Lib. 2. c. 58). The practice of erecting statues, temples, and altars to Roman governors was the invention of the

fears and of the gross adulation of the Greeks. Under the emperors it was carried still further. When Cicero was governor of Cilicia, he had the decency to forbid it. (Ad Attic. v. 21.)

When Verres landed in Sicily the island was probably in a more prosperous state than it ever was before, or ever has been since, unless perchance in the time of Augustus, or under the mild and prudent administration of the Antonines. Since the overthrow of the Carthaginian power and the suppression of the servile revolts, it had enjoyed many years of tranquillity, being united under one government, which allowed no tyrant but itself. Under the system of farming, which employed large capitals, the produce was greatly increased. It had an extensive commerce and various manufactures. Malta, a dependency of Sicily, was famed for its fine linen. The industrious Greeks of Sicily produced excellent household furniture, and numerous articles of domestic use of exquisite taste. Couches, candelabra, carpets, plate of excellent workmanship, carved work in ivory, bronzes, pictures, and statues were the evidence of the wealth, the taste, and the artistic skill of the population of the island.

Dureau de la Malle (Économie Politique des Romains), whose work I have already cited, has many useful remarks on the condition of Sicily in the time of Cicero; but he is chargeable with inexactness in some particulars. The following passage, for the accuracy of which I will not vouch, relates to the population of the island (Vol. ii. p. 379): "We have the means of estimating accurately the annual produce of wheat in that portion of Sicily which formed the ancient kingdom of Hiero, which paid in kind the 'decumae' of wheat, and the extent of which did not comprise the third part of the island; for Cicero informs us in the third Verrine, named Frumentaria (c. 70), that the value of the tenths of the wheat in one year, during the praetorship of Verres, was 9,000,000 sesterces, which at three sesterces the modius makes 3,000,000 modii. Consequently, multiplying 3,000,000 by 10, we get for the produce of wheat in this part of Sicily 30,000,000 modii = 405,000,000 livres, poids de marc. Now the mean of the weight of a modius of wheat being 13½ livres, and the daily consumption of wheat by an individual being fixed at 2 livres, it is easy to deduce from it:

"1. The population of this portion of the island which formed the former kingdom of Hiero;

"2. The number of Roman citizens or inhabitants of Italy maintained by the exportation of the wheat of Sicily, which exportation was to the amount of 3,800,000 modii (51,300,000 livres), including in this amount the 800,000 modii of 'frumentum imperatum;' this number, I say, was in 681 of Rome, 50,340 persons. The population of this third of Sicily subjected to the payment of 'decumae' amounted to 396,864, and that

of all Sicily to 1,190,592 persons." It is easy to make several objections to these conclusions. Premises are assumed which cannot be admitted. For instance, who can assume that Hiero's part of the island was exactly one-third of the whole island, or rather that it contained exactly one-third of the population? I have no doubt that the relative population of Hiero's part was greater than that of the rest of the island.

It remains to make a few remarks on the object of the Romans in collecting the 'decumae' of Sicily, and the 'frumentum emptum.' The corn was for the supply of Rome, the city only as it seems. It was an old Roman policy for the state to look after the supply of corn for Rome. We cannot suppose that private enterprise did not partly supply the city; but in times of scarcity at least persons were appointed to buy on account of the state. Livy, on some authority we may presume, speaks of such purchases at an early period of Roman history (ii. 9, iv. 12); and in the second of these passages the creation of a 'praefectus annonae' is mentioned. On the occasion of a scarcity so early as the consulship of T. Geganius and P. Minucius (B.C. 492), Rome sent to seek for corn in Sicily (Liv. ii. 34). The possession of Sicily assured a large supply from the regular 'decumae,' and more could be had, if it was wanted, by a demand of the 'alterae decumae' and the 'frumentum imperatum.' The Lex Frumentaria of C. Gracchus (B.C. 123) substituted for the occasional and irregular distributions of corn at Rome, the sale of it at a low fixed price (Lib. 3. c. 70, note); and in this way the 'decumae' of Sicily seem to have been disposed of in B.C. 70, when Cicero prosecuted Verres. The gratuitous distribution of corn at Rome belongs to a later period in the life of Cicero, and not to the period of Verres, as Dureau de la Malle assumes. The discussion of the pauper system of Rome does not belong to this place.

XI.

"Non modo," &c.

The use of this form has been noticed several times in the commentary. It is one of the usual formulae of the Latin language. The common translation of 'non modo' is 'not only,' which will sometimes express the meaning of the Latin original, and sometimes it will not. 'Not only,' in English, implies that the thing of which a predication is made, in the clause which contains 'not only,' is not all; and that something further is going to be predicated. 'Not only' may sometimes[1] express 'non modo' in such forms as the following:—

Divin. c. 4.—"Hi sciunt hoc non modo a me petitum esse, sed ita saepe . . petitum ut," &c.

Act. i. c. 1.—"opinio . . quae non modo Romae sed et apud exteras nationes . . percrebuit," &c.

Divin. c. 5.—"cujus legis non modo a populo Romano sed etiam ab ultimis nationibus jampridem severi custodes requiruntur."

In these cases 'sed' is followed by 'et,' 'etiam,' or 'ita,' as in Divin. c. 4, and in Lib. 3. c. 88: "et id non modo fieri, sed ita fieri quasi liceat."

'Non modo,' so placed, does not differ in use from 'non solum,' followed by 'sed etiam' or 'verum etiam:'—

Divin. c. 13.—"non solum commoveor animo, sed etiam toto corpore perhorresco."

Act. i. c. 16.—"eosque ambos non solum deseruerit, sed etiam prodiderit."

Act. i. c. 18.—"ut homines miseri . . . non modo jus suum fortunasque . . . amittant, verum etiam deplorandi juris sui potestatem non habeant."

In the following passage 'sed' is not followed by any emphatic word:—Act. i. c. 3,—"Intelligit me ita paratum . . venire ut non modo in auribus vestris sed in oculis omnium sua furta atque flagitia defixurus sim." In the following passage (Divin. c. 14) also 'sed' is not followed by 'et' or 'etiam,' but there is the emphatic word 'ipso:' "ne ille non modo verbis te obruat, sed gestu ipso ac motu corporis praestringat aciem ingenii tui," &c. No variation is noted in this passage; and I doubt if 'non modo' can be translated 'not only.' There is a

[1] Not always. See Cic. Ad Attic. ii. 18, "non modo privatos," &c.; and Ad Div. xv. 6.

similar passage in Lib. 1. c. 46, where 'non modo ceteros' is followed by 'sed te ipsum.' There are other examples where 'non modo,' followed by 'sed' only, is, or seems to be, equivalent to 'non modo' followed by 'sed etiam.' (See Verr. ii. Lib. 2. c. 20; Pro Milone, c. 4; Pro Cluentio, c. 40; In Cat. ii. c. 12; Sallust, Cat. c. 18.)

In the following passage (Lib. 4. c. 41) 'non modo' cannot be rendered by 'not only,' and it confirms what I have said as to 'sed:' "Tu ista stultitia, nequitia, inertia, non modo totius Siciliae sed unius tenuissimi Siculi clientelam tueri potes?"

In the following passages also 'non modo' cannot be translated 'not only:'—

Divin. c. 18.—"quid habes quod possis dicere quamobrem non modo mihi sed cuiquam anteponare?"

Lib. 3. c. 31.—"An poterat non modo Apronius sed quivis, si exercitui metiendum esset, improbare Siculum frumentum," &c.

Divin. c. 8.—"quo tempore aut qua in re non modo specimen ceteris aliquid de te, sed tute tui periculum fecisti?"

The second instance, perhaps, shows most clearly how we must endeavour to express the 'non modo' in such cases as these: "I don't ask if Apronius could, but if any one could refuse to accept Sicilian corn?"

We must seek in the primitive meaning of 'modo' a solution for the true meaning of these expressions. 'Modo,' like several other words in an ablative case, is used as an adverb; it is a word of measure, and therefore of limitation. Professor Key remarks (Latin Grammar, § 794, 1st edit.) that 'modo' means literally 'by measure,' and "hence, with small quantities, mŏdŏ, *by measure*, may be translated by *only:* on the other hand, with great quantities, admŏdum, *up to the measure*, is equivalent to *full, quite.*" So Cicero says (Lib. 3. c. 5): "id fuit mihi gratum admodum:" 'that was agreeable to me, to the full, to the complete measure.' In Lib. 3. c. 97, he says, "Atque utinam posset aliqua ratione hoc crimen quamvis falsa, modo humana atque usitata, defendere," which means that Cicero would be glad if Verres could answer this charge in some way, as false as you like, within the limits of 'humanitas' and usage. So in Lib. 3. c. 87, there is "magnum praeclarumque vectigal, si modo salva provincia, si sine injuria sociorum percipere possumus[a]." Now here the 'modo' might be omitted, but it helps to express more clearly the condition or limitation, which limitation is the existence and integrity of the province. One more example may help to explain this. Lib. 3. c. 58: "hoc aut innocens homo perpeti potuisset, aut quamvis nocens, qui modo judicia Romae fore putaret,

[a] The usages of 'modo' in Terence may be compared. Caesar also uses 'admodum' in a way which shows its meaning, 'turres admodum cxx excitantur' (B. G. v. 40).

non aliqua simulatione existimationi se hominum venditasset?" Here the 'modo' might be omitted also, for 'qui . . putaret,' an ordinary formula in Cicero, would express what is meant, but with somewhat less precision than 'qui modo,' which limits more exactly the 'guiltiest man' to one of the class who believed that there would be judicial investigation at Rome[1].

The notion contained in this word 'modo,' then, is that of 'limit;' and 'non modo' is a negation of the limit. In such an expression as 'tantum modo,' we have the meaning 'so much, and no more;' or 'that is all.' Now the only difficulty lies in seeing how the notion contained in this 'non modo' is to be combined with the notion contained in the other words which it is intended to qualify. In the Divin. c. 4, 'hi sciunt hoc,' &c., the notion contained in 'a me petitum' is not the measure or limit: there was more than that. In Lib. 3. c. 31, 'an poterat non modo Apronius,' &c., Cicero's question of the possibility of rejecting this corn is not limited to Apronius, it extends to any body and every body.

If I should be asked what is the best translation in all these instances, I should answer that I do not know. I merely mean to say that 'not only,' which happens to fit some cases, will not fit all cases; and I would not quarrel with any translation of 'non modo' in any given case, if it expressed the meaning with precision. There are numerous expressions of common occurrence in modern languages, which we find as difficult to express in our language as many of those which occur in Roman writers, though we have the advantage of having the precise force of such modern expressions explained by a living teacher. Some of those words called adverbs and conjunctions, which are used very frequently, are perverted by usage in such a way that it is hard to seize their precise meaning, and trace it up to the original signification of the word.

There is another use of 'non modo,' followed by 'ne quidem,' which requires a few words. In such cases as the following, 'non modo' is said to be used for 'non modo non,' an explanation which may lead to misunderstanding:—

Act. I. c. 38.—"Non modo proditori, sed ne perfugae quidem locus in meis castris cuiquam fuit."

Lib. 3. c. 91.—"si hoc crimen non modo Marcelli facto sed ne Lepidi quidem potes defendere;"—and Lib. 4. c. 45, where there are two examples.

If we here translate 'non modo' by 'not only,' our idiom requires that we insert a negative which is not in the Latin, thus: 'not only no

[1] Compare Livy, xxii. 2: "Primi qua modo praeirent duces," &c.

traitor, but not even a deserter has ever found a place in my camp." But I do not think that this is a good form of translation.

Professor Key (Grammar, § 1415) observes that the "negative in 'ne . . quidem,' when followed by a common predicate, often extends its influence over a preceding clause beginning with 'non modo.'" He gives the following instance and translation:—

"Assentatio non modo amico sed ne libero quidem digna est" (Cic.): 'flattery is unworthy not merely of a friend, but even of a free man.'

He adds in a note: "It is in such passages as these that 'non modo' is said to be used for 'non modo non.'" The predicate contained in 'digna' is placed at the end of the sentence, but it applies equally to both parts of it; and the 'non modo' expressed to a Roman clearly enough, that what was going to be predicated was not limited to friend, but, as the next words show, extended even to a free man.

'Non solum' is used in the same way, as in the following example from the same Grammar: "Senatui non solum juvare rem publicam, sed ne lugere quidem licuit:" 'the senate were forbidden not merely to assist, but even to mourn over their country.'

In Lib. 3. c. 5, there is "ut eum facile non modo extra tectum, sed ne extra lectum quidem quisquam videret," which is another of these supposed examples of 'non modo' for 'non modo non;' and there are many other examples in these orations. But the supplying of another 'non' after the 'non modo,' and in the clause to which 'non modo' belongs, is contrary to the usage of the Latin language in such cases.

In the following instances however there is a double negative in the first clause, and yet there is 'ne . . quidem,' with the general predicate, in the second clause:—

Lib. 3. c. 48.—"multis autem non modo granum nullum sed ne paleae quidem . . relinquerentur."

Lib. 4. c. 22.—"non modo oppidum nullum, sed ne domus quidem ulla paulo locupletior expers hujus injuriae reperietur."

These are instances of the double negative, as it is called, the repetition of the negative, to give emphasis: "Not to speak of towns, of not a single town being exempt, I add, not even will a single house of the richer class be found to have escaped this wrong." Compare Lib. 2. c. 46: "quod non modo Siculus nemo sed ne Sicilia quidem tota potuisset." In the Pro S. Roscio Am. c. 52, there is "in quo non modo culpa nulla, sed ne suspicio quidem potuit consistere;" but in the Pro Murena, c. 33, Cicero writes "frequentiam in isto officio gratuitam non modo dignitati ullius unquam, sed ne voluntati quidem defuisse," and here no various reading is mentioned by the last editors of these orations.

The following case is different from those just given (Lib. 5. c. 18):

"nunc non modo te hoc crimine non arguo, sed ne illa quidem communi vituperatione reprehendo." Here each clause has its predicate, and if the 'non' before 'arguo' were omitted, the meaning would be so far just the opposite of what is intended.

If the predicate occurs in the first part of the sentence, and a negation is intended, the 'non' is necessary, though 'ne .. quidem' comes after (Lib. 3. c. 97): "non solum aestimandi frumenti modus non fuit sed ne imperandi quidem [4]."

There are many cases in which 'non modo non' occurs, but the reader must learn to distinguish them from the supposed case of 'non modo' being used for 'non modo non.' In Divin. c 9, "M. Caecilium .. non modo non adesse neque tecum tuas injurias persequi, sed esse cum Verre," where it is plain that the second 'non' qualifies 'adesse.' The assertion is not limited to a 'non adesse' at the trial, and a 'neque persequi' of Verres: it goes so far as to affirm an 'esse cum Verre.' In the following instance (Divin. c. 11), "facile omnes intelligent vobis inter vos non modo voluntatem fuisse conjunctam, sed ne praedam quidem adhuc esse divisam," a 'non' before 'conjunctam' would negative what Cicero affirms in that clause, 'that there was union of will, and that was not all.' In Lib. 1. c. 15, the true reading is "non modo non exsistit verum etiam opprimit antequam prospicere . . potueris," which passage some of the critics would corrupt by omitting the 'non' before 'exsistit;' and thus they would make Cicero write nonsense.

[4] Compare the instance in Cic. Ad Attic. I. 11.

NOTE.

As there is room here, I have a remark to make, which ought to be made somewhere. In a work of this kind numerous references are expected, and when they are exact, they are useful. I have examined every reference which I have made, and many of them twice; except in those cases where I had not the books and I was obliged to trust to others. These cases are not numerous, and I have always either directly or indirectly shown that I am not responsible for the accuracy of some references; or if I have not always done so, I intended to do it. This making and verifying of references is a most tedious, hateful toil, and I consider it more real trouble than all the rest. The causes of error, even when the references are most carefully examined, are many: for instance, a man does not always copy a reference truly, even if he has the passage before his eyes; and the most careful and exact of printers, and such is the printer of this book, may sometimes print incorrectly what is correct, and the editor may not discover the error, even if he be as careful as I affirm that I am, without meaning to say that some people with the same care might not be more exact. There are other causes of error well known to writers and printers, but on this head I have said enough.

I do not know how many references there are in this book. If they average ten a page, they will amount to more than six thousand, many of them references to Cicero himself, some of them dates, which imply reference, and others to numerous works and passages useful for the explanation of these orations.

INDEX TO THE NOTES.

THE REFERENCES ARE MADE TO THE PAGES.

END OF VOL. I.

www.ingramcontent.com/pod-product-compliance
Lightning Source LLC
Chambersburg PA
CBHW022121020426
42334CB00015B/714

* 9 7 8 3 7 4 2 8 4 4 1 5 6 *